DAY BY DAY

The Twenties

Day by Day: The Twenties

Copyright © 2008 by Infobase Publishing

Facts On File, Inc.
An Imprint of Infobase Publishing
132 West 31st Street
New York, NY 10001

Library of Congress Cataloging-in-Publication Data

Day by day : the twenties / Rodney P. Carlisle, general editor.
      v. cm.
      Includes bibliographical references and index.
      Contents: v. 1. 1920-1924 -- v. 2. 1925-1929.
      ISBN 978-0-8160-7183-8 (hbk. : alk. paper)
    1. Nineteen twenties-Chronology. I. Carlisle, Rodney P. II. Title: Twenties.
      D723.D43 2008
      909.82'2--dc22
          2007050850

Facts On File books are available at special discounts when purchased in bulk quantities for businesses, associations, institutions, or sales promotions. Please call our Special Sales Department in New York at (212) 967-8800 or (800) 322-8755.

You can find Facts On File on the World Wide Web at http://www.factsonfile.com

Photo Credits
Library of Congress: 1920 pages 2–3; 1921 pages 110–111; 1922 pages 238–239; 1923 pages 368–369; 1924 pages 480–481; 1925 pages 588–589; 1926 pages 702–703; 1927 pages 820–821; 1928 pages 928–929. Getty Images: 1929 pages 1034-1035

GOLSON BOOKS, LTD.
President and Editor	J. Geoffrey Golson
Creative Director	Mary Jo Scibetta
Managing Editor	Susan Moskowitz
Copyeditor	Jacqueline Frances Brownstein
Layout Editors	Kenneth Heller
	Susan Honeywell
	Stephanie Larson
Proofreaders	Julie Grady
	Joan K. Griffitts
Indexer	J S Editorial

Printed in the United States of America

VB GB 12 11 10 9 8 7 6 5 4 3 2 1

This book is printed on acid-free paper and contains 30 percent post-consumer recycled content.

The Twenties

VOLUME 2

1925–1929

Rodney P. Carlisle, Ph.D.

General Editor

Facts On File
An imprint of Infobase Publishing

CONTENTS

VOLUME 2

1925

March 4, 1925: The inaugural parade of President Calvin Coolidge.

	World Affairs	Europe	Africa & The Middle East	The Americas	Asia & The Pacific
Jan.	The second world opium conference opens in Geneva. The League-sponsored meeting continues into February.	Benito Mussolini dissolves parliament. He takes dictatorial control of Italy....Norway renames its capital Christiana to Oslo.	The Wahhabis begin a six-month siege of Jidda. They fail to oust Sharif Ali....Britain modifies Tanganyikan immigration policy. German settlers are allowed to return....France combines Damascus and Aleppo territories into Syria.	Costa Rica leaves the League. It cites League failure to resolve regional disagreements.	In the Treaty of Peking Japan gives the Seychelles back to Russia. The Russo-Japanese convention gives Japan oil and coal concessions on Sakhalin in return for withdrawal of Japanese troops. It resolves most outstanding disagreements between the two. Japan recognizes Russia.
Feb.	The opium conference rejects a U.S. proposal. The United States leaves the meeting.	Kurds rise against Turkish religious policy and demand autonomy. Kemal crushes the rising at great cost. His power grows more dictatorial....France suppresses the Vatican embassy. The anti-clerical policies of the government alienate the right. In April, France opens an embassy in Vatican City to pacify the conservatives.	The February 1925 issue of *National Geographic* is devoted to a 5,000 mile trip the length of Africa by train, boat, and foot. The article reveals cultural insensitivity by the author but helps to inform a public largely ignorant of Africa.	The baseball series between the All-Cuban and All-American teams begins with a Cuban victory. The U.S. will win the series 5-2-1.	
Mar.	The BBC leads in establishing the first international broadcasting convention. The International Broadcasting Union lasts until the 1950s.	*Pionerskaya Pravda* (Truth for Young Pioneers) debuts. It will be one of Europe's longest-running children's newspapers.	Walter Mittelholder becomes the first to fly over Iran's Demawend Mountain.		Japan's parliament accepts male suffrage....The U.S. annexes Swain's Island near American Samoa.
Apr.		Communists assault St. Nedelya Church in Sofia, Bulgaria. The attack kills 150 and injures another 500....Adolf Hitler forms the Schutz Staffel as his personal bodyguard. The SS will become the elite Nazi force....Hindenberg becomes Germany's president....Britain returns to the gold standard.	Abd-el-Krim rebels against France in Morocco.	Cuba's Club Femenino hosts the second National Women's Conference. Representatives of 71 organizations, 40 more than the first in 1923, hear President Machado promise female suffrage during his term.	The *Raifaku Maru* sinks with the loss of its crew of 38. One liner is damaged in the futile rescue attempt.
May	The League of Nations holds a conference on poison gas use and arms control.		The cornerstone for Hebrew University in Jerusalem is laid.	British explorer Percy Fawcett sends his wife a telegram. He then disappears into the Amazon—forever.	Japan enacts its General Election Law. It enfranchises all males 25 and older, approximately 12 million people or 20 percent of the population.
Jun.	Geneva hosts the first international feminist conference....At Geneva's International Arms Control and Trade Convention, nations agree to outlaw chemical and bacteriological weapons.	Kurdish rebels surrender to Turkish forces....The Netherlands returns to the gold standard.	The African Sleeping Sickness conference meets in London under League auspices....Britain cedes Italy a strip of land on the Juba River in Somaliland.	The International Red Cross recognizes the Panamanian Red Cross and authorizes Panama's use of the Red Cross flag.	Chinese riots in Canton begin. This is an expansion of the strike and boycott of British interests in protest of unfair treaty arrangements.
Jul.		The Telegraph Agency of the Soviet Union (TASS) begins operations....Mein Kampf appears....England enacts an unemployment insurance law....Czechoslovakia celebrates John Hus day. The Vatican severs diplomatic relations in protest.	Persian guru Meher Baba begins his 44-year silence. He will not speak again, communicating through an alphabet board or gestures....France arrests Druse leaders after inviting them to a Damascus conference. The Druse have previously claimed that France favors Christian Syrians. In Lebanon, Sultan Pasha leads the Great Druse Rebellion against France, rapidly controlling the countryside and threatening the cities....France and Spain agree to combine against the Rif in Morocco.	U.S. Marines activate the 2nd Battalion, 2nd Marines at Camp Haitian, Haiti. These and other Marine units will provide order in 1925 and 1926 and again in 1929–33.	A British warship fires on strikers in Hong Kong harbor.
Aug.	At Stockholm the ecumenical movement revives as delegates from various faiths around the world meet together.	France leaves Duisburg, Dusseldorf, and Ruhrort. It is finished evacuating the Ruhr....At Stockholm, delegates meet to revive the prewar ecumenical movement.		The Cuban Communist Party holds its initial meetings....U.S. Marines leave Nicaragua after 13 years.	

A	B	C	D	E
Includes developments that affect more than one world region, international organizations and important meetings of world leaders.	*Includes all domestic and regional developments in Europe, including the Soviet Union.*	*Includes all domestic and regional developments in Africa and the Middle East.*	*Includes all domestic and regional developments in Latin America, the Caribbean, and Canada.*	*Includes all domestic and regional developments in Asian and Pacific nations (and colonies).*

U.S. Politics & Social Issues	U.S. Foreign Policy & Affairs, Defense	U.S. Economy & Environment	Science, Technology & Nature	Culture, Leisure & Lifestyle	
During the January 27–February 1 Serum Run to Nome, dog sleds carry diphtheria serum across Alaska. Twenty mushers and 150 dogs cover the 674 miles to prevent an epidemic. Radio covers the effort, making mushers and dogs national heroes....Texas seats the first all-female state supreme court.	Frank Kellogg takes over as Secretary of State.	Congress holds hearings on the economics of radio. Writers and composers testify that radio is infringing on their copyrights.	The U.S. Navy airship *Los Angeles*, over Long Island, films a solar eclipse. The film lasts 2 minutes.	The college fashion craze is Oxford baggy pants.	Jan.
After 18 days of media circus, expert caver Floyd Colllins dies. Rescuers fail to get him out of Sand Cave, KY.	The United States signs a treaty with Canada that resolves outstanding disagreements over fishing.	The first waterless gas storage tank enters service in Michigan City, IN.	The first use of thermite is to break up an ice jam on the St. Lawrence River in Waddington, NY.	The *New Yorker* debuts. Under Harold Ross, it is the magazine for upscale sophisticates.....Art Gillham records the first Western Electric masters for Columbia records. Gillham is a leading radio crooner....The number one song is *Tea for Two*.	Feb.
Governor Austin Peay signs the Butler Act. Tennessee outlaws the teaching of evolution....Johnny Torrio moves to New York. The new head of the Chicago mob is Al Capone.	The United States annexes Swain's Island near American Samoa. The one-square-mile island remains under private ownership....The U.S. house votes overwhelmingly to back U.S. acceptance of the World Court protocol. Pressure is on the Senate to agree.	The United States establishes a standard national highway numbering system and the shield logo for highway signs.	The worst tornado in U.S. history, the Tri-State tornado, kills 695 people in Missouri, Illinois, and Indiana. The F5 tornado leaves a 219-mile path, the longest in the world.	Crossword puzzles become the newest craze.	Mar.
		The Chicago World's Fair opens its gates.	Imperial Airways introduces in-flight movies. The first film shown is First National's *The Lost World*....Victor replaces acoustic disks with electronic recordings. Columbia follows suit in May.	F. Scott Fitzgerald's *The Great Gatsby* appears. It has critical but not popular success....Frank Heath leaves Washington, DC, on his horse Gypsy Queen. They make a two-year ride through all 48 states.	Apr.
At Dayton, TN, authorities arrest John Scopes for teaching evolution.		Warner Brothers buys Vitagraph. It uses the $4.2 million asset to experiment with sound in film.	The sternwheel steamboat *M.E. Norman* sinks near Memphis, TN. Twenty-three drown but Tom Lee uses his rowboat to save 32 others.	Bruno Jacob of Ripon, WI, creates the National Forensic League. The league sponsors speech and debate for high school students.	May
	Secretary Kellogg accuses the Calles government of failing to protect U.S. citizens' rights and property. Relations, long strained, become more tense.	Walter Percy Chrysler forms the Chrysler Corporation. Chrysler previously worked for Buick, Willys-Overland, and Maxwell....Warner Brothers and Western Electric form the Vitaphone Company to work on sound on disk technology. An 11-member Bell Labs team uses the Vitagraph studio.	Charles Francis Jenkins transmits synchronized pictures and sound. Jenkins in 1923 transmitted silhouettes in front of witnesses. This transmission of a windmill in motion is seen by officials of various government agencies....A 6.3 intensity earthquake destroys downtown Santa Barbara, CA.	Charles Mellor wins the 29th Boston Marathon. Time is 2:33:00:6....Peter DePaolo becomes the first to average over 100 mph at the Indianapolis Motor Speedway.	Jun.
The Scopes trial takes place. A jury finds Scopes guilty and fines him $100.	The first transcontinental airmail plane lands at Mather Field, CA. A crowd of 4,000 watches.	Boston's Dreyfus Hotel collapses, killing 44		Paris hosts the *Exposition Internationale des Arts Decoratifs et Industriels Modernes*. The first comprehensive fair of the style features Style Moderne works. Style Moderne will be renamed art deco in the late 1960s.	Jul.
A Klan march in Washington, DC brings 40,000 hooded marchers.... The Brotherhood of Sleeping Car Porters organizes in Harlem.	The United States and Belgium agree on terms for Belgian repayment of war debts.	The original Hetch Hetchy powerhouse goes on line at Moccasin, CA. Moccasin is a company town owned by San Francisco to house power company workers.		Chaplin's *The Gold Rush* premiers....The first proposal for Mount Rushmore appears.	Aug.

F	G	H	I	J
Includes campaigns, elections, federal-state relations, civil rights and liberties, crime, the judiciary, education, healthcare, poverty, urban affairs, and population.	*Includes formation and debate of U.S. foreign and defense policies, veterans affairs, and defense spending. (Relations with specific foreign countries are usually found under the region concerned.)*	*Includes business, labor, agriculture, taxation, transportation, consumer affairs, monetary and fiscal policy, natural resources, pollution and industrial accidents.*	*Includes worldwide scientific, medical and technological developments, natural phenomena, U.S. weather and natural disasters.*	*Includes the arts, religion, scholarship, communications media, sports, entertainment, fashions, fads, and social life.*

	World Affairs	Europe	Africa & The Middle East	The Americas	Asia & The Pacific
Sep.	International jurists convene in London to develop a means of preventing future wars....The League ends control of Austrian finances.	Albania sets up a national bank. Italy provides assistance and loans.		Although the U.S. declines to support Colombia's effort to establish a Caribbean air route, it does stir itself to push Pan American to move to the Caribbean, which it does in 1928.	Gandhi founds the All-India Spinners Association....Australia enacts legislation authorizing the governor-general to bar any group of aliens he chooses. Rarely used, the act does bar Italians opposed by organized labor.
Oct.	The Treaty of Locarno is signed. Rightwing Germans object. The "Spirit of Locarno" is the basis for interwar European stability, but it fails to stop German expansionist efforts and French use of bilateral treaties	Portugal exposes Alves Reis' forgery of escudos in the Portuguese Bank Note Crisis. When the scale of the forgery becomes known, the government loses confidence, and it falls the next year.	Italy takes Somalia.	Canada's Dr. Julius Lilienfield applies for the first patent on a transistor....Emiliano Chamorro begins a rebellion against the government of Carlos Solarzano. Vice President Sacasa resigns. U.S. intervention will resume.	
Nov.	The League holds a conference to establish standard measurement of ship tonnages.	The German parliament ratifies the Treaty of Locarno.	Abd-al-Aziz ibn Saud signs treaties with Iraq and Britain. The former establishes treatment of tribal minorities while the latter defines borders with Transjordania and Hejaz-Nejd.		Prajadhipok as Rama VII becomes King of Siam. He is Siam's last absolute monarch and first constitutional monarch. He abdicates in 1935....Gandhi begins writing his autobiography, *The Story of My Experiments with Truth.*
Dec.	Piuis XI publishes *Quas Primas.* The encyclical rejects modernism and reiterates Christ the King....The League gives Iraq most of the disputed oil territory in Mosul. Turkey objects.	Russia's Communist Party announces plans to industrialize and deemphasize agriculture....Belgium, France, Great Britain, Italy, and Germany sign treaties guaranteeing Germany's borders with Belgium and France.	Excavation of the Sphinx is finished....Ibn Saud captures Jidda. His control of Arabia is firmed.		Colombo Radio begins broadcasting. It will later be Radio Ceylon.

A	B	C	D	E
Includes developments that affect more than one world region, international organizations and important meetings of world leaders.	*Includes all domestic and regional developments in Europe, including the Soviet Union.*	*Includes all domestic and regional developments in Africa and the Middle East.*	*Includes all domestic and regional developments in Latin America, the Caribbean, and Canada.*	*Includes all domestic and regional developments in Asian and Pacific nations (and colonies).*

U.S. Politics & Social Issues	U.S. Foreign Policy & Affairs, Defense	U.S. Economy & Environment	Science, Technology & Nature	Culture, Leisure & Lifestyle	
Xavier University in New Orleans opens. The school is all black.	The U.S.S. *Shenandoah* breaks up in Ohio on the way to Scott Field, IL. Twenty-nine survive, but thirteen and the commander die. The commander's superiors earlier overrule his protests against making a promotional flight in thunderstorms.	Hoover advocates a self-supporting aviation industry but establishes a federal role under the postmaster general. He also asks municipalities to assist in airport construction.		Film debut of the month is Harold Lloyd's comedy, *The Freshman.*	Sep.
Texas outlaws the teaching of evolution.			John Logie Baird creates the first television transmitter in Britain and in his laboratory becomes first to transmit in halftones. Straight electronic systems will eventually replace his electromechanical one.	Fred Waller patents water skis.	Oct.
The American Association for the Advancement of Atheism forms.	Italy and the United States agree on repayment of Italian war debts. The United States requires interest of 0.4 percent.		Robert Millikan says he has discovered cosmic rays.	Barn Dance, renamed Grand Ole Opry in 1927, debuts on WSM, Nashville....Josephine Baker, expatriate American, begins her "jungle" numbers in the *Revue Negre* at the Theatre des Champs-Elysees. Her risqué performances make her the rage of all Europe....The popular dress style is the flapper.	Nov.
Billy Mitchell is court martialed for insubordination.	The Philippine legislature submits a petition for independence to the U.S. Congress.	Arthur Heinman opens a motor court in California. He coins the name "motel."		Sergei Eisenstein's movie *Battleship Potemkin* premiers.	Dec.

F	G	H	I	J
Includes campaigns, elections, federal-state relations, civil rights and liberties, crime, the judiciary, education, healthcare, poverty, urban affairs, and population.	*Includes formation and debate of U.S. foreign and defense policies, veterans affairs, and defense spending. (Relations with specific foreign countries are usually found under the region concerned.)*	*Includes business, labor, agriculture, taxation, transportation, consumer affairs, monetary and fiscal policy, natural resources, pollution and industrial accidents.*	*Includes worldwide scientific, medical and technological developments, natural phenomena, U.S. weather and natural disasters.*	*Includes the arts, religion, scholarship, communications media, sports, entertainment, fashions, fads, and social life.*

	World Affairs	Europe	Africa & The Middle East	The Americas	Asia & The Pacific
Jan. 1	Costa Rica withdraws from the League of Nations because of that organization's failure to resolve regional disputes.	The British government assures the United States that it will raise no objections if the United States grants a moratorium or a lower interest rate on France's World War I debts to the United States...Germany's President Friedrich Ebert states that the past year has been one of economic progress for Germany's recovery from the war....In his New Year's Day address, Czechoslovak President Jan Masaryk defends a government initiative to separate church and state.	The British government allows German settlers to return to Tanganyika, a German colony until the end of World War I.... France creates the Mandate territory of Syria combining the old Ottoman provinces of Aleppo and Damascus.		
Jan. 2	U.S. President Calvin Coolidge states that he is opposed to a proposal for the United States calling an international and armament conference to meet in the United States preferring that the League of Nations sponsor the conference.	Italy states that it will pay all of its war debts as soon as possible, despite opposition within the country....Yugoslavia bans activities by Croatian nationalists which it states are supported by the Soviets....Anti-Fascist rioting throughout Italy with Benito Mussolini calling on all parties to cease fighting.		Carlos Solarzano is inaugurated as President of Nicaragua for a four-year term....Heavy snowstorms dump at least nine inches in the Northeast, paralyzing the region.... An explosion in the Boston subway, caused by the explosion of movie film, injures 30 people.	U.S. Marines land at the Chinese city of Nanking to preserve order and prevent looting.
Jan. 3		Benito Mussolini announces that he will use force to crush all opposition to the Fascist government.	The Spanish Army evacuates 40,000 men from Morocco as part of an effort to reduce Spanish garrisons in this occupied territory.		It is announced that Dr. Sun Yat-Sen, leader of the government of Southern China, will undergo treatment for a serious liver aliment.
Jan. 4		The German Reichstag meets to form a government after previous efforts to build a ruling coalition have failed....The Estonian government accuses the Soviet government of supporting an attempted revolt in December 1924....A flood strikes the city of Leningrad forcing the population to evacuate the city.			
Jan. 5	Ambassadors of the United States, France, and Britain announce they will not withdraw their occupation troops from the German city of Cologne on January 10, as previously agreed.	Germany and France break off negotiations to establish a post-Versailles Treaty trade agreement....Benito Mussolini rebuilds Italian government cabinet appointing all Fascists.			
Jan. 6		The Yugoslav government denies that it has been sending raiding parties into Albania....The Soviet Union accuses the British government of actively working to subvert the Soviet government....The British Ministry of Labor announces that unemployment increased 10 percent at Christmas 1924, totaling 1,272,600 unemployed.			British authorities capture Abdul Karim Khan, pretender to the Afghan throne on Northwest Frontier in India.
Jan. 7		Socialist Paul Loebe is elected as President of Reichstag while the German cabinet has still not yet been assembled as a coalition group....The German Navy launches a cruiser, *Emden*, one of six allowed under the Versailles Treaty.			

A	B	C	D	E
Includes developments that affect more than one world region, international organizations and important meetings of world leaders.	Includes all domestic and regional developments in Europe, including the Soviet Union.	Includes all domestic and regional developments in Africa and the Middle East.	Includes all domestic and regional developments in Latin America, the Caribbean, and Canada.	Includes all domestic and regional developments in Asian and Pacific nations (and colonies).

U.S. Politics & Social Issues	U.S. Foreign Policy & Affairs, Defense	U.S. Economy & Environment	Science, Technology & Nature	Culture, Leisure & Lifestyle	
			Photographs are successfully transmitted from California to Chicago by telegraph to the *Chicago Tribune* for use in the newspaper.	Tenor John McCormick and soprano Lucrezia Bori perform on a radio broadcast that reaches an estimated 6 million listeners.... Notre Dame and Stanford play at the Rose Bowl.	Jan. 1
While awaiting sentencing, anarchist and convicted killer Bartolomeo Vanzetti, is transferred from his cell and to Bridgewater Asylum for the Insane for observation....Cardinal Hayes of the Archdiocese of New York sends a message stating that the new ideas of personal freedom are a form of lawlessness and detrimental to society.	A special board prepares its final report to President Calvin Coolidge assessing the relative value of airships, battleships, and submarines in order to determine allocating defense expenditures.	Plans are announced to begin an airline that will eventually have 20 dirigibles in service to transport passengers domestically and overseas....Radio stocks increase in value.		American tenor Lawrence Tibbett performs at the Metropolitan Opera House in New York and receives a standing ovation.	Jan. 2
President Calvin Coolidge discusses the possibility of delivering relief to livestock farmers.	.	The Jubilee Auto Show opens in New York City with more than 300 cars on display....The State of New Hampshire expresses interest in purchasing the rock formation, "The Old Man of the Mountain."...The New York Stock exchange records the greatest trading in 18 years, radio stocks raise dramatically in price....The American Chemical Society announces that gasoline consumption may use up all existing oil supplies in 10 to 20 years.	The U.S. Department of Interior announces that it will protect dinosaur tracks discovered near the Grand Canyon, AZ.	German conductor Wilhelm Fuertwaengler makes his American debut, conducting works by Brahms and Richard Strauss.	Jan. 3
Nellie Taylor Ross is sworn in as Governor of Wyoming becoming the first woman to be a governor in the United States...The warden of the New York State Penitentiary in Ossining announces that the year 1924 saw a 37 percent increase in the number of convicts over 1923.				The film, *The Thief of Baghdad,* starring Douglas Fairbanks is playing at American theaters....Polish Harpsichordist Wanda Landowska performs a concert on the seldom-heard harpsichord in concert....Composer Igor Stravinsky arrives in New York City where he will give several concerts....Palm Beach, FL, announces it will ban flesh-colored stockings worn with bathing suits and one-piece bathing suits.	Jan. 4
Chicago coal drivers go on strike, halting all deliveries except those to hospitals....Harlan Fisk Stone is nominated to the U.S. Supreme Court by Calvin Coolidge.	The Atlantic Division of the U.S. Navy (30 ships) leaves Norfolk, VA, for a cruise to Cuba and then Panama to participate in maneuvers with the Pacific Division.		The French government establishes an Antarctic game sanctuary.	New York University begins offering courses over the radio.... Finnish runner Paavo Nurmi ("The Flying Finn") competes in and wins two races at Madison Square Garden.	Jan. 5
Progressive Senators Bob LaFollette, Lynn Frazier, and Edwin Ladd removed from Republican Party by Senate caucus....Samuel Spachia, an official of the United Mine Workers is shot and killed during a coal strike in West Virginia....Hiram Bingham (Yale professor who discovered Inca city of Machu Picchu in 1911) sworn in as Governor of Connecticut.... The six textile workers unions of Fall River, MA accept a 10 percent wage reduction.	U.S. Army and Navy commanders in Panama announce that there are several important flaws in the Canal zone defenses.				Jan. 6
	President Calvin Coolidge states that he will not approve of the Navy Board's recommendation to build additional ships or to modernize already existing battleships.	An earthquake hits Eastern Massachusetts and New Hampshire for only the fifth time in New England's recorded history.		Al Jolson, in blackface, opens a new musical, *Big Boy.*	Jan. 7

F	**G**	**H**	**I**	**J**
Includes campaigns, elections, federal-state relations, civil rights and liberties, crime, the judiciary, education, healthcare, poverty, urban affairs, and population.	*Includes formation and debate of U.S. foreign and defense policies, veterans affairs, and defense spending. (Relations with specific foreign countries are usually found under the region concerned.)*	*Includes business, labor, agriculture, taxation, transportation, consumer affairs, monetary and fiscal policy, natural resources, pollution and industrial accidents.*	*Includes worldwide scientific, medical and technological developments, natural phenomena, U.S. weather and natural disasters.*	*Includes the arts, religion, scholarship, communications media, sports, entertainment, fashions, fads, and social life.*

	World Affairs	Europe	Africa & The Middle East	The Americas	Asia & The Pacific
Jan. 8	The Comintern (Communist International) announces that its efforts in building organizations in France and Germany has made a great deal of progress.	The Portuguese government promises that it will reconsider its decree forbidding the importation of any cars manufactured outside of Portugal....There is significant opposition to Benito Mussolini in the Italian Parliament as a bloc known as the Aventine Opposition announces it will boycott the Parliament.			
Jan. 9	Economist John Maynard Keynes suggests that the United States and Britain restructure the war debt plans to make it easier for France and Italy to pay.	Italian government forces raid Communist organizations said to be planning an armed revolt....Adolf Joffe, Soviet Ambassador to Austria states that the Balkan states are threatening the Soviet Union to solidify their internal political control.			A severe earthquake strikes Tokyo, followed by a series of severe aftershocks; there is little damage.
Jan. 10	An agreement is reached that will allow France, Italy, and Belgium to pass their reparations money from Germany directly to the United States to pay their war debts.	The post-war political unit of France-Saarland is formed....As part of a crackdown on opposition, the Yugoslav government arrests large numbers of ethnic Croats, Germans, and Hungarians....Germans observe a day of mourning to protest the failure of the Allies to withdraw their occupation troops from the German city of Cologne....Romanian labor unions accuse the government of actively suppressing the workers.	The first radio station in Turkey is installed with plans to commence broadcasting at the end of the month.		Japanese Premier Kato Takaaki is the object of an unsuccessful assassination attempt.
Jan. 11		The first French Ambassador arrives to open the embassy in the Soviet Union.			In the latest development in the Chinese Civil War, the city of Shanghai is seized by a rebel army.
Jan. 12		Benito Mussolini introduces a bill into Parliament aimed at making the Masons illegal but which includes all organizations that might be considered "secret."... French reports claim that literature for children in the occupied Rhineland is being distributed to German children to regard France as their enemy....The Soviet government states that in the forthcoming elections opposition parties will be allowed as long as they do not clash with the Soviet government's general policy.	Howard Carter succeeds in negotiating an agreement from the Egyptian government concerning how the artifacts are to be split up and is now ready to renew his excavations at Luxor.		American warships are sent from Manila to Shanghai to protect foreigners in that city.
Jan. 13		The French government warns the Soviet government that it must stop ordering French Communists to spread anti-government propaganda....The skeleton of a German aviator killed in World War I, is found in France, the latest in many discoveries that continue to be made.	The French government announces that it will no longer sentence military prisoners to convict camps in North Africa but will imprison them in France instead....Dr. Chaim Weizmann in a speech describing Zionist colonization in Palestine announces that 2,000 Jews arrive there each month....Sir Leonard Wooley, excavating at Ur in Mesoptamia describes finding the remnants of business accounts scratched on clay tablets.		
Jan. 14		Italian Communists, ending a two-year boycott of Parliament, as part on increased opposition to Benito Mussolini....The German government announces that a new cabinet has been formed with a majority being made up of Nationalists and right-wing politicians.		Orders are prepared for the last American Army unit in Nicaragua to return to the United States indicating the end of the American intervention in that country.	

A	B	C	D	E
Includes developments that affect more than one world region, international organizations and important meetings of world leaders.	*Includes all domestic and regional developments in Europe, including the Soviet Union.*	*Includes all domestic and regional developments in Africa and the Middle East.*	*Includes all domestic and regional developments in Latin America, the Caribbean, and Canada.*	*Includes all domestic and regional developments in Asian and Pacific nations (and colonies).*

U.S. Politics & Social Issues	U.S. Foreign Policy & Affairs, Defense	U.S. Economy & Environment	Science, Technology & Nature	Culture, Leisure & Lifestyle	
Dr. John Locke of Denver Colorado, Grand Dragon of the Ku Klux Klan, is arrested on charges of kidnapping and conspiracy.	The U.S. Navy Board announces its future sea policy placing more emphasis on aircraft and submarines while keeping the battleship as the key component.		Professor Albert Michelson of the University of Chicago announces the recently concluded experiments provide a confirmation of Albert Einstein's theory of relativity.	Romanian composer Georges Enesco arrives in the United States to begin a tour....American painter George Bellows dies.	Jan. 8
			Scientists at the American Museum of Natural History state that the Japanese beetle, which has been in America for only a few years, might become one of the worst insect infestations.	American songwriter Irving Berlin states that Jazz is true American folk music and will eventually be sung in opera houses.	Jan. 9
The Kansas supreme court issues a writ banning the Ku Klux Klan in that state....The Chicago Crime Commission announces that the year 1924 saw a dramatic rise in the crime over the previous year.					Jan. 10
In a trend that is tied to Prohibition, Chicago Health Commissioner Hermann Bundesen states that 390 people in that city died of alcohol poisoning in 1924.	Secretary of State Charles Evans Hughes resigns; President Calvin Coolidge nominates Frank Kellogg to replace him.		The Field Museum of Chicago announces that it will send out 14 expeditions in 1925 to include to Peru, Bolivia, and Mongolia.	French Composer, organist, and teacher Nadia Boulanger appears at the first of several concerts she will give in the United States.... Russian Bass Feodor Chaliapin gives a concert at New York's Metropolitan Opera House.	Jan. 11
U.S. Senator William Borah in a speech urges his fellow Republicans to honor their election pledges and to create a program to aid farmers.			The most powerful railroad engine in Europe, designed and built in France, is tested and reaches speeds of 75 miles per hour.	Austrian conductor and composer Richard Strauss announces he will return to Vienna to run the University of Music and the Vienna Opera.	Jan. 12
	The U.S. submarine, S-19, runs aground in a storm off the Massachusetts coast; the crew is rescued.		A radio listener in France succeeds in talking to other radio operators on five continents in one day.		Jan. 13
A congressional committee begins a public investigation into what must be done to develop American commercial aviation which is currently less developed here than in Europe.			Obsolete planes are purposely crashed at Wilbur Wright field in Ohio; films are made of the crashes to assist in developing safety features.		Jan. 14

F	G	H	I	J
Includes campaigns, elections, federal-state relations, civil rights and liberties, crime, the judiciary, education, healthcare, poverty, urban affairs, and population.	Includes formation and debate of U.S. foreign and defense policies, veterans affairs, and defense spending. (Relations with specific foreign countries are usually found under the region concerned.)	Includes business, labor, agriculture, taxation, transportation, consumer affairs, monetary and fiscal policy, natural resources, pollution and industrial accidents.	Includes worldwide scientific, medical and technological developments, natural phenomena, U.S. weather and natural disasters.	Includes the arts, religion, scholarship, communications media, sports, entertainment, fashions, fads, and social life.

	World Affairs	Europe	Africa & The Middle East	The Americas	Asia & The Pacific
Jan. 15	The Soviet Union announces that it expects diplomatic recognition by the United States, a story denied by the U.S. government....The League of Nations attempts to resolve a conflict between Poland and the Free City of Danzig; Poland claims that it has the right to operate a postal service within the city and threatens to invade to exercise that right.	Fascist and anti-Fascist forces through out Italy continue to riot in the streets; the University of Naples is closed in response to fighting there.	Howard Carter states that he may need up to two years to complete taking all artifacts out of the tomb of Tut-ankh-Amon.	The Mexican government announces that it will sponsor extensive excavations of Maya sites in Yucatan.	U.S. forces land in the Chinese city of Shanghai to protect American citizens.
Jan. 16		Leon Trotsky is removed from his position as Commisar for War by Josef Stalin....Benito Mussolini's position is upheld by a large majority in a confidence vote in the Italian Parliament....The Soviet government begins a purge of college students and government officials with ties to landowners or opposition political groups....The French Parliament consider a measure that would make it illegal for Deputies to assault each other while in session....The German government announces that nearly half of its revenues go to paying veteran pensions and benefits from World War I.		Mexico's Minister of Foreign Relations denies that there are bad relations with Nicaragua.	
Jan. 17		American archaeologists find the remains of a Greek colonial town in Spain....France and Germany agree to a trade agreement that will avoid high tariffs.		Nicaragua opens its first radio station....An attempted coup against the Brazilian government is stopped....The Dean of McGill University in Montreal reassures a meeting of the Canada Society that there is no sentiment in the United States to annex Canada.	Three additional American warships are ordered to reinforce the naval force stationed near Shanghai.
Jan. 18		The German government reports that the number of unemployed grew by 31,289 in one month raising the total to 458,125....Five men and one woman, alleged to be members of the Irish Republican Army are arrested for attempting to blow up British warships.	The Persian Minister of the Interior and other officials are arrested on suspicion of aiding the Soviets....The Spanish Air Force bombs Moorish rebels in Spanish Morocco.		
Jan. 19		Benito Mussolini and King Victory Emmanuel attend the memorial service of composer Giacomo Puccini who died the previous month....Britain's *X-1*, the largest submarine in the world at 350 feet in length, completes a series of performance tests.			
Jan. 20		The League of Nations assumes responsibility for supervising the German Navy.		U.S. Secretary of State Charles Evans Hughes declares that the Monroe Doctrine of protecting the hemisphere does not mean that the United States wants to rule Latin America and that the burden of hemispheric defense should be shared by those countries.	The Japanese and Soviet governments restore diplomatic relations and recognize the treaties ending the Russo-Japanese War of 1904–05....The British agree to recognize Chinese sovereignty with the Anglo-Chinese Treaty of Peking.
Jan. 21		A Yugoslav court clears Croatian leader Stefan Raditch and others of being illegally detained. Yugoslav government indicates it will re-arrest these opposition leaders upon their release....The National Assembly of Albania proclaims that the country is now a republic....At ceremonies on the first anniversary of Vladimir I. Lenin's death, Leon Trotsky who has been removed from his earlier posts is attacked by name.		The U.S. Senate ratifies a treaty with the Dominican Republic to evacuate U.S. soldiers that have been performing peacekeeping duties there.	Japan recognizes the Soviet Union.

A	B	C	D	E
Includes developments that affect more than one world region, international organizations and important meetings of world leaders.	Includes all domestic and regional developments in Europe, including the Soviet Union.	Includes all domestic and regional developments in Africa and the Middle East.	Includes all domestic and regional developments in Latin America, the Caribbean, and Canada.	Includes all domestic and regional developments in Asian and Pacific nations (and colonies).

U.S. Politics & Social Issues	U.S. Foreign Policy & Affairs, Defense	U.S. Economy & Environment	Science, Technology & Nature	Culture, Leisure & Lifestyle	
			Francis Jenkins, an inventor, announces plans to develop the ability to transmit movies over the airwaves similar to radio, using what he terms "radio vision."	A controversy heats up between owners of U.S. baseball teams who want the government to directly run professional baseball and those opposed to it.	Jan. 15
	The U.S. Army Air Force stationed in the Philippines begins its largest series of maneuvers which will last for 10 days to practice an aerial defense of the islands.	Eighty cities on the Great Lakes denounce the city of Chicago for its failure to install a new sewage system that would not lower the levels of Lake Michigan.		Reports from Paris indicate that very short ("bobbed") hair is falling out of fashion.	Jan. 16
The Coast Guard reports that iceboats with sails capable of reaching high speeds are being used extensively to smuggle from Canada to the United States along the Great Lakes....Senator James Wadsworth of New York states that he is opposed to an Equal Rights Amendment for women to be added to the Constitution.	At a meeting of American news editors, Calvin Coolidge announces that the "The business of America is business."	American banks announce that they will make a $50 million loan to the Polish government....The Department of the Interior announces that that logging in the National Parks in 1923 exceeded any previous year's total....A sharp advance in stock prices on Wall Street is greeted as good news although not universally seen as the beginning of a trend toward generally higher prices.		The New York Times reviews the new novel by Thomas Mann, The Magic Mountain....A new book of drawings by the French author and artist, Jean Cocteau is published.	Jan. 17
				Spanish cellist Pablo Casals gives a concert in New York's Town Hall....The U.S. Commerce Department reports that the number of woman smokers has increased 400 percent in the last 10 years.	Jan. 18
The Commissioner General of Immigration reports to Congress that approximately 20,000 Europeans are currently in Cuba, looking for an opportunity to enter the United States illegally.	The first metal amphibian plane to be manufactured is delivered to the U.S. Army Air Corps.				Jan. 19
The U.S. Senate condemns the leasing of U.S. Navy oil fields, the main cause of the Teapot Dome scandal.		The Department of Commerce announces that the United States leads the world in the consumption of cotton, averaging 30 pounds per person.		A group of American writers and composers appears before a Congressional committee asking that copyright protection be extended to the lifetime of the author plus 50 years....The French national Tourist Office announces that a record number of Americans (135,000) visited France in 1923.	Jan. 20
					Jan. 21

F
Includes campaigns, elections, federal-state relations, civil rights and liberties, crime, the judiciary, education, healthcare, poverty, urban affairs, and population.

G
Includes formation and debate of U.S. foreign and defense policies, veterans affairs, and defense spending. (Relations with specific foreign countries are usually found under the region concerned.)

H
Includes business, labor, agriculture, taxation, transportation, consumer affairs, monetary and fiscal policy, natural resources, pollution and industrial accidents.

I
Includes worldwide scientific, medical and technological developments, natural phenomena, U.S. weather and natural disasters.

J
Includes the arts, religion, scholarship, communications media, sports, entertainment, fashions, fads, and social life.

	World Affairs	Europe	Africa & The Middle East	The Americas	Asia & The Pacific
Jan. 22		Aviator, poet, and leader of the Italian seizure of the city of Fiume, Gabriele D'Annunzio is rewarded by the King of Italy with a villa near Rome.		Formal relations are reestablished between the United States and Honduras.	
Jan. 23					
Jan. 24		Bavaria reaches a formal agreement with the Vatican concerning schools in the German state; the agreement is criticized by many in Germany because it was reached without the consent of the Federal German government.		Currently ruling military junta of Chile is overthrown by a group of Army officers who promise democratic reforms.	Another earthquake strikes Tokyo.
Jan. 25		The German government expresses alarm at the possibility of the Polish Army entering and occupying the free city of Danzig....Irish political leader Eamon de Valera protests the planned visit of the Prince of Wales to the Irish Free State.	The Turkish Republic declares that all foreign diplomats must have their residences in the new capital of Ankara instead of Constantinople which had formerly been the capital....A French aerial exploration completes the first leg of its journey, landing in the Sahara its first stop.		
Jan. 26		The Yugoslav government launches a wide-ranging offensive against opposition political parties.	Elections to the parliament of British-run are postponed owing to a list of 10 million registered voters in a population of three million.		A British aviator lands at Darjeeling with the intent to perform a survey of possible air routes over the Himalayas.
Jan. 27		In response to a query by the League of Nations, the Greek government states that its naval armament program aims not to expand but to modernize already existing levels.	The Turkish government issues a law requiring all government employees to wear only clothes made in Turkey....The League of Nations reports that all ethnic Greeks have now left Turkey.	The U.S. Public Health Service, in response to an outbreak of diphtheria in Nome, Alaska, orders one million units of medication.	Representatives of several Western nations inform the Chinese government of its responsibilities to protect all foreigners residing in China....The British government defends its policies concerning opium, noting the opium eating is not abused in India more than drinking in some countries.
Jan. 28		Stripped of his war minister portfolio, Leon Trotsky leaves Moscow for southern Russia for medical treatment.		Dog sled teams that will haul diphtheria medication to Nome, leave Anchorage in the first stage of the journey.	
Jan. 29		The Irish government sends aid to western Ireland where poor harvests for two years and a particularly bad potato crop have caused severe hardship....Political prisoners held in the Lubianka prison in Moscow stage a revolt which is broken after suffering many casualties....The League of Nations reports that many Germans are migrating to the Sarre region with the idea of eventually making the area German once again when a plebiscite is held in 1936.			There is rioting in Shanghai as victorious troops in the civil war attempt to disarm their adversaries.
Jan. 30		Winston Churchill (chancellor of the Exchequer) and First Sea Lord David Beatty openly clash on the subject of reducing Naval expenditures.	The government of the Turkish Republic exiles Constantine VI, the Greek Orthodox Patriarch of Constantinople....The former Premier of Egypt protests to the British government that their policies will result in an eventual separation of Egypt and Sudan.	While dog sled teams continue to bring diphtheria medication to Nome, Alaska, the epidemic becomes worse....The bones of prehistoric mammals and human remains are found in southern Argentina.	British authorities raid Communist Party offices in Cawnpore, India, confiscating copies of their newspaper.

A	B	C	D	E
Includes developments that affect more than one world region, international organizations and important meetings of world leaders.	Includes all domestic and regional developments in Europe, including the Soviet Union.	Includes all domestic and regional developments in Africa and the Middle East.	Includes all domestic and regional developments in Latin America, the Caribbean, and Canada.	Includes all domestic and regional developments in Asian and Pacific nations (and colonies).

U.S. Politics & Social Issues	U.S. Foreign Policy & Affairs, Defense	U.S. Economy & Environment	Science, Technology & Nature	Culture, Leisure & Lifestyle	
				A French medical student is expelled from school when it is discovered he was wearing a wireless radio set that allowed his girl friend to broadcast answers to him....New York theater producer, Lee Shubert, states that the novelty of radio will wear off and people will return to theaters in large numbers.	Jan. 22
Former Presidential candidate William Jennings Bryan states that neither Republican nor Democratic parties have dealt with the nation's vital interests.		The Burroughs Adding Machine Company wins a suit against the National Cash Register Company in a patent case revolving around which company first invented the adding machine.		Doctor Sigmund Freud turns down an offer from Samuel Goldwyn to make movies....Several Seventh Day Adventist groups predict that the world will end on February 6,1925.	Jan. 23
The Internal Revenue Service issues a statement warning taxpayers to be careful not to overpay their income tax....Chicago gangster Johnnie Torrio is shot and killed in the latest occurrence of a gang war in Chicago that has been going on for two months.	The U.S. House of Representatives raises the money limit for the construction of two aircraft carriers to $34 million each.		A total eclipse of the sun occurs, visible through most of North America....The largest group of U.S. aircraft since World War I takes off from an airfield in New York to make observations.	Champion swimmer Johnny Weismuller completes the 150 yard freestyle, cutting a full second off his world record for that event.	Jan. 24
			A French military pilot breaks the aerial speed record for 500 kilometers.		Jan. 25
				Author Booth Tarkington wins a lawsuit brought against him for plagiarism.	Jan. 26
				The German silent film, *The Last Laugh*, is shown in New York City.	Jan. 27
The American Federation of Labor and other labor organizations state that they will continue the fight to get child labor laws passed.		U.S. gas prices rise as both stockpiles and production drop; prices of petroleum stocks advance....US Steel announces it will no longer manufacture horseshoes.			Jan. 28
House Republicans ban members of the party who label themselves as "Progressive" from the party caucus.	The second American submarine in a month, the *S-48*, runs aground off the New Hampshire coast.				Jan. 29
	The crew of the *S-48* is rescued by the Coast Guard....The *S-19*, grounded since January 13 is still aground.	Radio Corporation of America announces that its gross income doubled to $54,848,131 in 1924 compared to 1923.	William Easton of the Westinghouse Electric and Manufacturing predicts that the spread of radio will one day make English the world's universal language.	Kentucky cave explorer Floyd Collins becomes trapped while exploring Sand Cave....All American halfback Harold (Red) Grange turns down an offer to make movies at a $2,000 a week salary.	Jan. 30

F	G	H	I	J
Includes campaigns, elections, federal-state relations, civil rights and liberties, crime, the judiciary, education, healthcare, poverty, urban affairs, and population.	Includes formation and debate of U.S. foreign and defense policies, veterans affairs, and defense spending. (Relations with specific foreign countries are usually found under the region concerned.)	Includes business, labor, agriculture, taxation, transportation, consumer affairs, monetary and fiscal policy, natural resources, pollution and industrial accidents.	Includes worldwide scientific, medical and technological developments, natural phenomena, U.S. weather and natural disasters.	Includes the arts, religion, scholarship, communications media, sports, entertainment, fashions, fads, and social life.

	World Affairs	Europe	Africa & The Middle East	The Americas	Asia & The Pacific
Jan. 31		From Berlin there are reports that the famine in the Soviet Union is so bad that farmers are locking themselves and their families in buildings and burning them down....An influenza epidemic in Britain has resulted in 200 deaths in the past week....Plans to reduce the Italian Defense budget are defeated in Parliament.	Prince Habib Lotfallah, Arabia's envoy to Europe states that all of the Arab nations between Egypt, Persia, and Turkey must unite into one nation.	The U.S. Secretary of the Navy states that the Navy cannot provide either a surface ship or aircraft that would succeed in getting the medication to Nome.	
Feb. 1	The Turkish government indicates that it may expel more Greek Church officials as mass demonstrations are held in Athens protesting the expulsion of the Patriarch from Turkey....The British government announces that it is likely that the Allied governments will have to intervene in the current Turkish-Greek crisis....The British Foreign Secretary states that unrest in France and Italy coupled with Germany's response to the Allied failure to end its occupation of Cologne have unsettled the general political atmosphere in Europe.	The German government reports that its balance of trade for the year 1924 was unfavorable with imports greatly exceeding exports....Poor harvests in the Balkan states in 1924 have forced the importation of wheat into those countries at double previous prices....The Soviet government announces that it will set aside areas in the Crimea for the purpose of establishing Soviet Jewish colonies....Reports from Vienna indicate that the earthquake that struck Hungary on January 31 was more serious than previously thought.	In Egypt, the tomb of Pharaoh Shepses-ka-f is discovered....In addition to fighting the Spaniards in Morocco, the Moors under Abd-el-Krim are fighting other tribes; reports indicate that the former warlord Raisuli and his followers have been captured by the Moors.		An organization called the Revolutionary Party distributes pamphlets calling for the violent establishment of a Communist government appears in several cities in India and Burma....Dr. Sun Yat-sen, leader of South China, recently hospitalized for liver cancer is reported to be much weaker....A military conference opens in Beijing to discuss disarming the various factions currently fighting.
Feb. 2		The French government closes the Vatican Embassy as part of its anti-Catholic clergy policy.			
Feb. 3	The Turkish government announces it will not submit its expulsion of the Greek Patriarch to the World Court for arbitration.	The French government issues statements to contradict rumors in Germany that graves of German soldiers killed in France during World War I have been neglected and vandalized....Sir Philip Dawson, a British politician returns from a tour of the Russian borderland and states that the men running the current Soviet government are the "most unscrupulous set of individuals the world had ever seen."	Spanish forces are actively on campaign in Spanish Morocco while local tribes appear to be joining together to resist them.... The Nilometer, a column in Cairo built in the 8th century c.e. to measure the depth of the Nile is sinking, prompting a committee to be named to attempt to save it.	The situation is tense in Chile as political opposition to the former President Arturo Allesandri, who relies upon a large working class political base, is planning to resort to violence upon his return.	The Indian Legislative Assembly passes a bill for reciprocal action against the United States and other nations that treat Indian nationals as inferiors.
Feb. 4	The League of Nations opens a major health conference in the city of Singapore to coordinate efforts at fighting disease in Asia....The Turkish government protests to the League of Nations in the drawing up of the boundary between Turkey and the province of Mosul in Northern Iraq.	The Polish Senate ratifies an agreement consolidating its war debt to the United States....The Italian government orders the commencement of tests to determine the feasibility of archaeological excavations at the Circus Maximus, in Rome....Germany announces that it will resume trade talks with France.	Primary elections are held in Egypt with only a minimal amount of rioting in one city.	Brazilian coffee growers express concern about the economic consequences of a rumored American coffee boycott.	
Feb. 5	The U.S. Senate passes an amendment to the yearly Naval bill that will lead the way to an international Naval Arms conference....The Polish government protests against the League of Nations decision that there can be only one official Polish mail station in the free port city of Danzig.	Fifteen earthquakes, some of them severe, are recorded in Norway....Reports from the Soviet Union indicate uprisings on the part of peasants against Soviet tax collectors....The Soviet Union announces that it will expel from the party and all governmental positions anyone adhering to the ideas of Leon Trotsky....Unemployment in Austria reaches 290,000 an all-time high since the end of World War I.	The French Army sends reinforcements to French Morocco to prevent the Spanish actions against the Moors to create destabilization in their own area....Moorish chief Abd-el-Krim marries the daughter of his rival, Raisuli, as part of his efforts to unite all natives in the area against the Spanish....A large belt of platinum ore is discovered in South Africa.	Canada registers with the League of Nations a fisheries treaty it signed with the United States; by registering it independently of Britain, Canada indicates the level of independence it has assumed as a country.	The Civil War in China continues as forces under General Chen Chiung-Ming begin an assault on the city of Canton....Representatives of Dr. Sun Yat-sen's party, the Kuomintang, announce that they will withdraw from the Chinese Unification Conference because no provision has been made for a "people's conference" to be held....News that the U.S. Senate has approved a measure that will make a Naval Armaments Conference possible is greeted enthusiastically by Japan.

A	B	C	D	E
Includes developments that affect more than one world region, international organizations and important meetings of world leaders.	Includes all domestic and regional developments in Europe, including the Soviet Union.	Includes all domestic and regional developments in Africa and the Middle East.	Includes all domestic and regional developments in Latin America, the Caribbean, and Canada.	Includes all domestic and regional developments in Asian and Pacific nations (and colonies).

U.S. Politics & Social Issues	U.S. Foreign Policy & Affairs, Defense	U.S. Economy & Environment	Science, Technology & Nature	Culture, Leisure & Lifestyle	
				Serge Kousevitsky leads the Boston Symphony Orchestra in a premier of Modest Mussorgsky's *Pictures at an Exhibition* in an orchestration by the French composer Maurice Ravel....Boxer Jack Dempsey announces that he has not retired and intends to fight again, to defend the title of world's heavyweight boxing champion....Babe Ruth leaves New York for a four-week visit to a spa in Arkansas before beginning spring training.	Jan. 31
A mass meeting on the anniversary of Vladimir I. Lenin's death attracts 15,000 participants in New York City....The number of deaths in the diphtheria epidemic in Nome, Alaska, reaches 100; Medication is on the way but storms have prevented communication to determine where the sled teams are.	Secretary of Navy Curtis Wilbur states that predictions that cities will be destroyed by aerial bombs are ridiculous and that the next war will involve "comparatively few people."	The U.S. Agriculture Department predicts that 1925 will be a good year for farmers although that trend may not continue.	Scientists report that heavier than usual snowfall and extremely cold temperatures are keeping deer in Alaska from moving to their usual feeding grounds with the result that many are starving.	A group of at least 200 men have arrived at Sand Cave, Kentucky, in an attempt to free cave explorer, Floyd Collins....The American National Baseball League celebrates its 50th anniversary at its annual meeting of club owners....A commission admits that St. Paul's Cathedral in London is in need of repairs but rumors that it is in danger of collapse are untrue.	Feb. 1
Andrew Volstead (creator of the act creating Prohibition) announces that he approves of the addition of jail time in addition to fines for violating the act.	Testifying before Congress, admirals attack the plan of creating a unified American Air Force as is proposed by General Billy Mitchell.	The Burley Tobacco Growers Association announces that American Tobacco companies have just purchased 60 million pounds of tobacco in one of the largest sales ever recorded.		Rescuers in Cave City, KY, have failed to rescue Floyd Collins and are now bringing in machinery in an attempt to pull him out from where he is stuck with his foot pinned.	Feb. 2
Newark NJ attempts to schedule the opening and closing of factory shifts in an effort to prevent traffic congestion....Sled driver Gunnar Kasson arrives in Nome, AK, with diphtheria medication, crediting his lead dog, Balto with the success. Completing a 650 mile run, delivering the first 35,000 of 300,000 units....An election in Anaheim, California, recalls all city trustees affiliated with the Ku Klux Klan....It is announced that while a special session of Congress will be convened on Inauguration day (March 4) to confirm President Calvin Coolidge's cabinet nominations.		A raise in wholesale and retail gas prices is announced bringing prices to their highest level since 1923; wholesale prices are now 19 cents a gallon.	American Roy Chapman Andrews completes negotiations with the Mongolian government to conduct another expedition to find dinosaur fossils....Sir Leonard Wooley discovers in Mesopotamia the remnants of a school and museum dating to approximately 500 B.C.E....Two French airmen leave Paris by plane to fly to Dakar in Western Africa to set a new record for non-stop flight.	Representatives of the music industry testify in Congress against a proposed copyright bill, accusing modern composers of plagiarism citing the resemblance of *Yes We Have No Bananas* to Handel's *Halleluiah Chorus*....West Virginia takes disciplinary action against woman students caught smoking....A French scientist announces that he has found a way to distinguish natural from cultivated pearls, earlier a French court had decreed that they were not as valuable.	Feb. 3
Police in Nashville, Tennessee, are called in to suppress a demonstration by African-American students protesting the actions of the President of Fisk University....While no new diphtheria cases have been reported in Nome, Alaska, an additional one million units of diphtheria medication are being shipped to that city.	The Secretary of the Navy begins motions to remove Rear Admiral William Moffett, the Navy's Chief of aviation from his position as he is considered too progressive and had advanced opinions about aviation similar to those of General Billy Mitchell.	The General Electric Company pays out $1 million bonus to all employees who have served five years or more.	The North Sea has eroded nearly all of the land near the German town of Hohenneuendorff while not far away currents are in the process of creating a new island on the German coast.	French aviators are forced to land almost 500 miles short of their objective in Dakar due to fuel problems....The U.S. Bureau of Mines sends engineers to assist in the attempts to rescue Floyd Collins.	Feb. 4
In the state of Missouri, 45 doctors who have been found to have fraudulent diplomas will lose their licenses to practice medicine.	A House of Representative committee announces that it will question General Billy Mitchell on his views as to the importance and usefulness of air power.	A dam in Oregon bursts as the result of flooding causing over $250,000 in losses.		Rescuers still have not yet pulled Floyd Collins from Sand Cave; some rescuers express the fear that he may be dead. Work now focuses on digging a shaft from the hillside to Collins, bypassing where a slide sealed him off.... Two French aviators, who were unable to make a nonstop flight from Paris to Dakar, finally reach their destination....Robert Reidt, of Patchogue, NY, who had predicted the end of the world on February 6, announces that the end may occur a week later than he thought.	Feb. 5

F	G	H	I	J
Includes campaigns, elections, federal-state relations, civil rights and liberties, the judiciary, education, healthcare, poverty, urban affairs, and population.	*Includes formation and debate of U.S. foreign and defense policies, veterans affairs, and defense spending. (Relations with specific foreign countries are usually found under the region concerned.)*	*Includes business, labor, agriculture, taxation, transportation, consumer affairs, monetary and fiscal policy, natural resources, pollution and industrial accidents.*	*Includes worldwide scientific, medical and technological developments, natural phenomena, U.S. weather and natural disasters.*	*Includes the arts, religion, scholarship, communications media, sports, entertainment, fashions, fads, and social life.*

	World Affairs	Europe	Africa & The Middle East	The Americas	Asia & The Pacific
Feb. 6	The United States withdraws from participation in the World Opium Conference because opium-producing nations will not agree to controls over the distribution of raw opium.	The German government states that it is not secretly creating an air force in violation of the Versailles treaty....The Soviet Union announces that it will initiate rail service from Riga, Latvia to Vladivostok on Russia's Pacific coast....Romania states that it should not pay its war debts to the United States and Britain until its reparations for damages have been paid by Germany and Austria.		The President of Mexico announces that all authorities in Mexico will step up their activities to curb drug trafficking.	
Feb. 7		Germany states that it will not assume liability for damages that Romania claims as a result of World War I....The Italian government announces that the last year's harvest will be sufficient to meet the nation's needs....Voters in Serbia are to decide whether the confederated Yugoslav nation will remain or if a Greater Serbia will come into existence....Irish government officials deny that crop failures in western Ireland have resulted in famine and deaths.... The current leader of the Soviet State Police is assigned responsibilities as second in command of both Army and Navy.	Leonard Wooley, finding evidence of war in the excavated city of Ur in Iraq, speculates that war and the capture of the city may have caused the prophet Abraham to leave that region....Three Communists are arrested in French Tunisia resulting in reprisal attacks on French authorities.... The Turkish government suspends talks for air service between Italy and Turkey unless the route is direct and does not have a stop in Greece.		The Maharaja of Nepal decrees an end to slavery.
Feb. 8	As the Turkish-Greek crisis continues, Greek Army troops are rumored to be concentrating on the Turkish-Greek border.	The heaviest vote in Yugoslavia results in a win for the Serbian Party of Premier Pasic, defeating Croatian nationalists as well as Communists and Socialists....The Soviet government sentences seven factory managers for corruption and mismanagement.... Unrest continues in rural villages in the Soviet Union as Soviet government observers in the villages are attacked....Soviet leaders acknowledge a problem but refuse to consider sharing power with the peasants.			The Soviet government announces the finds made by an archaeological expedition in Mongolia the previous year, particularly many artifacts unearthed from burial places.
Feb. 9	The Prime Minister of Greece states that because Turkey has refused arbitration in the current crisis that he will take his nation's case to the League of Nations.	Josef Stalin grants what is probably his first interview with a reporter and states that Germany will not see a Socialist revolt against the government....The Comintern announces that it will be sending a grant of 1,500,000 francs to assist the French Communist Party.	Most of the Riff Army which is fighting against the Spanish Army in Morocco is concentrated against the new Spanish defensive lines....Estimated Spanish losses the retreat to their new lines in Morocco are set at 5,500, 2,000 of them prisoners of war.		
Feb. 10	The Italian government announces that a direct transoceanic cable has been completed between Italy and the United States.	Rioting in the French Port of Marseilles between Catholics and Communists results in two dead and 100 injured....Reports from Moscow indicate that the state police have shot a largest than normal number of accused former Czarists....The personal train Leon Trotsky used on missions throughout the Soviet Union is broken up and the cars dispatched to Soviet railroads, another sign that Trotsky's position in the Soviet Union is no longer significant.	The Premier of Persia addresses the national Assembly stating that it must choose between himself and the Shah as the nation's leader.	The United States and Canada sign a fishing rights treaty....The Mexican government's Treasury Department states that for the first time in the current administration it has a surplus and has been able to cover all government salaries.	Japan formally states that it does not consider the current U.S. naval maneuvers in the Pacific to be a threat, also stating that the proposed British naval base in Singapore would have an effect on Japan but would probably not be a threat.

A	B	C	D	E
Includes developments that affect more than one world region, international organizations and important meetings of world leaders.	*Includes all domestic and regional developments in Europe, including the Soviet Union.*	*Includes all domestic and regional developments in Africa and the Middle East.*	*Includes all domestic and regional developments in Latin America, the Caribbean, and Canada.*	*Includes all domestic and regional developments in Asian and Pacific nations (and colonies).*

U.S. Politics & Social Issues	U.S. Foreign Policy & Affairs, Defense	U.S. Economy & Environment	Science, Technology & Nature	Culture, Leisure & Lifestyle	
	General Billy Mitchell testifies to Congress that U.S. air forces rank fifth in the world and the fault lies with the Secretaries of the Navy and War....Secretary of the Treasury Andrew Mellon states that Italy's war debt to the United States is $2,097,347,122.		An airplane is flown using a single piece propeller made of magnesium, most propellers at this time are made of wood.	College attendance in the United States rises by 8.5 percent over enrollments in the 1923–24 school year....Another rockslide increases the difficulties of the rescuers searching for Floyd Collins, additional soldiers are sent to keep order around the cave.	Feb. 6
Although no new outbreaks of diphtheria are being reported, additional units of medicine are being flown into the city.	U.S. submarine, S-48, is refloated and brought in for repairs at Portsmouth, NH.	Secretary of Commerce Herbert Hoover announces that the United States currently has 503 radio stations operating or under construction.	The Surgeon General of the United States announces that there may be signs of bubonic plague in New Orleans, Los Angeles, and Oakland....Scientists prepare for tests measuring earth temperature after an eclipse of the moon predicted to occur in the late afternoon.	Tests at Sand Cave indicate that the shaft being drilled will reach Floyd Collins....Nicholas John, King of the Gypsies of the United States is buried in a New York cemetery....Helena Normanton, a lawyer from Britain announces at a function in the United States that New England pie and American chicken could cure Bolshevism.... Robert Reidt continues his watch for the end of the world, attracting crowds of hundreds at his New York home, states that the end was delayed by the large amount of artificial lighting reporters and photographers had installed in front of his house.	Feb. 7
African-American activist and leader Marcus Garvey enters the Federal Penitentiary in Atlanta after being convicted of mail fraud....The United States Employment Service announces that it assisted 2 million Americans in getting jobs in 1924.		The London Times discusses the great extent to which American banks have invested in Germany which while it has helped German industry has caused some concern in Germany about the amount of debt owed to the United States.... The Department of Commerce announces that the United States exported $1 billion worth of food world wide in 1924.	A wireless operator in London succeeds in relaying a message to a Royal Geographical Society expedition exploring the Amazon.	There are now approximately 10,000 sightseers at Cave City, Kentucky, to watch the rescue efforts to retrieve Floyd Collins.... Violinist Fritz Kreisler performs to a standing room only crowd in Carnegie Hall....The opera Cavelleria Rusticana is broadcast on the radio....Results of a three-year experiment by Seattle High Schools in which students are grouped according to ability is reported as a great success....Roget's Thesaurus gains new popularity as a result of the cross word puzzle craze.	Feb. 8
	In a radio address General Billy Mitchell states that New York City is extremely vulnerable to destruction by air attack.			The President of the New Jersey Clothiers and Furnishers Association states the in the coming year men and women will wear light-colored clothing as a result of general prosperity and light-heartedness....Rescuers at Cave City still have not reached Floyd Collins; the Governor of Kentucky launches an investigation to determine whether Collins is actually in the cave.	Feb. 9
	President Calvin Coolidge states that he is against any policy of returning private German property seized by the United States during World War I....President Calvin Coolidge states that for reasons of economy, the inaugural parade and other festivities will be kept to a minimum.	A minor earthquake is reported in San Francisco.	Doctor William Beebe departs New York on the ship Arcturus to confirm the existence of the Sargasso Sea and investigate it vegetation and animal life....A 10,000 year-old shoulder blade from a mammoth is found in London....Astronomer Edwin Hubble is awarded the annual award from the American Association for the Advancement of Science.	Rescuers continue to dig a tunnel to reach Floyd Collins; the Lieutenant-Governor receives a telegram alleging that Collins has actually been kidnapped and is being held in Kansas.	Feb. 10

F	G	H	I	J
Includes campaigns, elections, federal-state relations, civil rights and liberties, crime, the judiciary, education, healthcare, poverty, urban affairs, and population.	Includes formation and debate of U.S. foreign and defense policies, veterans affairs, and defense spending. (Relations with specific foreign countries are usually found under the region concerned.)	Includes business, labor, agriculture, taxation, transportation, consumer affairs, monetary and fiscal policy, natural resources, pollution and industrial accidents.	Includes worldwide scientific, medical and technological developments, natural phenomena, U.S. weather and natural disasters.	Includes the arts, religion, scholarship, communications media, sports, entertainment, fashions, fads, and social life.

	World Affairs	Europe	Africa & The Middle East	The Americas	Asia & The Pacific
Feb. 11		The Austrian government announces that a plot exists to being back the Habsburgs to rule the country....Riots in Prague to protest the high cost of living are broken up by police who shoot at and wound eight....Catholic-Communist rioting continues in France, spreading to the city of Avignon....An explosion causes a collapse of a mine in Dortmund, Germany, trapping miners.			
Feb. 12	The League of Nations announces it will negotiate a settlement between Greece and Turkey in the current crisis originating in Turkey's expulsion of the Greek Patriarch.	Reports indicate that as many as 200 miners may have died in the mine cave-in at Dortmund, Germany.			
Feb. 13		The suicide rates in Vienna and Budapest continue to grow, averaging five deaths a day in each city; shortage of housing and the cost if living are given as the primary reasons....Benito Mussolini achieves a significant political victory as his proposed bill governing the national rules for national elections is passed by the Italian Senate....The Italian government states that the new agreement between Albania and Anglo-Persian oil company presents a danger to Italy's ability to have access to oil.	Using cavalry and airplanes, Italian troops in Tripoli, north Africa, launch a successful campaign against rebels....The Spanish outpost of Saasa in Morocco is captured by the Moor rebels.		
Feb. 14	France and Siam sign a treaty whereby France's previous rights in the area are waived and all disputes between the two nations will be submitted to arbitration....Reports indicate that as a result of the Naval Arms Limitation Treaties, the navies of Britain, France, the United States, Japan, and Italy are moving away from battleships and larger vessels that count against the limitations and designing and building small ships such as cruisers and destroyers.	Leon Trotsky is removed from his last post in the Soviet government, a fact announced overseas but not within the Soviet Union itself....Turkish Deputy Halid Pasha dies after having been shot by Deputy Ali Afium during a session of the National Assembly.	The Sultan of Morocco states that he believes that France will not allow the fighting in neighboring Spanish Morocco to affect his region.		
Feb. 15		It is announced in Moscow that a huge center for guests from Asia will open there in order to provide accommodations for visitors and to provide instruction in Communist practice and theory....Reports from the Soviet Union indicate that the harvest of 1924 decreased 11 percent from 1923....Political assassinations of Bulgarian politicians continue; the rise in violence is blamed on Communist and Macedonian nationalists....A new government is formed in Portugal after the previous government received a no-confidence vote by the Chamber of Deputies.	The Spanish government announces that its army in Morocco, using extensive machine gun and air support, has successfully repelled a series of attacks by the Moors.	Cuban and American officials hold a ceremony commemorating the sinking of the USS *Maine*, which had precipitated the Spanish American war of 1898.	
Feb. 16		Former German Ambassador to the United States, Count Johann Bernstorff, announces that Germany will probably enter the League of Nations within the next year.			

A	B	C	D	E
Includes developments that affect more than one world region, international organizations and important meetings of world leaders.	*Includes all domestic and regional developments in Europe, including the Soviet Union.*	*Includes all domestic and regional developments in Africa and the Middle East.*	*Includes all domestic and regional developments in Latin America, the Caribbean, and Canada.*	*Includes all domestic and regional developments in Asian and Pacific nations (and colonies).*

U.S. Politics & Social Issues	U.S. Foreign Policy & Affairs, Defense	U.S. Economy & Environment	Science, Technology & Nature	Culture, Leisure & Lifestyle	
The U.S. Congress officially counts the electoral ballots from the 1924 Presidential election and certifies that Calvin Coolidge is President of the United States				A revival of Eugene O'Neill's *The Emperor Jones* opens in New York starring Paul Robeson....Inventor Thomas A. Edison celebrates his 78th birthday as he is vacationing in Florida with Henry Ford.	Feb. 11
The Tennessee House of Representatives tables a bill that would forbid anyone from teaching who did not believe in God and Jesus Christ.	General Billy Mitchell testifies that because the Navy has neglected air power, it could be destroyed by almost any nation.			A Lincoln's birthday celebration is held in New York City includes both Confederate and Union veterans.	Feb. 12
		A thaw hits the northeast, casing floods throughout New England and New York as rivers reach flood tide.			Feb. 13
Documents found in Berlin, Germany, indicate that Comintern intends to begin a large campaign to provoke a Communist revolution in the United States...Former head of the International Workers of the World, "Big Bill" Haywood is reported to have returned to Chicago and will turn himself in to Federal officials; he had been convicted of attempting to obstruct the U.S. war effort.	At the Foreign Policy Luncheon American and Japanese speakers discuss the relations between the two countries and assert that war will not come largely because the United States will tend to defer to what ever Japan wants....The USS *Patoka*, tender ship for the Navy dirigible *Los Angeles* arrives in Bermuda, preparatory to the airship landing there.		Scotland Yard announces that its success in installing radios in police cars has been a great success.	The Commerce Department announces that the per capita consumption of coffee in the United States in 1924 was about 500 cups, a slight decrease from the previous year....Runner Paavo Nurmi runs two miles in eight minutes, 58 seconds, setting a new world's record.	Feb. 14
Republican senators, faced with the threat of a Democratic filibuster to prevent several of pieces President Calvin Coolidge's legislation are searching for strategies to pass the legislation before the session ends.			The French government begins experiments of flying bombers entirely by radio control with no crew members on board....The London Zoo announces it will install lights to diminish the effect of fog on the animals.	The Isabella Stewart Gardner Museum, a private residence converted to a public art gallery, opens for the first time in Boston.	Feb. 15
The last member of the party of Union soldiers who hunted down presidential assassin John Wilkes Booth dies....Congress approves a survey that will result in the creation of national parks in the Smoky Mountains of North Carolina, Virginia's Shenandoah Valley, and Mammoth Caves in Kentucky.				Would-be rescuers at Cave City, Kentucky, find Floyd Collins, apparently dead for at least 24 hours.... A 13-year-old in Pennsylvania dies in an abandoned mine in an attempt to imitate Collins.	Feb. 16

F	G	H	I	J
Includes campaigns, elections, federal-state relations, civil rights and liberties, crime, the judiciary, education, healthcare, poverty, urban affairs, and population.	Includes formation and debate of U.S. foreign and defense policies, veterans affairs, and defense spending. (Relations with specific foreign countries are usually found under the region concerned.)	Includes business, labor, agriculture, taxation, transportation, consumer affairs, monetary and fiscal policy, natural resources, pollution and industrial accidents.	Includes worldwide scientific, medical and technological developments, natural phenomena, U.S. weather and natural disasters.	Includes the arts, religion, scholarship, communications media, sports, entertainment, fashions, fads, and social life.

	World Affairs	Europe	Africa & The Middle East	The Americas	Asia & The Pacific
Feb. 17	Romania is expelling German citizens in its territory as reprisal for Germany's failure to pay Romania reparation for damage caused in the war.	Communist-inspired demonstrations continue in Czechoslovakia, a military force in the town of Losocz fires on the crowd, wounding 20....Airplanes are used to search for and drop food to three skiers lost in the Alps.	The Shah of Persia, vacationing in Nice France, refuses to answer messages from the Prime Minister.		
Feb. 18	Informal responses to President Calvin Coolidge's efforts to negotiate new Naval Treaties are beginning to indicate that France, Italy, Britain, and Japan may look at the proposals favorably....Italy sends a new envoy to the United States to discuss issues of resolving Italy's war debt, immigration, and dual citizenship.	Negotiations between the Italian government and Anglo-Persian Oil continue with the Italians hinting at an offer to allow Anglo-Persian to drill for oil in Italy in return for concessions in Albania....Anti-Semitic rioters in Budapest attack Jewish men and women in the street, killing one and injuring several.	The Shah of Persia indicates that he will assume command of all Persian forces and is invited by the government to take this job.	The Japanese Ambassador to America leaves home prepared to discuss the possibilities of new Naval Treaties with the United States as well as American immigration exclusion clauses aimed at Japanese businessmen.	
Feb. 19	The Turkish government sends more troops to the Greek Turkish border; discussions begin to renew a Turkish-Yugoslav defensive alliance....The Romanian government states that it would be interested in having the United States act as arbiter in its disputes with Germany....Official statements from France express skepticism of a new Naval Treaty, citing their concern that submarines should not be part of the negotiated tonnage amounts.	Josef Stalin, becoming more prominent as a spokesperson for the government states that to maintain order, the government may make concessions to the peasants similar to concessions made earlier under the New Economic Policy.			
Feb. 20	Italy requests that the Egyptian government to cede Oasis Jarabub, on Libya's eastern frontier; Egypt refuses.	The Bulgarian government expresses concern over the recent series of assassination of various politicians, Communist agitation....The British government states that it will begin decreasing both expenditures and the number of men in the British Army....Strikes against the Soviet government take place in the Urals, 40 strikers are killed, and detachments of state police are sent to quell the rebellion.			
Feb. 21		The Soviet Union begins investigating its personnel at embassies in an effort to remove all Trotsky sympathizers.	The Premier of the state of Transjordan is deposed in a coup although the king's position is untouched.		
Feb. 22		The British government acknowledges that while the cost of living did not change in the month of January, unemployment has risen....Raiders from Yugoslavia cross the border into Bulgaria and raid several towns.	The Moors attack several Spanish outposts in Morocco but are repulsed with heavy casualties.	The United States states that it will offer Mexico a "more than adequate supply of water" for irrigation in return for being able to construct a dam on the Colorado River.	
Feb. 23	Turkey accepts an invitation from the League of Nations to discuss a conference for the limitation of arms.	A gang posing as Allied representatives has claimed money from various German merchants claiming they were collecting war reparations....German President Friedrich Ebert is rushed to the hospital for appendicitis.	Official population returns indicate that 11,851 Jewish immigrants entered Palestine in 1924, the increase being three times the population growth in 1923.	One woman is killed and three are injured when a riot over rival Catholic factions breaks out in Mexico City.	Prime Minister Stanley Baldwin of Britain defends the decision to build a Royal Navy base in Singapore, stating that responsible opinion in Japan is not opposed.

A	B	C	D	E
Includes developments that affect more than one world region, international organizations and important meetings of world leaders.	*Includes all domestic and regional developments in Europe, including the Soviet Union.*	*Includes all domestic and regional developments in Africa and the Middle East.*	*Includes all domestic and regional developments in Latin America, the Caribbean, and Canada.*	*Includes all domestic and regional developments in Asian and Pacific nations (and colonies).*

U.S. Politics & Social Issues	U.S. Foreign Policy & Affairs, Defense	U.S. Economy & Environment	Science, Technology & Nature	Culture, Leisure & Lifestyle	
	The Navy Department certifies that it has scrapped 27 ships in to conform with the Naval Limitation Treaty....President Calvin Coolidge states that the United States will not recognize Russia and begin diplomatic relations.	A new type of locomotive that burns diesel oil instead of coal, halving the cost of fuel, is under development at the Baldwin Locomotive Works in Philadelphia.		Officials determine that the body of Floyd Collins cannot be brought up, the cave is sealed, and a funeral service is held outside.	Feb. 17
	A report is issued that states the Navy's policy that the battleship can successfully survive air attacks and will remain the backbone of the fleet and that in future wars, aviation will not be a critical factor at sea.		After a search of three years, naturalists from the American Museum of Natural History capture a pink headed duck in India....A 13-mile tunnel to channel flood waters to provide electrical power for the San Joaquin valley in California is completed.	Charles Ponzi, financier and inventor of the scheme to defraud that bears his name is on trial for defrauding investors of $9 million....The Anderson Aeroplane Corporation of New Jersey states that it will soon build aircraft capable of holding one person and selling for $400.....Italy reports that American tourists are the third largest group visiting behind Britain and France.	Feb. 18
The second strike in two days against garment manufacturers begins with more than 15,000 on strike for higher wages and recognition of the union.	The American-German Mixed Claims Commission decrees that five outstanding claims for the loss of loved ones, totaling 61,000 must be paid by Germany....Billy Mitchell continues his speeches on the need for airpower, stating that Japan could capture both Hawaii and the Philippines in two weeks and that efforts must be made to protect Alaska....Rear Admiral Charles Hughes reveals that when bombs were dropped in an attempt to sink two old battleships as a test that he and another officer had been on one of the ships to demonstrate their confidence that air power could not damage battleships.	According to the President of the Asiatic Petroleum Company, American drivers used more gasoline in August 1924 than were used in all of Britain for the whole year.	Henry Ford buys a set of tools formerly belonging to Thomas Edison that he will put on display in his planned museum in Michigan.	The National Safety Council announces that 20,00 people were killed in auto accidents in 1924, up from 5,000 in 1914; the report also goes on to say that there are 17,700,000 card registered in the United States, one for every 6.2 persons....The first day of a three-day annual international dog sled race in Quebec concludes.	Feb. 19
				New York District Attorney Joab Banton demands that producers rewrite or take plays off the stage in an attempt to censor language and content; the producer of Eugene O'Neill's Desire Under the Elms state that they will not close their production.	Feb. 20
The South Dakota House of Representatives defeats a bill that would allow women to sit on juries.	The Congressional hearings concerning air power and American Defense at which Billy Mitchell and other military leaders have testified is abruptly cancelled. The official reason is lack of funds.	The Great Lakes Carriers' Association announces that more ships were lost in storms on the Great Lakes since 1913, a loss of 16,450 tons....The New York Merchants Association announces that New York City must have an airport near the city if it is to ensure that the city will have adequate civilian air service.		The first issue of The New Yorker is published....The New York Times reviews a translation of A Death in Venice and other short stories by the German writer Thomas Mann....A dig team from Manitoba wins the three-day Quebec dog team races.	Feb. 21
Members of the Ku Klux Klan cross the Delaware River as part of a Washington's Birthday rally.	The U.S. Navy begins extensive war games with two opposing fleets in the Pacific off the California coast.		Scientists from Chicago's Field Museum discover extensive fossilized remains of mastodons and other animals in Bolivia.		Feb. 22
Senator William Borah proposes an amendment to repeal a recent salary increase Congress has voted for itself....Former Congressman Walter Chandler attacks the lack of freedom of speech in Russia and suggests that "Red" demonstrations in the United States be broken up and their leaders jailed.	Lieutenant Eric Nelson, one of several officers to have been part of the Army's 1924 round the world flight becomes supervisor of an aircraft assembly plant....The Navy informs the House Appropriations Committee that the earlier estimate of $68 million for the two aircraft carriers under construction did not include equipment, the total cost will be $86 million.		Goodyear and the Zeppelin Company announce plans to construct the world's largest dirigible that will provide transatlantic service by 1926....A severe earthquake causes damage in Seward and Anchorage, AK.	Former boxing champion Jack Johnson testifies in the Court that he was offered a bribe if he would provide false testimony in the conspiracy to defame trial of developer W.E.D. Stokes.	Feb. 23

F	G	H	I	J
Includes campaigns, elections, federal-state relations, civil rights and liberties, crime, the judiciary, education, healthcare, poverty, urban affairs, and population.	Includes formation and debate of U.S. foreign and defense policies, veterans affairs, and defense spending. (Relations with specific foreign countries are usually found under the region concerned.)	Includes business, labor, agriculture, taxation, transportation, consumer affairs, monetary and fiscal policy, natural resources, pollution and industrial accidents.	Includes worldwide scientific, medical and technological developments, natural phenomena, U.S. weather and natural disasters.	Includes the arts, religion, scholarship, communications media, sports, entertainment, fashions, fads, and social life.

	World Affairs	Europe	Africa & The Middle East	The Americas	Asia & The Pacific
Feb. 24		King Boris of Bulgaria meets with government officials to resolve the recent series of assassinations ands raids without taking extreme measures such as imposing the death penalty.	Kurdish rebels in Turkish Kurdistan launch a rebellion against the Turkish government.		The former emperor of China who had been overthrown in 1924 flees Chino for the Japanese-held territory to avoid being killed.... Albert Sarraut, former French Minister of Colonies states that western nations must beware of the "Yellow Peril."
Feb. 25		Josef Stalin announces that the current economic crisis in Russia may necessitate some cooperation between the government and private capitalists....A French court sentences nine German officers in absentia for their destruction of French property during the war.			Edsel Ford, son of Henry Ford, announces that Ford Motor Company will establish a Japanese company and assembly line in Yokohama, Japan.
Feb. 26	Faced with a major distraction with the Kurdish rebellion, the government of Turkey states that it will look to find a new solution to the crisis instigated by its expulsion of the Patriarch.	Engineers announce that the leaning tower of Pisa's slant has increased, leading to an investigation to see what engineering projects may be required to stop it from leaning any further.	The Turkish government deploys almost 40 percent of its Army to deal with the Kurdish rebels.... Viscount Edmund Allenby, who captured Jerusalem in World War I, resigns his post as British High Commissioner in Egypt.		
Feb. 27		Adolf Hitler resurrects the NSDAP, giving his first speech since his release from prison....The Soviet government orders all former landlords to hand over whatever remaining property they have to the state.		The U.S. Marines land in Panama in response to an Indian uprising under the leadership of an American explorer.	
Feb. 28		President Friedrich Ebert of Germany dies; concern is expressed in France that his death may mean the end of the German republic and a return of the German Royal family to power....France and Germany sign a trade agreement and will continue to negotiate a permanent trade treaty....The Soviet Union announces that it will allow girls to marry at age 15 and a half and boys at and a half, to both encourage population growth as well as to legalize many marriages that have already taken place.		The Panamanian Indian revolt continues, Indians demand assistance from the United States and independence from Panama....A huge explosion of gunpowder and gasoline stored on an island near Rio de Janeiro kills six people and creates a property loss estimated at over $1 million.	A British court sentences four men to die and nine to serve life terms for inciting a religious riot in Lahore, India, that killed 21 and injured 34.
Mar. 1		Two major stock markets in Central Europe (Budapest and Vienna) are weak with declining prices; Prague is the exception to this trend with a much stronger market.... Following the death of Germany's President Friedrich Ebert, British politicians express concern that that there will be a resurgence of the monarchy.	The French government announces that authorities in French Guinea have captured, convicted, and executed six cannibals.	Mexico City's transit workers shut down the city's trams and claim that supporters in other unions will shut off power and light as well....Reports from Rio de Janeiro indicate that an explosion on a nearby island where gunpowder is stored has killed eight and injured 600; there are still 300 people unaccounted for.	
Mar. 2		Mikhail Frunze, successor to Trotsky as Minister of War, states that the current size of the Red Army (562,500 men) is not large enough to defend the Soviet Union from attack....The German government doubles the tax on beer; opposition is vocal in Bavaria where it is predicted that reaction will be more serious than the 1923 Hitler-Ludendorff putsch....Benito Mussolini succeeds in neutralizing the political effectiveness of veterans groups that have been opposing the Fascist Party.	Reports on the extent of the Kurdish revolt in Turkey are vague but there are reports that Turkish aircraft and local units are having success against the rebels.	Reports continue to come in about the February 28 earthquake in eastern North America; seven are reported to have been killed in Quebec.	Reports describe a rumored revolt against the Soviets in the Pacific port city of Vladivostok....The All-India Committee's plans to build Hindu-Muslim unity break up citing serious differences; Mohandas Gandhi declares that any sort of agreement is impossible in the current set of circumstances.

A	B	C	D	E
Includes developments that affect more than one world region, international organizations and important meetings of world leaders.	Includes all domestic and regional developments in Europe, including the Soviet Union.	Includes all domestic and regional developments in Africa and the Middle East.	Includes all domestic and regional developments in Latin America, the Caribbean, and Canada.	Includes all domestic and regional developments in Asian and Pacific nations (and colonies).

U.S. Politics & Social Issues	U.S. Foreign Policy & Affairs, Defense	U.S. Economy & Environment	Science, Technology & Nature	Culture, Leisure & Lifestyle	
Mrs. Edgar Shumway of the Brooklyn Woman's Club testifies to the New York Legislature that a proposed child labor amendment to the Constitution is a Communist plan that "comes straight from Moscow."			The first telephone conversation between London and New York is successfully made.		Feb. 24
			The British government announces that it is in the process of designing an airship, one to be built by the government, the other to be built by a private company. It will service Asia and Australia.		Feb. 25
			Doctor William Beebe finds the Sargasso Sea characterized as a mass of floating seaweed that moves about in the Atlantic.	James Michael Curley, Mayor of Boston hits a hole-in-one while on vacation in Florida....The Salvation Army in London states that working men in Britain have developed greater interest in listening to the radio causing the amount of drunkenness to decrease....Henry Ford announces that he will build a large museum near his home in Dearborn, MI.	Feb. 26
A federal judge denies a request to delay the beginning of the Tea Pot Dome scandal trial over misuse of government leases in federal oil fields.			Glacier Bay National Monument in Alaska is dedicated.	Sculptor Gutzon Borglum is arrested for having destroyed models for the Stone Mountain Confederate Memorial in Georgia, which he was working on after having been fired by the memorial commission.	Feb. 27
Although he fails to get the congressional pay increase repealed, Senator William Borah manages to get a vote for the record.		The Georgia Attorney General announces that he will begin an investigation to determine why gasoline prices are so high and asks Georgia congressmen to investigate as well.	Earth tremors are felt along the east coast from the province of Quebec, Canada, to Alabama.	Radio stations KDKA of Pittsburg and WBZ of Boston announce that they will begin to broadcast educational courses over the air....The Robert Morris Hotel in Philadelphia has installed radio receivers in every guest room.	Feb. 28
The Washington, DC police are launching a campaign to ensure that the Prohibition is strictly enforced during the inauguration of President Calvin Coolidge to avoid any incidents....Groups of Republican and Democratic women address the New York State legislature asking it to ratify the Child Labor Amendment to the Constitution....A U.S. Customs agent is killed at Niagara Fall, NY, when his car is blown up by liquor smugglers.	War games between the "Blue" and "Black" fleets of the U.S. Navy continue in the Pacific Ocean off the coasts of Mexico and California.	The Studebaker Corporation announces that its profits from auto sales dropped from 145,167 in 1923 to 110,240 in 1924....The U.S. Department of Agriculture announces that the world crop for sugar in 1924 was 24,671,000 tons, a record....The economic outlook for the western U.S. is seen as very good for the coming year based on steel production and increases in dry goods sales.	Ottawa, Canada reports a seismic shock, the most severe in the city's history....A Franco-American archaeological expedition in Tunis begins excavation of the city of Utica.	George Bernard Shaw announces that because of his advanced age (68), he will not be writing any more plays....It is announced that Portugal will compete in the Davis Cup tennis competition for the first time....Jose Fonseca, known as "the Mexican Daredevil," and one of the first wing walkers, dies in a plane crash.	Mar. 1
Organizations in New York City campaign to get 100 more policewomen on the force....Harlan Stone is sworn in as Associate Justice of the U.S. Supreme Court.	In Pacific fleet maneuvers during a smoke screen exercise, a destroyer rams an aircraft carrier support ship.			In a story that is unfortunately very common, the New York Times describes how five people have died overnight of suffocation when their gas jet lighters leaked....Babe Ruth and Earl Combs are the center of attention as the New York Yankees open the first day of Spring training at St. Petersburg, FL.	Mar. 2

F	G	H	I	J
Includes campaigns, elections, federal-state relations, civil rights and liberties, crime, the judiciary, education, healthcare, poverty, urban affairs, and population.	Includes formation and debate of U.S. foreign and defense policies, veterans affairs, and defense spending. (Relations with specific foreign countries are usually found under the region concerned.)	Includes business, labor, agriculture, taxation, transportation, consumer affairs, monetary and fiscal policy, natural resources, pollution and industrial accidents.	Includes worldwide scientific, medical and technological developments, natural phenomena, U.S. weather and natural disasters.	Includes the arts, religion, scholarship, communications media, sports, entertainment, fashions, fads, and social life.

	World Affairs	Europe	Africa & The Middle East	The Americas	Asia & The Pacific
Mar. 3		Albania's minister of Finance is assassinated while visiting Italy....The Soviet government begins efforts to excavate beneath the Kremlin in an effort to find the library of Czar Ivan ("The Terrible")....Reports from the Soviet Union describe the murder of four children by their father in order to keep them from growing up to be Communists.	In a sign that the Kurdish revolt may be more serious than has been admitted, the Turkish Cabinet resigns after a no-confidence vote.		Sir Harcourt Butler, Governor of Burma, describes his recent trip in the interior where the Naga tribemen declare that they will not give up slavery or human sacrifice.
Mar. 4	Brazil signs the League of Nations anti-narcotic opium convention bringing the total of signatories to 16.				British Prime Minister Arthur Balfour once again defends the British government's plans to build an extensive naval base at Singapore, repeating that Japan has indicated that it has no objections.
Mar. 5	President Calvin Coolidge officially signs his arbitration order for the border dispute between Peru and Chile; a plebiscite will be held to determine full sovereignty over this area.	German Monarchists are campaigning for the Crown Prince of the Hohenzollern family to run for president.	The Turkish government admits that Kurdish rebels have seized towns in eastern Turkey....Italian troops from garrisons in Libya are reported fighting with Bedouins well within Egyptian territory.	Earth tremors continue to be felt in Quebec province....A representative of American banks in Mexico states that the current financial reforms are placing Mexico on its soundest financial footing in the past ten years....A treaty is signed between the Panamanian government and the San Blas Indians who had recently rebelled.	An armed group opposed to universal male suffrage breaks into the home of Japan's Premier Kato Takaaki to protest. The forces of Dr. Sun Yat-Sen defeat their main rival in a battle at the city of Swatow.
Mar. 6		The German government proposes a readjustment of borders that will take land away from Poland....The Estonian government denies a claim by the Soviet Foreign Minister that Estonia offered Britain a naval base in return for promises to defend the country from the Soviets....A report indicates that the cost of living in Britain rose in the month of February.	The Turkish National Assembly passes a bill forbidding the publication of articles critical of the government.		The Chinese government agrees to pay damage claims to Americans resulting from an armed bandit attack on a train in 1923.
Mar. 7	Lithuania announces that it will request the Vatican to intervene in returning the Lithuania city of Vilnius, seized by Poland after World War I....Poland announces it will not allow any changes in its border with Germany.	A bill is introduced in the Italian House of Deputies that would regulate the activities of all foreign correspondents....Both Monarchists and Communists are very active in Germany's Presidential elections but the Middle Parties claim that they are in control of the political situation.	The British Commissioner of Palestine announces that Haifa has been selected over Jaffa as the site for modern port expansion and construction....The Turkish ambassador to Germany is recalled back home to lead a military expedition against Kurdish rebels.	The U.S. High Commissioner for Haiti states that nation is making progress in political and financial stability....The Mexico City transit strike continues with workers refusing to allow food and water to reach company guards safeguarding engines and rolling stock in the car barns....Ray Chapman Andrews and his party that will explore the Gobi desert for dinosaur fossils, leave San Francisco.	The lower house of the Japanese legislature passes a bill banning all Communist activity....The U.S. State Department announces that it has been informed that Japanese Naval expenditures for the coming year will be 20 percent less than they were last year.
Mar. 8		The Polish Prime Minister announces to the Polish legislature that he has been given assurance from France that Germany will not adjust the border with Poland....Business conditions in Germany are good with fewer bankruptcies and unemployment slightly decreasing; wages, however, are not rising....Catholic demonstrations in France protest what is considered to be persecution by the government's anticlerical policies.	The Boston-Harvard archaeological expedition in Egypt announces that it has cleared further areas around the Great Pyramids at Giza finding many additional tombs of minor members of the Egyptian Royal families.		The Japanese government announces it has made five arrests connected to a series of bombings and attempted assassinations of the previous summer.
Mar. 9	Yugoslavia becomes the most recent nation to sign the League of Nations anti-opium convention.	The Prince of Wales prepares for an overseas tour of the Empire; logistical problems involved include stowing 400 trunks belonging to the Prince on the battleship *Repulse*....The British armaments manufacturer, Vickers, agrees to build a factory in Romania.	A tomb discovered at Giza, Egypt is claimed, by the archaeologist E.A. Wallis Budge to be the tomb of the Pharaoh Sneferu.		

A	B	C	D	E
Includes developments that affect more than one world region, international organizations and important meetings of world leaders.	*Includes all domestic and regional developments in Europe, including the Soviet Union.*	*Includes all domestic and regional developments in Africa and the Middle East.*	*Includes all domestic and regional developments in Latin America, the Caribbean, and Canada.*	*Includes all domestic and regional developments in Asian and Pacific nations (and colonies).*

U.S. Politics & Social Issues	U.S. Foreign Policy & Affairs, Defense	U.S. Economy & Environment	Science, Technology & Nature	Culture, Leisure & Lifestyle	
President Calvin Coolidge signs a bill signs a bill raising the salaries of members of Congress from $7,500 to $10,000 a year.			Roald Amundsen announces that he will attempt to fly to the North Pole, land and take observations, and then return; flight is scheduled for May.	The state of Nevada allows licensed gaming—roulette, twenty-one and other games—previously only poker had been allowed.	Mar. 3
Calvin Coolidge is inaugurated as president of the United States for a second term.			The French government announces that it will build a meteorological and seismograph lab near the Swiss border; it will also have a large wireless installation there as well....President Calvin Coolidge's inauguration is broadcast nationwide, the first time an inauguration has been broadcast by radio.	Finnish runner Paavo Nurmi sets two new world records for the mile and an eighth and the 2,000 yard.	Mar. 4
The Republican Party announces that it is dropping Senator LaFolette, a reformer from Wisconsin from the Republican caucus.	Secretary of State Frank Kellogg states that American foreign policy will remain continuous in Calvin Coolidge's second term and there will be no sharp departures.	Ford Motor Company states that it paid $253,001,528 in salaries and wages in 1924....After some losses, the New York Stock Exchange recovers, mostly on the strength of industrial and specialty stocks; the market as a whole, however, seems irregular.		The two major league baseball teams in St. Louis (the Browns and the Cardinals) agree to rebuild the current baseball park in that city to expand capacity.	Mar. 5
President Calvin Coolidge denies that he is opposed to appointing women to high government offices.	The Department of the Navy announces that submarines will be constructed in New Hampshire and California while a light cruiser will be built in New York City....General Billy Mitchell, advocate of air power is reduced in rank to Colonel....In a demonstration of the effectiveness of anti-aircraft fire against airplanes, none of the "attacking planes" are hit.	The U.S. Census Bureau reports that the output value of American shirt manufactures rose 18 percent in 1923 over 1921....In a survey released by the Long Island Railroad, Long Island's building activities were greater in 1924 than in any year of its history.	For the first time in history, parachutes save the lives of two aviators when their aircraft collide at Kelly Field in Texas.		Mar. 6
James Weldon Johnson, president of the NAACP, makes a public a letter he sent to President Calvin Coolidge protesting the lynching of an African American in George on March 2.	Dr. Harrison Howe of the American Chemical Society states that the U.S. military lags behind other nations in developing both offensive and defensive chemical capabilities.	The U.S. Commerce Department announces that German shipping activities through the Panama Canal has increased, now ranking fourth after the United States , Britain, and Japan....The Baldwin Locomotive company sues the nation of Romania for $2 million worth of locomotives delivered but not paid for....The Curtiss Aeroplane Company announces that in 1924 it grossed $3,385,850 for 1924 with a $156,228 net profit....A geological survey party leaves Seattle to explore potential Naval Petroleum reserve tracts in Alaska.	Chinese radio broadcasts from Beijing are heard in Germany for the first time.	Paavo Nurmi, once again breaks a record, this time for the mile, running it in 4:12....The New York Times reviews Arrowsmith, the latest novel by Sinclair Lewis....Czech composer Leos Janacek is made an honorary Doctor at Masaryk University in Brno....A census of automobiles worldwide indicates that there are 21,360,779 cars in the world.	Mar. 7
The Teapot Dome Trial, focusing on corruption in letting government oil leases begins.				The Daughters of the American Revolution announce that they will place markers to identify historic sites through the United States.	Mar. 8
Governor Miriam Ferguson of Texas signs a bill into law prohibiting the wearing of masks in public as a means of stemming Ku Klux Klan activity....The city budget for New York City is estimated to be $7,500 a minute.		The American Railway Association announces that thus far in 1925, freight traffic is breaking all previous records....George Eastman, President of the Eastman Kodak camera company announces he will retire as of April 7.	At a meeting of the International Geodetic and Physical Union, the world's diameter is officially stated to be 7,926,678 miles at the equator.	President of the Boston Braves, Christy Mathewson, announces that the Braves will begin a high school that will train baseball players.	Mar. 9

F	G	H	I	J
Includes campaigns, elections, federal-state relations, civil rights and liberties, crime, the judiciary, education, healthcare, poverty, urban affairs, and population.	Includes formation and debate of U.S. foreign and defense policies, veterans affairs, and defense spending. (Relations with specific foreign countries are usually found under the region concerned.)	Includes business, labor, agriculture, taxation, transportation, consumer affairs, monetary and fiscal policy, natural resources, pollution and industrial accidents.	Includes worldwide scientific, medical and technological developments, natural phenomena, U.S. weather and natural disasters.	Includes the arts, religion, scholarship, communications media, sports, entertainment, fashions, fads, and social life.

	World Affairs	Europe	Africa & The Middle East	The Americas	Asia & The Pacific
Mar. 10		Reports have reached Berlin that there is rioting in the streets of Leningrad due to unemployment and shortages of food requiring troops to break up the crowds....The Soviet government announces that it will not grant oil concessions in the Transcaucasus to any foreigners.	The famous Irish woman explorer, Mrs. Green, is killed by a rhinoceros on her trip walking across Africa....The British Royal Engineers are setting up barricades to keep crowds of tourists from overrunning the excavation site at the tomb of Pharaoh Sneferu....Sir Leonard Wooley's archaeological expedition in northern Iraq uncovers an ancient industrial center with many business records on clay tablets.		
Mar. 11	Lithuania breaks off diplomatic relations with the Vatican over what is perceived as support for Poland's policies to include the annexation of the Lithuanian city of Vilnius.	Italy succeeds in gaining concessions to drill for oil in Albania....Mikhail Frunze orders the activities of civilian political commissars in the Red Army to be curbed in order to eliminate civil interference and increase efficiency....The French General Statistics Service reports that the cost of living in Paris is five times what it was in 1914.		A Mexican newspaper, *El Globo*, reports that approximately 90 percent of the population in southern Mexico suffer from malaria....A general strike is called in Peru to protest the results of the border arbitration with Chile settled by President Calvin Coolidge.	Dr Sun Yat-sen, leader of the South Chinese government dies of cancer.
Mar. 12		Paris police arrest nine Communists, some of them armed, at a demonstration....Bulgaria seeks permission from the Allied Commission to raise an additional 4,000 men for its army to fight Communist sympathizers.			
Mar. 13	The League of Nations requests that the World Court arbitrate the dispute between Poland and Germany over the Free City of Danzig.	The campaign for president of Germany opens with five candidates seeking office; the election is to be held on March 29....The French government announces that in its Paris-to-Prague flights it will no longer fly over German territory owing to problems created by the German government when French planes have had to land at German fields.	Returns from parliamentary elections in Egypt are almost even with the probably outcome that the current government will remain in power.		Lord Thomson, former British Secretary of State predicts that there will be regular air service between the United States and Australia.
Mar. 14		The Archbishop of Alsace calls for a three-day strike in schools in response to a French law that forbids the teaching of any religion in school.			
Mar. 15		King Victor Emmanuel of Italy dedicates a monument to those killed in World War I.	A large four-engined Italian aircraft is found in the desert near the Libyan-Egyptian border is found; none of the crew members are located....The Turkish Assembly votes additional funds to meet the threat of the now apparently widespread Kurdish revolt against the Turkish government.	The Chilean government deports several opposition politicians.	Civil war continues in China despite the recent successes of Sun Yat-sen's factions; fighting is particularly fierce in Hunan province.
Mar. 16		Irish politician Eamon de Valera delivers a St. Patrick's Day message to Irish living abroad, asking their support to counter what he claims are English efforts to subvert the Irish Republican movement....It is formally announced that the recent infrequent appearances of Benito Mussolini in public were due to a serious illness, a severe bleeding ulcer....German newspapers express discontent with remarks made by President Calvin Coolidge that he hoped Germany could learn from America's experience in democracy.		Chilean President Arturo Alessandri, on his way back to Chile to resume his presidency, arrives in Argentina where he is warmly greeted.	The new Japanese ambassador arrives in Washington and is received by President Calvin Coolidge.

A	B	C	D	E
Includes developments that affect more than one world region, international organizations and important meetings of world leaders.	Includes all domestic and regional developments in Europe, including the Soviet Union.	Includes all domestic and regional developments in Africa and the Middle East.	Includes all domestic and regional developments in Latin America, the Caribbean, and Canada.	Includes all domestic and regional developments in Asian and Pacific nations (and colonies).

U.S. Politics & Social Issues	U.S. Foreign Policy & Affairs, Defense	U.S. Economy & Environment	Science, Technology & Nature	Culture, Leisure & Lifestyle	
Secretary of the Navy Curtis Wilbur suggests that schoolchildren of America, using pennies, fund the restoration of the ship, USS Constitution in Boston.		The Flatiron Building, one of New York City's most famous skyscrapers is sold at an estimated value of $2,025,000.	Sergeant Wernert of the French Air Forces sets a world record for glider flight, soaring for nine hours and 17 minutes.	The Washington Senators baseball club asks President Calvin Coolidge to toss the first ball of the season on April 22....Opera star Luisa Tetrazzini sings on a radio broadcast reaching an estimated audience of 10 million.... Monsignor John C. York of New York City criticizes women who go to the movies in the afternoon and then purchase canned goods to make the evening meal.	Mar. 10
	Naval maneuvers continue in the Pacific with submarines playing an active and successful role in defeating the "invading" fleet.		Two army aviators flying at an altitude of several thousand feet and flying five miles apart succeed in talking to each other using the radio, a first....The planes that will be used by Roald Amundsen in his planned flight to the North Pole leave by steamship from Italy.		Mar. 11
President Calvin Coolidge submits the name of Charles Warren for Attorney General even though he has been rejected once before for the post....28 people in Chicago die of influenza epidemic brining the 12 day total to 279 deaths.		Henry Ford opens a lawsuit to prevent a Realty Company from using the term "Ford Houses" to describe a type of quickly and cheaply built houses....American Tobacco nets $20,784, 870 in profits for 1924, its largest earnings ever.	Dr. William Beebe's scientific expedition in the Sargasso Sea continues, hampered by heavy seas although the scientific work is continuing.	Charles Scribner's Sons defends its new version of the Bible which has eliminated all references to wine, saying that it does not contain any prohibition bias.	Mar. 12
			A burial urn, estimated to be 2,000 years old, is found north of Phoenix, AZ.		Mar. 13
30,000 unionized women's garment workers agree to end their strike and return to work.			The U.S. Department of the Interior announces that prehistoric mosaics have been discovered at the Casa Grande National Monument in Arizona....Scotland Yard and the police Department of New York announce that they will soon be testing the transmission of fingerprints by radio.		Mar. 14
The Worker's Party of America holds its parade at Madison Square Garden, carrying broomsticks because they have been prohibited from marching with rifles....The debate in Congress continues over Calvin Coolidge's selection to be Attorney General; opponents are vowing to continue the fight in opposing Coolidge's choice.			The Boston and Maine Railroad tests a train powered by gasoline instead of coal to reduce costs.		Mar. 15
	The U.S. government orders 85 new airplanes for the Army totaling $1,100,000.		An undersea cable providing direct communications between Italy and the United States begins operations.	The U.S. Department of Agriculture reports that consumption of ice cream in the United States in 1924 was 285,550,000 gallons, down nine million gallons from the year before, largely due to cooler weather throughout the country.	Mar. 16

F	G	H	I	J
Includes campaigns, elections, federal-state relations, civil rights and liberties, crime, the judiciary, education, healthcare, poverty, urban affairs, and population.	Includes formation and debate of U.S. foreign and defense policies, veterans affairs, and defense spending. (Relations with specific foreign countries are usually found under the region concerned.)	Includes business, labor, agriculture, taxation, transportation, consumer affairs, monetary and fiscal policy, natural resources, pollution and industrial accidents.	Includes worldwide scientific, medical and technological developments, natural phenomena, U.S. weather and natural disasters.	Includes the arts, religion, scholarship, communications media, sports, entertainment, fashions, fads, and social life.

	World Affairs	Europe	Africa & The Middle East	The Americas	Asia & The Pacific
Mar. 17	President Calvin Coolidge repeats that any disarmament conference to be held in Washington would be for naval arms only and would not discuss land warfare.	France responds favorably to the proposed naval disarmament conference but says before it negotiates anything its security concerns about Germany must be resolved....An article published by well-known German military historian Hans Delbruck states that had Germany moved first against Russia and then France in 1914, Germany would have won World War I....Demonstrations continue in Leningrad over the scarcity of bread.		The American embassy in Lima, Peru is attacked in protest by Peruvians angry over President Calvin Coolidge's arbitration of the Peru-Chile border dispute.... Statistics released on usage of the Panama Canal indicate that a record amount of cargo (25,892,134 tons) was transported even though the number of ships passing through in 1924 declined.	
Mar. 18		The Soviet embassy in Paris is burglarized; Soviet officials express concern about the sensitivity of some documents that may have been stolen....Large-scale strikes continue in northern Italy; Fascist labor unions have returned to work but Socialist unions are still on strike....Campaigning for the Presidency of Germany continues with one candidate denying that he wants the monarchy to return while simultaneously claiming that the Kaiser's departure was bad for the country.		Trujillo, the third largest city in Peru, has been destroyed by floods, forcing 11,000 to leave their homes.	A fire in Tokyo destroys 2,600 buildings, leaving 12,000 homeless.
Mar. 19		Lord Curzon, former Viceroy of India, dies at the age of 66....The British Admiralty announces that it has thus far scrapped 400,000 tons of warships as part of the Naval Disarmament Treaty.... Reports from Berlin indicate that Soviet newspapers are admitting the serious problems from famine and that as many as 750,000 children may be staving in southern Russia....Italian strikers return to their jobs in the city of Milan although strikes continue in Turin and other cities.	Italy reports that in a recent battle with Libyan opponents to the Italian colonial government, Ibrahim Scetoui, commander in chief of the Arabs, has been killed.	Factories in Sao Paolo, Brazil, announce they will cut the number of hours their employees are working due to declining sales.	
Mar. 20		The Soviet government announces that it will import both grain and flour to ease the current food shortages in the Soviet Union.... General Erich Ludendorff, a fellow conspirator with Adolf Hitler in 1923, declares his intention to run for the presidency of Germany.... Children playing in Budapest discover golden dishes, estimated to date from 800 B.C.E.			The town of Talifu in Western China is completely destroyed by earthquakes and fire.
Mar. 21		A team for the League of Nations with the mission to study boat traffic flow on the Danube arrives in Vienna on....Italian strikers announce that they will all return to work tomorrow.	Two French explorers attempting to cross the Sahara from the Atlantic coast to the Red Sea are reported missing; no word has been heard since March 2.		
Mar. 22		Appearing in a Fascist Black shirt, Benito Mussolini delivers a speech to crowds in Rome as he announces the end of his convalescence.... Germany, which is near admission into the League of Nations, states that its entry will require a security treaty guaranteeing parity with France and England....British unemployment increased slightly in February and is higher than it was a year ago....German unemployment in February decreased.	The Turkish government announces that it expects that all foreign embassies will move from Constantinople to the new capital at Ankara.		

A	B	C	D	E
Includes developments that affect more than one world region, international organizations and important meetings of world leaders.	Includes all domestic and regional developments in Europe, including the Soviet Union.	Includes all domestic and regional developments in Africa and the Middle East.	Includes all domestic and regional developments in Latin America, the Caribbean, and Canada.	Includes all domestic and regional developments in Asian and Pacific nations (and colonies).

U.S. Politics & Social Issues	U.S. Foreign Policy & Affairs, Defense	U.S. Economy & Environment	Science, Technology & Nature	Culture, Leisure & Lifestyle	
Dr. Haven Emerson, former Commissioner of Public Health states that the neglect of the U.S. government has resulted in very high death rates among Native Americans as well as a very high infant mortality rate.	Japan's new ambassador states that he will not reopen the question of loosening immigration restrictions in the United States on Japanese seeking entry.	The Wright Aeronautical Corporation declares a profit for 1924; while commercial aviation is beginning to provide a significant business the company states it still must look to government support....A mine explosion in West Virginia traps an estimated 33 men....The Soviet Union at a trade fair announces that it will purchase large lots of American cloth dyes, citing their superiority to European dyes.	Austrian scientists find human bones in a cave that are an estimated 250,000 years old as well as many animals bones from about the same date....A Swiss scientist states that lead particles from gasoline are now commonly found in road dust and are poisoning the atmosphere.	The Maine legislature passes a bill forbidding the imposition of daylight saving time in the state of Maine....Harvard University awards the construction for the construction of Harvard Business School on the banks of the Charles River for an estimated $5 million.	Mar. 17
Federal Prohibitions Officers seize $100,000 in liquor while arresting three bootleggers....The state of New Hampshire defeats the proposed Child Labor Constitutional Amendment.	The U.S. Navy orders that its current training planes manufactured by the Boeing Corporation will undergo some structural changes.	Police are investigating yesterday's mine explosion in West Virginia which may have been purposely bombed; three men are held on suspicion of setting the blast.... A tornado strikes Illinois, Indiana, and Missouri, killing an estimated 950 and injuring 2,700.	13 passengers fly in an aircraft designed and built by the Sikorsky corporation that is completely enclosed—twin engined, no one exposed....Bulletproof glass is shown to be a practical invention after it saves the life of a bank patron during a holdup in St. Louis, MI.	The Belgian Olympic commission declares that at the meeting of the world Olympic organization next week it will oppose the removal of tennis as an Olympic event.... Madame Tussaud's wax museum in London burns with extensive damage....Mrs. Sophie Hazel, of Medina, OH, admits to poisoning 17 relatives, three of whom have died.	Mar. 18
Senator William Borah, chairman of the Senate Foreign Relations Committee reports that that between December 12, 1924 and March 18, 1925, the Senate had ratified 19 foreign treaties, a record....The State of New York reports that 131 people were killed in the state due to industrial accidents....President Calvin Coolidge orders the Red Cross to mobilize and aid the Midwest after the tornado.	The Distinguished Service Medal is awarded to eight Army fliers who flew around the world in 1924.	Wall Street activity is characterized by a rise in stocks, particularly manufacturing; announcements of lower gas prices have not affected any petroleum stocks....Estimates of the tornado damage in the Midwest indicate that the number of deaths exceeds 820 with the total of injured approaching 3,000....At a conference in Atlantic City, NJ, the National American Wholesale Lumber Association requests that the U.S. government establish limits as to how much can be cut in order to keep the supply from far exceeding the demand.	The city of Philadelphia begins an experiment where burglar alarms will be directly connected to police stations.		Mar. 19
	The U.S. Navy announces it is planning to construct five more aircraft carriers similar to the Lexington and Saratoga which are due to be launched next month....Senator William Borah declares that he will oppose U.S. entry into the World Court because of its domination by the European powers.	The U.S. Census Bureau reports that cotton harvest in 1924 was the largest in 11 years.			Mar. 20
	Admiral Bradley Fiske of the U.S. Navy in a speech warns that the next war will result from U.S., British, and Japanese competition in the Pacific.	The Fifth Avenue Association of New York City announces its opposition to proposed measures that would eliminate restrictions on the height of skyscrapers.		The city of Palm Beach announces that new hotel construction to replace several hotels that have just burned will be of fireproof construction....The Barnum and Bailey, Ringling Brothers Circus begins its tour by performing in Madison Square Garden, enlarging its show to five instead of the usual three rings.	Mar. 21
The U.S. Controller General states that Congressmen must take their newly increased paychecks but if they want, they can return the excess.		Sinclair Oil Company in a court case against the Soviet Union is claiming full rights to drill on the island of Sakhalin in the pacific coast and will not accept the refund of its $100,000 deposit.	Army fliers disprove the theory that a long free fall will result in unconsciousness when they jump out of planes at 3,000 feet and open their chutes at 2,000 feet.	The Metropolitan Museum of Art opens a special exhibition of clay seals found in Iraq.	Mar. 22

F	G	H	I	J
Includes campaigns, elections, federal-state relations, civil rights and liberties, crime, the judiciary, education, healthcare, poverty, urban affairs, and population.	Includes formation and debate of U.S. foreign and defense policies, veterans affairs, and defense spending. (Relations with specific foreign countries are usually found under the region concerned.)	Includes business, labor, agriculture, taxation, transportation, consumer affairs, monetary and fiscal policy, natural resources, pollution and industrial accidents.	Includes worldwide scientific, medical and technological developments, natural phenomena, U.S. weather and natural disasters.	Includes the arts, religion, scholarship, communications media, sports, entertainment, fashions, fads, and social life.

	World Affairs	Europe	Africa & The Middle East	The Americas	Asia & The Pacific
Mar. 23	President Calvin Coolidge appoints General John Pershing as head of the commission that will administer the territorial plebiscite resulting from Coolidge's arbitration of the Peru-Chile border dispute.... The League of Nations Malaria Board announces it will expand its activities into Egypt, Turkey, Sicily, Corsica, and Spain.		The Turkish government announces its intention to build the most powerful radio transmitting station in the world at its capital, Ankara.	The Panamanian government banishes American Richard Marsh for his activities in instigating the revolt of the San Blas Indians in Panama in recent weeks.... Canadian officials state that the recent bans on immigration in the United States will result in a significant influx of settlers coming to Canada.	The Japanese legislature passes a bill forbidding foreigners from owning land in Japan.
Mar. 24	France states that it will not bring up the matter of the United States occupying the Haiti to the League of Nations because as a member of the League, Haiti can bring up the issue itself if it wishes.	Archaeologists in Budapest find six stone coffins, each containing bones that are tentatively dated to be 2,000 years old.	The Egyptian Ministry of Foreign Affairs sends a note directly to the League of Nations fueling speculation that Egypt is trying to exercise some degree of independence from the British....The Turkish government extends the application of martial law in response to the Kurdish revolt.	Albert Einstein arrives in Buenos Aries to begin a series of lectures.	
Mar. 25	Peru accuses the Chilean government of atrocities on civilians in the border area now under dispute.	The Italian government burns 100 million lire in an effort to decrease the amount of currency in circulation....The Director of the Vienna Medical College alleges that a new drug, coming from America, has been instrumental in the increased number of suicides and insanity cases in Vienna; he will not identify the drug, however....The Soviet Union announces that it seeks to establish trading relations with France....Germany states that it will not pay any reparations directly to Poland but that Poland must get its share from the general pool of reparation payments that Germany is making to the Allied powers.	The French Colonial Ministry announces that two explorers, who were crossing the Sahara by auto and reported lost, have been located and will reach their destination on the Red Sea.	American diplomats meeting in Mexico City are attempting to construct a pan-American policy on curbing arms sales; Mexico states that it is studying the proposals and favors the prohibition of selling arms to revolutionary movements.	Dispatches from British administrators in Calcutta describe an incident of human sacrifice to combat demonic possession; the father and two of the brothers are sentenced to death....Crowds in Tokyo, showing continued opposition to the Universal Male Suffrage proposal attack and damage the home of representatives who have gone on record as having supported the measure....The Australian government announces that it will order two submarines to be constructed in Britain.
Mar. 26		A member of the French chamber of Deputies in a corruption trial refuses to swear on a Bible but places his hand on a hammer and sickle instead....A fistfight between Fascist and Socialist Deputies breaks out in the Italian legislature....A member of the French Chamber of Deputies calls for censorship, particularly of advertisements for their "corrupting character."	French diplomats are opening discussions with Turkey creating the rumor that the two nations may between the two....Lord Balfour, creator of the Balfour Plan to create a homeland in Israel for Jews arrives in Jaffa to begin a tour of Palestine.		Japan announces that it will not raise the issue of the British base at Singapore in any naval disarmament talks.
Mar. 27	The International Birth Control Conference approves a resolution to ask the League of Nations to study birth control as a means of preventing war.	Retired Field Marshal Paul von Hindenburg asks his former partner, ERich Ludendorff to withdraw from the German presidential elections because he may take votes away from the Rightist elements....Germany announces that it still intends to see border changes that will incorporate territory now claimed by Poland.	The level of conflict between the Moors in Morocco and Spanish and French soldiers is declining sharply as Ramadan, the month of fasting, is approaching.		
Mar. 28	Sweden registers it latest treaty with the United States. The treaty is criticized by the League of Nations because it allows wide latitude as to whether arbitration will be used for all disputes.	The British government protests a new Romanian law that effectively puts a curb on emigration from Romania to the United States as it will affect British shipping which provides most of the sea transportation from Romania.... Although he has been stripped of all his offices, Leon Trotsky appears at the Soviet Congress in Moscow....In Hamburg, Germany, 72 Communists inmates end their two-week hunger strike.... The Czechoslovak government reduces the length of time to be served in the Army, substantially decreasing the number of troops on active duty.	Arab organizations in Palestine send official protests to the League of nations over the visit of Lord Balfour.	Rumors that the American directors of the National Bank of Nicaragua creates a mass run on the bank.... Mexico announces that it will not participate in the arms sales talks with other American nations because it was not specifically invited to the discussions by the League of Nations....Argentina reports that in 1924 it increased its favorable trade balance, increasing its exports and decreasing its imports.	China protests recent Soviet diplomatic relations with Japan on the grounds that this is against the agreement that the Soviets would not establish relations with countries that disputed China's rights.

A	B	C	D	E
Includes developments that affect more than one world region, international organizations and important meetings of world leaders.	*Includes all domestic and regional developments in Europe, including the Soviet Union.*	*Includes all domestic and regional developments in Africa and the Middle East.*	*Includes all domestic and regional developments in Latin America, the Caribbean, and Canada.*	*Includes all domestic and regional developments in Asian and Pacific nations (and colonies).*

U.S. Politics & Social Issues	U.S. Foreign Policy & Affairs, Defense	U.S. Economy & Environment	Science, Technology & Nature	Culture, Leisure & Lifestyle	
The Governor of Tennessee signs a bill banning the teaching of evolution....The U.S. Supreme Court announces it will not review the conviction of Marcus Garvey's conviction on mail fraud.	President Calvin Coolidge announces that national Guard troops will not be paid for their monthly drills until he determines that money is not being wasted.	Humble Oil, part of Standard Oil of New Jersey declares 1924 profits of $9,835,194 which is an increase over 1923's profits of $5,058,192.	The U.S. Navy will begin airplane flights to provide data that it will send to the Weather Bureau to add to their data for forecasting.	The Austrian composer Richard Strauss announces that he has written a piano concerto to be played on one hand, composed specifically for Austrian pianist Paul Wittgenstein who lost an arm in World War I.	Mar. 23
	Assistant Secretary of the Navy Theodore Robinson states in a speech to an aviation group that airplanes could never be a deciding factor in any future war.	An area of more than 75 square miles is found to be covered with poisonous capsules intended to kill fur bearing animals, resulting in a Massachusetts law to ban this activity.	The U.S. Department of Agriculture reports that American per capita consumption of meat decreased slightly in 1924.	The American Geographical Society shows a film of the Mount Everest ascent that claimed the lives of Mallory and Irvine in the e unsuccessful attempt to climb in 1924....California farmer, Herman Schalow dies as a result of being branded as part of a cult ceremony....A very large response (215 men) meets Notre Dame football coach Knute Rockne's call for spring drill.	Mar. 24
Members of the Coast Guard report receiving death threats as a result of their activities in intercepting liquor smugglers.	In the U.S. Navy fleet maneuvers off the coast of California, surface ship anti-aircraft batteries fail to score any hits against "attacking" airplanes.		The Norwegian government will send a naval transport ship north to Spitzbergen to support the planned exploratory flight by Roald Amundsen.		Mar. 25
Puera Johnson, the first woman minister of any denomination on the East Coast of the United States is accepted as a preacher in the Methodist Episcopal Church in Newark, NJ....Arguments by prosecution and defense end in the Teapot Domes corruption trial....A truce ending a tong war among Chinese in the United States end a conflict that has killed 50 since October 1924.			A Conference of 25 news agencies is meeting to create laws covering copyright, transmission, and interception of radio news.	The Board of Trustees of the Harding Memorial Association announces that they will soon begin construction of the memorial to the late president....The Postmaster General announces that the government will issue a new set of commemoratives in April to commemorate the 150th anniversary of the battles of Lexington and Concord.	Mar. 26
In an effort to unionize the coal mine workers in West Virginia, a coal strike is called by the United Mine Workers....The National Association Against the Prohibition Amendment predicts that whiskey supplies from Canada will be cheap and plentiful in the coming months.			Photographs of people in different emotional states are being taken at the experimental psychology lab in Princeton to determine if there is universal recognition of emotions as shown by facial expression.		Mar. 27
Police in Washington, DC, break up a Communist demonstration at the Polish Legation.	The War Department announces that civilian aircraft can no longer use military airfields except in emergencies.	Ford Motor Company announces that it sold 2,100,000 cars in 1924 and made a profit of $47 for each car....A spreading forest fire threatens the trees at Sequoia National Park.		Dionysus in Doubt, a book of new poems by Edward Arlington Robinson is reviewed by the New York Times.	Mar. 28

F	G	H	I	J
Includes campaigns, elections, federal-state relations, civil rights and liberties, crime, the judiciary, education, healthcare, poverty, urban affairs, and population.	Includes formation and debate of U.S. foreign and defense policies, veterans affairs, and defense spending. (Relations with specific foreign countries are usually found under the region concerned.)	Includes business, labor, agriculture, taxation, transportation, consumer affairs, monetary and fiscal policy, natural resources, pollution and industrial accidents.	Includes worldwide scientific, medical and technological developments, natural phenomena, U.S. weather and natural disasters.	Includes the arts, religion, scholarship, communications media, sports, entertainment, fashions, fads, and social life.

	World Affairs	Europe	Africa & The Middle East	The Americas	Asia & The Pacific
Mar. 29	Protesting Chilean activities on its border, the government of Peru requests that President Calvin Coolidge send American troops to take over and keep peace in the border area.	The Austrian government reports that in January it took in more revenue that it spent....The results from the first round of the German Presidential elections are in; as no candidate has received a majority vote, a second election is scheduled for April 26....The German government approaches France on commencing talks concerning security and fixing the border between France and Germany.	The Kurdish revolt in Turkey continues but contradictory reports make it unclear whether the revolt is expanding or if the Turkish government is successfully containing it.		
Mar. 30		Italian Field Marshals Cadorna and Diaz speak publicly in opposition to a proposed bill that would cut the size of the Italian Army....Reports from Constantinople indicate that thousands are being executed by the Soviet police in Soviet Georgia....The court-martial of Captain Jacques Sadoul begins; he is accused of sending information to the Soviets.	Lieutenant Colonel Ali Ruhi of the Turkish Army is court-martialed and sentenced to seven years in prison for expressing opinions favorable to the Kurdish rebels....An Italian archaeological expedition near Aswan Egypt discovers an early Christian Coptic Monastery....A Franco-American archaeological expedition begins its work in excavating the Forum of Carthage....Spanish troops recapture the town of Alcazar Seguir in Morocco from the Arabs.	Serious flooding has washed out roads, bridges, and buildings through out the northeastern United States and in Quebec province; some rivers are reported at 15 feet above flood stage.	
Mar. 31		The Tashkent Express crashes into a Moscow commuter train, killing at least 50 and injuring 100....During training maneuvers, 67 German soldiers are killed when a pontoon bridge they are building collapses throwing them into the Weser River.			Ray Chapman Anderson's expedition in search of dinosaur fossils departs from the Chinese city of Shanghai for Mongolia.
Apr. 1	The debate continues about what should be discussed in any international arms agreements; France goes on record as saying that airplanes should not be part of any arms limitation discussions.	The British Parliament votes down a bill to abolish the death penalty in the British Army....A vote to decrease the size of the Italian Army is put off but will be debated and probably defeated later....Rumors that Leon Trotsky has disappeared or been killed are denied by the Soviet Union....Czechoslovakia's Foreign Minister, Jan Benes, attacks the idea that Germany and Austria combine into one country.	Britain's Lord Balfour, on tour in Palestine, dedicates Hebrew University in Jerusalem.	President Marcelo de Alvear sends a bill to the Argentine Congress proposing currency reforms. The former President of Uruguay, Baltasar Brum, suggests a Pan-American League of Nations, adding it would not interfere with the role of the United States in Latin America.	
Apr. 2	The Peruvian government delivers a note to President Calvin Coolidge concerning his recent arbitration of the Peru-Chile border, requesting if the United States will not send troops to guard the border that a special border unit be formed....The French and Turkish governments agree that the city of Alexandretta on the Turkish-Syrian border will be autonomous.	German and Austrian diplomats are indicating that they might be receptive to a unification of the two countries....Benito Mussolini addresses the Italian Parliament expressing his opinion that instead of considering the reduction of Italy's military, more wars will come and Italy should be prepared.			
Apr. 3	President Calvin Coolidge informs the Peruvian government that while U.S. troops will not guard the Chilean-Peru border, enough safeguards have been put into place to assure Peru's interests.	A union of broadcasters in Europe is formed in Geneva to promote cooperation among the broadcasters of Europe.	The Turkish General Staff declares that it is making excellent progress in suppressing the Kurdish revolt....The South African government sends troops into the Southwest African former German colony to suppress a tribal revolt there....Archaeologists in Utica, Tunis, North Africa find baby bottles estimated to be 2,000 years old.		The Japanese government announces that it is planning to build 22 additional ships: 11 cruisers, 10 destroyers, and an airplane mother ship....The Afghan government announces that its troops have killed or wounded 1,575 rebels in the Khost District.

A	B	C	D	E
Includes developments that affect more than one world region, international organizations and important meetings of world leaders.	Includes all domestic and regional developments in Europe, including the Soviet Union.	Includes all domestic and regional developments in Africa and the Middle East.	Includes all domestic and regional developments in Latin America, the Caribbean, and Canada.	Includes all domestic and regional developments in Asian and Pacific nations (and colonies).

U.S. Politics & Social Issues	U.S. Foreign Policy & Affairs, Defense	U.S. Economy & Environment	Science, Technology & Nature	Culture, Leisure & Lifestyle	
The Republican Party leaders are beginning discussions of who might run in 1928 for the presidency; Calvin Coolidge and Herbert Hoover are mentioned as likely candidates.		The U.S. Northeaster Forest Experiment Station reports that a bud worm infestation has destroyed 40 percent of Maine's spruce trees since 1910....The wheat commodities market which has seen significant price increases crashes; the price drops to $1.25 per bushel, considerably lower than the $2 a bushel price that was expected.	The Soviet scientist/explorer Colonel Kozloff leaves Moscow to head another expedition, this time from Mongolia to Tibet on a trip that is expected to go on until 1927.	Henrietta Perkins, an editor of a student publication at Boston University is forced to resign for running articles critical of ROTC.... While the Catholic Church in the United States has gained 94,241 in the past year, it is the smallest increase in several years....Dr. D. S. Pritchett, President of the Carnegie Foundation states that overemphasis on sports in college, to include paid coaches and professional training methods.	Mar. 29
The Red Cross is continuing to both distribute aid to Midwestern tornado victims as well as to solicit contributions nationwide.	Colonel (formerly General) Billy Mitchell reports to his new assignment to duty as air officer of VIII Corps at Fort Sam Houston, TX.	The U.S. Commerce Department reports that U.S. exports to Europe grew in 1924 while imports from Asia increased as well.	Arctic explorer Donald MacMillan advises President Calvin Coolidge that the United States should send an expedition to the North Pole in order to claim additional territory, citing Denmark's claims of land in Greenland.	In response to concerns expressed about how it will affect children in the audience, the Barnum and Bailey Ringling Brothers Circus announces it will no longer have wild animal acts in the arena.... Fans of the Detroit Tigers baseball club wait in line all night for opening day tickets....The Boston Museum of Fine Arts buys a painting, *Emma and Her Children*, painted by George Bellows who had recently died.	Mar. 30
Seven members of the American Civil Liberties Union are convicted for conducting a meeting with strikers the previous October.		W. A. Harriman, an investment company in New York announces its plans to finance an airline making regular runs between Boston and New York.		The American Painter, Childe Hassam creates controversy in displaying a painting of Adam and Eve in a setting identified as being Montauk Point, NY.	Mar. 31
New Mexico newspaper editor Carl Magee, in a speech, warns that corporations that can withhold advertising to influence editorial policies, present a danger to freedom of the press.		Miners in West Virginia begin a strike that will involve 4,500 miners....The New York, Pittsburgh, and Chicago Railroad announces plans to build a 344-mile stretch of line, most of it in Pennsylvania.		Movie cowboy, Tom Mix is in New York City preparing for his European tour....British pianist Dame Myra Hess gives a concert in New York's Aeolian Hall.	Apr. 1
A report from the U.S. Board of Education describes conditions in high schools which are characterized by gambling, cheating, forgery, and cutting classes.	Senator William Borah declares his opposition to the idea of a World Court until there is some recognized body of international law.		The British successfully test a new landing mast for the dirigible *R-33*.		Apr. 2
The NAACP states that it will fight a recently passed Texas Law that forbids African Americans from voting in primaries....The West Virginia legislature defeats the proposed Child Labor Law amendment to the U.S. Constitution.... Massachusetts reports a sharp increase in the numbers of driver's licenses revoked for reckless and drunk driving....The California Board of Education votes in favor of teaching evolution in California schools but only as a theory....The warden at the Federal Penitentiary in Atlanta states that the prison will no longer send its baseball team to inter city league play; additionally prisoners will no longer receive packages, to curb narcotic traffic in the prison.	A U.S. fleet of 96 ships, having completed maneuvers off the California and Mexican coasts sails to Hawaii where it will conduct combined sea and land exercises.	The Department of the Interior announces that gasoline production for the month of February was the greatest on record.... Phillip K. Wrigley of the chewing gum company announces that he will join Edsel Ford in establishing a commercial airplane project.		Film star, William S. Hart joins United Artists, along with Douglas Fairbanks, Mary Pickford, Rudolph Valentino....In Cave City, KY, workers begin the task of recovering the body of cave explorer Floyd Collins who died in February.... Dean Arthur Greene of Princeton states that engineers should study the classics as well as a scientific and engineering curriculum....Tom Mix, still preparing for his tour of Europe broadcasts appears on the radio; Mix addresses the audience in place of Tony, "the intelligent horse," who, it was feared, would not whinny on cue.	Apr. 3

F	**G**	**H**	**I**	**J**
Includes campaigns, elections, federal-state relations, civil rights and liberties, crime, the judiciary, education, healthcare, poverty, urban affairs, and population.	*Includes formation and debate of U.S. foreign and defense policies, veterans affairs, and defense spending. (Relations with specific foreign countries are usually found under the region concerned.)*	*Includes business, labor, agriculture, taxation, transportation, consumer affairs, monetary and fiscal policy, natural resources, pollution and industrial accidents.*	*Includes worldwide scientific, medical and technological developments, natural phenomena, U.S. weather and natural disasters.*	*Includes the arts, religion, scholarship, communications media, sports, entertainment, fashions, fads, and social life.*

	World Affairs	Europe	Africa & The Middle East	The Americas	Asia & The Pacific
Apr. 4		Following their fistfight in Italy's Chamber of Deputies, two Deputies fight a duel with swords until the Fascist is wounded in the arm....Field Marshal Paul von Hindenburg states that he will run for the Presidency of Germany....France announces it will allow up to 10,000 Austrians a year to enter the country as laborers....Anarchist Emma Goldman, formerly resident in the United States, has left the Soviet Union and attacks it for its attacks on personal liberties....Benito Mussolini announces that recent pay increases to the Italian Civil Service mark the limits as to what the government will do and that state employees should not consider strikes....In a speech in Vienna, the Vice-Chancellor of Austria expresses the hope that Austria and Germany will unite.	The League of Nations boundary commission leaves Alexandria, Egypt, after completing its survey of what will be the border between Turkey and northern Iraq; their recommendations will be presented to the League....The Prince of Wales continues his tour of Africa, stopping at Gambia where he revives the regional chiefs.	The Pope announces that he will canonize Isaac Jogues, Jean Brebouef, and other Jesuits who served in Canada as missionaries, as Saints....Reports indicate that radio is becoming more common in Latin America with 12,000 radios in Mexico City and 3,000 in Havana.	
Apr. 5		Italy declares that its imports are exceeding its exports and show a substantial increase over last year....Large demonstrations are held in Moscow to protest the killing of Communists in Poland....Germany reports that general business continues to improve, especially in the area of engineering where Germans are successfully competing with Britain.	Reports from Constantinople indicate that Kurdish rebels are making a last stand and Turkish forces are in pursuit despite the mountainous terrain and snow....Lord Balfour goes to Haifa, the next stop on his Middle east Tour, on his way to Damascus, Syria.		
Apr. 6	Norway and Abyssinia announce that they will participate in the League of Nations arms control talks that will be held in May....A committee of the League of Nations agrees on a set of topics that will be discussed to help begin to define a code in International Law.	Karl Radek, a member of the higher ranks of the Soviet government has his position reduced and it is rumored he will soon be following Trotsky into political oblivion....The first trade statistics made public concerning trade between Italy and the Soviet Union indicate Italy is taking in more imports than sending exports to the Soviet Union.	Three provinces of Turkey are declared to be completely cleared on Kurdish rebels....The Prince of Wales's tour stops at the port of Freetown in Sierra Leone.	Leonard Seppalla, who was prominent in bringing the diphtheria serum to Nome, wins the annual Kennel Club dogsled race.	The Robert Dollar Company, a shipping company, announces that it will no longer provide transportation on the Yangtze River.
Apr. 7		G. C. Haas of the U.S. Department of Agriculture opens an office in Vienna from which he will survey agriculture in Austria, Hungary, Yugoslavia, Czechoslovakia, Bulgaria, and Romania with particular interest in identifying markets for American farmers.			
Apr. 8	Japan states that even though France has expressed reservations about naval disarmament talks, it is still very interested in pursuing the discussion.	Although French Premier Edouard Herriot's government has received a no confidence vote, he states that he will not dissolve the government but will attempt to complete his financial reform program....French detectives arrest Michel Lezinski, a Soviet spy, who was attempting to leave the country with airplane plans....Poland's commanding General states that Poland is ready to fight to defend its borders with Germany.	The Count de Prorok continues his archaeological expedition inn North Africa, looking for traces of Roman or Carthaginian towns that disappeared....Despite continued assurances by the Turkish government, the revolt in the Kurdish region continues and the government finally admits that the situation is "grave."...Continuing his tour of the Middle East, Lord Balfour's visit to Damascus prompts riots throughout the city.	The Cuban ambassador in Ottawa, Canada, successfully calls his government in Havana, the call taking only 15 minutes to go through....The Mexican government states that it will return National Railway Lines to its original owners which had been nationalized.	
Apr. 9	President Calvin Coolidge states that he will make no changes in his arbitration of the Peru-Chile border dispute and will not send U.S. troops; he will, however, send General John Pershing to supervise and assures all parties that it will be done equitably....France and Turkey continue to negotiate a treat that will guarantee the territorial sovereignty of Syria.	General Primo de Rivera, de facto ruler of Spain, announces that reforms and the return of government to civil control will be delayed....Representatives of British trade unions agree that they will support the efforts of Russian Trade Unions....In Italy continued fighting between Fascists and Communists in the streets with at least five dead.	Two are killed and nine injured in the riots in Damascus protesting the visit of Lord Balfour; Balfour is secretly taken out of the city to save his life.		

A	B	C	D	E
Includes developments that affect more than one world region, international organizations and important meetings of world leaders.	Includes all domestic and regional developments in Europe, including the Soviet Union.	Includes all domestic and regional developments in Africa and the Middle East.	Includes all domestic and regional developments in Latin America, the Caribbean, and Canada.	Includes all domestic and regional developments in Asian and Pacific nations (and colonies).

U.S. Politics & Social Issues	U.S. Foreign Policy & Affairs, Defense	U.S. Economy & Environment	Science, Technology & Nature	Culture, Leisure & Lifestyle	
Senator William Borah, in a speech, calls on Americans to recover the rights they have lost to an increasingly bureaucratic Washington with its tendency to peer into the private lives of Americans....Private Paul Crouch of the U.S. Army has been sentenced to 40 years in, prison for his efforts to launch a Communist plot in Hawaii.	Ammunition and other supplies are ordered to supply the military citizens training camps that will open throughout the United States in the summer....The 27th Infantry Division, New York's National Guard Division will mobilize in 1926 for maneuvers; it is the first time that the entire division has been mobilized since World War I.	The City of Chicago takes over 75 acres of land to create an airport for the city; it is expected that it will be ready to handle aircraft in two weeks and will be expanded by an additional 300 acres.	It is announced that an international conference will be held in May to investigate the best ways that radio can support police work.	Atlantic City announces that it will remove restrictions on women's bathing suits other than that the skirt must be at least 11 inches long....American composer Aaron Copland writes a letter to The New York Times in which he defends the music of Gustav Mahler saying that even when his musical ideas are not original, his means of expressing them are....Obeying orders from the Baltimore Police Department, the dancers in a show entitled "Seduction" dance with tin pie plates between their chins and waists in order to avoid charges of indecency.	Apr. 4
		The American Engineering Council states that it will begin campaign to examine how the government does business and to maker recommendations to eliminate waste.			Apr. 5
The Catholic Welfare Workers declare that no American labor unions will support any birth control initiatives.		A Federal District Court in Tennessee declares that the Piggly Wiggly Stores Corporation can recover more than $1.6 million from its founder.		Ed "Strangler" Lewis successfully defeats Joe "Toots" Mondt in a 48-minute wrestling match held in Tulsa, OK....German conductor, Otto Klemperer, is announced to be the guest conductor of the New York Symphony Orchestra....The League of Nations announces that it will issue a list of the best 600 books published each year.	Apr. 6
		The Studebaker Company announces that because its output of 600 cars a day exceeds demand, it will go into the bus manufacturing business....President Calvin Coolidge announces to a meeting of cotton merchants that he is opposed to raising protective tariffs on imported goods.	In Lexington, KY, archaeologists discover the skeletons of 21 Native Americans, thought to have belonged to a prehistoric tribe.	It is announced that The Makropoulos Secret, a play by Czech writer Karel Capek who wrote Rossum's Universal Robots, will soon be produced in New York City.	Apr. 7
			A professor from Johns Hopkins University, Robert Wood, states that infrared light can be used effectively for military signaling as well as detecting forgeries.... Secretary of the Navy Curtis Wilbur appoints Commander Richard Byrd to command the Navy unit that will accompany the Macmillan expedition to the North Pole.	McKinley, the last surviving horse of Wild Bill Cody, dies in his stall, eight years after his master's death....Mrs. Mary Saunders, the first woman to ever make a living as a typist (1875–1906), dies at the age of 73.	Apr. 8
	The Navy dirigible Los Angeles is still undergoing repairs and will not leave Lakehurst, NJ, today.		Austrian engineers test a new form of turbine to generate electric power from the Danube River....The Naval officer ion charge of radio communications for the Macmillan polar exploration team says that the group will issue daily progress bulletins on a daily basis....The British polar expedition, which will rely on using a blimp, is also making preparations for its late May departure.	Students at the University of Chicago stay awake for 115 hours as part of an insomnia study....Silent film star Ben Turpin announces that he will retire from the movie industry in order to take care of his wife who is recovering from a series of strokes.	Apr. 9

F	G	H	I	J
Includes campaigns, elections, federal-state relations, civil rights and liberties, crime, the judiciary, education, healthcare, poverty, urban affairs, and population.	Includes formation and debate of U.S. foreign and defense policies, veterans affairs, and defense spending. (Relations with specific foreign countries are usually found under the region concerned.)	Includes business, labor, agriculture, taxation, transportation, consumer affairs, monetary and fiscal policy, natural resources, pollution and industrial accidents.	Includes worldwide scientific, medical and technological developments, natural phenomena, U.S. weather and natural disasters.	Includes the arts, religion, scholarship, communications media, sports, entertainment, fashions, fads, and social life.

	World Affairs	Europe	Africa & The Middle East	The Americas	Asia & The Pacific
Apr. 10		The Soviet Union announces it will begin publishing a newspaper in Paris.	Continuing his tour of Africa, the Prince of Wales meets with Ashanti chiefs.		
Apr. 11		The Zeppelin company announces it may move from its current facilities in Friedrichshafen in Germany to Switzerland.			The China Inland Mission says that one of its missionaries who was captured by bandits has been released.
Apr. 12	Switzerland, France, Sweden, and Britain officially protest actions by the U.S. government to gather information in their countries that will be used to determine whether the United States will impose protective tariffs.	An editorial in a German newspaper attacks the candidacy of Paul von Hindenburg for president especially as he has huge support from the pro-Monarchist faction....Austria's heavy imports which have created a serious trade imbalance are reported to be decreasing while its exports increase.		Mexico's most famous bullfighter, Rodolpho Gaona, retires at the age of 38 after a career of 18 years....The authorities in Tampico, Mexico, are taking measures to safeguard the health of the city after a rat with symptoms of bubonic plague has been caught.	
Apr. 13		Officials in London state that because the prime minister's quarters at No. 10 Downing Street are so old and in such disrepair, they may tear the building down and provide another house for the prime ministers to live in.			France joins the nations that have signed the Nine-Power Treaty which will regulate customs agreements between the Chinese and western nations.
Apr. 14		Officials from the Austrian government state their intention to bring a proposal to the League of Nations to united Austria and Germany....After more than 35 political assassinations in the past few months, terrorists attempt to kill Bulgaria's King Boris.	A Franco-American archaeological expedition in Tunis reports that it has found a cluster of prehistoric homes....The Prince of Wales leaves the Port of Accra on the Gold Coast as he continues on his tour....Lord Balfour leaves Alexandria to conclude his tour of the Middle East.	The Colombian Army attempts to overthrow the government fails when several of the leaders are arrested....The government of Honduras declares martial law to counter an attempt to overthrow the government.	
Apr. 15		Paris Police foil an attempt by a Russian emigré to assassinate the Soviet Ambassador to France....The Danish press criticizes Arctic explorer Donald MacMillan for his earlier comments that Denmark's control of Greenland could cause problems for the United States.	Unconfirmed reports indicate that the Turkish Army may have captured Sheik Said, the leader of the Kurdish rebels....The Turkish National Assembly has accepted a government proposal to give free land to establish embassies in the new capital of Ankara.	General Gerardo Machado, President of Mexico visits President Calvin Coolidge while on tour in the United States.	
Apr. 16	The Italian government denies that there are problems in the negotiations it is conducting with Egypt to determine the border between Egypt and the Italian possession of Libya....The League of Nations is told that if the boundary commission's report about fixing the borders between Turkey and northern Iraq are unsatisfactory, the Turkish Army will mobilize and invade.	In the wake of the assassination attempt against Bulgaria's King Boris, there is new rioting in the capital of Sofia; at least 20 have been killed when a bomb explodes in Sofia's cathedral....The Polish government prohibits the sale of several Jewish newspapers.		The Argentine government has accepted an invitation to a League of Nations conference on controlling arms trafficking....The U.S. government protests the seizure by the Mexican government of an American-owned power plant....Guatemala refuses permission to enter the country to a group of labor leaders who are trying to create labor unions in the country....Nicaragua and Honduras announce their cooperation in patrolling their mutual border to clear it of revolutionaries and bandits.	

A	B	C	D	E
Includes developments that affect more than one world region, international organizations and important meetings of world leaders.	*Includes all domestic and regional developments in Europe, including the Soviet Union.*	*Includes all domestic and regional developments in Africa and the Middle East.*	*Includes all domestic and regional developments in Latin America, the Caribbean, and Canada.*	*Includes all domestic and regional developments in Asian and Pacific nations (and colonies).*

U.S. Politics & Social Issues	U.S. Foreign Policy & Affairs, Defense	U.S. Economy & Environment	Science, Technology & Nature	Culture, Leisure & Lifestyle	
In Jasper, Alabama, Homer Sanderson, a member of the Ku Klux Klan, is found guilty of flogging a man who made derogatory comments about the Klan.			The National Geographic Society announces that it believes that because the Macmillan polar expedition will be exploring in the summer that it may well find land in the north pole region....Paleontologists in Utah discover the skeleton of a dinosaur that they estimate to be 16 million years old.	Miners are still working at getting to the body of Floyd Collins from the cave where he died.... President Calvin Coolidge denies that he spent $65 for a suit for Easter, stating that he already has an adequate supply of suits.	Apr. 10
			Doctor William Beebe makes radio contact with the naval Station at Balboa, Panama, stating that the exploration is going well.	Over a million radio listeners listen to a program asking for donations to save and restore Jefferson's home at Monticello and turn it into a National monument.	Apr. 11
				Over 200,000 participate in the Atlantic City Easter Parade....The Easter Parade in New York City on Fifth Avenue is the largest since World War I.	Apr. 12
		Ford's Air Service between Chicago and Detroit begins air service, which it will continue on a daily basis....Auto manufacturers ask the U.S. Secretary of the Treasury to eliminate federal taxes on autos which would decrease the price per car by $31....The Postmaster General issues new regulations that will allow companies that provide air mail service to the government can now carry passengers and freight as well.	Roald Amundsen arrives at Spitzbergen from which he will begin his polar expedition.		Apr. 13
Madge Oberholtzer, who took poison after being assaulted by former Ku Klux Klan Grand Dragon, D.C. Stephenson, dies.		The National Biscuit Company declares a profit of $2,877,031 profit in the first quarter of 1925.	Since the beginning of the year, Philadelphia has reported more than 100 cases of smallpox while nearby Camden, NJ, has reported even more cases.	Will Rogers and Harry Houdini are among the stars appearing at a benefit for a Children's Clinic in New York City....Tom Mix arrives in England to begin his European tour.	Apr. 14
A vigilance committee of 250 men in Kansas City, Kansas is issued weapons to protect banks from being robbed.	Lucille Atcherson is named as appointed to the U.S. Legation in Berne, Switzerland, making her the first woman named to a U.S. diplomatic post....President Calvin Coolidge declares that National Guard pay which had been stopped in March will be continued for the remainder of 1925....The U.S. Pacific Fleet, now numbering 127 ships approaches the island of Hawaii as it begins preparations for the land and sea maneuvers that will take place there.	The petroleum industry announces that while production has been higher than ever, the great use of fuel in the past months has offset that resulting in higher prices.	A new type of loudspeaker using a paper cone is tested and is demonstrated at the Institute of Electrical Engineers....An x-ray photograph of a hand is transmitted by wire from New York to Chicago in a process lasting only seven minutes.	To pay their way through school, 150 University of Michigan students are giving blood transfusions, as needed....Hungarian composer and conductor Ernst von Dohnanyi discusses his plans when he will assume duties as Guest Conductor for the State Symphony Orchestra in New York....American artist John Singer Sargent dies at the age of 69....Evangelist Billy Sunday opens a revival in New York City fir the first time since 1917 as the first stop on a six-week tour.	Apr. 15
Senator Bob LaFollette criticizes the Coolidge administration and the Republican Party for giving "the country four years of government in the interests of big business."	Approximately 12,000 U.S. Army troops in Hawaii are put on alert as the planned war games and simulated invasion are about to begin.	Dr. William Beebe, aboard the *Arcturus* discovers two new volcanoes off the Galapagos islands.	The *R-33*, Britain's dirigible tears loose from its mooring mast and is blown out to sea by a gale; it returns but in a damaged state....Dr. William Sadler states that a condition he calls "Americanitis" which combines heart disease, strokes, and high blood pressure claims at least a quarter million unnecessary deaths a year....Fokker Aircraft experiments with a new safety device that will improve stability and safety in flight.		Apr. 16

F	G	H	I	J
Includes campaigns, elections, federal-state relations, civil rights and liberties, crime, the judiciary, education, healthcare, poverty, urban affairs, and population.	Includes formation and debate of U.S. foreign and defense policies, veterans affairs, and defense spending. (Relations with specific foreign countries are usually found under the region concerned.)	Includes business, labor, agriculture, taxation, transportation, consumer affairs, monetary and fiscal policy, natural resources, pollution and industrial accidents.	Includes worldwide scientific, medical and technological developments, natural phenomena, U.S. weather and natural disasters.	Includes the arts, religion, scholarship, communications media, sports, entertainment, fashions, fads, and social life.

	World Affairs	Europe	Africa & The Middle East	The Americas	Asia & The Pacific
Apr. 17		Reports from Moscow indicate that some of the Soviet leaders are prepared to make a peace with Leon Trotsky and restore him to a position of power....The death toll in Sofia in the wake of the bomb blast in the Cathedral is now estimated to be 150 dead; police have not yet located the individuals who tried to kill King Boris.			
Apr. 18	A League of Nations report indicates that little progress has been made in reducing arms and armies worldwide.	A revolt against the Portuguese government begins; the president and cabinet leave Lisbon, but shortly return....The attempt to assassinate King Boris and set off the bomb is Sofia Cathedral is identified as a Communist plot.	The Prince of Wales arrives in Nigeria, receiving the local chiefs and reviewing a parade of 20,000 troops.	Mexico states that it will not attend the League of Nations conference on curbing the arms trade....Women in the British possession of Bermuda fail to get the vote.	Japanese police have made several arrests in a plot to bomb the port of Osaka.
Apr. 19	The Turkish and Japanese governments renew diplomatic relations.	German Presidential Candidate Paul von Hindenburg is cheered at a rally; he has a great deal of pro-Monarchist support....Reports from Vienna indicate that the Bulgarian government has executed 400 Communists so far after the attempted assassination of the ing and a bomb blast in Sofia's cathedral....German iron and steel production continue to increase due mostly to the auto and railroad industries.	Turkish journalists are being held for trial for writing articles that are considered to be prejudicial to the maintenance of order....A riot involving 4,000 Africans breaks out in the Orange Free State, South Africa.	The Mexican government announces it may begin to draft citizens into the Army.	
Apr. 20	The Commission on Hygiene of the League of Nations, already tasked with cancer research takes on the added assignment of investigating cures for tuberculosis.	Soldiers and police continue to search for conspirators and have sealed off the City of Sofia....Echoing Mexico's objections, the Soviet Union states that it will not participate in any arms control talks sponsored by the League of Nations.		Brazil's President Artur Bernardes states that he will not grant any pardons to any individuals who have rebelled against the government....The U.S. Navy lands a force of 165 men in Honduras to protect American lives and property during the revolt in that country.	
Apr. 21		Reports from London and Vienna describe a recent meeting of the Communist Third International (Comintern) in which their most recent plans are to establish a Soviet state along the Danube River and the Balkans....The Yugoslavian government issues a denial that it is planning to invade Bulgaria during its internal rioting and violence.	Aga Khan, a prominent Indian Muslim, states that if the British do not lift their restrictions on Indians traveling to British possessions in Africa that they will go and work in the French possessions that need their labor....Moroccans attack French troops, marking a new development in a war in which their fighting has been against the Spanish in that region.	Dr. L. S. Rowe, Director General of the Pan-American Association states that on a recent trip to Latin America he found a tendency to equate American investment wit as a form of imperialism....The uprising in Honduras spreads; the American government states that it will land troops again if it feels that Americans and their property need protection.	
Apr. 22		The Allied Council of Ambassadors authorizes Bulgaria to increase its army by an additional 7,000 men to keep order in the recent wave of bombings and terrorist attacks....The Soviet newspaper, *Pravda*, issues an angry denial that the unrest in Bulgaria has been initiated or encouraged by the Soviet Union.	The city of Johannesburg in South Africa prepares the expected visit of the Prince of Wales.		
Apr. 23		The Vatican denies that it is intervening in German politics that it is coming out on the side of Paul von Hindenburg....The Greek government mobilizes its troops and deploys them on its border with Bulgaria in response to the fighting in that country; Romania does the same.	The French Army sends troops into the border area between French and Spanish Morocco in an effort to put pressure on the Moors in that region that are fighting both the Spanish and French governments.	The Mexican newspaper *El Globo* ceases publication, claiming that the Mexican government pressured advertisers to stop supporting the newspaper.	

A	B	C	D	E
Includes developments that affect more than one world region, international organizations and important meetings of world leaders.	Includes all domestic and regional developments in Europe, including the Soviet Union.	Includes all domestic and regional developments in Africa and the Middle East.	Includes all domestic and regional developments in Latin America, the Caribbean, and Canada.	Includes all domestic and regional developments in Asian and Pacific nations (and colonies).

U.S. Politics & Social Issues	U.S. Foreign Policy & Affairs, Defense	U.S. Economy & Environment	Science, Technology & Nature	Culture, Leisure & Lifestyle	
The home of D.C. Stephenson, former Ku Klux Klan Grand Dragon who is under indictment for kidnapping Madge Oberholzer is fire bombed; Stephenson is now being investigated and will probably be indicted for murder.				The *Harvard Lampoon* is banned from sale in Boston and Cambridge because of its cover of Washington Crossing the Delaware may be considered a violation of the flag law.	Apr. 17
Former Grand Dragon of the Ku Klux Klan, D.C. Stephenson is indicted for the murder of Madge Oberholzer....The Legislature of the State of Delaware votes to retain the whipping post for crimes; there were nine whippings in 1924.	The Plattsburg, NY, military training camp for the summer of 1925 is rapidly approaching its quota of 4,700 young men....The new Italian Ambassador to the U.S. states that America's mass output and the high quality of Italy's production complement each other and he looks forward to good economic relations between the two nations.	The New York Traffic Commission reports that 364,000 commuters come into New York City each day....Edsel Ford predicts that in the "not too distant future" individuals will own airplanes.		In an interview, Dean Howard McClenahan blames the auto for the shift in moral codes and the use of drugs, and decrease in church attendance....A massive rally is held in Atlantic City to protest the Volstead (Prohibition) Act as it currently stands.	Apr. 18
D.C. Stephenson surrenders to police to face trial for the murder of Madge Oberholzer.	The United States will meet with Mexico to discuss an anti-smuggling treaty (liquor and drugs).	Business leaders express fears that the recent U.S. postal rate raises will harm the economy	A French inventor describes his latest invention, an anti-aircraft shell containing a large net that will either catch propellers or break the wings of overhead aircraft.	F. Scott Fitzgerald's new novel, *The Great Gatsby* is reviewed in The *New York Times*.	Apr. 19
In a speech to the Daughters of the American Revolution, President Calvin Coolidge defends immigration limits, stating that lowering restrictions would allow too many aliens into the country.	U.S. Secretary of State Kellogg issues a statement to American diplomats abroad that there will be no change in the U.S. policy toward the Soviet Union; there will be no recognition of the Soviet Union.		With a now recorded 129 victims, the smallpox outbreak in Philadelphia continues; the previous average has been 15 cases a year.	The Boston Marathon takes place with 120 runners entered; Charles Mellor wins the 26-mile race running it in two hours and 33 minutes....The Associated Press celebrates its 25th anniversary....Reenactors at Lexington and Concord Massachusetts celebrate the 150th anniversary of the battles that began the American Revolution.	Apr. 20
The U.S. government announces that it is starting schools to train Volstead (Prohibition) agents for the government.		The Secretary of the American Dairy Federation in a speech states that big business is attempting to centralize power in the White House and "exploit the federal government for the benefit of the strong."...The Department of Agriculture completes its plans for using aircraft to patrol for forest fires in the western United States.	A new two-way radio record is established when communications occur between the U.S. Naval Observatory in Washington and an experimental laboratory in Sydney, Australia.		Apr. 21
The Attorney General of Wisconsin states that the Ku Klux Klan cannot legally incorporate in that state.			At a meeting of the American Institute of Architects, Harvey Corbett predicts that by 1975 there will be no cars on the streets of New York City and that people will travel through pneumatic tubes.	President Calvin Coolidge throws out the first pitch for the Washington Senators who beat the New York Yankees 10-1....A group of ministers in New Bedford, MA, protests the public reading of *Desire Under the Elms* by Eugene O'Neill and get the subject matter changed.	Apr. 22
			The U.S. Department of Agriculture describes its recent experiments to kill rodents by the use of carbon monoxide by hooking up cars that running to tubes....Sigmund Freud, in his just-published autobiography states that he never received the credit owed him for his discovery of cocaine as a local anesthetic.	Actor George Arliss states that among current evils in the theatre is the search for plays of the Elizabethan era with their themes of revenge, violence, and immoral behavior....Rogers Hornsby, star hitter of the St. Louis Cardinals is hospitalized after a concussion resulting from being hit on the head by a baseball.	Apr. 23

F	G	H	I	J
Includes campaigns, elections, federal-state relations, civil rights and liberties, crime, the judiciary, education, healthcare, poverty, urban affairs, and population.	*Includes formation and debate of U.S. foreign and defense policies, veterans affairs, and defense spending. (Relations with specific foreign countries are usually found under the region concerned.)*	*Includes business, labor, agriculture, taxation, transportation, consumer affairs, monetary and fiscal policy, natural resources, pollution and industrial accidents.*	*Includes worldwide scientific, medical and technological developments, natural phenomena, U.S. weather and natural disasters.*	*Includes the arts, religion, scholarship, communications media, sports, entertainment, fashions, fads, and social life.*

	World Affairs	Europe	Africa & The Middle East	The Americas	Asia & The Pacific
Apr. 24		Czechoslovakia signs a series of agreements with Poland concerning trade and the settlement of border questions....Reports indicate that in violation of the treaty agreements that ended World War I, German planes have been violating French airspace....The Soviet government announces that it will allow additional factories to operate privately, without direct government supervision.	The League of Nations commission charged with studying the border between Iraq and Turkey begins its reports.		
Apr. 25	The League of Nations announces that several of its bodies will meet in May to include Control of Arms Traffic, others include Commissions on White Slavery and protections of children, economics, and mutual assistance in the event of natural catastrophes.	Rome celebrates its 2,878th anniversary; accompanying the celebrations is a Fascist declaration claiming that extralegal activities on the part of the Fascists have been necessary to defend Italy's freedom....The presidential election in Germany is held today.... New outbreaks of violence occur in other cities outside of Sofia, Bulgaria.	General Primo de Rivera of Spain rules out an attempted conquest of all of Morocco due to the large number of troops such a campaign would entail.		
Apr. 26	Cuba's President Gerardo Machado, at a luncheon given in his honor in New York, endorses arbitration as a means of eventually outlawing war.	Election returns indicate that Paul von Hindenburg is elected as president of Germany....British observers as well as those from France and Italy express dismay over this result, principally because of the support Hindenburg received from the pro-Monarchist faction....In Berlin, two men are killed and scores injured as a result of election day rioting; other riots and disturbances are reported throughout the country.	The Turkish government is sending in additional troops with artillery and air support to combat the continuing Kurdish revolt.	A general strike in the Mexican City of Puebla has paralyzed the city; thus far three have been killed and three injured.	
Apr. 27		The results of the presidential election in Germany indicate that 3,500,000 more voters participated than had voted in the primary....Ex-Kaiser Wilhelm II states he is very happy with the election and would return from exile to Germany if he were asked to.			
Apr. 28	Representatives of the League of Nations express fear that the election of Paul von Hindenburg as president of Germany will lead to a dangerous escalation in German nationalism.	Both censorship and martial law are lifted as the Portuguese government regains control after the attempted revolt.			
Apr. 29		Archaeologists find a Roman mosaic near Budapest....The French government announces that it may to turn to the gold standard as the basis for its currency, as the British are now doing; analysts predict that Italy and Belgium will soon follow suit.	Moorish raiders in Morocco have stepped up their raids against the French in that region.		
Apr. 30		The Soviet government announces that it has signed a 50-year contract with a British company to exploit the gold fields of Siberia.... Police throughout Europe are preparing for what they fear will be widespread disorder during the May Day parades to be held tomorrow....Latvian police raid a Communist operation that has been manufacturing false passports....In a book published in London, Max Eastman asserts that shortly before his death, Vladimir I. Lenin wanted Josef Stalin and others removed from positions of responsibility in the Soviet government.	The Prince of Wales lands at Capetown, South Africa, as he continues his tour of Africa.	The Brazilian government states that rebels in the state of Sao Paulo who were earlier defeated are now reviving their activities.	

A	B	C	D	E
Includes developments that affect more than one world region, international organizations and important meetings of world leaders.	Includes all domestic and regional developments in Europe, including the Soviet Union.	Includes all domestic and regional developments in Africa and the Middle East.	Includes all domestic and regional developments in Latin America, the Caribbean, and Canada.	Includes all domestic and regional developments in Asian and Pacific nations (and colonies).

U.S. Politics & Social Issues	U.S. Foreign Policy & Affairs, Defense	U.S. Economy & Environment	Science, Technology & Nature	Culture, Leisure & Lifestyle	
Anarchist Bartolomeo Vanzetti is returned to prison after being held for psychiatric evaluation; he and Nicola Sacco have been convicted for murder and are awaiting the results of their appeal.		Radio Corporation of America (RCA) reports that its gross income for the first quarter of 1925 is $15,229,923, an increase over the last year.	It is announced that a party of 90 German climbers will launch a climbing expedition on Mount Everest in July....Doctor William Beebe's exploration of the ocean continues, most recently in studying sea life as his assistants fight off sharks that wander too closely to him....The third earthquake since January hits southern New England.	Boxer Jack Dempsey states that he believes that Gene Tunney is the chief contender for a title battle....For the first time since the end of the war in 1865, Civil War veterans in White Plains, NY, will not march in the Civil War memorial parade; there are few survivors and those remaining are in poor health.	Apr. 24
	The U.S. Fleet and Army maneuvers continue in the Pacific with a mock attack on the island of Oahu.	Warner Brothers movie company buys the Vitagraph Recording Company....The Patent Bureau is transferred to the Department of Commerce in a move that is seen to speed up the process for approving patents.	In an article published in a German science magazine, the diminishing gorilla population is blamed on hunters working for museums in America and Europe.	It is estimated that as many as 200,000 Americans will travel to Europe in the next three months, setting a record....The Atlantic City Beauty Pageant (later to be known as the Miss America contest) bars widows and married women from participating....The New York Times reviews Edith Wharton's newest novel, The Mother's Recompense.	Apr. 25
A drive among African Americans with the support of several politicians begins to have Frederick Douglass placed in the U.S. Hall of Fame.	In the Pacific Fleet, maneuvers the "invading" fleet scores a significant victory over the defenders and captures the Hawaiian airfields according to the maneuver's umpires; Oahu has still not been "captured."			The Pulitzer Prizes for 1924 are awarded; the winners include Edna Ferber for her novel, So Big, Edward Arlington Robinson for his book of poems, The Man Who Died Twice, and Sidney Hoard's Play, They Knew What They Wanted.	Apr. 26
Of the 4,293,000 men and women eligible to apply under the U.S. government Bonus Act, 2,972,425 have applied for relief; this bill had passed over President Calvin Coolidge's veto.	The Pacific Army and Navy maneuvers end with the "invading" fleet landing U.S. Marines "captures" the island of Oahu; the maneuvers used large numbers of submarines and airplanes as well as battleships, cruiser, and other traditional ships.		Donald MacMillan, who is preparing an arctic expedition that will soon depart, states that controversy about Robert Perry wrong and that there is no doubt that Perry reached the North Pole in 1909.... Over 800 specimens of fossils from South America are brought to the Field Museum in Chicago.		Apr. 27
More than 150 members of the Ku Klux Klan are held prisoners by more than 200 anti-Klan sympathizers who have surrounded them and will not let them depart.					Apr. 28
Cigarette smugglers are increasing their activities across the U.S.-Canada border as cigarette smuggling is more profitable than bringing in illicit liquor.	The Navy reports that Japanese vessels followed and observed the U.S. Fleet while on maneuvers from the Coast of California to the conclusion of the war games.			Paavo Nurmi, racing in Los Angeles breaks the record for the 1.5 mile race.	Apr. 29
		The Boston and Maine Railroad announces that it is launching a lawsuit to prevent bus lines from establishing a route along rail lines operated by the B&M.... Secretary of Commerce Herbert Hoover states that Britain's return to the gold standard as the basis for its currency will benefit the world economy.	Smallpox outbreaks in Washington, DC have resulted in 19 deaths since the beginning of the year; the head of Public Health requests that the 62,000 civil service employees in the city be vaccinated.	Dancer Isadora Duncan announces that she has bought a theatre in Nice, France, to provide a venue for those who do not like jazz.	Apr. 30

F	G	H	I	J
Includes campaigns, elections, federal-state relations, civil rights and liberties, crime, the judiciary, education, healthcare, poverty, urban affairs, and population.	Includes formation and debate of U.S. foreign and defense policies, veterans affairs, and defense spending. (Relations with specific foreign countries are usually found under the region concerned.)	Includes business, labor, agriculture, taxation, transportation, consumer affairs, monetary and fiscal policy, natural resources, pollution and industrial accidents.	Includes worldwide scientific, medical and technological developments, natural phenomena, U.S. weather and natural disasters.	Includes the arts, religion, scholarship, communications media, sports, entertainment, fashions, fads, and social life.

	World Affairs	Europe	Africa & The Middle East	The Americas	Asia & The Pacific
May 1		Other than the huge celebrations held in the Soviet Union, May Day celebrations in Europe are more peaceful than had been anticipated by law enforcement officials....May Day celebrations in Italy are quiet and not well attended; peaceful demonstrations are held in Germany, France, Britain, and Denmark....The tension between Germany and Poland continues: a train wreck in the Polish Corridor bordering on Germany kills 25 and is blamed by the Germans on Polish incompetence.	The Prince of Wales, now in Capetown, South Africa leads a parade and is enthusiastically received....An archaeological expedition in Tunis uncovers at least 4,000 archeological specimens at a prehistoric settlement.		
May 2		President of the Directory that rules Spain, General Primo de Rivera states that Spain wants to halt the fighting in Morocco as soon as possible....The Italian government announces that it will form a new cabinet-level Ministry of Aviation.			Two Lutheran missionaries in China are kidnapped by bandits.
May 3	Delegates of 42 nations meet under the Sponsorship of the League of Nations to discuss controlling the flow of arms from one nation to another.	Reports from Belgrade indicate that the Yugoslav government will be demanding an accounting from the Austrian government about why Vienna has become the headquarters of Communist anti-government activity throughout eastern Europe....In local elections in France the Socialists do very well, defeating many Communist candidates....Italy reports that thus far in 1925 it has imported far more than it has exported.	French troops succeed in driving back Moors under Abd-el-Krim in the area near the city of Fez....The Prince of Wales meets with South African Nationalists who wish to secede from the Dominion, delivers a speech in Dutch, and receives an enthusiastic reception.		
May 4			In a day along the Moroccan front that is relatively quiet, French units manage to resupply small outposts that had been surrounded by the Moors.		Emilio Aguinaldo who formerly led opposition to the Americans in the Philippines at the turn of the century, urges that Filipinos support the current U.S. administration.
May 5		Newly elected German President Paul von Hindenburg leaves the possibility open that he will grant an amnesty to certain political prisoners shortly after he assumes office....The German Communist Party announces it will conduct a 24-hour strike on the day that Hindenburg enters Berlin.			
May 6		The Bulgarian government outlaws the Communist Party....Reports from the Soviet Union describe "armies of children" who are orphaned, without shelter, and starving....Socialists and other political parties in Germany assert that Paul von Hindenburg's election was a fraud and demand that the election results be invalidated....According to reports, the political exile of Leon Trotsky is to end and he will return to Moscow today.	French soldiers are continuing their fight with the Moors who number approximately 20,000 and, according to some reports, have European advisors assisting them....A tribunal condemns two Armenians to death for plotting to assassinate Turkey's Premier, Ismet Pasha.	Labor Unions in Peru show their support of the Peruvian-Chilean border arbitration and support the plebiscite to determine which country will claim the Tacna-Arica border provinces.	The two missionaries captured by bandits in Hunan province are returned unhurt.
May 7	At the Geneva Conference, the U.S. representative proposes a complete ban on the transportation of poison gas from one nation to another....Britain surprises delegates at the arms convention by proposing that warships not be considered as part of the arms manufactured in one country and sold to another that would be regulated by the League convention currently under discussion.	Bulgaria proposes a union of all Balkan countries to oppose the Communists....Czechoslovakia's Foreign Minister, Eduard Benes, has cancelled his visit to Vienna; most observers see it as a sign of the worsening relations between Austria and Czechoslovakia.... Leon Trotsky returns to Moscow but receives a very cool reception from leaders of the Soviet Union; there is to be further discussion of what, if any position he will be offered.	Marshal Louis Lyautey, the French Commander in Morocco tells the French government he cannot succeed with the number of troops he currently has and that he needs reinforcements; reports indicate that the Moors are receiving aid from German military advisors and the French government is investigating the sources of advisors and weapons that the Moors currently have.		A great deal of unrest is gwoing in China with warlords and bandits raoming through the countryside, especially in Szechuan province and Manchuria....Premier Kato Takaaki of Japan, who has been attacked in his home and faces significant opposition for wanting to extend voting rights, is currently opposed by Baron Tanaka, who plans to succeed to the premiership.

A	B	C	D	E
Includes developments that affect more than one world region, international organizations and important meetings of world leaders.	Includes all domestic and regional developments in Europe, including the Soviet Union.	Includes all domestic and regional developments in Africa and the Middle East.	Includes all domestic and regional developments in Latin America, the Caribbean, and Canada.	Includes all domestic and regional developments in Asian and Pacific nations (and colonies).

U.S. Politics & Social Issues	U.S. Foreign Policy & Affairs, Defense	U.S. Economy & Environment	Science, Technology & Nature	Culture, Leisure & Lifestyle	
May Day rallies in the United States include a Communist rally held at the Metropolitan Opera House in New York where both capitalists and Socialists are condemned.	The U.S. Army and Navy convene that largest post-war games study they have ever held to examine what lessons can be learned from the recent Army and Navy maneuvers in Hawaii.	Mail order houses report significant increases in sales so far in 1925; Sears, Roebuck & Co reports a gain of over 8 percent over what it sold at this time in 1924....The U.S. Treasury Department admits that its efforts to circulate silver dollars is unsuccessful and people would rather use paper money than dollar coins.	A Navy airplane, being tested for a planned flight from California to Hawaii remains aloft for at least 16 hours and is still flying.		May 1
		Crude oil output is at its highest since 1923....The National Automobile Chamber of Commerce announces that U.S. auto production in 1924 numbered 3,243,285 cars and 374,317 trucks.	The Navy conducts experiments using short wave radio on board aircraft; signals from an aircraft flying in Minnesota are heard in Florida.	An article in The New York Times describes the four year-old development of Coral Gables, FL; the area now comprises 16-square-miles with 100 miles of paved roads....German tourist agencies and hotels are preparing for a large influx of tourists, many of them from America.	May 2
In Berlin, Massachusetts, a gathering of 300 members of the Ku Klux Klan is surrounded and stoned by local residents.			The Wright aircraft company announces that it has developed an air cooled engine, called the Cyclone, providing great power and weighing at least 200 pounds less than conventional liquid-cooled engines.		May 3
			Earthquake tremors are once again felt in the Northeastern U.S.		May 4
	The conference of Navy and Army officers meeting in Hawaii to discuss the lessons learned of the current maneuvers come to the conclusion that Hawaii is poorly defended and that it does not have the facilities required to adequately support the Navy.	Railroads of the eastern U.S. ask the Interstate Commerce Commission not to cut rates for hauling freight; Western U.S. railroads petition to have their rates increased.		A boxing match held at Madison Square Garden in New York is the last event held there before it is to be demolished later in the week....In a game against the St. Louis Browns, Detroit's Ty Cobb hits three home runs, tying the major league record for home runs in one game.	May 5
	Senator William Borah is forced to clarify his earlier remarks about nations not paying their war debts to the United States; he asserts he did not mean that the United States should go to war to get the money back....Admiral Bradley Fiske, in a speech to the New Jersey Chamber of Commerce, states that he was responsible for the American victory in World War I as Woodrow Wilson and his Naval Secretary, Josephus Daniels, were pacifists and were not interested in preparedness.	The All America Cables Company celebrates its 47th birthday and announces that its total amount of cable in operation is 28,300 miles throughout North and South America....The national Petroleum Institute announces that crude oil production for the week ending May 2 was 2,182,850 barrels, an increase of 26,400 barrels over the previous week.		Ty Cobb sets a major league record by hitting two home runs for a total of five home runs in two consecutive games.	May 6
At Howard University, 400 students strike over the imposition of compulsory ROTC training....The American Federation of Labor in extending its organization announces it will make a serious effort to incorporate African-American workers.	President Calvin Coolidge receives the first diplomat from Austria to be stationed in the United States since World War I.		Photos of the recent war games are transmitted by radio to California, a distance of over 5,000 miles in 20 minutes for each picture.		May 7

F	G	H	I	J
Includes campaigns, elections, federal-state relations, civil rights and liberties, crime, the judiciary, education, healthcare, poverty, urban affairs, and population.	Includes formation and debate of U.S. foreign and defense policies, veterans affairs, and defense spending. (Relations with specific foreign countries are usually found under the region concerned.)	Includes business, labor, agriculture, taxation, transportation, consumer affairs, monetary and fiscal policy, natural resources, pollution and industrial accidents.	Includes worldwide scientific, medical and technological developments, natural phenomena, U.S. weather and natural disasters.	Includes the arts, religion, scholarship, communications media, sports, entertainment, fashions, fads, and social life.

	World Affairs	Europe	Africa & The Middle East	The Americas	Asia & The Pacific
May 8	France and Norway state their opposition to Britain's proposal excluding warships from the convention regulating the transportation of arms; Britain's proposal is supported by Italy and Japan.	Benito Mussolini announces that in addition to his current responsibilities, he will become the Minister of the Navy; he also is Minister of Foreign Affairs, Army, and Air....A Reichstag committee has investigated the Paul von Hindenburg election and concluded that it is valid and that irregularities in the elections were too few to actually affect the result....Bulgarian military courts sentence 20 anti-government conspirators to death.	Hussein Jahid Bey is convicted of criticizing the government and is sentenced to life-long exile in a small town in Turkey's interior.	Nicaragua announces that it has rejected a project to dig a canal across Nicaragua from the Atlantic to Pacific oceans.	
May 9	In the conference on purchasing and transporting arms, small nations have won the right, with some restrictions, to import arms; this is seen as preferable to more nations starting up armaments industries.	After being offered a plan that will cut their wages, 93 percent of all Belgian miners vote to go on strike....The Greek government votes to provide funds to restore the Parthenon....Foreign Ministers of the "Little Entente" (Czechoslovakia, Yugoslavia, and Romania) are holding a meeting in which they discuss the effects of events in Bulgaria, Hungary, and the proposed Union of Germany and Austria....The Italian government begins preparation for a new defense law that will make any comments critical of the government a punishable offense.	Abd-el-Krim, in the midst of his successes against both the French and Spanish, has stated that he wishes to establish a form of self-government for his countrymen....While a French unit manages to relieve a military outpost, the Moors manage to capture and destroy another....The Makwar Dam on the Blue Nile is completed; the dam will make it possible to use an additional 300,000 acres for growing cotton in the Sudan.	A plot is reported of Mexican generals having had a conference in Phoenix, Arizona, to overthrow the Mexican government.... Conferences between labor unions and farmers groups in Mexico to determine the political activities of each group have broken off.... Mexico signs a treaty pledging to aid the United States in cutting down drug trafficking....The state of Maine issues a statement that it should receive a share in the power produced at a Canadian power station on the St. John River in New Brunswick....The Panamanian government expresses concerns that the San Blas Indians who recently revolted and were pacified may be planning another uprising.	
May 10		Joan of Arc Day passes in France without the fights between Catholics and Communist that were anticipated....35 days after its cabinet resigned, Belgium is still without a government as a new cabinet has yet to be called together; this is the longest period that this has ever happened in that country....The Little Entente meeting continues with the Foreign Ministers of the member states that Hungary has failed to disarm since World War I.	Estimates of the number of French troops it will take to pacify Morocco have now reached 100,000.		
May 11		President–elect Paul von Hindenburg enters Berlin; Pro-Monarchists express their approval....10,000 police on duty Communist demonstrations have been barred in the city.	France's difficulties with the Moors is compounded by the fact that the Moors often escape into Spanish territory where they are not being pursued and where the French cannot follow.	A new gold field has been discovered in the northwestern portion of British Columbia, Canada.	
May 12		Paul von Hindenburg takes the oath of office as President of the German Republic....France's Finance Minister states that the current economic crisis may result in additional taxes being levied....In a speech to the Federal Congress of Soviets, Josef Stalin declares that Communism is winning despite the successes of capitalism around the world.			Japan and the Soviet Union agree to allow all nationalities the use of public properties as the island's Japanese garrison is withdrawn and the Soviet Union takes possession.
May 13		As part of his restructuring of the Italian government, Benito Mussolini combines the Ministries of War, Navy, and Air into a single Ministry of National Defense which he will personally head.	The Prince of Wales arrives in Port Elizabeth South Africa on his tour of Africa, where he is serenaded by local railroad workers....There are 12 French outposts in Morocco that are surrounded by the Moors; efforts are being made to relive those stations.		

A	B	C	D	E
Includes developments that affect more than one world region, international organizations and important meetings of world leaders.	*Includes all domestic and regional developments in Europe, including the Soviet Union.*	*Includes all domestic and regional developments in Africa and the Middle East.*	*Includes all domestic and regional developments in Latin America, the Caribbean, and Canada.*	*Includes all domestic and regional developments in Asian and Pacific nations (and colonies).*

U.S. Politics & Social Issues	U.S. Foreign Policy & Affairs, Defense	U.S. Economy & Environment	Science, Technology & Nature	Culture, Leisure & Lifestyle	
New York City police investigate an "infantrium" that provides day care based on complaints that 22 children have died there in the past year.		The U.S. winter wheat crop for 1925 is the poorest since 1917, more than 115 million fewer bushels than last year's harvest.... A survey party of engineers is on board a government boat, The *Norman*, on the Mississippi River near Memphis when it capsizes and sinks; four drown and 14 are missing....A federal court upholds the rights of the United Mine Workers to recruit members into the union.	Roald Amundsen's planned flight to the North Pole has been delayed because of bad weather.	France and Italy advance to the next round of the Davis Cup Tennis competition, eliminating Hungary and Portugal.	May 8
	No more applications are being taken for the summer military training camp to be held at Plattsburgh, NY, as all 1,800 vacancies have been taken.	An article in The *New York Times* describes the efforts of the American Engineering Standards Committee in attempting to define and impose standardization to eliminate waste in American industry....The U.S. Interstate Commerce Commission places a value of $189,257,789 on the Chesapeake and Ohio Railroad.... The World Advertising Convention, opens its six-day convention in Houston, TX, where they will discuss topics such as advertising as a means to world progress.		The *New York Times* reviews Bruce Barton's *The Man Nobody Knows*, a book comparing Jesus Christ to modern American businessmen.	May 9
		In the United States, cattle prices are higher and hogs are at the highest price in 10 years, although lamb prices have dropped.	An archaeological expedition in Iraq reports on its findings which include toys, hand mirrors, and statues, as well as fish hooks, which were totally unexpected.	Brooklyn leads the National League standings followed by St. Louis, and Boston; The Philadelphia Athletics lead the American League followed by the Washington Senators and the Detroit Tigers.	May 10
The Commerce Department estimates that approximately $40 million in liquor has been smuggled into the United States.	The U.S. government has let out contracts for devices that can detect the location of aircraft at considerable distances by sound.... Senator William Borah continues to express his opposition to the United States joining the World Court as it now stands; he states it must be independent of the League of nations before the United States could join.	The State of Arizona has seen a 215 percent increase in its manufacturing capacity since 1921 according to the U.S. Census Bureau....The United States is now the world's leading investor nation; current American overseas investments total more than $9 billion.		Gunnar Kasson, one of the dog sled drivers who brought anti-diphtheria medication to Nome has informed the California Labor Department that the film company that contracted for him, Balto, and the rest of the dog team has not paid him.	May 11
William Jennings Bryan is asked if he will assist the prosecution team in the upcoming Scopes evolution trial in Tennessee and he agrees as long as the state of Tennessee does not object....An international Conference of over 500 police chiefs is being held in New York City.				Poet Amy Lowell dies at the age of 51.	May 12
In a speech in Philadelphia, William Jennings Bryan accuses American scientists of being "dishonest scoundrels" who are "stealing away the faith" of children. ...Further investigations into the "infantrium" which now seems to have been responsible for at least 44 infant deaths.	While the Panama Canal is considered still to be the most important overseas strategic point, the Army and Navy are in the process of making recommendations to improve the defenses of Hawaii.	Henry Ford has indicated that is interested in buying 400 surplus ships from the U.S. Shipping Board; he will keep several of them for business use and scrap the remainder.			May 13

F	G	H	I	J
Includes campaigns, elections, federal-state relations, civil rights and liberties, crime, the judiciary, education, healthcare, poverty, urban affairs, and population.	Includes formation and debate of U.S. foreign and defense policies, veterans affairs, and defense spending. (Relations with specific foreign countries are usually found under the region concerned.)	Includes business, labor, agriculture, taxation, transportation, consumer affairs, monetary and fiscal policy, natural resources, pollution and industrial accidents.	Includes worldwide scientific, medical and technological developments, natural phenomena, U.S. weather and natural disasters.	Includes the arts, religion, scholarship, communications media, sports, entertainment, fashions, fads, and social life.

	World Affairs	Europe	Africa & The Middle East	The Americas	Asia & The Pacific
May 14		New German President Paul von Hindenburg addresses the diplomatic community in Berlin and tells them that Germany wishes to work peacefully with other nations....Spain's Duke of Alba in an effort to establish his own land reform will allow his tenants to buy the land that they work on; he will be dividing two of his estates among 400 new landholders.	The excavating season for the archaeologists in Tunis exploring the ruins of Carthage comes to an end; it is believed that because of the demand for real estate so close to the cities that the archaeologists may not be able to return the following year.		
May 15			Three more isolated French military outposts are relieved as the Moors continue their attacks on French positions throughout Morocco; the French Air Force is flying many support missions.	Investigators from Brazil are in the United States to determine exactly why there has been a substantial decrease in coffee drinking based on fears that the coffee market is collapsing.	Reports from China state that an earthquake that occurred in mid-March appears to have claimed at least 65,000 lives and that 100,000 are homeless.
May 16		Communist rebels in Portugal ambush the country's chief of police; he is wounded but not seriously....A group of 31 planes, paid for by individual worker contributions is presented to the Soviet government.	American tourists in Egypt have spent an estimated $4 million while touring the area; excursions have included tours of the pyramids, railway trips to Jerusalem, and auto trips to Baghdad.		
May 17		Communists rebels in Bulgaria launch a series of raids outside the city of Sofia....France send representatives to Spain in order to get Spanish assistance in fighting the Moors in Morocco.	Students from the British School of Archaeology discover a cave in Palestine with artwork and other traces dating back to the Paleolithic era, indicating that Palestine was inhabited earlier than was previously thought.	Mexican army clashes with agricultural rebels and kills 13 near Guadalajara.	
May 18		Although he has some opposition, mostly from the navy, Benito Mussolini gets formal approval for the defense reorganization he has been carrying out....Gustav Streseman, Foreign Minister of Germany states that his country will fulfill all of its obligations to pay war reparations.		Mexican Communists state that if the oil facilities in Tampico are shut down, they will seize them and operate them on their own.	Japan's Baron Tanaka who is presumed to be the next Premier of Japan states that he favors closer political and business relationships with the United States...The Filipino Scouts, who form part of the American administration of the Philippines report that three of their men were murdered by local bandits.
May 19	Czechoslovakia's Foreign Minister, Eduard Benes is elected to head the League Committee on International Labor....Hungary and Mexico open discussions to establish diplomatic relations between the two nations.	Finland declares the Communist Party to be illegal....Italy bans Freemasons and all other societies deemed to be secret....France announces that it will open negotiations with the United States to settle its wartime debt.		Canada requests an interpretation of the U.S. Supreme Court ruling of the diversion of water from the Great Lakes buy the city of Chicago....Argentina appoints an envoy to the League of Nations, ending a four-year boycott....The president of Mexico issues a statement forbidding a general labor strike in that country, especially the oil workers in Tampico.	
May 20	The International Conference for controlling shipping of Arms is having difficulties, mostly based on the demand by smaller nations that weapons in larger countries be subjected to controls....Germany and Poland have submitted to the World Court their dispute concerning the shipment of coal from Polish Silesia to Germany without paying any kind of protective tariff.	Britain states it opposition to the Bulgarian Army extending the time that it can use the extra troops allowed it to put down Communist rebellions....Austria's Foreign Minister denies that Vienna has become the center of Communist activity designed to subvert the nations of Central Europe and the Balkans....M. Valline, First Secretary of the Soviet Embassy in Paris, leaves France as demanded by the French government for his encouragement of Communist anti-government parties....The French government is expressing grave concern about the mounting costs of the war against the Moors in Morocco.	The National Assembly of Persia approves a measure that would hire 12 additional American officials to assist the Persian Department of Finance....A Mexican-American boundary Commission is working on settling the border lines but may not publicize its findings until both nations have concluded a border treaty.		

A	B	C	D	E
Includes developments that affect more than one world region, international organizations and important meetings of world leaders.	Includes all domestic and regional developments in Europe, including the Soviet Union.	Includes all domestic and regional developments in Africa and the Middle East.	Includes all domestic and regional developments in Latin America, the Caribbean, and Canada.	Includes all domestic and regional developments in Asian and Pacific nations (and colonies).

U.S. Politics & Social Issues	U.S. Foreign Policy & Affairs, Defense	U.S. Economy & Environment	Science, Technology & Nature	Culture, Leisure & Lifestyle	
		The World Advertising Convention continues with the conference stating that war is the "foe of trade" and endorsing the efforts of peace organizations....Consumption of cotton in April has the effect of raising current cotton prices.... U.S. Commerce Secretary Herbert Hoover begins plans to conduct a survey to determine if government assistance in commercial aviation would be practical.		Sir H. Rider Haggard, author of *King Solomon's Mines* and *She* dies at the age of 68....Grover Cleveland Alexander, pitching for the Chicago Cubs defeats the Philadelphia Phillies four to two.	**May 14**
	The U.S. Navy launches two aircraft that will be sent to support the MacMillan Polar expedition.... President Calvin Coolidge states that the U.S. Navy will not be used to hunt down and capture liquor smugglers, saying that the fleet is not to serve as a police force.	The American Railway Association announces that the railroads of America will be spending $750 million for improvements in the coming year; they also announce that operating costs have decreased significantly in the past year.			**May 15**
It now seems likely that J. T. Scopes will be defended in his evolutionary law case by Clarence Darrow who offered his services when it became known that William Jennings Bryan would be assisting the prosecution....The Coast Guard breaks up a group of Long Island residents who have gone "bottle fishing," going out in boats to bring up cases of liquor dumped by smugglers.		The U.S. Department of Commerce announces that it will give favorable consideration to radio stations applying to increase their power and broadcasting range.... The city of Chicago opens a new train terminal at a cost of $75 million.	Roald Amundsen's planned departure for his aerial expedition to the North Pole is still delayed although he expects to leave as soon as good weather arrives.	Flying Ebony wins the Kentucky Derby; for the first time the race is broadcast by radio....The *New York Times* reviews the novel, *The Mistress of Husaby* by Sigrid Undset....British players eliminate Poland in the Davis Cup tennis competition....Tenor Beniamino Gigli is in Berlin, performing in *Tosca, Rigoletto*, and *Traviata*.	**May 16**
		U.S. Secretary of Labor James Davis addresses the Brotherhood of Railroad Trainmen and claims that there are 1 million illegal aliens currently in the country, most of these Mexicans although laborers from China are being smuggled in as well.	The Engineering Economics Foundation reports that the eight recent earthquakes felt in the eastern U.S. are indicative of a massive earthquake that could occur at any time, wiping out many port cities on the east coast.	Holland beats Czechoslovakia in the Davis Cup matches.	**May 17**
Union Army veterans state that they are opposed to any U.S. coins that will display the Confederate monument at Stone Mountain, GA.	Senator William Borah states that war should be outlawed as a crime and he attacks both the League of Nations and the World Court as relics of the old imperialism and unable to bring about justice which is the first requirement for world peace.	The W. A. Harriman Company of New York is continuing negotiations with the Soviet government to develop a manganese mining concession in Siberia.	Scientists at Providence, RI, are observing a newly discovered comet, named *Orkisd*, which was first sighted in Denmark last month; it is not visible to the naked eye.		**May 18**
Fistfights break out in Northbridge, Massachusetts between members of the Ku Klux Klan and anti-Klan groups....The population of Dayton, TN. is expressing anger at the possibility that anti-evolutionary trials might be held in Chattanooga instead of Dayton.	Naval officers will be court-martialed for the grounding of the U.S. submarine, *S-19*, which was run aground off the Massachusetts coast the previous January, where it remained for two months.	The American Railway Association announces that loading of revenue freight in the past week was greater than at any time this year....A U.S. court once again informs that United Mine Workers that they have no right to use "peaceful persuasion" to recruit members into the union.	The U.S. government announces that it will construct a government radio center at Fort Leavenworth in Kansas.	Actor Charlie Chaplin wins a lawsuit in which it is decided that his costume is distinctive to him and is therefore private property.	**May 19**
Six candidates for city offices endorsed by the Ku Klux Klan win election in Denver, Colorado....In the continuing investigation of the Geisen-Volk "infantrium," a woman admits that she purchased a baby there for $75.		The Interior Department abolishes an embargo established in 1896 that prevented granting rights for storage and diversion of water on public lands near the Rio Grande and Colorado Rivers....F.W. Woolworth Stores announce that their sales from 1,356 stores in the first four months of 1925 have shown a 10.4 percent increase over last year's sales....Total sales on the New York Stock Exchange pass the two million mark for the first time since mid-March.	A German inventor demonstrates what he calls "bottled wireless" a system constructed of wires and magnets that records sounds from the radio and allows the listener to play them back later....A cable, designed by Doctor Vannevar Bush at the Massachusetts Institute of Technology that can duplicate the conditions of transatlantic cables.		**May 20**

F	G	H	I	J
Includes campaigns, elections, federal-state relations, civil rights and liberties, crime, the judiciary, education, healthcare, poverty, urban affairs, and population.	*Includes formation and debate of U.S. foreign and defense policies, veterans affairs, and defense spending. (Relations with specific foreign countries are usually found under the region concerned.)*	*Includes business, labor, agriculture, taxation, transportation, consumer affairs, monetary and fiscal policy, natural resources, pollution and industrial accidents.*	*Includes worldwide scientific, medical and technological developments, natural phenomena, U.S. weather and natural disasters.*	*Includes the arts, religion, scholarship, communications media, sports, entertainment, fashions, fads, and social life.*

	World Affairs	Europe	Africa & The Middle East	The Americas	Asia & The Pacific
May 21			French troops are sent into a new sector of the front in Morocco but for the most part, the French force of 50,000 is occupying defensive positions.		
May 22			The Prince of Wales, on tour in Africa, is greeted by a group of 40,000 natives near the town of Umtata in the Union of South Africa.		
May 23		German reactionaries express anger over a speech by Germany's Foreign Minister Gustav Streseman in which he admits that Germany may have some guilt in starting World War I....The Austrian government has banned the Hackenkreuzler Party, a political group that models itself on Adolf Hitler's Nazi organization.	A small Turkish coastal steamer capsizes and sinks in the Bosporus Strait, killing 44.	U.S. postal officials are planning to establish service from Colombia to Havana to Key West....America's ambassador to Mexico is leaving that country to report to the U.S. government on the situation of U.S. property being seized by Mexican authorities.	
May 24		In another political fight in Vienna, members of the Hackenkreuzler Party fight with members of the Social democrats as well as attacking anyone they find in the Vienna parks....Reports indicate that Austria's economy is improving in that its import surplus is diminishing while its exports are increasing....In the Netherlands, imports have also decreased while exports are greater than last year.			In a speech, Josef Stalin encourages the students of Asia to resist the imperialists and do everything possible to get them out of China as well as other countries.
May 25			David Lloyd George, formerly Prime Minister of Britain states that regardless of what party in in power in Britain that the promises to establish a Jewish homeland in Palestine will be kept....In a radical departure from his previous policy, Bulgaria's King Boris signs the death warrant of three individuals convicted of bombing the Sofia cathedral.		There reports that the arsenal in Mukden, Manchuria, has blown up, killing 300 people....An earthquake in Japan kills an estimated 278 persons with at least 500 injured and over 2,7000 houses damaged.
May 26	The League of Nations convention on the transportation of weapons will not ban the transport of poisonous gas which had been proposed by the United States; instead a total ban on the use of gas will be taken up as a separate convention.		French authorities in Morocco are reportedly cutting off the heads of rebels and displaying them in the city of Fez to discourage others from rebelling against French rule.	In a lecture at Edinburgh University, Sir Robert Falconer says that the United States exerts a great cultural influence on Canada, primarily through films, radio, and drama.	
May 27		The German Communist Party publishes an article accusing the German government of maintaining a secret army which is funded by money not shown in the annual budget reports....Italy states that it wants a moratorium on the payments it owes the United States; Italy states that it would not be possible to make the payments for several years.			

A	B	C	D	E
Includes developments that affect more than one world region, international organizations and important meetings of world leaders.	*Includes all domestic and regional developments in Europe, including the Soviet Union.*	*Includes all domestic and regional developments in Africa and the Middle East.*	*Includes all domestic and regional developments in Latin America, the Caribbean, and Canada.*	*Includes all domestic and regional developments in Asian and Pacific nations (and colonies).*

U.S. Politics & Social Issues	U.S. Foreign Policy & Affairs, Defense	U.S. Economy & Environment	Science, Technology & Nature	Culture, Leisure & Lifestyle	
The first big Ku Klux Klan rally of the year in the northeast is held near Port Washington, New York; more than 3,000 attend.... Large groups of Americans are now crossing into the Province of Ontario to buy beer which is prohibited in the United States....A mob of approximately 300 men attempt to break into a Dallas jail and lynch two African-Americans accused of murder; the crowd is driven back with five injured and 100 arrested.			Roald Amundsen, in his two aircraft party, departs Spitzbergen on his way to land at the North Pole....It is assumed that the trip will take approximately eight hours....Dr. William Beebe's scientific expedition continues taking many pictures underwater as part of a study of sharks and eels.		May 21
Because its five courts are granting 200 divorces a month, Philadelphia is being called by some "The American Paris."	President Calvin Coolidge, in discussing the debts owed the United States by the nations of the First World suggests that the United States may make a distinction between war loans and relief loans in restructuring payments.	Representatives of the garment industry appeal to New York Governor Al Smith that they be granted relief from demands made by the unions.	At the Convention of the American Laryngological, Rhinological, and Otological Society, Dr. John Mackenty suggests that the increase in exhaust from vehicles and consumption of bad liquor are responsible for the increase in throat problems.	John Philip Sousa, the composer of marches, is suing the Lorillard Tobacco Company for the unauthorized use of his name as they are selling three-cent cigars with his name and picture; he is asking for $100,000 in damages.	May 22
The town of Dayton, Tennessee, is in the process of finding tents and Pullman cars to accommodate the anticipated crowds that will be attending the anti-evolution trial.		The price of raw rubber is showing signs of increasing; it is now at its highest price since 1919.	A seven foot fluctuation in the water level of Lake Huron occurs within a few hours; government officials say its cause was a change barometric pressure; this was greater than any variation ever recorded on the lake....In New Mexico, miners find a skeleton estimated to be 2,000 years old.		May 23
An unidentified infant who died at the Geisen-Volk "Infantrium" is determined not to be the child whose disappearance led to the investigations of this center.			The Norwegian government states that it is planning a relief expedition to find and rescue Roald Amudsen....Requests have been made of the U.S. government to send one of its dirigibles, the Los Angeles or the Shenandoah to assist in the rescue efforts.	The Metropolitan Museum of Art in new York acquires a large collection of armor dating to the 15th century after a series of negotiations that have taken 30 years to complete....The Philadelphia Athletics, followed by the Washington Senators, and New York Yankees lead the American League; the Boston Red Sox, Detroit Tigers, and St. Louis Browns are at the bottom of the standings....The New York Giants and Brooklyn Robins lead the National League; the Cubs are in last place.	May 24
			Today is the coldest May 25th in New York's recorded history with temperatures at 40 degrees; snow is falling in upstate New York and New England.		May 25
			A physician in Chicago reads a cardiogram of a patient in New York; the cardiogram had been transmitted by radio.		May 26
			A broker purchases 500 shares of stock by radio while flying in the dirigible, Los Angeles, a first for that type of transaction.	Future Hall of Famer Ty Cobb records his 1,000th career extra-base hit in a game against the Chicago White Sox, breaking the all-time record held by Honus Wagner.	May 27

	World Affairs	Europe	Africa & The Middle East	The Americas	Asia & The Pacific
May 28	The League of Nations is drawing up plans to create an international organization that will aid victims of catastrophes; as planned it would act in coordination with the Red Cross and other agencies.	Universities in Vienna are closed as a result of the activities of the Hackenkreuzler Party....Engineers in Spain are planning to create an artificial lake on the Ebro River that will supply electrical power to the northeastern part of Spain.	The Emir of Afghanistan has ordered the execution of 60 rebels; it is anticipated that there will be more to follow....Spanish air squadrons are concentrating their forces to bomb centers of activity occupied by the Moors.	The Mexican government is on the alert as it has intercepted plans for a military coup against the current President.	Viscount Shimpei Goto denies that he made statements that a war with America was quite possible if the United States did not change its immigration laws.
May 29		The Austrian government indicates that it understands that it will have to report to the League of Nations concerning its financial state for some time to come, despite improvements in the Austrian economy.			
May 30		The Council of Ambassadors representing the Allied nations orders Bulgaria to disband the additional troops it called into action when the Communist outbreak started....An air race that will be run over a 3,500 miles course begins in Germany with 90 planes participating....The Allies warn the German government that it must make its reparation payments on time; at the same time France and Britain are near an agreement on a border accord they will offer to Germany.		Another earthquake is felt in Quebec province; although there is no damage this is the latest in a series of earthquakes that have been felt since February....The Nicaraguan Congress passes legislation that will increase the investment of foreign capital in that country; railway materials and any other goods used to develop factories will not be taxed over the next three years....The Mexican Army has been given orders to disarm all civilians in an effort to reduce violence, particularly among the agrarians who have been opposing the government.	British Indian police at Shanghai fire into a crowd of strikers in Shanghai, killing at least six; a foreign volunteer group with artillery and armored cars has been called into action to assist the police in keeping order.
May 31		Reports from Germany indicate that there is an increase in savings although income from capital investments is still only a quarter of what it was in 1914....The Soviet Union delivers an optimistic report on its ability to conduct international trade, stating that Soviet productivity is at 70 percent of what it was in 1914, compared with 40 percent a year ago.	Using a massive concentration of troops, the French claim victory in their latest battle with the Moors in French Morocco....Egyptian police in a series of raids have arrested eight suspected Communists.		
Jun. 1	The League of Nations Legal and Military Commissions drop 11 articles of a proposed arms ban treaty concerned with restrictions on wartime zones and transportation through the zones.	Leon Trotsky having returned to Moscow is named to head the Scientific and Technical Branch of the Supreme Council....French Premier Paul Painleve in a speech in Strasbourg, France, makes an appeal for reconciliation between France and Germany on the eve of negotiations negotiation of the Rhineland peace treaty.	The Moors attacking French positions are now using heavy artillery with great effectiveness.		Japan's current cabinet, under Premier Kato Takaaki is expected to fall any day under the attacks by Baron Tanaka's party, primarily over the nations' budget....Rioting in Shanghai continues with at least 16 killed.
Jun. 2		The French government makes arrests in Marseilles of individuals suspected to conveying military information to the Moors fighting the French and Spanish in Morocco....In Hungary a former government Minister is arrested for publishing an article critical of Admiral Miklos Horthy, Hungary's regent and de facto ruler....A strike by seamen in Denmark has shut down all maritime traffic in that country.	The Prince of Wales continues his tour of Africa, visiting Spion Kop and other battlefields of the Boer War....French officers are calling for additional troops but also the most modern equipment available to fight the Moors in Morocco, especially light tanks, aircraft and cannon that can fire at high elevations.	Mexican National Railways announces that it will adjust its schedule to eliminate long stops at stations in an effort to bring more tourists to Mexico....Canada's Minister of the Interior states that Canada's claim of territory extends all the way to the North Pole.	Riots and strikes continue in Shanghai; Italian, American, and British land; foreign troops are using machine guns to clear the streets....The Soviet Union predicts that there will be increased violence in China over foreign holdings there; most foreign observers believe that the current unrest is the result of Communist agitation....The British send forces to India's Northwest Frontier which borders on Afghanistan in order to maintain order in the wake of a rumored uprising there instigated by Soviet Agents.
Jun. 3		The League of Nations reports that it is sending a two-man team to investigate and evaluate Austria's economy and its progress toward post-war reconstruction....By a vote of 261 to 4 the Italian Chamber of Deputies adopts a commercial treaty with the Soviet Union.	What is reported as the oldest stone building in the world (more than 5,000 years old) has been discovered 15 miles outside of Cairo.	The French and Spanish governments are reported near reaching a deal on how they will handle the rebellion in Spanish and French Morocco that have effected both their armies.	Unrest is China is spreading; strikers in Shanghai are estimated to be 50,000 to 100,000 and anti-foreign riots have claimed several lives....One British cruiser has arrived in Shanghai harbor and another British ship as well as American and Japanese ships are expected soon.

A	B	C	D	E
Includes developments that affect more than one world region, international organizations and important meetings of world leaders.	Includes all domestic and regional developments in Europe, including the Soviet Union.	Includes all domestic and regional developments in Africa and the Middle East.	Includes all domestic and regional developments in Latin America, the Caribbean, and Canada.	Includes all domestic and regional developments in Asian and Pacific nations (and colonies).

U.S. Politics & Social Issues	U.S. Foreign Policy & Affairs, Defense	U.S. Economy & Environment	Science, Technology & Nature	Culture, Leisure & Lifestyle	
A street parade is being planned to be held in Neptune, New Jersey, featuring the women of the Ku Klux Klan....Liquor smugglers are now using seaplanes as well as cigarette boats to smuggle rum into the United States			Dr. Alexander Rice who is exploring the Amazon River has been in radio contact with an operator in Philadelphia; Dr. Rice reports that all of his objectives have been accomplished.	Denmark is eliminated from the Davis Cup final after it lost to Britain....The famous Spanish matador, Jan Belmonte who retired in 1921 returns to the bullring for a contracted 20 appearances.	May 28
300 Union veterans of the Civil War participate in a memorial Day march....In a funeral procession of 30 autos carrying flowers, Angelo Genna, reputed mob executioner with 20 murders, is buried in a silver coffin; 20,000 spectators watch.	The Naval War College at Newport, Rhode Island graduates a class of 67 officers who have focused their studies on conducting future wars in the Pacific.	The National Coal Association states that it wants to reduce the number of lives lost to one miner for every one million tons of coal produced instead of the current three lives lost per one million tons.	Roy Chapman Andrews discovers more fossilized dinosaur eggs but also more recent ostrich eggs and some human remains as well.		May 29
In his Memorial Day address at Arlington Cemetery, President Calvin Coolidge states that there should be a return in this country to states rights and that the United States should learn to govern itself before it attempts to direct the rest of the world....A study indicates that Americans trail far behind the rest of the world in popular voting; New Zealand and Queensland hold the record for participation but Britain and Germany are near the top.		It is predicted that 10 billion gallons of oil will be needed to meet the needs of the United States for the remainder of 1925, an increase of 155 over last year.	The State of New York is investigating the possibility of installing a photostat recorder to take pictures of documents and save the time and expense of having them typed.	The *New York Times* reviews *The Common Reader* by Virginia Woolf....The number of students from foreign countries has increased substantially; currently there are 7,518 foreign students at American colleges and universities.	May 30
		U.S. steel producers are currently working at 70 percent capacity and see no reason to expect a decrease in output.			May 31
Members of the Coast Guard stationed near New York City state that as their enlistments run out they will not reenlist; their main reason is that their duties of keeping rum runners from brining liquor in has become too difficult and too dangerous.		Dun's Review reports that in the month of May, 1767 businesses failed, a decrease from April and the smallest number of failures since November 1924.			Jun. 1
				Ground is broken for the buildings that will constitute Harvard Business School; most of them anticipated to be completed within the next year....New Jersey Police state that they have found Blakley Coughlin, a child who had been kidnapped in June 1920 and are guarding him in a town in northern New Jersey.	Jun. 2
Former Republican, now Socialist Congressman, Fiorello LaGuardia is being suggested as the Socialist candidate for the Mayoral race in New York City....Governor Austin Peay, of Tennessee states that the planned trial of J.T. Scopes for breaking the law by teaching evolution will take only 30 minutes.		Near-record temperatures, the highest in 30 years, are responsible for two deaths in New York City....The Federal Reserve deposits of all member banks in the U.S. Reserve increased by $3 billion in 1924, mirroring the strong state of the U.S. economy.	Efforts continue to find Roald Amundsen; an aerial expedition is launched from Norway that will patrol the edge of the ice, their range of observation is expected to be 130 miles.	New Jersey Police continue to maintain that they child they have found is Blakley Couglin who the alleged kidnapper said he had killed five years before; his parent remain skeptical, believing their son was killed at the time of his kidnapping....Jack Johnson, formerly heavyweight boxing champion, undergoes an operation in Chicago for appendicitis.	Jun. 3

F	G	H	I	J
Includes campaigns, elections, federal-state relations, civil rights and liberties, crime, the judiciary, education, healthcare, poverty, urban affairs, and population.	*Includes formation and debate of U.S. foreign and defense policies, veterans affairs, and defense spending. (Relations with specific foreign countries are usually found under the region concerned.)*	*Includes business, labor, agriculture, taxation, transportation, consumer affairs, monetary and fiscal policy, natural resources, pollution and industrial accidents.*	*Includes worldwide scientific, medical and technological developments, natural phenomena, U.S. weather and natural disasters.*	*Includes the arts, religion, scholarship, communications media, sports, entertainment, fashions, fads, and social life.*

	World Affairs	Europe	Africa & The Middle East	The Americas	Asia & The Pacific
Jun. 4	There is a great deal of optimism in London that the recent discussions between Aristide Briand of France and Neville Chamberlain of Britain will result in security proposals that will also be acceptable to Germany.	A German People's League is launched in Vienna with an estimated one million members; their purpose is to create a union between Germany and Austria.			The situation in Shanghai has temporarily calmed down but the foreign nations have informed the Chinese government that Communist agitators have been responsible for the disturbances.
Jun. 5	On the suggestion of the American representative to the current arms discussions, a protocol will be drawn up that will call for an immediate ban on using poisonous gas in wartime....Britain and France are preparing their note which calls for Germany to disarm; immediate German reaction is not positive.	Benito Mussolini states that Italy opposes any kind of union between Austria and Germany and Italy must be consulted in any merger efforts....Spanish police find and defuse bombs which were meant to kill King Alfonso.	The Moors under Abd-el-Krim launch their heaviest attack yet against the French troops guarding the city of Fez in Morocco.... Over 25,000 Zulu warriors greet the Prince of Wales; as a preventive measure they are allowed to bring their clubs but not their spears as they greet the Prince.		Along with an estimated 150,000 workers on strike, 500 Chinese police also strike in Shanghai; American troops arrive in the city to help keep order....The U.S. State Department discounts predictions that this latest conflict will turn into a civil war but are still watching the situation very closely.
Jun. 6		The continued fighting which does not appear to be ending anytime soon in Morocco is having an effect on the current French government, hindering its efforts at financial reform....Leon Trotsky and Grigory Zinoviev in Moscow state that the recent outbreaks of violence in China, along with disturbances in Bulgaria are signs that a new battle with capitalism is approaching.	The Red Sea port of Rabach has been bombarded by troops under the command of Ibn Saud and King Ali of the Hejaz.	The Argentine government reports that is has raised its exports and that public revenue is rising although its stock market is currently weak....A major feature of the upcoming 100th anniversary of the creation of Bolivia will be an industrial exhibit; the exhibit is planned to open August 1.	The strikes in Shanghai are growing and civil war has been declared in Canton.
Jun. 7	The final week of the League of Nations Conference on regulating arms trafficking begins with the delegates close to significant agreements on manufacturing and international transport of weapons.	Wine growers of France claim that combined with the loss of both their Russian and German markets, Prohibition in the United States may cause them to have to give up wine making entirely....The Soviet Union sends messages to rebels in China encouraging them in thier strikes and revolt....King Victor Emmanuelle of Italy celebrates his 25th anniversary as King and is cheered by crowds in Rome.	Reports from Morocco indicate that the Moors are massing for another substantial attack on French positions.	Reports from Mexico indicate that the greater part of one town and entire families have been lost in severe flooding....A revolt in the northern provinces of Chile has been defeated by the government; at least 30 rebels have been killed and 400 taken prisoner.	Japan denies that it has threatened the Chinese government with quelling the disturbances in Shanghai if the Chinese could not or would not....The Japanese government sends four destroyers to Shanghai and another two ships to Canton....Fighting increases in Canton while gunboats steam up and down the river shooting at targets; despite the heightened combat, casualties are reported to be relatively light.
Jun. 8		Seven are killed in further violence in Sofia including a member of Parliament; police report that the home of a leader of one of the political parties was dynamited....One person is killed and nine are injured when a group of Communists clashes with a rifle club near Berlin....Britain states that it will defend France in case it is attacked with all of its naval, military, and air resources.	Reports from Fez in Morocco indicate that it is no longer in danger of being captured by Abd-el-Krim's Moors but those forces are still very active....Three Italian crewmen whose plane was forced down in the desert near the Libyan-Egyptian border have been found, apparently starved to death; their abandoned airplane had been found on March 15.	At least 100 people in Mexico drown as the result of floods; some cities are reported as being nearly submerged....A serious earthquake hit Bogota, Colombia, with considerable damage but little loss of life....The United States, which has been holding jewels of prominent Paraguayan families since 1883 returns them to the Paraguayan government....Canada announces that a combined expedition of scientists and Mounties will leave on a mission on July 1, to establish Canada's territorial claims in the far north.	Fighting continues in Canton, by both land forces and gunboats but there are few casualties reported....Plans are announced for a National Humiliation Day to be held in Japan on July 1 to mark the anniversary that the U.S. Immigration Act became effective, barring immigrants from Japan. ...The Japanese Navy is preparing its budget and is seeking the equivalent of $320 million to be sent over five years in a special armaments program for 40 ships.
Jun. 9		The Minister of Commerce for the Irish Free State declares Ireland is prospering and that rumors concerning famine are untrue; there is nothing occurring in Ireland that should deter visitors from the United States from arriving....The Soviet Union approaches the Baltic states of Estonia, Latvia, and Lithuania to remain neutral in the event if war between the Soviet Union and other countries; none of the Baltic states reply to the offer.	The Moors are continuing their attacks on French and Spanish positions; the air forces of both nations are cooperating very closely in providing support to their besieged outposts....An American destroyer, after taking on supplies in Tunis is reportedly sailing toward Morocco.	Nicaragua's cabinet resigns in order to give President Carlos Solorzano the ability to restructure and reorganize the government.	American and Filipino troops engage in a small battle with Moro rebels, killing eight....An Amrican woman is wounded in the fighting around Canton and U.S. Marines have landed to protect other Americans.

A	B	C	D	E
Includes developments that affect more than one world region, international organizations and important meetings of world leaders.	*Includes all domestic and regional developments in Europe, including the Soviet Union.*	*Includes all domestic and regional developments in Africa and the Middle East.*	*Includes all domestic and regional developments in Latin America, the Caribbean, and Canada.*	*Includes all domestic and regional developments in Asian and Pacific nations (and colonies).*

U.S. Politics & Social Issues	U.S. Foreign Policy & Affairs, Defense	U.S. Economy & Environment	Science, Technology & Nature	Culture, Leisure & Lifestyle	
		The massive heat wave is affecting parts of the country other than the northeast; in Washington, DC, where the temperature is 99 degrees, there have been three deaths thus far....The death toll from the heat in New York City is now nine people.	An archaeological expedition from the American Museum of Natural History finds the skeletons of 29 Native Americans along with approximately 2,000 objects in 50 rooms they have thus far excavated of a prehistoric complex.	Over 100,000 children march in New York City in the 96th annual parade of the Brooklyn Sunday School Union....The parents of Blakely Coughlin, who was kidnapped and assumed killed five years before, confirm that the child New Jersey police found is not their son.	Jun. 4
J. T. Scopes and his lawyers are meeting with representatives of the American Civil Liberties Union to plan his defense; possible members of his defense team may include Clarence Darrow and Felix Frankfurter.	The U.S. Navy selects three officers who will make a flight later this year from San Diego, CA, to Hawaii.			Heavy weight boxer, Gene Tunney defeats Tom Gibbons and states that he now wants to fight Jack Dempsey.	Jun. 5
The Democratic National Party announces that it has paid all of the debts it incurred in the 1924 presidential election.		Oil stocks jump in response to a new round of price increases and consumption for gas increase....The nationwide toll of deaths from the heat wave has now reached 300; record or near-record temperatures are reported in New York, Boston, Chicago, Baltimore, and Pittsburgh....The legislature of Montana states that the 400,000 wild horses that roam in the state and destroy property can be shot....Ford Motor Company announces that it is negotiating with the Finnish government to open an assembly plant there.	A panel of seven experts has been named who will study to determine if lead in gasoline is harmful and report their findings to the Surgeon General of the United States...The Norwegian government combined naval and aerial expedition to locate Roald Amundsen departs for Spitzbergen which will be the search base of operations.	The New York Times reviews a new book of poems, The Pot of Earth, by Archibald MacLeish.	Jun. 6
		In New York City the heat wave is broken, the temperature dropping 15 degrees in 15 minutes....Yesterday's death toll for deaths in New York City was 63 for a total of 162 during the recent hot weather; in addition the number of drownings as people go the beach because of the heat has increased; 13 people drown at Coney Island. Philadelphia counts 71 that have died from the heat. Some estimates place the loss of crops in the Midwest as a result of the hot weather to up to half of the total harvest.			Jun. 7
The U.S. government announces a budget surplus of $120 million almost twice of what had been estimated.		Further rains have accelerated the drops in temperature definitely bringing the heat wave to an end; one location in New Jersey reports a drop of 48 degrees in 12 hours.	Secretary of the Navy Curtis Wilbur refuses to send the U.S. Navy dirigibles Shenandoah or Los Angeles to assist in the efforts to find Roald Amundsen, citing the dangers that the extreme weather would pose to the airships. Commander Donald B. Macmillan states that he will search for Amundsen as part of his expedition in August if Amundsen has not been found by then. Macmillan is asking the State Department for a ruling on how he should claim any land he finds in his North Pole expedition.		Jun. 8
	The U.S. Fleet Submarine, JSSV-3, the third of its class which are the largest submarines in the U.S. Fleet is launched at Portsmouth, NH.				Jun. 9

F	G	H	I	J
Includes campaigns, elections, federal-state relations, civil rights and liberties, crime, the judiciary, education, healthcare, poverty, urban affairs, and population.	Includes formation and debate of U.S. foreign and defense policies, veterans affairs, and defense spending. (Relations with specific foreign countries are usually found under the region concerned.)	Includes business, labor, agriculture, taxation, transportation, consumer affairs, monetary and fiscal policy, natural resources, pollution and industrial accidents.	Includes worldwide scientific, medical and technological developments, natural phenomena, U.S. weather and natural disasters.	Includes the arts, religion, scholarship, communications media, sports, entertainment, fashions, fads, and social life.

	World Affairs	Europe	Africa & The Middle East	The Americas	Asia & The Pacific
Jun. 10		The number of unemployed in Britain increases by 60,000; a large part of this is due to decreased activity in the cotton industry.... In Germany, there is a great deal of popular feeling that France is looking to begin another war while Britain is trying to avoid future conflicts.	The Moors attack French positions on a 60-mile front and capture several outposts; counterattacks by French planes are successful to some degree.		
Jun. 11		A cabinet in Belgium is finally formed, a coalition that includes both Socialists and Catholics.... King Ferdinand III of Romania is reportedly in very poor health and may go to France for an extended rest.	The French government is increasing its efforts to have a cooperative agreement with Spain to combine their forces against the Moors.	Analysis of the drinking water in Mexico City finds that it is infected and the city faces a potentially devastating epidemic.	Anti-foreigner riots begin in Hankow, China; British troops use machine guns to protect their armory while American gunboats are fired on....The shipping strike in Shanghai continues....The Chinese government in Beijing states that the presence of foreign police and military has been the cause of the unrest in Shanghai.
Jun. 12		Benito Mussolini declares that increasing grain production is one of Italy's most significant problems and one that will be the objective of a new government campaign.	The Spanish government announces that Spanish troops were attacked by the Moors but have successfully defended their positions....Arrests are made in Turkey to foil a plot that would overthrow the Republic and reestablish Sultan Wahid el Din.	The Mexican Telephone and Telegraph company announces that it is making large scale improvements to its 37-year-old phone system.	The Kuomintang faction and its allies succeed in driving invaders from Canton.
Jun. 13	The League of Nations upholds Germany's right to be treated as an equal nation and not as a conquered territory.	The French government announces that it will begin installing a large system of radio beacons to assist aerial navigation.	French Premier Paul Painleve has arrived in Morocco to personally inspect the troops and the operations in the region.	The Peruvian government approves conducting the plebiscite that will determine whether Chile or Peru will own the Tacna-Arica border area.	Reports are coming from Canton indicating that the Kuomintang victory was bloody and that many atrocities were committed on the retreating troops....British and Japanese consulates in the Chinese city of Kiu-Kiang are attacked and destroyed; Japanese troops land to restore order there.
Jun. 14		The Turkish and Greek governments are near to completing an accord over the exchange of populations....The Soviet government is predicting that the harvests of 1925 will be significantly better than last year's....The German government will begin the first official census in 15 years to determine not only population figures but its industrial and agricultural holdings.		The Mexican government, in response to the U.S. warnings concerning the protection of American lives and property, states that no country has the right to interfere with Mexico's internal affairs.	
Jun. 15		The Yugoslav government concludes a successful set of negotiations with the United States, to which it owes more than $65 million in debt; payments will be made to the United States after the country's debt to France and Britain is settled.		A member of the Peruvian Senate, on vacation in New York states that other nations in Latin America do not resent America's stand that Mexico must protect U.S. lives and property.	The Japanese government has ordered four more destroyers to be sent to Shanghai to protect Japanese property and lives.... Reports from Hong Kong indicate that over 700 inhabitants of Canton were massacred by the victorious troops of the Kuomintang faction.
Jun. 16		A Croatian politician is selected to be president of a Yugoslav committee to plan a monument for the late King Peter; this step is seen as an important step to bring Serbs and Croats within Yugoslavia together by participating in government projects....King Alfonso broadcasts delivers a speech inaugurating a new Spanish radio station located in Madrid.	An unknown person attempts to kill the British governor of the Southern District of Palestine.		Chinese authorities in the city of Hankow execute a man who is supposedly a Communist agent inciting disorder....Reports state that the Communist wing of the Kuomintang Party's army are now in control of Canton; additionally there are reports that there are Russian soldiers in the city who may be sent out very soon.... A general strike has broken out in the port city of Swatow and a British ship has been sent there to protect property; the Royal marines have been landed at Nanking and U.S. Marines are currently patrolling Kiu-Kiang.

A	B	C	D	E
Includes developments that affect more than one world region, international organizations and important meetings of world leaders.	Includes all domestic and regional developments in Europe, including the Soviet Union.	Includes all domestic and regional developments in Africa and the Middle East.	Includes all domestic and regional developments in Latin America, the Caribbean, and Canada.	Includes all domestic and regional developments in Asian and Pacific nations (and colonies).

U.S. Politics & Social Issues	U.S. Foreign Policy & Affairs, Defense	U.S. Economy & Environment	Science, Technology & Nature	Culture, Leisure & Lifestyle	
			The government of New Zealand's Minister of Health proposes to sterilize individuals it considers to be unfit, especially epileptics and the mentally ill or retarded....The *Ingertre*, a Norwegian ship being used to search for Roald Amundsen crosses the arctic circle.		Jun. 10
In the 24-hour period ending at 3 o'clock in the afternoon, New York City police have filed 63 missing persons reports, the largest number ever reported in a 24-hour period.					Jun. 11
	Secretary of State Frank B. Kellogg warns Mexico that it cannot allow American citizens to be killed and American businesses must be protected by the Mexican government; otherwise, the current government will receive no support from the United States			France, Hollland, and India advance to the next round of the Davis Cup tennis competition....The Metropolitan Museum of Art purchases "The Cloisters" in New York City which it will use as a museum showcasing medieval art.	Jun. 12
		The U.S. Bureau of Mines is investigating the possibility of extracting oil from shale and whether such a process would be cost-effective.	The ship containing the planes that will be used to search for Roald Amundsen arrives on Spitzbergen.	Gertrude Ederle, an American swimmer, has announced that she intends to swim across the English Channel later in the year....Arturo Toscanini announces he will be conducting in New York City during the 1925–26 season....Italy and Sweden are eliminated in Davis Cup play and France and Britain are scheduled to face each other in the next round.	Jun. 13
		The New York Central Railroad's 20th Century Limited celebrates its 23rd birthday, having traveled over 16 million miles and carrying over 11 million passengers.		The result of a poll in New York restaurants over a three-week periods shows that corned beef and cabbage is the favorite dish.	Jun. 14
		The North American Company, a consortium of utility companies in describing the progress of electrification in America, states that a single sign on Broadway gives off more illumination than all the lights of Milwaukee had in 1892.	Professor William Campbell of the University of California states that every planet may be inhabited but that the life forms may be significantly different from human beings....The Royal Geographical Society states that if it is given the consent by the government of Tibet, that it will mount another expedition to climb Mount Everest.	In London, Luigi Pirandello's play, *Six Characters in Search of an Author* is presented in Italian, with a general explanation provided in English to get around a censor's ruling that the play could not be presented in translation.	Jun. 15
		A train wreck occurs at Rockport Sag, NJ; eventually there will be 51 fatalities....The department of the Interior announces that it will give away 670,510 acres as homestead lots; the government also adds one million acres to the Tongass national Forest....President Calvin Coolidge states that while government activities such as building dams for flood control are a good use of government resources, the government should not go into the business of developing and selling electrical power.	Commander Donald B. MacMillan leaves Boston to begin his polar expedition.		Jun. 16

F	**G**	**H**	**I**	**J**
Includes campaigns, elections, federal-state relations, civil rights and liberties, crime, the judiciary, education, healthcare, poverty, urban affairs, and population.	*Includes formation and debate of U.S. foreign and defense policies, veterans affairs, and defense spending. (Relations with specific foreign countries are usually found under the region concerned.)*	*Includes business, labor, agriculture, taxation, transportation, consumer affairs, monetary and fiscal policy, natural resources, pollution and industrial accidents.*	*Includes worldwide scientific, medical and technological developments, natural phenomena, U.S. weather and natural disasters.*	*Includes the arts, religion, scholarship, communications media, sports, entertainment, fashions, fads, and social life.*

	World Affairs	Europe	Africa & The Middle East	The Americas	Asia & The Pacific
Jun. 17	An arms agreement sponsored and conducted by the League of Nations controlling the manufacture and transportation of arms is signed by 18 nations....29 nations sign a similar agreement banning the use of poison gas in wartime.				A general strike of all Chinese workers is set to begin on June 25....The Kuomintang Party has abolished the civil government in canton and replaced it with a commission of seven officials.
Jun. 18		The situation in Morocco has created problems for the French left-wing parties as those wishing to withdraw from Morocco are labeled as Communists.			The Chinese government in Beijing is considering the demands for order being expressed by the foreign governments; Army forces are being brought into Beijing to protect the President....Chinese professors address a request to Pope Pius to use his influence to bring about a peaceful solution.
Jun. 19		A note from the Yugoslav government to the Austrian government is made public which asks the Austrians to stop the Communist International activities that are going on in that city and which affect all of central Europe....Benito Mussolini gets approval from the Chamber of Deputies to remove anyone in a government job if he disagrees with their political beliefs.	French and Spanish warships begin their blockade of the Morocco coast....In addition to using air support to fight the Moors, the French have been using aircraft extensively as ambulances to transport wounded soldiers.		
Jun. 20		In Britain, miners threaten to go on strike in response to mine owners' proposals to increase hours while reducing pay....A new trade agreement is signed between France and Belgium which will allow a greater number of French exports than before.	Reports from Morocco state that the chieftains who tried unsuccessfully to overrun French positions have had their ears cut off and are being forced to wear women's clothes.	An American engineer claims to have found skeletons in a cave in Mexico that measure 10 to 12 feet in height....Reports from Chile indicate that a Communist revolt was crushed; the number of dead is placed at between 500 and 1,000.	
Jun. 21		Fascist deputies gather in the chamber to celebrate their recent successes in consolidating the Fascist control of the state.	A French blockhouse in Morocco, when surrounded by the Moors, is blown up by the 23-man garrison when it appears that they can hold it no longer rather than surrender....As part of his tour, on his last day in South Africa, the Prince of Wales places a wreath on the grave of Paul Kruger who had led the Boer resistance.	President Augusto Leguia of Peru issues a manifesto that although Peru is disappointed in the results of the Peru-Chile border dispute, enough safeguards were set up to allow a fair plebiscite to be conducted and that he would never place arbitration in any hands other than the United States.	The possibility of general strike now appears in Hong Kong where strikes against foreign employers have begun.
Jun. 22					Martial law is imposed in Shanghai; 7,000 Chinese troops are called into the city to keep order....Four more American destroyers have arrived at Chinese ports....French and British gunboats are now at Canton and are assisting in the evacuation of foreigners from the area; popular discontent among the Chinese is still focused on the British and Japanese while Americans appear to be well treated.
Jun. 23		The Allied armies that have occupied the Ruhr region of Germany since the end of World War I will be out within eight weeks; it expected that the occupation of Cologne will end before the end of the year....In Vienna large crowds demonstrate in favor of a German-Austrian union.	Wahibi tribesmen who have been laying siege to the Arabian city of Jeddah have suddenly ended the siege and are believed to be returning to the city of Mecca.	The Premier of Canada announces that Canada will be sending an official envoy to the United States very soon.	British and French marines use machine guns on anti-foreign groups in Canton led by Chinese soldiers; American missionaries in the region have been ordered to leave.

A	B	C	D	E
Includes developments that affect more than one world region, international organizations and important meetings of world leaders.	Includes all domestic and regional developments in Europe, including the Soviet Union.	Includes all domestic and regional developments in Africa and the Middle East.	Includes all domestic and regional developments in Latin America, the Caribbean, and Canada.	Includes all domestic and regional developments in Asian and Pacific nations (and colonies).

U.S. Politics & Social Issues	U.S. Foreign Policy & Affairs, Defense	U.S. Economy & Environment	Science, Technology & Nature	Culture, Leisure & Lifestyle	
		Higher oil prices, due to decreased production are predicted by analysts and prices for the summer will be even higher....The Department of Agriculture states that there will be enough labor available for farm work in the summer, an increase from last year....Bureau of Labor statistics claim that there was a slight drop in employment (.7 percent) in April but wages rose.	University of Michigan archaeologists reopport finding more than 2,000 objects of the Greco-Roman period in Egypt....Otto Koller, a German engineer claims that he will build an airplane capable of going 400 miles per hour, significantly faster than the fastest American plane which has been clocked at 266 miles per hour.		Jun. 17
Senator Bob Lafollette of Wisconsin, reformer and progressive candidate for the presidency, dies at the age of 80.			Roald Amundsen who departed on his polar expedition on May 21, and has not been heard from since returns to Spitzbergen; coming to within 150 miles of the North Pole his party ran low on fuel and had to return.....A piece of a skull of a Neanderthal type has been found in a cave in Palestine where earlier this month, artwork and tools were found.		Jun. 18
William Jennings Bryan denies that the Scopes evolution trial in which he will assist the prosecution is about free speech; it is, he claims, based on the right of the state to determine what will be taught in its schools.		The Marshall Field weekly review of dry goods indicates that sales are better than they were at this time in 1924.			Jun. 19
In New York City, a group of Communists attempts to join the combined Socialist and American Parties in selecting a candidate for Mayor; a fight ensues and the Communists are thrown out of the building.	The largest air show and demonstration ever given of American military aircraft is presented at Staten Island, NY; more than 142 aircraft participate.		J.A. Higgins announces he has developed a new type of lubricating oil for aircraft engines that will allow them to fly across the country without changing their oil.	A total of 5,030 people were killed in auto accidents in 1924; In 1923 in the same cities, the death toll was 4,908.	Jun. 20
The Coast Guard adds 14 new boats to its station in Swampscott, MA, in order to better track and capture liquor smugglers.		U.S. anthracite coal miners will meet in Scranton, Pennsylvania, to demand a 10 percent pay increase; the mine companies are expected to demand a 15 to 20 percent cut in pay....The United States leads the world in both the number of oil tanker ships (402) and in gross tonnage (2,507,854).			Jun. 21
President Calvin Coolidge announces that he will ask Congress for a tax cut in the next session....A Department of Agriculture report states that in Chicago, Birmingham, New Orleans, Oklahoma City, Baltimore, Washington, and Detroit that meat packing plants do not enforce already established standards for sanitation.		The Curtiss Aircraft Company announces that it is receiving many inquiries about commercial aircraft and sees that 1925 will be a very good year for the company....The famed Smackover oil field reaches a new low in crude oil production, dropping 48 percent.		*George White's Scandals of 1925* opens in New York and receives excellent reviews.	Jun. 22
		Crude rubber prices in the United States are at their highest since 1917 due in large part to a shortage created by the need for auto tires.	The Roy Chapman Andrews expedition in Mongolia searching for dinosaur fossils has had to interrupt its expedition due to the civil war spreading to the region where he is working....Dr. John P. Sutherland of Boston University School of Medicine suggests that milk may be harmful and should not be drunk by anyone beyond infancy.		Jun. 23

F	G	H	I	J
Includes campaigns, elections, federal-state relations, civil rights and liberties, crime, the judiciary, education, healthcare, poverty, urban affairs, and population.	Includes formation and debate of U.S. foreign and defense policies, veterans affairs, and defense spending. (Relations with specific foreign countries are usually found under the region concerned.)	Includes business, labor, agriculture, taxation, transportation, consumer affairs, monetary and fiscal policy, natural resources, pollution and industrial accidents.	Includes worldwide scientific, medical and technological developments, natural phenomena, U.S. weather and natural disasters.	Includes the arts, religion, scholarship, communications media, sports, entertainment, fashions, fads, and social life.

	World Affairs	Europe	Africa & The Middle East	The Americas	Asia & The Pacific
Jun. 24		Germany expresses that it is pleased with the French plan to evacuate the areas occupied since the end of the war, although there is some skepticism as to whether the French will actually evacuate.		Reports from Mexico describe a situation in which increasing unemployment has resulted in an increase in deaths by hunger and disease....Reports from Honduras describe a large army assembling there but it is not clear whether its intent is to support the government or the rebels.	British Indian troops have landed at the foreign section of Canton as reinforcements after yesterday's fighting; all foreigners from the region have been evacuated to Hong Kong....Several Europeans have been killed as new fighting breaks out in Canton, said to be led by Russians.
Jun. 25		German cities are now looking to U.S. banks for loans, getting the money as bond issues; the recent loans to Berlin are being followed by a similar loan to Cologne.... German Army officers, who make up the first German military mission in the United States since World War I complete a tour of American military posts....A military coup overthrows the Greek government.	The Moroccan front has been relatively quiet for some days; no progress has been made in planning combined Spanish-French operations against the Moors.		Yelling "Death to the British," 20,000 students demonstrate in Beijing....Large numbers of Chinese troops are reported gathering near the foreign settlements in Canton.
Jun. 26			Harvey Firestone completes negotiations for concessions in Liberia to establish large scale rubber plantations; $5 million will be provided to Liberia for internal improvements.	Chile refuses permission for a Soviet ship to dock or communicate with the shore.	Both Canton and Shanghai are reported calmer but the strikes are continuing.
Jun. 27		The Irish language is made a compulsory subject in Irish schools.... King George V and the Queen witness an air show demonstrating the latest aircraft in service by the Royal Air Force.	The Moors launch a massive attack on the French positions around Fez while similar attacks are launched against Spanish positions....Thousands are homeless after extensive flooding in Armenia.		
Jun. 28		The German government has decided to continue negotiations with France and Britain in the area of security of borders in western Europe; French and British diplomats concede that one factor that bothers them is the extent to which Germany could negotiate some kind of understanding with the Soviet Union....Italy's foreign trade balance is improving with estimates that in the rest of 1925 exports will exceed imports.	The French report that during the past four days of fighting that they have successfully defended their positions against attacks by the Moors.	A Mexican rail strike that is also backed by telegraph operators, mechanics, and dispatchers begins....The Honduran government denies that it has been fighting antigovernment rebels but instead has been dealing with an uprising by the native population.	A serious typhoon strikes the Philippines, killing more than 20 people....The Home Rule Party in India's new leader is Sen Gupta; it had been thought that Mohandas Gandhi would assume that role.
Jun. 29		Reports from Moscow indicate that the Communist International is funding activities all over the world to bring about a Communist revolution....The French government begins its evacuation of occupation troops from Germany's Ruhr region; the withdrawal is supposed to be complete by August 15, 1925....American banks agree to lend $15 million to the German government.	Britain cedes a portion of territory in British Somaliland to Italy to fulfill a promise made in 1915.... The latest fighting in Morocco has resulted in heavy losses for the Moors and some recovery of territory by the French.	Officers from the Peruvian Navy arrive in the United States to direct the construction in Connecticut of submarines for their navy....The Honduran government winds a battle against anti-government rebels while the Nicaraguan government sends its troops to the border to seal off any avenues of escape....A severe earthquake hits the Canadian province of Alberta while a storm described as a hurricane strikes Edmonton, Alberta.	Strikes continue in Shanghai and observers describe the general atmosphere as "ominous."
Jun. 30	U.S. Senator William Borah, Chairman of the Foreign Relations Committee, embarks on a nationwide speaking tour aiming to educate the public on the perceived woes of the U.S.'s potential membership in the Permanent Court of International Justice.	The French government offers to reduce the war debt owed by the Soviet Union by a third; the Soviets reject the offer saying that is still too much....The Bulgarian government orders its army garrisons to take all precautions to eliminate anti-Semitic attacks throughout the country....Germany is presented with a note from the Allies stating that it must restrict its current aviation development programs as they are in violation of the Versailles Treaty.			

A	B	C	D	E
Includes developments that affect more than one world region, international organizations and important meetings of world leaders.	Includes all domestic and regional developments in Europe, including the Soviet Union.	Includes all domestic and regional developments in Africa and the Middle East.	Includes all domestic and regional developments in Latin America, the Caribbean, and Canada.	Includes all domestic and regional developments in Asian and Pacific nations (and colonies).

U.S. Politics & Social Issues	U.S. Foreign Policy & Affairs, Defense	U.S. Economy & Environment	Science, Technology & Nature	Culture, Leisure & Lifestyle	
	The United States and Hungary in a treaty of friendship, commerce, and consular rights, giving Hungary most-favored nation status.				Jun. 24
Clarence Darrow announces the list of 11 scientists who will testify on behalf of J.T. Scopes in the upcoming evolution trial.	Aviation training on a voluntary basis will be offered to all Army officers in the combat branches as well as students at the Army's Command and General Staff School.		Engineers of the American Society for Testing Materials have devised an improved method of making concrete that will make roads significantly better.		Jun. 25
An NAACP attempt to cancel a parade permit issued to the Ku Klux Klan for a monster rally to be held in Washington on August 8 fails.		Copper produced in the United States in 1924 exceeded both the gross output and value of 1923.... General Motors has expressed interest in a merger of the auto manufacturer and the Yellow Cab Company in what is estimated to be a $50 million deal.	Fridtjof Nansen and Hugo Echener announce plans to construct a 100,000-cubic-meter zeppelin that will be used on an expedition to the North Pole.		Jun. 26
The governor of Wisconsin vetoes a bill that would allow the forced sterilization of the mentally ill.		Earthquakes are felt in almost two thirds of Montana; no deaths and only a few injuries but damage estimates are put at $500,000.	The Tulane University expedition to Mexico and Honduras reports the discovery of a solid stone altar, a tomb and several carved figures.... Excavations at Corinth, Greece, have revealed a large painting depicting gladiators.		Jun. 27
		Sales for radios in 1924 were $300 million up from $2 million in 1920; there are 2.5 million radios in use in the country....Navy aviators will be used to map and survey shale oil fields; the surveys will be performed in western Colorado.... Beef and hog prices rise in the commodities markets while a surplus has dropped corn prices.	Engineers report discovering a large pre-Maya city near Vera Cruz with four pyramids and more than 100 underground chambers....The Soviet Union announces that it is planning a polar expedition and has called explorer Fridtjof Nansen has been called in as a consultant....The Engineering Economics Foundation suggests that the government should send aerial survey teams to map the area in Montana struck by the earthquake.	Antonio Ascari, driving an Italian car, wins the Grand Prix of Europe, trvaelling the 800 kilometers in six hours and 42 minutes.	Jun. 28
The defense team for J. T. Scopes is in the process of finishing its list of prospective witnesses; The state of Tennessee agrees to assist the town of Dayton in providing services and facilities for the many people expected to come to the town to observe the trial.		The Postmaster General of the United States announces that bids are now open for eight new air mail routes to include New York-Hartford-Boston, Los Angeles-Las Vegas-Salt Lake City, and St. Louis-Springfield–Chicago....A severe earthquake hits Santa Barbara, CA; 12 people are killed and property loss is estimated in the millions....Damage from the Santa Barbara earthquake seems to be restricted to the area near the city; no damage has been reported in central or northern California.	Arthur Hunter of the New York Life Insurance Company states that there is no basis in assuming hereditary factors to have any bearing on the incidence of cancer.		Jun. 29
		The United Mine Workers accuse the railroads and mining companies of trying to destroy the mining unions; John L. Lewis of the UMW states that the miners will not accept the proposed wage cuts especially working under conditions where 500 are killed each year and 22,00 are injured.... Overnight airmail service between New York and Chicago begins.		Gene Tunney and Jack Dempsey have agreed to hold a boxing match, the date will be July 4, 1926.	Jun. 30

F	G	H	I	J
Includes campaigns, elections, federal-state relations, civil rights and liberties, crime, the judiciary, education, healthcare, poverty, urban affairs, and population.	Includes formation and debate of U.S. foreign and defense policies, veterans affairs, and defense spending. (Relations with specific foreign countries are usually found under the region concerned.)	Includes business, labor, agriculture, taxation, transportation, consumer affairs, monetary and fiscal policy, natural resources, pollution and industrial accidents.	Includes worldwide scientific, medical and technological developments, natural phenomena, U.S. weather and natural disasters.	Includes the arts, religion, scholarship, communications media, sports, entertainment, fashions, fads, and social life.

	World Affairs	Europe	Africa & The Middle East	The Americas	Asia & The Pacific
Jul. 1	A League of Nations commission completes a draft plan which will be submitted in September to implement international aid in the case of natural disasters.	The Austrian government reports a revenue surplus and that exports now exceed imports....The Parliament of Greece votes confidence in the new Revolutionary cabinet under Premier Theodoros Pangalos.			Hong Kong is fairly quiet and there are no fresh strikes; the supply of fresh vegetables has been cut off but the supplies of food are generally good....The British government denies that its proposed naval base in Singapore will be large but that it will be a relatively minor establishment.
Jul. 2		A Soviet Court sentences three men to be executed for attempting to kill Josef Stalin, Leon Trotsky and other Soviet leaders....A nationalist German newspaper reports that both Czechoslovak and Polish troops are massing on the border, preparing to invade Germany....A tariff war has begun between Poland and Germany; Poland will not allow any goods from Germany and Germany has ordered similar measures....The Belgian Chamber of deputies approves the new cabinet which was formed on June 17.		Tolls for the Panama Canal for the fiscal year ending June 30 were $21,400,523, almost $3 million less than the previous year....The U.S. Marines leave Nicaragua, ending a 13-year peacekeeping mission.	Despite earlier signs of improvement, the situation in Hong Kong has become worse as strikes are spreading and strike leaders use armed guards to prevent workers from returning; it is estimated that over 100 have been killed and 200 injured in Canton....A riot in Calcutta results in 36 injured.
Jul. 3		French Communists plan to order a general strike protesting French involvement in Morocco....The German government indicates that it has doubts about negotiating a security treaty with France and Britain....The Spanish government asks for assistance from both France and Britain in fighting the Moors in Spanish Morocco.	The Turkish government accuses Britain's King George V and David Lloyd George of inciting the Kurds to revolt against the Turkish government.	Canada's Dominion Bureau of Statistics estimates that the Canadian wheat crop for 1925 will be in excess of 350 million bushels, 10 million bushels above the harvest average of the past five years.	
Jul. 4		The Greek government announces that it will begin an engineering project to dam the waters of the Marathon River in order to create a water supply for the city of Athens....The British Cabinet prepares a diplomatic note to the Soviet Union, telling it to stop instigating unrest in both China and Britain....The new German census is released indicating a total population of 63.25 million, 4.75 million fewer than just before World War I.	Reports indicate that the French-Spanish blockade of Morocco is having good effects although Abd-el-Krim is still very active in recruiting local tribes to his revolt....The Sultan of Morocco has ordered his military forces to assist the French against Abd-el-Krim.	The Argentine government completes its census, recording 2,310,441 inhabitants in Buenos Aires, making it the world's sixth-largest city.	The Methodist Board of Missions publicizes a report that includes descriptions of the effects of current unrest in China citing the benefits of missionaries and others reevaluating their relationships with the native Chinese as well as a request that the United States to back away from its "ever-growing tendency toward imperialism....Chinese soldiers in the city of Chunking attack and wreck western oil offices until put to flight by British Marines.
Jul. 5	Fridtjof Nansen, explorer and League of Nations Relief Commissioner returns from a two-week investigation of Armenia to see about possibility of a colony for refuges from Soviet Armenia.	Polish and Soviet forces clash; Polish forces burn a Soviet border station after a Soviet Group crosses the border to kidnap a Polish officer....The *Economist* Index of wholesale prices indicates the British wholesale prices are continuing to decline.	The Prince of Wales, touring the colony of Rhodesia addresses groups of natives and goes hunting, successfully killing a wildebeest.		The Soviet Union protests the arrest in Hong Kong by British authorities of a Soviet agent there; in retaliation, the Soviet Union is now refusing travel visas to all British subjects who wish to use the trans-Siberian railroad....The U.S. Destroyer, *Simpson*, rescues a group of American missionaries after being threatened; labor unrest in Shanghai continues.
Jul. 6	An organization of 21 nations calling itself the International Entente Against the Third International," circulates a petition to all nations asking them to banning all Communist activities.	The Madrid Conference between France and Spain continue to work out issues in determining their joint agreement and strategy to combat Abd-el-Krim....The British parliament debates whether to intervene in the Moroccan revolt, assisting Spain and France, without coming to a decision.	The French government is evacuating civilians from the Moroccan city of Taza due to danger of Abd-el-Krim moving his forces near this city....There are reports that Abd-el-Krim is holding local chieftains as hostages until they agree to support him.	A fire in the Colombian city of Manizales destroys 32 acres in the center of the city and kills at least 30 people.	

A	B	C	D	E
Includes developments that affect more than one world region, international organizations and important meetings of world leaders.	*Includes all domestic and regional developments in Europe, including the Soviet Union.*	*Includes all domestic and regional developments in Africa and the Middle East.*	*Includes all domestic and regional developments in Latin America, the Caribbean, and Canada.*	*Includes all domestic and regional developments in Asian and Pacific nations (and colonies).*

U.S. Politics & Social Issues	U.S. Foreign Policy & Affairs, Defense	U.S. Economy & Environment	Science, Technology & Nature	Culture, Leisure & Lifestyle	
The State of Kansas Charter Board refuses a charter to the Ku Klux Klan because it is not a benevolent association as stated in its petition.		The American Petroleum Institute announces that daily crude oil production over the past week has dropped significantly; the national total is 2,173,850 barrel for the week....Santa Barbara's death toll from the earthquake now reaches 11; Marines arrive in the city to ensure public order....President Calvin Coolidge announces that he will act to avoid a coal strike.	The Baldwin Locomotive Company announces that after 10 years its experiments with building a diesel oil burning locomotive are a success; it is estimated that replacing coal with these engines will result in a 25 percent cost savings.	Today is a big day for home runs in American baseball; 20 are hit (12 in the National League, seven by the New York Giants alone) and eight in the American League, including two by Babe Ruth.	Jul. 1
Despite protests by Catholics, Jews, and African Americans, President Calvin Coolidge says he cannot cancel the planned "monster rally" of this Ku Klux Klan in Washington in August; he says he will not review the parade....The Scopes evolution trial may be moved from Dayton, TN, to Nashville as the defense lawyers are preparing to argue before a federal rather than state court.	The Secretary of War announces that a special group of 20 officers will be appointed to investigate and eliminate waste within the army.	The new mail service between Chicago and New York now makes it possible to have a letter that leave Chicago at 7 p.m., arrive at its destination by 9 a.m. the following morning.... The Department of Agriculture announces that 1925 will be a record year for the cotton harvest with over 14.3 million 500-lb bales....A new record is broken for the price of a seat on the New York Stock Exchange: $122,000.... Auto manufacturers report that business in June was excellent and that several manufacturers are behind in meeting orders.			Jul. 2
		The newly established night mail flights between Chicago and New York are considered to be a success and preliminary plans are being made to establish passenger traffic soon....In the 2nd quarter of 1925, 111 banks failed, a decrease from the 1st quarter of this year and the 2nd quarter of 1924.		Impresario Sol Hurok announces that he will be sending concert tours later in the year featuring Feodor Chaliapin, Misha Elman, and the dancer Pavlova.... Motorcyclist Jim Davis breaks the world land speed record for the third time in three days, going 113 miles an hour....The Washington Senators baseball team are so sure of their chances of making the World Series that they have begun to sell tickets to the games.	Jul. 3
Eugene V. Debs, leader of the U.S. Socialist Party sends a letter to the president of Mexico congratulating him on his rebuke to American statements about Mexico.... Tennessee prosecutors state that the Scopes Trial, which will begin tomorrow, must be tried in a state and not a federal court as that would violate state sovereignty.	The 4th of July is also Defense Day; 8,040,395 men including the Regular Army and the National Guard as well as private citizens take part in exercises throughout the country.	The U.S. Department of Agriculture forecasts that except for winter wheat, the harvests for 1925 will be excellent....The U.S. Department of Commerce estimates that American industries lose $30 billion due to waste.... The city of Santa Barbara is hit by another shock, the 96th tremor in the past several days.	Frederick Kiesler, a Viennese architect, predicts that future houses will be built on platforms several hundred feet above the ground.	The American Auto Association states that education of passengers to not be a distraction is essential to cutting down on the number of auto accidents. ...Traffic north from New York City for the holiday weekend is very heavy; police in Peekskill, New York count 100 vehicles a minute, passing in both directions.	Jul. 4
		U.S. merchants are divided over whether businesses should be closed all day on Saturdays; several are opposed because fewer open hours during the week would result, they say, in a higher cost of living.	Roald Amundsen, returns from his voyage to the North Pole, arrives in Oslo, and receives a medal from Norway's king....More than 40 American universities begin to participate in a program that will conduct widespread archaeological investigations in the city of Athens.	The building containing Boston's Pickwick Club collapses killing at least 41; rescue crews are hampered by looters, four of whom are arrested....After defeating the Cuban team yesterday for the singles in the Davis Cup Competition, Spain once again defeats Cuba, this time in doubles competition.	Jul. 5
		General Electric and Westinghouse announce that they will manufacture standard sizes and wattages for electric light bulbs, reducing the number of designs from 45 to five....As new tremors bring the week's total; to 100, engineers estimate that the damage caused by quakes in Santa Barbara will cost an estimated $10 million.	A British inventor, F. H. Wallis, is at work on a small airplane that can carry one person and fly at 70 miles an hour.	The Chicago White Sox forbid radio station WMAQ from broadcasting games; this brings Chicago into compliance with American League policy which bans all radio broadcasts.	Jul. 6

F	G	H	I	J
Includes campaigns, elections, federal-state relations, civil rights and liberties, crime, the judiciary, education, healthcare, poverty, urban affairs, and population.	Includes formation and debate of U.S. foreign and defense policies, veterans affairs, and defense spending. (Relations with specific foreign countries are usually found under the region concerned.)	Includes business, labor, agriculture, taxation, transportation, consumer affairs, monetary and fiscal policy, natural resources, pollution and industrial accidents.	Includes worldwide scientific, medical and technological developments, natural phenomena, U.S. weather and natural disasters.	Includes the arts, religion, scholarship, communications media, sports, entertainment, fashions, fads, and social life.

	World Affairs	Europe	Africa & The Middle East	The Americas	Asia & The Pacific
Jul. 7		The Soviet Union announces that beginning with the next school term all young men in high school will be required to study military subjects and spend three months in military camps for training....An unnamed German politician speaking on condition of anonymity states that the western nations will eventually attack the Soviet Union and that Germany will get a share of Siberia....The German government indicates that it will not agree to restrictions on aviation that the Allies wish to impose.	The Spanish government announces that the Army has just successfully defeated a party of Moor rebels in Morocco....The Prince of Wales arrives in Salisbury, Rhodesia, the latest stop on his African tour....A French Army Captain reaches Cape Town, South Africa in a car from Oran in North Africa, a drive of 23,000 kilometer that takes eight months.		Reports from Manchuria indicate a high level of Soviet military and political activity resulting in extensive control over the Outer Mongolia....The British Secretary of State for India states that Britain is willing to revise its government of India but will not be coerced into giving independence.
Jul. 8		Kaiser Wilhelm II, in exile in the Netherlands since the end of World War I states to visiting friends that he hopes to be Kaiser of Germany once again....Despite protests by the British Treasury the Royal Navy announces that it will soon begin construction of four additional cruisers....The Spanish government announces a program that will create 1000 new schools in Spain, bringing to a total of 2500 schools constructed under the Directorate of General Primo de Rivera.	France and Spain sign an agreement by which they will impose a land blockade on Morocco; another agreement defining political collaboration between the two nations is expected to be signed as well....A French military news release states that an expected 10,000 Moors are on their way to attack the city of Fez....The Palestine government is studying whether outlying villages can withhold their water from the city of Jerusalem in times of drought.		The Civil Governor of Canton, China, is wounded by an assassin, perpotedly a former Army officer.
Jul. 9		Italy and Yugoslavia announce a series of agreements between the two countries on border issues, choice of nationality, and financial issues....Tension between Germany and Poland increases as the two nations cannot agree on tariffs for coal and livestock.	Abd-el-Krim's forces are gathering and moving in the general direction of French lines near the city off Fez in Morocco....Dr. Edward Ross of the University of Wisconsin states in a report to the League of Nations that the African colonies of Portugal are the victim of misrule and that slavery, abuse, and starvation are widely employed.	Agrarian rebels in Mexico have seized lands owned by the native Mexicans; the government is investigating these reports....Fighting breaks out in Buenos Aries between pro- and anti-Fascist Argentine-Italians.	
Jul. 10					The British Consulate in Canton warns all foreign women and children to leave for Hong Kong immediately.
Jul. 11		Reported outbreaks of bubonic plague in Southeast Russia have claimed 43 lives....The Soviet Union predicts that that harvests this year will be more than 20 percent greater than last year's....The German government announces that anyone can purchase and own a radio as long as they purchase a government license....British miners state that they will not meet with mine owners unless the wage reduction is withdrawn.	The French government announces it has successfully stopped a Moorish offensive near the major railway line leading to the city of Fez.	The Canadian province of Nova Scotia anticipates that its growing amount of paved roads will be attracting American tourists with autos....The Nicaraguan government announces that Colombia's claims to islands considered to be part of Nicaragua are invalid and the Colombians must evacuate the islands.	The city of Canton is currently quiet but posters have appeared throughout the city inciting violence against foreigners.
Jul. 12		Harvests reported in Central Europe are extremely good and estimated crop yields are expected to range anywhere from 7 to 15 percent better than last year....In a celebration of the anniversary of the Battle of the Boyne Catholics and protestants riot in the city of Glasgow; over 100 are injured.	The census of the Statistical Section of the Palestine Zionist Executive indicates that the Jewish population there has increased 100 percent in the last four and a half years; the current population is 115,000....The French government announces that it will initiate non-stop flights from Paris to Aleppo in French-controlled Syria, then eventually Paris to Baghdad.		An intense anti-foreigner campaign, concentrating mostly on British and Japanese has been launched in some of China's provinces.

A	B	C	D	E
Includes developments that affect more than one world region, international organizations and important meetings of world leaders.	Includes all domestic and regional developments in Europe, including the Soviet Union.	Includes all domestic and regional developments in Africa and the Middle East.	Includes all domestic and regional developments in Latin America, the Caribbean, and Canada.	Includes all domestic and regional developments in Asian and Pacific nations (and colonies).

U.S. Politics & Social Issues	U.S. Foreign Policy & Affairs, Defense	U.S. Economy & Environment	Science, Technology & Nature	Culture, Leisure & Lifestyle	
William Jennings Bryan, in a speech given in Dayton, TN, states that the Scopes Trial will be a duel to the death as both evolution and Christianity cannot survive together.		General Motors announces that it has acquired a controlling interest in the Yellow Cab Manufacturing Company which is not only a leading manufacturer of taxis but busses as well.	A presentation is given at the Conference of the national Association for the prevention of Tuberculosis that the use of gold injections may be an effective treatment....Commander Richard Byrd conveys to the Navy the message that the MacMillan Polar exploration party has encountered heavy ice in the waters off Newfoundland.	Articles in the Paris press are extremely critical of the large numbers of American soldiers who married French women during the war, only to abandon them.	Jul. 7
Tony Genna, the third member of the Genna crime family to die in recent days, is ambushed and killed in Chicago, presumably by followers of the late Dion O'Bannion....William Jennings Bryan states that he will begin a nationwide campaign to bar the teaching of evolution and that he will also campaign to have the Bible put into the Constitution of the United States.		The Mining and Metallurgical Society of America announces that peak production of oil in the United States reached its peak in 1923 and because demand exceeds supply, it may be necessary to import oil.	The MacMillan Polar expedition reaches the town of Hopedale, Labrador, and prepares for the next stage toward the Greenland coast....Burglars at a bank in Elnora, IN, are forced to leave the bank they are robbing when their entry triggers the release of Lewisite, up to that time the most poisonous gas known; other banks are studying the possible use of poison gas to foil robberies.	Soprano Luisa Tetrazzini announces that she will make a farewell concert tour in the United States and Australia later in the year.... Babe Ruth, who has been ill most of the season, hits a home run contributing to a 6–4 victory over the St. Louis Browns.	Jul. 8
Over 20,000 garment workers gather at Yankee stadium and state that they will strike if the new leadership of the union agrees to new terms set by the employers.		The American Rubber Association announces that it will begin efforts to curb rubber production in an effort to bring the price of raw rubber down; the price of rubber has increased about 400 percent since Spring 1924....The Department of Labor announces that between May 15 and June 15 the cost of food rose one to four percent in 23 cities.	The Health Commissioner of New York City starts an investigation to determine the extent to which carbon monoxide emitted by autos is damaging to health....An Austrian inventor has developed an airplane with a rotor like that on a helicopter and a single propeller that will allow it to go 300 miles an hour.	Paragon Park at Nantasket Beach, MA, installs smoking benches reserved for women in response to the great demand by its patrons.	Jul. 9
The jury of 12 that will try the J.T. Scopes trial is selected in just a few hours.	President Calvin Coolidge and Secretary of State Frank B. Kellogg discuss possible solutions for restoring order in China; earlier Coolidge had proposed an international conference to resolve issues of contention which was not enthusiastically received by Britain or the other powers with interests in China.		The skull of a prehistoric man is found in a cave in Palestine, near the city of Tiberias....The MacMillan Polar expedition, now having left Labrador reports that their progress along the coast is hampered by the large number of ice flows.	Henry Ford gives a party at his home where the music is entirely waltzes, polkas, and quadrilles in attempt to revive their popularity and combat the growing influence of jazz.	Jul. 10
J.T. Scopes announces that after the trial, he would not teach in Dayton again, even if asked.... The atmosphere in Dayton, TN is becoming more tense as the ending of the Scopes trial approaches and partisans for each side are becoming more contentious....A grand jury in Boston indicts nine individuals for the collapse of the Pickwick Club which has thus far killed 44.	The army and navy announce that increased radio communications saved the government over $1 million in the past year by using telephones less.	The United Mine Workers president states that the average miner' wages are $2,000 a year, a figure that the mine owners dispute, stating that it exceeds $2,500. The Interstate Commerce Commission announces that the total of railway workers in the United States is 1,745,643; current wage is 58 cents an hour....The oil industry expects that 1925 will be the best year on record; it is expected that more than 10 billion gallons will be required.	Roald Amundsen and the president of the Zeppelin corporation, Hugo Eckner, announce they will meet to make plans for a polar zeppelin flight.	Charles Ponzi, confidence man and inventor of the "Ponzi scheme," is sentenced in Boston to seven to nine years for larceny....Although Charlie Chaplin was upheld in a lower court about his costume being proprietary material belonging exclusively to him, a Superior Court judge announces that he is not entitled to exclusive use of baggy pants, hat, moustache, and characteristic walk....The Paris Exhibit of Decorative Arts, which is defining the term, "Art Deco."	Jul. 11
Despite the imposition of prohibition, deaths from alchohol increase; in May, 79 New Yorkers died from consuming alcohol, 11 times the number that had died of the same cause in May 1920....Dr. Harry Goldsmith, a Baltimore psychiatrist states that the dramatic increase in insanity in Maryland is a direct result of Prohibition and effects of World War I.	President Calvin Coolidge announces that the Chinese government has an obligation to fully protect all foreigners.	In the past week, cotton prices which were dropping dramatically, have increased....Another heat wave in the northeast kills at least three people in the New York area....Beef prices are the highest since 1920....Rubber prices throughout the world are rising dramatically as consumption increases; consumption for June was 35,000 tons and it is anticipated that demands in this country will exceed the total available supply.	The navy announces that it has completed a map made entirely of aerial photographs of the Lake Okeechobee region in Florida.... The Greek government announces that while it has not yet made any definite concession to any particular American school to excavate in Athens, it will allow work by any competent archaeological team to work in the city.	Holland Beats India in Davis Cup competition.	Jul. 12

F	G	H	I	J
Includes campaigns, elections, federal-state relations, civil rights and liberties, crime, the judiciary, education, healthcare, poverty, urban affairs, and population.	Includes formation and debate of U.S. foreign and defense policies, veterans affairs, and defense spending. (Relations with specific foreign countries are usually found under the region concerned.)	Includes business, labor, agriculture, taxation, transportation, consumer affairs, monetary and fiscal policy, natural resources, pollution and industrial accidents.	Includes worldwide scientific, medical and technological developments, natural phenomena, U.S. weather and natural disasters.	Includes the arts, religion, scholarship, communications media, sports, entertainment, fashions, fads, and social life.

	World Affairs	Europe	Africa & The Middle East	The Americas	Asia & The Pacific
Jul. 13		A young woman claiming to be the Anastasia, a daughter of the late Russian czar, is visited by a German Crown Princess in Berlin to see if she is indeed the Grand Duchess.	The current French government is under increasing criticism by opposition groups for its efforts to see about a peace on Morocco....Yeta III, Paramount Chief of Barotsa in Southern Africa, travels 300 miles with his retinue to meet with the Prince of Wales who is now in Rhodesia as part of his tour.	An attempt at climbing Canada's highest mountain, Mount Logan is currently blocked by a blizzard after reaching a height of 19,000 feet.	
Jul. 14			The French Premier announces that he will accept the offer of American veteran aviators to form an escadrille to fly in support of French forces on Morocco....The Afghan government has not replied to Benito Mussolini's demands for reparations after the Afghan government executed an Italian engineer.	The Canadian Alpine Club announces that its group scaling Mount Logan have successfully reached the summit.	
Jul. 15	The League of Nations Iraq Boundary Commission finishes a draft of its report; the League will not work on this boundary dispute between Iraq and Turkey in August but will wait until the December session....The League of Nations announces that it will investigate charges that Portugal allows slavery in its African possession.	The Soviet Union announces that its Baltic Fleet will be on maneuvers and will visit several Swedish and Norwegian ports....The departure of French troops occupying the German Ruhr Valley since the end of the war continues....Anti-Fascist members of the Italian Chamber of Deputies issue a statement opposing Benito Mussolini, accusing him of instigating violence against their leaders.			Floods in Korea are reported to have resulted in over 3,000 deaths....Civil war breaks out in the Chinese province of Szechuan.
Jul. 16		On a tour of America, Italy's delegate to the League of Nations, Count Cippico states that the victory settlement after the end of World War I was unfair to Italy which had fought with the Allies and had suffered heavy casualties.	Colonel Charles Sweeney, who commanded an infantry regiment in World War I, will command the American volunteers flying for France in Morocco....The French government sends Field Marshal Philippe Petain to take command of operations in Morocco.	The Urubu tribe in Brazil attacks coffee plantations, killing four people; local inhabitants are asking the government for protection.	
Jul. 17		Reports describe a gunfight in the streets of Warsaw between Communists and police; two are killed and nine are wounded.... A soccer match between Bologna and Genoa is cancelled as many fans have brought guns to the game....The Portuguese cabinet, which has been in existence for only two weeks, resigns following a no-confidence vote.	The French government announces that it will make heavy use of airplanes to subdue the rebels in Morocco....Moors under Abd-el-Krim manage to cut off the roads to the city of Fez, isolating the city....So far, French casualties in this war have totaled 707 killed, 2,775 wounded, and 666 missing.	Argentina's current wheat acreage is the largest on record for that country.	
Jul. 18		French and Belgian troops continue to evacuate from their garrison in the Ruhr Valley ending their 19-month occupation....The publication, *Electrical World* reports that Norway, which has a surplus of electricity from its hydroelectric dams, plans to build transmission lines to sell power to Germany, Denmark, and Sweden....A consensus is building among all political factions in Britain that government spending has become excessive largely because of recent increases in navy budget but the concern is also based on other factors.	The text of the Turkish accusations that Britain has been conducting reprisals against Turkish sympathizers in northern Iraq is published and distributed at the League of Nations....France's president announces that the American aviation volunteers who are assisting the French in Morocco will retain their own command structure so as not to jeopardize their American citizenship.	The American vice consul at Aguascalientes, Mexico, is shot in the back; the American Secretary of State orders a complete investigation.	The Han River in Korea floods as a result of heavy rains, breaks its dikes leaving 1,000 dead and over 300,000 homeless.

A	B	C	D	E
Includes developments that affect more than one world region, international organizations and important meetings of world leaders.	Includes all domestic and regional developments in Europe, including the Soviet Union.	Includes all domestic and regional developments in Africa and the Middle East.	Includes all domestic and regional developments in Latin America, the Caribbean, and Canada.	Includes all domestic and regional developments in Asian and Pacific nations (and colonies).

U.S. Politics & Social Issues	U.S. Foreign Policy & Affairs, Defense	U.S. Economy & Environment	Science, Technology & Nature	Culture, Leisure & Lifestyle	
The heat in Dayton, TN prevents many people from attending the latest session of the trial of J.T. Scopes; fortunately they are able to listen to the proceedings over the radio.		Dodge Brothers, a manufacturer of cars announce that their earnings for the first six months of 1925, a net profit of $16,487,891 for the first six months....The American Engineering Standards Committee reports that increasing standardization in U.S. industries is saving millions of dollars....Standard Oil announces that it will reduce the 12-hour day of its employees to eight hours a day.			Jul. 13
William Jennings Brian attempts to clarify remarks attributed to him several days before and denies that he wanted to put the Bible into the U.S. Constitution....Two chimpanzees are brought to Dayton, TN, along with other visitors; one of them is introduced to William Jennings Bryan who listens to a description of how chimpanzees may be descended from man instead of the other way around.	President Calvin Coolidge states that the United States, Britain, and Japan must as well as other nations that have signed extraterritoriality agreements with China to continue to proceed under those agreements and to adjust, as needed to current developments in China.	The American Telephone and Telegraph Company announces that its income for the first half of 1925 is more than $52 million, almost $10 million more than the first half of 1924....The Ford Motor Company announces that there will be no shutdowns of any manufacturing plants and that there will no major changes such as the rumored six-cylinder model.		It is reported that nearly every day on Long Island, NY, a motorist smashes through a railway crossing gate.	Jul. 14
Mrs. Helen Geisen-Volk under investigation for questionable activities in her "infantrium" pleads guilty to attempting to substitute a baby she was caring for....Clarence Darrow introduces scientific evidence as part of his defense of J.T. Scopes in the evolution trial.		Steel production in the United States is at 60 percent of capacity, a much higher amount than is usual in the summer....The J. C. Penny Company announces that it will open 100 stores in the United States and has selected the locations of 78 of those stores, for a total of 667 stores....The American Westinghouse Corporation, announces that it will be forming a Japanese subsidiary in Japan.		The National Baseball League announces that the so-called "Rabbit ball" which has been held responsible for so many home runs will continue to be the official ball of the League.	Jul. 15
In denying a proposed new utility, the New Jersey Public Utilities Commission states that competition among utilities is not in the best interest of the people....In his speech to the jury in the J.T. Scopes evolution case, William Jennings Bryan that the Tennessee law is clear and that in teaching evolution, Scopes broke the law....The Commissioner of the New Jersey State Department of Institutions and Agencies states that crime nationwide costs the nation $3.5 billion a year.		The New York Parks Conservation Association reports that the beaches of Long Island are covered with New York City garbage that has been dumped at sea.		Spain wins its first two matches against Mexico in the Davis Cup matches....Lillian Harrison of Argentina attempts to swim the English Channel but after almost nine hours in the water, and five miles from the end, she must stop; she intends to try again in August....MGM Studios sells 40 movies to distributors in Germany which will show the films next year.	Jul. 16
Clarence Darrow, defending J.T. Scopes attacks a decision by the judge to bar the testimony of scientists in the evolution case; Darrow is held in contempt of court....William Jennings Bryan says he regrets that the scientists will not be able to testify in the case.	The navy dirigible *Shenandoah* returns to its hangar in Lakehurst, NJ, after riding out a storm at sea.	President Calvin Coolidge declares that the government will intervene to prevent a possible strike by anthracite coal miners.		Detroit Tiger manager and player, Ty Cobb is suspended by the American league president after arguing with an umpire.	Jul. 17
	The Chief of naval Operations, after observing operations of the U.S. Navy dirigible, *Shenandoah*, states that he is not convinced that dirigibles are capable rendering real assistance in a future naval war.	The Pennsylvania Department of Mines announces that in the year 1924, 496 miners died while mining 87,277,499 tons of anthracite coal....The Department of Agriculture reports that the number of farm laborers now totals 3,085,000, 109,000 less than last year....B.F. Goodrich announces that it will increase the price of pneumatic tires by 10 to 15 percent and solid tires by 10 percent; all tubes will increase in price by 15 percent.	The government of Germany announces its is proposal for construction of a zeppelin that would drop an exploration party at the North Pole and return in six months to pick them up; the plan depends on whether the allies will allow Germany to build a zeppelin large enough to carry a party of eight with their equipment....The British Medical Research Council announces that it is working p on a vaccine against cancer....The U.S. Secretary of the Navy states that the navy is not interested in a proposed joint German-American journey to the North Pole by dirigible.	The Extension of Columbia University announces that it will offer 759 courses in the 1925–26 academic year; courses in ancient and medieval art, English Literature and European politics will be taught while a course in auto salesmanship has been dropped....France defeats Holland in the Davis Cup singles.	Jul. 18

F	G	H	I	J
Includes campaigns, elections, federal-state relations, civil rights and liberties, crime, the judiciary, education, healthcare, poverty, urban affairs, and population.	Includes formation and debate of U.S. foreign and defense policies, veterans affairs, and defense spending. (Relations with specific foreign countries are usually found under the region concerned.)	Includes business, labor, agriculture, taxation, transportation, consumer affairs, monetary and fiscal policy, natural resources, pollution and industrial accidents.	Includes worldwide scientific, medical and technological developments, natural phenomena, U.S. weather and natural disasters.	Includes the arts, religion, scholarship, communications media, sports, entertainment, fashions, fads, and social life.

	World Affairs	Europe	Africa & The Middle East	The Americas	Asia & The Pacific
Jul. 19		France reports that its economy is improving as its exports increase in value and volume and its imports decrease....France and Italy estimate that the tourist trade is bringing in near-record sums....For the second time in three months, the Portuguese Army has attempted to overthrow the government; the plot fails.			Chinese national leaders state that they are looking toward the United States to exercise leadership in restoring order to China in its relations with outside powers.
Jul. 20	The League of Nations Temporary Committee on Slavery in its report states that there is slavery in the Philippines and in several Central American nations.		Assisted by artillery and aircraft, French cavalry manage to counterattack the Moors; the first American veterans to volunteer for French service as pilots leave the United States.		The Japanese government makes public a note it sent to the Chinese government demanding that it must suppress all disturbances against foreigners.
Jul. 21		Portugal's Premier Antonio da Silva presents his resignation to the President after losing a no-confidence vote by the Chamber of Deputies.	France now has a force of 150,000 men in Morocco to fight the adherents of Abd-el-Krim. Spain sends an envoy to talk directly with Abd-el-Krim to discuss peace terms.	Mexico's War Department states that there are no bands of rebels operating within the entire republic and a few small groups of bandits are being eliminated by federal troops.	
Jul. 22		The Paris Council votes to restrict access to Parisian cemeteries such as Pere La Chaise by tourists as they are disrupting funerals....President Manuel Gomes of Portugal refuses to dissolve the Portuguese Chamber of Deputies as he searches for a new Premier; martial law is made somewhat less restrictive.	Riots in Beirut over increasing rents result in three dead and several others injured....French forces receive an additional 30 tanks to reinforce their soldiers currently massing for an offensive....Spain's General Primo de Rivera states that he will consult with France's Marshals Philippe Petain and Hubert Lyautey over possible peace proposals.		In Canton six strikers are killed as rival striking factions fight in the streets and are driven from the streets by the Chinese Army.
Jul. 23		The Economist John Maynard Keynes declares that Britain's return to the gold standard has resulted in a deliberate increase in unemployment....The governments of Yugoslavia, Czechoslovakia, and Romania (known as "the Little Entente") are reported to b working on a plan to for a centralized general staff for their armies and may even adopt a single uniform for the three armies.			
Jul. 24		The British government has taken steps to intervene and possibly head off a threatened coal mine strike in Britain.	French forces, backed by heavy artillery support have succeeded in pushing back Abd-el-Krim's forces all along the frontline in Morocco; in the meantime the French cabinet declares that Marshall Philippe Petain will be the supreme French Commander in Morocco.	An American church in Nicaragua is bombed and the three missionaries have been threatened and have had their residence stoned.	President Manuel Quezon of the Philippines denies that differences between Muslim and Christian Filipinos have caused the problems created recently by the island's Moro population.
Jul. 25	Reports from Stockholm describe a new international effort by the Soviet Union to open new propaganda centers world wide to include Buenos Aries, Constantinople, Alexandria, Teheran, and Tangier.	The Italian government cuts 20 million lira off the price of a piece of property that the Vatican wishes to use as the site of its proposed American College.			The 900-year-old Japanese classic, *Tale of the Genji* is published in an English translation by Arthur Waley....The Japanese government announces that it will begin extensive fleet maneuvers in September.

A	B	C	D	E
Includes developments that affect more than one world region, international organizations and important meetings of world leaders.	Includes all domestic and regional developments in Europe, including the Soviet Union.	Includes all domestic and regional developments in Africa and the Middle East.	Includes all domestic and regional developments in Latin America, the Caribbean, and Canada.	Includes all domestic and regional developments in Asian and Pacific nations (and colonies).

U.S. Politics & Social Issues	U.S. Foreign Policy & Affairs, Defense	U.S. Economy & Environment	Science, Technology & Nature	Culture, Leisure & Lifestyle	
Clarence Darrow and other prominent lawyers open the offices of the League for the Abolition of Capital Punishment in New York City....As the result of many complaints, the New York State Department of Health orders that hot dog stands are to be inspected....Court is not in session today for the J.T. Scopes trial; Clarence Darrow is making preparations for his final argument which is scheduled the next day and weighing how to handle his threatened contempt of court charge.			The Curtis Aircraft company christens a new airplane, named "Fox News," designed to send photographers to news scenes and back at high speeds (750 miles in less than seven hours)....A concentrated form of insulin is found by scientists at Johns Hopkins University that has been isolated from the commercial product; it is expected that the manufacture of synthetic insulin will be possible because of this development.		Jul. 19
Clarence Darrow apologizes to the court and avoids a contempt of court charge....Clarence Darrow calls William Jennings Bryan to the stand as an expert witness on the bible as the Scopes trial reconvenes.		Lawrence, MA, cloth mills announce that they will cut pay to their employees by 10 percent....The International Match Company announces that it is taking over the entire match manufacturing business in Poland in exchange for stock.	The MacMillan Arctic expedition is currently in Labrador; the Inuit who have visited the explorers are given demonstrations of the wireless radio....Dr. A. B. Nosque, head of the Polyclinical Hospital of Havana, Cuba, proposes that cancer cures under development should be tested on criminals as it would be unfair to inoculate healthy volunteers.		Jul. 20
J.T. Scopes is found guilty of breaking Tennessee law by teaching evolution; he is fined $100; an appeal is planned....John Washington Butler, author of the anti-evolution law expresses his satisfaction with the verdict but believes that Scopes should have been fined $500....The Republican Club of St. Thomas and St. John begins a campaign to grant citizenship to residents of the U.S. Virgin Islands.				Gertrude Ederle begins her training to swim across the English Channel.	Jul. 21
Pittsburgh sees several racial riots in outlying sections of the city....The Everett Mills in Lawrence, MA, closes its doors and will be closed for five weeks because of economic conditions instead of reducing wages.	The navy announces that ships will patrol the route of a planned flight from California to Hawaii, currently scheduled for September 2.				Jul. 22
10 miners are trapped while fighting a fire in a coal mine at Rockwood, TN....The Blackfoot, Blood Piegan, Gros Vent, and Nez Perce tribes are suing the U.S. government for land claims in Montana, Wyoming, Idaho, and Washington; the value of the lands at the center of the lawsuit is $68,707,343.		The Radio Corporation of America announces the first deficit in its history for the quarter ending in June....The U.S. Commerce Department announces that grain and grain products worth $535 million were exported during the fiscal year that ended in June.		The Metropolitan Opera in New York announces that Lauritz Melchior, the Danish tenor will appear in a to perform in several of Wagner's operas.	Jul. 23
William Jennings Bryan in an interview states that he favor an extended debate on evolution although he cautions the discussion would be more appropriate for adults than schoolchildren....The Workers Party of America demonstrates in New York City, denouncing U.S. policy in China and declaring their support of the Soviet Union.		Dun's weekly report on consumer prices indicates that in the past week most food has become more expensive....President Calvin Coolidge states that he will not intervene in a threatened coal strike, stating intervention before all other measures are exhausted would be harmful.	A new star, designated as Nova Pictoris has been discovered by a telegraph operator in South Africa.	In practice sessions for her proposed cross-Channel swim, Gertrude Ederle impresses all observers with her speed and endurance.	Jul. 24
A report in the New York Times describes the trend in increased unemployment insurance across the country and suggests that this may be the next significant labor reform in the coming years.		The National Board of Fire Underwriters announces that fire destroys 618 homes daily.		Beauty shop operators in Atlantic City, NJ, report the number of men asking for hair permanents equals that of women.	Jul. 25

F	G	H	I	J
Includes campaigns, elections, federal-state relations, civil rights and liberties, crime, the judiciary, education, healthcare, poverty, urban affairs, and population.	Includes formation and debate of U.S. foreign and defense policies, veterans affairs, and defense spending. (Relations with specific foreign countries are usually found under the region concerned.)	Includes business, labor, agriculture, taxation, transportation, consumer affairs, monetary and fiscal policy, natural resources, pollution and industrial accidents.	Includes worldwide scientific, medical and technological developments, natural phenomena, U.S. weather and natural disasters.	Includes the arts, religion, scholarship, communications media, sports, entertainment, fashions, fads, and social life.

	World Affairs	Europe	Africa & The Middle East	The Americas	Asia & The Pacific
Jul. 26		Italy announces a budget surplus which it will maintain into the next year....Portugal terminates military rule and will see a new cabinet formed within the week.	From Beirut come reports that a rebellion has broken out among the Druze tribesmen against French rule.		
Jul. 27		Socialist election victories in France threaten the stability of Premier Paul Painleve's government.	Britain's Committee on Imperial Defense announces that it will keep military forces in Egypt to safeguard its access to the Suez Canal....The building permits department of the city of Tel Aviv must close in order to review the largest number of building applications (208) that they have ever received in a one-month period.		Japanese Premier Kato Takaaki's government, which has come under increased pressure by the factions supporting opposition leader Tanaka is attempting to hold his cabinet together despite the anticipated resignation of three of Tanaka's supporters.
Jul. 28	Professor Schultze-Gavernitz becomes the first German appointed to a League of Nations office; he is named as Chief of the League of Nations' Section of Science which will soon open in Paris.	In a speech at Williams College in Massachusetts, British General Frederick Maurice states that currently Europe is as much an armed camp as it was before the war but he does not see that there will be a war within the next 20 years.	The League of Nations Commission on the Iraqi-Turkish border dispute states that if Mosul is to be an integral part of Iraq, the British Mandate must continue beyond the four year that has been agreed upon; if the British do not remain, the recommendation is that the northern Mosul region be incorporated into Turkey.		
Jul. 29		Britain's House of Commons approves the proposed naval construction program that will result in new battlecruisers despite arguments that the nation cannot afford it.	The Prince of Wales ends his tour of Africa, leaving the port of Cape Town; he is now on his way to South America and is expected to reach the port of Montevideo in mid-August.		
Jul. 30		Work in Romania's Moreni oil field comes to a halt as the result of an oil gusher which has caught fire and is sending flames 200 feet into the air....In Italy the price of all cereal products including bread and pasta has increased about 10 percent as a result of due to the reimposition of an import tax on wheat.	French troops are mobilizing to crush a rebellion in Syria; the Army has not yet encountered the rebels but French aircraft are bombing villages.	Property owners in Mexico's San Luis Potosi state send a complaint to the federal government that Governor Manrique is openly backing a syndicate of workers who are spreading Communist propaganda.	
Jul. 31		Members of Austria's Hakenkreuzler Party visit the Foreign Minister to protest the holding of the International Zionist Conference in Vienna....5,000 Germans have already left Poland with another 15,000 on the way to being deported; in reprisal for Poland's expulsion of Germans living in western Poland's Silesia, Germany deports 20,000 Polish coal miners.	Persia announces that it will establish a permanent delegation at the League of Nations....Marshal Philippe Petain returns to France after inspecting the Moroccan front....Spain's air force bombs several targets in Morocco while the Spanish Army employs heavy artillery barrages to dislodge snipers.		
Aug. 1		Celebrating the 25th anniversary of his accession to the throne, Italy's King Victor Emmanuele signs an amnesty freeing all political prisoners as well as criminal acts other than murder and homicide....A new cabinet is formed in Porigasl....Baron and Baroness de Valsco receive the first divorce in Spanish history....America's first representative to Albania is received by President Ahmed Zog....The final German refugees from Poland arrive in Germany, 7,000 in all....At midnight, the last French soldiers who had been occupying Germany's Ruhr Valley since early 1923 are withdrawn.	Threatening a combined Spanish and French offensive, France's President Paul Painleve warns Abd-el-Krim that he must make peace now and cease the conflict in Morocco.	In Nicaragua, the economy shows signs of strength as its entire coffee crop has been exported with some decline in imports....Mexican newspapers accuse the American Minister to Guatemala has been implicated in an attempt to get the Mexican state of Chiapas to secede from Mexico.	Japan's Premier Kato Takaaki is reappointed and makes only minor changes to his cabinet; new elections will take place next winter and are expected to be closely contested.

A	B	C	D	E
Includes developments that affect more than one world region, international organizations and important meetings of world leaders.	*Includes all domestic and regional developments in Europe, including the Soviet Union.*	*Includes all domestic and regional developments in Africa and the Middle East.*	*Includes all domestic and regional developments in Latin America, the Caribbean, and Canada.*	*Includes all domestic and regional developments in Asian and Pacific nations (and colonies).*

U.S. Politics & Social Issues	U.S. Foreign Policy & Affairs, Defense	U.S. Economy & Environment	Science, Technology & Nature	Culture, Leisure & Lifestyle	
William Jennings Bryan, three-time Presidential candidate, former Secretary of State, and most recently assistant to the prosecution in the J.T. Scopes evolution case, dies of a stroke at the age of 65.		The Federal Reserve Board reports that although there has been a decline in production, it is only a seasonal adjustment and production is still greater than it was that this time last year.			Jul. 26
					Jul. 27
			The MacMillan Arctic Expedition leaves Greenland for the next stage of its attempt to reach the North Pole.	The Boy Scouts of New York announce that they have planted 126,000 trees in the past three years.	Jul. 28
	The U.S. Navy announces that although it is following the experiments of Dr. Edwin Scott as he seeks to develop a "death ray" weapon but has not decided to allow him the use of a battleship for experimental purposes....The annual military training camp at Plattsburgh, NY, closes.		A 17th century ship, the second discovered in two days, is dug up in New York City's South Street.	The Soviet State Museum announces that an archaeological expedition in the vicinity of Irkutsk has discovered a Neolithic cemetery containing a 5,000 year old skeleton and approximately 2,000 objects.	Jul. 29
			William Beebe, completing his scientific exploration and survey on board the Arcturus, returns to New York City.	Washington Police are struggling how to interpret a city ordnance banning "indecent music"; attempts are being made to define the law in order to better enforce it and consensus seems to build that "hoochy-kootchie intonations" and "tom-tommy sort of Oriental music," are what is meant.	Jul. 30
William Jennings Bryan is buried at Arlington National Cemetery.		The Remington Cash Register Company wins a suit against the National Cash Register Company restraining an infringement on Remington's patents and ordering payments in excess of $1 million....U.S. production and consumption of gasoline reached new records in June with 994 million gallons produced that month. ...The Massachusetts Utilities Commission grants New England Telephone and Telegraph permission to increase telephone rates by 20 percent.		France's Premier Paul Painleve thanks U.S. Secretary of Commerce Hoover for sending a delegation to the Decorative Arts Exhibition, the exhibit that is defining Art Deco design....Swimmer Johnny Weissmuller breaks the world record for swimming 100 yards, completing it in 50.4 seconds.	Jul. 31
Commentator Will Rogers declines an offer to run for the Governorship of Arkansas....Two former Army privates who have been convicted of attempting to start a Communist-inspired mutiny at their barracks in Hawaii will be sent to California to serve their prison sentence.	The U.S. Navy, in exercises off the Hawaiian Islands stages a mock air battle to test the ability of land based anti-aircraft guns to protect the American bases.	The failures of business in America numbered 1,685 for the month of July, the fewest in any month this year....Secretary of Commerce Herbert Hoover meets with President Calvin Coolidge as part of an effort to see if the government can prevent a strike by anthracite coal miners.	Archaeologists find skeletons of mastodons and other animals in Mexico's Chihuahua state.... Archaeologists begin excavating an early iron age town in Sweden.... The Smithsonian Institution announces the airplane, Chicago, which flew around the world, will be on display at the museum in Washington.	Gertrude Ederle's planned attempt to swim across the English Channel is delayed by bad weather....Tris Speaker of the Cleveland Indians and Rogers Hornsby of the St. Louis Cardinals lead, respectively, the American and National Leagues in batting....Eugene O'Neil's play, Desire Under the Elms is banned from the British stage.	Aug. 1

F	G	H	I	J
Includes campaigns, elections, federal-state relations, civil rights and liberties, crime, the judiciary, education, healthcare, poverty, urban affairs, and population.	Includes formation and debate of U.S. foreign and defense policies, veterans affairs, and defense spending. (Relations with specific foreign countries are usually found under the region concerned.)	Includes business, labor, agriculture, taxation, transportation, consumer affairs, monetary and fiscal policy, natural resources, pollution and industrial accidents.	Includes worldwide scientific, medical and technological developments, natural phenomena, U.S. weather and natural disasters.	Includes the arts, religion, scholarship, communications media, sports, entertainment, fashions, fads, and social life.

	World Affairs	Europe	Africa & The Middle East	The Americas	Asia & The Pacific
Aug. 2		Camps are being set up in Germany for refugee that have been forced to leave Poland....The general economic situation in Central Europe is very good, based in large part on favorable harvests reports. ...An American company is now in negotiations with the government of Romania to provide electrical power to the country....Stressing world hostility toward the Soviet government, the Soviets announce that the government will call up all men born in the year 1903.	Fighting at isolated outposts continues in Morocco; after capturing a fort held by the rebels, the French find over 150 dead Moors.	The cabinet ministers of the Nicaraguan government have quit and a new government is being formed.	The strike in Shanghai enters its 10th week with no indications that it will halt any time soon.
Aug. 3	Tensions between Greece and Bulgaria have reached the point where war is possible; Greece has indicated that it may appeal to the League of Nations.	An earthquake strikes southern Italy in the city of Cerignola.	A large force of tanks leads an assault on the Moors in Morocco is successful but French authorities say that if the war is to be concluded successfully this month, more troops are needed....Reports from Paris state that Abd-el-Krim may have received some airplanes to help him in his struggle against France and Spain.	American General John Pershing begins his duties of mediating and enforcing the border dispute between Chile and Peru....After 13 years of keeping the peace, the U.S. Marines depart from Nicaragua.	
Aug. 4		British economist John Maynard Keynes marries dancer Lydia Lopoukhova....A plot has been uncovered in which Communist agents would have killed Tamas Masaryk, President of Czecoslovakia....Kaiser Wilhelm II, still in exile in the Netherlands tells an interviewer that he is "an instrument of God," and is waiting for his opportunity to regain his throne.	Landing on the Island of St. Helena, where Napoleon had been exiled, the Prince of Wales makes a stopover on his tour, now traveling from Africa to South America....Two detachments of American volunteers leave Paris going to Morocco where they will fly as volunteers for French forces there fighting Abd-el-Krim.		
Aug. 5			Another American group, this one flying six airplanes, departs to fight with the French in Morocco.... Spanish forces in Morocco capture a rebel force coming from Tangier; French aircraft spot and bomb Moorish positions.		
Aug. 6	The League of Nations commences a worldwide study designed to determine whether motion pictures have a negative impact on the minds of young children.	The German government announces that it will evict Polish nationals working in that country as Poland recently did to German workers.... Riots by over 600 striking miners in Wales result in 118 reported injuries.		The coffee-growing states of Brazil announce that they will restrict exports in order not to flood the world market and lower prices.	
Aug. 7		Italy's former Prime Minister Vittorio Orlando resigns his seat in the Chamber of Deputies in protest against the actions of the Fascist government....The Soviet War Commissar Mikhail Frunze is the object of an assassination attempt when a train is blown up; he is unharmed.	Reports indicate that there is no action on the Moroccan front; replacements are being sent to the front lines to allow troops that have been holding their positions to rest....Reports from Syria state that 200 French have been killed by rebel Druze tribesmen.	The city of Guadalajara reports serious flooding as the result of a severe rainstorm; at least five are reported killed....Mexico City is hit by earthquake tremors.	The Chinese government in Beijing reports that it has received word from local organizations in Kwantung Province that the Communists are very active there.
Aug. 8		As 6500 new officers are accepted into the Red Army, Soviet Minister of War Mikhail Frunze warns the Western Powers that the strength of the Army "cannot be shattered."... Spanish police raid a Communist cell in Saragossa, arresting six and capturing a great deal of political literature....Reports state that children are starving in Tiparary in the Irish Free State.	The French government admits that the situation in Syria is serious; 500 soldiers originally to have been sent to the fighting in Morocco have been diverted to Syria....In Morocco, the rebels of Abd-el-Krim have launched an attack on Spanish positions.... Wahhabis under the leadership of Ibn Saud have advanced toward the city of Jeddah on the Arabian Peninsula; foreigners are leaving the city....French troops capture the rebel fortress of Ameryou in Morocco.		

A	B	C	D	E
Includes developments that affect more than one world region, international organizations and important meetings of world leaders.	Includes all domestic and regional developments in Europe, including the Soviet Union.	Includes all domestic and regional developments in Africa and the Middle East.	Includes all domestic and regional developments in Latin America, the Caribbean, and Canada.	Includes all domestic and regional developments in Asian and Pacific nations (and colonies).

U.S. Politics & Social Issues	U.S. Foreign Policy & Affairs, Defense	U.S. Economy & Environment	Science, Technology & Nature	Culture, Leisure & Lifestyle	
The Chicago Crime Commission announces that so far this year there have been 227 murders in that city, more than one a day and the greatest number thus far of any year....A riot between members of the Ku Klux Klan and anti-Klan protesters breaks out with at least 20 injured and several arrested of the nearly 2,000 involved in Westwood, Massachusetts.	The military training camp at Plattsburgh, NY, receives an additional 500 men for training, raising the current program to 2,000 enrolled in the program.	President Calvin Coolidge announces he will not interfere in any strike against coal mines until it actually happens.		Gertrude Ederle once again postpones her swim across the English Channel due to weather.	Aug. 2
The Commerce Department announces that 418 people were killed in auto accidents in 57 cities for a total of 2,511 since the beginning of the year.				Charlie Chaplin arrives in new York City for the premier of his film, *The Gold Rush* which will open on August 15.	Aug. 3
	The Executive Committee of the American Chemical Society denounces discussions in Geneva that would ban the use of poison gas in warfare.	Negotiations are completed which will result in what will be New York's largest office building to date, a 30-story structure that will cost $19 million and be completed in 1927....The Soviet government announces that its trade with the United States has broken all records in the first six months of 1925....President Calvin Coolidge urges American railroads to merge to keep freight rates low....A strike by anthracite coal miners now seems inevitable as the Miners Union breaks off negotiations.	Commander Donald B. Macmillan makes the first of several aircraft flights that will be part of his Polar expedition.	Jeanne Sion attempts to swim the English Channel and comes within 1¼ mile of the English coast when she gives up.	Aug. 4
It is expected that 50,000 members of the Ku Klux Klan may arrive in Washington for their planned march on August 8; 43 trains have been reserved for the travelers coming in to Washington and the city. Police have called up their reserves.	The Department of the Navy announces that its dirigible, *Shenandoah* will be an armed craft with 10 guns while there will be no armament for the other Naval dirigible, the *Los Angeles*.				Aug. 5
President Calvin Coolidge announces he may stay at the summer White House in Swampscott, MA, for another month.	President Calvin Coolidge is told that any efforts to further economize within the army and navy will result in serious problems.	The New York Central railroad announces that it will install automatic signals on 2,600 miles of track....In the fiscal year that ended on June 30, 1925, a total of 9,445 miles of Federal aid highways have been built in the United States.	Members of the Macmillan sailing in kayaks off their ship, *Peary*, are attacked by a herd of about 100 walrus; continued flights by the party are beginning to annoy the local Eskimos who do not understand how the aircraft can stay up in the air.		Aug. 6
At least 20,000 members of the Klan arrive to march in Washington with more expected....In an act witnessed by passengers on a train, an African American is lynched by a crowd of 1,000 in Excelsior Springs, MO.			The Passaic Valley Sewerage Commission announces that since it installed a new sewer in 1924, that fish and plants have returned to the Passaic River.	Comedian and singer Eddie Cantor returns from a tour of Europe; he plans to star in a new Ziegfeld production, *Kid Boots*, in September.	Aug. 7
The Klan's planned march in Washington takes place with an estimated 40,000 marching....The U.S. government is sending 300 additional agents to patrol the border with Canada to cut smuggling and rum running....After 52 years of conflict, representatives of the Native American Pawnee and Sioux tribes have signed a peace agreement at Massacre Canyon, NE.	The flight of Navy airplanes from the West Coast of the United States to Hawaii will be monitored by ships which will relay radio messages to the crews.			In Great Britain, the official Censor bans the performance of *Six Characters in Search of an Author* by Luigi Pirandello.	Aug. 8

F	G	H	I	J
Includes campaigns, elections, federal-state relations, civil rights and liberties, crime, the judiciary, education, healthcare, poverty, urban affairs, and population.	*Includes formation and debate of U.S. foreign and defense policies, veterans affairs, and defense spending. (Relations with specific foreign countries are usually found under the region concerned.)*	*Includes business, labor, agriculture, taxation, transportation, consumer affairs, monetary and fiscal policy, natural resources, pollution and industrial accidents.*	*Includes worldwide scientific, medical and technological developments, natural phenomena, U.S. weather and natural disasters.*	*Includes the arts, religion, scholarship, communications media, sports, entertainment, fashions, fads, and social life.*

	World Affairs	Europe	Africa & The Middle East	The Americas	Asia & The Pacific
Aug. 9		The French government announces that it will abolish six war cemeteries in France, requiring the removal of the bodies of 5,000 British soldiers....Fighting breaks out in Berlin where the veterans group, *Stahlhelm* attacks a group of the Reichsbanner organization; there is one dead and many are injured....The French government announces that due to the projected harvest, France will have to import food....German bankers predict that the current shortage of credit in Germany will last for some time into the future.	Turkey announces that it will issue new stamps that have been solely designed by Turkish artists....A severe earthquake strikes the Turkish coastal city of Smyrna....Marshal Philippe Petain reports that efforts in Morocco will lead to success, that latest attempts by the Moors have failed and more reinforcements from France on the way....Druze rebels in Syria are succeeding in keeping their hold over a French garrison, foiling rescue attempts by French forces.		
Aug. 10		Italian poet Gabriele d'Annunzio cancels a flight he had been planning to commemorate the tenth anniversary of his bombing raid on Vienna during the war....The final disputes between the Italian government and Anglo-Persian oil company over oil in Albania is resolved; Italy will receive revenues from about half of what the British company extracts from Albania....Britain's Chancellor of the Exchequer Winston Churchill denies having said that the government's assistance in resolving a mining strike was cheaper than having a revolution.	French troops fall back to new positions after having lost 100 men in the fighting in Syria against the Druze rebels; British soldiers using armored cars and airplanes have assisted the French by keeping the rebels from entering Transjordan....Abd-el-Krim states that his aim is independence and that he will not enter into any negotiations with either the French or the Spanish unless they first recognize that fact.		General Leonard Wood, American Governor of the Philippines names new members to his cabinet; it is generally assumed that the Philippine Senate will not approve of his selections.
Aug. 11	The League of Nations announces that it will discuss an American proposal to encourage nations that grow poppies for heroin production to try alternate crops.	The Polish government announces that although it is not responsible for what happens to any German nationals it considers staying in Poland illegally, it will give them every assistance to leave Poland and go to Germany....The Austrian government prohibits the practice spiritualism and occult research.	French and Spanish forces join together and announce that they will be behind a major offensive soon; French forces now total over 50,000 men after a recent reinforcement of 15,000 troops.	The Argentine government announces that it will liquidate two short term debts by raising new bonds equal to $25 million.	Chinese soldiers fire on strikers and demonstrators in the Chinese city of Tientsin.
Aug. 12		The Czechoslovak government takes over and nationalizes the spa of Marienbad which had formerly belonged to the Catholic Church....The German legislature passes a high protective tariff on food articles from other countries....The American Red Cross announces that it will appropriate $5,000 to assist refugees coming into the country from Macedonia....Great Britain and France reach an agreement that will lead to a general agreement in Europe concerning security in Europe to include guaranteeing the borders of Poland and Czechoslovakia.	Great Britain announces that it planning to raise an army of 20,000 men to keep order in and defend the territory of Iraq; it will report to King Faisal but all officers will be British....Marshall Philippe Petain is expected to leave France soon to lead French forces in Morocco in person....The French government announces that in the fighting in Syria, there have been over 840 French casualties, killed, wounded, and missing.		Riots break out in Tientsin, China, in response to yesterday firing on strikers; in the fighting today 300 are arrested while a large number of strikers are wounded and some killed.
Aug. 13			The American aviators who have joined the French Service to fight against Abd-el-Krim formally enter French service as Squadron 19 of the French Air Service.		A severe hailstorm in Siberia ruins thousands of acres of crops in Siberia, also killing two and injuring several.
Aug. 14		The three-week old British textile strike ends with approximately 200,000 workers returning to work.	French President Paul Painleve rejects any consideration to be given to the suggestion that the Moors in Morocco be given independence.	The Prince of Wales arrives in the port of Montevideo, Uruguay, to begin his tour of Latin America.	The British government Air Ministry signs a contract with Imperial Airways to begin air service between Egypt and India.

A	B	C	D	E
Includes developments that affect more than one world region, international organizations and important meetings of world leaders.	Includes all domestic and regional developments in Europe, including the Soviet Union.	Includes all domestic and regional developments in Africa and the Middle East.	Includes all domestic and regional developments in Latin America, the Caribbean, and Canada.	Includes all domestic and regional developments in Asian and Pacific nations (and colonies).

U.S. Politics & Social Issues	U.S. Foreign Policy & Affairs, Defense	U.S. Economy & Environment	Science, Technology & Nature	Culture, Leisure & Lifestyle	
William Green, President of the the American Federation of Labor, warns African Americans that they should not attend a meeting of the American Negro Labor Congress because the meeting has been called by Communists.		Secretary of Commerce Herbert Hoover announces that because the government has cut taxes and maintained its protective tariffs that the nation can look forward to prosperity.	The MacMillan polar expedition, currently in Greenland flies over explores the site of the Greely camp where 18 died of starvation in 1884....In Rhodesia, archaeologists find copper bangles and other items estimated to be 10,000 years old....The Ford company announces that it has built the longest locomotive in the world, 117 feet long and can pull a train a mile and a half long....Two French pilots establish a new world record for endurance in flight, flying without stopping for 45 hours and 11 minutes....In New York state the average age has risen from 24 years in 1840 to 30 years in 1925.	Irish poet, William Butler Yeats states that "the day or oratory is past," and that under these circumstances the Irish theater must teach clarity of expression.	Aug. 9
In Framingham, MA, five men are shot in the wake of a riot following a Ku Klux Klan meeting.		The National Fire Protection Association announces that fire losses in the United States amount to $1,044 a minute....Standard Oil Company of New York announces it will cut two cents off the retail price of gasoline.	The Macmillan Polar expedition has yet to find in its aerial surveys a place to establish an advanced base camp.	British poet Thomas Hardy will be assisting in the London production of an adaptation of his novel, *Tess of the D'Urbervilles*....Lillian Harrison of Argentina attempts to swim the English Channel fails in the attempt, nearly drowning and having to be rescued eight miles from the English coast.	Aug. 10
Professor Edward East of Harvard states that immigration into the United States must be restricted.		The Department of Agriculture announces that the number of farms in the United States decreased by 30,000, estimated to be 25 million acres.	The Soviet Union announces that to celebrate the 200th anniversary of the Russian Academy of Science, it sill send out several scientific and exploration expeditions.	Johnny Weismuller sets a new world record for the 100-yard swim, completing it in 52 seconds.	Aug. 11
In Reading, Massachusetts an estimated crowd of 1,000 including members of the Ku Klux Klan and their opponents results in rioting with shots fired and bombs thrown; about 20 are arrested....In Scobey, MS, Sidney Towns is taken from the custody of the sheriff after an arrest for murder and is killed by a crowd....The United Mine Workers deny that they are using the threat of a strike against anthracite coal mines as a means to get consideration for their grievances in the bituminous coal industry....Two men who were charged in the July 4th collapse of the Pickwick Club in Boston which killed 44 are acquitted.		The American Petroleum Institute announces that oil production in the past week was 24,800 barrels greater than the week before.	Two French aviators complete a three-day flight around Europe flying from Paris to Belgrade to Constantinople, Moscow, Copenhagen before returning to Paris....A group of several record companies announce that they have invented a record disk that can play a whole symphony... Pilots of the Macmillan expedition aircraft discover a site for an advanced base camp.	"Roxy" Rothafel announces that he will open a new theatre on Broadway that will open in 1926; the cost of the theatre is estimated at $7 million....Gertrude Ederle resumes her training in her attempt to swim across the English channel....A record number of Americans have traveled to Oxford to participate in the Oxford Summer Extension School.... In Davis Cup play, Canada plays Australia and Japan plays Spain.... Japan beats Spain in the Davis Cup match; they will face Australia next....Australia defeats Canada in the Davis Cup championships.	Aug. 12
	After a tour of the Middle East and the Balkans, Senator King of Utah announces that the Soviets have great influence in Turkey, that the Turks are not complying with treaties imposed after the war and that he doubts the value of opening relations between the United States and Turkey.	The H. C. Frick Company begins to fire up 265 ovens used for making coke that will be used for the manufacture of steel; the reopening of the ovens is taken as a sign that the economy is doing better.	The MacMillan expedition broadcasts a concert of Inuit musicians giving a concert that is heard by radio operators in Chicago....A skull found in Palestine in June which was estimated to be 40,000 years old is being studied; scientists have detected that shows signs of surgery to relieve pressure on the skull.	The Salzburg Music Festival begin today with thousands of visitor attending the concerts and other productions....The Brooklyn Edison Company announces that it will give an award to any employee who saves a life; almost 3,000 employees have received first aid training.	Aug. 13
Lela V. Scopes, sister of J. T. Scopes who was convicted for teaching evolution in Tennessee signs a contract to teach school in Tarrytown, NY; she had been refused a contract at her school because she accepted the theory of evolution.	Mock night attacks by bombers are conducted at Camp Dix, NJ to test sound detecting equipment and searchlights....The Navy dirigible, *Shenandoah*, leaves its base in Lakehurst, NJ. for its first flight as an armed aircraft.	The Commerce Department announces that the cotton year 1924–25 which ended on July 31st. with 15,635,674 bales, an increase over the previous year by over 3 million bales.	George Washington University students volunteer for a sleep deprivation test staying awake and performing their jobs during a 66-hour period without sleep.		Aug. 14

F	G	H	I	J
Includes campaigns, elections, federal-state relations, civil rights and liberties, crime, the judiciary, education, healthcare, poverty, urban affairs, and population.	*Includes formation and debate of U.S. foreign and defense policies, veterans affairs, and defense spending. (Relations with specific foreign countries are usually found under the region concerned.)*	*Includes business, labor, agriculture, taxation, transportation, consumer affairs, monetary and fiscal policy, natural resources, pollution and industrial accidents.*	*Includes worldwide scientific, medical and technological developments, natural phenomena, U.S. weather and natural disasters.*	*Includes the arts, religion, scholarship, communications media, sports, entertainment, fashions, fads, and social life.*

	World Affairs	Europe	Africa & The Middle East	The Americas	Asia & The Pacific
Aug. 15	The International Chamber of Commerce reports that finances in several countries to include England, Germany, Italy, Austria, Hungary, and Poland have been improving since the end of World War I.	The Yugoslav royal family visits the Croatian city of Zagreb; the king is enthusiastically received....Poland's Foreign Minister, in Paris after his visit to the United States, says that Americans are aware of Europe's problems and will not pursue a policy of isolation....Police in Berlin state their greatest problem currently is the prevalence of cocaine and that its use rivals bootleg liquor in the United States.	Some reports indicate that the current revolt in Syria against the French Mandatory government has been instiated by King Faisal who is ruling Iraq under the auspices of a British-administered League of Nations mandate.	The Canadian government announces that it is considering dropping all control of railroads and privatizing them instead....Chilean and Peruvian diplomats are still contesting the details of the arbitration that will be conducted to settle their border dispute.	Cholera has broken out in Shanghai; there are approximately 1,000 cases....Observers returning from China state that they believe Chinese hostility toward Americans is substantially less than that toward the British and Japanese.
Aug. 16					
Aug. 17		In an interview, Benito Mussolini declares that Caesar is his hero and the idea of liberty exists only in the minds of philosophers.			
Aug. 18		Belgium signs an agreement with the United States in which Belgium will repay its war debt to the United States over a 62-year period and will not have to pay interest on any loans made before the armistice that brought the war to a halt.	Liberia notifies the League of Nations that it will adhere to the League-sponsored Arms Control Convention.	The Mexican government states that the next session of the national legislature will clarify laws on oil and property and especially those applying to drilling rights.	The Chinese government invites the major powers to a conference to discuss Chinese autonomy in tariffs and other matters involving trade....The Afghan government agrees to pay an indemnity to the Italian government in compensation for having executed an Italian engineer.
Aug. 19		The British government approves an appropriation equivalent to $5 million to restore and preserve the British House of Parliament....The Soviet government predicts an increase in trade in the coming year, up to $1 billion in foreign trade.		Puerto Rico is hit by an earthquake, the tremors are recorded in the United States, Canada, Italy, and England....The Prince of Wales visits the Argentine city of La Plata and is greeted by schoolchildren singing, "God Save the King."...Police in Havana, Cuba, seize the entire issue of *El Heraldo*, a newspaper that has been critical of the government.	
Aug. 20			France and Spain recall their delegates engaged in peace negotiations with Abd-el-Krim and are determined to impose a military solution on the rebels....General Primo de Rivera sends for additional troops from Spain to reinforce the forces already in Morocco.	Armando Andre y Alvarado owner of the Cuban newspaper *El Dia* is shot and killed; he had actively opposed the government's efforts to clean up gambling and other vice in Havana.	Britain, Japan, and the United States will meet to discuss China's request to exercise customs autonomy within its own territory rather than having this totally controlled by outside powers....The Chinese government puts into effect new regulations discriminating against British and Japanese commercial interests....Chinese bandits kidnap an Anglican bishop and seven others in Szechuan province.
Aug. 21		The first month of the fiscal year in Italy shows surplus as opposed to a deficit for the first month of the last fiscal year....King Gustav of Sweden visits Finland, the first time a Swedish monarch has visited that country since 1809....French organizations are protesting deforestation of French land that has been purchased by American timber companies.	Druze rebels in Syria ambush a French general wounding him slightly; reports indicate that while French leaders are talking with rebel leaders, fighting continues....Marshal Philippe Petain of France and General Primo de Rivera of Spain meet to discuss strategy for the upcoming joint campaigns against Abd-el-Krim.	The Mexican government announces it will review its land distribution policy as a result of recent dramatic drops in agricultural production....General John Pershing, in his capacity of arbitrating the treaty and border dispute between Peru and Chile breaks up an anti-Peruvian demonstration that started over the stories in a Peruvian newspaper.	Reports from Shanghai indicate that 50,000 workmen may return to work in the cotton mills....The Soviet Union accuses Britain of imperialist actions in China....Although British merchants who have been affected by the boycott of Hong Kong, are calling for strong military measures to stop the unrest in Canton, the British government is refraining from using force.

A	B	C	D	E
Includes developments that affect more than one world region, international organizations and important meetings of world leaders.	Includes all domestic and regional developments in Europe, including the Soviet Union.	Includes all domestic and regional developments in Africa and the Middle East.	Includes all domestic and regional developments in Latin America, the Caribbean, and Canada.	Includes all domestic and regional developments in Asian and Pacific nations (and colonies).

U.S. Politics & Social Issues	U.S. Foreign Policy & Affairs, Defense	U.S. Economy & Environment	Science, Technology & Nature	Culture, Leisure & Lifestyle	
12,000 members of the Ku Klux Klan hold a rally, parading in a motorcade through several cities and towns in New Jersey.	Edwin R. Scott of San Francisco has requested the use of Naval battleships and aircraft to test a new weapon that he says is not a death ray but which uses ultra violet or infrared rays for destructive force; the Navy does not lend him the equipment he requests.	The Better Business Bureau in New York City begins an information campaign that will make people aware of deceptive advertising.	The MacMillan expedition establishes a new base in its effort to get closer to the North Pole....The city of New York announces that it has been able to reduce the child death rate from tuberculosis by 76 percent since 1898.	The *New York Times* publishes an article describing the currently held Paris Exposition of the Decorative Arts, a collection of industrial and object design that is defining what is considered to be "Art Deco."	Aug. 15
		A survey of the use of appliances in the United States finds that 29 percent of all American homes have washing machines which average $150 each.	The expedition of Troy Chapman Andrews in Mongolia has found animal bones estimated to be 20,000 years old.	The Catholic Church performs the beatification of Father Isaac Jogues, a step in the formal process of sainthood, for the priests who was killed by native Americans in 1632.	Aug. 16
	The Navy Department publishes the itinerary of the dirigible, *Shenandoah,* which will tour the Midwest starting September 1, and will visit 35 cities and five state fairs.	Between 5,000 and 6,000 bituminous coal miners in southern Illinois are called back to work as six large coal mines in that region are reopened.			Aug. 17
		The U.S. Shipping Board's Bureau of Research announces that of all American ships, 93 percent are currently working while two-thirds of government ships are not being used....Alvin Fuller, Governor of Massachusetts calls for a conference of New England governors to discuss plans in the event of an anthracite coal strike.	Commander Donald B. MacMillan, commander of the Naval-National Geographic expedition to explore the North Pole by air, has discussions with the Secretary of the Navy and admits that he may have to stop the expedition....Captain George Wilkins, a British polar explorer announces that he is planning an Antarctic expedition which will include an aerial survey.	Gertrude Ederle attempts to swim the English Channel; at one point as she is coughing because of water in her throat here trainer pulls her toward the pace boat, disqualifying her at 6-1/2 miles off the English coast....Babe Ruth hits his 12th home run of the year; the Yankees beat the Tigers 5-2....The Field museum in Chicago has purchased a collection of over 1,900 statues, weapons, and works of art made in Africa....Producer William Brady states that he will be producing six new plays to include a dramatization of *The Great Gatsby* later in the year.	Aug. 18
			Commander Donald B. MacMillan officially abandons the effort to reach the North Pole by airplane and will begin the return trip to the United States....The Mongolian government banishes American scientist Roy Chapman Andrews, accusing him of spying and spreading propaganda that is anti-Communist among the Mongolians he has met....Ales Hrdlicka, investigating in South Africa, states that he has found new evidence that will provide more information on early man in this area of the world.	Cricketer Jack Hobbs records his 127th century in a single game, surpassing an all-time record set by W.J. Grace.	Aug. 19
In Burgettstown, PA, hooded men kidnap Robert Norris, tar and feather him, and throw him from a moving vehicle on Main Street.			Archaeologists from Tulane University report on their results of their expedition in Guatemala and Mexico where their discoveries included temples and astronomical observatories....Commander Donald B. MacMillan decides against attempting another flight as part of his expedition because of the bad weather.	Gertrude Ederle states that she will make one more attempt to swim the English Channel setting the date for August 31 or September 1.	Aug. 20
.		New England governors meet to develop plans to counter the threat of a fuel shortage as a result of the pending anthracite coal strike.		Australia beats Japan to capture the Davis Cup.	Aug. 21

F	G	H	I	J
Includes campaigns, elections, federal-state relations, civil rights and liberties, crime, the judiciary, education, healthcare, poverty, urban affairs, and population.	*Includes formation and debate of U.S. foreign and defense policies, veterans affairs, and defense spending. (Relations with specific foreign countries are usually found under the region concerned.)*	*Includes business, labor, agriculture, taxation, transportation, consumer affairs, monetary and fiscal policy, natural resources, pollution and industrial accidents.*	*Includes worldwide scientific, medical and technological developments, natural phenomena, U.S. weather and natural disasters.*	*Includes the arts, religion, scholarship, communications media, sports, entertainment, fashions, fads, and social life.*

	World Affairs	Europe	Africa & The Middle East	The Americas	Asia & The Pacific
Aug. 22		The electrification of the Soviet Union is progressing at a very good rate according to the Soviet government, although some peasants are not enthusiastic, as they believe electric lights to be the work of evil spirits.	Sir George Goldie, founder of the British colony of Nigeria dies at the age of 79....The current Turkish government discourages women from wearing veils and encourages women in athletic contest as part of its modernization program....The city of Medina in the Arabian Peninsula is bombarded by the Wahhabi forces of Don Saoud; among the damaged structures is the tomb of Mohammed.	The Mexican government announces that it will bar African Americans from entering the country to work at harvest time.	The Chinese government at Canton announces that American goods can enter China if they do so on Russian and Chinese ships and avoid Hong Kong.
Aug. 23			In Cairo, Egypt, seven men are hanged for the murder of Sir Lee Stack, the Governor General of Sudan....The Labor and Immigration Department of the Zionist Executive in Palestine states that immigration into Palestine averages 3,000 a year.		
Aug. 24		Grand Duke Cyril Romanoff claims to be the new czar and in an interview states that while he will not lead a White Army against the Communists, he is waiting for a call to the throne.			
Aug. 25		The International Socialist Congress adopts a resolution urging the adoption of a universal eight-hour work day and that no unjustified overtime be permitted....Mount Vesuvius has resumed eruptions although observers do not believe that there will be any danger to nearby cities and towns....Reports from Berlin claim that Germany's President Paul von Hindenburg has met with the former Crown Prince.	While the Spanish Navy is bombarding the coast of Morocco, French forces are beginning a new offensive.	After a two trip into the countryside, the Prince of Wales arrives in Buenos Aries as he continues his South American tour.	The Soviet Union's diplomacy in Asia has been emphasized quite heavily in attempts to reach commercial and other agreements with Japan.
Aug. 26		Despite rumors of bad weather, the Soviet government remains optimistic about its harvest and is preparing to export it overseas....General Primo de Rivera, head of the Directorate that is the real ruler of Spain states that the Directorate will quit once it has accomplished its objectives in Morocco.	The Syrian city of Deir-ez-Zor is reportedly been captured by the Druze rebels.	The town of Rama, in Nicaragua has been completely destroyed by a fire....The president of Bolivia prevents his successor from taking office; using troops he prevents the inauguration.	There is continued rioting in Shanghai with two killed and four injured....There is some fear that the continued unrest may result in armed intervention by the Japanese, British, and other powers.
Aug. 27		A strike by 30,000 Belgian metal workers comes to an end after a month....A Soviet judge condemns nine military contractors to death for corruption; 34 are sentenced to prison and 23 are acquitted....Bulgaria's government announces that its wheat surplus this year will be 300,000 tons, about half of the surplus in the years before the war when more land was under cultivation.	Reports in Paris are indicating that Communists located in Lisbon, Portugal, are assisting the rebels under Abd-el-Krim against the Spanish and French in Morocco.... A French attack along a 15-mile front in Morocco captures its objectives.		A planned conference is scheduled to open on October 20 that will discuss a Russo-Japanese railroad link....Mongolians in Moscow are stating that despite his denials, Roy Chapman Andrews was actually conducting espionage and not scientific expeditions when he was banished from the country....A group of military students, known as the Whampoa Cadets with a reputation for being Communist sympathizers have occupied buildings and arrested more than 100 government officials.
Aug. 28		The Soviet Union accuses rich peasants of holding grain so as to increase prices even though one-third of the population cannot buy the food they need.	American aviation volunteers see action for the first time against the Moor rebels in Morocco....The largest French battleship, Paris, has left the port of Toulon; speculation is that its orders are for it to sail to Syria, accompanied by two destroyers.	In a speech in Washington, Mexico's Minister of Labor asserts that there are few Communists in Mexican labor unions....The Nicaraguan government once again announces that a new cabinet has been formed....Great Britain and Mexico agree to resume diplomatic relations after 10 years.	

A	B	C	D	E
Includes developments that affect more than one world region, international organizations and important meetings of world leaders.	Includes all domestic and regional developments in Europe, including the Soviet Union.	Includes all domestic and regional developments in Africa and the Middle East.	Includes all domestic and regional developments in Latin America, the Caribbean, and Canada.	Includes all domestic and regional developments in Asian and Pacific nations (and colonies).

U.S. Politics & Social Issues	U.S. Foreign Policy & Affairs, Defense	U.S. Economy & Environment	Science, Technology & Nature	Culture, Leisure & Lifestyle	
An estimated 4/5 of the poorer residents of Santa Barbara, CA, are now on assistance because of the losses they suffered in the recent earthquake....The successful development of plastic surgery in the years after World War I has created problems for law enforcement as criminals are now making increased use of it to change their appearance....Clyde Osborne, Grand Dragon of the Ku Klux Klan in Ohio declares that the Klan will take up the torch of William Jennings Bryan in promoting religious fundamentalism.	The Naval Dirigible *Shenandoah* goes on a test flight from Lakehurst, NJ, for a series of acceleration trials in preparation for its planned flight to several cities in the U.S. Midwest.				Aug. 22
		The Interstate Commerce Commission reports that 1,767,292 men are now working on major railroads in the United States, an increase of over 21,000 from the previous month.		Attendance records are shattered at the Polo Grounds in New York City as 51,200 people witness a game between the Pittsburgh Pirates and the New York Giants.	Aug. 23
		President Calvin Coolidge approves a plan for a Federal program to assist the development of commercial aviation....Coal dealers in the northeast sate that they have no worries about a fuel shortage in the wake of an anthracite coal strike.	The Macmillan expedition begins its return to the United States from the coast of Greenland.		Aug. 24
	Naval officials have been forced to cut $50 million from their annual budget, reducing it to $310 million a budget that will require closing some installations.		Alphonse Duby, an aviation inventor from Worcester, MA, commits suicide, despondent over the failure of his flying machine which consisted of a pair of wings which were to be flapped like a bird.		Aug. 25
		With a strike looming in the immediate future the Lehigh Valley roadway breaks all 1925 records when it sends 925 cars of coal to market.	The Macmillan expedition ships continue on their trip home, seeking to get away from the coast of Greenland....The U.S. Army Air Service invents a new compass to be used on aircraft that counteracts the affects of the iron and tell of the engine on magnetic compasses.		Aug. 26
William Joyce, Chairman of the National Surety Company, states that bands of western criminals are beginning to move to the eastern U.S. and it may be necessary to form vigilantes in the east to combat that menace.	Retired Rear Admiral W. S. Sims states in an article published in *The Aero Digest* that battleships are doomed and will be replaced by aircraft as naval weapons.		The MacMillan polar expedition's return voyage is marked by difficulties; the ship *Bowdoin* grounds on a reef during a 50 mile-an-hour gales.	Robert Nichols, British writer, attacks American movies noting American "hicks" always demand a happy ending.	Aug. 27
Representative of the Hip Sing and On Leong tongs agree on a truce at a meeting convened by a U.S. district attorney.	Secretary of the Navy Curtis Wilbur announces the crew of the *Shenandoah* which will begin its tour of the American Midwest on September 1.	Long Island, NY now has 500,000 telephones installed and operating....Profits for American railroads increased in July, totaling almost $81 million, $20 million more than in July of 1924....Reports have reached the Labor Department that bituminous coal miners may join in a sympathy strike if anthracite miners go on strike.			Aug. 28

F	G	H	I	J
Includes campaigns, elections, federal-state relations, civil rights and liberties, crime, the judiciary, education, healthcare, poverty, urban affairs, and population.	Includes formation and debate of U.S. foreign and defense policies, veterans affairs, and defense spending. (Relations with specific foreign countries are usually found under the region concerned.)	Includes business, labor, agriculture, taxation, transportation, consumer affairs, monetary and fiscal policy, natural resources, pollution and industrial accidents.	Includes worldwide scientific, medical and technological developments, natural phenomena, U.S. weather and natural disasters.	Includes the arts, religion, scholarship, communications media, sports, entertainment, fashions, fads, and social life.

	World Affairs	Europe	Africa & The Middle East	The Americas	Asia & The Pacific
Aug. 29		The Rumanian government announces that its forecast for the yearly harvest will meet requirements for internal food and enough for export as well....The Polish and Soviet governments approve an agreement that will resolve recent border disputes.... As part of the Paris Exhibition of Decorative Arts, the Eiffel Tower has been covered with 250,000 electric lights....Taxes in Germany have yielded a government surplus equivalent to $100 million.... Disabled French war veterans at a congress issue a declaration that the League of Nations should have its own army to prevent war.		A new radio station opens in Hialeah, FL, that will communicate directly with Colombia, Costa Rica, Nicaragua, Panama, Honduras, Guatemala, and the Bahamas.... The United States announces that it will not officially recognize the government of Ecuador which has come into result of a coup d'etat....The Mexican government announces that it will reduce illiteracy in the country forcing all of those 18-year-old men who cannot read and write into the Army where they will receive schooling as well as military training.	
Aug. 30		Observers are generally agreed that the harvests are expected to be very good; stock exchanges are influenced by the good expectations....A tablet is unveiled at the house where Benito Mussolini was born....The Lithuanian government bans a performance of *Saint Joan* by George Bernard Shaw.	Reports in Syria indicate that the Druze rebels lost 700 in a recent raid on Damascus and the city is currently quiet....The Turkish government is meeting with great success in changing the dress in the country with the fez being rapidly replaced by Panama Hat.	As part of vigorous anti-Chinese sentiment in Mexico, the Mexican government reports that 40 Chinese laborers have been kidnapped in the state of Sonora.	
Aug. 31		The Italian navy announces that one of its submarines, on maneuvers off the east coast of Sicily, is missing....The Irish Free State announces that it will send a representative to the League of Nations.	The British government states that it fears war will break out between Turkey and Britain over the dispute over the Turkish-Iraqi border.	The U.S. Treasury announces that it is placing $5 million to the credit of Colombia as part of the $25 million payment the United States made for rights to separating Panama from Columbia as part of the Panama Canal project.	In the Dutch East Indies the first electric motor car transporting passengers as public transportation goes into operation.
Sep. 1		For the first time, a formally agreed upon set of radio frequencies is used in Europe to minimize interference between the current 70 stations that operate on the continent....German President Paul von Hindenburg issues a decree allowing former German Army officers to wear their uniforms.	Action on the Moroccan front continues; French attacks on the front lines are meeting with some success and once the current set of objectives is reached the terrain will cease to favor the defense allowing the French to advance more rapidly.	The Bolivian Congress annuls the recent election of Jose Gambino Villanueva who has recently been elected as president....Colombia announces that its national budget for this year is balanced.	A Soviet plane flying from Peking to Tokyo becomes separated gets lost, and lands in a restricted Japanese military area creating a possible diplomatic incident.
Sep. 2		Benito Mussolini indicates that he may represent Italy in the forthcoming meeting of Allied Foreign Ministers discussing a proposed security compact with Germany.... Western reporters describe the increasing cult of Vladimir I. Lenin growing throughout the Soviet Union.	The League of Nations declares that it will begin discussions concerning the border between Turkey and northern Iraq....The British Navy holds naval maneuvers in the Aegean Sea, not far from the Turkish coast.	A demonstration supporting regulation of health insurance and sick benefits for workers attracts a crowd of 25,000 in Mexico City.	
Sep. 3		Reports from Bulgaria claim that King Boris has been poisoned.... A commercial treaty between Yugoslavia and Austria goes into effect, based on mutual reduction of tariffs....The Berlin police begin to use aircraft to monitor the city in an effort to stop an epidemic of arson....Britain launches what is up to now the world's largest warship, the HMS *Nelson*.	The French government denies that Syrian rebels have captured the city of Suedia....France and Germany agree to resume trade talks that will take place in September....The French fleet opens a barrage against Moorish rebel positions in Morocco as Philippe Petain begins a new offensive.	The Chilean government once again expresses its dissatisfaction with the implementation of the Peruvian-Chilean border established by President Calvin Coolidge.	
Sep. 4		Recently reinstalled, Leon Trotsky is actively in supervising industrial activities although he no longer holds any real political power.... The Bulgarian government officially denies that King Boris has been poisoned.	The Turkish government issues a decree closing all Dervish monasteries in the country and banning the orders in addition, all government officials must wear western clothing....French and Spanish officials state that their joint planning efforts for conducting the war against the Moorish rebels in Morocco are now complete.	Mexican Labor Federation officials indicate that they have no interest in accepting an invitation from the Soviets to join forces....The Bolivian government announces that it has assembled a new cabinet and the president of the Senate will act as interim president until new elections are called....Five governors in Mexico face charges by the federal government that they abused their positions of authority.	Reports from Shanghai indicate that a severe typhoon has resulted in great losses exceeding $1 million in cargo....The Japanese Foreign Office makes public a note it sent to the Chinese government demanding that the Chinese preserve order and protect foreigners.

A	**B**	**C**	**D**	**E**
Includes developments that affect more than one world region, international organizations and important meetings of world leaders.	Includes all domestic and regional developments in Europe, including the Soviet Union.	Includes all domestic and regional developments in Africa and the Middle East.	Includes all domestic and regional developments in Latin America, the Caribbean, and Canada.	Includes all domestic and regional developments in Asian and Pacific nations (and colonies).

U.S. Politics & Social Issues	U.S. Foreign Policy & Affairs, Defense	U.S. Economy & Environment	Science, Technology & Nature	Culture, Leisure & Lifestyle	
The war between the rival Chinese tongs in the United States, the Hip Sing and On Leung, breaks out in several cities.	Colonel Billy Mitchell claims that it is possible to fly a plane from the United States to Paris, varying a one-ton lead of bombs but that the U.S. government will not take the steps necessary to develop it.	The anticipated strike of anthracite coal miners will not only affect the 150,000 men who walk out on the job but at least 10,000 railroad employees....The output of barrels of crude oil in 1924 was 713,940,000 barrels according to the U.S. Bureau of Mines....B. F. Goodrich Rubber Company reports that its profits for the first six months of 1925 were $60,434,755, an increase of $9,751,924 over the previous year.		Babe Ruth is suspended from playing and fined $5,000 for misconduct.	Aug. 29
			Archaeologists in Cadiz, Spain, have discovered the remains of Roman and Phoenician cemeteries....The MacMillan Polar expedition visits Viking ruins in Greenland.	Babe Ruth states that if the manager of the Yankees remains in place, he will not play for the club....At a testimonial celebrating his 20 years in baseball, Ty Cobb is presented with a check for $10,000.	Aug. 30
	Two Navy planes, *PN-9 No. 1* and *PN-9 No. 3* leave from California to begin their flight to the Hawaiian Islands.			Colonel Jake Ruppert, owner of the New York Yankees states that in any conflict between his manager, Huggins, and any player, even Babe Ruth, he will back the manager.	Aug. 31
Income tax amounts paid by Chicago corporations is released to the public; the Oscar Meyer Company paid $18,984, Sears and Roebuck paid $2,259,713, Florsheim Shoe Company paid $313,334, and Swift and Company paid $2,391,000....Publicized income tax returns include those of actor Douglas Fairbanks ($182,190), Charlie Chaplin ($345), and Gloria Swanson ($57,075).	War Department officials are expressing disapproval of a recent book published by Colonel Billy Mitchell in which he not only attacks War Department aviation policy but also ridicules the Secretary of War....The naval plane *PN-9 No. 1*, flying from San Francisco to Hawaii on a non-stop flight is reported missing.	Dun and Company reports that the total of business failures in August was the smallest since September 1924 when there were 1,396 failures....Loading of revenue freight for the week ending August 22 is reported at 1,080,107 railroad cars, the greatest weekly total for this year....The American Federation of Labor begins a campaign to fight against the importation of foreign goods.		Although Babe Ruth has apologized to Manager Miller Huggins and the owner of the New York Yankees, he is still not allowed to play as a result of comments he made about the manager.	Sep. 1
Charles Evans Hughes, Secretary of State in the first Coolidge administration delivers a speech in which he expresses his fears about intolerance toward minority opinions and that civil liberties must be protected against bureaucracy.	The U.S. Navy dirigible *Shenandoah* passes over Pennsylvania on its trip from the naval station at Lakehurst, NJ, to Minneapolis and St. Paul....U.S. Navy craft continue their search for the *PN-9 No. 1*.	Earth tremors are reported in South Illinois and Indiana and western Kentucky....Figures for the month of July show that July 1925 exceeded all records for both gasoline production and consumption.	British scientist Oliver Simmons predicts that aircraft will be designed that can carry 100 passengers from Europe to America in 36 hours....The ship *Bowdoin* of the MacMillian arctic expedition reaches Greenland.	Gertrude Ederle postpones her attempt to swim the English Channel due to severe storms.	Sep. 2
	During a storm over Ohio the dirigible *Shenandoah* breaks apart and crashes killing 14 and injuring two severely; efforts to secure the area are hampered by large numbers of local sightseers and looters.	The Department of Commerce declares that although imports from Europe increased, they are still less than American exports....The level of building construction in the United States continues at a great rate leading experts to predict that the record highs of the amounts of construction set in 1924 will be surpassed this year.	San Francisco is now linked to London by means of the world longest telegraph circuit.		Sep. 3
The National Convention of the Veterans of Foreign Wars calls on the government to pay its promised veterans compensation in 1928.	The navy continues its investigation into the *Shenandoah* crash; in the meantime looters have stolen the aircraft's instruments, the covering, and pieces of the framework....President Calvin Coolidge announces that government will build a new dirigible for military purposes....The search for the *PN-9* expands and 18 ships are now engaged in the search.	The southern United States is undergoing the worst drought in 50 years.	A proposed flight from London to Cape Town is announced, the trip, to be accomplished in 23 stages, will begin on November 1.	Rogers Hornsby leads the national League in batting with .387; Tris Speaker leads with in the American League with an average of .380.	Sep. 4

F	G	H	I	J
Includes campaigns, elections, federal-state relations, civil rights and liberties, crime, the judiciary, education, healthcare, poverty, urban affairs, and population.	Includes formation and debate of U.S. foreign and defense policies, veterans affairs, and defense spending. (Relations with specific foreign countries are usually found under the region concerned.)	Includes business, labor, agriculture, taxation, transportation, consumer affairs, monetary and fiscal policy, natural resources, pollution and industrial accidents.	Includes worldwide scientific, medical and technological developments, natural phenomena, U.S. weather and natural disasters.	Includes the arts, religion, scholarship, communications media, sports, entertainment, fashions, fads, and social life.

	World Affairs	Europe	Africa & The Middle East	The Americas	Asia & The Pacific
Sep. 5		A statue commemorating Czech Reformer Jan Hus is erected in Prague's Old Town Square, 510 years after his death.... Czechoslovakia announces that it will set up a new national bank w that will manage the country's currency.	The French Army executes 11 Syrian rebels.	Nicaraguan government officials state that the nation is looking for a source of loans to finance the construction of a new railroad.	
Sep. 6	The 6th Assembly of the League of Nations, with its 54 member convenes today.	The German government announces that the president of the Reichsbank, Hjalmar Schacht will visit the United States and denies that the visit is political in any way.		Members of the Mexican Congress state that they are ready to enact a law forbidding anyone from carrying weapons into the building when Parliament is in session.	Two British journalists are seized by crowds of strikers in Canton and confined in a cage where they are put on public display before being released.
Sep. 7		Two Macedonian leaders are killed in a fight on the Yugoslav-Bulgarian border by Bulgarian police....German president Paul von Hindenburg announces that he will make a tour of the Ruhr valley....A parade of 100,000 children in Leningrad opens the 200th anniversary celebrations commemorating the Science Academy.	The Spanish government begins preparations for staging a large amphibious landing on the coast of Morocco....The French air force launches bombing raids against the Moors in Morocco; dropping two tons of bombs.	The Prince of Wales arrives in Santiago, Chile, where he is given an enthusiastic welcome.	British police fire on a mob of strikers in Shanghai, wounding three who attempted to break into the international section of the city.
Sep. 8			Initial reports indicate that the Spanish amphibious landing on Morocco's coast has failed with great losses to both men and ships....The Turkish government announces that it may reject the League of Nations decision concerning fixing the boundary between Turkey and northern Iraq.	The Cuban government announces that Cuban sugar mills will be required to pay an additional tax of two percent.	
Sep. 9		Poland and Czechoslovakia seek to join in the European Security talks; Allied powers are willing to admit them to the discussions but state that their participation is based on Germany's decision.	Great Britain rejects Turkey's statements about the Iraq-Turkey boundary stating that a plebiscite within the Mosul area cannot be considered again....Rumors of a Spanish failure in their amphibious landing are proven to be untrue; French and Spanish troops are now claiming significant advances against the rebels. ...Arab leaders in Palestine say they will stop smoking and encourage others to do so, using the money to create a fund to "save Palestine from the Zionist menace."	A fortress in Nicaragua, held by a renegade general for 10 days is handed back to the President of Nicaragua, a sign that political tensions in the country are diminishing.	Native leaders in the Philippines indicate very strong opposition to the imposition of prohibition there.
Sep. 10		The Belgian government orders the deportation of several accused Communists....Reports from the Soviet Union indicate that bonuses to encourage workers are now being paid....The British government announces that it will sell 17 of its destroyers built during World War I....A three-hour strike is conducted by 10,000 Austrian civil servants who walk off their jobs in Vienna.	A massive bombardment by the French Army is begins a large offensive; some observers are stating that although the French and Spanish are making progress they may not successfully end the war until next year.	Agrarian rebels in Mexico kill the mayor of San Cristobal in the state of Vera Cruz.	

A	B	C	D	E
Includes developments that affect more than one world region, international organizations and important meetings of world leaders.	Includes all domestic and regional developments in Europe, including the Soviet Union.	Includes all domestic and regional developments in Africa and the Middle East.	Includes all domestic and regional developments in Latin America, the Caribbean, and Canada.	Includes all domestic and regional developments in Asian and Pacific nations (and colonies).

U.S. Politics & Social Issues	U.S. Foreign Policy & Affairs, Defense	U.S. Economy & Environment	Science, Technology & Nature	Culture, Leisure & Lifestyle	
	Colonel Billy Mitchell once again attacks the manner in which military aviation is managed; he states that the recent crash of the Shenandoah and the apparent loss of the *PN-9* are examples of incompetence and gross negligence....Investigators of the *Shenandoah* disaster are beginning to agree that the reason for the crash was the dirigible being caught in a storm....The YWCA reports that a survey of 320 women college students shows that during the summer they had earned $11.50 a week as waitresses as well as living expenses.	The Bureau of Commerce reports that the Philippine Islands hold the best possible solution to the increasing world-wide rubber shortage; currently the United States uses 80 percent of the world's rubber....Reports indicate that during the month of August, New York City awarded 912 contracts for building with a planned expenditure of more than $140 million....The U.S. government announces that it will begin purchasing land in Minnesota to be used as a wildlife refuge....Gas prices in the mid-Atlantic states fall by one cent a gallon.	The New York City Library has established a "photostat" office that makes copies of pages from books for its patrons.	The *New York Times* reviews *The Professor's House*, a new novel by Willa Cather....New York Yankees Manager, Miller Huggins, accepts Babe Ruth's apology but still will not allow him to play....The fall foliage season begins in New Hampshire with many motorists touring the area.	Sep. 5
President Calvin Coolidge announces that he will end his vacation in Massachusetts this week.	The War Department announces that it will court-martial Colonel Billy Mitchell for his comments following the *Shenandoah* crash....An airplane, perhaps the *PN-9 No. 1* has been reported adrift near Hawaii; the navy is sending ships into the area.	The U.S. is not the only the world's lead producer of copper but also the leading user, consuming 686,364 tons in 1924, compared with 362,125 tons in 1913.	The first birth of a musk-ox calf in captivity occurs at the Brooklyn Zoo....From Greenland, Commander MacMillan reports that he has observed great numbers of birds beginning their migration south to avoid the polar winter.	*The Phantom of the Opera*, starring Lon Chaney, opens in New York, City....France and Australia play in the Davis Cup match; France wins.	Sep. 6
A gathering of 10,000 members of the Ku Klux Klan meets in Somerville, NJ....William Green, president of the American Federation of Labor states that the Unions will never cease in its efforts to drive Communists out of the American labor unions....New immigration laws have resulted in a 68 percent drop in immigration to the United States.	W. B. Shearer, an expert on aviation, reports that the Japanese have a much stronger air force than the United States.	Rains in South and North Carolina and Tennessee help to break the severe drought in that area....A flash flood in Washington state kills 17....Four men are arrested for derailing the Louisville and Nashville train in a wreck that killed one and injured 29.	The *New York Times* reports on the efforts of a woman chemist, Grace McGuire, who and her efforts to discover what enzymes are.	The writer, Thomas Hardy, attends a dramatization of his book, *Tess of the D'Urbervilles* in London....Babe Ruth is allowed once again to play; the Yankees still lose 5–1 to Boston.	Sep. 7
	Colonel Billy Mitchell, who will soon be brought to court-martial states that the United States must have a separate air force administered by a Secretary of the Air....Navy Secretary Curtis Wilbur orders that, although it seems the aircraft is lost, searching will continue for the *PN-9 No. 1* which went down between San Francisco and Hawaii....Naval officials state that the next dirigible to be put into construction will be twice the size of the *Shenandoah*, giving it a five million cubic foot capacity.		The Soviet government announces that a scientific expedition will be sent to Mongolia to make a geological survey at the request of the Mongolian government.		Sep. 8
The Osage tribe of Oklahoma announces that it will invest $3 million in Liberty Bonds from the government, one of the largest single transaction using Native American funds.		The state of Oregon protests U.S. government efforts to expand the Crater Lake National Park by taking over land held by the State....The American Railway Association announces that shippers and railroads saw 23 percent fewer losses than the in the first six months of 1924.	Roald Amundsen announces that his next trip to the North Pole will be accomplished using an Italian dirigible.	While making a movie, actor Rudolph Valentino falls from his horse and is dragged for a short distance....Poet Thomas Hardy announces he will soon publish a new volume of poetry.	Sep. 9
					Sep. 10

F	G	H	I	J
Includes campaigns, elections, federal-state relations, civil rights and liberties, crime, the judiciary, education, healthcare, poverty, urban affairs, and population.	*Includes formation and debate of U.S. foreign and defense policies, veterans affairs, and defense spending. (Relations with specific foreign countries are usually found under the region concerned.)*	*Includes business, labor, agriculture, taxation, transportation, consumer affairs, monetary and fiscal policy, natural resources, pollution and industrial accidents.*	*Includes worldwide scientific, medical and technological developments, natural phenomena, U.S. weather and natural disasters.*	*Includes the arts, religion, scholarship, communications media, sports, entertainment, fashions, fads, and social life.*

	World Affairs	Europe	Africa & The Middle East	The Americas	Asia & The Pacific
Sep. 11		German President Paul von Hindenburg attends the annual German Army maneuvers dressed in his old uniform; he is enthusiastically received by the soldiers.	The French and Spanish advance continues with the French now establishing their old defensive line which they occupied before the recent rebel attacks....Diamonds have been discovered in the British colony of Tanganyika.		The Chinese government appeals to the League of Nations for support in its efforts to curb the power of foreign governments within China's borders.
Sep. 12	The Sixth Assembly of the League of Nations reports progress in several areas thus far to include a security treaty for Europe and advances in agreements concerning finance, health, national disputes and protection of women and children....The League issues a statement that it will not hold an arms conference for 12 months but will call one as soon as the European Security Pacts are finalized.	An attempt to assassinate the King and Queen of Romania is stopped....Switzerland reports that its budget for 1925 is nearly balanced....Investigators from Scotland Yard are searching for a group of women crooks going by the name of "the 40 elephants," thus far without success.	French and Spanish authorities once again claim to be making progress in Morocco; the combined armies are said to number 200,000 against the 50,000 rebels under the command of Abd-el-Krim....British representatives will meet with representatives of King Hussein of the Hedjaz and Ibn Saud of the Wahhabi tribesmen in an effort to broker a peace between those two parties.	A strike against the Aguila Oil Company in Mexico begins....The Mexican government announces that it will begin to broadcast classes over the radio.	Japan and the Soviet Union are reported nearing an agreement on oil and coal concessions in the Sakhalin Islands.
Sep. 13		Bulgaria has applied to the Allied Commissioners for the military commission to leave the country as Bulgaria has honored all of its disarmament commitments following World War I.	Syrian rebels ambush and kill a French officer....The French government states that its forces in Morocco are advancing while Spain reports that its troops are coming under heavy attack by the rebels.		The Chinese government has begun to buy goods from the Soviet Union and indicates that trade may continue and expand.
Sep. 14		Two French aviators in an attempted flight from France to Baghdad crash in Germany; one is killed and the other imprisoned by German authorities....Former German Crown Prince Wilhelm visits East Prussia where he is enthusiastically received.			
Sep. 15		Bulgaria reports nine political murders in the past three days; the assassination include that of Todor Alexandroff, leader of the Internal Macedonian Revolutionary Organization (IMRO)....Reports in Ireland describe a possible effort to establish a trans-Atlantic port on the western coast of Ireland.		A new telegraph cable between the United States and the Dominican Republic goes into operation.	The Japanese government protests to the Chinese government concerning the recent serious unrest in Manchuria....Reports from Beijing indicate wider unrest throughout northern China as government and anti-government forces mass their forces.
Sep. 16		Austria and Hungary express satisfaction that their financing efforts have been approved by the League of Nations....The Ulster government reaffirms its earlier decision not to accept the Border Commissions proposals for the Ulster-Irish Free State border....Reports from the Soviet Union describe a revolt, precipitated by poor food supplies that has now spread to the Crimea.		The Brazilian government says that rebels have captured several federal garrisons.	Reports have been received that there has been serious fighting between government and anti-government forces in northern China; the British and U.S. governments protest that they cannot accept a ban on their citizens from traveling in several provinces....Heavy fighting, principally by means of heavy artillery duels takes place near Shanghai.
Sep. 17		Police arrest 100 Communists in Florence, Italy....Shaking hands in Italy has fallen out of favor and is replaced by the Fascist salute.	Spanish forces are coming under heavy attack in Morocco although they are able to call on some support by aircraft as well as naval gunfire against the Moor attacks.	Abnormally large coffee crops are causing a sharp decrease in the price of Brazilian coffee.	
Sep. 18		It is announced that the killers of Italian Socialist Deputy and opponent of Benito Mussolini, Giaccomo Matteotti will be brought to trial in 1926....Czechoslovakia's government budget shows a surplus for the first time since the country was established.	The French Army admits that it has lost approximately 20 aviators to as casualties of the rebels in Morocco.	The government of Bolivia declares a siege in three provinces and its president-elect flees to Chile.	Japan's House of Peers and House of Representatives are destroyed in a fire.

A	B	C	D	E
Includes developments that affect more than one world region, international organizations and important meetings of world leaders.	Includes all domestic and regional developments in Europe, including the Soviet Union.	Includes all domestic and regional developments in Africa and the Middle East.	Includes all domestic and regional developments in Latin America, the Caribbean, and Canada.	Includes all domestic and regional developments in Asian and Pacific nations (and colonies).

U.S. Politics & Social Issues	U.S. Foreign Policy & Affairs, Defense	U.S. Economy & Environment	Science, Technology & Nature	Culture, Leisure & Lifestyle	
Native Americans of the Nez Perce tribe describe at a Congressional hearing how they have not received the money owed them through the Bureau of Indian Affairs....Nathan Leopold and Richard Loeb, convicted and sentenced to life sentences for murdering Bobby Franks have been promoted from performing menial tasks in prison.	The crew members of the Naval airplane, *PN-9 No. 1* are rescued by a naval ship; the aircraft still afloat and the crew all alive.		An American expedition reaches the city of Dar-es-Salaam, Kenya, with two gorillas it captured in the Congo intending to bring one to New York and the other for Antwerp.	Miss California wins the Miss America competition at Atlantic City, NJ....In an interview, American actor Paul Robeson states that he wants to be a singer and specialize in African-American spirituals.	Sep. 11
	Navy Secretary Curtis Wilbur congratulates the crew of the *PN-9 No. 1* for their efforts and for surviving 10 days at sea....The *New York Times* reviews a novel entitled *The Great Pacific War*, which describes Japan launching a war against the United States, opening with an attack on the Philippines and the Panama Canal.	Manufacturers report that the cost of manufacturing a locomotive has more than doubled since 1914....A new book, *The Present Economic Revolution in the United States* by Thomas Caver predicts that America will become a financial utopia and that the difference between capital and labor will disappear.	A British Naval officer states that better weather reporting could have prevented the crash of the *Shenandoah*....The volcano on the island group of Santorini in the Aegean erupts and forms a new island....C. Francis Jenkins predicts that soon miniature motion picture screens will be attached to radio sets allowing people to watch movies broadcast over the air.	Walter Naumberg begins what will be the annual Naumberg Competition for young musicians in honor of his late father.	Sep. 12
					Sep. 13
Over 450 Chinese are seized in New York City as authorities attempt to put a halt to the war between the On Leong and Hip Sing tongs; in a related development a meeting is held between the two groups that is also attended by new York authorities and the Chinese Consulate to reach a peace.	The United States announces that it will restructure the payments France is making for its war debt in order to make the next few payments easier.	A merger that will involve the power plants in five states in the northeast is being planned and will go into effect before the end of October....At a meeting of the National Association of Credit Men, the widespread use of installment selling is said to be harmful and leads to extravagance.			Sep. 14
The National Women's Party announces that it will launch a campaign that a woman may retain her own name and will not have to take her husband's name.		The six New England states report that their international exports have increased, amounting to $90 million in the first six months of 1925.	A French engineer, Etienne Oehmichen wins a prize of 40,000 francs from the French government for the operation of his helicopter which successfully lifts 220 pounds.	Frank Chance, baseball player and manager who led the Chicago Cubs to their last World Series championship in 1908, dies at the age of 47.	Sep. 15
In Kammerer, Wyoming a mine explosion kills 33 men; 12 manage to come out of the tunnel....African Americans ask President Calvin Coolidge to make a statement against the Ku Klux Klan, a request he does not respond to....Senator Jones of New Mexico charges that President Calvin Coolidge's figures on employment data are wrong and that the number of employed and their wages have dropped since 1920.	President Calvin Coolidge announces that he favors a relaxed payment plan for France's and Italy's war debts....Coolidge has recalled Naval Secretary Curtis Wilbur from his round of speeches on the west coast due to his attacks on the Japanese.			Baseball Commissioner Kennesaw Mountain Landis announces that he will set the dates for the upcoming World Series.	Sep. 16
		The International Harvester Company says that the prospects for selling farm equipment in the next year are excellent.			Sep. 17
					Sep. 18

F
Includes campaigns, elections, federal-state relations, civil rights and liberties, crime, the judiciary, education, healthcare, poverty, urban affairs, and population.

G
Includes formation and debate of U.S. foreign and defense policies, veterans affairs, and defense spending. (Relations with specific foreign countries are usually found under the region concerned.)

H
Includes business, labor, agriculture, taxation, transportation, consumer affairs, monetary and fiscal policy, natural resources, pollution and industrial accidents.

I
Includes worldwide scientific, medical and technological developments, natural phenomena, U.S. weather and natural disasters.

J
Includes the arts, religion, scholarship, communications media, sports, entertainment, fashions, fads, and social life.

	World Affairs	Europe	Africa & The Middle East	The Americas	Asia & The Pacific
Sep. 19		German President Paul von Hindenburg completes his successful tour of the Ruhr Valley which has recently seen French and Belgian occupiers leave....Italian police arrest 158 Communists and seize large amounts of printed propaganda.	The French government announces that its forces in Morocco will advance no further for the rest of the year and keep winter quarters at their present positions....The Syrian city of Suedia, manned by a French garrison continues to ensure its siege by rebel Druze tribesmen.		Military intervention by the outside powers in China is ruled out as it is estimated that bringing order to China in this way would take 10 years and cost $3 billion.
Sep. 20		Soviet leadership admits that is losing ground in managing the central economy because of the success of small-scale businesses....An additional tax on horsemeat has drawn widespread opposition among the population and may result in a political crisis.	The Spanish section of the front against Abd-el-Krim is coming under major attacks; the French segment of the line is inactive.... The Archbishop of Hauran, Syria, warns the French government that the present rebellion poses a grave threat to the Christian population in the region an that the French government must do more to intervene.	The Prince of Wales completes the Chilean segment of his tour of South America and crosses the border to Argentina.	
Sep. 21	Experts are generally agreed that the world's wheat harvest this year will be significantly larger than that of 1924.	In France, the U.S. State Department comments on American volunteers not being allowed to fly for France is construed as an insult and is seen as part of an overall offensive against France at a time when it is trying to renegotiate its war debts.	Reports have been received that Abd-el-Krim is planning a major offensive that will be aimed at the international city of Tangier.	The Aguila Oil Company states that it will refuse all orders, even from the Mexican government, for oil until the strike is settled.	The government of Canton is still successfully maintaining its boycott of the English port of Hong Kong.
Sep. 22		The Soviet Communist Party has reportedly begun a purge to eliminate all members who have any kind of "bourgeois taint."...The British government announces that it will begin a crackdown on Communist agitators and has already identified over 40 who will be deported.	The Turkish government reiterates its position that it will not back down from maintaining the border with Iraq and is prepared to go to war....Turkish authorities report that smoking is on the rise; it is estimated that 2,179 cigarettes are smoked in Constantinople each day.	The Nicaraguan government announces that it is annulling the contract with the American form that has been running the Nicaragua-Pacific Railway since 1919; no reason for the change is given....U.S. warships *Denver* and *Tulsa* which have been stationed off the coast for Nicaragua to help keep order for the past nine days are ordered to depart from their stations.	Four Soviet trade unionists are visiting Japan where their activities are closely monitored; the Japanese government has forbidden all demonstrations by labor groups in Japan.
Sep. 23		A joint German-Soviet effort to provide air service from Berlin to Tokyo is planned....Hungarian police arrest 42 Communists including future Hungarian leader Matyas Rakosi....Local Communist Party elections are conducted in the Soviet Union.	Moroccan rebel Abd-el-Krim announces that he will pay a reward for every captured American pilot volunteer.... Although American fliers have been told by the U.S. State Department that they cannot serve in the French Army, the fliers state that they will do so regardless of government orders....The League of Nations announces it will listen to British charges against the Turkish government in the ongoing Iraq-Turkey border dispute.		Twelve Chinese robbers are publicly executed in Shanghai; Chinese officials state that they will continue to hang six a day until 180 have been executed....Rioting breaks out in Teheran, Iran over shortages of bread.
Sep. 24		War games in England conclude with a combined infantry and tank force saving London from the "invaders."....German President Paul von Hindenburg announces that he will not now make an issue of admitting Germany's war guilt as a prerequisite for security negotiations with the western Allies.	The League of nations announces it will investigate charges that Syrian Christians are being forcibly deported from Iraq.		Japan is now increasing its imports from the United States, seven times as much as was the case in 1914....Chinese general Chang Tso-lin announces that he will not allow the Communists to succeed in China and calls upon the Japanese to assist him in his campaigns.
Sep. 25		Although there are over already 200 dance bands in London, the number is growing in anticipation of a record dancing boom expected for the winter season at clubs and restaurants....Hungarian Communist, Bela Kun, who led Hungary for three months in 1919 is reported as having been seen in Vienna.	The French report that they have succeeded in breaking up the Druze rebels in Syria.		

A	B	C	D	E
Includes developments that affect more than one world region, international organizations and important meetings of world leaders.	Includes all domestic and regional developments in Europe, including the Soviet Union.	Includes all domestic and regional developments in Africa and the Middle East.	Includes all domestic and regional developments in Latin America, the Caribbean, and Canada.	Includes all domestic and regional developments in Asian and Pacific nations (and colonies).

U.S. Politics & Social Issues	U.S. Foreign Policy & Affairs, Defense	U.S. Economy & Environment	Science, Technology & Nature	Culture, Leisure & Lifestyle	
An additional 72 Chinese, alleged members of the Tongs and engaged in the recent war have been put on a list of people to be deported....The City of Indianapolis and Marion County, IN, will begin setting up approximately 300 crosses to indicate where people have been killed in auto accidents....An exposition of Women in Arts and Industry begins in New York and will continue for the next week.		In the first eight months of 1925, 2,644,583 autos were manufactured in the United States, a gain of 12 percent over 1924.	Earth tremors and heavy snow are reported in Montana while Chicago begins a severe heat wave.	The Pittsburgh Pirates need only four games to win the National League pennant; The Washington Senators who lead the American League need six games to secure their title....It is estimated that 40,000 people are night students in New York colleges....The *New York Times* reviews *Dark Laughter*, a new novel by Sherwood Anderson.	Sep. 19
		In a listing of 25 railroads, all but four show increased revenues for 1925; the Atchison, Topeka, and Santa Fe leads the list with a stated income of $4,573,000 for the first seven months of 1925.	Radio Station WGY in Schenectady, NY, announces that it will begin broadcasting using high power (50,000 watts).		Sep. 20
	The first session of the inquiry to determine the causes of the *Shenandoah* crash is held in Lakehurst, NJ.		An astronomer in the Soviet Union detects Brook's Comet which generally appears every seven years although it missed detection in 1918....In a 3,000-mile motor trial held in the Soviet Union, Americans win 11 out of 20 trophies.	President Calvin Coolidge accepts a wallaby presented to him by an American living in Tasmania; it will not reside at the White House and will be given to the Washington Zoo.	Sep. 21
	President Calvin Coolidge states that he will not do anything to discourage the proposed Disarmament Conference that the League of nations plans to have but that the U.S. government will do nothing to support it and will not participate....Navy Secretary Curtis Wilbur states that planes are an integral part of the Navy and creating a totally separate air force would damage the Navy's capabilities.	The Skenandoa Corporation buys a factory in Utica, NY, where it will manufacture artificial silk....The Department of Agriculture announces that there are 400 million chickens in the United States, which would form a line 100,000 miles long.			Sep. 22
John Hulbert who has performed 140 executions at Sing Sing Prison since 1914 announces he will retire next June.	Investigations into the *Shenandoah* crash publicize a letter by its commander expressing reluctance to fly under bad weather conditions.	The anthracite coal strike continues; railroad officials estimate their loss in revenue has been $3.5 million a week and they have had to lay off almost 15,000 rail workers.		The Pittsburgh Pirates win the National League pennant....Gertrude Ederle announces that she will again make the attempt to swim the English Channel next year.	Sep. 23
The Anthracite Committee of the United mine Workers sends a telegram to coal dealers stating that since mine operators will not honor arbitration they will not accept it wither....In Genesee county of upstate New York, reports indicate that recent months 3,500 members of the Ku Klux Klan have quit, leaving only about 50 active members.	The Secretary of the Navy announces that there will be no more attempts to fly from California to Hawaii until at least January 1926....Senator Hale of Maine states that the best guarantee for world peace is for the United States and Britain to continue to control the oceans.	Bath Ironworks, a major shipyard in Maine, is sold for $193,100.		The Washington Senators capture the American League pennant....The City of Boston announces that it will not allow the play, *What Price Glory* to be shown unless some of the offensive language is deleted.	Sep. 24
	The U.S. submarine *S-51*, sailing off the coast of Rhode Island is rammed by a steamer, *The City of Rome* and sinks; only three men are rescued.		The Macmillan Arctic expedition sends word that its ship, the *Bowdoin*, has survived a gale off the coast of Greenland which had cut off communications for 48 hours.	College Football season opens on today; games scheduled include Notre Dame vs. Baylor, North Carolina vs. Wake Forest, and Dartmouth vs. Norwich.	Sep. 25

F	G	H	I	J
Includes campaigns, elections, federal-state relations, civil rights and liberties, crime, the judiciary, education, healthcare, poverty, urban affairs, and population.	Includes formation and debate of U.S. foreign and defense policies, veterans affairs, and defense spending. (Relations with specific foreign countries are usually found under the region concerned.)	Includes business, labor, agriculture, taxation, transportation, consumer affairs, monetary and fiscal policy, natural resources, pollution and industrial accidents.	Includes worldwide scientific, medical and technological developments, natural phenomena, U.S. weather and natural disasters.	Includes the arts, religion, scholarship, communications media, sports, entertainment, fashions, fads, and social life.

	World Affairs	Europe	Africa & The Middle East	The Americas	Asia & The Pacific
Sep. 26	At the close of its 6th Assembly the League of Nations announces that it will begin several new projects that will lead to economic and disarmament conferences.	Earth tremors are felt throughout central France....Although Italy's population is increasing unemployment, has dropped and fewer Italians are leaving the country.... General Primo de Rivera announces that civil rule may return to Spain the following week although he will remain as cabinet head.... The Dutch government announces it will begin a project to reclaim a further 1,000 square miles by damming off and draining the Zuyder Zee.	The Turkish government announces that astrology is illegal; it also bans performances by dancing bears and monkeys in the streets on Constantinople....Riots in Teheran, Persia, are described by the British officials there as a provocation by the Soviet government....Mustafa Kemal states that Turkey and its Army will be ready to fight and will not concede British claims in Northern Iraq's Mosul province.	The Consul General of Nicaragua, at a luncheon in Washington, DC, states that contrary to what Americans have been told, Nicaraguans do not want American troops occupying their country.	The Soviet Union protests the arrest in Manchuria of a Soviet citizen by Chinese officials.
Sep. 27		The state government of Bavaria begins to negotiate a loan of $15 million from American banks.... Officers and soldiers of the Portuguese Army are acquitted of treason as a result of their attempted rebellion against the government in April.	The Spanish Army is planning to establish a new aviation base to support its Moroccan forces; in the meantime in a small action, Spanish forces capture an objective that will improve their defensive positions.	Peru accuses Chile of attempting to influence the upcoming plebiscite to determine the exact placement of the Peruvian-Chilean border....The Prince of Wales leaves Argentina, concluding his six-week tour of South America.	The British government states that it intends to keep its large commercial operations operating in China although there is some disagreement as to the best way to do this and the extent to which native reform is to be encouraged.
Sep. 28	Professor Manley Hudson, professor at Harvard Law School and a member of the League of Nations Law Section, states that the League of Nations has become a success, indicated by the increasing support it receives each year from it member nations.	Benito Mussolini indicates that he is interested in forming some sort of alliance with Germany and the Soviet Union.		Alberto Pani, Mexico's Minister of Finance travel to the United States to negotiate loan agreements.	The American governor of the Philippines, Leonard Wood, states that there is little popular response to a non-cooperation program initiated by anti-American elements.... Governor Wood is sponsoring an appeal to get funds to take care of the 4,000 Filipino children who have been abandoned by their American soldier fathers....The breaking of a dike in the Yellow River, China, has resulted in a flood that has killed 100 and ruined crops in a 1,500-square-mile area.
Sep. 29		Workers voice strong opposition to the Irish government's practice of entering into labor contracts with foreign companies....Albania's President Ahmed Zog (later to become King Zog I) is in the process of forming a new cabinet.	Italy and Egypt indicate that they will begin negotiating the boundary between Libya and Egypt.		An American gunboat is ordered to protect an American-owned steamboat on the Yangtse River when it is fired upon and hit by Chinese troops.
Sep. 30		The Soviet Foreign Minister warns Germany that its entry into the League of Nations will be interpreted as a hostile act toward the Soviet Union....Publication of Turin's newspaper, Stampa, is suspended by Italian authorities in retaliation for articles critical of the Army.	The Turkish government calls up all eligible recruits aged 22 to 25 years to serve in the Army immediately....Moors ambush a group of American fliers who escape with no casualties....French forces dismantle their fort at Suedia, Syria as preparation for offensives in a new direction.		
Oct. 1		The Bank of England cuts its discount rate for loans from 4.5 percent to 4 percent.	Spanish forces are advancing against Abd-el-Krim as the French also advance; letters have been found on prisoners and on dead Moors describing orders that the rebels kill their wives and children rather than surrender.	President Arturo Alessandri of Chile resigns his post and names a successor.	
Oct. 2		Germany and the Soviet Union are close to completing a trade treaty....The Soviets issue a statement that attacks Britain for its hostility while speaking of desired friendship between the Soviets and the United States.	Madrid is the scene of large celebrations for the Spanish and French victories in Morocco....The Archbishop of Canterbury sends a letter to British Prime Minister Baldwin that Christians in Iraq should be protected by the British forces there.	Reports from Costa Rica indicate that it may reconsider its decision to withdraw from the League of Nations.	

A	B	C	D	E
Includes developments that affect more than one world region, international organizations and important meetings of world leaders.	Includes all domestic and regional developments in Europe, including the Soviet Union.	Includes all domestic and regional developments in Africa and the Middle East.	Includes all domestic and regional developments in Latin America, the Caribbean, and Canada.	Includes all domestic and regional developments in Asian and Pacific nations (and colonies).

U.S. Politics & Social Issues	U.S. Foreign Policy & Affairs, Defense	U.S. Economy & Environment	Science, Technology & Nature	Culture, Leisure & Lifestyle	
In a speech to 25,000 in West Virginia, United Mine Workers President John Lewis declares the effort to unionize will continue, despite court orders.	Efforts begin immediately to rescue the crew of the S-51; Naval vessels are present to attempt to lift the submarine....The U.S. State Department announces that it will take no actions against the American fliers who have volunteered to serve in the French armed forces against the rebels in Morocco.		Archaeologists from the University of Pennsylvania and the British Museum announce that they hope to find the Library of Ur in Iraq during the upcoming season of excavations.	A survey made public by the Department of Agriculture states that only 8.5 percent of farms (553,003) have radios....The Federal government announces that roads in the United States will now be designated as numbered routes: even numbers assigned to east-west routes and off numbers for north-south.	Sep. 26
The Anti-Dry League of New Jersey announces that it will begin a campaign to have wine and beer legalized....Every person in New York City is estimated to create 1,605 pounds of garbage a year.	The U.S. Navy begins its inquiries in Boston concerning the sinking of the S-51; navy divers are now certain that there are no survivors aboard the sub.	Consumption of steel in the United States exceeds previous estimates with steel plants working at 20-25 percent, greater than is usually the case at this time of year....American wheat prices are currently the highest in the world; experts see possible competition in world markets from Canada and Argentina.		The New York Times reviews The Venetian Glass Nephew, a novel by Elinor Wylie.	Sep. 27
	Testifying at a the Aircraft Board of Inquiry called by President Calvin Coolidge, all of the Army flyers state that they would like to see a separate service for the air corps....Admiral Harley Christy orders all available aircraft to assist in the effort assist in the effort to find bodies of S-51 crew members; rescue efforts are continuing but divers have not yet been able to open any hatches.	The Baltimore and Ohio Railroad reports that its August revenues for August were $4,940,913, a substantial increase over the revenues of August 1924 which were $4,211,437....The Scranton, PA, Chamber of Commerce is attempting to reopen negotiations to put an end to the anthracite coal strike.	Roald Amundsen announces that he will definitely be using an airship instead of an airplane for his proposed arctic expedition next year, the trip which will start in Spitzbergen, Norway, and finish in Alaska.		Sep. 28
	Bad weather prevents rescue crews from raising the sunken S-51 although divers manage to recover two bodies....Colonel Billy Mitchell asserts that the United States is at the mercy of an enemy air attack, that current equipment is worn out and that the senior officers in charge of the air services are incompetent.	70railroads report their profits for the month of August 1925; they made $24 million than they did in August 1924....An interstate symposium opens in New York City to discuss plans for oil and gas conservation.			Sep. 29
	Secretary of the Navy Curtis Wilbur overrules Admiral Christy and orders that rescue attempts must continue for the crew of the S-51....Commander Rodgers of the navy's NP-9 No.1 arrives in Washington to testify before Congress on the events of the flight....In the lead up to the upcoming court martial of Colonel Billy Mitchell, the War Department releases figures of aircraft production which they claim proves he is wrong.	The massive Smackover oil field in Arkansas which has been declining in its output now reports that it's most recent weekly output is down by 7,200 barrels, for a total of 174,000 barrels....A Cocoa Exchange opens in New York City; it is anticipated that the city will become the world's cocoa trade center.	An Egyptian temple, dating to 1200 B.C.E. is discovered in Palestine....Commander Donald B. MacMillan announces that he hopes to return to Wiscasset, ME, around October 10.	Notre Dame's football coach, Knute Rockne tells reporters that he is very optimistic about the coming game with Army and the season as a whole.	Sep. 30
	U.S. Navy fliers attack the current aviation system in as being run by officers who have no knowledge of aviation and declare support of a separate branch of the military to do aviation.		Commander Donald B. MacMillan and his polar exploration party on their return to the United States have landed at Battle Harbor in Newfoundland....Three six-wheeled autos which will be used in the Prorok expedition across the Central Sahara are christened and begin the trip to the starting point at Algiers.	There are indications that the record attendance of 10 million spectators at college football games last year will be exceeded by between 25–50 percent this year....Most observers believe that the Washington Senators will beat the Pittsburgh Pirates in the World Series.	Oct. 1
The evangelistic campaigns of preacher Billy Sunday are attacked by some religious leaders because the campaigns lack permanence and many who convert return to their old ways when the evangelists leave town.	Divers attempting recovery efforts on the S-51 find that the entire submarine is full of water and 33 of the crew died.	The output of oil in August is reported as having fallen by one percent, in a report by the Bureau of Mines.	The French Institute of Oriental Archaeology in Egypt announces that it has found a temple, several burial; places and an entire town.		Oct. 2

F	G	H	I	J
Includes campaigns, elections, federal-state relations, civil rights and liberties, crime, the judiciary, education, healthcare, poverty, urban affairs, and population.	Includes formation and debate of U.S. foreign and defense policies, veterans affairs, and defense spending. (Relations with specific foreign countries are usually found under the region concerned.)	Includes business, labor, agriculture, taxation, transportation, consumer affairs, monetary and fiscal policy, natural resources, pollution and industrial accidents.	Includes worldwide scientific, medical and technological developments, natural phenomena, U.S. weather and natural disasters.	Includes the arts, religion, scholarship, communications media, sports, entertainment, fashions, fads, and social life.

	World Affairs	Europe	Africa & The Middle East	The Americas	Asia & The Pacific
Oct. 3	Delegates from the various countries are beginning to arrive in Locarno, Switzerland, to begin diplomatic discussions covering a wide range of topics but mostly border security between Germany and France.	Louis Brennan, an aviation expert in Britain, predicts that large helicopters will be used to protect London from aerial raids in the future....Members of the British Fascist Party announce they will assist local police in suppressing any activities by local Communist groups.		The Canadian government announces an arrangement with the Canadian Pacific and Canadian National Railroads to select immigrants and transport and settle them in Canada.	
Oct. 4		Italy reports that its public revenue for June and July exceeded the projected income; at the same time last year there was a serious deficit....A Communist conspiracy to kill the King and Queen of Romania has been discovered....The large grain harvests in Central Europe are having an effect on prices; the harvests have been large but the quality has not been consistent and prices are falling....An unnamed Finnish gunboat sinks while conducting maneuvers; the entire crew of 47 is drowned.	Moorish leader Abd-el-Krim retreats to a new position where he is making preparations for defense against the French and Spanish forces that are in pursuit.		
Oct. 5	The Locarno Conference begins....Germany announces that it will join the League of Nations	In street fighting between Fascists and anti-Fascists, three are killed in Florence, Italy....General Primo de Rivera denies that there will be a transition to a civil government in Spain and that his directory will continue for at least five more years....British dirigible R-33 goes out for a 24-hour test run with a crew of 40 for the first time since its accident last April.	France's premier announces that he is launching an investigation into the conduct of the Syrian campaign to include the reasons behind a massacre of 3,000 French by Druze rebels....Spanish advances in Morocco are so rapid (the last being 20 miles in one day) that they are surprising not only the Moors but their French allies as well.	There is great opposition in Mexico to revise the Constitution to allow General Alvaro Obregon to serve once again as President....One of the largest cotton mills in Mexico closes; 400 are unemployed....An archaeological expedition announces that it will leave Mexico City in mid-October to explore what are believed to be pre-Aztec ruins in the Mexican state of Guerrero....In Chile all political factions have at least temporarily united behind Emiliano Larrain as the next President of the country following the resignation of Arturo Alessandri.	
Oct. 6		Reports from Moscow indicate that sales of pre-war strength vodka are brisk and that the city has seen an increase in civil disorder....Sources in Vienna allege that the Romanian government has been campaigning against U.S. oil interests and recently forged documents showing Standard Oil had been planning to sabotage Romania's oil industry.	The American aviators who volunteered to serve France in Morocco are scheduled to be transferred to a more active sector.		Muslims in Calcutta, India, have threatened to riot if the body of a saint who died last is moved from the marketplace where it has lain for the past year.
Oct. 7		The Fascist Council approves a plan that will abolish the current political parties in Italy and that the executive branch of the government in the person of Benito Mussolini will be strengthened....Briand and Luther of France and Germany meet to talk apart from the general meetings at Locarno to discuss security and better relations between Germany and France....The Romanian cabinet has significantly reduced the export taxes on agricultural products so Rumanian farmers can export more food.	Abd-el-Krim's prestige in the wake of recent defeats has been weakened; not only are the Spanish and French forces after him but his followers are being killed by members of rival tribes....British Prime Minister Stanley Baldwin is on his way to the Conservative Party's convention in which he will address the general situation in northern Iraq.	A plot is discovered to kill Mexico's President Plutarco Calles.	
Oct. 8	At the Locarno Conference, Germany states that it is dropping any conditions it might have had before joining the League of Nations.	The Catholic bishops of Ireland issue a statement that modern dances are an "imported evil" and recommend that these dances be banned in Ireland.			

A	B	C	D	E
Includes developments that affect more than one world region, international organizations and important meetings of world leaders.	Includes all domestic and regional developments in Europe, including the Soviet Union.	Includes all domestic and regional developments in Africa and the Middle East.	Includes all domestic and regional developments in Latin America, the Caribbean, and Canada.	Includes all domestic and regional developments in Asian and Pacific nations (and colonies).

U.S. Politics & Social Issues	U.S. Foreign Policy & Affairs, Defense	U.S. Economy & Environment	Science, Technology & Nature	Culture, Leisure & Lifestyle	
The Sacco and Vanzetti Defense Committee reports that it has spent $282,715 to defend the two anarchists who are awaiting execution in Massachusetts....The city of Venice, CA, votes to become part of Los Angeles.	The navy is retiring its last surviving monitor, the USS *Cheyenne*, built in 1904.	The Soviet Union offers contracts totaling $160 million in orders in the United States for machinery bit states that it will require substantial credit over a long terms....The city of New Orleans reports its greatest prosperity since the end of World War I due partly to farm profits as well as a large building program.		It is announced that Italian composer Ottorino Resphigi will visit the United States and make a concert tour staring in new York....The Operetta, *The Student Prince* will be broadcast over radio station WJZ within the next two weeks to see how well stage shows can be broadcast....Harpsichordist Wanda Landowska is awarded the French Legion of Honor for her services not only in revising the harpsichord but in resurrecting French composers of the 18th century.	Oct. 3
	Senator William King of the Senate Naval Committee states that the Panama Canal Zone lacks an air defense after a conference with Naval experts....Colonel Billy Mitchell's contention that the Navy dirigible *Shenandoah* was violating the law by flying over land is countered by a legal opinion obtained for the navy and there is no law barring naval aircraft from flying over land.	Reports from Pittsburgh, PA, indicate that steel mills are operating at a high rate of production.	American archaeologists in Palestine discover the Temple of Astaroth, mentioned in the Old Testament....Commander Donald B. MacMillan continues his return voyage, departing Newfoundland and heading for the port of Sydney in Nova Scotia.	Members of the Washington Senators baseball club arrive in Pittsburgh; they will practice tomorrow.	Oct. 4
In West Virginia, 53 miners plead their case in court, accused of violating an injunction against picketing; they have no defense attorneys because the judge would not appoint one because the county would have to bear the cost....The main Post Office in Boston is fortified in an effort to combat higher crime in that city and to protect federal facilities.	The Naval hearings being held at Lakehurst, NJ, to investigate the *Shenandoah* crash adjourn and will now move to Washington to conclude the hearings....Colonel Billy Mitchell receives the details of the charges that will be presented at his court-martial.	The State of New Jersey reports 144 cases of Typhoid, twice that of September 1924....On a trip to Omaha, NE, President Calvin Coolidge announces that he believes that there is wide and continued prosperity in the country based on both agriculture and industry.	A group of European scientists announce that they have organized an expedition to Sumatra where they will study an eclipse of the sun on January 14, 1926.	Poet Archibald MacLeish writes a letter to the *New York Times*, rebutting its recent criticism that one of his poems reviewed in the paper has no meaning....George M. Cohan's latest play, *American Born*, is well received by critics although they note that his acting makes the play seem better than it is....Ty Cobb's batting average for 1925 is .380, making it 20 years in a row that his average has been at least 300.	Oct. 5
William Roth of St. Louis dies of tuberculosis first contracted as the result of his agreeing to be used for poison gas experiments during the war.	Colonel Billy Mitchell defies President Calvin Coolidge's ban on "propaganda" by delivering a speech to the American Legion advocating a unified air defense for the United States.	The Department of Justice announces that its new policy in anti-trust cases is that it will pursue only what it considers to be serious violations of the law....Secretary of Commerce Herbert Hoover will call a conference on November 9 to discuss the distribution of stations over the available band of frequencies.	Commander Donald B. MacMillan states that airplanes have no place in a polar expedition and that the best way to explore is still dog sled; his expedition was conducted in what was the worst recorded summer in the arctic.	The Pittsburgh Pirates are said to be the 11 to 10 favorites to win the World Series....New York radio stations will carry the World Series although localities where there is no radio coverage will get their updates using playerboards that show the progress of the games.	Oct. 6
President Calvin Coolidge delivers a speech in Cincinnati tackles the topic of tolerance and the activities of the Ku Klux Klan in a speech at Omaha in which he attacked the Klan, a position he did not take during the election.	In conjunction with air races that are being held in the New York City area, a large segment of the Army Air Force is at Mitchel Field to prepare for a mock war.	U.S. iron production on September increased to 3,632 tons a day, a four percent increase over August....The output of crude oil drops during the week ending October 3....As a result of the strike that began on September 1, there is now a 30-day supply of anthracite in the United States.	20 monkeys have been sent to Johns Hopkins University to assist in the study of evolution.	The Washington Senators win the first game of the World Series....Baseball hero of the early part of the 20th century and president of the Boston Braves Christy Mathewson dies of tuberculosis, brought on by exposure to poison gas during World War I.	Oct. 7
	Colonel Billy Mitchell, who has been called to testify at the Shenandoah hearings, refuses to testify as he says it could prejudice his rights at his forthcoming court-martial.		Explorer Roald Amundsen discusses his plans for another trip to the North pole, probably next May in an Italian airship, traveling from Norway to Nome Alaska.	The Pittsburgh Pirates win the second game of the World Series against the Washington Senator, 3–2; the MacMillan Polar exploration party which is near Nova Scotia on its way back to the United States hears the scores over the wireless radio.	Oct. 8

F	G	H	I	J
Includes campaigns, elections, federal-state relations, civil rights and liberties, crime, the judiciary, education, healthcare, poverty, urban affairs, and population.	Includes formation and debate of U.S. foreign and defense policies, veterans affairs, and defense spending. (Relations with specific foreign countries are usually found under the region concerned.)	Includes business, labor, agriculture, taxation, transportation, consumer affairs, monetary and fiscal policy, natural resources, pollution and industrial accidents.	Includes worldwide scientific, medical and technological developments, natural phenomena, U.S. weather and natural disasters.	Includes the arts, religion, scholarship, communications media, sports, entertainment, fashions, fads, and social life.

	World Affairs	Europe	Africa & The Middle East	The Americas	Asia & The Pacific
Oct. 9		Czechoslovakia and the United States agree on a payment plan in which Czechoslovakia will pay its $185 million debt to the United States over a 62-year period....The French wheat crop for this year is estimated at 8,980,000 tons, an improvement over the crop of 1924....Three members of the Fascist are cleared in the murder of Giacomo Matteotti, a Socialist deputy killed in 1924.	Spanish position at the city of Ajdir, recently captured from Abd-el-Krim, are attacked by Moorish reels.		The Chinese Ministry of Justice has accused Westerners in China who have judicial power of corruption and also accuses westerners of committing murder and other offense and not being punished....The city of Nigata, Japan is the scene of a fire that kills eight people, destroys 600 houses and causes $1 billion in damage.
Oct. 10	The World's wheat crop for 1925 is estimated to be 851 million bushels, exclusive of the Russian and Chinese harvests, a substantial worldwide gain....The Rhine compact which is an important part of the Locarno Conference negotiations is accepted by Italy.	The Italian government announces that the trial for the murder of Socialist Deputy Giacomo Matteotti may be held in December....The French government announces that it will increase the pay of its Civil Service by 25 percent.	French cavalry is said to be advancing toward the recently captured Moorish stronghold of Ajdir.		All of the outside powers, except for Italy and Portugal agree to meet on December 18 to discuss Chinese autonomy issues.
Oct. 11		Soviets in Moscow state that the current unrest in China is only the beginning of what will be a large-scale social revolution....Storms in the Leningrad area have created rising water which is now seven feet higher threatens to damage the city....In Britain the Anti-Rodent Society has begun its push to "do your rat killing early," and to not wait for National Rat Week which is customarily held in late November....The French Communist Party orders a 24-hour general strike to protest the war in Morocco.		In Mexico City, it is the opening day of the winter bullfight season, two bullfighters, Joselito de Malaga and Juan Silveti, are seriously gored.	Japan announces it will withdraw its objections to an American radio station in Shanghai but declares it must be subsidiary to the Japanese station built by Mitsui in Beijing....In Canton, China, the strike against foreigners continues while wounded soldiers from battles being fought for the control of the city are arriving for treatment.
Oct. 12		Poland and the Soviet Union reach an agreement on freight and passenger traffic between the two countries....A three-month, partial strike by British seamen ends. ...Leon Trotsky is again reported to be ill and on enforced convalescent leave in the Crimea....Germany and the Soviet Union sign a commercial trade treaty....Two are dead and many are injured in the wake of a general strike in Paris; the strike is not as widespread as its organizers had hoped.	France announces it will disband the American volunteer squadron that had organized to assist France in the Moroccan campaigns.	A new direct cable between Italy and Argentina is opened....Extended unrest breaks out in Panama City after rent riots; U.S. troops are called in to keep order in the streets.	
Oct. 13		In the wake of the rioting in Paris yesterday, the French government arrests 50 Communists....Romania funds its war debt to Britain which it will pay over a period of 40 years....The Soviet Union announces that it will build a large marble tomb to house the body of Lenin....Several Fascists have been expelled from the party as a result of recent disorders in Florence and other locations.	An attempted attack on French positions in Morocco by the Moors meets with failure with heavy casualties.		Five deaths and 11 new cases of cholera have been reported in the Philippines.
Oct. 14	Germany announces that it will accept all Allied terms that have to do with relations between Germany and the Allies in the occupied Rhineland, setting the state for the successful conclusion of the Locarno Conference and the entry of Germany into the League of Nations.	A Royal Decree in Spain forbids the teaching of subjects considered to be anti-social and anti-national.	Trolley cars in Constantinople now have reserved seats for women and women may now sit side by side with men.	Earth tremors are felt in northern Argentina.	A mission from the Chinese government is on a world tour to spread the Chinese government's point of view; the group is now in Paris and states that the powers that outsiders have in China have made the work of the Chinese government more difficult.

A	B	C	D	E
Includes developments that affect more than one world region, international organizations and important meetings of world leaders.	*Includes all domestic and regional developments in Europe, including the Soviet Union.*	*Includes all domestic and regional developments in Africa and the Middle East.*	*Includes all domestic and regional developments in Latin America, the Caribbean, and Canada.*	*Includes all domestic and regional developments in Asian and Pacific nations (and colonies).*

U.S. Politics & Social Issues	U.S. Foreign Policy & Affairs, Defense	U.S. Economy & Environment	Science, Technology & Nature	Culture, Leisure & Lifestyle	
	The American Federation of Labor renews its battle to eliminate Child Labor in the United States by means of an amendment to the Constitution.		Earth tremors are felt in Maine and New Hampshire;' tremors are also felt in Santa Barbara, CA.	Rain results in a postponement of the World Series; the third game is scheduled tomorrow.	Oct. 9
Sing Sing's Warden Lewis Lawes announces he has received 35 applications for the post of executioner when current executioner John Hulbert retires.	The United States and Germany ratify a commercial trade treaty.	The American government announces that it will not lift its embargo on grapes grown in Spain's Almeira province....The Baldwin Locomotive Company has completed a diesel electric locomotive with 1,000 horsepower; it has been able to pull trains weighing 1,000 tons....Baking bread has become a large business, compared by some to the Steel and Oil Industries; foremost among these is the General Baking Corporation which is valued at $400 million and controls 157 baking factories.	A "mystery" plane is said to be a British entry into the air races to be held at Mitchel Field, NY; it's speed is said to have been 226 miles an hour in earlier trials....The expedition in Mongolia headed by Roy Chapman Andrews found the skull of a prehistoric two-horned animal which will be placed on display at the Museum of Natural History in New York....Lieutenant Commander Richard Byrd defends the use of aircraft in polar exploration even though it did no succeed in this most recent attempt.	Hungarian composer Bela Bartok has completed a new work, The Miraculous Mandarin, which will be performed in Budapest this season; his colleague Zoltan Kodaly has also completed a work, Hary Janos, which will also be performed in the coming season....The Washington Senators defeat the Pittsburgh Pirates in the 3rd game of the World Series by a score of 4–3.	Oct. 10
The Massachusetts Institute of Technology states that it will allow women to smoke at dances; Goucher bans women from smoking at any location or event....Citing the Ku Klux Klan, Prohibition, and the Scopes Trial, Dr. Livingston Farrand, president of Cornell University criticizes the growth of intolerance in the United States in recent years.		U.S. auto makers sent 26,516 autos overseas in August.		Washington beats the Pirates 4–0 in the fourth game of the World Series....John Philip Sousa and his band open a new concert hall in New York City.	Oct. 11
The trial of D.C. Stephenson, former Grand Dragon of the Ku Klux Klan, for the murder of Madge Oberholtzer has begun; jurors have not yet been selected....A group of Italian-Americans in black Fascist uniforms march in the New Haven, CT, Columbus Day parade.	At the Shenandoah hearings, testimony is given that the airship gave way at the top of the craft, although eyewitnesses disagree.	At a regional meeting of the Advertising Clubs of the World, speakers praise honest advertising and that only truthful messages should be tolerated.	Lieutenant Cyrus Bettis, flying at 249 miles per hour wins the Pulitzer Air race at Mitchel Field, NY....The MacMillan polar expedition finally returns to the United States, landing at Wiscasset, Maine....The Prorok expedition which will cross the Sahara over a distance of 1,500 miles has arrived in Algeria and is ready to begin.	The Pittsburgh Pirates defeat the Washington Senators in Game 5 of the World Series by a score of 6–3.	Oct. 12
	The army general staff announces its policy that infantry is the dominant branch in the U.S. Army and that all other branches, especially aviation, are to support infantry in its dominant role.		The Prorok expedition begins, leaving the city of Constantine, Algeria....A new comet as been discovered which is visible in the Pegasus constellation.	The Pittsburgh Pirates beat the Washington Senators 3–2 in the sixth game of the World Series; the teams are now tied.	Oct. 13
Workers on the Western Maryland railway refuse the terms offered them and announce they will go on strike....The American Federation of Labor which supports the anthracite coal strike, charges that mine owners have been forcing dealers to accept a plan that would raise the cost of coal.		Secretary of the Treasury Andrew Mellon will propose a $250 million tax cut to the House Ways and Means Committee....The Firestone Company announces that it will plant one million acres of rubber trees in Liberia.	Another temple in the region of Palestine where the Ashtaroth temple was recently found has been discovered by the Philadelphia Museum expedition....Explorer Benjamin Burbridge returns to the United States with Congo, the only female gorilla in captivity.		Oct. 14

F	G	H	I	J
Includes campaigns, elections, federal-state relations, civil rights and liberties, crime, the judiciary, education, healthcare, poverty, urban affairs, and population.	Includes formation and debate of U.S. foreign and defense policies, veterans affairs, and defense spending. (Relations with specific foreign countries are usually found under the region concerned.)	Includes business, labor, agriculture, taxation, transportation, consumer affairs, monetary and fiscal policy, natural resources, pollution and industrial accidents.	Includes worldwide scientific, medical and technological developments, natural phenomena, U.S. weather and natural disasters.	Includes the arts, religion, scholarship, communications media, sports, entertainment, fashions, fads, and social life.

	World Affairs	Europe	Africa & The Middle East	The Americas	Asia & The Pacific
Oct. 15	As part of the Locarno Conference, Germany and France state that they will never go to war and that there will be a neutral zone between the countries and that they will accept arbitration in all disputes; observers see this as an important first step toward beginning a general disbarment of Europe.	The success of diplomatic meetings that formed the Locarno Conference is being enthusiastically received in France.		The United States and Mexico agree on a new border convention that will curb smuggling across the border.	
Oct. 16	The Locarno Conference ends. Among the effects of the Locarno Conference is a treaty between Germany and Czechoslovakia in which disagreements will be arbitrated....A mutual guarantee between Czechoslovakia, France, and Poland in case Germany is an aggressor is also signed at Locarno.	Germany signs an agreement where it will buy 75,000 tons of benzene from the Soviets each year....The Prince of Wales returns to Britain, having concluded his tours of Africa and South America....Police arrest 500 bakers in Berlin for overcharging for bread....A mine collapses in Austria trapping 300 men; rescuers have been able to send food to the trapped men and rescue efforts continue.			Shanghai has been captured by a new military ruler; the solders holding Shanghai for the past nine months have retreated into the interior of the country.
Oct. 17		In an interview, Benito Mussolini states that his revolution in Italy is only beginning and repeats his earlier belief that liberty "turns to license."...French courts are now deliberating on whether a woman must have her parents' consent to have her hair bobbed....A French journalist is attacked and beaten by Italian Fascists at the Locarno Conference....Exiled Kaiser Wilhelm II warns that Europe will be overrun by China and Japan.	It is now required that only priests can wear turbans in Turkey and the wearers must obtain a license to do so.	General John Pershing announces that he will remain in Chile to continue to manage the plebiscite to determine the border between Chile and Peru.	The American Guardian Association of Manila is beginning a fund drive to care for an estimated 18,000 children of American servicemen.
Oct. 18		Holland and Switzerland announce they will underwrite a municipal loan to the city of Berlin....The French government announces that its tax revenues are less than half of what they were in 1924.	The World Court states that it will begin deliberations on the border dispute between Iraq and Turkey.		The conflict in China continues; the cities of Soochow and Wusih have been captured by warlords.
Oct. 19			Italian troops occupy all of Somaliland, part of which had been treated as a protectorate with the natives given a large degree of autonomy.		In fighting in the region of the Yangste River between rival warlords, several groups are now retreating north beyond the river.
Oct. 20		Soviet authorities state that they are considering eliminating the censorship of articles written by foreign journalists....Because harvests have been disappointing, Soviet leadership announces it will send commissioners to western nations in an effort to obtain financial credits.	Officials of the Near East Relief organization are held up by bandits in Georgia, near Tbilisi.		The Japanese government expresses concerns of a possible war with the Soviet Union over Manchuria.
Oct. 21		A new campaign in Italy is being initiated by King Victor Emmanuele to outlaw profanity....British forces which have been occupying the German city of Cologne, are preparing to withdraw and return to Britain.	American destroyers in the Mediterranean have been ordered to be prepared to assist any American citizens caught in the fighting in Syria.	The Chilean government will be receiving a number of British Naval officers to assist instruction and professional development in the Chilean Navy.	Chinese soldiers fire on a Japanese steamer sailing near Shanghai.
Oct. 22		Reports indicate that the Greek Army which has invaded Bulgaria is making rapid progress. Bulgaria is appealing to the League of Nations for assistance....The Soviet Union announces that priests cannot have the same rights as other citizens.	The rebels of Abd-el-Krim are still fighting; four French artillery batteries have been captured and there are reports that a Spanish garrison has been captured and the soldiers massacred....France declares martial law in Syria.	A trade agreement is signed between Jamaica and Canada with the hope that Canada will grant preference to Jamaican oranges.	14 of 18 Chinese provinces are now in revolt with warlords attempting to set up rival governments.

A	B	C	D	E
Includes developments that affect more than one world region, international organizations and important meetings of world leaders.	Includes all domestic and regional developments in Europe, including the Soviet Union.	Includes all domestic and regional developments in Africa and the Middle East.	Includes all domestic and regional developments in Latin America, the Caribbean, and Canada.	Includes all domestic and regional developments in Asian and Pacific nations (and colonies).

U.S. Politics & Social Issues	U.S. Foreign Policy & Affairs, Defense	U.S. Economy & Environment	Science, Technology & Nature	Culture, Leisure & Lifestyle	
	The U.S. submarine *S-25* is hit by the minesweeper USS *Ortolan* not far from San Diego; no lives were lost and damage is reported to be minimal....The Navy begins its official inquiry into the loss of the submarine *S-51* which was struck by the freighter *City of Rome* on September 25.			The first concert of the New York Philharmonic's new season is given, featuring the Brahms Second Symphony and *Don Quixote* by Richard Strauss....Charlie Chaplin arrives in Hollywood and that he will close up his operations in California and move to New York....The Pittsburgh Pirates defeat the Washington Senators in the seventh and final game of the World Series. Pittsburgh wins 9–7, due to a three-run eighth inning.	Oct. 15
Yale University lists the selling of blood as an established occupation for students; many apply to do it and it is "very remunerative."... Injunctions on the behalf of nearly every mine in West Virginia have been issued against the United Mine Workers for having formed a monopoly to control labor.	President Calvin Coolidge's Aircraft Board reports that the Army lacks the funds for building an aviation presence and that to allocate the funds needed would take all available funds from other branches of the Army.	President Calvin Coolidge states that the federal government should decrease the amount of aid it gives to states to construct and maintain roads.	The Prorok expedition has been encountering heavy rains; the resulting mud has made the trip go more slowly than planned.		Oct. 16
		The price of vegetables and fruits in the northeast has gone up in the past year despite the fact that a greater amount of produce is now shipped to the region from the south and the west....U.S. railroads have placed orders for 147 locomotives in the past week.	The skeleton of a mastodon has been discovered in Middletown, NY, the New York Museum of Natural History has sent experts to evaluate the find.	An estimated 500,000 people view twenty football games throughout the United States; the largest crowd was 80,000 seeing Army beat Notre Dame....Bonuses of $5,700 will be paid to each of the members of the victorious Pittsburgh Pirates; each of the Senators will receive $3,800.... The *New York Times* reviews a new book, *Dialogues in Limbo*, by George Santayana.	Oct. 17
		A surplus of livestock cuts the price for beef and hogs although sheep prices remain at the same level.			Oct. 18
The U.S. Supreme Court declares that a minimum wage law passed by Arizona is illegal because it invades contract rights and is unconstitutional.	Senator William Borah responds to the ex-Kaiser's comments about China and Japan saying the Wilhelm's wish for the white race to dominate would result in a global race war.	Railroads carried more freight in the month of August than in any month of any year except 1920....Members of the Retail Coal Dealers state that the current anthracite coal strike will be the last as substitutes are being developed.			Oct. 19
	The court-martial of Billy Mitchell has been set for October 28 with a panel of 12 generals.	Crude oil production in the United States continues to drop; the daily average is currently 2,062,900 barrels a day.		A census in Putnam County, NY, reports that deer are increasing there at a faster rate than human beings.	Oct. 20
The Ku Klux Klan opens new expanded headquarters in Washington, DC....The Otis Mills of Ware, MA, closes for an indefinite period of time; 500 men and women are out of work.	Lieutenant Fred Nelson of the Army Air Corps is charged by federal game officials for purposely running his plane into geese in flight to kill them.				Oct. 21
Chicago garment workers on strike throw acid bombs at strikebreakers attempting to enter the factory.	Salvage and recovery operations on the sunken sub, *S-51*, continue; another body is recovered....The army announces that the Billy Mitchell court-martial will be held in public.		Physicians at Memorial Hospital in New York are reporting success in using radiation to cure cancer.		Oct. 22

F	G	H	I	J
Includes campaigns, elections, federal-state relations, civil rights and liberties, crime, the judiciary, education, healthcare, poverty, urban affairs, and population.	*Includes formation and debate of U.S. foreign and defense policies, veterans affairs, and defense spending. (Relations with specific foreign countries are usually found under the region concerned.)*	*Includes business, labor, agriculture, taxation, transportation, consumer affairs, monetary and fiscal policy, natural resources, pollution and industrial accidents.*	*Includes worldwide scientific, medical and technological developments, natural phenomena, U.S. weather and natural disasters.*	*Includes the arts, religion, scholarship, communications media, sports, entertainment, fashions, fads, and social life.*

	World Affairs	Europe	Africa & The Middle East	The Americas	Asia & The Pacific
Oct. 23		The Greek army has renewed its attacks on Bulgaria; reports indicate that at least 15,000 Bulgarian soldiers have retreated from the front lines....Gustav Streseman, Germany's foreign minister, states that there was no talk at the Locarno Conference of developing an anti-Russian bloc.			The Maharajah of Nepal has already spent $2 million to free 53,000 slaves as his effort to end slavery in his country.
Oct. 24	The League of Nations states that it will impose peace on the Greeks and Bulgarians.	Reports from Vienna state that Bulgaria is mobilizing its army and moving it to the Greek border; further reports state that the Greek army was ordered to advance on and invade Bulgaria....Soviet authorities arrest 80 officials and contractors on the charge of extensive bribery.		Unrest in Panama City in the wake of the rent riots has quieted down and U.S. troops are being withdrawn....General Emiliano Chamorro, former President of Nicaragua, launches a coup and is president once again.	Japanese representatives are in Moscow to discuss the establishment of a direct rail route from Tokyo to Paris by way of Riga.
Oct. 25		Unemployment in Germany has risen from 3.5 percent to 5 percent although informal reports since the release of this figure indicate that there may be improvements.			The Chinese Customs Conference begins in Beijing today....Soviet troops are sent into Mongolia as a result of the fighting in neighboring China.
Oct. 26	The League of Nations delivers an ultimatum to both the Greek and Bulgarian governments that they must stop fighting and that all troops withdraw within 60 hours; mediation will be effected by Romania.	Although the Communist Party Congress will not open until December there are already substantial criticisms of Gregory Zinoviev, President of the Communist International that may become an issue in two months.			The Chinese Customs Conference which will decide the extent to which the Chinese government can collect import customs again after 80 years opens, accompanied in Beijing by large scale rioting.
Oct. 27		At an official German inquiry into the reasons Germany lost World War I, soldiers who were at the front state that the arrival of the Americans and the probability that they would be coming in increased numbers had a great deal to so with the end of the war....The Italian government has announced that it will impose press censorship.	Reports from Damascus indicate that a new uprising against the French government has started; estimates of those killed have varied from 1,000 to 8,000.		Civil war continues in China with substantial troop movements reported throughout the country.
Oct. 28		The Greek government reports that there is still fighting going on with Bulgarian troops near the border with Macedonia....Greece reports to the League of Nations that it has fulfilled its requirements from the League concerning hostilities with Bulgaria....The Spanish government announces it will purchase a collection of letters from Ferdinand and Isabella to Columbus....There are celebrations in Italy as the Fascists commemorate the third anniversary of their march on Rome in which they took power.	French troops in Syria are being moved to provide additional defenses for the city of Damascus which is still under attack by Druze rebels....The American consulate in Damascus advises Americans to leave Syria.	Elections are held in Canada to elect members to the House of Commons.	
Oct. 29		Hostilities between Greece and Bulgaria come to an end when a truce is signed....Hungarians in Parliament are openly critical of the League of Nations and move to have Hungary withdraw from the organization; the motion is later withdrawn....All Greek soldiers have been withdrawn from Bulgaria.		An oil well in Argentina has been producing 2,300 barrels a day for the past two days, a national record.	
Oct. 30		British commentators state that a reverse Monroe Doctrine should be applied to the United States to keep it from meddling in Europe's affairs....Kaiser Wilhelm II states that he still believes that his exile is only temporary and he will return to rule Germany.	General Maurice Sarrail who has been in charge of military and government operations during the revolt in Syria, is recalled back to France.		

A	B	C	D	E
Includes developments that affect more than one world region, international organizations and important meetings of world leaders.	Includes all domestic and regional developments in Europe, including the Soviet Union.	Includes all domestic and regional developments in Africa and the Middle East.	Includes all domestic and regional developments in Latin America, the Caribbean, and Canada.	Includes all domestic and regional developments in Asian and Pacific nations (and colonies).

U.S. Politics & Social Issues	U.S. Foreign Policy & Affairs, Defense	U.S. Economy & Environment	Science, Technology & Nature	Culture, Leisure & Lifestyle	
	President Calvin Coolidge states that he wants to have a memorial at the Tomb of the Unknown soldier and not a simple slab marking the grave.			The Dean of Princeton's Graduate School states that that approximately one million are studying Latin.	Oct. 23
The American Legion is stating that new laws should be passed to provide disability pay for veterans on an extended basis....The Tennessee Supreme Court rules that the exceptions in the Scopes trail will be ruled out; this means the testimony about evolution will be stricken and the center of the case will rest on whether Scopes broke the law.	Billy Mitchell's defense states that it will use the right of free speech as the cornerstone of its defense when the trial opens in a few days.	American aircraft companies are receiving significant amounts of order for aircraft engines by companies in Europe....The anthracite coal strike continues with estimated loses of $165 million to include $78 million in lost wages by miners and railroad workers....The number of American-owned vessels engaged in overseas trade has increased from 117 to 134 in the period 1 July to October 2.	A study at Colgate University states that while men and women share intelligence equally, men are more emotionally stable, though hysteria is equally common in both sexes.	Rose Taibbe of New York City picks up a lit bomb thrown into her tenement building, places it in a sink and prevents it from exploding; police believe it may have been left in the building as the result of a feud....William Randolph Hearst sells The *Fort Worth Record* to Amon G. Carter after having owned the newspaper for three years.	Oct. 24
		Severe storms strike the eastern and southern U.S., with dead reported in the northeast and a tornado in Alabama; 60 mph winds wreck 17 navy seaplanes in Maryland and barges on Lake Champlain in New York are sunk.		Scholars in Vienna find a manuscript of a mass by Composer Carl Maria von Weber which was supposed to have been lost in a fire in 1803.	Oct. 25
		The Pierce Arrow auto company reports that its profits in the quarter ending in September were $405,777....Coca-Cola reports that its quarterly profits were $3,345,980.	The inner sarcophagus of Tutankhamen is opened and revealed; it is expected that the tomb will be a great tourist attraction during the coming tourist season.		Oct. 26
President Calvin Coolidge states that more power should be granted by the states and that there should be less centralization at the federal level.	The court-martial of Billy Mitchell on the charge of speaking out when he was ordered not to by the president opens in Washington, DC....Lieutenant Jimmy Doolittle breaks the world record for speed by a seaplane when he reaches a speed of 245 miles an hour.		The Prorok Expedition in the Sahara has discovered a cliff containing messages etched on the floors of surrounding caves; in another cave the explorers also find pictures of camels and gazelles.	Boxing Champion Jack Dempsey on a tour of Mexico states that his nose is real and not made of wax and he will let anyone twist it to prove that point.	Oct. 27
	The court-martial of Billy Mitchell begins; he attempts to dispute the jurisdiction of the court and successfully challenges three of the generals appointed on the panel....At a naval inquiry, the captain of the ship *City of Rome* blames the captain of the *S-51* for the collision which sank the sub with nearly all hands.	The Department of Commerce reports that at least 250 organizations will participate in the Radio Conference being called by Commerce Secretary Herbert Hoover....Once again railroad car loadings have exceeded a million in a week; this is the 13th week in a row that a million or more cars have been loaded.			Oct. 28
A meeting of the American Negro Labor Congress adopts a resolution calling for "full social equality" for African Americans; the American Federation of Labor has accused the Congress of being a Communist organization.	Colonel Billy Mitchell loses his appeal to have his court-martial dismissed on the grounds that he was entitled to free speech.		A new safety device is tested that will warn engineers of possible disaster and then automatically applies the brakes if the engineer does not....Sir Richard Redmayne, former chief inspector of British Mines predicts that the United States will run out of oil in 25 years and that the world's oil supply will be used up in 80 to 100 years.		Oct. 29
The Court in the Stephenson murder case states that it will accept the dying declaration of Madge Oberholtzer against D.C. Stephenson and two others of murdering her.					Oct. 30

F	G	H	I	J
Includes campaigns, elections, federal-state relations, civil rights and liberties, crime, the judiciary, education, healthcare, poverty, urban affairs, and population.	Includes formation and debate of U.S. foreign and defense policies, veterans affairs, and defense spending. (Relations with specific foreign countries are usually found under the region concerned.)	Includes business, labor, agriculture, taxation, transportation, consumer affairs, monetary and fiscal policy, natural resources, pollution and industrial accidents.	Includes worldwide scientific, medical and technological developments, natural phenomena, U.S. weather and natural disasters.	Includes the arts, religion, scholarship, communications media, sports, entertainment, fashions, fads, and social life.

	World Affairs	Europe	Africa & The Middle East	The Americas	Asia & The Pacific
Oct. 31	The League of Nations' prestige is at an all time high as a result of the Locarno Conference and its successful efforts to stop a war between Greece and Bulgaria.	The Polish government announces that it will dedicate its Tomb of the Unknown Solider in Warsaw.... The French government announces that it will select recruits to serve in Morocco on the basis of a lottery.... A woman and three men are convicted in a Soviet court as spies serving Poland and are executed.... Mikhail Frunze, head of the Soviet Army, dies while being operated on for an ulcer.	The League of Nations commission to investigate deportations of Christians by Turks in the Mosul region has arrived has arrived in Mosul, to be chaired by a member of the Estonian Army.... The Permanent Mandates Commission of the League of Nations is asking the French government to answer questions about the recent disorder in Syria.	American Ambassador James Sheffield is received by Mexican President Plutarco Calles.... In the Mexican state of Tabasco, five priests are arrested because they have refused to marry in violation of a new Mexican law that states all priests must be married if they are to exercise their duties.	Edward Wood is named by King George V and Stanley Baldwin as the new Viceroy of India.... The Persian National Assembly by a vote of 80 to five has deposed the Shah; the country will be ruled by its Premier, Reza Khan.
Nov. 1		The state government of Prussia announces that it is willing to award the Kaiser's family $2 billion for their lands and other property as a settlement for losses by the family.... British aircraft manufacturers are expressing dissatisfaction with the British Air Ministry's latest preference for buying American aviation equipment.... A Fascist catechism has been printed and approved by Benito Mussolini which states that Italy will make good its claims to Malta, Corsica, and Nice, part of Switzerland, and part of Yugoslavia.	Druze rebels are raiding settlements on the outskirts of Damascus, Syria but the town itself is now returning to normal.... Reports from Morocco indicate that the forces of Abd-el-Krim have received assistance from a former German Army officer who acted as military advisor and a former Colonel in the Serbian army directed artillery.	Santos Chocana, Poet Laureate of Peru, shoots another writer, Edwin Elmore, over a literary dispute.	The China Customs Conference has been proceeding for a week without interruption; American diplomats believe that the Conference will be a success if it is not ended by the currently raging civil war.
Nov. 2		Police in France claim they cannot cope with increased crime that is the result of a large alien population; politicians have suggested that France should revise its immigration policy.... All wireless operators in London walk out on a strike.	Arabs in Palestine are calling for a general strike protesting against granting of a Zionist homeland and against French policies in Syria.... British observers express grave concern over the removal of the Shah of Persia and the interest the Soviet government has shown in the area.... Reports from Palestine indicate that in Syria, the French have lost control over large parts of the region.	Five people are killed and 27 injured during elections in the Mexican state of Yucatan.	Strikers clash with police in Freemantle, Australia; 100 arrests are made and several strikers shot.
Nov. 3		A strike of all 90,000 Austrian civil servants is called.... Britain's Labour Party gains gain 135 seats in local municipal elections.... The President of the Irish Free State announces a bill that will make education compulsory.	American pilots attached to the French Army have landed in neutral Tangier after a bombing raid against the rebels in Morocco.... French authorities in Syria are sending arms to Europeans in villages in Syria so they can defend themselves.		Chinese government forces under General Chang Kai-shek have captured the city of Swatow as the Canton government consolidates its control in the Kwantung Province.... China's desire to have the autonomy to collect its own customs after 80 years will be granted by 1929 as a result of the recent Chinese Customs Conference.
Nov. 4		The Spanish government reports that 40,000 American tourists visited that country in 1924, compared with 3,000 in 1923.... By offering a 28 percent pay increase to its civil service, the Austrian government prevents a strike.	American fliers who volunteered to fight for France in Morocco are now returning to France by way of Barcelona, Spain.		Canton, China, is reported to be a very active Communist center.
Nov. 5		The Commission to settle the border between Northern Ireland and the Irish Free State is due to report its findings in two weeks.... Soldiers are called into Madrid on rumors that there may be an attempt to overthrow General Primo de Rivera.... An attempt to kill Benito Mussolini is foiled.	The Lafayette Squadron, a group of volunteers serving the French against the Moors in Morocco will withdraw entirely from the front by November 15.	Chile announces it will accept the rules of the plebiscite to determine its border with Peru.	A compromise within the Japanese cabinet over naval expenditures prevents a split that would result in having to form a new cabinet.... Both the Soviet Union and Britain recognize the new Persian government under Reza Khan.
Nov. 6		Klimint Voroshilov is named head of the Soviet Armies, replacing Mikhail Frunze who died last month.	The city of Damascus in Syria is still held by the French but is now reported to be isolated; Arabs have now joined the Druze tribesmen in the revolt against French rule.... Reza Khan states that he will rule Persia as a monarch.		Khai Dinh, ruler of the French protectorate of Annam in southeast Asia dies; he had succeeded to the throne in 1916.... The Crown Prince of Japan, on his American tour arrives in Washington to meet with President Calvin Coolidge.

A	B	C	D	E
Includes developments that affect more than one world region, international organizations and important meetings of world leaders.	*Includes all domestic and regional developments in Europe, including the Soviet Union.*	*Includes all domestic and regional developments in Africa and the Middle East.*	*Includes all domestic and regional developments in Latin America, the Caribbean, and Canada.*	*Includes all domestic and regional developments in Asian and Pacific nations (and colonies).*

U.S. Politics & Social Issues	U.S. Foreign Policy & Affairs, Defense	U.S. Economy & Environment	Science, Technology & Nature	Culture, Leisure & Lifestyle	
New York City reports that 43 of its policemen have been killed in the past 10 years and that 28 have been killed in the last five years.... In New York state, the State Association of Children's Court Judges endorses a bill that would prohibit marriage under 16 without the approval of a Children's Court Judge although the state legislature recently killed the bill.		The President's Commission on Recreation has suggested adding approximately 300,000 acres to Yellowstone Park.	Yale University announces that it will establish a psychiatry course of study for physicians....German scientists at the University of Leipzig announce that they will attempt to send messages and photographs by air to the United States.	Filming continues for the spectacle film, *Ben Hur;* filming is done on the chariot race scene using 42 cameras; none of the 48 horses were injured during the making of the scene.	Oct. 31
	The defense in the Billy Mitchell court-martial will seek to prove that all of Mitchell's criticisms of the government aviation policy are true although many observers believe that he will not get a chance to do this in court.	German stock exchange experts express doubts that the American stock market will be able to sustain its growth and prosperity indefinitely....Massachusetts banks are warning investors from that state to exercise caution in Florida land investments; it is estimated that since June, Massachusetts investors have spent $20 million on Florida land deals....New York City now manufactures 60 percent of the entire total of clothing manufactured in the United States.	Professors from Harvard University's Observatory will be delivering 15-minute lectures twice a week from a radio station in Boston.	An American, Harry Pidgeon, who taught himself navigation completes his solo sailing voyage of circling the globe, doing it in four years.	Nov. 1
President Calvin Coolidge states he will not become involved in the resolution of the anthracite coal strike and will not assume responsibility for dictating the level of wages....Department of Commerce statistics for the month ending October 10 indicate that 59 American cities reported 455 auto fatalities, a very slight decline in the previous month's total.	The American scouting fleet which has spent time in Jamaica will leave there to return to the Naval base at Guantanamo, Cuba.... Colonel Billy Mitchell demands that the Secretaries of War and the Navy testify at his court-martial.	Stock sales at the New York Stock Exchange total 2,279,722 shares, the greatest number ever sold in one day; prices are generally higher....The United States leads the world in exports to the Soviet Union for the first nine months of 1925, accounting for 35 percent of that country's imports.	New York Health Commissioner Frank Monaghan announces that there is no danger to the public from heavy auto exhaust fumes although two researchers from Yale report that the fumes may present a hazard.	The Nobel prize organization states that there will be no awards of the Nobel prize for literature, medicine, physics, or chemistry; the Nobel peace prize may be awarded for peace may still be awarded....Concert pianist Paul Wittgenstein who lost an arm in World War I gives a one handed piano recital playing music especially composed for him by Richard Strauss.	Nov. 2
Jimmy Walker, a self-avowed member of Tammany, becomes Mayor of New York City winning by 400,000 votes.	Judges at the Billy Mitchell court-martial rule that he is within his rights in requesting a list of 70 persons be called as witnesses for his defense although the motion to dismiss the case for lack of evidence is not granted.	Output of U.S. oil has decreased in the past week by 2,100 barrels a day.	The Prorok Expedition across the Sahara arrives at a French Fort in the Sahara after escaping from a band of hostile Arabs.	Writer Ring Lardner is threatened with arrest if he ever returns to Chicago due to an unpaid $50 fine from six years ago....Film star Rudolph Valentino has left Hollywood for New York but says he will not visit his wife on his way to Europe; they will not see each other as long as she wishes to work in motion pictures.	Nov. 3
Several local elections around the country indicated that candidates backed by the Ku Klux Klan did not do well....The state rests its case against D.C. Stephenson, former Klan Grand Dragon, alleging that the wounds Madge Oberholtzer received as a result of her kidnapping and assault were responsible for her death.	The war department announces that army aircraft will not be flown at air shows on Sundays.		Experiments at the University of Chicago indicate that fasting for long periods reduces mental quickness....Roy Chapman Andrews whose expedition to Mongolia was cut short by political factors states that he believes that man originated in the Mongolian region of Asia.	Women in Paris are continuing to wear small hats (cloches) and continuing the fashion for short (bobbed) hair.	Nov. 4
John L. Lewis of the United Mine Workers declares that full responsibility for the current anthracite coal strike rests entirely on the mine operators.		President Calvin Coolidge refusal to act on the current anthracite strike has encouraged some members of Congress to suggest Secretary of Commerce Herbert Hoover as a mediator....The Department of Agriculture announces that there will be no shortage of turkeys for Thanksgiving.	Anthropologists in Czechoslovakia find a human skeleton of an estimated 20,000 years of age.... Howard Carter working at the tomb of King Tutankhamen has uncovered the third coffin, covered entirely in gold.		Nov. 5
The Ku Klux Klan announces that it opposes the World Court.		Production of steel ingots reaches the highest level in the previous month than at any time since March; the total output is 3,125,418 tons.		Broadway producer Phillip Goodman sues actor W.C. Fields for $100,000 over an alleged breach of contract.	Nov. 6

F	G	H	I	J
Includes campaigns, elections, federal-state relations, civil rights and liberties, crime, the judiciary, education, healthcare, poverty, urban affairs, and population.	Includes formation and debate of U.S. foreign and defense policies, veterans affairs, and defense spending. (Relations with specific foreign countries are usually found under the region concerned.)	Includes business, labor, agriculture, taxation, transportation, consumer affairs, monetary and fiscal policy, natural resources, pollution and industrial accidents.	Includes worldwide scientific, medical and technological developments, natural phenomena, U.S. weather and natural disasters.	Includes the arts, religion, scholarship, communications media, sports, entertainment, fashions, fads, and social life.

	World Affairs	Europe	Africa & The Middle East	The Americas	Asia & The Pacific
Nov. 7		Army officers are arrested held for plotting to overthrow the current government of Spain....An outbreak of hoof and mouth disease among cattle in Britain may prevent the usual round of livestock shows that take place in December....The Fascist Party asserts that the recent attempt to kill Benito Mussolini was a Masonic plot.	Nationalists in Syria are supporting the recent rebellion against the French by Arabs and Druze and are demanding independence for Syria....Recently proposed legislation in Turkey includes an income tax as well as taxes on domestic animals, entertainment and catering, and sales of businesses.	Canada's national debt now stands at $2,360,022,809, an increase in the past month but not enough to make it an increase for the year.	The head of Nanking University states that China depends upon the United States to ensure justice for China in its relations with other countries.
Nov. 8		Europe's wheat harvest for 1925 is 26.5 percent greater than last year and only about 5 percent less than pre-war levels....Weapons have been found in Italy leading to speculation that they were intended for a revolt against the government; 50 suspects are arrested in Livorno....The Finnish government arrests 30 Communists suspected of attempting to spy on the Finnish military....Although a recovery is expected, prices on the Berlin stock market have fallen drastically and are barely what they were in January.	There are public executions in Damascus, Syria, of Druze rebels who have been caught; there is further fighting south of the city and an estimated 200 rebels have been killed....Reports from Egypt are claiming that the French in Syria have been committing atrocities and robbing the population under the guise of keeping order and searching for suspects.		
Nov. 9		Grock, "the funniest clown in the world," has decided to leave Britain forever because of the high tax rate....The French government proposes hat the League of Nations conduct a study before drastic arms limitation programs are discussed....Prices in France have been rising, principally due to rising costs in raw materials.		The Colombian government announces that it will seek a $45 million loan from the United States.	
Nov. 10		Restrictions imposed on occupied Germany will be relaxed by the French and British....A French Fascist movement counting 10,000 followers is launched in Paris.	The French government is set to launch a new offensive in Syria while rebels are edging closer to Damascus....Italians in Somaliland occupy a settlement as they extend their holdings in the area.	The Canadian government estimates that this year's wheat crop will be the second largest on record.	Fighting continues in the Chinese civil war with armies reported to be near Beijing.
Nov. 11	Today is Armistice Day, the anniversary of the end of World War I....All of Britain stops and pauses for several minutes of silence at 11 o'clock in the morning.		Druze rebels in Syria are attacking a French outpost near Damascus.		Reports from Shanghai claim that China's President Tuan and his Minister of War have been taken prisoner in Beijing.
Nov. 12		The British submarine *M-1* is sunk 12 miles off the English coast with a loss of all 69 crew members....An attempted uprising against the Directorate of General Primo de Rivera in Barcelona is crushed....The German Reichstag Judiciary Committee has been debating whether Army Officers should be allowed to hold duels....A Soviet government commission is taking measures to halt corruption in the civil service which has grown significantly.			The agreements that were being developed at the Chinese Customs Conference may be in danger as China's President is imprisoned; in the meantime, there is a great deal of troop movement and some fighting throughout China....The boycott of Hong Kong called by the Chinese government is waning and Canton is said to be willing to discuss the resumption of trade talks.
Nov. 13		Poland's Prime Minister Wladyslaw Grabski resigns bringing to an end the longest running Polish government between the two world wars (23 months)....British authorities believe that the *M-1* cannot be recovered, that it was probably crushed by water pressure.	Druze rebels in Syria are expanding their activities and have raided several more towns; Beirut is now the center of refugees fleeing from the western part of Syria.	The Mexican Chamber of Deputies passes a bill that places restrictions on land ownership by foreign individuals and corporations.	

A	B	C	D	E
Includes developments that affect more than one world region, international organizations and important meetings of world leaders.	Includes all domestic and regional developments in Europe, including the Soviet Union.	Includes all domestic and regional developments in Africa and the Middle East.	Includes all domestic and regional developments in Latin America, the Caribbean, and Canada.	Includes all domestic and regional developments in Asian and Pacific nations (and colonies).

U.S. Politics & Social Issues	U.S. Foreign Policy & Affairs, Defense	U.S. Economy & Environment	Science, Technology & Nature	Culture, Leisure & Lifestyle	
John Burkman, 86, a trooper of the 7th Cavalry who saddled Custer's horse commits suicide; he had recently been refused entry in the California Soldiers Home.	The navy announces it may try another attempt at sending sea-planes from California to Hawaii on a nonstop flight next year.	The Florida land boom continues with active land speculation and rising prices....The National Association of Broadcasters plans to petition the U.S. government to amend copyright restrictions on the mechanical reproduction of music.	The tusk of a mastodon has been uncovered in Middletown, NY.		Nov. 7
President Calvin Coolidge in a speech praises the American press as a safeguard against bigotry and oppression; the speech is well received by many organizations across the United States.	The court-martial of Billy Mitchell continues with the prosecution arguing that Mitchell may call his witnesses only to mitigate whatever sentence he is given and not to prove his innocence.				Nov. 8
At the D. C. Stephenson murder trial three defense witnesses testify that Madge Oberholzer was not forced into Stephenson's private train....The trial has revealed that that several political leaders of Indiana were frequent visitors to Stephenson's office and that most of the candidates Stephenson had supported in 1924 won their elections.	Judges in the Billy Mitchell court-martial have allowed Mitchell the ability to call witnesses on his behalf to prove the truths of his statement criticizing American air policy....During the trial, Mitchell accuses the navy of a cover up in investigating the *Shenandoah* crash.	The Radio Conference called by Secretary of Commerce Herbert Hoover convenes.	A new process for developing steel using an electric furnace develops steel directly from ore; the process has been developed in Sweden.		Nov. 9
President Calvin Coolidge states that he hopes the entire country will observe a few minutes of silence at 11 o'clock tomorrow in honor of Armistice Day.	A witness at the Billy Mitchell court-martial testifies that 505 U.S. air men have been killed flying obsolete aircraft; four additional officers confirm this fact.	The Department of Agriculture reports that the total harvest of corn in the United States was 3,013,390 bushels, the fifth largest in U.S. history.	At a speech at the Museum of Natural History, Roy Chapman Andrews descries how was able to bring back the fossils of 40 dinosaur eggs and the skulls of six new types of mammals on his recent expedition to Mongolia.... The Prorok Expedition crosses the Hoggar mountain range and meets with Taureg tribesmen.	More than 100,000 Christmas trees will be shipped from Vermont to markets this year....Some colleges announce that they will include intelligence tests based on psychological questions as part of the admissions process.	Nov. 10
Governor Gifford Pinchot of Pennsylvania is continuing his efforts to broker an end to the anthracite Coal strike; Pinchot has a successful meeting with the United Mine Workers and will see the mine operators today.	The U.S. Lightship *Hedge Fence* is rammed and sunk by the Danish steamer, *M.C. Holm*; no lives are lost.			Actress Theda Bara, the original "vamp" announces that she will become a comedienne and will make a comedy next month with Hal Roach.	Nov. 11
The Prosecutor in the murder trial of D.C. Stephenson begins his closing statements.	The United States offers better terms to Italy to pay its war debt to the US; the amount to be paid is $2.5 billion over a 70-year period.		British aviator Alan Cobham announces that next week he will make the first flight from London to Capetown, South Africa, an 8,000 mile trip over mostly unexplored territory.		Nov. 12
Governor Alvin Fuller of Massachusetts warns 12,000 state employees planning to form a union that they will not receive favorable consideration.			The process of unwrapping the mummy of King Tutankhamen proceeds slowly; experts estimate that his age was 15 at the time of his death.		Nov. 13

F	G	H	I	J
Includes campaigns, elections, federal-state relations, civil rights and liberties, crime, the judiciary, education, healthcare, poverty, urban affairs, and population.	Includes formation and debate of U.S. foreign and defense policies, veterans affairs, and defense spending. (Relations with specific foreign countries are usually found under the region concerned.)	Includes business, labor, agriculture, taxation, transportation, consumer affairs, monetary and fiscal policy, natural resources, pollution and industrial accidents.	Includes worldwide scientific, medical and technological developments, natural phenomena, U.S. weather and natural disasters.	Includes the arts, religion, scholarship, communications media, sports, entertainment, fashions, fads, and social life.

	World Affairs	Europe	Africa & The Middle East	The Americas	Asia & The Pacific
Nov. 14		Travelers to Albania report that the country is over run by bandits and that travel in the countryside is very dangerous....The British government announces it will cease its occupation of Cologne by December 1....During an election in Slovakia, peasants attack Socialists and cut off their ears.... The financial crises in France this year have caused several government agencies to seek new methods of taxation....Italy reports that its wheat crop is 41 percent greater than last year's.	Soltan Pasha, leader of the Druze rebellion against the French states that the rebellion will continue until the French leave....French reinforcements have begun to arrive in Syria....Observers estimate that the French will need to send 50,000 additional men to restore order in Syria.	Members of the Canadian Boards of Trade and Chambers of Commerce are meeting in Winnipeg to define a new economic policy for the country.	There is now general agreement at the Beijing Conference on China's rights to collect customs and a more generalized autonomy to follow....The Japanese cabinet forces the navy to delay on its plans to construct four new cruisers....A halt in fighting during the Chinese Customs Conference has helped the government negotiate and observers predict the regime will last at least into the spring of 1926.
Nov. 15		General elections for the national Assembly are held in Czechoslovakia....A demonstration in Paris by approximately 4,000 French Fascists demands a dictator for France....Germany reports an increase in its auto manufacturing of 45 percent.	The Turkish government authorizes a plan for the paper money that will replace the old currency of the Ottoman Empire.		In an effort to influence events in China, the Soviet Union is sending delegations there while continuing to provide training to several groups of Chinese civil and military leaders in Moscow.
Nov. 16		The Italian government has issued an appeal for 5 million citizens to give the equivalent of $1 a year fto pay the debt installments that Italy owes the United States for its war debt....Appearing in public for the first time since the attempt on his life, Benito Mussolini speaks to the Italian Senate.	British troops have been sent to patrol the Palestine-Syria border to ensure that Druze rebels fighting the French do not enter the British Mandate....Druze rebels are marching toward the Lebanese city of Sidon, after seizing a village where they burned 500 houses and where 200 were killed....The Wahhabi faction under the leadership of Ibn Saud has captured "the Prophet's City," Medina, in Arabia.	Railway workers in Mexico deny that they will call a general strike when the government returns the state railways to private owners.... Aurelio Manrique, Governor of the State of Potosi and known as a Communist is deposed by the State legislature....The President of Mexico announces he is planning to introduce legislation that will restrict the use of alcohol in that country.	Reports from China describe a mutiny of the 5th Shantung Division which fired on the Russian White Brigade which had been attached to them; most of the 3,000 Russians are reported to be dead.
Nov. 17		Women's suffrage is being debated in the Italian Senate with the likely result that women will be allowed to participate in municipal elections.	The Lebanese port of city of Beirut has come under heavy artillery fire by the Druze rebels; French troops are sent to Sidon which is also threatened by the rebels.		At a lecture at the Royal Asiatic Society, Professor Ernst Herzfield describes finds in India's northwest that he says prove that the region was once Persian....Japanese naval officials state very strongly that they do not favor abolition of submarines.
Nov. 18	The League of Nations announces that it will open a special session in February 1926 to admit Germany as a member.	Britain's House of Commons ratifies the Locarno Treaty....All five major political parties have retained their seats in the recent Czechoslovak elections meaning that the current coalition running the country will continue....The French government states that it wants submarines for its navy and does not understand the logic behind American desires to ban the weapon.	In the wake of reports describing successes of Druze rebels against the French in Syria, the French government is asking Britain for assistance....Large numbers of refugees from Syria are entering Palestine.	Mexico's Federation of Labor calls a general strike to begin on November 19.	
Nov. 19		Reports from Budapest indicate that former Archduke Albert Habsburg wishes to come back to Hungary and establish a Fascist style government on the Italian model devised by Benito Mussolini.	Reports from Lebanon state that even as French reinforcements are arriving in the area, the Druze rebels are beginning to retreat from Beirut....In Syria itself reports describe new attacks by a force of 4,000 rebels....The League Nations states that it will not receive the leader of the Druze rebels who is on his way to seek redress against the French.	The Villes des Cayes, a Haitian steamer traveling to Cuba with workers for the cane fields, sinks taking with it at least 200; only three are saved.	Reports from the Caucasus region claim that there will be an anti-Soviet revolt in the Spring of next year; the revolt will center in Georgia and Azerbaijan....The city of Chihli, 100 miles southwest of Beijing, has fallen to yet another warlord, looting the city after capturing it.
Nov. 20		Benito Mussolini is attacked by Socialists in Germany's Reichstag for his oppressive policies in Italy which have had a bad effect on German-Italian trade agreements....In Dublin, a theater showing a British war film, Ypres, is bombed.	French troops in a massive operation have counterattacked Druze rebels and using a force of 400 autos have enveloped the rebels.		

A	B	C	D	E
Includes developments that affect more than one world region, international organizations and important meetings of world leaders.	Includes all domestic and regional developments in Europe, including the Soviet Union.	Includes all domestic and regional developments in Africa and the Middle East.	Includes all domestic and regional developments in Latin America, the Caribbean, and Canada.	Includes all domestic and regional developments in Asian and Pacific nations (and colonies).

U.S. Politics & Social Issues	U.S. Foreign Policy & Affairs, Defense	U.S. Economy & Environment	Science, Technology & Nature	Culture, Leisure & Lifestyle	
The anthracite coal miners strike continues although the nation's supply is rapidly decreasing; observers note that the unions have never been so entrenched and solid as they are this time....An Indiana jury convicts D.C. Stephenson, former Klan Grand Dragon of second degree murder in the death of Madge Oberholzer and sentence him to serve 20 years.		New England shoe manufacturers who have seen their business move to the U.S. Midwest predict a return of business due to an improved labor situation and new merchandizing methods.	The Prorok expedition continues its expedition in the Sahara, looking for traces of human tribes that lived in the area....Archaeologists in Siberia have discovered human skeletons estimated to be 30,000 years old as well as the remains of wolves, bears, and mammoths.	Film comedian Ben Turpin is operated on for appendicitis and is currently under observation....It is announced that Russian bass Feodor Chaliapin will present a matinee performance of *Boris Godunov* as a benefit for schools in the southern U.S.	Nov. 14
Textile mills in Massachusetts state that unless the 48-hour work week is repealed and they are allowed to go back to a 54-hour hour week, they will move their operations into southern states.	Senator William Borah, Chairman of the Senate Foreign Relations Committee endorses a campaign to ban the use of submarines that would extend to war itself.... According to standing agreements, 19 nations that owe the United States for war debts will pay $180,282,628 in 1926; these nations include Britain, Italy, Czechoslovakia, and Belgium.	The price of a share of Coca-Cola drops to $6 after a peak of $9 a share.	A report is issued describing the latest discoveries concerning the mummy of Tutankhamen which includes the body is wearing gold sandals and gold finger covers.	The movie, *Stage Struck* opens in New York City, starring Gloria Swanson.	Nov. 15
The anthracite coal strike ends its 12th week with no resolution; several groups are asking President Calvin Coolidge to intervene to end the strike.				Metro-Goldwyn-Mayer and United Artists announce that they will form a merger of the distributing companies that the studios own....In Prague, a new chemical element named dvimagan is discovered (it will later be renamed rhenium)....American poet, Edgar Lee Masters, author of *The Spoon River Anthology* delivers a eulogy at the funeral of his father in Springfield, IL.	Nov. 16
John L. Lewis of the United Mine Workers announces that he is willing to discuss a one-to-five year contract arrived at by collective bargaining.	A large part of the defense strategy in the Billy Mitchell court-martial depends on testimony to show his criticism is correct; witnesses for the defense testify that flying has been dangerous for the officers involved because of old equipment....President Calvin Coolidge favors a ban on submarines but that a world wide sentiment must occur before that can happen.	A large fire along the New Orleans waterfront destroys five blocks and causes $2 million damage.... This is the 7th week in a row that oil production has dropped in the United States; only fields in Wyoming and Oklahoma are increasing their output.			Nov. 17
While not giving any details, Senator William Borah announces he has a plan for ending the anthracite coal strike....Saugus, MA, announces it will plan to arm 100 citizens to patrol the streets of the town....Dr. Clarence Little, President of the University of Michigan urges the sterilization of "mental and criminal defectives."			Dr. Koshinsky of the Soviet Union claims to have been able to transfer human thoughts to animals even at great distances by telepathy from a specially constructed iron box.		Nov. 18
According to Dr. Archibald Henderson of the University of North Carolina, H.L. Mencken, most recently famous for his commentary on the Scopes Trial has done more harm than good to Southern culture by his comments.	Thirteen American aviators, all veterans of World War I, issue a statement in Paris after having served the French in the recent war in Morocco, stating they will return if they are needed.		Howard Carter completes unwrapping the mummy of Tutankhamen, Carter and the others are able to determine that the portraits of the Pharaoh actually portrayed his facial features quite accurately.	Buck Weaver, former third baseman for the 1919 Chicago White Sox loses his lawsuit to obtain $20,000 back pay from the team's owner....The film, *The Big Parade*, based on a story by Laurence Stallings, directed by King Vidor, and starring John Gilbert, opens in New York.	Nov. 19
Mine operators sate that they will "fight to the finish" over coal wages and will wait until there is a proper state of mind before reaching any settlement.				Thomas Duffy of Tarrytown, NY, has been confined to his home to recuperate from back injuries caused by dancing the "Charleston."	Nov. 20

F	G	H	I	J
Includes campaigns, elections, federal-state relations, civil rights and liberties, crime, the judiciary, education, healthcare, poverty, urban affairs, and population.	Includes formation and debate of U.S. foreign and defense policies, veterans affairs, and defense spending. (Relations with specific foreign countries are usually found under the region concerned.)	Includes business, labor, agriculture, taxation, transportation, consumer affairs, monetary and fiscal policy, natural resources, pollution and industrial accidents.	Includes worldwide scientific, medical and technological developments, natural phenomena, U.S. weather and natural disasters.	Includes the arts, religion, scholarship, communications media, sports, entertainment, fashions, fads, and social life.

	World Affairs	Europe	Africa & The Middle East	The Americas	Asia & The Pacific
Nov. 21	Recent successes by the League of Nations have given it added prestige in Europe with many hoping that the next step will be a comprehensive disarmament.	Latvia announces it will seek a $10 million loan from the United States....The British Admiralty reports that the lost submarine, *M-1*, did not sink by mechanical defects but was rammed by a Swedish steamer.	The World Court decides that the League of Nations has the right to determine the borders between Iraq and Turkey by a unanimous vote of the Council.... French forces in Lebanon are able to suppress an attempted rebellion in Lebanon, started by Druze tribesmen in that region.	Brazil denies that it is trying to fix coffee prices but that its regulation of exports prices is only to stabilize prices.	
Nov. 22		Although some buying by American investors has helped stock prices somewhat, the stock exchange in Berlin reports that its prices are at the lowest they have been all year....France's coal output is now breaking all records with an average of 2,730 tons a day greater than previous totals.	Reports from Morocco describe how defeated remnants of Abd-el-Krim's army now wander through the countryside begging for food.		
Nov. 23		Maxim Litvoniff of the Soviet Union states that the Soviet Union will not join the League of Nations, despite rumors to the contrary.	The French Army opens a new offensive in Syria while it opens an offensive to push the Druze rebels out of Lebanon.	The Mexican Biological Department states that Mexico City has the world's highest infant mortality rate due to many mothers drinking pulque, an alcoholic beverage.	
Nov. 24		Austria's Minister of Commerce announces that the country's foreign trade is improving and that its exports have increased.... Germany's foreign Minister, Gustav Streseman claims that the success of the Locarno Treaty avoided an anti-German alliance from forming.			Supiyalat, former Queen of Burma dies; she had been dethroned by the British in 1885 and was commemorated in the Rudyard Kipling poem, *Mandalay*.
Nov. 25	The League of Nations Committee to investigate the recent war between Greece and Bulgaria and will deliver its report of December 7.	The Polish legislature authorizes the government to seek a $102 million loan to be secured by government monopolies....Winston Churchill testifies in a law suit trying to determine claims of various inventors for their part in developing tanks during World War I for Britain.	French reports state that their troops have managed to force Druze rebels to retreat from villages they had captured; the French accuse the rebels of burning villages and killing women and children.	A new congress has been elected in Chile but shows little change from the last elected Congress.	The Japanese government announces that it will begin a program of tax reform that will give relief to the middle and lower classes.
Nov. 26		Russian exiles in Paris claim that Soviet reports of the harvest are exaggerated and that famine will occur....Visiting his home town of Xeres, Spain, General Primo de Rivera declares that Abd-el-Krim has been beaten and Spanish troops will leave Morocco in December.	Damascus is quiet following the imposition of martial law; French troops claim to have defeated the Druze rebels in a battle in which 300 rebels were killed....A League of Nations investigator in northern Iraq reports that the Turks have been committing atrocities against Christians in the Mosul area near the Turkish border.		Japan announces that it is beginning a new 10-year program that will pull up all American-made railroad rails in the country and replace them with rails of European manufacture....The King of Siam dies with no heir; his brother succeeds to the throne.
Nov. 27		Opposition parties in Hungary protest the restrictions placed on the number of Jews allowed in universities....In what is called the first of the important Fascist reforms, the Italian Chamber of Deputies has eliminated self-rule in 7,500 of Italy's 9,000 towns and cities; locally elected officials will be replaced by appointed officials....By a vote of 291 to 174, the German Reichstag approves the Locarno Treaty.	Fresh rebel activity is reported near the city of Homs in northern Syria; Christian refugees are going either to missionary stations or toward the ports in Lebanon; the French claim to have restored access to the Aleppo-Damascus railroad which had been in the hands of rebels....Turkey declares that it will not accept compulsory arbitration by the League of Nations over the Iraq-Turkish border.		Customs and autonomy talks between China and the outside powers are expected to continue despite the increased fighting throughout the country....Japan is acting as a mediator in the Soviet-Chinese deadlock on running a railroad through Chinese territory to the Soviet Union.

A	B	C	D	E
Includes developments that affect more than one world region, international organizations and important meetings of world leaders.	Includes all domestic and regional developments in Europe, including the Soviet Union.	Includes all domestic and regional developments in Africa and the Middle East.	Includes all domestic and regional developments in Latin America, the Caribbean, and Canada.	Includes all domestic and regional developments in Asian and Pacific nations (and colonies).

U.S. Politics & Social Issues	U.S. Foreign Policy & Affairs, Defense	U.S. Economy & Environment	Science, Technology & Nature	Culture, Leisure & Lifestyle	
In a bipartisan effort Congress is developing what is hoped to be a $300 million tax reduction....The Democratic Women of New York City announce that they will drive to have at least one woman in an important position in each department of New York City under the administration of the new mayor, Jimmy Walker....State representative Emmitt Williams of Georgia condemns the methods used to punish convicts in Georgia camps to include "sweatboxes" and hanging a prisoner by his arms.	Secretary of the Navy Curtis Wilbur sends letters of Commendation to Commander Rogers for his Pacific Flight earlier in the year and to Lieutenant Commander Richard Byrd for his flights in the MacMillan Polar expedition.	The New York Times estimates that over 15 million Americans own some shares of stock in American companies....The National Association of Real Estate Boards estimates that the year 1925 will record a $5 billion building program, the largest in U.S. history....Turkeys are now on sale in American markets for Thanksgiving, the most expensive are selling at 55 cents wholesale.	A German astronomer, Max Valier, plans to fly to the moon using a rocket based on the design of Robert Goddard of Clark University....The Chicago Museum of Natural History acquires the stuffed and mounted remains of two famous lions, the Maneaters of Tsavo....The Prorok expedition has found a prehistoric collection of jewels and small sculptures and a tomb and skeleton.	The Seaboard Air Line's new train, the Orange Blossom Special, leaves New York for its first trip reaching West Palm Beach, FL, in less than two days....Because colleges cannot satisfy the demand for football, a professional league is being formed with teams in cities such as Chicago, Canton, Green Bay, Buffalo, Cleveland, and Detroit....The Harvard and Yale football game is a tie at 0–0.	Nov. 21
Senator William Love, of Brookline, NH, condemns that state's revival of its policy of sentencing prisoners to solitary confinement.			Dr. Edward Trudeau is praised for his work in operating the Tuberculosis Sanitarium in Saranac, NY, which has been operating for 40 years....A new comet is discovered by Polish astronomers; this is the eighth comet to have been discovered this year, an unusually high total.		Nov. 22
Bryn Mawr College announces it will allow its students to smoke, overturning an 1897 ban....President Calvin Coolidge announces he will not intervene in the potential soft coal strike just as he has not intervened in the anthracite coal strike.	Billy Mitchell testifies, defending his charges against the aviation system, emphasizing that his comments were not aimed at individuals but the nation's aviation system as a whole.			The Federal Bureau of Education has compiled a list of 40 books that all children should read before the age of 16; the list includes Little Women, Robinson Crusoe, Uncle Remus, Tom Sawyer, Captains Courageous, and Howard Pyle's Merry Adventures of Robin Hood.	Nov. 23
President Calvin Coolidge acknowledges he received a letter from the United Mine Workers over a possible soft coal strike; he says he is displeased by what he considers the threatening tone of the letter.	In his court-martial Colonel Billy Mitchell states that both army and navy have failed in their responsibility to defend the country; defense witness Fiorello LaGuardia, a former aviator, declares that anti-aircraft guns would be inadequate to protect cities.	The Aunt Jemima Milling Company of St. Joseph, MO, is sold to Quaker Oats for $4 million.		Edgar White Burrill of Yale will broadcast the Longfellow poem, Evangeline, accompanied by an orchestra; schools are notified so that students can tune in and listen to the performance....Russian bass Feodor Chaliapin states he will not be returning to Moscow.	Nov. 24
A proclamation by the National Anti-Saloon League states that national prohibition is a total success.	The defense rests in the Billy Mitchell court-martial; the prosecution opens its case.				Nov. 25
The Ku Klux Klan burns crosses at Hammonton, NJ.			The New York Tuberculosis and Health Association advises people to sleep with their windows open to avoid contracting the disease.		Nov. 26
Governor Gifford Pinchot of Pennsylvania calls for a new round of discussions to end the anthracite coal strike; the mine operators respond by saying they cannot get their committee together to discuss the proposal.	The Secretary of War claims that the United States could raise an army of four million more rapidly and more cheaply than has ever been the case in any country.			The President of Wellesley College states that many students cannot read and write well and cannot adequately summarize a book they have just read....British conductor and composer, Eugene Goosens, accepts an invitation to conduct the Boston Symphony Orchestra.	Nov. 27

F	G	H	I	J
Includes campaigns, elections, federal-state relations, civil rights and liberties, crime, the judiciary, education, healthcare, poverty, urban affairs, and population.	Includes formation and debate of U.S. foreign and defense policies, veterans affairs, and defense spending. (Relations with specific foreign countries are usually found under the region concerned.)	Includes business, labor, agriculture, taxation, transportation, consumer affairs, monetary and fiscal policy, natural resources, pollution and industrial accidents.	Includes worldwide scientific, medical and technological developments, natural phenomena, U.S. weather and natural disasters.	Includes the arts, religion, scholarship, communications media, sports, entertainment, fashions, fads, and social life.

	World Affairs	Europe	Africa & The Middle East	The Americas	Asia & The Pacific
Nov. 28	League of Nation Commissioners investigating the recent war between Greece and Bulgaria have completed their work and are preparing a report blaming Greece for starting the war.	Sweden is using an underground cable to carry electricity generated there to Denmark....The Italian Chamber of Deputies passes a law confiscating the property of Italians abroad who criticize the government and removing their ability to vote....The city of Berlin announces that it will levy a tax on each dog equal to $17.50; the tax will be placed on all 205,000 dogs living in the city.	Ibn Saud and the British government reach an agreement on the frontiers between Arabia, Transjordan, and Iraq....British engineers are considering how they might be able to install irrigation reservoirs and canals in Iraq to use the Tigris and Euphrates Rivers....In Palestine, the introduction of crushing machinery has caused an upsurge in the olive oil production in the region.	Peru's President Augusto Leguia condemns Chile's attitude in the recent border disputes and praises General John Pershing for his role in settling the dispute....Canada's exports to the Soviet Union have now increased to $14 million a year.	The Japanese navy has ordered a destroyer to move from Port Arthur to the Chinese coast to protect Japanese nationals in China....In Beijing, a mob estimated to number 1,500 wrecks the homes of government officials as part of an anti-government protest which is said to have been instigated by Communists.... Opponents of giving the Philippines independence are suggesting that the question of granting it be settled by a nationwide referendum in the United States.
Nov. 29		Austria announces that the current wheat crop has allowed it to limit its wheat imports and that rye and oats will be exported....The German government is expressing optimism in light of the acceptance within the country of the Locarno Conference results and unexpectedly good foreign trade showing a decrease in imports and an increase in exports....Winston Churchill, current Chancellor of the Exchequer, warns in a speech against Socialists and Communists and says that despite their differences, they seek to destroy British society.	The Head of the Near East Organization has arrived in Beirut to see what can be done for an estimated 45,000 refugees that have been displaced because of the Druze revolt against the French in Syria....Christians in Syria are accusing the Druze tribesmen of committing atrocities against Christians.		Mohandas Gandhi is once again on a hunger strike against British rule in India; he is currently unable to speak; the fasting is supposed to continue until tomorrow.... Japanese railroads have decided to buy English rails instead of the American product to replace rails already in service....Riots continue in Beijing and an anti-Communist newspaper office is set on fire and destroyed.
Nov. 30		In Athens, women cannot go out in public if their skirts are more than one foot above the ground....Leon Trotsky returns early from convalescent leave and is believed by some to be wielding great power within the Soviet leadership.	Observers in Britain expect that Turkey will invade Iraq if the border in the Mosul region is not settled favorably to Turkey.... French troops in Syria are on the move in an effort to surround the Druze reels.		Japan and the Soviet Union complete three months of negotiations over exploiting oil and royalty payments for drilling in the Sakhalin Island oil field.
Dec. 1		Romania and the United States agree that Romania will pay its $44.5 million debt to the U.S. over a 62-year period....The Allied evacuation from the Rhineland which has been under Allied occupation continues; British, French, and Belgian troops are leaving with their places taken by German authorities.	Druze rebels attack a French detachment in a suburb of Damascus.	The Chilean government states that it will protest to the League of Nations that General John Pershing's actions in administering the border plebiscite are preventing a solution.	The U.S. Navy sends three destroyers from Manila to Shanghai because of the unrest in that city.
Dec. 2		The birth rate in Britain is now the lowest since the war at 18.8 per 1,000, slightly below France's birth rate of 18.9 per 1,000....General Primo de Rivera resigns as dictator of Spain; the Directory is being replaced by a civil government with de Rivera as premier.	Anticipating fierce fighting to keep Damascus, the French authorities have warned foreign consulates that there will probably be heavy bombardments during the fighting....Modernization in Turkey progresses although with some opposition: a man attacking the government's policy of outlawing the fez and wearing western-style hats has been arrested and executed.	Chile disclaims its earlier accusations of obstructionism by General John Pershing in the border dispute.	
Dec. 3		A secret tribunal in Romania has tried and convicted 85 peasants accused of assisting Soviet cross-border raids last year; they are sentenced to between two and 20 years....The League of Nations finds Greece guilty of provoking the war with Bulgaria and orders it to pay a fine of $219,000.	A two-pronged attack by the French against Druze rebels in Syria has had the effect of driving them back although they appear to have had some reinforcements.		According to the official Japanese census, the population is 59,736,794, an increase of four million in the last five years.
Dec. 4		The British dirigible *R-31* successfully launches and then takes on a plane in mid-air by using a trapeze-like device.		The Ecuadorian government denies reports that it has asked the United States to mediate a border dispute with Colombia.	

A	B	C	D	E
Includes developments that affect more than one world region, international organizations and important meetings of world leaders.	*Includes all domestic and regional developments in Europe, including the Soviet Union.*	*Includes all domestic and regional developments in Africa and the Middle East.*	*Includes all domestic and regional developments in Latin America, the Caribbean, and Canada.*	*Includes all domestic and regional developments in Asian and Pacific nations (and colonies).*

U.S. Politics & Social Issues	U.S. Foreign Policy & Affairs, Defense	U.S. Economy & Environment	Science, Technology & Nature	Culture, Leisure & Lifestyle	
The anthracite coal strike which is now entering its fourth month has cost the nation an estimated $260 million and shows no signs of being resolved.	The army now is linked by radio, using a network of 12 major and 60 auxiliary stations that handle traffic of 800 messages a day.	New York banker Otto Kahn states that he believes that the next six months will be very prosperous for the United States, with only farmers not sharing in the general prosperity.	The *New York Times* reviews a book entitled *Almost Human* by Robert Yerkes which discusses the intelligence of baboons, monkeys, and gorillas....Doctors in Worcester, MA, launch an appeal by radio to find blood donors for a seriously injured woman; a satisfactory donor is found in less than four hours.	A new breed of dog, the Schnauzer, is becoming very popular in America....Army beats Navy, 10–3 in the annual game before a crowd of 60,000 at the Polo Grounds in New York....Charles Scribner's Sons is publishing a new 32-volume South Seas Edition of the works of Robert Louis Stevenson, costing 90 cents a volume....The American Auto Association states that it will fight the proliferation of speed traps as a means of gathering revenue for towns.	Nov. 28
The United Mine Workers announce that they are willing to participate in talks with the mine operators according to an agreement that they will work at 1923 wages leaving a decision for an increase to be settled later; the mine operators have not yet commented on the proposal.	The war department reports that the death rate for soldiers fell in 1924 with a rate of 3.83 per thousand that year as opposed to 3.91 in 1923 which was the first year the rate had dropped below 4 percent.				Nov. 29
In Chicago, 200 gravediggers go on strike demanding $6 for an eight-hour day....Governor Gifford Pinchot expresses disappointment but makes no further comment upon receiving word that the mine operators have refused his proposed solution which the United Mine Workers have tentatively accepted.	Senator William Borah states that he will fight the United States joining a World Court that is associated with the League of Nations but supports joining it as it is now constituted....The war department is constructing an airplane it claims will be able to climb to 50,000 feet.	Gasoline prices in the northeast are 17 cents a gallon wholesale, a rise of 1 cent since the previous week....Miami, FL, is flooded after 14 inches of rain in 12 hours.	The Prorok expedition arrives safely at a French settlement after passing through one of the worst sandstorms in years.	A group of 11 original letters written by Benjamin Franklin sells for $2,900.	Nov. 30
	Billy Mitchell's defense challenges one of the judges at the court-martial for bias but is overruled by the court.	There were 1672 business failures in the United States in November; the total thus far in 1925 is 19,332....Secretary Commerce Herbert Hoover states that there is a need for more purely scientific research that is not industrially based.	The Prorok expedition discovers what it claims are the bones of Tim Hinan, the goddess and ancestor of the Taureg tribesmen; the skeleton is covered with jewels and bracelets.	*The Best Bad Man*, starring Tom Mix opens in New York.	Dec. 1
Most people in the anthracite coal mining region believe that the miners' strike will last all winter and be the longest on record; many coal miners are going to Pittsburgh in an effort to find work.		A shipment of 4,000 tons of anthracite coal arrives in Boston from Germany....The shipping season on the Great Lakes ends with the highest total transported on record: 98 million tons.			Dec. 2
The United Committee for Prohibition Enforcement, which represents 26 prohibition organizations, criticizes President Calvin Coolidge for not doing enough to enforce the Dry Laws.	Former Secretary of the Navy, Josephus Daniels, suggests that the Departments of War and the Navy be disbanded and replaced with a single Department of Defense....Major General Amos Fries, head of the Army Chemical Warfare Service states that there is no truth to the stories that tuberculosis results from having been exposed to poison gas.		Dr. William McGovern of Oxford, who set out in May to explore the headwaters of the Amazon, is believed to be lost; no word has been received since August 20.		Dec. 3
The population in Florida has expanded so quickly that many people there cannot find homes; approximately 600,000 are living in camps throughout the state posing a health problem for the state.			A Czechoslovakian archaeological expedition in western Turkey has found the remains of a temple in the ancient city of Kyme.	George Gershwin's "Piano Concerto in F" premiers with the composer playing with the New York Symphony Orchestra.	Dec. 4
F Includes campaigns, elections, federal-state relations, civil rights and liberties, crime, the judiciary, education, healthcare, poverty, urban affairs, and population.	**G** Includes formation and debate of U.S. foreign and defense policies, veterans affairs, and defense spending. (Relations with specific foreign countries are usually found under the region concerned.)	**H** Includes business, labor, agriculture, taxation, transportation, consumer affairs, monetary and fiscal policy, natural resources, pollution and industrial accidents.	**I** Includes worldwide scientific, medical and technological developments, natural phenomena, U.S. weather and natural disasters.	**J** Includes the arts, religion, scholarship, communications media, sports, entertainment, fashions, fads, and social life.	

	World Affairs	Europe	Africa & The Middle East	The Americas	Asia & The Pacific
Dec. 5	The League of Nations prepares to discuss the recent conflict between Bulgaria and Greece; complicating matters is the role of the Macedonians who claim autonomy.	Germany's Chancellor Hans Luther resigns, leaving President Paul von Hindenburg to select a new cabinet....Benito Mussolini addressing an education group demands that fascism be taught in all schools....Reports from the Soviet Union describe how large numbers of homeless children are starving to death or else wandering about in packs "like wolves."	American destroyers USS *Coghlan* and USS *Lamson* are withdrawn from the Beirut area as they are no longer needed to protect American citizens....France claims that it has cleared Lebanon of Druze rebels although Damascus may once again be under attack....Turkey announces that it will soon be using the Gregorian calendar.	The Mayan city of Chichen Itza is being restored by several American organizations working with the Mexican government.	A former American teacher in China, Raymond Rich states that the influence of the Communists in China has grown substantially and that there is a great deal of distrust of America....Imports into the Philippines from the United States have increased by 50 times in the first 25 years of American rule there according to the American Chamber of Commerce.
Dec. 6	The French Prime Minster suggests that navies be included in the upcoming disarmament talks now being discussed.	Eamon De Valera gives a speech against the partition of northern Ireland and the Irish Free State, calling it a dismemberment of Ireland....The city of Berlin has recorded 9,921 more deaths than births in the past seven years; in 1913 there were 27,000 more births than deaths.	Although heavy fighting continues in the area around Damascus, Syria, fighting in Lebanon has ceased....American Red Cross efforts in Lebanon are encountering great difficulties; estimates are that 30,000 people were driven from their homes in addition to 105,000 refugees in Syria before the Druze revolt.		Japanese reports sate that Chinese General Chang Tso-Lin has surrendered and attempting to make peace with other warlords.
Dec. 7	It is understood that the Nobel Peace prize for 1926, which carries a cash award of $160,000 will be awarded to British Foreign Minister Austen Chamberlain and French Premier Aristide Briand for their work at the Locarno Conference.	Opinion in Britain is thus far opposed to any restrictions on naval arms in coming disarmament talks....A group of 15 executioners from the time of the Czar in Russia are executed by the Soviets for having killed 500 revolutionaries....Germany's President Paul von Hindenburg is constructing a new coalition cabinet to rule Germany in the wake of the resignation of Chancellor Hans Luther.	Egypt and Italy agree on a new border with the Oasis of Jarabub going to Italy and a portion of the coast going to Egypt.		
Dec. 8	The League of Nations formally invites the United States to the Disarmament Conference as well as asking Germany and the Soviet Union to attend.	Members of the Liberal Party running for Parliament state that they support the proposed land reforms of former Prime Minister David Lloyd George which would result in increased availability of land....Yugoslavia's government has arrested a group of 20 anti-government conspirators in southern Serbia.	Druze rebels in Syria are said to be planning for a large attack near Damascus while French forces are preparing to crush the rebellion.	The Spanish government announces that it will open an air route from Seville to Buenos Aries, Argentina.	
Dec. 9		As a result of elections held in November the Agrarian Party receives a majority and forms a new government in Czechoslovakia.	French newspapers state that American oil interests are behind Turkey's efforts to incorporate the Mosul region of northern Iraq into its borders.		Despite denials of involvement, Japanese military units are active in Manchuria, busy securing area s near Japanese-owned businesses; at the same time they are providing financial support to General Chang Tso-Lin.
Dec. 10		Cambridge beats Oxford in the 50th annual rugby game....Manuel Teixera Gomes, President of Portugal resigns for reasons of ill health....The President of the German Reichsbank, Hjalmar Schacht, states that America's interest in Europe is based on good motives and not just materialistic objectives.	Turkey states it will not continue League of Nations discussions on northern Iraq and leaves the Conference.		American soldiers are assigned to guard the train line between Beijing and Tientsin as opposing armies are only 15 miles apart in this region and part of the track has been blown up....The Soviet Union is preparing a protest against increased Japanese forces in Manchuria.
Dec. 11		The President of Austria, having been called, "an old jackass," by a former Finance Minister challenges him to a duel....While introducing a law that will recognize only the Fascist Labor Union, Benito Mussolini states that Italy is "in a permanent state of war."	There is a rumor that northern Iraq could be administered directly by the League of Nations without British control under the Mandate.	Restrictions have been removed from Cuban sugar mills and sugar exports increase.	Americans aboard the international train between Beijing and Tientsin are fired upon by warring factional armies.

A	B	C	D	E
Includes developments that affect more than one world region, international organizations and important meetings of world leaders.	*Includes all domestic and regional developments in Europe, including the Soviet Union.*	*Includes all domestic and regional developments in Africa and the Middle East.*	*Includes all domestic and regional developments in Latin America, the Caribbean, and Canada.*	*Includes all domestic and regional developments in Asian and Pacific nations (and colonies).*

U.S. Politics & Social Issues	U.S. Foreign Policy & Affairs, Defense	U.S. Economy & Environment	Science, Technology & Nature	Culture, Leisure & Lifestyle	
Six states, California, Wyoming, Utah, Nevada, Colorado, and New Mexico are asking Congress to approve construction of the proposed Boulder Dam.	In the Billy Mitchell court-martial, Admiral Edward Eberle denies that he forced the commander of the airship *Shenandoah* to fly but left departure up to the commander's discretion.		Count de Prorok returns to Paris with, among other relics, what is believed to be the oldest sculpture in the world, the so-called "Libyan Venus."	Polish novelist and poet, Wladslaw Reymont, winner of the 1924 Nobel Prize for Literature dies at the age of 57.	**Dec. 5**
				W.P.G. Myers wins the flapjack eating contest in Groton, SD, eating 43 five-inch pancakes....Former college football star, Red Grange makes his first professional appearance in New York, playing for the Chicago Bears in their victory over the Giants; his pay for the day is approximately $30,000....Richard Wagner's son, Siegfried, condemns jazz as a "barbaric noise."	**Dec. 6**
At the Farmer's Convention in Chicago, President Calvin Coolidge urges the imposition of tariffs to protect American farmers....Boston Mayor, James Michael Curley demands an apology from Reverend John Haynes of New York who said that Boston had been dominated by Catholics and disgraced by them....A new radical political magazine, entitled, *The New Masses* will soon appear it is announced; Contributors will include Eugene O'Neil, Van Wyck Brooks, and Sherwood Anderson.	A witness for the prosecution in the Billy Mitchell court-martial takes issue with Mitchell's opinions stating that an invading force would have to have a navy three times larger than the U.S. Navy.	The airliner, *Miss Keylargo City* takes off from New York City on its first voyage to Miami.	Charles Marvin of the Weather Bureau states that the government withholds funds from the weather service when more efforts should be made toward expanding weather reporting for aviation.	The first opera, *Orfeo*, composed by Claudio Monteverdi in 1607 is produced at Oxford University; critics state that they find the music to be "surprisingly competent," despite its age.	**Dec. 7**
	Generals Ely and Allen, testifying for the prosecution in the Billy Mitchell court-martial state that the air service was not singled out for economies but all branches of the army had to undergo reductions.		The U.S. Weather Bureau and the Smithsonian Institution are engaged in a controversy concerning the degree to which the sun affects the weather....The Bureau states that it has no effect while the Smithsonian states that solar activity to include sunspot activity does affect the earth's atmosphere....In Denmark, the fossil of a prehistoric whale has been found 24 miles from the coast....French aviators state that dirigibles and other lighter-than-air craft will never be replaced by airplanes.	American poet Carl Sandburg gives a recital of his poems at Pelham Manor, NY....The British novelist, Cosmo Hamilton, states that the day of reading is over; he says he will be broadcasting one of his own books, abridged to 15 minutes in length over the radio....A study conducted by 160 engineering schools reports that 60 percent of all engineering students do not complete the courses.	**Dec. 8**
	The War Department is cutting the pay of the regular Army by $487,469 which will mean the elimination of part of the lower enlisted ranks or a reduction in the number of senior sergeants.				**Dec. 9**
Samuel Browne, an African-American letter carrier files a suit for $100,000 against neighbors in the Castleton Hill district of Staten Island, NY, for attempting to drive him out of the neighborhood; he and his a family are the only African Americans in the area.	Senator William Borah, Chairman of the Senate Committee on Foreign Relations offers three bills: one would recognize the Soviet Union, one would repeal restrictions on aliens who had sought to overthrow the U.S. government, and one would provide a means to assist aliens regain property seized by the United States.			The English poet Alfred Noyes speaks to students at Princeton, telling them that formlessness in poetry will eventually pass away.	**Dec. 10**
The Boston and Maine Railroad receives a court injunction to prevent it from reducing its work force in New Hampshire....Relief workers retrieve the bodies of 51 miners who died in an mine explosion in Alabama.					**Dec. 11**

F	**G**	**H**	**I**	**J**
Includes campaigns, elections, federal-state relations, civil rights and liberties, crime, the judiciary, education, healthcare, poverty, urban affairs, and population.	*Includes formation and debate of U.S. foreign and defense policies, veterans affairs, and defense spending. (Relations with specific foreign countries are usually found under the region concerned.)*	*Includes business, labor, agriculture, taxation, transportation, consumer affairs, monetary and fiscal policy, natural resources, pollution and industrial accidents.*	*Includes worldwide scientific, medical and technological developments, natural phenomena, U.S. weather and natural disasters.*	*Includes the arts, religion, scholarship, communications media, sports, entertainment, fashions, fads, and social life.*

	World Affairs	Europe	Africa & The Middle East	The Americas	Asia & The Pacific
Dec. 12	Latvian police have uncovered a white slavery ring in which young women from Russia are being transported and sold throughout Central and Latin America.	The French government opposes any attempts to ban submarines.... Women in Italy who are war widows and mothers gain the right to vote in municipal elections.... Former British Prime Minister David Lloyd George begins a campaign for land reform to make it easier to obtain....The Spanish Directory under the leadership of General Primo de Rivera is planning to allow greater autonomy to towns and cities in the country.... Two young girls are reported to have been eaten by wolves in Bosnia-Herzegovina.	The capture of Medina in Arabia by Ibn Saud's Wahhabis is looked on as a possible threat to Europeans in the region, especially in Transjordan, Syria, Iraq, and Palestine....According to the World Zionist Organization the Jewish population in Palestine had doubled since World War I and now stands at 133,000....The Turkish government has banned all dervish groups, approximately 200, in the country	The Palace of Justice in Santo Domingo, Dominican Republic, is destroyed by fire....Imperial Oil has organized a new oil company that will begin drilling for oil in Alberta.	A group of 20 Americans on a train are caught in the middle of fighting between Beijing and Tientsin, China....Japan's Foreign Minister states that there is a significant military presence in Manchuria, enough to protect Japanese interests there....Having a license to carry a pistol is now seen as a status symbol in the Philippines.
Dec. 13		A Balkan defensive pact originally proposed by Greece is not meeting with favorable reception as several countries to include Bulgaria, Macedonia, and Romania serious disagreements on several issues.... Germany's shipping has grown to 15,245,116 tons for the year so far, exceeding shipping tonnage in 1913.	The Turkish government has proposed that northern Iraq by made into a neutral demilitarized zone.	Delegates from 20 nations meet in New York City for the tenth annual session of the Pan American Commercial Congress.	
Dec. 14			Druze rebels raid French posts in Syria near the city of Homs.		
Dec. 15	The League of Nations is assembling a preparatory committee that will plan an economic conference to be held in 1926.	People in Britain and Germany are able to listen to jazz orchestras over the radio from New York and Pittsburgh....Because of treaty restrictions resulting from the war, the German Dornier aircraft manufacturing company announces it will move operations to Switzerland....British unemployment decreases but the nation still has 1,161,000 without jobs.... A new German Cabinet, this one containing four former Chancellors has been formed.	Heavy fighting continues in Syria with substantial damage from artillery shelling reported in Damascus....Britain will continue to administer the Mosul territory which according to the League of Nations will become part of northern Iraq....Estonia's General Johan Laidoner, who has been investigating in northern Iraq for the League completes his report which states that the Turks have committed atrocities against the Christians in the area.	The total value of Canada's agricultural crops this year is estimated at over $1 billion, the largest on record.	Additional Japanese troops are sent to Manchuria to protect the rail lines against damage by opposing warlords.
Dec. 16		Britain announces that it does not anticipate war between it and Turkey over the border determined by the League of nations but it will honor all of its obligations to both Iraq and the League regardless of what happens....France denies that it has signed an accord with the Soviet Union although it has been conducting some diplomatic discussions....The Italian Senate votes in press censorship without affording any legal appeals to the process.	Sources in Turkey report that country is seeking assistance from the Soviet Union in the event of a war over the Turkish-Iraqi border.	The Canadian government announces it will join in the Pan-American Commercial Congress.... The Mexican government denies all accusations that Soviet activities have been significant in South and central America and especially Mexico.	
Dec. 17		The new German Cabinet that has been assembled under Erich Koch must be built again as Socialists within the cabinet will not cooperate with other members of the coalition....The Bulgarian government is planning a Christmas amnesty for political prisoners.... The British Navy launches the warship HMS *Rodney*....Henri Haeberlin is elected as President of Switzerland and will assume office in 1926.	In answer to a question in the House of Commons, British Prime Minister Stanley Baldwin states that Britain will stay in Iraq in its Mandatory role for only a short time....Syrians appeal to U.S. President Calvin Coolidge to assist them against the French invaders.		The city of Mukden in Manchuria is occupied by Japanese soldiers in order to protect Japanese and other foreign lives and interests.... It is now eight days since the last train passed on the Beijing-Tientsin rail line; Beijing is effectively cut off from the outside world.

A	B	C	D	E
Includes developments that affect more than one world region, international organizations and important meetings of world leaders.	Includes all domestic and regional developments in Europe, including the Soviet Union.	Includes all domestic and regional developments in Africa and the Middle East.	Includes all domestic and regional developments in Latin America, the Caribbean, and Canada.	Includes all domestic and regional developments in Asian and Pacific nations (and colonies).

U.S. Politics & Social Issues	U.S. Foreign Policy & Affairs, Defense	U.S. Economy & Environment	Science, Technology & Nature	Culture, Leisure & Lifestyle	
A mine workers meeting held to discuss proposals made by some business men is conducted without any substantial progress toward resolving the anthracite coal strike.	A defense for the prosecution in the Billy Mitchell court-martial disputes Mitchell's statements about the defense plans for Hawaii in 1923....The defense in the Mitchell court-martial scores when a witness states that even 10,000 anti-aircraft guns could not adequately defend Washington from aerial attack.		Pollution on along the mid-Atlantic U.S. coast is becoming a serious problem, resulting in diminished numbers of shad, sturgeon, and bluefish....The Department of Agriculture reports that there are now 553,000 radios on farms and that 24 Agricultural Colleges operate radio stations.		Dec. 12
W. W. Inglis, Chairman of the Mine Operators Wage Negotiating Committee denies reports that the mine owners and operators have not been honest in their recent financial statements.	A special committee of the House of representatives reports that America does not yet understand the importance of air power and that, at best, the United States ranks third in the world.			The British Museum has acquired two chapter's from the first draft of the novel *Persuasion*, making it the owner of the only known Jane Austen manuscript in existence.	Dec. 13
In his continuing efforts to bring an end to the anthracite coal strike, Governor Gifford Pinchot of Pennsylvania asks the mayors of 83 towns and cities to meet; the Mine operators and owners state that they will not be "stampeded" by any of the Governor's efforts....Robert LaFollette, Jr., a reform Republican has been admitted into the ranks of the Republican regulars and receives three committee assignments.	The British government pays an installment of $92 million of its war debt to the United States....U.S. Congressman Hamilton Fish of New York states that Benito Mussolini must not be allowed to create Fascist centers throughout the United States as he has stated he would do.	The Ford Motor Company signs a $6 million contract to sell 10,000 Ford tractors with plows and spare part to the Soviet government....Standard Oil of New Jersey announces that it will soon be acquiring Humble Oil Company.		The new Madison Square Garden formally opens tonight featuring a hockey game between New York and the Montreal Canadiens.	Dec. 14
			Britain's Air Ministry announces it will abandon wooden aircraft and will begin to construct all-metal aircraft; the conversion is expected to cost the equivalent of $20 million.	A monument to Balto the sled dog who brought the serum to Nome earlier this year is unveiled in Central Park; Balto is present at the ceremony.	Dec. 15
		Gasoline price wars are ending and several oil companies are raising the price for gas....Wisconsin will soon be linked into an electrical power system that will extend through eight states....Arrangements have been finalized to merge two typewriter companies, the L.C. Smith Company and the Corona Company.		Arne Borg and Johnnie Weismuller set new swimming records for the 400 free-style and 100-yard freestyle.	Dec. 16
At least 511 people have died from poisoning as a result of drinking illegal alcohol this year; since Prohibition, deaths from industrial and poisoned alcohol have increased significantly.	Colonel Billy Mitchell is convicted for insubordination and conduct prejudicial to good order and military discipline and suspended from holding all rank and pay for a period of five years....Now that his court-martial is over, Colonel Mitchell has been summoned to testify at the navy's inquiry into the *Shenandoah* crash.		Archaeologists near Jaffa, Palestine, discover a mausoleum with a hall, two chambers, and a niche.	John L. Griffith, athletic director of the Western Conference states that through its greed, professional football has ruined any chances it had to become a major element in this country; professional football, he says, "had died."... The Division of Manuscripts of the Library if Congress announces that after an extensive search of 15 years, it has found the papers of President Chester Arthur.	Dec. 17

F	G	H	I	J
Includes campaigns, elections, federal-state relations, civil rights and liberties, crime, the judiciary, education, healthcare, poverty, urban affairs, and population.	*Includes formation and debate of U.S. foreign and defense policies, veterans affairs, and defense spending. (Relations with specific foreign countries are usually found under the region concerned.)*	*Includes business, labor, agriculture, taxation, transportation, consumer affairs, monetary and fiscal policy, natural resources, pollution and industrial accidents.*	*Includes worldwide scientific, medical and technological developments, natural phenomena, U.S. weather and natural disasters.*	*Includes the arts, religion, scholarship, communications media, sports, entertainment, fashions, fads, and social life.*

	World Affairs	Europe	Africa & The Middle East	The Americas	Asia & The Pacific
Dec. 18		The 14th Communist Party Conference begins....On their appearance in the Czechoslovak Chamber of Deputies, the new cabinet is pelted by heavy bundles of paper and told to resign.	The French begin construction of a number of fortified stations that will surround Damascus and protect it from Druze attacks....A force of 2,000 French soldiers is currently advancing on the Syrian City of Homs, an important position in French defenses....Italy has destroyed Bergal, the capital of the Sultanate of Mijertins in Italian Somaliland as a reprisal for the killing of two soldiers.		The Burmese government is buying slaves from their owners in an effort to stamp out slavery within the country....The Warlord Feng Yu-hsiang is reportedly losing battles despite aid received from the Soviet Union.
Dec. 19		The French government has approved a protocol to be used in discussing trade agreements with Germany....Several Jewish groups in Hungary state that they do not want outside interference concerning Hungarian laws which have created limits on how many Jews can attend universities....Benito Mussolini's latest plans to develop a new Italian Empire are receive approval from both the King of Italy and the Vatican....The Soviet Union announces that it will accept the invitation from the League of Nations to participate in the coming disarmament conference.	The state of the Sphinx in Egypt is causing great concern; engineers surveying the statue have state that erosion may cause the head to fall off....News of Northern Iraq's award to Britain as part of its mandatory responsibility brings a mixed response in Britain; the possibility of access to oil is cheered by some while others believe that Iraq's administration is a needless expense.... Indications from Turkey are that there is a diminished likelihood of Turkey invading the Mosul region of Iraq.	The Panamanian government has closed one of its Atlantic seaports, Puerta Obaldia closed to foreign trade....All America Cables, Inc., announces its plans to add 2,000 miles of additional cables to link Cuba and Panama, Peru and Chile at a cost of $1.5 million.	The Chinese government is requesting a new conference to demand equality with all nations and a stop to extraterritoriality, by which outside nations have controlled other Chinese government and finances.
Dec. 20		Josef Stalin predicts a peaceful assimilation between the Soviet Union and the capitalist countries.	King Ali of the Hedjaz who has been under siege in the Arabian City of Jeddah, has surrendered to the Wahhabis and will abdicate the throne.		Part of the anti-foreign feeling in China is an increase in anti-Christian sentiments; reports are being heard that there will be demonstrations planned for Christmas Day....Increased fighting breaks out again in Manchuria as rival Chinese factions seek to control the country.
Dec. 21		Police in Budapest arrest a former government Minister and other individuals on the suspicion of being Communists....The House of Commons votes to accept the award of Mosul as part of the Mandate Britain administers in Iraq....During the Communist Party Congress, arguments over the suppression of rich farmers (kulaks) becomes a point of contention; Gregory Zinoviev shakes his fist at Stalin.	The Turkish government as part of its westernization program is continuing to mete out punishment to me who continue to wear the fez instead of western hats; in a village near Trebizond on the Black Sea, two men are hanged for not abandoning the fez and several others have been sentenced to hard labor....French authorities express pleasure at the award of Mosul to Britain, stating it will make their situation in Syria easier.		During a fight in Tokyo among contract laborers, 1,000 police are called in to restore order; 100 of the laborers are shot and several killed.
Dec. 22		Germany reports that its trade balance for December will be favorable for the first time in 18 months.	Turkey and the Soviet Union sign a peace past in which each country promises not to attack the other for three years.	The Brazilian state of Sao Paulo has asked the legislature for a loan to be used to protect the price of coffee....Officials predict that Peru will win the plebiscite over its border with Chile but that Chile will not honor the agreement.	
Dec. 23			The French government lists its casualties in its Moroccan war this year: 10,199 dead and wounded.		20 fishing boats carrying a total of 150 fishermen are reported lost off the coast of Northern Japan in the wake of a severe storm.
Dec. 24		Albania makes good on its promises (such as honoring U.S. passports) which they made in return for recognition by the United States; Albania will now receive Most Favored nation trading status....Pope Pius XI closes the Holy Year 1925 in a ceremony before 75,000 onlookers in St. Peter's Basilica.	French officials are now negotiating an armistice in the conflict with rebels in Syria....An article in The New York Times describes Gertrude Bell, an Englishwoman, as the "right-hand man" of King Feisal of Iraq.	The Mexican Chamber of Deputies accepts Senate amendments to a bill defining property rights of foreigners in Mexico.	The Chinese government in Canton is protesting Japanese involvement in the Chinese Civil War.

A	B	C	D	E
Includes developments that affect more than one world region, international organizations and important meetings of world leaders.	Includes all domestic and regional developments in Europe, including the Soviet Union.	Includes all domestic and regional developments in Africa and the Middle East.	Includes all domestic and regional developments in Latin America, the Caribbean, and Canada.	Includes all domestic and regional developments in Asian and Pacific nations (and colonies).

U.S. Politics & Social Issues	U.S. Foreign Policy & Affairs, Defense	U.S. Economy & Environment	Science, Technology & Nature	Culture, Leisure & Lifestyle	
			Edwin Belin, announces to members of the Society of French Photography that he has succeeded in finding a solution to the problem of "television," giving a demonstration of his instrument, however, his invention is not a "radio television" device.	The Mayor of Atlantic City states that it is likely that the Miss America pageant will not be held in the city next year....Violinist Josef Szigeti performs at Aeloian Hall in a concert of pieces by Bach, Tartini, Mozart, Bloch, and Prokofiev.	**Dec. 18**
Lindsay Coleman, an African American, is lynched in Clarksdale, Mississippi, moments after having been acquitted of murdering a local plantation store owner.... Barnard College reports that of its 987 woman students, 125 are currently enrolled in government and politics courses.	U.S. Congressman Sol Bloom of New York proposes to lift immigration restrictions in some cases to help ease the critical shortage of domestic servants in the United States....The guilty verdict in the Billy Mitchell court-martial is attacked by Congressman Tilman of Arkansas; he demands that President Calvin Coolidge mitigate the sentence....Admiral William Moffett of the navy reports that the number of naval fliers is far below what it should be.	According to the Engineer News Record, 270,000 buildings were built in 1925 for a total value of $5.61 billion which breaks all previous records....It is estimated that approximately $350 million of business was done by sales of radios, and advertising during the year 1925....In Colorado, the First National Bank of Rifle closes, the sixth bank to do so in Colorado in three days.	An expedition to be sent by the U.S. National Museum in Washington will be using aircraft in New Guinea to search for a "lost race" of pygmies...."British writer H. G. Wells states that he sees no future in air travel, that it is unpunctual and untrustworthy.	American Kees Hermsen has purchased a painting just authenticated to have been painted by Pieter Brueghal; the painting, Peasants Wedding Feast, will be soon shipped to New York....The New York Times reviews Robert Benchley's latest comic novel, Pluck and Luck....David Sarnoff, Vice President and General Manager of the Radio Corporation of America predicts that in the future, radio will not just have established stars but will search the country for new voices in entertainment....Pola Negri's latest film, A Woman of the World opens in New York.	**Dec. 19**
		Railroads in the United States set several records in 1925 including the greatest freight traffic in history, the greatest single amount of traffic in any month ever (October), and the greatest amount of railroad taxes paid ($360 million)....A new air route is to be opened in Florida between Tampa, Fort Myers, and Miami, starting on January 1, 1926.			**Dec. 20**
President Calvin Coolidge sends a message of gratitude to the 125,000 surviving Civil War veterans.	A meeting between the coal miners and the operators and owners is out off; the strike continues.... A congressional committee recommends that improvements be made to the naval base at Pearl Harbor, Hawaii.	All indications are that 1925 will be an excellent Christmas shopping season....The "back home pilgrimage" across the country begins today.	British aviation engineers and designers are conducting several experiments including the development of an automatic pilot for aircraft of Imperial Airways.	In Indiana, 3,000 physicians endorse basketball when accompanied by physical examinations.	**Dec. 21**
	The navy's investigation of the Shenandoah crash of September is completed....The board states that it was "inevitable" and that the commander of the craft did everything possible to try and save it.				**Dec. 22**
Vice President Charles Dawes meets with the Senate pages and advises them not to swear, drink, or smoke.		Stockholders approve the merger of the Jell-O Company with the Postum Cereal Company.			**Dec. 23**
President Calvin Coolidge lights the White House Christmas Tree.... Sheriff S. W. Glass of Coahoma County, three deputies, and five other men are indicted for the lynching of Lindsey Coleman after Coleman had been acquitted in a murder trial.					**Dec. 24**

F	G	H	I	J
Includes campaigns, elections, federal-state relations, civil rights and liberties, crime, the judiciary, education, healthcare, poverty, urban affairs, and population.	Includes formation and debate of U.S. foreign and defense policies, veterans affairs, and defense spending. (Relations with specific foreign countries are usually found under the region concerned.)	Includes business, labor, agriculture, taxation, transportation, consumer affairs, monetary and fiscal policy, natural resources, pollution and industrial accidents.	Includes worldwide scientific, medical and technological developments, natural phenomena, U.S. weather and natural disasters.	Includes the arts, religion, scholarship, communications media, sports, entertainment, fashions, fads, and social life.

	World Affairs	Europe	Africa & The Middle East	The Americas	Asia & The Pacific
Dec. 25		Imperial Airways announces that it will regularly fly night freight between Paris and London starting January 15, 1926.			Six American destroyers with U.S. Marines on board leave Manila and sail to China to keep order there....Severe earth tremors are recorded in Persia.
Dec. 26	There is discussion at the Vatican about holding an Ecumenical Conference, the first to be held since 1870....Spain and Portugal announce that they will submit their dispute concerning rights to the Guadiana River to an international tribunal at the Hague.	Soviet authorities admit that they have not been able to export as much grain as planned largely because villagers are hoarding their harvests....An amnesty for 10,000 Bulgarian political prisoners and exiles has been proposed....Work subsidized largely by American donors is begun to rebuild the Library of Louvain, Belgium, destroyed by Germany in 1914....Elections in the German state of Prussia indicate that the pro-Monarchist faction is not as large as expected.	Druze rebels in Syria have accepted peace proposals offered by French authorities....France and Spain announce they have no intention of opening discussions with Abd-el-Krim and that the war in Morocco is virtually over....A clause in the new Turkish Civil Code allows women in Turkey to have divorce rights equal to those of men.	The Bermuda Parliament decides to keep its ban on motor vehicles....The government of Peru will exile several Army officers involved in a plot against the government.	Reports from Japan indicate that as civil war in China has become more desperate and bitter, the numbers of executions in the wake of battles is likely to grow....Muslims in India state that they will assist Turkey if it goes to war with Britain....The Chinese city of Tientsin is currently quiet; non-Chinese troops guarding the foreign quarter have been withdrawn....Japan announces it may withdraw some of its troops from China as an economy measure.
Dec. 27		Italian newspapers state that the upcoming disarmament talks will be of no practical value, that Italy wants more armaments, and will not accept any agreement that leaves other nations with military power superior to Italy....The balance of trade in Germany for this past November shows a significant decline in imports....French Fascists declare that they wish to combine in a "Latin Bloc" with Italy that will rule with Benito Mussolini as a Caesar.	In the background behind the Turkish-British border discussions is the belief in the west that Turkey and the Soviets have concluded a secret military treaty which the Turks could call on if needed in their dispute over the Iraqi border.	Erath tremors are felt in several places in Mexico including Vera Cruz.	The Chinese government criticizes Japan's involvement in Manchuria; the Customs and autonomy conferences between China and the outside powers will continue.
Dec. 28		Rumania's Crown Prince Carol renounces his right to the succession to the throne in favor of his son, Michael....The British Communist Party states that it favors home rule and independence for India....The French government is indicating unease over disarmament talks and wants to know the probable attitudes of the Soviet Union, Germany, and the United States.	There is optimism that Turkey, which has softened its stand on the Iraq-Turkish border dispute, and Britain may soon reach an agreement....Reports from Morocco indicate that more tribesmen who had been part of Abd-el-Krim's forces are now leaving their units and returning home.	The White Engineering Corporation announces it will begin a $30 million project to build an irrigation system in Mexico....The Mexican government indicates it will loosen some restriction on foreign ownership of land.	Soviet troops have attacked and captured an Afghan outpost near the Russian border; British officials indicate they are alarmed that this may lead to more hostilities.
Dec. 29		The Austrian government's statistical bureau notes that since divorce laws have been liberalized there is one divorce for every eight marriages (earlier the ration was 1 to 70); at the same time marriages have decreased by 8 percent.			Sir Eric Geddes of Imperial Airways announces that a new route will be opened for flights from Cairo to Karachi, Bombay, Calcutta, Rangoon, Singapore, and other Asian locations.
Dec. 30		The governments of France, Britain, and Italy announce they will end their inter-allied military control in Bulgaria as that nation ha s fulfilled all of its treaty obligations.....At the Communist Party Conference Josef Stalin speaks against world revolution while the Lev Kamenev and Grigori Zinoviev factions are losing support.	French Premier Aristide Briand refuses to discuss any peace offers with Abd-el-Krim.		In Madras, India, Mrs. Annie Besant, President of the Theosophical Society announces that a world teacher will soon arrive from the Himalayas.
Dec. 31	The worst flooding in Europe in many years is causing severe damage. The level of the Rhine River has risen by 30 feet....Flooding in Belgium is the worst since 1876.... In Coblenz, Germany, 1,200 are homeless while in Trier, officials fear the entire city will be under water.	The 14th Communist Party Conference ends; Two major figures, Lev Kamenev and Grigori Zinoviev are defeated by Stalin in their attempt to contest the current industrialization plan; Zinoviev is demoted from the Politburo....In Germany there is optimism even though unemployment is rising; the currency has been stabilized and local governments are on a good financial footing....Benito Mussolini announces a project that will clean up Rome and restore its monuments and create new buildings.	Mount Kilimanjaro has been climbed successfully for the first time by G. Londt of Capetown, South Africa.		

A	B	C	D	E
Includes developments that affect more than one world region, international organizations and important meetings of world leaders.	Includes all domestic and regional developments in Europe, including the Soviet Union.	Includes all domestic and regional developments in Africa and the Middle East.	Includes all domestic and regional developments in Latin America, the Caribbean, and Canada.	Includes all domestic and regional developments in Asian and Pacific nations (and colonies).

U.S. Politics & Social Issues	U.S. Foreign Policy & Affairs, Defense	U.S. Economy & Environment	Science, Technology & Nature	Culture, Leisure & Lifestyle	
The car of Andrew Mellon, Secretary of the Treasury is stolen while he is delivering a radio message to the nation; the car has not been recovered.		A new radio station, KMOX in St. Louis, MO, begins operations.	A fossilized prehistoric fish, estimated to be more than 50 million years old, is found in Vermont.	A drawing of the god Apollo by Albrecht Durer has been found in an art library in Zurich, Switzerland.	Dec. 25
It is announced that, using a special mallet to prevent further damage, the Liberty bell will be rung and the sound broadcast over the radio on New Year's Eve....Marjorie Carlough, 24 years old, dies from the effects of radiation poisoning, the seventh employee of United States Radium Corporation to die in three years.	The United States has lodged a diplomatic protest against German restrictions on showing American films....Colonel Billy Mitchell writes a letter to a Florida newspaper; he states that he will continue to fight for an improved national defense.	Large segments of the country are hit by cold weather; the temperature is just below zero in Chicago where six people have died and 30 degrees below zero in Minnesota....The Southern Bell Company's projected budget for operations is $33 million in 1926, the largest it has ever spent.	The Governor of Algeria is seeking the Count de Prorok, accusing the Count if having taken artifacts from the country without permission during his archaeological expeditions....Astronomers state that there will be a total eclipse of the sun on January 14, 1926 visible from Indian Ocean, Sumatra, and eastern India....Industry experts are predicting that with the development of new types of tubes that television could become a reality in 1926.	*The Memoirs of William Jennings Bryan* is published....The *New York Times* reviews a collection of essays, *Reflections on the Death of a Porcupine*, by D. H. Lawrence and *Gentlemen Prefer Blondes* by Anita Loos.	Dec. 26
Despite some predictions that the anthracite coal strike will end soon, the strike continues with no obvious resolution in sight.	An article in *Aero Digest* Magazine states that within three years Japan will have a larger air force than the United States.	The U.S. Commerce Department reports that in 1924 the nation's death rate fell slightly in 1924 compared to 1923 but was still higher than 1921.		Violinist Efrem Zimbalist performs the Brahms Violin Concerto with the New York Philharmonic Orchestra.	Dec. 27
	General Smedley Butler, recent Director of Public Safety for Philadelphia withdraws his resignation from the U.S. Marines after a conference with Major General John Lejeune of the Corps....The Navy announces that it will soon release its findings on the sinking of the submarine *S-51* and the crash of the airship *Shenandoah*.	More mail was sent for the Christmas season in 1925 than any previous year; more than 7 million letters were sent in Chicago and 75 million pieces were sent in New York....Bitterly cold weather has claimed 40 lives in recent days; in Chicago, 17 have died of the cold.		The Chicago Opera company announces it will begin a tour in January visiting Boston, Miami and several other cities....A new musical, *Tip-Toes* opens on Broadway with lyrics by Ira Gershwin and music by George Gershwin.	Dec. 28
Jimmy Walker is sworn in as mayor of New York City.		The Industrial Commissioner of New York reports that wages in New York factories were the highest in five years and the average weekly income for November was $28.65, an increase of $1 from 1924.	The Peabody Museum of Yale, which has the stated of demonstrating evolution, is dedicated.	Rudyard Kipling celebrates his 60th birthday....Paul Whiteman gives a concert in New York featuring compositions by American composers Deems Taylor and George Gershwin.	Dec. 29
Labor Unions announce they will keep u the fight to get a Constitutional Amendment to ban child labor stating it will eventually win.		Film Companies Universal, Famous Players, and MGM complete a deal with the German film company, UFA, to distribute American films in Germany....President Calvin Coolidge confers with Commerce Secretary Hoover over plans to develop civil aviation in the United States and the best way for the government to support these efforts.	Dr. Hornell Hart states that by the year 2000, the mean life expectancy should be around 100 with many people living to be 200.	The film, *Ben Hur*, starring Francis X. Bushman which cost $3 million to make, opens in New York City.	Dec. 30
During the year 1925 there were 18 lynchings according to the NAACP, an increase of two over the previous year; Mississippi led with six....During the year 1925 traffic deaths killed 370 people in Manhattan while 106 were shot and 78 died from other crimes....The anthracite coal strike, begun in September is still not ended with 158,000 miners still out of work....Mine owners are still in favor of arbitration; coal miners are seeking collective bargaining.	Vice President Charles Dawes states that he sees 1926 as a year which will usher in an era of peace.	Shipbuilding in the United States 1925 grew 31 percent.	The Count de Prorok and the Algerian government clear up the controversy over from relics that the Count brought to France after his expedition this year.	Mrs. Mary Jones, 122, who was born a slave, dies in Charleston, WV....Sergei Essenin, regarded by many as Russia's best poet is buried in Moscow in the wake of his suicide for which many of his friends are blaming Isadora Duncan.	Dec. 31

F	G	H	I	J
Includes campaigns, elections, federal-state relations, civil rights and liberties, crime, the judiciary, education, healthcare, poverty, urban affairs, and population.	Includes formation and debate of U.S. foreign and defense policies, veterans affairs, and defense spending. (Relations with specific foreign countries are usually found under the region concerned.)	Includes business, labor, agriculture, taxation, transportation, consumer affairs, monetary and fiscal policy, natural resources, pollution and industrial accidents.	Includes worldwide scientific, medical and technological developments, natural phenomena, U.S. weather and natural disasters.	Includes the arts, religion, scholarship, communications media, sports, entertainment, fashions, fads, and social life.

1926

Results of the Miami hurricane that struck September 18, 1926.

	World Affairs	Europe	Africa & The Middle East	The Americas	Asia & The Pacific
Jan.		Ireland's first radio station begins broadcasting. 2RN will later become Radio Eireann....Turkey converts from the Julian to the Gregorian calendar. Using Europe's calendar is one of Ataturk's reforms.	Abdul Aziz ibn Saud becomes king of the Hejaz. He renames it Saudi Arabia....The Makwar Dam on the Egyptian Nile in the Anglo-Egyptian Sudan is finished. The dam stores water for cotton farms. Egyptians object that the dam diverts water they need.	Emiliano Chamorro's revolution succeeds in Nicaragua. The United States declines to recognize his government.	Bao Dai (Nguyen Vinh Thuy) ascends the throne of Vietnam He is the last emperor of Vietnam, leaving for exile in 1945.
Feb.	Germany's parliament votes to ask League membership.	The Irish Free State establishes the Committee on Evil Literature. Seeking to toughen laws against obscene print material, the committee reports to the government and disbands at the end of the year....Austria's chancellor Seipel indicates that he wants Austria to join Germany.	Italy uses Fiat 3000 tanks in Libya. Based on a French Renault model, the tanks will be used again against Ethiopia in 1935.	Mexico nationalizes Catholic Church property. The measure is part of the government's anti-clerical policy.	Preparations to implement the new Indochinese faith, Caodaism, are finished. They begin in 1925 when a group of Saigonese visit the leader, Ngo Minh Chieu, for spiritual guidance.
Mar.	China requests a seat on the security council. Spain and Brazil block Germany's attempt to join the League....They disagree on who will hold permanent seats.	Fire destroys the 1879 Shakespeare Memorial Theater at Stratford-on-Avon....The replacement theater opens in 1932....Denmark begins to disarm unilaterally....Eamon de Valera resigns as head of Sinn Fein.	Franco-Moroccan peace talks take place but prove inconclusive.		Manchuria receives a new governor whose mandate is to keep the army supplied. His excesses cause the economy to collapse.
Apr.	The League convenes a conference in Paris to discuss world traffic problems.	Italy implements the corps of force to crush the unions....Greece elects dictator, Theodora Pangalos, as president....An assassination attempt against Mussolini fails....Germany and Russia extend the 1922 Rapallo treaty of friendship and neutrality.	Reza Khan becomes Shah of Iran. His royal name is Pahlevi....France and Morocco begin peace talks. The talks are inconclusive.	A train wreck in San Jose, Costa Rica, kills 178 people.	Hindus and Muslims riot in Calcutta.
May	The League hosts a conference in Geneva to promote theater and drama....The preparatory Commission on Disarmament meets for the first time. The United States and Russia will attend later meetings.	A British coal miners' strike mushrooms into a general strike. The government declares martial law....Josef Pilsudski's coup is successful in Poland....Portugal's Manuel Gomes de Costa establishes the *Ditadura Nacional* (National Dictatorship.) It precedes Antonio de Oliveira Salazar's *Estado Novo*.	Syrian Druse rebels launch a second offensive. The French bomb Damascus....Lebanon adopts its new constitution....In Morocco, Spain and France resume the offensive against the Rif. With the Rif's defeat, leader Abd el Krim is exiled to Reunion Island.	Sandino begins a rebellion against the Chamorro government. Nine months after leaving Nicaragua, U.S. Marines return. They will remain until 1933.	
Jun.	Spain leaves the league but returned later. Brazil leaves the League effective in 1928....The economic reconstruction of Hungary is ended. The League relinquishes control.	Germany holds a referendum on whether to compensate for expropriated princely estates.	Ethiopia protests the Angl0o-italian note of 1925 as a threat to Ethiopian sovereignty. Both England and Italy reassure Ethiopia that its sovereignty is secure.	Canada's new prime minister is Arthur Meighen, back for a second term. The first prime minister from the west, he only serves until late September.	
Jul.	Austria's economy is recovering. The League ends oversight of Austria's finances.	Antonio Carmona overturns the government of Portugal and becomes the new dictator....The Briand government falls in France after a devaluation of the franc brings its value to 2 cents....Bavaria enacts a law regulating gypsies, vagabonds, and idlers, which have become a "plague."...Having ousted the internationalist Trotskyites, Stalin begins consolidating "socialism in one country."...Bulgarian Macedonians begin raids into the Kingdom of the Serbs, Croats, and Slovenes. Balkan border problems proliferate.	England and Portugal agree to a border between Southwest Africa and Angola. The boundary is the Kuene River.	Canada returns to the gold standard....Mexico enacts anti-clerical laws that threaten to rupture relations with the Vatican.	The Kuomintang begins an attack on the north. The goal is unification. When finished in October, Chiang controls Hankow and Wuchang.... The Bombay Electrical Supply Company begins running buses. Originally a tramway company, BEST became the municipal utility at the turn of the century.
Aug.		Georgios Kondylis overturns the Pangalos dictatorship in Greece. Three days later Pavlos Kountouritis becomes president, after declaring the dictatorship ended....London installs traffic lights on Piccadilly Circus....Italy and Spain sign a peace treaty.	Lebanon becomes a republic. First president under the French mandate is Charles Debbas....The Shah of Iran faces a rising....Italy signs a friendship pact with Yemen. This is Italy's first effort to extend its influence east of the Red Sea.	Violence breaks out in central and western Mexico. The Cristero rising is a protest of government anti-church policies.	Afghanistan signs a treaty of neutrality and non-aggression with Russia.

A	B	C	D	E
Includes developments that affect more than one world region, international organizations and important meetings of world leaders.	Includes all domestic and regional developments in Europe, including the Soviet Union.	Includes all domestic and regional developments in Africa and the Middle East.	Includes all domestic and regional developments in Latin America, the Caribbean, and Canada.	Includes all domestic and regional developments in Asian and Pacific nations (and colonies).

U.S. Politics & Social Issues	U.S. Foreign Policy & Affairs, Defense	U.S. Economy & Environment	Science, Technology & Nature	Culture, Leisure & Lifestyle	
	The Senate votes to join the World Court. The court members accept most U.S. reservations but reject the U.S. position on advisory opinions. The United States does not join the court at this time.	Ford implements the previously announced eight-hour day at a minimum $5 a day.	John Logie Baird demonstrates television in London. His mechanical device is the first television, but electronic technology will supersede it.	*Sam 'n Henry* debuts. Starring white Freeman Gosden and Charles Correll as black Harlemites, the radio program is a precursor to *Amos 'n Andy*....George Burns and Gracie Allen marry.	Jan.
Chicago business leaders ask Congress to investigate lawlessness in their gang-dominated city.	The United States refuses to recognize the Chomorro government, contending that it has seized power illegally in Nicaragua.	A parcel of land at Broadway and Wall streets sells for a record $7 a square inch.	A Sap Gulch, UT, avalanche buries 75. Forty die.	The Charleston is the rage. Three men dance non-stop for 22 hours.	Feb.
The United States hosts the first lip-reading tournament.		The Dow bottoms out with industrials at 135.20 and rails at 102.41 before resuming the climb to the crash of 1929.	At Auburn, MA, Robert Goddard launches his first liquid fuel rocket. It travels 56 meters.	At Miami, FL, the International Greyhound Racing Association forms....America hosts the first lip-reading tournament.	Mar.
	The United States reaches an agreement on terms of repayment of France's war debt. The term is 62 years at 1.6 percent.	New York's attorney general estimates that bootlegging in the United States is a $3.6 billion a year business.	Goddard launches his second liquid fuel rocket.	The Book of the Month Club's debut selections are Sylvia Townsend Warner's *Loving Huntsman* and *Lolly Willowes*....Canada's Johnny Miles wins the 30th Boston Marathon in 2:25:40:4.	Apr.
The Air Commerce Act becomes law. It licenses pilots and airplanes. The Railway Labor Act also goes into effect. It promotes bargaining and mediation in place of strikes.	Congress establishes the U.S. Customs Court. The court replaces the board of appraisers established in 1890 to settle customs disagreements.		Admiral Richard Byrd claims the dirigible *Norge*, under his commanded and piloted by Floyd Bennett, becomes the first to fly over the North Pole. The claim later comes under a cloud when Byrd's diary indicates otherwise. Roald Amundsen flies over the pole three days later.	Evangelist Aimee Semple McPherson disappears. She will reappear months later with a tale of abduction and torture....Blind Lemon Jefferson, the decade's most popular blues performer, records *Long Lonesome Blues*. This is the first of his recordings for Chicago's Paramount Records....Gene Austin's *Five Foot Two, Eyes of Blue,* is number one.	May
Mordecai Johnson becomes the first black president of Howard University, the historically black college established during Reconstruction.		New Yorkers can get home telephones for $4 a month.	The Rhodes earthquake causes damage in Anatolia, Egypt, and Crete as well as Rhodes.	The Philadelphia World's Fair opens.	Jun.
	The Army Air Corps becomes operative. Congress authorizes the Distinguished Flying Cross.	Fox buys Movietone patents for putting sound on film....Southern Bell Telephone and Telegraph opens for business.	A lightning strike in Lake Denmark, NJ, destroys an ammunition dump. It kills 21 and does $75 million in damage.		Jul.
	The U.S and Panama negotiate a treaty obligating the U.S. to defend the canal in time of war.		The National Aeronautics Administration transmits a weather map for the first time. The signal leaves the NAA offices in Arlington and reaches the Weather Bureau office in Washington, DC.	New York's Gertrude Ederle swims the English Channel from France to England. She is the first woman to do so. Her 14 hour, 31 minute swim garners her a New York ticker tape parade....Warner Brothers premiers vitaphone. The film is Don Juan starring John Barrymore....Rudolph Valentino dies. A hundred thousand mourn.	Aug.

F
Includes campaigns, elections, federal-state relations, civil rights and liberties, crime, the judiciary, education, healthcare, poverty, urban affairs, and population.

G
Includes formation and debate of U.S. foreign and defense policies, veterans affairs, and defense spending. (Relations with specific foreign countries are usually found under the region concerned.)

H
Includes business, labor, agriculture, taxation, transportation, consumer affairs, monetary and fiscal policy, natural resources, pollution and industrial accidents.

I
Includes worldwide scientific, medical and technological developments, natural phenomena, U.S. weather and natural disasters.

J
Includes the arts, religion, scholarship, communications media, sports, entertainment, fashions, fads, and social life.

	World Affairs	Europe	Africa & The Middle East	The Americas	Asia & The Pacific
Sep.	Spain withdraws from the League to protest Germany's membership.... The League enacts a convention banning slavery in all forms. Twenty nations are signatories.	Turkey approves civil marriage.		William Lyon Mackenzie-King replaces Arthur Haighen as Canadian prime minister.	Italy and Yemen sign a treaty.
Oct.	At the Imperial Conference that runs into November, British nations establish that they are equal dominions tied by their common sovereign, the British monarch.	Josef Pilsudski becomes Poland's prime minister....British miners agree to end their strike....Italy bans women from holding public office....The Politburo throws out Leo Trotsky and the Trotskyites.		A hurricane strikes Cuba. The death toll exceeds 650.	Mohammed Nadir Khan's rising begins in Afghanistan. It will kill 1,200....A troop ship sinks in the Yangtze, killing 1,200....After Britain relents on the "unequal treaties" China ends a boycott of British goods.
Nov.	Pope Pius XI issues an encyclical on state suppression of the church in Mexico.	Italy revives the death penalty. It also arrests all Communist deputies....Catalonians based in France attempt a coup against the Spanish government.		Brazil's new president will serve until 1930, building highways while juggling a crushing foreign debt burden.	Michinomaya Hirohito becomes Japan's 124th emperor....A Communist rising begins in Java. The Dutch have difficulty repressing it. They crush it only in July 1927....The Statutory/Simon Commission begins its inquiry into the government structure of India. Its omission of Indian representatives fuels Indian nationalism and boycotts.
Dec.	Pius XI condemns fascism in Italy. The Vatican proscribes the works of French Fascist Charles Maurras.	Stanley Baldwin ends martial law, instituted due to the mine strike.		Nicaragua's congress installs a new government. The selection of conservative Adolfo Diaz alienates liberals and provokes the return of the liberal exile Sacasa and renewal of the civil war.	Michinomaya Hirohito becomes Japan's 124th emperor on the death of Taisho....Mail service by air begins between England and India.

A	B	C	D	E
Includes developments that affect more than one world region, international organizations and important meetings of world leaders.	*Includes all domestic and regional developments in Europe, including the Soviet Union.*	*Includes all domestic and regional developments in Africa and the Middle East.*	*Includes all domestic and regional developments in Latin America, the Caribbean, and Canada.*	*Includes all domestic and regional developments in Asian and Pacific nations (and colonies).*

U.S. Politics & Social Issues	U.S. Foreign Policy & Affairs, Defense	U.S. Economy & Environment	Science, Technology & Nature	Culture, Leisure & Lifestyle	
The O'Banion gang, in retaliation for the murder of the leader, attacks Capone headquarters. Twelve carloads of gangsters fire on the Hawthorne Inn near Chicago. Only one of Al Capone's gangsters is wounded.	The U.S. withdraws all forces but a small contingent to protect the Hankow legation. The troops have been in China since August.		A hurricane destroys much of Miami, FL, killing 100. It also damages the Bahamas and Alabama and helps to end the Florida land boom.	Outdoors, in a deluge with 130,000 fans watching, Gene Tunney defeats Jack Dempsey. He becomes the world heavyweight boxing champion....*Gentlemen Prefer Blondes* premiers on Broadway.	Sep.
	The Coast Guard establishes an airways division under the lighthouse service. The new unit is responsible for runways and navigational aids.			Harry Houdini dies from complications after his appendix ruptures.... Benny Goodman makes his first recordings. He is a member of Ben Pollack's band.	Oct.
California's "Gorilla Man" rapes and kills his ninth victim.		Route 66 comes into being.... Westinghouse, General Electric, and RCA combine forces to create NBC. The new network has 24 stations.	Vesuvius erupts in Italy.	The restoration of Colonial Williamsburg begins. Critics say the Rockefeller-driven project better depicts the 1930s than the 1730s....Ernest Hemingway publishes *The Sun Also Rises*. A. A. Milne publishes *Winnie the Pooh*.	Nov.
	The commission headed by Carmi Thompson reports that the Philippines are unready for independence. The commission recommends more self-rule and the removal of government ownership of businesses.		A patent is issued for the gas refrigerator.... The FAA makes its first aircraft airworthiness inspection prior to delivery of an American plane to a Canadian firm.	The *Chicago Tribune* claims that the Tigers threw a 1917 series that allowed the White Sox to reach the World Series. The claim remains unproved.	Dec.

F
Includes campaigns, elections, federal-state relations, civil rights and liberties, crime, the judiciary, education, healthcare, poverty, urban affairs, and population.

G
Includes formation and debate of U.S. foreign and defense policies, veterans affairs, and defense spending. (Relations with specific foreign countries are usually found under the region concerned.)

H
Includes business, labor, agriculture, taxation, transportation, consumer affairs, monetary and fiscal policy, natural resources, pollution and industrial accidents.

I
Includes worldwide scientific, medical and technological developments, natural phenomena, U.S. weather and natural disasters.

J
Includes the arts, religion, scholarship, communications media, sports, entertainment, fashions, fads, and social life.

	World Affairs	Europe	Africa & The Middle East	The Americas	Asia & The Pacific
Jan. 1		German President Paul von Hindenburg addresses diplomats at a New Year's event wearing evening clothes rather than his military uniform, a gesture meant to signify his nation's commitment to democracy....Flooding on the Rhine forces approximately 50,000 people from their homes; total damage is estimated at $7 million. Much of the city of Cologne is underwater.	Turkish President Mustafa Kamal presses his country's claims to the city of Mosul in the British mandate of Iraq.		
Jan. 2		Joseph Stalin is re-elected as General Secretary of the Communist Party in the Soviet Union. Leon Trotsky regains his seat as one of nine members of the party politburo, while long-term member Leon Kamenev is ousted from power.			
Jan. 3		Belgian officials appeal for aid for thousands of victims of flooding on the Meuse River....Prime Minister Theodoros Pangalos declares himself dictator of Greece, seven months after staging a coup against the parliamentary government.... Two Russian peasants in the village of Zikleev are executed for practicing sorcery.	A joint expedition sponsored by the British Museum and the Museum of the University of Pennsylvania announces discovering an ancient boat, dated to 3000 B.C.E., in Iraq.	The Insular Government of Puerto Rico, in conjunction with the New York Botanical Garden, announces plans to carry out a survey of the island's indigenous flora, in an attempt to apply the theory of evolution to plant life.	
Jan. 4	President Coolidge urges that the United States attend a League of Nations disarmament conference, recommending a $50,000 appropriation for expenses. The move is widely interpreted as a sign that the United States is becoming more receptive to the League....Secretary of the Treasury Andrew Mellon urges Congress to ratify wartime-debt funding agreements reached with Italy. He warns senators that they might impoverish Italy if they insist on stringent terms.	Officials in Hungary and Romania estimate that as many as 1,000 people died in recent flooding, primarily along the Theiss River....The King and Queen of Belgium donate 2 million francs, their silver wedding anniversary gift, to their nation's flood victims.	Several Jabal Druze chiefs agree to stop fighting against French troops in Syria, but Sultan Pasha al-Atrash refuses all peace overtures.		Chinese General Zhang Zuolin demands punishment for eight followers of defeated rebel General Guo Songling who have sought refuge in the Japanese Consulate.
Jan. 5	U.S. congressmen take up the issue of Italy's treatment of Freemasons. American Masonic officials charge that the Mussolini government has systematically persecuted their Italian fraternal brethren, "even to the extent of murder."	The Supreme Chief of the State Police is the latest high-ranking Hungarian official arrested for his role in a counterfeiting ring, said to involve 300 conspirators....A dam on the Nethe River in Belgium bursts, submerging hundreds of homes, while floodwaters from the Oise River inundate several French towns.	Cereal magnate W. K. Kellogg announces that he will finance an expedition to Arabia to import pure-blooded Arabian horses.		
Jan. 6	Missouri Senator James Reed calls for an investigation into alleged propaganda efforts by the World Court to pressure the United States into canceling European war debts.	The Seine River floods low-lying suburbs around Paris....Centrist political leaders in Germany warn that the country could become a military dictatorship unless parliamentary rifts are healed....The Soviet government sets aside 400,000 acres in the Don region to colonize Jews.			
Jan. 7	British port officials search the crew and cargo of a Soviet ship, the Ilitch, for propaganda literature, but find nothing.	The Thames River swells dangerously after a two-hour downpour in London, while steady rains in France cause the Seine to continue to rise....German publishers release a book about Judaism with an article by former Kaiser Wilhelm, in which he urges, "Our slogan must be 'Away with Judaism,' with its Jehovah."	The American Embassy files a protest against the Turkish government's special customs tax on U.S. commodities, seen as retaliation for failed commercial negotiations.	The Mexican Army puts down uprisings in Chihuahua against the government of President Plutarco Calles.	

A	B	C	D	E
Includes developments that affect more than one world region, international organizations and important meetings of world leaders.	*Includes all domestic and regional developments in Europe, including the Soviet Union.*	*Includes all domestic and regional developments in Africa and the Middle East.*	*Includes all domestic and regional developments in Latin America, the Caribbean, and Canada.*	*Includes all domestic and regional developments in Asian and Pacific nations (and colonies).*

U.S. Politics & Social Issues	U.S. Foreign Policy & Affairs, Defense	U.S. Economy & Environment	Science, Technology & Nature	Culture, Leisure & Lifestyle	
U.S. President Calvin Coolidge greets and shakes hands with 3,130 White House visitors during a New Year's reception for the general public.			An attempt to hold a worldwide New Year's celebration through radio transmissions is a partial success. Listeners in England, France, and Argentina tune in for a U.S. broadcast, but atmospheric interference prevents Americans from hearing the midnight tolling of London's Big Ben.	The University of Alabama, the first Southern team ever invited to the Rose Bowl, upsets the University of Washington by the score of 20–19....Robert Reidt, a Long Island house painter and Seventh-Day Adventist known as the "Prophet of Doom," predicts for the second straight year that the world will be destroyed in February.	Jan. 1
A mob of 300 men in Evansville, Indiana, kidnap five "scab" workers from a coal mine during a strike....City patrolmen, striking coal miners, and the miners' wives clash in Scranton, Pennsylvania, where three women are among those arrested following a fifteen-minute melee.		U.S. Postmaster General Harry New signs orders denying the use of the mail to two companies accused of real estate fraud. The companies have sold unimproved, inaccessible lots in central Florida to buyers by using brochures with "beautiful faked pictures."		Chicago officials report that 8,143 cars were stolen in the city in 1925, an increase of 35 percent from the previous year.	Jan. 2
The Anti-Saloon League of America reports that progress has been made in prohibition enforcement, citing the 38,925 convictions of offenders on federal charges in 1925.		Secretary of Commerce Herbert Hoover observes that the consumer practice of "installment purchasing" is a cause for concern.	German engineer Hugo Eckner suspends plans to build a super-Zeppelin to explore the North Pole. His attempts to raise funds have been hindered by Germany's financial straits.		Jan. 3
A Ku Klux Klan unit in New Haven, Connecticut, votes to disband, accusing the national organization of widespread graft....W.K. "Bill" Hale, a prominent Oklahoma rancher, is arrested on suspicion of plotting the murders of several Osage Indians.				The defense counsel for biology teacher John Scopes files final arguments on his behalf with the Tennessee Supreme Court....Tin Pan Alley composer Irving Berlin marries New York City socialite Ellin Mackay in an impromptu wedding.	Jan. 4
	Due to budget constraints, the War Department cuts the number of non-commissioned Army officers by 4,347. Total troop strength for 1926 will be 118,750 soldiers.	Three clergymen meet with United Mine Workers president John L. Lewis, pleading with him to call off a five-month-long strike in Pennsylvania's anthracite region.	The first train telephone system operates in Germany.	The Prince of Wales is cited by the International Association of Clothing Designers as the primary trend-setter in male fashions....Evelyn Nesbit, who gained notoriety in the 1906 "Crime of the Century" Stanford White murder trial, attempts suicide in Chicago after being fired from a vaudeville show.	Jan. 5
Ohio State University begins an investigation into alleged Communistic activities and prohibition violations at the school, with the focus on a recently arrested faculty member....Police in Paterson, New Jersey, destroy a brewery hidden in a one-story garage, with the capacity to produce 1,000 gallons of beer per day.		Secretary of Commerce Hoover condemns foreign "trusts" that regulate the distribution of important products such as crude rubber and phosphates. He singles out the Stevenson Act in England, which has driven up the price of rubber by restricting shipments from the British East Indies.			Jan. 6
American playwrights form a closed shop to protect their financial interests against theater managers, who have profited from selling the rights to plays to Hollywood....The Indiana Democratic Party passes a resolution castigating the role of the Ku Klux Klan in the state's politics.			A Detroit manufacturer announces plans to build a giant all-metal dirigible, "equipped as luxuriously as a Pullman."	Yale University alumni demand that professional football cease offering money to recruit college players before they have graduated.	Jan. 7

F	G	H	I	J
Includes campaigns, elections, federal-state relations, civil rights and liberties, crime, the judiciary, education, healthcare, poverty, urban affairs, and population.	Includes formation and debate of U.S. foreign and defense policies, veterans affairs, and defense spending. (Relations with specific foreign countries are usually found under the region concerned.)	Includes business, labor, agriculture, taxation, transportation, consumer affairs, monetary and fiscal policy, natural resources, pollution and industrial accidents.	Includes worldwide scientific, medical and technological developments, natural phenomena, U.S. weather and natural disasters.	Includes the arts, religion, scholarship, communications media, sports, entertainment, fashions, fads, and social life.

	World Affairs	Europe	Africa & The Middle East	The Americas	Asia & The Pacific
Jan. 8	The House Ways and Means Committee urges ratification of debt agreements with Italy, but several Democrats, led by Cordell Hull, oppose the measures as debt "cancellation."	The rains stop in France, but flood damages are estimated at $17.5 million....Film audiences in Bergamo, Italy, upset that Rudolph Valentino has applied for American citizenship, boo his film "Monsieur Beaucaire" off the screen.			Japan seeks to redivide seal hunting territories, requesting a new agreement with the United States and Russia....A Manila City Council member in the Philippines is jailed for using insolent language toward Governor General Leonard Wood. He called Wood "a big tree without a shadow."
Jan. 9		Berlin officials report that because of rampant unemployment, 36,000 residents are living on city-provided relief.		The U.S. government formally protests a new Mexican land law and petroleum bill, which are both seen as inimical to American investor interests....Mexican bandits in Michoacan massacre 50 train passengers, but allow several foreign female passengers to escape unrobbed and unharmed.	Feng Yuxiang quits as head of the National People's Army of the Republic of China. Duan Qirui announces his resignation as Chief Executive of the republic, but does not fix a date.
Jan. 10	The American Legion endorses U.S. membership in the World Court, calling the court an "American idea" with no connection to the League of Nations.	Metropolitan Peter, head of the Russian Orthodox Church, is arrested by Soviet authorities in Moscow.		The Mexican foreign minister, insisting on the sovereignty of his nation, tells the American ambassador that Mexico will pass whatever land laws it pleases.	
Jan. 11	British trade minister Leland Summers dismisses as "spoofing" the Coolidge Administration's protests about high rubber prices. He cites America's own repeated use of the protective tariff....The American Jewish Joint Distribution Committee announces plans to provide a million dollars in relief for starving Polish Jews.	Monarchist politicians in Berlin issue a manifesto calling for the dissolution of the German parliament....In the German province of Saxony, a Communist plot to foment mass rioting by unemployed factory workers is uncovered....The former king of Greece, George II, announces plans to build a vacation home near Fort Lauderdale, FL.		The Coolidge Administration reasserts that the Mexican government may not retroactively confiscate lands in which other nations have made lawful investments.	The ultranationalist Black Dragon Society in Japan demands the recall of a Brazilian ambassador for his disrespectful behavior during a procession for Crown Prince Hirohito. The ambassador hit a policeman with his cane.
Jan. 12		A "moveable school" for gypsy children opens in Surrey, England.... Pope Pius XI rejects Fascist calls for "collaboration" between the Italian government and the Holy See.	British archaeologists announce that they have unearthed Sumerian pictographic tablets outside Baghdad.	Mexican Federal troops have successfully apprehended the Michoacan train bandits, killing most of them and executing several suspected accomplices.	
Jan. 13	The U.S. House debate over Italian debt repayments intensifies. Some representatives call Mussolini a murderer, while New York Representative Fiorello LaGuardia cites Italy's allied role in the Great War....In a delaying tactic, Senate Democrats call for the preparation of a State Department information index before any American commitment is made to the World Court.	German Chancellor Hans Luther announces the formation of a new cabinet, although only three political parties, accounting for less than a third of the Reichstag vote, are represented.			Experts at a foreign affairs conference at Radcliffe College cite Japan's overpopulation problem as an international concern, because the country may use force to seize more land.
Jan. 14		Seven Rhine and Ruhr steel companies in Germany merge, forming a conglomerate worth an estimated $150 million.			Warlords in North China continue to muster troops. General Li Chin-ling is readying an attempt to retake the port city of Tientsin, which he lost to Marshal Feng Yuxiang in December. A large number of White Russian soldiers are said to be joined with the general.

A	B	C	D	E
Includes developments that affect more than one world region, international organizations and important meetings of world leaders.	Includes all domestic and regional developments in Europe, including the Soviet Union.	Includes all domestic and regional developments in Africa and the Middle East.	Includes all domestic and regional developments in Latin America, the Caribbean, and Canada.	Includes all domestic and regional developments in Asian and Pacific nations (and colonies).

U.S. Politics & Social Issues	U.S. Foreign Policy & Affairs, Defense	U.S. Economy & Environment	Science, Technology & Nature	Culture, Leisure & Lifestyle	
The U.S. Supreme Court hears a segregation case originating in New York City, in which an African-American woman was denied home ownership in a neighborhood with a compact against selling to blacks....Theater owners respond to the new playwrights union. "The authors take themselves too seriously, anyway," says spokesman Al Woods. "They don't do the work; the managers do that. All they do is write plays."		President Coolidge rejects plans to use government funding, in tandem with private investment, to develop a U.S. crude rubber industry in the Philippines....Sears, Roebuck & Co. executive Julius Rosenwald turns a profit of $6.75 million in a deal involving his option on 50,000 shares of company stock....Talks between the United Mine Workers and anthracite operators are reported at a standstill.	Mount Vesuvius spews lava, and a violent earthquake shakes Tuscany.	Henry Ford announces that he will establish a replica Pilgrim-era colonial village in Sudbury, MA.	Jan. 8
		The president of the National Automobile Chamber of Commerce predicts a record year for foreign purchases of American cars.	A tidal wave strikes a small harbor in Bernard, ME.	Large crowds pay fifty cents a head to tour the Cornelius Vanderbilt mansion in New York City, soon to be torn down to build a skyscraper....The National League and American League are unable to reach an agreement on a closing date for the coming baseball season; the National League insists on October 4, while the American League wants September 26.	Jan. 9
The Assistant Secretary of the Treasury announces that Americans may make cider and fruit juices with an alcohol content of no more than one-half of one percent by volume, provided the beverages are not used to cause intoxication.		Anthracite miners vote down a plan to allow former Secretary of State Charles Evans Hughes to arbitrate a strike settlement.		Administrators at a high school in Fall River, Massachusetts, ban jazz at school dances, calling the style a "travesty on music."	Jan. 10
Representative John Langley of Kentucky, a member of the congressional "dry bloc," is forced to resign his seat. He has been convicted for conspiring to sell whiskey....The Women's Trade Union League begins a drive to establish the forty-eight hour work week for women and children in New York State....An outbreak of smallpox in Tampa, FL, leads to the emergency inoculation of 30,000 children.		John L. Lewis, citing the no-arbitration policies followed by major industrialists such as John D. Rockefeller, defends the United Mine Workers refusal to arbitrate....Pan American Petroleum and Transport, with a large stake in Mexican oil, suffers a sharp drop in its stock price.		Richard Strauss's "Rosenkavalier" is performed in Dresden, accompanied by a film; the famous composer predicts that fusing music and the moving image will lead to a new era in the arts....Actress Mary Pickford forms her own film production company, investing a million dollars....Helen Keller visits the White House to "listen" to President Coolidge by holding her hand to his lips. "They say you are cold, but you are not," she tells him. "You are a dear President."	Jan. 11
Republican Gerald Nye is appointed senator of North Dakota, filling a vacancy. Known as a supporter of Senator Robert La Follette, his appointment raises the possibility of a Democratic-Progressive Republican coalition....Buffalo, NY, opens an institute for rehabilitating hoboes.		The Nash Motors Company announces a nine-for-one stock split. The stock closes at an all-time high, at $517 per share....Parley talks are suspended between anthracite miners and operators after two weeks of negotiations....A large Scranton, Pennsylvania, department store files for bankruptcy, citing the lack of customers in coal country.		Paul Robeson sings spirituals before 1,200 members of the Institute of Arts and Sciences....Chicago Bears star Red Grange acknowledges that he will earn $200,000 from his new movie contract.	Jan. 12
Ninety-three miners, most of them African-American, are feared dead after an explosion in a Wilburton, Oklahoma, coal mine....The Massachusetts Supreme Court hears final arguments in the appeals trial of Nicola Sacco and Bartolomeo Vanzetti, convicted for murder in 1921. Their defense has tried to show that the pair were found guilty because of their political radicalism.	Serious rifts are reported in the Navy Department over the subject of dirigibles. Rear Admiral William Moffett seeks funding to build a massive airship, while other authorities question the airship's military importance. The debate takes place against the backdrop of budget cuts.	The Federal Reserve Board reports that the United States in 1925 set records for manufacturing output, construction activity, and automobile production....Pearl Kramer becomes one of the first women named to the board of directors of a major Wall Street bank.		The president of Rutgers University praises football for building "sound manhood in American youths."	Jan. 13
A lead and zinc mine is Picher, Oklahoma, proves to be a "front" for an elaborate whiskey distillery, complete with electrical hoists and pumps, huge copper stills, and multiple secret entrances.		Five hundred miners crowd into the lobby of a hotel in Hazleton, Pennsylvania, to cheer John L. Lewis for his handling of their strike.... Pennsylvania state senators propose several amendments favoring the operators.	From the vantage point of Sumatra, an expedition of Swarthmore College students uses a 62-foot-long camera to photograph a total solar eclipse.	Hollywood stars Douglas Fairbanks and Mary Pickford have hired an armed guard to protect them from "all the nuts who come to Los Angeles," according to Fairbanks.... New York Yankees star Babe Ruth, strenuously working out in an effort to lose weight, has dropped 23 pounds in the past month.	Jan. 14

F	G	H	I	J
Includes campaigns, elections, federal-state relations, civil rights and liberties, crime, the judiciary, education, healthcare, poverty, urban affairs, and population.	Includes formation and debate of U.S. foreign and defense policies, veterans affairs, and defense spending. (Relations with specific foreign countries are usually found under the region concerned.)	Includes business, labor, agriculture, taxation, transportation, consumer affairs, monetary and fiscal policy, natural resources, pollution and industrial accidents.	Includes worldwide scientific, medical and technological developments, natural phenomena, U.S. weather and natural disasters.	Includes the arts, religion, scholarship, communications media, sports, entertainment, fashions, fads, and social life.

	World Affairs	Europe	Africa & The Middle East	The Americas	Asia & The Pacific
Jan. 15	The U.S. House of Representatives ratifies the Coolidge Administration's debt settlement with Italy; in the party-line vote, Democrats favor rejection.	Soviet officials arrest several priests in Kiev, accusing them of manipulating peasant superstitions.	Turkish President Mustafa Kemal's westernization efforts continue. His government adopts the Swiss Civil Code and bans the practice of polygamy.	President Coolidge insists that Chile and Peru must stick to their agreement to hold a plebiscite, supervised by General John Pershing, about the disputed Tacna-Arica region.	
Jan. 16		Grand Duchess Olga insists that the woman she has interviewed at a German sanitarium is not the Grand Duchess Anastasia, daughter of Tsar Nicholas, reportedly killed during the Russian Revolution. The woman in Germany persists with her claims.	The Turkish government has introduced the first electric street signals in Constantinople. City policemen, who wore fezes before a general ban last year, are now adorned in crimson-and-brass helmets.		Roman Catholics in Shanghai begin publishing a newspaper supporting current Chinese institutions. The paper editorializes against Chinese nationalist aspirations and warns against the influence of Bolshevism among the Chinese intelligentsia.
Jan. 17		Germany plans to reopen the issue of "war guilt" before the League of Nations. German jurists will call for a neutral court to decide ultimate responsibility for the Great War....G.Y. Sokolnikoff is removed from his position as Commissar of Finance in the Soviet cabinet.	A French explorer shoots two crocodiles near a waterhole in the middle of the Sahara Desert, raising questions about the region's geological history....The Carnegie Endowment for International Peace announces intensive data-collection plans focused on Middle Eastern social and political movements.		
Jan. 18	By a vote of 359 to 1, the House of Representatives approves appropriations for the United States to attend the League of Nations disarmament conference....Idaho Senator William Borah leads Progressive Republicans and Democrats in opposing a vote on U.S. membership in the World Court.	Berlin decides to build a subway system as a public works project, hoping to relieve as many unemployed workers as possible....A proposed tax law will fall heavily on the 67,000 American expatriates living in France. All foreigners in the country will be required to pay income taxes; the rate will require a millionaire to pay $800,000 per year.			General Zhang Zuolin, angry that the Japanese Consulate refuses to surrender eight supporters of the defeated General Kuo, responds by making illegal all foreign leases on Manchurian lands....The Anti-Bolshevist General Wu Pei-fu is accumulating power in South China.
Jan. 19		The Swiss branch of the Italian Chamber of Commerce defies Mussolini's direct orders to disband....Soviet police in Odessa announce the discovery of a massive monarchist plot and arrest dozens, including several tradesmen.		Mexico's foreign affairs minister insists that oil and land laws have been misinterpreted by Americans. He claims the laws are not retroactive or confiscatory and will not prohibit foreigners from owning land. He points out that U.S. immigration laws are more restrictive, requiring legal residence to acquire real property.	
Jan. 20	Anti-World Court senators use delaying tactics—such as reading lengthy magazine articles—during floor debate, prompting Vice-President Charles Dawes to criticize them in a radio broadcast....The French ambassador discusses the issue of war debts with President Coolidge....The Soviet Union threatens to send the Red Army into China unless Chinese soldiers cease seizing trains in Manchuria.	Reports from Moscow indicate that Leon Trotsky remains without substantial power, although he has regained his Politburo seat. Joseph Stalin is now regarded as the most significant leader in the Communist Party, although he prefers to remain in the background....Commander Ramon Franco makes final preparations for his attempted flight from Spain to Argentina, by way of the South Atlantic.	Twenty-one Turkish "reactionaries" have been hanged in the past few weeks.		
Jan. 21	Senate "irreconcilables," led by Senators Reed and Borah, continue to successfully filibuster against the World Court vote.	Soviet authorities remove jewels, crowns, and other ornamental objects from the tombs of the Russian emperors and empresses buried at the Church of St. Peter and St. Paul in Leningrad. According to reports, some of the jewels will be housed in museums; the rest will be sold to private foreign buyers.	The British High Commissioner of Egypt inaugurates the Makwar Dam on the Nile River, which is anticipated to irrigate three million acres.		Chinese troops have been seizing trains operated by the Chinese Eastern Railway in Manchuria and assaulting Soviet passengers, according to a formal protest by the Soviet ambassador.

A	B	C	D	E
Includes developments that affect more than one world region, international organizations and important meetings of world leaders.	*Includes all domestic and regional developments in Europe, including the Soviet Union.*	*Includes all domestic and regional developments in Africa and the Middle East.*	*Includes all domestic and regional developments in Latin America, the Caribbean, and Canada.*	*Includes all domestic and regional developments in Asian and Pacific nations (and colonies).*

U.S. Politics & Social Issues	U.S. Foreign Policy & Affairs, Defense	U.S. Economy & Environment	Science, Technology & Nature	Culture, Leisure & Lifestyle	
Harvard Professor Albert Bushnell Hart, in a public speech, supports banning Japanese, Chinese, and Hindu immigrants from the United States, observing that they are unassimilable and will "plague our posterity."			Forty-five bicyclists suffer from falls on a slippery London street during a major snowstorm.	A $10 million hotel and country club opens in Coral Gables, Florida....Jim Thorpe announces his retirement from professional sports. The 40-year-old American Indian has most recently punted for a football team from St. Petersburg, Florida....The New York Yankees sell their popular first baseman, Wally Pipp, to the Cincinnati Reds. Pipp lost his starting job last season to the young star Lou Gehrig.	Jan. 15
W. E. B. DuBois observes that the black labor movement is becoming increasingly radicalized. Noting that black workers are often denied membership in mainstream unions, he warns, "If you kick them out of the trade unions, you kick them into Communism."		Several senators criticize President Coolidge's inaction on the coal strike, urging him to adopt Theodore Roosevelt's "Big Stick" approach.... The New York Stock Exchange reports that $4,277,249,907 in new stock and bond securities were traded in 1925.		The Army basketball team runs up the score in a lopsided game, defeating Georgetown University 47–20.	Jan. 16
The National Women's Party marches on the White House to petition President Coolidge to back an Equal Rights Amendment for female workers.			Daniel Guggenheim gifts $2.5 million to promote aeronautics, with the goal of establishing passenger and freight airline services on "a self-supporting basis."	A counsel for the Unitarian Layman's League files a brief on behalf of John Scopes. The Unitarian denomination is the only Christian body in the United States to officially aid the defense in the case.	Jan. 17
President Coolidge responds to yesterday's petition by female activists. Noting women's family duties, he states that safeguarding women in the workplace will also safeguard "the American home."			Work begins on the Christian Missionary Building on Broadway in New York City, planned to be the world's tallest. At a cost of $14 million, the skyscraper will be 8 feet higher than the Woolworth Building....The Osage Indians in Oklahoma are reported to have earned almost $30 million in oil revenues in the past year.		Jan. 18
Four Ohio State University professors deny that they are Communists.... Eighty-eight-year-old William Mack Lee, the personal manservant of General Robert E. Lee, becomes the first African-American since Reconstruction to speak in the Virginia State Capitol Building. He delivers a reminiscence about his former master.		In an effort to improve transparency, the Federal Reserve and the New York Stock Exchange announce that broker loans will be publicly reported....Sears, Roebuck & Co. reports record profits in 1925.... President Coolidge continues to refuse to intervene in the anthracite coal strike.	Scientists have dismissed the popular notion that lightning causes radio static.	The autograph of Button Gwinnett, one of the signers of the Declaration of Independence, fetches $22,500 at an auction in New York City.	Jan. 19
A Detroit judge decides a child custody case by secretly filming the disputants. With the birth mother and the foster mother in court, he announces that the child will be institutionalized. Hidden cameras record each woman's reaction. According to psychologists, the film shows that the foster mother has a more "biological emotional reaction"; the judge awards her the child.	Secretary of War Dwight Davis rejects the notion of fusing the army and navy departments, telling the House Military Affairs Committee that the branches have separate missions and needs.		France leads the world with 45 aviation records, while the United States is second with 33.	Americans are estimated to consume 400,000,000 quarts of soft drinks per year....Promoters announce that Jack Dempsey will defend his heavyweight boxing title against Gene Tunney in Jersey City in August....The British government abandons efforts to impose a quota system to limit the booking of American films in England.	Jan. 20
Disagreement breaks out between the National Women's Party and several groups representing women in organized labor. American Federation of Labor representatives observe that the proposed Equal Rights Amendment would negate existing laws that provide special protections for laboring women, particularly the 48-hour workweek guaranteed to female textile workers.			Two French aviators successfully complete an 80-hour nonstop flight from Paris to Tehran and back.... Astronomer Edwin Hubble speculates that another galaxy, similar to the Milky Way, may exist 700,000 light years away.		Jan. 21

	World Affairs	Europe	Africa & The Middle East	The Americas	Asia & The Pacific
Jan. 22		Commander Franco's seaplane successfully completes the first leg of its flight plan, landing in the Canary Islands.....Monarchists in the German Reichstag are said to be openly conferring with a military captain who helped lead the Kapp Putsch against the Weimar Republic in 1920.		The Coolidge Administration will send 20 officials to oversee voting during the Tacna-Arica plebiscite.	
Jan. 23		Cardinal Mercier, the Primate of Belgium known for his leadership during the Great War, dies.		Explorers report that they have discovered a Polish colony with 1,000 inhabitants in Brazil. The group has been living in isolation since 1873.	Five American tourists are arrested in Java for using a hammer to deface an ancient temple....Japan has rejected overtures from the Soviet Union that the two nations act jointly against aggression in China.
Jan. 24		Centrist political leaders in Berlin seriously consider backing a Socialist-Communist plan to confiscate all property owned by former royal families; leftist groups agitate for the plan with a house-to-house campaign in worker districts.			Chinese troops have seized telegraph lines and isolated the Soviet Consulate in Harbin, Manchuria.
Jan. 25	A successful Senate closure vote brings to an end the debate over the World Court. A resolution on U.S. adherence to the World Court protocol is expected within days.	Inmates stage an uprising at a London prison, attempting to attack the prison governor during a Sunday chapel service. They protest the treatment of an inmate who had committed suicide.		The Coolidge administration refuses to recognize the week-old government of General Emiliano Chamorro, who has come to power in what is believed to be a coup. Secretary of State Frank Kellogg reiterates the American commitment to "constitutional government and orderly procedure in Central America."	
Jan. 26	Britain reaches an accord with Italy over debt repayments. The terms granted the Italian government are more lenient than those permitted by the U.S.–Italy accord.	A rabies epidemic around Moscow claims several lives. People report being bitten by vagrant dogs and cats; a pack of wolves has killed a man on the city's outskirts.			
Jan. 27	The U.S. Senate votes to join the World Court by a margin of 76–17.	60,000 Communists in Berlin mark former Kaiser Wilhelm's birthday by hanging him in effigy and calling for his death.			The Premier of Japan, Viscount Takaaki Kato, dies from influenza. Kato has been known in America for his hostility to U.S. exclusion policies toward Japanese immigrants.
Jan. 28	World leaders, including French Premier Aristide Briand, hail U.S. adhesion to the World Court. Briand calls it a "first step" toward joining the League of Nations.	German Chancellor Luther receives a vote of confidence from the Reichstag, winning by the narrow margin of ten votes. Socialist representatives abstain from voting....A play satirizing the Scopes trial will be performed in Moscow. Actors reproducing key episodes from the trial will appear as monkeys....The Soviet Union plans to produce 75 million gallons of vodka in 1926 for the Russian market....Italy bans jazz dancing and conducts a series of raids on dancehalls.	A Harvard expedition in Cairo resumes excavating a tomb dated to Egypt's Fourth Dynasty....Turkish officials are accused of discriminating against American firms in Constantinople. The behavior is seen as an attempt to pressure the United States to sign the Treaty of Lausanne, which legitimated the Republic of Turkey.		

A	B	C	D	E
Includes developments that affect more than one world region, international organizations and important meetings of world leaders.	Includes all domestic and regional developments in Europe, including the Soviet Union.	Includes all domestic and regional developments in Africa and the Middle East.	Includes all domestic and regional developments in Latin America, the Caribbean, and Canada.	Includes all domestic and regional developments in Asian and Pacific nations (and colonies).

U.S. Politics & Social Issues	U.S. Foreign Policy & Affairs, Defense	U.S. Economy & Environment	Science, Technology & Nature	Culture, Leisure & Lifestyle	
President Coolidge supports the repeal of inheritance taxes, as recently proposed in Congress.... The Interior Department determines that American Indians who conduct all of their business on reservation lands do not have to pay federal income taxes....Palm Beach, Florida, is experiencing a crime wave. Several homes have been burgled in the past week, with a quarter of a million dollars in gems stolen.		The St. Louis-San Francisco Railroad purchases majority rights in the Chicago, Rock Island & Pacific Railway Company, creating the largest railway system, in terms of mileage, in the world....Hopes are briefly raised, then dashed, about a possible anthracite settlement. John L. Lewis accepts the "Lynett plan," a newspaper editor's plan for a temporary work resumption, but the operators refuse.	British inventor John Baird has reportedly perfected mechanical television. While he speaks before his transmission apparatus, his face and words can be seen in another room.	President Coolidge's father, a steadfast opponent of the telephone, finally allows one to be installed in his home because of his lengthy illness....Yale University offers their expertise to other schools on implementing motion pictures as a teaching tool in the classroom.	Jan. 22
Several leading publishers and editors of Southern newspapers call for better educational facilities throughout the South, to undergird the region's rapid industrial and commercial growth.	Statistics from the U.S. Army Air Service indicate that flying is becoming safer. Since 1922 nearly eight million miles have been flown and 10 Army pilots have been killed, a considerable improvement over statistics from the 1918–21 period.		The Department of Commerce releases a report anticipating dramatic growth in air transportation.	The American Automobile Association reports that drunk driving is prevalent across the United States and notes the lack of serious law enforcement....President Coolidge authorizes a President's Cup in his name, to be given to the champion in competitive speedboat races....John Barrymore stars as Captain Ahab in "The Sea Beast," Hollywood's adaptation of Herman Melville's novel Moby-Dick.	Jan. 23
More than 3,500 American Communists rally at meetings in New York City in honor of the second anniversary of Vladimir Lenin's death. Picture postcards of Lenin are sold for 5 cents apiece.			An attempt at international radio broadcasting is unsuccessful. American listeners are able to hear only brief snippets of English broadcasts. The experiment is interrupted when a ship's SOS distress call off the Delaware coast forces all Atlantic Seaboard stations to remain silent....American chemists have improved processes for manufacturing nitrates, used in high explosives, to the extent that the United States is no longer dependent on foreign sources.	A butler is shot dead upon answering the door of a brownstone on Fifty-Fourth Street in New York City; John D. Rockefeller and former senator Chauncey DePew own homes on the same block....The Julliard Musical Foundation announces plans to create a major center for the advancement of music in the United States....Reports indicate that there were 21,000 automobile deaths in the United States in 1925, an increase of 5 percent from the previous year.	Jan. 24
A doctor practicing for a quarter-century in the Ozark Mountains of Arkansas, thought to be a man, is revealed to be a woman....Jewish leaders express their interest in constructing a National Synagogue in Washington, DC.	President Coolidge modifies the court-martial sentence of Colonel William Mitchell, former Assistant Chief of the Army Air Service, allowing him half-pay. Mitchell had been court-martialed for publicly charging the War Department with incompetence and negligence following the destruction of the airship Shenandoah in 1925.		A hurricane causes havoc in the North Atlantic. Two men on the U.S. liner President Roosevelt are lost during a rescue attempt of a distressed British freighter.... International radio tests are again interrupted by SOS signals on the Atlantic Seaboard, but listeners in the Midwest report hearing broadcasts from as far away as Buenos Aires and Prague.	A New York City Board of Education proposal that would require the Ten Commandments to be read weekly in public schools is vigorously attacked by opponents.	Jan. 25
Sixty individuals, including thirteen Coast Guardsmen, are indicted for their roles in the Dwyer liquor syndicate, a major coastal rum-running operation. Among the conspirators is a pilot, the first "air bootlegger" ever charged.		Miners and anthracite operators resume talks, but the "Lynett plan" is permanently tabled.	A hurricane, with 50-foot seas, continues to batter the North Atlantic. Only six sailors have been rescued—by the German liner Bremen—from two distressed British freighters. Several dozen men are said to still be adrift.		Jan. 26
Senate Progressives vow to fight an effort to repeal estate taxes.	Colonel William Mitchell submits his letter of resignation from the U.S. Army, pending President Coolidge's approval.	The F. W. Woolworth Company reports record profits in 1925.	The President Roosevelt manages to rescue the entire crew from the British freighter Antinoe; two dozen men on another ship are presumed drowned.		Jan. 27
		Secretary of Labor James Davis arrives in Philadelphia in an effort to exert federal pressure on coal strike negotiations....The Pennsylvania Railroad reports record profits for 1925.	The final night of international radio testing is more successful than previous evenings. New York listeners report clearly hearing jazz music from Lisbon.		Jan. 28

F
Includes campaigns, elections, federal-state relations, civil rights and liberties, crime, the judiciary, education, healthcare, poverty, urban affairs, and population.

G
Includes formation and debate of U.S. foreign and defense policies, veterans affairs, and defense spending. (Relations with specific foreign countries are usually found under the region concerned.)

H
Includes business, labor, agriculture, taxation, transportation, consumer affairs, monetary and fiscal policy, natural resources, pollution and industrial accidents.

I
Includes worldwide scientific, medical and technological developments, natural phenomena, U.S. weather and natural disasters.

J
Includes the arts, religion, scholarship, communications media, sports, entertainment, fashions, fads, and social life.

	World Affairs	Europe	Africa & The Middle East	The Americas	Asia & The Pacific
Jan. 29		A papal spokesman in Paris disparages rumors of a concordat between the Italian government and the Vatican. He sarcastically refers to Mussolini's "new Roman Empire."…The Soviet Commissariat of Education orders all male university students to participate in compulsory military training on campus.			Chinese General Zhang Zuolin continues to arrest Soviet citizens in Harbin, and the Soviet Foreign Commissar has demanded the general's removal.
Jan. 30		Commander Franco successfully executes the most difficult segment of his flight from Spain to Argentina, landing on an island off the coast of Brazil after traveling more than 1,400 miles.	The Turkish government institutes the Roman alphabet in place of Arabic lettering.	The U.S. Senate launches an investigation into the deportation and subsequent execution of Mexican Colonel Manuel Demetrio Torres, a participant in the failed De la Huerta revolution in 1924 who had sought asylum in San Antonio, TX.	Japan passes an edict abolishing voting property-holding requirements, extending suffrage to an estimated 10 million voters. Women still cannot vote….Chinese provincial assemblies call for a national conference to undertake a truce between various warring generals and elect a president and parliament, to replace the provisional government at Peking.
Jan. 31		Commander Franco completes his journey from Spain to South America when he lands safely in Brazil….Soviet officials announce plans to sell or trade tsarist crown jewels and old master paintings by Rembrandt and Raphael in the United States. They want to receive tractors and locomotives in trades.		Mexican President Calles and the American ambassador meet to discuss the continued deadlock over land and oil laws.	Nationalist students in Peking establish the Anti-Red Imperialism Foundation to denounce meddling by the Soviet Union in Manchuria.
Feb. 1		Hungarian Prince Windisch-Graetz has been indicted as the ringleader of a counterfeiting scheme. Over the past three years the prince and his co-conspirators, operating from the Hungarian Cartographical Institute, have produced an estimated 30 million individual false bills, primarily crowns and francs.		Six former Mexican government officials, now all political refugees living in Texas, protest to President Coolidge that the deportation of recently executed General Manuel Demetrio Torres was a violation of international rights.	In Harbin, Manchuria, 500 Chinese women riot to protest the arrest of several Communist youths.
Feb. 2	President Coolidge asserts that U.S. adherence to the World Court protocol should in no way be considered a preliminary to joining the League of Nations.	In Leningrad, 48 people, including a priest and four women, are on trial for conspiring to destroy the nation's infrastructure, such as munitions plants and bridges. Most of them face the death penalty….Leon Trotsky has published Whither England?, a book that calls for a general strike in Great Britain as a prelude to revolution.	The Turkish government is severely truncating traditional wedding practices. Under new laws, the usual weeklong feast has been reduced to one day, wedding gifts are banned, and no more than five carloads of celebrants may follow the bride to her new home.	The Mexican government insists that General Torres was executed for being a "dangerous train robber," not for his political activities. An investigation into the U.S. handling of the case has revealed that Torres was handed over to Mexican authorities without the benefit of formal extradition proceedings.	
Feb. 3			Spanish and French military strategists are conferring about how to best subdue the rebellious activities of tribal groups in Morocco. Abd-el Krim, a Berber guerilla leader, continues to present problems. Approximately 250,000 combined French and Spanish troops are operating in the Rift region of Morocco.	Mexican President Calles insists that his country's land and oil laws will remain unchanged, regardless of pressure from Washington.	Chinese officials at a Nine Powers customs conference in Peking demand full autonomy to set tariffs.
Feb. 4			Druse tribesmen have requested direct peace negotiations with the French military in the mandate of Syria.		

A	B	C	D	E
Includes developments that affect more than one world region, international organizations and important meetings of world leaders.	Includes all domestic and regional developments in Europe, including the Soviet Union.	Includes all domestic and regional developments in Africa and the Middle East.	Includes all domestic and regional developments in Latin America, the Caribbean, and Canada.	Includes all domestic and regional developments in Asian and Pacific nations (and colonies).

U.S. Politics & Social Issues	U.S. Foreign Policy & Affairs, Defense	U.S. Economy & Environment	Science, Technology & Nature	Culture, Leisure & Lifestyle	
	Secretary of War Davis accepts Colonel William Mitchell's resignation from the military. It is widely expected that Mitchell will continue his advocacy for aviation reforms.	The United Mine Workers makes its first important concession in negotiations with anthracite owners. They accept the idea of arbitration by a fact-finding panel headed by Charles Evans Hughes. They refuse the operators' demand that the arbitration decision must be final and binding.	Two air mail pilots set a new record for night flying, completing their route from Chicago to New York—which typically takes more than seven hours—in only five hours and twenty-four minutes. The pilots' average speed is 134 miles per hour....A military pilot sets an American altitude record, reaching a ceiling of 35,900 feet, in a CZO-5 plane featuring new principles of wing engineering....An enormous ice jam upriver has caused Niagara Falls to temporarily go dry.		Jan. 29
Leading penitentiary officials scorn the idea of holding music concerts in prisons. "I have no patience with the uplifter and social worker who would turn our prisons into recreation centers," one official remarks.			Aviator Richard Byrd announces his intentions to explore the North Pole by air, although he is uncertain whether he will use a plane or a dirigible.	Sailors from the President Roosevelt are feted as heroes upon landing in Queenstown Harbor....Canadian professional hockey players, citing their low salaries in comparison to hockey players in American leagues, plan to unionize.	Jan. 30
			An astronomer in Johannesburg announces the discovery of a sextuple star, composed of three double stars.	American tennis champion Helen Wills, playing in the Riviera, has won nine straight sets against highly-ranked rivals.	Jan. 31
Masked gunmen pull off a daring robbery of the central post office in Pawtucket, Rhode Island, making off with $265,000 in stamps and registered mail....Progressive Republican senators pledge full deliberations, including a filibuster if necessary, on the tax reduction bill before Congress.	The U.S. Marine Corps has granted the Metro-Goldwyn Picture Corporation exclusive rights to make films featuring Marines. The studio will remake the hit war picture "The Big Parade" as "Tell It to the Marines," with real Marines performing formations. The remake is intended as a recruiting vehicle for the Corps.	Several senators attack the proposed merger of two large baking companies into the Ward Food Products Corporation. If the merger proceeds, the "bread trust" will be worth $2 billion and consolidate most of the wholesale bakeries in the United States....The New York City store Lord & Taylor celebrates its centennial.			Feb. 1
The capital trial of African-American Ed Harris, who has confessed to assault and murder, is completed in 16 minutes in a Lexington, Kentucky, courthouse. After Harris pleads guilty, the jury takes 3 minutes to decide on the death penalty. Nearly 1,000 soldiers guard the courthouse outside against potential lynch mobs.		Negotiations between coal miners and operators break down again over the issue of voluntary versus compulsory arbitration.		Professional baseball celebrates its 50th anniversary with a gala event in New York City, with several senators, governors, and presidential cabinet members in attendance.	Feb. 2
The Church Temperance Society of the Protestant Episcopal Church declares Prohibition a failure. Their report insists that the Volstead Act has actually bred intemperance and an atmosphere of disdain for the law.		Under heavily armed guard, a record shipment of gold bars from South America, worth $10 million, arrives in New York City from Chile and is transported to the Federal Reserve Bank....More than 10,000 workers are striking the woolen mills in Passaic, NJ.		The American Cinema Association, a group of independent film producers, distributors, and exhibitors, calls for family-friendly comedies and melodramas to replace Hollywood's "sex" pictures.	Feb. 3
The Senate skirmishes over a tax reduction bill, with Progressive Republican George Norris leading efforts to preserve provisions that require Treasury tax return information to be open to public inspection...."Dry" leaders from several organizations, including the Anti-Saloon League and the Christian Endeavor Society, criticize the Episcopalian stance on Prohibition.	Six soldiers at Schofield Barracks in Honolulu die from accidentally drinking wood alcohol, which was sold to them as bay rum....The Navy Bureau of Aeronautics has submitted a request for $250 million to bolster the nation's aerial defenses. They plan to build 1,250 new fighter planes.	The Goodyear Tire and Rubber Company reports record net profits in 1925....Two Chicago bootleggers, under arrest, admit to the Internal Revenue Service that they earned $1.5 million for one year as illegal beer brewers. They offer to pay back taxes.	A major winter storm whips the Atlantic Seaboard. The city of Boston is brought to a standstill, and eight people are killed when a snow-heavy roof collapses at a manufacturing plant in New Britain, CT....Germany introduces the in-flight movie to air travel, as the American film "The Lost World" is shown to passengers over Berlin. Radio is used to provide musical accompaniment.		Feb. 4

F	**G**	**H**	**I**	**J**
Includes campaigns, elections, federal-state relations, civil rights and liberties, crime, the judiciary, education, healthcare, poverty, urban affairs, and population.	Includes formation and debate of U.S. foreign and defense policies, veterans affairs, and defense spending. (Relations with specific foreign countries are usually found under the region concerned.)	Includes business, labor, agriculture, taxation, transportation, consumer affairs, monetary and fiscal policy, natural resources, pollution and industrial accidents.	Includes worldwide scientific, medical and technological developments, natural phenomena, U.S. weather and natural disasters.	Includes the arts, religion, scholarship, communications media, sports, entertainment, fashions, fads, and social life.

	World Affairs	Europe	Africa & The Middle East	The Americas	Asia & The Pacific
Feb. 5	Germany announces plans to apply for membership in the League of Nations, making the United States and the Soviet Union the only major countries that continue to refuse membership.	Officials in Berlin are investigating the "Feme murders," a series of politically motivated killings attributed to a shadowy paramilitary organization, the Black Reichswehr....Soviet officials have put on public display the house where Tsar Nicholas II and his family were murdered. Tourists can visit the basement execution room and meditate at a "Square of National Vengeance" outside.		In an interview, Mexican President Calles dismisses notions that he is anti-American. He declares that he will not be affected by widespread rumors that the U.S. State Department plans to withdraw recognition of his government.	
Feb. 6		Italian Premier Mussolini berates Germany for protesting his government's treatment of German-speaking Italians in the Upper Adige region. He calls the German "concern" for these inhabitants a pretense; what Germany really wants, he insists, is to claim the territory. Among other belligerent remarks, he declares a new policy for his country: "Two eyes for an eye and a whole set of teeth for just one tooth."		A gold strike in Red Lake, Canada, 150 miles north of Winnipeg, has brought a sudden influx of prospectors and dog sled teams. More than 1,000 are expected this spring with better weather.	
Feb. 7		French officials have dropped plans to charge an income tax on the revenue of foreigners, but other taxes penalizing foreigners have been proposed.		A major Mexican newspaper closely aligned with the government publishes an editorial that calls the United States "a selfish and dominating country without windows abroad."	
Feb. 8			College students in Cairo attempt to wear western-style clothing to classes, but are denied admittance by police. The Ministry of Education threatens to expel them unless they wear proper Egyptian garb.	The Coolidge Administration ratchets up tensions with Mexico, declaring that the Calles government has failed to live up to the terms of the 1923 U.S.-Mexican Claims Commission, which guarantees indemnities to Americans who have suffered physical or property damage in past Mexican revolutionary conflicts....An expedition of American scientists reports discovering an ancient Mayan city in Cozumel, Mexico.	
Feb. 9		The president of the Reichstag reads a formal declaration denouncing Mussolini's "attacks and sneers" against Germany. Citing the mistreatment of Germans living in the Italian Southern Tyrol, he demands justice for "racially related minorities" living under foreign sovereignty....After 18 straight days of rain, the Lea River floods several London suburbs.			
Feb. 10		Mussolini delivers a sarcasm-tinged speech against the German Reichstag. He reiterates his pledge of last week that Italy is prepared "to carry her flag beyond the present frontiers." This has been widely interpreted as an inflammatory threat to Italy's neighbors....Seven separate failed assassination attempts have been perpetrated in recent days against Spanish Premier Miguel Primo de Rivera, allegedly by syndicalists.		England has formally protested the Mexican anti-alien land and oil laws, similar to the American stance.	The two major Philippine political parties are forming a coalition to pursue a common goal, independence from the United States.

A	B	C	D	E
Includes developments that affect more than one world region, international organizations and important meetings of world leaders.	Includes all domestic and regional developments in Europe, including the Soviet Union.	Includes all domestic and regional developments in Africa and the Middle East.	Includes all domestic and regional developments in Latin America, the Caribbean, and Canada.	Includes all domestic and regional developments in Asian and Pacific nations (and colonies).

U.S. Politics & Social Issues	U.S. Foreign Policy & Affairs, Defense	U.S. Economy & Environment	Science, Technology & Nature	Culture, Leisure & Lifestyle	
Eighteen Episcopalian bishops reject the Church Temperance Society's call for changes to Prohibition law....The Dramatists Guild demands 50 percent of money obtained from movie rights for their plays....Progressive Republican James Couzens and Democrat Kenneth McKellar speak for almost five hours on the Senate floor against repealing income tax publicity.		The National Better Business Bureau and the Florida State Chamber of Commerce announce a joint campaign to stamp out real estate flimflammery in Florida.			Feb. 5
Congress debates creating a Bureau of Prohibition, which would take up enforcement duties from the Internal Revenue Service. "Wets" in the Senate attack the proposal and cite the Episcopalian report in their call for Prohibition reform.		Operating under new transparency rules, the New York Stock Exchange announces that brokers borrowed $3.5 billion in January for speculative and investment purposes. Call loans account for 70 percent of this total.		The National Football League bans collegiate athletes from playing in pro games until after their class has graduated....Red Grange applies for ownership of his own pro football franchise, with plans to play at Yankee Stadium....Playwright George Bernard Shaw denounces audience applause during plays, believing that it distracts from the creative process.	Feb. 6
Rebutting efforts by the American Federation of Labor to guarantee overtime pay for government employees, Representative Martin Davey of Ohio calls the typical government clerk a "loafer, time-killer, and buck-passer."...Pittsburgh police conduct a liquor raid on the famous Americus Club, which for decades has hosted senators, diplomats, and cabinet members.		Figures indicate that American railroad companies earned more than $1 billion in 1925, an industry record....The Justice Department has launched an investigation into the proposed Ward Food Products Corporation....Labor Bureau statistics indicate that American average wages are keeping pace with the cost of living. Both increased by 3 percent in 1925.	Chicago introduces the world's largest coordinated system of traffic lights. The system controls the flow of traffic at 49 street intersections....Henry Ford plans to operate an express passenger airline, with service linking cities such as New York and Boston.	French tennis champion Suzanne Lenglen and her doubles partner Baron Henri de Morjurgo defeat Helen Wills and Charles Aschlimann in straight sets before a French Riviera crowd....Director Robert Flaherty's film Moana, featuring Samoan nonactors playing themselves, has been released. A reviewer in the New York Sun coins a new term to describe the movie—"documentary."	Feb. 7
By a vote of 49–32, the Senate kills Senator Norris's "tax publicity" amendment, ensuring that the new revenue law will repeal this mechanism of disclosure....President Coolidge is nearly hit by a delivery truck while attempting to cross a street by the White House....During the trial of Henry Butler, an African-American accused of attacking a 12-year-old girl, the state militia must use tear gas to stop a mob from storming the courthouse in Georgetown, Delaware. Butler is found guilty and sentenced to hang. The girl is recovering from a skull fracture.		The U.S. Government files suit to stop the creation of the Ward Food Products Corporation, alleging that the giant company would form a nation-wide monopoly.... Shares in food and baking companies drop precipitously on the New York Stock Exchange....Citing difficult conditions in the nation's Northeast brought on by severe winter weather and fuel shortages, several members of the U.S. House of Representatives urge President Coolidge to intervene in the coal strike.	The United States Weather Bureau has introduced a new term, "smog," to describe the combination of fog and smoke created by human activity.	A distinctly American ballet with syncopated music, John Alden Carpenter's Skyscrapers, is set to debut at the Metropolitan Opera House in New York City....Helen Wills needs 15 minutes to defeat a British opponent 6–0, 6–0 at Cannes....The British film industry remains interested in imposing a quota on foreign films. The latest plan states that one British film must be exhibited for every seven foreign films shown during the coming year.	Feb. 8
The Virginia state legislature is considering a Racial Integrity bill that will class as "colored" any white person with a known "admixture of Indian or Negro blood." State patriotic societies are protesting, because several prominent Virginia families are descended from unions of white settlers and Indians during the 17th century.	President Coolidge upholds the court martial death sentence of Second Lieutenant John Thompson, who has been convicted of murdering an 18-year-old American woman in Manila....The British government in India will permit the creation of a Royal Indian Navy, with a certain number of officer commissions reserved for Indians.	The Senate passes a non-binding resolution in an effort to pressure the Coolidge Administration to settle the coal strike. In the House, Democratic representatives claim that the administration's "masterful inactivity" is rooted in its alignment with large national financial interests that seek to break the union....Previously convicted swindler Charles Ponzi has been indicted again for fraud.		Immigration officials detain a British aristocrat, the Countess Cathcart, for questioning at Ellis Island upon her first visit to the United States. She has been through a well-publicized divorce involving adultery, an act viewed as "moral turpitude" under U.S. immigration laws.	Feb. 9
By a two-to-one margin, the Senate votes to abolish estate taxes. In addition, the so-called "nuisance levies" on automobiles and theater admissions are repealed....The governor of Arizona accuses California of committing "rapine" in seeking to divert waters from the Colorado River.	Army Air Service Major General Mason Patrick has reportedly been pressing to establish an independent air corps, angering Secretary of War Dwight Davis and other War Department top brass.	The former beer brewery Anheuser-Busch in St. Louis, struggling with Prohibition, announces plans to produce and market yeast. Other sales commodities include ice, cattle feed, and soft drinks. The company, which once employed 7,000 workers, has cut staff to 1,800....The Pullman Company has given its maids and porters a substantial pay increase; their wages are now 141 percent higher than in 1913.			Feb. 10

F	G	H	I	J
Includes campaigns, elections, federal-state relations, civil rights and liberties, crime, the judiciary, education, healthcare, poverty, urban affairs, and population.	Includes formation and debate of U.S. foreign and defense policies, veterans affairs, and defense spending. (Relations with specific foreign countries are usually found under the region concerned.)	Includes business, labor, agriculture, taxation, transportation, consumer affairs, monetary and fiscal policy, natural resources, pollution and industrial accidents.	Includes worldwide scientific, medical and technological developments, natural phenomena, U.S. weather and natural disasters.	Includes the arts, religion, scholarship, communications media, sports, entertainment, fashions, fads, and social life.

	World Affairs	Europe	Africa & The Middle East	The Americas	Asia & The Pacific
Feb. 11	Germany, Spain, Poland, and Brazil are all candidates to hold permanent seats on the Council of the League of Nations. Germany has been assured a seat upon admission to the League, which will threaten French influence on the Council; the composition of the others seats has therefore become an important political issue.	Sean O'Casey's play *The Plough and the Stars*, newly premiered in Dublin, provokes an audience to riot. During the third act, members of the audience assault two female performers onstage. The play casts a critical eye on Irish nationalist aspirations during the 1916 Uprising.		The Mexican government announces that all church properties will be seized and nationalized. In addition, all foreign priests are to be arrested and deported. Several priests from Spain and Ireland have been rounded up by police.	Golf is reportedly becoming a favorite sport in Japan. An expert from the Japanese government has recently completed a world tour to study the game.
Feb. 12					Reports indicate that Chinese nationalist students on Hainan Island have attacked an American mission, beating the Chinese menials who work there and ripping down an American flag....Chinese general Wu Pei-fu, who had been confined to the south, is now making advances northward and has captured the large central Chinese city of Hankou.
Feb. 13		British historian Sir William Ashland defends the recent spate of sales of British historical documents to American libraries. He cites the many promising young historians working in American academia, who are bringing "fresher and more open minds" to Old World materials....London's trolley system is teetering on the verge of bankruptcy. Reports indicate that 6,500,000 fewer people rode the trolleys in 1925 than in the previous year.			Soviet officials believe that the British have signed a secret treaty with Zhang Zuolin. According to their allegations, the British will send 100,000 troops to China to bolster Zuolin's leadership against both Bolshevist and Chinese nationalist influences. British officials deny the Soviet claims.
Feb. 14		In an abrupt turnabout in policy, Soviet authorities forbid members of the Young Communist Party to stage anti-religious agitprop plays. The authorities are reportedly concerned that such works will provoke the anger of the nation's peasants.	John D. Rockefeller donates $10 million to Egypt to build a national archaeological museum.... Archaeologists from the British Museum and the University of Pennsylvania have found evidence in Iraq of what they believe to be a pre-brick civilization, dating to well before 3300 B.C.E.		
Feb. 15			British Lieutenant Colonel T.E. Lawrence has published *The Seven Pillars of Wisdom*, about his experiences during the Arab Revolt of 1916–18....Ibn Saud, leading a large force of Salafist followers, is operating in the Emirate of Transjordan near the border of Syria. He poses a threat to both British and French control of the region.		
Feb. 16		Chancellor of the Exchequer Winston Churchill reports that the British national debt stands at nearly £8 trillion.		The Mexican government is closing all schools, both religious and secular, run by foreigners.	The three provinces in Manchuria have demanded autonomy and will unite in a federation under Zhang Zuolin. They cite the weakness of the central government in Peking and the continued influence of the Soviets in Manchuria as reasons to "take independent steps."
Feb. 17		An English country mansion with 150 rooms outside of London is destroyed in a fire—becoming the seventh such mansion to burn down in the past two months.			

A	B	C	D	E
Includes developments that affect more than one world region, international organizations and important meetings of world leaders.	Includes all domestic and regional developments in Europe, including the Soviet Union.	Includes all domestic and regional developments in Africa and the Middle East.	Includes all domestic and regional developments in Latin America, the Caribbean, and Canada.	Includes all domestic and regional developments in Asian and Pacific nations (and colonies).

U.S. Politics & Social Issues	U.S. Foreign Policy & Affairs, Defense	U.S. Economy & Environment	Science, Technology & Nature	Culture, Leisure & Lifestyle	
		The largest banking merger in the nation's history is announced. The Chase National Bank and the Mechanics and Metals National Bank intend to consolidate, creating an entity with more than $1 billion in assets....Department of Commerce statistics indicate that 1925 was a record-setting year for U.S. oil production and consumption. The U.S. output of crude oil increased 7 percent over 1925.		Citing her "crime involving moral turpitude," immigration officials order the deportation of the Countess Cathcart.	Feb. 11
The Senate votes 58–9 in favor of a tax reduction bill worth $456 million. Nevertheless, the Treasury expects a $67 million surplus for the 1926 fiscal year.		The anthracite coal strike, which has lasted five months, involved 158,000 miners from 828 mines, and cost an estimated one billion dollars, is finally settled. The United Mine Workers wins a contract guaranteeing five years of fixed wages.		George Bernard Shaw has admitted being offered a million dollars by Hollywood mogul Samuel Goldwyn for the film rights to his plays. Shaw turned the money down.	Feb. 12
Although generally supportive, members of the House of Representatives question some aspects of the Senate tax reduction bill. They contend that cuts are too deep and will result in a federal budget deficit. The Senate's repeal of the estate tax is not likely to survive in the House version of the bill.		The U.S. government files an antitrust suit against the National Food Products Corporation, accused of trying to establish a monopoly over milk and ice cream manufacture and distribution....The National Association of Real Estate Boards acknowledges the problem of real estate fraud and calls for investor protections, which will in turn protect the industry's reputation.	A wireless telephone is successfully used to transmit a transatlantic conversation between Rugby, England, and Long Island.	Guy Massey, the alleged author of the first "hillbilly" song to become a major hit in the United States, has died. "The Prisoner's Song," recorded by Massey's cousin, singer Vernon Dalhart, has sold more than five million copies in the past two years. Massey has been embroiled in controversy over his authorship claim; many insist that "The Prisoner's Song" is actually an old-time song that has been circulating for years.	Feb. 13
			Five people are drowned during severe storms in the mining town of Coaldale, KY.	Immigration officials have received hundreds of protest letters and wires from women who point out the moral "double standard" involved in deportation proceedings against the British countess. The Earl of Craven, the co-respondent in her divorce case, has already been admitted to the United States with no legal entanglements.	Feb. 14
The House Committee on Immigration estimates that there are as many as 1.3 million illegal immigrants in the United States. Most of them reside in the major Atlantic Seaboard cities and in Pittsburgh, St. Louis, Chicago, and Detroit. Rounding up and deporting them will cost $25 million.	Citing the perils of isolationism, education leaders at the Forum on Foreign Affairs have called on the United States to develop more university schools of diplomacy.	The bears are loose on Wall Street, as most industrial issues drop 4 to 5 points. It is the worst day for stocks since November 1925.	Boston is facing a serious rat infestation, the result of heavy snowfalls and high tides that have driven the rodents from their habitat in the Charles River and Boston Harbor.	A copy of the Gutenberg Bible sells at a public auction in New York City for $106,000, and is thought to be the highest price ever paid for a book....Showman Florenz Ziegfeld announces plans to build a lavish million-dollar theater in Miami.	Feb. 15
A wholesale grain alcohol ring with profits of $140 million, centered in Philadelphia, is being investigated by a federal grand jury. More than 200 people, including four millionaires, are being indicted.	Congress passes appropriations for $660 million for national defense. In addition, $100 million is earmarked for a five-year aviation buildup, to include a thousand new airplanes, two giant dirigibles, and a metal-clad dirigible.	Anthracite miners have officially ratified the agreement reached by the Joint Negotiating Committee of Miners and Operators in Philadelphia. The miners will start back to work tomorrow.		Six-time Wimbledon champion Suzanne Lenglen defeats 20-year-old American star Helen Wills 6–3, 8–6, at Cannes. The match draws a huge crowd, including the King of Sweden and numerous British aristocrats. Wills leads in both sets before Lenglen rallies.	Feb. 16
A caucus of Republican Senators is determined to limit the number of congressional investigations, citing the public expense....Treasury Prohibition officials are advocating a plan to buy all of the nation's medicinal whiskey, at a likely expense of $400 million, to prevent legal alcohol from being diverted for illegal uses.			An avalanche destroys the hamlet of Highland Boy, Utah, killing at least 30 people.	Secretary of Labor Davis upholds the decision by immigration officials to deport the Countess Cathcart....The poet Carl Sandburg has published his biography *Abraham Lincoln: The Prairie Years*, to critical acclaim.	Feb. 17

F	G	H	I	J
Includes campaigns, elections, federal-state relations, civil rights and liberties, crime, the judiciary, education, healthcare, poverty, urban affairs, and population.	*Includes formation and debate of U.S. foreign and defense policies, veterans affairs, and defense spending. (Relations with specific foreign countries are usually found under the region concerned.)*	*Includes business, labor, agriculture, taxation, transportation, consumer affairs, monetary and fiscal policy, natural resources, pollution and industrial accidents.*	*Includes worldwide scientific, medical and technological developments, natural phenomena, U.S. weather and natural disasters.*	*Includes the arts, religion, scholarship, communications media, sports, entertainment, fashions, fads, and social life.*

	World Affairs	Europe	Africa & The Middle East	The Americas	Asia & The Pacific
Feb. 18	While Germany expects a permanent seat on the Council of the League of Nations, German officials insist that no other expansions of the Council should be made to accommodate countries such as Spain or Poland.		The British House of Commons votes to ratify the Iraq Treaty, which extends the British mandate over Iraq for 25 more years.	The Mexican Secretary of the Interior denies that the government has closed several Catholic orphanages. He claims that Catholic administrators, not the government, have turned out orphans into the streets, "with the object of creating a bad impression on the public to appear as victims."	In the U.S. House of Representatives, Charles Underhill of Massachusetts criticizes Filipino leaders in their drive for independence. He notes that he recently visited the Philippines, where he found the population "no more fit for self-government than a bunch of schoolchildren."
Feb. 19		A major German newspaper has investigated the claims of a female sanitarium patient, Frau von Tschaikovsky, that she is in fact the Grand Duchess Anastasia. The paper insists that "beyond doubt" the woman's story is true.		Members of the U.S. House Foreign Affairs Committee urge the Coolidge Administration to be more aggressive in protecting the rights of Americans in Mexico. Representative Benjamin Fairchild calls Mexico "a sore fist thrust up into the very bowels of the United States." He speculates that Mexico may need "a permanent cure."	Fourteen Japanese seamen, adrift for more than a month on a disabled steamer, are rescued in the mid-Pacific. The men had been without water for the past five days and subsisted on eating rats and the ship's cat.
Feb. 20		Germany announces plans for the world's most ambitious commercial aviation program. Forty-two routes will connect Germany to cities such as London, Paris, and Moscow. Seventeen separate flights will depart from Berlin every day—an unprecedented number.			
Feb. 21	Senators William Borah and James Reed have taken to the streets and the radio airwaves to denounce the recent Senate vote to join the World Court. A parade today in Chicago featured 3,000 automobiles, festooned in anti-Court slogans, traveling 35 miles to greet Borah upon his arrival in the city.	Grigory Zinoviev, chairman of the Communist International in Moscow, admits that exporting world proletarian revolution may be difficult. He cites challenging circumstances for communism in the United States and Japan, but he sees South America and especially China as more fertile ground....Although unemployment remains high, the financial picture in Germany is beginning to improve. Capital scarcity is no longer a concern.			American missionaries have been trapped for several days between opposed Chinese armies near Sinyanchow.
Feb. 22		Pope Pius XI dismisses Mussolini's efforts to achieve a rapprochement between the Italian government and the Vatican as a "policy of blandishments."...American efforts to persuade the Pope to build a six-hole golf course on the Vatican grounds have failed....Jewelers from London, Paris, Antwerp, and New York bid vigorously on tsarist gems in Moscow; the winning bid, placed by French jewelers, is worth $3 million.			French authorities stop an attempted prison break by Chinese convicts in Shanghai, killing 15 inmates....After hiding from troops, eight American missionaries have successfully reached Hankow, where they report on the activities of Wu Pei-fu's army. His men have been indiscriminately murdering civilians and confiscating all food supplies; many civilians are dying from starvation.
Feb. 23				A riot, primarily involving women, breaks out at the Catholic Church of the Sacred Family in Mexico City. Worshippers hinder efforts by government agents to arrest Spanish priests at the church for deportation. A large mob of several thousand people then marches to a government office to protest policy. Police efforts to quell the mob result in two deaths.	

A	B	C	D	E
Includes developments that affect more than one world region, international organizations and important meetings of world leaders.	Includes all domestic and regional developments in Europe, including the Soviet Union.	Includes all domestic and regional developments in Africa and the Middle East.	Includes all domestic and regional developments in Latin America, the Caribbean, and Canada.	Includes all domestic and regional developments in Asian and Pacific nations (and colonies).

U.S. Politics & Social Issues	U.S. Foreign Policy & Affairs, Defense	U.S. Economy & Environment	Science, Technology & Nature	Culture, Leisure & Lifestyle	
Omaha is being terrorized by a sniper who fires into buildings with lighted windows. Two men have been killed and one wounded in the past week.				The prominent attorney Arthur Garfield Hayes, who has also defended John Scopes and Sacco and Vanzetti, has been hired to fight against deportation for the British countess. The case has become a rallying cry for women's groups, who are flooding her with supportive mail....Violinist Jascha Heifetz is the rage of Paris.	Feb. 18
The Omaha sniper has struck again, shooting a railroad detective six times. Unlike in the other shootings, the detective was outside, not in a lighted building. Miraculously, he has survived....Negotiations between the Senate and the House have resulted in an agreement on the tax reduction bill. The Senate has been forced to give up the desired repeal of the estate tax.		Statistics indicate that there were 10 percent fewer business bankruptcies nationally in January 1926 than in January 1925.	The National Research Council, by measuring levels of radioactivity in lead-uranium, has estimated that the earth is one billion years old.	The cast of Eugene O'Neill's play Desire Under the Elms is arrested in Los Angles on obscenity charges. Their production had been attended by several ministers and members of the Parent-Teachers' Association.	Feb. 19
A survey indicates that the Ku Klux Klan is waning as a national organization. Membership remains strongest in the North and West, although it has fallen dramatically. For example, in New York State there are approximately 100,000 members, down from 200,000; in Texas there are 18,000 members, down from 100,000.		Harvard professor William Ripley criticizes public utilities corporations, suggesting that their financing is "extremely unwise and liable to grave abuses." While the primary corporations may appear financially sound, subsidiary companies are often heavily indebted. Utilities magnate Samuel Insull has dismissed such criticisms as "sob stuff."		Following negotiations with officials, Arthur Garfield Hayes announces that the Countess Cathcart is likely to be freed within a few days. She has signed a contract to star on the American stage....Yale University plans to build a major research library, the Sterling Memorial Library. Among the most important collections will be those devoted to the Orient, Johann Wolfgang Goethe, James Fenimore Cooper, and rare coins.	Feb. 20
Pro- and anti-Prohibition forces celebrate Washington's Birthday by attempting to co-opt the first president. The Association Against the Eighteenth Amendment notes that Washington wrote his own beer recipe, while the Anti-Saloon League observes that he had his soldiers whipped for drunkenness.				Immigration officials grant the Countess Cathcart a 10-day permit to leave Ellis Island....Swedish actress Greta Garbo has made her American film debut in The Torrent....The American Medical Association is investigating the impact of having a modishly "boyish" figure on women's health.	Feb. 21
Congressional leaders hope to pass a constitutional amendment that will change the date that the president and Congress take office following an election. Currently, after a November election, the president assumes office in March, while Congress does not convene until the following December. The amendment would require both branches to take power in January. The change is intended to shorten the length of "lame duck" presidencies and Congresses....Police capture the Omaha sniper, a 45-year-old farm hand who is suspected of being insane.				The Bishop of London has applauded the arrests of actors in a Los Angeles production of Desire Under the Elms....In a 300-mile automobile race in Florida, Peter de Paolo wins $30,000 and averages 129.29 miles per hour, setting a world record for the distance. More than 30,000 fans watched the race along the route....In Palm Springs, Florida, 5,000 high society members attend a ball to celebrate Washington's Birthday. The dining hall is decorated to resemble the Street of Abundance in the ancient city of Pompeii, featuring Mount Vesuvius in the distance.	Feb. 22
The U.S. House of Representatives passes the tax reduction bill by a landslide vote of 354 to 28.	President Coolidge opposes a substantial expansion of the air force, fearing that this would inaugurate a period of competitive international military buildups.	The International Ladies' Garment Union calls off a threatened strike of 22,000 workers at a thousand dress shops....Through an innovative employee stock-purchasing plan, Standard Oil Company workers own title to $40 million in company shares, almost 5 percent of the company's outstanding stock.		Metropolitan Opera star Beniamino Gigli hastily leaves Detroit under guard, breaking a concert commitment. The Detroit Chief of Police has received a threat against him, which states: "There are ways of slicing canary throats." Gigli has been targeted by ultranationalist Italian groups that deem him unsuitably patriotic about Mussolini's government.	Feb. 23

F	G	H	I	J
Includes campaigns, elections, federal-state relations, civil rights and liberties, crime, the judiciary, education, healthcare, poverty, urban affairs, and population.	Includes formation and debate of U.S. foreign and defense policies, veterans affairs, and defense spending. (Relations with specific foreign countries are usually found under the region concerned.)	Includes business, labor, agriculture, taxation, transportation, consumer affairs, monetary and fiscal policy, natural resources, pollution and industrial accidents.	Includes worldwide scientific, medical and technological developments, natural phenomena, U.S. weather and natural disasters.	Includes the arts, religion, scholarship, communications media, sports, entertainment, fashions, fads, and social life.

	World Affairs	Europe	Africa & The Middle East	The Americas	Asia & The Pacific
Feb. 24	Germany announces that its membership in the League of Nations hinges on Poland being denied a permanent seat on the League of Nations Council. France reportedly wants Poland, its ally, to be given a seat to offset the German vote. Germany considers the French machinations to be an act of bad faith.	A French military aviator successfully executes a stunt where he flies through an arch at the base of the Eiffel Tower. His plane then hits a wire, crashes, and explodes, killing him.			
Feb. 25	Knowledgeable observers believe that Germany is using the Poland issue as a tactic to negotiate the removal of all Entente occupational forces from the Rhineland.	In the British House of Commons, politicians protest the fact that Hollywood film companies pay no English income tax on movies exhibited in England.	Spain has ordered military officers on leave to report to Morocco; an offensive by the Berber forces under Abd el-Krim is believed imminent.	Several prominent Catholic women in Mexico have petitioned President Calles about the government's treatment of Catholics. A major newspaper editorializes that the country will remain Catholic "whatever the laws, as one cannot change the soul of the people with decrees."	
Feb. 26	Mussolini, warning against a resurgent Germany, insists that Poland be given a permanent seat on the League of Nations Council to counteract German admission. He speaks of the need to find the right balance between the three European "races," Latin, Germanic, and Slav.				
Feb. 27					The Maharajah of Indore, Tukoji Rao III, renounces his rulership under British pressure. He has been the central figure in a scandal involving the disfigurement of a dancing girl and the murder of her male companion.
Feb. 28	China is pressing for a seat on the Council of the League of Nations, observing that Europe is overrepresented.	British multimillionaire hotelier Sir Henry Lund announces plans to surrender his entire fortune, except $2500 annually, to establish an organization devoted to church unity and world peace....The Italian government establishes the National Institute for Collective Ownership, which rejects private property.			
Mar. 1			Berber leader Abd el-Krim has attacked a force of Mtioua tribesmen and French troops. During the winter, the Mtioua tribes had agreed to submit to French rule. The Berbers have reportedly destroyed several Mtioua villages.	Senator George Norris demands the release of all State Department correspondence pertaining to the diplomatic imbroglio with Mexico. He accuses the United States of deliberately stoking anger against the Mexican government. The goal, he asserts, is to gain greater U.S. control over Mexican oil.	

A	B	C	D	E
Includes developments that affect more than one world region, international organizations and important meetings of world leaders.	*Includes all domestic and regional developments in Europe, including the Soviet Union.*	*Includes all domestic and regional developments in Africa and the Middle East.*	*Includes all domestic and regional developments in Latin America, the Caribbean, and Canada.*	*Includes all domestic and regional developments in Asian and Pacific nations (and colonies).*

U.S. Politics & Social Issues	U.S. Foreign Policy & Affairs, Defense	U.S. Economy & Environment	Science, Technology & Nature	Culture, Leisure & Lifestyle	
The Senate passes the revised tax reduction bill, with no estate tax repeal, by a vote of 61 to 10.			New York City officials have proposed replacing the city's trolley lines with an extensive bus system.	Baseball fans are mourning the death of Eddie Plank, a former star pitcher for the Philadelphia Athletics.	Feb. 24
		Secretary of Commerce Herbert Hoover predicts continued prosperity for the country and states that there has not been an unhealthy boom in stock market speculation.		William Faulkner's debut novel, *Soldier's Pay*, about disillusioned World War I veterans, is published....The Everglades Club in Palm Springs holds the most glamorous ball of the season, one-upping all previous efforts. Women arrive at the costume party dressed as "Poor Little Rich Girl," "Mme. Pompadour," and "Starry Night." Most of the men are dressed as pirates and devils.	Feb. 25
President Coolidge signs the tax relief bill of 1926, bringing to $700 million the total amount of tax cuts during his presidency. He warns Congress that it must be fiscally prudent to avoid a deficit.		The stock market takes a considerable hit, with 177 individual companies reaching yearly lows. Industry professionals call the decline a necessary correction.	The French are building a giant airplane, described as a "flying cottage," for nonstop transatlantic passenger flights. The plane is expected to fly 120 mph and will have two cabins that can hold 19 people.	Louis Armstrong and His Hot Five record the songs *Muskrat Ramble* and *Heebie Jeebies* in Chicago. *Heebie Jeebies* introduces a new style of jazz singing, called "scat."	Feb. 26
Vice-President Charles Dawes urges the Senate to investigate links between Chicago city officials and organized crime. His petition alleges that Cook County State's Attorney Robert Crowe was a guest at a banquet held by known gangster Tony Genna, who has since been slain. Several politicians, judges, and policemen have reportedly been seen at the funerals of crime bosses.			Passenger plane service has begun to remote Red Lake, Ontario, the scene of a gold strike.	164 horses, a record number, have been applied for entry into this year's Kentucky Derby....The typical senior at Yale University can expect to earn $1,600 as starting pay upon graduating and taking a job.	Feb. 27
		The National Industrial Conference Board has released an extensive report about the difficulties facing the U.S. agricultural sector. Foreign competition and high overhead capital costs are imperiling the farmer. In 1921 the per capita income for farmers was $186, compared to $701 for the rest of the nation.	Lieutenant Commander Richard E. Byrd announces plans to explore the North Pole by airplane.	Resorts in the Swiss Alps are reporting record crowds of skiers from England and the United States. A favorite tourist event has been fox-trotting on ice to orchestral accompaniment....The Pittsburgh Pirates baseball team announces a hike in ticket prices for the 1926 season. Box seats will be $1.75 and general admission will be $1.15. The owner cites his $2 million investment in the club as the reason for the increase.	Feb. 28
General Lincoln Andrews, in charge of Prohibition enforcement, has vexed his superior, Secretary of the Treasury Andrew Mellon, by proposing a commission to investigate the public reaction to dry laws. Andrews believes that an investigation will help enforcement officers to better understand "actual conditions" in the country.	The United States has developed a five-inch-caliber anti-aircraft gun for battleships, the largest in the world, with the capability to shoot down airplanes six miles aboveground.			Riviera merchants are selling a new fad item: the "Helen Wills eyeshade," similar to the sun visor the tennis star wears on the court.... The Women's International League for Peace and Freedom challenges toy manufacturers to end the production of tin soldiers and toy guns and swords. The organization has threatened a boycott.	Mar. 1

	World Affairs	Europe	Africa & The Middle East	The Americas	Asia & The Pacific
Mar. 2					
Mar. 3		Parisian high society is engrossed by "La Croisiere Noir," a film documenting the ten-month Citroën Central African expedition in 1925.			Tibetans transporting electrical equipment from England to Tibet for factory construction are slaughtered in the "Forbidden City" of Lhasa. The attack reflects the nation's antipathy for outside influences.
Mar. 4		Soviet officials claim that the Red Army has been cut recently to 560,000 troops, but some sources allege the number is actually more than one million.		Cuba has agreed with U.S. Prohibition authorities to help fight liquor smuggling into Florida.... Secretary of State Kellogg, bypassing the U.S. Ambassador to Mexico, directly addresses a protest note to the Mexican Foreign Office. His neglect of the usual protocol indicates the seriousness of the impasse.	
Mar. 5	The White House has summoned home the Ambassador to Great Britain, Alanson Houghton, to confer about the current situation regarding the League of Nations. The Coolidge administration is concerned that European wrangling over seats on the permanent council will ultimately hinder U.S. naval disarmament efforts.	French premier Aristide Briand and his cabinet are forced to resign suddenly after failing to reach an agreement with Nationalists and Socialists on a fiscal plan to reduce the national deficit. The country has been staggering under the burden of war debts. . . Pope Pius XI issues an encyclical letter declaring that "dark skinned races" possess the same mental capacities as "white races."			The Methodist Episcopal Church in the Philippines, with 63,000 members, formally adopts a resolution calling for national independence.... A coalition cabinet representing three major parties has been formed in Peking in an effort to bolster support for the Chinese government.
Mar. 6		British newspapers complain about the number of American "bagmen" invading England, peddling shares in fake real estate and oil companies.			Tensions over the Chinese Eastern Railroad in Manchuria have abruptly eased. Zhang Zuolin has released all arrested Russians and agreed to fire several anti-Soviet Chinese officials. Diplomatic observers speculate that Russia has made some kind of behind-the-scenes deal with the Manchurians.
Mar. 7	The League of Nations opens in Geneva under unfavorable circumstances. Germany insists that it will join only if given the sole new permanent seat on the Council; Spain threatens to quit the meeting unless also given a permanent seat, and China, Poland, and Brazil press their claims. French leader Aristide Briand is a crucial player in deliberations, but he has just lost his premiership and is without authority.			The Mexican Federation of Labor accuses Soviet diplomats of spreading Bolshevik propaganda to undermine the Calles government.	General Wu Pei-Fu, leading forces hostile to the government at Peking, now controls most of the Henan province in East Central China.
Mar. 8	German envoys are threatening to leave Geneva. They refuse to make any compromises regarding the composition of the Council of the League of Nations.	French political leaders now regret the treatment of former premier Aristide Briand and are entreating him to return to the job. Briand has refused, telling reporters, "They broke a platter on my head, and now they are counting on me to stick the pieces together."	Druse rebels are dealt heavy losses during a French air raid in Syria, with more than 150 men killed.		Warships aligned with Zhang Zuolin shell the port city of Tietsin, where troops loyal to the government in Peking are garrisoned.

A	B	C	D	E
Includes developments that affect more than one world region, international organizations and important meetings of world leaders.	*Includes all domestic and regional developments in Europe, including the Soviet Union.*	*Includes all domestic and regional developments in Africa and the Middle East.*	*Includes all domestic and regional developments in Latin America, the Caribbean, and Canada.*	*Includes all domestic and regional developments in Asian and Pacific nations (and colonies).*

U.S. Politics & Social Issues	U.S. Foreign Policy & Affairs, Defense	U.S. Economy & Environment	Science, Technology & Nature	Culture, Leisure & Lifestyle	
The *Chicago Tribune* has published a photograph showing State's Attorney Robert Crowe, the Illinois secretary of state and lieutenant governor, and several other government officials at a banquet thrown in 1924 by the Genna brothers, notorious mobsters....The Senate Immigration Committee unanimously rejects Vice-President Dawes's petition for Congress to investigate crime in Chicago. The committee advises that the city's problems are its own.		The Interstate Commerce Commission rejects the proposed merger of five major railroads in Virginia and the Great Lakes region. The move is unexpected, because the Coolidge administration's policy has supported consolidating railroads into regional groups....The New York Stock Exchange witnesses a frenzied sell-off during the last hour. In that period, 1.5 million shares are traded. Losses across the board range from 5 to 18 points.	Three separate expeditions from three nations, using three different forms of modern transport, will explore the Arctic this summer. The Norwegian Amundsen-Ellsworth expedition will use a dirigible; the American Byrd expedition will use airplanes; and a French group will use motor-powered sledges, with airplanes in support.	Babe Ruth reports for spring training practice wearing a Helen Wills sun visor and a sweat-inducing rubber shirt, intended to help him burn fat.	Mar. 2
Policemen on motorcycles charge a crowd of snowball-throwing textile strikers in Passaic, beating them with clubs. Several newspaper photographers attempting to record the incident are also beaten.		More than 3.7 million shares are sold in a record-setting day for volume on Wall Street. Heavy losses for individual stocks range from 5 to 50 points; there are no rallies during the day. Much of the loss stems from margin speculators being forced to sell.		Helen Wills defeats German tennis champion Nelly Neppach in straight sets at the Mentone tennis tournament in France....On the final day of her temporary release from Ellis Island, the Countess Cathcart rehearses her play "Ashes of Love" and awaits word from immigration authorities about her status.	Mar. 3
Three thousand strikers, some of them equipped with gas masks, march at "Trouble Corner," the street intersection in front of the Botany Worsted Mills in Passaic. Police allow them to picket unmolested.		The stock market rebounds vigorously, with the typical issue advancing 5 points. Nevertheless, the market has shed $4 billion in value in the past month, the sharpest decline in history....Under federal scrutiny for violating the Clayton Anti-Trust Act, the proposed National Food Products Corporation merger is called off.	For the first time, the engine car and the caboose on a train are able to communicate directly by telephone. The Pennsylvania Railroad successfully tests a line on a 75-car train.	Bishop William Manning decries the prevalence of divorce in the United States. He cites statistics indicating there is one divorce for every seven marriages in the country. He singles out the bad example set by "high social leaders," whose divorces are heavily publicized.	Mar. 4
Eight gunmen in Chicago take ten minutes to commit a midday robbery at an International Harvester tractor factory, making off with $80,000 in company payroll....The Department of Labor reports that 29,733 alien immigrants were permitted to enter the United States in January, while 15,081 immigrants left the country.	President Coolidge opposes the proposed five-year buildup of the military's aviation program, citing deficit concerns.	President Coolidge, Secretary of the Treasury Mellon, and Secretary of Commerce Hoover all affirm that the U.S. economy remains fundamentally sound, regardless of recent turmoil on Wall Street.		Immigration officials give up their efforts to deport the Countess Cathcart, ruling that she may stay in the United States indefinitely and do as she pleases.	Mar. 5
			A cold wave has gripped New England, with temperatures reaching 30 degrees below zero in some places....A Viennese ear specialist, Dr. Fritz Pfuffer, predicts that the noise pollution of urban life, which forces people to strain to catch the spoken word, will cause the human race to develop extremely large ears.	King Vidor's film version of *La Boheme*, starring Lillian Gish and John Gilbert, is receiving strong reviews....F. Scott Fitzgerald has published his short story collection *All the Sad Young Men*.... Hollywood stars Rudolph Valentino and Pola Negri are deeply in love and planning marriage, according to Negri.	Mar. 6
The National Industrial Conference Board issues a report on the increasing political radicalism of Midwestern farmers. Farmers have become frustrated that Eastern political and financial elites are ignoring their policy concerns. Statistics indicate that the number of farm failures rose 1,000 percent between 1910 and 1924.			American scientists announce their breakthrough success in developing biological stains for use in the pathological study of disease states.... Telephone researchers hold a successful four-hour wireless conversation between New York City and London, following more than three years of experimentation.		Mar. 7
Textile strikers in Passaic, New Jersey, again skirmish with police....Twenty-eight coal miners are believed dead in an explosion at Eccles, WV.			Chemists at the University of Illinois announce the discovery of what they believe to be unknown element No. 61.	The Master Hairdressers' Association of America reports that 60 million customers patronized beauty salons in 1925, producing $390 million in revenue.	Mar. 8

F	G	H	I	J
Includes campaigns, elections, federal-state relations, civil rights and liberties, crime, the judiciary, education, healthcare, poverty, urban affairs, and population.	*Includes formation and debate of U.S. foreign and defense policies, veterans affairs, and defense spending. (Relations with specific foreign countries are usually found under the region concerned.)*	*Includes business, labor, agriculture, taxation, transportation, consumer affairs, monetary and fiscal policy, natural resources, pollution and industrial accidents.*	*Includes worldwide scientific, medical and technological developments, natural phenomena, U.S. weather and natural disasters.*	*Includes the arts, religion, scholarship, communications media, sports, entertainment, fashions, fads, and social life.*

	World Affairs	Europe	Africa & The Middle East	The Americas	Asia & The Pacific
Mar. 9		Aristide Briand has once again accepted the post of premier of France. He has created a new cabinet in Paris and will leave immediately for Geneva to engage in pressing League of Nations matters....French royalist youths armed with blackjacks and weighted canes storm a meeting of 1,400 leftist workers in Paris, injuring several.... Another English country mansion—the ninth so far this year—has been destroyed in a fire.		An American Protestant minister in a Mexican village is severely beaten by a mob for distributing pamphlets, which the villagers perceive as anti-Catholic.	The Indian government is considering a bill to ban the export of opium, except for medicinal purposes.... Russians in Mongolia report that many nomadic tribesmen are now bobbing their hair, in the popular style of American women.
Mar. 10		German Communists are accusing royalists, aided by the Black Reichswehr, of a 1923 plot to overthrow the government, murder the president and several ministers, and reinstate the monarchy.	Ibn Saud is making the cost of pilgrimage to Mecca as inexpensive as possible. Pilgrims are now paying $2.50 for transport by camel or automobile, compared to prices around $100 formerly.		The port city of Tietsin has been cut off from Peking; the harbor and waterways have been mined, and all means of communication are being interfered with by troops.
Mar. 11	A potential hitch has emerged regarding American adherence to the World Court protocol. The United States has attached reservations insisting that the Court may not offer an advisory opinion on a case involving the United States without the consent of the American government. Several jurists in Geneva are said to be balking at this stipulation.	Two major American corporations, General Electric and Westinghouse, are in negotiations with the Soviet government to develop power on the Dneiper River and electrify Moscow suburban trains....A high official with the Soviet Cinematograph Department has reportedly approached Hollywood stars Douglas Fairbanks and Mary Pickford about appearing in two Russian films.	The Council of the League of Nations awards the Mosul region of Iraq to Great Britain. The region is claimed by Turkey, which protests by refusing to attend the meeting.		
Mar. 12	Germany has rejected a compromise proposal made by Aristide Briand that Poland receive a nonpermanent seat on the Council of the League of Nations.		Archaeologist Howard Carter and the Antiquarian Society of Egypt, which represents the Egyptian government, are at loggerheads over handling artifacts from King Tutankh-amen's tomb. All excavation work has stopped.	In the town of Jalisquello, Mexico, three officials, including a congressman and a mayor, are killed and mutilated during an unsuccessful effort to close down a local Catholic church.	Manchurian warlord Zhang Zuolin is shelling Lanchow, near Tietsin, incurring heavy civilian casualties....Fourteen foreign nations, including England and Japan, have formed the Constitutional Defense League in Shanghai to warn against Bolshevist influences in China.
Mar. 13	Germany and France face off over the League of Nations Council seats. A major French newspaper refers to Germans as a "people of aggression, driven by pride," who have "not accepted their defeat of 1918."		Turkish President Mustafa Kemal is erecting a statue of himself in the harbor at Constantinople—in contradiction to Muslim laws against idolatrous images of the living.... Nearly 140,000 Jews are now living in Palestine, an increase of 60 percent over the last three years.		
Mar. 14		An Englishman is sentenced to eight months in prison in Italy for making derogatory remarks about Premier Mussolini, even though the court acknowledges that he was in an "irresponsible condition" at the time....More than 7 million votes have been cast in a German referendum on compensating royal family members for seizing their property; the vote is overwhelmingly against compensation, which is seen as a major victory for the Socialist and Communist parties that advocate seizure.	At least 600 Berber troops have been killed in recent fighting against Spain and France in Morocco, but a lull is expected to commence tomorrow with the start of Ramadan.	Two hundred forty-eight Costa Ricans are killed when a passenger train wrecks on a bridge; one overloaded car hurtles 50 feet into a river....The Emergency Foreign Policy Conference in Chicago, with a membership including 14 U.S. congressmen, condemns "the tendency of the State Department of the United States to interfere with the internal affairs of Mexico."	The National Geographic Society has taken the first known photographs of Tibetan Buddhist religious ceremonies in a remote province of China.
Mar. 15	Aristide Briand has successfully engineered a compromise with Germany over the composition of the Council of the League of Nations. Germany and Poland will be given permanent seats, and in exchange Czechoslovakia and Sweden will give up theirs. But this arrangement is threatened because Brazil is now demanding a permanent seat.			U.S. congressmen deny any involvement in the Emergency Foreign Policy Conference that issued the statement yesterday denouncing State Department policy toward Mexico.	

A	B	C	D	E
Includes developments that affect more than one world region, international organizations and important meetings of world leaders.	Includes all domestic and regional developments in Europe, including the Soviet Union.	Includes all domestic and regional developments in Africa and the Middle East.	Includes all domestic and regional developments in Latin America, the Caribbean, and Canada.	Includes all domestic and regional developments in Asian and Pacific nations (and colonies).

U.S. Politics & Social Issues	U.S. Foreign Policy & Affairs, Defense	U.S. Economy & Environment	Science, Technology & Nature	Culture, Leisure & Lifestyle	
		The House Committee on Agriculture is considering a farm relief proposal by which a government agency would be created to fix the prices of staple commodities.		The Chicago Board of Education reports that city schoolboys are playing "gangsters and hijackers," not "cowboys and Indians."…The American Historical Association announces plans to create a million-dollar endowment to fund research on the nation's history.	Mar. 9
Congress engages in lively, daylong debate over proposed modifications to Prohibition laws.…City councilwoman Bertha Landes is elected the first female mayor of Seattle.		The Florida real estate boom is apparently coming to a close. Real estate speculators are focusing on Long Island as the possible site of a new boom during the coming summer.	Bell Telephone Laboratories has developed an ultraviolet microscope that can magnify to 9,000 diameters.	Rudolph Valentino denies that he and Pola Negri intend to marry.	Mar. 10
The National Woman's Party announces plans to send two members on a national automobile tour to scout for suitable female congressional candidates. Only three women currently serve in Congress.…The U.S. Marshal in Chicago has released crime statistics for the city. In the past 18 months, 30 train carloads of criminals have been shipped to federal penitentiaries, 1,500 buildings have been padlocked for Prohibition violations, and 18 breweries have been shut down.		The J.C. Penney Company reports gross sales in 1925 of $91 million, an increase of almost 20 percent from the previous year.			Mar. 11
Sixty-nine people, ranging from a Philadelphia millionaire to a truck driver in St. Paul, are arrested for their alleged roles in a nationwide bootleg liquor conspiracy.… Congressional leaders have decided not to pursue farm legislation in upcoming sessions.				In fallout from the Countess Cathcart case, the Commissioner of Immigration at Ellis Island resigns.…The National Academy of Design honors painters Childe Hassam and Kyohei Inuka and sculptors Attillio and Horatio Piccirilli.	Mar. 12
				Douglas Fairbanks's colorful adventure film *The Black Pirate* has opened at theaters.	Mar. 13
Wisconsin dairy farmers issue a statement opposing the reintroduction of beer, which they believe will compete with their own products.…The strike by more than 10,000 New Jersey textile workers is now eight weeks old.	Huff Daland Airplanes, Inc., is constructing a new single-engine bomber for the U.S. Army Air Service. The plane will be the largest and fastest bomber used by the military, with a payload capacity of 9,000 pounds.			The biggest surprise of major league baseball spring training is 17-year-old phenom Mel Ott with the New York Giants. Manager John McGraw is contemplating promoting Ott immediately to the majors, without a single game of minor league experience.	Mar. 14
		The Department of Labor reports near-full employment in many regions of the United States, based on February statistics. Among the industrial sectors singled out as particularly healthy are automobile manufacturing, the boot and shoe industry, and steel and iron mills.	More than 5,000 songbirds and several monkeys suffocate in a fire at the "House of Pets" store in New York City. More than a thousand Easter chicks and rabbits and hundreds of small dogs and cats survive the blaze in the four-story building.	The Camp Fire Girls announce a national membership of 158,521.… The Countess Cathcart's autobiographical play, "Ashes of Love," makes its debut in Washington, DC. to negative reviews and mediocre box office; the audience reportedly titters during her most tragic moments onstage.	Mar. 15

F	G	H	I	J
Includes campaigns, elections, federal-state relations, civil rights and liberties, crime, the judiciary, education, healthcare, poverty, urban affairs, and population.	Includes formation and debate of U.S. foreign and defense policies, veterans affairs, and defense spending. (Relations with specific foreign countries are usually found under the region concerned.)	Includes business, labor, agriculture, taxation, transportation, consumer affairs, monetary and fiscal policy, natural resources, pollution and industrial accidents.	Includes worldwide scientific, medical and technological developments, natural phenomena, U.S. weather and natural disasters.	Includes the arts, religion, scholarship, communications media, sports, entertainment, fashions, fads, and social life.

	World Affairs	Europe	Africa & The Middle East	The Americas	Asia & The Pacific
Mar. 16		The Soviet government is offering for sale or lease to foreigners several tsarist palaces in Leningrad.	Abd el-Krim publishes a letter in the *London Times* insisting on rights for his people and decrying French and Spanish arrogance. Newspapers that carry the letter remark on its "quaint Oriental language."		
Mar. 17	The League of Nations adjourns without having reached a final agreement on the composition of the Council. Brazil is blamed for the last-minute difficulties.				The United States, Japan, and England have threatened naval action unless Tietsin is reopened to foreign shipping. The Chinese government in Peking has agreed to take the necessary steps.
Mar. 18	Before departing Geneva, the League of Nations Council invites the United States to send representatives to a September 1 conference to discuss American reservations about adherence to the World Court.		Druse rebels in Syria have successfully ambushed a French military detachment, killing 42 of the 50 soldiers.		Students in Peking demonstrate against the government's acquiescence to the foreign-powers ultimatum on Tietsin. The protest turns bloody when guards open fire, killing approximately 40 students.
Mar. 19	Senators opposed to American adherence to the World Court are adopting a "told you so" attitude about yesterday's League of Nations invitation. They have long insisted that participation in the Court will inevitably lead to entanglement with the League.	The French franc has fallen to a record low, which economists are blaming on the nation's recent political uncertainty....The Spanish government is undertaking efforts to eradicate leprosy from its population. More than 1,000 cases have been reported, the majority in the Canary Islands.	The French and Spanish armies have amassed 250,000 troops to fight Abd el-Krim in Morocco. They suspect that the Berber leader is being secretly supplied by the Soviet Union and Turkey.	Stone-throwing Catholics and machine gun–wielding soldiers clash over the closing of churches in San Luis Potosi, Mexico.	The Chinese government in Peking arrests several education officials, including the Director of the Sino-Russian University. They are accused of provoking yesterday's fatal protest.
Mar. 20		The Soviet Union is the first country to use airplanes to transport convicts, sending political prisoners to the penal colony on Solovetsky Island in the White Sea....Russia continues to suffer from a rabies epidemic, with 820 cases reported in the past two months.	The French War Ministry is reportedly negotiating with Abd el-Krim in the hope of averting warfare. France is struggling with the financial costs of their troop buildups in Morocco and Syria.		
Mar. 21	European newspapers are in an uproar over statements attributed to Alanson Houghton, the U.S. Ambassador to Great Britain who reported to the Coolidge administration last week on European conditions. Houghton allegedly told European journalists about the contents of his report: he spoke of Europe's nationalistic selfishness and unwillingness to disarm and the possible dissolution of the League of Nations.	Powerful right-wing newspaper magnate Alfred Hugenberg is reportedly politicking to become the leader of the German Nationalist Party. He intends to unite the country's various anti-Weimar factions and create a Fascist dictatorship.		Several prominent U.S. oilmen are attending a hastily called meeting with government officials in Mexico City to discuss the new petroleum regulations.	The armies of three warlords are on the move in China. Wu Pei-fu continues to push north, while Manchurian general Zhang Zuolin has been harassing the area around Tietsin. Feng Yuxiang, whose Kuominchun army is allied to the government in Peking, is now hemmed in by the other warlords.
Mar. 22	U.S. senators debate the alleged Houghton statements about Europe. Those in favor of the World Court blast the Coolidge administration for attempting to undermine American adherence; the "irreconcilables" against the Court reassert their arguments about European dysfunctionality.	Grigory Zinoviev is replaced as head of the Leningrad Soviet for "heretical" remarks he has made recently.	Abd el-Krim is said to be in difficult straits in Morocco, with ongoing supply problems. A Spanish general predicts a quick victory over el-Krim this spring....Aristide Briand is being criticized for undertaking negotiations with el-Krim. One newspaper insists on punishing el-Krim as an example for other Moroccan leaders and attacks Briand's "false humanitarianism."		The city of Tietsin has fallen to the armies of Manchurian general Zhang Zuolin. Kuominchun forces loyal to the government have evacuated the city and are retreating toward Peking, less than 100 miles away.

A	B	C	D	E
Includes developments that affect more than one world region, international organizations and important meetings of world leaders.	*Includes all domestic and regional developments in Europe, including the Soviet Union.*	*Includes all domestic and regional developments in Africa and the Middle East.*	*Includes all domestic and regional developments in Latin America, the Caribbean, and Canada.*	*Includes all domestic and regional developments in Asian and Pacific nations (and colonies).*

U.S. Politics & Social Issues	U.S. Foreign Policy & Affairs, Defense	U.S. Economy & Environment	Science, Technology & Nature	Culture, Leisure & Lifestyle	
The Indianapolis City Council, backed by the White People's Protective League, has passed an ordinance strictly segregating residence in the city....The Committee of Twenty-Two, representing the interests of farmers in several Midwestern states, has presented a proposal for farm relief to members of the House Agriculture Committee. The congressmen, observing that the proposal is tilted to favor corn growers over the producers of other basic commodities, dismiss it as "absurd."		Senators Robert La Follette and William Borah have taken up the cause of the New Jersey textile strikers. Borah points to their average weekly wage of $17 and occasional 18-hour workdays. Senator Edward Edwards of New Jersey denies the allegations, insisting that the workers have been "never better treated" and that they have been misled by Communist propaganda.			Mar. 16
A grand jury in Williamson, West Virginia, spends two minutes deliberating before sentencing to death an African-American man who has pled guilty to assaulting a white woman.		The Federal Reserve Board releases statistics indicating that the United States is in a period of "almost unprecedented prosperity." The board cites low interest rates, record corporate profits, and no evident strain on the nation's credit facilities.	German medical scientists believe they have discovered a method for detecting early-stage cancer by spectroscopically examining the patient's blood....American doctors at the Cancer Research Institute doubt that cancer is hereditary; British scientists believe that cancer is caused by a germ.	Richard Rodgers and Lorenz Hart's musical The Girl Friend debuts on Broadway, featuring the song The Blue Room.	Mar. 17
President Coolidge's father has died.			German scientist Max Born presents his theories about quantum mechanics to Princeton faculty members, who hail his work on atomic structure.	The National Bureau of Economic Research estimates the U.S. population at 115,940,000, up 10 million from the 1920 census. The bureau reports that immigration has played no meaningful role in recent growth.	Mar. 18
The Passaic textile strike has again turned violent. After allowing picketing for several weeks, police changed tactics today and used their nightsticks to disperse a crowd of 2,000 strikers and onlookers. Several news reporters and cameramen were among those beaten in the fracas.					Mar. 19
An ore-melting furnace at the Woodward Iron Company in Brimingham, Alabama, explodes, killing 21 workers instantly....Strike leaders in Passaic intend to beef up their picket lines in the coming week, in an effort to shut down three mills completely. The strikers have lost $1.75 million in wages so far, but they are receiving $10,000 in aid weekly from other union groups.				Multiple-unit apartment buildings are becoming a popular dwelling in major U.S. cities, faced with expensive home prices and increasing populations....The Department of Agriculture reports that Americans ate a record amount of red meat in 1925, consuming 63.1 pounds per capita....Four jockeys and three horse owners have been banned for life for fixing races at Kentucky and Coney Island tracks.	Mar. 20
The leading Catholic priest in Passaic condemns the "outside revolutionaries" who have fomented the textiles strike, telling an audience of strikers that they have been duped....One hundred fifty men are the first graduates from "Hobo College" in Chicago, a philanthropic venture.				Langston Hughes publishes his first book of poetry, The Weary Blues....The National Association of Broadcasters supports a bill before the House Committee on Patents that would require radio stations to pay a royalty for broadcasting copyrighted music. A regularized government tax is preferable to the current ad hoc system, in which music companies can charge exorbitant rates.	Mar. 21
		An international deal has reportedly been reached by U.S., British, German, Belgian, and French steel companies regarding the trade in steel rails. The deal will substantially increase U.S. access to European export markets.	Oil City, Pennsylvania, has been flooded by the Allegheny River, causing $5 million in damage.... Russian physicist Maria Levitskaya has discovered electromagnetic waves measuring less than four-tenths of a millimeter.	The Football Rules Committee has decided to impose a five-yard penalty on the offensive team for each incomplete forward pass....Protests in Emporia, Kansas, have led to the cancellation of a touring Ziegfeld's Follies show, which featured too much "kicking" by the dancers.	Mar. 22

F	G	H	I	J
Includes campaigns, elections, federal-state relations, civil rights and liberties, crime, the judiciary, education, healthcare, poverty, urban affairs, and population.	Includes formation and debate of U.S. foreign and defense policies, veterans affairs, and defense spending. (Relations with specific foreign countries are usually found under the region concerned.)	Includes business, labor, agriculture, taxation, transportation, consumer affairs, monetary and fiscal policy, natural resources, pollution and industrial accidents.	Includes worldwide scientific, medical and technological developments, natural phenomena, U.S. weather and natural disasters.	Includes the arts, religion, scholarship, communications media, sports, entertainment, fashions, fads, and social life.

	World Affairs	Europe	Africa & The Middle East	The Americas	Asia & The Pacific
Mar. 23	President Coolidge, typically placid even after yesterday's Senate attacks, insists that there will be no change in U.S. policy regarding European countries, the World Court, or the League of Nations.	The U.S. State Department is investigating complaints by Americans who own real estate in Germany that their property has been seized....Lock Ah Tam, a prominent Chinese businessman well-known for aiding Chinese immigrants to the United States and England, is hanged in Liverpool for murdering his Welsh wife and children.		American oil executives and Mexican government officials have failed to reach an understanding about new oil laws....An American railroad worker is stoned to death by a mob in the Mexican state of Nayarit. This is the third reported attack on Americans in the past week.	Burma has freed the last of its slaves, under pressure from the British government. Naga chiefs in the Hukwang Valley released 3,487 slaves today.
Mar. 24	Secretary of the Treasury Andrew Mellon offers a vigorous defense of U.S. war debt policies toward Europe. He disagrees with congressmen who call for more stringent payments. "We have a surplus," he observes, "and to dispose of this surplus we must reach markets abroad." Leniency on war debts will enable Europe to be America's "best customer," a healthy, solvent market.	British Chancellor of the Exchequer Winston Churchill criticizes American war debt policies, suggesting that the United States has profited by "squeezing" war-weakened European nations.			
Mar. 25		British newspapers attack Secretary Mellon's debt speech yesterday. Several editorials denounce the American refusal to forgive war debts, when the European Allies paid "something more precious than dollars" during the war—"the blood of our people."...An outbreak of the bubonic plague in the Ural region of the Soviet Union has killed 28 people. The disease is being spread by marmots.	French troops have driven Druse forces from the town of Nebk, a rebel stronghold in Syria. However, the French sustained heavy casualties. Druse attacks in the city of Damascus are becoming more brazen and frequent.		
Mar. 26		British coal miners warn of a strike if the government attempts to reduce their wages....Italian Premier Benito Mussolini celebrates the seventh anniversary of the Fascist movement....The Soviet Union has banned monasticism, insisting that all monks must take up useful livelihoods.	Wealthy Syrians have been abandoning Damascus, where street fighting between the Druse and the French has intensified.	The Mexican government again insists that it will not budge on the issue of oil laws.	
Mar. 27		The American Jewish Joint Distribution Committee reports that in some districts in Poland up to 85 percent of Jewish workers are unemployed, the result of discrimination and difficult economic conditions....Novelist Grazia Deledda and poet Ada Negri have been named to academic "chairs" by Mussolini—the first Italian women to attain this status in the nation's universities.	Druse rebels are attacking rail lines outside Damascus and have adopted trench warfare in their positions around the city. "They have learned some sense now and are done with rushing our positions and losing a lot of men for nothing," a French officer observes.	Attacks on Americans in Mexico continue. In Durango, several American mining engineers have been kidnapped, prompting the U.S. ambassador to demand that Mexican authorities respond quickly to acts of banditry.	All communications between Tietsin and Peking have reportedly been cut off.
Mar. 28		France is adding a 25 percent tax to the hotel bills of tourists.	The French army has stationed machine gunners in the minarets of mosques in Damascus, where an estimated 1,000 Druse fighters have been launching attacks on the city.		South Chinese Communists attack an American mission in Kwelin. Their stated goal is to drive all Christians out of the country.
Mar. 29				Mexico's land laws are officially in effect. The regulations severely restrict the ownership of property by foreigners. There is disagreement about how to interpret the laws: Mexico insists that they are not retroactive and thus will not impact pre-existing foreign land interests, while the United States believes several articles are retroactive and punitive.	Manchurian warlord Zhang Zuolin has reportedly skirmished with government troops twenty miles outside Peking.

A	B	C	D	E
Includes developments that affect more than one world region, international organizations and important meetings of world leaders.	Includes all domestic and regional developments in Europe, including the Soviet Union.	Includes all domestic and regional developments in Africa and the Middle East.	Includes all domestic and regional developments in Latin America, the Caribbean, and Canada.	Includes all domestic and regional developments in Asian and Pacific nations (and colonies).

U.S. Politics & Social Issues	U.S. Foreign Policy & Affairs, Defense	U.S. Economy & Environment	Science, Technology & Nature	Culture, Leisure & Lifestyle	
			American aviator Alfred Lawson announces plans to build a double-decker passenger airplane.		Mar. 23
"Wets" in Congress have proposed a nationwide referendum on Prohibition during the 1928 elections. The idea is under consideration by the Senate Judiciary Committee.		For the third time this month, the New York Stock Exchange has nose-dived. All sectors of the market were hit today, with American Can and General Electric bearing particularly large losses. A total of 115 securities reached their yearly lows.		Helen Wills has completed her tennis season in the French Riviera, having won trophies in eight of nine singles tournaments. She is now leaving for a sightseeing art tour of Italy, where Benito Mussolini has arranged for her to play special exhibitions for him.	Mar. 24
Twenty policemen confront 1,500 textile strikers as they march across a bridge in Passaic, beating some of them with clubs and making several arrests. Strikers began picketing a new mill today, where the large majority of loom workers have remained at their jobs....Debate opens in the Senate over ratification of the Italian war debt agreement, which the House passed in January.				"Uncle Bunt" Stephens, a Tennessee fiddler who won a nationwide contest sponsored by Henry Ford, is making guest appearances in New York City.	Mar. 25
Textile strike leaders in Passaic are in talks with the Associated Silk Workers of America to expand the walkout to include silk and dye workers in Paterson, New Jersey.... The House Immigration Committee hears testimony from groups criticizing alien deportation laws.			Norwegian explorer Roald Amundsen has arrived in King's Bay, Spitzbergen, to begin preparations for his summer dirigible flight to the North Pole.	Queens, New York, has experienced a series of daring burglaries committed by the "radio robber," who steals only radio sets and children's book bags. The robber has also shot and wounded three policemen in narrow escapes from the law.	Mar. 26
The American Civil Liberties Union plans to file civil lawsuits against the police chief of Passaic, in response to complaints of "atrocious assault and battery" against strikers. The textiles strike is entering its 10th week.			Johns Hopkins University researchers are studying sleep by measuring the body's resistance to electrical currents during slumber. The scientists believe that there are two distinct stages of sleep....The University of Paris plans to establish a "museum of the spoken word," which will use cylinder recording technology to collect hundreds of languages and dialects.		Mar. 27
Several thousand textile workers in Lawrence, Massachusetts, are planning to walk out of their mills, in a show of unity with strikers in Passaic....Chicago Election Commissioners, responding to complaints of widespread voter fraud, have stricken 215,217 "suspect" names from registration lists.... "Wets" intend to make modification of Prohibition laws the centerpiece of U.S. Senate campaigns this fall.		European economists are pointing to the excessive use of credit on Wall Street as the reason for recent stock market instability.	The National Farm Radio Council reports that radio has become an indispensable tool for American farmers. Farmers rely on the radio to receive market reports two days faster than previously....The Surgeon General is now regulating the ventilation of automobile parking garages, where carbon monoxide inhalation is a persistent danger.	Police in Queens believe they have apprehended and killed the "radio robber." They found the suspect with four radio sets in his home; he was shot trying to escape from custody.	Mar. 28
African Americans in Brooklyn protest the city's failure to prosecute a white policeman who has allegedly assaulted a black woman. "Two colored men in Kentucky and Delaware were tried and convicted in less than fifteen minutes for assaulting white women," the pastor leading the protest observes. "Why shouldn't we have equal justice in this city?"		Wall Street experiences widespread selling, with 231 individual stocks hitting yearly lows. Financial experts suggest that the sell-off is a necessary correction after last year's rampant speculation.	Food researchers at Columbia University believe that canned vegetables retain more vitamins than cooked vegetables; raw vegetables are superior to both as a source of nutrition.		Mar. 29

F	G	H	I	J
Includes campaigns, elections, federal-state relations, civil rights and liberties, crime, the judiciary, education, healthcare, poverty, urban affairs, and population.	Includes formation and debate of U.S. foreign and defense policies, veterans affairs, and defense spending. (Relations with specific foreign countries are usually found under the region concerned.)	Includes business, labor, agriculture, taxation, transportation, consumer affairs, monetary and fiscal policy, natural resources, pollution and industrial accidents.	Includes worldwide scientific, medical and technological developments, natural phenomena, U.S. weather and natural disasters.	Includes the arts, religion, scholarship, communications media, sports, entertainment, fashions, fads, and social life.

	World Affairs	Europe	Africa & The Middle East	The Americas	Asia & The Pacific
Mar. 30	British Foreign Secretary Austen Chamberlain insists that Brazil acted alone at the recently ended League of Nations sessions. He asserts that Brazil was not led into intransigence by Great Britain, France, or any other power in an effort to thwart German membership.			The U.S. House Foreign Affairs Committee hears testimony alleging that nuns in Mexico have been arrested and threatened with being sold into prostitution.	
Mar. 31		The cabinet of French premier Augustin Briand has won a tax bill to balance the national budget, bringing to a close three months of political fighting.	Unconfirmed reports indicate that Abd el-Krim is actively pursuing a peace settlement with France.		
Apr. 1				Upon a close reading of the Spanish text of the new land regulations, the U.S. State Department determines that the Mexican land law is not retroactive or confiscatory.	
Apr. 2	President Coolidge opposes American participation in a League of Nations conference to discuss the U.S. reservations attached to World Court adherence. He points out that the United States has no obligations to the League, but only to the member nations of the Court.	A German right-wing newspaper accuses the United States of aggressive behavior in the world, pointing for evidence to the Boy Scouts as an early training ground for militarism.	French troops have initiated an offensive against Druse rebels operating in Southern Lebanon. The Druse continue to attack trains in Syria.		President Coolidge is sending a representative on a fact-finding tour of the Philippines, to ascertain Filipino readiness for self-government....British officials have refuted an Indian prince who argues that Indian and British governors are equivalent in authority. Britain responds that no Indian ruler can negotiate "on an equal footing" with the English crown.
Apr. 3			The Turkish government plans to spend half the national budget for 1926 on a military buildup.	General Angel Flores, a popular conservative general who ran for the Mexican presidency against General Calles, has been murdered through arsenic poisoning.	
Apr. 4			Abd el-Krim has launched an offensive against tribal groups that recently allied with the French.... The American Protestant Episcopal Church urges the U.S. Senate to refuse to ratify the Treaty of Lausanne, which legitimates the Republic of Turkey. Episcopal bishops point to the Turkish genocide against Christian Armenians in the early 1920s.		Two large American-operated hospitals in South China are forced to shut down, following armed blockades by Chinese Communists....Muslims and Hindus in Calcutta have been warring for several days; at least 40 people have been killed and more than 500 wounded.
Apr. 5	Pope Pius XI urges the world's Catholics to offer special prayers for the "cessation of the persecution of Catholics in Mexico."		Egyptian officials are uncertain of John D. Rockefeller's motives in offering to build them a $10 million antiquarian museum. The project has largely been kept under wraps, and the officials suspect it may be intended as a "national bribe" for an unspecified purpose. They are likely to reject Rockefeller's offer.	The Tacna-Arica plebiscite, intended to settle a boundary dispute between Chile and Peru, is proving to be an impossibility. Observers believe that the U.S. plebiscite commission will not be able to ensure a fair vote.	General Wu Pei-fu is negotiating terms with government-allied Kuominchun forces to recognize his control over South China. Manchurian warlord Zhang Zuolin's armies continue to press south toward Peking.

A	B	C	D	E
Includes developments that affect more than one world region, international organizations and important meetings of world leaders.	Includes all domestic and regional developments in Europe, including the Soviet Union.	Includes all domestic and regional developments in Africa and the Middle East.	Includes all domestic and regional developments in Latin America, the Caribbean, and Canada.	Includes all domestic and regional developments in Asian and Pacific nations (and colonies).

U.S. Politics & Social Issues	U.S. Foreign Policy & Affairs, Defense	U.S. Economy & Environment	Science, Technology & Nature	Culture, Leisure & Lifestyle	
In Passiac, members in the Kiwanis, Lions, and Rotary clubs give their support to police actions and insist that the textile strike is being instigated by Communists.		The stock market plunges again, with railroad shares suffering the heaviest losses. Stocks of 295 companies close at yearly lows. The situation is described as "confused and extraordinary"—shares of both strong and vulnerable companies are jettisoned. Trading volume for the day reaches more than 3 million shares for the eighth time in history; three of those days have occurred this year.	A March-end winter storm hits much of the South and Midwest, with heavy snows blanketing an area stretching from southern Texas and Mississippi to the Great Lakes....The British government is sponsoring an expedition to study whales in the hope of saving the species from extinction.		Mar. 30
		Wall Street bounced back today, experiencing the first significant rally in eight trading days.	Pennsylvania is suffering through a serious measles outbreak, with 12,000 cases reported.	According to statistics, the murder rate in the United States increased significantly in 1925. In 77 cities, the rate was 11.1 murders per 100,000 people.	Mar. 31
The U.S. House of Representatives votes to impeach George W. English, a federal judge in the Eastern District of Illinois. English has been accused of "tyrannical" behavior and various improprieties on the bench, such as threatening to jail jurors who fail to pass sentence according to his wishes.				Statistics for New York City indicate that 80 percent of crimes are committed by individuals under the age of 22....Hollywood couple Douglas Fairbanks and Mary Pickford are embarking on a world tour, which they say may last for two years.	Apr. 1
John T. King, the former national committeeman of the Republican Party, is indicted for income tax fraud.			Minneapolis physicians believe they have developed an effective anti-toxin treatment for early stage pneumonia.	The office of the U.S. Attorney General rules that California schoolchildren cannot be given assignments to write essays on communism....The American Bible Society distributed 9 million Bibles in 1925 in 150 different languages, an increase of 2.5 million Bibles from 1924.	Apr. 2
The Federal Census Bureau has compiled statistics on insanity in the United States. Nearly 300,000 Americans are institutionalized. There are far more foreign-born insane inmates than native-born; for example, in Oregon there are 849 foreign-born insane per 100,000 population, compared to the national average of 241.	The U.S. War Department has developed an .80-caliber bullet with a range of 5,500 yards—compared to 3,500 yards for the most recent model.	A federal court judge orders that the "bread trust," the Ward Food Products Company, be dissolved. The government will then drop its suit against the company for violating the Sherman Anti-Trust Act.		Parisian film enthusiasts are establishing a theater devoted to cinema classics, although the art form is only a few decades old. The films chosen to inaugurate the theater include three American productions: "Robin Hood," with Douglas Fairbanks"; "Little Lord Fauntleroy," starring Mary Pickford; and Charlie Chaplin's "The Kid."	Apr. 3
E. Y. Clarke, formerly the publicist for the Ku Klux Klan, has founded the Supreme Kingdom in Atlanta. The organization is devoted to stamping out the teaching of evolution in public schools. Clarke believes that his public relations campaign, yoking Darwinism, atheism, and "the peril of Redism," will be more effective than anti-evolution legislation.		The U.S. Treasury Department anticipates a federal budget surplus of $270 million for the 1925–26 fiscal year....The Botany Consolidated Mills in Passaic, the flashpoint of the ongoing textiles strike, reports a $1 million profit for 1925.		American Mercury editor H. L. Mencken is in Boston, where he will attempt to sell copies of the magazine on street corners. The April issue has been banned there because of a story, "Hatrack," by the author Herbert Asbury, about a prostitute in small-town Missouri. A Boston moral-watchdog group has judged the story "obscene" and pressured local retailers into not selling the issue.	Apr. 4
Congressional leaders are foot-dragging on the issue of reapportioning the U.S. House of Representatives to reflect the 1920 census. The current 435 members could leap to 483. California, which stands to gain several seats, demands reapportionment....The United States Children's Bureau has released statistics indicating that juvenile delinquency has declined since 1920 in nine major cities.		The United Front Committee, representing the Passaic strikers, condemns yesterday's Botany Mills earnings report. A spokesman declares that the company's profits were actually $5 million; he compares this to the typical employee wage of $12 to $22 per week.	Aviator Richard E. Byrd and 47 volunteers have departed from New York City on the first leg of their airplane expedition to explore the Arctic.	National Vaudeville Artists' Week, one of the highlights of the theater season, kicks off in New York City. Among the headliners are Sophie Tucker, Marie Dressler, Olga Petrova, George Jessel, Anatol Friedland, and Jack Benny....H. L. Mencken, seeking a court case, is arrested after selling a copy of the American Mercury to the president of the New England Watch and Ward Society—the organization that had the magazine issue banned.	Apr. 5

F	G	H	I	J
Includes campaigns, elections, federal-state relations, civil rights and liberties, crime, the judiciary, education, healthcare, poverty, urban affairs, and population.	Includes formation and debate of U.S. foreign and defense policies, veterans affairs, and defense spending. (Relations with specific foreign countries are usually found under the region concerned.)	Includes business, labor, agriculture, taxation, transportation, consumer affairs, monetary and fiscal policy, natural resources, pollution and industrial accidents.	Includes worldwide scientific, medical and technological developments, natural phenomena, U.S. weather and natural disasters.	Includes the arts, religion, scholarship, communications media, sports, entertainment, fashions, fads, and social life.

	World Affairs	Europe	Africa & The Middle East	The Americas	Asia & The Pacific
Apr. 6	Several European countries, including England and France, are reportedly balking at the reservations the United States has attached to World Court adherence.	A Soviet court sentences to death Ukrainian bandit Nicholas Trapishkin, found guilty of murdering approximately 100 persons during a six-year spree....In response to continued U.S. Senate debate over Italian war-debt repayments, Fascist black shirts have organized attacks against American naval personnel in Venice, beating up several sailors.			
Apr. 7		A 50-year-old Irish woman attempts to assassinate Benito Mussolini in Rome, shooting him with a small revolver at close range, the bullet grazing his nose. "A woman!" Mussolini shouts. "Fancy, a woman!" He is slightly wounded....Approximately 10,000 Soviet doctors, many of them women who have recently graduated from medical schools, are unemployed.	In a battle in Bayas in Syria, the French suffer one soldier killed, compared to 204 Druse killed....The French have constructed more than 1,200 miles of highway through Algeria and Tunisia; they are used primarily by American automobile tourists.		
Apr. 8	President Coolidge affirms that the cornerstone of U.S. foreign policy is noninterference in the political affairs of other countries.	The British Miners Federation flatly rejects mine owner proposals for reduced pay, increased hours, and the discontinuation of a national minimum wage. The British coal industry, facing economic doldrums for the past several years, is being subsidized by the government. The subsidy is due to expire on May 1, and a strike is expected immediately thereafter.	John D. Rockefeller announces that his proposed archaeology museum in Egypt will revert to the nation's control after 30 years. In the meantime, the museum will be primarily run by American, French, and British archaeologists, who will train Egyptians in the methodologies of Egyptology. Egyptian authorities have not decided whether to accept this arrangement....The Spanish government is concerned that France may negotiate a separate peace with Abd el-Krim in Morocco.	Puerto Rico is exporting three million bees to the U.S. Midwest. Puerto Rican bees are free of a bacterial disease that afflicts most of the world's bee populations.	
Apr. 9		The Soviet Foreign Commissariat is reportedly engaged in diplomatic discussions with Poland and Finland. The Soviet government seeks pacts that recognize existing borders and guarantee nonaggression.	The Tigris River has floods much of Baghdad, causing numerous deaths and $5 million in damage.	Latin American Communist organizations have broken with the leadership of the Third International. At a recent party meeting, members from Argentina, Brazil, and other countries condemned the "criminal banditti policy" of the Soviet Union.	
Apr. 10		Five British airmen perish when two planes collide during parachuting exercises in Bedfordshire. The accident marks the worst loss of life for the British Air Force since the Great War....Benito Mussolini is undertaking a tour of the Italian colonies of Tripoli and Libya. He is interested in Africa as a site for Italian immigration settlement, a safety valve for overpopulation at home.			A bloodless coup d'etat in Peking by Kuominchun officers ends the presidency of Tuan Chi-jui, who has been under political pressure following the recent massacre of student demonstrators. General Wu Pei-fu is invited to "restore the political situation."
Apr. 11		Statistics indicate that 60 percent of French tax revenues are spent on paying the nation's debt.	France and Spain have officially sent envoys to negotiate a settlement with Berber rebels in Morocco. Meanwhile, their amassed force of 250,000 troops is poised to attack if the parleys fail.	A prominent Mexican bishop has been indicted for urging his parishioners to resist the recent flurry of anti-Catholic laws....The entire nine-member board of aldermen of Oyotempantecali, Mexico, in the state of Puebla, is assassinated while taking the oath of office.	China watchers believe that a confrontation between Wu Pei-fu and Zhang Zuolin is in the offing, as the armies of both warlords approach Peking.
Apr. 12	The Rockefeller Foundation reports a $200 million endowment, with large expenditures fighting hookworm and malaria internationally.	Irish communities along the Connemara Coast are suffering from severe malnutrition and tuberculosis, following a year of hardship in the fishing industry.	Syrian Druse rebels have lost 700 men in recent fighting, compared to 18 French soldiers killed....The president of the Mandates Commission of the League of Nations observes that the Druse are "nothing but big children. It must be admitted, however, they undoubtedly have their grievances."		The first segment of the Sutlej Valley irrigation project in India is officially opened by the British governor of Punjab.

A	B	C	D	E
Includes developments that affect more than one world region, international organizations and important meetings of world leaders.	*Includes all domestic and regional developments in Europe, including the Soviet Union.*	*Includes all domestic and regional developments in Africa and the Middle East.*	*Includes all domestic and regional developments in Latin America, the Caribbean, and Canada.*	*Includes all domestic and regional developments in Asian and Pacific nations (and colonies).*

U.S. Politics & Social Issues	U.S. Foreign Policy & Affairs, Defense	U.S. Economy & Environment	Science, Technology & Nature	Culture, Leisure & Lifestyle	
Approximately 35 percent of the prisoners in U.S. federal penitentiaries are serving sentences for drug trafficking and possession....There have been more clashes between police and strikers in Passaic. The strikers throw rocks and bottles, occasionally knocking a policeman unconscious; the police use clubs.	Secretary of War Davis is developing a preparedness plan that will enable the quick mobilization of the nation's industries in the event of an emergency. Before the House Military Committee, Davis observes that "modern warfare is no longer a matter for the army and navy. It is a matter for all the resources and activities of the country."	British consumers are rejecting American-grown apples, which are sprayed with a small amount of arsenic as a pesticide. American apple wholesalers insist that the apples pose no health threat.		The Montreal Maroons defeat the Victoria Cougars to win the National Hockey League's Stanley Cup.	Apr. 6
Preacher Billy Sunday announces that he will run for president in 1928 if Prohibition faces repeal. His theme will be "to hell with booze."...Federal attorneys estimate that bootlegging is a $4 billion annual industry.		Unlike most American automakers, the Ford Motor Company reports decreased earnings in 1925 against the previous year.	Lightning strikes touch off an inferno at oil reservoirs in San Luis Obispo, California, causing $10 million in damage. Approximately 4 million barrels of oil are ignited.	The U.S. radio-listening audience is estimated at 27 million; they own 5 million radios....The Department of Agriculture reports that the nation's farming population decreased by 500,000 in 1925....A Boston judge rules that the *American Mercury* is not indecent. "This magazine appeals to the intelligent and the open minded and apparently is issued with no other purpose in view," he observes.	Apr. 7
Two foreign oil tankers collide and explode in the Mississippi River near New Orleans, reportedly killing dozens....The House of Representatives votes by a 265–87 margin against reapportioning U.S. congressional districts based on the 1920 census. Several representatives insist that reapportionment is not mandated by the constitution.			Roald Amundsen's dirigible, the *Norge*, leaves Rome on the first leg of its attempted flight to the North Pole.	Contradicting the judge's ruling in Boston, the Solicitor of the U.S. Post Office Department rules that the April issue of the *American Mercury* is obscene. Mailing the issue will be regarded as a federal offense.	Apr. 8
		The Standard Oil Company reports record profits for 1925, with net earnings of $31 million, a 16 percent increase from the previous year.	Smithsonian Institution researchers believe that Tibetans and North American Indian tribes are closely related. The researchers note striking similarities in the speech intonations of both peoples.	The trial for the entire 17-member cast of a production of Eugene O'Neill's *Desire under the Elms* begins in Los Angeles. The cast is accused of staging an "immoral" play.	Apr. 9
			After conducting experiments on himself, a German doctor believes that cancer is not contagious. The doctor has injected himself with cancer bacilli and transferred cancerous tumors from a patient to his own skin. He finds that the cancer cells quickly die.		Apr. 10
An American oil tanker explodes while docked at Port Arthur, Texas, killing 25 men sleeping below deck....The Roman Catholic Church in the United States added nearly 225,000 members in 1925, more than any other Christian denomination.	The Naval Bureau of Aeronautics has been conducting experiments to break up fogbanks over airfields. Scientists project electrically charged waves of air into fog, which causes it to precipitate. This will open paths for safe runway landings.		Luther Burbank, an American amateur botanist credited with creating more than 800 strains and varieties of plants, including the Russet-Burbank potato, has died.	Will Rogers plays to a packed house at Carnegie Hall in New York City, performing lasso tricks while philosophizing on the issues of the day: flappers, Prohibition, evolution, the Ku Klux Klan, and Florida real estate. He observes that the Florida state emblem is the all-day sucker.	Apr. 11
The cities of Passaic and Garfield in New Jersey are under martial law following picketing outside the Fortstmann & Huffmann textile mill. Police use riot guns and clubs to disperse 5,000 strikers; most of the strike leaders, including Nancy Sandowsky, called the "Joan of Arc" of the workers, are arrested.	The House of Representatives votes to fund a five-year buildup of the nation's military aviation program, with the goal of adding 1,000 planes. A House committee observes that among the current force of 993 planes, 398 are obsolete.			Most experts pick the New York Giants to win the National League pennant in the upcoming major league baseball season. The American League favorites are the New York Yankees and the Washington Senators....At the *Desire under the Elms* trial in Los Angeles, a police officer testifies that he was "painfully shocked" by the play, particularly a scene with an actress wearing a long flannel nightgown.	Apr. 12

F	G	H	I	J
Includes campaigns, elections, federal-state relations, civil rights and liberties, crime, the judiciary, education, healthcare, poverty, urban affairs, and population.	Includes formation and debate of U.S. foreign and defense policies, veterans affairs, and defense spending. (Relations with specific foreign countries are usually found under the region concerned.)	Includes business, labor, agriculture, taxation, transportation, consumer affairs, monetary and fiscal policy, natural resources, pollution and industrial accidents.	Includes worldwide scientific, medical and technological developments, natural phenomena, U.S. weather and natural disasters.	Includes the arts, religion, scholarship, communications media, sports, entertainment, fashions, fads, and social life.

	World Affairs	Europe	Africa & The Middle East	The Americas	Asia & The Pacific
Apr. 13		A right-wing German newspaper announces the founding of an organization called Horticulture, intended to cultivate the image of the nation's deposed royalists....Three militarist youth groups in Germany, the Steel Helmets, the Young German Order, and the Werewolf, have set aside their differences and coalesced around the idea of establishing a nationalist dictatorship.			The Chinese General Chambers of Commerce publishes a full-page manifesto in major national newspapers, demanding racial equality and full civil rights for the Chinese in the foreign districts of Shanghai.... Warlord Zhang Zuolin insists that he has no designs on becoming president of China, "my business being entirely in Manchuria."
Apr. 14	A health report issued by the League of Nations notes that international infant mortality rates are decreasing.	.			
Apr. 15		The French franc has reached a new historic low. Experts cite as a primary concern the heavy French war-debt payments—primarily owed to the United States—that are coming due....British authorities expect a strike by coal miners. The main point at issue is a minimum wage: the miners want a fixed minimum wage applied nationally, while mine owners believe the minimum wage should vary according to district.	French premier Aristide Briand is concentrating on attaining a quick peace settlement with Abd el-Krim at the Oudjda conference in Morocco....A University of Chicago archaeological expedition, financed by John D. Rockefeller, begins the largest excavation to date in Palestine. They are using 300 Arab laborers to examine a mound in Megiddo with relics dating to the 10th century B.C.E.		Zhang Zuolin's forces have pushed to within 15 miles of Peking and are shelling the city heavily; Kuominchun forces loyal to the government have reportedly abandoned the city.
Apr. 16		The Soviet Union is actively pursuing negotiations with Germany, in an attempt to establish mutual neutrality in the event that either nation becomes involved in conflict with other countries.			Some of Zhang Zuolin's forces have entered Peking. The Kuominchun have withdrawn to northwest of the city.
Apr. 17		In London, 20,000 women, the majority of them working class, march in protest against labor strife. They carry banners with slogans such as "The Strike is a Two-Edged Sword" and "The Only Solution of Unemployment is Work."	Foreign banks and businesses in Turkey have been ordered to employ at least 50 percent Muslim Turkish workers on their staffs. Violators will be shut down by the government.		
Apr. 18	Columbia University president Nicholas Murray Butler, speaking for the Carnegie Endowment for International Peace, notes the problem of rising despotism. He observes that nationalist dictators maintain their power by arousing cultural xenophobia and international jealousies.	Germany observes "Health Week," a celebration of the human form, exercise, fresh air, and clean moral living. A kickoff parade in Berlin feature 5,000 female gymnasts and several thousand muscular young men.	French and Spanish diplomats are surprised by the attitude of tribal representatives at peace talks in Morocco. The European strategy is to negotiate directly with the tribes, "over the head" of leader Abd el-Krim, in an attempt to siphon off support.		
Apr. 19	Secretary of State Kellogg formally notifies the League of Nations that the United States will not participate in the September conference on American reservations to World Court adherence. He states that the reservations are "plain and unequivocal."	Berlin is experiencing a strange fad: spectator fasting. Participants spend weeks sealed in glass cages, where they refrain from eating. The foodless record is 45 days. Spectators buy tickets to watch the caged fasters, who have become celebrities. Several have received multiple marriage proposals. Police intend to ban the "sport."		Secretary of State Kellogg meets with ambassadors from Peru and Chile in an effort to solve the Tacna-Arica crisis.	

A	B	C	D	E
Includes developments that affect more than one world region, international organizations and important meetings of world leaders.	Includes all domestic and regional developments in Europe, including the Soviet Union.	Includes all domestic and regional developments in Africa and the Middle East.	Includes all domestic and regional developments in Latin America, the Caribbean, and Canada.	Includes all domestic and regional developments in Asian and Pacific nations (and colonies).

U.S. Politics & Social Issues	U.S. Foreign Policy & Affairs, Defense	U.S. Economy & Environment	Science, Technology & Nature	Culture, Leisure & Lifestyle	
A county sheriff election in Herrin, Illinois, ends in bloodshed. Armed with pistols and machine guns, members of the Ku Klux Klan and anti-Klansmen have a shoot-out in front of the town Masonic temple; three men from each side are killed....The Senate Judiciary Committee hears testimony about the impact of Prohibition on the nation's coal-mining districts, where pastimes among young people reportedly include "liquor joy rides" and "Fatty Arbuckle parties."		General Motors reports that March 1926 has been their record month for automobile sales, with 106,051 cars sold. Their previous high was set in April 1923.		Opening day attendance for major league baseball is reported at 223,000. The day's largest crowd—45,000 at the Polo Grounds in New York City—witnesses the Brooklyn Robins shut out the New York Giants by the score of 3–0....Police in Queens apprehend the "radio burglar" at the Polo Grounds. He admits to one murder, several other shootings—and the burglary of 14 radio sets. Police now believe they were mistaken in apprehending and shooting dead another suspect on March 28.	Apr. 13
Well-known Socialist Norman Thomas is arrested in Garfield, NJ, which remains under martial law. He is in town to contest the ban on public meetings. Police continue to closely monitor the streets; strangers are told to "walk out of town, or you'll be in the hospital in two minutes."				Fred and Adele Astaire make a dozen curtain calls after their opening night performance in the musical *Lady Be Good* in London.	Apr. 14
Minnesota congressmen vow not to permit Congress to adjourn until a farm relief bill has been enacted. A proposal favored by the Coolidge administration will establish a revolving fund intended to stabilize the price of agricultural commodities....The House Committee on Education considers a bill that would enable the federal regulation of movie content.			Mauna Loa, the largest volcano on the island of Hawaii, is erupting, with a river of lava threatening local communities.	The cast of *Desire under the Elms*, on trial in Los Angeles, performs the entire play for the judge and jury.	Apr. 15
		The Pan-American Petroleum Company reports record profits for 1925....The Department of Commerce reports that coal, oil, lumber, and cotton production are up in first quarter of 1926 from the same period in 1925. The use of electrical energy by U.S. industries is up approximately 10 percent, indicating substantially increased activity.		The U.S. Post Office stands by the decision to bar the April issue of the *American Mercury* from the mails, despite a personal appeal by editor H. L. Mencken....New York Supreme Court justice Harry E. Lewis attributes immorality in part to the dim lighting in restaurants and clubs.	Apr. 16
The textile strike in Passaic is now 13 weeks old. The town of Garfield remains under martial law, with all meetings—even private ones—forbidden. Hundreds of armed guards patrol the mills, and 10,000 workers remain idle.				The president of Beaver College for Women in Jenkintown, PA, citing the "general Bowery-dancehall atmosphere" of fraternity events, has barred his students from attending University of Pennsylvania dances....The *Desire under the Elms* trial in Los Angeles ends in a hung jury. The judge will schedule a retrial.	Apr. 17
		American dye production increased substantially in 1925 compared to 1924, with the export trade growing by 25 percent.	The entire Hawaiian village of Hoopulos has been swallowed by a fifty-foot-deep river of lava from the Mauna Loa volcano.		Apr. 18
			The Norwegian whaler *Sir James Clark Ross* has brought home a record haul in whale oil: 39,000 barrels, worth an estimated $1.2 million. The ship spent nine months in Antarctic waters and killed 531 whales.	Novelist Sinclair Lewis. speaking at a church in Kansas City, berates fundamentalist Christianity and dares God to strike him dead.... British trade officials are concerned that Hollywood films are undermining their colonial empire.	Apr. 19

F	G	H	I	J
Includes campaigns, elections, federal-state relations, civil rights and liberties, crime, the judiciary, education, healthcare, poverty, urban affairs, and population.	*Includes formation and debate of U.S. foreign and defense policies, veterans affairs, and defense spending. (Relations with specific foreign countries are usually found under the region concerned.)*	*Includes business, labor, agriculture, taxation, transportation, consumer affairs, monetary and fiscal policy, natural resources, pollution and industrial accidents.*	*Includes worldwide scientific, medical and technological developments, natural phenomena, U.S. weather and natural disasters.*	*Includes the arts, religion, scholarship, communications media, sports, entertainment, fashions, fads, and social life.*

	World Affairs	Europe	Africa & The Middle East	The Americas	Asia & The Pacific
Apr. 20			The French have been unable to dislodge Druse fighters from two strongholds in Syria. Druse sources claim that the French have sustained more than a thousand casualties.		
Apr. 21	The U.S. Senate votes 54–33 to ratify the Italian war-debt repayments.	Italy holds a gala celebration recognizing the 2680th anniversary of the founding of Rome. Tens of thousands of Fascists, including many common laborers marching in military formation, pay tribute to Benito Mussolini as the "Caesar of the Modern Empire." The day's festivities emphasize competitive sporting events, which Mussolini intends to make a central facet of Italian life. During the evening Rome is lighted by thousands of incandescent globes.			Reports indicate that before evacuating Peking, Kuominchun forces executed 395 of the 400 guardsmen who fired on student protestors last month.
Apr. 22		An audience riots at the Comédie Française in Paris, the French national theater, where the play *La Carcasse* is found to be demeaning toward the French army....The Soviet Foreign Office announces its willingness to enter into non-aggression compacts with all nations, including the United States and Great Britain.			Dutch soldiers have been attacked several times recently by the indigenous populations of Sumatra and the Dutch East Indies. One patrol of 12 soldiers was massacred by sword-wielding Achine natives. Dutch authorities blame the unrest on Communist propaganda.
Apr. 23		Soviet officials are in the United States seeking funding for a proposed $70 million hydroelectric project on the Dnieper River in Ukraine....The Moskava River is rising quickly with the late spring thaw, flooding parts of Moscow....The Polish government is contemplating appointing a Jewish finance minister to the national cabinet, an idea that is causing controversy....The British government is seriously considering renewing the coal subsidy in an effort to ward off the impending strike.	The Standard Oil Company and three European petroleum companies have won the right to undertake oil exploration in Iraq.		A major Japanese newspaper editorializes about current plans to build up the U.S. Air Force. "Such a plan must be taken as a manifestation of positive militarism by America," the paper observes. Many Japanese believe that the United States dissimulates when advocating international disarmament.
Apr. 24		Germany and the Soviet Union sign a mutual neutrality treaty. The countries agree that neither will enter into military or economic aggression against the other....The Italian government has denounced all efforts at birth control, calling them "insidious, practical, pseudo-scientific, neo-malthusian propaganda."	Peace talks between representatives of Abd el-Krim and Franco-Spanish diplomats have broken down. A French official warns that "it will soon be the turn for the cannon to speak."	A U.S. fact-finding committee, including a former governor of Colorado and a Jewish rabbi, returns from Mexico City describing President Calles as a "tolerant man." The Calles government's policies are intended to improve educational opportunities for Mexicans; the country's entrenched institutions, particularly the Catholic priesthood, are seen as obstacles to progress.	
Apr. 25		The American Bible Society has received permission to distribute Bibles in the Soviet Union....Violinist Jascha Heifetz is honored by France with the Cross of the Legion of Honor. At age 26, he is the youngest civilian recipient of the award.	French troops have succeeded in taking the Syrian Druse stronghold of Soueida, following a ferocious six-hour battle.		Clashes between Hindus and Muslims continue in Calcutta, with at least 11 people killed.

A	**B**	**C**	**D**	**E**
Includes developments that affect more than one world region, international organizations and important meetings of world leaders.	*Includes all domestic and regional developments in Europe, including the Soviet Union.*	*Includes all domestic and regional developments in Africa and the Middle East.*	*Includes all domestic and regional developments in Latin America, the Caribbean, and Canada.*	*Includes all domestic and regional developments in Asian and Pacific nations (and colonies).*

U.S. Politics & Social Issues	U.S. Foreign Policy & Affairs, Defense	U.S. Economy & Environment	Science, Technology & Nature	Culture, Leisure & Lifestyle	
Some U.S. senators point to Benito Mussolini's ambitious rebuilding plans for Rome as evidence that Italy does not need lenient terms for debt repayment.			Herbert Hoover is heading the National Research Endowment, a campaign to provide $20 million to support pure scientific research in American universities.	Babe Ruth hits his first home run of the season, a monster shot off Washington Senators pitcher Walter Johnson. He also contributes two doubles and two singles in the Yankees' 18–5 win.	Apr. 20
The U.S. Circuit Court of Appeals rules that Prohibition agents may not seize foreign rum runners beyond the three-mile coastal waters territorial limit....Law enforcement statistics indicate that 1 in every 110 murderers in America is punished with the death penalty. In England virtually all murderers are executed; however, there are approximately 10,000 murders in the United States annually compared to 100 in Great Britain.			Roald Amundsen's dirigible arrives in King's Bay, Spitzbergen, which will be the launching place for his proposed flight over the North Pole....Researchers at the Washington Navy Yard have developed a sonic depth finder for measuring distances to the ocean floor.	Jack Dempsey will receive a $450,000 purse for defending his heavyweight title this September.	Apr. 21
The House Immigration Committee approves a bill facilitating the rapid deportation of aliens convicted of bootlegging, prostitution, opium dealing, or carrying a concealed weapon.			At the American Medical Association Conference in Dallas, Dr. Mazyck Ravenel of the University of Missouri School of Medicine muses on the subject of medical care for "incompetents." "There are more people unfit mentally and physically than are good for the community," he remarks. "They tend to multiply at a rate faster than the fit. The population of the world has already reached the saturation point in many countries." He recommends that it may be unwise to save "incompetent" lives.		Apr. 22
President Coolidge, concerned about a budget deficit, threatens to veto several appropriations being pushed by Congress. Among the threatened measures are a pension bill for Spanish-American War veterans and the Civil Service Retirement bill.			Scientists have determined that watching movies does not cause eye strain or vision damage.		Apr. 23
American Indians in Oklahoma are suffering from widespread trachoma, an infectious eye disease that can cause blindness. Approximately 20 percent of the Indians in the state have the disease.			Johns Hopkins University researchers believe that high-frequency sound waves can be used to treat arthritis. Experiments show that circulation is improved when an arthritic joint is placed in water stimulated by sound waves.	William Henry Johnson, better known by his performing names "Zip the Pinhead" and "What-Is-It," has died. He was one of the most popular stars in P. T. Barnum's circus, dating to the 1860s.	Apr. 24
Several Republicans are said to be mulling a presidential run in 1928, including Vice President Charles Dawes, Speaker of the House Nicholas Longworth, Senator William Borah, and Secretary of Commerce Herbert Hoover....The president of the American Farm Bureau lambastes the Coolidge administration for making empty gestures toward agricultural relief. Washington's solution for the farmer's surplus problem, he says, is "give them a Federal Board."		American investments in foreign corporations have surpassed $10 billion for the first time.	The Western Electric Company and Warner Brothers Pictures announce the successful development of a sound synchronization system for motion pictures. They believe sound will revolutionize the industry.	Giacomo Puccini's unfinished opera *Turandot* receives its posthumous premiere in Milan, with Arturo Toscanini conducting....The American Association of University Professors issues a report criticizing college football as a distraction on most campuses. The professors cite the atmosphere of the big game, when the "hysteria" is "a bad thing for intellectual balance and morale." Students neglect their coursework and sometimes partake in drinking and gambling. Compared to academics, football assumes a "false importance"; "the sheer physical size of the stadium dwarfs the significance of the library....and lecture hall."	Apr. 25

F	G	H	I	J
Includes campaigns, elections, federal-state relations, civil rights and liberties, crime, the judiciary, education, healthcare, poverty, urban affairs, and population.	Includes formation and debate of U.S. foreign and defense policies, veterans affairs, and defense spending. (Relations with specific foreign countries are usually found under the region concerned.)	Includes business, labor, agriculture, taxation, transportation, consumer affairs, monetary and fiscal policy, natural resources, pollution and industrial accidents.	Includes worldwide scientific, medical and technological developments, natural phenomena, U.S. weather and natural disasters.	Includes the arts, religion, scholarship, communications media, sports, entertainment, fashions, fads, and social life.

	World Affairs	Europe	Africa & The Middle East	The Americas	Asia & The Pacific
Apr. 26		Anna Serebryakova, a tsarist police spy who posed as the hostess of a salon for leftist revolutionaries, is sentenced to death at a trial in Moscow.	The French are making increased efforts at peace talks in Morocco, advancing negotiations with the Berbers from the preliminary to the plenary stage. Observers note that Abd el-Krim's apparent strategy, to open a rift between French and Spanish diplomats, is working; the French are much more conciliatory than the Spanish.		Japan has formed a national news agency, modeled on the Associated Press in the United States.
Apr. 27	Several American economists and bankers are concerned that the issue of war debt repayments will unsettle international relations for decades. They point out that the United States will continue to be blamed by debtor European nations for financial problems.	Chancellor of the Exchequer Winston Churchill has proposed a tax on betting, provoking a firestorm of criticism in England. Bookmakers fear they will lose their livelihoods; church leaders believe the tax will give government sanction to gambling....An American Harvard graduate is arrested after making an insulting comment about Mussolini at a Vatican museum.			
Apr. 28		The negotiations in England between coal miners and owners are failing; the primary sticking point is the owners' desire for a lengthened workday....The Reichstag has been unable to negotiate a compromise between leftist and conservative politicians over the expropriation of royalist lands. More than 12.5 million voters signed a referendum to hold a plebiscite on the issue, which will take place in mid-May.	John D. Rockefeller withdraws his offer to build a $10 million antiquities museum in Egypt.		
Apr. 29	President Coolidge and French Premier Briand sign a compact on war debt repayments, which will require France to pay $6.8 billion spread over the next 62 years.	A railroad bridge collapses over a flooded river near Leningrad, killing 50 commuters.	Peace talks in Morocco have once again stalled. Abd el-Krim is demanding autonomy for his confederation of Arab tribes; French and Spanish negotiators are offering a measure of home rule.		
Apr. 30	Yesterday's Franco-American agreement on war debts is receiving negative reviews on both sides of the Atlantic. French newspapers complain that the agreement amounts to the United States "trying to establish everywhere its hegemony—to reign as an imperialistic democracy which must bend the old Continent to its economic will."	Mussolini is cracking down on the Sicilian Mafia, arresting 450 suspected members.			
May 1		As British coal miners prepare to strike, the General Council of the Trades Union Congress announces a sympathy walkout, with potentially enormous repercussions: more than 4 million workers may take part in the general strike set to begin Monday May 3. The British government has declared a state of emergency....May Day, the European version of Labor Day, turns bloody in Poland when Socialist and Communists clash during a Warsaw parade.	The British government in Egypt has uncovered a Soviet plot to foment unrest in Cairo.		

A	B	C	D	E
Includes developments that affect more than one world region, international organizations and important meetings of world leaders.	Includes all domestic and regional developments in Europe, including the Soviet Union.	Includes all domestic and regional developments in Africa and the Middle East.	Includes all domestic and regional developments in Latin America, the Caribbean, and Canada.	Includes all domestic and regional developments in Asian and Pacific nations (and colonies).

U.S. Politics & Social Issues	U.S. Foreign Policy & Affairs, Defense	U.S. Economy & Environment	Science, Technology & Nature	Culture, Leisure & Lifestyle	
Progressive Democratic senator Burton Wheeler attacks President Coolidge and the Congress for being "subservient" to large corporations....A white mob in Carteret, New Jersey, torches an African-American Baptist church and forces more than 100 black families to leave town. The rioting is provoked by a scuffle between whites and blacks, which leaves one white man dead.			French researchers propose the theory that cancer is caused by mildew.	Vaudeville actor Mae West makes her mainstream theatrical debut in the play Sex.	Apr. 26
William H. McSwiggin, known in Chicago as "the hanging prosecutor," is machine-gunned to death with three other men outside a tavern in Cicero, Illinois.			Scientists have found significant variations between the sexes in one-celled organisms; female cells have considerably more chemical activity and oxidizing power.	Belle Moskowitz, a Democratic Party organizer affiliated with New York governor Al Smith, tells a women's political conference in New York City that their sex's "intuitive sense is the biggest thing that they bring to politics....They are not the intellectual equals of men."	Apr. 27
The murder of William McSwiggin is raising questions in Chicago. The states' attorney was in the company of Myles "Klondike" O'Donnell, a well-known bootlegger and bitter foe of gangster Al Capone; O'Donnell apparently escaped alive from the assault. The other three men who died were all known criminals. Police are uncertain why McSwiggin was with them and what they were doing in Cicero, the heart of Capone's gangland territory. Police report that the weapon used in the killings was a military-issue Thompson machine gun, capable of spraying 1,500 rounds per minute.			Harry Guggenheim, president of the Daniel Guggenheim Fund for the Promotion of Aeronautics. insists that the United States must strive to keep pace with European advances in aviation. He finds that Germany is the world leader in commercial flight, and France and England have become the technological innovators. These countries benefit from government-subsidized aviation programs, which the United States lacks.	Cleveland Symphony Orchestra conductor Nikolai Sokoloff is at loggerheads with his musicians, who have signed a petition accusing him of abusive conduct....The Greenwich Theater in New York City, devoted to experimental plays, announces its new season. The lineup includes Viva Mexico, by Communist author Michael Gold; Sumpin' Like Wings, by Cherokee Indian author Lynn Riggs; and When in Rome, by antiwar playwright Laurence Stallings.	Apr. 28
Admissions officials at Columbia University and Brown University deny that they discriminate against Jewish students, although Columbia admits using a quota system for Jewish applicants....Eleven senators from agricultural states "revolt" against the Coolidge administration, insisting that they will block congressional adjournment until farm relief measures are enacted.		The Federal Reserve Board announces a robust first quarter of 1926 for retailers. Department store sales are up five percent from the same quarter last year.		The United Artists film studio signs a contract with the largest German theater chain, ensuring that United Artists films will play in more than 1,200 theaters in Germany.	Apr. 29
New York City actresses protest the derogatory use of the phrase "chorus girl" by newspapers and magazines. The actresses, who work in theatrical chorus lines, complain that "chorus girl" has been linked in the public mind with scandalous divorces....The American Civil Liberties Union obtains an injunction ending martial law in Garfield, New Jersey, permitting 2,000 strikers to hold a meeting.		A total of 224 American companies pay out dividends to their shareholders—a Wall Street record.	The Radio Corporation of America successfully transmits a "radio picture" from London to New York City. A photograph is translated into radio impulses, then transmitted and reproduced, using a stylus on hot wax. Because of climatic interference, the process takes nearly two hours; researchers believe 20 minutes will be more typical....The works of Russian psychologist Ivan Pavlov are being translated for the first time into English.		Apr. 30
Alabama authorities are investigating the state's system of leased convict labor. An incident in 1924, when an inmate died while being tortured by guards through "dunking" in a water barrel, has spurred the investigation.	The U.S. Navy is busy readying two aircraft carriers, the Lexington and the Saratoga, for commission by early next year. Each ship will carry between 80 and 100 aircraft.		A German inventor has developed a hand-held device that enables the user to apply electrical shocks with a touch of the hand. The German police are negotiating to use the device.	Approximately 80,000 fans watch a 300-mile race at the Atlantic City Motor Speedway, as six world speed records are broken. The victor, Harry Hartz, averages 134.1 miles per hour.	May 1

F	G	H	I	J
Includes campaigns, elections, federal-state relations, civil rights and liberties, crime, the judiciary, education, healthcare, poverty, urban affairs, and population.	Includes formation and debate of U.S. foreign and defense policies, veterans affairs, and defense spending. (Relations with specific foreign countries are usually found under the region concerned.)	Includes business, labor, agriculture, taxation, transportation, consumer affairs, monetary and fiscal policy, natural resources, pollution and industrial accidents.	Includes worldwide scientific, medical and technological developments, natural phenomena, U.S. weather and natural disasters.	Includes the arts, religion, scholarship, communications media, sports, entertainment, fashions, fads, and social life.

	World Affairs	Europe	Africa & The Middle East	The Americas	Asia & The Pacific
May 2		Negotiations between British Prime Minister Stanley Baldwin and union leaders break down entirely, setting the stage for an unprecedented nationwide general strike. The government is scrambling to set up emergency committees to provide basic services, such as transportation and food distribution. Military troops are being stationed in coal mining regions in anticipation of unrest....German unemployment continues to be a serious issue, with more than 1.8 million workers idle.	Still reeling from their defeat at Soueida, Druse rebels meet in council and vote to fight "to the bitter end" against the French....The American Committee Opposed to the Lausanne Treaty publishes a pamphlet claiming that 100,000 Christian women are held captive in Turkish harems. The pamphlet is endorsed by New York Episcopal Bishop William Thomas Manning.	A Catholic laymen's organization has collected 500,000 signatures petitioning the Mexican government to modify stringent religious laws.	For the first time, women are eligible for election to public office in India.
May 3		At the toll of midnight, the British general strike begins. More than 2.5 million workers participate, including 1.1 million miners and 860,000 transportation employees. Prime minister Baldwin warns the House of Commons that the British constitution is being threatened and civil war may result; by a vote of 308–108, the House backs his views. Thousands of Londoners, many of them women, apply as volunteers to keep the city functioning during the strike.		The Mexican government arrests several prominent individuals linked to the 1913 assassination of President Francisco Madero. The attorney general is reportedly planning to request the extradition of former U.S. ambassador Henry Lane Wilson for his role in the murder plot.	China makes no progress toward assembling a new central government in Peking. Neither of the dominant warlords, Wu Pei-fu and Zhang Zuolin, appears to be interested in assuming the presidency.
May 4	President Coolidge praises Secretary of the Treasury Andrew Mellon for successfully negotiating war-debt repayment settlements with all the major debtor nations, with the exception of Russia.	With public transportation at a standstill, London is snarled by a traffic jam and hundreds of thousands of people walk to work, but conditions are generally calm....The Soviet government issues a proclamation: "The struggle has begun. Millions of the English proletariat have risen as one man against the exploiters. All workers, regardless of factions, must stand with our struggling brothers."			
May 5		British prime minister Baldwin announces he will only negotiate with strikers after the general strike has been ended....President von Hindenburg causes an uproar in Germany by approving the display of a black, white, and red flag at the nation's foreign embassies; the design is strikingly similar to the former monarchical flag....The Polish cabinet resigns because of financial policy wrangling....The value of the French franc, which has already reached historic lows this year, tumbles again.			Generals Wu Pei-fu and Zhang Zuolin are said to be deadlocked over the issue of reviving the Chinese parliament; Zhang is reportedly opposed. In the meantime, China has no functioning central government.
May 6		There are skirmishes involving public transportation in working-class neighborhoods of London, Edinburgh, and Glasgow, but predictions of widespread unrest have not come to pass in England.	The peace talks in Morocco have failed. French and Spanish troops are ready to begin an offensive against Abd el-Krim. A spokesman for el-Krim remarks, "They wanted only to force us to make peace like beaten rebel tribesmen."...Druse rebels conduct nighttime raids on French army posts, killing eight soldiers and capturing more than 20.		
May 7		The British government is mobilizing the military and recruiting a force of emergency police constables. There is concern that strikers might try to interfere with food supply lines, although strike leaders promised not to do this. Disturbances continue to be limited, although 89 people are arrested in Glasgow and Edinburgh....Observers of German politics believe the recent flag ruling is a maneuver by the Luther cabinet to gain more support from the country's nationalist elements.		A Nicaraguan rebel group storms a branch of the national bank and steals more than $160,000.	

A	B	C	D	E
Includes developments that affect more than one world region, international organizations and important meetings of world leaders.	*Includes all domestic and regional developments in Europe, including the Soviet Union.*	*Includes all domestic and regional developments in Africa and the Middle East.*	*Includes all domestic and regional developments in Latin America, the Caribbean, and Canada.*	*Includes all domestic and regional developments in Asian and Pacific nations (and colonies).*

U.S. Politics & Social Issues	U.S. Foreign Policy & Affairs, Defense	U.S. Economy & Environment	Science, Technology & Nature	Culture, Leisure & Lifestyle	
Chicago police believe that state's attorney William McSwiggin was an accidental victim in last week's gangland murders. Their theory is that Al Capone was hunting his rival, Miles "Klondike" O'Donnell, and had no idea McSwiggin was with O'Donnell's group in Cicero.… The American Negro Labor Congress protests the lack of response by state and local authorities to the race riot in Carteret, NJ.		The U.S. merchant fleet totals 1,068 ships, with a gross tonnage of 5.6 million.…The Council of the American Bankers Association, addressing the recent stock market downturn, believes that the United States economy is fundamentally sound.	The New York Building Congress announces 13 winners of their "Certificate of Craftsmanship," given to workers of special distinction in the building trades. Among the winners are a hodcarrier, a glazier, and a bricklayer.	Former heavyweight champion Jack Johnson, now 48-years-old and fighting in Mexico, wins a 15-round bout against Pat Lester.… Preseason National League favorites the New York Giants drop their fourth game in a row, although rookie Mel Ott, in his debut, hits a pinch single and drives in a run.	May 2
A special grand jury convenes to investigate the recent spate of gangland killings in Chicago. There have been at least 20 so far this year.			Researchers announce their ability to measure the flow rate of blood through the human body, by injecting active radium.…The American Bankers Association urges the federal government to become more active in fostering civil aviation.	The Pulitzer Prizes for 1925 are announced. Among the winners are Sinclair Lewis for his novel *Arrowsmith*, George Kelly for his play *Craig's Wife*, Edward Channing for his *History of the United States*, and Amy Lowell (posthumously) for her poetry volume *What's O'Clock*.	May 3
John D. Rockefeller purchases an entire city block of slum dwellings in Harlem, with the intention to build modern low-cost housing for African Americans.…The House Committee on Education shelves a bill supporting federal movie censorship, in part because of the Coolidge administration's opposition.…The Passaic textiles strike is now 100 days old.		The Nash Motor Company reports record earnings for the first quarter of 1926.…President Coolidge believes the British general strike will not impair the U.S. economy. He emphasizes that there is no parallel between British and American labor conditions.	The Atlantic seaboard experiences a May cold snap, with temperatures in the 30s.		May 4
Two wardens have been arrested in Alabama in connection with several convict deaths in the state's prisons.…Vanderbilt University professor Edwin Mims describes the modern South as swinging between genuine progress and "political and social immobility and decadence." He observes that the American popular mind is fixated by "caricature, satire and sentimentalism" about the South, which only serves to reinforce the region's conservatism.		Stock market activity has dwindled because of uncertainty surrounding the British general strike. Today 660,000 shares were traded; the average this year has been between 2 and 3 million shares daily.…The United States produced more pig iron this April than in any month since 1923.		Sinclair Lewis refuses to accept the Pulitzer Prize for his novel *Arrowsmith*, objecting to one of the terms of the prize, that the book should represent "the highest standards of American manners and manhood." In his letter rejecting the award, he observes that this phrase means books are selected not for literary merit but "in obedience to whatever code of good form may chance to be popular at the moment."	May 5
"Flying squads" of policemen conduct raids in New York City, padlocking 50 places of business found in violation of Prohibition, including a leading French restaurant, several night clubs, three drugstores, and a sacramental wine shop.		Gasoline prices are up this year, selling at an average of 18 cents per gallon wholesale.…The U.S. Anaconda Copper Mining Company gains rights to the world's second largest zinc deposit, in Poland and Germany.	The American Society for the Control of Cancer seeks a million dollars to promote cancer awareness. A spokesman notes that many people with early-stage cancer are unaware they have the disease.	The Provincetown Playhouse in New York City's Greenwich Village, where noted literary figures Eugene O'Neill and Edna St. Vincent Millay began their careers, is struggling financially and may close.	May 6
President Warren G. Harding's attorney general, Harry Daughtery, is indicted for accepting bribes in 1921 from Swiss businessmen connected to the American Metal Company.…Officials at Harvard University acknowledge that race plays a role in admissions. "Extreme racial characteristics" that might prevent a student from partaking fully in university fellowship are a factor.		The Commerce Department announces that U.S. business activity for 1926 is outpacing the previous year, with the dollar volume of trade up considerably.…Statistics show that the United States owns 82 percent of the world's automobiles.		Henry Ford personally directs firefighters in stopping a blaze that threatens his antiques-filled historic Wayside Inn in Sudbury, MA.	May 7

F	G	H	I	J
Includes campaigns, elections, federal-state relations, civil rights and liberties, crime, the judiciary, education, healthcare, poverty, urban affairs, and population.	Includes formation and debate of U.S. foreign and defense policies, veterans affairs, and defense spending. (Relations with specific foreign countries are usually found under the region concerned.)	Includes business, labor, agriculture, taxation, transportation, consumer affairs, monetary and fiscal policy, natural resources, pollution and industrial accidents.	Includes worldwide scientific, medical and technological developments, natural phenomena, U.S. weather and natural disasters.	Includes the arts, religion, scholarship, communications media, sports, entertainment, fashions, fads, and social life.

	World Affairs	Europe	Africa & The Middle East	The Americas	Asia & The Pacific
May 8		There are rumors that British troops have fired on violent strikers, but the English government insists they are untrue. There has been only one fatality in the general strike so far. "It is a truly remarkable," a spokesman notes, "how little serious disorder has occurred in an industrial conflict of this magnitude."	The French launch a surprise pre-dawn attack against Berber rebels, driving them out of their network of mountain trenches....French troops and Syrian Druse clash in the suburbs of Damscus.		The Smithsonian Institution launches an expedition into the mountains of Dutch New Guinea, the home of a pigmy population. The Smithsonian describes the region as "the world's last great unknown land."
May 9		The British government appears to be winning the strike. With a large cadre of citizen volunteers, transportation has not been significantly impeded and food distribution is perhaps at 90 percent capacity. The government is making efficient use of 200,000 trucks to deliver goods.	The French military shells the Midan Quarter of Damascus, where approximately 200 Druse insurgents have barricaded themselves in houses. The French allow civilians a half hour to evacuate before the bombardment begins; 15 hours of steady shelling follows. According to press reports, "Women and children rushed aimlessly through the streets to fall victims to stray rifle shots, bursting shells, and collapsing houses." Three hundred homes in the quarter are demolished and more than 500 civilians killed.		
May 10		Reports indicate informal talks have begun to end the British general strike....Benito Mussolini greets Hollywood stars Douglas Fairbanks and Mary Pickford in Rome....A 1st-century B.C.E. subterranean fort has been discovered near Bourdeaux, France.	The French drive the Druse from Damascus, after killing approximately 90 rebels in yesterday's intense bombardment.		
May 11	In Geneva, Brazil presses once again for a permanent seat on the League of Nations Council.	The British Trades Union Congress calls out 100,000 Scottish shipbuilders and engineers from their jobs, apparently ratcheting up the general strike....Violinst Jascha Heifetz is greeted with rapturous applause after performing at the Paris Opera House.	Spanish troops advance significantly in Morocco, cutting off several tribal groups from their allies.		
May 12		The British Trades Union Council calls off the general strike, although the coal miners' walkout continues. Observers note that the general strike failed to win the support of the British public....Marshal Józef Pilsudski stages a *coup d'etat* in Poland.	French troops have recently pacified 25 Syrian villages and report that 80 percent of the nation is under their full control.		
May 13		Polish president Stanislaw Wojciechowski is forced to step down and arrested by Marshal Pilsudski, who has 2,500 troops in Warsaw. Pilsudski's men battle with loyalist troops in the city's streets, with 200 reported killed.... Chancellor of the Exchequer Winston Churchill is winning great acclaim for his role in the government's effective handling of the strike.			A temporary cabinet is established in Peking, but the post of president remains vacant.
May 14		Polish loyalist reinforcements are reportedly on the move toward Warsaw, although a strike called by Socialist railway workers is retarding their progress....British prime minister Baldwin decides to personally mediate between coal miners and coal owners. Neither side embraces his proposals....The Italian lire declines again, while the French and Belgian francs reach new historic lows.			

A	B	C	D	E
Includes developments that affect more than one world region, international organizations and important meetings of world leaders.	Includes all domestic and regional developments in Europe, including the Soviet Union.	Includes all domestic and regional developments in Africa and the Middle East.	Includes all domestic and regional developments in Latin America, the Caribbean, and Canada.	Includes all domestic and regional developments in Asian and Pacific nations (and colonies).

U.S. Politics & Social Issues	U.S. Foreign Policy & Affairs, Defense	U.S. Economy & Environment	Science, Technology & Nature	Culture, Leisure & Lifestyle	
The U.S. House of Representatives is debating proposed farm relief measures. Democrat Andrew Somers from New York observes that the farmer must "work out his own salvation."			Bengali scientist Jagdish Chandra Bose's experiments suggest that plant life has a nervous system, similar to animals and humans, and is capable of experiencing pleasure and pain.	Members of the World War Veterans Light Wines and Beer League unfurl 60-foot black streamers from the crown of the Statue of Liberty, in protest against their "loss of liberty."...Thornton Wilder has published his debut novel, *The Cabala*.	May 8
Irish-American politicians take issue with the new "national origin" provision of U.S. immigration law, set to go into effect next year. The provision stipulates that immigrant quotas by nationality should be set to reflect the population composition of the 1790 U.S. census; the current practice is to fix quotas by the 1890 census. By switching to 1790, the number of Irish immigrants permitted in the country will drop from 28,530 to 8,330 per year. The Ku Klux Klan strongly supports the "national origin" provision.	.	The National Association of Credit Men has conducted surveys indicating that businessmen rely heavily on the financial opinions of newspapers and trade periodicals. The association warns against this tendency toward "mob-thinking."	Richard E. Byrd successfully flies his three-engine Fokker airplane across the North Pole, circling several times. The polar journey takes 15 hours and 51 minutes before he touches down again in Kings Bay, Spitzbergen. He beats his own expected trip time of 24 hours.	The New York Yankees play before their largest home crowd—55,000 fans—since 1924, but Ty Cobb smacks two homeruns and the Detroit Tigers win, 14–10.	May 9
U.S. congressmen hail Richard E. Byrd as a national hero....The National Woman's Party, meeting in Baltimore, reports that during the past five years there have been 506 bills drafted by state legislatures to reduce discrimination against women.			Robert Guthrie, a metallurgist, succeeds in photographing the structure of a microscopic piece of steel, magnified at 15,500 diameters.	Salmon's Display wins the Preakness at the Pimlico Race Course in Baltimore....The National Fire Protection Agency estimates that 6 percent of fires in the United States are caused by careless cigarette smokers.	May 10
Henry Patterson, an African-American living in Labell, FL, is shot dead and subsequently hanged by a gang of whites. Patterson had inadvertently frightened a white woman....The Forstmann & Huffmann Company in Garfield, New Jersey, obtains an injunction against strikers, limiting the number of picketers outside their factory to eight.		The U.S. total output of motor vehicles in 1925 was 4,157,830, a 6.9 percent increase from 1923.	Roald Amundsen's dirigible the *Norge*, with a crew of 16, begins its polar flight from Kings Bay, Spitzbergen, in fair weather....The International Health Bureau convenes in Paris, with representatives from 65 nations. Their object is to draft a world health plan; many of the delegates are most concerned with exterminating rats worldwide, as a primary carrier of dangerous diseases.	Richard Rodgers and Lorenz Hart's musical *Garrick Gaieties* opens on Broadway, featuring the song *Mountain Greenery*....Yankees manager Miller Huggins calls his outfielder Bob Meusel "the greatest player in the American League."... A federal judge issues an injunction against U.S. Post Office officials, enabling the April *American Mercury* to finally be mailed.	May 11
Final appeals for Nicola Sacco and Bartolomeo Vanzetti are denied by the Massachusetts Supreme Court....The U.S. Coast Guard seizes an American freighter 60 miles off the New Jersey coast. The ship holds a $1.5 million cargo of champagne and whiskey, and the entire crew is reported "roaring drunk."			The missing dirigible the *Norge* radios that it has reached the North Pole, but a few hours later all contact with the dirigible is lost....A French polar expert speculates that Richard E. Byrd may not have actually reached the North Pole, but instead drifted to either side of the summit.	The Philadelphia Athletics win their ninth straight baseball game, led by stars Al Simmons and Mickey Cochrane.	May 12
Former Republican National Committeeman John T. King, indicted a few weeks ago for fraud, has died....Statistics indicate that there are 5.5 million elderly (aged 65 and older) in the United States, constituting approximately five percent of the population. Almost 80 percent live in dependence on family, pensions, or some form of relief.			There is no word from the missing dirigible the *Norge*.		May 13
Approximately 25,000 Americans were killed and 700,000 injured in automobile accidents in 1925.... There are more confrontations between strikers and policemen in Passaic.		The Federal Reserve Board notes that there has been a gradual decline in commodity prices. Many industries, operating on narrower price margins, are dependent on greater output, which has reached record levels. But distribution and consumption have matched the pace, and the nation's economic outlook is good.	The *Norge* has now been out of radio contact for more than 48 hours. Experts suggest that the dirigible may be caught in a polar storm over the southern Arctic.		May 14

	World Affairs	Europe	Africa & The Middle East	The Americas	Asia & The Pacific
May 15		Marshal Pilsudki completes his coup, as all loyalist opposition folds.	French and Spanish troops are engaged in a pincher-like operation in Morocco, with plans to converge in the Nekour Valley. French movement has been unopposed recently, and the mountain passes are clear of rebels.	The Calles government deports the papal representative to Mexico, claiming that he has entered the country under false pretenses.	A man-eating tiger in India's Allahabad district, notorious for more than 200 human kills, is shot to death by a British officer.
May 16		Rumors abound about "Frau von Tschaikovski," the woman being treated in a Berlin sanatorium who claims she is Russian Grand Duchess Anastasia. The woman is said to have bullet scars on her scalp and abdomen. Royal relatives of the tsar are employing detectives to investigate her case.		The papal representative to Mexico denies the allegations of the Calles government, but leaves the country.	
May 17		Wilhelm Marx becomes the new chancellor of Germany....The French franc continues to slide, now valued at less than 3 cents on the New York foreign exchange market. Financial experts are perplexed, because the French economic picture has been improving recently. The Italian lire and the Belgian franc also fall. The American dollar and the British pound are the two strong currencies.	The population of Fez, Morocco, is suffering through a typhus outbreak.	A bomb explodes at the U.S. embassy in Buenos Aires, Argentina. Evidence suggests the perpetrators are radical sympathizers with Sacco and Vanzetti....The Mexican government is now expelling Protestant ministers. One minister will be allowed to remain in Mexico City, but he must refrain from preaching.	
May 18		The French franc is depressed even lower, reaching a value of 2.72 cents....The Society for the Prevention of Cruelty to Animals in Germany seeks to ban the films of director Hans Schwartz. Schwartz forced two young horses to run over a 50-foot cliff while shooting a Western movie, then spent hours filming them while they suffered with broken bones.		The National Catholic Welfare Conference writes to President Coolidge about the situation in Mexico. They decry the existence of a North American government "that explicitly denies the principles which we believe are the very life of our country."	
May 19		Coal miners and owners in Britain make no headway, despite the negotiating assistance of prime minister Baldwin....Benito Mussolini insists that the democratic state, "weak and agnostic, is no more." In its stead rises the Fascist state.	French troops drive almost six miles in less than a day in their steady advance against Berber rebels.		The Japanese province of Shinchiku is suffering in a famine.
May 20	At a preparatory meeting for the League of Nations Disarmament Conference, several small nations point out that disarming would leave them vulnerable to aggressive larger nations. They want their security safeguarded first.		Following a series of withdrawals, Berber rebels launch a sneak attack against Spanish-held territory in Morocco, torching a dozen villages.		
May 21		British coal miners and coal owners remain deadlocked; the proposals advanced by prime minister Baldwin have been rejected....The French government draws on its gold reserves to support the franc, which experiences an uptick in value.	French and Spanish armies advance convincingly against Abd el-Krim, capturing more than a third of his own tribal territory.		

A	B	C	D	E
Includes developments that affect more than one world region, international organizations and important meetings of world leaders.	*Includes all domestic and regional developments in Europe, including the Soviet Union.*	*Includes all domestic and regional developments in Africa and the Middle East.*	*Includes all domestic and regional developments in Latin America, the Caribbean, and Canada.*	*Includes all domestic and regional developments in Asian and Pacific nations (and colonies).*

U.S. Politics & Social Issues	U.S. Foreign Policy & Affairs, Defense	U.S. Economy & Environment	Science, Technology & Nature	Culture, Leisure & Lifestyle	
The Southern Baptist Convention passes a resolution declaring evolution a heresy.			Although beset for a full day by an Arctic storm, the Norge successfully lands in Teller, Alaska. The dirigible took 71 hours to travel 2,700 miles....American eugenicist and paleontologist Henry Fairfield Osborn is elected to fellowship in the Royal Society of England.	Babe Ruth hits his fourth home run in the past three games, giving him 12 already for the season.... Bubbling Over wins the Kentucky Derby handily, with the second-place horse finishing behind by five lengths.	May 15
The Southern Baptist Convention passes a resolution castigating beauty contests as "evil and evil only." Other sources of evil: card playing, dancing, "late joyriding," and "general mixed bathing."	The House of Representatives passes the "Equalization" bill, which provides naval staff officers with the same promotional opportunities as their contemporaneous line officers.				May 16
Social workers in New York City are troubled by a phenomenon they observe in immigrant homes. Damaging rifts develop between foreign-born mothers and their more Americanized children. The social workers cite a "lack of understanding" from the mothers and a "lack of respect" from the children. Juvenile delinquency among immigrants is attributed to this trend.		Secretary of Commerce Hoover observes that the United States has moved away from a desire for trust-busting toward a recognition that the "business stability" provided by large corporations is to the public benefit.		The St. Louis Cardinals beat the Boston Braves for their fourth consecutive win, with National League home run leader Jim Bottomley contributing his seventh homer of the year.	May 17
The House is preparing to vote on farm relief legislation. Two bills are being considered. The Tincher bill, advocated by the Coolidge administration, would establish a Federal Farm Board and a revolving fund of $100 million, which will be loaned to farmer cooperatives for the purpose of buying and holding crop surpluses. The competing Haugen bill provides $375 million for the same purpose but also enables the government board to buy surpluses outright, in order to maintain prices. President Coolidge will likely veto the Haugen bill if passed.				The House District of Columbia Committee, considering a bill to ban the commercial practices of astrologers and mediums in the nation's capital, hears testimony from Harry Houdini. Houdini calls them all "frauds." One witness testifies that President Coolidge holds "table-tipping séances" in the White House. The loud hostility between Houdini and the fortune tellers in the audience finally forces the committee to adjourn.	May 18
A mediator committee appointed by the New Jersey governor has met with both sides in the textiles strike. The committee finds that the mill owners are adamantly prejudiced and will under no circumstances negotiate with the strikers' United Front Committee.				Babe Ruth smashes two more home runs, giving him 14 for the season. He is running six games ahead of his record-setting pace in 1921, when he hit 59 homers. The Yankees win their eighth game in a row....New York stage actor Humphrey Bogart, currently appearing in the play Cradle Snatchers, is set to wed actress Helen Menken.	May 19
Popular evangelist Aimee Semple McPherson vanishes mysteriously from a beach in Santa Monica, CA. Her followers believe she has drowned, but a police detective claims to have seen her in an automobile after the time she went missing.		Wall Street behaves erratically over news of a dividend paid out by the Hudson Motor Car Company. Heavy selling begins with a news report that the dividend will be modest. The report proves to be false, and many stocks rebound wildly when a larger dividend is actually declared.	Thomas Edison predicts that talking pictures will fail to catch on with American audiences. He believes that filmgoers prefer "a restful quiet" in the theater.	Al Jolson resigns from an exclusive New York country club because the management objects to one of his guests. The entertainer is told flatly, "We don't want any Jews here."... The Yankees win their ninth game in a row, as Babe Ruth hits his fifteenth home run.	May 20
By a vote of 212–167, the Haugen farm bill is defeated in the House of Representatives. The Coolidge administration has made it clear that the bill would be vetoed if passed. The Tincher farm bill is also dropped....President Coolidge issues an executive order enabling state officials to also serve as federal Prohibition enforcement agents. The order is roundly denounced from both parties as an unconstitutional infringement on state rights.	The U.S. War Department invites historians to research its archives, which include Revolutionary War documents and the papers of several Civil War generals.		A University of Pennsylvania pathology professor warns that smoking poses a grave health hazard, often causing cancer of the mouth.... French researchers believe that some forms of cancer can be treated by applying extreme cold.	The movie Aloma of the South Seas, starring dancer Gilda Gray—known as the inventor of the "shimmy"— proves to be a major Hollywood hit....The Yankees take their tenth game a row, led by the pitching of Herb Pennock. Babe Ruth is walked three times.	May 21

F	G	H	I	J
Includes campaigns, elections, federal-state relations, civil rights and liberties, crime, the judiciary, education, healthcare, poverty, urban affairs, and population.	Includes formation and debate of U.S. foreign and defense policies, veterans affairs, and defense spending. (Relations with specific foreign countries are usually found under the region concerned.)	Includes business, labor, agriculture, taxation, transportation, consumer affairs, monetary and fiscal policy, natural resources, pollution and industrial accidents.	Includes worldwide scientific, medical and technological developments, natural phenomena, U.S. weather and natural disasters.	Includes the arts, religion, scholarship, communications media, sports, entertainment, fashions, fads, and social life.

	World Affairs	Europe	Africa & The Middle East	The Americas	Asia & The Pacific
May 22	President Coolidge strongly supports U.S. ratification of the Treaty of Lausanne, which extends recognition to the Republic of Turkey. William Borah is expected to be the most forceful advocate for the treaty in the Senate. Several prominent Christian groups, concerned about Turkish treatment of Armenians, pressure senators to oppose ratification.		Many of the routed Berber tribes submit to the European armies in Morocco. A widespread rumor holds that Abd el-Krim's own men have turned against him and taken him captive. El-Krim has issued a proclamation permitting his followers to lay down arms.	Chile and Peru remain at an impasse over the disputed Tacna-Arica territory; Secretary of State Kellogg has expended considerable effort on the issue, to no avail....A Mexican official in the United States insists that "systematic one-sided propaganda" prevents Americans from understanding the reform efforts of the Calles government. He says the government is intent on providing better education for the country's lower classes—"about 90 percent of the population."	
May 23		The Soviet Union blames reduced industrial productivity on workers drinking vodka. Drunkenness is believed to be the cause of absenteeism and "loafing," which are especially evident after paydays....The Italian lire has recovered to its usual value.	A principal Berber city, Targuist, falls to French troops.	Two American mining engineers are kidnapped in Mexico.	
May 24		Approximately 200,000 Communists and 100,000 Steel Helmets hold competing rallies in Berlin over the issue of confiscating former royal properties.		The Mexican government deports ten nuns.	
May 25			Abd el-Krim has petitioned the French for an armistice, which the French cabinet refuses. Premier Briand calls it a desperate ploy with "one object—to gain time and enable him to gather together his warriors in some fortified position." Across Morocco, Berber rebel activity has dwindled.		At least 900 people die in Japan when the Mount Tokachi volcano, thought to be extinct, erupts suddenly. A large mountain lake is emptied, and the combined lava, water, and mud crash down on several villages.
May 26		Hungary expels 7,000 Chinese, many of whom entered the country after being expelled from other European nations. The Hungarian police claim the Chinese are Communist propagandists.	On horseback, Abd el-Krim rides into a French military camp and gives himself up.	A prominent Mexican bishop is found guilty of protesting against the constitution's religious clauses. He awaits sentencing.	
May 27		The British government begins rationing coal to households, as the coal strike is now 27 days old....The French franc has rebounded 20 percent in the past few days.		Two American oil workers are kidnapped in Mexico, making a total of six American kidnap victims for the week. The American ambassador lodges a formal demand with the Mexican government for their release.	General Wu Pei-fu's armies are now fighting in the southern China province of Guangdong.
May 28		A matrimonial eugenics bureau in Berlin will counsel couples on their physical adequacy for marriage and parenthood.			

A	B	C	D	E
Includes developments that affect more than one world region, international organizations and important meetings of world leaders.	Includes all domestic and regional developments in Europe, including the Soviet Union.	Includes all domestic and regional developments in Africa and the Middle East.	Includes all domestic and regional developments in Latin America, the Caribbean, and Canada.	Includes all domestic and regional developments in Asian and Pacific nations (and colonies).

U.S. Politics & Social Issues	U.S. Foreign Policy & Affairs, Defense	U.S. Economy & Environment	Science, Technology & Nature	Culture, Leisure & Lifestyle	
		According to the latest statistics, U.S. automobile production is finally slowing.	Congress has passed legislation creating the Great Smoky Mountains National Park in Tennessee.	Down 6–2 in the seventh inning, the New York Yankees come back to defeat the St. Louis Browns 7–6, for their eleventh win in a row....The bob has become a trans-Pacific haircut, worn by women in the Philippines, Guam, Panama, Hawaii, and San Francisco's Chinatown.	May 22
The search continues along a California beach for missing evangelist Aimee Semple McPherson, but no trace of her has been found....A parade of 20,000 strikers and sympathizers, including many clergymen, marches in Passaic. The textiles strike is entering its 18th week.	The Navy Department is experimenting with using a helium-oxygen mixture to prevent deep-sea divers from experiencing the "bends."	Delegates from 11 nations will meet in Washington, DC, this summer to discuss the problem of oil pollution in navigable waters.			May 23
The U.S. Supreme Court upholds the right of white homeowners to form covenants or indentures forbidding the sale of neighborhood property to African-Americans. .... Socialist Norman Thomas observes that radio broadcasting reinforces the status quo and denies a voice to organized labor and leftist groups....Robert Whitman, who pretends to be the English aristocrat "Lord Beaverbrook," is arrested in Philadelphia. Authorities learn that he has at least nine wives and has possibly swindled various women out of $1 million.			Speaking at the Northern Baptist Convention in New York City, Reverend T.T. Shields lays blame for many of the country's social ills on the public's acceptance of the theory of evolution.		May 24
President Coolidge, feeling heat from Congress, defends his executive order regarding state officials and Prohibition enforcement, but also seems unlikely to implement the measure....President Coolidge signs a bill appropriating $165 million for the construction of new federal government buildings across the country....The Forstmann & Huffmann mill in Passaic is the one holdout among local mill employers that refuses to allow workers the right to organize.			Mammoth Cave in Kentucky is designated a national park.	A symphony violinist in Milan sues conductor Arturo Toscanini for his abusive behavior. Toscanini allegedly called the violinist a "weakling" and "feeble" during a rehearsal.... A collection of rare Elizabethan and Early Stuart books brings $642,687 at auction in New York City....The Yankees sweep a doubleheader from the Boston Red Sox, running their winning streak to 15 games. Babe Ruth smashes his 16th homer of the season.	May 25
			Engineers are conducting experiments that enable synchronized radio broadcasts over the same wavelength. Stations in nearby towns may be able to broadcast on the same wavelength without the effects of "squealing" and "fading" that currently pester radio listeners.	A Baltimore bank clerk admits to stealing $200,000 from his employer to play the horses, losing an average of $3,000 per day over three years....A total of 692 golfers—the largest number ever—have entered the U.S. Open.	May 26
			Some experts doubt that aviator Richard E. Byrd was at the North Pole long enough to take an accurate reading of his position, given the Arctic's observational challenges. Byrd circled the pole for 14 minutes.	Hannibal, MI, honors the literary achievements of Mark Twain with life-size statues of Tom Sawyer and Huckleberry Finn.	May 27
Farmers and government irrigation officials are in standoff in Nebraska's North Platte Valley. The cost for irrigation water has increased, and many farmers are in arrears; the officials refuse to provide water until the farmers pay. Today the farmers hanged in effigy Secretary of the Interior Hubert Work.		The Department of Commerce announces that manufacturing rates in April were the highest of the decade.		The Yankees are finally beaten, losing 2–1 to the Philadelphia Athletics, ending their winning streak at 16 games.	May 28

F	G	H	I	J
Includes campaigns, elections, federal-state relations, civil rights and liberties, crime, the judiciary, education, healthcare, poverty, urban affairs, and population.	Includes formation and debate of U.S. foreign and defense policies, veterans affairs, and defense spending. (Relations with specific foreign countries are usually found under the region concerned.)	Includes business, labor, agriculture, taxation, transportation, consumer affairs, monetary and fiscal policy, natural resources, pollution and industrial accidents.	Includes worldwide scientific, medical and technological developments, natural phenomena, U.S. weather and natural disasters.	Includes the arts, religion, scholarship, communications media, sports, entertainment, fashions, fads, and social life.

	World Affairs	Europe	Africa & The Middle East	The Americas	Asia & The Pacific
May 29		The British public, which had no great enthusiasm for the general strike, has been busily collecting subscriptions for families involved in the coal miners' strike....The Soviet Union is suspicious of Marshal Pilsudski, concerned that he is supported by British interests. The Soviets believe Pilsudski will interfere with their own efforts to develop friendly relations among the Baltic nations....The Russian town of Kopeln is destroyed in a fire, with many deaths reported.			
May 30		A bloodless military coup leads to the resignation of Portuguese prime minister Antonio Maria de Silva....Some British coal miner leaders urge renewed negotiations, hoping to achieve reasonable terms as quickly as possible....France recognizes the Mother's Day holiday for the first time.	Abd el-Krim is a prisoner of war in the hands of the French....Henry de Jouvenal, the French high commissioner in Syria, excuses his nation's shelling of civilians in the Midan Quarter of Damascus on May 9. "It was a choice between the Midan Quarter and Damascus," he says, "and we chose to protect Damascus."		
May 31		The Polish National Assembly elects Marshal Pilsudski president, which he promptly turns down. Observers suggest that he wants constitutional changes made that will significantly increase the president's power, whereupon he will accept the position.	Reports indicate that Spanish troops have attacked a Berber tribe that already offered to submit to the French....French military authorities, who have been pleased with Abd el-Krim's treatment of their prisoners, anticipate that he will be exiled to France.	Mexico plans to beef up border security to prevent the entry of "undesirables."	The Kuominchun are on the move again in China, occupying an area 20 miles from Peking. A soldier mutiny near the capital has caused a cessation of railroad traffic.
Jun. 1		Ignacy Moscicki, a politician believed to be a puppet of Marshal Pilsudski, is elected president of Poland....Russians in the city of Astakhan work desperately to construct temporary earth-and-stone dams to hold back Volga River floodwaters.		The Mexican secretary of the interior decides to jail rather than expel Catholic and Protestant priests.	
Jun. 2		Left-leaning French premier Aristide Briand is receiving significant support from the nation's right, due to his willingness to work with financial experts in coping with the country's massive internal debt and devalued currency. Leftist politicians, angry at his reliance on bankers, are increasingly voting against him.	The Spanish army in Morocco reports atrocities committed by Berber rebels. They have evidence that the Berbers murdered 22 Spanish prisoners of war in April.		A tidal wave on the Burmese coast kills at least 2,800 people.
Jun. 3		The French National Tourist Office estimates that American tourists spent $226 million in France during 1925.		The Guatemalan government begins to deport priests.	
Jun. 4				A bomb explodes at the U.S. legation in Uruguay, in continued South American protest against the conviction of Sacco and Vanzetti. Handbills appear throughout the city of Montevideo proclaiming "North American justice is soon to commit the most horrible of crimes."...Catholic churches in Mexico City are packed as a particularly large crowd observes Corpus Christi Day.	General Wu Pei-fu has apparently stymied a planned coup by one of his subordinates, the governor of Honan province.

A	B	C	D	E
Includes developments that affect more than one world region, international organizations and important meetings of world leaders.	*Includes all domestic and regional developments in Europe, including the Soviet Union.*	*Includes all domestic and regional developments in Africa and the Middle East.*	*Includes all domestic and regional developments in Latin America, the Caribbean, and Canada.*	*Includes all domestic and regional developments in Asian and Pacific nations (and colonies).*

U.S. Politics & Social Issues	U.S. Foreign Policy & Affairs, Defense	U.S. Economy & Environment	Science, Technology & Nature	Culture, Leisure & Lifestyle	
Asa Bartlett, a Ku Klux Klan leader in Muskegon, Michigan, is arrested for killing a bride and groom with a mail bomb on the eve of their wedding. Bartlett is a political foe of the woman's father.			Dutch aircraft designer Anthony Fokker is designing a jumbo airplane that will provide sleeping berths for up to 40 passengers....Construction is almost complete on the Holland Tunnel beneath the Hudson River, which will enable 46,000 vehicles to pass daily between New York and New Jersey. The total cost of the project is approaching $50 million.		May 29
The governor of Kentucky commutes the 40-day jail term of a woman sentenced for slapping a preacher who criticized her bobbed hair.				An estimated 450,000 people descend on Coney Island to enjoy Memorial Day....The General Federation of Women's Clubs conference in Atlantic City condemns Hollywood films for glamorizing the lives of "crooks."...Former heavyweight champion Jack Johnson is knocked out in the seventh round of a bout in Juarez, Mexico.	May 30
The American Civil Liberties Union cites California as the worst U.S. state for protecting civil rights. Among 76 individuals deemed "political prisoners" in America, 72 are incarcerated in California.				Frank Lockhart wins the Indianapolis 500, which is reduced to 400 miles because of hazardous thunderstorms. More than 150,000 sopping-wet fans watch the truncated race....The Sesquicentennial Exposition opens in Philadelphia, with 100,000 in attendance.	May 31
The home of a relative of one of the principle witnesses in the trial of Sacco and Vanzetti is dynamited in West Bridgewater, Massachusetts. No one is injured. The convicted murderers are awaiting sentencing....The appeal of convicted science teacher John Scopes goes to the Tennessee Supreme Court. The State argues against teaching the "animal dogma' of evolution; Clarence Darrow, one of six members on the defense team, calls for the "intellectual freedom of man."					Jun. 1
Prosecutors are determined to speed up the sentencing of Sacco and Vanzetti, following yesterday's dynamite attack.			The American Neurological Association declares that nervousness is a desirable modern condition. "Nervousness follows culture, for culture develops the power to react quickly to thoughts and emotions," a spokesman relates. "The more highly civilized we become, the more nervous we find ourselves."	A cash prize is being offered for the best translation of Don Quixote into Esperanto.	Jun. 2
	The Senate takes only 16 minutes to approve an $85 million appropriation to build up the Navy Air Service.		A German glider pilot stays airborne for 9 hours and 21 minutes, shattering the world record.	Theatrical producer Earl Carroll is sentenced to a year in prison for perjury. He has been convicted of lying to a federal grand jury investigating the use of liquor at a party held at Carroll's New York theater in February, at which a 17-year-old girl was reportedly bathing nude in a champagne-filled bathtub as the center stage attraction.	Jun. 3
A grand jury in Chicago investigating the murder of prosecutor William McSwiggin notes the "conspiracy of silence" that accompanies most gangland slayings. There have been nearly 100 during the past two years, but most have proved unsolvable.				Frank Lloyd Wright is arrested in Spring Green, Wisconsin, on a peace warrant obtained by his estranged wife.	Jun. 4

F	G	H	I	J
Includes campaigns, elections, federal-state relations, civil rights and liberties, crime, the judiciary, education, healthcare, poverty, urban affairs, and population.	Includes formation and debate of U.S. foreign and defense policies, veterans affairs, and defense spending. (Relations with specific foreign countries are usually found under the region concerned.)	Includes business, labor, agriculture, taxation, transportation, consumer affairs, monetary and fiscal policy, natural resources, pollution and industrial accidents.	Includes worldwide scientific, medical and technological developments, natural phenomena, U.S. weather and natural disasters.	Includes the arts, religion, scholarship, communications media, sports, entertainment, fashions, fads, and social life.

	World Affairs	Europe	Africa & The Middle East	The Americas	Asia & The Pacific
Jun. 5	The Women's Suffrage Alliance, meeting at conference in Paris with delegates from 40 nations, debates an array of subjects: the rights of female aviators; the need for police-women in all countries; and the unsuitability of domestic science as a feminist topic. The conference proposes to censure the League of Nations for attempting to protect women in industry, because this relegates female workers to a seg-regated, unequal status.	Viennese newspapers are publish-ing stories about atrocities com-mitted by Italian Fascists against Germans living in the Italian-con-trolled South Tyrol. The unconfirmed stories may be propaganda....Marshal Pilsudski is having difficul-ties pacifying Poland; there is unrest in the Vilna province, where two companies of military recruits have mutinied....Germany is struggling with a legacy from the Great War: the 679,410 Germans maimed or diseased during the war who are now fully dependent on the govern-ment for care.		Marriages in Mexico City must be approved by the government Sanitary Department, which will determine if men and women are physically capable of having chil-dren. The mortality rate in Mexico for children under the age of one year is approximately 83 percent.	
Jun. 6		Marshal Pilsudski seeks to severely weaken the Polish National Diet and give parliamentary author-ity to a cabinet of his own appoin-tees....The Bank of France refuses to use its gold reserves to further stabilize the franc, despite pres-sure from the Briand cabinet....The Catholic Church in Germany urges voters to reject the confiscation of former royal lands, arguing that this amounts to stealing. The ref-erendum on the issue is scheduled for June 20.	Bennet Doty, the only American member of the French Foreign Legion, is arrested and condemned to death for desertion in Syria. He reportedly fired on French troops sent to retrieve him while he hid in the Hauran mountains. He is sched-uled to be shot in two days.	The Mason-Spinden Expedition to Yucatan, Mexico, has proved to be an ornithological treasure trove. Expedition naturalists report the discovery of seven previously unknown bird species.	
Jun. 7	The fortieth session of the League of Nations Council convenes in Geneva, with hangover problems from the spring session on the agenda. Brazil and Spain expect permanent seats on the council.	The Austrian Pan-German Party declares its "Anschluss will"—its desire for political union with Germany—at a congress in Innsbruck.	England will use African-American primary schools in Alabama and Georgia as a model for their schools in East Africa.		
Jun. 8		A lengthy negotiating session between British coal miners and coal owners achieves nothing. The miners have adopted a guiding slo-gan: "not a penny off pay, not a minute on the day."...The French Central Detective Bureau estimates there are several thousand American thieves and swindlers operating in Continental Europe. They primarily prey on wealthy American tourists, staying at the same resorts and hotels and watching for opportuni-ties to pilfer jewelry.	The French military, with 30,000 troops stationed in Syria, believes that 20,000 more may be necessary to fully impose order. The military must contend with the organized Druse rebels while stamping out "brushfire" bandit attacks through-out the country....Tribal rivalries in Morocco lead to multiple killings at a Berber garrison in Chechaoune. Djebala tribesmen, targeted this past spring in raids by Abd el-Krim, carry out the revenge attack.	The Mexican government is final-izing new regulations on religious activities. Priests and ministers must be native Mexicans to legally practice their calling. Any priest or minister who criticizes the govern-ment or foments disobedience of the religious laws is subject to up to five years imprisonment.	
Jun. 9	The U.S. State Department warns American diplomats abroad to take necessary precautions, following the multiple bombings related to the Sacco and Vanzetti case.	Authorities have uncovered a movie piracy ring operating in Eastern Europe. Prints of Hollywood movies are stolen at night, then dupli-cated; hundreds of prints are then circulated, often before a movie opens legitimately. The United States lacks copyright protection treaties with the 11 countries impli-cated....Benito Mussolini returns to Rome following a three-day holiday during which he drove his sports car around Italy visiting family members.	The French War Minister intervenes to spare the life of Bennet Doty, the American French Legionnaire due to be executed today for desertion.		
Jun. 10	Denied a permanent seat on the Council of the League of Nations Council, Brazil quits the council. Brazilian diplomats insist that South America is being discriminated against. But Germany will only join the league if it is given the sole new permanent seat on the council, and Germany's participation is consid-ered crucial to the league's disarma-ment mission. Therefore, German demands take precedence.	President Hindenburg's letter opposing the seizure of royal prop-erty is causing an uproar in the German Reichstag, where mem-bers from both the left and center attack him for attempting to sway the referendum process....Marshal Pilsudski quickly ends a strike by iron workers in Galicia. Shortly after the walkout begins, soldiers are summoned and open fire, killing three strikers and convincing the rest to return to work.	The French town of Salies de Bearn has offered the War Ministry an 18th-century château for Abd el-Krim's use in exile.	American officials have determined that the Tacna-Arica plebiscite will be impossible to carry out, due to Chile's inability to ensure fair elections.	Japanese colonial officials use 25,000 police to control mourners in Seoul, Korea, during the funeral of Prince Yi, a member of the dynas-tic family that ruled the country until 1910. Hundreds of students are arrested for possessing anti-Japanese literature.

A	B	C	D	E
Includes developments that affect more than one world region, international organizations and important meetings of world leaders.	*Includes all domestic and regional developments in Europe, including the Soviet Union.*	*Includes all domestic and regional developments in Africa and the Middle East.*	*Includes all domestic and regional developments in Latin America, the Caribbean, and Canada.*	*Includes all domestic and regional developments in Asian and Pacific nations (and colonies).*

U.S. Politics & Social Issues	U.S. Foreign Policy & Affairs, Defense	U.S. Economy & Environment	Science, Technology & Nature	Culture, Leisure & Lifestyle	
	American schoolchildren are rallying to save "Old Ironsides," the U.S.S. *Constitution*, from scrapping. More than five million children have made donations to restore the ship.	The F. W. Woolworth Company is the largest chain discount retailer in the United States, with 1,423 stores.		A 16-year-old Cincinnati woman dies of heart failure after winning a Charleston dance- endurance contest....U.S. Post Office authorities ban *The New Masses* from the mail, after deeming a poem by a Yale University English professor to be "lewd and obscene."...The New Jersey Board of Education rules on a case involving a woman who was denied teacher certification by the State Board of Examiners because she is a chain smoker. The board finds in her favor.	Jun. 5
War hero Sergeant Alvin York is raising funds to build an industrial institute for educating rural Tennesseans living in the Appalachian Mountains.			The Mellon Institute of Industrial Research in Pittsburgh is conducting studies on sleep. Among their findings is that sleepers change position every 11 minutes on average, a total of 33 times nightly.		Jun. 6
The House of Representatives passes a bill that facilitates the deportation of aliens judged to be insane.			On the inaugural run of the air mail service between Minneapolis and Chicago, the pilot crashes and dies.	A New York City citizen's play jury, empowered by the district attorney to root out indecency on the stage, votes to close *The Bunk of 1926*, which features nudity.	Jun. 7
An insurgent underdog Republican candidate for senator defeats two strong mainstream candidates in the Iowa primary; the vote is seen as a response to the Coolidge administration's agricultural policies....Congress will wait for official data on aviator Richard E. Byrd's polar flight before making him an honorary rear admiral.			The Smithsonian Institution has received "fossil footprints," believed to be millions of years old, uncovered at the Grand Canyon.	Babe Ruth smacks two homeruns, his 20th and 21st of the season, as the Yankees defeat the Detroit Tigers.	Jun. 8
The Prudential Insurance Company has compiled suicide rates for 75 cities in the United States. San Diego has the highest suicide rate, with 39.6 per 100,000 population. In comparison, Brooklyn has a rate of 10.6. East Coast rates are much lower than West Coast rates, and men are more than three times as likely to commit suicide as women. African Americans have a substantially lower suicide rate than whites.	.		A Russian anthropologist claims to have found a fossilized prehistoric brain in a clay pit outside Moscow.	The summer entertainment on stages in New York City includes *Paris, London, and New York*, a musical revue; *The Cocoanuts*, starring the Marx Brothers; *Thieves*, a murder melodrama starring Judith Anderson; and British female impersonator Bert Errol....The American Historical Association will offer guidelines to overhaul how history is taught in U.S. public schools, intended to meet the "increasingly complex problems" of America in the world.	Jun. 9
The Senate considers the Haugen farm bill, recently defeated by the House and opposed by President Coolidge....New York City police are aware of a new panhandling method, by which beggars hide one or more limbs under bandages and clothes and pose as maimed war veterans.			Plans to build the tallest building in the world, a 65-story skyscraper to be called the Christian Missionary Building, are dropped. Two 15-story apartment buildings will go up in its place in New York City.	The St. Louis Cardinals defeat the New York Giants behind the pitching of Flint Rhem, who leads the National League with a 10–1 win-loss record....In a 15-round bout in the Bronx, Paul Berlenbach, "the Astoria Assassin," defeats W. L. "Young" Stribling to become the Light Heavyweight Champion of the World.	Jun. 10

F	G	H	I	J
Includes campaigns, elections, federal-state relations, civil rights and liberties, crime, the judiciary, education, healthcare, poverty, urban affairs, and population.	*Includes formation and debate of U.S. foreign and defense policies, veterans affairs, and defense spending. (Relations with specific foreign countries are usually found under the region concerned.)*	*Includes business, labor, agriculture, taxation, transportation, consumer affairs, monetary and fiscal policy, natural resources, pollution and industrial accidents.*	*Includes worldwide scientific, medical and technological developments, natural phenomena, U.S. weather and natural disasters.*	*Includes the arts, religion, scholarship, communications media, sports, entertainment, fashions, fads, and social life.*

	World Affairs	Europe	Africa & The Middle East	The Americas	Asia & The Pacific
Jun. 11	In Geneva, the Military Committee of the Preparatory Disarmament Commission, a subcommittee of the League of Nations, has spent two weeks debating how the word *armaments* will be defined and understood in their sessions.	The British government confronts the Soviet Union about funding sent to England to support last month's general strike....The rabies outbreak in the Soviet Union has reached a "plague state," according to health officials.			
Jun. 12	Several Italian attachés to the League of Nations are arrested in Geneva for their role in a brawl after they interrupt a Socialist meeting. One of the Socialists shouts, "Mussolini is an assassin!," which provokes a violent response from the Italian diplomatic staff members.	The British Trades Union Congress insists that no money was accepted from the Soviet Union during the general strike, because such an action would be "willfully misrepresented" by the British government in an effort to paint the strike leaders as Communists....Meletius Metaxakis is elected patriarch of the Greek Orthodox Church of Alexandria.		The Mexican government bans schoolteachers and professors from engaging in politics.	
Jun. 13		The British pound sterling has remained strong throughout the coal strike, even while Continental European currencies have recently struggled....Marshal Pilsudski has accepted the role of permanent Commander in Chief of the Armies—making him Poland's dictator.			
Jun. 14	Brazil formally resigns from the League of Nations.			The Federation of Mexican Societies, representing the interests of tens of thousands of Mexican farmers who fled to the United States during the Mexican Revolution, is working with the Mexican government on the issue of repatriation. The government hopes to bring back the farmers, who have learned American agricultural and business techniques, to repopulate villages that are now almost deserted.	
Jun. 15		French Premier Aristide Briand is once again forced out of office, along with his cabinet. He has lost the support of his leftist followers in his handling of the nation's currency crisis; his finance minister, faced with a franc worth 2.7 cents, has resigned. Briand fully expects to be called on soon to form yet another cabinet.		Chile announces the intention to withdraw from U.S.-mediated negotiations with Peru over the Tacna-Arica territory. The American chairman of the Plebiscitary Commission, Major General William Lassiter, charges the Chileans with fostering a "state of terrorism," deporting and violently intimidating Peruvians in advance of a vote.	
Jun. 16		A day after his government collapses, Aristide Briand reassumes the French premiership. He seeks to assemble a cabinet that includes center and right elements, because his former allies on the left have proved obdurate in his battle to save the franc.	The Spanish military in Morocco reports that the Berber rebellion is finished, as the few straggling tribes are now negotiating for submission.	Major General Lassiter calls for terminating the Tacna-Arica plebiscitary proceedings.	
Jun. 17		In the British House of Commons, Labour Party leader Ramsay Macdonald points out that individual Russian trade unions, not the Soviet government, donated money to the general strike. In rebuttal, conservative members note that "the Soviet government and Soviet organizations were the same." A total of 380,000 pounds came from Russia during the strike.	In the Rankus region of Syria, 107 Druse rebels are killed in intense fighting with the French.	Major General Lassiter is hissed by a crowd of Chileans outside his home in Arica; he plans to leave for the United States in a few days.	Rioting between Hindus and Muslims in the Rawalpindi district of India leave 14 individuals dead.

A	B	C	D	E
Includes developments that affect more than one world region, international organizations and important meetings of world leaders.	Includes all domestic and regional developments in Europe, including the Soviet Union.	Includes all domestic and regional developments in Africa and the Middle East.	Includes all domestic and regional developments in Latin America, the Caribbean, and Canada.	Includes all domestic and regional developments in Asian and Pacific nations (and colonies).

U.S. Politics & Social Issues	U.S. Foreign Policy & Affairs, Defense	U.S. Economy & Environment	Science, Technology & Nature	Culture, Leisure & Lifestyle	
A mini-riot occurs at a public school in an Italian-American neighborhood in Brooklyn after several schoolboys begin shouting "Black Hand!," a reference to the well-known Italian extortion racket. Children rush out of the school, their mothers in the neighborhood rush to the school, and the police are called in to restore order.			The World Health Congress adjourns in Paris. The congress identifies the Far East and all international shipping as hot spots for the outbreak of diseases.	American "jazz king" Paul Whiteman entertains audiences in Vienna....Babe Ruth is arrested in Howell, Michigan, for catching several bluegills out of fishing season....The National Hosiery and Underwear Exposition chooses a "Queen of Hosiery," the woman with the most beautiful ankle.	Jun. 11
Chippewa and Ojibwa Indians in Michigan are pressing their claim to compensation for the Detroit waterfront, which they say is due them according to the terms of early 19th-century treaties.				Movie "czar" Will Hays, proselytizing for his industry, remarks on the power of the motion picture to shape modern "habits, ideals, and customs." "I do not mean that it takes the place of the home or of religion," he observes, "but except for these there is nothing comparable to it in influence."	Jun. 12
Celebrating Flag Day, Secretary of Labor James Davis asserts that the lowly American hobo is a "better asset to a nation than a grumbling and discontented Communist."		Statistics indicate that one of the wealthiest communities in the United States is the farming village of Garnavillo, Iowa—population 340—where the citizens have bank deposits totaling $2.5 million.		The Salvation Army observes that nearly half of the unmarried mothers who receive assistance from their organization are of high-school age. According to their survey, many of these women "attribute their difficulties to automobile flirtations."	Jun. 13
Secretary of the Treasury Andrew Mellon launches a frontal attack on the Haugen Farm Relief bill, which is due for a vote in the senate....Violent unrest in the 21-week-old New Jersey textiles strike assumes a new form. A homemade bomb is tossed onto the porch of a mill employee who has refused to strike. Police say the weak-impact bomb was intended to frighten him....A coke oven explodes at an Illinois Steel Company plant in Gary, IN, killing more than a dozen workers....Henry Ford is awarded an honorary doctorate in engineering by the University of Michigan.			Thunderstorms in the Midwest kill 12 people, primarily in Chicago.... The Rockefeller Foundation spent in excess of $9 million in 1925 fighting diseases; the foundation reports major worldwide successes in eradicating yellow fever as a health threat.	Relatives of the late tenor singer Enrico Caruso, some in the United States and some in Italy, are battling in court over approximately $1 million in royalties.	Jun. 14
President Coolidge opposes compulsory military drilling for high school and college students. He suggests this might promote a dangerous martial spirit in the young.		Oil stocks have been the strongest plays recently on the U.S. stock market.		American Impressionist artist Mary Cassatt dies....The College Entrance Examination Board will administer a new test, called the "Scholastic Aptitude Test," for 21,700 students across the nation next week.	Jun. 15
Two bombs explode in Garfield, New Jersey, as the textiles strike continues. Some picketers are using automobiles to parade in front of the mills.		Western congressmen have introduced a bill that would enable oil exploration on 22.5 million acres of unallotted Indian land.	The Soviet government, in collaboration with the American Association for the Advancement of Atheism, is sponsoring research in West Africa to prove the link between humans and apes. They hope to achieve "the artificial hybridization of the human and anthropoid species."	In a tight race, the Pittsburgh Pirates have taken the lead in the National League. Team star outfielder Kiki Cuyler has hit safely in 22 straight games....Big Ten universities are conferring 13,300 degrees this week, an 8 percent increase over last year.	Jun. 16
			The Medical Society of New Jersey emphasizes the importance of preventive—rather than curative—approaches in dealing with diseases such as high blood pressure. Individual human behaviors, such as eating a "rational diet" and fixing bad teeth, can prolong life.	American amateur golfer Bobby Jones, playing in a qualifying event for the British Open, compiles an aggregate score of 134 for 36 holes. The record low score for a single round at the Open is 68; Jones scores 66 and 68 back-to-back.	Jun. 17

F	G	H	I	J
Includes campaigns, elections, federal-state relations, civil rights and liberties, crime, the judiciary, education, healthcare, poverty, urban affairs, and population.	Includes formation and debate of U.S. foreign and defense policies, veterans affairs, and defense spending. (Relations with specific foreign countries are usually found under the region concerned.)	Includes business, labor, agriculture, taxation, transportation, consumer affairs, monetary and fiscal policy, natural resources, pollution and industrial accidents.	Includes worldwide scientific, medical and technological developments, natural phenomena, U.S. weather and natural disasters.	Includes the arts, religion, scholarship, communications media, sports, entertainment, fashions, fads, and social life.

	World Affairs	Europe	Africa & The Middle East	The Americas	Asia & The Pacific
Jun. 18		British trade is beginning to seriously suffer as the coal strike becomes prolonged. Industries are experiencing fuel shortages and a lack of raw materials.	An assassination plot against Turkish President Mustafa Kemal fails in Smyrna.	Chile formally notifies the U.S. State Department that it is withdrawing from the Tacna-Arica plebiscite negotiations, ending four years of endeavor.	
Jun. 19		British Chancellor of the Exchequer Winston Churchill joins the vehement Conservative attack on the Soviet Union, denouncing "those miscreants who have ruined their own country and are tireless in their efforts to ruin ours."…On the eve of Germany's referendum on royal property confiscation, several people are beaten on the streets for wearing political paraphernalia.	Forty people have been arrested in the plot to kill President Kemal, including two members of the Turkish National Assembly.		
Jun. 20		The effort for royal property seizure goes down to defeat in Germany. The national referendum procedures require that 50 percent of qualified voters must cast ballots; although 15 millions votes are cast, that figure falls short by 5 million. Most opponents of the measure simply stay home to ensure its failure.			
Jun. 21		The Reichstag is acting quickly to pass a bill ensuring the private property rights of the former German ruling families.…Radziwill Oskilko, a Ukrainian leader known for his anti-Bolshevik views, is assassinated in Poland.	An estimated 2,000 Druse rebels are still ensconced in the suburbs of Damascus, which the French are bombarding daily. Two thousand shells and bombs have been fired at these neighborhoods in the past week.		
Jun. 22		British women plan to agitate to change the country's suffrage laws. Women under the age of 30 are prohibited from voting, while men over the age of 21 can vote.	In Morocco, Abd el-Krim orders several suits of clothes from French tailors.	At the Pan-American Conference in Panama, several delegates advocate for forming a "League of American Nations."	W. W. Ken, who has been serving in the weakened position of premier of the Chinese national government in Peking, resigns after just a month in office. The warlords still dominate the nation's political scene.
Jun. 23	Spain refuses to participate in any League of Nations commissions unless given a permanent seat on the council; the Spanish delegates argue that the league must decide if their policies will recognize countries for their "moral importance" or their military power.…Following their attaché rumpus on June 12, Italy warns Switzerland that it will abide no more organized anti-Fascist activities in Geneva.	The entire Polish Diet resigns from office, enabling Marshal Pilsudski to fashion his own parliament.			
Jun. 24		Although German Socialists were handed a defeat by the property referendum, they are forming a substantial bloc with Catholic centrists, who voted heavily in favor of confiscation.…Germany is being inundated with severe rainstorms, which have caused an estimated $10 million in damage to crops.	Berber resistance in Morocco has stiffened, due to a false rumor spreading that Abd el-Krim's surrender has been a French lie.	A dam breaks on the Lerma Santiago River in Mexico, causing an 8-foot wall of water to slam into the city of León during the night. The death toll is estimated around 1,300.	

A	B	C	D	E
Includes developments that affect more than one world region, international organizations and important meetings of world leaders.	Includes all domestic and regional developments in Europe, including the Soviet Union.	Includes all domestic and regional developments in Africa and the Middle East.	Includes all domestic and regional developments in Latin America, the Caribbean, and Canada.	Includes all domestic and regional developments in Asian and Pacific nations (and colonies).

U.S. Politics & Social Issues	U.S. Foreign Policy & Affairs, Defense	U.S. Economy & Environment	Science, Technology & Nature	Culture, Leisure & Lifestyle	
Following a series of bombings of worker homes in Garfield, New Jersey, 800 citizens petition the local government to reimpose martial law....There were 22,500 automobile- related deaths in the United States in 1925, a 10 percent increase from the previous year.		According to statistics, American consumers spend $5 billion annually through installment payments. Of this total, $3 billion is spent on installments for automobiles; in comparison, $112.5 million is spent on pianos.			Jun. 18
More than 20,000 American Indians gather at the Little Big Horn battle-field in Montana to commemorate the fiftieth anniversary of General George Custer's demise.		During the franc's valuation struggles, France has experienced a "flight of capital." There have been extremely large French deposits made in American banks....Henry Ford decries the American reliance on installment-plan buying. "Debt has become a national industry," he observes.	American meteorologists are attempting to dismiss the popular idea that radio waves are responsible for extreme weather conditions.	Golf historians have been unable to find any scores that match Bobby Jones's 134 over two straight rounds in England.	Jun. 19
A crowd of 200 strikers in Garfield throws bricks at police before being dispersed. Prospective Garfield policemen say they are turning down the job because the pay does not equal the physical risk....With $100,000 in funding from the Rockefeller Foundation, the University of Hawaii is undertaking a study of the "biological, mental, ad social characteristics" of the island's indigenous peoples.	A Marine Corps commissioned officer and nine of his men are arrested for rum-running out of a military base in San Diego.			A teenager dancing the Charleston in a rowboat causes it to capsize, leading to six drowning deaths in the St. Mary's River in Michigan.	Jun. 20
The textile strikers' General Relief Committee seeks to place 5,000 children of workers in sympathetic, comfortable homes for the summer....Two 14-year-old boys run through h a New York City public school shouting, "Look out, Black Hand!" and are promptly arrested for juvenile delinquency.		The U.S. Treasury Department announces a $390 million federal surplus for the fiscal year.	Swiss engineers have built the world's largest electric locomotive. Powered by six engines, the locomotive is 65 feet long.	The pennant race in the National League is turning into a close battle between the league-leading Cincinnati Reds, the Pittsburgh Pirates, and the St. Louis Cardinals.	Jun. 21
The Haugen Farm Relief bill is generating support in the Senate. Democrats and Western Republicans would like to place President Coolidge in a position where he must make good on his threat to veto the measure.				Will Hays, president of the Motion Picture Producers and Distributors of America, agrees to prolong his term for ten more years....The 10-year-old daughter of Broadway impresario Florenz Ziegfeld is robbed of $10,000 in jewels in New York City....At the Eucharistic Congress in Chicago, with a roster of international Catholic dignitaries, more than 325,000 people throng Soldiers' Field to attend services.	Jun. 22
The State Department reports that 18 foreign nations have already filled their immigration quotas for 1926. ....Missing evangelist Aimee Semple McPherson turns up at a hospital in Los Angeles, where she tells reporters that she was kidnapped off a beach, held for a $500,000 ransom in Mexico, and tortured by being burned with cigarettes before she finally managed to escape.		A mild recession has hit the automobile industry due to an inventory backlog. Automobile companies continue to produce at a fast clip: more than two million units have been manufactured this year, up 250,000 from the same period last year.			Jun. 23
The Haugen Farm Relief bill is defeated in the Senate by a vote of 45–39....Aimee Semple McPherson, several Los Angeles police detectives, and assorted reporters are in the border town of Agua Preita, Mexico, searching for the shack where she says she was held captive.		Although the United States refuses to extend political recognition to the Soviet government, scruples do not prevent Americans from trading with the Communists. The United States is the Soviet Union's largest trade partner, providing more than a quarter of its imports.		Americans Bobby Jones and Bill Melhorn lead the British Open golf tournament....The U.S. Post Office cracks down on the Scientific Research Laboratories of New York City for using the mail to sell bogus anti-fat remedies.	Jun. 24

F	G	H	I	J
Includes campaigns, elections, federal-state relations, civil rights and liberties, crime, the judiciary, education, healthcare, poverty, urban affairs, and population.	*Includes formation and debate of U.S. foreign and defense policies, veterans affairs, and defense spending. (Relations with specific foreign countries are usually found under the region concerned.)*	*Includes business, labor, agriculture, taxation, transportation, consumer affairs, monetary and fiscal policy, natural resources, pollution and industrial accidents.*	*Includes worldwide scientific, medical and technological developments, natural phenomena, U.S. weather and natural disasters.*	*Includes the arts, religion, scholarship, communications media, sports, entertainment, fashions, fads, and social life.*

	World Affairs	Europe	Africa & The Middle East	The Americas	Asia & The Pacific
Jun. 25		The British House of Commons continues to debate terminating relations with the Soviet government. Foreign Secretary Austen Chamberlain explains that the British government intends to continue relations. The day ends with a general disorder, forcing the suspension of the session.		Jamaicans are using coconuts as containers to smuggle whiskey into the United States.	
Jun. 26		The Elbe and Oder rivers in Germany are flooding, overwhelming dams and dikes; 15 people have drowned, and damages are estimated at $30 million....African-American spirituals and work songs are a hit with German audiences.	The Zionist Organization of America reports that 33,000 Jews settled in Palestine in 1925.	The Mexican government bans the importation and use of foreign currencies....The Panama Canal was used to transport 26.7 million tons of goods in 1925, a record for tonnage.	
Jun. 27		Germany's reserve of foreign currency has been cut in half recently, as debt obligations have come due....British stocks have held up well during the coal strike, although the economy has taken a substantial hit. For example, British railroads, which were running a net revenue gain for the year before the strike, are now 10 million pounds in the red.			General Zhang Zuolin, with a bodyguard of nearly 50,000 troops, arrives in Peking to discuss forming a new government with General Wu Pei-fu.
Jun. 28		The International Chamber of Commerce counsels that European financial conditions have become "extremely critical." The organization cites the problems of destabilized currencies and excessive tariffs and trade barriers. Their report states: "Prompt remedies are essential if eventually an economic disturbance, which would affect all countries in succession, is to be avoided."			
Jun. 29	More than 150 prominent church leaders urge the U.S. Senate to ratify the Lausanne Treaty and recognize the Republic of Turkey.				An American doctor in Canton, China, the directing physician at a hospital, is told by authorities to immediately surrender his post. He will be succeeded by a Chinese doctor.
Jun. 30		The Italian government announces plans to reduce all newspapers to no more than six pages. There will be almost no foreign news reported, and only a bare-bones recitation of domestic information; the sports and arts sections and all evidence of personal journalism and opinion will be phased out.	Moroccans in Tangier charge that European police officials use torture to extract confessions....Turkish president Kemal is fining Muslim women who object on religious grounds to new dress reforms, such as the government's condemnation of the veil and sanctioning of short skirts.		
Jul. 1	A League of Nations committee of naval experts, working on the issue of disarmament, cannot agree on a standard by which to discuss fleet reductions. The majority wants to use total fleet tonnage as the standard, while the minority, including the United States, insists that the tonnage of individual classes of warships must also be considered.	A report indicating a spike in French government debt leads to an international sell-off of the franc, sending the currency to a new record low....Several British trading firms rebuff Winston Churchill for his recent hostile stance toward the Soviet Union, citing the close economic ties between the two nations.			Prominent French novelist Pierre Benoit, recently in Japan, warns that the country's naval buildup is a threat to world peace. "Her eighty million inhabitants have no room on her islands," he observes. "She obviously aims to seize Hawaii and Manila and also to colonize China."...Two earthquakes strike the same area of Sumatra in a three-hour period, leveling the city of Padang and killing hundreds.

A	B	C	D	E
Includes developments that affect more than one world region, international organizations and important meetings of world leaders.	*Includes all domestic and regional developments in Europe, including the Soviet Union.*	*Includes all domestic and regional developments in Africa and the Middle East.*	*Includes all domestic and regional developments in Latin America, the Caribbean, and Canada.*	*Includes all domestic and regional developments in Asian and Pacific nations (and colonies).*

U.S. Politics & Social Issues	U.S. Foreign Policy & Affairs, Defense	U.S. Economy & Environment	Science, Technology & Nature	Culture, Leisure & Lifestyle	
				Amateur golfer Bobby Jones wins the British Open, with Americans also finishing second and third.... The Women's Sport Federation of France rules that French female athletes must wear knickers below the knees and dark-colored, sleeved tunics rather than "trunks" and white sleeveless shirts. Bras are required....Florenz Ziegfeld, who introduced nudity to the Broadway stage, rails against the "dirt and filth" evident in the revues of the past two seasons.	Jun. 25
Evangelist Aimee Semple McPherson has located her shack outside the border town of Agua Prieta, Mexico. Police detectives find evidence—strands of rawhide, a broken window—that corroborate parts of her story.			German airlines are installing wireless telephones for passengers.	Atlantic City hosts the fourth annual National Marble Championship, with 47 children from across the country competing. There are two Chinese Americans and one girl, who beat out 16,000 players to win the local Cleveland title.	Jun. 26
The National Association for the Advancement of Colored People, meeting in Chicago, announces plans to raise $1 million to fight segregation. Secretary James Weldon Johnson assails the U.S. government's fixation on Prohibition and lack of interest in civil rights. "The federal government will use a navy to prevent a man from taking a drink," he remarks, "but will not empower a deputy marshal to protect the negro's ballot."			A large earthquake with an epicenter in the Eastern Mediterranean sends out shock waves that are felt as far away as Sumatra and Singapore.	A crowd of 400,000 horse-racing fans witnesses Take My Tip win the Paris Grand Prix....Babe Ruth blasts his 25th home run of the season as the Yankees defeat the Boston Red Sox.	Jun. 27
		A "run" on two banks in West Palm Beach, FL, forces them to temporarily close.		The American Society of Dancing Teachers convention is divided as to the future of the Charleston: half the members believe the dance is dead, while the other half see opportunities for its steps to evolve. A guest artist, the director of the National Opera ballet in Paris, traces the Charleston to 18th century French dances.	Jun. 28
Another farm relief measure, the Fess proposal, which President Coolidge supports, goes down to defeat in the Senate in a 56–24 vote....African-American historian Carter Woodson receives the Spingarn Medal from the NAACP in recognition for his distinguished service to his race.		U.S. steel common reaches a record high price.	The National Geographic Society verifies aviator Richard E. Byrd's polar calculations.	The New Jersey Department of Motor vehicles is cracking down on car owners who display small metal signs bearing "expressions that in many cases are most indecent." Drivers in violation will risk losing their license.	Jun. 29
The International Ladies Garment Workers Union has declared a strike for 40,000 female workers in the cloak industry in New York City.					Jun. 30
Progressive Republican Gerald Nye is elected U.S. Senator from North Dakota, filling the vacancy caused by the death of Senator Edwin Ladd in 1925. The election result is seen as evidence that western farmers are rejecting the policies of the Coolidge administration....The American Federation of Labor condemns the Passaic textiles strike as "Communistic."	The Navy Submarine School in New London, CT, is training a large class of 55 officers in intensive submarine tactics.	The Treasury Department reports a federal budget surplus of $377,767,816 for the 1926 fiscal year. Total ordinary receipts have increased $200 million over fiscal year 1925.		The American Institute of Homeopathy recommends regular health examinations for all individuals as a way to increase the national average lifespan, currently at 58 years....The National Education Association plans to build "teachers homes" for retired unmarried schoolteachers with low incomes, "to prevent loneliness and grief."	Jul. 1

F	G	H	I	J
Includes campaigns, elections, federal-state relations, civil rights and liberties, crime, the judiciary, education, healthcare, poverty, urban affairs, and population.	Includes formation and debate of U.S. foreign and defense policies, veterans affairs, and defense spending. (Relations with specific foreign countries are usually found under the region concerned.)	Includes business, labor, agriculture, taxation, transportation, consumer affairs, monetary and fiscal policy, natural resources, pollution and industrial accidents.	Includes worldwide scientific, medical and technological developments, natural phenomena, U.S. weather and natural disasters.	Includes the arts, religion, scholarship, communications media, sports, entertainment, fashions, fads, and social life.

	World Affairs	Europe	Africa & The Middle East	The Americas	Asia & The Pacific
Jul. 2		Torrential thunderstorms in Serbia cause an estimated fifty people to die in lightning strikes....A group of North Dakota farmers reports success in teaching Russian peasants American methods for growing grain. The American-organized Russian Reconstruction Farms Company cultivates 23,000 acres and runs an agricultural school.	Franco-Spanish authorities have determined that Madagascar will be the site of Abd-el Krim's exile.		
Jul. 3		A committee of French financial experts urges a series of draconian measures to stabilize the French franc, including slashing government expenditures. Their report predicts that economic recovery will require "difficulty and suffering" for the nation....American suffragists rally at Hyde Park in London, protesting Britain's suffrage law that forbids women to vote until the age of 30.		The Calles government issues a series of thirty-three decrees cracking down on religious activity in Mexico. Under the new laws, all church property will be confiscated and parochial education is banned. Ministers are forbidden to wear clerical garb in public or to hold political views. Monasteries and convents are dissolved.	Chinese warlords Wu Pei-fu and Zhang Zuolin parley in Shanghai, a meeting characterized by observers as "farcical" and "perfunctory." No progress is made toward establishing a government in Peking.
Jul. 4		America's 150th Independence Day is celebrated in several European countries, including France, Poland, and Czechoslovakia....The Swedish government, citing an average annual death toll of 340 persons due to drowning, declares that all students must learn to swim in order to pass their school exams.		Prominent Catholic organizations in Mexico condemn the new Calles religious decrees as government persecution. Among other groups, the Knights of Columbus plans to openly defy the proscriptions.	
Jul. 5		Widespread unemployment is reported among German artists; in a single district in Berlin, more than 1,600 are on the dole, including 200 opera singers and 55 dancing teachers....Germany is pelted by hen's-egg-size hail during a powerful storm that kills 31 people across the country.			A Smithsonian Institution expedition is using airplanes to track down tribes of pigmies in a remote area of New Guinea. The planes are used to spot evidence of campfires and village clearings....Another killer earthquake shakes Sumatra, with the death toll estimated in the hundreds.
Jul. 6		The Italian government suspends all provincial, communal, and municipal elections. Fascist leaders are reportedly concerned about local politicians balking at national initiatives....The Soviet Union reports a budget surplus of 117.8 million rubles, with the state telegraph and railroad industries posting particularly strong receipts.			
Jul. 7	U.S. Senator William Borah announces he will embark on a nationwide speaking tour aiming to convince the public that U.S. entry into the World Court is a grave mistake.	The newspaper *Pravda* warns against the growth of a peasant bourgeoisie under the Soviet Union's New Economic Policy. The *kulaks* (well-to-do peasants) are becoming politically influential, "striving to penetrate every pore of our administrative apparatus," an editorial observes. "The correct policy of our country can be ensured only by reinforcement in a proletarian direction."			

A	B	C	D	E
Includes developments that affect more than one world region, international organizations and important meetings of world leaders.	Includes all domestic and regional developments in Europe, including the Soviet Union.	Includes all domestic and regional developments in Africa and the Middle East.	Includes all domestic and regional developments in Latin America, the Caribbean, and Canada.	Includes all domestic and regional developments in Asian and Pacific nations (and colonies).

U.S. Politics & Social Issues	U.S. Foreign Policy & Affairs, Defense	U.S. Economy & Environment	Science, Technology & Nature	Culture, Leisure & Lifestyle	
As the U.S. Congress plans to recess until winter, President Coolidge touts two major accomplishments: the Senate ratification of the World Court Protocol and the enactment of the Tax Revision bill....Jane Addams defends Prohibition, insisting that suppressing working-class saloon culture has given the average worker more money and "a completer life."		Panicked runs by depositors force four suburban Miami banks to temporarily close.		The Cincinnati Reds defeat the Chicago Cubs 6–1, increasing their lead in the National League pennant race to four and a half games....Golfer Bobby Jones, returned from his victory at the British Open, is feted with a ticker-tape parade down Broadway in New York City, complete with rebel yells and a band playing "Dixie." The taciturn Jones, from Georgia, briefly explains that he was "just lucky."	Jul. 2
Grumbling at his workload, President Coolidge signs a total of 153 bills in a rush during the last day of the congressional session....A white woman in New Jersey is deemed mentally incompetent and placed in a home for the feeble-minded after she applies for a license to marry an African-American man.				More than 18,000 American passengers embark from New York Harbor on steamliners for ports in Europe, the West Indies, and South America—a seasonal record....The town of Bristol, New Jersey, enacts an ordinance permitting "noiseless spooning" in automobiles; however, noisy spooning will be stopped by the police.	Jul. 3
				An estimated 600,000 celebrants spend the Fourth of July at Coney Island. New York governor Al Smith seizes the opportunity to shake voter hands on the boardwalk. A mini-stampede starts when a low-flying plane drops candy samples along the beach; in the rush for candy, a woman is trampled, breaking her arm.	Jul. 4
The Passaic textiles strike is entering its 24th week, with little evidence that worker determination is flagging. Strike leader Albert Weisbord, a 25-year-old Communist and Harvard graduate, is credited with maintaining their morale. Established union organizers from the United Textile Workers and the American Federation of Labor have no role in the strike.				At midseason in major league baseball, the New York Yankees hold a dominant ten-game lead in the American League. In the National League, the Pittsburgh Pirates, Cincinnati Reds, and St. Louis Cardinals are poised for a tight pennant race.	Jul. 5
Evangelist Aimee Semple McPherson is subpoenaed to appear before a Los Angeles County grand jury investigating the circumstances of her kidnapping and reappearance....At the First World Conference on Narcotic Education in Philadelphia, experts admit that no reliable statistics are available on drug addiction.		The U.S. Commerce department reports that one in every six Americans owns an automobile. In contrast, international statistics indicate that one in every 31,871 people in China owns a car, while in Afghanistan the ratio is one to 1.2 million....The J. C. Penney Company reports a 29.17 percent increase in sales for the first six months of 1926 over the same period last year.		The mother of actress Pola Negri predicts a 1927 wedding for her daughter and matinee idol Rudolph Valentino....Statistics indicate that the cancer death rate in 73 American cities has climbed steadily during the past two decades. The rate was 74.5 deaths per 100,000 population in 1906, compared to 114 per 100,000 in 1925.	Jul. 6
The Coast Guard reports seven fully laden "rum runners" anchored eighty miles off the coast of Boston, beyond the jurisdiction of authorities....The American Federation of Labor is vigorously opposing a plan by some affiliated union leaders to send a delegation to the Soviet Union to observe economic and working conditions....The Citizens' Committee of Three Hundred is formed in Passaic; the organization calls strike leader Albert Weisbord a "harpy" preying on a "peaceful, decent community."...President Coolidge begins his summer vacation in the Adirondack Mountains.		American chain stores report robust sales for the first six months of 1926, led by the F. W. Woolworth Company, with $107 million in earnings for the year. The next closest chain competitor, the McCrory Stores, has earned $14 million.		The Rockefeller Foundation identifies Detroit as the American city with the worst prostitution problem....Acclaimed German film director F. W. Murnau announces plans to make a movie, Sunrise, for the Fox Film Corporation.... Egyptian fakir Rahman Bey, a rival of Harry Houdini, fails in his attempt to remain for an hour in a cataleptic trance in a bronze casket at the bottom of New York City's North River. Just 19 minutes into the feat, his emergency bell rings and he is pulled to the surface. Best known for forcing hatpins through his cheeks—without bleeding—on the New York stage, Bey is apparently in his trance when the casket is opened and insists he did not ring the bell.	Jul. 7

F

Includes campaigns, elections, federal-state relations, civil rights and liberties, crime, the judiciary, education, healthcare, poverty, urban affairs, and population.

G

Includes formation and debate of U.S. foreign and defense policies, veterans affairs, and defense spending. (Relations with specific foreign countries are usually found under the region concerned.)

H

Includes business, labor, agriculture, taxation, transportation, consumer affairs, monetary and fiscal policy, natural resources, pollution and industrial accidents.

I

Includes worldwide scientific, medical and technological developments, natural phenomena, U.S. weather and natural disasters.

J

Includes the arts, religion, scholarship, communications media, sports, entertainment, fashions, fads, and social life.

	World Affairs	Europe	Africa & The Middle East	The Americas	Asia & The Pacific
Jul. 8		The French franc plunges in value from 37.36 to 39.80 to the dollar, its greatest depreciation in a single day, while the Italian lira also declines precipitously.			
Jul. 9		Italian labor leaders express their opposition to the government's recent imposition of a nine-hour workday....The London Times excoriates the British film industry for lagging far behind Hollywood. An editorial calls industry leaders "men without taste or culture, content to imitate the worst that comes from America, incapable of original thought themselves."	A Harvard Medical School expedition is studying sleeping sickness along the Congo River.		
Jul. 10		Premier Aristide Briand wins a vote of confidence from the French parliament by a narrow margin of 269 to 247. His government will proceed with attempts to stabilize the franc and negotiate war debt repayment terms with England.			Central Sumatra is again struck by a series of temblors.
Jul. 11		In Paris, more than 20,000 army veterans, many of them maimed, march to a statue of George Washington to protest U.S. policy regarding the settlement of war debts.		The Mexican Board of Biological Studies announces that infant mortality in the State of Chihuahua averages 65 percent. Across Mexico, 60,000 babies die annually from stomach infections.	The Territory of Hawaii reports that tourism has increased 20 percent during the past year, with more than 13,500 American and 400 Asian visitors in 1925.
Jul. 12		Based on dental records and extensive interviews, authorities in Berlin have concluded that the mystery woman hospitalized in a local sanitarium is not the Grand Duchess Anastasia of Russia....A pet monkey breaks into a restaurant in Berlin that caters to aristocrats. The monkey proceeds to wreak havoc, throwing glasses and bottles and overturning tables. It takes several policemen and firemen to finally subdue him.			A newspaper story about an American missionary has caused outrage in Korea. The story, which has been verified, describes how the missionary used acid to brand a Korean boy on the cheeks with the word "thief" after catching him stealing apples.
Jul. 13		The British government agrees to cancel three-fifths of French war debt obligations—terms that are much more lenient than the American/French debt settlement....The Belgian parliament grants King Albert dictatorial powers in an effort to save the nation's economy. The Belgian franc, like the French franc, has been in a freefall.			

A	B	C	D	E
Includes developments that affect more than one world region, international organizations and important meetings of world leaders.	Includes all domestic and regional developments in Europe, including the Soviet Union.	Includes all domestic and regional developments in Africa and the Middle East.	Includes all domestic and regional developments in Latin America, the Caribbean, and Canada.	Includes all domestic and regional developments in Asian and Pacific nations (and colonies).

U.S. Politics & Social Issues	U.S. Foreign Policy & Affairs, Defense	U.S. Economy & Environment	Science, Technology & Nature	Culture, Leisure & Lifestyle	
At a workers' meeting in Passaic, Albert Weisbord denies that the textiles strike is "Communistic." He asserts that the strikers have "bona fide trade union demands" and are fighting for the right to organize....The U.S. Circuit Court of Appeals rules that the Coast Guard can seize any American vessel suspected of rum-running, no matter how far from the nation's coast. The decision overturns a lower court ruling that limited seizures to 12 miles offshore.	The U.S. Navy successfully raises the *S-51* submarine that sunk in Long Island Sound last September after a collision with a merchant steamer. The bodies of 18 sailors are found aboard.	The Commerce Department reports that the state of North Carolina has experienced the most rapid economic development in the United States during the past decade. The largest migration in the country has been to Los Angeles, where a million people have moved.		College football officials announce that seats for the Army-Navy game on November 27 at Soldier Field in Chicago will sell for $10 per person, a record price for college athletics. The anticipated $400,000 gate will also set a college record....A New York City movie studio, Tec Art, is sued by 137 extras from the film *Oh Baby*. The plaintiffs claim that their vision has been damaged from the studio's use of Klieg lights, for which they received inadequate protection.	Jul. 8
Federal authorities plan to make greater use of airplanes to combat bootleggers. Aerial photography has proved useful for pinpointing the location of illegal stills....In Lansing, Kansas, 372 convicts, working in a prison mine, refuse to return to the surface in protest of their living conditions. Their demands include running water in their cell house and "three square meals a day."				Babe Ruth launches his 27th home-run of the season as the Yankees trounce the Cleveland Indians, 8-2.	Jul. 9
In Union, New Jersey, Prohibition agents are confronted by an angry mob after destroying 12,000 gallons of beer from a wildcat brewery. More than 500 local residents wield sticks and stones during the standoff, yelling about the waste of good beer.	The naval munitions depot at Lake Denmark, New Jersey, experiences a series of devastating shell explosions after it is struck by lightning during a summer storm. Homes in nearby towns are rocked from their foundations; in a community four miles away, every plate glass window is blown out, and falling debris is spotted 22 miles away. Twenty-one people are killed, dozens are seriously injured, and the damage is estimated at $84 million.		Eight Philadelphians die from the sweltering heat, as temperatures reach 97 degrees.	A circuit judge in Chicago decries the city's courts as a "divorce mill." "Our sacred marriage law has become a jazz, just as much a prostitution of morals and ethics as jazz is a prostitution of music," he remarks....The Metropolitan Museum of Art in New York City is struggling with an outbreak of "bronze disease," which is severely discoloring their collections of ancient bronze statues. Museum officials blame the summer humidity.	Jul. 10
The recently ended Sixty-Ninth Congress passed 700 new laws and $4.4 billion in appropriations. The tax reduction bill slashing $319 million from federal treasury coffers is cited by many political observers as the major accomplishment.	Secretary of War Dwight Davis inspects the damage at the Lake Denmark naval depot, where shells are still exploding. Communities in a 15-mile area around the depot are damaged and deserted, as refugees flee numerous fires.		The Ford Motor Company reports successfully testing a three-engine, all-metal airplane. The Stout plane, with room for eight passengers, will be used for commercial travel.	The favorite Parisian beach style for women features an all-white ensemble, with "overblouse, knickers, cap, and circular cape." To add a splash of color, women wear a wide red belt that ties in the front in an "immense bow."...The University of Illinois bans students from operating automobiles. The university sends a letter to parents that cites reduced scholastic scores by car owners. "The owning of automobiles has involved a constant and serious waste of time," the letter states.	Jul. 11
The Justice Department identifies an international heroin smuggling operation that links New York City, China, and Germany. The drugs are hidden in shipments of novelty items such as bowling pins....The Texas State Textbook Commission has ordered chapters on evolution to be omitted from biology books intended for Texas public schools.				The American Historical Association seeks to standardize history teaching methods across the nation, insisting that "a clear course must be steered" in training U.S. citizens....Will Hays, president of the Motion Picture Producers and Distributors of America, announces that jokes about Prohibition will be forbidden in Hollywood movies.	Jul. 12
Former Assistant Secretary of the Navy Franklin D. Roosevelt, in Warm Springs, GA, for his health, predicts that the Democratic Party will take control of the U.S. Senate in this fall's elections.				John D. Rockefeller, Jr. announces that newspaper photographers will not be allowed to take pictures of his teenaged sons. Such press attention, he believes, might cause his boys to gain an exaggerated sense of their own importance.	Jul. 13

F	G	H	I	J
Includes campaigns, elections, federal-state relations, civil rights and liberties, crime, the judiciary, education, healthcare, poverty, urban affairs, and population.	*Includes formation and debate of U.S. foreign and defense policies, veterans affairs, and defense spending. (Relations with specific foreign countries are usually found under the region concerned.)*	*Includes business, labor, agriculture, taxation, transportation, consumer affairs, monetary and fiscal policy, natural resources, pollution and industrial accidents.*	*Includes worldwide scientific, medical and technological developments, natural phenomena, U.S. weather and natural disasters.*	*Includes the arts, religion, scholarship, communications media, sports, entertainment, fashions, fads, and social life.*

	World Affairs	Europe	Africa & The Middle East	The Americas	Asia & The Pacific
Jul. 14		The Italian government is cracking down on local politics. An official Fascist paper criticizes the "local Tom, Dick, or Harry" who focuses on "the horizons of their individual town" at the expense of "Fascism's national and international activity."…London is experiencing a "heat wave," to the amusement of American tourists used to more formidable summers. The temperature reached 85 degrees Fahrenheit today.	The French Army has launched a new military offensive against holdout tribes in the mountainous regions of Morocco. The peace following the surrender of Abd-el Krim has proved to be short-lived.… Thirteen men, including a former Minister of the Interior and five parliament members, are executed by hanging at street corners in Smyrna, Turkey, accused of conspiring to assassinate President Kemal.		
Jul. 15	Statistics indicate that for the first time since the end of the Great War, the world's trade volume has attained pre-war levels.	The economic situation in France remains perilous. The franc has fallen to 40.80 to the dollar, and the Briand government has been forced to borrow heavily during the past week to stay solvent.…The Italian government announces plans to create its own national jazz music, in an effort to cut down on expenses for foreign products.	The Sultan of Morocco. Mulai Yusef, is in France to preside at the official opening of the Grande Mosquée de Paris, built by the French government in gratitude for African Muslim military participation against Germany during the Great War.		Moro Muslims in the Philippines appeal to the Coolidge administration to establish a separate Moro state.
Jul. 16			Bennet Doty, the Tennessean charged with deserting the French Foreign Legion while serving in Syria, is sentenced to eight years of hard labor.	Reports indicate that 150 nuns, all of them involved in child education, are in the process of leaving Mexico due to the new religious regulations.	
Jul. 17		For the third time this year, Premier Augustin Briand's government falls in France. By a vote of 288 to 243, the parliament refuses to endorse a plan to salvage the franc, forcing the Briand cabinet to resign.…A massive landslide buries a passenger train near Sarajevo, Bosnia, killing 117 people.…The Danube River in Yugoslavia is flooding following repeated downpours. Women and children are reported stranded on the rooftops of houses, which later collapse into the floodwaters.		Mexican Catholics plan to launch a widespread economic boycott beginning August 1 to protest the religious decrees instituted by the Calles government.	The movie business is booming in Japan, where there are five production companies. An American film salesman notes that the Japanese closely copy Hollywood films. "There is an impersonator on the Japanese screen of every one of our major stars. Chaplin, Pickford, Valentino, Fairbanks, Barthelmess, all have their duplicates in Japan."
Jul. 18		French parliamentary president Èdouard Herriot, who spearheaded the demise of the Briand government, is appointed to lead a new cabinet.…British newspapers at-tack the United States for its role in Briand's fall. The *Daily Mail* editorializes: "There would have been none of this miserable debt-collecting business which is causing so much harm in France and Italy if the United States had agreed to general cancellation of war debts."…The Pan-German Gymnast Festival in Vienna includes a three-hour parade featuring 33,000 gymnasts carrying Austrian and German flags.			
Jul. 19		British Chancellor of the Exchequer Winston Churchill criticizes American Treasury Secretary Andrew Mellon for his approach to the issue of war debt repayments.			

A	B	C	D	E
Includes developments that affect more than one world region, international organizations and important meetings of world leaders.	Includes all domestic and regional developments in Europe, including the Soviet Union.	Includes all domestic and regional developments in Africa and the Middle East.	Includes all domestic and regional developments in Latin America, the Caribbean, and Canada.	Includes all domestic and regional developments in Asian and Pacific nations (and colonies).

U.S. Politics & Social Issues	U.S. Foreign Policy & Affairs, Defense	U.S. Economy & Environment	Science, Technology & Nature	Culture, Leisure & Lifestyle	
Joseph Ciccone, a lieutenant with the Genna organized crime family in Chicago, is gunned down at his home. The gang, which once controlled the city's Little Italy neighborhood, has lost much of its influence after warring unsuccessfully against northside mobster Bugs Moran and southside boss Al Capone.				Will Rogers signs a contract to appear in the British film *Tip-Toes*.	Jul. 14
A grand jury witness testifies that he saw evangelist Aimee Semple McPherson accompanying a man in Salinas, California, during the time when she was allegedly being held captive by kidnappers in Mexico. Semple and the man have also been traced to a hotel in San Luis Obispo, where they registered under the names of Mr. and Mrs. Frank Gibson....President Coolidge passes the day fishing in the Adirondacks, where he catches 30 brook trout.	The city of Baltimore is demanding that the War Department remove millions of pounds of explosives stored at Curtis Bay, a few miles from the downtown area.	A total of 64 state banks have failed in Georgia in recent days, tied to bankruptcy proceedings against the Bankers Trust Company of Atlanta.		Among the new revues opening in New York City is "1926 Bare Facts, or Nothing to Wear," at the Triangle Theater in Greenwich Village. Among the vaudeville shows announced to open soon are "Light Wines and Beer," "Wine, Women, and Song," and two shows featuring all-African American casts, "Watermelons" and "Lucky Sambo."	Jul. 15
Don R. Mellett, the publisher of the *Canton Daily News* in Canton, Ohio, is shot to death outside his home. He had crusaded successfully against political corruption, exposing links between prominent officials and Canton's notorious criminal underworld. The city police announce that they have no suspects.				Challenger Jack Delaney defeats Paul Berlenbach in a 15-round decision to win the light-heavyweight boxing championship. The match at Ebbets Field in Brooklyn draws an unusually large number of women spectators. Delaney, a handsome French-Canadian, has a following of female fans, known as Delaney's Screaming Mamies.	Jul. 16
San Francisco police warn that further bloodshed is likely in the war between two rival Chinese tong societies. Killings have occurred recently in Sacramento, Santa Barbara, Seattle, Portland, and San Francisco.		Seven eastern states agree to sign a compact to combat pollution in rivers and streams. The Potomac River, where coal gas waters and pulp wastes are routinely dumped, has been singled out as being particularly polluted.		The Department of Agriculture reports that American salad consumption has more than quintupled in the past decade....Among the novelties in French furs are giraffe skin capes and pony skin coats.	Jul. 17
Citizens in Canton, Ohio, are angry that the police have made no progress toward making an arrest in the murder of publisher Don R. Mellett. Many are convinced that the police are implicated in the murder. An attorney remarks, "There is no doubt in any one's mind that the killing of Mellett was due to his eight months' campaign against rampant vice, lack of law enforcement and political factions in the Police Department."		The Department of Agriculture reports that the nation's farming population has dropped by almost a half million people during the past year....A major forest fire is raging out of control on the Klamath reserve in California. Authorities believe an arsonist is responsible; several local men have grievances against the U.S. Forest Service.	There are 39 aircraft factories in the United States, which employ 2,657 workers, according to the Commerce Department. In 1925 the industry produced 621 airplanes, an increase of 20 percent over 1924.	The New York Yankees fail to score a run for the first time this season, shut out by pitcher Tom Zachary and the St. Louis Browns, 4–0.	Jul. 18
The Passaic textiles strike has now lasted half a year.		Federal Reserve statistics indicate that the national debt has been cut $5.842 billion since 1920....Eight people die in Chicago as a result of the summer heat, which reaches 94 degrees.	Researchers at the University of Chicago have observed that human blood and chimpanzee blood react similarly to invading bacteria. Their immunological tests indicate that "the bloods of anthropoids are more closely related to human blood than the bloods of horses and donkeys are related to each other."	A farmer from Keokuk, Iowa, known for breaking up automobile "petting parties" and blackmailing couples for money by threatening to hand them over to police for his interference, is shot dead....Babe Ruth pays a $25 speeding fine at a New York City traffic court. He was driving his roadster 33 miles per hour.	Jul. 19

F	G	H	I	J
Includes campaigns, elections, federal-state relations, civil rights and liberties, crime, the judiciary, education, healthcare, poverty, urban affairs, and population.	Includes formation and debate of U.S. foreign and defense policies, veterans affairs, and defense spending. (Relations with specific foreign countries are usually found under the region concerned.)	Includes business, labor, agriculture, taxation, transportation, consumer affairs, monetary and fiscal policy, natural resources, pollution and industrial accidents.	Includes worldwide scientific, medical and technological developments, natural phenomena, U.S. weather and natural disasters.	Includes the arts, religion, scholarship, communications media, sports, entertainment, fashions, fads, and social life.

	World Affairs	Europe	Africa & The Middle East	The Americas	Asia & The Pacific
Jul. 20	Only three nations—Cuba, Greece, and Liberia—have accepted the U.S. Senate reservations to the World Court protocol.	The French franc reaches yet another historic low, shedding 12 percent of its value during the day....Felix Dzerzhinsky, former head of the feared Cheka secret police in the Soviet Union, dies in Moscow.			The Soviet Union is concerned that the Japanese-financed railroad being built in Northern Manchuria is the "thin edge of a wedge," presaging Japanese control of Asian mainland resources.
Jul. 21		Only two days after assuming the premiership of France, radical leader Èdouard Herriot is forced from office. He is met with lusty boos in parliament as he is voted down by a coalition of center and rightist politicians....The French franc rises in value to 2.20 cents. Recently it has been hovering below 2 cents....The Soviet government has supplied British coal miners with $2.1 million in strike assistance, according to an International Miners' Federation report.			
Jul. 22		The newest French premier, Raymond Poincarè, is attempting to create a strong coalition government. He has invited five members of the Radical Socialist party to hold cabinet positions, along with his own conservative allies. Based on these improved prospects, the French franc rallies in value to 44 to the dollar....American tourists in a "See-Paris-by-Night" tour bus are surrounded and detained for several minutes by an angry French crowd, who jeer American war debt policies.	The French have launched a new offensive near Damascus against insurgent Syrian Druses. The French report that the Syrians have suffered heavy losses, with more than 150 killed.		
Jul. 23		Raymond Poincarè has successfully gathered six former premiers in his cabinet, which ranges across the political spectrum....Italian Fascist premier Benito Mussolini comments on his country's expansive aims. "We are thirsting for the power, for the riches and the prosperity so long denied us," he asserts. He goes on to explain that "our imperialism poses no threat to the world's peace."	The French Army reports success in pacifying Morocco, where 2,000 families have recently submitted.... Five American oil companies have bought interests in the British-controlled Turkish Petroleum Company, with plans to aggressively explore for oil in Iraq near Mosul.	The Calles government issues a new decree forbidding the teaching of religion in private schools. Several leaders of the Young Men's Catholic Association, who have been instigating an economic boycott, are arrested. The government is carrying out mass vaccinations at churches in Mexico City, often using the same needle on multiple parishioners.	The Japanese government announces plans to colonize the northern island of Hokkaido. They envision relocating 1.8 million farmers to the island in the coming years, although recent emigrants have balked at the typical sub-zero temperatures.
Jul. 24		Prominent Soviet leader Grigory Zinoviev is expelled from the Politburo, accused of fomenting factional activities. The move is seen as further cementing the power of Central Executive Committee general secretary Joseph Stalin.			The Japanese government decrees that thousands of small shrines devoted to the worship of animals such as foxes and snakes be demolished.
Jul. 25	U.S. senators William Borah and Hiram Johnson, Republican "irreconcilables," have issued blistering statements responding to the European criticism of American war debt policies. "The United States is the pariah among nations, openly accused of being a moneybag and a Shylock," Johnson contends. In return, he promises to lead efforts to pull the United States out of the World Court.	Paris newspapers are decrying the recent anti-American mob scenes, and the police have promised to protect tourists. Nevertheless, the "See-Paris-by-Night" bus tours have been suspended indefinitely....The Spanish government is launching a campaign against widespread illiteracy. More than 1.5 million children lack adequate schooling, and the national illiteracy rate is 45 percent.		On the final Sunday before government anti-religious decrees go into effect, Mexican Catholics throng the nation's churches. The Shrine of Guadalupe draws an especially huge crowd. Church officials issue a pastoral letter in which they announce that all Catholic services will be suspended effective July 31 in protest of the regulations.	
Jul. 26		The British Board of Trade estimates that the ongoing coal strike has cost the nation a total of £148.5 million in lost earnings capacity. Heavy industry has been deprived of 1 million tons of pig iron and 1.2 million tons of steel.	The French Army claims great success in recent operations in Syria and denies having killed 400 civilians during an artillery "clean-up" of Damascus.		

A	B	C	D	E
Includes developments that affect more than one world region, international organizations and important meetings of world leaders.	Includes all domestic and regional developments in Europe, including the Soviet Union.	Includes all domestic and regional developments in Africa and the Middle East.	Includes all domestic and regional developments in Latin America, the Caribbean, and Canada.	Includes all domestic and regional developments in Asian and Pacific nations (and colonies).

U.S. Politics & Social Issues	U.S. Foreign Policy & Affairs, Defense	U.S. Economy & Environment	Science, Technology & Nature	Culture, Leisure & Lifestyle	
The Corn Belt Committee, composed of leading midwestern farmers from eleven states, passes a resolution condemning the Coolidge administration for supporting "the industrialization of the nation at the expense of the farmers."		Thirty banks in Florida have closed in the past seven weeks, caused by the failure of the chain bank system controlled by the now-bankrupt Bankers Trust Company of Atlanta.		Rudolph Valentino challenges a *Chicago Tribune* writer to a fight after the newspaper publishes an editorial about the American male becoming a "pink powder puff." Valentino is identified as the prototype.	Jul. 20
Eleven Canadian teenagers drown on Balsam Lake in Ontario after their "war canoe" capsizes in a squall....Cleveland is on the alert for a sniper who uses a high-powered rifle to shoot randomly into store windows from a speeding automobile....Nine coal miners in Blocton, Alabama, die when a gas pocket explodes.		New Yorkers are warned against swimming in three of the city's bays, which have been found to be sources of typhoid, skin diseases, and other pollution-related illnesses.		Theatrical impresario Florenz Ziegfeld predicts that the tide is turning in favor of plumper women. "Women are too thin," he observes. "Many who have achieved the false ideal of extreme thinness look half-starved. The thing has been greatly overdone." He anticipates the return of "curves within reason."	Jul. 21
Police in Canton, Ohio, make a few arrests while investigating the Mellett slaying, but soon release the suspects. Citizens are angered at their desultory efforts. Several private detectives are in town, lured by a $27,000 reward for identifying the murderer....A tourist bus full of women and children skids on a wet road and overturns near Sparkill, NY, killing ten.	Eleven members of the U.S. Coast Guard are arrested on the charge of accepting bribes from rum runners.			Babe Ruth catches a baseball dropped from an airplane flying at 300 feet—after failing to catch six balls dropped from higher altitudes.	Jul. 22
A mob in Corning, Iowa, has a tense standoff with a group of Ku Klux Klansmen on their way to attend a meeting.				The Liberty Mutual Insurance Company has determined that 250,000 automobiles were stolen in the United States in 1925. Around 80 percent were eventually recovered.	Jul. 23
The police chief of Canton, Ohio, is placed on thirty-day suspension by the city mayor, for his failure to apprehend the murderer of publisher Don R. Mellett. National Guardsmen have been assigned to the homes of several city officials who have received anonymous mailed warnings to not participate in the investigation.		For the first time, the number of American workers in the construction trades unions has surpassed one million members.		American League baseball president Ban Johnson issues a directive to his umpires to quell Detroit Tigers manager Ty Cobb's frequent outbursts on the field, which are prolonging the length of games.	Jul. 24
				Film producer Samuel Goldwyn declares that the "nude or semi-nude female's form" in movies is "passé." He predicts that "the day when you could substitute legs for brains in the motion pictures has gone forever."	Jul. 25
Miriam "Ma" Ferguson, the first female governor of Texas, loses the Democratic primary....Robert Todd Lincoln, the last surviving child of President Abraham Lincoln, dies at the age of 82.	The Naval Board of Investigation examining the circumstances of the Lake Denmark depot explosion has received more than 3,000 property damage claims from neighboring residents.	President Coolidge is meeting with Edsel Ford, the son of Henry Ford, about potential government aid for the development of commercial aviation.			Jul. 26

F	G	H	I	J
Includes campaigns, elections, federal-state relations, civil rights and liberties, crime, the judiciary, education, healthcare, poverty, urban affairs, and population.	*Includes formation and debate of U.S. foreign and defense policies, veterans affairs, and defense spending. (Relations with specific foreign countries are usually found under the region concerned.)*	*Includes business, labor, agriculture, taxation, transportation, consumer affairs, monetary and fiscal policy, natural resources, pollution and industrial accidents.*	*Includes worldwide scientific, medical and technological developments, natural phenomena, U.S. weather and natural disasters.*	*Includes the arts, religion, scholarship, communications media, sports, entertainment, fashions, fads, and social life.*

	World Affairs	Europe	Africa & The Middle East	The Americas	Asia & The Pacific
Jul. 27		The Poincarè cabinet's fiscal plan is greeted with resounding support in the French parliament, approved by a vote of 358 to 131. The proposed measures include a large tax increase and new bank credits.			
Jul. 28		The Poincarè government has decided to shelve the controversial issue of war debt repayments for the near future. Recent accords reached with the Unites States and England will not be submitted to the French parliament until the fall.		A hurricane lashes the Bahamas, drowning an estimated 150 people and causing $8 million in damage....Mexican Catholic women are successfully boycotting large stores in Mexico City, where sales have been halved.	
Jul. 29			Much of the city of Damascus lies in ruins following extended warfare between Syrian Druse rebels and the French Army. The city has essentially been in a state of siege for the past ten months.	The Mexican government orders all Catholics to be disarmed. There are rampant rumors that Catholic groups are secretly plotting against the government.	
Jul. 30				On the order of the Archbishop of Mexico, this is the last day before Catholic services will be suspended in protest of the Calles government's religious decrees. Churches across the country are packed; at a cathedral in Yucatan, 3,000 people are confirmed or baptized....Catholic protests turn violent in Mexico City. A large crowd of worshippers refuses to vacate the Church of San Rafael; police open fire on the church, wounding nine. Elsewhere, irate crowds hurl stones at justice department employees.	Flooding in Japan kills 400 people in the Niigata Prefecture.
Jul. 31		The French parliament approves the Poincarè cabinet's plan for a substantial tax increase, which will add 11.5 billion francs to government coffers over the next two years.		The Mexican government proceeds with taking over Catholic churches across the nation. Many of the buildings are patrolled by government troops.	
Aug. 1		During "Colonial Week" in Hamburg, Germans rally to demand the restoration of all the country's former colonies, which were stripped away at the end of the World War.	Contrary to French reports, eyewitnesses in Damascus claim that the French Army offensive is going badly, suffering heavy losses.	An estimated 50,000 people parade through the streets of Mexico City to show their support for the Calles government. They carry banners with slogans such as "The Clergy Are Rich, the People Are Poor." Very few spectators watch the parade; there have been rumors of impending violence....Mexican officials have difficulty clearing a church in Pachuca. When the parishioners rush to hold the church doors against government agents, 12 women and children are suffocated....Nine people in Mexico City, said to be "religious fanatics," are arrested and charged with plotting to assassinate President Callas.	

A	B	C	D	E
Includes developments that affect more than one world region, international organizations and important meetings of world leaders.	Includes all domestic and regional developments in Europe, including the Soviet Union.	Includes all domestic and regional developments in Africa and the Middle East.	Includes all domestic and regional developments in Latin America, the Caribbean, and Canada.	Includes all domestic and regional developments in Asian and Pacific nations (and colonies).

U.S. Politics & Social Issues	U.S. Foreign Policy & Affairs, Defense	U.S. Economy & Environment	Science, Technology & Nature	Culture, Leisure & Lifestyle	
The investigation of Canton publisher Don R. Mellett's murder is being impeded by members of the city's underworld, locally called the "Jungle." None of them has provided necessary information about the case.		President Coolidge believes that the nation's business is "proceeding along healthy, progressive lines" and that general prosperity will continue....General Motors reports record earnings for the first six months of 1926. The net earnings of $93 million almost doubles the figure for the same period in 1925.		The New York Yankees win their sixth game in a row, as Babe Ruth bashes his 31st homerun of the season.	Jul. 27
Iowa Democrats are calling for a national "tariff war," uniting the agricultural Midwest and South against the industrial East, as a central theme in upcoming elections.		The Census Bureau reports that American land in agricultural production has dropped during the past five years by 19 million acres.	Edsel Ford announces his intention to inexpensively mass-produce airplanes, with the ultimate goal of making "the American people a nation of flyers."		Jul. 28
Al Capone is freed after spending one night in jail on the charge that he murdered assistant state's attorney William McSwiggin. The warrant is dismissed for lack of evidence....A Chicago grand jury indicts 42 Cook County election officials and poll workers for committing vote fraud....Prominent Texas fundamentalist preacher J. Frank Norris is charged with murdering a man at his church office in Fort Worth. The victim was a friend of the city mayor, a Catholic who has been targeted for criticism by Norris.				Led by the powerful bat of Lou Gehrig, the New York Yankees win their eighth straight game.	Jul. 29
			Emil Wolff-Heide, a German photochemist, has developed a relatively inexpensive and efficient process for producing color movies.	A leading cosmetician warns that gum chewing causes the face to harden. "Many a modern woman has a face as hard as the crockery of a railroad lunch counter," she declares, "and the reason is chewing gum."	Jul. 30
				The National Safety Council estimates that 10 Americans die in accidents every hour. The American accidental fatality rate is the highest in world, 50 percent greater than the next highest country. The vast majority of deaths are caused by automobiles, but the United States also leads in fatalities caused by falls and burns....The New York Yankees win their tenth game in a row, led by Babe Ruth, who contributes his 33rd homerun.	Jul. 31
The Iowa Republican Convention endorses President Coolidge to run for another term, raising hopes among his supporters that there will be no serious "corn belt revolt" against his policies. Coolidge has not divulged his intentions to even his closest advisers....Boston Cardinal William O'Connell condemns the Mexican government as "a clique of atheists" and suggests that President Calles has links to the Soviet Union. He calls the Catholic Church "the most powerful bulwark" that society has "against rapine, robbery and anarchy."		The Anaconda-Harriman Syndicate takes over management of the sprawling Giesche zinc and coal mines in Poland—the largest European industrial enterprise ever owned and operated by American businessmen.		The New York Yankees win their eleventh straight game, with star pitcher Herb Pennock notching his seventeenth victory of the season....Jewish author Israel Zangwill, best known in America for his popular play about the immigrant experience, The Melting Pot, has died.	Aug. 1

F	G	H	I	J
Includes campaigns, elections, federal-state relations, civil rights and liberties, crime, the judiciary, education, healthcare, poverty, urban affairs, and population.	Includes formation and debate of U.S. foreign and defense policies, veterans affairs, and defense spending. (Relations with specific foreign countries are usually found under the region concerned.)	Includes business, labor, agriculture, taxation, transportation, consumer affairs, monetary and fiscal policy, natural resources, pollution and industrial accidents.	Includes worldwide scientific, medical and technological developments, natural phenomena, U.S. weather and natural disasters.	Includes the arts, religion, scholarship, communications media, sports, entertainment, fashions, fads, and social life.

	World Affairs	Europe	Africa & The Middle East	The Americas	Asia & The Pacific
Aug. 2		Premier Mussolini asks the Italian people to eat "war bread," which uses less wheat, in order to cut the nation's import expenses....Will Rogers observes that Ireland is the friendliest country these days for American tourists: "They don't owe us and they don't hate us."		Mexico City is quiet today, although seven more people, all of them teenagers, are arrested for conspiring to kill President Calles. In some provincial towns Catholics are wearing their mourning clothes and draping their homes in black.	The Pan-Asiatic Conference in Japan rejects Esperanto as a common language for all Asian nations, dismissing it as a "white man's language."
Aug. 3		The Mussolini cabinet has decided to reorganize the Italian Football Federation, the National Pugilistic Federation, and the Automobile Club of Italy. In general, sporting events in the country have been judged insufficiently Fascist. There is too much violent rivalry between local groups of fans, and too many ceremonies commemorating individual rather than national achievements.	Forty-nine prominent Turkish citizens, including editors, writers, politicians, and the former chief of police of Constantinople, are being tried for plotting a *coup d'état*.		
Aug. 4		British civil service employees are forbidden to join unions....The French government is concerned that the weak franc has made the nation's industries attractive takeover targets for foreign investors. One of the country's largest dye companies is now controlled by German businessmen.		The Calles government issues a statement insisting that it has no desire to interfere with the spirituality or governance of the Catholic Church. Many Catholics interpret this to mean that the government will back down in the current controversy.	
Aug. 5				The Knights of Columbus are pressuring President Coolidge and the State Department to intervene actively in the Mexican situation. Although President Calles is not a Communist, the organization argues that he is ruled by the "Soviet philosophy" and attempts to "Russianize" Mexico.	Several dikes along the Yangtze River in China burst, flooding 2,000 square miles of land and drowning an estimated 3,000 people.
Aug. 6		The French franc has rebounded smartly since the Poincarè government came to power, rising from a value of 48 to the dollar to 35.		Responding to the Knights of Columbus, President Coolidge asserts that unless the Calles government violates American property rights, his policy toward Mexico is hands-off.	
Aug. 7		The Italian government issues a decree urging citizens to replace spaghetti with potatoes as a staple of their diet, in an effort to reduce expenses for wheat.		The Mexican Department of Health bans the Charleston in dance halls, arguing that it can cause heart failure.	A cholera outbreak in Shanghai is resulting in more than 1,000 deaths daily.
Aug. 8		The prolonged British coal strike is providing one benefit for everyone: the air in London this summer is noticeably cleaner....Theatrical producer Max Reinhardt's production of the 15th century morality play *Everyman* is a smash success at the Salzburg Festival in Austria; 25,000 playgoers have descended on the town.		In an interview, Mexican president Calles explains his attitude toward the Catholic Church hierarchy: "The Catholic clergy has never been a factor in the development or uplift of the nation. There also has been a tendency to keep political power in their hands. This is the origin of the difficulties."	

A	B	C	D	E
Includes developments that affect more than one world region, international organizations and important meetings of world leaders.	*Includes all domestic and regional developments in Europe, including the Soviet Union.*	*Includes all domestic and regional developments in Africa and the Middle East.*	*Includes all domestic and regional developments in Latin America, the Caribbean, and Canada.*	*Includes all domestic and regional developments in Asian and Pacific nations (and colonies).*

U.S. Politics & Social Issues	U.S. Foreign Policy & Affairs, Defense	U.S. Economy & Environment	Science, Technology & Nature	Culture, Leisure & Lifestyle	
Passaic strike leader Albert Weisbord has received death threats from the Black Hand Society....Thirty-five American Indian tribes sue the United States for $1.2 billion, citing a series of fraudulent land treaties dating back to the presidency of Andrew Jackson.		General Motors has been the hottest stock on Wall Street. Shares were up to $201 per share today; earlier this year the stock sold for $113.		The Pittsburgh Pirates are in first place in the National League, with a game-and-a-half lead over the Cincinnati Reds. The St. Louis Cardinals are lagging in third place, having lost four straight games.... The New York Yankees finally lose a game, stopped by the Chicago White Sox, 2–1.	Aug. 2
The Passaic Strikers' Milk Fund is being supported by a benefit concert featuring the Metropolitan Opera Company and 100 musicians from New York City's principal orchestras....A leading "dry" evangelist in Morgantown, Kentucky, is shot dead by moonshiners while leading a revival meeting....Investigators in the Hall-Mills case believe that love notes between the two victims, found ripped up and strewn around their dead bodies, are a direct link to the murderer or murderers. Two suspects are reportedly under surveillance.	A U.S. Navy court determines that no human is culpable for the Lake Denmark ammunition depot disaster. However, the court advises that the depot is "too near inhabited land for the safe storage of more than a small amount of large explosives."	General Motors stock surges upward again, climbing to $213 per share. Speculation is at a fever pitch in Detroit, where local shareholders have reportedly made $10 million in the past two weeks....New York City health officials attribute more than 100 typhoid cases to swimming at the city's beaches.	The French Academy of Science believes that diabetes can be treated by injecting small amounts of nickel and cobalt under the skin.	French tennis champion Susanne Lenglen announces her intention to turn professional, after being offered $200,000 to undertake a four-month tour of the United States. There are only a handful of female professional tennis players in the United States, and experts doubt that the International Lawn Tennis Association will sanction amateur-professional matches for Lenglen. "What I am doing is something new in tennis," she says proudly.	Aug. 3
Prohibition officials are cracking down on "prescription bootlegging." A grand jury indicts 57 doctors and druggists for abusing their right to prescribe or distribute medicinal whiskey. An estimated half million gallons were issued through spurious prescriptions last year.			Lee De Forest, one of the primary inventors of radio technology, sues the top executives at his own company, the De Forest Radio Company, for gross financial mismanagement.	Heavyweight champion Jack Dempsey is mobbed by a crowd upon arriving at New York City's Pennsylvania Station. His fight with challenger Gene Tunney is scheduled for September 16 at Yankee Stadium.	Aug. 4
Birth control advocate Margaret Sanger urges a plan that will provide pensions to "defectives" in exchange for their forgoing procreation, citing the high national cost of caring for the insane and feeble. She remarks: "When we realize that a moron's vote is as good as that of an intelligent, educated, thinking citizen, we may well pause and ask ourselves, 'Is America really safe for democracy?'"		American railroads report all-time record earnings for the first half of 1926. Southern railroads servicing Florida have been particularly profitable, benefiting from the mania for Florida real estate.		Harry Houdini stays submerged for 91 minutes in an airtight metal casket at the bottom of a hotel swimming pool in New York City....The Westerners' Protective Association, a group of horsemen who frequently portray cowboys in movies, are protesting the increased use by Hollywood of rented U.S. cavalrymen to perform horse-riding stunts.	Aug. 5
			Warner Bros. introduces the Vitaphone, a phonographic disc process that enables movies to be synchronized with sound. In the technology's debut in New York City, the film *Don Juan*, starring John Barrymore, is shown to a rapt audience.	Gertrude Ederle becomes the first woman to swim the English Channel. The 20-year-old American completes the swim in 14 hours and 31 minutes—smashing the previous Channel record, set by a man, of 16 hours 23 minutes.	Aug. 6
A U.S. district court awards damages to a Japanese man who was denied employment with a lumber company in Toledo, Oregon, by the local white population, which threatened him with violence. The case is seen as upholding the workplace rights of Japanese immigrants.		American farmers are increasingly joining cooperative associations. More than 2.5 million farmers belong to such organizations, a 300 percent increase in the past decade....England is the largest foreign customer for American candy, purchasing 5.3 million pounds of confections in 1925, most of it chewing gum.		Swimmer Johnny Weissmuller sets a new world record for the 330-yard freestyle.	Aug. 7
Bishop Adna Leonard of Baltimore castigates New York governor Al Smith, who is reportedly interested in running for the White House in 1928. "No Governor can kiss the Papal ring and get within gunshot of the White House," the bishop insists. "The United States is ... a Protestant nation and, as long as the English language is interwoven with the word of God, America will remain Protestant."		General Motors reports $535 billion in sales for the first six months of 1926—a figure that nearly matches their total sales for all of 1925.		Atlantic City draws its largest crowd of the summer, an estimated 500,000 people, who mill about the boardwalk and beach. Train service is packed from New York City, Baltimore, Washington, and New Jersey; more than 40,000 passengers arrive from Philadelphia.	Aug. 8

F	G	H	I	J
Includes campaigns, elections, federal-state relations, civil rights and liberties, crime, the judiciary, education, healthcare, poverty, urban affairs, and population.	Includes formation and debate of U.S. foreign and defense policies, veterans affairs, and defense spending. (Relations with specific foreign countries are usually found under the region concerned.)	Includes business, labor, agriculture, taxation, transportation, consumer affairs, monetary and fiscal policy, natural resources, pollution and industrial accidents.	Includes worldwide scientific, medical and technological developments, natural phenomena, U.S. weather and natural disasters.	Includes the arts, religion, scholarship, communications media, sports, entertainment, fashions, fads, and social life.

	World Affairs	Europe	Africa & The Middle East	The Americas	Asia & The Pacific
Aug. 9		Former French premier Georges Clemenceau, a close American ally during the World War, has written a letter to President Coolidge urging him to reconsider the issue of war debt obligations. He questions America's insistence on a "money peace." Observers believe that the letter will only harden the attitude of U.S. Senate "irreconcilables," led by William Borah. For his part, Coolidge chooses to ignore the letter.		The Vatican announces that there will be no negotiations with the Mexican government as long as "persecutive religious laws" are in effect....A group of American Protestant ministers, calling themselves the "Good Will Mission," issues a report from Mexico that praises President Calles for undertaking "a program of education and social reform, necessary for the rehabilitation of Mexico."	
Aug. 10					
Aug. 11		Senator William Borah goes on the offensive against former French premier Clemenceau for his "cruelly misleading" letter. He wonders why France, so eager to have its own war debts dismissed, will not set an example by relieving Germany of its reparation obligations.		A Mexican archbishop claims that two Catholic priests and approximately three dozen Catholic citizens in provincial towns were executed by the military during unrest on August 1 and 2....The Calles government proceeds with plans to confiscate rural estates owned by the Catholic clergy, worth more than $12.5 million.	
Aug. 12	Germany remains adamant that it must be the only country given a new permanent seat on the Council of the League of Nations.			Mexican military authorities strongly deny that any priests or other Catholic citizens have been executed during the recent unrest.	
Aug. 13	The U.S. State Department has stipulated that all American embassies must be furnished solely with American-produced items. U.S. textile firms have been concerned that diplomats will prefer Oriental rugs to the American article.			Dignitaries in the Mexican Catholic Church meet and determine to make no compromises with the Calles government. They release a statement which asserts that no argument against the Church is credible, "since truth and justice are on its side."	
Aug. 14		Another significant leader in the Soviet Union is ousted from power: Economic Council member Georgy Pyatakov.		The Catholic economic boycott has cut substantially into the business of department stores and wholesale trade houses in Mexico City.	Generals Wu Pei-fu and Zhang Zuolin, who have largely defeated the Kuominchun national army, are making no effort to establish a central Chinese government in Peking.

A	B	C	D	E
Includes developments that affect more than one world region, international organizations and important meetings of world leaders.	*Includes all domestic and regional developments in Europe, including the Soviet Union.*	*Includes all domestic and regional developments in Africa and the Middle East.*	*Includes all domestic and regional developments in Latin America, the Caribbean, and Canada.*	*Includes all domestic and regional developments in Asian and Pacific nations (and colonies).*

U.S. Politics & Social Issues	U.S. Foreign Policy & Affairs, Defense	U.S. Economy & Environment	Science, Technology & Nature	Culture, Leisure & Lifestyle	
				Director Victor Seastrom's film adaptation of *The Scarlet Letter*, starring Lillian Gish, has opened to strong critical praise.	Aug. 9
In their battle against bootleggers, Prohibition agents plan to increase the poison content of industrial alcohol. Currently the government "denatures" industrial alcohol by poisoning it, making it too dangerous to drink; however, bootleggers have discovered chemical "renaturing" methods, counteracting the poison and making the alcohol drinkable.		American banks have a billion dollars more in assets through June 1926 than during the same period last year.	Scientists have developed a new process for film emulsion, which uses inexpensive chemicals instead of expensive silver salts. This is expected to drive down the cost of movie film stock.	Director Cecil B. DeMille has screentested more than 200 actresses in England and America in his attempt to find the perfect Mary Magdelen for his upcoming epic *The King of Kings*. All so far have failed; his manager notes that the challenge is to find a "great actress of whom nothing derogatory has ever been published."	Aug. 10
The husband of murder victim Eleanor Mills now admits that he knew all along about her affair with Reverend Edward Hall. He says that they were planning to run off together. In the previous investigation of the case, he had claimed to be ignorant of the full extent of their relationship.	The War Department rolls out the Huff-Daland XHB-1 "Cyclops" bomber plane. The plane features a single engine and can carry four men; an unusual benefit is that half of its flying weight can be utilized for "useful load"—bombs and other munitions.			United Artists announces plans to start its own movie theater chain, with operations in cities such as Chicago and Detroit. The circuit will have preferential access to United Artists movies, with their roster of stars including Rudolph Valentino and Douglas Fairbanks.	Aug. 11
Five coal miners are dug out alive from the caved-in section of a zinc mine in Salem, Kentucky, after spending more than six days trapped underground....The New Jersey state police arrest two men, the brother and cousin of Frances Hall, and charge them with helping her to murder Reverend Edward Hall and Eleanor Mills.				A Yale University law professor, William Vance, attributes the increase of crime in the United States to the culture's distorted "sentimentality." He points to media portrayals of criminals on trial as the underdog. "In some strange manner," he suggests, "popular psychology comes to see the defendant as a martyr to the cause of liberty."	Aug. 12
The Republican Party is concerned about possible defections from its ranks among rural voters. Responding to constituent opinion, Republican congressmen from seven agricultural states plan to push hard for resurrecting the McNary-Haugen bill. The Coolidge administration is working to craft an alternative farm relief plan....At the Hall-Mills hearing today, the state's star witness, Jane Gibson, a hog farmer popularly known in newspapers as "the pig woman," describes what she saw on the night of the murder. Her testimony—about pistol shots, a woman crying "Don't!" three times, and two likely assailants, a white-haired woman and a man who "looked like a colored man"—impresses the judge.			Secretary of Commerce Herbert Hoover outlines an ambitious plan for the federal government to aid in the development of commercial aviation. The government will provide vital infrastructure—lights for landing fields, charts of air routes, radio information, and the like. "No one private company could afford to provide these services for a great national system," he observes. Private enterprise will fund two new airlines, Transcontinental Airway and Southwestern Airway. The goal is to establish the world's most comprehensive air service within three years.	The International Lawn Tennis Association comments on Susanne Lenglen turning professional: "Her years of unchallenged supremacy have made her too arrogant for ordinary handling." The association welcomes her withdrawal from amateur status and tournaments such as Wimbledon....Although the Pittsburgh Pirates are in first place in the National League, the team has been riven with dissension. Team captain Max Carey is suspended indefinitely without pay after he leads a player revolt against club Vice-President Fred Clarke.	Aug. 13
Observers believe that President Coolidge is gearing up for a 1928 reelection run; his own meticulous silence on the subject is viewed as positive evidence....Chicago utilities magnate Samuel Insull donated $200,000 to various political campaigns during the recent primaries....A grand jury in Canton, Ohio, is investigating whether city police knew of a bootlegger plot to assassinate publisher Don R. Mellett and have since been protecting the murderers.			Entomologists have determined that mosquitoes and flies are more attracted to blondes than brunettes.	The town of Pittsfield, MA, bans women from wearing knickers in public. The law is rushed into effect after female tourists scandalize a local hotel by wearing "knickers rolled up and stockings rolled below the knee."	Aug. 14

F	G	H	I	J
Includes campaigns, elections, federal-state relations, civil rights and liberties, crime, the judiciary, education, healthcare, poverty, urban affairs, and population.	Includes formation and debate of U.S. foreign and defense policies, veterans affairs, and defense spending. (Relations with specific foreign countries are usually found under the region concerned.)	Includes business, labor, agriculture, taxation, transportation, consumer affairs, monetary and fiscal policy, natural resources, pollution and industrial accidents.	Includes worldwide scientific, medical and technological developments, natural phenomena, U.S. weather and natural disasters.	Includes the arts, religion, scholarship, communications media, sports, entertainment, fashions, fads, and social life.

	World Affairs	Europe	Africa & The Middle East	The Americas	Asia & The Pacific
Aug. 15		Spurred by Senator William Borah's critical comments, the Poincarè government is said to be seriously considering the possibility of relieving Germany of most of its war debts and reparations....Berlin has been tormented recently by unusually large swarms of mosquitoes.	Spain plans to demand that Tangier, currently an "international" city, be placed under its protectorate in Morocco, as recompense for policing the zone for the past 17 years....The French Army claims to have completely driven out Syrian rebels holed up in the suburbs of Damascus.		
Aug. 16				Thirty women are arrested in Saltillo, Mexico, after they hurl stones and bricks at a parade of marchers supporting the Calles religious decrees....The FBI arrests General Enrique Estrada, a former secretary of war in Mexico, on the charge of plotting an insurrection against the Calles government.	Chinese generals Wu Pei-fu and Zhang Zuolin have taken the strategically important Nankow Pass, one of the last redoubts of the Kuominchun national army.
Aug. 17		A leading Polish envoy to the Soviet Union reports that the country's "old guard" revolutionaries, devoted to spreading international Communism, are being driven from influence by the Stalin government. He also detects growing anti-Semitism in Soviet policy.		Mexican bishops meet to discuss possible negotiations with the Calles government....Despite pressure from American Catholic groups, President Coolidge is holding to his policy of non-interference in the internal affairs of Mexico.	
Aug. 18				The Catholic hierarchy in Mexico sends an official letter to the Calles government, offering to negotiate modifications of the government religious decrees. The letter surprises and upsets supporters who have urged the Episcopate to stand firm....Canada pledges to fully aid the United States in enforcing the Volstead Act.	
Aug. 19		An attempt to reopen negotiations between British coal miners and coal owners quickly fails. However, a group of 17,000 miners, bucking the union federation, accepts an offer to return to the pits.		President Calles rejects overtures from the Catholic Episcopate, refusing to modify any of his government's religious laws. He advises the bishops to seek redress through the courts or a congressional amendment.	
Aug. 20		"Old Bolshevik" Lev Kamenev, a recent opponent of Joseph Stalin, is removed from his position on the Soviet Council of Labor and Defense....Soviet officials fly to Berlin to expel several prominent German Communists from the party, including vocal leader Ruth Fischer.		Mexican church leaders are optimistic about comments made yesterday by President Calles. They believe the current religious controversy will soon be worked out in the Mexican Congress.	The Kuominchun national army continues to be routed in China, forced to evacuate the city of Kalgan.
Aug. 21		The Soviet government is struggling to part peasants from their grain. The state grain purchasing program has met less than half of its quota for August. The peasants prefer to build up personal reserve stocks, threatening government efforts to plan the nation's economy.			

A	B	C	D	E
Includes developments that affect more than one world region, international organizations and important meetings of world leaders.	Includes all domestic and regional developments in Europe, including the Soviet Union.	Includes all domestic and regional developments in Africa and the Middle East.	Includes all domestic and regional developments in Latin America, the Caribbean, and Canada.	Includes all domestic and regional developments in Asian and Pacific nations (and colonies).

U.S. Politics & Social Issues	U.S. Foreign Policy & Affairs, Defense	U.S. Economy & Environment	Science, Technology & Nature	Culture, Leisure & Lifestyle	
A masked mob barges into a jail in Wytheville, Virginia, and shoots dead an African-American man charged with as saulting a white woman; the body is later hanged from a tree....Polling by the National Economic League indicates that only 43 percent of Americans favor retaining the Volstead Act.			The Aeronautical Chamber of Commerce announces aviation figures for 1925: the United States operated 13 air transport routes, 200,000 passengers flew during the year, and 112 tons of air express mail were delivered.	Screen star Rudolph Valentino is reported in fair condition at a New York City hospital, following emergency surgery for acute appendicitis and a gastric ulcer. The actor collapsed suddenly at his apartment. His doctors expect him to recover....Babe Ruth cracks his 39th homerun of the season.	Aug. 15
President Coolidge is given a 46-pound cherry pie by the Grand Traverse Cherry Growers of Michigan.				At his training camp in Saratoga Springs, NY, heavyweight champion Jack Dempsey convincingly batters several of his sparring partners.	Aug. 16
Canton underworld kingpin Louis Mazer is arrested on the charge of murdering publisher Don R. Mellett.				Rudolph Valentino's doctors say that the next 48 hours will determine his prospects for recovery. The actor told his manager this morning that he feels "marvelous."	Aug. 17
	The War Department appropriates $7 million in funds to build permanent housing structures at 17 army posts, where many of the 40,000 enlisted men currently sleep in tents.		The University of Illinois is offering a course of study in aviation and aeronautical engineering, attracting hundreds of students.	Rudolph Valentino is in serious but favorable condition. The telephone switchboard at his hospital is receiving 2,000 calls per hour from his fans....The St. Louis Cardinals are advancing in the National League pennant race, trailing the first-place Pittsburgh Pirates by only a half game.	Aug. 18
The U.S. Circuit Court of Appeals in Boston rules that the Coast Guard may not search or seize American watercraft located more than 12 miles from the coast, contradicting an earlier decision by the U.S. Circuit Court of Appeals in New York City. The issue is likely to wind up before the Supreme Court....The Negro Business League of Detroit reports that more than 12,000 African-Americans are now employed by the Ford Motor Company.		Promoters connected to two projected Florida resort communities, Fulford-by-the-Sea and Arcadia, are indicted for mail fraud. The 42 real estate officials have received more than $10 million for lots over the past five years.		Rudolph Valentino's doctors report that he is now out of danger, "unless some unexpected development occurs." The actor releases a statement thanking his fans for their well wishes, which he says have hastened his recovery....In London, Will Rogers notes that "you can pick an American bootlegger out of a crowd of Americans every time. He will be the one that is sober."	Aug. 19
President Coolidge, citing anti-trust proceedings against the National Food Products Corporation and the Ward Products Corporation, denies that his administration is in cahoots with Wall Street.	The Bureau of Aeronautics places a large order for new navy airplanes, including 27 battleship fighting planes.		Secretary Hoover advocates a program to build "super highways," with as many as six to eight lanes. Reports indicate that the United States loses $19 million a day because of poor road conditions, including lost man-hours due to traffic congestion and wear and tear on automobiles from stopping and starting.	Rudolph Valentino continues to improve, although his doctors are monitoring him closely. After he pesters them incessantly for a cigarette, they allow him to smoke.... The Cincinnati Reds win their fourth game in a row. The National League pennant race is tight: the St. Louis Cardinals are in first place, the Pittsburgh Pirates are a half game back, and the Reds trail by just one game.	Aug. 20
Following negotiations led by Senator William Borah, amateur strike leader Stanley Weisbord agrees to relinquish his position in the Passaic textiles strike. The American Federation of Labor will take over the effort. The mill owners refused to negotiate with Weisbord, charging him with communism; it is hoped that the more mainstream AFL will be able to win permanent recognition for the workers' union.	.	Statistics indicate that the United States accounts for six percent of the world's total population and possesses 40 percent of the world's total wealth.		Rudolph Valentino's condition has worsened significantly. He has developed pleurisy and is running a temperature of 104 degrees. His doctors are considering a blood transfusion....Edna Ferber's novel *Show Boat* is now in bookstores.	Aug. 21

F	G	H	I	J
Includes campaigns, elections, federal-state relations, civil rights and liberties, crime, the judiciary, education, healthcare, poverty, urban affairs, and population.	Includes formation and debate of U.S. foreign and defense policies, veterans affairs, and defense spending. (Relations with specific foreign countries are usually found under the region concerned.)	Includes business, labor, agriculture, taxation, transportation, consumer affairs, monetary and fiscal policy, natural resources, pollution and industrial accidents.	Includes worldwide scientific, medical and technological developments, natural phenomena, U.S. weather and natural disasters.	Includes the arts, religion, scholarship, communications media, sports, entertainment, fashions, fads, and social life.

	World Affairs	Europe	Africa & The Middle East	The Americas	Asia & The Pacific
Aug. 22	The League of Nations will meet on September 1 to consider the American reservations to the World Court protocol. The most difficult issue is expected to be the demand that the World Court may not offer an advisory opinion on any dispute or question involving the United States, without American consent.	Theodoros Pangalos, dictator of Greece since January, is toppled in a military coup....There are approximately 3,000 destitute American tourists living in Paris; many came to the country to "enjoy life," used up their savings, and are now unable to afford the return home.		Mexican Catholic leaders have been in talks with President Calles; a church spokesman calls the meetings "truly satisfactory" and indicates that the settlement of grievances may be near. The nation enjoys a strife-free Sunday.	
Aug. 23					
Aug. 24		British coal miners who wish to return to the pits are being intimidated and harassed. Mass picketing in Nottinghamshire has convinced several hundred men to stay away; some of their homes have been vandalized with painted messages such as "Scab lives here."...Statistics indicate that for every new church built in England, there are 10 new cinemas and 100 new branch banks constructed.			
Aug. 25		Switzerland expels from the country a "nature" sect given to meandering in the woods and singing hymns while naked.			
Aug. 26		Observers of the Soviet Union point out that numerous commissariats have been subsumed under the centralized power of the Supreme Economic Council, in an effort to increase efficiency and production. This is seen as an indication that the leadership is now focused on developing "Socialist" capitalism.			
Aug. 27		The British coal miners' strike is now 120 days old.	Four prominent Turkish leaders, including a former minister of finance, are hanged for plotting to overthrow the government of President Kemal....A new French high commissioner is appointed in Syria; coinciding with the announcement, rebel tribesmen launch raids in three different regions of the country....Abd-el Krim begins his exile from Morocco.		

A	B	C	D	E
Includes developments that affect more than one world region, international organizations and important meetings of world leaders.	Includes all domestic and regional developments in Europe, including the Soviet Union.	Includes all domestic and regional developments in Africa and the Middle East.	Includes all domestic and regional developments in Latin America, the Caribbean, and Canada.	Includes all domestic and regional developments in Asian and Pacific nations (and colonies).

U.S. Politics & Social Issues	U.S. Foreign Policy & Affairs, Defense	U.S. Economy & Environment	Science, Technology & Nature	Culture, Leisure & Lifestyle	
A freight train wrecks near Wyanet, Illinois, killing eight hoboes who were riding in a boxcar....The National Industrial Conference Board reports immigration statistics for the 1925–26 fiscal year. There has been a notable uptick in the emigration of European professionals to the United States, said to be the result of the continent's continued postwar economic difficulties.				Rudolph Valentino is weakening, but his doctors are giving him "a fighting chance." The actor is apparently unaware of the severity of his condition; he has been talking of plans to go fishing in Maine. The hospital switchboard has been receiving 10 phone calls per minute....Influential educator and former Harvard University president Charles William Eliot dies....The Philadelphia Athletics play the first-ever Sunday ballgame in Philadelphia.	Aug. 22
Recently placed on suspension, the chief of police of Canton, Ohio, has now been fired for failing to expedite the murder investigation of publisher Don R. Mellett. The police chief is widely suspected of having ties to the Canton underworld. Investigators continue to look for evidence of police involvement in the murder.			The American Society of Composers, Authors and Publishers plans to sue the creators of the Vitaphone movie sound-synchronization process for copyright infringement. The first Vitaphone feature, Don Juan, utilizes two copyrighted songs.	Screen star Rudolph Valentino dies at the age of 31; the cause of death is peritonitis and septic endocarditis, an infection of the heart tissues. "He passed peacefully," his doctor tells reporters. "He didn't know he was going." Although the young actor earned $1 million annually, he leaves little in the way of an estate.	Aug. 23
A would-be bank robber in Pittsburgh blows himself up with 50 sticks of dynamite after his demand for $2,000 is refused. A bank security officer is also killed; 120 people are wounded.		Harvard economist William Ripley criticizes American corporations for their lack of financial transparency. He says that stockholders are not "intelligently informed" through complete company reports about balance sheets and dealings. Advance copies of his article about the problem, to be published in the Atlantic Monthly, cause a sharp selloff on Wall Street.	The president of the American Chemical Society asserts that chemical warfare has been unfairly stigmatized. Pointing to the use of mustard gas to clear out machine-gun nests during the World War, he says that such gases are important defensive weapons that ultimately save lives.	Rioting starts outside a church in New York City, where Rudolph Valentino's body is on display. Approximately 75,000 people, most of them women and girls, wait for hours to file past his remains....The streaking Cincinnati Reds have won ten straight games and are in a second-place tie with the St. Louis Cardinals. The Pittsburgh Pirates are in first place.	Aug. 24
Secretary of Agriculture William Jardine seeks to persuade leading bankers to aid farmers in solving their credit problems. He notes that "there will be a farm problem as long as the farmer's dollar is at a discount to purchasing power."			German photographers have developed a process for color photography, using red, yellow, and blue plates....The chief of the Division of Chemistry of the U.S. Public Health Service makes a plea for scientific freedom, uninfluenced by legislatures and philanthropists pushing for "practical results."	The public is barred from viewing Rudolph Valentino's body. The actor's manager cites yesterday's unruly crowd, which became "a three-ring circus." There is also a fear that Fascists and anti-Fascists may clash at the church; both groups are claiming Valentino's legacy....A movement to open 100 playgrounds in New York City is credited with halving the number of children killed or injured in street accidents.	Aug. 25
In Clymer, Pennsylvania, 44 coal miners are killed in an explosion. ...Bail is denied to "Willie" Stevens, the brother of Frances Hall; a card found at the scene of the Hall-Mills murder bears his fingerprint. He is incensed in court today when the special prosecutor notes that his hair and complexion make him "look like a colored man," fitting the description of the assailant given by star witness Jane Gibson.		Industrial production has remained strong this summer, in contrast to the usual seasonal decline.	A Dutch K-XIII submarine successfully navigates the 10,000 miles from Holland to San Francisco, setting a record for submarine travel without a convoy escort.	Two fine new film comedies have debuted: Ernst Lubitsch's urbanely witty So This Is Paris and Buster Keaton's gag-filled Battling Butler....Novelist Carl Van Vechten has published his novel Nigger Heaven, about African-American life in Harlem....Catholic priests in the Newark diocese are forbidden to own or operate automobiles.	Aug. 26
	Navy commander John Rodgers, who unsuccessfully attempted the first trans-Pacific flight from California to Hawaii in 1925, dies after crashing his plane into the Delaware River.	President Coolidge believes in safeguarding the rights of stockholders, but he is not certain the Federal Trade Commission has the legal right to require corporations to provide detailed reports of their financial activities.		Jack Dempsey is favored by two to one odds in his upcoming heavyweight title bout with Gene Tunney....The German Tennis Association has ruled that amateur players cannot compete against professionals, forcing several players to withdraw from the St. Moritz tournament, where Susanne Lenglen plans to play. She charges that she is being "persecuted."	Aug. 27

F	G	H	I	J
Includes campaigns, elections, federal-state relations, civil rights and liberties, crime, the judiciary, education, healthcare, poverty, urban affairs, and population.	Includes formation and debate of U.S. foreign and defense policies, veterans affairs, and defense spending. (Relations with specific foreign countries are usually found under the region concerned.)	Includes business, labor, agriculture, taxation, transportation, consumer affairs, monetary and fiscal policy, natural resources, pollution and industrial accidents.	Includes worldwide scientific, medical and technological developments, natural phenomena, U.S. weather and natural disasters.	Includes the arts, religion, scholarship, communications media, sports, entertainment, fashions, fads, and social life.

	World Affairs	Europe	Africa & The Middle East	The Americas	Asia & The Pacific
Aug. 28		The British Miners' Federation makes a significant concession in their coal strike: they offer to negotiate on wages, but remain firmly opposed to working longer hours.		At the request of the governor of Nicaragua, U.S. Marines land to protect "foreign life and property" in the country. Rebels have been harassing the government, which cannot guarantee the safety of Americans.	A new power is emerging in China: General Chang Kai-shek, who leads the southern Cantonese army. General Wu Pei-fu is reportedly in Hankow attempting to repel an invasion of the southern forces. There is still a political vacuum in Peking.
Aug. 29					The government of Nepal has completed a program to liberate the country's 51,782 slaves. Owners are compensated $35 for adult females and $26 for adult males under the age of 40; older slaves are discounted by 50 percent.
Aug. 30	After lobbying by Secretary of State Frank Kellogg, seven countries, including Luxembourg and Albania, have accepted the U.S. reservations to the World Court protocol. None of the major nations has agreed.				
Aug. 31		At least 300 people drown at the port of Leningrad when an overloaded steamship rams into a breakwater and quickly sinks.			Hankow has reportedly fallen to troops under General Chiang Kai-shek.
Sep. 1		The Mussolini government is undertaking a deflation strategy in an attempt to bolster the Italian lira. Their plan calls for immediately withdrawing 3 billion lire from circulation and significantly increasing the national gold reserve.	A former governor of Angora is hanged for conspiring to overthrow Turkish president Kemal.		
Sep. 2	In Geneva, many nations are taking a conciliatory stance toward the U.S. reservations to the World Court protocol. However, Canada, Sweden, and New Zealand all oppose the fifth reservation, which they claim would give the United States a "veto" over the court.	Italian officials admit that their deflation plans may precipitate an unemployment crisis. "The working classes will suffer, but we are sure all classes will support the Government with full faith in Mussolini's sagacity," a spokesman observes....The British miners' strike may soon be settled. By a majority of more than 300,000 votes, the Miners' Federation authorizes its leaders to negotiate a national agreement.	Following Turkey's example in abandoning the fez, many Egyptians are now wearing European hats rather than the traditional tarboosh.		There are conflicting reports about the fate of General Wu Pei-fu: stories indicate that he has been shot in the chest and killed or, alternately, overthrown by his subordinates and imprisoned in a warship.

A	B	C	D	E
Includes developments that affect more than one world region, international organizations and important meetings of world leaders.	*Includes all domestic and regional developments in Europe, including the Soviet Union.*	*Includes all domestic and regional developments in Africa and the Middle East.*	*Includes all domestic and regional developments in Latin America, the Caribbean, and Canada.*	*Includes all domestic and regional developments in Asian and Pacific nations (and colonies).*

U.S. Politics & Social Issues	U.S. Foreign Policy & Affairs, Defense	U.S. Economy & Environment	Science, Technology & Nature	Culture, Leisure & Lifestyle	
The American Civil Liberties Union has taken up a case in the state of Washington involving a 9-year-old boy whose parents belong to a religious sect, the Elijah Voice Society, who believe that saluting the American flag is an act of idolatry. The boy has refused to participate in patriotic exercises at school.	U.S. soldiers are paid more than any army in the world. The U.S. government spends an average of $2,000 annually per soldier for compensation and subsistence; in comparison, France spends less than $500.	In an effort to supply water for the city of Los Angeles, CA, Senator Hiram Johnson is pushing to build a dam in Boulder Canyon on the Colorado River. Seven western states are jockeying to claim the river's resources.	A hurricane kills dozens of people along the Louisiana coast; seaplanes spot refugees on rafts, as well as bodies floating in the Gulf of Mexico.	In this year's Davis Cup final, France, led by René Lacoste and Henri Cochet, will meet the United States, led by Bill Tilden....Babe Ruth hits his 40th homerun of the season....Fans of heavyweight challenger Gene Tunney are growing concerned: while he has been cut and bruised by his sparring partners, he has yet to deliver a "really telling blow" on any of them. Meanwhile, Jack Dempsey has knocked down several of his training partners.	Aug. 28
Newton Baker, the Secretary of War during the Wilson presidency, urges mutual war-debt cancellation by the United States and its allies. To do otherwise, he warns, will "sow seeds of international distrust, ill-will, and selfishness." He believes Germany should also be forgiven part of its reparation burden....Political observers believe control of the U.S. Senate could switch to the Democrats in the fall elections. Four states are seen as crucial battlegrounds: New York, Missouri, Ohio, and Illinois.				The new edition of the Encyclopedia Britannica features dozens of distinguished contributors, including George Bernard Shaw, H. L. Mencken, Sigmund Freud, Ramsay MacDonald, Leon Trotsky, five members of President Coolidge's cabinet, and 17 Nobel prize-winning scientists.	Aug. 29
Strike sympathizers in Manville, Rhode Island, throw rocks through windows and attempt to set fire to a textile mill. Damages are estimated at $1,000....A white man accused of murder is lynched in Waycross, Georgia....The Children's Bureau of the Labor Department reports that approximately 100,000 babies below the age of one month die in the United States annually. In addition, the nation's maternal mortality rate is among the highest in the industrialized world, at 6.8 per 1,000 live births.			Austrian specialists have determined that cigarette smoking enlarges women's vocal cords, making the female voice "harsh and guttural, instead of soft and sweet."	Babe Ruth signs a contract for $100,000 to tour for twelve weeks this winter on the Pantages vaudeville circuit....The Independent Theaters Clearing House reports a renaissance in regional "little" theaters. There are more than 1,000 theatrical groups performing in the United States, supported by $5 million in annual funding....A German swimmer, Ernst Vierkoetter, sets a new record for swimming the English Channel, beating by almost two hours Gertrude Ederle's mark established earlier this month.	Aug. 30
Citing his obligations to the American taxpayer, President Coolidge rejects Newton Baker's idea to cancel war debts....The NAACP reports that there were 20 lynchings in the nation during the past twelve months, including two lynchings of white men....Police open fire on a crowd of 1,800 textiles strikers in Manville, Rhode Island; no one is killed.				The U.S. Congress is considering setting aside twenty vaults at the Archive Building for the preservation of historically important films, such as footage of William McKinley's inauguration and the signing of the Versailles Treaty....The St. Louis Cardinals sweep the Pittsburgh Pirates in a doubleheader, taking a half-game lead in the National League.	Aug. 31
		Commercial bankruptcies in the United States have declined for four straight months....Utilities expert Henry L. Doherty challenges the national oil conservation policy advocated by the American Petroleum Institute, headed by former secretary of state Charles Evans Hughes. The Hughes plan calls for the oil industry to regulate itself, without federal oversight.		More than 150,000 spectators turn out for a costumed baby parade in Asbury Park, NJ, featuring 750 marching toddlers. Among the popular themes are children dressed as English Channel swimmers, Arabian sheiks, and hooded Ku Klux Klan members. The parade is marshalled by Jackie Ott, a boy from Miami Beach advertised as "the perfect child."	Sep. 1
President Coolidge pays a visit to the American Legion Convalescent Hospital in upstate New York, which cares for World War veterans suffering from tuberculosis. Characteristically, he displays no emotion, although he does salute one bed-ridden soldier.		Leading American tire companies report record production during the summer.		Heavyweight challenger Gene Tunney dismisses reports of opponent Jack Dempsey's ferocity in training sessions. "Dempsey knocks out his sparring partners indiscriminately," Tunney says. "There's no sense in that. I use my sparring partners to practice blows on."	Sep. 2

F	G	H	I	J
Includes campaigns, elections, federal-state relations, civil rights and liberties, crime, the judiciary, education, healthcare, poverty, urban affairs, and population.	Includes formation and debate of U.S. foreign and defense policies, veterans affairs, and defense spending. (Relations with specific foreign countries are usually found under the region concerned.)	Includes business, labor, agriculture, taxation, transportation, consumer affairs, monetary and fiscal policy, natural resources, pollution and industrial accidents.	Includes worldwide scientific, medical and technological developments, natural phenomena, U.S. weather and natural disasters.	Includes the arts, religion, scholarship, communications media, sports, entertainment, fashions, fads, and social life.

	World Affairs	Europe	Africa & The Middle East	The Americas	Asia & The Pacific
Sep. 3	President Coolidge expresses confidence that Geneva will accept the American reservations to the World Court protocol. He points out the issue is one of equality. The League of Nations Council requires unanimous votes, which means that each member nation has a de facto veto when matters contradict its own interests; to join the World Court, the United States simply seeks the same kind of protection....The Canadian *Daily Standard* editorializes about the American "veto": "In international relations the United States wishes to be and intends to be a law unto itself. It is prepared to play only when the play suits it."	In an official letter to Chancellor of the Exchequer Winston Churchill, the British Miners' Federation states its willingness to negotiate about reducing labor costs.		The Catholic Episcopate in Mexico is drawing up a petition proposing changes to the Calles religious laws, to be presented to the national congress. Many observers believe that the church will make little headway; congressional politicians recently cheered a presidential message denying the importance of Catholic concerns.	Chiang Kai-shek's Cantonese army is threatening to overrun the important Central Chinese "triple cities" of Hankou, Wuchang, and Hanyang, which are part of the foreign concessions. The Japanese have mobilized gunboats to protect its nationals.
Sep. 4	Germany is formally offered the sole new permanent seat on the League of Nations Council....Spain's request for a permanent seat is denied. The Spanish government refuses to attend the current sessions, insisting that it must maintain "an attitude of dignified abstention."...Turkey officially requests to enter the League as "representative of the Muslim interests of the world."...A League of Nations special committee begins making a juridical assessment of the American World Court reservations.	The recent conciliatory moves by the British Miners' Federation are rejected by the mine owners, who turn down Winston Churchill's offer to mediate negotiations. The owners are adamant that they will not accept a blanket national strike settlement; rather, they wish to negotiate separate district agreements....Rumors out of Spain indicate that General Miguel Primo de Rivera's government is on the verge of toppling.			Another Chinese general has entered into the warlords' contest for power: Sun Chang-fang, who controls five eastern provinces, is now on the move in central China....A typhoon devastates Japan's east coast, killing 50 passengers on a Tokyo train that overturns.
Sep. 5		General Primo de Rivera declares martial law in Spain. Artillery Corps officers and a garrison of military cadets are reportedly mutinying against the government.			Contrary to earlier reports, General Wu Pei-fu has not been killed in recent fighting, although his forces are collapsing in Central China.
Sep. 6		Winston Churchill is pressuring British mine owners to abandon their intransigent position in the coal strike....A makeshift movie theater—in a garage loft—in the village of Dromcolliher, Ireland, catches fire; 47 people are trampled to death trying to escape....The Berlin premiere of the Hollywood movie Ben Hur is attended by dignitaries including Chancellor Marx and several diplomats, attracting a huge crowd outside the theater.			Two British warships draw heavy gunfire on the Yangtze River near Hankou in China. In recent days two British merchant steamers on the Yangtze were seized, allegedly by forces loyal to Wu Pei-fu, who has previously been regarded as an important British ally.
Sep. 7	Spain announces that it is resigning from the League of Nations.	The uprising of artillery officers against the Spanish government has been quelled. The country's state of martial law is lifted.		The Mexican Catholic Episcopate submits a petition to the national congress, requesting "liberty for all religions" and several modifications of the Calles laws. Simultaneously, the Episcopate releases a pastoral letter to the faithful urging them to resist the laws.	Seven British sailors are killed attempting to liberate the two merchant vessels seized near Hankou.
Sep. 8	The special commission at Geneva is deadlocked on the issue of the American World Court reservations.	The Soviet press has been unusually outspoken about mismanagement of the national economy, particularly by the Foreign Trade Monopoly Department. Not coincidentally, the department was administered until recently by Lev Kamenev, ousted from power by Joseph Stalin.		The Mexican Episcopate has granted permission to 38 priests to leave the country for dioceses in Europe and Cuba. Observers believe that the church hierarchy expects a protracted struggle with the Calles government.	

A	B	C	D	E
Includes developments that affect more than one world region, international organizations and important meetings of world leaders.	*Includes all domestic and regional developments in Europe, including the Soviet Union.*	*Includes all domestic and regional developments in Africa and the Middle East.*	*Includes all domestic and regional developments in Latin America, the Caribbean, and Canada.*	*Includes all domestic and regional developments in Asian and Pacific nations (and colonies).*

U.S. Politics & Social Issues	U.S. Foreign Policy & Affairs, Defense	U.S. Economy & Environment	Science, Technology & Nature	Culture, Leisure & Lifestyle	
				Chicago is enforcing a new curfew law for children under the age of 16. Several married women in their twenties, wearing bobbed hair, rolled stockings, and short skirts, have been mistaken for children and inadvertently arrested....Harry Greb, a former middleweight boxing champion, is unimpressed with Jack Dempsey's recent workouts. "He is missing too much and he is being hit too often by sparring partners who are not particularly brilliant. He impresses me as all dried out," Greb observes.	Sep. 3
President Coolidge does not believe that any amendments are necessary to current American anti-trust laws, which he finds are "fully protective of the public."	The U.S. Army is using correspondence courses to train 23,000 reserve officers.	Twelve utilities conglomerates control approximately two-thirds of the American power supply. Samuel Insull's interests control more than 10 percent....According to statistics, the American farmer's dollar is worth 87 cents in purchasing power.		As the follow-up to his bestseller about Jesus, *The Man Nobody Knows*, Bruce Barton publishes *The Book Nobody Knows*, about the Bible.	Sep. 4
A speeding tourist train derails and plummets into a river bed near the Royal Gorge in Colorado, killing at least 20 people....From the presidential camp in the Adirondacks, the Coolidge administration has transmitted news dispatches totaling 1.2 million words. Five telegraph operators have maintained around-the-clock service.		The stock exchange index reaches a yearly high....The Federal Oil Conservation Board estimates that the United States has 4.5 billion barrels of oil reserves—a six years' supply. The board warns that new conservation and consumption measures—or increased foreign trade and exploitation of foreign fields—will be necessary to meet future demand.	Swiss physicians believe they have developed a method that will enable animal blood to be safely transfused into humans.	Football star Red Grange makes his movie debut, starring in *One Minute to Play*....Cleveland Indians first baseman George Burns sets a major league record when he hits his sixtieth double of the season.... In Paris, a French father commits suicide after his two daughters bob their hair against his command.	Sep. 5
The Chicago Federation of Musicians is on strike, with more than 3,000 members walking out of movie houses, dance halls, radio stations, and orchestra pits. Labor Day audiences are drastically smaller at the city's 400 movie theaters, which are forced to post "Pictures Only; No Music" notices.		The Bureau of Foreign and Domestic Commerce finds that American international trade has catapulted in recent years. Exports to South America have increased by 250 percent since 1922; during the same timeframe, sales to South Africa have increased 168 percent. On the other hand, exports to Europe during the past year have declined.		Following in the footsteps of Suzanne Lenglen, Mary Browne, a former U.S. tennis champion, announces that she is turning professional....A 15-year-old New Jersey girl commits suicide after she is unable to get a bobbed haircut for her first day of classes in high school.	Sep. 6
A corruption trial begins for Harry M. Daugherty, Warren Harding's attorney general, and former alien property custodian Thomas W. Miller; the men are charged with defrauding the government and taking approximately $450,000 in kickbacks in connection with a 1921 alien property case.		Prominent Wall Street speculator W. C. Durant predicts an impending "great bull market," even though there has already been a substantial run-up in stock prices. He observes: "Several of America's leading corporations have gained public confidence and good-will to such an extent that, greatly increased values may consistently be expected for many years to come."	The American Academy of Physiotherapy prescribe golf as the best form of exercise for people suffering from high blood pressure.	"Dr. Sterling C. Wyman," who spoke frequently with reporters about Rudolph Valentino's funeral arrangements, has been revealed to be a chronic impersonator, known to authorities under eleven different aliases. He is actually Ethan Weinberg, who will now be under the care of a psychologist.	Sep. 7
Senator Irvine Lenroot from Wisconsin, a Republican with close ties to the Coolidge administration, is defeated by his primary challenger, Progressive John J. Blaine. The loss is seen as further evidence that the balance of Republican power is shifting to Progressives and that Democrats may gain control of the Senate in the upcoming election.			The General Electric Research Laboratory has developed an atomic-hydrogen flame, "the hottest flame known," which will enable the welding of metals that have been considered impossible to fuse.		Sep. 8

F	G	H	I	J
Includes campaigns, elections, federal-state relations, civil rights and liberties, crime, the judiciary, education, healthcare, poverty, urban affairs, and population.	*Includes formation and debate of U.S. foreign and defense policies, veterans affairs, and defense spending. (Relations with specific foreign countries are usually found under the region concerned.)*	*Includes business, labor, agriculture, taxation, transportation, consumer affairs, monetary and fiscal policy, natural resources, pollution and industrial accidents.*	*Includes worldwide scientific, medical and technological developments, natural phenomena, U.S. weather and natural disasters.*	*Includes the arts, religion, scholarship, communications media, sports, entertainment, fashions, fads, and social life.*

	World Affairs	Europe	Africa & The Middle East	The Americas	Asia & The Pacific
Sep. 9	The League of Nations Military, Naval, and Air Preparatory Committee, working on the issue of international disarmament, has made little progress and decides to adjourn until next year.				
Sep. 10	British economist John Maynard Keynes argues that the Dawes war reparations plan has become an exercise in circularity, creating an artificial equilibrium. "America lends to Germany, Germany transfers the equivalent to the Allies and the Allies pay it back to Washington—nothing real passes and nobody is a penny the worse."	The Poincarè government in France is implementing a series of cost-reducing measures. These range from closing down dozens of military installations to requiring bread loaves to use less flour....A Frenchman, Georges Michel, sets a new record for swimming the English Channel—the third time the record has been broken in the last five weeks.		Officials in the Calles government assert that President Coolidge's hands-off stance toward Mexico is proof of the government's legitimacy. Calles policies are "based strictly upon the principles of international law." Mexican Catholics are angered that the American government has not exerted pressure in the religious controversy.	The United States has ordered four gunboats to Hankou to protect American citizens along the Yangtze River. There is reportedly intense animosity in the region toward the British.
Sep. 11		An anarchist throws a bomb at Premier Mussolini's motor car; it bounces off the left side and explodes in the street, seriously injuring eight bystanders. Mussolini is unharmed....General Primo de Rivera is holding a nationwide plebiscite that will allow Spanish voters to express their opinion of his government. Observers point out that this amounts to a "solemnly organized vote of self-confidence" for Primo de Rivera, with the result a "foregone conclusion." The plebiscite will enfranchise women above the age of 18—the first time they have been able to vote in Spain.			
Sep. 12					Three Chinese generals, Wu Pei-fu, Zhang Zuolin, and Sun Chang-fang, are apparently banding together to fight against the Cantonese army of Chang Kai-shek.
Sep. 13		British mine owners again reject Winston Churchill's efforts to open government-mediated talks to settle the coal strike....Speaking about the repeated failed assassination attempts against him, Mussolini remarks: "My stars protect me as Italy is protected. I shall die a natural death."...German police have uncovered a narcotics ring, believed to be the major supplier of cocaine to the United States. Among those arrested are Berlin's official chemist and two Russian noblemen.			
Sep. 14		In England, 977,600 unemployed claimants were on the dole in 1925, paid an average of $5 per person weekly.	The Egyptian government is being pressured to prosecute an Egyptian University professor who published a controversial book on pre-Islamic poetry. Muslims regard the book as an insult to their religion. A stormy parliamentary session ends with the cabinet refusing to take action.		

A	B	C	D	E
Includes developments that affect more than one world region, international organizations and important meetings of world leaders.	*Includes all domestic and regional developments in Europe, including the Soviet Union.*	*Includes all domestic and regional developments in Africa and the Middle East.*	*Includes all domestic and regional developments in Latin America, the Caribbean, and Canada.*	*Includes all domestic and regional developments in Asian and Pacific nations (and colonies).*

U.S. Politics & Social Issues	U.S. Foreign Policy & Affairs, Defense	U.S. Economy & Environment	Science, Technology & Nature	Culture, Leisure & Lifestyle	
		The Treasury Department reports that there are more than 11,000 millionaires in the United States. New York is the state with the most, at an estimated 2,800; North Dakota is the only state with none.	French pilot Rene Fonck plans to make a non-stop flight from New York to Paris in the enormous three-engine Sikorsky plane, which is capable of generating 480 horsepower. An American military observer notes that current bomber planes can "just stagger off the ground" with one 4,000 pound bomb, whereas Fonck's plane can "easily take up two 4,000-pound bombs and gasoline sufficient for a long flight."	In the opening singles matches of the Davis Cup final, Americans Bill Tilden and William Johnston easily dominate French players Jean Borota and Rene Lacoste....French tennis star Paul Feret announces that he is signing on with Suzanne Lenglen's promoter and turning professional....Danish critic Georg Brandes's controversial book *Jesus: a Myth* is published in English translation.	Sep. 9
President Coolidge will not interject himself into the fall elections and will not speak about any candidate.				Norma Smallwood from Tulsa, OK, wins the Miss America Pageant in Atlantic City. Stage personality DeWolf Hopper serves as the emcee,....For the seventh straight year, the U.S. tennis team wins the Davis Cup.	Sep. 10
Four Franciscan nuns from Massachusetts are arrested for attempting to smuggle $5,000 in fine laces, hidden in their clothes, across the Canadian border.		Business theorist Roger W. Babson predicts an economic recession and "possibly a panic" in the United States within the next three years. While he acknowledges that present business conditions are good, he points to "three flies in the ointment": "first, the foreign situation, which is still very bad; second, installment buying, which is eating the vitals out of the American people, and, third, the fact that manufacturing capacity of almost all industries exceeds consuming power."	The United States operates 80,000 public transportation buses, compared to 4,500 buses in France and 18,000 in England....New American automobiles are getting 30 miles to the gallon of gasoline and require only four oil changes per year.	The Department of Agriculture reports that five-cent cigars are hugely popular; more than 281 million were produced during July alone. Meanwhile, chewing tobacco use has declined.... Acclaimed Southern novelist Ellen Glasgow publishes *The Romantic Tragedians*....Prominent British music critic Ernest Newman, writing in the *Sunday Times*, lambastes American jazz. "The brains of the whole lot of [jazz composers] would not fill the lining of Johann Strauss's hat."	Sep. 11
Chicago gunmen steal $135,000 from a federal mail car....In the recent U.S. Senate primaries, candidates typically spent less than $10,000. For example, Smith Brookhart's successful Republican campaign in Iowa spent $1,479, and Alabama Democratic winner Hugo Black spent $8,700.					Sep. 12
A Ku Klux Klan national parade in Washington, DC., draws only 15,000 marchers–fewer than half the number that participated in last year's march....Lawyers for Nicola Sacco and Bartolomeo Vanzetti petition the Superior Court of Massachusetts for a retrial; their action is based on a confession by Celestino Madeiros, a condemned murderer, that his gang committed the payroll killings for which Sacco and Vanzetti have been convicted.				The American musical comedy *Rose Marie* plays its 625th show at London's Drury Lane Theater, setting a performance record. The play has drawn more than a million theatergoers during its run.... Neither the St. Louis Cardinals or the Cincinnati Reds has been able to pull away in the National League pennant race. The Cardinals just lost three out of four games against the Boston Braves, while the Reds have followed four straight losses with five straight wins.	Sep. 13
President Coolidge conferences with Herbert Tily, president of the National Retail Dry Goods Association. Tily tells Coolidge that businessmen prize stability: "We feel that legislation destined to reach down and change fundamental things, of an experimental nature, would be exceedingly bad."			The British freighter *Loyal Citizen*, 400 miles off the coast of Florida, signals an SOS that its "rails [are] awash." There have been reports from steamships about a huge tropical storm brewing in the Caribbean.	The General Federation of Women's Clubs believes that club training will prepare women to be successful political activists. "The modern, efficient, studious clubwoman is not easily fooled," a spokeswoman notes. "The trained mentality of millions of women directed toward better laws, backed by the power of the vote, will be a thing to reckon with."...The Cincinnati Reds take a slim half-game lead in the National League.	Sep. 14

F	G	H	I	J
Includes campaigns, elections, federal-state relations, civil rights and liberties, crime, the judiciary, education, healthcare, poverty, urban affairs, and population.	Includes formation and debate of U.S. foreign and defense policies, veterans affairs, and defense spending. (Relations with specific foreign countries are usually found under the region concerned.)	Includes business, labor, agriculture, taxation, transportation, consumer affairs, monetary and fiscal policy, natural resources, pollution and industrial accidents.	Includes worldwide scientific, medical and technological developments, natural phenomena, U.S. weather and natural disasters.	Includes the arts, religion, scholarship, communications media, sports, entertainment, fashions, fads, and social life.

	World Affairs	Europe	Africa & The Middle East	The Americas	Asia & The Pacific
Sep. 15		Spanish officials estimate that some 6 million people—more than half of eligible voters—took part in the plebiscite affirming General Primo de Rivera's government. Whether that number is satisfactory is debatable: negative votes were not allowed to be cast, and the results can be interpreted as meaning that almost half the nation stayed away from the polls in rejection of the government.			
Sep. 16		During the past year there have been 120 books published in Germany on the topic of the United States, with titles such as *America, Thou Art Happier Than We!* Many of the books discuss the American "economic miracle," which is attributed to industrial standardization and the average citizen's "naivete" about work, regarding it "not as an inevitable evil but as good 'fun,' a means of getting some 'thrill' out of life."			
Sep. 17		Arkansas Senator Thaddeus Stevens, recently returned from Europe, reports that the French are desecrating the graves of American servicemen. "Go into these cemeteries and you will find ribald and insulting remarks chalked or penciled on many of the little white crosses," he states.	Spain withdraws its demand that Tangier be incorporated into its protectorate in Morocco.		In Tokyo, an Asian man attempts to assassinate the visiting Princess Louise of Sweden, throwing a knife at her during a luncheon. The knife strikes an ambassador's son, who survives....There have been a series of agitations and boycotts against the British in Chinese port cities.
Sep. 18	A World Court commission guarantees the United States full equality with other members of the Council of the League of Nations. The commission sees this as an acceptable substitute for America's fifth reservation.	The French are complaining about new government food policies that require them to eat "adversity bread," made with cornmeal, potatoes, and limited flour.			Southern Cantonese troops besiege the city of Wuchang, near Hankou; 21 Americans are reportedly trapped there, with a dwindling food supply.
Sep. 19					
Sep. 20	President Coolidge opposes Geneva's counter-proposal to the U.S. World Court reservations. Dismissing the offer of "equality," Senator Frank Willis, a close Coolidge ally, observes: "If we wanted to be on an equal footing we could join the League of Nations. We are not a member of the League, nor are we going to become a member."				Cantonese troops open fire on a U.S. gunboat on the Yangtze River, wounding three sailors.

A	B	C	D	E
Includes developments that affect more than one world region, international organizations and important meetings of world leaders.	*Includes all domestic and regional developments in Europe, including the Soviet Union.*	*Includes all domestic and regional developments in Africa and the Middle East.*	*Includes all domestic and regional developments in Latin America, the Caribbean, and Canada.*	*Includes all domestic and regional developments in Asian and Pacific nations (and colonies).*

U.S. Politics & Social Issues	U.S. Foreign Policy & Affairs, Defense	U.S. Economy & Environment	Science, Technology & Nature	Culture, Leisure & Lifestyle	
In Colorado, Republican senator Rice Means, heavily supported by the Ku Klux Klan, is defeated in the state primary. Political observers believe this demonstrates the Klan's growing weakness; Colorado has been seen as an organizational stronghold.			The largest radio hook-up yet attempted, with 33 stations covering the entire nation, successfully broadcasts the Radio Industry Dinner from the Hotel Astor in New York City, where keynote speaker Vice President Charles Dawes delivers an address attacking the use of filibusters in the Senate.	Among popular vaudeville acts in New York City are Borrah Minnevitch's harmonica players, the illusionist Long Tack Sam, the Yip Yip Yaphankers, and the Dancers from Clownland.	Sep. 15
The Quapaw Indian tribes of Oklahoma file suit against several mining companies, alleging that former Secretary of the Interior Albert Fall leased tribal lands with valuable lead and zinc ore deposits to the companies over Quapaw protests.		Kansas senator Arthur Capper observes that 23 percent of the nation's wealth is concentrated within a 500-mile radius of New York City, while the western states possess 14 percent of the national income.	The National Weather Bureau warns of an approaching hurricane, now passing the Bahamas.	Bill Tilden, for six straight years the U.S. Open tennis champion, is finally defeated by Henri Cochet of France....Even though the Cincinnati Reds shut out the New York Giants, the St. Louis Cardinals regain their first-place tie after sweeping a doubleheader from the Philadelphia Phillies.	Sep. 16
Arrest warrants are issued for evangelist Aimee Semple McPherson, her mother, and five associates. They are charged with intent to carry out a criminal conspiracy regarding McPherson's alleged kidnapping. It is believed that she spent much of her "captivity" at a cottage in Carmel, CA, with a companion, Kenneth Ormiston.		Federal Trade Commissioner William Humphreys announces plans to "war" against false advertising in American newspapers and magazines.			Sep. 17
Prosecutors have outlined their case for the upcoming Hall-Mills murder trial: they believe that Frances Hall's two brothers, Henry Stevens and Willie Stevens, were the killers. A week before the slayings, the family had learned about the Hall-Mills relationship and confronted the minister, who announced that he wanted a divorce. On the night of the murder, the brothers trailed Hall to his assignation with Mills, shot him three times, and slit her throat. Frances Hall and a cousin, Henry Carpender, were "passive" participants at the scene.			A hurricane with 130-mile-per-hour winds and 20-foot waves strikes Miami. Reports are still sketchy, but it is believed that at least 75 people died and 2,000 buildings were destroyed. The town of Miami Beach is under three feet of water, and every boat in the harbor has been sunk.	Among the notable people who will attend the Dempsey-Tunney bout on the 23rd are Vice President Dawes, three members of the Coolidge cabinet, two senators, five state governors, four members of the Roosevelt family, actors Charlie Chaplin and Tom Mix, Broadway impresario Florenz Ziegfeld, publisher Joseph Pulitzer, and 2,000 millionaires....Rene Lacoste wins the U.S. Open tennis championship.	Sep. 18
Herbert Hoover, who has gained a reputation as a "one-man cabinet," the most active member of the Coolidge administration, will campaign for Republican congressional candidates this fall. His itinerary calls for him to deliver speeches in several midwestern and western states, where he has taken a leading role in developing aviation and irrigation projects.	In conjunction with the Navy Department, Yale University has established a four-year course of study in naval science and tactics.		Yesterday's hurricane rampaged for nine hours, destroying cities and towns for sixty miles along the Atlantic Coast from Miami to Palm Beach. The death toll is estimated at between 500 and 1,000, with perhaps 3,000 people injured and 38,000 left homeless.	Mary Pickford is starring in the film *Sparrows*.	Sep. 19
Extensive flooding in Sioux City and other parts of Iowa have caused $10 million in damage....Gunmen in several automobiles rake Al Capone's Hawthorne Inn in Chicago with machine-gun fire; two people are shot, but the mobster, eating in a nearby café, is unharmed.			The hurricane is now over Alabama and Mississippi, losing power as it moves inland. The death toll in Miami is estimated at 325, many of them swimmers who had gone to the beach, believing the storm was ended when they were in the "eye." President Coolidge appeals for relief contributions, to be administered through the Red Cross....The city of San Francisco is planning to build a bridge across San Francisco Bay to Oakland, at an estimated cost of $100 million.	"Hobo" writer Jim Tully has published his hard-boiled novel *Jarnegan*....Singer Kate Smith is getting rave notices for her Broadway debut in the musical comedy *Honeymoon Lane*....Several college football teams have decided to use the "huddle system" this year in running their offenses.	Sep. 20

F	G	H	I	J
Includes campaigns, elections, federal-state relations, civil rights and liberties, crime, the judiciary, education, healthcare, poverty, urban affairs, and population.	Includes formation and debate of U.S. foreign and defense policies, veterans affairs, and defense spending. (Relations with specific foreign countries are usually found under the region concerned.)	Includes business, labor, agriculture, taxation, transportation, consumer affairs, monetary and fiscal policy, natural resources, pollution and industrial accidents.	Includes worldwide scientific, medical and technological developments, natural phenomena, U.S. weather and natural disasters.	Includes the arts, religion, scholarship, communications media, sports, entertainment, fashions, fads, and social life.

	World Affairs	Europe	Africa & The Middle East	The Americas	Asia & The Pacific
Sep. 21	President Coolidge insists that the World Court reservations are non-negotiable. He says that the fifth reservation clearly states that the Court council cannot provide advisory opinions on any matter in which there is a U.S. interest without American consent. The reservation is intended as a bulwark for the United States against the Court's decisions.				
Sep. 22		For the sixth time since late April, King George declares a state of emergency in England due to the ongoing coal strike.			The Chinese city of Nanchang has been occupied by the Cantonese army. Rumors indicate that Wu Pei-fu has fled far to the north, effectively removing him as a political force.
Sep. 23				By an overwhelming majority of 171 to one, the Mexican Chamber of Deputies rejects the Catholic Episcopate's petition to revise the Calles religious laws.	
Sep. 24	The Coolidge administration is pessimistic about America joining the World Court.	The African-American musical revue *Blackbirds*, starring Florence Mills, is a smash hit in London.			
Sep. 25	The League of Nations adjourns, proclaiming Germany's entry as a major accomplishment advancing international understanding.	The British Board of Trade estimates that the coal strike has now cost the country $1 billion.			The Chinese Encyclopedia is being republished—at 800 volumes and 800,000 pages....More than 700,000 workers have joined labor unions in southern China during the past two years.
Sep. 26		The British coal strike has precipitated a depression in the nation's heavy industries, which lack necessary fuel. Other sectors of the economy, including chemicals, shipping, and the cotton and woolen trades, are holding up fairly well.			
Sep. 27		British prime minister Stanley Baldwin rebukes mine owners for turning down the government's offer to establish a national arbitration tribunal to settle the coal strike. "They acted with stupidity and want of courtesy to the Government," he tells Parliament, to cheers.		Following their failure in the national congress, Mexican Catholics are launching a major grassroots effort—featuring parades, petitions, circulars, and public meetings—to demand a "fair deal." The Mexico City press is sympathetic.	

A	B	C	D	E
Includes developments that affect more than one world region, international organizations and important meetings of world leaders.	Includes all domestic and regional developments in Europe, including the Soviet Union.	Includes all domestic and regional developments in Africa and the Middle East.	Includes all domestic and regional developments in Latin America, the Caribbean, and Canada.	Includes all domestic and regional developments in Asian and Pacific nations (and colonies).

U.S. Politics & Social Issues	U.S. Foreign Policy & Affairs, Defense	U.S. Economy & Environment	Science, Technology & Nature	Culture, Leisure & Lifestyle	
There will be 27 Republican Senate seats in play during the fall elections, and the Republican Senatorial Campaign Committee expects to retain almost all of them. "Coolidge and prosperity" is the party's refrain.		The insurance industry expects to pay out $175 million to hurricane victims in Florida.	French pilot Rene Fonck's attempt to fly his huge Sikorsky airplane from New York City to Paris quickly ends in disaster. The overloaded plane is unable to take off and crashes just beyond the runway, bursting into flames and killing two crew members....Reports indicate that no building is left intact in Fort Lauderdale following the hurricane.		Sep. 21
The National Democratic Senatorial Committee asserts that Republicans are "whistling to keep up their courage" about the upcoming congressional elections. A spokesman points to depressed conditions in agriculture and the textiles industry, compounded by the Coolidge administration's "do-nothing attitude."		Cotton prices have continued to decline, reaching a seasonal low today....The automobile industry sets a seasonal production record, rolling out 429,394 vehicles in August.	Thomas Edison predicts that there is no future for music on the radio. The sound quality is poor and badly distorted, he asserts, noting that the radio medium is better suited for news reports and ballgames. Once the "radio fad" passes, he is certain that Americans will return to the superior-sounding phonograph.	Boxing experts uniformly expect Jack Dempsey to win tomorrow's heavyweight bout. He features a devastating left hook and is judged to have superior speed, strength, and endurance. Gene Tunney is viewed as a defensive boxer, a "counter-fighter" with the bad habit of telegraphing his punches.	Sep. 22
The Red Cross has collected $1.7 million in private donations to help Florida hurricane victims, although at least $4 million is necessary to provide suitable relief....The state of Florida is conscripting the unemployed to haul off hurricane debris. People on the streets in Miami unable to show proof of employment are being put to work by deputized American Legionnaires.			Rene Fonck is being criticized for his lack of experience as an experimental test pilot, especially flying heavy planes. Fonck has enjoyed a successful career as a decorated fighter pilot.	Fighting in a rainstorm, Gene Tunney wins the world heavyweight boxing championship, defeating Jack Dempsey in a ten-round decision. Tunney dominates the entire match, surprising his critics with his aggressiveness, while Dempsey seems listless. "I have no alibis," the ex-champ says afterward....Tunney earns $250,000 for the fight, compared to Dempsey's $700,000 payout.	Sep. 23
In Ironwood, Michigan, 43 iron miners are trapped 700 feet below the surface after a cave-in....Four textile workers are being held in Passaic, New Jersey, on the charge that they set off bombs to intimidate non-strikers....An Episcopalian newspaper moralizes that the Florida hurricane was a divine judgment on the nation's "lavish, quick prosperity."		The Rockefeller Fund is financing a massive study of petroleum and its chemical properties, to be undertaken by Princeton University and the American Petroleum Institute.... There is an early snowfall today in the Midwest.		The St. Louis Cardinals clinch their first-ever National League pennant by winning seven of their last ten games. Meanwhile, the rival Cincinnati Reds have been in a tailspin, losing six straight. The Cardinals did not even reach first place in the tightly contested race until August 23.	Sep. 24
Construction engineers believe that Florida's poor-quality housing stock—primarily cement block buildings and wooden bungalows thrown up during the real estate boom—was a major contributor to the hurricane's destructiveness. Total building losses are estimated at $50 million.			The American Society for the Control of Cancer, bringing together 100 international experts, releases a statement describing generally accepted opinions about the disease. While admitting that the cause of cancer is not understood, specialists agree that it is not hereditary, infectious, or contagious and that early detection and treatment are paramount for recovery.	Big Ten college football officials ban ticket scalping, gambling, and "violation of the Prohibition law" by fans....The National Hockey League admits two new teams, the Chicago Black Hawks and the Detroit Cougars....Some American colleges and universities report receiving far more student applications than they can accept.	Sep. 25
Rescue crews in Ironwood, Michigan, believe they have heard tapping on water pipes—a sign that the trapped iron miners are alive....American automobile death rates continue to climb. According to the Commerce Department, in 66 major cities this year there have been 18.9 fatalities per 100,000 population compared to 17.9 for last year.				The major league baseball season ends, with the New York Yankees and St. Louis Cardinals headed to the World Series. Babe Ruth's 47 homeruns dwarf the output of his peers; the next highest total is 21 homers, posted by Hack Wilson of the Chicago Cubs. Heinie Manush finishes with the highest batting average at .378; Ruth is close behind at .372. Among the pitching stars are Herb Pennock, George Uhle, Ray Kremer, and Flint Rhem. Paul Waner is the outstanding rookie, with a .336 batting average.	Sep. 26
The town of Moore Haven, Florida, in the Everglades, was the worst hit by the hurricane per capita. Almost the entire population was affected: 160 are dead, 150 are missing, and most of the rest are injured....Florida citrus groves suffered $15 million is damage.		Texas has surpassed California as America's leading oil-producing state.		Among the new football rules this season is one declaring the ball dead when it goes out of bounds....Dancer Adele Astaire predicts that the rage for the Charleston will continue, as the dance evolves into new forms such as a "kickless" version.	Sep. 27

F	G	H	I	J
Includes campaigns, elections, federal-state relations, civil rights and liberties, crime, the judiciary, education, healthcare, poverty, urban affairs, and population.	Includes formation and debate of U.S. foreign and defense policies, veterans affairs, and defense spending. (Relations with specific foreign countries are usually found under the region concerned.)	Includes business, labor, agriculture, taxation, transportation, consumer affairs, monetary and fiscal policy, natural resources, pollution and industrial accidents.	Includes worldwide scientific, medical and technological developments, natural phenomena, U.S. weather and natural disasters.	Includes the arts, religion, scholarship, communications media, sports, entertainment, fashions, fads, and social life.

	World Affairs	Europe	Africa & The Middle East	The Americas	Asia & The Pacific
Sep. 28			Confusion over French and Spanish territorial borders in Morocco is causing problems with rebellious tribesmen. A tribal group claiming French affiliation recently attacked a Spanish army contingent attempting to occupy their land.		The situation in China continues to deteriorate for westerners. British residents are evacuating Szechwan province, the center for American and English missionary activities. There are reports that six missionaries have been kidnapped, while 500 missionaries serving in the region are isolated and unable to evacuate. Rumors hold that a Chinese secret society will pay $50 for every foreigner killed.
Sep. 29					
Sep. 30					A typhoon along the Ianton River in Hong Kong drowns 2,000 fishermen.
Oct. 1	President Coolidge reasserts that only "unconditional acceptance" by Geneva of the American World Court reservations is acceptable. He will make no final decision about the issue before conferring with World Court backers in the U.S. Senate.	The school year opens in Spain, where the large majority of students will be unable to attend classes because of the insufficient number of grammar schools.			
Oct. 2		British foreign secretary Austen Chamberlain is in Italy meeting with Premier Mussolini. He tells reporters that while he finds Fascism "unsuited" for England, he admires Mussolini's forceful patriotism and personal charm....The Italian government reinstitutes capital punishment, which has been banned in the country since 1888. The measure is taken to deter would-be assassins of Mussolini....French premiere Poincare admits that the government was on the verge of bankruptcy when he took office in July.	Prince Faisal, the son of Hussein bin Ali, the King of the Hedjaz, is forbidden to take part in inauguration ceremonies at the new mosque in Southfields, England. The ceremonies will be open to unbelievers, an action that orthodox Muslims find heretical.		Besieged troops defending the city of Wuchang in China open fire on Red Cross ships intended to rescue women and children; there are no reported casualties.
Oct. 3		Four major opposition figures in the Soviet Union—Leon Trotksy, Grigory Zinoviev, Karl Radek, and Lev Kamenev, all recently removed from positions of influence by Joseph Stalin—are speaking out against the Communist Party's autocratic leadership....A beneficiary of the British coal strike is the German steel industry, where production is up significantly for the year.	Only one rebellious district remains to be pacified by the Spanish Army in Morocco, where more than 30,000 rifles have been recently confiscated....A statue of Turkish president Kemal is unveiled in Constantinople, defying Muslim beliefs about blasphemous human images.		Three American missionaries are kidnapped in Hunan province in China.

A	B	C	D	E
Includes developments that affect more than one world region, international organizations and important meetings of world leaders.	Includes all domestic and regional developments in Europe, including the Soviet Union.	Includes all domestic and regional developments in Africa and the Middle East.	Includes all domestic and regional developments in Latin America, the Caribbean, and Canada.	Includes all domestic and regional developments in Asian and Pacific nations (and colonies).

U.S. Politics & Social Issues	U.S. Foreign Policy & Affairs, Defense	U.S. Economy & Environment	Science, Technology & Nature	Culture, Leisure & Lifestyle	
A federal circuit court rules on the Teapot Dome case, finding that the leasing of public lands to a private oil company in 1922, arranged by the Harding administration, was fraudulent. Former Secretary of the Interior Albert B. Fall is specifically cited for corruption....The Indiana Senate is investigating state political corruption linked to former Ku Klux Klan Grand Dragon D. C. Stephenson....The 43 iron miners in Ironwood, MI, are rescued after spending 120 hours trapped below ground.				Anita Loos's comedy *Gentlemen Prefer Blondes* makes its Broadway debut....The International Motion Picture Congress, an offshoot of the League of Nations, meets in Paris. Most of the congress's energies are devoted to denouncing the American film industry.	Sep. 28
The Miami Citizens' Relief Committee has established a commission to punish landlords seeking to profiteer from the homeless situation. There have been thousands of complaints of gouging in the past few days.			Western businessmen are pressuring the Coolidge administration to provide more federal funds for forest fire prevention. In the past year there have been 7,400 forest fires in the northwestern states, causing more than $5 million in timber losses. Private interests have footed approximately 85 percent of the costs for fire prevention in the region.	Columbia University president Nicholas Murray Butler warns against "specialization" in education, noting that students are neglecting the liberal arts to concentrate on "the business at hand." "The student who surrenders to specialization may get a practical training, an efficient training, but not an education."	Sep. 29
Floridians are angry at Governor John Martin and the State Drainage Board, accusing them of failing to maintain a safe water level at Lake Okeechobee, which had been reported as dangerously high in the weeks before the hurricane. More than 400 residents in the area died in the flooding.			The International Union against Tuberculosis gathers 500 health care workers from 22 countries in Washington, DC. Approximately 75,000 Americans died from tuberculosis last year, although the death rate has dropped by more than 60 footed approximately 85 percent in the past quarter century.	Vincent Richards, the third-ranked tennis player in the United States, turns professional.	Sep. 30
Prohibition enforcement head Lincoln Andrews is banning his agents from entering homes without search warrants. Public hackles have been raised by several instances when private dwellings have been invaded without due process....The chairman of the American Red Cross accuses Florida governor John W. Martin of hindering the $5 million relief campaign for hurricane victims.				French authors are commenting on the phenomenon of American "hero worship," exemplified by the recent mass celebrations for Gene Tunney and Gertrude Ederle and the near-riot conditions that followed the death of Rudolph Valentino. "Here one saw the American people," author Robert de Beauplan writes, "replete with a facility of juvenile admiration, with a collective and docile infatuation for any one who can boast of having accomplished something."...Yale University is no longer making daily chapel service mandatory for students.	Oct. 1
Despite four jury investigations, the murder of assistant state's attorney William McSwiggin in Chicago remains unsolved.		According to Treasury Department statistics, the citizens of three states—New York, Illinois, and Pennsylvania—pay almost half of the nation's federal income tax.... Nash Motors announces record profits for the month of September. The company's automobile production is up 33 footed approximately 85 percent for the year.	The Henry Phipps Institute at the University of Pennsylvania finds that tuberculosis treatment among African Americans improves markedly when African-American doctors are on staff. Fewer than 100 black patients a year received care at the institute when only whites were employed there; with black physicians now employed, 2,600 black patients are treated annually.	Herb Pennock limits the St. Louis Cardinals to three hits—only one after the first inning—as the New York Yankees take the World Series opener, 2–1....More than 10,000 baseball fans gather before New York's City Hall to watch game updates on two scoreboards, while peanut vendors work the crowd.... The Channel Swimming Association is established in London. The organization seeks to define and codify "true" English Channel swims. Crossings from France to England—the route taken by recent successful swimmers—will not qualify.	Oct. 2
The American Federation of Labor, meeting at its annual convention in Detroit, announces plans to demand a five-day workweek.... At Aimee Semple McPherson's Angelus Temple in California, several thousand churchgoers view a special tableau, "The March of the Martyrs," showing scenes of religious persecution throughout history, beginning with Christ and ending with the present day.			Statistics suggest that the tuberculosis death rate among African Americans is three times higher than that for whites. The areas with the highest tuberculosis death rate in the United States are the industrial cities of the south.	Led by Grover Alexander's four-hit pitching, the St. Louis Cardinals take game two of the World Series, 6–2. A record series crowd of 63,600 attends Yankee Stadium....French tennis champion Rene Lacoste rejects the recent trend toward professionalism in his sport....French playwright Jacques Deval describes New York City as a "mass of banality, and the most exhausting city in the world."	Oct. 3

F	G	H	I	J
Includes campaigns, elections, federal-state relations, civil rights and liberties, crime, the judiciary, education, healthcare, poverty, urban affairs, and population.	*Includes formation and debate of U.S. foreign and defense policies, veterans affairs, and defense spending. (Relations with specific foreign countries are usually found under the region concerned.)*	*Includes business, labor, agriculture, taxation, transportation, consumer affairs, monetary and fiscal policy, natural resources, pollution and industrial accidents.*	*Includes worldwide scientific, medical and technological developments, natural phenomena, U.S. weather and natural disasters.*	*Includes the arts, religion, scholarship, communications media, sports, entertainment, fashions, fads, and social life.*

	World Affairs	Europe	Africa & The Middle East	The Americas	Asia & The Pacific
Oct. 4	"Irreconcilable" senator William Borah announces that he stands with President Coolidge in his refusal to compromise on the World Court reservations.	The Communist Party Central Committee in Moscow issues a statement denouncing the Trotskyite opposition as "baneful violators of party discipline." The committee urges all Communist organizations to guard against "the fever of discussion with which these disrupters endeavor to infect and split the party."			A contingent of Wu Pei-fu's soldiers attempts to break out of the besieged city of Wuchang; all 500 troops are killed by the surrounding Cantonese army....Two influential newspapers in London, *The Times* and *The Daily Telegraph*, are advocating joint British-American military intervention in China.
Oct. 5			The Spanish Army announces that hostilities have ceased in Morocco, where the last two rebel tribes have laid down their arms. A dispatch notes: "For nearly the first time in seventeen years Spanish soldiers are able to make ordinary daily marches unmolested."		Some Christian missionaries oppose the use of gunboats by western powers to tamp down unrest in China. Sending a few boats up the Yangtze River tends "to aggravate instead of pacify conditions," imperiling the missionaries, one organizer asserts. "The powers either should intervene outright with sufficient forces to effect reforms or abandon the pretense of protecting their nationals."
Oct. 6					Japanese investors in the Philippines now control between 50 and 75 percent of the Davao province's lucrative hemp trade, with a major market in the United States.
Oct. 7		Five members of a family in Turkestan are executed for murdering another family member, a young woman who had embraced Communism. She had vocally supported Soviet decrees against polygamy and the sale of infant girls into marriage, practices that are widespread in Turkestan. Disgraced by her behavior and her rejection of religious and parental teachings, the family ritualistically stabbed her to death.	Jews in Palestine protest a contract given to an Arab firm to make repairs on the tomb of Rachel, a Jewish holy site.		The Red Cross has successfully rescued 38,000 women and children from the besieged Chinese city of Wuchang. However, several hundred people have reportedly been trampled to death scrambling for places on the Red Cross ships.
Oct. 8					There are reports that 10,000 people have starved to death in Wuchang since late August, when the city was boxed in by the Cantonese army.
Oct. 9			An enormous explosion at a coalmine in Dannhauser, South Africa, kills all 125 men working on the night shift.	American immigration authorities believe that an international ring has been smuggling lower-class European immigrants into the United States over the Mexican border. There are reportedly 8,000 Europeans currently waiting in Mexico City to be brought across.	Northern troops surrender the city of Wuchang to the Cantonese army.
Oct. 10		The Politburo in Russia cites the Trotsky-Zinoviev oppositional faction for insubordination. Political observers in Moscow believe that Trotsky has such a strong following in the Communist Party that he is immune from any "drastic action."...The French government is attempting to expedite the citizenship process for foreigners. With a steadily declining birthrate among the native French, there is unease about the nation's "unnaturalized" population of 4 million.			

A	B	C	D	E
Includes developments that affect more than one world region, international organizations and important meetings of world leaders.	Includes all domestic and regional developments in Europe, including the Soviet Union.	Includes all domestic and regional developments in Africa and the Middle East.	Includes all domestic and regional developments in Latin America, the Caribbean, and Canada.	Includes all domestic and regional developments in Asian and Pacific nations (and colonies).

U.S. Politics & Social Issues	U.S. Foreign Policy & Affairs, Defense	U.S. Economy & Environment	Science, Technology & Nature	Culture, Leisure & Lifestyle	
A gas explosion at a coal mine in Rockwood, TN, leaves 28 men dead....The Charity Organization Society charts the effect of Prohibition on working-class families. According to their statistics, in 1916, before the Volstead Act, alcoholism was a factor in 19.9 percent of family cases handled by social workers.	The U.S. Navy Department is working to develop goggles that prevent "aviator's blindness," caused by sun glare.			In response to criticism that America dominates the world's film output, Will Hays points out that major actors, directors, and cinematographers from 22 nations are employed in Hollywood....Frank Harling's "native opera" *Deep River* opens in New York City.	Oct. 4
Henry Suzzallo, the president of the University of Washington, is ousted from office by state governor Roland Hartley. The two men have been involved in a dispute dating back to the World War, when Suzzallo advocated an eight-hour workday for lumbermen, vigorously opposed by Hartley, a wealthy timber owner. Hartley recently replaced five members of the university board of regents with his own appointees, who have now forced Suzzallo's dismissal.		Wheat prices have been declining.		The Cardinals take the lead in the World Series by defeating the Yankees, 4–0. Pitcher Jesse Haines is the star of game three, tossing a shutout and hitting a homerun.... The Woman Citizen Corporation, the first publishing company owned and financed exclusively by women, will publish the magazine *Woman Citizen*.	Oct. 5
The Ku Klux Klan suffers another electoral setback, this time in Georgia, where their slate of favored candidates is trounced.		American chain stores continue to report increasing sales. For eleven chains during the first nine months of 1926, profit increases over last year range from five to 59 percent....The National Automobile Chamber of Commerce anticipates a record year for American automobile production.		Babe Ruth pounds three homeruns—setting the World Series record for a single game—as the Yankees easily handle the Cardinals, 10–5, to even up the series. The St. Louis fans surprise New Yorkers by cheering Ruth's homers.	Oct. 6
Republican nervousness about the upcoming elections is exemplified by the roster of heavy hitters who will speak on the campaign stump. Six members of the Coolidge cabinet and approximately 100 sitting or former senators and representatives have been called upon to make speeches for candidates—an unprecedented number.			The Westinghouse Electric Company uses short-wave transmissions to successfully broadcast to Sydney, Australia, a radio show that originates in Pittsburgh.	After defeating the Cardinals in ten innings, 3–2, the Yankees have a clear advantage in the World Series. St. Louis must now return to New York, facing elimination with one more loss....The mayor of Philadelphia declares the Sesquicentennial International Exhibition to be a flop. Expected to attract 25 million visitors, the exhibition has drawn fewer than 5 million. Concessionaires have been complaining, and the city has $3 million in unpaid bills.	Oct. 7
In Aiken, South Carolina, a black woman and two black men, suspected of murder, are pulled from their jail cells by a large mob, taken to the outskirts of town, told to run, and shot dead. Approximately 1,000 people gather to watch.	General John Pershing condemns military budget cuts. He warns that saving "a few million dollars a year" on the peacetime army will only result in spending "many billions in an emergency … to make up deficiencies."	The Department of Agriculture forecasts a record cotton crop of 16,627,000 bales. The anticipated glut sends the price of cotton down to $4 per bale, much lower than the cost of production.	The Cardinals' Special—the train carrying the St. Louis Cardinals baseball team—sets a speed record for the run between St. Louis and New York City, at 21 hours and 20 minutes. The route typically takes more than 24 hours for even the fastest trains.	An anonymous New Yorker is having a chateau, built in 1640 in France, disassembled and completely rebuilt, stone by stone, on Long Island.	Oct. 8
At a coroner's jury investigation in Aiken, South Carolina, town law enforcement officers claim that they were unable to recognize any members of the mob—estimated at 150 people—that carried out yesterday's lynching. The jury returns the verdict that the deaths were caused by "unknown parties."				The St. Louis Cardinals win game six of the World Series, scoring three runs in the first inning on the way to a 10–2 victory. Grover Alexander, the 39-year-old pitcher who was picked up off waivers earlier in the season, wins his second start of the series.	Oct. 9
	The American Legion opposes any ban by the League of Nations on the use of poison gas on the battlefield. A spokesman cites statistics indicating that only 2 percent of those gassed during the World War died. Gas is "one of the most humane weapons of warfare," he says, enabling combatants to be disabled from action without dying. The Legion attributes the movement to abolish poison gas to pacifists; "practical soldiers," who know better, do not support the effort.	Henry Ford says he supports the five-day workweek because it provides workers with the leisure time to "cultivate a higher standard of living" and become more active consumers.		The St. Louis Cardinals win their first world championship by defeating the New York Yankees, 3–2. Grover Alexander is once again the hero, entering the game as a reliever with the bases loaded in the crucial seventh inning and striking out Yankee slugger Tony Lazzeri....While the seven-game series seesawed between the two teams, an estimated $20 million changed hands in heavy betting.	Oct. 10

F	G	H	I	J
Includes campaigns, elections, federal-state relations, civil rights and liberties, crime, the judiciary, education, healthcare, poverty, urban affairs, and population.	Includes formation and debate of U.S. foreign and defense policies, veterans affairs, and defense spending. (Relations with specific foreign countries are usually found under the region concerned.)	Includes business, labor, agriculture, taxation, transportation, consumer affairs, monetary and fiscal policy, natural resources, pollution and industrial accidents.	Includes worldwide scientific, medical and technological developments, natural phenomena, U.S. weather and natural disasters.	Includes the arts, religion, scholarship, communications media, sports, entertainment, fashions, fads, and social life.

	World Affairs	Europe	Africa & The Middle East	The Americas	Asia & The Pacific
Oct. 11					
Oct. 12		The Grand Condé diamond, an internationally famous jewel worth an estimated $2 million, is stolen in a daring burglary at a national museum in France. Other jewels worth $1 million are also taken.		More than 100,000 worshippers attend consecration anniversary ceremonies at the shrine of the Virgin of Guadalupe in Mexico.	
Oct. 13				The archbishop of the city of Puebla in Mexico is arrested, along with 10 Catholic priests, and charged with conspiring against the Calles government.	In Shensi province in China, 51 western missionaries are rescued, while three refuse to leave their posts.
Oct. 14		Former British prime minister H. H. Asquith resigns his leadership position in the Liberal Party, reportedly because his strong opposition earlier this year to the general strike placed him at odds with the party membership.			
Oct. 15					
Oct. 16		Membership in the Italian Fascist Party passes 1.5 million. In addition, approximately 3 million Italian workers belong to Fascist trade unions....The Soviet Commissar of Education is urging a campaign against "that wild beast called anti-Semitism," but there is much circumstantial evidence that anti-Semitism is becoming prevalent in the Communist Party. Many of the high-ranking officials recently purged are Jews.			A munitions-laden troop ship on the Yangtze River in China explodes, killing 1,200 soldiers.
Oct. 17		Leon Trotsky and other members of the opposition in the Soviet Union publicly repudiate their recent actions. They acknowledge their error in attempting to split the Communist Party and unconditionally submit themselves to party discipline. Moscow political observers, who had expected Stalin to be forced into a compromise with Trotsky, say the confession represents "complete defeat" for the opposition.			

A	B	C	D	E
Includes developments that affect more than one world region, international organizations and important meetings of world leaders.	*Includes all domestic and regional developments in Europe, including the Soviet Union.*	*Includes all domestic and regional developments in Africa and the Middle East.*	*Includes all domestic and regional developments in Latin America, the Caribbean, and Canada.*	*Includes all domestic and regional developments in Asian and Pacific nations (and colonies).*

U.S. Politics & Social Issues	U.S. Foreign Policy & Affairs, Defense	U.S. Economy & Environment	Science, Technology & Nature	Culture, Leisure & Lifestyle	
The corruption trial of former attorney general Harry M. Daugherty and former alien property custodian Thomas W. Miller ends in a hung jury. The final votes are 7–5 for the conviction of Daugherty and 10–2 for the conviction of Miller. In none of the balloting do a majority of jurors find either man innocent.		The American Banker Association reports that 250 leading U.S. companies earned $568 million during the first half of 1926—an increase of 21 percent over the same period in 1925.		A critically acclaimed adaptation of Theodore Dreiser's novel An American Tragedy is playing on Broadway....The American Dietetic Association recommends any of the following items as suitable lunch fare for a "white collar man": "Cheese or meat sandwich, vegetable salad sandwich, creamed soups, stewed fruit, ice cream, buttermilk."	Oct. 11
President Coolidge approves plans to build a dam on the Owyhee River in Oregon, expected to provide irrigation for 124,000 acres in Oregon and Idaho.				D. W. Griffith's film The Sorrows of Satan is in theaters....Popular stage comedian Eddie Cantor makes his movie debut in Kid Boots.	Oct. 12
Prisoners at a county jail in Media, PA, riot to protest overcrowded conditions. There are 196 inmates housed in 65 cells....Libraries in Kansas City, KS, are experiencing a spate of vandalism: books on evolution have been ripped apart and covered with Bible quotations.		The Department of Agriculture anticipates that American farm income for 1926 will decrease by $400 million from the previous year.		A recent survey shows that pie is the most popular food in the United States. Food experts point to the scarcity of regional dishes on the list of favorites as evidence of "the nationalization of our food taste."	Oct. 13
Armed bandits steal $300,000 from a U.S. mail truck in Elizabeth, NJ, shooting the driver dead. The robbers are believed to be members of the locally notorious James Cuniffe gang, wanted for four previous robbery-murders....Missouri senator James Reed announces that he will lead a senate investigation into the alleged ties between Indiana politicians and the Ku Klux Klan.		The Irving Bank and Trust Company and the American Exchange-Pacific National Bank announce a planned merger, which will create the nation's third largest financial company.			Oct. 14
The Red Cross acknowledges that it has raised only $3 million of the $5 million needed for Florida hurricane relief—the first time in the organization's history that it has failed to reach a primary fund-raising goal. A month after the hurricane, donations have slowed to a trickle.		Prominent banker Jules Bache takes issue with pessimists who anticipate a downturn in the American economy. "Bad times usually come to a nation when speculation is rife," he states. But in America, "there is little speculation, and we are buying what we need and no more."		Douglas Fairbanks and Mary Pickford are building a million-dollar "dream home" on 800 acres near San Diego....Philip Barry's satire White Wings debuts on Broadway....An American, Herbert Weinig, wins the International Oratorical Contest in Washington, DC, with President Coolidge and several foreign dignitaries in attendance. The prize-winning speech is on the U.S. Constitution; the runner-up, from Mexico City, speaks about Simon Bolivar.	Oct. 15
Responding to the New Jersey mail truck robbery, President Coolidge calls out 2,500 marines to guard federal mails throughout the country.		Cotton prices continue to plummet.		Married women are increasingly finding work in American department stores. One general manager notes that the peak hours for trade in the late morning and early afternoon fit well with the schedules of married women.	Oct. 16
The Kellogg Switchboard and Supply Company in Chicago is robbed of $100,000 by a contingent of 16 burglars, who overpower the employees and spend eight hours cracking safes in the plant.			The National Research Council believes that European nations, suffering economically in the aftermath of the World War, can no longer afford to sponsor advanced scientific research. Although America has traditionally trailed behind Europe in scientific knowledge, the onus is now on the United States to support the pure sciences.	After 665 performances, the American musical No, No, Nanette completes its run in London. The play's hit song, "I Want to Be Happy," has been sung on the Palace Theatre stage an estimated 10,625 times.	Oct. 17

F	G	H	I	J
Includes campaigns, elections, federal-state relations, civil rights and liberties, crime, the judiciary, education, healthcare, poverty, urban affairs, and population.	Includes formation and debate of U.S. foreign and defense policies, veterans affairs, and defense spending. (Relations with specific foreign countries are usually found under the region concerned.)	Includes business, labor, agriculture, taxation, transportation, consumer affairs, monetary and fiscal policy, natural resources, pollution and industrial accidents.	Includes worldwide scientific, medical and technological developments, natural phenomena, U.S. weather and natural disasters.	Includes the arts, religion, scholarship, communications media, sports, entertainment, fashions, fads, and social life.

	World Affairs	Europe	Africa & The Middle East	The Americas	Asia & The Pacific
Oct. 18					
Oct. 19	Leading bankers and industrialists from sixteen countries issue a newspaper appeal, "For the Removal of Restrictions upon European Trade." The widely published document warns that international trade has been dangerously hampered since the World War by high protective tariffs.	British coal miners continue to abandon the strike, including 19,478 who return to the pits today. The total number of miners now back at work is 238,669.			
Oct. 20					
Oct. 21		The Y.M.C.A. has been expelled from the Soviet Union....The dachshund is featured in a British dog show for the first time since 1913. The dog breed had fallen into disrepute in England during the World War because of its association with Germany.		A hurricane strikes Cuba, killing at least 650 people in Havana....The Mexican government upholds its ban on displaying the crucifix in the nation's schools.	
Oct. 22			The international slump in cotton prices is having political ramifications in Egypt, where the premier may resign.	A British freighter sinks during the hurricane in the South Atlantic, with an estimated 100 crewmen dead.	The Cantonese army, behaving less despotically than the northern forces, is gaining popularity with Chinese civilians.
Oct. 23		An earthquake in Armenia leaves at least 300 people dead, destroying the city of Leninakan and several towns. More than 100,000 people are homeless.	Eastman Kodak president George Eastman, just returned from a safari in East Africa during which his party bagged sixteen lions, observes that the region's big game is being rapidly depleted.	Brazil plans to build "a tropical Washington" in the heart of the country, replacing Rio de Janeiro as the nation's capital.	
Oct. 24					
Oct. 25		In an effort to stabilize its national currency, Belgium goes on the gold standard and borrows $100 million from American and English banks.... In the British House of Commons, members debate whether too many of them are "drunkards."			

A	B	C	D	E
Includes developments that affect more than one world region, international organizations and important meetings of world leaders.	*Includes all domestic and regional developments in Europe, including the Soviet Union.*	*Includes all domestic and regional developments in Africa and the Middle East.*	*Includes all domestic and regional developments in Latin America, the Caribbean, and Canada.*	*Includes all domestic and regional developments in Asian and Pacific nations (and colonies).*

U.S. Politics & Social Issues	U.S. Foreign Policy & Affairs, Defense	U.S. Economy & Environment	Science, Technology & Nature	Culture, Leisure & Lifestyle	
		U.S. cigarette consumption has increased significantly for six years running—and 1926 numbers are outpacing record-setting sales figures for 1925. Last year American companies produced 88 billion cigarettes.		George Hossfeld wins the World Professional Typewriting Championship at Madison Square Garden in New York City before 30,000 spectators. He types 132 words per minute.	Oct. 18
		American bankers are divided on the issue of installment buying. Defenders point out that the practice has been essential to America's economic boom, since wages have not kept pace with the rapid increase in production; deferred payments enable consumers to purchase goods that would otherwise remain unsold. Detractors insist that the installment plan represents "nothing more nor less than a first mortgage on salaries not yet earned."	Major companies such as Standard Oil and Southern Pacific have begun distributing a pamphlet, "Warning to Stockholders," to their investors, providing useful tips on how to avoid stock fraud.	German chefs at Europe's largest restaurant are studying methods of food service in the United States; they say they want to emulate the American "speed" ethic.... Theodore Roosevelt Jr., the son of the president, advocates more playgrounds and organized recreation for children as a means to prevent crime. "Young criminals are created by what is done in their leisure hours," he observes.	Oct. 19
Labor leader and former Socialist presidential candidate Eugene V. Debs dies.		The Phillips Petroleum Company reports record net earnings for the past quarter....A federal court finds that General Motors's 1922 Buick model automobile infringes on two internal-combustion engine patents.		Six professional tennis engagements featuring Suzanne Lenglen and Vincent Richards have drawn 41,000 spectators; promoters expect the entire tour to gross close to $700,000.	Oct. 20
Architect Frank Lloyd Wright is arrested in Minneapolis, along with his companion Olga Milanoff, on the charges of violating the Mann act and committing adultery....Among the pool of 60 potential jurors for the Hall-Mills murder trial, there are 21 farmers and no women.	.	The Bureau of Consumer Research is established at Boston University to enable manufacturers to better tailor their products to women shoppers. A spokeswoman notes that because women "spend five out of every seven dollars in the national pay envelope," companies need to understand "her point of view when she buys."			Oct. 21
Nicola Sacco and Bartolomeo Vanzetti are denied a retrial by the Superior Court of Massachusetts. The judge finds that Celestino Madeiros, who claims to have committed the killings for which Sacco and Vanzetti have been convicted, is a liar.		Southern Pacific Railroad reports its best monthly profit since 1923.		Princeton University is investigating "Buchmanism" on campus—a Christian evangelical practice, founded by Frank Buchman, which detractors claim involves occultism and hysterical emotionalism.	Oct. 22
Police chiefs in New Jersey hope to fight crime in the state by establishing a telephone and radio circuit that will relay up-to-the-minute information to 43 separate jurisdictions.		Conservation officials at the Stanislaus National Forest in California have completed a two-year deer eradication program, wiping out the entire population of 25,000 in an effort to prevent the spread of hoof and mouth disease. The disease was passed to the wild deer from cattle herds.		Neurologist Joseph Collins publishes his book The Doctor Looks at Love and Life, in which he diagnoses the American condition of "adult-infantilism." He writes that Americans are infantile in their responses "to the demands and obligations of life," evident in their suggestibility, conformity, possessiveness, and constant preference for amusement.	Oct. 23
The major issues in the U.S. Senate campaigns this fall are farm relief, opposed "wet" and "dry" agendas, the influence of the Ku Klux Klan in politics, and tariff reform. Neither party is particularly interested in discussing the World Court.		The National Hardware Association condemns installment buying. "With everything from hairnets to country estates offered on easy terms," an official remarks, "a devastating disease is slowly but surely undermining the moral sense of responsibility of our people."		The Metropolitan Life Insurance Company reports that deaths due to alcoholism among its 17 million policyholders have increased 14 percent during 1926....German film star Emil Jannings has signed a three-year contract with the Famous Players-Lasky Corporation in the United States.	Oct. 24
The U.S. Supreme Court delivers its opinion on Myers v. United States, an important case about the separation of powers. The Court rules that the president has the sole authority to remove executive branch officials from office.				Western artist Charles Marion Russell, known for his painting of cowboys and American Indians, has died.....Magician Harry Houdini, suffering from acute appendicitis, undergoes emergency surgery in Detroit and is reported in grave condition. He began to suffer pain after a fan jokingly punched him in the stomach.	Oct. 25

F	G	H	I	J
Includes campaigns, elections, federal-state relations, civil rights and liberties, crime, the judiciary, education, healthcare, poverty, urban affairs, and population.	Includes formation and debate of U.S. foreign and defense policies, veterans affairs, and defense spending. (Relations with specific foreign countries are usually found under the region concerned.)	Includes business, labor, agriculture, taxation, transportation, consumer affairs, monetary and fiscal policy, natural resources, pollution and industrial accidents.	Includes worldwide scientific, medical and technological developments, natural phenomena, U.S. weather and natural disasters.	Includes the arts, religion, scholarship, communications media, sports, entertainment, fashions, fads, and social life.

	World Affairs	Europe	Africa & The Middle East	The Americas	Asia & The Pacific
Oct. 26		At the opening of the All-Russian Communist Party Congress, Joseph Stalin uses his address to castigate the "heresies" of the Trotsky-Zinoviev opposition. The party elects 37 members to the Praesidium, including Stalin and his close protégés....The American Embassy in Paris has received numerous threats of "punishment" if Sacco and Vanzetti are executed. The American diplomatic corps is under heavy police protection.	The French Army, facing another flare-up in the area around Damascus, kills 90 Syrian Druses rebels.		
Oct. 27					
Oct. 28			In an effort to curtail cotton production, the Egyptian government slashes by two-thirds the amount of cultivatable acreage that may be used for cotton.	The Mexican government calls in several bishops and priests from the provinces and asks them to remain in Mexico City, ostensibly to protect them from ill-treatment by local authorities. Observers believe the government wants to concentrate the Catholic hierarchy in one place.	
Oct. 29		The French Army cancels all athletics, reasoning that soldiers should instead devote themselves to military training.	Egyptian literary professor Taha Hussein is on trial for defaming Islam in his book about pre-Islamic poetry. His study suggests that the Quran cannot be considered a literal historical account.		British gunboats and Chinese army patrols continue to exchange gunfire in China's Szechuan province.
Oct. 30		The city of Paris enacts a law forbidding "Broadway style" electric lights along the rooflines of buildings.			Pope Pius XI consecrates six Chinese bishops—the first native Chinese to be so appointed.
Oct. 31		Benito Mussolini survives another assassination attempt, the third made against him in six months. As the premier stands in an open automobile amid a crowd in Bologna, an 18-year-old boy fires at him from close range; the bullet tears through Mussolini's coat but leaves him untouched. The assailant is tackled by bystanders and soon killed.			

A	B	C	D	E
Includes developments that affect more than one world region, international organizations and important meetings of world leaders.	Includes all domestic and regional developments in Europe, including the Soviet Union.	Includes all domestic and regional developments in Africa and the Middle East.	Includes all domestic and regional developments in Latin America, the Caribbean, and Canada.	Includes all domestic and regional developments in Asian and Pacific nations (and colonies).

U.S. Politics & Social Issues	U.S. Foreign Policy & Affairs, Defense	U.S. Economy & Environment	Science, Technology & Nature	Culture, Leisure & Lifestyle	
Gang warfare erupts in Herrin, Illinois, leaving two bootleggers dead. The rival Birger and Shelton gangs have been skirmishing with machine guns and armored trucks in the small towns of southern Illinois; it is believed that seven members have been killed in recent months....There are currently 6,696 prisoners serving in the nation's three federal penitentiaries.				Mary A. Sullivan becomes the first female detective on the New York City police force....The National Association of Audubon Societies reports there are more than three million schoolchildren enrolled in junior Audubon clubs, with a large growth spurt in membership during the past year.	Oct. 26
In a speech before the American Association of Advertising Agencies, President Coolidge calls advertising one of the central drivers of American prosperity, creating the mass demand upon which mass production depends. Declaring that prosperity has become a general condition in the country, he points to the millions of automobiles, radios, and telephones sold as evidence that Americans no longer fear "being exploited by large aggregations of wealth."		United States Steel Corporation chairman Elbert Gary offers his opinion about the five-day work-week. He believes that American industry will not be able to compete with European competitors "if American labor worked only five days while they worked six." He questions whether American consumer demand can still be met through the output of a shortened week.		Women in the United States spend an estimated $5 million per day on cosmetics. Last year 20 million boxes of rouge and 40 million packages of cold cream were purchased over the counter.	Oct. 27
A U.S. senate committee hears evidence that Indiana senator James E. Watson has been until recently a card-carrying member of the Ku Klux Klan....In New Jersey, the body of Eleanor Mills is exhumed for a new autopsy....Civic boosters in the Miami area insist that the city is ready to accommodate an expected 200,000 winter season visitors.... Harry Hull, the U.S. Commissioner General of Immigration, believes that 3 million illegal immigrant reside in America.	The American Legion condemns recent military budget cuts and demands that the United States maintain a standing army of 125,000.	The price index for all agricultural goods has dropped four percent during the past month.	Nobel Prize-winning physicist Robert A. Millikan has been in Bolivia conducting studies to confirm the existence of cosmic rays.	A Pennsylvania county court rules that the Philadelphia Athletics may not play baseball, defined as "a worldly employment," on Sundays in violation of blue laws. The club plans to appeal the decision to the state supreme court....The College of William and Mary imposes a rule forbidding female students with low test scores from dating and enjoying other social privileges; the same rule is not applied to male students.	Oct. 28
Oklahoma rancher William K. Hale, known as the "King of the Osage Hills," is convicted to life in prison for murdering an Osage Indian in 1923. Hale is believed to have murdered as many as two dozen members of the Osage tribe, in an effort to terrorize them and seize their oil wealth....Police are searching nationwide for a Memphis bank teller who embezzled $463,967 and then disappeared.		Florida businesses reassure investors that although many small homeowners were wiped out by the hurricane, "99 percent of [the Miami area's] taxable value remains intact and uninjured."	The American College of Surgeons is sponsoring a program that seeks to use film as a method for teaching surgical techniques.	Harry Houdini undergoes a second operation, although his doctors give him a slim chance for recovery.	Oct. 29
The Republican National Party faces a daunting task in the upcoming U.S. Senate elections: 15 of their seats are considered vulnerable. Moreover, several of their candidates are identified as Progressives, who typically vote against the Coolidge administration....Seven Democratic senators are up for reelection, but all of these seats are from Southern states considered "safe."				Ernest Hemingway publishes his masterpiece, The Sun Also Rises.... In college football, Army whips Yale 33–0—the first time Army has beaten the Elis since 1911. Defying prevailing trends, the Army offense does not attempt a forward pass for the entire game....There are approximately 350 correspondence school in the United States, with two million students enrolled in courses.	Oct. 30
Eight states are holding referendums on Prohibition in the upcoming elections....Among the Senate contests expected to be close are the races in Massachusetts, Illinois, and Ohio....James Cunniffe, the New Jersey criminal wanted for the recent U.S. mail robbery, is shot to death by another gangster in Detroit.		Corn prices are at a seasonal low, the result of a record yield and few interested buyers.		Magician Harry Houdini dies in Detroit....John Gilbert is starring in the film Bardelys the Magnificent, directed by King Vidor.	Oct. 31

F	G	H	I	J
Includes campaigns, elections, federal-state relations, civil rights and liberties, crime, the judiciary, education, healthcare, poverty, urban affairs, and population.	Includes formation and debate of U.S. foreign and defense policies, veterans affairs, and defense spending. (Relations with specific foreign countries are usually found under the region concerned.)	Includes business, labor, agriculture, taxation, transportation, consumer affairs, monetary and fiscal policy, natural resources, pollution and industrial accidents.	Includes worldwide scientific, medical and technological developments, natural phenomena, U.S. weather and natural disasters.	Includes the arts, religion, scholarship, communications media, sports, entertainment, fashions, fads, and social life.

	World Affairs	Europe	Africa & The Middle East	The Americas	Asia & The Pacific
Nov. 1	Germany is pressing to regain former colonies lost at the end of the World War, insisting that they need raw materials for their industries. But the colonies were assigned as mandates to other western powers, who now regard their oversight role as a sovereign right.	Italian Fascists hold mass rallies condemning the recent spate of assassination attempts on Benito Mussolini. Leaders exhort the huge crowds to be on the lookout for traitors.			
Nov. 2		Italian police are making a sweep for Communists, oppositionists, and other suspected plotters against Mussolini; more than 100 have been arrested. Whipped into a frenzy by yesterday's demonstrations, mobs have wrecked the homes of several well-known oppositionists, and publication has been suspended at twelve opposition newspapers. Angry Fascists also attack French consulates in Tripoli and Ventimiglia; France is widely seen as a haven for Italian expatriate anti-Fascists.			Western reporters in China are frustrated by what they call "the babel of false propaganda" from both northern and southern forces, rendering their reporting unreliable.
Nov. 3		The Soviet Communist Party Congress votes to censure Leon Trotsky, Lev Kamenev, and Grigory Zinoviev.			
Nov. 4		Ricciotti Garibaldi, the grandson of the famous Italian patriot, is arrested in France on suspicion of being an agent provocateur for Benito Mussolini. Garibaldi has reportedly been working with a network of anti-Fascists in France, Spain, and Italy, then exposing them to the Italian secret police.		The U.S. State Department denies entry into the country to Alexandra Kollantai, the Soviet Union's newly appointed diplomat to Mexico. She seeks to enter Mexico through the United States but is barred because of her affiliation with Communism.	
Nov. 5		The Italian government passes measures aimed at stamping out all opposition activities, punishable in most cases by two to five years of imprisonment. One decree stipulates up to fifteen years in prison for spreading "false or exaggerated" news abroad about conditions inside Italy.			
Nov. 6		Because of the British coal strike, European nations are expected to experience a 100-million-ton coal shortage during the coming winter....France demands an apology for Italy's recent provocations, including the foiled Garibaldi plot and the anti-French embassy riots.			Belgium refuses China's request to renegotiate a treaty from 1865 based on "equality and reciprocity"; the Chinese government responds by promptly annulling the treaty.... Chiang Kai-shek's Cantonese forces have been consistently outsmarting their northern enemies. They recently reported that Chiang Kai-shek was dead and began what seemed to be a full-fledged retreat from Kiangsu Province; they then abruptly turned on their heels and attacked, occupying the city of Kiukiang.

A	B	C	D	E
Includes developments that affect more than one world region, international organizations and important meetings of world leaders.	Includes all domestic and regional developments in Europe, including the Soviet Union.	Includes all domestic and regional developments in Africa and the Middle East.	Includes all domestic and regional developments in Latin America, the Caribbean, and Canada.	Includes all domestic and regional developments in Asian and Pacific nations (and colonies).

U.S. Politics & Social Issues	U.S. Foreign Policy & Affairs, Defense	U.S. Economy & Environment	Science, Technology & Nature	Culture, Leisure & Lifestyle	
The campaign season is drawing to a close, with 35 Senate seats and the entire House of Representatives to be determined at the polls tomorrow. Eight states are holding nonbinding referendums on Prohibition....The U.S. Supreme Court rules in *Herbert v. Louisiana* that an individual can be tried in both state and federal court for breaking a Prohibition law. The defense in the case has argued that this violates the constitutional protection against double jeopardy.				The Times Building in New York City will use an elaborate system of searchlight signals to provide election returns. For example, a searchlight making semicircles to the east means that James Wadsworth has been elected New York senator, while a searchlight to the west means Robert Wagner has defeated Wadsworth and a searchlight to the south means Ogden Mills is the new governor.	Nov. 1
President Coolidge loses his friendly senate in the midterm elections. Seven incumbent Republicans are defeated, while the Democratic Party retains all of its incumbents. The U.S. Senate will now feature a balanced distribution of 48 Republicans, 47 Democrats, and one Farmer-Laborite....The Republicans maintain their large margin in the U.S. House of Representatives, with 238 seats to 194 for the Democrats; the Democrats manage to pick up nine seats.		Wall Street statistics indicate that there are an estimated 15 million individual stockholders in the United States. A recent phenomenon is employees who invest in their own company's stock; for example, 160,000 workers at American Telephone & Telegraph buy shares through methods such as the company installment plan. More than 70 American companies now have more than one million outstanding shares; the largest of these companies are Standard Oil of New Jersey, with 20 million shares, and Willys-Overland Motors, with 12 million.		Three New York City radio stations broadcast election bulletins every few minutes, beginning at 6 p.m. and continuing until midnight. Reports from the Atlantic seaboard and the Midwest are relayed by stations in Pittsburgh and Chicago. One station employs statisticians to provide expert analysis for listeners.	Nov. 2
Consistent in victory and defeat, President Coolidge displays no emotion about the congressional election results....The chairman of the Republican Senate Campaign Committee asserts that the results "can in no way be construed as party repudiation."			French astronomers are perplexed by an "extraordinarily brilliant spot" that recently appeared on the planet Mars. The spot fluctuated in brightness for three days, then disappeared.	Baseball great Ty Cobb retires after 22 seasons with the Detroit Tigers....Champion sharpshooter Annie Oakley dies.	Nov. 3
Nellie Tayloe Ross, the first American female state governor, concedes defeat in her reelection bid in Wyoming....Pig farmer Jane Gibson, the State's star witness in the Hall-Mills murder trial, is said to be gravely ill and may not be able to testify....African-American educator Mary McLeod Bethune points to a growing interest among Southern educational authorities in giving black and white children equal opportunities in school.				The American Medical Association publishes a study on marijuana use in the state of Louisiana. The drug is primarily imported from Mexico; it is sold on the street under the names "muggles," "moota," and "bombalachi." Thousands of young men and women in the state are believed to smoke marijuana cigarettes regularly.	Nov. 4
President Coolidge plans to use the budget surplus to provide a 10 percent income tax rebate for Americans....A deputy Prohibition administrator and three of his agents are fired for their conduct during an automobile search in Washington, DC.			The Central Petroleum Committee of the National Research Council is undertaking an ambitious study of the geological processes related to petroleum.		Nov. 5
There will be seven Progressive Republicans serving in the new Senate, clearly holding the balance of power in a body split evenly along party lines.		During the first ten months of 1926, nearly a billion dollars in building contracts are awarded in Manhattan, surpassing last year's record-setting pace by 16 percent.	William H. Welch of Johns Hopkins University is appointed professor of the history of medicine—the first time this specialty is recognized with an endowed chair in American education.	The anthology *American Literature*, selected by University of Cincinnati professor Robert Shafer, is published. The book offers 55 American writers deemed to be of "high national value"; among current authors making the cut are Rachel Lindsay, Sherwood Anderson, and Eugene O'Neill.	Nov. 6

F	G	H	I	J
Includes campaigns, elections, federal-state relations, civil rights and liberties, crime, the judiciary, education, healthcare, poverty, urban affairs, and population.	*Includes formation and debate of U.S. foreign and defense policies, veterans affairs, and defense spending. (Relations with specific foreign countries are usually found under the region concerned.)*	*Includes business, labor, agriculture, taxation, transportation, consumer affairs, monetary and fiscal policy, natural resources, pollution and industrial accidents.*	*Includes worldwide scientific, medical and technological developments, natural phenomena, U.S. weather and natural disasters.*	*Includes the arts, religion, scholarship, communications media, sports, entertainment, fashions, fads, and social life.*

	World Affairs	Europe	Africa & The Middle East	The Americas	Asia & The Pacific
Nov. 7					A typhoon and accompanying tidal wave have struck the Philippines, killing at least 300 people....Tokyo is experiencing a serious increase in nonviolent crime, with more than 50,000 people convicted of offenses such as petty theft and blackmail over the past twelve months.
Nov. 8		Continued earthquakes near Leninakan, Armenia—several after-shocks a day, ongoing now for more than two weeks—has persuaded the Near East Relief organization to evacuate their orphanages to a different area.			
Nov. 9		Benito Mussolini formally apologizes for recent Italian behavior toward the French at Tripoli and Ventimiglia.	French authorities in Morocco have been imposing laws that impact Berber marriage customs. One decree requires a husband to pay alimony for three months and three days if he divorces his wife—the amount of time before she is regarded as marriageable again under Islamic law. Husbands are also now obligated to pay child support.		
Nov. 10		The Fiske Jubilee Singers perform African-American spirituals for a large audience in Paris, en route to a five weeks' concert tour of Spain....England appoints its first female sheriff.			
Nov. 11		On Armistice Day, England honors the nation's million war dead by observing two minutes of silence. London is strewn with red, as much of the population wears a red poppy, recalling the common flower of French battlefields....At a Communist Party conference in Moscow, Joseph Stalin denounces Leon Trotsky as a grandstanding "cinema revolutionary" and Lev Kamenev as "Trotsky's porter."			
Nov. 12	Indian writer Dhan Gopal Mukerji calls the League of Nations "a purely European house party," with no sense of the issues that concern India and other Asiatic nations.... Five nations—Cuba, Greece, Liberia, Albania, and Luxembourg—have notified the U.S. State Department that they accept the World Court reservations.	The 28-week British coal strike may finally be nearing an end. The Miners' Federation has signed a "memorandum of settlement" that concedes a major negotiation sticking point, allowing for individual district settlements. In return, the district settlements must follow national guidelines, with the British government providing oversight to ensure adherence....Henry Ford has become a popular hero in the Soviet Union, where his name often adorns banners at workers' meetings and parades.			

A	B	C	D	E
Includes developments that affect more than one world region, international organizations and important meetings of world leaders.	Includes all domestic and regional developments in Europe, including the Soviet Union.	Includes all domestic and regional developments in Africa and the Middle East.	Includes all domestic and regional developments in Latin America, the Caribbean, and Canada.	Includes all domestic and regional developments in Asian and Pacific nations (and colonies).

U.S. Politics & Social Issues	U.S. Foreign Policy & Affairs, Defense	U.S. Economy & Environment	Science, Technology & Nature	Culture, Leisure & Lifestyle	
The mayor of Colp, Illinois, is machine-gunned to death in the street—the latest victim in the bloody Birger-Shelton bootlegger war. Hundreds of shots are fired at him from four automobiles outside a roadhouse....Prohibition agents raid Chicago's city hall and arrest three clerks who are keeping liquor in their lockers.		Community chests across the country pool their fund-raising knowledge in a campaign to raise $40 million in 150 cities.	Scientists are meeting at the Carnegie Institute of Technology to discuss alternative energy sources to coal, such as natural gas, coke, gasoline, and fertilizers....The East Tennessee Development Company is undertaking a $2 million survey of eleven possible dam sites along the Tennessee River.		Nov. 7
The U.S. Senate is planning to investigate two senators-elect, William S. Vare of Pennsylvania and Frank L. Smith of Illinois, on charges that they committed fraud during their primary campaigns. The two men allegedly benefited from huge slush funds....A group of 13 convicts succeed in overpowering guards and escaping from the Ohio Penitentiary in Columbus, only to be caught within a few hours.	Due to budget cuts, four navy battleships may be placed on reserve status next year. The navy brass, unhappy with the budget, estimates that only 80,000 enlisted men can be maintained given the strictures.		A U.S. Navy Curtiss R-C34 seaplane attains a speed of 256 miles per hour, unofficially setting a new world's record.	A famous Catholic shrine in Quebec, the Basilica of Ste. Anne de Beaupré, is gutted by fire, destroying several valuable relics.	Nov. 8
Senate "insurgent" Republicans are reportedly planning to use the filibuster in the upcoming short congressional session, to delay essential fiscal business and force President Coolidge to call a special session for the summer. While in session, the senators will have a public forum from which to attack Coolidge and perhaps impact his 1928 renomination chances.			The British Admiralty is developing an emergency instrument for distressed submarines that are unable to surface. A buoy, filled with compressed air and equipped with a telephone, lights, and a signal bell, can be released from the submarine, bobbing to the surface and marking the craft for rescuers.		Nov. 9
The American Legion castigates a variety of women's organizations for being insidiously leftist. "We don't fear the acknowledged radicals," a spokesman says. "The danger lies in organizations like the Women's International League for Peace, in the churches, the schools, and the women's clubs." He singles out settlement house founder Jane Addams for trying to "strip the uniforms from our cadets at West Point, to deprive our colleges of military training and leave America undefended."		Several prominent national business associations, including the National Manufacturers Association and the American Mining Congress, are banding together to pressure Congress to repeal various corporate income taxes. They argue that the tax on the corporation is actually a tax on the nation's 15 million stockholders.	Astronomer F. G. Pease, who has already designed the 100-inch telescope at California's Mount Wilson Observatory, is now planning a giant telescope with a 25-foot mirror, anticipated to be three times as powerful.	The National Institute of Arts and Letters elects its first female members, the novelists Edith Wharton, Mary E. Wilkins Freeman, Margaret Deland, and Agnes Repplier. Member playwright Owen Davis wonders why it has taken so long. "A writer is a writer, and that is all there is to it," he says....Harry Houdini's will includes a bequest of his personal library, worth an estimated $500,000, to the Library of Congress and the American Society of Psychical Research.	Nov. 10
President Coolidge delivers his Armistice Day address in Kansas City with 175,000 people in attendance. Along with describing America's interest in promoting international goodwill, he states, "Our main responsibility is for America....We are a creditor nation. We are more prosperous than some others. This means that our interests have come within the European circles where distrust and suspicion . . . have been altogether too common."			The American Museum of Natural History has been studying the migratory patterns of birds and fish in Alaska's Bering Sea region.	Radio programs across the United States offer a full slate of Armistice Day programming. Radio events include a program of popular tunes from the World War era; a children's show, portraying a typical American family reacting to the events and personalities involved in the Armistice; an antiwar play,	Nov. 11
European nations react negatively to President Coolidge's Armistice Day speech. "It is a view of the situation," a French newspaper remarks, "devoid of all idealism, which subordinates the whole of American politics to the question of money."...The ongoing feuding between bootlegger gangs in southern Illinois has now escalated into aerial warfare. Two members of the Shelton gang use an airplane to drop three bombs, each containing twenty sticks of dynamite, on Jack Birger's cabin but miss, hitting a nearby tree and a cock-fighting shed instead. None of the crudely made bombs explodes.			Researchers at the University of British Columbia believe that handshaking is a primary means of spreading germs between people.	George Bernard Shaw wins the Nobel Prize for literature....The first hot dog company is registered in England, in an effort to capitalize on a popular quick-lunch trend.... Princeton University announces that it will no longer participate in athletic competitions with Harvard University, citing the "atmosphere of ill-will" that exists between the schools. A particular thorn is a recent edition of the undergraduate magazine The Harvard Lampoon. The magazine features satirical doggerel and jokes deemed offensive, such as this one: "Are you a Princeton man?" "No, I was kicked by a horse."	Nov. 12

F	G	H	I	J
Includes campaigns, elections, federal-state relations, civil rights and liberties, crime, the judiciary, education, healthcare, poverty, urban affairs, and population.	Includes formation and debate of U.S. foreign and defense policies, veterans affairs, and defense spending. (Relations with specific foreign countries are usually found under the region concerned.)	Includes business, labor, agriculture, taxation, transportation, consumer affairs, monetary and fiscal policy, natural resources, pollution and industrial accidents.	Includes worldwide scientific, medical and technological developments, natural phenomena, U.S. weather and natural disasters.	Includes the arts, religion, scholarship, communications media, sports, entertainment, fashions, fads, and social life.

	World Affairs	Europe	Africa & The Middle East	The Americas	Asia & The Pacific
Nov. 13	Experts in international finance believe that more nations will attempt to stabilize their currency and balance their budget by operating on the gold standard. England, Germany, Japan, Belgium, and Norway have all adopted the exchange in the past two years.	Unemployment in the Soviet trade unions is up 19 percent over last year; more than 1.18 million workers are without jobs....Berlin police authorities announce a three-day rat extermination drive; homeowners and landlords who do not participate will be fined....Premier Mussolini is defying would-be assassins by ramping up his public appearances, with the help of a full contingent of police agents in every crowd. He often walks the streets of Rome near his home. "Risk should not be the spice but the staff of life for a ... nation which dares to be strong," he declares.			By specializing in making imitations of American and German toys, Japan has become the world's third-largest toymaker. Toy production, all of it handmade, is provided by women and children working at home.
Nov. 14		In a close vote of 432,000 to 352,000, British Miners' Federation delegates recommend acceptance of the "memorandum for settlement," which will now be voted on by the districts. Critics point out that the proposed arbitration board ensuring national guidelines will only sit for six months, rendering it almost useless.			
Nov. 15		The South Wales Miners' Federation, a militant participant in the British coal strike, agrees to return to work. The 250,000-member federation is expected to influence the decision of other districts....The rapid rise of the French franc is causing a decline in the nation's exports, particularly textiles....The German economy is benefiting enormously from the British coal strike; coal exports for the first nine months in 1926 totaled 204 million tons, compared to only 10 million tons at the same point last year.		Adolfo Diaz is inaugurated as president of Nicaragua. He professes his close friendship with the United States and his worry that Mexico will attempt to "force on Nicaragua Mexican influence."...The Calles government plans to enact a law banning African Americans from entering Mexico, citing an influx through southern California.	Foreign observers in China believe that the nation's railroads are retarding economic development. They are a flashpoint for the endless "petty wars" fought by the nation's many generals, who seize the lines as a means of warfare. "I used to worry about deterioration of railways here," one foreign official notes. "Now I begin to think it would be better to destroy them altogether."
Nov. 16					Senator William Borah warns against American military intervention in China, arguing that "China for the Chinese" has become a legitimate and unstoppable aspiration in a nation of 400 million people. He sees China as an "acid test" for whether the major powers will seek to solve international crises through justice or force.
Nov. 17		The French franc continues to recover quickly, at almost exactly one-and-a-half times its value on June 20, when it reached a historic low....Stalin loyalists have been agitating among university students and Red Army officers, calling for "ruthless eradication" of the Trotsky-Zinoviev opposition....The Soviet Union announces plans to create an autonomous Jewish "territorial unit," where the nation's Jews can live without being assimilated.		The United States officially recognizes the government of Adolfo Diaz in Nicaragua. Secretary of State Frank Kellogg, echoing the new president, warns against "interference from outside sources."	
Nov. 18				The U.S. State Department is interested in brokering peace between the new conservative government in Nicaragua and the opposition liberal party. American officials are certain that Mexico has been running guns to rebels in Nicaragua.... Mexican officials react incredulously to charges of military interference in Nicaragua.	

A	B	C	D	E
Includes developments that affect more than one world region, international organizations and important meetings of world leaders.	Includes all domestic and regional developments in Europe, including the Soviet Union.	Includes all domestic and regional developments in Africa and the Middle East.	Includes all domestic and regional developments in Latin America, the Caribbean, and Canada.	Includes all domestic and regional developments in Asian and Pacific nations (and colonies).

U.S. Politics & Social Issues	U.S. Foreign Policy & Affairs, Defense	U.S. Economy & Environment	Science, Technology & Nature	Culture, Leisure & Lifestyle	
In the Hall-Mills trial, Frances Hall sits quietly but flushed as the prosecution reads from love letters by her dead husband, Reverend Edward Hall, to Eleanor Mills, many of them addressed "Dear True Love."		Michigan is undertaking the nation's most ambitious reforestation program, planting 12,000 acres this year. Around 10 million acres in the state have been cleared by the lumber industry and now lie idle.... Americans hold more than $24 billion in savings deposits, an increase of $3 billion in the last twelve months....The price of wheat hits a new yearly low.	Westinghouse Electric is providing radio news broadcasts to fur trappers and Canadian Mounties in the Canadian Arctic.	A display home in Fieldston, New York, intended to be "an American standard," has been visited by thousands of women. The brick house is described as "spacious yet cozy," featuring a living room with 18th century Georgian-style furniture; a Colonial American–style dining room; a kitchen with all the modern amenities, including a device that performs 30 separate actions, such as chopping and mixing; assorted bedrooms and four bathrooms; a nursery; and a two-car garage. The model was conceptualized by the New York State Federation of Women's Clubs.	Nov. 13
Citizens in Herrin, Illinois, are appealing for national guardsmen to patrol Southern Illinois. Bootlegger gang domination of the region has reached the point that sheriffs, prosecuting attorneys, and potential witnesses will not act "for fear of their own lives being taken."...The Ford Motor Company reports success in its transition to the five-day workweek.		The J. C. Penney Company is enjoying the most robust sales among the nation's leading chain stores.			Nov. 14
			The Coolidge administration plans to turn over New York-Chicago postal air routes to private enterprise. Officials reiterate that the government is not an aviation operating agency.		Nov. 15
Pennsylvania senator-elect William Vare files a financial statement that shows he spent $7,668 on his general election campaign; the Senate committee investigating him believes that he spent $600,000 on his earlier primary run.		The Great Lakes Harbors Association, representing the interests of Milwaukee, Toledo, Toronto, and other Great Lakes cities, denounces Chicago as "an outlaw city" that brazenly diverts water resources with no regard to laws and rights.	The Commerce Department admits that the nation's radio airwaves are becoming unmanageable. Experts feel that the nation's bandwidth capability will permit 178 properly spaced radio stations across the entire United States, while there are 595 stations already broadcasting, with 40 more due to go on the air.		Nov. 16
A Chicago grand jury indicts 75 people—most of them involved in law enforcement—for conspiring to violate Prohibition laws. The roster of alleged criminals includes a municipal judge, two police captains, a dozen other police officers, several former police officers, and a court bailiff....Benjamin Purnell, fugitive leader of the House of David commune, is captured by police in Benton Harbor, Michigan. Purnell has been wanted for four years on immorality charges.		According to the Agriculture Department, Thanksgiving dinners will be less expensive for American consumers this year, given the strong harvests in cranberries, potatoes, lettuce, and pumpkins. Texas, the nation's largest source of turkeys, has increased production 115 percent over last year, driving down consumer costs.		British physiologist Leonard E. Hill avers that scanty clothing is good for female constitutions. "Talk of 'pneumonia blouses' is all nonsense," he says. "No girl ever caught pneumonia wearing a low blouse. It hardens her and helps her to resist such diseases."	Nov. 17
Jane Gibson is wheeled into the courtroom on her hospital bed at the Hall-Mills murder trial, where she gives her testimony. Raucous crowds, many of them mocking her, turn out to watch Gibson's ambulance—followed by six carloads of newspaper reporters—on its 60-mile journey to Somerville, New Jersey. "Ooh, the Pig Woman'! Do yer squealin'I," is a typical taunt.		Sugar prices reach a yearly high, based on market rumors that Cuba plans to limit the sugar cane crop....International wheat prices have still been dropping.		The Paramount Theater in New York City's Times Square opens for business. The movie palace features an enormous organ, Italian marble columns, a "Hall of Nations" with stones from 17 countries, 58 individual paintings, a Peter Pan statue, and a "Powder Puff" room for women.	Nov. 18

F	G	H	I	J
Includes campaigns, elections, federal-state relations, civil rights and liberties, crime, the judiciary, education, healthcare, poverty, urban affairs, and population.	Includes formation and debate of U.S. foreign and defense policies, veterans affairs, and defense spending. (Relations with specific foreign countries are usually found under the region concerned.)	Includes business, labor, agriculture, taxation, transportation, consumer affairs, monetary and fiscal policy, natural resources, pollution and industrial accidents.	Includes worldwide scientific, medical and technological developments, natural phenomena, U.S. weather and natural disasters.	Includes the arts, religion, scholarship, communications media, sports, entertainment, fashions, fads, and social life.

	World Affairs	Europe	Africa & The Middle East	The Americas	Asia & The Pacific
Nov. 19	Disarmament negotiators at the League of Nations are concerned about the German government's ability to control the country's popular martial patriotic organizations.	The British Miners' Federation is recommending that all recalcitrant striking districts open negotiations with the owners.		A spokesman for the opposition in Nicaragua accuses the United States of "dollar diplomacy"—using support for the Diaz regime as a means to assert authority over the nation's railways and banks.	
Nov. 20		England declares its dominions to be equal and autonomous nations within the British Commonwealth, although they will lack independent constitutions. Observers point out that the decision reflects the English belief that "the Empire is most united when the ties binding it are the loosest." Due to preexisting arrangements, India is not included in the new compact.			
Nov. 21		The French franc has rebounded so quickly that it has caused a serious slowdown in the country's export trade....Large crowds are descending on the Mona Lisa at the Louvre. Cynics suspect that the current authenticity debate is a publicity stunt.	J. P. M. Hertzog, premier of South Africa, is credited with convincing England to declare equality for the dominions. He believes that "nothing has ever been accomplished so calculated to lay a deep and enduring foundation for national cooperation between the members of the British Commonwealth."		Foreign businesses operating in China are facing a quandary: the officially recognized Peking national government has essentially ceased to operate, while the Cantonese army—which refuses to recognize "unequal" foreign trade treaties—has begun to take on several of the functions of government. There is uncertainty about whom to deal with.
Nov. 22	German foreign minister Gustav Stresemann demands that Germany, now a full member of the League of Nations, be given equal treatment. "It is impossible and incompatible with equality to permit the continuance of general freedom of armament while dictating complete military impotence to one particular State," he asserts. Germany wants the Allied Military Commission of Control, in place since the end of the war to provide oversight for German armaments, to be disbanded.	The Soviet Union is attempting to reengineer the daily habits of government office workers by requiring them to be on the job at 9 a.m. Common practice since the tsarist era has been that office workers do not arrive until noon....The Moscow Clowns' Academy opens, with the purpose to train comics in "ironical satirization" of the bourgeoisie.			
Nov. 23		Rumors hold that Italian Fascists are preparing to conduct raids into France to kidnap leading Italian expatriate anti-Fascists....The town of Altdorf, Switzerland, is taxing women who wear bobbed hair....Soviet opposition leader Grigory Zinoviev resigns from his position as president of the Communist International.		The Mexican Catholic Episcopate accuses the Calles government of attempting to construct a "Communistic Utopia of socialism, free love, and the subjection of religion to the State."	Newspapers in India are angered that the country has not been granted dominion status in the British Commonwealth; one editorial observes that India will now be "subordinate in a household in which there are six mistresses instead of one."
Nov. 24		The American ambassador to France, Myron Herrick, tells an audience in Paris that recent accusations of American empire-building are absurd. "The United States has not the slightest desire for the throne of the universe or any other throne," he says. "We chiefly ask now, as always, simply to be let alone."			Agitators in Hankow are pressuring customs administration employees to strike, in an effort to shut down all foreign trade in the region.
Nov. 25			The president of American University in Cairo believes that movies and automobiles are helping to westernize Muslims. The turning point, he says, was the World War, during which Muslims who fought for the allies developed a taste for western values and goods.		

A	B	C	D	E
Includes developments that affect more than one world region, international organizations and important meetings of world leaders.	Includes all domestic and regional developments in Europe, including the Soviet Union.	Includes all domestic and regional developments in Africa and the Middle East.	Includes all domestic and regional developments in Latin America, the Caribbean, and Canada.	Includes all domestic and regional developments in Asian and Pacific nations (and colonies).

U.S. Politics & Social Issues	U.S. Foreign Policy & Affairs, Defense	U.S. Economy & Environment	Science, Technology & Nature	Culture, Leisure & Lifestyle	
				To ensure that his biblical epic *King of Kings* is adequately reverent, director Cecil B. DeMille is employing expert consultants including several church leaders, a rabbi, a biblical scholar, and Bruce Barton, author of *The Man Nobody Knows*.	Nov. 19
A Norwegian oil tanker explodes at a dry dock in Baltimore, killing at least 40 workmen....Confederate president Jefferson Davis's mansion in Mississippi has been reopened as a home for Confederate Army veterans.			According to statistics, around 60 percent of America's industries are now electrified.	The film adaptation of the hit anti-war play *What Price Glory*, directed by Raoul Walsh and starring Victor McLaglen, is now playing....The Carnegie Corporation has donated $4.5 million in the past year to improve American library service; plans are afoot to found a new graduate library at the University of Chicago.	Nov. 20
Jewish philanthropist Nathan Straus accuses Henry Ford of anti-Semitism, carried out in a "campaign of slander against the Jewish people" in his newspaper the *Dearborn Independent*.					Nov. 21
The U.S. Supreme Court rules that an automobile used to illegally transport liquor can be seized, even if the owner is "innocent of wrongful intent."...Oregon Senator Gilbert Haugen is working on a streamlined version of the McNary-Haughen farm relief bill that failed in the last congress....The jury is selected for the trial of Albert Fall, the secretary of the interior during the Harding administration, and oil magnate Edward Doheny. The defendants are charged with conspiracy in the 1922 Elk Hills oil reserve scandal.			The *Scientific American* reports that a psychic medium in Attleboro, MA, has been receiving messages from dead magician Harry Houdini.		Nov. 22
				Noel Coward's play *This Was a Man* opens on Broadway.	Nov. 23
Many Republican senators support using the federal surplus to pay down the national debt....Nine days after a coal mine in Hazleton, Pennsylvania, is flooded, five miners are pulled out alive....Statistics indicate that 70 percent of American men between the ages of 20 and 24 are unmarried, while 32 percent of men between the ages of 25 and 34 are bachelors.			A joint panel of engineers from the United States and Canada has determined that the St. Lawrence River can be "canalized," with a deepened 25-foot channel, to provide a waterway from the Great Lakes to the Atlantic Ocean. The estimated cost of the project runs between $350 and $650 million.	The Thomas Lawrence painting *Pinkie* sells at public auction in London for $377,000—a world record-setting price for an auction sale....More than 1.5 million fans attended Big Ten college football games during the season just completed. The largest paid attendance was 94,000 for the Ohio State–Michigan game.	Nov. 24
Alabama governor-elect Bibb Graves, reputedly a member of the Ku Klux Klan, has appointed another reputed Klansman to be the state's assistant attorney general....A Thanksgiving Day attack on the southside O'Donnell Brothers gang in Chicago fails to kill anyone, although two bootleggers and a bystander are wounded. More than 100 machine-gun rounds are fired at the victims from an automobile.			Tornadoes touch down in a half dozen different places in Arkansas, killing 34 people on Thanksgiving.	Department of Commerce statistics indicate that the American divorce rate outpaced the marriage rate in 1925: divorces were up 2.7 percent, while marriages were up a fraction of one percent. The states with the highest percentage increases in divorce were Utah and Florida, at over 20 percent.	Nov. 25

F	G	H	I	J
Includes campaigns, elections, federal-state relations, civil rights and liberties, crime, the judiciary, education, healthcare, poverty, urban affairs, and population.	Includes formation and debate of U.S. foreign and defense policies, veterans affairs, and defense spending. (Relations with specific foreign countries are usually found under the region concerned.)	Includes business, labor, agriculture, taxation, transportation, consumer affairs, monetary and fiscal policy, natural resources, pollution and industrial accidents.	Includes worldwide scientific, medical and technological developments, natural phenomena, U.S. weather and natural disasters.	Includes the arts, religion, scholarship, communications media, sports, entertainment, fashions, fads, and social life.

	World Affairs	Europe	Africa & The Middle East	The Americas	Asia & The Pacific
Nov. 26		France is experiencing a spike in unemployment related to the new-found strength of the franc and the resulting dip in exports.		All of the British oil companies operating in Mexico have complied with the new Calles petroleum laws, but only a few American companies have done so. U.S. Secretary of State Frank Kellogg explains America's objection. The laws provide confirmation of oil rights for a period "not more than fifty years from the time exploitation work began"; this means that the Mexican government wants American companies to exchange their unlimited rights for time-limited concessions "of manifestly less scope and value."	The strikes in Hankow now involve servants, washmen, rice dealers, and railwaymen; a general strike and boycott against the British are expected.
Nov. 27		The city of Leningrad is being plagued by hooliganism, with more than 12,000 acts recorded in the past six months, many of them committed by young unemployed males against women and girls. Newspapers blame peasants who move to the city with no sense of "revolutionary order and discipline."			Foreigners in Shanghai hope that an anti-Communist northern general, Chang Chung-chang, prevails in the current unrest, but the majority of the city's Chinese population hates and fears the northern armies and supports Cantonese general Chiang Kai-shek.
Nov. 28			The Carnegie Endowment for International Peace releases a pessimistic report about the Jewish movement to colonize Palestine, anticipating that it will "bring more unhappiness for both the Jew and the Arab, … accentuating at each step bitterness that already lies just below the surface." The idea of a Jewish homeland in Palestine aggrieves the Arabs, "who demand to know, and with some reason, what is to become of them."	Skirmishing continues between rebels and government troops in Nicaragua.	
Nov. 29			The World Zionist Organization responds to yesterday's report by the Carnegie Endowment for International Peace, which called Jewish homeland aspirations in Palestine "unfortunate and visionary." A spokesman points to new industrial enterprises that will improve the standard of living for both Jews and Arabs.	The Mexican minister of foreign relations reports that American, British, and French oil companies are experiencing little difficulty in complying with the country's new oil regulations. However, American oil companies deny that they have adhered to the laws.	British journalists in China describe the current anti-foreign unrest as "the gravest crisis since the Boxer rebellion." British shipping in the upper stretches of the Yangtze River may be halted; Chinese military authorities are firing on the ships daily, forcing them to pay bribes and commandeering them as troop transports. There is concern about Chiang Kai-shek's recent insistence that "unequal" treaties with foreign powers must be abrogated.
Nov. 30					The entire cabinet of the Chinese national government in Peking quits, citing a lack of funding to "carry on even the most elementary functions."…The United States dispatches two naval destroyers to the upper Yangtze River near Hankow.
Dec. 1		King Vidor's powerful war film *The Big Parade* premieres in Paris, playing to a house packed with dignitaries and World War veterans. It is hoped that the film can serve a diplomatic purpose, evoking a sense of wartime comradeship for audiences amid recent tensions between France and the United States.	John Vandermerwe, a champion South African big game hunter with 38 lion kills to his credit, is mauled to death by a lion.	Secretary of State Frank Kellogg offers a possible solution to the ongoing Tacna-Arica dispute between Chile and Peru: sell the contested provinces to Bolivia.	The American Extraterritoriality Commission in China has published a report condemning the "illegal and brutal actions" of the Chinese generals, who continue to destabilize the country. Chinese nationalists are angered by the report, which they say demonstrates Western disdain for Chinese rights. American and British observers are concerned about the recent successes of Cantonese general Chiang Kai-shek, who is said to be influenced by Bolshevism.…Amid heckling at the House of Commons, British foreign secretary Austen Chamberlain asserts that the Chinese situation does not merit military intervention.

A	B	C	D	E
Includes developments that affect more than one world region, international organizations and important meetings of world leaders.	*Includes all domestic and regional developments in Europe, including the Soviet Union.*	*Includes all domestic and regional developments in Africa and the Middle East.*	*Includes all domestic and regional developments in Latin America, the Caribbean, and Canada.*	*Includes all domestic and regional developments in Asian and Pacific nations (and colonies).*

U.S. Politics & Social Issues	U.S. Foreign Policy & Affairs, Defense	U.S. Economy & Environment	Science, Technology & Nature	Culture, Leisure & Lifestyle	
Florida's Seminole Indians, who have never officially made peace with the United States following warfare in the early 19th century, finally swear alliance to the American flag and petition for citizenship rights.		Nineteen banks in Iowa are forced to close to ward off runs by depositors....The Scripps-Howard Newspapers chain continues to expand; recent purchases have given the company 25 newspapers in cities ranging from Baltimore to Albuquerque.	Best-selling author and explorer William Beebe announces the development of a deep-sea submersible, capable of withstanding pressure a mile below the ocean surface, with plans for tests along the Equator next year.		Nov. 26
	According to military budget statistics, the United States spends 52.3 cents per day to feed a navy sailor, 49.7 cents to feed a marine, and 31.5 cents to feed an army soldier.			The biggest college football game of the year, between archrivals Army and Navy before 110,000 fans at Soldier Field in Chicago, ends in a hard-fought 21–21 tie....Columbia University Teachers' College is hosting 27 international education administrators in the United States to study methods for teaching immigrants in large cities, poor whites and blacks in the South, "and other problems of like nature."	Nov. 27
A survey of 4,700 male community leaders in the National Economic League identifies "disrespect for the law" as the most pressing problem facing the nation.		Secretary of Commerce Herbert Hoover releases a report on economic conditions during 1926, concluding that America's current prosperity is unsurpassed in the nation's history. He cites high wages, virtually full employment, and manufacturing productivity up seven percent for the year....In a contrasting view, Iowa senator Smith W. Brookhart asserts that "America's much-vaunted prosperity means sheriff's sales for the farmer."		Paul Robeson and Lawrence Brown perform African-American spirituals and folk songs at a joint concert in New York City.	Nov. 28
The U.S. Supreme Court upholds Prohibition limitations on the use of medicinal whiskey. The law permits doctors to prescribe no more than one pint for a patient every 10 days.				Ethel Barrymore is starring in W. Somerset Maugham's comedy The Constant Wife on Broadway....Star centerfielder Tris Speaker retires from major league baseball after a 19-year career.	Nov. 29
		The state of Idaho hopes to purchase 8,000 acres of prime land in Yellowstone National Park to build a reservoir to assist beet farmers.		Warren Griffin, a 15-year-old from Oscar, Kentucky, wins the title of the nation's healthiest farm boy at the International Live Stock Exposition in Chicago.	Nov. 30
The United States has deported 10,994 illegal aliens during the past year—a record number. The majority are Europeans who passed into the country through Canada.		Wall Street financial firms, flush with profits, are expected to hand out $35 million in Christmas bonuses this year.	A cold wave descends on the Midwest, causing temperatures in Iowa to plummet 50 degrees in 24 hours. The thermometer in one Minnesota town registers at 26 below zero.	Stage actor Rudolph Zaslavsky, known as the "Edwin Booth of the Soviet Union," is in Brooklyn appearing in Yiddish plays. He describes the challenges facing Russian actors under Communism: they appear in State dramas before peasant audiences, who pay them with onions and eggs....A Rudolph Valentino look-alike has recently arrived in New York City from Hungary; according to his handlers, the young actor has already received offers from Universal and Paramount studios....Charlie Chaplin and his second wife, Lita Grey, have separated.	Dec. 1

F	G	H	I	J
Includes campaigns, elections, federal-state relations, civil rights and liberties, crime, the judiciary, education, healthcare, poverty, urban affairs, and population.	Includes formation and debate of U.S. foreign and defense policies, veterans affairs, and defense spending. (Relations with specific foreign countries are usually found under the region concerned.)	Includes business, labor, agriculture, taxation, transportation, consumer affairs, monetary and fiscal policy, natural resources, pollution and industrial accidents.	Includes worldwide scientific, medical and technological developments, natural phenomena, U.S. weather and natural disasters.	Includes the arts, religion, scholarship, communications media, sports, entertainment, fashions, fads, and social life.

	World Affairs	Europe	Africa & The Middle East	The Americas	Asia & The Pacific
Dec. 2		Leon Trotsky continues in his fall from power in the Soviet Union: he has now been removed from a minor office, as head of a provincial hydroelectric power works....The British Miners' Federation derides the lack of support shown by the American Federation of Labor during the coal strike. The AFL contributed less than £20 thousand to the effort, compared to £1.8 million that came from the Soviet Union.			Five northern Chinese generals band together in an effort to stop the southern Cantonese army. Zhang Zuolin, the generalissimo of the united forces, proclaims that he will "relieve the distress of the people, exterminate rebels and strengthen the nation's foundations." Wu Pei-fu, who recently controlled much of Central China, is absent from the union, evidence that he has lost his influence.
Dec. 3		The Soviet Union is actively buying American-made tractors and other farm equipment.			
Dec. 4		Although the Soviet Union controls the Siberian fur industry, it is primarily financed by the United States. This year U.S. business interests will provide around $6 million to outfit fur trappers in the Siberian Arctic. American women are the largest consumers of Siberian pelts....Italy plans to establish a national theater, with playwright Luigi Pirandello as the director.			China announces that it will no longer submit to unequal treaties with the sixteen countries that possess treaty rights in China, including the United States, England, and Japan. All new treaties must be based on equality and reciprocity....Former British prime minister Lloyd George castigates the nation's conservative press, which has been calling for military intervention in China.
Dec. 5		The British coal situation is improving; the industry is now producing an estimated 2 million tons per week, although the typical pre-strike output was 5 million....The London Stock Exchange remains flat, as most sectors of the national economy continue to feel the strike's aftereffects....French Impressionist painter Claude Monet dies....British police authorities announce that mystery writer Agatha Christie has disappeared from her home in Sunningdale.	Turkish newspapers are pushing to rename Constantinople after President Kemal....A newly discovered chamber of King Tut-ankh-amen's tomb in Egypt is yielding treasures.	The Chilean government tentatively accepts Secretary Kellogg's proposal to end the Tacna–Arica dispute by selling the region to Bolivia.	
Dec. 6		Judging domestic coal stocks to be sufficient, the British government authorizes the renewal of coal exports....The Italian government institutes a tax on bachelors between the ages of 25 and 65, in an effort to pressure them to marry. Unmarried women are exempt, Premier Mussolini declares, because "the failure to contract matrimony often does not depend on the desires of women."		Pointing to Soviet embassy activity in Mexico, the U.S. State Department insinuates that the Calles government has Bolshevist ties. The Mexican president responds that the charge is pure propaganda.	The Cantonese army carries a manual that teaches: "Who are your chief enemies? Great Britain and Japan."
Dec. 7		A British newspaper responds to President Coolidge's budget message, which considers various options for using the federal surplus: "To the impoverished tax-crushed people of Europe such discussions seem like those of the ancient gods on Mount Olympus, impervious to mere human suffering....No power gives Olympians the gift to see themselves as others see them."		Mexico officially recognizes rebel leader Juan Sacasa and his government in Nicaragua.	

A	B	C	D	E
Includes developments that affect more than one world region, international organizations and important meetings of world leaders.	*Includes all domestic and regional developments in Europe, including the Soviet Union.*	*Includes all domestic and regional developments in Africa and the Middle East.*	*Includes all domestic and regional developments in Latin America, the Caribbean, and Canada.*	*Includes all domestic and regional developments in Asian and Pacific nations (and colonies).*

U.S. Politics & Social Issues	U.S. Foreign Policy & Affairs, Defense	U.S. Economy & Environment	Science, Technology & Nature	Culture, Leisure & Lifestyle	
The defense rests in the Hall-Mills murder case. Throughout the trial, Frances Hall's counsel has focused on inconsistencies in the rambling testimony of the prosecution's star witness, Jane Gibson. Today the defense attacks Gibson as an eccentric with a "rambling, dreaming, visionary mind," compelled by the spotlight to create multiple versions of the murder story, "each one better and more graphic."				The 1926 college football season earned $30 million for the nation's universities. Five eastern schools—Harvard, Yale, Pittsburgh, Pennsylvania, and Columbia—were the biggest draws....Sidney Howard's play *Ned McCobb's Daughter*, starring Alfred Lunt and Clare Eames, has opened in New York City.	Dec. 2
The three defendants in the Hall-Mills case are found not guilty. The lack of credibility of witness Jane Gibson proves to be the determining factor. While the case has been hashed out on the front pages of newspapers for months, the jury needs only five hours to make its decision.	Bond prices are skyrocketing, and the volume of bond trading has reached an all-time high. During the past week, Wall Street sold $250 million in new bond offerings; typically $100 million is regarded as a busy week....A pool of investors led by Chicago commodities trader Arthur W. Cutten has earned $10 million during the past month on Baldwin Locomotive stock; from a low of 92, shares closed yesterday at 165.			Circus founder Charles Ringling dies.	Dec. 3
	Two army generals criticize the Coolidge administration for failing to meet the goals of the 1920 National Defense Act. The current size of the army in 131,000; the legislation had called for a buildup to 280,000.			Notre Dame meets the University of Southern California in college football for the first time, winning 13–12 before a crowd of 76,500 in Los Angeles....The U.S. Postal Service explains procedures for mailing Christmas letters and packages, including reminding immigrants to write the name of their destination country in English, "as all clerks cannot read foreign languages."	Dec. 4
A pastor in New York City responds to the Hall-Mills media frenzy: "We cannot but wonder why the papers gave such space or why the crowds read the inane, cheap and nauseating evidence. Let us now have a few columns of optimism, of recounting good deeds."		The Plate Glass Manufacturers of America announces a record year in production, surpassing 135 million square feet. Five years ago the total was less than 55 million square feet. The upsurge is attributed to the recent popularity of plate glass in new office buildings and hotels.	The American Telephone and Telegraph Company will inaugurate transatlantic radiophone service between the United States and England. Calls will cost $15 per minute....The United States Biological Survey reports that only one jaguar remains in the state of Arizona; a hunter killed its mate yesterday.	Golden Rule Sunday is observed in churches across the United States to raise money for Armenian earthquake victims....Soviet director Sergei Eisenstein's masterpiece *The Battleship Potemkin* is publicly screened for the first time in the United States.	Dec. 5
Returned from a five-month break, the U.S. Congress prepares for a short session that will end in early March....The American Farm Bureau convenes at its annual convention in Chicago. Leaders insist that farmers are being punished for their own success, as bumper crops produce low prices. Cooperative marketing is seen as the mechanism to solve the surplus problem.		National City Bank announces new capitalization plans that will make it the largest bank in the world.		According to the National Industrial Conference Board, a working-class family of three can maintain "a fair American standard of living" in Brooklyn for $25.94 per week. Expenses include $7.50 for rent and $10.25 for food. Brooklyn is the least expensive of New York's five boroughs.	Dec. 6
President Coolidge's annual budget message is read before Congress. The president advises following a moderate course, reminding congressmen that major legislation will be hard to enact during the upcoming short session. "What the country requires," he states, "is not so much new policies as a steady continuation of those which are already being crowned with such abundant success."			The United States Public Health Service advises that airborne coal smoke is a leading cause of pneumonia.		Dec. 7

F	**G**	**H**	**I**	**J**
Includes campaigns, elections, federal-state relations, civil rights and liberties, crime, the judiciary, education, healthcare, poverty, urban affairs, and population.	*Includes formation and debate of U.S. foreign and defense policies, veterans affairs, and defense spending. (Relations with specific foreign countries are usually found under the region concerned.)*	*Includes business, labor, agriculture, taxation, transportation, consumer affairs, monetary and fiscal policy, natural resources, pollution and industrial accidents.*	*Includes worldwide scientific, medical and technological developments, natural phenomena, U.S. weather and natural disasters.*	*Includes the arts, religion, scholarship, communications media, sports, entertainment, fashions, fads, and social life.*

	World Affairs	Europe	Africa & The Middle East	The Americas	Asia & The Pacific
Dec. 8		A Polish diplomat in the United States attributes acts of persecution against Jews in his country to Jewish "aloofness." Problems can be alleviated, he says, when the Jewish population engages in "sincere cooperation" with other Poles....The French franc is now worth more than four cents, its highest valuation this year.		The U.S. State Department announces that it will closely monitor Juan Sacasa's rebel government. There are currently five American naval ships off the east coast of Nicaragua, near the rebel "capital."	
Dec. 9		The recent uptick in Royal Air Force aviation fatalities—there have been 83 so far this year—is discussed by the British House of Commons. A third of the accidents have occurred in older model aircraft that have been in service since before 1917.	Liberia grants one million acres to the Firestone Tire and Rubber Company to construct a rubber plantation.		
Dec. 10	The 1926 Nobel Peace Prize is awarded to American vice-president Charles Dawes and British foreign secretary Austen Chamberlain.	The British Advisory Committee on Spoken English directs broadcasters to use proper pronunciation for several words, rejecting the American variants. For example, the first syllable of "patriot" must rhyme with "hat."...The first British national polo team to feature Indian Army officers, due to play next year for the International Cup, is being sponsored by a flood of contributions from throughout India.			
Dec. 11				Nicaraguan president Adolfo Diaz requests American intervention in his country, charging that Mexico is planning to send troops and gunboats to assist the rebels in toppling his government.	
Dec. 12		A manhunt is underway for Agatha Christie, the mystery novelist who has been missing now for nine days. At least 10,000 searchers and several packs of bloodhounds are sweeping Sussex Downs in England. Police are frustrated that many of the searchers seem to be there in a "holiday spirit," serving no purpose other than to create traffic jams with their automobiles and bicycles.		Mexico's Foreign Office dismisses Adolfo Diaz's charges of their military threat to Nicaragua.	
Dec. 13	The "Big Five" allied powers agree to cede control of German armaments beginning on January 31 next year.	Italy launches the passenger ocean liner *Augustus*, at 33,000 tons the largest diesel-driven ship in the world.	The Kemal government in Turkey is attempting to convince Islamic women to no longer wear the traditional veil. Officials argue that the practice is unhygienic. Turkish women, particularly from the lower classes, will not be swayed.		Australia is fighting an outbreak of bush fires near the town of Dubbo. Six people and tens of thousands of sheep have been killed.

A	B	C	D	E
Includes developments that affect more than one world region, international organizations and important meetings of world leaders.	Includes all domestic and regional developments in Europe, including the Soviet Union.	Includes all domestic and regional developments in Africa and the Middle East.	Includes all domestic and regional developments in Latin America, the Caribbean, and Canada.	Includes all domestic and regional developments in Asian and Pacific nations (and colonies).

U.S. Politics & Social Issues	U.S. Foreign Policy & Affairs, Defense	U.S. Economy & Environment	Science, Technology & Nature	Culture, Leisure & Lifestyle	
A conference meeting in Washington, DC called the Conference on the Cause and Cure of War, brings together representatives from nine national women's organizations from across the political spectrum. These include the American Association of University Women, the General Federation of Women's Clubs, and the National Woman's Christian Temperance Union. A major topic of discussion at the conference is the "irreconcilable" U.S. Senate attitude toward the World Court.	The House Naval Committee takes issue with statements made by President Coolidge during his recent budget message. The president noted that there would be no funds made available to build three new light cruisers, which were originally authorized in 1924. Citing the United States involvement in preliminary negotiations on international naval disarmament, Coolidge advised that it "would be unfortunate and not in keeping with our attitude toward these negotiations" to proceed with ship construction. Several congressmen are upset with the president's apparent lack of a sense of urgency about military matters.			American newspapers used 18 percent more newsprint during the first nine months of 1926 than during the same time period in 1925....The German film *Faust*, directed by F. W. Murnau and starring Emil Jannings, has been released in the United States.	Dec. 8
Kenneth Ormiston, the former consort of evangelist Aimee Semple McPherson, wanted by authorities for his participation in her kidnapping hoax, is caught in Harrisburg, Pennsylvania. Living under assumed names, he eluded detectives for six months....A coal mine fire in Princeton, Indiana, kills 26 miners.		Secretary of the Treasury Andrew Mellon predicts continued prosperity in 1927. He points to the economy's broad-based health. Average Americans are being prudent, building up their savings accounts and buying more life insurance policies and bond securities, even as they spend more than ever before as consumers.	The American College of Surgeons announces plans to utilize film technology. Medical movies will record surgical techniques, the progression of diseases, and the functions of human organs....The American Society for the Control of Cancer maintains that all cancers can be cured if treated in the earliest stage.		Dec. 9
President Coolidge meets at the White House with 600 women delegates from the Conference on the Cause and Cure of War....Prohibition head Lincoln Andrews acknowledges that the federal government should not encroach on law-enforcement powers that belong to local police jurisdictions. "But I am charged with enforcement of the [Eighteenth Amendment], so what can I do?" he asks.		More than two-thirds of the world's life insurance protection, worth $63.8 billion, is held in the United States.		The seafaring adventure movie *Old Ironsides*, starring Charles Farrell and Wallace Beery, is playing in theaters.	Dec. 10
Republican members of the House Ways and Means Committee have rejected President Coolidge's proposal to provide income-tax refunds out of the federal surplus. The congressional preference is to use the surplus to pay down the national debt....The Federal Council of Churches issues demands for stiffer Prohibition enforcement, federal lynch laws, greater cooperation with the Calles government in Mexico, and resolution of the "comparatively unimportant" objections preventing America from joining the World Court.				Many college football teams are naming a lineman as their team captain for next year—a significant change from the usual practice of choosing a halfback for the role....The film *His Busy Hour*, with a cast of deaf actors, is exhibited at the Lexington School for the Deaf in New York City. The premise behind the movie is that deaf people are particularly adept at pantomime and might find careers on the screen.	Dec. 11
New Jersey police authorities, who irregularly enforce the state's Sunday blue laws, perform a surprise crackdown on the town of Irvington. They net 98 lawbreakers at their jobs, including taxi drivers, cigar storekeepers, bootblacks, trolley drivers, and newspaper reporters.			The Smithsonian Institution is undertaking an extensive study of solar radiation.		Dec. 12
The ten-month Passaic textiles strike has ended, with a good measure of success for the workers. Under the aegis of the American Federation of Labor, the union is now officially recognized by the mill owners and guaranteed the right of collective bargaining. The Botany Worsted Mill, the site of much labor unrest this past spring, has begun to accept back workers.	Members of the House Naval Committee sharply question President Coolidge's unwillingness to provide funds for three new naval cruisers.		A major winter storm hits the Rocky Mountain states, snarling train traffic and bringing air mail service to a halt.	A nationwide newspaper survey of religious attitudes finds that 89 percent of Americans believe in God and 70 percent worship regularly....Pope Pius XI attacks women's modern clothing trends as "an ugly, ruinous, catastrophic tendency, which Catholic husbands, fathers and brothers should attempt to check at all costs."	Dec. 13

F	G	H	I	J
Includes campaigns, elections, federal-state relations, civil rights and liberties, crime, the judiciary, education, healthcare, poverty, urban affairs, and population.	*Includes formation and debate of U.S. foreign and defense policies, veterans affairs, and defense spending. (Relations with specific foreign countries are usually found under the region concerned.)*	*Includes business, labor, agriculture, taxation, transportation, consumer affairs, monetary and fiscal policy, natural resources, pollution and industrial accidents.*	*Includes worldwide scientific, medical and technological developments, natural phenomena, U.S. weather and natural disasters.*	*Includes the arts, religion, scholarship, communications media, sports, entertainment, fashions, fads, and social life.*

	World Affairs	Europe	Africa & The Middle East	The Americas	Asia & The Pacific
Dec. 14		Mystery writer Agatha Christie, missing since December 10, is located at a Yorkshire spa, where she is staying under an assumed name. Christie's husband tells reporters that his wife had lost her memory. Skeptics wonder at all the newspaper attention given to her "mysterious disappearance," pointing out that she had notified a relative about her plans to stay at a spa.			Anti-British agitation has erupted again in Hankow, where strikers have forced British-American Tobacco Company facilities to close.
Dec. 15		Newspaper magnate William Randolph Hearst has purchased a 10th-century cloister, located in Segovia, Spain, and is having it disassembled piece by piece and shipped to California for rebuilding. This has prompted the Spanish government to pass a law forbidding the exportation of valuable national art and architecture.		Rebel forces are reportedly advancing on the Nicaraguan capital of Managua.	
Dec. 16			The American Red Cross declines an appeal for aid to victims of an ongoing famine in Syria. The organization's mandate limits it to providing relief in "sudden" emergency situations.	The Calles government reminds American companies that the deadline to comply with the new Mexican oil laws is December 31. The Americans have protested that the laws do not adequately safeguard their pre-existing commercial and land rights.	
Dec. 17		German chancellor Wilhelm Marx receives a no-confidence vote in the Reichstag and is forced to resign.... The government of Lithuania is toppled in a coup d'etat, carried out by groups hostile to the country's growing links to the Soviet Union.			Cantonese forces have reportedly captured the city of Yichang on the upper Yangtze River, where they have fired on Japanese and British steamers.
Dec. 18		The Mussolini government temporarily lifts limitations on the use of wheat flour so that bakers can make sweet breads and cakes for Christmas.		President Adolfo Diaz expresses his frustration that the United States will not send troops to aid him in Nicaragua. "I cannot believe," he says, "that the United States government will stand aloof and allow Mexico to overthrow a Nicaraguan government recognized by the United States."	
Dec. 19		Pope Pius XII offers thanks for Benito Mussolini's life after recent assassination attempts, calling his survival the "almost visible intervention of Divine Providence." The pope then goes on to condemn Mussolini's Fascist government for making "the State an end in itself and citizens mere means to that end."			

A	B	C	D	E
Includes developments that affect more than one world region, international organizations and important meetings of world leaders.	Includes all domestic and regional developments in Europe, including the Soviet Union.	Includes all domestic and regional developments in Africa and the Middle East.	Includes all domestic and regional developments in Latin America, the Caribbean, and Canada.	Includes all domestic and regional developments in Asian and Pacific nations (and colonies).

U.S. Politics & Social Issues	U.S. Foreign Policy & Affairs, Defense	U.S. Economy & Environment	Science, Technology & Nature	Culture, Leisure & Lifestyle	
Plans are announced that a new two-year junior college for women, to be called Sarah Lawrence College, will be opened in Bronxville, NY, in 1928....The mayor and the chief of police of Edgewater, NJ, are indicted for their roles in a $2 million rum-running operation.					Dec. 14
The U.S. Senate rejects a request by Prohibition head Lincoln Andrews to appropriate $500,000 in funds to employ anonymous "undercover" men, who would amass evidence against bootleggers while remaining off the official government payroll.		The U.S. Chamber of Congress urges President Coolidge to take advantage of the federal budget surplus to slash the corporate income tax.		Three college football teams, Alabama, Stanford, and Lafayette, finish the season with undefeated records, although Navy is widely regarded as the strongest team in the nation....College football officials are seriously considering eliminating the point-after-touchdown kick; detractors argue that football is a team sport and too many games are being determined by the success or failure of a single player, the kicker.	Dec. 15
A jury finds former secretary of the interior Albert Fall and oil tycoon Edward Doheny not guilty of conspiracy charges related to the Elk Hills oil reserve scandal. However, Fall will be tried again next month for his central role in the Teapot Dome scandal....The jury decision is decried by newspapers across the country; former secretary of the navy Josephus Daniels calls the jury members "mental inepts."	President Coolidge is conferencing with the chairman of the House Naval Committee on the issue of military spending. Congressmen are concerned that the U.S. Navy will fall behind the navies of Great Britain, Japan, and France if adequate funding is not provided.	Automobile sales have slowed noticeably since late October, and many car dealers report lots full of new cars. Many Detroit companies plan to close for the holidays to lessen production.		Major league baseball owners reelect Kenesaw Mountain Landis to a second term as commissioner....British novelist Rebecca West announces plans to relocate from England to New York City, citing America's "vitality." Among other subjects, she discusses the Hall-Mills murder trial. She found the atmosphere to be "delightfully light-hearted." "Everybody in New York seemed to be going up for the trial, all one's friends," she says.	Dec. 16
		Wall Street is enjoying a pre-Christmas bull run, with three 2,000,000-share trading days during the past week.	A national medical conference on rabies advocates mandatory pet immunizations and the destruction of stray dogs. Statistics for one state, New Jersey, indicate that there were 202 cases of rabies in dogs during the past year, with seven people dying from rabid dog bites.	An issue in pulpits and newspapers this Christmas season is whether "Xmas" is an irreverent abbreviation....Lewis Mumford publishes The Golden Day, his study of American literary transcendentalism.	Dec. 17
A debate team from Lincoln University, an African-American school, defeats debaters from England's Oxford University. The country's first international interracial debate is held at an African Methodist Episcopal church in Baltimore.	President Coolidge signals his approval of $140 million in expenditures to build ten new 10,000-ton cruisers for the Navy. The legislation is introduced by Thomas Butler, the chairman of the House Naval Committee. The president had earlier supported the idea that postponing new naval construction might spur international disarmament talks....The U.S. Navy has contracted with two companies, Curtiss and Boeing, to build fighter planes that will use all-metal construction, rather than wood-and-wire fuselage frames. A shipboard fighter plane is also being flight tested.	Shares of U.S. Steel close at an all-time high following a wild day of speculative buying. More than 600,000 shares exchange hands, the largest daily volume for the stock since 1916. The frenzy is fueled by the company's announcement of a substantial dividend increase.... R.H. Macy & Co. in New York City is employing 12,000 workers in 156 store departments for the Christmas season. There are 29 information clerks on hand to answer shopper questions. The company utilizes 355 delivery trucks, which transport up to 75,000 packages daily.	Plans have been filed in New York City to build the world's tallest building, a 110-story skyscraper in Times Square to be called the Larkin Tower Building.	The heavily accessorized doll is the most popular toy for Christmas this year. "One can buy for it now not only shoes, dresses, and millinery," a department store spokesman relates, "but also rainy-day outfits, umbrellas, vanity sets, trousseaus, hot-water bottles, eyeglasses, sun visors and wrist watches."... Department store Santa Clauses in New York City are drawing an estimated 5,000 children daily.	Dec. 18
The National Negro Development Union meets in Harlem to protest the Aiken, South Carolina, lynchings in October. Among the topics of discussion are white author Carl Van Vechten's Harlem novel Nigger Heaven. A Wilberforce College professor reads pages from the book deemed offensive, rips them out, and burns them onstage. He calls for blacks to form their own protective association, to be called the "Black Hawks," to counter the Ku Klux Klan.		Statistics indicate that Americans invested a billion dollars in foreign countries during 1926. Investment centered in Europe, but South America has become an important market.	According to radio retailers, consumers are becoming more savvy about radio technology. Whereas a few years ago they bought inferior equipment simply to have a radio, today they insist on high-quality name brands and in-store demonstrations.	French author Maurice Muret's treatise The Decline of the White Race is published in America....Among the Christmas gifts received so far this year at the White House are a pair of boxing gloves for President Coolidge, with a note to "use them on Congress," and a ceremonial Indian robe for First Lady Grace Coolidge from the Camp Fire Girls.	Dec. 19

F	G	H	I	J
Includes campaigns, elections, federal-state relations, civil rights and liberties, crime, the judiciary, education, healthcare, poverty, urban affairs, and population.	Includes formation and debate of U.S. foreign and defense policies, veterans affairs, and defense spending. (Relations with specific foreign countries are usually found under the region concerned.)	Includes business, labor, agriculture, taxation, transportation, consumer affairs, monetary and fiscal policy, natural resources, pollution and industrial accidents.	Includes worldwide scientific, medical and technological developments, natural phenomena, U.S. weather and natural disasters.	Includes the arts, religion, scholarship, communications media, sports, entertainment, fashions, fads, and social life.

	World Affairs	Europe	Africa & The Middle East	The Americas	Asia & The Pacific
Dec. 20		A Paris hotel chambermaid bites into an apple, which she pilfered from a suitcase, and discovers the Grand Condé diamond, stolen from a museum in October. Police apprehend the suspected burglars; their first question is, "Do you like apples?"			Tokyo is at a virtual standstill today, as Japan keeps a vigil for the invalid Emperor Yoshihito, who is critically ill.
Dec. 21		Several well-known French actors have quit the famous Comédie Française in Paris, where some remuneration schedules have not been changed since the theater was founded under Napoleon.			
Dec. 22		German department stores, using the installment plan for the first time since the World War, are enjoying brisk Christmas sales.			
Dec. 23		The Mussolini government implements a Fascist calendar, which gives both regular years and years marked from the "birth date" of Fascism in Italy in 1922. According to the calendar, 1926 is Fascist year IV.		American forces land in Nicaragua, in what is described as a precautionary measure to protect American lives and property.... Senator William Borah charges that the United States is using Nicaragua to ignite a "shameless, cowardly little war with Mexico," to protect American oil interests.	
Dec. 24					
Dec. 25		Champagne in France costs double what it did last year, contributing to a less festive Christmas atmosphere in Paris.		The American military command in Nicaragua demands that rebel leader Juan Sacasa and his followers immediately disarm.	Japanese Emperor Yoshihito dies at the age of 47.
Dec. 26		British coal production is almost back to normal. Miners continue to return to the pits, with 150,000 starting work again this week, bringing the total to 886,500 employed.			The British Foreign Office plans to take a more conciliatory approach to China's nationalist movements. In a major policy memorandum, recently released to the public, England recognizes the growing importance of the Cantonese army and recommends revising the five-power treaties with China.
Dec. 27		The Soviet Union will provide better pay to military officers, reportedly in an effort to quell grumbling in the Red Army....According to his physician, Benito Mussolini takes no more than three minutes to eat his meals; the dictator is otherwise in good health.			

A	B	C	D	E
Includes developments that affect more than one world region, international organizations and important meetings of world leaders.	Includes all domestic and regional developments in Europe, including the Soviet Union.	Includes all domestic and regional developments in Africa and the Middle East.	Includes all domestic and regional developments in Latin America, the Caribbean, and Canada.	Includes all domestic and regional developments in Asian and Pacific nations (and colonies).

U.S. Politics & Social Issues	U.S. Foreign Policy & Affairs, Defense	U.S. Economy & Environment	Science, Technology & Nature	Culture, Leisure & Lifestyle	
In a statement released by the White House, President Coolidge sends Christmas greetings to the nation's veterans....A Hudson River ferry taking workers to a linseed oil plant hits an ice floe and quickly sinks, drowning at least 35 men.				Just months after winning the World Series, the St. Louis Cardinals trade their manager and biggest star, Rogers Hornsby, to the New York Giants for second baseman Frank Frisch. The deal was spurred when Hornsby demanded a $150,000 contract over the next three seasons.	Dec. 20
New York City Prohibition officials clamp down on "wet" Christmas cheer by padlocking 58 of the city's most popular night spots.	An article in The Century magazine, "Our Crumbling National Defense," by a brigadier general, discusses the impact of military budget cuts on U.S. Army morale. Statistics show that more than 1,000 enlisted men deserted from the army monthly during 1926.			Baseball commissioner Kenesaw Mountain Landis is investigating former star players Ty Cobb and Tris Speaker, both newly retired, on the charge that they conspired to fix a 1919 game between the Detroit Tigers and the Cleveland Indians. The pair have been accused by former player Dutch Leonard.	Dec. 21
A Chicago judge offers to release 54 husbands—in jail for their failure to provide support for their families—to their wives for Christmas; 44 of the women refuse the gift.				Recent studies of the nation's working married women—estimated at two million in the 1920 census—reveal wide discrepancies in middle-class and working-class home life. The Bureau of Vocational Information finds that middle-class women can usually hold their jobs and "run a comfortable, contented, happy home besides," with the full support of their husbands. But working-class wives experience tensions with their husbands and sometimes neglect their children.	Dec. 22
Two passenger trains collide head-on outside Rockmart, Georgia, killing 20 people and injuring 65.				The most popular toy in Paris this Christmas is a pink velvet stuffed-animal dog. "Countrified cat" stuffed animals are second in popularity.	Dec. 23
A former president of the American Medical Association is testing an experimental drug, narcosan, on 366 prisoners at Welfare Island in New York City. He reports that the drug may be a cure for addictions to cocaine, morphine, heroin, and alcohol....Retail experts judge the Christmas trade this year to be about as strong as last year.				John Philip Sousa and Leopold Stokowski lead 1,400 singers in a Christmas Eve program of carols and "The Stars and Stripes Forever" at Philadelphia's Independence Square.	Dec. 24
The National Woman's Party agitates for the right of women to perform jury duty in New York state. Twenty-two states now allow women to sit on juries.				Among the choices in a "Best Similes of 1926" contest are "Empty as a Detroit stable," "Impersonal as a department store window," and "A flapper is like a bungalow, painted in the front, shingled in the rear and nothing in the attic."	Dec. 25
				French ethnographer Lucien Lévy-Bruhl publishes How Natives Think in an American edition.	Dec. 26
		Chairman Elbert Gray of the U.S. Steel Corporation tells stockholders during a year-end meeting that "there is no reason why prosperity during 1927 will be seriously interrupted."			Dec. 27

F	G	H	I	J
Includes campaigns, elections, federal-state relations, civil rights and liberties, crime, the judiciary, education, healthcare, poverty, urban affairs, and population.	Includes formation and debate of U.S. foreign and defense policies, veterans affairs, and defense spending. (Relations with specific foreign countries are usually found under the region concerned.)	Includes business, labor, agriculture, taxation, transportation, consumer affairs, monetary and fiscal policy, natural resources, pollution and industrial accidents.	Includes worldwide scientific, medical and technological developments, natural phenomena, U.S. weather and natural disasters.	Includes the arts, religion, scholarship, communications media, sports, entertainment, fashions, fads, and social life.

	World Affairs	Europe	Africa & The Middle East	The Americas	Asia & The Pacific
Dec. 28					Japanese Emperor Hirohito delivers his first imperial message, calling for national devotion to progress, improvement, and peace.
Dec. 29		German poet Rainer Maria Rilke dies.	The Turkish National Conservatory disbands its Department of Oriental Music. Native Turkish music will no longer be taught, replaced by European music studies exclusively.		
Dec. 30				With the Calles government's oil laws set to go into effect tomorrow, U.S. State Department officials are not divulging what actions could be taken if Mexico seizes foreign-owned oil properties.	
Dec. 31		British prime minister Stanley Baldwin acknowledges that he is eager to leave behind "a year of unhappy discord and industrial depression." England faces 1927 with a considerably enlarged deficit, a product of the coal strike....Soviet officials suspect that Russian peasants are intentionally sowing less grain to protest higher prices for goods; in some regions the amount of land sown during the fall was down 40 percent.		President Calles reconfirms that his government will protect lawful oil interests. American companies, with $700 million in oil wealth in Mexico, have refused to file the "confirmatory concessions" now required by Mexican law.	

A	B	C	D	E
Includes developments that affect more than one world region, international organizations and important meetings of world leaders.	Includes all domestic and regional developments in Europe, including the Soviet Union.	Includes all domestic and regional developments in Africa and the Middle East.	Includes all domestic and regional developments in Latin America, the Caribbean, and Canada.	Includes all domestic and regional developments in Asian and Pacific nations (and colonies).

U.S. Politics & Social Issues	U.S. Foreign Policy & Affairs, Defense	U.S. Economy & Environment	Science, Technology & Nature	Culture, Leisure & Lifestyle	
A U.S. attorney in Illinois estimates that $30 million in graft is paid out annually in Chicago. As an example, he points to $1 million in cancelled checks recently seized in Cicero, Al Capone's stronghold, payable to various public officials. "The influence of $30 million of yearly graft money is a force to be reckoned with in politics," he warns. "It reaches into high places. It finances campaigns."				New York City mayor Jimmy Walker, responding to reports of nudity and lewd dialogue on local stages, summons a group of leading impresarios and threatens them with censorship.	**Dec. 28**
Prohibition officials are doubling the wood alcohol content in industrial alcohol, increasing the lethality in an effort to stymie bootleggers; a repulsive-smelling compound is also being added to ward off potential drinkers....In New York City there were an estimated 800 deaths in 1926 from drinking poisonous industrial alcohol.			Westinghouse Electric announces the invention of the Osiso, a pocket-sized oscilloscope intended to enable deaf people to "hear" music and speech. The device translates sound into visible waves.	Theologian Reinhold Niebuhr warns that Americans are confusing national power with comfort and "buying a bigger car." "The only determining factor in the attitude of the United States is that we are rich and Europe is poor, that we do not need the world, but the world needs us," he declares.	**Dec. 29**
	The League for Industrial Democracy condemns universities that permit military training on campus, calling this evidence of "bureaucratic control" in education.			Researchers at the Yale University Psycho-Clinic are studying the "plasticity" of the mental makeup of children younger than the age of five.	**Dec. 30**
President Coolidge urges the American press to support the nation's foreign policies. Citing current difficulties in Mexico and Nicaragua, he says that newspapers should strive to provide a "correct representation of the American attitude," so as not to give foreign governments the impression that Americans are divided about administration policy....The American Association of University Professors is forming a national organization to coordinate efforts challenging state-level anti-evolution legislation.		Secretary of Commerce Herbert Hoover offers a year-end snapshot of national and international economic activity. He sees one potential trouble spot in the American economy: the agricultural sector, where production costs exceed crop prices. Otherwise, the year 1926 brought "more and better homes, more electric lights and power, more transportation, more roads, more substantial buildings, more radios and automobiles, more savings, more life insurance, and more of a lot of things." Internationally, he believes that nations are beginning to recover from the World War, taking the necessary steps to pay down their debts and stabilize their currencies.		Under a steady drizzle, crowds gather in New York City's Times Square, waiting for the midnight ball to drop.	**Dec. 31**

F	G	H	I	J
Includes campaigns, elections, federal-state relations, civil rights and liberties, crime, the judiciary, education, healthcare, poverty, urban affairs, and population.	*Includes formation and debate of U.S. foreign and defense policies, veterans affairs, and defense spending. (Relations with specific foreign countries are usually found under the region concerned.)*	*Includes business, labor, agriculture, taxation, transportation, consumer affairs, monetary and fiscal policy, natural resources, pollution and industrial accidents.*	*Includes worldwide scientific, medical and technological developments, natural phenomena, U.S. weather and natural disasters.*	*Includes the arts, religion, scholarship, communications media, sports, entertainment, fashions, fads, and social life.*

HOME COMERS
e for every State

1927

Charles A. Lindbergh speaking
from a flag-draped podium, with
Calvin Coolidge in 1927.

	World Affairs	Europe	Africa & The Middle East	The Americas	Asia & The Pacific
Jan.	The League hosts a Paris conference on child health and welfare.	The Inter-Allied Commission ends its activity in Germany. The League now has jurisdiction on issues of German rearmament.	Harvey Firestone reports that rubber trees planted in Liberia in 1910 are mature, with harvesting to begin in 1932. Firestone plans to develop the full 1 million acre plantation.	Mexico implements land and petroleum laws that reduce foreign exploitation. The Calvo Clause prohibits foreign oil concerns from appealing to their home governments the restriction of oil leases to 50 years. Land reform reduces large foreign holdings. U.S.–Mexico relations sour.	The Nationalist Chinese establish their new government at Hankow.
Feb.	The League's Opium Advisory commission asks members to control illicit drug traffic. The request has no enforcement provision, so nations do as they please.	A 10-day rising against Portugal's dictatorship fails at the cost of over 1,000 lives.	Airline service from Germany to Persia begins. Junkers flies to Baku, Tehran, Esfahan, and Bashire. Service ends in 1932....The Tangier Conference attracts international delegates to discuss Spain's claim that Tangier should be part of Spanish Morocco.	The Catholic Church rejects the new Mexican Constitution, which contains anti-clerical provisions.... Mexico begins confiscating church property, closing parochial schools, and banishing clerics.	At the Indian-South Africa Conference India and South Africa agree to methods of making return to India easier for those who choose to leave and making life less restrictive for those who choose to stay in South Africa....Britain agrees to end its concessions in Hankow and Kiukiang. The British intent is to counter growing Soviet influence.
Mar.	A British white paper reveals that Britain has 67 cruisers while Japan has 39 and the U.S. 37. There will be much scrapping of warships to meet the 5:5:3 ratio.	Germany reports that meat consumption in Berlin returned almost to the prewar level in 1926. Per capita consumption of 126 pounds is only 12 pounds below the 1914 rate.	Italy revokes Libyan self-government.	Nicaragua is in the middle of a civil war with both sides having occasional success.	Communists seize Nan king from the Nationalists, killing six foreigners. The International community raises a force of 40,000 to safeguard Shanghai...In accord with treaties with foreigners, Siam ends extraterritoriality. It closes consular courts and establishes its own tariff policy.
Apr.	Aristide Briand announces his plan to outlaw war. His ideas are the product of March consultations with Columbia University's James T. Shotwell.	Britain grants suffrage for women between 21 and 30, adding 5 million new voters	South African Prime Minister Hertzog requests laws to segregate, establish economic ceilings, and remove civil rights for South Africa's 5.5 million blacks, reversing 25 years of incorporating blacks into white society and 50 years of a black franchise.	Mexico deports the head of the Catholic Church, accusing him of fomenting rebellion.	Chiang Kai-shek splits with the Communists. He purges the Hankow government of Russian and Communist influences and moves his government from Hankow to Nanking.
May	An international economic conference in Geneva attracts delegates from 50 nations.	Black Friday brings the German economy to the brink of collapse. The crisis threatens to spread through Europe....Britain abrogates its 1924 trade agreement with Russia. The cause is Communist agitation in London; the consequence is breaking of relations between the two governments.	Under the Anglo-Nejd Treaty, Britain recognizes the sovereignty of ibn Saud's new government in Saudi Arabia.		Japanese troops enter Shantung. By situating themselves to protect Tsinan, they impede the Nationalist advance on Beijing....An earthquake in Nan Shan kills 200,000 Chinese.
Jun.	Britain, Japan, and the United States open three-power arms reduction talks. France and Italy do not participate and the United States and Britain stalemate over cruisers, so the talks fail and end in August.	The Kingdom of the Serbs, Croats, and Slovenes (Yugoslavia) severs ties with Albania after a series of cross-border raids beginning in May.	The Druse rising that began in 1925 is finally fully ended. A large-scale French campaign drives the Druse into Transjordan.	In Montevideo, Uruguay, a League-sponsored conference on the welfare of children convenes.	In Samoa, natives protest New Zealand's administration. An investigation finds that foreigners, mostly Germans, have instigated unrest, so New Zealand expels the foreigners and takes their property.
Jul.	Naval reduction talks begin with easy agreement on submarine limits but quickly stalemate over cruiser tonnages.	After European powers intervene, Yugoslavia and Albania restore relations....Czechoslovakia implements reforms to appease Ruthenians and Slovaks, who have complained about unequal treatment by the central government. Reforms give the two groups greater self-rule.... Austrian Socialists riot and burn the Palace of Justice.	The last resistance of the Rif ends in Morocco....Egypt and Britain agree to a draft treaty making administrative changes and ending the British occupation in 10 years....Belgium and Portugal agree to the boundary between Angola and the Belgian Congo. Belgium gives up 480 square miles of territory for a single square mile it needs to finish the Matadi-Stanleyville Railway.		
Aug.	League-sponsored conferences deal with communications and transport as well as the press and journalism.	Allied military control of Hungary ends.		The International Peace Bridge between the United States and Canada opens. It ties New York and Ontario....Brazilian Communists strike. President Luis Pereira de Souza outlaws strikes and represses Communists.	
Sep.	The League sponsors an international anthropology conference.	Germany's President Hindenburg repudiates the war guilt clause of the Versailles Treaty.	Sierra Leone outlaws slavery.		The United States and Mexico establish long-distance telephone service.

A	B	C	D	E
Includes developments that affect more than one world region, international organizations and important meetings of world leaders.	*Includes all domestic and regional developments in Europe, including the Soviet Union.*	*Includes all domestic and regional developments in Africa and the Middle East.*	*Includes all domestic and regional developments in Latin America, the Caribbean, and Canada.*	*Includes all domestic and regional developments in Asian and Pacific nations (and colonies).*

U.S. Politics & Social Issues	U.S. Foreign Policy & Affairs, Defense	U.S. Economy & Environment	Science, Technology & Nature	Culture, Leisure & Lifestyle	
Massachusetts requires auto insurance. It is the first state to do so.	Panama rejects the treaty of 1926 because it infringes on Panamanian sovereignty. Panama submits the issue to the League, which fails to act....The U.S. Senate votes to arbitrate disagreements with Mexico arising from Mexico's new petroleum laws.	Building and loan associations begin providing mortgages that make borrowers members of the association. The duration of the note is 12 rather than the customary 4 years.	Fox debuts Movietone. The technology synchronizes film and sound.... The first commercial transatlantic telephone service ties London and New York.	Baseball commissioner Landis holds hearings on charges that the 1917 White Sox threw four games with Detroit....Fritz Lang's anti-technology film, *Metropolis*, debuts....The Daddy and Peaches trial opens.	Jan.
Coolidge creates the Federal Radio Commission to regulate the airwaves, where anarchy and overlapping frequencies are rampant.	President Coolidge appoints William Phelps as first minister to Canada....Coolidge calls for a five-power meeting to discuss disarmament issues neglected in the 1921 agreements. He wants limits on cruisers, destroyers, and submarines. The meetings convene in June.	Colorado's Moffat Tunnel through James Peak opens. It is seven miles long and costs $12 million.		The New York customs inspector rules that sculptures by Constantin Brancusi are not art.	Feb.
The Supreme court overturns a Texas law that bars blacks from voting in party primaries....Pittsburgh is the site of the first armored car holdup in U.S. history.		Pan American Airlines incorporates.	Major H.O.D. Segrave sets a world land-speed record at Daytona. His auto attains a speed of 203.79 miles per hour.	Babe Ruth signs for $70,000. He becomes baseball's highest paid player....The first golden gloves boxing tournament takes place.... Jose Capablanca of Cuba wins a 33-day chess tournament.	Mar.
Nicola Sacco and Bartolomeo Vanzetti receive death sentences.	New U.S. immigration law requires entrants from Canada, Mexico, and Cuba to have visas and work papers and pay a head tax.	U.S. oil production gluts the market.	The first international rabies conference opens under League auspices....The first public long distance television transmission features commerce secretary Hoover....The Mississippi River floods. Eventually it will cover 4.4 million acres and do $300 million in damage.	Johnny Weissmuller sets records in 100 and 200 meter freestyle swimming....Mae West receives a 10-day sentence for obscenity in her Broadway show, *Sex*....Clarence Demar of Massachusetts wins the Boston Marathon. His time is 2:40:20.2.	Apr.
	Henry Stimson arbitrates an end to the Nicaraguan war. The agreement allows Diaz to end his term while liberals disarm. The United States will oversee new elections.	Ford produces its 15 millionth Model T. A few days later, it ends production of the Model T.	Charles Lindbergh flies solo across the Atlantic Ocean, becoming the first to do so....Philip Drinker and Louis Shaw invent the iron lung.	Number one on the charts is Ben Bernie's *Ain't She Sweet?*	May
	Briand submits a draft of the war-banning treaty he has developed in collaboration with Secretary of State Kellogg.		The first flight to Hawaii from the west coast occurs.		Jun.
The League for American Citizenship reports that half of all those seeking citizenship are illegal, with the British and Germans the most numerous.		When Ford shuts down to retool, the economy enters a recession that lasts through the end of the year.	Kilaeau erupts after a long dormancy. Hawaiians offer Pele berries and other gifts.	Ban Johnson resigns as American League president after 34 years.	Jul.
Governor Fuller rejects Sacco and Vanzetti's clemency effort and the state supreme court refuses to intervene. The two are executed along with Celestino Madeiros, who confessed in 1925.	The U.S. Army reorganizes. It also reveals that its actual manning is only 119,000 people, down from 185,000 in 1920.	American auto sales are at record levels, with Hudson and Nash and Essex reporting records in July or August.	An air-powered car proves a hoax. Investigators find batteries hidden in the upholstery.	*Wings* starring Clara Bow, premiers. The movie earns $3.8 million and receives the first academy award for best picture.	Aug.
Federal marshals arrest Harry Sonenshine for flying banned fight films across state lines. Interstate movement of boxing film became illegal in 1912.		U.S. blacksmiths number 70,000, and they are seeking new recruits.	A St. Louis, MO, tornado kills 85.	Isadora Duncan dies when her scarf gets entangled in a car wheel....In the "long count" fight, Dempsey fails to recover his title against Tunney....Babe Ruth ends his 60-homer season, breaking his previous record of 59.	Sep.

F	G	H	I	J
Includes campaigns, elections, federal-state relations, civil rights and liberties, crime, the judiciary, education, healthcare, poverty, urban affairs, and population.	*Includes formation and debate of U.S. foreign and defense policies, veterans affairs, and defense spending. (Relations with specific foreign countries are usually found under the region concerned.)*	*Includes business, labor, agriculture, taxation, transportation, consumer affairs, monetary and fiscal policy, natural resources, pollution and industrial accidents.*	*Includes worldwide scientific, medical and technological developments, natural phenomena, U.S. weather and natural disasters.*	*Includes the arts, religion, scholarship, communications media, sports, entertainment, fashions, fads, and social life.*

	World Affairs	Europe	Africa & The Middle East	The Americas	Asia & The Pacific
Oct.	League conferences deal with easing of trade barriers and promotion of international commerce as well as control of disease and epidemics.	Bulgaria declares martial law on its border with Yugoslavia. The hope is to end Macedonian border incursions.	Persia signs a non-aggression pact with Russia.		
Nov.	Canada becomes a member of the League Council....The Preparatory Commission on Disarmament rejects Maxim Litvinov's proposal for immediate and total disarmament as mere Communist propaganda.	France and Yugoslavia sign a treaty intended to counter growing Italian influence in the Balkans. Italy and Albania counter by signing the Second Treaty of Tirana, a 20–year military alliance.	King Faisal of Iraq visits Britain. He seeks British backing for immediate entry of Iraq into the League.... Persia claims Bahrain. The sheikh of Bahrain is under British protection but his land is rich in oil.	The Mexican Supreme Court overturns the new petroleum laws.	Britain announces the commission to explore Indian self-determination will meet 2 years early. Indian nationalists protest the absence of Indian representatives on the committee
Dec.		The 15th Communist Party congress rejects Trotskyite deviationism, expels Trotskyites from the party, and banishes Trotskyites to the provinces. Stalin's victory is complete.	Britain grants Iraq independence but retains a military presence. Britain agrees to support Iraqi admission to the League in 1932. In return, Britain receives 3 bases in Iraq and the right to train Iraqi army officers.	Mexico modifies its petroleum law to make it more acceptable to American interest. It recognizes concessions predating the 1917 constitution.	Chiang Kai-shek breaks relations with Russia. He also overthrows the Hankow government as he consolidates his power.

A	B	C	D	E
Includes developments that affect more than one world region, international organizations and important meetings of world leaders.	*Includes all domestic and regional developments in Europe, including the Soviet Union.*	*Includes all domestic and regional developments in Africa and the Middle East.*	*Includes all domestic and regional developments in Latin America, the Caribbean, and Canada.*	*Includes all domestic and regional developments in Asian and Pacific nations (and colonies).*

U.S. Politics & Social Issues	U.S. Foreign Policy & Affairs, Defense	U.S. Economy & Environment	Science, Technology & Nature	Culture, Leisure & Lifestyle	
Mississippi recognizes only black and white. The state supreme court rules that Chinese are black and must attend black schools.	President Coolidge appoints Dwight Morrow as ambassador to Mexico. Morrow has better rapport than his predecessor and has some success in easing friction between the two states.	Ford's new car has not yet been revealed. Advance orders top 350,000, many prepaid.	Fox Movietone presents the first sound newsreel in New York.	*The Jazz Singer* premiers in New York. The first talking picture stars Al Jolson....The Yankees sweep the Pirates in baseball's 24th World Series.	Oct.
	Although urged to support the Briand peace plan, Coolidge remains aloof, fearing foreign entanglements.		The first underwater tunnel, the Holland Tunnel opens. It ties New York and New Jersey....A tornado strikes Washington, DC.	Carl Eliason of Sayner, WI, receives the first snowmobile patent.	Nov.
	Morrow's intervention produces an improvement in relations between the Mexican government and the Catholic Church....Secretary Kellogg announces that he will negotiate a treaty to outlaw war. After talking with Sen. Borah he submits a multilateral note rather than a bilateral pact.	Ford debuts the Model A at $385. Immediately the company has orders for 50,000 of them.	The submarine *S-4* sinks after an underwater collision. All 34 aboard perish.	The first radio broadcast of the Grand Ole Opry takes place in Nashville, TN.	Dec.

F	G	H	I	J
Includes campaigns, elections, federal-state relations, civil rights and liberties, crime, the judiciary, education, healthcare, poverty, urban affairs, and population.	Includes formation and debate of U.S. foreign and defense policies, veterans affairs, and defense spending. (Relations with specific foreign countries are usually found under the region concerned.)	Includes business, labor, agriculture, taxation, transportation, consumer affairs, monetary and fiscal policy, natural resources, pollution and industrial accidents.	Includes worldwide scientific, medical and technological developments, natural phenomena, U.S. weather and natural disasters.	Includes the arts, religion, scholarship, communications media, sports, entertainment, fashions, fads, and social life.

	World Affairs	Europe	Africa & The Middle East	The Americas	Asia & The Pacific
Jan. 1			Egypt denies a visa to Shapurgi Saklatvala, a Communist. Saklatvala is an Indian member of the British parliament....The Jordan River is to be harnessed to provide electricity to Palestine.	Earthquakes rock southern California and Mexicali, Mexico. Damage is estimated at $2.5 million....Mexican laws go into effect limiting oil concessions to 50 years. Laws also deny companies the right to appeal to their home governments and restrict foreign ownership of Mexican land.	Dutch labor unions in the East Indies create a central organization to represent their interests at the Hague. Because the unions regard them as unready; native workers are excluded....Filipinos on Batanes are near starvation due to the lack of a relief ship.
Jan. 2			Chaim Weizmann of the World Zionist Organization announces his goal. He wants 500,000 Jews in Palestine by 1937.		
Jan. 3	Vice President Charles Dawes receives $16,000 as his share of the Nobel Peace Prize for the Dawes Plan.	The *reichsmark* is stable; as specified by the Dawes Plan, the United States resumes gold shipments to Germany....The Hungarian *Pengo* enters foreign exchange.		A Canadian commission reports that liquor smuggling is widespread. Canada vows to clamp down on rum-runners....American oil companies report that their Mexican operations are unaffected by political unrest.	In Hankow, China, British police and military forces ward off an attack on the British concession. Nationalist speakers arouse the Chinese by recalling British abuses. The number of Chinese dead reported vary from 300 (British report) to 2,000 (Chinese report.)
Jan. 4		A phone line links Vienna and Berlin. It allows the German and Austrian presidents to converse....France provides public works employment. Few unemployed French are interested.		Concerns are increasing about Mexican banditry. Plutarco Calles orders the Mexican courts to proceed against oil companies not in compliance and seize their lands if necessary....The Argentine meat wars end. Argentina's three major producers agree to share the British market.	The Chinese mob takes the Hankow concession. British troops withdraw as agreed with the Chinese government.
Jan. 5		Northern Albanians rise against the government. They protest in the Italo-Albanian treaty....Under last year's agreement, five German officers are allowed to take civilian flight training at their own expense. Germany has two dozen military pilots.	Ethiopian Christians led by Haile Selassie threaten to break with the Egyptian Coptic Church. Abyssinian and Egyptian Copts dispute ownership of a church in Jerusalem.		Hankow rioters fight Chinese troops. Foreign missionaries withdraw from the interior, women prepare to evacuate, and American and British troops are standing by ready to intervene.
Jan. 6				Mexican forces fight rebels. The government charges that Catholic priests are leading the Parras rising.	British troops take control of the Hankow concession.
Jan. 7		The Soviet Union mandates that citizens help the police. Those who fail to assist risk arrest themselves.		The Willacy County, Texas, sheriff is among seven charged with murdering five agricultural workers. Some of the arrested are also charged with peonage. Mexico claims one worker is its citizen, but Texas denies that.	Chinese loot at Kiukiang. Others harass missionaries in Fukien Province.
Jan. 8		The Czar's state executioner dies in solitary confinement in Moscow. He was responsible for over 600 executions.		Nicaragua accuses Mexico of aiding the rebels.	Five U.S. warships arrive in Shanghai....The rising in Padang, Sumatra has resulted in 100 deaths and 550 arrests so far.
Jan. 9	The Warsaw government and European and American utilities agree in principle to a $25 million electrification project for Poland. ...Canada and England are linked by radiotelephone.	The economic downturn in France is easing as the government buys gold. The total is $56.7 million to date and leftists gain seats in the Senate....Italy's economy is at a three-year low. It remains stronger than those of Germany and England.		Mexico arrests two priests as rebels.	Chinese forces abandon the Hankow concession. British troops venture out to test the mood of the mobs.

A	B	C	D	E
Includes developments that affect more than one world region, international organizations and important meetings of world leaders.	Includes all domestic and regional developments in Europe, including the Soviet Union.	Includes all domestic and regional developments in Africa and the Middle East.	Includes all domestic and regional developments in Latin America, the Caribbean, and Canada.	Includes all domestic and regional developments in Asian and Pacific nations (and colonies).

U.S. Politics & Social Issues	U.S. Foreign Policy & Affairs, Defense	U.S. Economy & Environment	Science, Technology & Nature	Culture, Leisure & Lifestyle	
Herbert Hoover, concerned that the immigration law due to become effective July 1 might prohibit "desirable" aliens, asks the commission establishing quotas to suspend its work....Al Smith, at his fourth inaugural as governor of New York, provides his plans for the 1928 presidential race.		The average farmer works 11.4 hours a day while his wife works 11.3 hours. Average farm family size is 4.5 persons, and average annual living expense is $1,598....New mortgage loans provided by building and loan associations make borrowers into members. They also allow mortgages of 12 years rather than the normal four year loan.	The United States implements standard warning signs and a highway numbering system for 80,000 miles of roadway. Even numbered highways run east to west and odd numbered ones run north to south....Vulcanology becomes a recognized science. Vulcanologists announce that they can now predict eruptions.	Ferenc Herczeg announces that "Monkey Business," his comedy based on the Scopes trial, will begin rehearsals shortly....Alabama and Stanford tie, 7–7, in the Rose Bowl....Baseball Commissioner Kenesaw Mountain Landis holds hearings on corruption in baseball. He hears testimony that the White Sox bought four games with the Tigers in 1917.	Jan. 1
Walter White of the NAACP urges the organization to fight for passage of the Dyer anti-lynching bill. South Carolina Governor Thomas McLeod failed to act in the three Aiken lynchings of October 1926.	An ecumenical group of protesters in New York City calls on the United States to intervene in Romania on behalf of persecuted Romanian Jews. A spokesperson denounces the Romanian charge that the protest was Communist inspired.	24 banks refuse veterans loans backed by the Veterans' Bureau. Reportedly, they fear that honoring up to 3 million certificates worth $200 million might hurt their ability to take care of their customers.	Archaeologists report finding a tablet showing the computation of cube roots in Ur....Captain William P. Durtnall of Britain announces invention of a low-voltage train system. His system allows long distance train service because it does not need frequent power substations.	World War I veterans make do. A blind captain and a one-legged major box to a draw.	Jan. 2
The Supreme Court rules that Rhode Island cannot tax electricity sold to Massachusetts because that trade is interstate commerce. The court also rules against Florida's claim that a federal estate tax is unconstitutional.	Among the Navy ships in need of repair are the *Nevada* and *Oklahoma*....Senator Burton Wheeler says that the United States should leave Nicaragua. He argues that the Nicaraguan election the White House objects to was legal.	Famous Players denies Federal Trade Commission charge that it has a monopoly on motion pictures.... General Motors reports $100 million in overseas business for 1926. The U.S. gold supply grew $100 million in 1926. This compares to a loss of $134 million in 1925.	Zoologist Ernest W. MacBride warns the Eugenics Society that civilization is at risk from the continued breeding of degenerates. He decries the complacency of the "Nordic" races.	Hair stylists meet in Vienna, Austria. They announce that 1927's styles will include bobbed hair and curls.... Pittsburgh's president claims the New York Giants baseball players paid Brooklyn Robins players to beat Pittsburgh in 1921.	Jan. 3
Courts order a halt to implementation of the new formula for poisoning alcohol. The government poisons alcohol to reduce consumption by drinkers.	U.S. marines are in Managua. This is their first return since 1925....The House appropriations committee agrees to fund the cruisers. It also authorizes giving eleven vessels gun range equal to that of the British.	Cotton prices rise after weeks of wet weather and reports of lowered cotton ginnage....Daily oil production is 2.388 million barrels....A treasury surplus of $218 million for the first half of the fiscal year produces a projection the annual surplus will reach $500 million.		The College of St. Elizabeth bans rolled stockings, short skirts, and lipstick for its 300 women. Many St. Elizabeth women are daughters of wealthy and prestigious families.	Jan. 4
	President Calvin Coolidge lifts the ban on arms to Nicaragua.	Bankers agree to expedite veterans' loans.		Ty Cobb is among the 29 baseball players who deny fixing of 1917 games.	Jan. 5
	Calvin Coolidge sends additional ships and marines to Nicaragua.... Over Calvin Coolidge's objections, the House committee includes three cruisers in the naval bill. Provision is made for a dirigible as well.		Palmer H. Craig of Mercer University invents a series of bismuth plates that will replace radio batteries and tubes. Westinghouse offers $100,000....Transatlantic radiophone service begins with calls to London.	Gene Tunney signs for a million dollar bout in September. His opponent is to be determined....In Mexico mobs throng to the site where the Virgin of Guadalupe reappears....A New York cop climbs 32 flights to capture a human fly.	Jan. 6
	The full house backs Calvin Coolidge on the naval appropriations bill. It cuts the cruisers but keeps the dirigible.		Westinghouse denies that it offered Palmer Craig $100,000 for his invention that would replace radio tubes and batteries.		Jan. 7
The chancellor of Lincoln Memorial University, Tennessee, claims that 72 percent of the mountaineers in Appalachia are illiterate. He is seeking funds for his university, which serves Appalachia.	Congressional Democrats attack the Calvin Coolidge administration's "bullying" in Mexico and Nicaragua.		Standard equipment most on 1927 cars includes balloon tires, four wheel brakes, and three speed transmissions.	Rogers Hornsby signs with the New York Giants for $40,000 a year, making him number two to Babe Ruth in salary.	Jan. 8
A roadhouse near Marion in southern Illinois is bombed and burned. Three men are machine gunned in the ongoing war between rival bootlegger gangs.		New York reports that 1926 is a record year with over 26,000 incorporations. Real estate offices are up and beauty parlors down....The War Department reports that the Muscle Shoals sold Alabama Power $826,000 worth of hydroelectric and steam-generated electricity in 1926.	A Chicago to New York mail flight sets a record of four hours and 20 minutes....The closely guarded Wright Cyclone engine for army and navy planes produces 525 horsepower.	King George of England bans shingle cuts and bobbed hair at court. ...Enrollments in U.S. colleges are up 11 percent from 1925–26, with Columbia the largest at 30,526, followed by California's two-campus system and Illinois. The smallest of the top 25, the University of Missouri, has fewer than 4,000 students.	Jan. 9

F	G	H	I	J
Includes campaigns, elections, federal-state relations, civil rights and liberties, crime, the judiciary, education, healthcare, poverty, urban affairs, and population.	Includes formation and debate of U.S. foreign and defense policies, veterans affairs, and defense spending. (Relations with specific foreign countries are usually found under the region concerned.)	Includes business, labor, agriculture, taxation, transportation, consumer affairs, monetary and fiscal policy, natural resources, pollution and industrial accidents.	Includes worldwide scientific, medical and technological developments, natural phenomena, U.S. weather and natural disasters.	Includes the arts, religion, scholarship, communications media, sports, entertainment, fashions, fads, and social life.

	World Affairs	Europe	Africa & The Middle East	The Americas	Asia & The Pacific
Jan. 10	World leaders applaud the accomplishments of the seven-year-old League of Nations. They bemoan the absence of the United States.	German President Paul von Hindenberg calls on Julius Curtius to form a new center-right coalition government. The coalition excludes the Socialists, the largest party in the *reichstag*. The coalition requires Christian Democrat support, but the Christian Democrats are reluctant.		In El Paso, TX, Rene Capistran Garza declares a Mexican rebellion. Mexico arrests five bishops and expels a representative of the episcopate to Cuba for abetting the rebels.	The Majarajah of Cochin and the Gaekwar of Baroda indicate they will step down. Old-style rulers are slowly giving way to demands by Indians for more modern governments and fears of British intervention in states that do not reform.
Jan. 11	The president of the U.S. shipping board asks for subsidies. He tells Congress that American shipping cannot compete against other nations' subsidized shipping.	Spain, Switzerland, and France are hardest hit of the European nations suffering a flu epidemic. Spain's mortality rate is doubled, but the outbreak is much less than that of 1918–19....Russia begins registering men from 24–34 under its 1925 draft registration law....Fernand Bouisson is the first Socialist to head the French senate.	Prof. W.A. Hall, expert on Syria and head of the America University in Beirut, dies at age 55.	Central Americans in Mexico urge a boycott of the United States in retaliation for U.S. involvement in Nicaragua.	Bandits massacre 1,000 Chinese and destroy their village, Wangchihpao. The village is fifty miles from the birthplace of Confucius....An Australian labor leader reports that Papuan gold miners are risking group extinction. The miners are burdening their wives with 130-pound loads and treating the women as slaves.
Jan. 12		A border clash with Soviet troops kills one Romanian soldier....Italy bans nightclubs.	Chaim Weizman, leader of the World Zionist Organization, meets with Calvin Coolidge....Harvey Firestone, vice president of Firestone Plantations, reports plans to develop the full million-acre Liberian rubber concession and build a harbor at Monnrovia. Trees planted in 1910 are mature and ready for harvesting in 1932. ...Under the Cape Town Agreement, South Africa agrees not to enact reservations. India agrees to repatriate its nationals voluntarily.	The Mexican cabinet is in crisis over the religious and oil laws. Business is at a standstill.	Cantonese troops are seizing American property in Fukien province as missionaries evacuate there and other provinces....British ships are at Kiukang and in the Yangtze River.
Jan. 13	The Soviet Union seeks closer ties with foreign governments. Accordingly, it indicates it will allow national Communist parties greater autonomy.	In Moscow "Big Bill" Haywood, former head of the Industrial Workers of the World, reveals he married a Russian woman weeks back. Neither speaks the other's language....European trade unions maintain their refusal to talk with Soviet unions....Benito Mussolini warns currency speculators that reductions in the supply of notes are coming.		Costa Rica offers a negotiated peace in Nicaragua....Mexico denies U.S. claims that the Soviet Union is involved in Mexican affairs.	China suggests that the powers should return their concessions, valued in the billions of dollars. China also raises taxes and Chinese workers threaten to strike....In Kabul, Afghanistan, the German envoy rescues a woman from the slave market by buying her.
Jan. 14	The Allies meet with the Germans in Berlin to discuss German manufacture and export of arms. Germany agrees not to export warships or large weapons but wants no restrictions on small arms and optics. Meanwhile, the League of Ambassadors is meeting in Paris to discuss Germany's eastern fortifications.	In Germany, Julius Curtius fails to attract the centrist parties. He notifies Paul von Hindenberg that he cannot form a cabinet....In a record-setting deal, Viennese banks Boden-Kreditanstalt and Union merge. B-K takes the smaller bank as payment for a $11.5 million debt.	The Royal Mail Line announces that the *Asturias* will stop at Tristan de Cunha in the South Atlantic en route from South America around Africa to Cape Town. Originally a British garrison established to keep Napoleon on St. Helena, Tristan de Cunha is off the main routes and hard to land at. It receives ships on average once a year.	Mexico refuses well drilling permits to companies not complying with the new laws. Mexico is also reported drafting convicts and arresting anti-Plutarco Calles priests. Nevertheless, tensions with the United States seem to be easing after Senator William Borah speaks on Mexico's behalf and Mexico denies the Communist involvement.	20,000 demonstrate at Hankow. They parade and hear speeches by Chiang Kai-shek and other Nationalists. Evacuations of foreign women and children continue as Britain and China negotiate the status of the concession. The Chinese use Sikh and Hindu speakers against imperialism Japan backs China.
Jan. 15		Maurice Boucher of Paris became the first known to commit suicide by leaping from an airplane. He jumped from a Toulouse-Casablanca passenger liner 2,000 feet over Alicante, Spain....Poland thwarts a Communist plot. Authorities arrest three deputies and 150 students.	South Africa is growing. Lumber imports set records in 1926 and are expected to continue record growth through 1927.	Sinclair Oil gets a court injunction against Mexico's cancellation of its drilling permit. The government is surprised while oilmen hope it is a precedent.	Australia announces it will preserve the story of its aborigines. Anthropologists will visit the fast-changing aboriginal population and document their physical traits, society, and culture before western society contaminates it. Scientists, concerned that aboriginal cultures have long been slighted, also plan to visit Papua, New Guinea, and other Commonwealth mandates.

A	B	C	D	E
Includes developments that affect more than one world region, international organizations and important meetings of world leaders.	Includes all domestic and regional developments in Europe, including the Soviet Union.	Includes all domestic and regional developments in Africa and the Middle East.	Includes all domestic and regional developments in Latin America, the Caribbean, and Canada.	Includes all domestic and regional developments in Asian and Pacific nations (and colonies).

U.S. Politics & Social Issues	U.S. Foreign Policy & Affairs, Defense	U.S. Economy & Environment	Science, Technology & Nature	Culture, Leisure & Lifestyle	
The prosecutor drops criminal conspiracy charges against evangelist Aimee Semple McPherson, her mother, and three others. He expresses skepticism about McPherson's claims she was kidnapped but indicates he lacks evidence to convict....The U.S. Supreme Court denies Harry Sinclair's appeal of lower court rulings that he must stand trial for contempt of Congress. Sinclair also has two other Teapot Dome trials pending.	In a message to Congress, Calvin Coolidge defends his Nicaraguan intervention and warns Mexico to stop its interference. He fails to pacify critics who claim there is no American interest at stake and no threat to the Panama Canal.	Cotton prices are up 20 points at New York and New Orleans on brisk activity....Western politicians urge Calvin Coolidge to act promptly on the Boulder Dam project.	French schools disinfect books to reduce school illness....An engineer forecasts that "radio movies" will be broadcast into homes shortly.	Designers reveal a pick-proof pocket for men....Actors Equity suspends over a dozen actors for violating the eight-performance-a-week clause....18-year-old Lita Grey Chaplin sues for divorce, citing abuses and infidelity. She wants custody of the two children, and half of Charlie Chaplin's $14 million.	Jan. 10
The American Federation of Labor's William Green advocates the five-day work week....Jury selection begins in the Fort Worth, TX, murder of fundamentalist Baptist leader, the Rev. J. Frank Norris. Veniremen are questioned about evolution, the KKK, and other issues.	Canada protests its citizens having to wait overnight. The United States agrees to allow immigrants to land as late as 8:30 p.m....Anti-American protests occur in Argentina and Chile.	Amherst College announces a tuition increase of $50 for September 1927. This increase comes on top of the increase from $200 to $250 in September 1926....All U.S. radio broadcasters took losses in 1926. When the National Broadcasting Corporation announces it will spend $3.8 million and advertisers will spend $1.5 million on entertainment in 1927, expectations are that 600-700 small broadcasters will cease operations.	The German military reports that it has a gas that neutralizes all known poison gases and another that can put an entire army to sleep for four hours. France and other Europeans are wary.	Broadway's "Abie's Irish Rose" celebrates its fifth year, 2,000th performance, a $5 million profit, and an imminent movie deal.... Gus Comstock of Fergus Falls, MN, regains his coffee drinking title from H.A. Streety of Amarillo, TX. Comstock downs 81 seven-ounce cups (21.25 quarts) in seven hours and 15 minutes. His goal is 100 cups, but he falls short.	Jan. 11
Rev. C.O. Thompson of Etowah introduces a bill in the Alabama legislature outlawing the teaching of evolution....The Hialeah, FL, race season gets under way despite a ban by Florida's governor....New York City denies licenses to indecent publications.	The United States accuses the Soviet Union of organizing Latin America against the United States and Mexico of shipping arms to Nicaragua.	Lieutenant Jimmy Doolittle, on leave from the army to counter European influence, wins Curtiss Aircraft's largest postwar contract. He impresses the Chilean government by flying with both his legs broken.	U.S. oil producers want restrictions on the waste of gas. They ask for standardized laws.	60 of 10,000 Americans attend college. In France the comparable number is 13; in England, 15.... British men are growing beards to combat the increasing masculinity of women....the president of Columbia Burlesque claims Equity is trying to kill low-priced drama.... Baseball Commissioner Kenesaw Mountain Landis exonerates the players accused of fixing 1917 games. At the same time he calls for a new baseball code.	Jan. 12
The Norris jury in Fort Worth is set. It includes one ex-Klansman.	The House's proposed $366 million army bill authorizes an increase from 115,000 to 118,750 men. This is larger than the administration requests.	The Great Northern and Northern Pacific seek a $1.6 billion merger. Combining the two smaller railways, will create the largest line in North America.	The U.S. Naval Academy rowing team begins tests of an aluminum shell. Built at the naval aircraft factory, the single-seater weighs half what cedar shells do....England tests high speed wireless to Australia.	West Point allows cadets and their dates to smoke between dances.... Charlie Chaplin declares he will counter-sue. After intensive adverse publicity, he asks a fair hearing for his side of the story.	Jan. 13
The Engineering Council asks the establishment of a new cabinet post. The Department of Public Works and Domain would take functions from the Department of Interior.		Other railroads object to the proposed Great Northern-Northern Pacific merger. The Southern Pacific announces a $100 million expansion. Merger critics refer back to the Gilded Age efforts to create railroad monopolies.		Scotland's distillers reveal plans to make wine from Greek currant juice. Scotch consumption continues to decline.	Jan. 14
Governor Miriam "Ma" Ferguson of Texas conditionally pardons a murderer but requires him to serve as her husband's chauffeur for six years. Conditional pardons usually specify payment, and the chauffeur will receive $15 a month, clothing, and board....John Scopes goes free. The Tennessee Supreme Court upholds the anti-evolution law but overturns the conviction for errors by the judge.		A survey of retailers reports dislike of "Fordized" manufactures. The retailers object to a system controlled by manufacturers that forces retailers to engage in high pressure tactics to move merchandise at high volume....William Green of the AFL denies bribery is involved in the New York furriers strike. He also rejects charges of Communist influence.	France reportedly has developed synthetic gasoline. Although expensive, the fuel will allow energy independence.	Forthcoming books include *Elmer Gantry* by Sinclair Lewis and a memoir by Luther Burbank. Also newly released is a United Daughters of the Confederacy-sponsored history of Reconstruction Arkansas by David J. Thomas....The American Library Association announces sales of its "Reading with a Purpose" pamphlet top 200,000. The pamphlets offer reading lists for self improvement.	Jan. 15

F	G	H	I	J
Includes campaigns, elections, federal-state relations, civil rights and liberties, crime, the judiciary, education, healthcare, poverty, urban affairs, and population.	*Includes formation and debate of U.S. foreign and defense policies, veterans affairs, and defense spending. (Relations with specific foreign countries are usually found under the region concerned.)*	*Includes business, labor, agriculture, taxation, transportation, consumer affairs, monetary and fiscal policy, natural resources, pollution and industrial accidents.*	*Includes worldwide scientific, medical and technological developments, natural phenomena, U.S. weather and natural disasters.*	*Includes the arts, religion, scholarship, communications media, sports, entertainment, fashions, fads, and social life.*

	World Affairs	Europe	Africa & The Middle East	The Americas	Asia & The Pacific
Jan. 16	French Marshal Ferdinand Foch and other allied military experts reject the German's proposed Konigsburg-Kestrin line. Germany claims the line complies with the Treaty of Versailles. The French note that the "defensive" line is capable of supporting half a million troops. The Treaty of Locarno protects Germany from Poland anyway.	Germany reports improved coal and iron output for 1926. Coal is higher than 1913, and iron exceeds the total for 1925. Germany also reports a budget surplus for 1926....The Polish budget anticipates a surplus, Czechoslovakia is rebounding, and the French stock market is rising after a year of stagnation.		American oil producers tell Congress that Mexico plans to confiscate their lands. The producers say that they bought or leased the lands properly under Mexican law.	Anti-missionary rioters in Foochow drag English and American women into the streets and beat them. Cantonese soldiers loot the YMCA, missions, and other Western facilities.
Jan. 17	The League of Nations Conference of Health Experts on Child Welfare in Paris convenes in Paris to address world child health issues.	Turkey captures the brother of the Kurdish chief who led the rising of 1923. Sheik Abdul Rahman has waged guerrilla war since his brother's rising was quelled. Rahman has stalled the Kemalist government's reforms of the east. To stabilize the region, Turkey will move 1,500 persons to the west.	The German cruiser *Emden* docks in Cape Town. Sightseeing crowds become unruly. The ship's captain directs the hose at the crowd to calm it and reduce the risk of women and children falling into the water due to the crush.... The World Zionist Organization announces the formation of a committee to investigate conditions in Palestine and to assist the British there. The 1927 quota for the United Palestine Appeal is announced as $7.5 million, $2.5 million from the United States.	The Catholic archbishop of Jalisco reportedly raises the banner of revolution. In clashes with Mexican troops, over 100 Catholic rebels die. In Tepatiplan, federal forces regain several towns....President Adolfo Diaz of Nicaragua rejects the Costa Rican offer of mediation. He claims Costa Rican bias against him. And he alleges that Costa Rica has allowed the rebels to base themselves there.	The British cabinet vows to protect its nationals in China. Britain remains willing to negotiate with the government but not with the mob. It will send 13 of its 31 cruisers to China if necessary. The Foochow mob burns itself out and the city is quiet, if uneasy.
Jan. 18	At the request of the U.S. Lawn Tennis Association England ends the ban on German players in its tournaments and English players in German events. The international tennis body approves the return of Germany by 45–12. Hungary and Austria are also reinstated. Turkey and Bulgaria remain excluded.	Italy outlaws anti-fascist seamen. Sailors expressing anti-government sentiments can be barred from the merchant marine for up to five years....The Montenegran Committee for National Defense agitates for independence and union with Herzegovina. Yugoslavia, which annexed Montenegro over Montenegrin protest in 1918, suspects that Italy is behind the move. Neighboring Albania and Romania are perturbed.	Near East Relief expenses total over $3.37 million for the year. Extraordinary expenses are due to the Albanian earthquake and the Druse revolt and consequent refugee movement.	Allegedly, American oilmen in Mexico are hiring gunmen. A Mexican newspaper charges that they are trying to foment unrest. Mexico remains firm that it will not relax the law unless ordered by the courts to do so....Both the Catholic church and the Mexican government deny the involvement of archbishops in the Jalisco unrest, but the government affirms that the troops are necessary to quell Catholic unrest.	India's viceroy opens Delhi House. The new structure is opulent and the ceremony is lavish, with British and Indian troops escorting the viceroy, whose arrival is announced by a flourish of trumpets.
Jan. 19	Belgium is in mourning. Charlotte, widow of Maximilian of Mexico and daughter of King Leopold of Beigium, dies of pneumonia. Mentally deranged, she returned home after the death of her husband in 1867.	Prospects for a new German cabinet under Wilhelm Marx are somewhat brighter. The Socialists indicate they will cooperate, but the nationalists are balky. The Reichstag cannot deal with important matters until the cabinet is set.	Rhodesians and South Africans pay tribute to the American band leader, Bert Ralston, of the Havana Band. Highly popular in South Africa, Ralston died in a hunting accident. The Salisbury, Rhodesia, funeral cortege is over a mile and a half long.	Mexico claims the Jalisco revolt is ended. Confusion remains about the role of the archbishop, with the army unable to confirm reports that he headed a 1,000-man army.	General Motors announces plans to build an automobile plant in Batavia. The plant will produce cars for Malaysia....Governor General Leonard Wood reports that finances are good in the Philippines. The treasury has a surplus and the sinking fund is sound.
Jan. 20	The Conference of health Experts on Child Welfare ends its meeting.	On the eve of his departure from Italy, British Chancellor of the Exchequer Winston Churchill praises fascism and Benito Mussolini as the right solution for Italy. Not only does fascism help to stabilize Italy's economy but it is an effective counter to Communism and an example to the world of how to deal with the red menace....Paul von Hindenberg requests that Wilhelm Marx form a nationalist-led cabinet. The sticking point remains centrist approval.		Mexico bans rumors of revolt and reports disruptive to the peace. Mexican women petition for peace and criticize oil companies. Mexican newspaper editors foresee successful negotiations.	Japan announces its financial plan for the coming fiscal year. It includes tax reform, railroad expansion, retirement of debt, improved housing, and colonization. The premier suspends the Diet for three days as a warning to the opposition to cooperate....Chinese unrest resumes. Spain sends ships to protect its missionaries as Portugal prepares to follow suit. Britain begins modifying a vessel into a troopship. Missionaries and YMCA employees evacuate Foochow and Hankow.
Jan. 21	The German foreign office says it will meet the disarmament clauses of the Treaty of Versailles by January 31. The allies should be withdrawing from Germany shortly thereafter. Germany will demand so.	Germany lists 1.8 million war-related pensions. Under 800,000 are for disabled veterans, while over a million are for children....The Soviet Union protests the Franco-Romanian treaty. The Russians claim it is an unfriendly act....Poland and Lithuania restore diplomatic relations. Both are in economic crisis and need each other. Poland promises to be nicer to its minorities.	A report reveals that as of September 1, 1926, Palestine's Jewish population is 158,000. The Christian population is 78,000, and there are 10,000 in the "other" classification. The Muslim population is 641,000.	The Mexican bishops deny complicity in the risings. They note that the government would have published evidence were there any. Mexican leaders call for an increase in the army by 75,000 troops, citing the risings as showing a need.	The Chinese situation deteriorates. The United States recalls its envoy and sends marines to the Philippines. The United States has 55 ships in the area and a commander authorized to take whatever measures he deems necessary. Britain is preparing to send marines but backs the nationalists and prefers a peaceful outcome.

A	B	C	D	E
Includes developments that affect more than one world region, international organizations and important meetings of world leaders.	*Includes all domestic and regional developments in Europe, including the Soviet Union.*	*Includes all domestic and regional developments in Africa and the Middle East.*	*Includes all domestic and regional developments in Latin America, the Caribbean, and Canada.*	*Includes all domestic and regional developments in Asian and Pacific nations (and colonies).*

U.S. Politics & Social Issues	U.S. Foreign Policy & Affairs, Defense	U.S. Economy & Environment	Science, Technology & Nature	Culture, Leisure & Lifestyle	
Representatives of the National Negro Development Union and the National Centre Political Party meet with President Calvin Coolidge. Coolidge decries the lynching of blacks and promises to talk with the attorney general about the possibility of martial law to prevent lynching....In Tennessee, attorneys for John Scopes ask to reopen the case. Although Scopes is not guilty on a technicality, the state's biology teachers lack a clear decision on evolution.		Reductions in the price of Southern pig iron make it competitive with Northern iron. A drop in pig iron prices from $20 to $18 a ton reverses several years when high coking coal prices made Southern iron more expensive than Northern.	The *Tampa*, America's first diesel-powered ship, arrives in New York from Bremen. The United States has committed $25 million to providing the *Tampa* and 13 other ships with diesel engines....The Associated Press implements wire service from New York to Havana. The service includes a 1915 mile cable link and printers generating 60 words a minute in English and Spanish.	17-year-old George Young of Toronto wins the Catalina swim and a $25,000 purse. He was in the water nearly 16 hours and was the only finisher of 102 entrants including the top marathoners. The two women in the race fell short, one coming within a mile of finishing.	Jan. 16
The Supreme Court rules that Congress can compel witnesses to testify. It is a necessary element of the legislative process. Harry Sinclair and Samuel Insull are among those Congress will compel.	Peru rejects Secretary of State Frank B. Kellogg's proposed solution of the Tacna–Arica dispute. In November Frank B. Kellogg asked Peru to sell the provinces to Bolivia. Chile and Bolivia agree. Peru claims it cannot alienate sovereign territory.	The Supreme Court rules that an Arkansas minimum wage for women is unconstitutional. The state welfare commission had ordered the minimum wage for an overall factory, the state supreme court upheld it, but the federal appeals court overturned the law.		Miami announces plans to build a $100,000 bike track. The track will allow Miami to hold bicycle races year-round rather than losing the event to Europe during the winter. Miami pastors protest the continuation of horse racing as a means to restore prosperity....Mrs. Chaplin gets $4,000 a month for maintenance of herself and the two children. Charlie Chaplin is also hit with a $1 million tax lien. The divorce trial is pending and Chaplin is in receivership.	Jan. 17
An anti-evolution measure introduced in the Missouri legislature would provide a $50–$100 fine and forfeiture of the contract of any teacher teaching other than the Biblical creation story. Laughter by House members greets the bill...."Ma" Ferguson gives her farewell address as Texas governor. She scores her opponents, portrays herself as a martyr. She pardons 143 more, bringing her total to almost 3,600.	The Senate restores the three cruisers cut by the House. Calvin Coolidge reiterates his opposition. He wants nothing to risk renewal of the arms race. Rather, he hopes for a new arms treaty....Secretary of State Frank B. Kellogg proposes arbitration with Mexico. Some Democrats move to his side, opposing those in their party who try to make it a religious issue.	Cotton attains a new high price. Domestic and foreign markets are strong....The weekly output of oil is 2.391 million barrels. Oklahoma production is up. California's output is down.	The Royal Air Force supports bubble gum. It helps to ease parched throats as flyers descend....French flyers predict that the Paris-New York flight will occur more than once in 1927. They cite the improvements in motors, fuel carrying capacity, and speeds. They also predict that the first flight will be by a Frenchman and that within three years the route will be routine.	Black and white hold their own in spring fashion. The tailored look and embroidery are in vogue. Colors are common in sportswear. Skirts remain short....Charlie Chaplin claims he has less than $100,000. Receivers find nearly $1 million in Chaplin assets.	Jan. 18
J.R. Allen of Healdton, OK, alleges that the directors of the Llano Cooperative Colony in Louisiana allowed immorality while using crooked mortgages to take communal property for themselves. Llano is among the last American utopian communities.		Cotton prices are lower. American buyers are spooked by estimates of the crop size, but Liverpool spot sales remain strong....The British war office buys 1.5 million tins of American beef. U.S. beef is safer than Australian tinned beef.		Arturo Toscanini, is not expected to perform as guest conductor this year. He is down with the grippe and preparing to return to Italy. Substitute guests are to be George Georgesco of Romania and Fritz Reiner of Cincinnati.	Jan. 19
Wayne B. Wheeler, General Counsel of the Anti-Saloon League, writes M. Louise Gross, president of the Women's Committee for the Modification of the Volstead Act. Wheeler affirms the league's commitment to prohibition and opposition to repeal or modification of the Eighteenth Amendment. He lists 14 points in favor of prohibition. ...New York garment workers stage mass protests against a takeover attempt by Communists. The AFL sends encouragement to the demonstrators. Police provide a barrier between demonstrators and a Communist counter-demonstration.	The U.S. Senate calls for arbitration of disputes with Mexico. Mexico expresses optimism that a arbitration will work....Calvin Coolidge meets with the new Nicaraguan envoy. He expresses optimism that peace will come to Nicaragua. The president says that the United States has no special interests and wants peace and prosperity for all of Latin America.		Dr. Michael Haberlandt of Innsbruck University reports progress on the sterilization of animals. He has located a hormone that can cause temporary sterility lasting months, permanent sterility if overdosed. He is optimistic that it can be of benefit to eugenics once it is available for human use.	Humid Bey, Indian fakir, breaks Harry Houdini's record for being buried alive. Bey remains underground for three hours with cotton stuffed into his mouth, nose, and ears.	Jan. 20
West Virginia defeats a bill banning the teaching of evolution in the public schools. The House of Delegates votes against the measure 57 to 36....The Texas legislature condemns "Pa" Ferguson's commercialization of his wife's just-finished governorship. It also condemns her abuse of her pardoning power and the squandering of millions. Impeachment is mentioned....Virginia outlaws Sunday baseball.	After the Senate calls for talks with Mexico, Calvin Coolidge opposes negotiation with Mexico. For him the real issue is the taking of American property. Senator Frank Norris asks Secretary Frank B. Kellogg to provide a list of oil concessionaires and their views on the Mexican law.		A radio broadcast of "Faust" is heard by 10 million. The production uses 15 microphones on stage. The applause in Chicago comes through clearly.	Recovered from his illness, Charlie Chaplin sues to get access to his assets. The government liens are also keeping his estranged wife from collecting her maintenance.... Racing at Tampa stops under court order until the courts can resolve the legality of racing in the face of Florida's law against it....American newcomer Fidel La Barba pummels Scotland's Elky Clark before 16,000 in Madison Square Garden. He wins the world flyweight championship. Each fighter weighs 111.5 pounds.	Jan. 21

F	G	H	I	J
Includes campaigns, elections, federal-state relations, civil rights and liberties, crime, the judiciary, education, healthcare, poverty, urban affairs, and population.	*Includes formation and debate of U.S. foreign and defense policies, veterans affairs, and defense spending. (Relations with specific foreign countries are usually found under the region concerned.)*	*Includes business, labor, agriculture, taxation, transportation, consumer affairs, monetary and fiscal policy, natural resources, pollution and industrial accidents.*	*Includes worldwide scientific, medical and technological developments, natural phenomena, U.S. weather and natural disasters.*	*Includes the arts, religion, scholarship, communications media, sports, entertainment, fashions, fads, and social life.*

	World Affairs	Europe	Africa & The Middle East	The Americas	Asia & The Pacific
Jan. 22	Princess Charlotte of Belgium, once Empress Carlotta of Mexico, is buried under Mexican and Belgian flags. Surviving soldiers of Maximilian's armies provide the escort. Crowds throng despite a blizzard.	Denmark returns to the gold standard....Germany's birth and death rates are both low. The labor force contains 1.7 million more workers than it did in 1914.		A Tampico court refuses to allow Sinclair Oil's request for a permanent injunction. Mexico's land law prevails....Calvin Coolidge's refusal to negotiate with Mexico causes worry in Mexico that its rebels might benefit through an influx of arms. At the same time, Mexico reports that the rebellion is waning.	Britain has four battalions ready to go to China. Also ready is an Indian brigade.
Jan. 23		Germany's economy is growing, with steel output in some cases exceeding supposed capacity. Germany proposes to borrow 1.5 billion *reichsmarks* to feed the expansion....Italy continues its slow deflation of its currency. Falling prices have not yet triggered trade problems or unemployment.	The Catholic Near East Welfare Association begins a drive to enroll 1 million members and raise 1 million dollars. The association replaces all other Catholic relief associations for the Near East. Pope Pius XI calls it a holy crusade....Howard Carter suspends the removal of treasures from the tomb of King Tutankhamen. The valuable items are in Cairo, and a photographer for the Philadelphia Museum has taken pictures of the other items in situ. Removal will resume in March.		China begins censoring overseas dispatches. Manchurian warlord Chang Tso-lin claims the Nationalist troublemakers are under Communist influence, puppets of Moscow.... Russia and Japan are establishing economic ties. They have agreements on coal, oil, and timber. Fishing is next.
Jan. 24	Russia informs the League that it will not attend the economic summit in Geneva. Russia is miffed with the League because it refuses to take sides in Russia's dispute with Switzerland over the assassination of envoy Vorowsky.	France expels an Italian agent. The self-professed fascist agent provocateur is caught at Nice....Germany accepts the allies' limits on armaments. The end of the allied occupation is near.		Mexican labor rallies against the United States. Leaders claim the United States is seeking any pretext for invading. Also, Mexico is Latin America's first line of defense.	In Kashmir near Chinese Turkestan, Major Kenneth Mason of the Royal Engineers reports discovering new tributaries to the Shaksgam River. The rivers run through an area untrod by Europeans since the 1880s....The Rockefeller Institute's study of Australian aborigines is finished. The team went to central Australia in 1926 to document the natives through photos, blood tests, and such before the "race" disappears.
Jan. 25		The Marx cabinet seems set. The nationalists and centrists are in, but the democrats are still in opposition....Russia reports epidemics of black plagues and flu. Sweden reports widespread flu.			A British armada is nearing Shanghai. It is the largest deployment outside home waters since the war. It carries 19–21,000 marines. The Chinese suspend their civil war to observe the western activity. The Indian assembly challenges the right of the government to send troops without the legislature's approval.
Jan. 26		Wilhelm Marx remains unable to form a cabinet. The nationalist royalists are unwilling to acknowledge the republic.			The United States promises a new Chinese agreement once stability returns....Evangeline Booth announces the Salvation Army will build a leper colony on the Ganges.
Jan. 27	Secretary of State Frank B. Kellogg calls for a meeting with all Chinese factions. Japan supports Kellogg's position. Japan also expects China to gain control of its tariffs and westerners to lose extraterritoriality.	The Spanish *peseta* is at a postwar high. Norwegian currency is also strong....A Soviet balloonist is missing. The Russians, fearing he has frozen, ask other nations to watch for him.		The warring factions in Nicaragua open talks. An American observer stands ready to assist.	

A	B	C	D	E
Includes developments that affect more than one world region, international organizations and important meetings of world leaders.	*Includes all domestic and regional developments in Europe, including the Soviet Union.*	*Includes all domestic and regional developments in Africa and the Middle East.*	*Includes all domestic and regional developments in Latin America, the Caribbean, and Canada.*	*Includes all domestic and regional developments in Asian and Pacific nations (and colonies).*

U.S. Politics & Social Issues	U.S. Foreign Policy & Affairs, Defense	U.S. Economy & Environment	Science, Technology & Nature	Culture, Leisure & Lifestyle	
John Scopes's attorneys elect not to seek a rehearing of his case. The state is also disinclined to pursue the matter. The constitutionality of the Tennessee anti-evolution law remains undecided....The long strike in San Francisco is over. It began in May 1926, turned violent, and accomplished nothing. The strikers return on the same terms as they left.		Average bond prices are the highest in 14 years for both foreign and domestic bonds. Volume is increasing and money is cheap, with the call rate 4 to 4.5 percent and foreign gold flowing into the United States....Buick reports that 1926 was a record year. Sales totaled 254,356 cars....Chain stores set records in 1926. Sales were up 14 percent.		W.C. Fields gets favorable reviews for his movie, *The Potters*. Fields is better known for his stage performances....Ten Baylor athletes die in a train-bus collision en at an unguarded crossing. Among the dead are two all-Southwest Conference backs....At the Brooklyn College Games, Bob McAllister of the Columbus Council, Knights of Columbus, lowers the 100 meter record a fifth of a second to 10.2 seconds.	Jan. 22
The American Bible Society reports that in 1926 it provided a million Bibles in 67 languages. The 1927 budget is $1 million to fight ignorance of the Bible. The Justice Department reports that it held 8,750 prisoners and housed another 6,500 in county jails as of January 1, 1926. More were in jail for narcotics violations than for alcohol violations. Narcotics violators decreased from 2,656 to 1,991; alcohol violators rose from 773 to 1,837....*Who's Who in American Jewry* is released. Nearly half of the 2,500 entries are New Yorkers.	Church and labor leaders as well as university professors call on Calvin Coolidge to arbitrate the oil dispute with Mexico. Calvin Coolidge refuses, indicating that the public apparently does not understand the issues. He says that agitation is bad because it leads Mexico to think that Calvin Coolidge lacks support.	Cotton exports continue up over 1926. Demand for manufactured goods is brisk both domestically and abroad. Corn growers seek government relief.		Promoter Tex Rickard rates the contenders. He chooses Gene Tunney over Jack Dempsey as top heavyweight....Ty Cobb is mulling an offer of $25,000 to play for the Baltimore Orioles of the International League. Cobb has been banned from managing in the American League for incompetence while managing the Detroit Tigers. Cobb and Tris Speaker are exonerated when the American league ousts its 27-year president, Ban Johnson, for intemperate attacks on baseball commissioner Kenesaw Mountain Landis.	Jan. 23
In Texas, the J. Frank Norris murder trial is winding down. The prosecution defines Norris as a dangerous man and dynamic speaker. The defense portrays his victim as violent when drunk....Strong speculation indicates that William G. McAdoo is preparing a run for the democratic nomination in 1928. Progressive dry backers want reform of the rule requiring the nominee to win two-thirds of the delegates.		Crude oil output drops below 2.4 million barrels for the week.	F.S. Lee says the demand for wood is too great for nature to supply. Reforestation requires laboratory research.	A Tampa, Florida, court sets aside the injunction against racing. The dogs races resume tomorrow, with horses the day after.	Jan. 24
Reverend J. Frank Norris is found not guilty of murder.	The Senate votes unanimously for arbitration in Mexico. It also calls for no more seizures of assets until arbitration is done (Senator Lenroot claims $166 million has already been taken.) The resolution is non-binding, and Calvin Coolidge does not indicate whether he will heed it.			Charlie Chaplin gets a temporary injunction against the receivers. His assets are free from the federal liens as well as the divorce claims of his estranged wife....Pasadena bans Chaplin films....Babe Ruth forfeits bond and has another warrant issued for his arrest in San Diego, California. He is charged with violating child labor laws in his vaudeville act....A former chess champion alleges clock manipulation and palming of gate receipts. Another player is accused of smoking in poorly ventilated rooms to overpower his opponents.	Jan. 25
The United Mine Workers, in convention, charge that anti-unionists are getting Communist money. The delegates reject John L. Lewis's call for a labor party. The majority denies the minority's charges of electoral fraud.	-General John Ross Delafield of the Reserve Officers Association says that only 50,000 men are ready for a military emergency. He encourages passage of the defense bills because they will improve rations and quarters and eliminate such embarrassments as artillery units without horses, officers who earn less than carpenters forced to pay their own travel expenses, and troops without full uniforms.	Construction problems cause a slip in completion of Germany's super zeppelin from August until mid 1928. When put onto the Spanish-South American route, the airship will have a ballroom as well as sleeping areas and a kitchen capable of serving 40 persons.	The tinless can has arrived after three years. It uses lacquered steel or iron. The big difficulty was finding a lacquer that would not spoil the contents. It should help to alleviate the tin shortage.	Paris evening styles for spring feature high fronts and remarkably low backs. New colors are bright, including banana red, vert d'eau, and cochineal.	Jan. 26
Florida prohibition enforcement agents capture 16 law enforcement officers. Allegedly the officers were on the payroll of bootleggers....The mine workers announce their largest organizing drive ever....Nicola Sacco and Bartolomeo Vanzetti ask the Massachusetts Supreme Court for a new trial. They cite a confession by another person to the murders and offer a local gang as culprit.	The United States acknowledges it is discussing the 1926 Panama treaty but says the modifications are minor. Panama rejects the treaty with the United States as infringing on its sovereignty	Gillette reports it sells a million razors a month. That mark was a record in 1917, but in 1927 it is standard. Gillette has doubled manufacturing capacity in four years but cannot keep up with demand for safety razors and blades....Prices for copper, lead, and zinc are at their lowest since 1924.	Radium overdose is the cause of death for a Waterbury, CT woman. She worked in a watch factory painting luminous dials....Lieutenant Commander Noel Davis announces plans to compete for the $50,000 prize for flying from New York to Paris. He will try this summer in a three-engine Huff-Deland bomber currently under development.	Baseball Commissioner Kenesaw Mountain Landis reinstates Ty Cobb and Tris Speaker. They are free agents but must sign with the American League. The Yankees express interest in buying both.... Based on number of states its students are from, Yale is the number one "national university" followed by Princeton and Harvard.	Jan. 27

F	G	H	I	J
Includes campaigns, elections, federal-state relations, civil rights and liberties, crime, the judiciary, education, healthcare, poverty, urban affairs, and population.	*Includes formation and debate of U.S. foreign and defense policies, veterans affairs, and defense spending. (Relations with specific foreign countries are usually found under the region concerned.)*	*Includes business, labor, agriculture, taxation, transportation, consumer affairs, monetary and fiscal policy, natural resources, pollution and industrial accidents.*	*Includes worldwide scientific, medical and technological developments, natural phenomena, U.S. weather and natural disasters.*	*Includes the arts, religion, scholarship, communications media, sports, entertainment, fashions, fads, and social life.*

	World Affairs	Europe	Africa & The Middle East	The Americas	Asia & The Pacific
Jan. 28		Wilhelm Marx finally forms a government. It includes nationalists, centrists, and populists. The government has a 40 member majority and meets Paul von Hindenberg's requirements of acceptance of the Locarno agreement and no civilian interference with the military.		Canada leads the world in production of newsprint. The number one consumer is the United States.	
Jan. 29	The special League court plans to hear reparations claims rules against Germany's objection to the Dawes reparations. The United States is entitled to nine billion gold marks.	Italy suppresses the YMCA The organization is accused of subverting patriotism and of proselytizing. The Roman Catholic Church supports the ban....France is skeptical over the new German cabinet. Difficulties over the Rhineland are anticipated....England identifies a need to provide its bobbies with motorcycles. Jewelry thieves use vehicles to escape bobbies who are on foot.	Two American archaeologists from the Pacific School of Religion, Berkeley, are returning to Palestine to find another "bobbed hair Venus." They found the first terra cotta Astarte, dating from 750 B.C.E., during their 1926 dig in Mizpah....Egypt and Germany disagree over possession of the bust of Nefertiti in the Berlin museum. Egypt is attempting to establish control over its territory....Drought in the Transvaal is killing thousands of cattle.	Mexico urges expedited appeals of oil cases to the supreme court.	
Jan. 30	British Communists try to stop the warships from sailing to China. Propaganda advocates a dock strike, but unionists ignore it. Chang Sha stores are looted and Swedish and Italian boats are taken. The Tibetan Tashi Lama condemns bolshevism.... Russia calls on the world's proletariat to stop the U.S. exploitation of Latin America.	European armies are stockpiling gas weapons. France is investing in flamethrowers....In Austria, 30 peasants sympathetic to fascism are arrested after they kill four Socialist paraders and injure 14 others.... Socialist and reactionary victories in Thuringia and rifts among the centrists, nationalists, and royalists threaten to undo the Marx coalition.		Liberals attack Rivas, Mexico, twice. Diaz forces drive them away. Mexico also tries to stem the leakage of gold to the United States and establishes customs houses in Baja Mexico to tax American fishing vessels.	
Jan. 31	THe Allies end military control of Germany. Despite no accord on fortifications, the seven-year oversight ends. Responsibility now lies with the League.	Spain's prime minister delays opening of the Cortes. A governmental crisis is feared....Yugoslavia forms a new cabinet. Croats and Slovene parties back it unanimously.	The high commissioner of Palestine receives American financier Felix Warburg. The American also meets with the Zionists. He recently donated $500,000 to Hebrew University.	Oil companies report that Mexico is reinstating some drilling permits.	Chinese pirates seize a British-flagged ship. The Chinese government acknowledges that British proposals have merit but is not pleased with the show of force that accompanies them.
Feb. 1	The League of Nations Opium Advisory Commission calls for an end to illegal drugs and trafficking. There is no enforcement provision, so governments are free to do as they please regarding illicit drugs.	Austrian Socialists protest the murder of their compatriots by fascists. The protest includes mass meetings and strikes....British flu deaths are 725 for the week. That's up from 470 the week before....The Marx cabinet divides over the agreement that rid Germany of the allies. Nationalists dislike the decision on the eastern forts.	A dig in Jerusalem is six weeks along in uncovering the walls of the ancient city. Details of the walls match the description in Josephus's history.	Bishop Diaz, expelled by Mexico, arrives in New York. He denies fomenting rebellion and promises that Catholics will prevail in Mexico....Mexico again blames American oilmen for shutting down work and trying to foment strife. Federals kill 16 rebels in Jalisco.	Negotiations between Britain and China break down. Britain continues sending more troops. Chen says signing with so many troops massed would amount to signing under duress. Civil war seems near.
Feb. 2		Italian Socialists abandon their opposition to fascism. They tout labor-capital solidarity and form a cultural society for the masses.		Mexico eases restrictions on oil wells, allowing drilling of those licensed before January 10. Mexican output has been falling for five years. Mexico also offers rebels amnesty and licenses Protestant clergy....The Nicaraguan leftist leader agrees to accept arbitration of the civil war.	
Feb. 3		Portuguese troops rise at Oporto. Fears are that other forces will join the effort to oust the dictator Carmona.		Jamaica objects to an unfair Cuban tariff. It also asks that Canada honor the current reciprocity agreement....Mexico bans private masses unless priests register. The Catholic Church refuses to allow its priests to register.	Opposing Chinese forces prepare for battle near Shanghai. The United States is sending another 1,200 troops, and will have 2,500 troops and 33 ships available.
Feb. 4	Italy's Benito Mussolini sends Britain's Chamberlain a note that he supports the British Far East policy. Italy also prepares to send forces to China.	The Portuguese rebellion expands in the north. Southerners engage in a sympathy general strike...,A Polish deputy says the fleet has 10 admirals for each unit.		Seven Mexican rebels are executed. Another 16 are prisoners.	The battle for Shanghai begins. Chinese armies clash 160 miles away, with 500 wounded. The British say they will not divert to a safer city.

A	B	C	D	E
Includes developments that affect more than one world region, international organizations and important meetings of world leaders.	Includes all domestic and regional developments in Europe, including the Soviet Union.	Includes all domestic and regional developments in Africa and the Middle East.	Includes all domestic and regional developments in Latin America, the Caribbean, and Canada.	Includes all domestic and regional developments in Asian and Pacific nations (and colonies).

U.S. Politics & Social Issues	U.S. Foreign Policy & Affairs, Defense	U.S. Economy & Environment	Science, Technology & Nature	Culture, Leisure & Lifestyle	
The Aiken County, SC, brings no indictments in the October 1926 lynchings of three blacks. The jury cites insufficient evidence....In Chicago, 16 police chiefs testify for a proposal to ban criminals' possession of guns. They agree also that there is no benefit in citizens having guns.	The United States reinstitutes the ban on sales of aircraft to Mexico after lifting it five months earlier. The ban on military equipment, dating to the Obregon coup of 1920, continues.		A hurricane blows through Great Britain. Eight are dead in Glasgow and 100 injured by the storm that carries 104 mph winds. Over all Great Britain, deaths are 20 and injuries 300....Noel Davis is not alone in the Paris-New York field. Several French flyers, including Rene Fonck who failed earlier, are preparing, too.		Jan. 28
Metropolitan Life reports that 1926 saw the highest number of alcohol-related deaths since prohibition began....The head of the National Liberty League says he supports free speech. During the Red Scare he backed the Lusk Committee and he currently supports loyalty oaths for teachers....The United Mine Workers Association votes to oust reds. Only 15 of 1,500 delegates oppose.		Motor boat sales reach $10 million.	California develops a plan to save its redwoods. A six-million-dollar bond issue will finance the establishment of a state park system.... William Reid of South Africa gets credit for finding his eighth comet.	The St. Louis Cardinals come to terms with Frankie Frisch....The other Babe Ruth, a Philadelphia boxer, loses a 10-round match by decision.	Jan. 29
Smuggled aliens are caught off Florida. Among them are three Polish opera singers.		Cigarette smoking in 1926 produced $371 million, up $28 million over 1925. Cigarettes brought in 72 percent of the total IRS tobacco revenue.		A new lawsuit in Tampa alleges conspiracy to violate state laws against gambling. The Tampa race club is still operating under a court order pending the outcome of a public nuisance suit.	Jan. 30
The New York Assembly asks Congress to ban poison liquor. After a two-day debate, the bipartisan vote also asks Congress to heed the New York referendum results. ...Republican committeeman for Texas R.B. Creager says that the Democrats are still dry and the anti-Catholic South will vote Republican if Smith wins the nomination.	Methodist Episcopal editors urge Calvin Coolidge to arbitrate with Mexico.	The Missouri Pacific issues $95 million in bonds, the second largest offering ever.	Surgeons decry the uninformed use of iodine to treat goiter. They say surgery is the only solution. Also, they say, untreated goiter may lead to cancer.	Races stop in Tampa. Operators are unwilling to risk arrest....The annual student oratory contest begins. Topic: the U.S. Constitution. The winner gets a trip to Europe.	Jan. 31
Missouri Democrats boost the presidential candidacy of Senator, Thomas Reed. Funding for the campaign comes from the $2.00 apiece backers pay to join the Reed for President Club.	Despite Calvin Coolidge's opposition, the Senate votes to add three cruisers. Coast state republicans join Democrats in a 49-27 authorization of $1.2 million to begin construction....The Senate votes to delay implementation of the new immigration quotas for a year. Critics say the quotas harm Germany, Scandinavia, and the Irish Free State.	Daily oil output is 2.37 million barrels, down 18,300 barrels from the previous week.	The White River breaks through its levees in northeastern Arkansas and inundates 100,000 acres. The American Red Cross and Arkansas National Guard are helping 1,500 homeless people.	Stanford women vote to allow smoking. Three sorority houses are exempt because their national rules prohibit smoking. The associated women of Stanford accept the ruling but indicate they prefer no smoking in public or on campus.	Feb. 1
Police in Amite County, MS, arrest two for enslaving five. The men kidnapped a black family and sold them for $20....Near Willis, Texas, an unmasked mob lynches a black after disarming his police protectors. In Willacy County, Texas, blacks tell of blacks and whites held in peonage.			A fast camera reveals that lightning spirals. The jagged edges are an illusion....Reportedly, smoke in New York cuts sunlight by 31 percent.		Feb. 2
Federal officers are in Louisiana checking on reports of peonage.		AT&T announces a $395 million expansion for 1927. Demand for telephones forces the largest expansion in AT&T's history....The Senate is ready to act on McNary-Haugen farm relief bill. Senators have the votes to invoke cloture if necessary.	France is testing a billion candle-power lighthouse. The purpose is to assist night flyers.	Yale announces it will experiment with scholastic aptitude tests to evaluate prospective students. Until the tests prove their worth, traditional measures will decide admissions.	Feb. 3
A Georgia man gets life for his role in a lynch mob last August. Eleven others are serving terms of four to 20 years.		Cotton prices reach new highs. Markets are buoyed by news that farm relief legislation is near.... U.S. Rubber declares a $5 million dividend.		The White House is to be renovated. Calvin Coolidge selects the four-story, 30-room Patterson mansion, designed by Stanford White, as his temporary residence.	Feb. 4

F	G	H	I	J
Includes campaigns, elections, federal-state relations, civil rights and liberties, crime, the judiciary, education, healthcare, poverty, urban affairs, and population.	Includes formation and debate of U.S. foreign and defense policies, veterans affairs, and defense spending. (Relations with specific foreign countries are usually found under the region concerned.)	Includes business, labor, agriculture, taxation, transportation, consumer affairs, monetary and fiscal policy, natural resources, pollution and industrial accidents.	Includes worldwide scientific, medical and technological developments, natural phenomena, U.S. weather and natural disasters.	Includes the arts, religion, scholarship, communications media, sports, entertainment, fashions, fads, and social life.

	World Affairs	Europe	Africa & The Middle East	The Americas	Asia & The Pacific
Feb. 5		France faces a wine shortage. The 1926 crop was short; prices have doubled and will rise 50 percent more....The Marx government survives a confidence vote. Leftist parties vote en bloc against Wilhelm Marx, and the Socialists accuse Interior Minister Walther Keudell of complicity in the Kapp putsch that tried to overturn the republic in 1920.			
Feb. 6		Ahmed Zog, president of Albania, announces he will marry a rich American. He renounces polygamy.	Rabbi Stephen Wise and Dr. Chaim Weizmann announce a joint effort by Zionists and non-Zionists to settle Palestine. Wise says immigration restriction in France, England, and the United States leave Palestine as the Jewish settlement option.	Mexican government forces say they have routed Yaqui Indian rebels, who have fled to the hills.	Nationalist forces win at Shanghai. Chang Tso-lin's armies withdraw to Hangchow....The Filipino Veterans Association re-elects Emilio Aguinaldo president. It expels Manuel Quezon, opponent of occupation.
Feb. 7	China and Britain are negotiating the fate of concessions. Expectation is that concessions will end within a year.	The Marx cabinet is unstable as Catholics threaten to split over the Keudell putsch involvement. ...The rebels continue to hold Oporto despite hundreds of casualties. Lisbon joins the revolt against Portugal's dictatorship.	The American Zion Commonwealth is in a financial bind. The primary colonizer of Jews in Palestine has overbought land just as Polish Jews, due to the Polish economic downturn, are unable to meet their financial commitments.	Mexican forces win at Piedras Negras. They also stop former generals with hand grenades at Tampico.	Aides advise warlord Chang Tso-lin to return to Manchuria. Meanwhile, Russians are rumored on the border, and the northern forces advance against the nationalist southerners. Western forces continue toward Shanghai as two American vessels come under fire....Two million Japanese line the streets. A mix of Shinto and martial elements mark the burial of modernizing Emperor Yoshishito.
Feb. 8		Although the forces under President Antonio Carmona have retaken Oporto at a cost of 200 lives, the Portuguese uprising continues. Britain sends warships. The American legation in Lisbon suffers damage and staff evacuate it.	Negotiations open on Spain's request for inclusion of Tangier in Spanish Morocco. Currently England and France control the city, which is theoretically under the Sultan of Morocco. Spain notes that international status helped the Rif rebels arm themselves in Tangier. The United States and Italy also want revision of the current arrangement.	In an ongoing effort to reduce the influence of the church in national affairs, Mexico thwarts two plots by the Religious Defense League. The battles in two Mexican states produce scores of dead federal military and Catholic priests.	
Feb. 9	The League Secretariat denies rumors that it will act on China. The Chinese delegation denies it has requested League action....The term of World War I Foreign Debt Commission expires by law. Established in 1922, it won over $11.5 billion in repayment agreements from 13 countries. Austria's debt is suspended until 1943, and Russia's is not negotiable because the United States does not recognize the Soviet Union.			Nicaragua's President Adolfo Diaz indicates he will resign if necessary to satisfy Calvin Coolidge. The conservative government also claims victory over the liberal rebels in Chinandega, with 330 dead and 500 wounded. Diaz indicates that he backs the U.S. Marine presence in Nicaragua. Calvin Coolidge is pleased....In Chile the War Minister forces the cabinet out. The new cabinet is strongly anti-Communist.	The Aga Khan makes his horse racing debut in New Orleans. His $48,000 horse, Amilcar, loses.
Feb. 10	While the debate over the size of the U.S. Navy continues in Congress, Calvin Coolidge asks the great powers to limit their auxiliary vessels. The powers and the League are skeptical. The initial Japanese reaction is favorable. Benito Mussolini has reservations but does not reject the concept....Calvin Coolidge proposes a 5-5-3 ratio for the United States, Britain, and Japan, with flexibility for France and Italy.	The last rebels in Lisbon surrender. The rebellion is ended. Casualties in Lisbon and Oporto total nearly 1000....The Soviet Union announces it will execute two kulaks who murdered two peasants during recent elections. Kulaks are barred from political participation.		Mexico's Catholic rebellion is over, with only a handful of holdouts. The agrarians who took the opportunity to attack ranches are fleeing federal forces. Most of Mexico is at peace.	The British win agreement for a concession in Hankow. The concession will be governed by a joint Chinese-British council, and the agreement goes into effect only when the entire dispute is resolved. The northern warlords start a drive to push the nationalists back to the mountains.
Feb. 11	Although some in the United States fear a renewed naval arms race, world reaction to the 5-5-3 proposal is mixed but mostly positive. Calvin Coolidge has indicated that he is flexible over details.	Wilhelm Marx tells the Reichstag that he will not remove interior minister Walter von Keudell. Leftists seeking to oust Keudell cite his role in the 1920 Kapp putsch....Germany's new minister of transportation calls for improved highways. He downplays the value of rail, canal, and air. He foresees a day when the automobile will be a necessity for Germany, as it is for the United States.		With the rebellion under control in most areas, Mexico's rebels reconstitute themselves in Aguascalientes.	

A	B	C	D	E
Includes developments that affect more than one world region, international organizations and important meetings of world leaders.	*Includes all domestic and regional developments in Europe, including the Soviet Union.*	*Includes all domestic and regional developments in Africa and the Middle East.*	*Includes all domestic and regional developments in Latin America, the Caribbean, and Canada.*	*Includes all domestic and regional developments in Asian and Pacific nations (and colonies).*

U.S. Politics & Social Issues	U.S. Foreign Policy & Affairs, Defense	U.S. Economy & Environment	Science, Technology & Nature	Culture, Leisure & Lifestyle	
Five Texans, including the Willacy County sheriff, are guilty of peonage. The sheriff arrested "vagrants" and had them work off their fines on local farms.	Secretary of State Frank B. Kellogg warns the Chinese factions that the powers will use all necessary force to prevent escalation of the conflict. He urges the factions to stop the fight for Shanghai.		National Guard Captain and airmail pilot Charles Lindbergh of St. Louis indicates that he might try the New York to Paris flight. He plans to go solo in a small plane.	John McCormack and Edward Johnson laud each other as world class tenors. Neither is willing to claim to be the best since Enrico Caruso....American tennis purges professionals from the rankings. Bill Tilden is number one for the seventh straight year. Due to illness, Helen Wills, the 1926 champion, does not make the list.	Feb. 5
200 people attend the first meeting of the Pioneer Negroes of the World, Inc. The founders indicate that the colonized races are rising against white domination. They also say the PNW will learn from Marcus Garvey's mistakes.					Feb. 6
In a speech seen as an effort to get Calvin Coolidge to commit, Nicholas Murray Butler says he does not believe Calvin Coolidge will run in 1928. Butler raises the specter of the third term. He expects a wet to win....The New York Senate votes unanimously to ask Congress to allow immigration of dependants of those who declare intent to become citizens. Congress is increasing immigration restrictions.	Frank B. Kellogg wants Shanghai as a neutral city. The Chinese factions unite in opposition to Frank B. Kellogg's proposal.		Electrical engineers in convention note the need for cheaper electricity. Standardization is also important to continued economic growth.	After 60 years' effort, Anglicans produce the first rewrite of their prayer book since 1662. "Obey" is deleted from the marriage ceremony, and the groom shares rather than endowing his bride with all his goods....Citing God-given voices and wasp waistlines, Diva Mary Garden says Fernand Ansseau and Charles Healey are superior tenors to John McCormack and Edward Johnson.	Feb. 7
The Texas legislature expels two members for taking bribes. Under the new administration, Investigations continue into abuses under former Governor "Ma" Ferguson....The widow of a War of 1812 veteran dies at age 108. 16 pensioners from that war remain alive.	Calvin Coolidge indicates that he will veto the Philippine legislature's September call for a referendum on independence. Philippine Governor Leonard Wood earlier vetoed the bill. Calvin Coolidge regards it as inappropriate "at this time."	With farm prices generally down from 1926, cotton prices rise on news that the McNary-Haugen farm reform bill is expected to pass the Senate. Calvin Coolidge marshals his forces to defeat the package in the House—or veto the bill if necessary.	Commander Richard E. Byrd announces he will vie for the $25,000 prize for the first to fly the New York–Paris route. Byrd will navigate. Bernt Balchen, the Norwegian polar explorer, will assist in navigation. Byrd's polar pilot, American Floyd Bennett, will fly the plane.	Ty Cobb signs with the Philadelphia Athletics. His one-year contract gives him a salary of $75,000. Connie Mack's Athletics have spent $250,000 on new players so far.	Feb. 8
States continue to debate evolution. The Arkansas house approves an anti-evolution law while New Hampshire rejects one, following Missouri's rejection yesterday. ...Congress announces that both houses will hold votes on the propriety of a third term. Republicans and Democrats refer to the Grant precedent of 1875 in indicating their opposition to a third term for Calvin Coolidge	The United States indicates that progress is occurring in the effort to resolve the Chinese crisis. China claims that Secretary Frank B. Kellogg bypassed his ambassador in demanding a neutral zone in Shanghai. Meanwhile, marines approach Shanghai. The Presbyterians indicate that the majority of their missions are unaffected....The Senate drops efforts to have the United States join the World Court. Because Britain will not accept U.S. reservations, U.S. participation is dead.	The California Avocado Growers Association asks for an end to the term "alligator pear," by which their fruit has been known since a 16th century misreading of "ahuacate." An avocado is neither alligator nor pear; the false label deters consumers and ruins the avocado business....Remington Typewriter, Rand Kardex, and three other office equipment companies with assets of $65 million merge into Remington-Rand office equipment company.		The Literary Guild defends its pricing of its one-year, 12-volume subscription at $18.00. Book dealers want the price raised to $30.00, but the Guild counters that the cost of producing a $2.00 to $2.50 book in lots of 25,000 is under 30 cents. The Guild seeks to attract readers deterred by traditional pricing.... Babe Ruth returns his $52,000 contract. He says he will quit first. the Yankees explain that the contract is just a formality to meet the deadline for an offer. With Cobb getting $75,000, Ruth will ask $100,000.	Feb. 9
The Arkansas Senate tables the anti-evolution bill passed by the House yesterday. The Southern Methodist education committee resolved on behalf of no restriction on the teaching of science....The House resolution against the third term is sent to committee, there to die from neglect.		The cotton market in the United States and Liverpool is down due to uneasiness over the fate of McNary-Haugen. Democrats are rumored to be split, leaving the final vote cloudy, and Calvin Coolidge is still on record as wanting to veto the bill.	A stout-Ford trimotor airplane on the Dayton to Detroit route becomes the first commercial craft to navigate by means of radio beacon. The army has experimented with the beacons, but never before has a flight relied on beacons at both ends. The radio emits morse code dots and dashes to inform the pilot if the plane is on or off course.	A court rules against an attempt by a business associate of Charlie Chaplin to vacate the receivership. Chaplin's estranged wife had won the receivership to protect her interests in his assets during the divorce dispute.	Feb. 10
	U.S. marines are at Shanghai. They will not leave their ships unless needed.	The Senate passes the McNary-Haugen agriculture bill with both parties split. In favor are 24 Republicans and 22 Democrats. Opposed are 22 Republicans and 17 Democrats. The majority is too small to withstand an expected Calvin Coolidge veto.	"Talkies" arrive. A private showing of a film synchronized with sound takes place in New York City. The talking movie is a joint effort of Radio Corporation of America, General Electric, and Westinghouse Electric and Manufacturing. RCA's head says it will be great for allowing broadcasts of presidential addresses.	William S. Hart, cowboy movie star, sets up a $103,000 trust fund for his ex wife in an easy divorce settlement. The Chaplin divorce continues, with the estranged wife demanding the Chaplin mansion and citing financial distress.	Feb. 11

F	G	H	I	J
Includes campaigns, elections, federal-state relations, civil rights and liberties, crime, the judiciary, education, healthcare, poverty, urban affairs, and population.	Includes formation and debate of U.S. foreign and defense policies, veterans affairs, and defense spending. (Relations with specific foreign countries are usually found under the region concerned.)	Includes business, labor, agriculture, taxation, transportation, consumer affairs, monetary and fiscal policy, natural resources, pollution and industrial accidents.	Includes worldwide scientific, medical and technological developments, natural phenomena, U.S. weather and natural disasters.	Includes the arts, religion, scholarship, communications media, sports, entertainment, fashions, fads, and social life.

	World Affairs	Europe	Africa & The Middle East	The Americas	Asia & The Pacific
Feb. 12	Opposition to Calvin Coolidge's plan firms up. Although Japan is willing to agree to anything he proposes, Italy and France, the two nations without firm numbers in the 5-5-3 ratio, find it unacceptable.	France cites world affairs as justification for its 7 billion franc fortifications project. Although Aristide Briand is speaking of peace, War Minister Paul Painleve notes the rise of the airplane, the eventual French evacuation of the Rhineland, and tensions with Italy and Germany.	Opening in New York is a display of 500 pieces of art collected in the Belgian Congo. African art started being noticed in Europe 15 years earlier, but it still is mostly neglected in the Western world.	The oil dispute in Mexico is in a truce. The government and producers are awaiting arbitration and the court decision.	The King of Siam receives a white elephant from the Borneo Company. He now has three of them as well as four pink ones. The elephants are sacred, as well as symbols of good fortune.
Feb. 13	Chicago's Sanai Temple hosts a meeting of 500 Protestants, Jews, and Catholics. Both black and white, delegates meet to discuss world unity. The movement plans several additional meetings before its world conference in November.	Italy's war factories are operating at 100 percent. Britain is wondering why.	An archaeological dig in Ur uncovers ancient vanity cases and other toilet items from the 12th century B.C.E. Also unearthed are records of Marduk Nadin Ahi.		The southern Chinese government bars religious teachings in schools, forcing Episcopal schools to shut down. New, mandatory rituals include bowing to the southern flag and the reading of parts of the will of Sun Yat Senator
Feb. 14	France rejects Calvin Coolidge's limitation plan, saying it prefers to deal through the League. Britain is also opposed....In China, Britain and China break off talks on concessions. British troops land and move toward Shanghai.	France and Germany have the same military budget. The French army counts 465,000 men while the German has only 100,000. Prices are higher in Germany.		In Nicaragua, Adolfo Diaz recants his decision to resign if necessary for peace. The conservative government prepares for the "decisive" battle against the liberals at Matagalpa.	
Feb. 15	Frank B. Kellogg refuses to accept French rejection of the American plan. He says that France misunderstands and will come around.	Stanley Baldwin says his nation will not cede poison gas research to the League. He notes that two of the world's largest powers are not in the League....German nationalists begin work to undo Versailles' decree of German war guilt.		The Puerto Rican legislature asks for home rule in internal affairs.	Northern warlords and Manchurian Wei pei fu combine forces and drive toward Hankow and Kiukang. Southerners relieve pressure on Shanghai. Both sides prepare for a major battle for China.
Feb. 16	The Chinese government in Peking brings its complaint against Britain to the League. China contends that the presence of British forces is a violation of the League Covenant and Washington Treaty.	Germany indicates it cannot meet its 1928 Dawes reparations obligations because that would disrupt the 1927 budget. Observers read this as a first step toward getting reparations reduced....A Belgian report indicates that the German army is actually 300,000, not the Versailles-mandated 100,000.	Italy demands the expulsion of Senussi tribesmen from Egypt and the jailing of others. Italy claims the Senussi are crossing the Tripolitan border and causing trouble in Italian territory.	When asked by Senator George Norris, Secretary Frank B. Kellogg writes President Calvin Coolidge that only four American companies are seeking concessions under the new Meixcan law. About 50 are ignoring the law. The 50 produce about 70 percent of Mexico's oil output. Kellogg denies U.S. government involvement.	Northern forces in Hangchow, blocking the route to Shanghai, suffer defeat at the hands of Nationalist southerners. Northern leaders blame southern propaganda for demoralizing the defenders.
Feb. 17				Canada's new budget includes a tax decrease of $27 million. Revenues are estimated at $394 million and the trade balance is favorable. The postwar depression is over.	
Feb. 18		Chancellor Wilhelm Marx denies that Germany intends to renege on its Dawes obligations.		Calvin Coolidge explains his reason for sending additional troops to Nicaragua. He says Americans there are alarmed that leftist rebels are getting additional arms. The liberal leader reiterates that Mexico is not aiding the rebels and says that American aid to the conservatives will only delay liberal victory.... Mexico claims American oil producers of 56 percent of the 1926 output are complying with the law. This in rebuttal to Frank B. Kellogg.	The southern offensive continues. British forces parade through the streets of Shanghai. Shanghai workers strike to weaken the northern defenders and demand that the northerners and British leave.
Feb. 19		The Soviet Union accepts defeat in its attempt to impose prohibition. Too many illicit stills make enforcement impossible.			

A	B	C	D	E
Includes developments that affect more than one world region, international organizations and important meetings of world leaders.	*Includes all domestic and regional developments in Europe, including the Soviet Union.*	*Includes all domestic and regional developments in Africa and the Middle East.*	*Includes all domestic and regional developments in Latin America, the Caribbean, and Canada.*	*Includes all domestic and regional developments in Asian and Pacific nations (and colonies).*

U.S. Politics & Social Issues	U.S. Foreign Policy & Affairs, Defense	U.S. Economy & Environment	Science, Technology & Nature	Culture, Leisure & Lifestyle	
The National Automobile Chamber of Commerce opposes mandatory car insurance. Among its arguments: it will make drivers careless because they no longer fear financial loss. The first state to mandate insurance is Massachusetts, but 22 other states have legislation in draft.			Cairns, Australia, suffers a hurricane. Damage is estimated at $5 million.	With $1.2 billion, Henry Ford is the world's richest person....Paris's spring styles feature skirts that barely cover the knees. Undergarments are scant, and bright colors in peasant motifs enliven women's clothing.	Feb. 12
Beverly Hills actors tell their mayor to choose between his career and his office. Eddie Cantor says Mayor Will Rogers is absent too often because he's on the road with his cowboy philosopher act....A Rand School of Social Science report says that American Communists total between 5,000 and 7,000. The party peaked in 1919 at 35,000, never the millions alleged in years past.	The navy reveals that it has five ships whose guns can fire over 34,000 yards. Britain has the second best range, but it is only 22,000 yards, and most of the United States' lesser ships can match that distance.	Southern university officials and professors oppose price supports. They also decry the South's dependency on one-crop agriculture and blame high interest rates, averaging 12-15 percent but reaching to 40 percent. They support farm cooperatives....The House begins debate on McNary-Haugin, with several days of discussion expected.	The president of the Illinois chiropodist association says that women's feet are turning into hooves. He blames high heels....A snowstorm in Niigate Prefecture kills 91. The blizzard is Japan's worst in 50 years.		Feb. 13
Evangelist Uldine Utley is selected to lead a revival in New York from May to November. After the meeting, the 14-year-old Utley left for a revival campaign through the southeast....President Calvin Coolidge receives a petition from 20,000 blacks asking him to end discrimination in the federal government and ask Congress to move on anti-lynching legislation. Calvin Coolidge is silent.	The Cantonese reject Frank B. Kellogg's proposal to neutralize Shanghai. The forces defending the city against Cantonese armies also reject Frank B. Kellogg's plan.			The author and cast of The Virgin Man are held on charges of indecency. Trials of two other plays, Sex and Captive, open. The arrests are part of a campaign to clean up the theater.	Feb. 14
After seven months of attempting to elude authorities, Charles Ponzi surrenders and begins serving a 7-9 year state sentence for postal fraud. Ponzi earlier serves a federal sentence for postal fraud related to his 1920 pyramid scheme.	1200 marines are preparing to embark at Philadelphia for Nicaragua. They are to serve as reinforcements as the United States expands its "safety zones" in the country.	The House accepts the Senate version of McNary-Haugen 201-62. Quick passage means Calvin Coolidge cannot pocket veto the bill....After price reductions of $10–$200, new Studebakers sell for $1,195–$1,585.	Coastal California is hit by an earthquake, a gale, and mudslides. Only one person dies....In a remote section of Yugoslavia, 600 are dead from an earthquake. Peasants reportedly think it's the end of the world.	In Paris, friends raise funds to buy the home of Isadora Duncan. They plan to establish a memorial dancing school.	Feb. 15
Over 1 million petition to the Massachusetts legislature in support of a referendum on the repeal of prohibition.	The United States sends another six planes and 100 ground troops to Nicaragua. The liberal rebels threaten action if the United States establishes additional neutral zones.	The East Coast Bank and Trust Company of Orlando, Florida, fails. This is the second failure in two days, another indicator that the Florida boom is over....The branch banking bill passes the Senate 71–17. Senator Carter Glass wants an inquiry into the expenditure of $100,000 by the American Bankers Association.	The wind, rain, and mudslides in the California storm area are the worst in California history. Adding to the misery are snowstorms in higher elevations. 10 people are dead in an avalanche....In Yugoslavia, another earthquake kills 96, razes a village, and causes a river to disappear.	A New York City alderman proposes to restrict six-day bicycle races to three hours in 24. He notes that riders use drugs as stimulants, a charge the race manager denies.	Feb. 16
	Calvin Coolidge, with the 5-5-3 proposal dead, consults with Frank B. Kellogg and other advisors on other options for arms reduction. The failure of his proposal due to France's refusal provides ammunition for those who want the three new cruisers and a larger navy.	McNary-Haugen passes 214-178 as critics assail its unconstitutional usurpation of presidential powers and the farm bloc's steamroller tactics. The Calvin Coolidge veto is still likely.		Deems Taylor's English-language opera, King's Henchman, receives raves at the Metropolitan Opera. Critics rate it as America's best.	Feb. 17
Tornadoes in Louisiana, Mississippi, and Alabama cause $400,000 in damage, kill 40, and injure 100, mostly black sharecroppers. Owners indicate they will not rebuild or repair plantation quarters.	The American High Commissioner at Constantinople and the Turkish Foreign Minister agree that the United States will enjoy most favored nation status until the two nations sign a treaty. The United States severed relations with Turkey in 1917 when it entered World War I.	Congress passes the bill to regulate commercial radio. More than 18,000 radio stations will now have to apply for federal licenses and bandwidth.		James Joyce threatens to sue for publication in the United States of Ulysses without permission or payment. John Galsworthy and Sherwood Anderson are among the authors who support his complaint against publication by Two Worlds Monthly of an expurgated version....Jim Maloney defeats light-heavyweight champion Jack Delaney in an elimination bout for the right to meet heavyweight champion Gene Tunney in the fall. An indoor record 20,000 paid an indoor record $200,000 to watch.	Feb. 18
The second annual National Negro History Week begins. The week is an accomplishment of Carter Woodson and the Association for the Study of Negro Life and History.		New Yorkers enjoy the season's first asparagus (from California, South Carolina, and Georgia), Illinois cucumbers, and Argentine grapes.	A report from Liverpool indicates that world cotton fabric sales are down 16 percent since the war. Synthetics are eroding the market for natural fibers.	The World's Chess Championship begins in New York City. It will continue until March 19. World champion is Cuba's J.R. Capablanca. Alexander Alekhine of Russia is the number one challenger....Canadian curlers beat the United States and win the Gordon Medal for this year.	Feb. 19

F	G	H	I	J
Includes campaigns, elections, federal-state relations, civil rights and liberties, crime, the judiciary, education, healthcare, poverty, urban affairs, and population.	Includes formation and debate of U.S. foreign and defense policies, veterans affairs, and defense spending. (Relations with specific foreign countries are usually found under the region concerned.)	Includes business, labor, agriculture, taxation, transportation, consumer affairs, monetary and fiscal policy, natural resources, pollution and industrial accidents.	Includes worldwide scientific, medical and technological developments, natural phenomena, U.S. weather and natural disasters.	Includes the arts, religion, scholarship, communications media, sports, entertainment, fashions, fads, and social life.

	World Affairs	Europe	Africa & The Middle East	The Americas	Asia & The Pacific
Feb. 20		One tangible fruit of the royal wedding of last November is that Sweden and Belgium agree never to go to war with one another. Sweden already has no-war agreements with all its Scandinavian neighbors but Norway, with whom negotiations are close to final.			The Shanghai walkout now involves 80,000. Police club a mob that stones British troops. The executioner beheads 20 in the street to stop the strike....In Turkestan, the Soviet Union agrees to rebuild historic mosques. The move is to conciliate its Muslims.
Feb. 21	Italy rejects Calvin Coolidge's request for great power naval restriction discussions. He finds the proposal insulting to Italy. The talks are effectively dead.	Russia reports a defense budget of over $350 million.		President Adolfo Diaz asks the United States to take virtual control of Nicaraguan affairs. U.S. troops have made safe zones of eight Nicaraguan cities and are replacing Diaz's troops....Mexico reports that five-sixths of oil companies are obeying the law. Over 14 million hectares of oil land are in compliance with the law. About half a million hectares are not.	Britain agrees to cede its Hankow concession. The city will be Chinese again. British conservatives call for severing relations with Russia for meddling in China. Shanghai remains paralyzed by the strike and shocked by the beheadings....Anti-Sikh demonstrations in Bombay'a Muslim quarter results in death for a Muslim and a Hindu and injury to 26 other Indians. The Sikhs refused to stop a noisy parade near a mosque.
Feb. 22	Britain's Stanley Baldwin expresses support for the Calvin Coolidge proposal to discuss naval restrictions.		Miners in southwest Transvaal find a gravel deposit 40 miles long. They plan to begin digging diamonds within the week.		Japan takes a hands-off position toward the Chinese disturbances. Japan also supports the great power talks proposed by Calvin Coolidge.
Feb. 23	League-sponsored meetings on tariff reduction and other restrictions open in Paris. Hopes are that reductions in trade and transport barriers erected to facilitate postwar recovery will improve trade among the 43 participating European nations.				Silver shipments from the United States to India for the week total about 1.8 million ounces, consistent with averages for the past year. Although the Indian government is considering a British recommendation that it switch from the silver to the gold standard, India remains heavily committed to silver for ornamentation.
Feb. 24					The competing Chinese armies are near Shanghai. The strike is over after 100 beheadings. Foreigners are armed and ready to defend their concessions. An anti-British general strike breaks out in Hankow.
Feb. 25		The Polish government seeks a $100 million loan. The government promises fiscal reforms. A group led by Morgan Bank will provide financing.	Transvaal authorities anticipate South Africa's last diamond "rush" to attract 10,000 miners. The total is 17,000. As 100,000 watch, 12,000 "Sooners" break through a 200-man police line 20 minutes before the starting time to stake their claims ahead of professional runners hired by the syndicates.	President Adolfo Diaz asks for a $20 million loan and offers to surrender much Nicaraguan sovereignty over military and financial matters. The proposal is similar to U.S. arrangements with Haiti and the Dominican Republic and the U.S. proposal for Panama.	
Feb. 26		Germany applauds French premier Aristide Briand for maintaining the spirit of Locarno. Germany takes his cooperative attitude as a sign that settlement of the Rhineland dispute is likely.			

A	B	C	D	E
Includes developments that affect more than one world region, international organizations and important meetings of world leaders.	Includes all domestic and regional developments in Europe, including the Soviet Union.	Includes all domestic and regional developments in Africa and the Middle East.	Includes all domestic and regional developments in Latin America, the Caribbean, and Canada.	Includes all domestic and regional developments in Asian and Pacific nations (and colonies).

U.S. Politics & Social Issues	U.S. Foreign Policy & Affairs, Defense	U.S. Economy & Environment	Science, Technology & Nature	Culture, Leisure & Lifestyle	
South Carolina begins enforcing blue laws enacted in 1922. Because work for profit or worldly entertainment is illegal on Sunday, closing is mandatory for cigar stores, gas stations, and drug stores.			An Atlantic storm lashes New York and New Jersey, with 80 mile an hour winds driving heavy rains. Thousands flee the resorts, with railways and highways under water and extensive property damage.		Feb. 20
The Supreme Court overturns Hawaii's 1920 law regulating Japanese foreign language schools. The court ruled that the state could not usurp rights of parents, teachers, and children....Congressman Benjamin Fairchild (R-NY) proposes to amend the Constitution to bar a third presidential term. The proposal is another attempt to head off a third-term try by Calvin Coolidge.		Senators from Utah and Arizona begin a filibuster of the Boulder Dam bill. Senator Johnson of California threatens cloture. The two states were among the western states that agreed in 1920 to build the $28 million dam on the Colorado River. They later decided that diversion of water to California's Imperial Valley was not in their interest.	Cuban naval lieutenant Pedro Audux invents an automated SOS. The radio weighs 50 pounds and allows anyone, not just operators trained in Morse Code, to transmit distress signals.		Feb. 21
The North Carolina Ku Klux Klan splits with national Klan leader Dr. Hiram Evans over Evans' promotion of anti-Catholic laws in the state legislature. The resigning head of the North Carolina Klan, a superior court judge, and other Klansmen object to attempts to regulate religion by law....Chicago's mayoral primaries feature shootings, kidnappings, stolen ballot boxes, fights, and police raids.	The Curtiss Aeroplane and Motor Company announces that it will test a plane capable of landing on water and ships. The plane can reach speeds of 180 mph. If the tests are successful, Curtiss will enter it into the competition for the navy pursuit plane to replace the Curtiss P1.	Negotiations between coal operators and miners over a new pay scale fail after weeks of futility. Refusing a pay cut, miners set a strike for April 1....Record production in Oklahoma's Seminole oilfields drop oil prices 15 to 39 cents a barrel. Prices range from $1.35 to $2.31 a barrel, with overproduction at 100,000-175,000 barrels a day.		A puzzlers convention in Newark, NJ, reports that anagrams and brain twisters are the new craze. They lead to good English. Crossword puzzles are passé.	Feb. 22
The U.S. Naval Academy resolves a cheating scandal by expelling the second-year man who cribbed answers. The four first-year students that bought his cribbed information are set back a year.	Britain notifies the United States that it may send a warship to Nicaragua. The 200 British nationals have no guarantees of protection from the Nicaraguan government. The notification is sees as support for Calvin Coolidge.	Miners agree to restrict their April walkout to the Central Field. They also promise to supply railroads with fuel.		Customs officials assess duties on a Constantin Brancusi sculpture. They say the work of Rodin's Romanian pupil is merchandise. One is quoted: "If that's art, I'm a bricklayer."	Feb. 23
New York Republicans claim that Tammany has shifted to a dry stance to support the presidential hopes of Al Smith.		The Alabama governor and Congressional delegation meet with Calvin Coolidge to press the state claim to ownership of the Tennessee River within its borders. The Wilson Dam, part of the Muscle Shoals project, is in Alabama, and Alabama is forcing settlement of the Muscle Shoals power plant dispute....A seat on the New York Stock Exchange sells for $185,000, the same as the previous sale.		The Chatauqua season includes 630 cities and a $5 million budget.... Bobby Jones gets his first hole in one. Reigning British and U.S. Open champion, the 25-year-old Jones has been playing golf for 20 years.	Feb. 24
The Oklahoma legislature demands that Governor Henry Johnston fire his secretary, Mrs. O.O. Hammonds. The woman claims spiritualist powers, and the governor believes in her. The legislators resent their loss of influence with the governor. ...Chicago gangsters fell three in a Philadelphia drive-by shooting. The shooters fire machine guns from a speeding car.	Calvin Coolidge supports the British move to send a ship to Nicaragua as haven for British nationals. Concerns for the breach of the Monroe Doctrine are minor.	Calvin Coolidge signs the branch banking law. National banks can expand and provide easier credit. The law also renews federal reserve bank charters due to expire in 1934....Calvin Coolidge vetoes McNary-Haugen because of unconstitutional price controls. Farm prices rise on heavy trading. The farm bloc vows to make the veto a presidential campaign issue.	France unveils a five-engine flying boat. The craft is the world's largest bomber, with a length of 85 feet and a weight of 25,000 pounds. It can fly seven hours at top speed. France is the world's military air leader, rumored able to field a force of 1,200 planes.	Baseball player Babe Ruth, recently cleared of California child labor charges for using children in his vaudeville act, is charged again in San Diego. Ruth meanwhile is in Hollywood working on movies.	Feb. 25
Officials at 35 colleges oppose students driving cars on campus. They cite safety, wasted time, negative impact on scholarship, and the risk to morals....Swarthmore raises annual tuition to $800.		The Senate defeats cloture. With only four days remaining in the session, the Boulder Dam bill is dead.... The United States has seven billion-dollar corporations. The largest at over $2 billion is AT&T. Following are U.S. Steel, General Motors, the New York Central/Pennsylvania Railroad, Standard Oil of New Jersey, and Ford Motor Company at barely $1 billion.	The Cleveland Railway Company ends a four-month test of an aluminum railway car. Production will begin shortly.	The New York Pubic Library, with a grant from the Carnegie Foundation, acquires the Schomberg black history collection. The 4,000 books, manuscripts, and documents provide the core for the library's black research facility....Marcel Duchamp defends Constantin Brancusi's sculptures, denigrated as not art by U.S. customs three days earlier.... Ruth reveals he wants $200,000 for two years and will retire if he does not get it.	Feb. 26

F	G	H	I	J
Includes campaigns, elections, federal-state relations, civil rights and liberties, crime, the judiciary, education, healthcare, poverty, urban affairs, and population.	Includes formation and debate of U.S. foreign and defense policies, veterans affairs, and defense spending. (Relations with specific foreign countries are usually found under the region concerned.)	Includes business, labor, agriculture, taxation, transportation, consumer affairs, monetary and fiscal policy, natural resources, pollution and industrial accidents.	Includes worldwide scientific, medical and technological developments, natural phenomena, U.S. weather and natural disasters.	Includes the arts, religion, scholarship, communications media, sports, entertainment, fashions, fads, and social life.

		World Affairs	Europe	Africa & The Middle East	The Americas	Asia & The Pacific
Feb. 27		French police guard the American embassy. French radicals are protesting U.S. treatment of Nicola Sacco and Bartolomeo Vanzetti, demanding either their release or their execution.	Italy establishes a "nobility of good conduct." Families with spotless records qualify....Ireland is preparing to abandon women on juries. The Free State constitution requires absolute equality of women with men, but women have the right to exemption from jury duty. Only 30 have served in two years.	Jewish and British leaders in Palestine honor the Jewish National Fund on its 25th anniversary. The fund pays for purchasing land in Palestine. Its 1927 fund is $2.5 million.	Larry Gains beats Soldier Jones for the Canadian heavyweight championship....Mexico imports oil. The new production restriction law leads to shortfalls.	
Feb. 28		Britain denies entry to Roger Baldwin, head of the American Civil Liberties Union and a leader of the International Committee for the Release of Political Prisoners. Baldwin has been supportive of the Soviet Union. Britain and Russia are in the middle of a diplomatic spat over Russian involvement in China.		The Cairo press wages a campaign against the exemptions from Egyptian law enjoyed by foreigners. The United States, Greece, Belgium, and Spain are willing to transfer drugs and white slavery from consular to mixed courts, but other European nations refuse....The British in India prepare for Russian-financed Communist strikes.		Five more U.S. destroyers are en route to China to join the seven already there. The nationalists are moving against Nanking while the northerners are moving toward Hangchow. Red infiltration of the Cantonese forces is problematic.
Mar. 1			The Spanish flu epidemic sweeps through Romania. Arad reports 12,000 cases. In some provinces, schools shut down.		After five years, the British Privy Council rules for Newfoundland in a dispute with Canada over the boundary of Labrador. Newfoundland gains 110,000 square miles of timber and mineral land valued at over $250 million.	
Mar. 2			Albania is unsettled by rumors of a coup by Zog. The fear is that the coup will give Italy an excuse to enter Albania.			After Muslim and Hindu religious processions clash in Ponabalia, India, a Muslim mob returns with spears. Police fire on the mob, killing 20 and injuring 40.
Mar. 3		Britain publishes a white paper showing comparative naval strength. Britain has 62 cruisers. Japan has 39. The United States has 37. Establishment of a 5-5-3 ratio would entail scrapping many ships.	Britain indicates that it is losing patience with the Soviet Union but will not sever relations just yet. Russian interference in China is the major cause of friction....British women march on the Commons. They demand the vote for women 21 and older.	Benito Mussolini denies that he plans to remove General Emilio De Bono, governor of Tripoli, for conspiring to make Mussolini king. The rumor has been circulating since it originated in a U.S. newspaper last September.		
Mar. 4		A new transatlantic cable links the United States and Germany. The cable transmits 1500 letters a minute and reestablishes U.S.–German communications severed during the war.	Turkish women resist government efforts to get them to abandon the veil. In some cases they use umbrellas to cover their faces. The end to the veil is supposed to be voluntary, unlike the earlier mandatory end of the fez....Budapest censors ban the Venus de Milo.	In Cairo archaeologists are attempting to find the mummy of Cheops's mother. They theorize that Cheops hid her somewhere in his pyramid....After the results of the earlier Transvaal rush are voided because of "sooners" jumping the gun, a new rush allows 25,000 to vie for coveted diamond claims. The rush is larger than the gold rushes in California and the Klondike.		The Chinese government is split between reds and nationalists. Two Communist factions are uniting to oust Chiang Kai-shek.
Mar. 5			Supporters of the Weimar Republic want royalist ostracism, which is particularly bad in the military, outlawed....Italians are training the Albanian military. They are also building roads, air bases, and other infrastructure....Moscow relaxes as tensions with the U.K. abate.	A cyclone in Madagascar kills 500. Two steamers collide and two sailing vessels are lost. Total storm damage is set at $4 million.	Mexico reports an outbreak of bubonic plague in Mazatlan, Sinaloa. The last time Sinaloa had plague, in 1903, it killed hundreds although authorities burned all the tenements....Panama invests $12 million in banana growing.	

A	B	C	D	E
Includes developments that affect more than one world region, international organizations and important meetings of world leaders.	Includes all domestic and regional developments in Europe, including the Soviet Union.	Includes all domestic and regional developments in Africa and the Middle East.	Includes all domestic and regional developments in Latin America, the Caribbean, and Canada.	Includes all domestic and regional developments in Asian and Pacific nations (and colonies).

U.S. Politics & Social Issues	U.S. Foreign Policy & Affairs, Defense	U.S. Economy & Environment	Science, Technology & Nature	Culture, Leisure & Lifestyle	
The U.S. Consulate in Juarez is processing hundreds of Mexican families who want to enter the United States. Labor recruiters are attracting men who seek work. The Mexican government is doing nothing despite a developing labor shortage on the haciendas.	The U.S. Army has a self-operated aerial camera capable of mapping 180 square miles at 15,000 feet from its fastest plane. Designed by Sherman M. Fairchild, the camera takes a series of photos and records the time it takes them.		Sinclair Oil reports a new oil discovery in Mexico. The new field is further south than oil was previously believed to exist.		Feb. 27
The Princeton student council resigns over the ban of autos on campus. The issue is a matter of principle not one of having car, the council says.		Packard reduces prices of its small sixes by $335. At $2,250 to $2,350, the prices are $2,700 lower than the factory price when the models were introduced in 1920. There is no price reduction for large six or eight-cylinder Packards.	Skelly Oil begins construction of a large gas processing plant in the Texas panhandle. Capable of processing 50 million feet a day, it is the world's largest.	Mrs. Chaplin indicates that she may change her complaint against the actor. She hints that she may implicate an actress in her divorce suit.... The U.S. team takes 9 of 10 games from Britain in the World Checkers Tournament.	Feb. 28
The cheating scandal at Annapolis reaches beyond the students. The teacher responsible for the crib sheet resigns....As Senator Reed of Missouri seeks to extend the life of his committee, opponents filibuster. Ending the Reed committee will end Insull's contempt charge as well as the inquiry into excessive campaign contributions.	The Senate agrees to give battleships *Oklahoma* and *Nevada* longer range guns and to complete aircraft carriers *Saratoga* and *Lexington* as well as a submarine.	The Supreme Court invalidates Edward Doheny's Teapot Dome related oil leases. The companies that got Elk Hills oil in the early 1920s now owe the government $10.5 million.		The Atlantic City Chamber of Commerce downplays criticism of its beauty pageants. Countering criticism by the General Federation of Women's Clubs and other women's organizations, the chamber notes that the 1926 winner, Norma Smallwood of Tulsa, OK, demonstrated not only beauty but intelligence, grace, and refinement.	Mar. 1
House proposes to liberalize immigration. It would allow entry by spouses and dependants of aliens. Also, women who lost citizenship by marrying aliens before the 1922 Cable Act may regain citizenship. ...Princeton undergrads roller skate on campus. They are protesting the ban of student autos....Calvin Coolidge vacates the White House to allow remodeling. The White House was last vacant during 1902 renovation.	Calvin Coolidge signs three naval bills, including the appropriations bill that includes the three new cruisers he opposed. France's opposition to naval limitation talks causes his change of heart.	Curtiss aircraft reports that its funded debt is down to $552,000. It made a profit of $413,000 in 1926, thanks largely to government orders. Airplanes are becoming a business, not just an adventure.		Babe Ruth settles for $210,000 for three years, not the $100,000 a year he asked. The entire Cincinnati payroll in the 1870s, when the first pro teams started, was $10,000.	Mar. 2
The new immigration legislation passes the House 232–111 and goes to Calvin Coolidge. If he signs, quotas based on 1890 numbers will be delayed until 1928.		First National Pictures, the Stanley Company, and East Coast Theaters combined owners of more than 350 theaters, merge. The new organization has assets of $100 million. It's the largest merger in film since Famous Players—Lasky merger of 1916, which led to antitrust investigations.	Royal Air Force experiments with aerial refueling are successful. The experiments involved a plane with spare tanks flying over another, matching speeds, and lowering a flexible hose to a mechanic who inserts the hose into the gas tank. Transoceanic flights are now possible.	15,000 fans see Jack Sharkey stop Mike McTigue in the 12th round. The up and coming Sharkey was behind the 38-year-old McTigue until the 10th....Babe Ruth is in the top shape of his Yankee career. His waistline is 38 inches, and he weighs only 218 pounds.	Mar. 3
Warren Harding's attorney general Harry Daugherty is found not guilty of conspiracy when one juror stands firm against conviction. Harding's alien property custodian Thomas Miller is guilty but plans to appeal....The Senate adjourns its session, leaving military and veterans legislation among its unfinished business. It failed to break the filibuster.			Thomas Edison reports success with Madagascar rubber trees on his Florida estate. He also has successfully grown rubber trees in New Jersey.		Mar. 4
Near Pittsburgh, prohibition officials seize two freight cars containing 117 barrels of beer listed as oil. This is the first confiscation of railroad cars or corporate property, but seizing of cars, wagons, boats, and other individual means of transporting alcohol are routine.				The racing season in Miami ends with a victory by War Eagle, three-year-old son of Man o' War, at Hialeah. The colt breaks the track record for a mile and a furlong.	Mar. 5

F
Includes campaigns, elections, federal-state relations, civil rights and liberties, crime, the judiciary, education, healthcare, poverty, urban affairs, and population.

G
Includes formation and debate of U.S. foreign and defense policies, veterans affairs, and defense spending. (Relations with specific foreign countries are usually found under the region concerned.)

H
Includes business, labor, agriculture, taxation, transportation, consumer affairs, monetary and fiscal policy, natural resources, pollution and industrial accidents.

I
Includes worldwide scientific, medical and technological developments, natural phenomena, U.S. weather and natural disasters.

J
Includes the arts, religion, scholarship, communications media, sports, entertainment, fashions, fads, and social life.

	World Affairs	Europe	Africa & The Middle East	The Americas	Asia & The Pacific
Mar. 6	Foreign ministers of the big five powers (Britain, Germany, France, Poland, Italy) arrive in Geneva for meetings on issues including Albania, the Saar, and other regional concerns. Fears are that the Chinese might intrude their issues into the deliberations.	Spain's first effort to humanize bullfighting draws jeers from a Madrid crowd. Rubber armor fails to protect horses, with bulls killing four of eight.	Excavations at Ur reveal a civilization rivaling that of Egypt. Archaeologists report that the deeper the layer the more sophisticated the arts, with delicate and intricate items dating to 3500 B.C.E....South Africa's leading expert on cave art reports that art in a Rhodesian cave is Egyptian. It depicts clothed figures with instruments unknown to Bushmen, whose cave art depicts unclothed figures.	A second British ship is headed for Nicaraguan waters. Meanwhile, a prominent liberal suggests that both the conservative and liberal leaders should step down and let the United States mediate.	
Mar. 7	American tourism in the French Riviera is slumping. Americans dislike high prices, required identity cards, and French anti-Americanism during the 1926 collapse of the franc. Benito Mussolini's Italy is drawing Americans now that Miami is closed to tourists.			The Mexican army gets orders to show "no quarter" to the rebels. The fighting is widespread. Arms and ammunition are due from Germany later this month.	
Mar. 8	The League hears that the Vatican is interested in membership. The problem is that only sovereign states are eligible.	A putsch attempt in Latvia fails. The officer who took a post office with 40 men is unbalanced.			A Japanese earthquake kills 2,600 and leaves 50,000 homeless....When a provincial warlord switches sides, the northern armies in Shanghai are surrounded on four sides by nationalist armies. Three Russians taken by Chang Tso Lin will be executed as spies despite Russian protests.
Mar. 9	The League prepares to release a report on white slavery and schedules a conference. Meanwhile it urges all nations to enforce current laws and conventions.		Italy tightens control over its Libyan territories. Cyrenacia and Tripoli, semi-autonomous since 1919, now have consultative powers only, and parliaments, suffrage, and other rights end.	Mme Kollontay, Russian envoy to Mexico, denies her legation is spreading Communist propaganda. She also indicates that Russia wants improved trade with Mexico.	After months of delay, the measure switching India from the silver to the gold standard passes 68 to 65 and awaits the viceroy's signature. The rupee rises on the news.
Mar. 10	Britain accepts an invitation to Washington for three-party talks on naval reductions. Japan is to follow suit. Optimism revives that Italy and France stop their opposition.		After months of winter fighting, Somali sultans concede defeat. Italy's conquest of Somaliland is complete.		
Mar. 11	Japan confirms that it will join the three-power talks. A 5-5-4 ratio is rumored.				
Mar. 12			The 40,000 member Industrial and Commercial Workers Union joins the International Federation of Trade Union with British unionist support. South Africa's white unionists are displeased and the press charges the black union, founded in 1919, is Marxist.	Greenland's free newspaper, *Atuagogulliatutit*, circulation 2500, is published in the native language for the island's population of 15,000 Eskimos. Because there is no route between east and west Greenland, the paper has to be shipped to Copenhagen, then to west Greenland.	

A	B	C	D	E
Includes developments that affect more than one world region, international organizations and important meetings of world leaders.	*Includes all domestic and regional developments in Europe, including the Soviet Union.*	*Includes all domestic and regional developments in Africa and the Middle East.*	*Includes all domestic and regional developments in Latin America, the Caribbean, and Canada.*	*Includes all domestic and regional developments in Asian and Pacific nations (and colonies).*

U.S. Politics & Social Issues	U.S. Foreign Policy & Affairs, Defense	U.S. Economy & Environment	Science, Technology & Nature	Culture, Leisure & Lifestyle	
A Georgia grand jury refuses to indict night riders. Rather it indicts the victim, a lawyer seized, taken to the countryside, and flogged. He is charged with possession of a firearm and liquor.		Vaudeville giant Keith's Orpheum announces plans to build new houses and remodel others. It plans a dual circuit—one class A vaudeville and the other including movies....General Motors gives a record dividend. The company reports 1926 sales almost matched the total GM's first 10 years.		Fifteen teams begin the 42nd annual six-day bicycle race at Madison Square Garden. Charlie Chaplin fires the opening gun....Otto Klemperer conducts his farewell concert with the New York Symphony....Rising-star Klemperer succeeded Wilhelm Furtwaengler. Next of this year's guests is Fritz Busch....Florida's Pompano track opens under court order. Anti-gambling forces had outlawed it.	Mar. 6
In *Tumey v. Ohio*, the Supreme Court rules that Ohio's liquor courts are invalid. Judges receive payment for convictions, a violation of due process....The Supreme Court rules Texas' white primary unconstitutional. White primaries in one-party states disfranchise blacks....Harry Sinclair's Teapot Dome related contempt trial opens.	The Navy solicits bids on six cruisers. Included are the three Calvin Coolidge did not want....The army reserve officers' association protests. New rules make promotion as hard for them as for regulars. Rules also establish an active and an inactive reserve.	White Motor Company reports profits down 51 percent in 1926. Used trucks were overpriced and credit sales resulted in losses.			Mar. 7
Former alien property custodian Thomas Miller receives a sentence of 18 months and a $5,000 fine for his role in the Harding scandals....Dr. T.T. Shields of Toronto tells the Baptist Bible Union of North America that Harry Emerson Fosdick is anti-Christian. Shields says Fosdick and other modernists empty churches and do not preach the Bible.	Secretary Frank B. Kellogg announces that the United States will not consider a protectorate for Nicaragua. This rebuffs President Adolfo Diaz' offer to allow the United States to control his country.	Cotton prices are off after several days of improving prices. Demand for exports, especially to India, is up 1.75 million bales from 1926....Oil output drops to 2.4 million barrels a week as Oklahoma producers cut back....Three Florida banks face runs. Miami bankers send $2 million to stabilize two Palm Beach banks and avoid spreading the run.		A judge rules *The Captive* is immoral and denies an injunction to allow performance during appeal. Another court denies jury trial to *Virgin Man* producers.	Mar. 8
Baptist Bible Union fundamentalists announce a purge of modernists and a plan to take their fight against false doctrine nationwide.			Massachusetts tests of hypnotism by radio are inconclusive. One subject seems to succumb, one is unaffected, and two respond partially.	With an 86-17 lead, the Americans clinch the world checkers title....The Florida supreme court shuts down horse racing at Pompano, Tampa, and Jacksonville because it uses "certificate" (pari-mutuel) wagering. Dog racing and jai alai are also affected.	Mar. 9
A gas bomb ends a rising by women at a Florida prison farm. The inmates wanted candy instead of cabbage. ...Black parents in Toms River, NJ, keep their children out of school. They sue to stop the transfer of the children from their integrated school to a new black school due to KKK influence.	Princeton faculty join with professors at Columbia in calling for a revision of the war debt agreements. The academics note that the terms seem lenient but do not fit reality.	Although Florida's bank run stops, hotel workers face hard times as a disappointing tourist season ends.	Chile announces a new process that cuts the cost of processing nitrate ore by 50 percent. Ores with as little as 15 percent are competitive in the production of artificial nitrogen.	Works at New York's independent artists show the influence of prohibition. One work tracks bootleg liquor from the speakeasy to Bellevue. Another shows eyes changing during a drinking bout.... The United States wins the checkers match 96–20 with 388 draws.	Mar. 10
The Department of Justice sends an attorney to Tampa to begin prosecutions of land fraud. The prosecutions will also extend into the Midwest under postal fraud statutes....In Pittsburgh gangsters dynamite an armored car, injuring 5. In Chicago the bootleggers' gang war resumes with 3 dead.	Japan's purchases of French planes total $7 million over the past 22 months. That price includes 172 planes, including 60 large bombers. The United States observes without comment.	Central Pennsylvania soft coal operators agree to maintain the current wage scale. Because of earlier agreement that the central settlement would apply throughout, the feared coal strike is averted.	Telephone lines link London and Havana, as the telephone links continue to spread. In yet another first-ever airplane flight, a Portuguese begins his trip from Africa to Brazil. Total time is 20 hours.	Pompano race track reopens—as does dog racing—with no betting. The courts rule that purses are legal....Boston bans nine books. Commonly, Boston censored a book now and then, but a backlog had developed after the death of the city's unofficial censor in 1926. Among banned titles: *The Plastic Age*, *The Hard-boiled Virgin*, and *The Beadle*.	Mar. 11
	The U.S. state department in a public note of thanks to Britain and Japan expresses regret that Italy and France are not attending the naval conference.	American income, according to the Bureau of Economic Statistics, was the world's highest in 1926. At $89.6 billion, it provided $2,010 for each "gainfully employed" person.		Wealthy Palm Beach residents meet to find another $3 million to save a local bank. The run is in its fifth day....Reggie McNamara's and his Italian partner, Franco Georgetti, wins the six-day races. This is "iron man" McNamara's 51st 2,340 mile race. He is 39 and began racing in 1913. His payout: $8,000 in prize money and incentives. Total payout for the racers: $75,000.	Mar. 12

F	G	H	I	J
Includes campaigns, elections, federal-state relations, civil rights and liberties, crime, the judiciary, education, healthcare, poverty, urban affairs, and population.	Includes formation and debate of U.S. foreign and defense policies, veterans affairs, and defense spending. (Relations with specific foreign countries are usually found under the region concerned.)	Includes business, labor, agriculture, taxation, transportation, consumer affairs, monetary and fiscal policy, natural resources, pollution and industrial accidents.	Includes worldwide scientific, medical and technological developments, natural phenomena, U.S. weather and natural disasters.	Includes the arts, religion, scholarship, communications media, sports, entertainment, fashions, fads, and social life.

	World Affairs	Europe	Africa & The Middle East	The Americas	Asia & The Pacific
Mar. 13		Germany's iron output is up 50 percent over 1926. The budget shows a surplus of 18 million marks for 10 months. Foreign trade is up, and rye prices fall, indicating that supports are ended....Italy's structured deflation continues. Prices are down over 14 percent since August. The stock market is up 25 percent since December. The central bank is reportedly stronger.		The Mexican war department announces a major drive against the Jalisco rebels. 68 are dead....In Nicaragua some troops are turned bandit. They hold up Americans taking supplies to Marines in Matagulpa.	
Mar. 14		Britain relents and allows Roger Baldwin to visit for two weeks. Baldwin had been earlier barred for his leftist sympathies.		Mexican attacks against Yaquis produce few casualties during a six-hour battle. Catholic bishops are again reported leading the rebels.	
Mar. 15		Avoiding a cabinet rupture over minor issues such as the number of Allied guards, the German cabinet, with royalists supporting the unanimous decision, agree to accept the French compromise on the Saar. The French Ruhr evacuation can now proceed.	The Rosenwald Library at Thebes, Egypt, opens. Attendees include archaeologist Howard Carter, the Czech minister, representatives of the Metropolitan Museum, and Egyptian dignitaries.	Fighting over a wide front in Nicaragua produces 300 casualties. Both liberals and conservatives have some success.	The American destroyer *Preble* fires its machine guns at Chinese after being fired on by infantry. The minister begins an inquiry. On other fronts the Chinese-on-Chinese fighting remains heavy. Chiang Kai-shek loses his offices amid speculation that reds unduly influence him.
Mar. 16	Geneva police uncover a Communist spy ring. They plan to expel Soviets spying on the League....Discussions begin on an American proposal that all defense budgets be public. Italy opposes. Other nations are noncommittal.	The French government is split on accepting Calvin Coolidge's invitation to the naval talks. Foreign minister Aristide Briand supports while Premier Raymond Poincare, Andre Tardieu, and Marin oppose.... Agriculture minister Martin Schiele calls for higher protective farm tariffs and says the Dawes payments are impossible for Germany to meet.			
Mar. 17	The United States rejects a League commission proposal on limiting preparations for war. Specifically, the United States maintains that training in poison gas warfare is not a crime.	France and Britain compete for tank supremacy. Each plans a high-speed (21–24 mph) machine with a six-inch gun. The speed is double the best current capability, which is four times that of World War I tanks.			Japan's peers reject a religion control bill. A month's pressure by Buddhists and Christians led to the rejection.
Mar. 18		Italy notifies the European powers that Yugoslavia plans to invade Albania. Italy may intervene.		Canadian Prime Minister William McKenzie-King tells his parliament that trade in natural products with the United States is consistent with dominion policy. He offers to meet with Calvin Coolidge on tariff reductions.	Nationalists drive on Soochow and Shanghai. The battle of Nanking is expected to prove decisive because the probable Nationalist victory will isolate the northerners in Shanghai.
Mar. 19		Warsaw turns out to celebrate Poland's "savior," Marshal Joseph Pilsudski on St. Joseph's Day. Highlight is a parade of 60,000 soldiers and 105 13-man detachments of the "civilian army" representing each Polish district. Rumor says Poland will use the day to invade Lithuania, but nothing happens.			A report for the Kahn Foundation says that Chinese will take over the Philippines if the United States leaves. Chinese businessmen already dominate. The report downplays the likelihood of Japanese aggression for the Philippines....The northern armies in Shanghai break. Nanking is also hard pressed.
Mar. 20		Yugoslavia denies warlike intentions toward Albania. As the powers begin investigating, Yugoslavia offers to let the League look into the matter....Poles in Upper Silesia celebrate the sixth anniversary of their inclusion in Poland.	Count Joseph Hunyady dies within sight of Khartoum. Descendant of kings and regents of Hungary and the final Lord High Steward for Charles of Austria, Hunyady was mauled by a lion in central Africa some weeks earlier....New gold from Africa is weakening the gold exchanges.	Border towns in Ontario report a building boom in hotels and cafes. An estimated 3.5 million Americans are expected, and the Detroit-Windsor ferry will run around the clock. A $2.00 drink permit qualifies as Canadian citizenship.	Nationalists take Shanghai. Foreigners guard their concessions.

A	B	C	D	E
Includes developments that affect more than one world region, international organizations and important meetings of world leaders.	*Includes all domestic and regional developments in Europe, including the Soviet Union.*	*Includes all domestic and regional developments in Africa and the Middle East.*	*Includes all domestic and regional developments in Latin America, the Caribbean, and Canada.*	*Includes all domestic and regional developments in Asian and Pacific nations (and colonies).*

U.S. Politics & Social Issues	U.S. Foreign Policy & Affairs, Defense	U.S. Economy & Environment	Science, Technology & Nature	Culture, Leisure & Lifestyle	
John H. Holmes calls for a middle way between theism and atheism. It is humanism. Bishop Manning says Christ is best guide. Meanwhile, atheists want the Uldine Utley revival stopped. They allege that the teen is just being exploited....Investigations reveal that Toombs County, GA, has hundreds of floggings.	Former Secretary of War Henry Stimson says that most Filipinos are content and not desirous of independence. Proper application of the Jones Act should satisfy most.		Noel Davis throws his plane into the New York-Paris sweepstakes. Formerly a leading aviator, Davis is now overshadowed by Rene Fonck and Richard Byrd. He will navigate while his pilot flies the plane.	Farmer's Trust Company of Palm Beach fails to reopen after the rich people's subscription falls short by over $1 million.	Mar. 13
The Ford-Sapiro million dollar libel suit opens in Detroit. Sapiro claims Ford libeled him in 1924–1925 when Ford's Dearborn Independent said Sapiro organized farmers' cooperatives for personal gain and as part of a "Jewish conspiracy."	The United States invites Italy and France to the three-power talks as informal participants. France agrees to send an observer. Italy is expected to follow suit.	General Electric reports that it has $137 million in life insurance on its employees. 83 percent of workers have coverage.	Vesuvius rumbles. Tremors are felt as far away as Norway.	Three more Florida banks close. Runs on two others abate....Blossom Seeley and Benny Fields head the bill at the Palace as vaudeville celebrates its centennial. Loews State has no particular celebration, but its headliners are Clayton, Jackson, and Durante.	Mar. 14
In Philadelphia, the musical *Lucky* eliminates its 15-foot Buddha. New York Buddhists protested because one scene involves an actress diving from Buddha's head.		The bond market reaches record highs as treasury bills recover from the recent slump. Foreign bonds are flourishing, particularly Belgian and French....Quarterly income tax receipts exceed the 1926 record and 1927 estimates. With $600 million anticipated, Congress begins considering tax cuts.		The Prince of Wales declares that the British army is becoming Americanized. Chewing gum is popular with the troops, who consume 3 million pieces a year.... Davis Cup tennis matches the 1925 record with 25 nations entered. Germany is back for the first time since 1914, but Australia is out for the second year.	Mar. 15
The court rules that the Jewish issue is not germane to the libel case against Henry Ford....Harry Sinclair is found guilty of contempt for refusing to answer Congressional questions during Teapot Dome hearings. Possible penalties include a jail term of one month to a year and/or a fine of $100 to $1,000.		AT&T stock rises 7¼ points, bringing the year to date rise to 16¼ points. The stock has not been this high since 1903.	Dr. Serge Voronoff predicts that humans will eventually have an active life of 125 years. After a three-month old age, they will die. Voronoff experiments on sheep and monkeys. He contends that glands wear out earlier than other body parts, which can last the 125 years.	Charlie Chaplin's wife, claiming the actor has not paid any support for their children since November and rebuffed by a court that declined to grant her $4,000 a month alimony pending settlement of the divorce suit, indicates she will return to acting....Black depositors begin a run on a Florida postal savings office. They withdraw $25,000 on a rumor that the post office was keeping their money in Florida banks.	Mar. 16
A millionaire cowboy fined for buying liquor on the *Leviathan* blames the stewards. The captain acknowledges the ship carries rum but denies that any is for sale.		*Daily Metal Trade* reports that Ford is lowering prices to clear inventories, designing a two-cycle engine, and ordering suppliers to get ready for a new model by April. Ford produces only half as many cars as General Motors.	A New York committee recommends that the city build an airport, preferably in the suburbs. Other options include a seaport, but the consensus is that the city needs a commercial aviation facility.	Jose Capablanca draws and clinches the world chess championship with a record of eight wins and nine draws. His prize: $2,000.... Yale in China announces that it will transfer to Chinese control with a Chinese president.	Mar. 17
Prohibition enforcement begins weeding out agents. Under the reform act, effective April 1 all agents must pass the civil service examination. The act separates liquor from internal revenue enforcement and requires a new commissioner.			August Heckscher announces that he has a new refrigeration process using carbon dioxide. Circulating "liquid air" will allow cheap mass-produced freezers.	Musical comedy star Eddie Cantor announces he is abandoning his $8,000 a week stage contract. He's heading for Hollywood to make moving pictures.	Mar. 18
		February gold imports are reported over $22 million. Major exporters are France, England, and China.	The Appalachian Scenic Highway is finished with selection of the Florida leg. The road stretches 2500 miles from Quebec to the Gulf of Mexico It is 85 percent paved or improved road, the brainchild of a Georgian and the non-governmental Appalachian Scenic Highway Association.	With over $86 million, Harvard is the United States's richest university....The sponsors of the Floranda resort put up $500,000 to repay losses of U.S. and British investors.	Mar. 19
Chatauqua's National Community Foundation indicates that it will spend $500,000 to expand its musical and dramatic programs in small towns. Road shows are fewer since the advent of the movies....Jane Addams indicates that her choice for president is Carrie Chapman Catt.	Senator William Borah, returned from a controversial investigative trip to Mexico, reports to a crowd of 5,000 that the Plutarco Calles government is free of Communist influence. Borah lauds Mexican land reform. He also blasts the League and says recognition of Russia is in order.	Arkansas assumes county road bonds and imposes a five cent a gallon gasoline tax to pay for bonded roads. This act switches the burden from property taxes.		Chicago's six-day race opens. The field of 28 includes 16 American and 12 foreign riders....*Sex* closes voluntarily but the producer blames the judge. The star, Mae West, is tired after a year's run.	Mar. 20

F
Includes campaigns, elections, federal-state relations, civil rights and liberties, crime, the judiciary, education, healthcare, poverty, urban affairs, and population.

G
Includes formation and debate of U.S. foreign and defense policies, veterans affairs, and defense spending. (Relations with specific foreign countries are usually found under the region concerned.)

H
Includes business, labor, agriculture, taxation, transportation, consumer affairs, monetary and fiscal policy, natural resources, pollution and industrial accidents.

I
Includes worldwide scientific, medical and technological developments, natural phenomena, U.S. weather and natural disasters.

J
Includes the arts, religion, scholarship, communications media, sports, entertainment, fashions, fads, and social life.

	World Affairs	Europe	Africa & The Middle East	The Americas	Asia & The Pacific
Mar. 21	Germany asks the League to intervene in the Italy-Yugoslavia dispute. France reads Italy as wanting control of the Straits of Otranto. Italy is slow to ask arbitration.	Italy eases restrictions on church lands. Improved relations with the papacy result.			Soviet attempts to impose women's equality in Samarkand and Tashkent lead to violence. Women without veils are put to death.
Mar. 22	French foreign minister Aristide Briand reports that the three powers—France, Britain, and Germany—defused the Albanian dispute between Italy and Yugoslavia. League involvement was unnecessary.	France and Italy begin discussions of Calvin Coolidge's proposed naval commission....France's Raymond Poincare delays state control of oil until 1929. He cites the burdensome start up costs of several billion francs....Poland outlaws the White Russian and Agrarian parties.		Canada reports that 1926 rail traffic. It increased 10,764,485 tons from 1925.	After the northern warlords lose shanghai, 150,000 strike, looting becomes common, and crowds storm the western concessions. British and Italian troops fire on the crowds and beat them back....In Japan, eight banks fail in a week. Post-earthquake stress causes bank runs.
Mar. 23		Meat consumption in Berlin is almost at the level that obtained prior to the war. The 1926 figure of 131 pounds per person is 12 pounds below pre-war consumption. Berlin also has to double its police force to counter attacks by reds and monarchists that kill one and injure 14.		The United States sells 200 machine guns, 3,000 rifles and 3 million rounds to the Diaz government in Nicaragua....A flyer calling for a boycott of American goods is in every Mexico City mailbox....Chile bars religion from school curricula. It is okay after hours though.	Nationalists take both Nanking and Chinkang. Earlier a northern warlord claimed that the fall of Shanghai was insignificant because Nanking would hold.
Mar. 24	As League officials indicate disappointment at the lack of movement on naval disarmament by the seven attendees, Sweden proposes exemption of the major powers from any agreement.	Prussia asks Germany to enact a law barring the return from exile of the ex-Kaiser. The current law ends in July.		Cuba outlaws poker, either using cards or dice.	The run on Japanese banks ends. Twelve banks fail due to earthquake liabilities....Nanking violence causes American casualties. More cruisers are en route.
Mar. 25		Germany indicates that it will have its zeppelin airline in operation in 1928. Service between Seville and Buenos Aires will commence on Columbus Day.	Egypt's legation to the United States will not be getting a new building. The committee assigned by the Chamber of Deputies to look into the matter sees no social or diplomatic need.	Police strike in Tampico. Their grievance is that they have not received their pay.	Nationalist forces in Nanking free western captives. They do so after the American commander threatens to shell the city.
Mar. 26	At Geneva disarmament talks are at a standstill. Britain insists that land and naval disarmament are separate issues. France wants both settled together.	For the fourth time, the French cabinet is unable to decide whether France should attend Calvin Coolidge's naval arms reduction talks.	Egyptians dispute polygamy. The government wants to require a man to get government permission to take a second wife. A committee of Alahzar University Ulemas determines that such a rule violates the Koran and is also socially and morally detrimental.	Negotiations over church autonomy in Mexico break up without results. The church maintains Rome must approve all agreements. Plutarco Calles, who says the church has influenced other nations to interfere in Mexico, wants the Mexican church to agree without Rome.	At the trial of Datu Tahil, the principal governor's testimony blames the Moro rising on American Dorr H. Malone. The Philippine constabulary major provided Tahil with several rifles and 600 rounds of ammunition for his failed rebellion.
Mar. 27	India's move to the gold standard is drawing down English gold supplies. The Bank of England is capable of handling increased demands for gold, but as more countries move to the gold standard the bank may become unable to maintain its reserves.	Italy celebrates the eighth anniversary of *fascismo* with pomp and pageantry. A major element is the admission of 80,000 18-year-olds to the *avanguardista*, the youth component of the party militia.		Mexico arrests two for spreading Communist propaganda. A theater owner is arrested for showing a "red" film and the printer who produced his advertisements is also jailed.	
Mar. 28	Lord Cecil fails to convince other nations to abandon conscription. Holland, Sweden, and Germany support the British position. The other nations like the idea of having millions of trained men in reserve.			Chile explains that its elimination of a state-paid Catholic clergy is not an attack on the church. It is merely ends the transitional time, which allowed payment of teachers and military chaplains, under the 1925 law separating church and state.	Chinese cities are turning red during an anti-Christian wave. Japanese and French concessions in Hangchow are under siege and consuls at Chunking and Changsha close.

A	B	C	D	E
Includes developments that affect more than one world region, international organizations and important meetings of world leaders.	Includes all domestic and regional developments in Europe, including the Soviet Union.	Includes all domestic and regional developments in Africa and the Middle East.	Includes all domestic and regional developments in Latin America, the Caribbean, and Canada.	Includes all domestic and regional developments in Asian and Pacific nations (and colonies).

U.S. Politics & Social Issues	U.S. Foreign Policy & Affairs, Defense	U.S. Economy & Environment	Science, Technology & Nature	Culture, Leisure & Lifestyle	
		Chateau Thierry is racing for San Francisco. Flu has killed five, with 67 down with flu and mumps. The ship carries 900 troops, 13 congressmen, and 125 dependants.		*Little Women* is more influential than the *Bible* with high schoolers according to a *Current Literature* poll. Third is *Pilgrims Progress*, with Helen Keller's life fourth.	Mar. 21
	As a warning to the Plutarco Calles government, the U.S. terminates its anti-smuggling agreement with Mexico. The arms embargo remains in effect so rebels cannot get American arms. But Calvin Coolidge can lift the embargo at any moment.		RCA introduces an alternating current tube that replaces batteries in its radios. This brings a successful end to the search for a means to tap into house current that began in 1920. The 6 million radios in use all require multiple batteries to operate.	Winter residents offer $400,000 to help Palm Beach banks. Florida banks are suffering in the aftermath of the real estate collapse.	Mar. 22
Philadelphia police announce they will use machine guns and armored cars against city bandits. New York already uses comparable forces in its effort to keep pace with gangster firepower....A federal court rules that Chicago clubs cannot allow drinking even for patrons who bring their own liquor. Another judge rules that grape juice turned to wine by nature is still illegal....Courts rule that New Jersey cannot establish a separate black school.	Secretary of State Frank B. Kellogg indicates that he is ready to deal over the issue of concessions in Shanghai. He wants an international settlement, not a bipartite one.	Edward Hatch again urges New York mayor Jimmy Walker to look into the possibility of a deep sea tunnel for disposal of the city's garbage. Hatch notes that the practice is common in Europe and is much better than having the current filthy river....Stocks are down to two-week lows, primarily due to weakness in the automobile industry.	The warden of the New York City's sanitarium lauds Narcosan as treatment for drug addiction. He says it makes the 600 patients in hospital wards calm and is much more humane than the previous practice of weaning addicts without any palliative treatment.		Mar. 23
With his candidacy gaining strength, Governor Al Smith receives request from Charles Marshall to declare his allegiance—to church or to state. Writing in *Atlantic Monthly*, Marshall cites historical papal acts and statements....A Tong war flares up in six cities. It has killed nine to date. Deportation is possible.	Vice President Charles Dawes arrives in Panama on vacation. Welcoming him are an infantry parade, a flight of 25 American planes and assorted American military and civilian officials as well as Panamanian dignitaries.	Minnehaha Falls is laughing again as heavy rainfall in the watershed bring natural water to the gorge. Last year the Mississippi was so low that falls were fed by well water.	German physicians report success with a bromine-based anesthetic. Bromine has potential end reliance on ether and chloroform.	After listeners vote 5–1 in its favor, Chicago broadcasters preserve "silent night." They do not air programs on Monday so that listeners can hear programs from far away.	Mar. 24
Saginaw, MI, becomes a boom town littered with derricks after an oil strike there....Operators in New York and eventually nationwide will end with "thank you." Repeating of the telephone number is deemed too slow....As two more die, Tong leaders deny there is a war. They say the killings are personal.		The National Broadcasting Company announces that it will establish a chain of seven west coast radio stations effective April 5. There is no word whether the west coast network will link with the eastern and midwestern ones....The Seaboard Air Line announces discount round-trip fares to Florida on April 2 and 14, good for 15 days. The fares, one and one-fifth the regular one-way first class fare, is good on all of the railroad's trains, including the Orange Blossom Special.	Psychology students at Western State, Gunnison, CO, report that a kiss shortens one's life by three minutes. The cause is increased heart palpitations.	12,000 Texans watch two Tarahumara Indians from Mexico race 83 miles from Austin to San Antonio in 14 hours, 46 minutes, the last 20 miles in a fog of auto exhaust. A third drops out. Their sisters race 26 miles.	Mar. 25
New York's Bureau of Preventable Diseases reports that the U.S. quarantine is effective in preventing the European flu epidemic from reaching the United States. There is no legal basis for the quarantine. Most cases are in England, France, and Switzerland.	The United States fires on Nanking and the crisis abates but the United States still asks China for details of the death of one American. Meanwhile, American marines are on the battle lines as the fight for Shanghai looms.	In moderate Saturday trading, the stock market ends the week up. Banks and chain stores show the best results.	Two German scientists report that they have produced helium from hydrogen. Never before has anyone produced a heavier atom from a lighter one. The possibilities for airships are significant because helium is not flammable, as hydrogen is.	The world chess tournament officially ends. Jose Capablanca, who wrapped up the title days ago, earns two additional prizes: for best played game and chess strategy.	Mar. 26
The Reed Committee reports that the Ant-Saloon League spent $13 million over the first six years of prohibition....The Welfare Council reports that employer bias hampers hiring of the handicapped. An exception is Henry Ford who has 13,000 handicapped workers.	The United States proves that Mexican documents are forgeries. The documents incite Mexicans to revolution. The United States suspects that they are intended to provoke a Mexican–U.S. war.	Detroit merchants begin a boycott of Ford, who has entered their business and undercut their prices for food, coal, clothing, and other merchandise. Merchants in other cities are considering a comparable boycott. Ford contends he is just countering profiteering.	Auburn, NY, reports no diphtheria deaths in three years. Auburn is a test city for the new Schick vaccine after recording 13 deaths in 13 cases in 1921. Overcoming initial parental objections, Auburn officials inoculated over 6,000 Auburn children from 1922.	Paris fashion as shown at the International Hairdressers Convention dictates that the boyish bob is out. The new look is the longer and more feminine Joan of Arc. Long hair is still unfashionable....Georgetti-Stockholm win the Chicago six-day bicycle race.	Mar. 27
China's consul ends the American Tong war unconditionally. He convinces the Tong leaders that Chinese in America cannot afford a bad image during the Chinese crisis.		A 30-story skyscraper is going up over the Morgan bank building. Morgan leased air space, allowing the 42-story Equitable Trust Building will rise from a truss bridging the Morgan building....The first daily freight flight from Detroit to Buffalo carries Ford parts.		The author and two producers of *Virgin Man* are found guilty. Their sentences are 10 days in jail. Seven cast members are found guilty but set free. Backers of the theater clean up drive claim a perfect score under the 20-year-old law.	Mar. 28

F	G	H	I	J
Includes campaigns, elections, federal-state relations, civil rights and liberties, crime, the judiciary, education, healthcare, poverty, urban affairs, and population.	Includes formation and debate of U.S. foreign and defense policies, veterans affairs, and defense spending. (Relations with specific foreign countries are usually found under the region concerned.)	Includes business, labor, agriculture, taxation, transportation, consumer affairs, monetary and fiscal policy, natural resources, pollution and industrial accidents.	Includes worldwide scientific, medical and technological developments, natural phenomena, U.S. weather and natural disasters.	Includes the arts, religion, scholarship, communications media, sports, entertainment, fashions, fads, and social life.

	World Affairs	Europe	Africa & The Middle East	The Americas	Asia & The Pacific
Mar. 29		France and England establish a board of control to manage Albania until the crisis is resolved. Yugoslavia is expected to make concessions to Italy in return for modification of the Treaty of Tirana. Albania claims that all is calm....Allied military control of Hungary ends.	African diamond fields are plagued with starvation and disease. Food and water are scarce, sanitation is poor, and children are dying of enteric fever. Failed and sick miners are leaving in droves....A report from Tunis indicates that tea has become a narcotic since its introduction during the war. Tunisians spend all their time and money on tea, drinking to the point of intoxication.	Uruguay's consul explains to a touring soccer team that the rules are different in the United States. The first Uruguayan goodwill matches ended with a riot and other disturbances.	A British officer and two others die in Burma in a fight to free slaves. The campaign against slavery, begun last December, has hitherto been peaceful, even when it entered the territory of the head-hunting Nagas, who practice human sacrifice.
Mar. 30			Senator William H. King of Utah tells the Women's Division of the United Palestine Appeal that Palestine can be home to a million Jews. Irrigation and reclamation projects like those in the western United States will be required.		France repels assaults on its Shanghai concession. Refugee Americans are stoned. Western vessels are fired on. A new general strike looms.
Mar. 31	Army limitation agreements come at Geneva. Parties agree to a French formula for restrictions on army size.	Fascist Italy wants a larger population. It regards emigration as evil. Italians abroad will be subject to control by Italian consuls....The Reichstag demands renegotiation of reparations. Deputies of all parties agree that the Dawes level is unworkable.			The prince of Kalat, Baluchistan, emancipates all slaves in his state. Owners receive no compensation as an age-old practice ends.
Apr. 1	At the Preparatory Disarmament Commission, France demands that civil aviation be included in arms limitation talks. The United States and Britain insist that talks address military aviation only....France also indicates that it will not be bound by joint negotiations on China.	British suffragists increase pressure on Parliament in reaction to Tory opposition to giving the franchise to women between 21 and 30. Tories note that women voters would outnumber men.	The African Broadcasting Company begins.		
Apr. 2	The French cabinet yet again is unable to decide whether to send a delegation to Calvin Coolidge's arms talks. One reason is the faltering arms talks currently under way in Geneva.	Acting on guidance from the Pope, the cardinal of Warsaw warns against the heretical and aggressive American YMCA but does not prohibit membership. The orgnaization in Poland is a postwar development. Many prominent Polish political leaders are on its board.		President Plutarco Calles sends the guard to Colima and Jalisco. Presidential guards win after lengthy battles. Calles also orders airplanes to seven states to fight the rebels. Calles also reassures American bondholders that Mexico will not default as rumored.	China and Australia call for a pan-Pacific labor meeting on China. Meanwhile, the nationalists are fighting themselves in Shanghai, and Chiang is vowing to eradicate the reds.
Apr. 3				Chile begins litigation against American bankers for violations in a $60 million loan. The bankers claim to be puzzled....Argentina's ambassador calls for liberalization of trade. He notes that tariffs might provide a short-term advantage but will result in declining trade in the long run.	A Japanese landing party fires on looters in Hangchow. Two are dead.
Apr. 4	Preparatory disarmament talks produce an agreement to treat both military and civil aviation but not to mingle the two. Nations agree tentatively not to create civil craft with easy capability for conversion from civil to military. Other rules draw clear distinctions between civil and military.	France declines its invitation to the Calvin Coolidge naval talks.	The British Colonial Office announces that it will let a concession for extraction of 100,000 tons of potash, bromine, magnesium, and salt from Jordan's Dead Sea. A 40-mile railroad spur will connect the extraction plant to existing railways to the coast.		Americans flee the north. Japanese in Hangchow continue to come under attack.
Apr. 5		Italy and Hungary sign a treaty of friendship. The issue of providing Hungary access to the sea through Fiume is unresolved.	Italy reveals that its forces are again battling Arab rebels in Cyrenaica. It reports a March 27 ambush but declines to give details.		Britain presents Canton with a note blaming the Nationalist government for damages in Nanking. Britain wants reparations. Japan says it will send no troops to China. It will let the situation stabilize itself.

A	B	C	D	E
Includes developments that affect more than one world region, international organizations and important meetings of world leaders.	*Includes all domestic and regional developments in Europe, including the Soviet Union.*	*Includes all domestic and regional developments in Africa and the Middle East.*	*Includes all domestic and regional developments in Latin America, the Caribbean, and Canada.*	*Includes all domestic and regional developments in Asian and Pacific nations (and colonies).*

U.S. Politics & Social Issues	U.S. Foreign Policy & Affairs, Defense	U.S. Economy & Environment	Science, Technology & Nature	Culture, Leisure & Lifestyle	
The United States prepares for at least a partial coal strike as the operators ignore the miners' offer to settle for the current wage structure. The central field is expected to be the site of the walkout.	Senator Edge, back from a junket to Nicaragua, blames U.S. critics of Secretary Frank B. Kellogg for encouraging the liberal resistance there. Edge reports that Nicaragua cannot escape future interventions until it establishes an effective system of elections.	General Electric reports that 1926 is a record year. Records are set in billings, orders, and profits. The company has $50 million in assets, $44 million in 1926 revenue, and a $103 million surplus....Award of the Chicago-New York air mail contract is delayed. One bidder allegedly gave gifts and that pilots promised to buy North American stock if the line got the contract.	A German seaplane sets a record for weighted flight. Carrying 500 kg, it flies 1,702 kilometers in 14 hours, eight minutes, doubling the American records....Cancer researchers in Britain report that a lead-selenium colloid injection holds promise.	Russia's state movie trust invites Charlie Chaplin to escape from "pious hypocrisy" brought on by his marital troubles. The Soviets also criticize the hypocritical moralizing of the women's group that objects to Chaplin's films.	Mar. 29
A survey of Dartmouth students reveals that although most believe in God and regard religion as a good thing to have, most do not believe in a divine or personal Jesus, immortality, or an inspired Bible. ...Henry Ford is injured in a car crash. Another vehicle attacks his in what he regards as an assassination attempt.	The Panama Canal is nearing capacity. During his vacation, Calvin Coolidge will study options including adding a third lock and creating a Nicaraguan canal.		George B. Kistiakowsky of Princeton debunks the claims of two Germans to have produced helium from hydrogen. He attributes the presence of helium to the leakage of air into the test apparatus.	Mrs. Louise Jaffer asks Calvin Coolidge and Congress to lift immigration quotas. She cites a shortage of servants. She particularly desires more white European women.	Mar. 30
Coal strikes begin as 200,000 walk out in the central fields. Major operators work strikebreakers. The United States has 80 million tons of coal in reserve. Calvin Coolidge keeps hands off because advisors say he lacks authority to intervene.		Adair Realty and Trust of Atlanta fails. The $2 million business has heavy losses in Florida real estate.		"Anastasia" is really Francisca Schnzkowski of Borowielasse, Germany. For seven years she claimed to be the youngest daughter of Russia's last czar.	Mar. 31
Henry Ford leaves the hospital in secrecy. He abandons his assassination theory but uses two ambulances, one as a decoy.	The United States is cooperating with other powers in negotiations with China, but Frank B. Kellogg says the United States will not be bound by the results and will do what is necessary to defend its citizens and negotiate claims arising from Nanking.	Standard of California cuts per-barrel price by 50 cents. Overproduction and lower prices for gasoline are causes. California crude prices are now in line with the national average as the oil market remains glutted.	The navy reports that manmade silk is superior to Japanese silk for parachutes. Speed of opening and rate of descent are comparable, and the artificial silk chutes oscillate less.	The world's smallest book, a Rubiyat of 5/16 square inches, sells for $1,050. Created in 1900, it is one of a run of 57.	Apr. 1
Calvin Coolidge officially overturns Warren Harding's leases of military oil reserves to Doheny-Sinclair. Return of Sinclair's Teapot Dome leases awaits the outcome of Sinclair's April 21 trial. Sinclair has another conviction on appeal.	Secretary Frank B. Kellogg announces that meetings are to begin with Canada on construction of a St. Lawrence Seaway. Backers of the project express concerns that it might get sidetracked by a Nicaraguan canal.	Fur dressers and dyers report that they used 37.8 million pelts in 1926, down nearly 2 million from 1925. Mole shows the greatest increase while muskrat and squirrel drop most. Furs gross $13 million a year.		Princeton announces plans to build an "open air" gym. Emphasis is on physical culture and life sports.	Apr. 2
Orthodox Jews announce that they will fight the reform domination of American Judaism. They contend that liberals have influence beyond their numbers.		The government charges 43 oil companies with illegal monopoly in price fixing. Among them are Standard of Indiana and New Jersey and the Texas Company....National Air Transport wins the disputed New York-Chicago airmail contract for $1.26 a pound. National, the winner, earlier protested pilots owning stock in low-bidder, North American. Government pilots are unemployed.	The Army reports success in using a radio dial for signaling planes. The technology is similar to that used in telephones.	Gene Sarazen beats Walter Hagen in match play golf. Sarazen outdrives his rival on 22 of 28 holes, but barely holds off Hagen's rally....10,000 watch the opening day outdoor races at New York's velodrome.	Apr. 3
Former governor Frank Lowden of Illinois agrees to run for the presidency if the people demand it. A committee on his behalf hopes to create a Midwestern boom for the Republican....One fourth of the immigrants over the past eight months settled in New York.	The United States indicates that it is not surprised at France's declining of the invitation to the naval talks. It expects Italy to decline also.	Cotton prices are down, but only slightly, as domestic and European demand decline. The boll weevil report shows the bug restricted to Louisiana....Ford says he will close his stores to the general public. Merchants' protests turn to cheers as Ford's agent announces that store trade will be for Ford employees only.	A German pilot sets a new record for a 1,000-kilogram deadweight load. He flies 2,020 kilometers in 14 hours, 29 minutes, shattering his old record of 1,400 kilometers in 10 hours.		Apr. 4
Massachusetts rejects the appeals of Nicola Sacco and Bartolomeo Vanzetti. Unless the federal courts intervene or the governor grants clemency, they will die....Chicago elects William Thompson mayor. Heavily armed police at the polls and on the streets prevent gangland violence. Thompson has gang ties. Chicago will be an open city.	The U.S. Army in New York state bars a black from a Civilian Military Training camp. Blacks protest. The army says it will build separate camps—in the South—where black youths may train at their own expense.	Six chain stores release quarterly sales figures. Sales continue setting records. F.W. Woolworth announces expansion in England, Germany, and the United States.		Sex goes to the jury, which finds 22 players including actress/author Mae West, guilty. Some see it as a vindication of police enforcement, obviating censorship....Florida sees improvement now that failures have purged banking and "surplus" workers have left due to the economic slowdown. Many cities face tax shortfalls however.	Apr. 5

F	G	H	I	J
Includes campaigns, elections, federal-state relations, civil rights and liberties, crime, the judiciary, education, healthcare, poverty, urban affairs, and population.	*Includes formation and debate of U.S. foreign and defense policies, veterans affairs, and defense spending. (Relations with specific foreign countries are usually found under the region concerned.)*	*Includes business, labor, agriculture, taxation, transportation, consumer affairs, monetary and fiscal policy, natural resources, pollution and industrial accidents.*	*Includes worldwide scientific, medical and technological developments, natural phenomena, U.S. weather and natural disasters.*	*Includes the arts, religion, scholarship, communications media, sports, entertainment, fashions, fads, and social life.*

	World Affairs	Europe	Africa & The Middle East	The Americas	Asia & The Pacific
Apr. 6	Socialist protests erupt throughout the world as Massachusetts prepares to execute Nicola Sacco and Bartolomeo Vanzetti....Aristide Briand suggests that the United States and France should sign a treaty outlawing war between the two. The suggestion receives no attention.			Speaker Rodolphe Lemieux of the House of Commons asks a ban on pornographic American newspapers. He notes that they harm Canadian youth. And even France prohibits them.	The Chinese government tells Chiang Kai-shek to return to the front and stay out of foreign affairs....With liabilities of $250 million, Suzuki & Co suspends business. Suzuki has 60–70 subsidiaries, and its suspension causes the yen to decline and Tokyo to retain its ban on gold exports.
Apr. 7		English suffragists petition Prime Minister Stanley Baldwin. They face Tory opposition.			Chinese police raid Russian offices in Shanghai. Russia protests. This comes on top of Chinese raids on British facilities in Peking. France and Italy also express outrage at Chinese behavior.
Apr. 8	The Preparatory Arms Convention takes up the matter of Germany's armaments. France notes that Versailles calls for reductions, not just limitations.	English M.P.s join the protests of the Sacco-Vanzetti decision....Austria and Czechoslovakia end trade negotiations. A Central European tariff war looms.		Strikers in Buenos Aires bring parts of the city to a halt. They are protesting the Sacco-Vanzetti execution decision.	Chiang Kai-shek blocks a red attempt to take over Shanghai. Then he goes to Nanking and says the Koumintang will announce its policies from there....Five powers prepare identical notes to Hangchow, with copies to Chiang Kai-shek in Nanking. The United States will not share the joint protest.
Apr. 9		All is quiet in Rome as the Sacco-Vanzetti protests fail to gain traction....Tourists from the United States and the United Kingdom return to Paris despite higher prices. Parisians are no longer hostile....Benito Mussolini announces excavations at Herculaneum. Plans include draining Lake Nemi to reveal the 2,000-year-old ships of Tiberius.		Government forces in Nicaragua have rebels pinned in the mountains.	Northerners turn suddenly, retake Yangchow and rout the Communist Pukow-Tientsen army. Refugees on the Yangtse report boatloads of Cantonese casualties.
Apr. 10	The international force in Chinese waters is the largest in Asian history. It includes 172 fighting ships and 30 auxiliaries from eight nations. Britain has the largest contingent, followed by Japan and the United States.	French authorities seize three Frenchmen and two Russians in a plot to sell military secrets. Authorities say the ring also plotted extensive sabotage.		Fascism spreads to the western hemisphere with the assumption of dictatorial powers by General Carlos Ibanez in Chile. Ibanez claims to be averting Communism in a country whose problems include inflation, depression in nitrates, and the still unsettled border dispute with Peru that provoked the Tacna–Arica War.	The five powers present Canton with their joint note on Nanking. The nationalists near a split and the powers may step in. Russia claims that the powers are trying to break Russian ties with China.
Apr. 11		Italy and France agree to share the costs of a tunnel through Mont Blanc.	A report from Palestine says that Arab–Jewish friction is declining; unemployment in Tel Aviv is decreasing. The Holy Land is being rebuilt.		With their forces in flight from the northerners over a wide front, Cantonese ask the powers for an inquiry into their allegations. Russian troops are on the border.
Apr. 12		The British cabinet approves the vote for women at 21. when Parliament passes the bill, Britain gains 5 million new voters....Anti-Soviet forces begin a sabotage campaign in the Ukraine. They blow up and burn factories and plants.		Conservatives rout a liberal army in Nicaragua.	The split between Chiang Kai-shek and the Reds is official as Chiang raids Red offices in four cities and declares martial law. Chiang says the reds caused nationalist outrages at Nanking to discredit him. The split is irreversible.
Apr. 13	The United States rejects any League control of its armaments, implying that there is no need. Italy rejects control also. Balkan nations fear the U.S. precedent might lead Russia to do the same.			Penn-Mex announces it will appeal a ruling that it must return lease land and compensate the owners for the oil it has extracted since 1924.	Japan denies it is reinforcing its troops in China. It is sending only replacements.

A	**B**	**C**	**D**	**E**
Includes developments that affect more than one world region, international organizations and important meetings of world leaders.	Includes all domestic and regional developments in Europe, including the Soviet Union.	Includes all domestic and regional developments in Africa and the Middle East.	Includes all domestic and regional developments in Latin America, the Caribbean, and Canada.	Includes all domestic and regional developments in Asian and Pacific nations (and colonies).

U.S. Politics & Social Issues	U.S. Foreign Policy & Affairs, Defense	U.S. Economy & Environment	Science, Technology & Nature	Culture, Leisure & Lifestyle	
	Calvin Coolidge vetoes the Filipino request for an independence plebiscite. He says disgruntled elements are slowing Filipino progress toward self rule.	William C. Durant of Durant Motors forms Consolidated Motors. THe Centerpiece of the possible rival to General Motors is the Durant Star Six. Durant recalls that GM used Buick as its core automobile in 1906....Ford earned $90 million in 1926. GM earns $50 million a quarter.			Apr. 6
		Despite four price cuts in six weeks, the oil market remains glutted. Seminole oil is half its price of November.	In a test, a picture of Herbert Hoover is transmitted from Washington to New York. Picture and sound are synchronized. The AT&T head sees it as a research triumph but commercial applications are doubtful.	U.S. yachts take the Bermuda series, 75½ to 67½. They pull out the victory over the Royal Bermuda Yacht Club with major wins on the final day after trailing earlier.	Apr. 7
Republicans debate prohibition. Butler wants it taken out of the Constitution; William Borah wants a 25-year test. Democrats worry that Calvin Coolidge-led Republicans will label Al Smith a big spender. Smith runs big-spending, big-sized New York.	The U.S. embassy presents Mexico with a note demanding punishment of the murderers of an American. This is the third victim in a month.	Canada protects its airwaves from piracy by putting violators of its six bands into a low frequency. Canada has the six bands due to a gentlemen's agreement with the United States as governments seek to unclutter previously unregulated broadcasting.	Floods in Kansas and Oklahoma kill 11, derail trains, and injure many. The Mississippi dikes are expected to be strong enough to hold when the floodwaters from tributaries arrive....J.L. Baird, British inventor of television, says he has already broadcast over the ocean.	Baseball bars Rogers Hornsby from playing for the Giants. Hornsby was traded to the Giants over the winter and refuses to divest himself of his 1,167 shares of the St Louis Cardinals for less than $105 a share. He may seek an injunction.	Apr. 8
James Joy Jeffries, the Railroad Evangelist, dies in Chicago. For five years he lived on $2.61 a week. He took no collections. His weight is 105 pounds and his estate is 75 cents and a Bible.		42 U.S. stations transmit over Canadian bandwidth. Only one indicates intention to appeal the requirement that they find new bandwidth immediately.	Experiments with lignite indicate that it has promise as fuel if carbonized. Lignite is partially developed coal; it makes up 1/3 of America's hard fuel.	Baseball writers pick Connie Mack's Athletics to take the AL. The Athletics get 29 of 43 votes. The Yankees get nine....Hornsby accepts $100,000 for his stock and is cleared to play.	Apr. 9
	A report for the Foreign Policy Association attacks American debt policy as harmful to the United States. It will lead to an unfavorable balance of trade and force governments to borrow, thereby moving debt from public to private control.	The radio board assigns the first 26 frequencies. It rejects split frequencies, a request for a waiver of the Canadian restriction and four others outside the authorized zone.	Commander Noel Davis, USN, is the frontrunner in the New York-Paris lineup. Davis has tested his biplane, "American Legion," and declares it ready to go. Dark horses are Bertrand Acosta and Charles Lindbergh.	The first American performance of George Antheil's *Ballet Mecanique* draws mixed reactions at Carnegie Hall. Audience reaction to Antheil's bells, car horns, propellers, whistles, anvils and such was a vocal mix of boos, catcalls, and applause. Antheil also premiers a black jazz symphony commissioned by Paul Whiteman.	Apr. 10
The Supreme Court rules that the United States can try British rum-runners. Britain has a treaty obligation to discourage violations of U.S. law.	The United States joins the powers in blaming the nationalist Chinese for the damage in Nanking. The U.S. document alludes to Soviet involvement.				Apr. 11
	William Thompson is sworn in as Chicago mayor. He takes in a ball game.	Cotton prices are up eight to 10 cents. British foreign trade news is one reason. The rising Mississippi is another....A mile-wide F5 tornado in Rock Springs, TX, kills 74. Hundreds are injured and 235 of 247 buildings are destroyed in the town of 800. Killer tornadoes strike in Oklahoma and Arkansas.	Admiral Richard Byrd's men arrange for his arrival in Paris. The French promise a huge welcome but still hope a French flyer will be the first to make the cross-Atlantic flight.... Europeans seek a solution to their radio problems. As does the United States, they have problems with interference due to sharing of frequencies.	Zeppo Marx marries. He is the youngest of the Marx Brothers.	Apr. 12
In Philadelphia, a running gun battle from speeding cars kills two gangsters. Police wound a moll holed up with another gangster. ...The Barnes Foundation of Merion, PA, announces that it will transfer its vast art collections to New York's Metropolitan Museum. It will convert to a national center for the advancement of African American art and intellect. Merion residents are almost unanimously outraged.	The United States holds half the world's gold. America's $4.6 billion far exceeds France's second-place $1 billion, and Britain's $712 million. The U.S. hoard is the largest in world history.	Oil production is down in the United States, particularly in Texas, and in Venezuela. Pennsylvania crude drops 25 cents, but the price adjustment is local only. 15 western independents are in the process of merging.	Bertrand Acosta and Clarence Chamberlin are aloft 38 hours. Having broken the American endurance record, they near that of the French....The United States has a third of the world's telegraph wires. Americans wired 200 million messages in 1926.	The Canandiagua Choral Society cancels its festival. Women skip rehearsals and go motoring....The Ottawa Senators beat the Boston Bruins to win their ninth Stanley Cup. The Senators win two games and tie two, making the final points 6–2 in their favor.	Apr. 13

	World Affairs	Europe	Africa & The Middle East	The Americas	Asia & The Pacific
Apr. 14		Italy charges that Yugoslavia is preparing to invade Albania. Italy says France is selling arms and supplies and Yugoslavia has $14 million set aside for the war.	A hurricane lashes Morocco, killing 20 sailors and causing $10 million in damage. the storm also hits Gibraltar and Spain....The heir to Ethiopia's throne sends a large consignment of animals to the Berlin Zoo and gives two zebras to Paul von Hindenberg.		The war halts as Southern chiefs meet at Nanking. Rumor is that Chiang made a deal with the northerners after destroying the Communists.
Apr. 15			Egyptian cotton is suffering because of depressed prices caused by the U.S. surplus and lowered worldwide demand. The government is paying small growers and holding their crops off the market.	Chihuahua's governor and Chihuahua City's mayor rebel against the Plutarco Calles government. Elsewhere, federals execute four rebels and kill another while restraining the mayor of Juarez.	An American destroyer fires on northern soldiers at Puchow. The nationalists begin uniting behind Chiang Kai-shek. The Chinese seem to be seeking to break the powers' unity rather than negotiating claims honestly.
Apr. 16		*Syndical Battles*, anti-fascist labor newspaper, resumes publishing in Belgium. The paper is the first to defy the November 1926 Fascist ban on opposition press....Germany tries to limit *wandervoegel*, weekend youth campers. The *wandervoegel's* exercise and health emphases make it susceptible to rightwing militarism.		Because of U.S. immigration restrictions, the Hebrew Sheltering and Immigrant Aid Society is redirecting Jewish migrants south. Latin American countries—particularly Mexico, Brazil, Uruguay, and Chile—welcome the new workers. HIAS assists with language training and job placement.	The Culion leper colony in the Philippines, begun in 1901 by a Catholic priest and several nuns, seeks $2 million in financial aid. The island colony has cured 1,000 lepers. It takes a third of the Philippines' public health budget and needs money to help its remaining 6,000 lepers.
Apr. 17	The League sees prospects for reopening of disarmament talks if Russia participates. Expectation is that Russia will choose regional arms agreements instead.	Fights break out between German and French rugby fans during the first match between the two nations since the war. After police restore order, France wins 30–5....Britain's Independent Labor Party votes not to send Ramsay MacDonald to the Labor Party convention. McDonald says the Socialists are only a small element of his party.	South African shipments of large amounts of gold to London create a large surplus at the Bank of England. Contributing factors to the surplus are lowered re-export demand and suspension of the requisition for India's switch to the gold standard.		The Bank of Formosa suspends operations for three weeks after the Japanese Privy Council refuses to extend $97 million in credit. The Japanese cabinet steps down over the financial crisis.
Apr. 18				A small contingent of 325 American Marines guard the safe zone city of Matagalpa as the rebels and government forces begin battling for it.	Chiang sets up his government in Nanking, but the nationalists fracture. Reportedly, every city has its warlord. The fighting continues.
Apr. 19	In preparation for a May 4 conference, the League issues a report on world population. It predicts 90 million U.S. workers in 1941. It also notes the need for markets for workers' output; lack of markets will threaten world peace.	Britain reports it will send a delegation to Europe to examine the steel cartel. Britain may join.	A. J. Klein, South African big game hunter, gets a license to wed in New York. He guides safaris and collects specimens for museums. ...Having driven him to resign by criticizing every niggling point of his administration, the Egyptian parliament wants Adly Pasha to rescind his resignation as prime minister. A cabinet crisis is likely otherwise.	Costa Rica asks Mexico to protest continuing the presence of U.S. Marines in Nicaragua. Costa Rica has sent comparable requests to other Latin American nations. "Bush Negroes" in Dutch Guinea learn of World War I. League officials tell them of work for peace.	Chinese reds declare war on Chiang. Rumors persist that he has joined forces with the northerners.
Apr. 20		Russia arrests anti-government plotters, allegedly followers of Count Nicholas. Russia blames foreign instigation and financing.		At Posoltega, Nicaragua, U.S. marines repel rebels with no casualties. They kill three.	The general strike ends, but Hankow has 200,000 unemployed and starving. Chiang executes 100, including the head of the Seamen's Union and detains 400 more. The party reaffirms ties to the Soviet Union.

A	B	C	D	E
Includes developments that affect more than one world region, international organizations and important meetings of world leaders.	Includes all domestic and regional developments in Europe, including the Soviet Union.	Includes all domestic and regional developments in Africa and the Middle East.	Includes all domestic and regional developments in Latin America, the Caribbean, and Canada.	Includes all domestic and regional developments in Asian and Pacific nations (and colonies).

U.S. Politics & Social Issues	U.S. Foreign Policy & Affairs, Defense	U.S. Economy & Environment	Science, Technology & Nature	Culture, Leisure & Lifestyle	
The *Christian Herald* reports that church membership rose half a million in 1926, half as much as in 1925. Catholics, totaling 16 million of the 47.5 million U.S. church members, had the largest increase. Evangelicals lost members.			New Orleans records 14.01 inches of rain in 24 hours, a record. The levees hold in New Orleans and Memphis, but the surge of flood water is still to the north....Bertrand Acosta and Clarence Chamberlin land after 51 hours, a new record. A French team announces plans to regain the record.		Apr. 14
Imperial Wizard Hiram Evans attacks the Catholic position that children of mixed marriages must be reared Catholic and the practice of annulling Protestant marriages. Evans says the Klan will get state laws barring the stipulations.			C.E. Levine, backer of the Bellanca plane that set the endurance record, says that his plane will race any other that attempts the New York-Paris fight. Either Bertrand Acosta or Clarence Chamberlin will pilot the Bellanca....The Mississippi inundates large sections of Arkansas. Kentucky is at risk....GE reports that shortwave radio is useful in rebroadcasting European programs.	Mary Pickford, Douglas Fairbanks, and Norma and Constance Talmadge leave their footprints and signatures in wet concrete. The footprints and those of other stars will provide an attraction for Sid Grauman's movie theater when it opens in May....The Miami Beach police chief closes 25 saloons. The city now recognizes prohibition.... Babe Ruth hits his first homer of the season.	Apr. 15
10,000 demonstrators gather at Union Square to protest the scheduled executions of Nicola Sacco and Bartolomeo Vanzetti. They hear speeches in four languages and a call for a general strike on execution day, June 15.		William Cramp and Sons' shipyard in Philadelphia closes after nearly a century of building naval and merchant vessels. Cramp has a single government and two private contracts and 2,000 laid off workers. The industry is able to absorb the 2,000 plus Cramp's 3,000 current workers.	Richard Byrd's plane crashes in test flights. Byrd has a broken wrist, and two others are injured. The pilot is unharmed and the plane is reparable, but the accident and injuries delay Byrd's flight....The great Mississippi flood begins—African Americans left behind as levees break on tributaries and heavy rains fall at New Orleans.	In major news for the entertainment business, Pathe and Cecil B. DeMille's Producers Distributing merge. The major player is the Keith-Albee-Orpheum, which owns half of Producer's Distributing.	Apr. 16
In the libel suit of the Alabama Grand Dragon against a Birmingham newspaper, an Alabama judge rules that the defense may call all members of the Robert E. Lee Klan who heard the Grand Dragon's speech. The Lee Klan includes most of Birmingham's money and political elite....Al Smith issues a statement that the nation comes before religion. He seeks to defuse the Catholic issue.		The two railroad presidents give stockholders additional time to deposit their stock. Once stock is deposited, they can ask the ICC to allow the merger of the Great Northern and Northern Pacific. They cite a $10 million savings from the proposed merger.			Apr. 17
The reaction to Al Smith's statement is almost universally favorable....10 of 11 surviving Sacco jurors say that they are still convinced the verdict was correct.		U.S. Steel passes $1 billion in capital. It is the largest corporation in the world.	The floods spread through the Mississippi and its tributaries as levees break, thousands work to shore up the system, tens of thousands are homeless, and people begin to die.	A federal court injunction halts the Jack Sharkey-Jim Maloney fight set for May 19. A rival promoter says he has Maloney's services for a Cleveland fight and Tex Rickard cannot have the boxer for a heavyweight elimination bout....Clyde Burrows sings in Esperanto. The new language is supposed to be the world's neutral universal tongue.	Apr. 18
Jesse Jones, Houston publisher and Democratic finance chair, reports that the South remains cool to Al Smith. The problem is not so much Smith's Catholicism as his wetness.	The governor of Chihuahua and mayor of Juarez are in Texas. El Paso immigration officials arrest then release them.	The radio board mandates separation of at least 50 kilocycles between stations to cut overcrowded bandwidth in major markets. New York and Chicago stations are affected....The cotton market fails to rise despite the flood news. Lancashire mills are closing and foreign demand is down generally.		Clarence De Mar, 38, wins his fifth Boston A.A. Marathon and his fifth straight marathon....Chaplin agrees to pay $1 million in taxes. The check for five years' arrears is in the mail, and Chaplin will be free of government liens. Now about that divorce proceeding....New York's boxing commission bans Delaney from Tex Rickard's elimination bouts. Delaney is a light heavyweight and cannot box out of class.	Apr. 19
The Red Cross and Army prepare to feed 50,000 of the 100,000 uprooted by the floods. Measles, mumps, and whooping cough affect 500 in refugee camps. Authorities rescue 600 flood-stranded Arkansans. Meanwhile, in Hot Springs, AR, society matrons hold a charity golf tournament....Republican national committee members from 23 states back a third term for Calvin Coolidge.		Cotton reacts as the flood spreads. Prices rise to record territory.... Magnolia Oil lowers prices for the sixth time since November. Rivals do not follow since prices are already below costs.	American Telephone and Telegraph reports it has successfully transmitted colored pictures from coast to coast. Eight cities have the capability to send three colors one at a time. Ghosts are now a problem.	*Goat Alley* opens to negative reviews. The play debuted in 1921 but its portrayals of life in black slums made more of a sociological than an artistic statement. This year's version lacks quality actors.... Mae West complains that prison wear is uncomfortable. She begins her 10-day sentence for *Sex*.	Apr. 20

F	G	H	I	J
Includes campaigns, elections, federal-state relations, civil rights and liberties, crime, the judiciary, education, healthcare, poverty, urban affairs, and population.	*Includes formation and debate of U.S. foreign and defense policies, veterans affairs, and defense spending. (Relations with specific foreign countries are usually found under the region concerned.)*	*Includes business, labor, agriculture, taxation, transportation, consumer affairs, monetary and fiscal policy, natural resources, pollution and industrial accidents.*	*Includes worldwide scientific, medical and technological developments, natural phenomena, U.S. weather and natural disasters.*	*Includes the arts, religion, scholarship, communications media, sports, entertainment, fashions, fads, and social life.*

	World Affairs	Europe	Africa & The Middle East	The Americas	Asia & The Pacific
Apr. 21	An otherwise dull arms meeting at Geneva passes the requirement to disclose the types and numbers of arms each nation possesses. Japan goes along reluctantly after getting assurance from France that disclosure will not imperil security.	To celebrate Rome's 2681st birthday, the Fascists issue their charter of labor. The document spells out rights and responsibilities of capital and labor under the state. Fascism means industrial peace....Russia provides a meeting place in Constantinople for Balkan Communists to consider a campaign in the Balkans.	The 1095 mile Paris–Oran flight takes nine hours and 25 minutes. This is the first nonstop flight between the two cities, another first for French aviation.		Chiang Kai-shek resumes his drive north to ease pressure on Nanking. In Hankow rioting and looting continue. The American contingent there is 85 people.
Apr. 22	The European powers ask Benito Mussolini not to invoke the Treaty of Tirana, which makes Albania a virtual Italian protectorate. The powers promise that if Italy enters Albania they will release Yugoslavia to take the issue to the League.		The Palestine Free Loan Society increases its funding from $100,000 to $250,000. The funds come from New York merchant Samuel Lamport.	Mexico deports Msgr. Mora y del Rio, head of the Mexican church, and five bishops to Texas for fomenting revolution, including a bloody rebel attack on a train. The clerics deny involvement in the episode, which killed hundreds. ...President Gerardo Machado of Cuba calls on Calvin Coolidge to invite the president and secretary of state to the Pan American Conference. He asks for revision of the Platt Amendment and greater autonomy for Cuba.	Japan is calm after announcement of temporary bank closings followed by a three-week moratorium. Several banks have failed and the yen has reached a record low for the year, but the government guarantees the Bank of Japan.
Apr. 23		Berlin's Communists call for violence against the Steel Helmet League, which will parade on May 8. France is looking for descendants of the Normans. England reports it can find none among its nobility.	South African Prime Minister J.B.M. Hertzog proposes four white bills. Collectively the four will segregate, establish economic ceilings, and remove civil rights for South Africa's 5.5 million blacks, after 25 years of incorporating blacks into white society and 50 years of a black franchise....The Egyptian parliamentary crisis nears an end as Sarwat Pasha agrees to form a government.	The first consignment of Ford parts arrive in Colon, Panama. Ford is testing the workability of assembling trucks and tractors for the central and northern south American market. Reports are that GM is also looking into setting up an assembly plant in Latin America.	Chiang Kai-shek says he will meet the powers' demands. Meanwhile, two red armies are marching against him and the Communists reveal papers that purport to show that Chiang received millions in Russian financing and Russian direction of his war against the north.
Apr. 24		France's deflation crisis is ended. Italy continues to deflate the lira.		Two more bishops and the monsignor arrive in Laredo as Mexico executes a rebel priest. Preparations are under way to bomb Jalisco from the air as infantry lays waste to the countryside.	
Apr. 25	U.S. Congressmen applaud Aristide Briand's proposal for a treaty outlawing war between France and the United States, the administration says it has no reaction because the idea is unofficial.		A.W. Pond says the 60,000 year old child's bones he found in Algeria support the theory that humankind began in Africa. Other theorists claim the Gobi Desert and other parts of the world.		
Apr. 26	After a month's effort to resolve issues such as the sizes of armies, disclosure of budgets, and such, the preliminary disarmament commission fails to reach agreement on any aspect, much less an overall disarmament plan. It does schedule another round of talks for November.	The European reaction to Calvin Coolidge's speech affirming the special role of the United States in Central America is negative. In Paris it still seems to be imperialism....Italy stands ready to discuss Albania. It will not abandon the Treaty of Tirana however.		Passengers on the Juarez-Mexico City train avoid the massacre suffered last week by passengers on a Guadalajara train. When rebels attack this time, federal troops on board are able to defend the train.	Americans fire on Chinese on the Yangtze River. Diplomatically, the Europeans are confused about what to do next while the Americans express no opinion.
Apr. 27	The League reaffirms that its invitation of Russia to the economic summit remains open. Russia wants a new invitation to the May 4 affair, claiming that the previous invitation is invalid because the Swiss had earlier blocked Soviet participation. The Americans will attend too, but Russia's participation is desirable.	Two Albanian deputies escape their guards and flee Italy. After motor boating across the Adriatic, they meet with other Albanian émigrés....The Polish government says it will back the Y.M.C.A. despite attacks on the organization by Catholics.		A woman arrested in Mexico for kissing her husband says that kissing should be banned on stage if it is immoral on the streets. She also objects to the 10 p.m. curfew for unescorted women and, in general, the outdated use of police as enforcers of morality.	Japan warns Russia to back away from its China policy. Continued interference imperils world peace, says Premier Giichi Tanaka....In China, fighting continues as the Peking government prepares to abrogate the treaty with Russia and take over the Chinese-Eastern Railway.
Apr. 28	Britain opposes Aristide Briand's proposal. It forms closer ties between France and Germany, and Britain wants tighter links to France herself.	Yugoslavia offers to negotiate with Italy over Albania. Yugoslavia is expected to seek treaties with Russia and Germany for protection against Italy.		The United States is pleased that Plutarco Calles seems unwilling to seize oil lands. With half his country in revolt, he really cannot anyway.	

A	B	C	D	E
Includes developments that affect more than one world region, international organizations and important meetings of world leaders.	Includes all domestic and regional developments in Europe, including the Soviet Union.	Includes all domestic and regional developments in Africa and the Middle East.	Includes all domestic and regional developments in Latin America, the Caribbean, and Canada.	Includes all domestic and regional developments in Asian and Pacific nations (and colonies).

U.S. Politics & Social Issues	U.S. Foreign Policy & Affairs, Defense	U.S. Economy & Environment	Science, Technology & Nature	Culture, Leisure & Lifestyle	
Aaron Sapiro's $1 million libel suit against Henry Ford collapses as the judge declares a mistrial. A Detroit paper's interview with a juror is his justification. One juror claims that all agreed Ford's defense was weak.		Cotton prices drop sharply. The rains are ending and forecasts are for fair and warmer weather. Also, profit taking occurs after earlier significant rises due to the floods.	The Mississippi floods have inundated 7500 square miles. Levees continue giving way as the surge nears New Orleans.		Apr. 21
William Green of the American Federation of Labor calls Benito Mussolini's labor charter autocracy gone mad. He equates Fascism with Communism, both being anti labor....A New York publisher is fined $100 for publishing Theodore Dreiser's *An American Tragedy*. Although on Boston's banned book list, the work is required reading at Harvard.	The new immigration policy requires that workers entering from Cuba, Canada, and Mexico have papers to work in the United States. They must pay an $8.00 head tax and have a visa from their home country. Those who have entered frequently since before 1924 will be grandfathered.		Thirty-two tent cities house flood refugees in four of the eight states hit by the flood. Calvin Coolidge names Herbert Hoover to head a joint government-Red Cross disaster relief committee. Also on the committee are the secretaries of war, navy, and treasury. The Red Cross is calling for contributions of $5 million.	Jack Dempsey begins working out as his comeback effort begins. He plans to face Gene Tunney for the heavyweight crown in the summer.	Apr. 22
31 New York cities begin daylight savings time. The experiment is in effect in 200 cities in Connecticut, Michigan, Massachusetts, Rhode Island, New Jersey, and Wisconsin.		Railroad stocks are on average lower than those of 1906. That was the year of the Harriman boom. The best stocks of 1906 are less attractive now, but there are more good railroad stocks than in 1906.	Airplanes fly low over the flood-ravaged areas of Arkansas. They spot the stranded and drop supplies. Rescue comes from boats however. Unofficial martial law is in effect, with seven government agencies involved. Relief workers need 40,000 vehicles.	Just released—*The Rise of American Civilization* by Charles and Mary Beard. Price is $12.50 for 1,624 pages.	Apr. 23
20,000 spectators watch as agents run a rumrunner to ground on Long Beach, NY. The cutter then captures another smuggler. Two other smugglers are in jail in Boston as their boat breaks up off Gayhead.	2,000 anti-fascist Italian Americans ask a change in U.S. policy toward Italy. They note that the fascist regime is repressive and that the Italian envoy is aiding U.S. fascists.	Soft coal output is down to 8 million tons in a week. This is off 200,000 tons....The Mississippi floods are affecting not only cotton prices but also wheat prices and Midwestern manufactures.	A breathalyzer involves mixing breath with sulphuric acid and potassium dichromate in a tube. A drinker's breath turns the chemicals green, with darker green meaning more alcohol....France tests a charcoal/coal auto fuel and claims it is more economical than gasoline.		Apr. 24
	Calvin Coolidge declares the United States has a special interest in Central America within the special interest in Latin America. The speech is hailed as a new corollary to the Monroe Doctrine.	On volume of 2.5 million shares, the market records its biggest drop since October. Causes include the floods, the Japanese economic situation, disappointing profits for Marland Oil, and China.	The flood crest passes Memphis. Displaced persons total 200,000. Relief donations total $1.2 million. Cities are under water and 13 million acres are in the flood's path.		Apr. 25
An open letter to Calvin Coolidge asks his intentions regarding a third term. *The Forum* says the other potential candidates need to know.			In its last test flight before the trans-Atlantic effort, the *American Legion* of Noel Davis and Stanton Wooster crashes in the Virginia marshes 15 minutes from Langley Field. At 17,000 pounds, the plane is overloaded. The two men die, but other contenders vow to press on.	Professor Blair Bell of Liverpool warns that pipes and cigarette holders are dangerous and may cause cancer of the mouth.	Apr. 26
The White House position is that Calvin Coolidge will not answer *The Forum's* call for him to state his presidential intentions for 1928.... Postmaster General New announces that a ban on firearms in the mails will go into effect May 10. Punishment may be up to $1,000 and two years in jail.	France is willing to consider an arbitration treaty, a mutual agreement, or an Atlantic accord. It wants the United States to take the first step in establishing the document that outlaws war.	West Coast Theaters takes over two other theater companies. The merger brings 300 theaters into one company valued at $270 million.	After touring the flood ravaged areas, Herbert Hoover says that proper engineering would have been less costly. The numbers of refugees and the costs of damages continue to rise as the flood crest moves south. Louisianans crowd the roads to New Orleans, trying to get there before the Poydras levee is cut to save the city.	Promoter Tex Rickard reveals Jack Dempsey's comeback schedule. First he fights Paulino. If he wins, he will take on the winner of the Sharkey-Maloney fight....Mae West finishes her 10-day sentence for *Sex*. After endowing the jail library, she heads for Chicago, talking of presenting *Sex* there.	Apr. 27
The Anti-Saloon League begins a national campaign against wet candidates. Among those opposed by the league are Governor Albert Ritchie of Maryland, Senator James Reed of Missouri, and Governor Al Smith of New York, all Democrats.			42,000 nurses are available to combat disease brought on by the spreading floods....Herbert Hoover says that $5 million will be inadequate. The Red Cross has raised $3.24 million.	Rene Acosta gives up his opportunity to fly the Bellanca to Paris. He agrees to assist with preparations. Clarence Chamberlin has the honors for the flight, due to occur the first week in May.	Apr. 28

F	G	H	I	J
Includes campaigns, elections, federal-state relations, civil rights and liberties, crime, the judiciary, education, healthcare, poverty, urban affairs, and population.	Includes formation and debate of U.S. foreign and defense policies, veterans affairs, and defense spending. (Relations with specific foreign countries are usually found under the region concerned.)	Includes business, labor, agriculture, taxation, transportation, consumer affairs, monetary and fiscal policy, natural resources, pollution and industrial accidents.	Includes worldwide scientific, medical and technological developments, natural phenomena, U.S. weather and natural disasters.	Includes the arts, religion, scholarship, communications media, sports, entertainment, fashions, fads, and social life.

	World Affairs	Europe	Africa & The Middle East	The Americas	Asia & The Pacific
Apr. 29	Russia announces that it will send a full delegation to the economic meeting. The United States will also have a large contingent but it has no economic policy to offer.	Evacuation of French troops from the Saar begins. The withdrawal will take three months, after which Germany will have control.	Excavations reveal the wall of Mizpah, 7 miles from Jerusalem and greater in size than the walls of Megiddo or Jerusalem. The wall dates to 1800 B.C.E. The city itself dates to 3000 B.C.E., before the Israelites.	The United States asks Panama to remove a rum smuggler from its registry. Panama declines, as it has in an earlier case, arguing that the ships' owners have rights to due process.	The civil war resumes in force as Chiang Kai-shek declares war on the red Hankow regime. He sends an army against Hankow but captures Chen Chien, perpetrator of the Nanking outrages, himself.
Apr. 30		French police discover a band of 1500 anarchists. The anarchists have a cache of bombs and arms and finance themselves through bank robbery. Most are Spanish or Italian….In Vienna a crisis is brewing over marriage. Socialists want state and city ceremonies, with no role for the church.	Archaeologists unveil the earth-works and massive stone monuments of the newly discovered city of the Olmeca, the "rubber people." Near Vera Cruz, the city dates to the 13th century. The Olmec used rubber in ceremony and for everyday uses.	Exiled churchmen in San Antonio denounce Plutarco Calles. They accuse him of torture, murder, and religious persecution. They deny that they fled to avoid prosecution.	
May 1					
May 2		Benito Mussolini enters his own wheat in a Ministry of National Economy contest for most improvement in a year. Reportedly, he plowed the land, sowed the seed, and then left the details to his peasants. Customarily, Benito Mussolini awards the prizes….Norway resumes liquor sales; prohibition began in 1914, as did smuggling and bootlegging.	The director of Chicago's Field Museum reports that the joint Field-Oxford excavation of a major temple to the earth goddess is finished. The Sumerian temple dates to around 3000 B.C.E. The Babylonian Nabodinus (father of Belshazzar, (noted in the Biblical book of Daniel) restored it 2,500 years later….The American Museum of Natural Science accepts the invitation of Belgium to study wildlife in the Congo. King Albert sets aside a large wildlife preserve.	Nicaraguans are unable to agree on whether Adolfo Diaz should retain the presidency until 1928. Liberals indicate to Calvin Coolidge's personal representative, Henry Stimson, that the conservative Diaz was instrumental in the 1927 coup that began the current war; consequently, he is unacceptable to them.	
May 3		A League of Nations report states that Europe's trade is still below 1913 levels. The war made former trading partners more independent of European manufactures		Former president Alvaro Obregon leads Coahiluan troops against General Valdes Caraveo, virtual dictator of Chihuahua. Caraveo and the Yaquis have risen against President Plutarco Calles. Fighting has already occurred near Sonora….A two day truce begins in Nicaragua. The truce is to allow Stimson and the liberals to meet safely.	Wealthy Chinese flee Nationalist extortion as Communists propagandize American sailors. Fighting remains intense.
May 4	The League's Economic Congress opens at Geneva with 1,000 delegates. France is prepared to submit a proposal for a United States of Europe. The United States is ready to defend itself if the issue of debt is not tabled.	European anti-prohibitionists organize the International League of Adversaries of Prohibition in Rome. The league calls for sensible use of alcohol. Italy's Minister of National Economy cites thousands of years of wine consumption without debilitation of the Latin "races."		President Emiliano Figueroa of Chile resigns in a dispute with Premier Carlos Ibanez. Figueroa, chief executive, and Ibanez, head of the government have been quarreling for a month since Ibanez demanded that Figueroa's brother resign from the Chilean supreme court. Figueroa cites ill health.	The British and Foreign Bible Society reports that 1926 sales in China were down over 100,000 from the 1925 record of nearly 4.3 million. Chinese unrest made travel difficult for the society's colporteurs, several of whom died in the violence.

A	B	C	D	E
Includes developments that affect more than one world region, international organizations and important meetings of world leaders.	*Includes all domestic and regional developments in Europe, including the Soviet Union.*	*Includes all domestic and regional developments in Africa and the Middle East.*	*Includes all domestic and regional developments in Latin America, the Caribbean, and Canada.*	*Includes all domestic and regional developments in Asian and Pacific nations (and colonies).*

U.S. Politics & Social Issues	U.S. Foreign Policy & Affairs, Defense	U.S. Economy & Environment	Science, Technology & Nature	Culture, Leisure & Lifestyle	
The government reports that farmers had 1.26 million radios in 1926....Indian guru Krishnamurti ends his American tour. He says that the pursuit of gold keeps Americans from finding religion. Americans are superficial, too.	The largest U.S. air force ever is assembling at San Antonio for maneuvers against the infantry. The combat force will total 100 planes. International observers will be on hand for the exercises, expected to demonstrate improvements in planes since the war and to alter American defense strategy.	Theater's Shuberts sue to overthrow the Dramatists Guild of the Artists League of America. Shuberts contend the guild is an illegal monopoly while the guild says it is a legal labor union entitled to bargain collectively.	Another Arkansas levee gives way. The Red Cross has 200,000 refugees on its hands. The Poydras levee is dynamited, taking six blasts, as thousands look on. Acknowledging that flood relief will top $15 million, Calvin Coolidge declines to call a special session of Congress. The people can donate the money.	With the Bellanca ready to take off in six days, the competitors are getting ready. France's Charles Nungesser says he will take off as soon as Clarence Chamberlin does. Charles Lindbergh, after barely averting a crash, is moving east....The court grants Mrs. Chaplin $1500 a month plus $4,000 in legal fees. It questions $8,600 in clothing bills.	Apr. 29
	The dreadnaught *Colorado* runs aground off the Brooklyn Naval Yard. A blast occurred on the *Langley* just days earlier.	April's money markets are stable, with trading over a narrow range. Contributors are the positive gold flow, a strong stock market, and government financing.	As houses and trees sweep through the widening Poydras breach, Herbert Hoover and Al Jolson broadcast over radio in an effort to raise funds for flood relief. Hoover says New Orleans is safe but the disaster is not yet done. Jolson asks for dimes.	Vernon Parrington's *Main Currents in American Thought* is published. Each of its two volumes costs $4.00. Total pages exceed 900....A coming sport for the college set is lacrosse. It strengthens footballers, and some predict that it will one day surpass baseball as the spring sport.	Apr. 30
Ella Boole, President of the Women's Christian Temperance Union, says the WCTU will oppose wet Catholic Democrat Al Smith. She reminds WCTU state presidents that the WCTU stopped Smith's presidential effort in 1924 and will not be fooled by his posturing as "damp" in 1928....Uldine Utley, 15-year-old evangelist, begins her summer revival in Carnegie Hall. 2,000 attend; 30 convert.	A high tide and 18 vessels are necessary to float the beached dreadnaught *Colorado*. After unloading fuel and ammunition to lighten the battleship, a 35-hour effort succeeds. Now the ship can enter drydock.		As flooding continues to spread, Commerce secretary Herbert Hoover and General Edgar Jadwin of the Corps of Engineers issue a joint statement that reservoirs at the headwaters and reforestation cannot prevent floods in the Mississippi Valley. The government must spend millions to6 raise the $100 million levee system to protect the farmlands reclaimed from swamplands.		May 1
In Little Rock, Arkansas, police hide 16-year-old Lonnie Dixon to save him from a 5,000-member lynch mob. Dixon, son of the black janitor at First Presbyterian Church, confesses to killing 11-year-old Floella MacDonald.	Secretary Herbert Hoover tells a Pan American conference that the United States will lend money for only productive works. Secretary Frank B. Kellogg says the state department has no such condition on its loans.			The Columbus, GA, *Enquirer Sun* wins the 1926 Pulitzer prize for its campaigns against the KKK, lynching, and anti-evolutionism. Among the other winners: Sinclair Lewis for *Arrowsmith*, Edward Channing for volume 6, *History of the United States*, and, posthumously, poet Amy Lowell for *What's O'Clock*.	May 2
The New York State Supreme Court agrees to hear arguments for and against teaching of religion in schools. Both religious and educational leaders assail the suit by White Plains freethinkers.	Calvin Coolidge officially opens the Pan American conference by declaring that the United States wants equality for and friendship with all American nations. The United States wants merely to help, not to control.	U.S. oil firms agree to pay Mexican export and production taxes in the United States. The tax bill is $8 million a year....The national debt is under $19 billion for the first time since the war. Reduction since 1919's peak is $7.6 billion.			May 3
U.S. Senator Royal S. Copeland and the niece of Indian poet Rabindranath Tagore are among the speakers who call for reversal of the Supreme Court decision barring Indians from U.S. citizenship. Arguments for reversal include the fine Hindu character, the fact that numbers are strongly limited by a 1917 immigration law, and Hindu membership in the Caucasian race....The Arkansas mob lynches Lonnie Dixon. The body is dragged through the streets before being burned in the "Negro quarter."	Treasury Secretary Andrew Mellon's statement that Britain collects more from others than it pays the United States in war debt provokes a strong British white paper. Winston Churchill points out that Mellon confuses the nation and the empire. The British want debt forgiveness all around. Mellon says he has erroneous data.	The west coast gasoline price war ends as companies reestablish March 1 prices. Prices are up 2.5 cents in Seattle to 5 cents in San Francisco. Los Angeles scale is 18.5 cents; San Francisco charges 19 cents.	An army balloonist sets a new altitude record of 41,000 feet. Captain Hawthorne Gray of Scott Field, IL, breaks the French record of 39,800 feet....The flood refugee camps still report typhoid, malaria, and smallpox. Increased outbreaks are likely in a week to ten days as the waters recede from the seven-state flood area. The Red Cross has inoculated 80,000 people to date.	While his divorce suit and back tax problems continue, Charlie Chaplin deals with another lawsuit. Leo Loeb wants $50,000 because, he alleges, Chaplin stole his *The Rookie* for *Shoulder Arms*....Douglas Fairbanks heads the newly established Hollywood Academy of Motion Pictures Arts and Sciences. The academy will issue awards for excellence in the industry.	May 4

F
Includes campaigns, elections, federal-state relations, civil rights and liberties, crime, the judiciary, education, healthcare, poverty, urban affairs, and population.

G
Includes formation and debate of U.S. foreign and defense policies, veterans affairs, and defense spending. (Relations with specific foreign countries are usually found under the region concerned.)

H
Includes business, labor, agriculture, taxation, transportation, consumer affairs, monetary and fiscal policy, natural resources, pollution and industrial accidents.

I
Includes worldwide scientific, medical and technological developments, natural phenomena, U.S. weather and natural disasters.

J
Includes the arts, religion, scholarship, communications media, sports, entertainment, fashions, fads, and social life.

	World Affairs	Europe	Africa & The Middle East	The Americas	Asia & The Pacific
May 5		Berlin police ban the National Socialist Party. At a mass meeting, party members beat non-members. 29 are charged with weapons violations. The "Hitler Youth" and Nazis have previously been banned in Limburg and Hessen for similar rowdyism.	Dr. J. Morton Howell, U.S. envoy to Egypt, resigns for the third time. This time Calvin Coolidge accepts, allowing Howell to return to the United States to his ailing wife.	Mexico claims that, after a five-day chase, federal troops have killed rebel General Jose Gallegos. The government also reports that 100 of those who attacked the Guadalajara train are dead. Sonoran fighting continues....After Canada eased rules for reestablishing citizenship, in 1926, 21,025 Americans emigrated to Canada. Over 2600 came from Michigan....Nicaragua's liberal rebels agree to cease fighting. They cite U.S. threats, which the United States denies.	Communists lose two cities in Kwantung. They evacuate a third. Reportedly, they are running out of money.
May 6		Berlin calls out 18,000 police for the mass demonstration of the Steel Helmets. The 78,000 veterans of the Kaiser's armies are expected to provoke Communist protests. Already, it has had to deny an anti-Semitic group claiming association with it.	An American woman, wife of a missionary en route to Burma, is shot in Palestine's Valley of the Bandits. The bandits kill the missionaries' native chauffeur.		
May 7		Germany in 1926 was the leading exporter of steel. It was 60 percent above England and double the United States....A Russian mechanic announces that he intends to fly a gasoline-powered rocket to the moon in September. Ivan Federof is a member of the All-Inventors Vegetarian Club of Interplanetary Cosmopolitans, whose several thousand members communicate using five vowels and five mathematical symbols....After seven years of negotiation, Hungary and Czechoslovakia sign a trade treaty.	Rev. Dr. Mark C. Hayward, head of a Baptist-based non-denominational church, the largest in the Ivory and Gold coasts, is in the United States seeking $500,000 for his church and school. The Gold Coast has school facilities for 40,000 of its 300,000 potential students. The Ivory Coast is even worse.	New evidence shows that Henry Stimson, as charged by the liberals, threatened the use of U.S. Marines if the rebels refused to disband. Liberal politicians protest; liberal generals continue to disarm. Smaller Latin American countries express concern.	Responding to threats to blockade him, Chen says Hankow can outlast the powers. He also claims that Chiang Kai-shek is labeling him a red in a move to take power. Chen wants U.S. friendship.
May 8		The Steel Helmets march to the jeers of Berliners who reject their monarchism. Occasional scrapes between Communists and steel helmets result in many Communist arrests....Five Italian shipping lines, with 80 vessels, merge. Now they have the size to build a 30-knot 48,000 ton ship.	Tunisian tea drinkers are drinking to excess. The result is an outbreak of theinism, tea poisoning.		The second son of the king, the Duke of York, unlocks Parliament House, making Canberra the new federal capital of Australia. American Walter Burley Griffin wins the design competition in 1911.
May 9			Palestinian Jews, Christians, and Muslims flock to an ancient Semitic temple uncovered by archaeologists at Tel en Ansheh. Beneath the 2,000 year old temple are the ruins of a still older one, perhaps predating Abraham.	Henry Stimson reports progress in disarming Nicaraguan rebels. 800 additional Marines are heading for Nicaragua. Their mission is "pacification." Liberal leader Sacasa warns that the Americans risk bloodshed if they persist in their unconstitutional support of the conservative Adolfo Diaz.	
May 10	The Pope declares war on immoral books. Noting that the world is overly prone to sin, he asks his bishops to issue lists of sensual books they ban in their parts of the world.	Soviet Communists split over support for China. Grigory Zinoviev says it's a turning away from Leninism. Nikolai Bukharin says it is appropriate to circumstances.			
May 11		Italy implements retail price cuts of 10 to 50 percent. Deflation remains the Italian policy....Germany announces it will protect youth from unhealthful amusements such as shows and dances. The Reichstag action comes on the heels of a ban on obscene and "trashy" literature.	British commander C. Crauford claims to have found the lost city of Ophir, home of Queen Sheba, in Arabia. Crauford says Palestine can rival the Transvaal as a source of diamonds and gold.	Former president Victoriano Huerta, from Los Angeles, reports that the Yaquis are demanding the surrender of federal troops dug in outside Nogales, Sonora. Huerta says he will return to Mexico when the time is right.	

A	B	C	D	E
Includes developments that affect more than one world region, international organizations and important meetings of world leaders.	*Includes all domestic and regional developments in Europe, including the Soviet Union.*	*Includes all domestic and regional developments in Africa and the Middle East.*	*Includes all domestic and regional developments in Latin America, the Caribbean, and Canada.*	*Includes all domestic and regional developments in Asian and Pacific nations (and colonies).*

U.S. Politics & Social Issues	U.S. Foreign Policy & Affairs, Defense	U.S. Economy & Environment	Science, Technology & Nature	Culture, Leisure & Lifestyle	
	After Andrew Mellon's retreat from his statement about Britain profiting from war debt, Britain and the United States let the war debt argument fade away. With British investors reassured, the British ease pressure for renegotiation or cancellation of some debt.	The week's gold imports total over $6 million.	The German Johannes Nehring sets a world glider mark. He stays aloft with a passenger for 5 hours, 20 minutes. This breaks the 1923 French record by 39 minutes....A German ship discovers the deepest spot in the ocean. A crevice off Japan is 34,210 feet deep....The flood crest is in Louisiana. The Red Cross is aiding over 300,000 refugees. Many Louisianans refuse to evacuate, and some are riding out the flood on rafts, wanting to stay near their farms.	Mrs. Chaplin says she'll settle for $1.25 million. Chaplin's lawyers say he does not have that much.... Harvard's Widener Library acquires 30,000 books and pamphlets from the collection of Comte Alfred Bolay de Meurthe. The collection on 19th century French religion and politics is Harvard's most important acquisition since the 1899 near eastern collection of Count Riant.	May 5
			The Mississippi is 40-miles-wide in areas. The crest is nearing the gulf, but New Orleans appears to be safe as the levees hold....The radio commission requires that all stations give their call letters every 15 minutes. The requirement may be waived when it would interrupt a speech or musical number.	In the 10th inning of an exhibition game, Babe Ruth steps to the plate, signals the crowd that the game is over, and hits a home run.	May 6
The Nevada state treasurer and two others are under arrest for embezzling. They stole $516,000 over eight years....2,000 protesters at Union Square demand that the United States withdraw from China. Black, Indian, and other speakers also demand an end to "oppressive" treaties and ties to Britain.	German Jews ask that the United States eliminate the religion entry on immigration forms. Since February Jews have had to identify themselves as Hebrew. They ask the right to identify themselves as German.	For the first time ever, Henry Ford settles a lawsuit out of court. A contractor, John M. Blair, sued in seven cases for $2 million, charging that Ford refused to pay for work and used injunctions to tie up Blair's equipment....An American Electrical Railway Association report shows that the increase in car miles in 1926 was due to increased bus service. True electric rail service declined, particularly in small cities.	Charles Nungesser takes off for Newfoundland from Paris. He plans to make the Paris-New York flight without a radio, which adds too much weight....The flood region suffers an earthquake and storms. In Louisiana anthrax threatens 55,000 cattle.	The Library of Congress receives the 5,000 volume Harry Houdini library on psychic lore and spiritualism. Included are many works debunking mediums and other charlatans....Customs is holding an edition of *Decameron*, awaiting a ruling on its decency under the 1922 law. The same edition has been imported without challenge for 30 years.	May 7
Although 1926 smallpox cases were fewer than those in 1925, the United States still had 33,352 cases, the highest total outside Asia. The American Association for Medical Progress blames anti-vaccine strongholds, including Southern California....American Fundamentalists announce a $24 million campaign against evolution and blames China's woes on modernism.			As part of a storm system that hits seven Rocky Mountain states with snow and rain, tornadoes in Kansas kill 11. The governor declares martial law....Separate scientific teams find a prehistoric fort in Kentucky and a mammoth skeleton in Oklahoma....New York prepares to welcome Charles Nungesser, now delayed. Stormy weather is reported in Nova Scotia.	Hundreds of tourists at Niagara Falls watch as an American commits suicide by wading into the water just above the falls. Before doing so, the man removes his topcoat and suitcoat.	May 8
Faculty members from 12 universities and a contingent of Swedes are the latest to petition the Massachusetts governor to review the Nicola Sacco and Bartolomeo Vanzetti death sentences. Pressure on the governor to overturn unjust verdicts continues to grow.		Another $6 million in gold comes to the United States this is the third shipment in two weeks. Since the beginning of the year, $105 million in gold has come to New York and $22 million has left, leaving a balance of $83 million. Money is easy on the New York market....22 chain store systems report sales up for April. Only one reports slower sales.	Tornadoes spread from Texas into five other states. 250 are dead, 40 in Poplar Bluff, MO, and several Arkansas towns are heavily damaged....With Charles Nungesser overdue, the navy begins searching the coastal waters. Meanwhile, rivals prepare their flights. Bellanca will try tomorrow. Charles Lindbergh is preparing to leave San Diego.		May 9
A New York court denies the claim of White Plains freethinkers that schools are unconstitutionally teaching religion by freeing children a half hour each week to receive religious training at the church of their parents' choice. The court notes that the practice is almost state-wide.	A board of inquiry reports that repairs to the *Colorado* will cost $100,000. Re-floating the vessel cost $70,000.	Since overcoming concerns about the workability of the veterans loan program in January, over 7,000 institutions have loaned $40 million to veterans with service certificates. The average loan is $88.	Another levee breaks in Mississippi. Doubts grow about the safety of the Louisiana levees. Thousands evacuate as 25,000 men fight to shore up the system.	Gertrude Ederle and Lotte Schoemell are among the entrants announced for the $10,000 July 14 Lake George, NY, 24-mile marathon. Ederle swam the English Channel. Schoemell swam the Hudson River from Albany to New York.	May 10
Henry Ford rejects Aaron Sapiro's offer to arbitrate his lawsuit. A mistrial had been declared in April in the $100,000 libel suit....Governor Alvan Fuller of Massachusetts says he may act this week on Nicola Sacco and Bartolomeo Vanzetti.	18 pursuit craft arrive in San Antonio after a 1300-mile flight from Detroit. Over 100 planes are now at Kelly Field for upcoming maneuvers. Observers are impressed with technological progress since the war.	The national broadcasters association says it wants to do away with radio call letters. It prefers names like those on ships and Pullman cars....Oil producers ask for help in curbing wildcatting and overproduction. The government notes the restrictions of antitrust law.	Charles Lindbergh arrives in St.Louis from San Diego. He sets a solo distance record of 1550 miles. Flying solely by compass, he makes the trip in 14 hours and five minutes.	Ban Johnson, president of the American League, censures manager Connie Mack and fines Ty Cobb and Al Simmons of the Philadelphia Athletics $200 each. The players were suspended for their roles in instigating a near riot by fans a week earlier against Boston.	May 11

F	G	H	I	J
Includes campaigns, elections, federal-state relations, civil rights and liberties, crime, the judiciary, education, healthcare, poverty, urban affairs, and population.	Includes formation and debate of U.S. foreign and defense policies, veterans affairs, and defense spending. (Relations with specific foreign countries are usually found under the region concerned.)	Includes business, labor, agriculture, taxation, transportation, consumer affairs, monetary and fiscal policy, natural resources, pollution and industrial accidents.	Includes worldwide scientific, medical and technological developments, natural phenomena, U.S. weather and natural disasters.	Includes the arts, religion, scholarship, communications media, sports, entertainment, fashions, fads, and social life.

	World Affairs	Europe	Africa & The Middle East	The Americas	Asia & The Pacific
May 12		London police raid the Russia's trading firm, the Arcos Agency, seizing documents and searching 1,000 employees. Labour and Russia protest, demanding to know the reason. The British government refuses to act, claiming it's a London matter.		Nicaraguan President Adolfo Diaz begins reorganizing his government and constabulary to return it to the form it had prior to the Chamorro coup. U.S. Marines are paying liberals $10 for each weapon they surrender. From Panama, liberal leaders refuse to support the government imposed by U.S. force.	Manchurian officials arrest 100 and execute 23 for complicity in a "Koumintang-Communist" plot to disrupt the Harbin Railroad. Nanking protests firing by American warships as gunfire resumes on the lower Yangtze River.
May 13		Britain supports German desires for troop reductions in the Rhineland. Britain suggests that the French reduce their 60,000 man contingent....Ministers of the Little Entente begin talks on the Balkans, Russia, and Italy. Entente members are Czechoslovakia, Romania, and Yugoslavia.		One of Canada's growth industries is manufacture of rayon and mixed cotton celanese using artificial silk. The industry uses over $4 million of artificial silk in the first nine months of fiscal 1927, compared with $3.7 million for all of 1926....All liberal Nicaraguan generals but one have surrendered. The war is over.	The three-week Japanese bank moratorium, imposed after a serious run on the Bank of Taiwan, ends. Business is heavy and stocks are steady as the government stands ready to intervene if a boom begins.
May 14	At the League's Commerce Commission, Sweden and Switzerland object to U.S. practices of checking the books of foreign firms in order to levy ad valorem taxes. Also, the commission schedules a November meeting to address Roland Boyden's subcommittee's recommendations for restoring production and international trade.	Rural parties win recent Austrian elections. They advise Chancellor Ignaz Seipel to take care of farm interests in the new parliament. Now *anschluss*, union of Austria with Germany, becomes probable because it will provide necessary markets....Germany bans grain exports due to shortages....Failing to reach political accord, the Little Entente becomes a union of commerce and culture.			
May 15		Britain reports that the Arcos trading company raids uncover lists of Soviet agents, state papers, and links on the continent. Mass protests occur in Russia.			Chiang Kai-shek begins a drive to the north, easing pressure on allied forces and citizens. Rumor has the Communist leader ready to flee to Russia....Authorities are cautious in enforcing an order committing the "emperor" of the Philippines to a mental institution. They fear provoking his followers, numerous and armed, who surround his bamboo "palace."
May 16	Viscount Ishi and Admiral Saito, several-time Minister of Marine, lead the Japanese delegation of 25 prominent individuals to the Naval Disarmament Conference set for June. The British delegation will be led by the First Lord of the Admiralty. The United States has no plans to upgrade its delegation until Ambassador Gibson returns from Switzerland.			Liberals sweep the Quebec elections with 72 seats. They reinstall Prime Minister Taschereau, who advocates big American projects with American money, and halve the conservative representation to 10 from the 20 elected in 1923. Two seats go to independent liberals.	
May 17	Italy advises Calvin Coolidge that it will participate in the naval conference. France has not yet changed its refusal to participate.	The Jewish colony of Djankey, near Novy Put, Ukraine, becomes Felix Warburg. Colonists are expressing their gratitude to the chair of the American Jewish Joint Distribution Committee	The Zionist-leaning Judea Life Insurance Company begins operation under a New York license. It is a subsidiary of the Palestine-based Judea Insurance Company Ltd, which since its 1925 founding has written over $2 million of coverage in Palestine, Egypt, and other Middle Eastern states.		Datu Tahil receives a 10-year sentence and a 20,000 peso fine for his treason in leading the Sulu uprising. His deputy receives five years and a 10,000 peso fine. His fourth wife, Princess Tarhata Karim, is under house arrest for blocking the constabulary from taking Tahil. She is the highly popular niece of the Sultan of Sulu.
May 18	The Inter-American Convention on Commercial Aviation drafts an agreement establishing that a state is sovereign over its air space. Commercial planes have rights of passage, but they cannot carry war material or transit war zones. The Pan American Conference in February 1928 will address the proposal....The Geneva economic conference is winding down with no agreement on cartels or rationalization.	The church and state join to restore a cross to the Roman Colosseum. The act commemorates the early Christian martyrs. The cross came off the Colosseum in 1870 with the loss of papal temporal powers....After a seven-year inquiry, the Reichstag declares that other than in trifles the World War I German army lived up to the rules of war.	The French open a new wireless station in Equatorial Africa. France already has links to Indochina, West Africa, and Madagascar. French Equatorial Africa is its most economically backward colony.	Costa Rica demands reparations from Adolfo Diaz for a raid by 70 Nicaraguan soldiers who stole farm animals, robbed farms, and wounded a Costa Rican constable. Costa Rica, although neutral in the Nicaraguan civil war, never recognized Diaz, and its citizens preferred Sacasa....In Tucson, AZ, former Mexican president Victoriano Huerta and four others are charged with arms smuggling.	

A	B	C	D	E
Includes developments that affect more than one world region, international organizations and important meetings of world leaders.	*Includes all domestic and regional developments in Europe, including the Soviet Union.*	*Includes all domestic and regional developments in Africa and the Middle East.*	*Includes all domestic and regional developments in Latin America, the Caribbean, and Canada.*	*Includes all domestic and regional developments in Asian and Pacific nations (and colonies).*

U.S. Politics & Social Issues	U.S. Foreign Policy & Affairs, Defense	U.S. Economy & Environment	Science, Technology & Nature	Culture, Leisure & Lifestyle	
The conservative Republican Union League Club resolves in opposition to a federal constitutional convention, fearing that it will disturb the prosperity and tranquility and produce radical change. 24 states have called for the convention, four short of the three-fourths required.... Franklin D. Roosevelt returns from the South. He says officials there want federal flood aid and support for Smith for president is growing.	The board of enquiry exonerates the *Colorado*'s captain, ruling that the grounding was unavoidable. The pilot, a civilian, is outside the board's jurisdiction.	Overproduction in Oklahoma remains uncontrolled. Oil companies seek a long term plan. In the short run they agree to the appointment of Ray Collins, independent out of Tulsa, as oil dictator for the Seminole field.	Charles Lindbergh arrives at Curtiss Field, having set a solo record of over 2500 miles and 21 hours, 20 minutes, solely by compass. Lindbergh's arrival spurs Clarence Chamberlin to get his Bellanca ready to fly tomorrow. Richard Byrd's Fokker is still undergoing tests.	The $50,000 Loeb plagiarism suit against Charlie Chaplin will be tried again. The first jury deadlocked.	May 12
Calvin Coolidge refuses to comment on allegations that in 1912 as a state representative he signed a petition seeking a Constitutional amendment against a third term. The goal in 1912 was to stop Teddy Roosevelt.	American businessmen back Panamanian protests that U.S. stores are unfair competition. Originally commissaries for those building the canal, the stores are now in general business. Calvin Coolidge defends the U.S. commissaries in the Panama Canal Zone as a treaty right.		Charles Nungesser is still missing. Bad weather grounds all the other flyers.		May 13
The Post Office intercepts a package of dynamite sent by a NIcola Sacco supporter to Governor Alvan Fuller of Massachusetts. Rumor says the governor will choose a commission to investigate the Sacco death penalty.	Secretary Frank B. Kellogg informs General Wu that the United States will negotiate only when all Chinese parties are represented. He also agrees to discussions on the issue of Panama Canal Zone commissaries.	The Businessmen's Commission on Agriculture, which has been exploring farm conditions since January, issues a preliminary report. It finds the U.S. agricultural depression is regional and temporary as well as long term elements. The commission can agree on no solutions.	The search for Charles Nungesser in Labrador ends. Reports of wreckage and other sightings will continue into July.	Philadelphia receives a $2 million bequest from Edwin Swift Balch, scientist, explorer, and author. The will specifies that his wife Emily holds the estate until her death. Then the funds will build a museum to house his art collection and his works. The Balch Institute for Ethnic Studies opens finally in 1976.... Linus McAtee rides Whiskery to victory in the Kentucky Derby.	May 14
The American Civil Liberties Union reports that the American Legion has replaced the Ku Klux Klan as the most repressive organization in the United States. The ACLU alleges the Legion and Fundamentalists are responsible for mandatory Bible reading, flag salutes, military drill and other denials of students' rights.			With the levee breached and the sugar growing region inundated, Louisiana releases 600 convicts to work on the honor system.	A Hopi Indian snake dancer and shaman, Quanowanu, wins the new York to Long Beach Marathon by 100 yards. The field of 136 confronted auto exhaust, heavy traffic, and 250,000 spectators.	May 15
Governor Alvan Fuller agrees to tests on the gun allegedly used by Nicola Sacco....A Klansman backed by Governor Bibb Graves and the state Grand Dragon loses the mayoral race in Montgomery, AL, by a 2 to 1 margin....The Supreme Court upholds California's anti-syndicalism law, denying that it is class legislation. Convictions of Charlotte Anita Whitney and William Burns are affirmed.	The quota list for next fiscal year's immigration opens. In Berlin 600 would be emigrants are put on the list for visas in July....War games begin in Narragansett Bay. Maneuvers continue in San Antonio.	Another $6 million brings the total gold arriving in the United States to $30 million since April 30. The amount matches what France received from England.			May 16
Calvin Coolidge remains silent on the 3rd term issue. Supporters deny he signed the 1912 petition against 3rd terms as alleged....Governor Alvan Fuller begins interviewing witnesses against Nicola Sacco.... Wets threaten to organize a third party for 1928 if the Republicans or Democrats do not stand against prohibition.			Calvin Coolidge reiterates that he sees no need to call Congress to deal with the flood crisis. The flood fund tops $12 million.	Eddie Cantor, after a year making three movies, re-signs with Florenz Ziegfield for five years, beginning with this season's follies. His salary is undisclosed but described as the highest ever paid a comedian.	May 17
The American Medical Association decrees that there will be no doctors on radio. It's unethical.	Benjamin Day, commissioner of immigration at the Port of New York, wants U.S. immigration quotas extended to Mexico. He also wants exemption from quotas for husbands and parents as well as wives and children. He notes that the New York immigration facility has 50,000 detainees, either criminal or mental.	The editor of the Dearborn *Independent*, a Ford spokesman, denies that the company will introduce a new car in the fall. He refutes a Detroit police spokesperson who claims the company plans a four-cylinder gear shift model. Ford has built 10 million Model Ts to date.	Flood waters inundate Acadian Louisiana, with millions of acres submerged. Two lakes on the western side of the Atchafalaya merge. Thousands flee a 30-foot wall of water. Franklin Roosevelt asks Calvin Coolidge to call a special session. Roosevelt says the combined efforts of the Red Cross, state banks, and the public are insufficient.		May 18

F	G	H	I	J
Includes campaigns, elections, federal-state relations, civil rights and liberties, crime, the judiciary, education, healthcare, poverty, urban affairs, and population.	*Includes formation and debate of U.S. foreign and defense policies, veterans affairs, and defense spending. (Relations with specific foreign countries are usually found under the region concerned.)*	*Includes business, labor, agriculture, taxation, transportation, consumer affairs, monetary and fiscal policy, natural resources, pollution and industrial accidents.*	*Includes worldwide scientific, medical and technological developments, natural phenomena, U.S. weather and natural disasters.*	*Includes the arts, religion, scholarship, communications media, sports, entertainment, fashions, fads, and social life.*

	World Affairs	Europe	Africa & The Middle East	The Americas	Asia & The Pacific
May 19	The Russian delegation asks economists to agree that the Communist and capitalist systems can coexist. They threaten to bolt if denied their way. Russia is also threatening to withhold reparations unless the allies provide new loans. And the Arcos crisis with Britain contributes to the friction. The majority of conferees are unsympathetic to Russia.				Anti-Communist forces mutiny in Hankow. Rich residents flee. A nationalist army is within 20 miles of the Communist capital.
May 20				After receiving a legislative resolution expressing satisfaction with the American government, Calvin Coolidge tells Puerto Ricans to avoid debt and learn English.	
May 21	With American backing, the Geneva economic meeting accepts the Russian position that two systems co-exist. The Americans argue that Communism exists, and only a fool would deny it.	Austrian nobility back the anschluss. They hope to regain their titles after the merger....Germany's attempt to get mandates provokes an editorial reaction. George Bernhard says the better approach is to ask an open door in the colonial world.	An archaeologist at a Palestinian dig near the Semitic temple finds a cache of pots in cisterns. The pottery includes types of Israeli work not previously known in the Near East.	Juan Sacasa leaves Nicaragua for Guatemala, ending the dual governments. His party expects to run liberal foreign minister Rodolfo Espinza in the 1928 Nicaraguan presidential election, held under U.S. guarantees.	The 1926 census reports that Australia's pureblood aboriginal population is down to 59,000, a drop of 3,000 from 1925. their death rate is up to 25 per 5,000 compared to 1 per 5,000 previously. The mixed population is up from 12,000 in 1924 to 15,000.
May 22	·	Russia declares a boycott of British goods. M. Mikoyan decrees that the Soviets will trade only with those who have proper trade relations and guarantee Russian safety. The move is seen as a reply to the Arcos raid.			In China, Hankow is less tense as the reds claim victories against the nationalists. The *Preble* engages in a gun battle. For five hours, with British aid, American sailors fight an oil tank fire started by a shell.
May 23	The Geneva economic meeting ends with a recommendation that the League continue the body with Russia and the United States as participants. The final report discusses the European depression, loss of purchasing power, and tariffs that strangle trade.			President Gerardo Machado of Cuba reveals that during his recent visit to the United States he brought up the subject of greater freedom from the United States. The U.S. State Department is silent on a possible renegotiation of the U.S.–Cuba treaty.	
May 24	The League Federation opens its 1927 meeting. The main topic is the status of minorities, and Germany says it will raise the issue of Lithuanian treatment of Germans in Memel.	Prime Minister Stanley Baldwin breaks relations with Russia. He discloses that the Arcos raid revealed a worldwide Soviet espionage network centered in London. He allows legitimate trade to continue.	The Palestine Arab Executive protests Zionism to the League's Permanent Mandates Committee. The executive also complains that there are too many British officials, too little Arab representation, and slights to the Arab language.		Japan halts gold exports. The government, which has been sending $4 million a month to stabilize exchange prior to returning to the gold standard, wants to make domestic adjustments after the bank crisis. Japanese gold in the United States totals $50 million.
May 25	Canada breaks relations with Russia. Trade representatives remain however. Russia severs trade ties with England. Maxim Litvinof says the English are trying to provoke a war.		Rabbi Stephen Wise and Sir Alfred Davies rebut Harry Emerson Fosdick, who argues that radicals are taking over the Zionist movement and that Palestine is not economically viable. Rather, Zionists are bringing new life to the country, and Arabs are adapting, even speaking idiomatic Hebrew.		
May 26	Chancellor Wilhelm Marx opens the eleventh annual meeting International Federation of League of Nations Societies. France criticizes arms resolutions and stands by Locarno. The minorities committee fails to agree on a position. Germany complains that it cannot be equal while parts of its territory are occupied.	Benito Mussolini announces that he will have an army of five million. Italy will also have a navy and air force that make its voice respected by 1940.	Tablets found in the Sinai that may hold clues to the origin of the alphabet. In Egypt archaeologists speculate that robbers destroyed the mummy of Queen Hetepheres in fear of King Cheops. They also say they are closer to understanding Egyptian mummification techniques.	Mexico has captured Los Altos. The Jalisco rising is over. Agricultural workers who helped the federals are released from duty.	
May 27	The Federation of League of Nations Societies hears an American defense of its immigration policy. Another issue is the status of Balkan Jews.			Ontario rejects the idea of being a "liquor oasis" for Americans. There will be no one-day citizenships, and the government will check permits.	Major fighting on the Plains of Honan destroys a large Hankow army. Southern moderates and radicals reach an accord....An Indian conference reports a plan to fight drug trafficking. The government would have sole control over opium.

A	B	C	D	E
Includes developments that affect more than one world region, international organizations and important meetings of world leaders.	*Includes all domestic and regional developments in Europe, including the Soviet Union.*	*Includes all domestic and regional developments in Africa and the Middle East.*	*Includes all domestic and regional developments in Latin America, the Caribbean, and Canada.*	*Includes all domestic and regional developments in Asian and Pacific nations (and colonies).*

U.S. Politics & Social Issues	U.S. Foreign Policy & Affairs, Defense	U.S. Economy & Environment	Science, Technology & Nature	Culture, Leisure & Lifestyle	
Tammany insiders report that William McAdoo has dropped out of the 1928 race. The way is clear for Al Smith to win the Democratic nomination.		General Motors is worth $198 million. Its stock tops 200 before dropping back to 198½.	Tens of thousands of Cajuns are stranded and still refusing to leave their homes. Breaks in the levees lower river levels, easing pressure downstream.		May 19
		A seat on the New York Stock Exchange sells for $215,000. This price is down $2,000 from yesterday's price. A seat on the Curb Exchange sells for $31,000, up from $22,000 in March but well off the 1925 record of $37,500.	Charles Lindbergh takes off and is over Newfoundland as the weather clears. The Bellanca flight is postponed due to high winds. Richard Byrd is set for a full-load flight test tomorrow.	Jack Sharkey stops 7–5 favorite Jim Maloney in the fifth round of a bout for the right to take on Jack Dempsey. Each boxer receives $49,228.	May 20
		A report reveals the economic limit to skyscrapers is 20 floors. After that the costs per cubic foot escalate rapidly.	Charles Lindbergh arrives in Paris. Crowds in the United States and France cheer. World reaction is excitement and delight. Prizes quickly surpass $100,000.		May 21
		The Great Northern-Northern Pacific merger committee extends until mid June the deadline for stockholders to show their support. The merger proposal continues until 1931, when it is withdrawn. The roads finally merge in 1970.	Charles Lindbergh gets a $500,000 movie offer and a $1300 tax bill for the Orteig Prize's $25,000. Acclaim continues to pour in.		May 22
Preliminary results of a survey of 6159 Episcopal clergy reveals they want to overturn prohibition. They form a temperance society to fight for moderation.	The army loses a blimp preparing to return to Illinois after maneuvers in Texas. While the army mourns the loss of 200,000 feet of scarce helium, the ship's captain notes this is the third blimp he has lost since 1922.	Calvin Coolidge approves a plan for the Farm Loan Board to help agricultural associations, bankers and businessmen to raise the funds to rebuild the flood ravaged regions. Half a million refugees are getting aid, with another 100,000 expected as rains aid the river against the levees.	The manufacturer of the magnetic compass used by Charles Lindbergh explains how it tracks a predetermined course against the earth's magnetic lines of force. He shows how it is uninfluenced by the motion of the aircraft.	Charles Lindbergh's mother refuses a $100,000 movie offer. Lindbergh himself is cold to the idea of making money off what he regards as a scientific venture.	May 23
Governor Alvan Fuller denies a request to argue for a Sacco commission. He says law prohibits him from delegating his review, which he continues.		Flood relief is just under $14 million. The Red Cross and state agencies combine to prevent epidemics.... The radio board reallocates band for 694 stations effective June 1. Protests are immediate, particularly from those given weaker lower bandwidths.	The fight to save the western sugar bowl fails as the Atchafalaya levee ruptures. Another 100,000 refugees are in flight as a 50-mile wide lake rushes toward the gulf and the Mississippi's level lowers.	Charlie Chaplin loses an attempt to strike most of the most scandalous charges in his divorce proceedings. The wife says she will name seven women, four of them actresses, if forced to depose.	May 24
Senator Simeon Fess (R-OH) uses history to argue for a third term for Calvin Coolidge. Fess says that Washington declined the third term not because he objected to three terms but because he was feeling old. Fess also references Jefferson, Lincoln, and Grant as unopposed to the third term. Fitness to serve, not tradition, should decide.		Ford announces a new model to be out within 90 days. There will be no shutdown of production lines.	In a lecture on the health crisis in the civilized world, Sir George Newman reports that the American maternal death rate is highest in the civilized world. The United States also has excessive deaths from automobiles, murders, and suicides.	Al Jolson, comedian and veteran of Vitaphone shorts, prepares to star in the screen version of "The Jazz Singer." George Jessel had the stage role.	May 25
	Despite U.S. government policy banning loans to governments that have not squared their wartime debts, American traders sell France $40 million of gold. France is stabilizing the franc in order to return to a gold standard. Gilt edge stocks in London respond favorably but the British government dislikes the tightening of money.	The treasury announces it will reduce the size of currency by a third. The dollar bill will be first. ...Remington Arms announces it will produce self-service vending machines for food, drugs, cigarettes, and such. The corner grocery will rival the automat.	Anticipating that the state will authorize a Bridge and Tunnel Authority, the New York Board of Estimates votes the first funds for the Tri-borough bridge, $150,000 for soundings and borings. The board declines funds for similar work on a vehicle tunnel under the East River....Eastman Kodak begins issuing four-minute films for home use.		May 26
Calvin Coolidge endorses a war on crime after states call for federal assistance.			Danes announce they have a process for producing color film.	After nearly a month of quiet on the censorship front, Boston booksellers withdraw Upton Sinclair's Oil. They fear that the new novel contains passages that violate Massachusetts' decency law.	May 27

F
Includes campaigns, elections, federal-state relations, civil rights and liberties, crime, the judiciary, education, healthcare, poverty, urban affairs, and population.

G
Includes formation and debate of U.S. foreign and defense policies, veterans affairs, and defense spending. (Relations with specific foreign countries are usually found under the region concerned.)

H
Includes business, labor, agriculture, taxation, transportation, consumer affairs, monetary and fiscal policy, natural resources, pollution and industrial accidents.

I
Includes worldwide scientific, medical and technological developments, natural phenomena, U.S. weather and natural disasters.

J
Includes the arts, religion, scholarship, communications media, sports, entertainment, fashions, fads, and social life.

	World Affairs	Europe	Africa & The Middle East	The Americas	Asia & The Pacific
May 28	Edward Bok's American Foundation, which sponsors a peace prize, releases a model treaty that outlaws war. The idea is to make Aristide Briand's proposal concrete.		Anglo-Egyptian relations are strained. Egypt seeks greater autonomy for its armed forces. Britain argues that oversight is hers under the 1922 independence agreement.		The northern offensive covers a 100 mile front. Japan sends troops to China, purportedly to protect Japanese nationals. Western diplomats contend it's a ploy to regain Shantung Province.
May 29		Premier Raymond Poincare speaks at Rouen as France observes Joan of Arc Day. The ceremony marks the 496th anniversary of her death on May 30, 1431.	The International Olympic Committee sanctions an African Olympics in 1929. The Alexandria, Egypt, event is open to African-born men only. It is separate from the 1928 Amsterdam and 1932 Los Angeles Olympics.		Admiral Kitelle reveals Russian-backed Chinese plotted to have Filipinos blow up the U.S. navy arsenal at Cavite. Kitelle tells the 2600 shipyard workers to model themselves on Aguinaldo, a model citizen, loyal to the United States.
May 30	The League Society concludes its Berlin meeting. It calls for all nations to outlaw war.		In response to the Egyptian attempt to take control of its army, Britain sends a warship to Cairo.		
May 31		The Comintern censures Leon Trotsky for deviations from party orthodoxy on war, Anglo-Russian relations, and China. He is not expelled, but the threat hangs over him.			Northern forces move to the defensive as they lose two provinces and southerners threaten Peking.
Jun. 1			France supports Britain against Egyptian efforts to take control of the military. The move is another indicator of revived Anglo-French entente. Where friction was the norm in Palestine, Transjordan, and Syria, now the two powers seem in accord throughout the Middle East.	President Plutarco Calles of Mexico embargoes American goods. The embargo is in retaliation for American refusal to allow arms shipments. The U.S. position is that the ban on arms aided Mexico against its insurgents.	As the northern defeat nears a rout, Marines move to Tientsen to protect American nationals. The United States ponders moving its legation from Peking, but the other powers are unwilling to leave.
Jun. 2	Unofficially, France tells the League it will send two observers to the Naval Conference. Italy has already taken observer status.	Italy sets the lira at 5.6 cents. The price will be stable through the fall.	France outlaws lip stretching, nose piercing, and tooth filing in its African colonies. Missionaries and military having failed to alter the practices, France now imposes sentences of two to five years (five to 10 years for family members) for those who disfigure in the name of beauty.	Senora Calles, wife of Mexico's president, dies of a heart attack. She dies in Los Angeles while convalescing from intestinal surgery.	Finance minister Korekiyo Takahashi resigns to protest Japan sending troops to China.
Jun. 3		Authorities say that White Russia is calm. They seek to dispel rumors of an anti-soviet rising in the region.	Egypt yields to English demands that it retain an English-model army and a British inspector general. A conference will deal with other issues....The South African winner of the $400,000 Calcutta Derby sweepstakes faces a fine of $1,000 or jail time for violating the anti-lottery law.	Chile names former president Emiliano Figueroa-Larrain as its envoy to the League of Nations. Figueroa-Larrain resigned only a month earlier due to ill health.	
Jun. 4		Romania's prince topples Alexandru Averescu's cabinet. The Stirbey government is expected to be friendlier to France....Greece seizes two deputies as Communists after disturbances at Salonika.	Syrian nationalists protest actions of the French mandatory government in suppressing a rising. The League replies that although the French should have not have used unsupervised auxiliaries and should have not used aerial bombing, overall the French suppression of the Syrian rising was not excessive.	Thousands line the streets as the body of Sra. Calles crosses into Mexico at Nogales. There she boards Porfirio Diaz' presidential train, the "Yellow Special," for her trip to Mexico City.	

A	B	C	D	E
Includes developments that affect more than one world region, international organizations and important meetings of world leaders.	*Includes all domestic and regional developments in Europe, including the Soviet Union.*	*Includes all domestic and regional developments in Africa and the Middle East.*	*Includes all domestic and regional developments in Latin America, the Caribbean, and Canada.*	*Includes all domestic and regional developments in Asian and Pacific nations (and colonies).*

U.S. Politics & Social Issues	U.S. Foreign Policy & Affairs, Defense	U.S. Economy & Environment	Science, Technology & Nature	Culture, Leisure & Lifestyle	
Young Women's Christian Association negotiations with Portland, OR, are at an impasse over segregation. The YWCA wants to hold its convention there but hoteliers refuse access to blacks.			As flood waters pour through Louisiana President Moton of Tuskegee heads a board to represent black interests before relief agencies. Herbert Hoover denies brutalities toward blacks in flood areas.	The American Society of Authors, Composers, and Publishers asks limits on broadcasts of music. ASCAP contends that the public quickly tires of hearing the same songs.	May 28
After dynamiting of the reservoir in the Owen Valley, Los Angeles sends sharpshooters to protect the Los Angeles Aqueduct. Owens Valley residents oppose the city's taking of their water and destruction of valley agriculture but also oppose saboteurs.	Armenian Americans protest the sending of Ambassador Joseph Grew to Turkey. The group contends that the United States recognizes Turkey in exchange for access to oil.			Mrs Edward W. Bok, daughter of publisher C.H.K. Curtis, donates $7 million to Philadelphia's Curtis Institute of Music, bringing the endowment to $12.5 million.	May 29
			With the floods receding everywhere except in lower Louisiana, attention turns to reconstruction. The flood-damaged area is estimated at 20,000 square miles.	The largest balloon race in U.S. history starts from Akron. 15 balloons are in the elimination race to determine the American entrant in September's international Gordon Bennett Cup. Storms quickly down most of the contenders.	May 30
The Supreme Court rules that the government can seize rumrunners, even outside the 12-mile limit.			Italy's Gabriele D'Annunzio sets a speedboat record of 78.9 mph. D'Annunzio is best remembered for seizing Fiume in 1919. He is also a poet, soldier, and flyer.	The 15th Indianapolis 500 draws a crowd of 100,000. George Souders in a Duesenberg leads a field of 33 and wins $30,000 of the $90,000 purse….A Boston court finds a clerk guilty of selling the immoral Oil.	May 31
While continuing his independent inquiry, governor A. Lawrence Lowell appoints a commission to conduct a complementary inquiry….The newly formed New York Anti-Third Term League includes former Bull Moosers, Democrats, and prominent Republicans. Speculation reads it as a campaign vehicle for, variously, Frank Lowden, Hiram Johnson, and Nicholas Longworth….In Tampa, 500 guardsmen contain rioters trying to lynch a confessed murderer of five. Three days of rioting produce four dead and 33 injured.	William Phillips, first Envoy Extraordinary and Minister Plenipotentiary from the United States to Canada, presents his credentials to Canadian Prime Minister William Mackenzie King. The United States has no legation because funds were tied up in a Senate filibuster.		As the waters recede in Louisiana, refugees begin returning.	Oxford men are fearful of a sex war now that the university has accepted women . The men want to set a ratio of women to men at one to four and limit female enrollment to 840.	Jun. 1
A ship's steward on the British steamship Lukin, details a smuggling ring. On trial in Philadelphia, he says 35,000 to 40,000 Russians are in Cuba awaiting the chance to circumvent U.S. immigration quotas.			Six scientists receive the John Scott Bronze Medal for inventions useful to humanity. Winners contribute to television technology, snakebite remedies, and other advancements. The prize dates to 1816.	Charlie Chaplin counters his wife's charges by charging misconduct, heavy drinking, and child neglect. He also says his income is $162,000…. Lizzie Borden dies, 33 years after being found not guilty of murdering her father and stepmother. The case is yet unsolved.	Jun. 2
Concluding a convention Caribbean cruise, homeopaths decry "socialization" of medicine. The American Institute of Homeopathy's 83rd convention resolves against medicine by large insurance companies and corporations.		Flood waters recede in the Mississippi Delta. Farmers resume planting in order to produce a cotton crop this year.	Louis B. Miller travels cross country by auto in 80 hours. He breaks his own record by three hours and immediately begins the drive back.	The United States leads Britain 3–1 in Ryder Cup golf. The gate is $8,000 with a crowd of 4,000.	Jun. 3
Evangelist Gypsy Pat Smith enters a Connecticut sanitarium recovering from a drug overdose. Smith cites an old war wound and an overdose of pneumonia medicine as causing his collapse….Governor Clifford Walker of Georgia professes skepticism but promises to investigate charges that W.R. King holds 50 black men in peonage under guard by 25 whites. James Felton of Virginia says he was shanghaied 18 months earlier after his car broke down. King faces a separate trial for holding both blacks and whites in peonage.	General Smedley Butler is en route to Peking. The United States will de facto recognize the nationalist government once it takes the northern capital, which will give it control of virtually all of China.	Dr. H.C. Taylor of Northwestern University reports that for the past five years farmers have received only 10 percent of U.S. income. Before the war, farmers got 20.5 percent.	In Berlin, Clarence Chamberlin is expected to receive a huge welcome because his flight is read as ending Germany's isolation. As the Bellanca flies over Newfoundland, Charles Lindbergh sails for the United States.	Helen Wills wins the North London tennis title handily. In beating Elizabeth Ryan 6–2, 6–2, Wills shows the form that made her U.S. champion. She has been allowing lesser opponents to take 4–6 games. Now she seems set for Wimbledon.	Jun. 4

F	G	H	I	J
Includes campaigns, elections, federal-state relations, civil rights and liberties, crime, the judiciary, education, healthcare, poverty, urban affairs, and population.	Includes formation and debate of U.S. foreign and defense policies, veterans affairs, and defense spending. (Relations with specific foreign countries are usually found under the region concerned.)	Includes business, labor, agriculture, taxation, transportation, consumer affairs, monetary and fiscal policy, natural resources, pollution and industrial accidents.	Includes worldwide scientific, medical and technological developments, natural phenomena, U.S. weather and natural disasters.	Includes the arts, religion, scholarship, communications media, sports, entertainment, fashions, fads, and social life.

	World Affairs	Europe	Africa & The Middle East	The Americas	Asia & The Pacific
Jun. 5		The English are displeased at French purchases of English gold without notifying the Bank of England. They see the stabilization of the franc coming at their expense.	Egypt reiterates that it will not have British command of its army. The expectation is that Britain will issue a strong note, leading to the fall of the Egyptian cabinet and the end of constitutional government.		China's anti-Communist groups begin discussions about joining forces against the Hankow reds. The end of the war is in sight.
Jun. 6		In Leningrad, the Unified State Political Administration (OGPU) executes workers for sending threatening letters. There are no trials.			
Jun. 7	In Paris, in light of the increased cordiality generated by the Charles Lindbergh flight, Minister Aristide Briand raises the matter of a treaty outlawing war. Ambassador Myron Herrick notifies Secretary Frank B. Kellogg.	The British Labour Party and commercial cooperatives of the Cooperative Union combine to create a five-million-person organization. British coops generate $1.5 billion annually.	The Persian minister to the United States says that Persian artists are returning to traditional designs. By trying to satisfy the western market, they lost their way.	Experts predict a bumper crop of Canadian wheat.	The lull in the Chinese war raises expectations of a stalemate, with the rivals producing a compromise peace. Japan halts troop movements.
Jun. 8	Britain announces that its participants at the Naval talks will include representatives from all dominions and India. After New Zealand unilaterally announces attendance, the other commonwealth nations—Canada, Irish Free State, Australia, and South Africa—follow suit. India is a diarchy, ruled by theoretically equal British and Indian governments.	Poland accepts Russia's demand for participation in the investigation of the murder of the Russian minister by a White Russian student in Warsaw. Poland is prepared to indemnify the family and has apologized, so there is no break in relations as occurred earlier when royalists killed the Russian envoy to Switzerland.		Three months after courts award the 110,000-square-mile Atlantic watershed to Newfoundland over Canada, International Paper offers $2.00 a mile for 10,000 square miles. Citing the depression in paper, the company wants the government to hold the entire 110,000 miles for five years. It also wants other concessions. Newfoundlanders are not amused.	
Jun. 9		Irish Free State elections are quiet, with heavy participation by women. Many former unionists vote for the first time. Proportional voting slows returns....Anarchist Gino Lucetti admits he attempted to assassinate Benito Mussolini on September 11, 1926. He attempts to clear his codefendants, saying he worked alone. Lucetti gets 30 years; they get 20 and 18.			Three days of Royal Air Force bombing in northwest India kills 50 invading rebels attacking Fort Shabkadr. The Mohmand sector has experienced unrest for several months after Kakir Sahib, the Stormy Petrel, declares jihad.
Jun. 10		Russia says the OGPU executed 20 in response to anti-red attacks and Britain is at fault. Germany says the killings are brutal and promises to help anti-red Russians.			
Jun. 11		The Irish Free State returns show the government failing. Greater success comes to Eamon De Valera's Fianna Fail and Captain Redmond's nationalist National League. In Paris, clashes occur among monarchists, Communists, and police as Leon Daudet, royalist writer, barricades his office and refuses to surrender. Daudet was convicted of libel for reporting that French police killed his father, Philippe, in 1923.	Amin Habib Kishmany, secretary to King Feisal of Syria, reports that Iraq is the safest and most modern of the Arab countries. It has a severe need for educational facilities and irrigation....A former South African planter warns the British Empire Service League of revived German imperialism. He sees Germany trying to reestablish influence in British-mandate Tanganyika. For each British settler there, 10 Germans come.	Argentina's president contracts with France for regular air/sea mail service. 20 percent by ship, the service covers the 1400 miles in 11 ½ days.	Australia's remote regions have a dearth of schools. Many rely for their education on correspondence courses.

A	B	C	D	E
Includes developments that affect more than one world region, international organizations and important meetings of world leaders.	*Includes all domestic and regional developments in Europe, including the Soviet Union.*	*Includes all domestic and regional developments in Africa and the Middle East.*	*Includes all domestic and regional developments in Latin America, the Caribbean, and Canada.*	*Includes all domestic and regional developments in Asian and Pacific nations (and colonies).*

U.S. Politics & Social Issues	U.S. Foreign Policy & Affairs, Defense	U.S. Economy & Environment	Science, Technology & Nature	Culture, Leisure & Lifestyle	
The Owens Valley war escalates after the fifth dynamiting. Farmers establish a 35-person armed force to counter a contingent of Los Angeles deputies.		Irate farmers dynamite the Los Angeles aqueduct for the third time in two weeks. The first two times were back-to-back on May 27 and 28.	Clarence Chamberlin lands 110 miles past Berlin, setting a new distance record, exceeding Charles Lindbergh by 295 miles. The flight takes 46.5 hours....Although flood waters are still rising in east Atchafalaya parishes, the flood surge is in the Gulf of Mexico.		Jun. 5
		The Seminole Oil Field sets a single day record of 374,000 barrels. The increase came from the Bowlegs district. Other districts in the field decreased.	RCA's new radios no longer require batteries. They operate on household electricity. They also feature improved speakers.	In Chicago, professional wrestler Demetral testifies that in 1924 he had to put up $5,000 and his house deed as trust that he would not throw a rival. Professional wrestling is rigged and operated by a trust. Legislators threaten to repeal the legalization of the sport.	Jun. 6
		The national daily output of 2,507,300 barrels is a new record. Seal Beach, California's increase of 10,000 barrels is mostly responsible....National building permits for the first five months are down 9 percent from last year. Total value is $1.15 billion. The 1926 amount was $1.27 billion....Average residential use of electricity in 1926 rose to 400 hours from 365 hours in 1925. Bills average $29.24 for the year.	A French mail carrier near Avignon demonstrates a model of an airplane that runs on compressed air. The plane also has vertical take off capability and wings that convert to parachutes....Two British flyers who failed to reach India non-stop return unnoticed. Lieutenants Carr and Gillman flew 3,400 miles before aborting their effort.	Greece asks England to return a caryatid and column of the Erechtheum. There is no expectation that Britain will return the Elgin Marbles. The British response is that it intends to keep the purchase intact.	Jun. 7
After hearing nearly 50 witnesses in the King peonage case, a Georgia jury finds the prominent doctor/landowner not guilty. James Felton recants his charge that King shanghaied him.		The stock exchange sets a record of 15 consecutive 2-million-share days. Total shares this year are a record 240 million, almost 50 million above the same time in 1926.		"Miss Universe" returns in triumph to New Jersey. Dorothy Britton of Jersey City recently won the title in Galveston, TX. The Galveston "International Pulchritude Pageant" started in 1920 and was one of the largest during the 1920s heyday of beauty contests. Britton is in Earl Carroll's Vanities in 1928, 1929, and 1930.	Jun. 8
			An additional 14 stations hook up to the network to broadcast the Charles Lindbergh welcome. With a total of 51 stations, it is the largest network to this time. The national hookup requires 12,000 miles of wire.		Jun. 9
A Maryland woman wins the Women's National Democratic Club contest for the 1928 Democratic slogan. "With eight years of Wall Street, now give Main Street a chance" earns her an etching of Woodrow Wilson's tomb and a poem by former Federal Trade Commissioner Huston Thompson....David Gordon begins serving an 18 month sentence in the New York City Reformatory. Gordon wrote an anti-American poem for the Daily Worker.	The court martial for negligence of Captain Franklin Karns of the Colorado, grounded on April 30, ends with no announcement. All guilty verdicts go to Washington, DC, for publication. The navigator's trial on the same negligence charge begins immediately.	Merchants in Harlem begin an advertising campaign. They anticipate that the opening of the Hudson River Bridge and the tri-borough bridge will make Harlem the commercial hub of three states.	General Electric presents findings on the use of neon lights to provide beacons for airmail flyers. The lights are better able to penetrate fog and are more distinct from city lights than the lamps currently in use.	22-year-old Helen Wills gains the final of the Kent Tourney by besting the American champion in 23 minutes. She earlier won over the South African champion in 20 minutes....Wimbledon begins a war on scalpers, who are asking $125 for $20 seats.	Jun. 10
Missouri escapes an effort by 150 inmates to blow a wall in the Jefferson City penitentiary and raid the city. A mother's plea convinces one of them to turn in his nitroglycerin and detail the plot.	Marines receive orders to leave Nicaragua. The first contingent leaves on 17 June. One squadron of airplanes will leave also. In July, Augusto Sandino, who was not invited to the liberal-conservative peace talks, will resume his guerrilla war.	The Consolidated Iron Works, birthplace of the Civil War Monitor, are no more. After a merger, its facilities are dismantled. At its end, the former shipbuilder is manufacturing gasworks.		The welcome home for Chalres Lindbergh begins when a flight of 65 army, navy, and airmail planes fly over his ship as it approaches Washington, DC. Record-shattering crowds of 300,000 turn out to welcome him....Helen Wills wins the Kent championship easily. Recovered from 1926's appendicitis, she seems the favorite for Wimbledon.	Jun. 11

	World Affairs	Europe	Africa & The Middle East	The Americas	Asia & The Pacific
Jun. 12	Gold is leaving London in amounts greater than France is taking. The Bank of England is becoming not only the guarantor of England's position but of other nations returning to the gold standard as well.	In an election seen as a test for 1928, defeating a Communist in the Aube takes a coalition of all other parties, including radicals and Socialists. Observers read a large French agricultural vote for Communists as a sign of discontent, not support for Communism.			
Jun. 13		Leon Daudet surrenders. Surrounded by police, firefighters, house and foot guards, he receives assurances of military honors, sends his army of 980 supporters out, and heads off to serve his five months....In Irish elections, the government has a narrow two-seat lead over Fianna Fail. Although this is a technical majority, coalition is probable.			Chang is headed for Mukden. His forces are in a sustained retreat as Chiang Kai-shek's forces take city after city.
Jun. 14	At the quarterly League of Nations Council meeting, Germany's Gustav Stresemann offers to ease demands for evacuation of the Rhineland in return for a German seat on the League mandates council. Aristide Briand unofficially indicates that France might be willing to reduce its Rhineland force if Germany agrees to inspections of fortifications.	In Ireland the government lead over Eamon de Valera is one seat with six seats undecided. The prospect of no majority is greater. Minority parties will decide the government.... Foreigners are leaving Moscow as executions pass 100 and women are training for the military. Also, thousands are sent to Siberia and 300,000 reservists are called up in the Ukraine.		A rising in Chihuahua City targets the local government. The rebels are of the Defensa Sociales. Government troops reportedly have them on the run.	In Shantung, the local forces fade away as Chiang Kai-shek approaches. The remaining defenders are White Russians.
Jun. 15		The final Irish tally gives W.T. Cosgrave's government 47 seats, Fianna Fail 44, and Labor 22. According to rule, Eamon de Valera's party and the six Sinn Fein will not take their seats because the members refuse to take the oath to the king. The total Dail has 153 seats, so Cosgrave will be without a majority even in the reduced body.			Japan is preparing for the naval conference with an open mind. The only firm Japanese demand is that there be no disparity in auxiliary ships.
Jun. 16		The light 15-year sentence of the Polish slayer of Russia's envoy angers Russia, which sees Britain's hand in it. Britain asks Germany to allow its troops to cross German soil to defend Poland if necessary. Britain also warns Italy not to create trouble in the Balkans.	Egyptian Premier Sarwat Pasha reveals that the Anglo-Egyptian crisis has passed after Egypt accepts the status quo. King Fuad can now visit England in July as previously planned.	Winnipeg captures, loses, and recaptures "the gorilla man." Virgil Wilson, a.k.a. Earl Nelson, is believed to have killed two Winnipeg women in the past week and as many as 20 Canadian and American women and children overall.	Chiang Kai-shek asks Americans to return, promising to safeguard them. He also announces that he will send an emissary to the United States seeking recognition.
Jun. 17	A fruitless League Council session ends with J. Austen Chamberlain and Gustav Stresemann exchanging charges about war materiel. Attendees are uneasy over the Polish-Russian friction.	Britain indicates it will maintain restrictions on rubber output despite the fall in prices. British producers are complaining of markets lost to the Dutch, and Americans are spreading rumors that the controls are about to end....Opposition parties propose backing W.T. Cosgrave despite his refusal to compromise.		Canada outlaws the third degree. The Supreme Court orders a new trial for Joseph Sankey, illiterate B.C. Indian, who signed a confession only on the fourth attempt, apparently under duress....Cuban President Gerardo Machado extends limits on sugar production to July 1928. Controls were instituted in 1926 after a glut dropped prices below costs.	The northerners pool their armies and make Chang Tso Lin dictator. A military regime will conduct a die-hard resistance in Shantung after peace talks with Chiang Kai-shek fail.
Jun. 18		Former Albanian premier Fan Noli calls for a Balkan federation of soviets. He says it is the only way to avoid Albania's falling under Italian domination. Bishop Noli was ousted by Albanian Muslims under Ahmed Zog in 1924.	Egypt announces that King Faud's visit to England on July 4 will mark the beginning of discussions of Egypt's status. Greater domestic autonomy for Egypt and guarantees of the Suez Canal are expected to result.	Federal agents in California capture two truckloads of arms intended for Mexico. At Santa Barbara they seize automatic pistols, rifles, machine guns, ammunition, and medical supplies valued at $50,000.	

A	B	C	D	E
Includes developments that affect more than one world region, international organizations and important meetings of world leaders.	*Includes all domestic and regional developments in Europe, including the Soviet Union.*	*Includes all domestic and regional developments in Africa and the Middle East.*	*Includes all domestic and regional developments in Latin America, the Caribbean, and Canada.*	*Includes all domestic and regional developments in Asian and Pacific nations (and colonies).*

U.S. Politics & Social Issues	U.S. Foreign Policy & Affairs, Defense	U.S. Economy & Environment	Science, Technology & Nature	Culture, Leisure & Lifestyle	
Seven thousand New England Klansmen swear opposition to Al Smith. At Springfield, MA, the Klansmen (and women) also swear opposition to the Pope and Catholicism....The Baptist Bible Union acquires Des Moines College. The fundamentalists take over and remove Modernists.	S. Parker Gilbert, administer of Dawes reparations, criticizes Germany. Gilbert says that Germany's problem is not lack of resources but excessive expenditures.			Upton Sinclair speaks before a crowd of 2,000 in defense of *Oil*. He challenges police to arrest him for speaking without a permit. They decline.	Jun. 12
The Calvin Coolidges leave the temporary White House for the new summer retreat in the Black Hills of South Dakota. They will be there for three months. The selection of the new vacation site took months of politicking....In Mississippi, a mob burns two blacks accused of murder. The sheriff is unable to protect the men.				As the Bellanca flyers receive a welcome in Baden Baden, Charles Lindbergh arrives in New York City. Four million line the streets to welcome him.	Jun. 13
On the 150th anniversary of adoption of the stars and stripes, the United States celebrates Flag Day with the first-ever vesper service in Washington, DC. Not only does John Philip Sousa lead the Marine Corps band in "Stars and Stripes Forever," but there is also singing by a 1,000-person choir and an address on "The Religion of the Flag."...Governor Alvan Fuller begins reviewing the Bartolomeo Vanzetti file.				The National Open Golf Championship opens at Oakmont Country Club near Pittsburgh. This is the first golf event on which a large gambling syndicate makes book. Bobby Jones is favored.... Warner M. Williams gets six months in Boston's house of corrections for blasphemy. *The Great Secret of Freemasonry* allegedly refers to Jesus as immoral.	Jun. 14
		The U.S. treasury takes in a record $2.5 billion on quarterly settlement day. Among others, revenue comes from the sixty companies that distribute dividends, the $500 million in due taxes, and reparations payments.	The new frequency allocations go into effect. The changes involve 697 radio stations. Harsh penalties are promised for violators of the federal attempt to cut chaos and poor reception in radio....The Red Cross reports it is still tending to 300,000 flood refugees in camps. Relief agencies are feeding 250,000 animals; 600,000 more refugees will require rehabilitation.	Helen Wills is seeded first at Wimbledon. Bill Tilden is second to the French star Rene Lacoste.... Gertrude Ederle signs a movie contract with Paramount. Ederle is the first woman to swim the English Channel.	Jun. 15
Frank Lund, chair of the Iowa Lowden-for-President League, launches the ex-governor's presidential campaign on a drizzly day to a crowd of 3,000. Lund scores Calvin Coolidge's failed agricultural policy.		More than three fourth of the world's life insurance is owned by Americans. According to New York State Superintendent of Insurance James Baha, the United States has 250 life insurance companies with combined assets of $13 billion. Over 100 million Americans have $80 billion in insurance....As a precaution, the $40 million rubber pool is extended until 1928. Formed to protect auto and tire manufacturers from high rubber prices in 1926, it seems moot with prices depressed in 1927.	The *Isle de France*, flagship of the French line, is open for viewing. 1,000 visit the liner. The ship features a glass-enclosed promenade, shops, second class cabins comparable to other liners' first-class accommodations, and state of the art technology. The 43,000 ton, 720 foot, vessel moves smoothly at 23 knots.	Tommy Armour ties Harry Cooper on the final hole of the U.S. Open, forcing a playoff. Defending champion Jones is eight strokes back.... The Lindbergh parade in Brooklyn draws 700,000. While in New York, Charles Lindbergh takes in a Yankees game but just misses Babe Ruth's 22nd homer.	Jun. 16
	Controversial James Sheffield, earlier believed involved in an aborted U.S. plan to invade Mexico and establish a more conservative government, denies that he has been removed as ambassador to Mexico. Mexican speculation is that Henry Stimson will replace him. For now, Sheffield is on vacation.	The opening of a new well in the Seminole field shows that the pool is larger than thought. The discovery increases the surplus that is already plaguing U.S. oil producers.	Broadcasters report that listener mail is favorable. Although some interference remains because stations have not all made the proper adjustments, reception is vastly improved.	Tommy Armour beats Harry Cooper 76 to 79 in the playoff. Cooper also is bitten by a mole he attempts to move from his putting line. Armour wins $700, a silver cup, and a gold medal....The Anglo-American Conference on English forms a conference of 50 from each country. The purpose is to study Anglicisms and Americanisms as well as to resolve usage disputes.	Jun. 17
Al Smith's religion becomes an issue as foes revive what they interpret as his advocacy of state aid to parochial schools in 1915. Supporters clarify that the proposal allowed state aid to all denominations' schools. The proposal died in committee anyway.		Herbert Hoover estimates the cost of the flood at between $200 million and $400 million. Refugees are slowly returning to their devastated farms....The United States has 80 percent of the world's 27.65 million vehicles.	French medical authorities call for vaccination of all children with the Calmette vaccine against tuberculosis. Developed by the Louis Pasteur Institute, the vaccine reduces mortality from 26 percent to 1 percent. European physicians support the vaccine (as they do those for smallpox and the like), but the general population resists.	Printed chiffons come in a wide variety of patterns and colors and prove ideal for afternoon wear. For the more athletic, women's sportswear is available from American manufacturers as well as French couturiers. Only seven or eight years earlier, sportswomen had to play in street clothes.	Jun. 18

F	G	H	I	J
Includes campaigns, elections, federal-state relations, civil rights and liberties, crime, the judiciary, education, healthcare, poverty, urban affairs, and population.	Includes formation and debate of U.S. foreign and defense policies, veterans affairs, and defense spending. (Relations with specific foreign countries are usually found under the region concerned.)	Includes business, labor, agriculture, taxation, transportation, consumer affairs, monetary and fiscal policy, natural resources, pollution and industrial accidents.	Includes worldwide scientific, medical and technological developments, natural phenomena, U.S. weather and natural disasters.	Includes the arts, religion, scholarship, communications media, sports, entertainment, fashions, fads, and social life.

	World Affairs	Europe	Africa & The Middle East	The Americas	Asia & The Pacific
Jun. 19		Thousands of Dubliners march on the Dail in support of Eamon de Valera's stance against the king....Central European stock exchanges sag due to sell offs by German speculators. Compounding the difficulties are the entangling tariffs barriers....Turkey's Women's Union elects delegates to meet with Kemal Pasha and ask a constitutional amendment granting woman suffrage.			
Jun. 20	At the naval reduction conference, the United States proposes a 5:5:3 ratio for small ships. The U.S. will eliminate 140,000 tons to the British 60,000 and the Japanese 40,000. Britain wants to reopen the Washington Treaty to lengthen the lives of vessels and reduce more large ships. Japan wants no radical changes.	After protests by the Soviet legation, Copenhagen police prohibit the display of caricatures of nine prominent Bolsheviks. The drawings are by a former white officer whose son died at the hands of the reds.	A German team claims to have found Noah's Ark and Moses' tomb on Mount Neboh. A.F. Futterer of the Los Angeles Bible Institute backs the German claim. The Bible institute is a Fundamentalist school, and the somewhat eccentric Futterer is known as the "Golden Ark explorer."		
Jun. 21		Conservative peers indicate their acceptance of the proposal to reduce the size of the House of Lords by over 150 seats, proposed yesterday by the government. Labor opposes any act that retains hereditary privilege, while the Commons opposes the peers' suggestion that displaced Lords enter the Commons. Both Liberals and Labor oppose the proposal that reform require Lords approval.	Having settled the military crisis, Egypt's parliament begins working on the defense budget. It retains funding for the British inspector general and provides provisional funding for the Sudanese defense. The provisions are that Egypt does not recognize that Sudan is no longer Egyptian, does not relinquish claims against Sudan, and does not recognize any Sudanese claims on Egypt.	Salvador, Guatemala, and Honduras establish an Entente Cordiale. The agreement is in response to American actions in Nicaragua. Costa Rica, which also disapproves the U.S. action, remains independent.	Leonard Wood is in the United States to meet with Calvin Coolidge and step down as governor general of the Philippines after six years. Wood is ailing. Wood's term has seen constant agitation for independence, but Wood does not regard the Filipinos as ready for that step. Wood dies August 7.
Jun. 22	Japan is close to agreement with the U.S. naval reduction proposal. Britain is a stumbling block because its measurement methods differ from those of the United States.	War Minister Paul Painleve says the rising of reservists is insignificant. Of the 20,000 called up for training, only 250 men at three locations sang the Internationale or otherwise showed support for Communism.		A Montreal manufacturer offers to buy the Newfoundland lumber mill that is part of the International Paper proposal. The Canadian offer includes none of the concessions demanded by the American firm.	
Jun. 23	Germany's Gustav Stresemann tells the Reichstag that the League is doomed unless the nations of the world disarm.	Britain's lords vote *viva voce* for reform of their chamber. Labor and liberal opposition grows. The Commons passes a hotly contested anti-labor trades union bill after liberals abandon labor. Labour vows to fight on against the bill that outlaws strikes....W.T. Cosgrave forms a cabinet without Eamon de Valera's Fianna Fail, whose party is frozen out for refusing to take the oath to the king. Anticipated disturbances fail to materialize....Turkey announces that small mosques are too expensive to maintain and will become schools. Secular Turkey owns all religious facilities.		General Arnulfo Gomez is nominated for president against Alvaro Obregon, not yet a declared candidate. Gomez is a strong Catholic and speaks for absolute freedom of religion and press. Reportedly, other Catholics have warned the government not to act against Catholics taken in the recent rising against the state.	Hankow's generalissimo Feng joins the southern nationalists and orders his people to expel the Russian reds in their midst. The southerners are united in what they expect to be the final push to oust northern warlord Chang Tso Lin. Former missionary schools begin to reopen, many under Chinese direction.
Jun. 24	Britain agrees to delay discussions of capital ships. Talks on limits of smaller vessels move to a series of technical committees.	Two towns are buried in a 10-foot flood of lignite muck after a dam breaks. Lignite is pre-coal.		Three Mexican agrarian conventions declare for General Alvaro Obregon, who remains quiet on his intentions. The field already includes generals Francisco Serrano and Arnulfo Gomez, both running on separation of church and state and individual freedoms.	
Jun. 25		French Premier Raymond Poincare indicates his support for the Aristide Briand peace plan. He tells the American Club of Paris that Charles Lindbergh's flight smoothed the way.	The Persian Caravan Company purchases 15 caterpillar trucks to replace camels on the 600-mile Trebizon-Tabriz Trail from the Caspian Sea to Tehran. The route dates to the time of Xenophon. The trucks carry 33 tons while a camel load is 400 pounds. In addition, trucks travel 50 miles a day to the camels' 20.	Argentina's Sacco-Vanzetti parallel is the case of Eusebio Manasco. The labor leader is charged with murdering a plantation manager. Argentina's unions are protesting that Manasco is being railroaded for successfully organizing plantation workers.	With the Chinese civil war winding down, missionary work prepares to resume. Fundamentalists oppose modernist missionaries, labeling them reds who deceive the world.

A	B	C	D	E
Includes developments that affect more than one world region, international organizations and important meetings of world leaders.	*Includes all domestic and regional developments in Europe, including the Soviet Union.*	*Includes all domestic and regional developments in Africa and the Middle East.*	*Includes all domestic and regional developments in Latin America, the Caribbean, and Canada.*	*Includes all domestic and regional developments in Asian and Pacific nations (and colonies).*

U.S. Politics & Social Issues	U.S. Foreign Policy & Affairs, Defense	U.S. Economy & Environment	Science, Technology & Nature	Culture, Leisure & Lifestyle	
Another blast rocks the Los Angeles aqueduct. The Owens Valley war shows no signs of abating.... In eastern Kentucky a new sect, The Unknown Tongue, worships by dancing violently to banjo music.				American lexicographers report that aviator Charles Lindbergh's fame has risen to the point where the word "lindy," a verb, is now under consideration to be officially included in the nation's dictionaries.	Jun. 19
		Production in the Seminole field sets a new record as drillers find the pool is larger than previously thought.		First day sales of the Lindbergh stamp exceed 100,000.	Jun. 20
In Kansas, 328 convicts rise, demanding cigarettes and refusing to mine coal. The convict miners take guards hostage and barricade themselves 720 feet below ground. Above ground, 310 convicts riot and attack warders. Gunfire ends the aboveground riots.	The United States informs France that it is ready to begin discussions in Paris of Briand's peace proposal.	Bellanca switches from exploration to commerce, announcing that New York to Chicago air service with five planes will begin in four months. Each plane can carry 12 passengers on the 7 ½ hour trip. Service to Miami is projected for the future.... Oil production sets a new record above 2.5 million barrels a day thanks to the Seminole field.		In Broadway news, after three years in London, Fred and Adele Astaire return to New York. The brother and sister singing and dancing team announce plans to appear in a new musical in the fall. Mexican American actor Leo Carrillo says he will switch from *Lombardi, Ltd* to *The Brigand* in the fall.	Jun. 21
A third of New York's Calvary Baptist Church's deacons resign in protest of John Roach Straton's Pentecostalism. Straton previously sought a high-rise church and sponsored evangelists J. Frank Norris and Uldine Utley.		The Radio Corporation agrees to license its patents to other radio manufacturers. RCA gains $1.25 million in royalties and ends the current round of litigation in the highly litigious radio industry.	The National Committee for the Prevention of Blindness reports that blindness due to ophthalmia neonatorum (infant conjunctivitis) is down 51 percent since 1906.		Jun. 22
The New York Chamber of Commerce calls for the extension of immigration quotas to all areas of the western hemisphere as well as Europe. Quotas date to 1924.		After Paramount-Famous-Players-Lasky announces across the board 10-percent salary cuts on June 22, 15 other studios follow suit. The measure, designed to reassure bankers worried by weak movie profits, causes studio stocks to drop on Wall Street....The Seminole pool has over 500 producing wells with another 450 in progress. Oil is discovered in Arkansas.	The Rockefeller Institute's attorneys are looking into the use of the institute's name in ads for the I-On-A-Co belt. Gaylord Wilshire, inventor of the $58.50 belt, has previously been investigated for stock fraud and has had publications barred from the mails for left-leaning tendencies.	Jack Dempsey and Jack Sharkey sign a contract to fight at Yankee Stadium on July 21. Expected gate is $1.25 million. The winner gets a shot at Gene Tunney.	Jun. 23
Immigration quotas for the fiscal year ending June 30 are filled for 25 countries. Large quotas include 51,000 for Germany, 34,000 for Northern Ireland and Great Britain, and 28,000 for the Irish Free State. Among the smaller quotas filled are Danzig's 228 and many of those limited to 100 per year....The Kansas convict miners surrender.	The commander of Crissy Field, CA, refuses to open his base to Pacific flyers Ernest Smith and Charles Carter. The commander denies that his refusal is because the army is sponsoring a rival flight to Hawaii. Smith and Carter threaten to appeal to the war secretary.	Charles Lindbergh announces that he will be involved in some capacity with a new air passenger service. Partners will include the National Air Transport Service, some of his St. Louis backers, and others. ...Another oil field opens in Montana. Oil interests admit that the compact to restrict Seminole production has failed....Consumer complaints about insurance companies' ruling that tornado damage is not wind damage lead to a call for standardization.	The first night baseball game proves a success. Lynn and Salem of the New England League play, with Lynn winning under floodlights with an estimated 26.64 million candlepower. Observers from the Red Sox and Senators express support for major league experiments with lights....The Metric Society opens its annual meeting. Melvil Dewey says he has been an advocate for 61 years. He also says teaching metrics could reduce a child's education by two years.	A crowd of 90,000 watches Harvard beat Yale in crew for the first time since 1920. Over 1,000 yachts salute the 1-length victory.	Jun. 24
The Black Hills, new home of the summer White House, are also the old home of the Sioux. The Indians are preparing an $800 million suit against the United States for failure to pay as promised under an 1876 treaty.		Texas Governor Daniel Moody leads a delegation of over 100 to New York for a tour of Wall Street and other sights. The delegation seeks northern investment, and reportedly some New England textiles have shown interest in relocating to the low wage state from their depressed area.	The Rawson-McMillan-Field Museum expedition leaves Maine to explore Labrador and Greenland. The 12-person expedition, Donald McMillan's eleventh, includes three ships and will spend 15 months investigating Eskimo culture and collecting meteorological data for use in aviation.		Jun. 25

F	G	H	I	J
Includes campaigns, elections, federal-state relations, civil rights and liberties, crime, the judiciary, education, healthcare, poverty, urban affairs, and population.	Includes formation and debate of U.S. foreign and defense policies, veterans affairs, and defense spending. (Relations with specific foreign countries are usually found under the region concerned.)	Includes business, labor, agriculture, taxation, transportation, consumer affairs, monetary and fiscal policy, natural resources, pollution and industrial accidents.	Includes worldwide scientific, medical and technological developments, natural phenomena, U.S. weather and natural disasters.	Includes the arts, religion, scholarship, communications media, sports, entertainment, fashions, fads, and social life.

	World Affairs	Europe	Africa & The Middle East	The Americas	Asia & The Pacific
Jun. 26	After a week the naval conference has accomplished nothing. The British are due to announce their plan soon. Notably, all delegations are using the press to make their cases daily.	Dutch bankers note that John Maynard Keynes's economic theory fails in Britain. Keynes theorized deflation caused low prices that produced unemployment. In fact, prices are lowest since the war while unemployment is lowest since 1921….The Soviet Presidium again votes to oust Leon Trotsky and Grigory Zinoviev for deviation.		Prince Edward Island votes to stay dry. It is the first of the nine Canadian provinces not to modify prohibition. Nova Scotia has not yet voted.	The world radio web has another strand. The first shortwave radio link to the Philippines opens. RCA's rates are 75 cents a word for "live" transmission and half that for delayed transmission.
Jun. 27	Japan shifts its position and backs the British demand for reopening of the Washington Talks limits on capital ships. Amid rumors of a Japanese-British deal on China, the United States says there is no way to reopen talks with two of the original participants absent.			President Carlos Ibanez of Chile banishes additional congress members and newspaper people for radicalism. Chile also denies rumors of a coup attempt….American and Canadian Iroquois meet at the Mohawk's Caughnagawa Reserve in Canada to seek ways to regain their lost glory. The four-day pow-wow will address such matters as how to get the governments to honor treaty obligations and recognize native religions.	
Jun. 28	Both the Japanese and Americans scoff at the rumored Japanese-British deal. Frank B. Kellogg reiterates that the United States will not reopen the Washington limitation agreement for capital ships.	France votes to reduce the military term to one year. The plan is contingent on the maintenance of an active force of 106,000.			After meeting with General Leonard Wood, Calvin Coolidge expresses support for civilian rule of the Philippines. He would transfer governance to the Department of the Interior.
Jun. 29		Centrists in the Reichstag coalition desert Wlihelm Marx on the issue of payment to princes. When the law lapses, German princes can sue to regain estates lost as long ago as 1848.		Three more oil companies concede to the Mexican government. They accept 50-year concessions for lands obtained before 1917…. Generals Arnulfo Gomez and Francisco Serrano promise that each will back the other against the candidacy of former president Alvaro Obregon. Many army officers are resigning to join their campaigns. Labor remains aloof.	Filipinos indicate that Calvin Coolidge's proposal is insufficient. Although pleased at the switch from a military administration, they see insular status under Interior as a step to being a permanent territory….New Zealand's Chamber of Commerce protests inclusion of New Zealand in "Australasia." Australia is 1,200 miles away and the offending term conceals New Zealand's distinct identity.
Jun. 30	Britain backs off and the conferees agree to limit destroyers to 1,500 tons. Next on the agenda are submarines.	Russia distrusts Marshal Pilsudski, saying Polish talk of friendship is only a smokescreen. The Soviet Union sees an English hand behind Poland's actions.		Canada celebrates 60 years of confederation.	
Jul. 1	Although conferees agree on submarines, naval reduction talks appear at risk. The United States says it will end them if Britain asks for 600,000 tons of cruisers, double the U.S. limit.	The world's smallest passenger plane, arrives in London. Only 24 feet long with a wingspan of 33 feet, it reaches speeds of 75 mph. The market for the German-made plane is private users.		To undermine American influence, General Augusto Sandino's liberal rebels seize a gold mine in Nuevo Segovia, Nicaragua. The mine's owner asks the United States to protect his $700,000 investment…. Columbia Phonograph announces a 14-station network to debut on September 4. Led by New York's WOR, the Columbia Broadcasting System will broadcast east of the Rocky Mountains.	An Adelaide radio station has to reassure listeners after broadcasting an overly realistic program portraying south Australia under air attack. At least one family prepares to evacuate and a fire brigade is called out while hundreds of anxious listeners call the station. The panic is reminiscent of a January 17, 1926 BBC broadcast of fake news items.
Jul. 2	Conferees put aside the cruiser issue for a day as news of the French submarine proposal leak. The United States, Britain, and Japan oppose France's requirement of 115,000 tons, 25,000 tons over the limit.		A South African doctor proposes to teach western medicine to Africans. Citing the experience of the Dutch East Indies, the Johannesburg doctor says the native doctors can treat their own people and reduce the dependence on witchcraft.	Manitoba votes in favor of beer by the glass. The province also gives Progressives 30 of the 55 seats in the legislature. Conservatives hold 13 seats.	

A	B	C	D	E
Includes developments that affect more than one world region, international organizations and important meetings of world leaders.	Includes all domestic and regional developments in Europe, including the Soviet Union.	Includes all domestic and regional developments in Africa and the Middle East.	Includes all domestic and regional developments in Latin America, the Caribbean, and Canada.	Includes all domestic and regional developments in Asian and Pacific nations (and colonies).

U.S. Politics & Social Issues	U.S. Foreign Policy & Affairs, Defense	U.S. Economy & Environment	Science, Technology & Nature	Culture, Leisure & Lifestyle	
		A report reveals that 207 Americans made over $1 million in 1925. New York is home to 96, more than the 75 total in the United States in 1924.	There are 4,000 airports in the United States. California has 100, with Texas next at 84. Seven of Chicago's 15 are city-owned. New York City has no municipal airport.	An American firm offers a $10,000 prize for a composer able to finish Schubert's unfinished symphony. Schubert was born in 1828.	Jun. 26
Former Oklahoma Senator and current president of the National Popular Government league Robert Owen defends the direct primary system. He counters Vice President Charles Dawes, who prefers to return to conventions, with machine politics and smoke-filled rooms.... Calvin Coolidge's tentative Indian nickname is "sullen warrior." The choice is in preparation for his induction into the Sioux tribe during the 1876 Deadwood celebration.				Helen Wills turns down a $210,000 movie offer and an offer of $100,000 to turn pro. Wills is 16.	Jun. 27
	Goodyear wins an army contract to build a dirigible capable of carrying and launching five army planes. With a capacity of 6.5 million cubic feet, the balloon will be nearly twice the size of the largest German balloon and much larger than the 5 million cubic footers the British are building.	The Seminole field sets another record, topping 418,000 barrels in 24 hours.	Professor Zoeller of Paris announces that tests show the efficacy of nasal inoculation for diphtheria and other diseases....After weeks of delay due to weather, Admiral Richard Byrd begins his flight across the Atlantic to Paris. His plane carries the first official American airmail to Europe. American and Canadian radio will track his flight.	Eleanor Holm breaks the 150-yard medley swim mark. Holm is 13 years old....Bill Tilden says he would not turn pro for $1 million—at least not right now.	Jun. 28
Governor Alvan Fuller gives Nicola Sacco and Bartolomeo Vanzetti a stay from July 10 to August 10 to finish reviewing 7,000 pages of evidence and interviewing 200 witnesses. He also postpones the execution of Celestino Madeiros, who has sworn that the Cherry Hill Gang committed the hold up and murders....In the Toms River case, the New Jersey Supreme Court bans classification based on race or nationality and orders the district to return black students to the schools that barred them.		A survey reveals that 84 percent of American urban homes have bathtubs, 96 percent have electricity, and 40 percent have automobiles. Half have no charge accounts and 16 percent have stocks. Only 11 percent have full time servants. Zanesville, OH, is the average city.	A team of army flyers arrives in Hawaii after a 26-hour flight from San Francisco. Rival planes dropped out before the flight....A solar eclipse is visible clearly in Germany and Sweden. The French, British, and Norwegian views are less spectacular.	Young Lou Gehrig hits his 24th homer, tying him with veteran Babe Ruth for the league leadership.	Jun. 29
Carrie Chapman Catt assails the Daughters of the American Revolution's "The Common Enemy." The pamphlet calls liberal women's and peace groups and leaders such as Jane Addams Communists.	The navy orders 54 planes from Martin. It holds an option on 96 more.	Stock market trading in June sets a record, as does trading for the first half of the year. Volume is 47.6 million shares, up 9.6 million from June 1926. Year-to-date volume is 271.3 million, up 52.6 million over 1926.	Richard Byrd's plane falls into the sea 120 miles from Paris. All aboard are safe....A Danish flyer parachutes safely after vibration at 400 mph destroys his Fokker.	Manhattan Mary and the Ziegfeld Follies" attract 1,000 chorus girls to their casting calls....Babe Ruth and Lou Gehrig each hit number 25....At Wimbledon, Bill Tilden falls. Helen Wills remains in the hunt for the championship.	Jun. 30
At a Queens, NY, meeting of the united Protestant Alliance, 3,000 members hear various Klan speakers. Also, Senator J. Thomas Heflin of Alabama tells the predominantly Klan audience that Al Smith cannot win because American protestants will not allow a Catholic president.		Sears Roebuck and Montgomery Ward report June sales up from the same month in 1926. Sears sales for the first half of the year are up $129.72 million from $126.6 million. Wards six-month total is $92.23 million, down from $93.21 million.	After ditching, Richard Byrd and his crew ride their raft the 120 yards to French soil. Despite falling slightly short, he and his crew become the first to cross the Atlantic in a multi-engine passenger-carrying airplane.	Lou Gehrig hits homer 26, taking the lead from Babe Ruth. This is the first time since 1922 that Ruth has been behind in home runs at this stage of the season.... As the Chaplin divorce case begins, Mrs. Chaplin denies infidelity while charging that Charlie Chaplin was unfaithful. She says Chaplin encouraged her to drink and smoke.	Jul. 1
		The Chicago Motor Club challenges the new Illinois gasoline tax in court. The club claims the tax unfairly exempts kerosene, a common motor fuel, and has other legal flaws.	Basking in triumph at Paris, Richard Byrd announces he will fly over the South Pole from New Zealand. He anticipates landing between South America or South Africa after a 2,000-mile flight.	Helen Wills beats Lili Alvarez in two sets, 6–2, 6–4. She is the first American woman in 20 years to win the tennis title at Wimbledon.	Jul. 2

F	G	H	I	J
Includes campaigns, elections, federal-state relations, civil rights and liberties, crime, the judiciary, education, healthcare, poverty, urban affairs, and population.	Includes formation and debate of U.S. foreign and defense policies, veterans affairs, and defense spending. (Relations with specific foreign countries are usually found under the region concerned.)	Includes business, labor, agriculture, taxation, transportation, consumer affairs, monetary and fiscal policy, natural resources, pollution and industrial accidents.	Includes worldwide scientific, medical and technological developments, natural phenomena, U.S. weather and natural disasters.	Includes the arts, religion, scholarship, communications media, sports, entertainment, fashions, fads, and social life.

	World Affairs	Europe	Africa & The Middle East	The Americas	Asia & The Pacific
Jul. 3		Yugoslavia backs away from its hard line over Tirana. Yugoslavia and Albania resolve their Tirana dispute amicably....Rumor holds that Constantinople will become Mustafa Kemal to celebrate the arrival of Kemal Pasha. The city has been Constantinople for 16 centuries.	Spanish forces in Morocco take Bad Taza, killing 50 and capturing 100 men and 1,000 cattle. Forces in Yebala and Gomera have met, forming a continuous front against the rebels.	Deportations of those opposed to President Carlos Ibanez continue. Protest by the Chamber of Deputies over loss of freedom stops some of the deportations. Tight censorship remains in effect....Mexico's Anti-Imperialist League calls a July 4 rally. Posters contrast 1776 with 1927.	
Jul. 4	After the American delegate indicates the United States can build more cruisers than the British, the British back down from 600,000 tons to 460,000. The United States offers 350,000 tons. Compromise seems likely.	Romania's former premier is accused of raiding the treasury on his final day for his own benefit. On his last day in office, he pays the coming year's salaries and other items totaling 12 billion lei. The lei is 1/160 of a dollar....King Fuad of Egypt arrives in London. Welcoming him are cheering crowds, the king, and the Prince of Wales.	Egypt is becoming a major cotton producer. The boll weevil follows the crop. The government is trying to destroy the pest on Lower Egypt's plantations.		
Jul. 5	The American cruiser compromise, which seems a final offer, is 400,000 tons. Japan backs it. The British delegate cites war damage to support his case for a larger tonnage.... In China, the future of the China Eastern Railroad generates tensions among the United States, England, Japan and Russia.			In Mexico, police break up a rally by 2,000 for Nicola Sacco and Bartoloemo Vanzetti....In Mexico City, a widow and her four children accidentally eat marijuana they collect with other herbs and vegetables for their supper. The mother is insane and the children are doomed to die, say doctors.	The Indian government considers censoring American movies for undermining morality. A Delhi crowd riots after a theater operator refuses to cease showing "Moon of Israel," which portrays Egyptian brutality toward Israelites. The audience takes it as a religious insult.
Jul. 6	The cruiser limit falls to 250,000 tons as the Japanese offer their solution. The British are stunned and regard the number as impossible.	The Anglican Church Assembly approves allowing use of either the new or the old Book of Prayer. Diehards predict the loosening of church ritual will provoke schism in the church....The U.S. embassy in Rome gets an official to handle the immigration quota under the new law.			
Jul. 7	The United States makes a new cruiser offer. Japan reopens the submarine issue. The conference is hanging in the balance....International bankers indicate that they will meet in August to get France back on the gold standard.	Italian fascists number over a million, including 960,000 men and 70,000 women. The greatest percentage is in Tuscany, but Lombardy has the greatest total. Membership is now closed to all but those who rise through the youth organizations.		Mexico denies that its disapproval of Transcontinental's drilling permits means that it's taking the company's drilling rights. That and other permit problems are tied to the litigation still in Mexican courts. Also, Mexican production is down because the American companies have ample supplies in the United States and elsewhere in Latin America. Low prices depress metal mining too.	Japan says it will defend Manchuria. It backs the moderates and will recognize any unified government, northern or southern.
Jul. 8					Northern forces retake Hanchwang, a key railroad center.

A	B	C	D	E
Includes developments that affect more than one world region, international organizations and important meetings of world leaders.	*Includes all domestic and regional developments in Europe, including the Soviet Union.*	*Includes all domestic and regional developments in Africa and the Middle East.*	*Includes all domestic and regional developments in Latin America, the Caribbean, and Canada.*	*Includes all domestic and regional developments in Asian and Pacific nations (and colonies).*

U.S. Politics & Social Issues	U.S. Foreign Policy & Affairs, Defense	U.S. Economy & Environment	Science, Technology & Nature	Culture, Leisure & Lifestyle	
20,000 protesters march in Philadelphia, demanding the release of Nicola Sacco and Bartolomeo Vanzetti. Protest organizers promise a turnout of 50,000 in New York on July 7....The American Federation of Labor calls for a world union to counter business' cartels....A delegation of The Women's Party vows to meet Calvin Coolidge and demand an equal rights amendment.		The Industrial Board reports that the United States has built a million miles of road since 1904. With annual expenditures of $1.5 billion, roads are the third largest public expense after schools and defense. Only 17 percent of the United States' 2.1 million miles of road is improved (surfaced, widened, straightened.)			Jul. 3
	In the most heroic exploit to date in the war on alcohol, Ensign Charles L. Duke of the Coast Guard single-handedly captures a rumrunner crewed by 22 Nova Scotians. The ensign knocks out a seaman, seizes the wheel, and runs the craft to ground. Then he holds the crew at gunpoint until help arrives.	The industrial workforce has decreased 11 percent since 1923, an average loss of 2 3/8 percent a year. Total payroll has declined less than 5 percent. The Labor Bureau does not know where the unemployed went—perhaps to casual labor, farms, public works, or unskilled labor.		Calvin Coolidge celebrates the 4th of July and his 55th birthday by dressing up in full cowboy regalia. He declines to mount a horse.	Jul. 4
Clarence Darrow offers to help the Association Opposed to Blue Laws fight a ruling against Sunday baseball in Pennsylvania....The National Education Association condemns states that bar teaching of evolution. It elects its first-ever classroom teacher as president, Cecilia Adair.		Chase National Bank reaches $1 billion in assets. It is the second U.S. bank to do so. National City Bank has $1.5 billion in assets.	A French inventor unveils his rudderless, dual-hulled, five-person torpedo boat. Built on hydroplane principles, it has a top speed of 40 knots. He plans a trans-Atlantic demonstration in mid August.... Missouri authorities take movies of bootleggers moving their goods.	Calvin Coolidge attends Old Frontier Days, a combined rodeo and Indian celebration. The Anti-Rodeo League protests.	Jul. 5
Illinois adopts the electric chair and prepares to install chairs at Joliet, Menard, and Chicago. Those awaiting death under previous sentences of execution by hanging will still be executed as prescribed....At Sugar Notch, PA, 800 miners strike. Layoffs hit 2,000. Ohio mine owners notify union miners the mines will reopen on July 15 with or without them. Operators offer $5 a day, the 1917 scale.	A subcommittee of the House Appropriations Committee visits Ellis Island, finding the food satisfactory and the facility solid. Members indicate that they are more concerned about smuggling from Canada and Mexico, the tens of thousands waiting in Cuba, and 150,000 convicts awaiting deportation when their sentences end.	An appeals court orders Albert Fall and Edward Doheny Jr to stand trial for accepting a $100,000 bribe. The court orders Edward Doheny, Sr. to stand trial for offering the bribe. The case, which arose during the Harding administration, previously ended when a jury found no conspiracy, just a legitimate loan....In the forgotten flood areas, farmers face a bleak winter with no crops and possible starvation.	The success of the Atlantic and Pacific flights spurs interest in civil aviation. The Commerce Department has over 2,000 pilot license applications as well as 1,500 applications for planes and 1,900 for mechanics.	A Boston judge finds a Framingham human fly's flagpole sitting endangers traffic. For spending two days 14 stories up, Frank Holl receives a $25 fine.	Jul. 6
Henry Ford orders the *Dearborn Independent* to stop its anti-Semitic attacks....The rally for Nicola Sacco and Bartolomeo Vanzetti in New York's Union Square ends in a riot. Six "reds" are arrested as the rally of 10,000 breaks up.	Ambassador Herrick and Secretary Frank B. Kellogg discuss the Briand peace treaty before presenting their assessment to Calvin Coolidge.	Five railroads consider having airline subsidiaries to provide enhanced passenger service. With fixed airmail routes due within a year and American Express linking to an airline, passenger service is inevitable.	After long dormancy, Kilauea erupts gloriously. Hawaiians offer berries and other items to Pele, the fire goddess.		Jul. 7
The Jewish community accepts Ford's apology for anti-Semitism in his newspaper. Aaron Sapiro indicates that he and Henry Ford are working on a settlement of his libel case against Ford....Ohio miners reject the owners' ultimatum about reopening on July 15 regardless. In Pennsylvania's anthracite fields, a mine foreman is injured by a blast at his home.	Ambassador James Sheffield resigns. His tenure in Mexico is marked by controversy and conflict with the Calles regime.	The Federal Power Commission approves construction of a dam in South Carolina. At 11 million cubic feet, the dam will be the largest in the world in cubic content. It will be 1½ miles long, 200 feet high, and create a lake 30 miles long and 14 miles wide. It will generate 200,000 horsepower, more than Muscle Shoals.		Ban Johnson, after 34 years in baseball, resigns as president of the American League. Johnson began in the Western League in 1893 and formed the American League in 1900.	Jul. 8

F	G	H	I	J
Includes campaigns, elections, federal-state relations, civil rights and liberties, crime, the judiciary, education, healthcare, poverty, urban affairs, and population.	Includes formation and debate of U.S. foreign and defense policies, veterans affairs, and defense spending. (Relations with specific foreign countries are usually found under the region concerned.)	Includes business, labor, agriculture, taxation, transportation, consumer affairs, monetary and fiscal policy, natural resources, pollution and industrial accidents.	Includes worldwide scientific, medical and technological developments, natural phenomena, U.S. weather and natural disasters.	Includes the arts, religion, scholarship, communications media, sports, entertainment, fashions, fads, and social life.

	World Affairs	Europe	Africa & The Middle East	The Americas	Asia & The Pacific
Jul. 9	Frank B. Kellogg rejects the British cruiser plan. He says any total above 400,000 is useless.	Belgium's chamber of deputies backs Foreign Minister Emile Vandervelde in his long-running dispute with Italy's Benito Mussolini. Italy has withdrawn its ambassador in protest of Vandervelde's outspoken anti-fascism.	Native troops under Ketama surrender to French forces. Thus ends the rising in Spanish Morocco, which has simmered since the surrender of the Rif chief, Abd-el-Krim.	Argentinians riot over their national anthem. Ten thousand protestors appear at the presidential palace to indicate their displeasure with the new anthem. When they perceive a presidential slight, they battle firemen and police, with 21 injured demonstrators....Mexico City bars burros from its streets other than early in the morning or late at night. The animals impede traffic.	
Jul. 10	The YMCA campfire in Great Britain, attended by representatives of 21 nations, ends. Hosted by King George on his Windsor estate, the 150 boys discuss peace, share sports, and live in tents, each housing a dozen nationalities....The British at Geneva seek a delay, perhaps a compromise, rather than failure of naval talks.	Three assassins kill Ireland's Vice president Kevin O'Higgins. En route to mass without an escort, he takes seven bullets but lingers for hours before succumbing. A strong opponent of Eamon de Valera, he is credited with restoring order, albeit harshly. Ireland has had many assassinations since 1919.	In Baghdad, Iraqi troops quell a riot of Muslims at the Kadhimain Mosque. Celebrating soldiers join a peaceful parade of civilians celebrating the martyrdom of Hussain. When a civilian and a soldier argue inside the shrine, the result is five dead and 49 wounded.		
Jul. 11		Authorities arrest nine in the Kevin O'Higgins murder. Eamon de Valera condemns the crime.	A South African sets a world mark in the 100-mile run. Arthur Newton finishes in 14 hours, 45 minutes. There is no previous record at this distance.		
Jul. 12	Lloyds reports that for the first time in world history motor tonnage being built exceeds steam tonnage. Under construction are motor vessels totaling 1.5 million tons and steam vessels totaling 1.3 million tons. Britain is building almost half the total.	Germany indicates suspicions of Belgian and French actions in the Rhineland. A French newspaper's slanders of Germany seem a tactic to delay evacuation as promised.... Radical Socialists agree to back Raymond Poincare. The government will not fall today.	An earthquake in Palestine kills 268, injures 823, and causes $1.25 million in damage. Aid is coming from Egypt and the United States.... Calvin Coolidge appoints William F. Francis, a Republican lawyer from Minneapolis, as minister to Liberia.	An American marine orders Augusto Sandino to surrender the American-owned mine he occupies or face an attack. Sandino's force numbers about 1,000 and includes four machine guns.	
Jul. 13					Floods in South Anwhei kill over 1,000 Chinese. Tens of thousands are homeless....Peking demands that Japan withdraw its troops from Shanghai.
Jul. 14	The naval talks are deadlocked as each of the three holds to its position.	Two wheat ships arrive in London with hundreds of bubonic plague infected rats aboard. Authorities block all escape by the rats into the city.			The Comintern accuses the Chinese Communist Party of counterrevolution. It orders the Chinese to quit the government in Hankow.
Jul. 15	Britain and Japan begin working on an acceptable compromise. Observers see Britain as needing a larger fleet due to greater obligations. The United States seems to be asking parity as a matter of prestige. A full solution is unlikely.	Chancellor Ignaz Seipel rejects outside offers of assistance as reds strike and riot in Vienna. Early casualty estimates from this effort to create a soviet Austria are 40 to 100 dead and 500 wounded. France and Britain worry that Germany or Italy might seize the opportunity.	British officials in Palestine solicit contributions to earthquake recovery. Estimated time for full recovery in Palestine and Transjordan is two years.		
Jul. 16		Prime Minister Carl Gustaf Ekman of Sweden says that the Scandinavians have already outlawed war among themselves and with other Europeans by mandating conciliation. The major powers might note their model.	The Baghdad Railway opens service to Aleppo, Syria. The Aleppo junction links Western Europe with India as well as Palestine, Egypt, Sudan, and, potentially, South Africa.	Bolivia reveals that it has arrested 20 and thwarted a Communist plot to seize or kill President Hernando Siles and place Jose Villanueva in power. Villanueva was elected in 1925, but the election was annulled.	New Zealand's rugby league is miffed at the English league's abandonment of the two-year residency requirement for colonial players to be eligible to play for English rugby teams. New Zealand threatens to join Australia in canceling its invitation to a touring English team.

A	B	C	D	E
Includes developments that affect more than one world region, international organizations and important meetings of world leaders.	Includes all domestic and regional developments in Europe, including the Soviet Union.	Includes all domestic and regional developments in Africa and the Middle East.	Includes all domestic and regional developments in Latin America, the Caribbean, and Canada.	Includes all domestic and regional developments in Asian and Pacific nations (and colonies).

U.S. Politics & Social Issues	U.S. Foreign Policy & Affairs, Defense	U.S. Economy & Environment	Science, Technology & Nature	Culture, Leisure & Lifestyle	
Illinois bituminous coal miners, on strike since April 1, are running out of money. The 90,000 strikers face an economic crisis by end of summer.	The army issues new standards for flight school. Married men are ineligible, as are those with high school only. The new standard is two years of college. The age range is 20-27, down from 20-28. The army also confirms that it will eliminate the hazardous wooden Jenny on September 1.	Chicago service station attendants halt the first such strike of the automobile era. After a one-day walkout, they receive a $5.00 a month raise, not the $10 they ask. Drivers get half their requested $15 a month increase but not the week's paid vacation they want. Attendants now make $145 a month and drivers earn $182.50. Chicago has 2,000 stations and 100,000 trucks and uses 700,000 gallons a day....The Federal Trade Commission rules that Famous Players is an illegal trust. It must cease block booking within 60 days.	San Franciscans are considering going to Congress. They are facing opposition from the navy, which does not want a bridge over the Golden Gate because it will hamper naval forces. San Franciscans need a replacement for the ferry system, which is inadequate, and a tunnel, which would be the longest of its time, is impractical.	The National Broadcasting Company announces that it will broadcast the 21 July Dempsey-Sharkey fight over its 30-station network. NBC indicates a possibility that it can link with the 7-station Pacific Coast Network too....Babe Ruth hits homers 28 and 29, regaining the lead over Lou Gehrig by one.	Jul. 9
The Klan governor of Alabama, Bibb Graves, denounces flogging. Masked men flogged a woman in Florence a few nights earlier....The head of the United Committee for Law Enforcement says that the president could end prohibition violations in a month if he really wanted to enforce the law. The United States has the resources but not the will.		The federal government estimates the cotton crop down over 12 percent from last year. Cotton prices rise sharply. The shortfall is due to the floods in the South, drought in Oklahoma and Texas, and the spreading boll weevil....Louisiana parishes continue under water and only dead animals populate the devastated area. Locals remain patient. Some murmur that the government should do something	Alan Burroughs, art expert, explains how he uses x-rays to detect forgeries. He says that there is always preliminary sketching and other alterations beneath the surface on an original. Fakes lack this evidence of an artist at work.		Jul. 10
Farm leaders meeting in St. Paul urge Congress to override Calvin Coolidge and pass McNary-Haugen farm relief.	The "flying battleship' survives its first air test at Mitchell Field. The Condor can carry passengers or up to eight tons of munitions.	Oil production declines in the Seminole fields after record setting weeks. California production is down for the fourth week.		Comedian Ethel Waters stars in *Africana.* The revue also includes Pickanninny Hill, world champion cake walker, and song, dance, and sketches.	Jul. 11
As the floodwaters continue to cover and ruin Louisiana farmland, W.S. Craig of the State Bank and Trust denounces farm credit associations. The associations do not lend to tenants, who are 95 percent of those in need.		The Commerce Department announces that it will send representatives abroad to 26 countries to promote American tobacco. A crop of 1.34 billion pounds pushes the effort to expand markets....Adolf Zukor of Famous Players defies the FTC, refuses to end its sales practices. A court showdown seems likely.	Orestes Caldwell of the Radio Conference announces that 40 nations will meet to resolve the conflict between ship and shore radio, whose bands overlap.		Jul. 12
	The Condor is just one of three bombers the army is testing for selection in 1928. The army air corps also is looking to the other army branches to supply men for its 1650 flying slots.	Banks report that 95 percent of veterans loans are in default. Veterans seem to regard the loans as their bonus.	The heat wave that earlier this year killed people in the Midwest is now in the east. 17 die in eastern cities.	The Aga Khan buys a son of Papyrus for $73,500. He outbid an American whose top offer was $67,500 for the son of the English Derby winner.	Jul. 13
The National Women's Party caravan stops at Rapid City. Still dust-smeared from the drive, they hold a rally at the city bandstand. They intend to see Calvin Coolidge and call for equal rights, not just suffrage.	The department of Interior agrees that after six years of control by Interior, the nation's oil reserves will once again be under the navy effective August 1.	New York's Corn Exchange Bank installs a night deposit chute for its customers. New to banking, chutes allow safer deposits after banking hours.	Researchers reveal that shirts wear out, not because the laundries are too hard on them, but because they are allowed to dry outside. Air-dried clothes pick up sulfuric acid from polluted air, hastening destruction of fiber.		Jul. 14
Calvin Coolidge receives the women's delegation, telling them that they need to create a majority if they expect to win equality. He is silent on his views of their cause.		The Seminole field records another record day's production, and drillers find another pool. The May limitation agreement is a dead letter....The Radio Board is still finding stations outside their assigned bands. More than a third of the 695 licensed stations have mechanical problems.	Late season Arctic ice captures the *Morrissey* off Labrador. After beaching the vessel for six days to make repairs to the propeller and tail shaft, the expedition heads for the Hudson Straits....American flyers, Ernest Smith and Emory Bronte, complete the San Francisco to Molokai flight in 25 hours, 38 minutes. The civilians beat the army time by 14 minutes.	A record crowd turns out at City College stadium for 'Flivver Ten Millions." Frederick Shepherd Converse's novelty classical piece honoring the ten-millionth Model T lasts only 13 minutes....Bobby Jones wins his second consecutive British Open with a record 285.	Jul. 15
After Ford apologizes for the anti-Semitic campaign of the *Dearborn Independent,* Aaron Sapiro drops his suit against Ford for libel. Sapiro denies rumors that money changed hands....W.G. Acree, Georgia flogger, gets a year on the chain gang and a $100 fine. A hung jury frees another hooded flogger and a different jury exonerates five more. Alabama indicts three.		Two more explosions along the Los Angeles aqueduct bring the total for the past two years to 11. The city's back up water supply will serve until the damage is repaired.		Men's resistance to paying high prices for shoes causes two thirds of the 25 prewar quality shoemakers to go out of business. A high price is $10; men prefer paying $3 or $4 and may stretch to $8.	Jul. 16

F	G	H	I	J
Includes campaigns, elections, federal-state relations, civil rights and liberties, crime, the judiciary, education, healthcare, poverty, urban affairs, and population.	*Includes formation and debate of U.S. foreign and defense policies, veterans affairs, and defense spending. (Relations with specific foreign countries are usually found under the region concerned.)*	*Includes business, labor, agriculture, taxation, transportation, consumer affairs, monetary and fiscal policy, natural resources, pollution and industrial accidents.*	*Includes worldwide scientific, medical and technological developments, natural phenomena, U.S. weather and natural disasters.*	*Includes the arts, religion, scholarship, communications media, sports, entertainment, fashions, fads, and social life.*

	World Affairs	Europe	Africa & The Middle East	The Americas	Asia & The Pacific
Jul. 17	The cruiser issue is close to compromise. Now the United States wants Britain to give up its western hemisphere bases in exchange for smaller guns asked by the British on warships.	Speaking in Belgium at the dedication of a monument to France's unknown soldier, Premier Raymond Poincare exonerates Belgium from war guilt. He is rebutting Professor Johann Bredt of the Reichstag commission on the war's causes, who charges Belgium provoked Germany by building illegal fortifications and allying with France....After the provinces and towns rally to Ignaz Seipel, calm returns to Vienna. Authorities charge 252 with conspiracy and station 10,000 troops in the suburbs.		40 Marines with heavy air support repel Augusto Sandino's assault. 50 to 300 Nicaraguan rebels are dead, mostly from U.S. bombs. The rebel army crumbles and Sandino goes into hiding.	
Jul. 18	England and Japan offer a 12-12-8 ratio and 500,000 tons. The U.S. sticking point is still gun size for the smaller vessels. France is surprised by what it sees as a revived Anglo-Japanese entente.		A newly-revealed Egyptian tomb appears to be that of a princess. The mummy wears gold and jeweled bracelets and a crown. The tomb dates to 1000—1100 B.C.E., but no dynasty is identified yet.	Pan American Airways gets a contract for 40.5 cents a pound to deliver mail from Key West to Havana. Flights will take one hour.	The Communists are gone from Hankow. Peking and Nanking are nearing a truce. Unified government is imminent....Samoans and some Australians are unhappy with the governor of the British protectorate. Major General Sir George Richardson has expelled several hereditary chiefs for disobedience. Critics decry the lack of English justice and open trials.
Jul. 19	Displeased with the American's statement that the terms are still unsatisfactory, Britain calls its delegates home for consultation.	European protests over Nicola Sacco escalate. A bomb explodes at the Nice American embassy. French police take precautions by rounding up radicals on the Riviera and preparing for a Paris demonstration.		A Marine private in Haiti will stand trial for shooting three Haitians. He leaves his post as legation guard at Port au Prince and roams the city before returning to the embassy and firing randomly. He kills one and wounds two.	Japan's Kawasaki and One Hundredth banks announce they will merge to counter losses from last spring's panic. Kawasaki is already the principal holder of One Hundredth. Under Bank of Japan oversight, the new bank will write off millions in bad loans.
Jul. 20		Romania's Ferdinand dies. Ion Bratiano bars Carol's return. Carol's five-year-old son, Mihai, is king. Bratiano rules.			
Jul. 21	Speaking before the Union German Societies in Berlin, Smith College professor Harry E. Barnes says Germany is not guilty of starting the war and acted honorably to prevent war in 1914. Barnes has been writing and speaking in exoneration of Germany for several years.	Carol proclaims himself king and awaits a call to Romania. This act defies Ferdinand's deathbed wish that Carol not provoke civil war by returning....In London's City Temple for the first time ever, a muezzin calls the faithful to prayer. The Fellowship of Faiths includes Jews, Hindus, Theosophists, Christians, Confucians, and Buddhists as well as Muslims.	Palestine receives its first shipment of new money to replace Egyptian money in the fall. The shipment of 430,000 pounds worth of silver, nickel, and bronze coins weighs 75 tons and comes in 1500 cases. The Palestine pound is divided decimally, unlike the British pound.	Eugene Dieudonne reaches Para, Brazil, after half a year in Brazil's jungles. Dieudonne, a member of the Parisian Apache gang of Jules Bonnot, escaped from France's penal colony in Guiana in December....In Washington, DC., the Pan-American Federation of Labor urges the United States to leave Nicaragua to work out its own affairs. It also asks pardons for Nicola Sacco and Bartolomeo Vanzetti.	Nipponphone workers strike to protest the sale of their company to English-owned Columbia Graphophone. They demand 500,000 yen compensation. Nipponphone president J.R. Geary fires three strike leaders, declares a three-day holiday and pays the workers full wages plus a bonus.
Jul. 22		Ireland's Public Safety Bill targets the Irish Republican Army. The government has powers to declare emergencies and martial law, deport individuals, proscribe organizations, and suppress publications.		Mexico orders emigration inspectors to insure that all workers have proper documentation before allowing them to leave. Workers must take documents to the Mexican consulate immediately on arriving in the United States.	
Jul. 23		France and Germany sign a commercial treaty. Most favored nation status will eliminate high tariffs and allow trade volume to increase greatly....Paris police thwart a crowd intending to storm the prison as a show of support for Nicola Sacco and Bartolomeo Vanzetti.	Palestinian Jewish labor leaders meeting in Tel Aviv ask an open door for immigration to Palestine. The federation also asks reductions in unemployment, state lands for Jewish immigrants, and Jewish service in the Palestinian military.	Ontario's government reports the new liquor law will net about $5 million in its first year. The legal alcohol trade should approximate the $30 million bootleg trade Ontario had under prohibition. American buyers will allow the province to balance its budget and cut taxes $2 million.	

A	B	C	D	E
Includes developments that affect more than one world region, international organizations and important meetings of world leaders.	*Includes all domestic and regional developments in Europe, including the Soviet Union.*	*Includes all domestic and regional developments in Africa and the Middle East.*	*Includes all domestic and regional developments in Latin America, the Caribbean, and Canada.*	*Includes all domestic and regional developments in Asian and Pacific nations (and colonies).*

U.S. Politics & Social Issues	U.S. Foreign Policy & Affairs, Defense	U.S. Economy & Environment	Science, Technology & Nature	Culture, Leisure & Lifestyle	
Herman Bernstein indicates that he will follow Aaron Sapiro's example and drop his libel suit against Henry Ford now that Ford has apologized for anti-Semitism. The $200,000 Bernstein suit dates to 1923....The Belleville, IL, bishop prohibits communion for women wearing make up or wearing low cut or sleeveless dresses.	The army makes rubber heeled garrison shoes standard issue. Soldiers no longer have to buy rubber heels to cover the leather ones that clatter so noisily.		A Milbank Fund report says that improvements in hygiene and public health can extend life expectancy 15 to 20 years. Despite billions in expenditures, distribution remains inefficient. Knowledge and use of new vaccines and health practices spread slowly and incompletely.	The shingle cut is giving way to the chignon. Hairdressers lay in "detachable transformations" (artificial hairpieces) and other supplies as Paris notes a shift to longer hair.	Jul. 17
Georgia State Senator J.C. Edwards introduces an anti-flogging bill after a series of floggings near his hometown. The bill includes harsh penalties up to 20 years and anti-mask provisions....Nicola Sacco and Bartolomeo Vanzetti are either on a hunger strike or suffering weak appetites due to the heat. Force feeding will begin at the warden's discretion.	Citizens Military Training Camp call-ups for August are issued. Voluntary no obligation training modeled after the Plattsburg Movement, the 30-day camps emphasize sports and recreation with instruction by professional soldiers in artillery, infantry, and other branches. Those who complete the basic red and white courses and a specialized blue camp may join the Officers Reserve Corps.	The Jackson and Eastern Railroad completes a 65-mile section between Decatur and Jackson, MS. The line significantly shortens the route from the Gulf, making New Orleans an attractive port for the Midwest, where grain producers will now realize significant freight savings.	Back in the United States to a tumultuous welcome, Richard Byrd turns his attention to his next venture, the Antarctic expedition set for the fall....New Yorkers continue to die from the heat. Hundreds of thousands flock to the beaches. Even a thunderstorm provides no relief, only humidity.	Babe Ruth trails Lou Gehrig once again in what is becoming a back and forth homer race. Ruth has 30, Gehrig 31.	Jul. 18
			C. Francis Jenkins, inventor of the reversible propeller, announces a portable runway that makes large airports unnecessary. The plane drops from 32 feet along a 100-foot ramp while revving its motor. It's on a turntable so the plane always launches into the wind. The reversible propeller allows split second stops.		Jul. 19
Republicans on the coasts prefer Herbert Hoover as president if Calvin Coolidge chooses not to run. Hoover backs Calvin Coolidge.	Under its five-year plan, the navy contracts for 54 planes and 48 Wright motors.	Herbert Hoover presents Calvin Coolidge with a ten-year $200 million flood control plan. Adequate relief funds are available.		Odds going into tomorrows fight favor Jack Sharkey 7–5. Few take Jack Dempsey, recovering from a recent injury.	Jul. 20
Ohio mine owners prepare to reopen their mines. They get restraining orders against workers and install machine guns at the mines.		Oklahoma's corporation commission temporarily halts drilling in the Seminole field. The commission sets a hearing for August 5.		Jack Dempsey stops Jack Sharkey in the seventh before 80,000 and a national radio audience. The purse tops $1 million. Dempsey earns a shot at Gene Tunney. If he wins, he will be the first heavyweight ever to regain the title. The previous Dempsey-Tunney fight gated $2 million....Evangelist Gypsy Pat Smith sues his wealthy wife for divorce, charging infidelity and cruelty. A month ago, she sued him for allegedly taking her home under false pretenses.	Jul. 21
Governor Alvan Fuller pays a surprise visit to Nicola Sacco, Bartoloemo Vanzetti, and Celestino Madeiros in prison. The review of the case is nearly finished.		The biggest technological change in steel in 175 years allows continuous machine manufacture of steel sheets, work previously done by hand. The two major rolling mills merge to meet soaring demand, already up to 5 million from 800,000 tons in 1902.		Controversy grows over alleged Jack Dempsey low blows. The referee affirms one, insufficient to disqualify Dempsey, Slow-motion films of the bout are not sufficiently clear to show others.	Jul. 22
American Slovaks announce plans to build a $1 million high school and college for Slovak boys near Harrisburg, PA. There is already a Slovak school for girls.		After the FTC ruling against Famous Players-Lasky, the Department of Justice orders an anti-trust investigation of the movie industry. The move comes after a consumers group charges that the attorney general has failed to investigate an industry headed by Will Hays, former attorney general.		Swedes ask that a rock in Yonkers on which Jenny Lind sang be preserved as her memorial.	Jul. 23

F	G	H	I	J
Includes campaigns, elections, federal-state relations, civil rights and liberties, crime, the judiciary, education, healthcare, poverty, urban affairs, and population.	Includes formation and debate of U.S. foreign and defense policies, veterans affairs, and defense spending. (Relations with specific foreign countries are usually found under the region concerned.)	Includes business, labor, agriculture, taxation, transportation, consumer affairs, monetary and fiscal policy, natural resources, pollution and industrial accidents.	Includes worldwide scientific, medical and technological developments, natural phenomena, U.S. weather and natural disasters.	Includes the arts, religion, scholarship, communications media, sports, entertainment, fashions, fads, and social life.

	World Affairs	Europe	Africa & The Middle East	The Americas	Asia & The Pacific
Jul. 24	King Albert of Belgium dedicates the British war memorial at Ypres, which bears the names of 58,000 dead in the four-year battle. Lord Plumer represents Britain. Crowds number 10,000.	Raymond Poincare asks Germany to accept that its Teutonic monarchy bears war guilt. He says France does not blame the people. Poincare also cites German atrocities at Orchies.	Egypt is on the verge of conquering the bell worm. Only 5,000 of the original 89,000 acres remain infested....Cairo records new earthquakes in Palestine.	In Mexico, 20,000 march in support of Alvaro Obregon.	General Leonard Wood asks $2 million to aid the leper colony in the Philippines....A radio message beamed from India reaches King George of England in 28 seconds.
Jul. 25		Berlin newspapers reject Raymond Poincare's charges, citing the official Reichstag report of French atrocities at Orchies. Germany merely responded....France sentences Russian spies to terms of two to five years. Paris warns Moscow to withdraw its agents.	French and Spanish officials ride the first train on the new Tangier-Fez line. Economic improvement in Morocco is expected.	Argentina holds Arcangel Roscigna for bombing the Buenos Aires statue of George Washington and the local Ford agency. The bombings protest the imminent executions of Nicola Sacco and Bartolomeo Vanzetti.	
Jul. 26		Romanian Premier Ion Bratiano indicates that Carol will not get his bequest if he makes trouble.... Russia has 2,500 men working on a hydroelectric project on the Dnieper River in Ukraine. When done in five years, the $70 million project will be one of Europe's largest....King Fuad leaves England for France.	Egypt's government announces that it will sell 25,000 tons of cotton to Russia. Egypt has previously been reluctant to deal with Russia but wants to unload stocks it bought to keep prices steady on the local market.		Chinese nationalists, having removed the Communists, begin fighting among themselves. The commander of the armies in Hankow and the son of Sun Yat Sen are among those who agree that fascist-leaning Chiang Kai-shek has betrayed the movement and must go.
Jul. 27	Amid signs that delegates are ready to return to the naval parley, Foreign Secretary Sir Austen Chamberlain says there is a likelihood of a temporary cruiser deal. The United States says that will not happen and sees little future in the meetings.	Simulated air raids destroy London. The three-day RAF exercises show that planes have advanced beyond the capability of anti-aircraft weapons. When the RAF finds a solution to cold at high altitudes, planes beyond anti-aircraft range can rain bombs on defenseless cities.	Franco-Spanish negotiations over Tangier deadlock. Primo de Rivera wants Tangier totally in Spanish Morocco. France wants joint control. During negotiations rumors spread of Spain ceding Morocco to Italy, removing troops from the bandit-dominated interior, or taxing French autos.		Up to 1,000 Indians are dead after a Baroda reservoir bursts out of its banks and floods several villages. Monsoon rains also flood Rangoon, Bengal, and Bombay presidencies, marooning a train and threatening a town, and destroying bridges and cattle.
Jul. 28	Meeting in Paris, leaders of Standard of New Jersey and Royal Dutch Shell reject business war over Russian oil. Controversy has been growing since Standard Oil of New York and Vacuum began buying Russian oil in the fall of 1926 for Egyptian and Far Eastern markets.	France reconsiders its withdrawal from the 1928 Olympic games. The French committee earlier withdraws after the Senate fails to provide funds. It reconsiders after Francois Coty's offer of a 1 million franc loan spurs the Senate to fund the teams.		Mexico prohibits politics in the army. The penalty for officers expressing a presidential preference is dismissal from service.	After communications are finally reestablished reports reach Shanghai that a May 23 earthquake in Kansu province causes 100,000 casualties. One city is buried under a mountain....Michael Borodin, Russian advisor to the Communist government in Hankow, leaves for Moscow. Soviet support ends.
Jul. 29	Hungary captures the international chess title with Denmark second. Individual winners are Miss Menchik, Russian émigré in London, and Sir George Thomas, who lost not a match.	Parliament ends its summer session after passing a new Trades Disputes Act and 93 other bills. Labour indicates that as soon as it takes power it will overturn the Trades Disputes Act, which bans strikes and intimidation, mandatory trade union levies, and civil servant unionism.	The Persian Mejliss asks the premier to manage national finances until it replaces Arthur Millspaugh. The American managed Persian finances for five years but declined to renew his contract when the assembly sought to reduce his autonomy.		
Jul. 30			The Abyssinian (Ethiopian) state church moves toward Catholicism, with Ras Tafari (Haile Selassie) waiting for a sufficient number of parishes to acknowledge Rome. Abyssinia has been Coptic under an Egyptian bishop since the 4th century.	The Canadian wheat pool with 142,000 members in western Canada is the world's largest cooperative. It controls 75 percent of Canada's wheat land, handles 200 million bushels a year, and has a cash turnover of $300 million. It sells in 51 ports.	
Jul. 31		Turkey's autocratic president, Kemal pasha, will select his own parliament. There will be no opposition—anti-government parties are illegal. Constantinople evicts 2,200 White Russian refugees, many of whom have been there for eight years.			

A	B	C	D	E
Includes developments that affect more than one world region, international organizations and important meetings of world leaders.	*Includes all domestic and regional developments in Europe, including the Soviet Union.*	*Includes all domestic and regional developments in Africa and the Middle East.*	*Includes all domestic and regional developments in Latin America, the Caribbean, and Canada.*	*Includes all domestic and regional developments in Asian and Pacific nations (and colonies).*

U.S. Politics & Social Issues	U.S. Foreign Policy & Affairs, Defense	U.S. Economy & Environment	Science, Technology & Nature	Culture, Leisure & Lifestyle	
The head of the National Association of Manufacturers John Edgerton says 1.5 million company union members know where their benefits are. William Green is just unhappy because AFL membership dropped from 4.1 million to 2.9 million since 1920....Bartolomeo Vanzetti ends his 8-day hunger strike. Nicola Sacco persists.		Ford has closed and is revamping its factories at a cost of $1 million a day. Details of the new car remain secret.			Jul. 24
Uldine Utley, 15-year-old evangelist, preaches in Wall Street. When she visits the Stock Exchange, she says she is impressed but at least half the workers there need to know God.... New York prepares for a strike by 26,000 transit workers. It cancels police leaves and imports 1,500 strikebreakers to keep its subways running.	Frederick Sterling, the first U.S. minister to Ireland arrives in Dublin. Welcomed by 100 members of the new Irish Free State Army and a crowd of 2,000, he will present credentials tomorrow.	John Hancock raises premiums for aviators' insurance, limits policies to $10,000 and prohibits double indemnity. Hancock is one of six aviator insurers. None insures stunt or exhibition flyers.		Four Chicago aldermen object to Jack Dempsey fighting in Soldier Field. Dempsey was a slacker during the war, and he should not be fighting in a war memorial, they say.	Jul. 25
Mayor Jimmy Walker averts the transit strike by getting the warring unions to agree to a truce while they negotiate unification. The strikebreakers get their pay and head for home.			A Spaniard invents an automaton that can play chess. It can also detect cheating. It can only play with half the full game's pieces however.	Both judges report to the state boxing board that Jack Dempsey hit Jack Sharkey low.	Jul. 26
Wisconsin's legislature upholds the governor's veto of the Duncan Beer Bill. The law would have allowed 2.75 percent beer.					Jul. 27
		Paramount-Famous Players-Lasky reports quarterly profits of $1.4 million. This is a 50 percent over profits in the second quarter of 1926.... Newly formed Union Tobacco buys American Tobacco's higher quality brands, freeing American to compete in the popular market.			Jul. 28
A statistician calculates Protestant denominations are losing half a million members a year. He attributes the loss to the war. 13 denominations combine efforts to reverse the trend....Denver's traffic code says that women always have the right of way.				Bobby Jones arrives in Atlanta. A brass band and American champion Tommy Armour welcome him.	Jul. 29
The president of the League for American Citizenship says that 43 percent of all aliens presenting themselves for citizenship in the first half of 1927 are illegal. British. Germans are second. Countries with the largest quotas have the largest number of illegal aliens.			A Ford engineer describes the planned "Pullman of the Air." Ford intends to build a 100-passenger airplane within a year. First Ford has to develop a 1,000 horsepower engine, for the Pullman will take six. Ford also will open a western airline in two months with Tri-motors.	The Biological Survey announces it will begin the first census of aquatic birds in August. Scheduled to run through January 1928, the survey will cover east, west, and gulf coasts as well as inland resting areas....Johnny Weissmuller wins the Chicago three-mile river swim in 54 minutes, 29 seconds. He sets a new record two minutes under the old time.	Jul. 30
A peaceful IWW meeting and parade in New York City in support of Nicola Sacco and Bartolomeo Vanzetti turns violent after 1,500 marchers refuse a police order to disperse.	Calvin Coolidge expresses disappointment at the collapse of the Geneva naval talks. He worries that the result will be large expenditures for a big navy. That would undo his economizing efforts....The army dirigible RS-1 sets a record, remaining airborne for 36 hours. The record is unintentional; bad weather forces the craft to remain airborne.	Calvin Coolidge proposes a $300 million farmer cooperative program to counter McNary-Haugen. Farmers would set their own prices, voluntarily limit production, and market their products cooperatively. Grain would be stored in cooperative warehouses.	The Morrissey mission pauses at Mill Island, Baffin Bay, where its crew explores Eskimo ruins. The expedition finds 1,000-year-old ivory miniatures of animals and other artifacts.	Jazz musicians are laborers, not artists. The head of the American Federation of Musicians wants the Department of Labor to protect Americans from cheap foreign players who come through exceptions in immigration and contract labor laws for artists.	Jul. 31

F	G	H	I	J
Includes campaigns, elections, federal-state relations, civil rights and liberties, crime, the judiciary, education, healthcare, poverty, urban affairs, and population.	Includes formation and debate of U.S. foreign and defense policies, veterans affairs, and defense spending. (Relations with specific foreign countries are usually found under the region concerned.)	Includes business, labor, agriculture, taxation, transportation, consumer affairs, monetary and fiscal policy, natural resources, pollution and industrial accidents.	Includes worldwide scientific, medical and technological developments, natural phenomena, U.S. weather and natural disasters.	Includes the arts, religion, scholarship, communications media, sports, entertainment, fashions, fads, and social life.

	World Affairs	Europe	Africa & The Middle East	The Americas	Asia & The Pacific
Aug. 1	The United States denies that it has ordered its representative to break off discussions at Geneva's naval parley. Secretary of State Frank B. Kellogg and the British ambassador meet.	Carol contends that his renunciation was forced. Carolists contend that he has the support of 80 percent of Romanians. They expect Bratiano to invite Carol to become king—eventually....Tergizno villagers evacuate as the lava flow from reawakened Vesuvius threatens their homes. Officials hope that forests will cool and slow the lava flow.			
Aug. 2	Japan makes a new offer. It preserves the status quo on cruisers while giving the United States and Japan an opportunity to catch up with Britain. The United States indicates skepticism because tonnages will be too high.	Foreign minister Rushdi Bey says that Turkey is 10 years away from being where it wants to be in the world. He also says that pork, taboo to Muslims, is among the best of meats....Vesuvius' lava flow slows, sparing Tergizno. Tourists return to the crater.	Benito Mussolini and King Victor Emmanuel greet Egyptian King Fuad in Rome. Thousands welcome Fuad, who spent several years in Italy as a military student and Italian artillery officer. Italy values Egypt as a trading partner and means of influence in the Middle East.		
Aug. 3	The World Conference on Faith and Order opens at Lausanne, Switzerland. The 19-day meeting has been in preparation for 17 years. Nearly 500 representatives of 90 churches, excluding Roman Catholics, seek Protestant unity.		Uganda, British East Africa, has 20,000 elephants according to the first report of the Uganda Game Warden. They are becoming a nuisance because reserves ended the indiscriminate killing that kept the population down. The white rhino population is 150 and gorillas number 100. The former species is protected; the latter should be.	The Nicaraguan government reports that Augusto Sandino has disbanded his forces and is in flight along the Honduran border. The marines are in pursuit.	Japan remains mired in depression. Rengo News Agency's précis of business conditions shows major industries down 15 to 50 percent, only of the 30 closed banks reopened, a large budget deficit that may require government borrowing, and rising unemployment.
Aug. 4	The naval meetings fail with an inconclusive final meeting.				
Aug. 5	World opinion on the affirmation of the Sacco-Vanzetti guilty verdicts is mixed. Guards appear around American embassies. Italians are hostile, so Americans head for Switzerland. Violence is minimal.		Iraq's King Feisal announces he will fly to London to agitate for an end to the mandate. He wants Iraq in the League. Sentiment in Britain is divided, but many want to lose the £3–4 million annual expense.		Japan announces it will build two planes and enter the trans-Pacific race in 1928.
Aug. 6		The only Jew in the Lithuanian foreign service Henrikas Rabinavicius resigns as Lithuanian consul general in New York. Prime Minister Wlademaras said in January that he wanted a Lithuanian, not a Jew, representing Lithuania. Historically, Lithuania has shown greater toleration of Jews than its neighbors have.	Reportedly the British government is awarding the Palestinian Dead Sea salts concession to Imperial Chemical Industries. Held off the market prior to the war, the salts will now break the Franco-German dominance of chemicals. The various salts have a value of $1.19 billion.	Bombs damage the Pergamino, Argentina, Ford plant as the general strike protesting Sacco-Vanzetti spreads.	General Leonard Wood dies in a Boston hospital after unsuccessful surgery to remove a skull cancer.
Aug. 7	Foreign protests of the Sacco-Vanzetti decision continue. Crowds boo in front of the London embassy. At Paris the demonstration by 10,000 is peaceful. Police break up riots in Munich.	The German Dye Trust reaches accord with Standard Oil of New Jersey to share patents for glycol-based medicines, synthetic gasoline from coal tar, and other oil-based products. Standard becomes tied to Soviet oil interests through German links.	In Casablanca, Morocco, a mob supporting Nicola Sacco and Bartolomeo Vanzetti attacks the American consulate and burns the American flag.	In one of the largest real estate deals ever in Havana, Bowman-Biltmore buys 4 ½ miles of beach from a Cuban company. The $7.7 million deal gives the American company the Jai Alai park, the racetrack, and other tourist properties. The company will build a new hotel as well.	Anticipated Indian silver sales cause prices to drop on the London market. Buyers are waiting for the India to release 9.2 million ounces to the market.

A	B	C	D	E
Includes developments that affect more than one world region, international organizations and important meetings of world leaders.	*Includes all domestic and regional developments in Europe, including the Soviet Union.*	*Includes all domestic and regional developments in Africa and the Middle East.*	*Includes all domestic and regional developments in Latin America, the Caribbean, and Canada.*	*Includes all domestic and regional developments in Asian and Pacific nations (and colonies).*

U.S. Politics & Social Issues	U.S. Foreign Policy & Affairs, Defense	U.S. Economy & Environment	Science, Technology & Nature	Culture, Leisure & Lifestyle	
Alabama records a "moral victory" by convicting five floggers. The state fails to get access to Klan records, and the three men and two women get only fines of $25 to $100 for flogging a woman for refusing to acknowledge scandalous behavior....Strike violence flares in Ohio when 200 unionists beat strikebreakers and burn a tipple. Governor A. Victor Donahey warns he may have to call in troops.	Western Union announces it will lay a cable to Asia at a cost of $10 to $16 million depending on the route selected. The stimulus is the shortage of cable capability between the United States and China during the recent crisis. The cable will increase capability from 200 words per minute to 2,500.	Hudson and Essex report record sales in July. Nash expects August to be its record month....Four Pittsburgh papers merge into two. The city now has one morning and two evening papers. Publishers include Scripps-Howard, William Randolph Hearst, and Paul Block. None is local, and all have extensive newspaper holdings elsewhere.	During a lull in the rain, Clarence Chamberlin takes off from the passenger ship *Leviathan*. He uses a runway rather than a catapult in becoming the first to take off from a civilian vessel.	Chicago's park board approves use of Soldier Field in September for the Dempsey-Tunney fight. With a top ticket price of $40, the fight is expected to draw 150,000 fans and $2 million.	**Aug. 1**
Calvin Coolidge announces he does not choose to run in 1928. His written statement is an ambiguous 12 words. Some see him as susceptible to a draft while others see the field open for all others. Herbert Hoover begins thinking it over....Nicola Sacco and Bartolomeo Vanzetti enter the death house amid reports of a newly discovered Vanzetti alibi and a new trial for Sacco.		Colonial Air Transport Company ends air passenger service between New York and Boston because trains are as fast as planes when including time to get to the airfield. Colonial will continue flying mail, which pays $600 for equivalent weight to a passenger paying $35....The ICC adjusts railroad coal rates to reduce disadvantage to the Midwest and South. Indiana and Illinois coal is depressed.	Dr. Leuman Waugh reports that Eskimos enjoy pain. Professor of orthodontia at Columbia, Waugh pulled teeth of nine men and women in Labrador and all said it did not hurt.	Favorite critics of 21 prominent Broadway actors are Alexander Woollcott and Robert Benchley.	**Aug. 2**
The American Anti-Bible Society asks the New York Supreme Court for permission to incorporate. The society wants repeal of laws enforcing religious teaching. The spark is the case of a parent who loses custody for refusing to send his child to Sunday school....Alvan Fuller announces that the Sacco-Vanzetti verdicts are right. Police guard the prison and Fuller's residence as the defense calls for a worldwide protest.		Colonial denies cutting passenger service. It will discontinue use of multi-motored planes....A regional report says that New York's metropolitan area has room for another century of growth, with 367,000 vacant acres. The report doubts that skyscrapers create more land value than they cost.	German scientists report that Therese Neumann is truly in a trance. They report she suffers and bleeds as Christ every Friday. She has attracted believers and debunkers as well as state and church investigators since 1918.	Lou Gehrig hits a pair of home runs. He leads Babe Ruth 37–34.	**Aug. 3**
An Alabama flogger gets eight years in prison for abducting a teen from church. The trial of another of the eight accused Klan members begins immediately....Calvin Coolidge dons a war bonnet and becomes a Sioux chief, "Leading Eagle."		To demonstrate nonstop delivery, a Ford "flying truck" drops a cargo by parachute from a height of 700 feet. Owned by Royal Typewriter, it will deliver 200 typewriters to Cuba.	Richard Byrd postpones his expedition to Antarctica until 1928. Bernt Balchen, Byrd's pilot, goes to Norway to collect men and supplies for the expedition. Byrd, having lined up Edsel Ford, is seeking other backers for the $250,000 expedition.		**Aug. 4**
Denying the American Anti-Bible Society permission to incorporate, the judge says the organization's purpose is "evil."...Sacco-protest bombs cause damage and injury in Philadelphia and New York.	The third competitor for the army bomber contract, Keystone, is ready to disassemble its plane for transport. The 90-foot plane carries 10 machine guns and 8,000 pounds of crew, fuel, and bombs.		Risticz and Edzard remain airborne for 52 hours. The Germans break Chamberlin's record by an hour....The *Morrissey* reaches the Arctic Circle and crew members explore uncharted Baffin Land.	Bertil Hult, University of Stockholm student, arrives in New York after completing an around-the-world bicycle trip. He began the ride, a research project for his senior thesis, in 1925.	**Aug. 5**
As a new defense team files for a new trial, the Baltimore mayor's home is bombed. Extra guards protect Calvin Coolidge as well as cabinet and supreme court members. Chicago, Albany, and other cities increase security, as does Wall Street....Ohio mine owners reject the governor's proposal for a wage conference after the mine workers' leader accepts.		California reports that its experience with the minimum wage after half a dozen years is that it has none of the ill effects on women's employment that critics predicted. Rather, companies and workers covered by the law have both increased, as has the average wage.			**Aug. 6**
		The National Retail Dry Goods Association and two rayon manufacturers report record 1926 rayon underwear sales records. Sales increase 45 percent, with slips up 57 percent. Women are learning to treat rayon as they do silk, so problems with runs are decreasing.	For the first time, all of Wisconsin's tuberculosis hospitals are at capacity with waiting lists. Dr. Hoye E. Dearholt blames pursuit of a boyish figure and scanty clothing, which reduce resistance in young women.	Tommy Armour wins the Canadian Open golf tournament. As American Open champion, he is the first to hold two titles in a single season....Eddie Foy, veteran of 57 years in show business, returns to the Palace. Lambs, Friars, the Cheese Club and other theatrical groups honor him.	**Aug. 7**

F	G	H	I	J
Includes campaigns, elections, federal-state relations, civil rights and liberties, crime, the judiciary, education, healthcare, poverty, urban affairs, and population.	*Includes formation and debate of U.S. foreign and defense policies, veterans affairs, and defense spending. (Relations with specific foreign countries are usually found under the region concerned.)*	*Includes business, labor, agriculture, taxation, transportation, consumer affairs, monetary and fiscal policy, natural resources, pollution and industrial accidents.*	*Includes worldwide scientific, medical and technological developments, natural phenomena, U.S. weather and natural disasters.*	*Includes the arts, religion, scholarship, communications media, sports, entertainment, fashions, fads, and social life.*

	World Affairs	Europe	Africa & The Middle East	The Americas	Asia & The Pacific
Aug. 8		English and Irish labor unions ask Governor Fuller for clemency for Nicola Sacco and Bartolomeo Vanzetti....Germany announces plans to sell synthetic gasoline this year. Domestic manufacture will allow reduced imports of the more-expensive foreign oil.	South African Communists protest the Sacco-Vanzetti ruling to the American consul.	Plutarco Calles has freed Catholic laymen because the Catholic revolt has ended. Presidential politics and foreign pressure clear the way for the bishops in San Antonio to return to Mexico.	
Aug. 9	The World Federation of Education Associations meets at Toronto. Proposals include universal teaching of Esperanto, already taught in many European cities, as a language of peace. Also proposed are teaching the worth of peace over war, greater academic freedom, and emphasis on foreign languages for English-speaking educators.	Chancellor Wilhelm Marx asks the minister of finance to investigate reports that the Reichswehr spent $1.3 million to subsidize military propaganda films....European consulates prepare for protests. Danes threaten to kill the American delegation. The British press asks clemency. Berlin police arrest 12. Nicola Sacco's father asks Benito Mussolini to intervene, but Il Duce says he has done all he can.		Paraguay and Uruguay join the call for amnesty for Nicola Sacco and Bartolomeo Vanzetti.	Mitsubishi Shoji Kaisha (the Mitsubishi Company) begins steamship service between Asia and the Pacific northwest. The *Coluimbia Maru* is due in Seattle on August 19.
Aug. 10		Britain's war minister, Lord Grey of Falloden, says Britain will not use the failure of the Geneva talks to begin a build up....Irish Republicans agree to take the oath. When they take their seats on August 12 and back a Labor Nationalist coalition, W.T. Cosgrove falls.		Bombs rock Buenos Aires. Argentineans applaud the stay of execution for Nicola Sacco, Bartolomeo Vanzetti, and Celestino Madeiros.	Chiang Kai-shek leaves Nanking for Shanghai after Sun's forces defeat his. Chiang plans to make a stand on the Yangtze River....Thousands attend the memorial for General Leonard Wood in Manila. Those raising $2 million for lepers use his final letter in their fundraising campaign.
Aug. 11		Avoiding expulsion from the party, Leon Trotsky instead gets the right to publish his views in the official party organs.	After American students protest being held in quarantine with blacks and Arabs, Egypt releases the students to the American consul. The students are arrivals from Iraq and Palestine, where cholera has broken out....Tangier talks close until October. France refuses to accept Spain's demand for what would be, in effect, total Spanish control of the area.	Bolivian Indians in the Pocoata Region rebel, killing several, and confront government forces. No motive is given for the rising in which thousands march on farmlands 200 miles southeast of La Paz.	
Aug. 12	The Lausanne meeting on church unity reaches a critical moment as the Lutheran delegation says that the apostolic succession gives primacy to the Pope. The Bishop of Bombay counters that the church is a monarchy, not a democracy.			The Bolivian rising now includes 80,000 Indians in Potosi, Cochabamba, and Sucre. Descended from the Incas, the Indians are desperately poor, from the 70 percent of Bolivians exploited by the dominant European and Creole 30 percent. They fight with clubs and slings against well-armed troops and already 100 have died.	
Aug. 13		British gasoline prices drop to their lowest level in 25 years. Causing the reduction is either U.S. overproduction or a worldwide gasoline war triggered by Russian price cuts to counter a British boycott....Portugal arrests the leaders of a failed military coup. This is the 18th try in 16 years.		A division of the army mobilizes to fight the Indian rising. The Indians now have firearms. Government officials accuse them of cannibalism.	Simla, India's legislature proposes banning *Mother India* because it libels Indians and promotes class hatred. The book by Catherine Mayo criticizes Hindu customs such as child marriage and contends that only the British presence prevents bloodshed.
Aug. 14		France modifies citizenship laws to allow women to retain their original nationality after marriage. French women deserted by foreign husbands after the war were without citizenship. They now can regain French citizenship.		In a move that helps revive Mexican democracy, Plutarco Calles cedes control of the budget to the legislature. He has had budgetary powers since almost the inception of his term....As the Bolivian rising grows, Peru increases troops along its border to head off the rising's spread.	Chiang Kai-shek surrenders his Nanking command and his aides join the Nationalists. Chiang appeals for unity against the north.
Aug. 15			The Egyptian Antiquities Service finds a major necropolis at Kharga Oasis. New York's Metropolitan Museum of Art unearthed a Christian necropolis, a Roman town, and two Egyptian temples in the area between 1909 and 1911.		

A	B	C	D	E
Includes developments that affect more than one world region, international organizations and important meetings of world leaders.	Includes all domestic and regional developments in Europe, including the Soviet Union.	Includes all domestic and regional developments in Africa and the Middle East.	Includes all domestic and regional developments in Latin America, the Caribbean, and Canada.	Includes all domestic and regional developments in Asian and Pacific nations (and colonies).

U.S. Politics & Social Issues	U.S. Foreign Policy & Affairs, Defense	U.S. Economy & Environment	Science, Technology & Nature	Culture, Leisure & Lifestyle	
Massachusetts refuses a new trial for Sacco-Vanzetti. Calvin Coolidge declines to intervene in a state matter. The ACLU, IWW, and AFL join the growing chorus of protests and strikes. Boston supporters prepare to march on the prison on the execution date. New York prepares 1,000 police for a 500,000 demonstration. Philadelphia arrests eight radicals and prepares for 50,000.		The radio commission rules that broadcasters must disclose when music is recorded rather than live.	An investigation reveals that the air-powered car of a Kansas City inventor is a fraud. It runs on batteries concealed in the upholstery.	With the 2239th performance, *Abie's Irish Rose* sets a new mark for longevity. Running since 1922, it surpasses *Chu Chin Chow*'s 2238 performance from 1916 to 1921 in London.	Aug. 8
Supporters claim 392,000 strike to support Nicola Sacco, but police claim crowds total 1,500 in Philadelphia and 15,000 in New York. Baltimore has bomb threats and a strike of 8,000 garment workers. At Jessup, PA, police charge and break up a march by miners. A mine explosion in Joplin, MO, injures six.	After meeting with Navy secretary Curtis Wilbur, Calvin Coolidge indicates his five-year plan will continue. He will not use the collapse at Geneva to begin a major buildup because he remains confident that reduction will come to pass.	Secretary Work tells Calvin Coolidge that the seven Colorado River states agree on a dam and will sign the Colorado River compact. The way is now clear for Congress to authorize the Boulder Canyon dam....With a drop of 7850 barrels, Oklahoma leads the reduction in oil output for the week. Standard Oil cuts gasoline 2 cents. Current price in New York is 17 cents.	Two planes drop out of the Dole air race from San Francisco to Honolulu; thirteen remain in the race.		Aug. 9
The second day of Sacco demonstrations turns into a riot in Rochester, NY. Boston arrests 39 and dampens protest ardor. New York is quiet after police routed snake-dancing demonstrators yesterday. Meanwhile, Massachusetts grants a 12-day stay of execution.		Edsel Ford says the new car can reach 65 mph and averages 55 mph over a two-hour test. Testing of components will continue however.	Calvin Coolidge dedicates the Black Hills monument on Mount Rushmore. Gutzen Borglem chisels the first line of George Washington's face....A Honolulu racer crashes in flames off San Diego. The two fliers die.		Aug. 10
Repairs to the White House are virtually finished. The $400,000 work includes replacing upper story beams and the roof. All that remains is minor interior work. Calvin Coolidge is free to return, having been away since mid-March.	Army reorganization adds three infantry and two cavalry divisions. Not an increase, the move consolidates units left scattered by unit deactivations as strength falls from 280,000 to 185,000 authorized and from 185,000 to 119,000 in actual strength between 1920 and 1927.	Women outnumber men as stockholders of major American corporations such as Westinghouse Airbrake, Southern Pacific, National Biscuit, General Electric, and others. Women investors have grown 25 percent in 10 years.		Another racer drops out as his plane crashes into the bay. The Honolulu race is delayed four days, a compromise between flyers who want two weeks and Honolulu backers who want the race to start on schedule—today.	Aug. 11
Removed from the death house, Nicola Sacco continues to fast while Bartolomeo Vanzetti takes light meals. The defense prepares its motion for a new trial and a picketer arrested in Boston files a test case.		The Red Cross reports that it is still providing aid to 130,000 flood victims....Southern coal operators request that the ICC provide them the same rates as it gives operators in the Midwest. Southerners still suffer a 48 cent a ton disadvantage against Northerners.	After a Fort Worth, TX, doctor reports success with cures from an inoculation against infantile paralysis, he receives an invitation from Franklin Roosevelt to bring patients to Warm Springs, GA, to test the efficacy of treatment there.	A third pilot dies as the Dole race field falls to nine.	Aug. 12
The Stone Mountain, GA, memorial to Confederate heroes is in trouble as backers fail to get eminent domain possession of the mountain. Urged by the United Daughters of the Confederacy, the state senate orders an audit of the Stone Mountain association's books.	The army requires soldiers stationed at Tientsin to learn at least 300 words of Chinese. Better communication should reduce fights and make soldiers more effective in the field.	U.S. investment in Latin America tops $4.8 billion. This is more than the $3.35 billion invested in Europe and $3.2 billion invested in Canada.	General Electric's atomic hydrogen welding technique passes hydrogen through the arc through two electrodes. The high heat produced allows welding of previously unweldable metals.		Aug. 13
	The navy begins the first-ever hydrographic survey of the Bay of Panama. The bay has potential as a base for submarines.	Railway freight traffic sets an all-time record. Traffic is up three percent for the first half of 1927 over the same period in 1926.	Germany's *Bremen* begins its trans-Atlantic flight. Its sister ship aborts due to weather. France's crew says it will not attempt to chase the Bremen.		Aug. 14
A federal court enjoins Ohio mine unionists from interfering with the reopening of six mines with non-union labor....Nicola Sacco sips broth, breaking his fast under threat of force-feeding.		Seminole oil production drops 40,000 barrels in 24 hours. The field is still 12,000 barrels over the 450,000 barrels producers set as their limit.	Weather forces the *Bremen* to turn back. The next opportunity is two days off. Courtney, the British flyer, postpones his effort indefinitely and considers a southern route to dodge North Atlantic weather....Eight planes are qualified for the Dole. A ninth has fuel capacity problems.	The world horseshoe-pitching champion is C.C. Davis of Columbus, OH. He defends his 1926 title at Duluth, MN.	Aug. 15

F	G	H	I	J
Includes campaigns, elections, federal-state relations, civil rights and liberties, crime, the judiciary, education, healthcare, poverty, urban affairs, and population.	*Includes formation and debate of U.S. foreign and defense policies, veterans affairs, and defense spending. (Relations with specific foreign countries are usually found under the region concerned.)*	*Includes business, labor, agriculture, taxation, transportation, consumer affairs, monetary and fiscal policy, natural resources, pollution and industrial accidents.*	*Includes worldwide scientific, medical and technological developments, natural phenomena, U.S. weather and natural disasters.*	*Includes the arts, religion, scholarship, communications media, sports, entertainment, fashions, fads, and social life.*

	World Affairs	Europe	Africa & The Middle East	The Americas	Asia & The Pacific
Aug. 16		W.T. Cosgrove wins a no-confidence vote in the Dail by the speaker's vote. The Dail adjourns until October 11....Italy and Albania clash at Scutari, with injuries.	Palestinian researchers report that manna, popular with tourists, is a product of insects, not tamarisk trees....A new diamond rush is on at Welverdiende, Transvaal.	Angry Panamanians storm the Buenaventura jail, seeking to lynch a police officer who killed a prominent citizen. Eight die in the riot.	
Aug. 17	Dr. Edward Alsworth Ross reports that the world is gaining 20 million people a year as births exceed deaths 3 to 2. He estimates that the 1.85 billion in 1926 will double in 60 years. When population exceeds food, population will crash, he says.	Premier Alexander Zaimis forms a new Greek cabinet. His previous cabinet dissolved last week due to a spat between two ministers. One of the ministers is in the new cabinet; Zaimis takes the other's post as well as his own.			
Aug. 18	Committees at the world faith conference complete their reports on sacraments and Christian unity. The Eastern Orthodox delegation announces it cannot support any but the one on the scriptures.	Lithuanian reactionaries made president Anton Smetona a dictator. Now they want to make him king. A simple living democrat, he demurs....Russia and Persia sign trade agreements worth 25 million rubles a year. Political clauses include one allowing pursuit of raiders across the border.	Fearing undue influence, in the new trade agreement France bars Germany from French Morocco. In return France drops the surtax on German imports to Morocco. Before the war, German colonists dominated French north Africa.... The Palestinian government reports a fiscal year 1927 surplus of $940,000.		Siberian floods on the Amur River kill 100 and leave 40,000 homeless.
Aug. 19		Rejecting British demands for force reductions, France insists on keeping 50,000 in the Rhineland, 5,000 more than it agreed to in 1925. France also reveals increases in the *Reichswehr* and Rhineland groups.... The Greek government repels a coup attempt by army non-commissioned officers. Followers of former dictator Theodoros Pangalos, the 31 men sought commissioned status.	*Le Matin* accuses Russia of attempting to disrupt the French empire by encouraging a new ruffian rising in Algeria. The newspaper says that Russian diplomats in France and Germany are supplying arms as well as propagandizing in Algeria, Tunis, and Morocco.	Mexico confirms a pre-1917 concession in Vera Cruz to the Texas Company. The decision is in keeping with the new petroleum law....Chile's ambassador to the United States steps down. Chile also recalls the second secretary. The two men are too conciliatory and willing to cooperate with the United States. Chilean policy on its dispute with Peru over Tacna-Arica takes a harder line.	The British repair a cut they made in a Chinese railway in retaliation for Chinese seizure of a British airplane for violating its air space. China's return of the plane defused the crisis.
Aug. 20		Macedonian students abroad protest against Serbian persecution in Yugoslavia. They claim that Serbs are brutalizing and torturing their young Macedonians in prison.			Cloistered in a Buddhist monastery, Chiang Kai-shek blames Japan for his defeat. He calls for unity against the north and promises to return.
Aug. 21		England's new craze is greyhound racing, with nightly crowds of 50,000 to 100,000. In 20 weeks 2.5 million attend. New tracks are going up.	The Fourth Pan-African Conference opens in New York City with W.E.B. DuBois presiding. Among the attendees is the ruler of the Gold Coast....Sheila MacDonald climbs Tanganyika's Mount Kilimanjaro, formerly in German East Africa. She is the first woman to do so.	A non-profit, non-political organization, The Pan-American Information Service, opens in New York. The goal is to improve exchange of information and trade relations between the United States and Latin America.	
Aug. 22	Representatives of every minority group in Europe meet in Geneva in advance of the League Assembly meeting. The purpose is air minority grievances and show leaving those grievances unresolved threatens peace.	Riots break out in London and Geneva. French crowds are quiet, expecting to the last minute a reprieve....France accepts the British plan and agrees to reduce its Rhineland force to 50,000 within a fortnight.	The Pan-African Conference continues. Speakers condemn white missionary prejudice against black mission workers.		The appeals court denies clemency to Kakori conspiracy plotters and affirms three death sentences and affirms or increases sentences of transportation. The 15 conspirators in 1924 plotted to create a United States of India.
Aug. 23	Reaction to the Nicola Sacco and Bartolomeo Vanzetti executions throughout the world is strong. Africa, Asia, Europe, and Latin America experience riots, protests, bombings, and burning of the American flag. In some cities, police fire on demonstrators, with deaths resulting.		Persia's director of internal revenue, Colonel D.W. MacCormack, sails for Geneva with the plan for eradication of the Persian opium crop. His approach is gradualist to minimize economic disruption.		

A	B	C	D	E
Includes developments that affect more than one world region, international organizations and important meetings of world leaders.	Includes all domestic and regional developments in Europe, including the Soviet Union.	Includes all domestic and regional developments in Africa and the Middle East.	Includes all domestic and regional developments in Latin America, the Caribbean, and Canada.	Includes all domestic and regional developments in Asian and Pacific nations (and colonies).

U.S. Politics & Social Issues	U.S. Foreign Policy & Affairs, Defense	U.S. Economy & Environment	Science, Technology & Nature	Culture, Leisure & Lifestyle	
The East Milton, MA, home of a Sacco juror is rocked by a bomb blast. The five-member family escapes unharmed.	Secretary Frank B. Kellogg and Ambassador Manuel Tellez sign a treaty extending the 1923 Mexican claims commission two years. Oil disputes are excluded.		The Dole field contains four planes. Two crash at the start while two others turn back....An army bomber hides the *Ile de France* under a smokescreen.	Babe Ruth hits the first homer out of White Sox Park. He still trails Lou Gehrig, 38 to 37....Odds makers favor Americans 6–5 over British in upcoming polo matches.	Aug. 16
		At Charlottesville, VA, an Institute of Public Affairs roundtable scores the ICC for its refusal to provide Southern shippers. Freight rate differentials are partially responsible for southern backwardness.	*Woolaroc* wins the Dole race in 26 hours, 17 minutes, 33 seconds. *Aloha* is two hours behind. Two of the Dole racers are missing at sea. The navy begins a search with five destroyers and two auxiliaries for seven missing flyers.	*Potiphar's Wife* shocks London theatergoers. The leading lady appears in scanty pajamas, and some of the language is blue. Two days later, the actress promises to wear more conservative pajamas in future performances.	Aug. 17
Strike sympathizers in Ohio evict non-union workers. They take 10 from their boardinghouse through persuasion, not violence.		The Radio Board refers a Louisiana broadcaster to the justice department for prosecution. His station exceeded authorized power output 40 days. He is subject to a $20,000 cumulative fine....Texas operators in the Pecos field use the Seminole approach to reduce output.			Aug. 18
Explosions damage the barracks of non-union black miners in Pennsylvania and North Carolina.... The state denies all Sacco-Vanzetti appeals and federal courts refuse the appeal. All that remains possible is a governor's stay. Federal authorities increase security in New York, Chicago, Philadelphia, Boston, and Worcester, MA....Mine union officials say men who join the unauthorized protest strike risk being fired.	Responding to recent calls for expanding the merchant marine, Calvin Coolidge reaffirms his decision to sell the U.S. merchant marine and get the government out of the money-losing business. He says the marine took a $3 billion loss during the war and remains a loser.... The army issues a revised mobilization plan that increases promotion opportunity for reserve officers. The plan counters rumors that the army intends to abandon the plan to field six wartime armies totaling two million men with 200,000 officers.	The postmaster general opposes airmail over the oceans. He says planes are too unreliable and carry too little.			Aug. 19
A Klan-backed measure under consideration in the Alabama legislature would outlaw press criticism of public officials. The measure provides trial in any county and prosecution for activities predating the law.	The United States has identified 99.9 percent of its war dead. The official total is 77, 771.	Made from seaweed, California agar is showing potential to replace Japanese agar. Important for chemistry and medicine as well as candies and jellies, California agar is more consistent, water-absorbent, and bacteria-free.	After spending $2.5 million, the United States has failed to control the corn borer in Ohio. Entomologists say the borer will survive as long as there is appropriate habitat and eradication efforts that depend on using machines such as stubble pulverizers, oil burners, trucks, and plows are futile.	Babe Ruth hits his 39th homer and ties Lou Gehrig again. The Yankees fall to the Indians, 14 to 8.	Aug. 20
Hundreds of intellectuals from 22 states sign a petition on behalf of Nicola Sacco and Bartolomeo Vanzetti. Alvan Fuller receives the petition....Former Senator Oscar Underwood backs *The Birmingham News* campaign against flogging and Klan control of the state Democratic Party. He calls for an anti-mask law.		An attempt to drop mailbags onto a liner at sea aborts after the pilot loses the ship in the fog.	The Rockefeller Foundation reports that its sanitation drive is succeeding. Now that it is traced to a single type of mosquito, malaria in the United States will soon be eradicated, as will hookworm....With no sign of the missing Dole flyers, the race—and the concept of such races—comes under criticism.		Aug. 21
		Ford announces that it will have a new truck with twice the power of the Model T. The truck will share technological improvements derived from work on the new car.		According to the Dancing Masters of America, the dance for 1927–28 is the Kinkajou. The Dixie Stomp, too violent, is out....The Chaplin divorce settlement includes $625,000 for the ex Mrs. Chaplin and 200,000 for the children....Babe Ruth hits number 40.	Aug. 22
All appeals fail, and there is no reprieve. Massachusetts executes Nicola Sacco and Bartolomeo Vanzetti. New York crowds are silent. Scores of protesters in Boston march into police arms, forcing their arrest.		Kapok is America's first choice as filler for upholstered goods and pillows. The Javanese plant fiber first came into use during the war. Kapok is light, soft, and water resistant.	The Pacific search contingent is now 60 vessels, including 15 U.S. destroyers. Occasional reports have sparked hope, but none has worked out.	Finland's Paavo Nurmi charges he lost a race to Germany's Dr. Peltzer because his competitor used pep pills. Peltzer challenges Nurmi to come to Germany for a rematch.	Aug. 23

F	G	H	I	J
Includes campaigns, elections, federal-state relations, civil rights and liberties, crime, the judiciary, education, healthcare, poverty, urban affairs, and population.	*Includes formation and debate of U.S. foreign and defense policies, veterans affairs, and defense spending. (Relations with specific foreign countries are usually found under the region concerned.)*	*Includes business, labor, agriculture, taxation, transportation, consumer affairs, monetary and fiscal policy, natural resources, pollution and industrial accidents.*	*Includes worldwide scientific, medical and technological developments, natural phenomena, U.S. weather and natural disasters.*	*Includes the arts, religion, scholarship, communications media, sports, entertainment, fashions, fads, and social life.*

	World Affairs	Europe	Africa & The Middle East	The Americas	Asia & The Pacific
Aug. 24	The League's first conference of news people opens in Geneva. Issues include support for news priority on the wires and opposition to favoritism toward government officials. Delegates are from 36 nations.	Leon Trotsky tells A.F.L. visitors that the ultimate goal is anarchy. The Soviet system is only an interim stage….Police in Paris quell red riots. Provincial riots continue. So far the riots have hurt 121 police and caused 4 million francs of damage.	The Pan-African Conference concludes. Final presentations deal with Africa as home of humanity and the need for black education.	Cuban police arrest three Greeks for smuggling immigrants into the United States….South American Gulf gets leases on 700,000 acres in Colombia. It buys out the Colombia Syndicate.	
Aug. 25		Britain disapproves the French plan to cut troops by 5,000. They want a greater cut in the Rhineland force…. In Irish by-elections W.T. Cosgrove wins two seats. The governor general dissolves parliament and calls for September 15 elections.		Mexico refuses American movie companies access to its mails. The government disapproves of the 19 companies' portrayal of Mexican life.	During night maneuvers, four Japanese warships collide. One sinks and three are damaged. More than 125 sailors are lost. This is the sixth fatal accident in seven years.
Aug. 26	Former League commissioner for Austria, Alfred F.M. Zimmerman, takes charge of the British-Mexican arbitration meetings. As agreed in December 1926, the meetings are to establish compensation by Mexico to Britain for losses during the 1910–20 revolution….The League meeting of news people resolves that information is property with monetary value and warrants safeguards from piracy.	Britain says it will keep troops in the Rhineland. France considers cutting its contingent by 10,000.		Argentina returns to the gold standard for the first time since 1914. Strong exports allow the move to a peso convertible to 44 gold centavos….Bolivia and Paraguay send troops to their disputed border. Two commissions are working to find a solution to the Chaco dispute, which involves oil, before it deteriorates into war.	With southern forces in disarray due to political infighting, Sun and the north threaten Shanghai. An American destroyer, the *Noa*, fights entrenched Chinese and eventually causes them to withdraw. It suffers damage to its armor plate.
Aug. 27		The Constantinople chamber of commerce asks Ankara to change the required holy day from Islam's Friday to Christianity's Sunday. Multiple days off reduce labor's output and are bad for business…. Germany faces a parliamentary crisis over its national and army flags. The Friedrich Ebert-mandated one is unacceptable to nationalists, and the nationalist preference is unacceptable to Socialists….Reversing policy, Russia allows the church to convene a synod. The church expresses loyalty.		29 American and British citizens hole up in Jalisco after "reds" take over three silver mines of the Amparo Mining Company. Federal troops are en route. The Southern Pacific railroad in western Mexico has come under attack by bandits twice during the past week with one fatality….United Fruit and Standard Fruit and Steamship agree that Panama is too small for both. One will buy the other or they will merge.	Japan awaits the arrival of an heir to the throne. The first child of the empress is a daughter.
Aug. 28		France bans government employee visits to Russia. Workers have been getting visas to spend their vacations learning about the Soviet system firsthand….Sinn Fein says that it will sit out the election. It lacks the finances.			
Aug. 29	The Geneva press meeting ends with a condemnation of censorship. Guatemala charges that U.S. diplomats tamper with news about American business in Latin America.			Louis Munoz-Marin arrives in the United States with an offer for the U.S. companies: help Puerto Rico's 200,000 unemployed and get a 10-year tax exemption and a free business site.	
Aug. 30	A new French peace plan involves a parliament of all property owners. The Federation of French Proprietors has opened a special department to work out the details.			Cuban police arrest Romanian alien smugglers.	Japan orders withdrawal of its Shantung forces within 10 days. Northerners suffer losses in trying to cross the Yangtze and take Nanking.

A	B	C	D	E
Includes developments that affect more than one world region, international organizations and important meetings of world leaders.	*Includes all domestic and regional developments in Europe, including the Soviet Union.*	*Includes all domestic and regional developments in Africa and the Middle East.*	*Includes all domestic and regional developments in Latin America, the Caribbean, and Canada.*	*Includes all domestic and regional developments in Asian and Pacific nations (and colonies).*

U.S. Politics & Social Issues	U.S. Foreign Policy & Affairs, Defense	U.S. Economy & Environment	Science, Technology & Nature	Culture, Leisure & Lifestyle	
Rev. Walter F. McMillin tells the General Bible Conference that God ordained capital punishment. McMillin sees a great crime wave flooding the world....Rev. Charles Stelzle reports that Protestantism is stagnating. Since 1900 growth has only matched population increases.	The Keystone SuperCyclops passes its first army flight tests. It gets high marks for ease of handling. The War Department accepts lightweight plane models for testing by the National Guard from Keystone, Curtiss, and Douglas. Guard planes date from the war.	Oldsmobile reports that July sales were an all-time record....Ford announces that it is testing a plane for private use. The tentative price tag is $11,000.			Aug. 24
Opponents of the Klan's newspaper silencing legislation defeat it by adjourning before it can pass....1,000 union miners decide not to invade Ohio's Pomeroy coal field after union leaders dissuade them. Some mines are working non-union labor and others are without funds to pay for private guards.			As the Pacific search widens, Paul Redfern sets off on a solo flight from Georgia to Rio de Janeiro. Flying across ocean and jungle without radio or other means of contact, he intends to set a non-stop distance record of 4600 miles. Another plane is in Maine, en route for Newfoundland, the staging base for a round-the-world flight.		Aug. 25
African-American Elks hear a report that the state of black health is the worst in U.S. history. Overcrowded and unsanitary urban environments and ignorant officials are to blame, according to a study of 400 cities.... Senator Pat Harrison (D-MS) says he opposes a Klan suggestion that the 1928 convention delegation be anti-Smith....Governor Hamill of Iowa refuses troops to mining areas. He tells owners and miners to settle their own problems.	The Army and Navy Joint Board establishes rules for wartime coordination between army and navy aviation. The instructions clarify which service commands in joint activities or when one aids the other, but it reaffirms that each air force is foremost an arm of its service.	A California judge ends the receivership of the Doheny oil leases. This is the final act in the restoration to the government of oil reserves improperly leased by Albert Fall during the Harding administration.	Britain develops wireless radio for tanks. The new technology allows communication despite the din of battle....A hurricane batters New England and Nova Scotia. The fishing fleet suffers major damage and loss of lives. Passenger ships have difficulties with 35-foot waves.		Aug. 26
Union miners prepare another march in Ohio. County officers and national guard are prepared....Overnight camps with bungalows are now common beside highways across the United States. The U.S. Chamber of Commerce reports 2,000 with $20 million in annual business. Also booming are conversions of large houses, particularly in New England, into inns and tearooms.	Army "chow," traditionally relied heavily on beans. It now features steak, chicken and other wholesome foods. The reason is the increase in the daily food allowance from 36 cents to 50 cents, effective July 1.	After U.S. Controller General McCarl refuses to allow transfer of $2 million in river funds to levee restoration, Louisianans express concern that flood relief might become a political football or that apathy might overtake the federal government. Doubts appear about Hoover's ability to get funds.	The final stage of the search for the Dole flyers is a retracing of their great circle route. Then the destroyers will return to San Diego but submarines will stand by in Hawaii. Redfern is missing over Brazil, but Schlee and Brock's round-the-world effort is over England....At the request of the Los Angeles chamber of Commerce, Sid Grauman cancels his $30,000 prize offering for a flight from Los Angeles to Tokyo. Cross-water flying is too risky.	Bobby Jones wins his third U.S. amateur golf title in four years, 8 and 7. He in now one short of Jerry Travers' record four U.S. amateur victories.	Aug. 27
Automobile deaths in the past year total 6993. Baptist Rev. G.H. Dowkontt says that radio is the tool of the Anti-Christ. Radio provides Babel of religious choices. Satan has become a radio preacher....The funeral procession for Nicola Sacco and Bartolomeo Vanzetti in Boston includes 7,000 marchers. Spectators top 200,000.		Strikes in bituminous are eroding anthracite overproduction. Oil is replacing bituminous as anthracite's rival, with home use up to 34 million barrels from 25 million in 1926 and 18 million in 1925....The Federal Trade Commission orders 8 oil companies to cease misleading and fraudulent practices in Texas. The FTC recently began investigating "blue sky" securities.	Schlee and Brock arrive in London after a 23-hour, nine-minute flight from Newfoundland. They survive gale winds and getting lost over England. Tomorrow they head to Germany....Redfern, now a day overdue, is presumed down somewhere. A search plane is standing by.	As the Yankees win their 17th straight over the Browns, Babe Ruth hits his 42nd home run. He is now up by two home runs over Lou Gehrig.	Aug. 28
Police break up a demonstration in Union Square. They use nightsticks and horses to scatter 10,000 marching for Nicola Sacco and Bartolomeo Vanzetti....Unionists fire the first shots in Ohio. They fire on non-union workers at Adena. None is injured. Police seize ammunition and a machine gun.	The United States and Canada begin talks on prohibition enforcement and border control. Not only is smuggling a problem both ways, but the configuration of border checkpoints is poor. Detroit is a major weak point.	The controller general rules that states that owe the federal government money are not eligible for federal aid. Tennessee, Montana, Louisiana, and North Carolina stand to lose $10 million. Debts date to the 1830s Indian wars or to this year's good roads. Land grant colleges may lose. Child welfare and maternity aid already have....New Jersey seizes 2 million counterfeit Gillette razor blades. Market value is $150,000.	Schlee and Brock reach Munich, stop overnight to avoid night flying in the mountains, and head for Constantinople. They would have landed in Stuttgart but they could not find the field.		Aug. 29
The Alabama senate passes an anti-flogging bill, 19-0. The bill now goes to the governor.		22 state legislatures want repeal of the federal estate tax, enacted in 1916.	The first flight from England to North America carries the first woman to try the Atlantic flight, a 62-year-old princess in an armchair, and 800 gallons of gasoline. William Brock and Edward Schlee are in Belgrade.	Helen Wills wins the U.S. tennis title at Forest Hills easily in straight sets. She regains the title she won three years consecutively but could not defend in 1926 due to illness.	Aug. 30

F	G	H	I	J
Includes campaigns, elections, federal-state relations, civil rights and liberties, crime, the judiciary, education, healthcare, poverty, urban affairs, and population.	Includes formation and debate of U.S. foreign and defense policies, veterans affairs, and defense spending. (Relations with specific foreign countries are usually found under the region concerned.)	Includes business, labor, agriculture, taxation, transportation, consumer affairs, monetary and fiscal policy, natural resources, pollution and industrial accidents.	Includes worldwide scientific, medical and technological developments, natural phenomena, U.S. weather and natural disasters.	Includes the arts, religion, scholarship, communications media, sports, entertainment, fashions, fads, and social life.

	World Affairs	Europe	Africa & The Middle East	The Americas	Asia & The Pacific
Aug. 31		The hand of Russia seems behind Poland deporting the editors of a monarchist newspaper....Two thousand Poles lose citizenship for failure to serve in the army. If they return from Germany and serve, they will become citizens again.		Mexico is reported as blocking aliens from entering. A 10,000-peso fee allows entry....Arnulfo Gomez and Francisco Serrano refuse to combine against Alvaro Obregon, ending speculation that one would give way to the other and make a two-candidate race.	U.S. trade with the Philippines is up. Doing particularly well are automobiles and cotton cloth.
Sep. 1		Germany fulfills its reparations obligations for the year. Improved German production, trade, and tourism make the 1.5 billion mark burden tolerable. The question is whether Germany can handle reparations in 1929, when the burden doubles.		In opening congress, President Plutarco Calles says that the deterioration in relations is because the U.S. is not clear about what it wants. He also asserts Mexico's right to enact its own laws, including the religious laws and those that expelled foreigners.	The nationalists in Hankow and Nanking merge into a single regime situated at Hankow. The merger is possible because the Communists are gone.
Sep. 2	A billion people live in 57 countries with regular broadcasting. 90 million have radios. All broadcast similar types of material. Europeans have more news, commercials, and government presentations.			Panama Canal traffic for August is 561 vessels, a record.	Cholera along the Yangtze is the south's ally. The disease forces Sun's army to retreat.
Sep. 3		Count Ignacio Thaon de Ravel has an audience with Benito Mussolini. He brings greetings from the American Blackshirts and a progress report on U.S. fascists, which Ravel heads....German manufacturers in convention reject mass production. They prefer quality....Kemal Pasha's hand-picked assembly candidates win unanimously. He allows no opponents.	The Syrian Independent Commission complains to the League that France is abusing its mandate. Rather than preparing Syria for independence, France is imposing its language and culture by force while neglecting economic development.	With the recent decision to complete the Hudson's Bay Railroad to Port Churchill, 25 years of western discontent should ease. First proposed in 1896 and begun in1908, the link will give western wheat producers a shorter, cheaper route to the east and to English markets. It should also promote migration to the west.	
Sep. 4	The League opens its meeting with the failed disarmament talks a major issue. In addition, the small nations are unhappy. After splits within French and English governments, the French representative says, the United States must get involved to reverse League "decrepitude."	Irish elections get under way. 249 candidates vie for 175 seats. The government labels Eamon de Valera's party perjurers....Spain imposes censorship of "disturbing" news after "pernicious" dispatches leak.			
Sep. 5	The eighth League Assembly chooses Uruguay's Alberto Guani president by one vote over Austria's Count Mensdorff. Six nations send no representative to a meeting with a light agenda.			An alert porter extinguishes the fuse at the last minute and prevents a bomb explosion at the West India Oil Company. West India is a Standard Oil subsidiary under boycott by labor. Buenos Aires police blame unionists.	The Nanking nationalists capture 10,000 northern soldiers and execute four northern generals. Britain continues fighting pirates.
Sep. 6		Hungary rounds up 250 Communists, with more raids promised. 14 reds admit to receiving Russian financing for their newspapers....In Moscow, Dutch-born M. Goier testifies that he served as a British spy in Leningrad between 1925 and 1927. He says he was preparing the way for a British invasion of Russia.		Nicaraguan rebel Carlos Salgado receives an ultimatum from American and Nicaraguan forces to surrender. An American-led constabulary wounds five bandits. Joint efforts against rebels Salgado and Augusto Sandino began after the two refused to recognize the liberal surrender.	Northerners hold the banks of the Yangtze. Japan continues evacuation from Shantung. Canton merchant hostages are free.

A	B	C	D	E
Includes developments that affect more than one world region, international organizations and important meetings of world leaders.	*Includes all domestic and regional developments in Europe, including the Soviet Union.*	*Includes all domestic and regional developments in Africa and the Middle East.*	*Includes all domestic and regional developments in Latin America, the Caribbean, and Canada.*	*Includes all domestic and regional developments in Asian and Pacific nations (and colonies).*

U.S. Politics & Social Issues	U.S. Foreign Policy & Affairs, Defense	U.S. Economy & Environment	Science, Technology & Nature	Culture, Leisure & Lifestyle	
	Mexico releases two army flyers who strayed across the border and landed in Chihuahua three days earlier. They report being well treated but the Mexican army still holds their plane....Army Jennies fly at Mitchell Field. Then the army retires World War I planes.	The National Zoo in Washington, DC, wins a French award for hatching blue geese. It is the first to hatch wild fowl.	Two naval lieutenants write in the U.S. Naval Institute Proceedings that the great circle route is the most perilous because weather data is scarce. They see cross-ocean routes in 15 years, probably by a more southerly route through the Azores. And safety requires seaplanes....William Brock and Edward Schlee make Constantinople.	Five-year-old Norma Dreyer, twice-winner of the Asbury Park baby parade, wins Baby Miss America over 26 other baby parade winners. The parade of 800 children draws 150,000 Asbury Park spectators, including the governor of New Jersey.	Aug. 31
After the U.S.–Canadian meeting on smuggling reduction, the U.S. doubles the number of border patrol agents to 400, with 50 at Detroit....The mine conflict in Ohio turns deadly. A trainman hauling coal from the disputed area is shot dead.	At the urging of the state department, a U.S. firm agrees to cancel shipment to Russia of 15,000 to 20,000 rifles. The government cannot force the cancellation because the 1922 Congressional resolution authorizing presidential embargoes does not cover Russia....Army Chief of Staff Major General Charles Summerall tells the Army War College future war will emphasize speed. Planes and tanks will reduce reliance on soldiers.		Werner Heisenberg details quantum theory to 200 scientists at the meeting of the British Association for the Advancement of Science. Among the 30 papers read were one about the inevitable extinction of the Eskimo and one on the existence of an Antarctic continent....Redfern is missing, and Brazil is searching. Princess Lowenstein-Wertheim is also missing off Canada. Since May, 15 flyers have been lost.	Eddie Rickenbacker closes a million-dollar deal for the Indianapolis speedway. Rickenbacker is head of the corporation and former car racer. He affirms the track will hold a single race each year, the 500-mile classic begun in 1911.	Sep. 1
The ACLU cites police abuse in quelling Sacco demonstrations in Boston. In Washington, Boston, New York, Chicago, Los Angeles, and Cheswick, PA, the ACLU documents denials of rights of assembly and speech....Health exams in Europe allow 175 third-class immigrants to bypass Ellis Island with 1,350 first-class passengers on the same liner.	President Calvin Coolidge says that the call by the International Economic Conference for tariff reduction applies to European tariff walls only. U.S. tariffs are not restricting trade, Calvin Coolidge says.		A solo British flyer takes off in a seaplane from Plymouth for North America. Eddie Stinson, whose company built Redfern's plane, says Stinson will build no more solo planes The American Bar Association says the government should regulate solo flights. The government says regulation would stifle initiative.	Babe Ruth hits homer 44. Lou Gehrig gets a pair but trails by one.	Sep. 2
Bar Harbor, ME, expects no black invasion after John Nail of Harlem buys property for black residences at Sorrento on Frenchman's Bay. Although eight miles by water, the property is 40 miles off by road.			Thanks to radio, Calvin Coolidge has spoken to more people than any other chief executive. His audiences total the U.S. population of 1865.	After weeks spent selecting the polo team and polishing it through exhibition matches, the United States is ready to take on Britain. The British team has a maharajah as advisor and a string of Indian polo ponies, but the U.S. is favored, 6-5....Port Jervis follows Beacon in banning rolled knickers. The police chief notes the town is not a bathing beach; women should cover themselves.	Sep. 3
A bomb damages the Brooklyn courthouse and hall of records. Radicals are suspected of making a Labor Day statement....William Z. Foster, U.S. Communist, points to unrest among the locomotive engineers. He tells the Workers Party convention the time is right to take over mining, metal, and transportation unions.	Senator William Borah asks Secretary Frank B. Kellogg to block a $100 million loan France is seeking. The Idaho senator wants French war debts settled first. He notes that France protests U.S. charges of 1 ¼ percent interest while accepting bankers' 6 percent. The government has no legal authority to stop the loan.	Secretary Herbert Hoover returns to the flood area. He finds the Red Cross still feeding 60,000, half of the area bankrupt, pellagra and malaria afflicting 50,000, and 300,000 in three states destitute and unable to pay their taxes.	British scientists the Bishop of Ripon advise them to cease work for a decade to allow the world to catch up. Sir Oliver Lodge counters that his grandmother felt that way about trains going 40 miles per hour. It is impossible to stop scientific advance....William Brock and Edward Schlee reach India in their round-the-world effort.	The second couple in 24 hours marries in an airplane over the Teterboro Air Show. Several thousand spectators listen as the plane shuts down its engines so the couple can hear the pastor.	Sep. 4
Population growth four times the New York rate in the past decade swells Harlem's population to 200,000. A seven-month study by 30 New York social work agencies reveals the area has high juvenile delinquency. It has poor play facilities, overcrowding and rent gouging and a high percentage of working mothers.				George M. Cohan takes the lead in "the Merry Malones." He replaces Arthur Deagon, who dies suddenly.	Sep. 5
		Newfoundland passes the final special interest law asked by International Paper. The American company now owns a paper mill with a daily output of 60,000 tons of paper and the right to build another near Gander Bay.	At the meeting of the British Association for the Advancement of Science, Sir Oliver Lodge says that electrons constantly in motion through the ether are the source of creation. Lodge accepts Einstein's relativity but also accepts ether, which Einstein ignores, and a "guiding mind."	Babe Ruth hits numbers 45, 46, and 47 and leads Lou Gehrig by two. He ties his 1926 total but is seven behind his 1921 record pace.	Sep. 6

F	G	H	I	J
Includes campaigns, elections, federal-state relations, civil rights and liberties, crime, the judiciary, education, healthcare, poverty, urban affairs, and population.	Includes formation and debate of U.S. foreign and defense policies, veterans affairs, and defense spending. (Relations with specific foreign countries are usually found under the region concerned.)	Includes business, labor, agriculture, taxation, transportation, consumer affairs, monetary and fiscal policy, natural resources, pollution and industrial accidents.	Includes worldwide scientific, medical and technological developments, natural phenomena, U.S. weather and natural disasters.	Includes the arts, religion, scholarship, communications media, sports, entertainment, fashions, fads, and social life.

	World Affairs	Europe	Africa & The Middle East	The Americas	Asia & The Pacific
Sep. 7	Another plane takes off from North America for Europe and another, *Old Glory*, broadcasts an SOS. Britain criticizes stunt flights. Australia restricts them....At the League meeting, Poland proposes outlawing war, Sweden objects to the big powers meeting privately, and Japan asks for arms reductions.	Turkey orders that all persons in Turkey on Friday, October 28, must be indoors for a census. The ruling excludes only passengers on steamers and express trains. Turkey wants to correct an undercount.		In Mexico, General Arnulfo Gomez denies saying that if elected he will shut down hostile papers. Press freedom is a campaign issue, and he has previously advocated it.... Chile is expected to ask Calvin Coolidge to withdraw in favor of the League as arbitrator of the Tacna-Arica dispute. Peru insists that Coolidge remain. The jurisdiction of the League in Latin America is in dispute.	After two days of Hindu-Muslim rioting in Nagpur, India, 25 are dead and hundreds injured. Police finally quell the disturbances, which began when Hindus disrupted a Muslim memorial service. Fired women stone to death their former boss.
Sep. 8	The League rejects Poland's proposal. Poland resubmits. The smaller nations remain unhappy with big power attitudes....Another flight from North America to Europe fails. Worldwide demands for cessation of flights grow as deaths increase. France and Germany join the anti-flight chorus.	British trades unions vote to sever ties to international Communism.... France implements new tariff rates that hit the United States hard and bring protests. Average tariff on electrical equipment rises 800 percent. Germany seems the beneficiary.	American companies receive the right to bid on the Palestinian Dead Sea salts concession. Under treaty, non-British companies have the same rights as British ones in the mandate territory.		
Sep. 9	Germany's Gustav Stresemann says reliance on war is foolish. Germany accepts Aristide Briand's arbitration plan. Poland submits its plan for outlawing war; Italy attacks it.	Paris begins purging its streets of radicals in preparation for the American Legion reunion. City police round up and expel or sequester 1,000 European and American reds. The Communist press, meanwhile, backs agitation for disrupting the veterans' return.			Ethnic violence in Kelaya, India, kills 600. Causes of the fighting that involves tens of thousands include Sunni-Shia and tribal differences plus the chance to claim spoils. Britain is considering what to do.
Sep. 10		After 25 years the Davis Cup comes to Europe. France celebrates the victory of Rene Lacoste and Henri Cochet over Bill Tilden and Bill Johnston. Enthusiasts rate the victory greater than Georges Carpentier's boxing victory over Jack Dempsey.... Moscow's Comsomol parade features not only red youth but also red sisters. Also in the parade is the first proletarian car, a prototype vehicle capable of 50 mph.	General J.C. Smuts, former president of the Union of South Africa, reiterates that South Africa will stand by Britain in event of war. He rebuts Interior Minister F. S. Malan, who contends that new status in the empire gives South Africa the option of declaring neutrality.	Fruit blight is destroying the banana crop in Panama and Costa Rica. Exports are off 90 percent as growers abandon infected fields. Attempts by United Fruit to replant fields in 1915 and 1916 failed. Although the fields lay fallow 30 years, the blight returned immediately.	
Sep. 11		A British naval reservist becomes first to cross the English Channel in a canoe. He paddles five hours in a blinding storm....In Lithuania a former army captain sacked for Communist activity leads 60 men in a robbery that nets $23,000. He also opens local prisons before fleeing arriving troops.		Augusto Sandino destroys a mine, takes the gold, and heads for the hills. He has money, arms, and provisions for a long stay.	
Sep. 12	Panama's Armando Morales takes his canal sovereignty dispute with the United States to the League. Not only is the presentation of Latin American disputes before the League, but airing disputes with the United States is unheard of. Most extraordinary, the League hears Panamanian claims. Frank B. Kellogg denies League jurisdiction.	Crimean earthquakes damage many houses at Sebastopol and elsewhere. Tremors are felt in the Caucasus.	The Zionist Congress reforms the Zionist Executive in Palestine. It consists of three English speakers not allied with any local faction. One member is Harriet Szold of the U.S., founder of Hadassah.		Anti-Japanese riots break out in Mukden after a month of unrest over northern-Japanese talks. Both Peking and Tokyo worry that this shows the people rejecting not only Japan but also Chang Tso Lin....In Raipur, India, disturbances between Muslims and Hindus injure 10. Hindus in procession with chanting and music disrupt Muslim prayers.

A	B	C	D	E
Includes developments that affect more than one world region, international organizations and important meetings of world leaders.	*Includes all domestic and regional developments in Europe, including the Soviet Union.*	*Includes all domestic and regional developments in Africa and the Middle East.*	*Includes all domestic and regional developments in Latin America, the Caribbean, and Canada.*	*Includes all domestic and regional developments in Asian and Pacific nations (and colonies).*

U.S. Politics & Social Issues	U.S. Foreign Policy & Affairs, Defense	U.S. Economy & Environment	Science, Technology & Nature	Culture, Leisure & Lifestyle	
Reports of a settlement in the Ohio coal strike prove premature. Talks continue. Meanwhile, in Pennsylvania, a non-union miner is killed and another wounded.	Mexico's consul hires an attorney to defend the five Latin Americans, four of them Mexican, accused of bombing the Brooklyn supreme court building and New York subway. The attorney says he wants to avoid another Sacco-Vanzetti....The army experiments with dying light horses darker shades. The hope is that camouflaging horses will hide them from aircraft surveillance.		The navy says it lacks the resources to search the Atlantic for Old Glory. Searchers must rely on civilian liners to spot the plane....Schlee and Brock are in Rangoon, having ridden out a monsoon.	Babe Ruth hits two more, tying a record with five homers in three games.	Sep. 7
		Chevrolet announces it will match any new Ford model in design and price. It guarantees its price to be within $50 of the new Ford....The Chicago reserve bank indicates it will take the Federal Reserve to court over the new rediscount rate forced on Chicago. The matter shows a rift between England-looking easterners and regionally focused midwesterners.	A German invents a car that flies. A New Yorker invents one lubricated by water instead of oil....John L. Baird, Scottish inventor of television, demonstrates his noctovisor by sending his face 200 miles from Leeds to London. The noctovisor uses infrared rays. Baird foresees it as more useful as a tool to warn ships at sea than as television.	Actress Valeska Suratt sues Cecil B. DeMille for $1 million. She says he stole her work for "King of Kings," and she wants his profits.	Sep. 8
The Calvin Coolidges end their summer vacation. They leave Rapid City, SD, by train....Indiana's governor is indicted for attempting to bribe a former governor. Others implicated include the mayor of Indianapolis, the head of the KKK, and state Republican leaders.	The navy bars its planes from flying over water and assisting contest flights. Cities including Boston and Philadelphia withdraw prizes and several would-be competitors cancel their flights....The United States protests France's new tariff. Frank B. Kellogg wants equality for U.S. goods.			Sixteen-year-old Lois Eleanor Delander, Miss Illinois, wins miss America. Moselle Ransome of Dallas, TX, is first runner up. The pageant also features a parachute drop form a dirigible and a prize for handsomest judge. Miss America 1926 denies she is a no-show because the pageant will not pay her.	Sep. 9
An Ohio federal judge enjoins foreign miners from picketing the Eastern Ohio field. The judge says non-citizens and non-English speakers will be deported. Owners in other Ohio fields ask similar injunctions.	New York appeals court justice Benjamin Cardozo declines an invitation from Calvin Coolidge to sit on the league's International Court of Arbitration. Offering the seat is Charles Evans Hughes, an American representative to the court. Cardozo sees a conflict between state and international service.	The new French tariff rates hit the United States hard as Germany begins dumping hides, silk, hardware, and electrical devices. The United States asks France to delay....The new cars are appearing. Cadillac and Packard feature low bodies. Ford has reportedly spent $15 million converting 15,000 machines, over half its production tools.	80,000 watch as Edsel Ford sends off the 15 entrants in the 16th annual Gordon Bennett Trophy. First off is the Spanish balloon. The first of three American entrants is fifth. Other entries are from Germany, Belgium, England, Italy, and Switzerland....William Brock and Edward Schlee are over Japan, halfway around the world, with a worn engine. They still plan to fly the Pacific.	The U.S.–Britain polo matches finally begin, with the British Army in India team against the United States' finest. The Tommy Hitchcock-led Americans take the first game.	Sep. 10
An Industrial Conference report shows English speakers increasing as a percentage of immigrants. They are 45 percent of those arriving since 1924, but there is a shift from England and Ireland to Newfoundland and Canada. Italian immigration remains heavy but shows a net loss of 30,000 over three years. Mexican immigration is rising rapidly, but overall numbers are below prewar levels.	At Camp Riley a 20-man U.S. army marksmanship team sets a record with 7,807 out of 8,000 in besting an English team. The United States regains the Dewar trophy, lost to Britain in 1926 after holding it since 1913.		Copdodger, a seemingly harmless powder, is the latest ploy smugglers use to fool customs. It converts into synthetic morphine when mixed with an innocuous looking liquid....William Brock and Edward Schlee are in Japan, stymied by weather that won't let them fly.		Sep. 11
The Second Annual Henry George Conference convenes in New York. Attendance is 300 Americans and Europeans. Their goal is a single tax. They hear of progress in China, Denmark, and Pittsburgh.	The United States gives France a draft treaty of amity and commerce asking most favored nation status. First of its kind, it is expected to encounter resistance....Secretary Dwight Davis unleashes efficiency experts on the War Department. The survey examines only administrative offices.	United Bank and Trust buys 11 California banks with a value of $9 million. The chain now owns 34 banks worth $104 million....Secretary of War Dwight Davis says repairs to the Mississippi system will continue despite Controller General McCarl's disapproval of transfer of $2 million but money will be gone in November.	A Detroit balloonist wins the Bennett trophy for flying the farthest, to Georgia. All 15 balloons land safely....Bell Laboratories scientists report they can measure a billionth of an inch and a millionth of a degree of temperature. The measurements will aid study of magnetism and sound transmission....The Morrissey expedition reports mapmakers have made Baffin Island 5,000 square miles too big.	Having switched to a more muscular lineup, the British polo quartet wins game 2....Musical comedy star Fannie Brice sues for divorce, claiming infidelity. She says her new nose makes her too beautiful and alienates her husband, ex-con Nicky Arnstein.	Sep. 12

F	G	H	I	J
Includes campaigns, elections, federal-state relations, civil rights and liberties, crime, the judiciary, education, healthcare, poverty, urban affairs, and population.	*Includes formation and debate of U.S. foreign and defense policies, veterans affairs, and defense spending. (Relations with specific foreign countries are usually found under the region concerned.)*	*Includes business, labor, agriculture, taxation, transportation, consumer affairs, monetary and fiscal policy, natural resources, pollution and industrial accidents.*	*Includes worldwide scientific, medical and technological developments, natural phenomena, U.S. weather and natural disasters.*	*Includes the arts, religion, scholarship, communications media, sports, entertainment, fashions, fads, and social life.*

	World Affairs	Europe	Africa & The Middle East	The Americas	Asia & The Pacific
Sep. 13	Persia agrees to try the League plan to replace opium with other crops, says Colonel Daniel MacCormack, technical advisor to the Persian government. He notes that drug-manufacturing states should lead the fight against narcotics. Among these states are France, Germany, Holland, Japan, and the United States.	Preparations are under way to handle 30,000 Legionnaires in Paris. American flags already overwhelm the quarter where the veterans will stay. Holders of the Croix de Guerre are providing French and American flags to all taxis and private cars that will carry the banners.	John Boyes, famous big game hunter in Kenya, proposes a hunt from airplane. He would have native beaters flush the lions, recover the animals shot from the air, and prepare the trophies. Boyes contends the recent British ban on hunting from automobiles does not apply.	A tidal wave hits west Mexico. After four days, rain ceases in central and southern Mexico. The rain and floods derail trains and cause extensive damage to cities and rural areas. Although the Grand Canal floods in several places and the Remedios River breaches along a 40-mile stretch, workers divert the floods before they inundate Mexico City.	A tidal wave and typhoon hit Kumamoto Prefecture, Kyushu, Japan. Floods destroy communications and rail and swamp Nagasaki and rich rice lands. Death reports vary from 100 to 1,000. At least 1,000 are missing.
Sep. 14		Bulgaria and Greece have League approval to borrow $50 million and $45 million respectively. Austria's request for $112 million is pending.... Swinemuende Bay hosts the largest German naval parade since the war. President Paul von Hindenberg and his army and navy chiefs review 35 ships and 7,000 men.		Quebec welcomes a 75-vehicle motorcade including the governor of Georgia and golfer Bobby Jones. The end of the 1,400-mile drive officially opens the Appalachian Scenic highway.	
Sep. 15	Seats on the new League Council go to Cuba and Canada, giving the Americas four seats. Finland replaces Belgium as the small nations seek greater rotation of seats.	Turnout in the Irish election is 70 percent. Early reports show W.T. Cosgrave gaining 14 seats and Eamon de Valera losing six. Official results will take about a week.		Canada imposes a 30 percent tariff on American magazines because they do not qualify as news sources. Among the 49 are *Argosy, Black Mask, Sweetheart Stories,* and other fiction magazines....Mexico prepares for independence day celebrations by increasing military presence. It seizes two men in a plot to assassinate Alvaro Obregon. Foreigners are leaving after the murder of an American and the seizure of an American mine.	
Sep. 16		The American Expeditionary Force and General John Pershing return to France. Enthusiastic crowds welcome the veterans at Cherbourg. Veterans stress Paris hotels and cause a soap shortage....Updated Irish returns show Eamon de Valera with 13 seats, W.T. Cosgrave with 12, and independents with five. Election fights kill two.			The new Japanese princess, a week old, receives the name Sachico Hisa, Steadfast Helper. Japan still has no heir.
Sep. 17	The League Council adjourns after a Romanian-Hungarian dispute over land law turns bitter. Canada shows its independence by backing the position contrary to that of Britain's representative.	A conservative attack on King Alfonso's veracity and legitimacy causes a crisis in Spain. Alfonso's government cries disloyalty....W.T. Cosgrave now has 49 votes in his coalition. His majority is one.			The Bank of Japan and other Japanese banks announce the formation of the Showa bank. The new bank will aid readjustment of banks that closed during the April panic.
Sep. 18		Eamon de Valera and W.T. Cosgrave each have 63 seats....A Communist paper in Berlin begins an anti-U.S. campaign portraying U.S. streets lined with machine guns. American troops are torturers.	The Palestine appeal urges payment of unpaid pledges within 12 days. The relief effort still has $350,000 unpaid.		
Sep. 19	Hungary rejects the League committee ruling in Romania's favor. The League accepts Poland's proposal outlawing aggressive war.	Nationalists applaud Paul von Hindenberg for rejecting German war guilt at the opening of the Tannenberg Memorial. Republicans fret that he is premature.	Egypt estimates this year's crop at 320,000 tons. This is the first year of crop restrictions, and planted area is down to 1.5 million fedans from 1.8 fedans in 1926. A fedan is roughly 1¼ acres.	Ford engineers in Brazil are testing the prospects for rubber plantations....in Los Angeles federal and local officers seize guns and ammunition and take 16 Mexicans into custody. 12 are released but four are held for plotting to attack Mexicali, Tijuana, and other cities in Mexico....An Argentine legislator introduces a bill raising tariffs on U.S. goods. He retaliates for U.S. barriers.	

A	B	C	D	E
Includes developments that affect more than one world region, international organizations and important meetings of world leaders.	*Includes all domestic and regional developments in Europe, including the Soviet Union.*	*Includes all domestic and regional developments in Africa and the Middle East.*	*Includes all domestic and regional developments in Latin America, the Caribbean, and Canada.*	*Includes all domestic and regional developments in Asian and Pacific nations (and colonies).*

U.S. Politics & Social Issues	U.S. Foreign Policy & Affairs, Defense	U.S. Economy & Environment	Science, Technology & Nature	Culture, Leisure & Lifestyle	
The mine strike continues in Illinois after negotiations fail.... Increasingly young men are seeking treatment for addiction, but not for heroin. Opium is popular. The new drug of choice is morphine, possibly because it is so easy to smuggle, possibly because $6 can buy a high that costs $15–$25 with heroin.	Canada detains the Coast Guard's anti-smuggling cutter *Crawford*. The vessel carries a 3-inch gun and fails to ask Canadian permission to proceed armed as required by the 1817 agreement between the United States and Great Britain....France agrees to delay implementing the new tariff. She will talk but expects something tangible for granting most favored nation status.	Crude oil output is down 21,600 barrels to 2,490,650. A large drop in Oklahoma is the main reason.... Calvin Coolidge urges shippers to support the Merchant Marine. He acknowledges that a $300 million building program is necessary but balks at the price.	Search teams find the wreckage of *Old Glory* and report that a 34 section of wing is severed from the plane. The search continues but with little hope for the flyers' survival.	Fannie Brice also sues the woman who alienated her husband's affections. She asks $250,000....Babe Ruth hits a pair. His home run total is 52.	Sep. 13
Senator Gerald Nye (R-ND) calls on Senate progressives to unite behind a program prioritizing farm and flood relief and rejecting a tax cut. He calls Senator George Norris (R-NB) to lead.	A Canadian businessman calls for U.S. tariff reform. He claims U.S. rates are discriminating against Dominion countries....France is reportedly willing to give most favored nation status but expects the United States to provide the same.	A seat on the curb exchange sells for $32,000. This is the year's top price but $5,000 below the record.	New York and Dallas establish a long distance link. Dallas is the hub for Texas cities. Repeaters in nearly a dozen cities along the way allow an uninterrupted circuit....William Brock and Edward Schlee announce they will ground the Pride of Detroit and take a steamer across the Pacific. Authorities express relief and celebrate the record-setting performance of the two.	Fannie Brice wins the $500,000 Chicago home in her uncontested divorce....Tommy Hitchcock and a great team effort bring polo victory to the United States....Isadora Duncan dies in Nice after her scarf is caught and drags her from a speeding car. Duncan is founder of modern dance....The Yankees win their 99th game and clinch the American League pennant—again.	Sep. 14
The Men's Church League begins a campaign to sign up a million U.S. and Canadian Protestant volunteers committed to converting one person a year until they have evangelized the entire world. The effort revives a 1924 campaign....The Grand Army of the Republic encamps at Grand Rapids, MI. The GAR consists of union veterans of the Civil War. Its major legislative goal is getting pensions for widows who married veterans after the war.	The United States says current law bars it from negotiating tariff terms with France so it must refuse reciprocity. France refuses the United States most-favored-nation status without a quid pro quo. A tariff war seems imminent.	Herbert Hoover reports that he has relief funds to last through the end of the year with a $1 million surplus. Ninety-two percent of the people are taking care of themselves. Food and health support is still going to 46,000. There is no need for a special congressional session.... Although Chicago's economy is good, the city counts 100,000 unemployed, with more arriving from the flood ravaged south, the agriculturally depressed midwest, and other cities.	The Federal Air Coordinating Committee advises Calvin Coolidge not to ban over-ocean flights. The committee says public opinion will discourage excessive risk taking.... Having remapped Fox Land, the *Morissey* begins its return from Labrador. The expedition discovers what seems to be a Viking settlement.	Ideal Sporting Goods withdraws its complaint against the New York Boxing Commission after that body withdraws its requirement that boxers purchase shorts of specific colors from Everlast Sporting Goods. Ideal's complaint is not that the commission favors another company but that many boxers in preliminary bouts box in homemade trunks because they receive poor pay or for sentimental reasons.	Sep. 15
Alabama indicts 18 men for conspiracy in a series of flogging incidents. The grand jury also scores overzealous fraternal organizations....Refuting recent reports of stagnation, the Federal Council of churches reports 50 percent growth over 20 years. 25 denominations show increases greater than population growth.		The government ends cotton price forecasts after one causes a sharp drop in the cotton market.		U.S. vaudevillians report that business remains strong. This after a report that vaudeville is in decline in England.	Sep. 16
William Gibbs McAdoo drops out of the race for the Democratic presidential nomination. He says he wants party harmony rather than the discord that wrecked the 1924 campaign.		The Florida East Coast Railway reports Miami almost fully recovered from the hurricane that struck exactly a year ago. Construction, bank clearings, and other indicators are at levels matching the pre-boom 1920s.	The German gyrostat provides automatic guidance for airplanes. It maintains stability and increases fuel efficiency.	Gene Tunney is favored 7–5 as experts anticipate a betting handle of $10 million for the championship bout....Rene Lacoste defeats Bill Tilden to retain his U.S. Open tennis title. This marks the first time in 46 years that a foreigner has held the title back to back.	Sep. 17
Smith forces fear William Gibbs McAdoo is trying to unite anti-Smith forces. The goal is a brokered convention....Los Angeles gets recognition as the most pedestrian-friendly city.		A Mississippi River boat experiments with powdered coal. The fuel is safe and economical.	26 planes take off in the Spokane Derby. The 2300-mile race has three categories—10-stop, 6-stop, and non-stop. The other two classes will take off later and fly different routes.	Babe Ruth hits number 54, tying his second best season, 1920. He still trails his 1921 record by five. The Yankees win number 104, one short of the league record.	Sep. 18
The Pittsburgh mayoral primary is ugly. Backers of Vare and Moore engage in fisticuffs and a gun battle....On trial for corruption, Indianapolis Mayor John Duvall says he appointed Klan backers before they met the grand jury but denies the Klan or any group owns him.	The United States agrees to participate in a Geneva trade conference in October. The meeting is to develop a treaty easing import/export restrictions, not to reform tariffs.	U.S. blacksmiths hold their annual convention at Jersey City. They number 70,000 despite the automobile and still are recruiting....Quaker Oats pays $2 million for Muffetts.... Leon Henderson of the Russell Sage Foundation tells the Better Business Bureau convention that salary buying causes 20–30 percent of bankruptcies. Payday loan usury leads 24 states to enact laws against salary buying.	A Chicago engineer says tests determine that the life of a spark plug is 10,000 miles....Ruth Elder flies twice with an inspector and once solo. She now has her pilot's license and can proceed with plans to co-pilot a trans-Atlantic flight.	Sir Henry Coward, English musician, says that whites must discard jazz. The music debases white culture, as do associated immodest dances.	Sep. 19

F	G	H	I	J
Includes campaigns, elections, federal-state relations, civil rights and liberties, crime, the judiciary, education, healthcare, poverty, urban affairs, and population.	*Includes formation and debate of U.S. foreign and defense policies, veterans affairs, and defense spending. (Relations with specific foreign countries are usually found under the region concerned.)*	*Includes business, labor, agriculture, taxation, transportation, consumer affairs, monetary and fiscal policy, natural resources, pollution and industrial accidents.*	*Includes worldwide scientific, medical and technological developments, natural phenomena, U.S. weather and natural disasters.*	*Includes the arts, religion, scholarship, communications media, sports, entertainment, fashions, fads, and social life.*

	World Affairs	Europe	Africa & The Middle East	The Americas	Asia & The Pacific
Sep. 20		W.T. Cosgrave has a 79–73 margin but some of his backers are undependable....After the opposition calls for an end to censorship of the press and speech, Marshal Pilsudski ends parliament....Authorities tie a gun battle in Constantinople to a soviet-backed plot to kill Kemal.		Mexico's Lerma River continues to flood for the third day. Cities are ruined and people are trapped on rooftops....Fighting in Telpaneca, Nicaragua, kills one marine and wounds another. Marines and militia kill 20 rebels and wound 50....The Texas Company begins wildcatting in Santo Domingo.	The new government—a council of five—replaces the old nationalist factions.
Sep. 21			After the Egyptian government's cotton estimate, prices drop $4 to $37.25 in three days. Analysts reduce the size of the crop.		
Sep. 22			Sierra Leone enacts legislation to free slaves. The British protectorate has 220,000 slaves and its supreme court last year overturned convictions of two owners who retrieved a runaway.	Reports from Mexico indicate that 10,000 are homeless and the flood has destroyed a third of Acambaro.	
Sep. 23		In the worst German air disaster, a Lufthansa plane crashes, killing the ambassador to the United States, Baron von Maltzan, and five others. Pilot failure, not rumored sabotage, is the cause. This is the second Lufthansa crash in two days.			
Sep. 24	The League Assembly votes unanimously to outlaw war. It accepts the Polish plan. Gustav Stresemann asks other nations to join Germany in abandoning the instruments of war.	German slaughterhouses announce success with stunning animals with electrical current before killing them. Plans are to implement this more humane procedure soon.		After initial skepticism, Mexican newspapers find new ambassador Dwight Morrow acceptable.	Bangkok reports that wild elephants used their trunks to douse a forest fire.
Sep. 25	The agreement to outlaw war revitalizes the League. Planning begins for arms restriction talks in the spring.	Italy's austerity measures have worked. Imports are down 26 percent while exports are down only 10 percent. Wholesale markets are equivalent with gold. France's budget balances. Germany finances its foreign trade deficit through borrowing.			
Sep. 26		A dam break on the Rhine floods virtually all of tiny Lichtenstein. Switzerland and Italy also suffer from floods.		Mexico's Panuco River is totally out of control. Floods reach Tampico. Oil production is affected.	A Muslim attacks Rajpal in Lahore and inflicts several non-lethal knife wounds. Rajpal's "The Merry Prophet" alienated Indian Muslims and Hindus and led to passage of a law banning writing against the founder of a religion....Communist capture of Swatow gives the reds a port for receiving Russian arms. Japanese troops are at Hankow and American vessels at Saigon.
Sep. 27	After working late into the evening selecting members of the security and disarmament committees, the League Council adjourns. Members express satisfaction with progress toward peace.	Communist French deputies Jacque Duclos and Andre Marty receive sentences of 30 and 10 years respectively. Both are convicted, as are two others, of fomenting army disorders, propagandizing about the Chinese civil war, and other anarchist activity. Four others are found not guilty.		Haiti releases three journalists arrested on September 19 for reporting that the United States and Haiti secretly negotiated a large U.S. army and navy base. Haiti and the United States denied the report and the journalists recanted....A Mexican army firing squad publicly executes 18 bandits. The bodies hang from trees as a warning. Bandit bands that attack trains have as many as 400 men.	

A	B	C	D	E
Includes developments that affect more than one world region, international organizations and important meetings of world leaders.	Includes all domestic and regional developments in Europe, including the Soviet Union.	Includes all domestic and regional developments in Africa and the Middle East.	Includes all domestic and regional developments in Latin America, the Caribbean, and Canada.	Includes all domestic and regional developments in Asian and Pacific nations (and colonies).

U.S. Politics & Social Issues	U.S. Foreign Policy & Affairs, Defense	U.S. Economy & Environment	Science, Technology & Nature	Culture, Leisure & Lifestyle	
Evangelical Lutheran ministers in synod hear that church members are casual. The reason is that too often clergy lack piety themselves.... The University of North Carolina has women faculty, the first in its 133-year history. The two are in the school of education.	Dwight Morrow resigns from J.P. Morgan to become U.S. ambassador to Mexico.		German ace Otto Koennecke heads over eastern Europe en route to the United States....Britain's E.F. Spanner says the airship has no future. It is dangerous, expensive, and commercially worthless.	Courts reject a minister's attempt to block the Dempsey-Tunney fight as "vulgar and brutal." Fans flock from Alaska and India and everywhere else to be gouged by Chicago hoteliers and watch the fight.	Sep. 20
Dr. Alexander Meikeljohn opens the University of Wisconsin experimental college with 125 students. Studying situations rather than subjects, students are to educate themselves....Long Island University opens. Brooklyn and Long Island, with a population greater than 38 states, now have a public university.	In Paris the American Legion calls for a separate cabinet department, a ministry of air. Former army flyer Billy Mitchell complains that "as soon as practicable" means not soon enough.	The director of the Radio World's Fair says that 25 major manufacturers have sold their entire output for the coming year. The director anticipates record sales.	New York and New Jersey governors speak over radio. Planes fly overhead. Mayors of New York and Fort Lee, NJ, break ground for the $60 million Hudson River Bridge, planned as the world's longest suspension bridge.	Columbia says it will broadcast the Dempsey-Tunney fight despite promoter Tex Rickard's opposition. Broadcasters prepare for an audience of 50 million over an 82-station network.	Sep. 21
Indianapolis mayor John Duvall is quickly convicted of corruption. His attorney blames a malicious press.... The Baltimore district naturalization officer causes a stir when he says American fascisti may lose their citizenship and face deportation. American fascist organizations protest that they are loyal to America before Italy.		The Pennsylvania Railroad announces discontinuance of local service on several branch lines in Maryland, Delaware, New Jersey, and Pennsylvania. Competition from private cars and buses is the reason.	Professor Hobbs and a crew of Eskimos and Americans establish a weather station on the Greenland icecap. The station detects gales and broadcasts alerts to ships. Hobbs is the first to radio from Greenland.	Jack Dempsey loses but says he will appeal the long count. Gene Tunney, he contends, was down 14-15 seconds in the 7th....In a game with seven triples, Babe Ruth hits his 56th homer and the Yankees tie the 1912 Red Sox record 105 wins. Lou Gehrig breaks Ruth's 1921 RBI record of 170.	Sep. 22
Federal marshals arrest Harry Sonenshine for attempting to fly Dempsey-Tunney films to Indiana, Michigan, and Ohio. Sonenshine says he is taking the film to Canada. The 1912 ban on interstate movement of fight film remains law until 1940.	Calvin Coolidge rejects a single defense department army and navy are one during war. He also rejects spending more on the navy than planned before naval talks failed. He might rebuild two former German ships for $6 million. New ships mean more mail revenue.		Dr. Chauncey Barber says nicotine poisoning kills 60 percent of smokers' babies by age two. He also says nicotine is the gateway drug for morphine, cocaine, and other drugs....Kansas City replaces its last fire horses, Jerry and Pete, with a fire truck.	Dean Gauss of Princeton says many parents are unfit to send their sons to college. He says their lack of knowledge of their sons means one-sixth of college students should not be there.	Sep. 23
Federal agents get 125 indictments and break up a four-state liquor ring. 71 of the indicted are in South Bend, IN.	The surprise plane in the Spokane race is the army's entry. The previously-unrevealed plane tops 200 mph.	Ford hires 4,000 more workers in anticipation of demand for its new car. The workforce is now 62,800.	Health officials are quick to challenge Barber's claims that maternal smoking kills infants. New York's health commissioner says he has never heard of a case.	The Illinois boxing commission rejects Jack Dempsey's claim of a long count. Gene Tunney shows bruises from Dempsey's low blows. The fight result stands.	Sep. 24
Begun in Boston in 1904, zoning is now used in 553 cities. 46 states allow cities to zone. New York is first to zone use, height, and area. The largest cities without regulation are Detroit and Philadelphia.... Louisiana Republicans begin efforts to oust blacks from their party. The target of the Pelican Club is wealthy black Walter Cohen, Harding-appointed collector of customs a New Orleans.		The New York Trust reports that the U.S. investment in Latin America is $4.5 billion, 50 percent greater than investment in Europe. Major imports are Colombian coffee and Columbian and Venezuelan oil. Imports from Cuba and Mexico are down due Cuban poverty and Mexican unrest.			Sep. 25
At Gary, IN, 800 of Emmerson High School's 1400 students walk out to protest enrollment of 24 blacks. Gary has another school, 50 percent white, but the black students are in the Emmerson district.			An outbreak of infantile paralysis closes Daviess County, KY, schools.	Babe Ruth is four homers shy of his record with four games to play—one against the Athletics and three against the Senators.	Sep. 26
With his corruption conviction on appeal, Indianapolis mayor Duvall faces a Democratic recall drive. His wife is city controller, and nine other family members work for the city. Combined salary of the mayor and family is $25,000....The secretary of a foundation that offers short religious movies to churches reports objections to movie portrayal of Jesus are waning.	Calvin Coolidge indicates he sees no benefit in U.S–Japanese naval talks as proposed by Admiral Saito. The Japanese government shares his disinclination to open discussions.		Professor Ludwig Mehely, racial biologist and new dean of philosophy, tells the faculty of the University of Budapest that mixed marriage imperils the human race. He contends that mixed offspring are degenerate. Mehely also wants reproduction for proletarians restricted.	Babe Ruth hits number 57. He has three games remaining. Lou Gehrig lags with 46.	Sep. 27

F	G	H	I	J
Includes campaigns, elections, federal-state relations, civil rights and liberties, crime, the judiciary, education, healthcare, poverty, urban affairs, and population.	Includes formation and debate of U.S. foreign and defense policies, veterans affairs, and defense spending. (Relations with specific foreign countries are usually found under the region concerned.)	Includes business, labor, agriculture, taxation, transportation, consumer affairs, monetary and fiscal policy, natural resources, pollution and industrial accidents.	Includes worldwide scientific, medical and technological developments, natural phenomena, U.S. weather and natural disasters.	Includes the arts, religion, scholarship, communications media, sports, entertainment, fashions, fads, and social life.

	World Affairs	Europe	Africa & The Middle East	The Americas	Asia & The Pacific
Sep. 28		Berlin bans Communists from marching in the Paul von Hindenberg birthday parade. The government fears disturbances....Britain records its millionth house built since the end of the war.		The United States provides Canada the largest number of non-British immigrants for the previous five months. Over 12,000 move to Canada. Immigration overall is up from 1926.	In Moscow, Eugene Chen, foreign minister of the failed Communist government, marries the widow of Sun Yat Senator Chen prepares a new Chinese rising with the aid of a large wedding present from the Communist International.
Sep. 29		Importers want Czechoslovakia to lift its 800-car-per-year limit on American cars, down from 1,600 last year. The government says it will allow 260 extra, but they will come out of next year's quota.			Australia increases the tariff on American cars $30–$125. The intent is to boost British imports and Australian manufactures.
Sep. 30		The Communist International removes Leon Trotsky and Vuyovitch from its executive. Trotsky defiantly charges the Stalinists are usurpers without authority from the masses. Thus, the expulsion is invalid.	Anxious to resolve the Tangier issue in Spain's favor, Primo de Rivera meets secretly with Austen Chamberlain to arrange a conference of interested parties—France, England, Italy, and Spain. This after several months of Franco-Spanish talks fail.	Rebellion resumes in Jalisco with heavy rebel casualties. The government seizes 25 Catholics in Mexico City.	
Oct. 1	The International psychic conference in Paris ends divided. Scientists want research with proper controls and reject phenomena such as the girl weeping blood and animals communicating their thoughts to humans.	The German celebration of Paul von Hindenberg's 80th birthday starts a day early. The occasion includes ceremonies, gifts, and amnesties of thousands. The Hindenberg Fund makes a preliminary $50,000 distribution to needy veterans. The fund receives voluntary contributions from Europeans and Americans, particularly Chicagoans.	Chamberlain is firm in rejecting Spain's proposal for a multi-power conference on Tangier. He explains that giving a single power too much control of Tangier will endanger the British interest in Gibraltar....South African Nationalists, advocates of independence from Britain, attack members of the South African Party of J.C. Smuts. Using chairs, clubs, and bottles, they force the SAP backers to flee and prevent Smuts from speaking.		The new KZRM, Manila, is broadcasting a 1,000 watt signal. The first broadcaster in the Philippines reaches throughout Asia and Australia with a consistent signal comparable in quality to signals in the United States.
Oct. 2	Britain protests payment to amateurs, halts fund raising for the Olympic Games, and considers a boycott. The British object to the payment of soccer players because it promotes professionalism. Britain boycotted soccer in the 1924 games.	75,000 Pan-Germans demonstrate in Vienna for union with Germany. The German envoy supports their position....Crowds for Paul von Hindenberg top 600,000.	Iran and Russia sign five accords. Among them are non-aggression and trade agreements. Others deal with fisheries, ports, and customs.		
Oct. 3	Prime Minister Stanley Baldwin calls Prime Minister William Mackenzie King. They inaugurate the new transatlantic cable linking England and Canada.	The British Labour Party convention opens. Its follows Trades Union Conference precedent and expels Communists. The opening session also sees the farewell of civil service unions such as the postal workers, prohibited by the Trades Unions Act from party membership....The nonchalant Spanish revolt is over. The military dictatorship has easily survived several risings in the past two years.	Iranian Kurds raid the Turkish frontier. Turkey protests to the Shah that the Kurds are under Persian military leadership.	Troops rebel in Mexico City, Torreon, and Vera Cruz. Plutarco Calles labels presidential rivals Francisco Serrano and Arnulfo Gomez leaders of the revolt. Government planes bomb the rebels. Rumor is that federal troops have captured and executed Serrano and Chiapas Governor Carlos Vidal.	
Oct. 4	The world radio conference opens with delegates from 70 countries. The goal is standardized radio policy.		Persia denies its officers are leading Kurdish bandits. In fact, the bandits have captured an officer and his men. Persia wants a joint effort against the bandits.	The rumors prove correct. Francisco Serrano and 13 others are executed after speedy trials. The rising fails and most of the 800 rebels in Mexico City have quit the battle.... Cuban President Gerardo Machado signs the sugar restriction law. Expectation is that an American will help administer the production and export limits. American companies have major stakes in Cuban sugar.	

A	B	C	D	E
Includes developments that affect more than one world region, international organizations and important meetings of world leaders.	Includes all domestic and regional developments in Europe, including the Soviet Union.	Includes all domestic and regional developments in Africa and the Middle East.	Includes all domestic and regional developments in Latin America, the Caribbean, and Canada.	Includes all domestic and regional developments in Asian and Pacific nations (and colonies).

U.S. Politics & Social Issues	U.S. Foreign Policy & Affairs, Defense	U.S. Economy & Environment	Science, Technology & Nature	Culture, Leisure & Lifestyle	
Federal agents in San Francisco arrest seven for showing fight movies. They issue a warrant for Tex Rickard and say they may also arrest Jack Dempsey and Gene Tunney.	The United States and Mexico inaugurate long distance service. The first call is between Calvin Coolidge and Plutarco Calles, with both presidents hoping for reduced future misunderstandings.	The Investment Bankers Association of America calls on the government to repair the flood damage as a national duty. Arkansas Governor John Martineau says over 10 percent of American investors have a stake in the flooded area. Repair costs are between $300 and $500 million.	Displays at a chemistry exposition include gears made of composites. Also featured are the use of perfume as insect bait and the use of ethylene to ripen fruit....Dr. Papez of Cornell reports that women's brains are not inferior to men's. He finds that the brain of Helen Gardener had more grey matter than most of the men in the university's collection.	Ring Lardner and George M. Cohan are collaborating on a baseball comedy. Lardner's "You Know Me, Al," stories, which first brought fame to Lardner, feature a hick baseball player.	Sep. 28
The Gary school strike ends in a "compromise." The city authorizes $15,000 to construct a separate building for the black students. Black aldermen say the deal is unconstitutional....The Girl Scouts abandon their khaki uniform as being too military. The new uniform is gray-green.	The navy approves a $7.6 million order for 146 planes and 505 air-cooled motors in the coming year.	*Factory News* reports that Ford paid $2 billion in wages during the 19-year life of the Model T. Total economic impact of the 15 million Model T's—including parts manufacture, service stations and garages and sales—exceeds $7 billion.	William Brock and Edward Schlee arrive in San Francisco—by boat. They plan to fly to Detroit and begin preparing for another around-the-world attempt....A tornado sweeps through the wealthy west side of St. Louis, killing 90 and causing $50 million in damage. Troops and police patrol against looters.	Babe Ruth hits two and ties his 1921 home run record with two games remaining.	Sep. 29
A federal judge in Pittsburgh enjoins striking miners from interfering with non-unionists. He rules the unionists are conspiring against interstate trade.	Having amended its constitution twice, Arkansas is preparing to issue bonds to pay Confederate veterans and widows pensions. The act also requires a ruling that pensions are not a debt incurred in support of the rebellion.		Synthetic wood and paper from cornstalks can be a $1 billion industry says Professor O.R. Sweeney of Iowa State College. He displays diabetic food, building blocks, embalming fluid and other products from the 200 million tons of waste available each year.	Babe Ruth hits number 60, driving in all Yankee runs in a 4–2 win.	Sep. 30
The coal strike finally ends in Illinois. Both sides agree to the old scale through next April, with negotiation in the meantime. The AFL's John L. Lewis anticipates similar results in the other strike areas.	France rejects the American request for most favored nation status. Frank B. Kellogg says he will release earlier correspondence. Offended at the American contention that she had no right to act as she did, France also asks that the United States not release its note without releasing France's reply at the same time.		The American Engineering Standards Committee announces its intention to standardize plumbing fixtures. The committee will begin with small parts such as faucet washers then work up to larger items.	Pittsburgh wins the National League and the opportunity to face the favored Yankees, winners of 110 games.	Oct. 1
		The United States prepares for a trade war as the Continental Steel Trust indicates it will compete in all U.S. markets with a unitary sales force like the one the wire trust uses successfully against U.S. firms. Europe has already made inroads into the U.S. trade with Asia and South America.	The Camden, NJ, hospital warns prospective buyers to beware guinea pigs. The 14 stolen from the hospital are tubercular.		Oct. 2
	Frank B. Kellogg releases the notes with France. The United States rejects the French claim that the president can reduce tariffs and makes no promises regarding treatment of specialty items or agricultural products.	American investors have purchased $975 million in foreign securities to date in 1927. this total is up $176 million from 1926.			Oct. 3
Informal polling shows Herbert Hoover is the second choice of Republican committee members, who have no interest in Charles Evans Hughes. Most prefer Calvin Coolidge....Sing Sing warden Lawes questions the death penalty. 53 reversals on appeal show errors in the system. He asks how many of the 261 executed by New York since 1889 might have been innocent.	Calvin Coolidge affirms that France is unfair in giving preferential treatment to other nations and not the United States. There will be no negotiation unless France ends this discrimination.		Prof. G.B. Vetter of New York University challenges the Cornell finding that women's brains are equal to men's. He says the appearance of a brain is no indicator of the quality of a mind.		Oct. 4

F	G	H	I	J
Includes campaigns, elections, federal-state relations, civil rights and liberties, crime, the judiciary, education, healthcare, poverty, urban affairs, and population.	*Includes formation and debate of U.S. foreign and defense policies, veterans affairs, and defense spending. (Relations with specific foreign countries are usually found under the region concerned.)*	*Includes business, labor, agriculture, taxation, transportation, consumer affairs, monetary and fiscal policy, natural resources, pollution and industrial accidents.*	*Includes worldwide scientific, medical and technological developments, natural phenomena, U.S. weather and natural disasters.*	*Includes the arts, religion, scholarship, communications media, sports, entertainment, fashions, fads, and social life.*

	World Affairs	Europe	Africa & The Middle East	The Americas	Asia & The Pacific
Oct. 5		A bomb outside the Nice Italian consulate is the fourth on the Riviera in recent weeks. Blamed on anarchist backers of Nicola Sacco and Bartolomeo Vanzetti, this one, unlike the others, harms no one....As the debt settlement dispute festers, France demands that Russia recall its minister, Christian Rakovsky. Russia ignored two previous notices that he is persona non grata....Poland arrests 20 Lithuanians in the ongoing dispute over ownership of Vilna.	Ceuta, Spanish Morocco, welcomes King Alfonso and Queen Victoria. Among the dignitaries are the sultan and representatives of all the tribes conquered by Spain.	Conflicting reports from Mexico say that the rebellion is either ended or spreading to 10 states. Reports say federal troops have executed Arnulfo Gomez, and the congress expels deputies who backed the revolt.	
Oct. 6	The world radio conference struggles with voting. Ireland wants one separate from Britain. Germany wants six.	Provincial Communists call on the central committee to expel Leon Trotsky and Grigory Zinoviev.... Assassination of Serb general Kovachevitch in Yugoslavia provokes anti-Bulgarian outbreaks and calls for war. Bulgarian and Macedonian irregulars are in a long-running conflict with Yugoslavia and Greece.		The United States says it will not recognize Emiliano Chamorro if he wins the Nicaraguan presidency. He is constitutionally ineligible because he had a previous term after his 1926 coup. That term ended when the United States refused to recognize him....Federal forces execute two more generals and 13 legislators. General Quijano of Mexico City dies before a crowd of 3,000, including bands and ice cream and candy vendors.	Solomon Islanders massacre a ship's crew, native police, and British officials. This is the largest loss to date in the Solomons and the first attack on government officials. Motive is unknown....The Communists are at risk of losing their capital in the revived civil war in China. All opposing forces are united under the Nationalist banner.
Oct. 7	The radio conference divides as the United States opposes government ownership. Canada, Cuba, and Mexico want more exclusive bandwidths than the United States wants to allow.	French auto dealers express concern at reports that U.S. makers have sold 100,000 vehicles in Europe this year.			
Oct. 8		France serves as peacemaker as Bulgaria sends Yugoslavia words of regret and promises to tighten up its border. Yugoslavia apprehends bandits on the Albanian border.		An Arnulfo Gomez backer says the general and 6,000 men avoided capture by the federals. He blames Plutarco Calles for forcing the rising by attempting to assassinate his rivals. Air chief Gustavo Salinas flees to the U.S. Border agents report Gomez has 30,000 troops.	Mohandas Gandhi acknowledges that Katherine Mayo's *Mother India* is true in many respects. He says, however, the book, which has inflamed Hindu passions for months and now causes controversy in Britain and the League, falls far short of reality.
Oct. 9		Britain joins France in advising Bulgaria to improve its border controls to reduce cross-border raids.... In Paris, 20,000 view the Nicola Sacco death mask. Police and Communists clash.	Jeremiah O'Connell reports to the U.S. shipping board on his trip to west Africa. He says American-West African Line vessels are obsolete and are losing trade to English and German diesels able to navigate west African rivers.	Arnulfo Gomez claims he has a good supply of weapons cached. Plutarco Calles says the rising is about done. San Antonio authorities arrest Calles detectives for spying on refugees and American citizens.	Courts sentence P. Sanhpe, Burma's "Robin Hood" to death for two murders. Sanphe has appeared in movies. He is a folk hero believed to be invulnerable to bullets and knives and able to become invisible.
Oct. 10	The U.S. delegation indicates it will back Britain in opposing proposed radio regulations. An Italian-led contingent wants implementation of the 1926 Cortina agreement's detailed radio code. The United States and Britain want minimal regulation at most. The United States also opposes tying radio conventions to the telegraph conventions of 1912.	The Spanish assembly convenes. The body has no powers. It may suggest, but the dictatorship may ignore....Constantinople's police chief denies a League representative's charge that Constantinople is a center of white slavery. The chief says the force tracks all women's movements. The representative is misreading the case of a Javanese seeking multiple brides, a search the police halted.		Plutarco Calles forces rout Arnulfo Gomez in a 6-hour battle, taking 600 prisoners. U.S. citizens flee Mexico by the trainload. Federal troops stop trains, search for "spies" and execute them. San Antonians suspect the abduction and execution of former rebel General Francisco Coss. Executions total 82.	Australia sends a cruiser to Malaita, Solomon Islands, to protect the remaining white population.
Oct. 11		Bulgarian measures against Macedonia are satisfactory to Yugoslavia. Negotiation of a treaty of accord resumes.	For six years a Russian with a British permit and a Greek with an Ottoman permit have sought a court determination of which can build a Palestinian power plant. The Permanent Court of International Justice rules itself incompetent to rule.	Henry Ford forms the company that will develop his 4 million acre Brazilian concession into a rubber plantation. His plan includes ships and planes to link the plantations with the auto factories.	

A	B	C	D	E
Includes developments that affect more than one world region, international organizations and important meetings of world leaders.	Includes all domestic and regional developments in Europe, including the Soviet Union.	Includes all domestic and regional developments in Africa and the Middle East.	Includes all domestic and regional developments in Latin America, the Caribbean, and Canada.	Includes all domestic and regional developments in Asian and Pacific nations (and colonies).

U.S. Politics & Social Issues	U.S. Foreign Policy & Affairs, Defense	U.S. Economy & Environment	Science, Technology & Nature	Culture, Leisure & Lifestyle	
Los Angeles police arrest Sid Bush outside the meeting room of the American Federation of Labor convention. Bush has Communist documents, including a letter from William Z. Foster, and is alleged to want Communist influence in labor councils.	Frank B. Kellogg promises Senator William Borah that Nicaraguan elections will be fair. The United States will provide observers.	Lloyd's Register reports that the conversion of U.S. ships from steam to diesel/electric is far behind the world. The current U.S. conversions will produce only 30 diesel vessels in a 500-ship fleet. New building and conversion for about 300 ships in the rest of the world is almost totally diesel.	The National Broadcasting Company provides the first nationwide network play by play of a world series. The Columbia Broadcasting System also provides U.S. coverage. Foreign coverage is by short wave radio.	The Yankees take game one of the series, 5–4, with Babe Ruth getting three hits.	Oct. 5
Exhibitors claim showing the Dempsey-Tunney films in New York is that the violation is in transporting them. Showing them violates no federal law. The district attorney says he will call all involved before a grand jury....In Ft. Lauderdale, prohibition agents seize a sheriff and deputy chief of police as well as 17 others on prohibition violation charges; 11 others accept arrest warrants.	A nationwide roundup snares 168 illegal aliens, including 50 women. Ellis Island houses them pending deportation. Officials say this is a normal effort now that the immigration service has better funding....The army demonstrates new coast artillery weapons at Aberdeen Proving Grounds. One gun shoots down a plane in the dark.	A gasoline price war begins in Detroit when Sinclair drops prices 2 cents and Standard of Ohio follows. Wars are under way in Louisiana, Ohio, and Michigan, with price reductions at the wellhead to follow....John P. Frey of the AFL Metal Trades Department dismisses talk of prosperity. He cites 1 million idle workers, 3.5 million underemployed, and wages rising 5 percent while productivity rose 49 percent since 1899.	Lee Deforest wins yet another patent suit over Westinghouse, General Electric and the U.S. government. The court affirms his claims to feedback and audion.	*The Jazz Singer*, starring Al Jolson, debuts. Vitaphone provides the sound, which critics find more satisfying for songs than for dialogue. The Vitaphone process is a year old....Babe Ruth is hitless but the Yankees take game two on superior pitching.	Oct. 6
The mine strike ends in Indiana. 25,000 return to work.			E.I. du Pont de Nemours and Company announces neozone. The product will extend rubber life by restricting oxidation....Postal telegraph officials say the Deforest victory will clear the way for short wave networks across the continent and around the world.	Detroit conductor Ossip Garbilowitsch resigns from the Schubert Centenary Committee. He says finishing Schubert's unfinished symphony is like putting arms on the Venus de Milo....Babe Ruth homers. New York wins game three, holding the Pirates hitless until the 8th inning.	Oct. 7
Pro-Klan, Fellowship Forum-owned Virginia station WTFF asks the FCC for 50,000 watts. That signal would drown out 18 other stations, so protests are inevitable. Only three U.S. stations broadcast at 50,000 watts.			Mrs. Elliott Lynn, English pilot, sets a new altitude record for light planes. She reaches 19,000 feet with a passenger. She set the previous mark, 16,000 feet, in May, but claims she actually exceeded 17,000 feet.	The Pirates falter in the 9th. Yankees sweep.	Oct. 8
		Chamber of Commerce leaders ask a $400 million tax cut, a top rate of 10 percent, and the end of nuisance levies such as the estate tax. The proposed cuts match the level Democrats seek. Republicans want $300 million.	Seven manufacturers enter the Daniel Guggenheim Safe-airplane competition. The $150,000 competition deemphasizes speed and performance. It seeks to reassure passengers deterred by frequent spectacular crashes.	The American Historical Association reports that less than a fourth of history Ph.D.s are productive scholars. The rest regard the degree as a teaching certificate. College presidents like the prestige of having Ph.D. faculty.	Oct. 9
The Mississippi Supreme Court bars Chinese children from white schools. In Mississippi, where people are either black or white, Chinese are now black—and segregated....Alabama demands that the federal government pay tax on Muscle Shoals. The courts will determine the Constitutionality of states taxing the federal government.... The Supreme Court cancels Harry Sinclair's Teapot Dome leases. The oil reserves are back in U.S. hands.	Secretary Frank B. Kellogg welcomes delegates to the Pan-American Conference on Simplification and Standardization of Consular Procedure. He tells them uniform consular headquarters are vital to international trade but regulation should be simple and minimal.	Advance orders for the new, unseen, Ford car top 350,000. Many orders include pre-payment.			Oct. 10
			Despite bad weather over the Atlantic, Ruth Elder and her co-pilot take off for Europe. She is attempting to be the first woman to cross the Atlantic.	The American League Most Valuable Player is Lou Gehrig. The American League rule is that no player can win the award, inaugurated in 1922, more than once.	Oct. 11

F	G	H	I	J
Includes campaigns, elections, federal-state relations, civil rights and liberties, crime, the judiciary, education, healthcare, poverty, urban affairs, and population.	Includes formation and debate of U.S. foreign and defense policies, veterans affairs, and defense spending. (Relations with specific foreign countries are usually found under the region concerned.)	Includes business, labor, agriculture, taxation, transportation, consumer affairs, monetary and fiscal policy, natural resources, pollution and industrial accidents.	Includes worldwide scientific, medical and technological developments, natural phenomena, U.S. weather and natural disasters.	Includes the arts, religion, scholarship, communications media, sports, entertainment, fashions, fads, and social life.

	World Affairs	Europe	Africa & The Middle East	The Americas	Asia & The Pacific
Oct. 12		In Ireland, after the Fianna Fail Party declines to contest for head of government, the Dail ratifies the Cosgrave cabinet. The rancor that characterizes the opening session gives way to reasonable good humor.		Now the sole presidential candidate, Alvaro Obregon at the border says he will continue enforcing the church laws.	
Oct. 13		Germany is reportedly investigating the electric chair as a replacement for the executioner's axe....Moscow avoids a break with France by recalling Rakovsky. Proposed replacement is Dovgalevsky, former representative in Tokyo, and reputedly not a propagandist....For the first time the Vatican lists specific requirements for establishing a new Papal state. With clear Papal demands, Benito Mussolini considers reestablishing the state lost in 1870.		Two Marine flyers are down and missing in Nicaragua. The rescue force battles 300 rebels to get to the site.	
Oct. 14	American nations unite against European radio rules. Meeting secretly they agree to oppose European efforts to take bandwidth currently used by U.S. shipping. The conference's technical committee votes 21–4 to establish itself as a permanent advisory body.	Albanian student Aghiad Bebi murders Tsena Bey, new Albanian minister to Czechoslovakia. Bebi says Bey wants to betray Albania to Czechoslovakia.	Continuing South Africa's rate war dating to April, Conference Lines offers to rebate 15 percent for wool shippers who use Conference exclusively. British and Continental promises to match Conference rebates although it regards them as illegal and may sue.	The government says it has trapped Arnulfo Gomez with 35 followers. Gomez backers at the border say the general has five generals behind him.	
Oct. 15		Germany and France form a chemical entente. Britain already has ties to Germany. The cartel will rival the U.S. chemical industry, which has grown greatly since the war disrupted the European industry.... Maneuvers with bicycle tanks and two deaths from phosgene gas bring warnings that Germany is rearming. Contrary opinion is that Germany is more interested in business, which, in fact, could readily convert to a war footing on a scale greater than in 1914.	Egypt has no radio station and Egyptians dislike European broadcasts within their range. The projected government radio station at Cairo will generate a boom in crystal radio sales. 85 percent of Egyptians live within 150 miles of Cairo.	Puerto Rican legislators ask Calvin Coolidge to help in their drive for an elected governor and general liberalization of the Organic Act. The request for greater freedom for these American citizens has been idling since 1924. Puerto Rico also wants greater economic assistance.	
Oct. 16		Spain honors Columbus with ceremonies throughout the kingdom, including 40,000 children at the Columbus Monument. The celebrations are belated because Spain recognized Soldiers Day, the end of the Moroccan war, on Columbus Day.	South African wool buyers reject the Conference Lines offer of a 15 percent rebate. They score Conference business methods as little better than intimidation. Meanwhile, a French importer refuses to sign any contract with Conference.		
Oct. 17		On the eve of the *Reichstag's* opening, the government faces a crisis. The Bavarian Party threatens to leave the coalition if it does not get more money. Other states are also unhappy with the way the federal government distributes funds.			A squadron of four fighting seaplanes leaves Plymouth, England, for a 25,000 mile trip via Karachi, Bombay, and Colombo and around Australia before reaching its permanent base at Singapore. The nine-ton duraluminum planes have sleeping and cooking facilities as well as a capability for hanging hammocks between the wings.
Oct. 18		Belgium joins the chemical trust. The four members have $1 billion in capital and $500 million in exports. It is a greater threat to U.S. business than the steel trust....Strikes in German lignite fields over wages spread. Coal shortages threaten Agfa photochemicals and Anhald sugar refineries....Spanish miners strike after the government lowers pay and extends their hours.		Seeking the two missing Marine flyers, 40 American and Nicaraguan forces come under attack by 400 guerrillas. Casualties include four constabulary and 67 rebels. The government is preparing a 600-man force to root out Sandino.	

A	B	C	D	E
Includes developments that affect more than one world region, international organizations and important meetings of world leaders.	Includes all domestic and regional developments in Europe, including the Soviet Union.	Includes all domestic and regional developments in Africa and the Middle East.	Includes all domestic and regional developments in Latin America, the Caribbean, and Canada.	Includes all domestic and regional developments in Asian and Pacific nations (and colonies).

U.S. Politics & Social Issues	U.S. Foreign Policy & Affairs, Defense	U.S. Economy & Environment	Science, Technology & Nature	Culture, Leisure & Lifestyle	
At Sedalia, MO, before a crowd of 12,000 to 15,000, Democratic Senator James Reed enters the presidential race with a blistering attack on Calvin Coolidge and Republican corruption.	The dedication of Wright Field as replacement of McCook Field as center of U.S. aviation includes the John L. Mitchell Trophy Race, with 15 pursuit planes entered, and a static display of the new bombers. The $10 million facility is on 5,000 acres donated by the people of Dayton, OH.	Movie industry meetings to establish self regulation falter over disagreements between distributors and exhibitors. Particularly contentious is the producers' plan to sell movies for home use, an idea exhibitors naturally oppose.	Although Ruth Elder's route takes her over the main shipping lane, no one has seen her for 28 hours.		Oct. 12
The American Federation of Labor convention denounces fascists and Communists and re-elects all officers of the Green presidency.... Senator John Sharp Williams presents a statue of Jefferson Davis to the United States at Vicksburg Federal Park, MS. The event is the culmination of the Confederate State Reunion.	Stirred by Frank B. Kellogg's approval of refunding of French debt by private bankers, Senator Carter Glass (D-VA) says the government should stay out of private business. He demands an investigation of the policy, which dates to the Harding administration.	A New York Stock Exchange seat sells for a record $265,000. The old record is $250,000. The profit of $245,000 is also a record. The owner bought the seat in 1893 when seats sold for $15,250-$20,000.	Ruth Elder ditches near the Azores, setting a distance record for a woman over water of 2623 miles. The plane burns, but she and her co-pilot are safe....Westinghouse exhibits a "mechanical man" that performs simple tasks when activated by human voice.	Ivy Gill, a 24-year-old typist, becomes the third woman to swim the English Channel this month.	Oct. 13
	Calvin Coolidge says the executive power to conduct foreign affairs includes overseeing loans. Senator William Borah of the western progressives supports Glass but declines to make an issue of it.... France agrees to return to old rates while negotiating new terms.	The new record price for an exchange seat is $270,000. Predictions are that seats will top $300,000 in a matter of weeks.			Oct. 14
Film distributors and exhibitors end their meetings inconclusively. They have no code of ethics and no agreement on block booking....An Alabama grand jury returns 102 true bills, indicts 36 Klansmen as floggers, and criticizes a preacher for distorting Jesus' teachings to impose his own morality.		Chain store sales for September are a record $80 million. Although 12 "5 and 10 cent" chains are down slightly, a dozen miscellaneous chains are doing well. "Miscellaneous" includes, among others, Penney's and Jewel Tea.		The first U.S. exhibition of French primitive paintings opens in New York. Primitives are 15th century court painters, first recognized in a 1904 Paris exhibit. Before then, authorities dated French painting's beginnings to the Fontainebleau school....Mona McLennan, really Dr. Dorothy Cochrane Logan, confesses that her record-setting 13 hour, 10 minute channel swim is a hoax. Gertrude Ederle's record stands.	Oct. 15
The Bookkeepers, Stenographers, and Accountants Union announces plans to organize 10,000 Metropolitan Life white collar workers, 70 percent women. Met Life president Harley Fisk says the workers are well paid at $12 a week. The union, backed by Eleanor Roosevelt, wants $21, overtime, and protection from summary firing.	The War Department announces the recipients of the first four Soldiers' Medals, established to recognize heroism outside war. Recipients include two who fight the Pig Point ordnance fire of Aug 18, 1926, and two who rescue drowning civilians.			New York's Veterans of Foreign Wars condemn the new history by Prof. J.H. Hayes and Thomas Parker Moon as having subtle pro-British biases. The organization says Modern History diminishes U.S. contributions and is unsuitable for school use.	Oct. 16
A first-of-its kind Pan-American hospital opens in New York. Staffed by Latin Americans, the 130-bed hospital provides Spanish- and Portuguese-language service to the area's 200,000 Latin Americans.... The Supreme Court upholds use of injunctions against striking mine union in West Virginia. It also lets stand Indianapolis convictions for talking to street railway workers about a strike.	Frank B. Kellogg defends state department review of private loans as within government's roles He also notes that the system is voluntary....Frank B. Kellogg indicates that French terms are unacceptable. The United States is unwilling to grant reductions and lift sanitary restrictions.	The railway association forecasts rail car requirements for shipping of 27 commodities in the final quarter will drop 174,000 cars to 9.236 million. Six of the regional commodities boards report increases and seven report decreases....A Statistical Service report that Ford could easily cut profit margins brings declines in stocks of GM and Hudson. The lesser companies would have to match Ford with fewer resources.		Yale announces that there will be no John Masefield prize in 1927. None of the poems submitted is of high enough quality.	Oct. 17
Jury selection is complete in the Fall/ Sinclair Teapot Dome fraud trial. Ten men and two women hear opening statements....Defenders of Nicola Sacco and Bartolomeo Vanzetti dine together and organize efforts to exonerate the two men. One restaurant refuses to seat them.		Six Ohio sheet steel companies merge. The combination of Waddell, Mansfield, Ashtabula, Falcon, Empire, and Thomas forms a $20 million company.	A 20-foot model of the new transatlantic liners reaches simulated speeds of 35 knots. Four-day crossings will be the norm for the new fleet. Mail airplanes will land on the ships, which will operate at 1.5 times the current speed with half the fuel and a third of the crew.		Oct. 18

F	G	H	I	J
Includes campaigns, elections, federal-state relations, civil rights and liberties, crime, the judiciary, education, healthcare, poverty, urban affairs, and population.	Includes formation and debate of U.S. foreign and defense policies, veterans affairs, and defense spending. (Relations with specific foreign countries are usually found under the region concerned.)	Includes business, labor, agriculture, taxation, transportation, consumer affairs, monetary and fiscal policy, natural resources, pollution and industrial accidents.	Includes worldwide scientific, medical and technological developments, natural phenomena, U.S. weather and natural disasters.	Includes the arts, religion, scholarship, communications media, sports, entertainment, fashions, fads, and social life.

	World Affairs	Europe	Africa & The Middle East	The Americas	Asia & The Pacific
Oct. 19	Bandits kill four escorts, steal an American mine payroll, and kidnap the British manager. The United States and Britain protest to Mexico.	Poland considers legislation that bars women under 21 from emigrating unless accompanied by family. Poland loses 40,000 young women a year. All emigrants must have government approval....Having seen the uniforms of American legionnaires, French Poilus demand livelier uniforms for themselves.	South Africa suspends debate on the new flag. For months controversy has raged as former president Smuts demands the inclusion of the Union Jack and flags of the two Boer republics in the new design. Premier Hertzog wants a flag without reference to South Africa's subservient history.	Recently expelled from the Baptists of Ontario and Quebec, Rev. T.T. Shields of Toronto leads other militant fundamentalist ministers into the new Regular Baptists of Ontario and Quebec. They object particularly to modernism at McMaster University.	
Oct. 20		Marshal Jozef Pilsudski locks the doors of parliament in Poland and posts a note that it is no longer in session. The Sejm had called itself into session but Pilsudski wants a session to address the budget only.		Panama warns Costa Rica to back away, talks of armed defense. Panama lacks an army but its police force has 500 rifles. The two countries have been at odds since 1921.	
Oct. 21		Revival of "The Grand Lady" by Szomory, a Jew, provokes anti-Semitic demonstrations in Budapest. Police arrest 65 and disperse a crowd of 2,000....The Vatican is disappointed at the Fascist newspaper's strong opposition to a Papal state. Observers see positives in the fact that the Vatican spelled out its requirements at last.		Dwight Morrow, new ambassador to Mexico, leaves San Antonio for Mexico City. From Laredo on, he travels on a special train with two armored cars full of machine guns and soldiers. Additional soldiers protect bridges and other sites vulnerable to rebel attack on his route.	Still fighting anti-Communist Chang Kai-shek in the north, the Nationalist south faces a rising by General Tang in Hankow. The nationalists are also seeking a $24 million loan. The United States will hold its forces at their present size, but Britain will cut its troops by 3,000 and discontinue airplane flights over Shanghai.
Oct. 22		Portugal's military dictatorship invites former president Gomes Da Costa to return. The dictatorship retains power, but political stability improves, enhancing Portugal's chance for foreign loans....The German coal strike ends after the government mandates arbitration.	The British bidder officially wins the Dead Sea concession over bidders from the United States and Europe. Development of vast potash and mineral salt resources is expected to drive Palestinian development.	The United States receives a copy of the new Cuban tariff schedule, in the works since 1926. Rates are highly favorable to the United States....From exile in Guatemala, Arnulfo Gomez asks the United States not to intervene in Mexico.	
Oct. 23		Dr. Joseph Rosen tells a Chicago conference of the successful Jewish Relief effort. Loans and grants allow 20,000 Russian and Polish Jews to leave cities, where they starve, for surplus agricultural lands, where they build farms, homes, and communities.	British negotiators head for Morocco's Atlas Mountains. They seek the release of the Steeg party, two men and two women, taken captive the previous day as "war prisoners."	Dwight Morrow arrives safely in Mexico City. Awaiting him are the land and oil disagreements. Mexicans are optimistic that a financier can resolve what are at bottom economic issues.	
Oct. 24				Abitibi Power and Paper takes over Spanish River and four other companies to create a $180 million pulp and paper company, Canada's third of this size. Independents are becoming scarce. Wood products are Canada's number one single export and seasonally exceed agricultural exports....The 1917 assassins of Bolivia's former president Pando draw lots to see which will face the firing squad. The youngest gets the black ballot.	
Oct. 25	At the World Radio Conference, after Germany, Britain, and Italy accept the U.S. position, conferees agree to privatized radio. Conferees ignore Russia's protest at its exclusion.	Romania declares martial law on the boy king's birthday and seals off all government buildings. The government alleges a Carolist plot to take the throne by plebiscite.	The British Anti-slavery and Aborigines Protection Society asks the British government to stop new legislation in Rhodesia allowing indenture with no age limit. In effect, child slavery is legal. Under the law Rhodesian mica mines use minor miners....J.B.M. Hertzog and J.C. Smuts compromise. The Union Jack will fly beside the new South African flag.	French-flagged Formose saves 720 of *Principessa Mafalda*'s passengers as the Italian liner sinks off Brazil. *Principessa Mafalda* carries 1,259, all but 110 immigrants, from Genoa to Buenos Aires. The final loss of life is 303.	

A	B	C	D	E
Includes developments that affect more than one world region, international organizations and important meetings of world leaders.	Includes all domestic and regional developments in Europe, including the Soviet Union.	Includes all domestic and regional developments in Africa and the Middle East.	Includes all domestic and regional developments in Latin America, the Caribbean, and Canada.	Includes all domestic and regional developments in Asian and Pacific nations (and colonies).

U.S. Politics & Social Issues	U.S. Foreign Policy & Affairs, Defense	U.S. Economy & Environment	Science, Technology & Nature	Culture, Leisure & Lifestyle	
Alabama Attorney General C.C. McCall, elected in a landslide with Klan backing, resigns from the Klan, saying the KKK no longer respects the law. KKK terrorists are chasing grand jury witnesses out of the state.	Frank B. Kellogg prepares another note to France. He clarifies that the United States asks not for most favored nation status but for a return to the previous French tariff schedule.	U.S. steel firms are operating at 64 percent of capacity. In 1926 they were at 85 percent. Prices are weak: Republic Steel's profit for the quarter is 21 cents per share—but demand is rising.			Oct. 19
A federal court rules that the showing of fight films is legal if they have not arrived in the state by common carrier. A grand jury will continue examining the means by which the Dempsey-Tunney film entered New York. The district attorney is satisfied.		American makers are alarmed when Switzerland increases duties on cars by 100 to 200 percent. The measure is for revenue, not protection.	Floods ravage New Jersey and the coal regions of Pennsylvania....A thinking machine quickly solves equations that humans take months to finish.	Mayor William Thompson of Chicago orders a search of the city's libraries for pro-British material. Historians find the mayor either ridiculous or amusing.	Oct. 20
University of Oklahoma students protest the banning of cars on campus. Chanting R-E-V-O-L-U-T-I-O-N, they also demand the right to date any night of the week and hold dances until midnight on Friday and Saturday. After 45 minutes, the 2,000 students return to class.... "Sport' Herrmann announces plans to burn British books on Chicago's lakefront.	The departments of state and agriculture agree to coordinate quarantines. Coordination will speed processing of imports, helping to satisfy French complaints about sanitary restrictions....Secretary of War Dwight Davis counters charges that payment for past wars and preparing for future ones takes 86 percent of the federal budget. His estimate is 30 percent, including pensions. Defense takes 13 percent of the budget.			Artists and art experts testify before the Customs Court of Appeals about the artistic merit of Constantin Brancusi's "Birds of Space." Because the customs officer did not recognize the work as a bird, customs is holding the sculpture pending payment of a $239 tariff as a miscellaneous metal object.	Oct. 21
Chicago Germans support William Thompson's purge of British books. The purge itself twists when searchers discover that Queen Victoria helped found the library, reestablished after the 1871 fire with a British donation of 7,000 books.				*Abie's Irish Rose* finishes its record run of 2,327 performances. In doubling the previous record, the play grosses $22 million from 11 million playgoers.	Oct. 22
Charles Lindbergh arrives in New York City after finishing his 22,350-mile triumphal tour. During the tour of 48 states, Lindbergh speaks 147 times and parades 1285 miles in 82 cities.	Immigration officials report that 170,000 people sneaked across U.S. borders in 1926, a record year. Agents caught 19,000 Canadians.	United Fruit Company begins weekly shipping from the tropics to San Francisco. Five steamers will provide the west service comparable to that enjoyed by the east coast.		Deans of the "seven sisters," say their women's colleges are not getting a fair share of money because graduates of men's schools control more resources than alumnae do. The deans say they are losing the middle class, which cannot afford tuition without aid.	Oct. 23
Two-week-old IWW-led strikes in Colorado's coal mines spread. As county jails fill to capacity with strikers arrested for picketing, Huerfano County commissioners want noncitizen miners deported....Sixty-nine Oklahoma legislators petition for a special session to investigate abuse of power by Governor Henry Johnston in six departments. A move to impeach the governor has already begun.		An Alaskan earthquake disrupts communications, rattles dishes and sets off alarms about a tsunami. Japanese fishermen catch unfamiliar deep sea creatures. An unusually active volcano season precedes the earthquake.			Oct. 24
A representative of the Brotherhood of Sleeping Car porters says Pullman's reliance on tipping as wages for porters saved it $150 million in payroll....Chicago mayor William Thompson says he never intended a book bonfire. A taxpayer seeks an injunction and an alderman intervenes on behalf of the library. In related matters, historians Mace and Schlesinger of Harvard testify in a libel suit against Thompson's book censor and the school board hearing on pro-British advocacy by the superintendent will resume tomorrow.	The army's first order for new National Guard planes goes to Curtiss. The 35 planes are O-II modifications of the O-I observation plane that showed well in the Spokane air race....The United States says it will recognize Moncada if he wins the Nicaraguan presidency. He is eligible because his coup failed.	Crude oil output for the week is 2.48 million barrels. Production continues to be down from record highs earlier in the year.		The Western Golf Association sets a minimum age for tour play. Girls under 16 must play the junior circuit whether they are prodigies or not.	Oct. 25

F	G	H	I	J
Includes campaigns, elections, federal-state relations, civil rights and liberties, crime, the judiciary, education, healthcare, poverty, urban affairs, and population.	*Includes formation and debate of U.S. foreign and defense policies, veterans affairs, and defense spending. (Relations with specific foreign countries are usually found under the region concerned.)*	*Includes business, labor, agriculture, taxation, transportation, consumer affairs, monetary and fiscal policy, natural resources, pollution and industrial accidents.*	*Includes worldwide scientific, medical and technological developments, natural phenomena, U.S. weather and natural disasters.*	*Includes the arts, religion, scholarship, communications media, sports, entertainment, fashions, fads, and social life.*

	World Affairs	Europe	Africa & The Middle East	The Americas	Asia & The Pacific
Oct. 26		Britain and France begin an airfare war. After Britain's Imperial introduces second class and cuts prices and travel times between London and Paris, French Air Union counters with lower fares, faster flights, and larger planes.			Japan uses airplanes for reconnaissance in large naval maneuvers. Results of the test remain secret.
Oct. 27		French and Senegalese troops block Catalans seeking to sneak through the Pyrenees and attack Barcelona. Cross-border raids are an ongoing problem, and a rising to create a Catalonian state is an annual event.		President Plutarco Calles ends the Mexican ban on government purchases in the United States. The embargo was a response to U.S. blockage of arms shipments to the Mexican government.	
Oct. 28		Today is census day in Turkey. For 12 hours, all persons are indoors and train, boat, and street traffic stops....Benito Mussolini celebrates his fifth year in power. He cites as accomplishments aqueducts, roads, and other infrastructure as well as revaluation of the lira, land reform, and the labor charter.	Conference Lines abandons its 15 percent rebate offer to South African wool shippers. Citing government opposition, the company sets fixed rates.		
Oct. 29			Lt. Bentley, flying a 40 hp Moth, arrives in Capetown after a 28-day, 8,100-mile flight from London. South Africa has used its air force since 1921 to keep the natives in check.	Governor M.L. Walker of the Canal Zone defers to Washington the decision over whether to allow a German Colombia-Panama airmail line to land in the Canal Zone. American interests worry that the line will block expansion of American airmail service in Latin America. The German counters that he has support from GE, DuPont, Baldwin Locomotive, and many other U.S. companies.	The Chinese government in Nanking announces a plan to eradicate opium use in three years. Effective January 1, all users must register, vendors must get licenses, and growing poppies will be illegal.... Manuel Quezon arrives in New York. He is en route to a meeting with Calvin Coolidge at which he will request Philippine independence once again.
Oct. 30		France signs a defense treaty with Yugoslavia. In combination with treaties with four other European states, this treaty effectively surrounds Germany.	King Armoah III of the Gold Coast's Fanti tribe speaks before the Nazarene Congregational Church. He cites the prevalence of religion through Africa and calls on African Americans to share their new world knowledge with Africa.... Negotiations for the ransom of the nephews of Governor-General Steeg begin. French troops patrol the area for bandits.	Msgr Drossaerts, Archbishop of San Antonio says Mexico is a shambles of blood and disarray. He asks why the U.S. press and public leaders are silent when religious persecution outrages Europeans.	At Yokohama, Hirohito reviews his entire navy, 172 vessels. Swarms of planes fly overhead. This is only the second such review in Japanese history. Reduced 100,000 tons by the Washington Conference, the fleet is less powerful offensively than the fleet reviewed by Hirohito's father in 1919, the fleet is otherwise more efficient, balanced, and suited to defense....Japan gets its first bishop, St. Francis Xavier, who brought Christianity to Japan in 1540.
Oct. 31	Russia advises the League that it will send delegates to the November world disarmament preparation meetings. The United States has already indicated that it will participate. Russia's move is seen as a sign the Communist nation is rejoining Europe.	Britain backs Benito Mussolini's claim, backed by sending warships, to a part of the administration of Tangier. France backs Spain's desire for single control....Romania denies rumors of a revolt. The government says all is so quiet that it is lifting censorship.			Harold Lamb, biographer of Genghis Khan, doubts the discovery of the conqueror's tomb by Professor Peter Kozloff. Lamb is particularly skeptical about the supposed 13th century Bible and the use of seven when the Mongol sacred number is nine.
Nov. 1					The Canton faction under Wang Cheng-wei is now dominant over those of Nanking and Hankow, which have been fighting each other. Chiang Kai-shek is poised to take command of a new offensive in the spring.

A	B	C	D	E
Includes developments that affect more than one world region, international organizations and important meetings of world leaders.	Includes all domestic and regional developments in Europe, including the Soviet Union.	Includes all domestic and regional developments in Africa and the Middle East.	Includes all domestic and regional developments in Latin America, the Caribbean, and Canada.	Includes all domestic and regional developments in Asian and Pacific nations (and colonies).

U.S. Politics & Social Issues	U.S. Foreign Policy & Affairs, Defense	U.S. Economy & Environment	Science, Technology & Nature	Culture, Leisure & Lifestyle	
Colorado's governor Adams warns the IWW that picketing is illegal. He will do whatever it takes to maintain the peace....Senate Majority Leader Charles Curtis (R-KS) is the first Republican to announce formally for the presidency.		Railroad income continues down. The top 26 lines have a combined September decrease of 5.5 percent from September 1926.		Alexander Alekhine wins the 21st game against world chess champion Jose Capablanca. The Russian leads 4-2. He needs two more victories to capture the title. Over the preceding two weeks the two played to eight consecutive draws and they have played 15 draws to date.	Oct. 26
Removed by the city council after the city treasurer refuses to accept vouchers he signs, Indianapolis mayor John Duvall barricades himself in his office. The mayor's bodyguards, a contingent of city police, profess to be ready to fight when the acting mayor attempts to take office.	Calvin Coolidge declines to overturn the war department reassignment of Rear Admiral Thomas Magruder, who over the past several months has been speaking harshly about waste and unpreparedness in the navy. This is the fourth time Calvin Coolidge has refused to hear a flag officer who appeals beyond the military structure.	A British government backed attempt to form a European tin pool fails when major companies decline to join small Dutch, British, and continental firms. Britain controls most of the world's tin. The United States is the largest user.	Austrian Dr. Julius Wagner-Jauregg wins the Nobel Prize for Medicine. His contribution is a method of inducing malaria to cure paralysis.	Florida governor John Martin says he will enforce the court ban on pari-mutuel betting. Hialeah, the Jockey Club, and three dog tracks indicate they will not open in the fall.	Oct. 27
The Federal Council of Churches of Christ in America sets February 12, Lincoln's Birthday, as Anti-lynching Day. Lynching declined to 16 cases each in 1924 and 1925 before rising to 30 in 1926 and 13 in the first 8 months of 1927....Mayor William Thompson takes his anti-British campaign to the nation. He charges $10 dues for members of his "America First Foundation."					Oct. 28
With the rival mayors sharing a desk, two additional claimants emerge. One is the appointee of the deposed mayor's wife, the city controller who in ordinary circumstances would have succeeded to the mayoralty, and the other is the loser in the 1925 election that seated Duvall. A judge is set to rule on Halloween.	Dwight Morrow presents his credentials to Plutarco Calles. Both speak of their hopes for amity in resolving outstanding issues.				Oct. 29
The New York Bible Society orders a million bibles in 22 languages. This is sufficient to provide a Bible to one in six New Yorkers. The society routinely provides Bibles in 67 languages and Braille.				More than 500 magicians, actors, and others turn out for the unveiling of the monument to Harry Houdini.	Oct. 30
The Indianapolis court rules in favor of the council designee. He will be mayor for the week before new elections. The pretenders vacate their claims.	The army successfully tests its new attack plane. The machine carries six machine guns, four of which are fired by electrical trigger, and a dozen 30-pound bombs.	September sees a slight rise in exports of automobiles and farm machines....Lost income, retooling, and other expenses for the new Ford model total $240 million. Ford absorbs the losses without resort to borrowing.		The Carnegie Hero Fund recognizes 46 individuals for acts of heroism in 1926. Survivors of 14 of the 18 who died in the effort receive pensions of up to $4,500 a year. Other heroes receive bronze or silver medals, some with cash, and some without.	Oct. 31
The New Jersey Supreme Court affirms the convictions of Roger Baldwin and seven other ACLU members. They participated in the 1924 Paterson textile strike, adjudged an illegal assembly. Baldwin's sentence is 6 months. The others receive $50 fines.		Chevrolet sales for September top 112,000, more than double the same month in 1926....Oil output is 2.46 million barrels, down on reduced Oklahoma production. Imports are at 1.534 million barrels.	A four-billion-candlepower beacon projects advertisements onto New York skyscrapers. Letters 150 feet high are too large for the largest skyscrapers, so the messages scroll. Plans are to drop smokescreens to provide a cloud-like backdrop for future ads.		Nov. 1

F	G	H	I	J
Includes campaigns, elections, federal-state relations, civil rights and liberties, crime, the judiciary, education, healthcare, poverty, urban affairs, and population.	Includes formation and debate of U.S. foreign and defense policies, veterans affairs, and defense spending. (Relations with specific foreign countries are usually found under the region concerned.)	Includes business, labor, agriculture, taxation, transportation, consumer affairs, monetary and fiscal policy, natural resources, pollution and industrial accidents.	Includes worldwide scientific, medical and technological developments, natural phenomena, U.S. weather and natural disasters.	Includes the arts, religion, scholarship, communications media, sports, entertainment, fashions, fads, and social life.

	World Affairs	Europe	Africa & The Middle East	The Americas	Asia & The Pacific
Nov. 2		Marshal Jozef Pilsudski declares his candidacy for president. He will run for the government party. The Polish Hindenberg, he is a unity candidate although before the war he was a Socialist.	An American company gets the $20 million contract to dam the Sudan for Ethiopia. The White Engineering Company will finance the dam itself, sell irrigation water to the British, pay Ethiopia a royalty, and eventually turn the dam over to Ethiopia.		
Nov. 3	At the International Conference for the Removal of Trade Restrictions, wine-growing nations protest the U.S. ban on intoxicants. France eases tension by recognizing the right of the dry U.S. to restrict imports of illegal products.			Jamaica's banana price is up. With the advent of the Cuyamel Fruit Company, United Fruit Company raises its offer from 4 to 6 shillings a bunch.	The newly centralized Canton regime declares war on pirates that have been interfering with Europeans.
Nov. 4	At the international Radiotelegraphic Conference Argentina prevails in the fight over presenting compulsory radio arbitration to the plenary session for final decision. Britain and Japan oppose and the United States wants voluntary arbitration. Seven nations fail to credential their delegations.		Africans await an American liberator. So says Oscar Crosby, just returned from a six-month foray into the back areas of South Africa, who also notes that black Africans are mostly satisfied with British rule....Britain says it will fight the American dam in Ethiopia. It claims treaty rights to a veto....The Moroccan kidnappers want 1.5 million francs and a phonograph.	Brazil buys $36 million worth of gold to back its return to the gold standard. The 1.8 million $20 gold pieces weigh 67 tons.	American companies gain rights to exploit oil at Mosul. The five companies have a 25 percent share. Others in the field are Dutch, British, and French....A cyclone in Nellore kills 300 Indians.
Nov. 5		The German labor sports society threatens to bar Russian athletes from international games unless the Russians convince German Communists to cease pro-Russian propaganda....Hungarian police rout Communists demonstrating at the dedication of the Kossuth memorial.	France backs England. The Paris government agrees that Ethiopia has no right to enter into a dam agreement with Americans.	The Mexican government displays the bodies of Arnulfo Gomez and his nephew, taken in ambush and executed by federal troops. Lucero, Almada, Aguila, and Medina remain at large.	British, Chinese, and American businessmen are relieved that the United States will pay only treaty levies, as Japan and Britain have previously decided. The Nanking government accepts the decision to ignore higher levies it tried to impose.
Nov. 6	Communists in Russia, the United States, and elsewhere celebrate the 10th anniversary of the Russian revolution.	The German stock market is reported at 28 percent below the year's high as bears reign.	The proposed Ethiopian dam alarms the Egyptian press and government. A dam outside Egyptian control, even in the hands of a supposed friend, threatens Egypt's existence.	Mexico reports that it has 15 columns in Vera Cruz searching rugged terrain for the remaining rebels. The army also says it has taken 500 former rebels prisoner.	
Nov. 7	Meeting at Geneva, trade delegates add a provision for equitable tariffs to the agreement for free trade. The United States protests, but 15 countries indicate they will sign.	Switzerland expels 14 members of the "Garden of Eden" group, including a countess, a baron, and a baroness. This is the third expulsion this year, The Garden of Eden has 250,000 German and Austrian followers....Romania arrests one Carolist officer and prepares the trial of another.	Ethiopia agrees to abandon the dam if Britain objects. The chief Ethiopian negotiator says the project is British.	The Panamanian government buys land at the head of the Chagres river to build a dam for drought relief and to insure adequate water for the canal. The $10 million dam is expected to be complete in three years. The canal still is not paying for itself....Mexico executes rebels Reyes and Garcia.	A cyclone in Madras kills hundreds. Cholera compounds the problem.... In Shanghai, 400 white Russian exiles, angered by celebrations of the revolution's 10th anniversary, storm the Soviet consulate. The Russian consul blames the British.
Nov. 8		Romania reimposes strict censorship in preparation for the trial. Premier Bratianu denies he is preparing to seize power....Leon Trotsky and others defy the party. They demonstrate in Moscow and Leningrad.	King Daudi Chwa, 32nd king of Buganda, opposes British plans for an East Africa Union. He fears loss of identity if Buganda federates with a large number of tribes. Buganda is the most westernized of the Ugandan kingdoms.	Liberals win by substantial margins in Nicaraguan local elections in 10 departments. The American officer overseeing the elections reports no difficulties.	Britain announces the Simon Commission to explore the possibility of independence for India will convene two years early. The government worries about Muslim-Hindu conflict under self rule. The commission has no Indian members.
Nov. 9		Amid Polish reports of hundreds of Romanian deserters, Ion Bratianu asks for greater powers for himself. He also introduces bills further restricting freedom of speech and press....France approves the use of movies in schools. Caution is urged; movies may harm nervous children....Italy orders the removal of German from Tyrolean grave markers. Italian is the replacement language.	Dr. Fitleef Nielsen, Danish archaeologist says the city of Petra is Mount Sinai. He also says that the ancient Hebrew religion has ties to Arabic moon worship.		Indian nationalists protest the exclusion of Indians from the self-determination commission. They call for a boycott of the proceedings.

A	B	C	D	E
Includes developments that affect more than one world region, international organizations and important meetings of world leaders.	Includes all domestic and regional developments in Europe, including the Soviet Union.	Includes all domestic and regional developments in Africa and the Middle East.	Includes all domestic and regional developments in Latin America, the Caribbean, and Canada.	Includes all domestic and regional developments in Asian and Pacific nations (and colonies).

U.S. Politics & Social Issues	U.S. Foreign Policy & Affairs, Defense	U.S. Economy & Environment	Science, Technology & Nature	Culture, Leisure & Lifestyle	
Jury tampering causes a mistrial for Albert Fall and Harry Sinclair. The two are on trial for conspiracy to defraud the government in Teapot Dome. The trial has not yet moved to the defense....Anti-dry women begin a campaign to overturn Volstead and the 18th Amendment. The women's Committee for Modification of the Volstead Act becomes the Women's Committee for Repeal of the 18th Amendment.	Church leaders memorialize Calvin Coolidge to accept the Aristide Briand peace proposal. The petition carries 700 signatures....Brassey's reports that the failure of naval limits has not produced an arms race. It also reports that the United States and Britain should unite against Japan in the Pacific.			New head of the American League is Ernest Barnard, who has been with the league since 1903. The league memorial to Ban Johnson is signed by all owners except Charles Comisky, who has never forgiven Johnson for his actions in the 1919 Black Sox scandal.	Nov. 2
In prison for life, William Loeb studies Latin through the Columbia University Home Studies Division. Loeb murdered Bobby Franks in 1924.	France insists on reciprocity as the basis for the new treaty. Frank B. Kellogg expects a temporary agreement that includes removal of temporary tariffs set when the new French tariff took effect....Manuel Quezon meets with Calvin Coolidge but fails to mention independence.	To reassure the motoring public that they can safely drive the new Holland Tunnel, officials set an automobile afire, creating a wall of flame that touches the roof. Firefighters extinguish the fire in 3.5 minutes.		A newly discovered diary seems to show that Barbara Fritchie did not really wave the American flag as reported in Whittier's poem. Rather, she sympathized with the Confederacy.	Nov. 3
Mayor William Thompson tells the library trustees to resign for spreading pro-British propaganda. He also attacks Edward Bok for backing a world court, Andrew Carnegie for seeking unity of all English speakers, and former ambassador Walter Hines Page for wanting early U.S. entry into the war on Britain's side....The jury tamperer appears to be an aide to Sinclair. A warrant is issued for Sinclair's arrest.	Calvin Coolidge is not willing to transfer control of the Philippines to the interior department, preferring war department administration.	Calvin Coolidge says he will back Treasury Secretary Andrew Mellon's $225 million tax cut. He will oppose anything greater.	Flooding in New England threatens to disrupt New York power. Vermont reports hundreds dead. Connecticut reports at least $1 million in losses. Earthquakes in California jar trains and ships at sea.		Nov. 4
		Gulf Oil discovers another pool in the Seminole field. Producers agree to maintain production caps through the end of the year.	With damage totals over $50 million, Calvin Coolidge orders troops, radios, and planes to flood-ravaged New England. The Red Cross is already working relief....Captain Hawthorn C. Gray sets a balloon altitude record of 44,000 feet. He dies after he cuts his oxygen tube by mistake.		Nov. 5
Mayor William Thompson announces that the America First Foundation will provide a $10,000 prize for a history that "tells the truth" about U.S. history....William J. Burns, head of the detective agency, is tied to the jury tampering that resulted in the Fall/Sinclair trial.	The Bank of America urges the United States to ratify League rules on shipping. The rules standardize bills of lading, insurance liability, and overall rights and immunities of ocean shippers. The United States is not a party to the agreement.		*Malaina*, a 95-foot yacht made in Germany and powered by a new small diesel engine, arrives in the United States. The diesel is more fuel efficient than gasoline motor, costing about a third to operate.... As the death total rises above 150, snowstorms hamper flood relief efforts in New England.		Nov. 6
Burns acknowledges his agents tailed jurors on Sinclair's behalf but denies tampering. He accuses the government.		Eighteen chains report October sales of $83 million, up over 7 million from October 1926. The 10-month rise is 12.5 percent, with Woolworth and National Tea leading the way.		Jose Capablanca and Alexander Alekhine draw in game 25 of their title match.	Nov. 7
In Colorado violence flares in the IWW mine strike as 400 miners battle police trying to break up a union meeting. Six police and two miners suffer injuries. Planes search for rumored IWW reinforcements.	Calvin Coolidge remains non-committal toward the Briand and other peace plans. He wants the United States as clear as possible of foreign involvements.		An autopsy on the brain of Anatole France reveals that his brain at 1,000 grams is well below the normal 1,300 grams for a man his age. However, the brain surface is great because it is extraordinarily convoluted.	Babe Ruth and Lou Gehrig finish a record-setting nine-state barnstorming tour. In 21 games, Ruth hits 20 homers, Gehrig 13. The largest turnout is 30,000 in Los Angeles.	Nov. 8
				Pittsburgh art lovers, after several years of accepting art they do not care for, challenge the award of a Carnegie International Art Exhibit prize to a painting in lurid colors. The painting is "Still Life" by Henri Matisse.	Nov. 9

F	G	H	I	J
Includes campaigns, elections, federal-state relations, civil rights and liberties, crime, the judiciary, education, healthcare, poverty, urban affairs, and population.	*Includes formation and debate of U.S. foreign and defense policies, veterans affairs, and defense spending. (Relations with specific foreign countries are usually found under the region concerned.)*	*Includes business, labor, agriculture, taxation, transportation, consumer affairs, monetary and fiscal policy, natural resources, pollution and industrial accidents.*	*Includes worldwide scientific, medical and technological developments, natural phenomena, U.S. weather and natural disasters.*	*Includes the arts, religion, scholarship, communications media, sports, entertainment, fashions, fads, and social life.*

	World Affairs	Europe	Africa & The Middle East	The Americas	Asia & The Pacific
Nov. 10	International radio conferees at Washington, DC., seeking to replace the 1912 radio convention, agree to 23 new radio rules. Most significant are the assignment of lower bandwidths and the regulation and licensing of amateurs.	Lord Wemyss demands that Britain reclaim its right to search neutral ships. Britain yielded the right under the Declaration of Paris in 1856. The declaration also banned privateering....The court martial of Manoilescu, charged as a Carolist conspirator, opens. He has 110 attorneys....Prominent Viennese offer the League a palace if it transfers from the Hague.	The head of Angola's bank says that Portugal must help its economically backward colony or risk disruption of relations with the colony. Angola is the outlet for railways proposed by Rhodesia and the Belgian Congo to the coast.	Mexico executes General Garcia after a court martial.	
Nov. 11	In London, in New York, and elsewhere, activity stops for two minutes at 11 o'clock. Today is Armistice Day.	Austria's high court rules that divorced persons can marry. They no longer require Vatican approval....Italy announces plans for one-party rule. Parliament will be smaller, with members subject to Benito Mussolini's approval. Only guild members can vote....France and Yugoslavia sign a treaty of mutual support and defense. The act is a blow to Italy, which sought to be signatory....The British pound trades at $4.87, its highest in 13 years.		At Arlington national cemetery, Canada unveils its cross in tribute to American war dead. The United States and Canada reaffirm their friendship.	Russian czarist general Peter Kozloff denies that he claimed to have found the tomb of Genghis Khan. Kozloff says the tomb he found is much too old. He recommends a year's research at the site.
Nov. 12		German cigar manufacturers announce they will lock out their 130,000 to 150,000 workers after wage negotiations stalemate. The workers want a 15 percent raise. The owners' offer is smaller....The Communist Party expels Leon Trotsky and 81 associates. The party claims the Trotskyites forced their hand by staging demonstrations.		Anticipating that the United States might not recognize Alvaro Obregon after the executions of his rivals as rebels, Mexican politicians rally behind the candidacy of the labor party's Luis Morones. Opposition to Obregon also comes from generals expecting to be fired and agrarians dissatisfied with Plutarco Calles' policies. Many see Plutarco Calles as a tool of Obregon.	Japan's new budget provides nearly 5 million yen for emigration. Most of the 1.45 million yen increase is for a museum providing information about destinations in Asia and Latin America. Japan also offers emigrant training schools, relocation services, and cheap or free fares. Japan wants to relocate disgruntled farmers, especially to Brazil.
Nov. 13		Russia says Poland is massing troops and ammunition on the Lithuanian border. Russia claims Poland's ultimate aim is to invade Russia.	Ruins uncovered at Bulawayo, South Africa, differ from those discovered 25 miles away at Zimbabwe, Rhodesia, in 1868. The inner walls of the former are angular while the latter are circular.	Would-be assassins throw two bombs from a moving car at Obregon's vehicle. A running gun battle ensues. Two attackers are wounded and one seized.	Only the Labor Party opposes New Zealand's contribution of a million pounds to the British naval base at Singapore. Prime Minister Joseph Coates denies that the base is an affront to Japan and affirms the friendship of the two nations.
Nov. 14		As German textile workers settle their strike, cigar makers walk out....Manoilescu is found not guilty of attempting to restore Carol to the Romanian throne....Poland denies any intention of invading Lithuania or anyone.	Stanley High says whites in Africa need to be more alert. Race war is likely because African nationalism is greater than that of India, China, or the Philippines....Negotiations between England and Ethiopia over the Lake Tsana dam resume. The threat of an American construction with no Anglo-Egyptian oversight brought Egypt around....Moroccan bandits say they will release the women in the Steeg party. They continue to hold Theodore Steeg.		Disarray in Hankow declines as Hankow and Nanking set a cease fire and open negotiations. Then Nanking takes Hankow peacefully.... A coastal vessel sinks near Bombay, with a loss of 135 lives.
Nov. 15	Cuba, Poland, Germany, and Czechoslovakia sign a pact to restrict sugar exports. Holland wants to sign too. Sugar prices rise.	Carolists claim the exoneration of Manoilescu is a blow to Ion Bratiano. Newspapers ask a lifting of censorship.			
Nov. 16		Polish paper money is sound. The government has gold and foreign currency worth 111 percent of paper issued....Spain is reportedly ready to rejoin the league. Italy and England are expected to support her bid for a seat on the permanent council....Northern Ireland's government rejects the franchise for women. Rather than follow the Free State, the decision is to wait on the imperial government.		General Juan Estrada, a liberal who led a revolution in 1909–1910 and was Nicaraguan president in 1910-1911, is appointed governor of the Bluefields Department. The cease fire brokered by Henry Stimson mandated that liberals govern liberal departments....Mexico accuses Hearst Newspapers of trying to destroy relations with the United States by manufacturing and publishing forged documents purportedly showing Mexican complicity in Nicaragua.	Northerners claim victory over the south and the halting of the southern drive outside the capital. After sporadic looting, Hankow is orderly.

A	B	C	D	E
Includes developments that affect more than one world region, international organizations and important meetings of world leaders.	*Includes all domestic and regional developments in Europe, including the Soviet Union.*	*Includes all domestic and regional developments in Africa and the Middle East.*	*Includes all domestic and regional developments in Latin America, the Caribbean, and Canada.*	*Includes all domestic and regional developments in Asian and Pacific nations (and colonies).*

U.S. Politics & Social Issues	U.S. Foreign Policy & Affairs, Defense	U.S. Economy & Environment	Science, Technology & Nature	Culture, Leisure & Lifestyle	
Oklahoma state Baptists in convention vote to withhold funds for seminaries in Ft. Worth and Louisville. By a 5–1 margin fundamentalists makes funding contingent on the seminaries espousing fundamentalist principles....Michigan banishes "King" Benjamin Purnell and places his 25-year-old religious colony in receivership. The "House of David" cult members may remain—but under state oversight.	At Portsmouth, NH, the navy launches V-4. The V-4 is the navy's first mine-laying submarine.	In Detroit revenue agents find a brewery. Valued at $500,000, it occupies a full block—and it is underground.	The Nobel Prize for Physics goes to American Arthur Compton and Englishman T.R. Wilson. Compton, father of the Compton Process, works with x-rays and Wilson with electrified particles....Three Studebakers set a record by traveling 25,000 miles in 25,000 minutes.	Alvin "Shipwreck" Kelly climbs a flagpole on a speeding plane. Kelly is the world champion flagpole sitter but declines to commit to setting an airborne record.	Nov. 10
	The German embassy in Washington, DC. flies the flag. No German embassy in another allied nation flies a flag. The flag is Germany's tribute to the United States for honoring all war dead. Other Allied nations celebrate their victory.	White fruit pickers in the Yakima Valley force Filipino pickers out of the valley. Filipino workers deny making advances to white women. White ranchers and local businessmen join the ant-Filipino move. The Philippines will file a protest with the AFL on 24 November.			Nov. 11
	France and the United States reach an accord on tariffs. France reestablishes the old rates pending negotiation of a formal agreement next year.	With an electrical assist from Calvin Coolidge, who throws a switch in Washington, New York and New Jersey dignitaries open the Holland Tunnel. Thousands of pedestrians tour the tunnel before automobile traffic begins at midnight.	Germany claims to have perfected synthetic rubber and medicines. The synthetics are, in many cases, cheaper than the products they replace.	Argentina refuses to let the chess championship end in a draw. Financing for an additional two months is available if necessary.	Nov. 12
Correspondents in the capital form the Foreign Press Association. Washington, DC., has become a news center equal to Paris, London, Berlin and other foreign capitals.		The Holland Tunnel handles 52,000 vehicles the first day. Over 200,000 people travel the tunnel. Tolls total $26,142.	Presbyterian Hospital classifies over 400 diseases and their symptoms. Defining bootlegging, cynicism, laziness, and other social problems as symptoms helps doctors understand social causes of disease.		Nov. 13
A gas explosion in Pittsburgh kills two dozen, injures hundreds, and levels blocks of the city, including Carnegie's mills. Red Cross relief begins almost immediately.		William Durant, creator of General Motors, provides details of a new company. Hupp is to be the nucleus of the $100 million company. Other makers include Moon, Chandler, Peerless, Star, Gardner, and Jordan.		The international Skating Union of America dissolves. Canada has already formed its own organization. The U.S. body is the Amateur Skating Union of the United States.	Nov. 14
Chicago Dutch want more mention of their contributions to U.S. history. Chicago Italians want guarantees that city Norwegians cannot supplant Christopher Columbus with Leif Erickson.	The National Industrial Congress calls for lower tariffs and freight rates. Calvin Coolidge says lower tariffs harm farmers by causing a depression. He is already working on freight rate reduction.	Although California and Texas panhandle output is down, total crude oil output is up 16,000 barrels. This is the first rise in 6 weeks. In 1926 foreign ships carried two-thirds of U.S. trade.		Jose Capablanca wins the 29th game in 70 moves. He trails the challenger 4–3.	Nov. 15
Representative Cordell Hull (D-TN) attacks Calvin Coolidge's tariff policy. He says high tariffs make European repayment of loans and war debts impossible.	The Saratoga joins the U.S. fleet. At 33,000 tons the $40 million aircraft carrier is the largest ship made in the United States.	The first fire in the Holland Tunnel is put out in less than a minute. In addition, to speed entry, tunnel authorities are selling tickets in books of 50....Pilots and passengers will have life and accident insurance. A group of 30 insurers agrees to provide it for those on a regular airline on a regular schedule from a regular airport with a licensed pilot. The single provider before this charges $5 for $5,000 of insurance.	Secretary Herbert Hoover tours flood-ravaged New England and meets with Vermont's governor.		Nov. 16

F	G	H	I	J
Includes campaigns, elections, federal-state relations, civil rights and liberties, crime, the judiciary, education, healthcare, poverty, urban affairs, and population.	Includes formation and debate of U.S. foreign and defense policies, veterans affairs, and defense spending. (Relations with specific foreign countries are usually found under the region concerned.)	Includes business, labor, agriculture, taxation, transportation, consumer affairs, monetary and fiscal policy, natural resources, pollution and industrial accidents.	Includes worldwide scientific, medical and technological developments, natural phenomena, U.S. weather and natural disasters.	Includes the arts, religion, scholarship, communications media, sports, entertainment, fashions, fads, and social life.

	World Affairs	Europe	Africa & The Middle East	The Americas	Asia & The Pacific
Nov. 17		The House of Commons passes a bill setting quotas for British films. By 1935 distributors will have to show 25 percent British movies. French exhibitors object to American movies because they portray French women as vamps and French men as villains....The birth rate for England and Wales for the third quarter is an all-time record low 16.7 per 1,000. Infant mortality is also at the lowest rate ever.	Alan Cobham and his wife leave England on the first leg of a projected 20,000 mile flight around Africa. Cobham's flying boat has a co-pilot and a crew of four. Lord Cobham seeks to improve communication and commerce with Africa....A mine disaster in South Africa buries 14 miners 3,000 feet below ground for 30 hours. Other shafts in the Crown mine collapse also, with several dead....France pays the Steeg captors $400,000 in gold and goods.	The Mexican supreme court rules in favor of two American companies. It overturns portions of the Mexican oil lease law and restores drilling permits. Although the ruling does not apply across the board, it seems a beginning to the complete reversal of Mexican oil law.	Under the replacement general for Chiang Kai-shek, nationalists lose half of Canton to a labor rising. Rumor says Chiang is coming back. In addition, famine confronts nine million Chinese.
Nov. 18	The League is in a quandary. The Chinese are due the presidency because of the rule that provides for alphabetical rotation. The Chinese claimant is representative of Peking's dictator, Chang Tso Lin, disliked as a bandit and tool of Japan.	France doubles tariffs on wheat and frozen meats. U.S. exporters are hurt, but because the tariff is across the board the U.S. government has no plans to protest....Yugoslavs demonstrate against Italy. Counter-demonstrators in Padua and Venice force police to protect the Yugoslav and French consulates....Brisk business at Ford's Paris plant fuels European concerns and raises the specter of higher duties on American cars.	The Moroccan sultan died yesterday. While the late sultan is laid to rest, at Fez. Moroccan *ulemas* meet to select the new sultan. Their choice is the 14-year-old third son of the sultan.	Mexico executes another Gomez general after summary court martial. Oscar Aguilar led infantry in Mexico City under General Hector Almada, still at large.	The Australian cruiser *Adelaide* returns from the Solomons. Most of the naval and civilian forces are finished punishing the Malaitan murderers but a contingent of 300 native police and carriers led by Australian officers is marching inland toward Suu.
Nov. 19		London detains purported German and Irish-American spies. Both have government documents and addresses in Germany and Holland....The first Turkish barbers' exposition reveals that older Turkish women are abandoning traditional hair-covering scarves. They are bobbing their hair and wearing Parisian hats.		The New Brunswick Supreme Court rules that prohibition, a wartime measure, is not in effect in Carleton County, which abuts Maine for 50 miles. Government liquor stores can now open there. Canadian bootlegging will decline.	Chiang Kai-shek indicates that he will take a high civilian post in the Nanking government and may take a military position too. He claims a unified south can beat the north in two months....China's northern government is entering the Manchurian railroad building competition aggressively. Japan attempts to enforce its treaty rights peacefully.
Nov. 20		Cook's Army enters London. After weeks on a 170-mile trek the army of unemployed demands Stanely Baldwin's ouster and jobs at decent wages....Turkey arrests nine Communists, including two Arcos employees, who infiltrate the tobacco workers. Turkey turns away from a friendship dating to the rise of Kemal.		Having won its court battle, Mexican Petroleum begins drilling again. Other companies are filing for drilling permits or preparing to drill. Within weeks Tampico will have 50 operating rigs.	
Nov. 21	Standard Oil of New Jersey signs a third contract for Russian oil. Royal Dutch Shell is displeased at the addition of the new oil to the world supply. A world oil war looms.	The Belgian government falls when Socialists refuse to compromise over the length of military service. A Catholic-Liberal coalition is probable but probably too weak to survive.	Morocco's new sultan enters the capital with auguries of good luck. Among them is torrential rain, a rarity in a capital where sun shines 300 days of the year.	Under a new agreement Nicaragua will spend $700,000 on guard forces that will take over police duties from U.S. Marines. American officers and NCOs will officer the new force....Reports indicate that Generals Almeda, Celes and other failed revolutionaries are in Texas.	Plague in Secunderabad, India, is taking 20 lives a day.
Nov. 22	In the run-up to the League disarmament meeting, France expresses skepticism about Russia's sincerity. The Soviets claim to want world peace but only with simultaneous world disarmament. They say less than total disarmament is a sign of hypocrisy.	Catholics, Liberals, and Christian Democrats are in the new government of Jaspers. The Socialists are in opposition and the coalition faces not only the military service issue but also deeper ethnic and language issues....Portugal is on alert for a possible revolution after bomb threats and reports of Communists in the army....Anti-Semitic Hungarian students bar Jews entry to schools. Some are armed.	Egyptian law requires new corporations to have two Egyptians on the board of directors. Egyptians must make up 25 percent of employees, and Egyptian capitalists must have opportunities to provide 50 percent of capital. British, American, and other foreign capitalists protest....Five thousand Wahhabis under Sheik Zobhar are in Kuwait preparing to raid Iraq. Countering them are Iraqi forces and the Royal Air Force.		At Tulagi, Solomon Islands, Australia jails Basiano and 40 followers who participated in the October Malaita massacre. Troops are patrolling the area, which is mostly peaceful with but an occasional confrontation.... A critic of Australia reports the indigenous population is 57,000. He says the number at Cook's arrival was 300,000....Europeans oppose Governor Jonkheer de Graaf's proposal for a native majority in Java's 10-year-old *volksraad*. They prefer the 35-25 European edge currently in place and disapprove even discussing it.

A	B	C	D	E
Includes developments that affect more than one world region, international organizations and important meetings of world leaders.	*Includes all domestic and regional developments in Europe, including the Soviet Union.*	*Includes all domestic and regional developments in Africa and the Middle East.*	*Includes all domestic and regional developments in Latin America, the Caribbean, and Canada.*	*Includes all domestic and regional developments in Asian and Pacific nations (and colonies).*

U.S. Politics & Social Issues	U.S. Foreign Policy & Affairs, Defense	U.S. Economy & Environment	Science, Technology & Nature	Culture, Leisure & Lifestyle	
Already implicated in the Fall-Sinclair jury tampering and under threat of additional obstruction and intimidation charges, the Burns Agency is subpoenaed by Calumet Baking Powder. In a case that has lingered for two years, two other baking powder companies are suing Calumet for illegal trade practices, and Calumet claims Burns engaged in industrial espionage.	Two destroyers, *Zeilin* and *Somers*, collide at top speed during torpedo drill off California. One is able to make port on its own, but the other requires a tow.	Ford purchasing agent Fred Diehl resigns. Coming on the heels of the resignation of Ford's sales manager, the resignation of Diehl sparks rumors that the new model A is encountering production delays.	A thunderstorm spawns a tornado that hits Washington, DC., and Alexandria, VA. The tornado damages 379 houses and the naval air station and causes $1 million in damage, but it kills only one person.	The Atlantic County Federation of Church Women tells pageant and Atlantic City officials that beauty pageants demean and corrupt women. The women say further that commercialization of the boardwalk damages the esthetics of the New Jersey seashore.	Nov. 17
An Indianapolis grand jury indicts four city council members for bribery in the effort to keep the former mayor.		Plans to list international stocks on the New York Stock Exchange suffer a setback when one of the first two invitees, an Amsterdam company, declines a NYSE invitation to list its stock. The NYSE sometimes lists American firms without their request but has no policy regarding foreign stocks, their listing being new.			Nov. 18
The American Eugenics Society reports that a survey of 499 institutions of higher education reveals that three-fourths of them offer courses in eugenics. Western sectarian and co-educational institutions are most likely to offer the course.... Representative Emmanuel Celler refutes claims that immigrant crime is higher than for native born.		Sikorsky reveals plans to build $1 million worth of planes. The company does not reveal buyers for the two dozen amphibians, but the navy is expected to be among them.	The Coast Guard reports success with experiments dropping a line from a plane to a vessel in distress and pulling the boat from shore. This method, it is hoped, will make rescue boats obsolete. The Coast Guard also notes that radio calls rather than flares are the common method to initiate rescues.	Three Chippendale chairs from the Alexander Hudnut collection bring $2,300 apiece at auction. A Duncan Phyfe breakfast table fetches $4,100. 92 objects bring $47,852.	Nov. 19
Presbyterians raise the base pay for missionaries by 10-20 percent. Chinese rates are $900 for single missionaries and $1680 for married ones. Indian rates are $1128 and $1884. The church has a deficit of $339,780 due to the raises and turmoil in China.			The former Princess Xenia of Russia runs a new-fantail-style passenger boat at an unofficial record of 60 kph. The boat carries 24 passengers. The navy is interested in the design as a torpedo boat auxiliary.	Princeton dean Fleming West reports that all overseas scholarships for the graduate college are taken, with six applicants for each position. Reversing the customary pattern, foreign students are coming to the United States for graduate study.	Nov. 20
Gang warfare in Chicago over control of gambling reaches the police precinct where officers nab two Capone men trying to blast a third out of the station. Police have been busy seizing stockpiles of weapons. The rump O'Banion-Weiss-Drucci gang plans to assassinate Capone....Colorado forces attack miners on the way to a demonstration. Five are dead and 20 wounded as police attack with machine guns. The national guard has planes and tanks in the area, which is under martial law.	American goods held up during the tariff spat begin arriving in Paris. The temporary lowered rates are in effect.	The Supreme Court rules that a retroactive federal gift tax, enacted in 1924, is unconstitutional. The court ties 4-4 and fails to rule on the Constitutionality of the tax itself. The court also rules that a lessee owes taxes on Indian oil lands. ...The New York merchants association redefines New York. Based on social and economic impact, the New York metropolitan area is 3,765 square miles with over 9.5 million people in New York, new Jersey, and Connecticut.	French professor Roubaude of the Pasteur Institute says that the way to stop the French Pyrale butterfly larva that is damaging corn is to use wormwood. The butterflies prefer the weed to the corn.	Now playing at the Palace are the Duncan Sisters with their new act and the perennial Fannie Brice.	Nov. 21
The court cites Burns and Sinclair for contempt but holds bribery and spying indictments in abeyance. A grand jury is still reviewing that matter....Chicago's William Thompson compiles a list of neglected American heroes.	Canada objects to an order restricting Canadian residents from commuting to the United States for work without having a visa and paying a head tax. The practice has become common because thousands of newly arrived Europeans are unable to make the quota. Now it is illegal under labor department General Order 86.	WTFF, the 50-watt Klan radio station outside the capital gets Radio Commission clearance to broadcast at 10,000 watts. Owners remain committed to 50,000 watts in the future.	The record setting boat with the new fantail design comes a cropper when its fantail breaks the propeller. The princess rigs a sail and gets it to dock.	The Amateur Athletic Union opposes pay for play and resolves to protest the international approval of paying soccer players in the Olympics for time lost from work.	Nov. 22

F	G	H	I	J
Includes campaigns, elections, federal-state relations, civil rights and liberties, crime, the judiciary, education, healthcare, poverty, urban affairs, and population.	*Includes formation and debate of U.S. foreign and defense policies, veterans affairs, and defense spending. (Relations with specific foreign countries are usually found under the region concerned.)*	*Includes business, labor, agriculture, taxation, transportation, consumer affairs, monetary and fiscal policy, natural resources, pollution and industrial accidents.*	*Includes worldwide scientific, medical and technological developments, natural phenomena, U.S. weather and natural disasters.*	*Includes the arts, religion, scholarship, communications media, sports, entertainment, fashions, fads, and social life.*

	World Affairs	Europe	Africa & The Middle East	The Americas	Asia & The Pacific
Nov. 23		George B. Shaw tells Britons to look carefully for a dictator. He notes that Benito Mussolinis are rare.... The government and opposition in Yugoslavia unite for the French treaty. They note that relations with Italy, where protests have occurred recently, are not perfect.		Mexico executes four for plotting to kill Alvaro Obregon. One is a priest.	
Nov. 24	The Soviet delegation arrives for dis-armament talks. Germany expects Soviet backing for its desire for arms parity. France will oppose. Britain and France expect the talks to be inconclusive.	Jon Bratianu dies of post-operative infection, sparking rumors of poison. His brother Vintila replaces him. Friends of Carol expect him to return....France announces a 20-year project to rebuild its 3.5 million ton merchant marine, which has not been rebuilt after the war ravaged it. The plan is to modernize 150,000 tons a year. The government will guarantee the first billion franc loan....Italy and Albania sign a mutual defense treaty. The pact counters the Franco-Yugoslav agreement.		Nicaragua's Emiliano Chamorro accedes to U.S. opposition to his candidacy. He will not run for president but indicates that he will be the power behind the throne if a conservative wins....Canada's immigration commissioner says the country needs European immi-grants. There is ample work that the English refuse to do.	Lord Birkenhead explains that Indians are not members of the Simon commission because he wants commissioners with no pre-conceived position. Besides, two thirds of Indians have no knowledge of the commission. Also, a commis-sion representing the many Indian positions would be unworkable.
Nov. 25	The Dutch opt not to join the sugar cartel. They do, however, indicate that they will support Cuban restric-tions—at least for a time....The world radio conference ends with the signing of the agreement on new regulations.	Former premier Alexadru Averescu backs the new premier Bratianu. He affirms that the 1926 act establish-ing the regency barred Carol from returning.	The estimated size of the South African wool crop is 240 million pounds. The International Institute of Agriculture also reports that quality is equal to or better than the 1926 clip.	20,000 line the streets for the funeral cortege of Father Projaurez and two of the other three execut-ed in the Alvaro Obregon assassina-tion attempt. Mourners toss flowers and cry, "long live the martyrs."	The U.S. state department indicates it has no objection to Morgan lend-ing the Japanese $30-$40 million to build a Manchurian railroad. China, on the other hand, finds the plan intrusive on its sovereignty.
Nov. 26	After protests that the League report on white slavery white-washes English-speaking nations, the commission agrees to review the already-published report. Lead complainant is Uruguay, which has fought the crime for two decades. Others include Italy, France, Poland, Brazil, and Argentina.	Germany prepares a 9.5 billion mark budget for the coming year. Thanks to an improving economy, the budget is in balance despite a 400 million mark increase in repara-tions....Eamon de Valera's attempt to promote Gaelic in the Dail found-ers. Too few know the language, and one even requests a translator.	The High Commissioner for Iraq reports that the British protector-ate is prosperous, with higher than anticipated revenues in 1926 and 1927, budget surpluses, little labor disturbance, and prosperous indus-try. Palestine, Egypt, and Syria are less fortunate.	The Canadian heirs of James Crook wait for the United States to pay their claim of $24,000. They are due the money for a ship seized by the United States and sunk by the British in 1812. The United States acknowledged the claim after a century but has not yet paid.	
Nov. 27			France demands the return of the ransom paid Moroccan kidnappers. French planes drop leaflets in the mountains notifying the inhabitants that they face a major offensive in the spring if they fail to return the 3 million francs and assorted booty.... Floods in Algeria kill hundreds as a dam breaks.		
Nov. 28	The pope appoints four new cardi-nals. The choices reduce the Italian majority to 33-32. It should help to defuse the issue of Italian domi-nance. The two French cardinals oppose L'action Francaise.	Fascist students at the German Technical Institute at Brunn remove Jews after the new president says he wants no Jews or Socialists at his inauguration. Czechs stand by, neu-tral, as students battle with guns and knives. Police finally break up the fighting.		Four more rebels are executed in Jalisco, Mexico. Plans are to begin a final assault on rebels in Jalisco, Aguas Calientes, and Michoacan. All other sectors are pacified.	
Nov. 29		Russia receives $40 million in cred-its for a steel factory at Makeyeva on the Don. Funding for expansion of the "Russian Pittsburgh" comes from American Percival Farquhar. It is the first break in the U.S. boy-cott of Russian projects....A long-rumored peasant rebellion in the Ukraine is confirmed. After three months and 5,000 dead, it is done.			Chang's aide denounces the U.S. loan for the Japanese Manchurian railroad. He insists Chang will not allow it.

A	B	C	D	E
Includes developments that affect more than one world region, international organizations and important meetings of world leaders.	*Includes all domestic and regional developments in Europe, including the Soviet Union.*	*Includes all domestic and regional developments in Africa and the Middle East.*	*Includes all domestic and regional developments in Latin America, the Caribbean, and Canada.*	*Includes all domestic and regional developments in Asian and Pacific nations (and colonies).*

U.S. Politics & Social Issues	U.S. Foreign Policy & Affairs, Defense	U.S. Economy & Environment	Science, Technology & Nature	Culture, Leisure & Lifestyle	
A Colorado coroner's jury acquits guardsmen in the deaths of miners. The jury finds that the guardsmen warned the miners to stop and did not use machine guns.... Calvin Coolidge commutes Marcus Garvey's sentence. Garvey will be deported under a 1925 order.	France releases Mississippi born deserter Bennett Doty from the Foreign Legion. He is pardoned then discharged because France does not want to create a *cause celebre* over an American....Army aviation chief Mason Patrick says the five-year plan is insufficient.	Seven distilleries merge into American Medicinal Spirits. The $15 million company has assets of over 60,000 barrels of bourbon....Both White Star and Cunard announce plans to build the largest ship afloat.		Alexander Alekhine wins the 32nd game. He leads Jose Capablanca 5–3 and needs one more victory for the chess title.	Nov. 23
Thanksgiving turns violent in Folsom (CA) Prison. 1,200 prisoners riot, with seven prisoners and two guards dead, but the attempted mass breakout fails....With the Colorado coalfields mostly quiet under martial law, demonstrators parade in New York against the Rockefeller-owned Colorado Fuel and Iron. The protesters claim the company controls the Colorado government.		Illinois farms lost $881 million in between 1921 and 1925. The five-year Missouri loss tops $960 million. Railroad workers make twice as much as Illinois farmers.			Nov. 24
After the warden threatens to flood the cellblock, prisoners surrender. Total fatalities are nine prisoners, two guards. 33 are wounded. Six ringleaders face murder charges.	Calvin Coolidge indicates that the United States cannot outlaw war through treaty. The war-making power lies solely with Congress. Still, he says signing the treaty might encourage others to support peace.	Continental Motors stock rises almost two points on news that Durant wants to include the company in his combination of small auto manufacturers.		Not only the audience but also the New York Symphony musicians applaud the performance of the Beethoven concerto. The performer is 11-year-old violinist Yehudi Menuhin.	Nov. 25
Nebraska nominates Norris, native-son presidential candidate, in its primary.	Senator William Borah says Calvin Coolidge is wrong. Signing a treaty outlawing war is constitutional and does not prevent Congress from declaring defensive war on violators of the pact.			The just-ended football season tallies 17 deaths and 100 injuries requiring hospitalization. The death total is up from 1926 but below 1925's record 20. New York hunting accidents kill 28. Football this year stresses safety, with rules changes protecting kickers and receivers of lateral passes. Goal posts are moved off the field of play.	Nov. 26
M.L. Kenner of the National Association for the Deaf contends that the deaf can drive safely. They are more attentive to the road. Kenner counters New York City Magistrate William McAdoo, who contends that the deaf are a menace because they cannot hear police whistles.	James Gerard, chair of the American Committee Opposed to the Lausanne Treaty, objects to the new Turkish envoy. Gerard says last year's modus vivendi with Turkey to put Lausanne into effect despite non-ratification is wrong. Additionally, the proposed ambassador is responsible for 30,000 Armenian deaths.			Football breaks records as attendance hits 30 million with $50 million gate receipts. Incalculable millions listen on radio....New basketball rules say no contact, no foul. The exception is blocking a player's progress.	Nov. 27
Democrats decline to organize the Senate, not wanting shaky control of one part of government during the remainder of the Calvin Coolidge administration. The Republicans have only 46 seats since the Senate refused to seat two contested Republicans. Democrats have 47, and one is a Farmer-Laborite.	A court rules that the United States can bar people from living in Canada and working in the United States. The judge provides that 600 working in Detroit can continue commuting if they pay the tax. Otherwise, they have to wait for quota-limited visas.			New salon cars feature brighter interiors contrasted with more subdued interiors. Features include spaces for golf bags and bars.	Nov. 28
Southern and western farm groups back McNary's proposal for crop controls. They tell Calvin Coolidge they oppose subsidies.	Safely in his Washington hotel after rumors of a plot against him, the Turkish ambassador declines to comment on charges that he is responsible for Armenian genocide.	Ford launches a $1.6 million advertising campaign for the new model, due out at the end of the week. Dealers handle a flood of inquiries.	United Cigar Stores begins experimenting with a vending machine that dispenses 11 brands of cigarettes and four types of pipe tobacco. The machine frees clerks from routine sales and allows them to assist customers with more complex transactions.	After 34 games and 74 nights, Alexander Alekhine wins, scoring equally from black and white Jose Capablanca helped Alekhine win his first major in 1909.	Nov. 29

F	G	H	I	J
Includes campaigns, elections, federal-state relations, civil rights and liberties, crime, the judiciary, education, healthcare, poverty, urban affairs, and population.	Includes formation and debate of U.S. foreign and defense policies, veterans affairs, and defense spending. (Relations with specific foreign countries are usually found under the region concerned.)	Includes business, labor, agriculture, taxation, transportation, consumer affairs, monetary and fiscal policy, natural resources, pollution and industrial accidents.	Includes worldwide scientific, medical and technological developments, natural phenomena, U.S. weather and natural disasters.	Includes the arts, religion, scholarship, communications media, sports, entertainment, fashions, fads, and social life.

	World Affairs	Europe	Africa & The Middle East	The Americas	Asia & The Pacific
Nov. 30	Litvinoff proposes the abolition of all armies, navies, and armaments. Briand questions how Litvinoff plans to get all to lay down arms simultaneously. The British press mocks the Soviet plan as no plan at all.	France and Germany sign the agreement that establishes the billion dollar dye trust. The Europeans will compete with the United States in Latin America and Asia.		Ontario offers $2 million in bonds to build a park at Niagara.	
Dec. 1	The League opens talks on how to mandate peace. Russia sends an observer but the United States refuses. As before, small nations want assurances of aid against aggressors. Large nations are reluctant to commit themselves. Conferees are looking for some means of enforcing non-war.	Aristide Briand's statement that he is willing to talk to Benito Mussolini sparks rumors that France might give Italy Syria. The transfer would ease France's mandate burden and reduce Italian hostility. Italy felt insulted by the 1919 mandate assignments and later failures in Albania and elsewhere. Italian reaction is skepticism....Poland charges that Lithuania is mobilizing under a madman. Lithuania denies the charge.	Algerian flood losses total over $23 million worth of property and 2,000 dead.		Chiang Kai-shek marries Meling Soong, the sister of Sun Yat Sen's widow. The bride is a Wellesley graduate. The wedding includes both a Methodist and civil ceremony. The marriage cements an alliance of two leading Chinese nationalist families.
Dec. 2	A $200 million cast iron pipe trust includes not only French, British, and German firms but U.S. ones as well. The four nations dominate the world market and establish world prices. Membership in the trust protects U.S. markets from the other trust members.	The Communist Party Congress convenes in Moscow for the first time since December 1925. Trotskyites maintain they are the true Leninists and will not leave. The Congress elects the Central Committee and Politburo....Debates over free speech and press deteriorate into fisticuffs in the Hungarian parliament. The precipitating issue is Bethlen's refusal to entertain debate on police attacks on 400 men.		Montreal's Protestant School Board contends before the Privy Council that its decision to bar Jews conforms to the Act of Confederation. The act of 80 years before established Protestant and Catholic systems but provided nothing for Jews, less than half a percent of the population. Jews argue that establishing their own system means degraded quality due to too many systems.	As the Kuomintang prepares to convene, Canton's Wang severs all ties with Communists. It warns Nanking that it must subordinate the military to the civil element if it expects Canton to join it....Sydney dockworkers strike rather than accept unwanted overtime. The tie up of shipping will cost another 10,000 jobs beyond the 3500 strikers.
Dec. 3	A German company will invest 8-10 million marks to build factory ships to allow processing of whales on the spot. Factory ships allow Norway to dominate whaling, with a 1 million kroner investment returning 23 million over two decades. Britain and Chile are other major whalers. A cartel is likely....The International Radio Conference sets "Mayday" as the shortwave radio SOS. Mayday is phonetic "M'Aider," help me.	Belgian demands for a larger quota threaten to break the steel cartel. France and Germany are strongly opposed. The cartel will meet on December 9....France and Italy sign a modus vivendi on the rights of each other's nationals. Aristide Briand and Austen Chamberlain discuss ways to mend relations with Italy.			
Dec. 4	At Geneva, Aristide Briand convinces Russia to join the peace process. He also extends a hand to Italy and makes progress on the Baltic and Polish-Lithuanian problems. Britain remains cold to Russia.		The University of Pennsylvania's excavations at Beisan, Palestine, of two temples dated to 1500 B.C. tie to passages in the Book of Samuel. The temples feature sacrifice of animals and, possibly, snake worship by Canaanites under Egypt's Tutmose III.		
Dec. 5	The report to the League on white slavery describes conditions in 28 countries, including the United States, Mexico, the Canal Zone, and Cuba have major problems while the United States has seen a switch from white slavery to bootlegging after passage of the Mann Act.	In an attempted assassination of a Bulgarian officer, Macedonians bomb a town café. Two bystanders die; others suffer wounds.			The Kuomintang unity conference falters as Nanking's representatives walk out. They claim that the Cantonese are still in thrall to the Communists after Canton refuses to support Nanking's desire for a new campaign against the north.

A	B	C	D	E
Includes developments that affect more than one world region, international organizations and important meetings of world leaders.	Includes all domestic and regional developments in Europe, including the Soviet Union.	Includes all domestic and regional developments in Africa and the Middle East.	Includes all domestic and regional developments in Latin America, the Caribbean, and Canada.	Includes all domestic and regional developments in Asian and Pacific nations (and colonies).

U.S. Politics & Social Issues	U.S. Foreign Policy & Affairs, Defense	U.S. Economy & Environment	Science, Technology & Nature	Culture, Leisure & Lifestyle	
In Alabama, the Attorney General quits the Klan flogging case. He claims the state police assisted the Klansmen. The solicitor general suspends cases against 31 after two are acquitted....A black man accused of murder in Kentucky is taken from jail and removed to Virginia. There he is shot and burned.	Frank B. Kellogg says limited transactions with Russia are okay but the U.S. policy remains in effect. He will permit no liquidation of securities.	Fifteen coal companies meet secretly to discuss a merger of up to 20 companies with $50 million capitalization. Many of the firms are not anti-union, and the two largest anti-union companies are not there....A seat on the curb exchange sells for a record $65,000....Ford prices are $385 to $570. Cars will be available in January. New Yorkers order 100,000 sight unseen. The stock market soars.	The British Royal Society presents medals to Americans W.D. Calvin Coolidge for work on x-rays, A.A. Noyes for physical chemistry. Canadian John McLennan receives a prize for spectroscopy and atomic physics....A London specialist warns smokers that pipes and cigarette holders promote cancer.		Nov. 30
Vice President Charles Dawes declares his non-candidacy for the Republican nomination. Charles Evans Hughes backers see the field clearing for their candidate. Herbert Hoover supporters wait for Calvin Coolidge to clarify his situation.	Frank B. Kellogg says the United States will not send an observer to the League commission drafting the treaty on arms limitation. The United States sees no benefit in joining talks on a treaty it cannot sign because it would place U.S. forces under international command.	The new Ford models—five cars and a truck—debut before admiring crowds. The only thing reminiscent of the flivver is the motor. Ford plans to rehire 75,000 workers....The ICC grants western shippers parity with those in the east on shipping to the south. The West has fought the 40 percent differential for 30 years.	The Radio Board says that it will begin eliminating 300 excess radio stations on February 1 by not renewing licenses as they come due. The move is necessary to reduce overcrowding of channels.		Dec. 1
A crowd of 500 blacks cheer Marcus Garvey as he leaves new Orleans for Jamaica.		Ford's New York showrooms attract 250,000 customers and 50,000 orders in a day. Comparable responses occur throughout the United States as the Ford market continues to move on Wall Street.		In a prototypical full "companionate divorce," a Cleveland couple divorce but continue living in the same house. Their agreement splits bills, sets wages for housework, and divides property. Custody of the three children living with them is not yet determined.	Dec. 2
New Jersey's education commissioner says drop out rates are too high, with 32 percent of 9th graders leaving before the 10th year and almost 2/3 gone by senior year. The system needs courses more attractive to students—and athletics integrated into the curriculum....Juries in Boston acquit Edna St. Vincent Millay and seven other Sacco protest marchers. Powers Hapgood is convicted of a minor charge, not riot.	Calvin Coolidge announces his new cruiser plan. World reaction is negative because it seems to seek parity with Britain and could generate arms buildups in land powers. The army announces the assignment of three officers and two enlisted mechanics to Cuba. Their mission is to assist Cuba in creating a flying school.		New York chemists ask for the reconvening of the World Congress of Chemists. The organization stopped meeting during the war.... India's Dr. Jagandis Chadra Bose reveals a device that can track the movement of plant cells. He reports that medicinal extracts can regulate the movement of the heart.		Dec. 3
The National Crime Commission calls for each state to establish a crime bureau and the sharing of information among the bureaus. The United States has the highest crime and worst data collection in the industrial world....The American Historical Association faults Mayor William Thompson's Americanism campaign. The AHA says hero worship generates false patriotism.	China attempts to get Frank B. Kellogg to block the Morgan loan for the Manchurian railroad. Chinese students in the United States protest the secretary's position that the loan is okay.	New York City breaks ground on the new Riker's Island prison, which replaces the 95-year-old facility on Welfare Island. When finished the $4–5 million facility will house 2400 inmates.		The annual Eddie Cantor benefit at the Ziegfield The4ter brings performers including Irving Berlin, Jackson and Jimmy Durante, George Jessel, and many more. The benefit allows poor east side boys to attend camp at Cold Springs, NY....Coach John W. Heisman retires at Rice Institute. His career at four schools lasts 36 years, second to Amos Alonzo Stagg.	Dec. 4
The Supreme Court settles the Texas–New Mexico border by ruling that New Mexico accepted the 1850 river location. It denies New Mexico's claim to the current river's location, which would give New Mexico 25,000 acres above El Paso valued at $2 to $3 million.	Secretaries Andrew Mellon and Frank B. Kellogg approve refinancing $19 million in Greek war debt at 3 percent over 62 years and new loans of $12 million over 20 years. The only remaining U.S. disagreements over war debts are with Armenia and the Soviet Union.	Two thousand farmers at the Chicago American Farm Bureau Federation support government aid, but not price controls or subsidies. They support protection and cooperatives. Average income for farmers in 1926 is $856; the national average is over $2,000....After two years a special master in chancery rules that 51 oil firms are not in violation of the Sherman Anti-Trust Act. The government contended that the companies acquired and held patents to block competitors..			Dec. 5

F	G	H	I	J
Includes campaigns, elections, federal-state relations, civil rights and liberties, crime, the judiciary, education, healthcare, poverty, urban affairs, and population.	*Includes formation and debate of U.S. foreign and defense policies, veterans affairs, and defense spending. (Relations with specific foreign countries are usually found under the region concerned.)*	*Includes business, labor, agriculture, taxation, transportation, consumer affairs, monetary and fiscal policy, natural resources, pollution and industrial accidents.*	*Includes worldwide scientific, medical and technological developments, natural phenomena, U.S. weather and natural disasters.*	*Includes the arts, religion, scholarship, communications media, sports, entertainment, fashions, fads, and social life.*

	World Affairs	Europe	Africa & The Middle East	The Americas	Asia & The Pacific
Dec. 6		After a six-week study, the American Committee on the Rights of Religious Minorities reports a disagreement between rhetoric and reality in Romania. A liberal constitution fails to protect Jews, Catholics, and Hungarian Lutherans in outlying regions.			
Dec. 7	As expected, Britain joins Germany and France in the chemical trust. Switzerland wants to join too. The next move is a nitrate cartel, but said cartel will not be able to achieve its goal of controlling the world supply unless the United States joins.	Friends of Dr. Joseph Eljas report that the Estonian chess player, who disappeared five weeks ago, is in a Leningrad prison being questioned by the Cheka. Russia claims Eljas' notebook of chess plays is cipher and that he is a spy for somebody.			
Dec. 8	The nitrate cartel talks begin in Europe with a U.S. representative. The cartel targets Chile, which controls the largest part of the world's nitrates.	An anti-war petition submitted to the government has signatures of 128,770 Britons. The signers oppose war and would refuse to serve in any manner if called. Many are veterans of the war....London begins expansion of Croydon Airdrome. When combined with Beddington, the new airport will be second in Europe only to Berlin's Templehof....Prussia votes Christmas advances for government officials. The advances range from $7.50 to $17.50.		Plans are announced for an Arctic expedition in April 1928; The explorers will use the *Morrissey* to find and examine natural Mongolian mummies, possibly the original Americans, in the Aleutians.	A fire in an overcrowded dwelling in North Calcutta kills 18. Three of the dead are women, five children.
Dec. 9	Calvin Coolidge proposes a world conference on aviation in 1928 to celebrate the 25th anniversary of flight.	Spain restricts emigration of laborers, minor males, and women under 25. Those who wish to leave must show they have support at their destination. Those who emigrate under this policy have a guarantee that Spain will pay for their repatriation if necessary.	Religious ceremonies in English, Hebrew, Arabic, Greek, and Armenian celebrate the 10th anniversary of the liberation of Jerusalem. Anglican, Orthodox, and Armenian clergy participate. In 1917 General Allenby took Jerusalem from the Turks.		In London high commissioners for New Zealand and India complain that the empire has suffered American films far too long. They cite American neglect of the British role in the war and the absence of elevating or informative content.
Dec. 10	A tense day and night of discussions defuse the Polish-Lithuanian crisis. At one point Pilsudski asks whether it will be peace or war. Aristide Briand eases tensions and the two governments agree to face-to-face talks with League mediation.			Marcus Garvey arrives in Kingston, Jamaica. A flag-waving crowd of supporters and a band escort him to Liberty Hall, headquarters of the Universal Negro Improvement Association.	The warring nationalist factions unify behind Chiang Kai-shek. They deny he is a dictator....Japan again warns China to stop building a railroad parallel to the South Manchuria Railroad. Since acquiring the road in 1906, Japan has built it to match the best of the west and kept it as a zone of peace despite war and banditry....New Guinea announces Pidgin is its official language.
Dec. 11	Having established the Polish-Lithuanian negotiation process, the League Council announces it will seek a meeting in Rome. The council hopes to defuse tensions between Italy and France.	Investigation reveals that reports of the Ukrainian rebellion are exaggerated. Although there are deportations and executions, there is no mass rising or massacre.			Chiang Kai-shek says the time has come for China to make new treaties and reestablish itself in the world. He rejects ties to the Soviets and indicates he is receptive to overtures from Western governments.
Dec. 12		U.S. filmmakers, Will Hays, and the state department watch with concern as France develops legislation that will require two of every three films to be produced domestically.... The galleries of the house of Lords are packed as debate begins on acceptance of the new, controversial, Book of Prayer. Opposition is strong, but approval is highly likely.		The annual ceremony at the Shrine of the Virgin of Guadalupe, Mexico's patron, attracts 100,000 but no priests, barred by Plutarco Calles's anti-Catholic law. Authorities detect a bomb disguised as a candle and remove it before it is lit....Mexico deports 50 American racetrack hangers-about from Tijuana. They cannot return to Mexico unless they show they have work.	Communists take Canton. Mobs rise in seven other Chinese cities as rebellion renews. The United States sends a third gunboat to back the two already at Canton.

A	B	C	D	E
Includes developments that affect more than one world region, international organizations and important meetings of world leaders.	Includes all domestic and regional developments in Europe, including the Soviet Union.	Includes all domestic and regional developments in Africa and the Middle East.	Includes all domestic and regional developments in Latin America, the Caribbean, and Canada.	Includes all domestic and regional developments in Asian and Pacific nations (and colonies).

U.S. Politics & Social Issues	U.S. Foreign Policy & Affairs, Defense	U.S. Economy & Environment	Science, Technology & Nature	Culture, Leisure & Lifestyle	
Calvin Coolidge officially bows out of the 1928 race. He tells the Republicans to find another candidate….The reconvened Senate begins debating whether to seat the two disputed Republican Senators, Vare of Pennsylvania and Smith of Illinois.	Ambassador Joseph Grew tells the Turkish press to relax. U.S. attacks on the new Turkish ambassador, Ahmed Moukhtar Bey, and the Treaty of Lausanne will not alter U.S.–Turkish relations.	The freighter *Mercer*, experimenting with a transatlantic crossing using pulverized coal, is a day out of Antwerp with no serious problems on her two-week voyage. Plans are to convert other vessels to the more efficient fuel.	Dr. R.R. Graves of the USDA's dairy bureau shows cattlemen how Mendel's theory of dominant and recessive genes can produce defectives from seemingly normal parents. From a talk about cattle he digresses to heredity's gamble with human beings.	Over the past five years, Notre Dame football has the best record, 42–5–2. Second is Southern Methodist at 34–5–7.	Dec. 6
Calvin Coolidge's 1928 budget totals $4 billion. It calls for a $225 billion tax cut while increasing the budget $244 billion over 1927. The federal debt has decreased $8 billion since 1920….Charles Evans Hughes also formally bows out of the 1928 race, reiterating that he is too old. Farmers boost John Pershing. The way is clear for Herbert Hoover….The Senate denies a seat to Al Smith, 50–32.	Colonel John Axton will retire as chief of army chaplains in April 1928. Axton, with the backing of the Federal Council of Churches, has been resisting retirement for some time. Brig. General Benjamin Foulois becomes deputy air chief. Foulois began his army career as a private.	A seat on the NYSE sells for $301,000.		Ground is broken at Philadelphia for the Mastbaum collection. The museum, a copy of the French museum at Meudon, will house the best collection of Rodin sculptures in the United States.	Dec. 7
An American-born woman faces deportation. When she married a Scot two years ago, she lost her citizenship because American law requires her to take her husband's citizenship. Since their 1925 divorce she has been on a series of visas, but the last expired and she is in the United States illegally….Rep William Sirovich (D-NY) introduces legislation for federal funding of one-third of the cost of state old age pensions, not to exceed $30 a month. He estimates annual costs of $30 million.	Insurgent Republican John Schaefer of Wisconsin, during the debate over spending for overseas deployments, criticizes the administration for sending troops to Nicaragua and China without Congressional approval. New York's Fiorello LaGuardia says Calvin Coolidge avoided Congress because he knew he would lose his request.	Cunard reduces its cabin fares to £27. It also cuts 2nd class fares to £20 and renames it tourist in hopes of attracting more middle class passengers. Third class, the old immigrant standard, remains as is….Henry Ford says his new model cost him $100 million. He also says he still has $250 million in the bank.	Calvin Coolidge submits a flood control plan costing $296 million over 10 years. State burden is $37 million. Critics want a $1 billion plan that includes reservoirs as well as the lateral floodways, Coolidge emphasizes. Critics also want a plan that covers the entire Mississippi and tributaries.	Nobel Peace Prizes go to 87-year-old Ferdinand Buisson of France and 70-year-old Ludwig Quidde of Germany. German nationalists are upset at the award to Quidde, who was ostracized after he questioned the Kaiser's sanity.	Dec. 8
The Senate rejects Vare. Regular Republicans agree to provide the five western insurgents with a timely hearing of their legislative proposals. United, Republicans have sufficient numbers to organize the Senate. Democrats are relieved not to have the responsibility.		Auto exports for October are almost $30 million, up 25 percent or $5.8 million over October 1926. Trucks are especially popular.	Roald Amundsen, explorer, resigns from the Royal Geographic Society over a supposed insult. Amundsen has previously had tiffs with the Explorers Club and Norwegian Aero Society over perceived slights….A cold wave kills 36 nationwide, nine in Chicago. It also disrupts Great Lakes shipping but ices over waterways that have been flooding New England.	Alexander Alekhine gets $5400 and a medal for his championship. Jose Capablanca receives $4600….After a multi-week jury trial, the owners of Peter the Great, one-time movie star, receive $125,000 from the man who killed him. Peter the Great is a dog.	Dec. 9
Oklahoma's house of representatives discusses impeachment of the governor. The session is questionable because the body lacks a quorum after 30 of the 82 members leave. They doubt the validity of a special session called by legislators rather than the governor.	Senate hearings open on controversial charges in the Hearst newspapers that Plutarco Calles put aside $1.2 million to pay four unnamed senators for supporting Mexico. The Mexican consulate and State Department indicate they will cooperate.	State governments in the Mississippi flood area indicate shock at Calvin Coolidge's requirement that they pay part of the recovery. They lack funds and say Herbert Hoover led them to believe the federal government would pay the full cost.			Dec. 10
The mayor-elect and three members of the city council of Reading, PA, explain how they won one of the largest victories in party history. They are Socialists, and they won by campaigning house to house on property taxes. Those of the wealthy had just dropped while those of the workers had risen.	Calvin Coolidge receives a petition from 395 leaders from both parties, all states and all walks of life. They ask him to break the impasse that keeps the United States from the World Court.	Prof. Irving Fisher, Yale economist, reports that U.S. incomes are rising, prosperity is spreading, and poverty is declining. He predicts poverty may be gone by 1932.	The Shipping Board announces that it will convert at least two more ships to pulverized coal. The board has 22 ships of the same class as the *Mercer*. Modernization also comes with the dieselization of 11 ships.	Rabbi Fineshriber endorses companionate unions. He tells his Philadelphia that honesty requires acknowledging what millions do surreptitiously.	Dec. 11
Troops block the entrance to the state legislature on Governor Johnston's orders. Legislators meet behind locked doors in a hotel to debate impeachment.	With the program due to close on 1 January, 525,844 veterans have not sought the bonus. Applications from 3.1 million veterans have taken all but $20,000 of the $3.6 million authorized….Calvin Coolidge's five-year naval plan is the largest since 1916. Costing $1 billion but staying within the 5–5–3 ratio, it includes 56 ships, including 26 cruisers, three carriers, and five submarines.	Labor secretary James John Davis once again begs coal operators to meet with unions. He indicates that, in order to bring peace to the coal states and resolve the crisis of overproduction, he will convene meetings on December 14, with or without the recalcitrant owners. He has held similar ownerless meetings before….Henry Leland's $6 million suit against Ford on behalf of Lincoln stockholders opens in Pontiac.			Dec. 12

F	G	H	I	J
Includes campaigns, elections, federal-state relations, civil rights and liberties, crime, the judiciary, education, healthcare, poverty, urban affairs, and population.	Includes formation and debate of U.S. foreign and defense policies, veterans affairs, and defense spending. (Relations with specific foreign countries are usually found under the region concerned.)	Includes business, labor, agriculture, taxation, transportation, consumer affairs, monetary and fiscal policy, natural resources, pollution and industrial accidents.	Includes worldwide scientific, medical and technological developments, natural phenomena, U.S. weather and natural disasters.	Includes the arts, religion, scholarship, communications media, sports, entertainment, fashions, fads, and social life.

	World Affairs	Europe	Africa & The Middle East	The Americas	Asia & The Pacific
Dec. 13		Government statistics show that British trade has nearly recovered. It is within 10 percent of the best prewar year.		Charles Lindbergh takes off for Mexico City, seeking to set another record.	Nationalists retake Canton, with rebels holed up in the police station. A preliminary estimate is that 4,000 die. Chiang breaks relations with Russia.
Dec. 14		A delegation of unionists just returned from the Soviet Union reports that the Soviets treat women better than the United States does.... Turkey admits its first two women to the bar. Turkey also has two women doctors and a dentist. Women still lack the vote.	Wahhabi raiders attack Bedur and Azzayed herders in the Nasiriyah District and seize their camels. British airplanes chase the Wahhabi off with one plane damaged and one mechanic injured.	El Salvador seeks former president Jorge Melendez. A coup attempt earlier in the week fails when one of the plotters talks too freely. Authorities execute 13 and impose martial law.	Native Koreans attack the Chinese over abuses of fellow Chinese in Manchuria. Southern Koreans are also boycotting Chinese establishments. Many Chinese are fleeing.... Henry Stimson says he admires the Filipino people. Aguinaldo, Rotas, and other leaders indicate they are pleased with the new governor.
Dec. 15		The House of Commons rejects the new book of prayer, 247-205. Supported by the great majority of the clergy, the book is the work of 21 years.	Professor Woolley unearths the tomb of King Meekalamdug of Ur. Although previously looted, the tomb still contains bodies and relics dating to before 3500 B.C.E.		Nanking severs relations with the Soviet Union after charging Russian complicity in the Canton rising. The Russians have a week to clear out. Trade relations are restricted too.
Dec. 16		France and Germany implement an entertainment entente. They exchange musical and theatrical artists, translate each other's plays, and eliminate material offensive to each other's citizens.		Charles Lindbergh continues his successful Mexico City stay. He hosts Mexican military officers, visits a school, and announces plans for goodwill flights to half a dozen Latin American capitals.	China begins a massive roundup of Communists. Nationalists raid the Hankow consulate, execute the Canton consul, and require Russians to register. Russia denies Chinese allegations it spreads propaganda and foments revolt.
Dec. 17		Dutch labor organizations demonstrate in three major cities. They oppose the death penalty. Their position coincides with that of the Socialist and Labor International. Holland abolished capital punishment in 1870 but the colonies still practice it.	British forces in the Sudan begin two punitive expeditions. One is to avenge the District Commissioner and a Greek trader. The other is to preclude the revival of human sacrifice.		En route to London to visit the queen, King Amanullah of Afghanistan preaches as an Imam in a Bombay mosque. He tells Indian Muslims to tolerate Hindus if they expect toleration.
Dec. 18	The U.S. Department of Commerce reports that there are 13 major cartels and untold numbers of smaller ones. Most date to after the war.	Moscow expels 98 Trotskyite leaders. The rank and file can remain; Moscow seeks to convert them.	Riots injure 15 Jewish men and women in Palestine. British authorities arrest 20 unemployed Jews for fighting imported Arab orange pickers....South Africa announces it will subsidize its own merchant fleet.		Madame Sun says her brother-in-law Chiang Kai-shek is at fault for breaking with the reds. She also says she will stay in Moscow until he reverses course. He says she can better serve China by coming home.
Dec. 19		Bishops meeting at London remain firm in support of a new book of prayer. They read parliament's acts as contradictory.			Angered by a recent climber's breach of faith, the Dalai Lama bars Everest to new explorers. The climber portrayed road workers as monks during a European speaking tour....Canton executes 600 reds. The act adds 20,000 refugees to the total.
Dec. 20	The League seeks clarification of the U.S. position on blockades. The League worries that two-party treaties on the American model will undercut a broad League peace covenant.	France indicates dislike of a formal anti-war agreement with cumbersome restrictions. The preference is for a simple non-aggression agreement. France also allocates resources for 15 new warships to maintain parity in the Mediterranean.... Grigory Zinoviev recants. The party tells him and Kamenev to wait six months before applying for readmission.			The Chinese executions now number over 2100. The government makes no effort to control the situation.

A	B	C	D	E
Includes developments that affect more than one world region, international organizations and important meetings of world leaders.	*Includes all domestic and regional developments in Europe, including the Soviet Union.*	*Includes all domestic and regional developments in Africa and the Middle East.*	*Includes all domestic and regional developments in Latin America, the Caribbean, and Canada.*	*Includes all domestic and regional developments in Asian and Pacific nations (and colonies).*

U.S. Politics & Social Issues	U.S. Foreign Policy & Affairs, Defense	U.S. Economy & Environment	Science, Technology & Nature	Culture, Leisure & Lifestyle	
A Reading Railroad conductor wards off 15 would-be robbers near Langhorne, PA. The veteran wounds one and saves a load of silk.... Oklahoma impeaches its governor.	Calvin Coolidge says reopening the issue of the World Court is futile because of Senate opposition. The White House also denies it approved a billion dollars for the navy.			Yehudi Menuhin's father says the prodigy will not perform again until 1929. Not even a $65,000 offer will distract Yehudi from his studies.	Dec. 13
Michigan's new gun registration law goes into effect. Police are surprised to learn that 48,000 Detroiters have weapons, including sawed off shotguns and large caliber pistols. Clergymen, notably, are armed.	Britain pays the United States $95.5 million, a semiannual payment on its war debt. The remaining balance is $4.8 billion.		After going missing for some time, Charles Lindbergh successfully completes his flight to Mexico. He reports getting lost in the fog, guiding himself by the gleam of breakers off the Pacific shore, and navigating carefully through the mountains.	Educators at a Swarthmore conference agree that the first two years of college are wasted. They contend that the colleges have to make up for deficient secondary education.	Dec. 14
Senators Borah, Heflin, Norris, and LaFollette deny receiving Mexican bribes. Hearst says his newspapers got the story from official Mexican documents but he personally does not believe the four took money.	The Sikorsky Guardian gets its first flight test and exceeds expectations for speed, lift, and landing. The plane has eight machine guns and a bomb load of 2,600 pounds.	Ford orders 32,000 tons of sheet metal from American Rolling Mills.			Dec. 15
Still barred by guardsmen from their chambers, Oklahoma legislators meeting secretly abandon their six-count impeachment bill. Instead, they accuse Governor Johnston of moral turpitude.	The Army sends Congress a proposal to increase retirements. Calvin Coolidge objects to the cost, but the Army needs to ease congestion at the lower grades....The House of Representatives begins debate on an alien property bill. The United States holds $270 million seized during the war, including German ships.	The president of the National Association of Music Merchants calculates that 1927 radio sales top $400 million. He defines radio as a musical instrument. With piano, it is bringing the family back home.		The West Point superintendent returns the 1928 Army-Navy contract unsigned. Army and Navy disagree on the number of years a player should be eligible.	Dec. 16
A report of a recent Mormon conference says that Heber Grant, successor prophet to Joseph Smith and Brigham Young, has expanded the definition of Zion. No longer just Utah, Zion is the United States. Mormons are already common in the rest of the West and returning to Missouri.	Congress receives a long-awaited world war pensions bill....Frank B. Kellogg indicates that the renewal of the Root arbitration treaty with France will include the Briand plan in part. The new treaty will also serve as a model for treaties with other major nations....A coast guard cutter rams the S-4 submarine, sending it to the bottom with 40 aboard.	The president of the American Rediscount Association says that installment buying is standardizing at a 33 1/3 percent down payment and 12 monthly payments. This standard minimizes defaults.			Dec. 17
The Reverend Dr. Steele of Philadelphia says Christmas is overly commercial, with the marketplace replacing the Christmas mass. Even the charitable aspects are burdensome as bonuses and handouts become a right....The National Association of Manufacturers says child labor laws keep mentally deficient 16- and 17-year-old students in school. As well as being a burden on schools, it promotes juvenile idleness and waste.	American Jews and students ask Frank B. Kellogg to intervene and stop the anti-Semitic Romanian riots. The students want intervention in anti-Semitic Hungary as well....A diver hears tapping from the forward compartment of the S-4. Six men are alive, but air is poor. Captain Ernest J. King, who supervised the retrieval of the S-51 submarine, is en route.		Tests using standard model American cars—Fords, Stutzes, and such—reveal that a gasoline-alcohol blend is more effective than gasoline-benzene or straight gasoline. It provides good acceleration, smooth ride, and no significant carbon buildup.	The first congressman intervenes in the Army-Navy football split. He asks the service secretaries to involve themselves and settle the split.	Dec. 18
Foes of a Herbert Hoover presidency begin hinting that he may be ineligible under the residency requirement. There is also whispering about a change to British citizenship during his time in India.	The airline to the S-4 snaps. The men are severely short of oxygen. Gale winds and ice hamper rescuers....Frank B. Kellogg rejects League proposals on classification of diplomatic officials, functions of consuls, and penal matters. He accepts a proposal on court jurisdiction in suits against states.	Chevrolet announces a $50 price cut and a new model with four-wheel brakes.		New York city officials accept a proposal for an $873,000 renovation of shabby Central Park. New paths, repaired walks, more gardens, and park police are among the improvements, but playgrounds and tennis courts are not.	Dec. 19
Before Congress, Robert Butler, suing for libel in the Times-Mexico forgery case, claims the forger is Joseph De Courcy, Times reporter expelled by Mexico. The Mexican government says forgery was not the reason for the deportation.	The House passes a $264 million alien property bill. It recognizes American claims against Germany totaling $247 million. It bars payment to draft evader Grover Cleveland Bergdoll and other fugitives....Hope for survivors of S-4 fades. The Navy effort continues.	Crude oil output is down 30,000 barrels. It is at the lowest level since February 5.	Ice, snow, and gale force winds paralyze continental Europe and the British Isles. Seventeen Yugoslav soldiers die of cold. Train and ship traffic are in disarray.		Dec. 20

F	G	H	I	J
Includes campaigns, elections, federal-state relations, civil rights and liberties, crime, the judiciary, education, healthcare, poverty, urban affairs, and population.	Includes formation and debate of U.S. foreign and defense policies, veterans affairs, and defense spending. (Relations with specific foreign countries are usually found under the region concerned.)	Includes business, labor, agriculture, taxation, transportation, consumer affairs, monetary and fiscal policy, natural resources, pollution and industrial accidents.	Includes worldwide scientific, medical and technological developments, natural phenomena, U.S. weather and natural disasters.	Includes the arts, religion, scholarship, communications media, sports, entertainment, fashions, fads, and social life.

	World Affairs	Europe	Africa & The Middle East	The Americas	Asia & The Pacific
Dec. 21		Anglican Bishops conclude their London meeting. They agree to modify the book and resubmit it to the Commons….Italy puts the Lira on the gold standard and sets its value at 1/19 of a dollar. English and American banks back $125 million in credits.		Inspired by Charles Lindbergh's visit, Mexico announces plans for a pilot training school and an air mail service. Mexico also indicates formation of a new department to prepare roads for tourist travel.	
Dec. 22					
Dec. 23	European and Latin American governments express condolences at the loss of the S-4.	A Silesian mother bears quadruplets. The four girls each weigh about 3 pounds. This is the fourth quadruple birth in Prussia this year.	Persia shuts down the American school at Hamadan. The school refuses to teach the Koran as required by a recent law.		Premier Stanley Bruce announces that Australia will reconsider the 1926 decision not to raise the status of its representative to the United States, currently a commissioner. Canada and Ireland have ministers to the United States, and the Australian commissioner has resigned, stating he is unable to work satisfactorily at his level.
Dec. 24	The League asks the United States to support a 13-month year popular with American business people. Each year will be the uniform, with Christmas on the same day and every Friday the 13th. The new month, Sol, is located between June and July.	Germany protests Raymond Poincare's call of yesterday for reparations of 132 billion marks. The Dawes Plan supersedes earlier plans and mandates only 2.5 billion marks.	Bethlehem attracts pilgrims from throughout the world. Churches offer services, and worshipers sing carols.		
Dec. 25					
Dec. 26		The archaeological find at Glozel, Vichy, disputed since 1924, continues to be controversial. Those who believe the find is a real sample of a civilization older than the Asian ones are accusing the debunkers of faking and altering evidence.		Cape Gracias, Nicaragua asks U.S. assistance against Sandino's forces. The residents will get marines and a gunboat.	
Dec. 27		A Berlin dancer dies in an explosion caused by the benzene she is applying to her hair….Gales in the English Channel sever telegraph lines and isolate England from the continent for the first time in 12 years.		The Mexican house passes a Calles-mandated bill favorable to U.S. interests on the issue of confirming land claims. The Senate will ratify shortly.	Famine spreads in China, with whole provinces depopulated. With 9 million starving, China appeals to the Red Cross.
Dec. 28		Native Scots seek to restrict immigration from Ireland. They fear Scots are becoming a minority in Scotland. In 1921 Irish were 1/8 of the population; a century earlier they were 1/30. In 1925 nearly 20 percent of Scotland's children were Irish.			The National Indian Congress calls for Hindus and Muslims to show each other greater respect and reduce intercommunity violence. It also calls for greater political rights for Indians in white-controlled Africa.

A	B	C	D	E
Includes developments that affect more than one world region, international organizations and important meetings of world leaders.	Includes all domestic and regional developments in Europe, including the Soviet Union.	Includes all domestic and regional developments in Africa and the Middle East.	Includes all domestic and regional developments in Latin America, the Caribbean, and Canada.	Includes all domestic and regional developments in Asian and Pacific nations (and colonies).

U.S. Politics & Social Issues	U.S. Foreign Policy & Affairs, Defense	U.S. Economy & Environment	Science, Technology & Nature	Culture, Leisure & Lifestyle	
Congress adjourns for the holidays.	The Navy sets a court of inquiry into the S-4 loss for January 4. Congress will also investigate. The S-19, companion to S-4, goes out on a trial run that tests the courage of its crew....The Navy announces plans to purchase 20 Loening amphibian planes. The price is $503,000.			Ignacy Paderewski is back in the United States. He has a schedule of 50 concerts.	Dec. 21
Oregon police capture William Edward Hickman. He denies murdering Marian Parker in Los Angeles but confesses to kidnapping her....Hiram Evans says the Klan will oppose Al Smith in 1928. The Klan rejects Smith as Catholic, wet, pro-immigration, and a machine politician.	Supreme Court Justice Thomas Crain proposes that European nations pay their war debts by giving West Indies and coast islands to the U.S. Islands would help to protect the Panama Canal from hostile Mexico and unstable Central America.	Kansas sets a record by planting 16 million acres of winter wheat. The U.S. total is 47 million acres.		Three social science research institutions merge to form the Brookings Institute, a national research and training center, in Washington, DC. The endowment is over three million.	Dec. 22
William Edward Hickman is guaranteed a speedy trial. The person he accuses of Marian Parker's murder has an alibi. Authorities deliberate over how to split the $90,000 reward.			Frances Grayson, real estate broker, lifts her amphibious plane toward Newfoundland in her fourth attempt to become the first woman to fly the Atlantic. Her pilot and navigator are experienced men aviators....Astronomers tend toward Skjellerup's Comet as the Star of Bethlehem. There are five other contenders.	New York's welfare office suspends its investigation of the Santa Claus Foundation until the U.S. Postal Service finishes its examination of the foundation's books. The foundation answers letters to Santa and provides gifts to needy children.	Dec. 23
A Midland, TX, deputy sheriff admits that he and another man duped three Mexicans into standing in front of a bank then killed two and wounded the third Mexican, claiming they were bank robbers. The deputy is trying to get a standing Texas Banker's Association reward of $5,000 for dead bank robbers.	Representative Emanuel Celler tells newspapers he has reliable information that administration policy is to bar immigrants from countries that refuse to accept U.S. deportees. He mentions Russia and Czechoslovakia specifically.	Chain stores offer efficiency. They train assistant managers in less than a year. Record sales for 1927 are up 15.7 percent over 1926.	Frances Grayson is 29 hours overdue. Her plane had fuel for 18 hours.		Dec. 24
William Edward Hickman is preparing to leave Oregon for California. He has attempted suicide twice since his capture.		Fresh off receiving a military contract, Loening announces that it will begin production of civilian seaplanes after the first of the year.	54 hours and no word from the Grayson plane. A report of wreckage on the Newfoundland coast proves false....Skjellerup's Comet fails to appear, raising doubts that it is the Star of Bethlehem.	Rabbi Stephen Wise says the Christian cross has evolved from a symbol of tolerance to a symbol of hate. He and Presbyterian Rev. Dr. Joseph W. Cochran share the podium at Carnegie Hall's Free Synagogue.	Dec. 25
A Civic Federation study of four states shows that poverty among the elderly is overstated. Of 14,000 surveyed, only 200 are in want. Widows are worst off....En route to California, Hickman confesses to murdering and dismembering Parker.		At South Pittsburg, TN, the militia steps in to impose order after violence virtually destroys the local police forces. A Christmas gun battle between city and county police kills five and wounds four. The underlying cause is that the city and county forces took opposing sides during a recent manufacturing strike.		Representative Frederick Britten (R-IL) says the army will be uncoordinated with other colleges if it persists in allowing four-year players. The move is to three-year eligibility....The West beats the East 16-6 in the annual charity football game at San Francisco. A crowd of 27,000 watch the West win its 11th of the 20 intersectional games.	Dec. 26
Welfare officials challenge the scope of the Civic Federation study. They also call for federal aid to the indigent elderly....Oklahoma's governor gets a second injunction. Both houses of the legislature are now enjoined from acting on his impeachment.	In an effort to catch up with the modern world, the War Department announces that all cavalry troops will have machine guns. They will also have motorized support.	Crude oil production is off another 24,750 barrels for the week. This is the lowest since February 5....U.S. Steel names J.P. Morgan chairman of the board but gives him no duties. The company splits the powers of late Judge Elbert Gary between two other directors, an executive and a finance officer.	Searches by naval and commercial vessels and a dirigible fail to turn up any sign of Frances Grayson's plane. A reported loud and clear "where are we" is downplayed; it originates in the same area as false reports of Charles Nungesser earlier this year.	In an apparent rebuttal of Representative Frederick Britten's claim that army football players resign their commissions as soon as possible, the Army Information Service documents that only eight of the 530 resignations since 1917 are football players. Average service before resigning is over three years....The Dolly Sisters announce their retirement.	Dec. 27
Meeting secretly in a hotel, the Oklahoma Senate defies the court and votes 24–2 to impeach Johnston. Troops continue to block access to the legislative chambers.		Packard reports quarterly earnings of $5.5 million. This is the best quarter in the company's history to date....Twenty-seven railroads issue earnings statements for the first 11 months. Almost without exception, gross and net income is down....Railroad purchases help lift the iron and steel slump. Ford's purchases are less than anticipated.	France is optimistic at reports that Calvin Coolidge is amenable to discussions of the entire foreign debt problem. The U.S. position remains that debt and reparations are two separate issues.	The National Amateur Athletic Federation and Amateur Athletic Union heal a yearlong rift. If the NCAA, YMCA, and Big 10 reunite with the AAU, the United States will present a united team at the 1928 Olympic Games. The AAU controls the American Olympic team.	Dec. 28

F	G	H	I	J
Includes campaigns, elections, federal-state relations, civil rights and liberties, crime, the judiciary, education, healthcare, poverty, urban affairs, and population.	*Includes formation and debate of U.S. foreign and defense policies, veterans affairs, and defense spending. (Relations with specific foreign countries are usually found under the region concerned.)*	*Includes business, labor, agriculture, taxation, transportation, consumer affairs, monetary and fiscal policy, natural resources, pollution and industrial accidents.*	*Includes worldwide scientific, medical and technological developments, natural phenomena, U.S. weather and natural disasters.*	*Includes the arts, religion, scholarship, communications media, sports, entertainment, fashions, fads, and social life.*

	World Affairs	Europe	Africa & The Middle East	The Americas	Asia & The Pacific
Dec. 29	The Student Volunteer Movement, with 3,000 attendees from four continents, hears a call to end racial snobbishness in missions. Speakers from Africa, Japan, and India tell the Detroit meeting that prejudice hampers mission work. Native missionaries are a critical need.	France responds to hints that the United States may raise import duties by indicating preparedness to retaliate. France raises, then suspends, duties on American automobiles....Italy announces it will have free ports. Elimination of customs duties improves Italy's competitiveness in world trade.			The foreign affairs and finance ministers resign the Nanking cabinet. The government's fall is imminent.
Dec. 30		France seizes 12 Alsatians in a plot to make Alsace autonomous. Among the leaders are a woman and a priest.		In his year-end message, Plutarco Calles cites improved foreign relations and decreased internal conflict. He denies religious ill feeling and calls for unity in 1928.... Canadian mineral production for 1927 reaches a record $241 million. Higher volume compensates for lower prices.	
Dec. 31		The Russian Red Cross releases a list of 47,000 names of children separated from their parents during pogroms, revolution, and other disturbance in Russia. In the United States the National Council of Jewish Women offers immigration assistance to parents finding a child on the list....Spain issues plans for tomorrow's nationalization of oil. The move affects English, Romanian, French and U.S. interests.	From Kenya come reports that man-eating lions are attacking villagers in packs of 20 to 30. Officials blame the glut of lions on the British taking arms from Masai warriors.		

A	B	C	D	E
Includes developments that affect more than one world region, international organizations and important meetings of world leaders.	Includes all domestic and regional developments in Europe, including the Soviet Union.	Includes all domestic and regional developments in Africa and the Middle East.	Includes all domestic and regional developments in Latin America, the Caribbean, and Canada.	Includes all domestic and regional developments in Asian and Pacific nations (and colonies).

U.S. Politics & Social Issues	U.S. Foreign Policy & Affairs, Defense	U.S. Economy & Environment	Science, Technology & Nature	Culture, Leisure & Lifestyle	
Pullman company officials deny rumors other racial groups will replace blacks as porters. The company also denies knowledge of reports that Filipinos and Chinese serve as club car porters on trains from Chicago....The Oklahoma Senate backs down, disavows House impeachment moves, and lets Johnston off the hook. The troops disperse, and Johnston declares vindication.		In the final legal action to cancel the Sinclair leases, a Cheyenne, WY, federal court denies Marathon Oil's request for return of a quitclaim deed valued at $1 million. Finally, the Navy has clear ownership of Teapot Dome again.	The U.S. Hydrographic Office issues its first air navigation chart. It recommends January transatlantic flyers take a Bermuda-Azores-England route. Monthly reports will continue providing safest route information....Astronomers finally get photos of the Skjellerup Comet. Its orbit is less than expected.	The NCAA rejoins the AAU Olympic body....The National Chess Federation forms with seven collegiate members. Princeton is chapter 1. Others are Chicago, Swarthmore, Allegheny, Rutgers, Penn, and Ursinus....The American Historical Association, one of 17 learned societies meeting under the auspices of the American Council of learned Societies, calls for honest texts, not false patriotism.	Dec. 29
Black New York University students allege discrimination in access to dorms and a physical education course. The university denies systematic discrimination but claims the right to select....New York's Association of Jewish Ministers protests showing of "The King of Kings" as arousing anti-Semitism. Bnai Brith and Will Hays have already agreed not to show it in European states where it might provoke anti-Jewish actions.	Calvin Coolidge says Mexico needs to fix land titles. He sees the recent oil laws as a positive step toward smoothing relations....Secretary Curtis Wilbur commits to calling a board to explore ways to improve submarine safety. The S-4 board extends its probe beyond the crash itself to the rescue efforts, still under way.	Year-end dividend and interest payments total $1 billion, up $75 million from 1926....Calvin Coolidge asks for an immediate $225 million tax cut. He says he did not ask for a delay until March....Another report shows rail revenues down 10 percent in November.		Prof. J.P. Baxter of Harvard tells the closing session of the AHA that France, not the United States, led in the development of ironclads. He also says that the Navy was not recalcitrant, as earlier portrayed, but in fact began seeking ironclads in 1861.	Dec. 30
	The Navy closes Teapot Dome. It is back in reserve....Senator William Borah issues a letter saying Herbert Hoover is eligible for the presidency. Borah seeks to quell rumors that Hoover's overseas time disqualifies him.			The Biscayne Bay Kennel Club wants telegraphic betting between Cuba and Florida and contends that it is interstate commerce, not subject to state or county law. A federal court declines to enjoin Florida from enforcing its ban on race betting.... After 70 years, the Oxford English Dictionary is at the printer.	Dec. 31

F	G	H	I	J
Includes campaigns, elections, federal-state relations, civil rights and liberties, crime, the judiciary, education, healthcare, poverty, urban affairs, and population.	Includes formation and debate of U.S. foreign and defense policies, veterans affairs, and defense spending. (Relations with specific foreign countries are usually found under the region concerned.)	Includes business, labor, agriculture, taxation, transportation, consumer affairs, monetary and fiscal policy, natural resources, pollution and industrial accidents.	Includes worldwide scientific, medical and technological developments, natural phenomena, U.S. weather and natural disasters.	Includes the arts, religion, scholarship, communications media, sports, entertainment, fashions, fads, and social life.

1928

The USS *Texas* entering Havana Harbor, Cuba, from Cabanas.

	World Affairs	Europe	Africa & The Middle East	The Americas	Asia & The Pacific
Jan.	Austria uncovers five carloads of arms and ammunition shipped from Italy to Hungary. After Little Entente protests, the League investigates.	The Soviet Union expels Leon Trotsky. He goes to Turkestan....The flooding of London's River Thames kills 14. A tidal wave floods the Tower of London's moat, which was drained and filled with grass in 1843....The allies end military control of Bulgaria.	The Senussi surrender in Cyrenaica. Libya is under Italian control.	The Sixth Pan American Conference legalizes the Pan American Union and establishes a series of conferences on various matters. The American delegate, Charles Evans Hughes, blocks an effort to ban interference with another country's internal affairs.	Afghanistan's King Amanullah and his wife begin a six-month tour of Egypt, India, and Europe. The king seeks aid in modernizing his country.
Feb.	St Moritz, Switzerland, is host to the Winter Olympics. Star of the games is 15-year-old Norwegian ice skater Sonja Henie, who wins the first of her three Olympic gold medals. Henie introduces short skirts and choreography.	Mussolini incorporates the Fascist militia into the Italian army.	The railway from Katanga Province to Portuguese East Africa through Rhodesia is finished. It gives the Belgian Congo an outlet to the Indian Ocean for its products.... Transjordania becomes independent with British oversight of its army and finances.	The Pan American conference concludes....At the Winter Olympic Games, Canada wins its third consecutive ice hockey gold medal.	Japan's Kyushu Medical School opens. It is a precursor to the private Kurume University.
Mar.	The League sponsors a conference on trade in hides and bones. The meeting is to lessen trade restrictions and promote the industry.... Spain cancels its withdrawal from the League.	A hailstorm in Britain kills 11 people....Malta becomes a British dominion.	France gives Spain control of Tangier....Egypt rejects the Anglo-Egyptian Treaty of 1927 as interfering with its sovereignty.		In Hangzhou the National Academy of Art opens. It later becomes the China Academy of Art.
Apr.		A bomb attack against Mussolini kills 17 bystanders.	British issue an ultimatum, forcing Egypt to restrict the right of free assembly.		The nationalists prepare an offensive against the north. Japan sends troops and seizes Chinese railways to forestall the offensive.
May	A League conference seeks a cure for syphilis.	Italy gives the vote only to men over age 21 who are in a high tax bracket....France convicts four Alsatians of seeking autonomy for Alsace.	Persia ends the capitulations and establishes new tariff rates. Led by Britain, other nations accept the changes.	A bomb attack against the Buenos Aires Italian consulate kills 22 and injures 41.	Australia begins the Royal Flying Doctor Service. The not-for-profit flying ambulance service provides medical care and education for remote areas....Chinese attacking Beijing clash with Japanese troops. The Japanese withdraw but angry Chinese boycott Japanese goods.
Jun.	A league conference deals with transit cards to speed the movement of emigrants across national borders....The Reparations Agent, representing the allies, demands that Germany make final payment of war reparations.	Medical doctors strike in Vienna.... In Yugoslavia, Macedonian Punica Rasic opens fire in parliament. He shoots three, including Croat Stjepan Radic, and injures three more. The shootings give King Alexander an excuse to abolish the parliament....To shrink its national debt, France devalues the franc 500 percent. The new value is less than 4 cents. The rentier class suffers.	France asks Syrians to draft a constitution. The drafters, mostly nationalists, create one that does not recognize France's mandate. France rejects the constitution.	In Argentina, Rosario University students take over the medical wing....Faced with competition from automobiles, Canada's Great Gorge and International Railway implements single-person crews on its Niagara Falls trolleys. Despite the cost cutting effort, the railway, which has an accident-prone history, folds in 1932.	The Nationalists take Beijing and end the Feng warlords' rule of the region. They rename the city Beiping. In Manchuria Chang tso Lin, under pressure from the nationalist armies, seeks to break ties with Japan. He is assassinated.
Jul.	The Amsterdam Olympic games introduce women's events.			Jose de Leon Toral assassinates presidential candidate Alvaro Obrregon.	Twelve states formerly led by warlords recognize the nationalist government. China nears unification. China unilaterally annuls "unequal" treaties with the west.
Aug.	Representatives of 15 nations sign the Kellogg-Briand Treaty. It outlaws aggressive war....The United States wins the Amsterdam Olympics. It totals 437 points. Germany returns to international competition after a 10-year absence.	*The Threepenny Opera (Die Dreigroschenoper)* by composer Kurt Weill and playwright Bertolt Brecht debuts in Berlin. The play captures the decadence of Weimar Germany....May Donoghue finds a snail in her ginger beer. The case of *Donoghue v. Stevenson* is a landmark in common law negligence cases.	Ethiopia signs a 20-year treaty of friendship with Italy. The pact lasts until Italy invades Ethiopia in 1936.		The Indian All-Parties Conference at Lucknow votes for the Nehru Plan. The plan seeks dominion status for India.
Sep.	The League Council holds its 52nd session.	Ahmed Zog declares that Albania is a monarchy and he is King Zog. As constitutional monarch dictator, Zog brings stability and dependence on Italy....The German people vote to build new battleships.	Haile Selassie becomes king of Ethiopia. He is not yet emperor.	Argentina nationalizes its oil industry. Because British interests are harmed, tensions between Argentina and Britain increase.	

A	B	C	D	E
Includes developments that affect more than one world region, international organizations and important meetings of world leaders.	*Includes all domestic and regional developments in Europe, including the Soviet Union.*	*Includes all domestic and regional developments in Africa and the Middle East.*	*Includes all domestic and regional developments in Latin America, the Caribbean, and Canada.*	*Includes all domestic and regional developments in Asian and Pacific nations (and colonies).*

U.S. Politics & Social Issues	U.S. Foreign Policy & Affairs, Defense	U.S. Economy & Environment	Science, Technology & Nature	Culture, Leisure & Lifestyle	
New York executes Ruth Snyder, murderer and adulterer, and her lover Judd Gray. A tabloid newspaperman surreptitiously photographs Snyder's electrocution. Snyder-Gray is the basis for a novel, a movie, and a play.		San Antonio, TX, opens the first U.S. air conditioned building.	A patent is issued for the first fully automated photographic film processing machine.	Eugene O'Neill's *Marco Millions* premieres in New York City	Jan.
Olmstead v. U.S. asks the Supreme Court to rule on the use of wiretap information in a criminal case. The court rules it admissible.			The Federal Radio Commission grants the first television license to Charles Jenkins Laboratories of Washington, DC. Call letters are W3XK. Jenkins uses mechanical technology similar to Baird's.	Mississippi John Hurt begins recording the "1928 Sessions" in Memphis, TN. He finishes the country blues sides in December in New York.	Feb.
		Wall Street has a record 4.79 million-share day on March 28.	California's St. Francis dam, built to provide Los Angeles with water, collapses. Between four and five hundred die as 12 billion gallons of water destroy towns in Los Angeles and Ventura counties.	The Dodge Victory Hour gives voice to silent stars. Among those broadcast are Mary Pickford, Charles Chaplin, Douglas Fairbanks, D.W. Griffith, Deloris Del Rio, and Gloria Swanson.	Mar.
Chicago holds the Pineapple Primary. The run-up to the Republican primary includes over 60 bombings and the deaths of two politicians.	Secretary Frank Kellogg responds to Briand's proposal to outlaw war by sending an offer to the Locarno Powers.		Two flyers complete the first transatlantic flight originating in Europe.	In London, Madame Tussaud's Waxworks opens.	Apr.
The Flood Control Act provides a 10-year, $325 million program of dam construction by the Corps of Engineers. The law is the result of 1927's disastrous Mississippi River flood.		General Electric introduces the first regularly scheduled television broadcasts. It airs programming in Schenectady, NY, Tuesday, Thursday, and Friday from 1:30 to 3:30 p.m....Wall Street sets another record with 4.82 million shares traded on May 16.	Max Knoll and Ernst Ruska invent the electron microscope. With the new device, viruses are now visible....The airship Italia crashes on a trip near the North Pole. Among the passengers is General Umberto Nobile, who piloted Amundsen's ship on the first flight over the pole. The first international polar rescue effort, including planes and an icebreaker, succeeds in June.	Mickey and Minnie Mouse debut in *Plane Crazy*, a take-off on the Lindbergh mania....Paramount, United Artists, and MGM receive licenses to use Movietone technology.	May
Democrats nominate Alfred smith for president. He is the first Catholic presidential candidate.	The preliminary Kellogg-Briand proposal goes to British, Italian, German, French, Dominion and Japanese governments.		Amelia Earhart is the first woman to fly the Atlantic.	Louis Armstrong records "West End Blues" for Chicago's Okeh Records.	Jun.
	The United States orders its troops to leave China.	Television sets go on sale in the U.S. Manufacturer is Daven Corp....Stocks decline sharply on July 11. Major stocks average 4.41 point losses....Dodge and Chrysler merge in a $160 million deal. The new company introduces the Plymouth, with the De Soto appearing in August.	The first televised tennis match airs....Emilio Carranza, Mexican aviator and hero, dies in a New Jersey plane crash after a goodwill trip to New York.	Warner Brothers premiers *The Lights of New York*. This is the first full talking picture.	Jul.
			The St Francis Dam collapse death toll continues to rise, reaching 385 this month. New bodies continue to be found into the early 1950s.		Aug.
	The United States recognizes the nationalist government of China.	Station W2XAD broadcasts the first play on television. The program is "The Queen's Messenger."...Motorola forms.	In London, Alexander Fleming discovers penicillin....The 160-mph Okeechobee hurricane strikes Florida. Over 2,500 die when the Okeechobee dike ruptures. Overall, the category 5 storm kills over 4,000 and destroys $100 million in property.	*The Singing Fool* stars Al Jolson.	Sep.

F	G	H	I	J
Includes campaigns, elections, federal-state relations, civil rights and liberties, crime, the judiciary, education, healthcare, poverty, urban affairs, and population.	Includes formation and debate of U.S. foreign and defense policies, veterans affairs, and defense spending. (Relations with specific foreign countries are usually found under the region concerned.)	Includes business, labor, agriculture, taxation, transportation, consumer affairs, monetary and fiscal policy, natural resources, pollution and industrial accidents.	Includes worldwide scientific, medical and technological developments, natural phenomena, U.S. weather and natural disasters.	Includes the arts, religion, scholarship, communications media, sports, entertainment, fashions, fads, and social life.

	World Affairs	Europe	Africa & The Middle East	The Americas	Asia & The Pacific
Oct.		Stalin announces his first five-year plan. The plan includes collectivization of private farms and emphasis on heavy industry.			Chiang Kai-shek wins the presidency of China.
Nov.	League conferences this month deal with economic statistics.	Turkey adopts the Latin alphabet. This is further westernization of the country.	The second League conference on African Sleeping Sickness convenes in Paris.		Manchuria recognizes nationalist rule. China is even more unified.
Dec.	The League hosts a printmakers' exposition....A Reparations Commission is established to determine if Germany has the capability of meeting its reparations obligations.	The Czech government arrests a Slovak on charges of Hungarian irredentism. Slovakian unrest grows.		Paraguay and Bolivia clash in Chaco. The Pan American Union attempts to mediate while awaiting Paraguay's appeal for League action.	The All-India Conference meets at Calcutta.

A	B	C	D	E
Includes developments that affect more than one world region, international organizations and important meetings of world leaders.	*Includes all domestic and regional developments in Europe, including the Soviet Union.*	*Includes all domestic and regional developments in Africa and the Middle East.*	*Includes all domestic and regional developments in Latin America, the Caribbean, and Canada.*	*Includes all domestic and regional developments in Asian and Pacific nations (and colonies).*

U.S. Politics & Social Issues	U.S. Foreign Policy & Affairs, Defense	U.S. Economy & Environment	Science, Technology & Nature	Culture, Leisure & Lifestyle	
President Hoover speaks about the American way, "rugged individualism."			Children's Hospital in Boston, is the first to use an iron lung. The device helps polio patients breathe.		Oct.
The sinking of the British Vestris off Virginia kills 113. The press plays the story sensationally....Hoover beats Smith for the presidency	President elect Herbert Hoover begins a seven-week goodwill tour of eleven Latin American countries. He returns in January 1929.		S.B. Eielson and Sir George Hubert Wilkins make the first airplane flight over Antarctica	Walt Disney's *Steamboat Willy* is the first fully synchronized sound cartoon. It premieres at New York's Colony Theater....Arnold Rothstein, notorious gambler, is shot dead at a New York poker game.	Nov.
Congress approves construction of the Boulder Dam in Nevada.	The state department's J. William Clark authors a memorandum saying that the Monroe Doctrine applies to Europe, not Latin America. In effect he refutes the Roosevelt Corollary, which allows U.S. intervention in internal Latin American affairs.	On Wall Street the market drops 22 points on December 8.	The first international dogsled mail begins between Minot, ME, and Quebec, CN.	The National League president proposes that designated hitters bat for pitchers	Dec.

F	G	H	I	J
Includes campaigns, elections, federal-state relations, civil rights and liberties, crime, the judiciary, education, healthcare, poverty, urban affairs, and population.	*Includes formation and debate of U.S. foreign and defense policies, veterans affairs, and defense spending. (Relations with specific foreign countries are usually found under the region concerned.)*	*Includes business, labor, agriculture, taxation, transportation, consumer affairs, monetary and fiscal policy, natural resources, pollution and industrial accidents.*	*Includes worldwide scientific, medical and technological developments, natural phenomena, U.S. weather and natural disasters.*	*Includes the arts, religion, scholarship, communications media, sports, entertainment, fashions, fads, and social life.*

	World Affairs	Europe	Africa & The Middle East	The Americas	Asia & The Pacific
Jan. 1		Edmund Schulthess becomes President of Switzerland, for his third one-year term in office....Austrian customs officials discover five railway trucks full of Italian-made machine-gun parts in a railway station at the Hungarian border at Szent Gotthard, which had been falsely declared on the customs manifest. The Hungarians claim they were being shipped to Poland as the number of machine guns that Hungary was allowed to possess was limited by the Treaty of Trianon.	Sheikh Shakhbut ibn Sultan Al Nahayan becomes ruler of Abu Dhabi, succeeding his nephew Shaikh Saqr bin Zayid who was assassinated....Bonded laborers who were effectively slaves numbering 200,000 are freed in Sierra Leone.	Juvenal Lamartine de Faria becomes governor of Rio Grande do Norte Province, Brazil, succeeding José Augusto Bezerra de Medeiros....George Albert Wenige becomes Mayor of London, Canada, for the second time....The opening of the Congress in Tegucigalpa, capital of Honduras, begins, with the government commandeering every vehicle they can for the imminent arrival of Charles Lindbergh who flies over San Salvador, capital of El Salvador, writing of his trip in the *New York Times*.	Burma police officer Eric Blair (George Orwell) puts in his resignation from the police....E.P. Fleming and H.E. Morton become Chief Commissioners of Sydney, Australia.
Jan. 2	The French government is critical of the plan by the U.S. Secretary of State Frank B. Kellogg to draw up a treaty outlawing war, citing the U.S. lack of involvement in the Treaty of Versailles as well as the U.S. non-participation in the League of Nations.	The German government issues a new plan, published in a Dusseldorf newspaper, to re-arrange the Dawes Plan and reduce overall world debt....The Spanish Premier, Miguel Primo de Rivera y Orbaneja, marqués de Estella, announces that he will continue with plans to draw up and implement a new constitution for Spain.		Charles Lindbergh flies into San Salvador, capital of El Salvador, praising the country, and then flies on to Tegucigalpa, Honduras.	Italian government protests over the murder of the Italian Vice-Consul to Baku in Russian Central Asia....Chinese General Chiang Kai-shek, in Shanghai, receives a telegram from the Nationalist government at Nanking urging him to return to his army position to begin the Northern Expedition to end warlord control of Peking.
Jan. 3	Pope Pius XI issues his encyclical "Mortabum Animos," denouncing ecumenical conferences.	The Polish and Soviet governments start an exchange of political prisoners....Spanish police arrest Senora Migual da Unamuno, wife of the controversial university professor and Liberal opponent of Primo de Rivera when she returns to Spain from France....Air Union announces the start of a daily passenger flight from London to Cannes, starting on March 1.	The leader of the Senussi in Cyrenaica surrenders to the Italians ending the war in eastern Libya and allowing the Italians to control the entire colony.	Monsignor Bernardo Herrera Restrepo, the primate and archbishop of Bogota, Colombia for 40 years, dies at the age of 83....Charles Lindbergh given a massive reception in Tegucigalpa, the capital of Honduras, although the aviator later describes the flight there as the "bumpiest" in his career.	
Jan. 4	The French foreign minister, Aristide Briand, sends a note to U.S. Secretary of State Frank B. Kellogg praising the idea to issue a pact to outlaw war, changing the stance of his country on the issue.	The British government announces that it wants to change some of the proposals by U.S. Secretary of State Frank B. Kellogg, in his planned anti-war treaty....Winston Churchill, the Chancellor of the Exchequer, sends an outline of his new budgetary plan to the British Prime Minister Stanley Baldwin.		Fighting escalates in Nicaragua....Charles Lindbergh is given a massive welcome by the Honduran Congress, followed by a lavish reception in the Presidential Palace. He is also invited to take part in hunting big game in Central Africa by French big game hunter Georges Petrognani.	General Chiang Kai-shek, accompanied by T'an Yen-k'ai, Yang Shu-chuang, Ch'en Li-fu and others leave Shanghai for Nanking.
Jan. 5	The sub-committee from the League of Nations to investigate plans by architects for a new headquarters on Lake Geneva reveals their selections which they made on December 22.	The British government introduces the first state pensions for people aged 65 or more years old....The German airline Deutsche Luft Hansa (now Lufthansa) starts its first service from Stuttgart, Germany, to Barcelona, Spain, where it connects with a service operated by its subsidiary Iberia, which flies from Barcelona to Madrid.	The Iraqi government announces that they will be sending a punitive expedition against a tribe which attacked over the border from Saudi Arabia.	Charles Lindbergh flies into Managua, capital of Nicaragua, avoiding flying near the battle zone, or volcanoes. He is greeted by a crowd of 35,000 people, the largest gathering in the city up to that point.	The Australian newspaper *Smiths Weekly* runs a spoof competition which it claims had come from *The Times* (London). This competition encourages readers to find a wife for Edward, Prince of Wales, "as he cannot or will not choose for himself."
Jan. 6		Flood on River Thames in London resulting in the drowning of 14 people over the next two days....A new plot to place Prince Carol on the Romanian throne is discovered by the Turkish authorities in Constantinople.		Charles Lindbergh is hailed by the Diaz Congress in Managua, Nicaragua, as an "envoy of peace."...Júlio Celso de Albuquerque Belo becomes acting governor of Pernambuco Province, Brazil, succeeding acting governor Júlio de Melo.	The forces of the Northern Coalition captured the city of Chochow from the Shansi troops who are supporting the Nationalists of Chiang Kai-shek....Colonel Hon A.G.A. Hore-Ruthven VC DSO is appointed as Governor of South Australia.
Jan. 7	A U.S. advisory committee on the codification of international law was organized at Cambridge, Massachusetts....The British government states their astonishment by the some of the clauses of the anti-war treaty.	The moat at the Tower of London, drained in 1843, is filled by flood water....The Polish government denies that the machine gun parts impounded by the Austrians at Szent Gotthard were destined for them. This rapidly becomes a major issue and is passed to the League of Nations.		Charles Lindbergh flies to San José, capital of Costa Rica, where he is cheered by 40,000 people. He describes the flight to San José as hazardous....The El Salvador and British governments conclude a commercial *modus vivendi*.	The Japanese Palace in Tokyo announces that Prince Chichibu, brother of the emperor, is marrying Setsu Matsudaira, daughter of the Japanese envoy to the United States, whom he met in Washington, DC, in 1927....Chinese general, Chiang Kai-shek formally resumes his position as Commander-in-Chief of the National Revolutionary Army.

A	B	C	D	E
Includes developments that affect more than one world region, international organizations and important meetings of world leaders.	*Includes all domestic and regional developments in Europe, including the Soviet Union.*	*Includes all domestic and regional developments in Africa and the Middle East.*	*Includes all domestic and regional developments in Latin America, the Caribbean, and Canada.*	*Includes all domestic and regional developments in Asian and Pacific nations (and colonies).*

U.S. Politics & Social Issues	U.S. Foreign Policy & Affairs, Defense	U.S. Economy & Environment	Science, Technology & Nature	Culture, Leisure & Lifestyle	
A newspaper plant for The *Scranton Sun*, in Scranton, Pennsylvania, is bombed injuring three New Years' Day revelers....The former home of Tammany Hall on 14th Street, New York, is sold to the Consolidated Gas Company.	Five U.S. Marines are killed and 23 are wounded in fighting with Nicaraguan rebels loyal to General Augusto Sandino, after they were ambushed.	Cold spell throughout the northern United States with the temperature in New York dropping to 12 degrees....Internal Revenue Bureau release figures showing that the number of Americans with an annual income of over $1 million had reached 228 in 1926, 21 more than in the previous year....Boeing Air Transport buys a majority shareholding in the U.S. airline Pacific Air Transport from Vern Gorst.		The Salvation Army announces that it will try to convert Greenwich Village, New York, by holding religious and other meetings....Maude Royden, the famous English woman preacher, announces that she will speak in Chicago in February and denies that the delay in her speaking engagements is because of her chain-smoking....*Time* magazine nominates aviator Charles Lindbergh as their first "Man of the Year."	Jan. 1
Harry Arista Mackey becomes Mayor of Philadelphia, Pennsylvania, taking over from W. Freeland Kendrick.	U.S. Marines fight another battle with rebels loyal to General Augusto (or Augostino) C. Sandino at Quilali, Nicaragua resulting in one more marine killed and five wounded....The U.S. State Department announces that it will receive applications for permits to export aircraft and related equipment to Mexico, ending the embargo which began in January 1924 over U.S. dissatisfaction with the political climate in Mexico.	Four people in New York die from cold spell.	Confirmation is received that the plane being flown by aviatrix Frances Grayson crashed into the sea off Cape Cod on December 23.	The pianist Ignace Jan Paderewski releases plans of his imminent visit to the United States.	Jan. 2
Republicans in New York oppose the plans by New York Governor Alfred E. Smith to push through changes in the management of water in the city.	U.S. government orders the sending of an additional 1,000 marines to Nicaragua to reinforce the existing 1,415 marines already there, as marines at Quilali build up their defenses expecting another attack from rebels loyal to General Augusto Sandino.			Mayor Jimmy Walker of New York announces that he would like to establish the Museum of the City of New York in Fifth Avenue....Archaeologists in Rome announce that they will recover the famous Ship of the Emperor Tiberius which had sunk in Lake Nemi.	Jan. 3
New York authorities release plans about the building of a new Nassau Jail....Judge Franklin Taylor, in the King's County Criminal Court, New York, congratulates traffic policeman August Schwalkman for recovering more than 100 stolen cars while guarding the Brooklyn end of the Williamsburg Bridge.	Divers from the U.S. Navy recover the first three bodies from the 40 who drowned when the *S-4* submarine was rammed and sunk by the coast guard destroyer *Paulding*, on December 17.	Postmaster General Harry S. New opens negotiations with the Mexican postal authorities about the feasibility of a regular air route from Washington, DC, to Mexico City, in addition to the planned routes from New Orleans to Brownsville, via Houston and Corpus Christi.	U.S. aviatrix Ruth Nichols of Rye, New York, makes the first non-stop flight from New York to Miami, accompanied by Harry Rogers, Air Line president, and owner of the Fairchild pontoon monoplane, and Major M. K. Lee, a retired businessman and sportsman.	Will Rogers appears on the radio of the National Broadcasting Company working from 47 radio stations which cover all 48 states of the United States....The England cricket team wins the second test match beating South Africa by 87 runs....The English evangelist A. Maude Royden, on her arrival in New York, defends her smoking.	Jan. 4
New York governor Al Smith indicates that he will deny pleas of clemency for Ruth Snyder and Henry Judd Gray, two murderers on death row found guilty of the murder of Snyder's husband Albert.	The U.S. Senate sidetracks a motion introduced by Democrat Senator Thomas Heflin of Alabama to attack the U.S. policy in Nicaragua.		Colonel Lawrence La Tourette Driggs, President of the American Flying Club and a director of the Colonial Air Transport Company, predicts that plans using diesel engines will become more popular, but also there will be the advent of much more deadly warfare as planes develop.	Edwin W. Marland, President of Marland Oil Company, and one of the wealthiest men in the South-West of the United States, confirms rumors mooted in newspapers that he will marry Lydie Miller Roberts, whom he had adopted in 1916, an announcement that came as a surprise to the mother of the bride.	Jan. 5
Calvin Coolidge issues a statement to newspapers saying that he is not alarmed at the increase in loans by brokers....The New York authorities announce that they are searching for an ex-convict Fred W. Edel in connection with the murder of actress Emma Briswalters Harrington.	The U.S. government announces that it is sending Major General John A. Lejeune to Nicaragua with marine units to try to stop increasing numbers of attacks by rebels loyal to General Augusto Sandino. This announcement coincides with further attacks by Nicaraguan rebels.	An oil tanker owned by the Sewell Oil Transportation Company founders off the Steeplechase Pier, at Coney Island, NY.	Dr. Elmer A. Sperry, inventor of the gyroscope compass, announces that he has perfected a diesel engine for air planes which will give the planes more power, using about one-fifth of the amount of fuel, making long haul flights easier, and also raising the possibility of increased military use of aviation.	Golfer Bobby Jones, winner of the United States amateur and also the British open golf championships announced that he will not accept the $50,000 house in Atlanta giving to him by an admirer even though the United States Golf Association states that this will not violate his amateur status.	Jan. 6
Senator Edward I. Edwards urges the Democratic Party to get a "real leader" who can lead the party to victory in the November elections.	Lieutenant Commander John S. Baylis, captain of the *Pauldling* is charged with his role in his coast guard vessel's collision with the *S-4* submarine on December 17, 1927, off Cape Cod, near Provincetown, MA, which resulted in the death of 40 submariners.	Stock on the New York Stock Exchange booms with sales being described as the second largest ever recorded on a Saturday....U.S. businessmen fly to Mexico City in two planes to try to rebuild business links with Mexico.	The prototype Polikarpov U-2 training biplane makes its first flight.	Some 8,795 people attended a concert held at the Metropolitan Museum of Art in New York, to hear Tchaikovsky's Fifth Symphony, and also military fanfares written by Russian composers Anatoly Liadov and Alexander Glazunov.	Jan. 7

F	G	H	I	J
Includes campaigns, elections, federal-state relations, civil rights and liberties, crime, the judiciary, education, healthcare, poverty, urban affairs, and population.	Includes formation and debate of U.S. foreign and defense policies, veterans affairs, and defense spending. (Relations with specific foreign countries are usually found under the region concerned.)	Includes business, labor, agriculture, taxation, transportation, consumer affairs, monetary and fiscal policy, natural resources, pollution and industrial accidents.	Includes worldwide scientific, medical and technological developments, natural phenomena, U.S. weather and natural disasters.	Includes the arts, religion, scholarship, communications media, sports, entertainment, fashions, fads, and social life.

	World Affairs	Europe	Africa & The Middle East	The Americas	Asia & The Pacific
Jan. 8	The King and Queen of Afghanistan arrive in Rome, Italy, to begin a tour of European capitals, visiting Italy, France, Belgium, Germany, Great Britain, Poland, Russia, Turkey and Persia, before returning to Kabul on July 1.	The British prime minister Stanley Baldwin starts the British general election campaign with a speech in his constituency at Bewdley.... The Polish and Lithuanian governments continue to feud over the problem of Vilna and whether or not it should become Lithuanian. The Lithuanian post office also states that it will not accept any mail which had the postal hand stamp Vilna on it, as this was tantamount to accepting Polish sovereignty over the city.		Charles Lindberg while in San José, Costa Rica, visits a bull fight.... For the first time in Canadian history, the income of the state of Newfoundland from fishery is exceeded by another sector, that of manufacturing paper pulp....The Mexican government announces that it will not sue the Hearst newspapers for printing stories against them which were found to have come from forged documents.	Thousands of soldiers are mobilized in Nanking, China, for a planned attack on northern warlords. Banners promoting Chiang Kai-shek and also the phrases of Abraham Lincoln "government of the people, by the people and for the people," are placed all around the Chinese Nationalist capital.
Jan. 9		The Central Committee of the French Communist Party denounces political alliances with any non-revolutionary parties....Large numbers of workers and volunteers in London start building many sand-bag walls to prevent another flood of London....British Chancellor of the Exchequer Winston Churchill goes to France to hunt boar with the Duke of Westminster.	Egyptologist Howard Carter announces that he has completed the work involved in clearing the fourth chamber of the tom of the Egyptian Pharaoh Tut-ankh-amen with the British newspaper The *Daily Express* being allowed to cover the details of the archaeological work.	Charles Lindbergh leaves San José, Costa Rica, in the morning, flying to Panama, flying off course because of cloud cover. He states that he can see Panama as a future air center for Central America. Lindbergh's arrival in Panama City is greeted by many Panamanians, including President Rodolfo Chiari.	Chiang Kai-shek announces, in a circular telegram, that he is resuming his post of Commander-in-Chief of the Nationalist armies and intends to resume hostilities against the Northern Coalition, and at the same time suppress Communism.
Jan. 10	A Papal Encyclical issued by Pope Pius XI condemns "Pan-Christian" attempts to find Church unity and says that the Roman Catholic dogma is inviolable. He also states that he will welcome "contrite dissidents."	Joseph Stalin orders the exile of Leon Trotsky to Alma-Ata, the capital of Kazakh SSR, along with 29 other anti-Stalin Bolsheviks, signifying the rise of Stalin and his triumph over Trotsky in the Bolshevik Party.... Anton Schreiner becomes Premier of Burgenland, Austria, taking over from Josef Rauhofer.		Charles Lindbergh takes President Rodolfo Chiari of Panama for a ride in his plane. Lindbergh goes on to praise Simon Bolivar, the man who led much of South America to independence from Spain.	The Australian postal authorities arrange for official mail to be carried on the first attempt to fly across the Tasman Sea between Australia and New Zealand. However aviators Lieutenant John Moncrieff and Captain George Hood, in their Ryan Brougham monoplane Aotearoa G-AUNZ are both lost at sea, some 400 miles from the New Zealand coast.
Jan. 11	U.S. Secretary of State Frank B. Kellogg publishes a draft treaty which outlines the proposal he and Aristide Briand, the French foreign minister, drew up to outlaw future wars.	Thomas Hardy, British novelist and author of *Jude the Obscure, Far from the Madding Crowd* and *The Mayor of Casterbridge*, dies at his home near Dorchester, England, aged 87....Lord Cecil addressing the League of the Nations Union at Sheffield, Yorkshire, England, speaks out critically of the U.S. stance on the proposed anti-war treaty.	Abdul Muhsin Bey al-Saadun becomes Prime Minister of Iraq for the third time, taking over from Jaafar al-Askari....A joint expedition by the British Museum and the University of Pennsylvania announce that they have found the tomb of the King of the Sumerian city of Ur in Iraq.	Charles Lindbergh arrives in the Panama Canal Zone where the speed limit of 18 miles per hour is lifted to allow motorcycle policemen running late to make up for lost time reaching speeds of over 40 miles per hour.	
Jan. 12		Negotiations are held between the French and the U.S. government over the payment of outstanding French war debts....Rumors reach Berlin that Leon Trotsky is still in Moscow and had not been purged....Two French Communist deputies who had been sentenced for incitement to rebellion are arrested after the Chamber of Deputies nullifies their parliamentary immunity.		Argentine and Mexican governments sign a treaty at Buenos Aires, capital of Argentina, regarding literary and artistic rights....Charles Lindbergh flies to Colon at the end of his time in the Panama Canal Zone....A British company, Bolivia Concessions Ltd, headed by Lord Askwith and Sir Martin Conway MP, outlines their plan for sending British settlers to Bolivia.	
Jan. 13	U.S. Secretary of State Frank B. Kellogg asks France to join with the United States in supporting the introduction of a multilateral agreement against war, to be proposed to the British, German, and Italian governments.	Allied military control in Bulgaria ends in accordance with the terms of the Treaty of Neuilly....Dr. Otto Gessler quits the German cabinet, citing health reasons.	Alphonse Choteau becomes Commissioner for Mauritania, French West Africa, taking over from Albéric Fournier who becomes Lieutenant-Governor of Upper Volta, French West Africa.... Adolphe Deitte becomes Lieutenant Governor of Chad, French Equatorial Africa.	French aviators Captain Dieudonne Costes and navigator Lieutenant-Commander Joseph Le Brix meet with Charles Lindbergh at Colon, Panama....Cuba declares a national holiday in honor of visiting Calvin Coolidge....Canada names a lake in the Red Lake district Lake Doran after missing aviatrix Mildred Doran.	

A	B	C	D	E
Includes developments that affect more than one world region, international organizations and important meetings of world leaders.	Includes all domestic and regional developments in Europe, including the Soviet Union.	Includes all domestic and regional developments in Africa and the Middle East.	Includes all domestic and regional developments in Latin America, the Caribbean, and Canada.	Includes all domestic and regional developments in Asian and Pacific nations (and colonies).

U.S. Politics & Social Issues	U.S. Foreign Policy & Affairs, Defense	U.S. Economy & Environment	Science, Technology & Nature	Culture, Leisure & Lifestyle	
Member of the House of Representatives George S. Graham from Philadelphia, Pennsylvania, is sworn in at his hospital bed in Mount Sinai Hospital where he was recovering from an operation. It was only the second time up until then that a U.S. member of the House was sworn in outside the House.	U.S. Marines in Nicaragua arrest eight men for their involvement in the death of murdered U.S. planter John Bolton, formerly from Wisconsin, but who had lived in Nicaragua for 37 years....General Augusto Sandino issues his Resolution Number 20 in which, as general in chief of the Autonomist Nicaraguan Army, he orders the confiscation of North American properties in Nicaragua.	Congress urges the U.S. Postal Service to reduce their postal rates....Four advisers give evidence to the House Irrigation Committee in favor of the building of the Boulder Canyon Dam (later the Hoover Dam).		Some 55,000 people head to Coney Island with warm weather also resulting in many other people flocking to the New Jersey seaside....A new movie, *Crooks*, is scheduled for release in Chicago concentrating on local gangsters and police.	Jan. 8
Ruth Snyder and Henry Judd Gray continue their pleas for clemency.		A large blast at the Industrial Coal Company's Mine No 18 at West Frankfort, Illinois, results in the death of 21 miners from the initial gas explosion.	The French Aero Club announces that of the first 101 men to qualify as pilots and receive licenses from them, some 77 are still alive and seven are still flying. In addition, 13 are still involved in the manufacture of aircraft.	Eugene O'Neill's *Marco Millions* premieres in New York City....The New York authorities announce that some 22,000 New York traffic police will attend courtesy schools where they will receive instructions on how better to deal with members of the public....The Union of Orthodox Jewish Congregations in America announce that they will urge the teaching of more history to their congregations.	Jan. 9
John Christian Lodge becomes Mayor of Detroit, Michigan, for the third time, taking over from John Smith....Al Smith refuses the pleas of clemency from convicted murderers Ruth Snyder and Henry Judd Gray saying that there were no extenuating circumstances....The Court of Appeals in Albany, New York, confirms the convictions of Phillip Ecker and Harry Vischnitzer for the murder of Morris Borkin, a New York policeman.		President Calvin Coolidge announces that the government will sell his trade fleet as quickly as possible, and the U.S. government will then give a ship subsidy for private owners....Al Smith in New York states that his state will not introduce a gasoline tax, but that his state will still have a $15 million surplus....U.S. banks urge for the sale of $500,000 worth of aircraft and parts overseas as part of a major export drive.	The French start work on building a ship that is planned to be able to make the Atlantic Ocean crossing from Cherbourg to New York in 60 hours. Unlike planes, it will be able to travel in rough weather but will only contain six men, and enough supplies for 10 days.	Rogers Hornsby, the highest-paid player in the National League goes to play for the Boston Braves "for the best interests of the New York Giants."...Historian and biographer Emil Ludwig arrives in New York for a lecture tour.	Jan. 10
Ruth Snyder wins a stay of execution for another day, with a federal plea for her co-defendant Henry Judd Gray.	President Coolidge announces that he will urge Pan-American Amity at the Havana Congress with problems arising over U.S. relations with Mexico and U.S. military involvement in Nicaragua....U.S. Marines involved in fighting in Nicaragua resulting in the defeat of Nicaraguan rebels during two attempts to ambush trains. 14 Nicaraguan rebels are claimed to have been killed.	The Volcano of Kilauea in Hawaii, the world's largest active volcano, starts glowing again, with evidence of some smoldering fire. Superstitious Hawaiians talk of the Goddess being angry.	U.S. aviators Clarence D. Chamberlin and Roger Quincy Williams in an attempt to break the air endurance record for being in the air for the longest period of time were forced to end their flight at Curtiss Field, Long Island, after four hours when their fuel pump started to have problems.		Jan. 11
Ruth Snyder is executed at Ossining, New York, dying in front of 24 witnesses. One of these, *Chicago Tribune* journalist Tom Howard, working for the *New York Daily News*, manages to smuggle in a small camera and photographs Ruth Snyder as she is being executed. Henry Judd Gray is executed 10 minutes later.	Calvin Coolidge sets out for Havana for the Sixth Pan-American Conference....U.S. Secretary for the Navy Curtis Wilbur declares that the navy, costing $129 million annually, needs an additional $2,580 million if it is to provide an effective defense role for the United States.			Princeton University creates Departments of Politics and Archaeology, offering many new courses previously unavailable. There is also the establishment of a graduate scholarship in vertebrate paleontology.	Jan. 12
The Jackson Day Dinner held in Washington, DC shows that many Democrats support the presidential candidacy of New York Governor Al Smith.	A number of Nicaraguan newspapers claim that some Conservatives including ex-President General Emiliano Chamorro, are supporting rebel General Augusto Sandino in his fight with the pro-U.S. government of President Adolfo Diaz, in a war that was costing the lives of many U.S. Marines. General Chamorro immediately denies these allegations.	In a dispute over oyster fishing in Virginia, the state militia was sent to Gloucester County....Calvin Coolidge signs a bill to beautify Washington, DC with $25 million to be spent to purchase private property south of Pennsylvania Avenue from the Botanic Gardens near the Capitol to the Treasury on Fifteenth Street.	Dr. E.F.W. Alexanderson of General Electric demonstrates television broadcasts to home receivers at Schenectady, NY.		Jan. 13

F	G	H	I	J
Includes campaigns, elections, federal-state relations, civil rights and liberties, crime, the judiciary, education, healthcare, poverty, urban affairs, and population.	*Includes formation and debate of U.S. foreign and defense policies, veterans affairs, and defense spending. (Relations with specific foreign countries are usually found under the region concerned.)*	*Includes business, labor, agriculture, taxation, transportation, consumer affairs, monetary and fiscal policy, natural resources, pollution and industrial accidents.*	*Includes worldwide scientific, medical and technological developments, natural phenomena, U.S. weather and natural disasters.*	*Includes the arts, religion, scholarship, communications media, sports, entertainment, fashions, fads, and social life.*

	World Affairs	Europe	Africa & The Middle East	The Americas	Asia & The Pacific
Jan. 14		Many people in Bavaria, Germany, take part in demonstrations against changes in the law which benefit Prussia, and issue a petition from Munich, the Bavarian capital, signed by many prominent Bavarians.	H. Hobart Porter, president of the American Water Works and Electric Company and his wife leave the United States to inspect their rubber plantations in Liberia and to continue to Central Africa where Mr. Porter plans to take part in hunting of big game.		Chinese academic Dr. Tehyi Hsieh in a speech in the Town Hall, New York, at an event organized by the League for Political Education, stated his support for U.S. policy in China claiming that the United States is not acting in an imperialistic fashion....The Imperial Household in Tokyo, Japan, starts drawing up the program for the forthcoming coronation of Emperor Hirohito.
Jan. 15	The Third National Congress on the Cause and Cure of War held at the Mayflower Hotel, Washington, DC under the auspices of nine U.S. women's groups.	In a statement from Moscow, the Soviet authorities claim that purged politician Leon Trotsky had tried to seize power....Several thousand Royalists taking part in a demonstration in Athens were dispersed by police using fire hoses....Italian leader Benito Mussolini reveals that he gave Prefect Mori a free hand to crack down on the Mafia in Sicily with Giuseppa Salvo, nicknamed the Queen of Guaci, being jailed for 25 years over her involvement with the Mafia.		Calvin Coolidge is given a warm reception when he arrives by ship at Havana for the Sixth Pan-American Conference in Havana, Cuba....Charles Lindbergh stops flying for a day to take part in hunting animals in the interior of southern Panama.	
Jan. 16	The Sixth Pan-American Conference, held at Havana, Cuba, starts meeting, but is not officially opened for another five days....Moves urged at Brussels, Belgium, to introduce laws to ban the use of poison gas in battle.	Leon Trotsky prepares for his exile in Alma-Ata, sending his luggage to the Moscow train station, and then is told that the journey has been delayed for two days....The Norwegian and Soviet governments conclude a agreement about reciprocal arrangements in connection with their nationals arrested in each other countries.	The term of office of the Earl of Athlone, the governor-general of South Africa, is extended for two years.	Senor Luis Dobles Segreda, the Costa Rican Minister for public Instruction, announces that his government spends more money on education than any other single item in its budget, with English taught to all schoolchildren. He suggests that American schoolchildren should also consider learning Spanish.	British barrister Sir John Simon KC MP announces his retirement from legal practice, shortly before being appointed to lead the Indian Statutory Commission....George Herbert Westcott DD, Bishop of Lucknow, India, dies, aged 65.
Jan. 17	The Brussels Conference about the possible use of poison gas in war discusses the idea of using cellars of buildings as refuges for civilians when a poison gas attack takes place.	In the morning, the OGPU arrest Leon Trotsky at his Moscow apartment, and escort him to the train leaving for Alma-Ata, with 1500 apparently watching him leave the Soviet capital. The Lithuanian government rejects a Polish plan about the future of the city of Vilna....The British government announces that it will abandon its plans to build a third cruiser.	A trial begins in Constantinople, Turkey, where 20 Communists are on trial facing accusations that the existence of the Communist Party is contrary to the Turkish Constitution.	Puerto Rico declares a national holiday to welcome Charles Lindbergh who arrives in San Juan, the capital of Puerto Rico....Nicaraguan rebel leader General Augusto Sandino sends a message to the 6th Pan-American Congress in Havana urging them to support him in his cause.	
Jan. 18		The Polish government expresses that it is perturbed that the Lithuanian government refused to meet at a conference in Riga, the capital of Latvia, to discuss the future of the city of Vilna....Coalition government in Germany in danger of falling over School Bill and Budget.		The British Colonial Office announces that the lease on Bouvet and Thompson Islands in the South Atlantic Ocean has been granted to a Norwegian firm, the island then being annexed by the Norwegian government to expand its whaling operations in the region.	Chiang Kai-shek urges the Central Executive Committee of the Kuomintang that they should only abrogate the "Unequal Treaties" by using peaceful negotiation whenever possible.
Jan. 19		Wilhelm Groener becomes Minister of Defense in Germany, replacing Dr. Otto Gessler....The French Chamber of Deputies adopts a bill reducing the length of military service from 18 months to one year.	The British government rejects the Persian note of November 22, 1927, whereby they claimed the Bahrain islands.	Charles Lindbergh begins his attempt to scale various mountains in Panama, taking a break from flying.	Plans in Tokyo to develop a Trans-Pacific plane near completion.
Jan. 20	Members states of the Sixth Pan-American Conference in Havana, Cuba, raise preliminary ideas about the legality of any rights of the United States or other countries to militarily intervene in other nation states.	A major scandal erupts in Germany after the Chancellor, Wilhelm Marx, announces that the government has lost several million marks through unauthorized subsidies of "national" films....French Prime Minister Raymond Poincaré defends his budget from attacks by his political opponents....The Soviet Union announces that it will sort out its budgetary problems to raise more money from sale of bonds....Admiral of the Fleet Sir John Michael de Robeck GCB GCMG GCVO, dies aged 65.	Yesif El-Jah, a Syrian seer in the United States, surrenders to police to face charges of involvement in kidnapping.		The Imperial Palace in Tokyo makes a formal announcement of the betrothal of Prince Chichu, brother of the Emperor, and the Heir Apparent to the Throne, to Sestu Matsudaira, the 18-year-old daughter of Tsuneo Matsudaira, the Japanese Ambassador to the United States. Calvin Coolidge sends a congratulatory message to the Emperor Hirohito of Japan....Over a hundred convicts in Allahabad, India, revolt and prison authorities open fire, killing one and wounding another 16.

A	B	C	D	E
Includes developments that affect more than one world region, international organizations and important meetings of world leaders.	*Includes all domestic and regional developments in Europe, including the Soviet Union.*	*Includes all domestic and regional developments in Africa and the Middle East.*	*Includes all domestic and regional developments in Latin America, the Caribbean, and Canada.*	*Includes all domestic and regional developments in Asian and Pacific nations (and colonies).*

U.S. Politics & Social Issues	U.S. Foreign Policy & Affairs, Defense	U.S. Economy & Environment	Science, Technology & Nature	Culture, Leisure & Lifestyle	
Catherine A. Smith, the wife of New York governor and presidential hopeful Al Smith recovers from an operation for appendicitis.... Five men tried for placing a bomb next to the Brooklyn Court Building are put on trial....Work starts on building a large convention hall, capable of holding 25,000, for the Democratic Party Convention to be held there in June.	The U.S. Naval Affairs Committee urges that the naval program should be completed in two years.	Calvin Coolidge lifts the ban on loans to French industry as a mark of increasing friendship between the two countries.	William P. Geddes, Vice President of the Radio Manufacturers' Association, claims that even though television will change many aspects of the radio, the radio service will continue to be more important for many decades to come....Three students from Harvard University train for a trip to the South Pole with Richard Byrd.		Jan. 14
A gathering takes place in New York organized by Under-Secretary of the Treasury Ogden L. Mills and others to start raising support for Republican Herbert Hoover for his presidential bid later in the year.... A blast of a furnace in the basement of a building in Broadway, New York, results in many people fleeing thinking that it was a bank robbery as dozens of police pour into the area.	Protests in the United States organized by Bernard G. Richards of Executive Secretary of the American Jewish Committee, and a delegate to the Conference on Jewish rights held in Zurich in 1927, over the discrimination against Jews in Romania.	New York Standard Oil, involved in a controversy about buying Soviet oil products, makes an open declaration of "war" on the Royal Dutch-Shell group of Europe, defending its own deal; with the Soviet Union....The Curtiss Aeroplane Corporation starts an export drive to sell some of its aircraft to Peru....The *Westminster Gazette* in Britain warns of a looming trade war between the major tobacco retailers.		The 13th edition of the *Encyclopedia Britannica* is launched. It runs to 32 volumes, with some versions being bound into 16 larger volumes.	Jan. 15
Theodore G. Bilbo becomes Governor of issippi, for a second time, taking over from Dennis Murphree....A large crowd attacks the jail in Flint, Michigan, where a confessed murderer of a five-year-old child is held. The murderer is taken away by National Guards after attempts are made to lynch him.	Preparations begin to hold an election in Nicaragua, a move which will affect the role of U.S. Marines in the country.	Al Smith finalizes his budget for New York State with a surplus expected of $36,860,540 at the end of the fiscal year.	Dr. Eckener in Germany announces that a new giant zeppelin will be ready on about May 1 for flights around the world.	Pan American Airways holds its first passenger service between Key West, Florida, and Havana, Cuba.... Boxer Jack Delaney lands a single punch on Sully Montgomery at a boxing match broadcast on Boxing from St. Nicholas Arena, knocking him out straight away in a bout that lasts 20 seconds.	Jan. 16
	The Conservative majority in the Nicaraguan House of Deputies voted to introduce a law which would eject the U.S. Marines from Nicaragua, and end much of the U.S. influence over the country.		French aviators Diedonne Costes and Joseph Le Brix fly to Venezuela, in a twelve hour flight from Colon, Panama....Richard Byrd announces that he will leave New York on September 10, and take a party of 60 to the South Pole.	Singer Dorothy Mirowsky, aged 30, soon after her first public recital held on January 15, falls into despair and commits suicide convinced that her performance was bad, and apparently not aware that it had won approval by the critics in the press.	Jan. 17
Senator Thomas Heflin of Alabama attacks the proposed presidential candidacy of Al Smith....Adolph Hotelling, the Owosso carpenter who pleaded guilty to the murder of a five-year old girl in Flint, MI, is sentenced to life imprisonment.	There are reports in Nicaragua that General Augusto Sandino, leader of the rebels, was killed after his jungle base was bombed by U.S. aircraft. This quickly turns out to be incorrect.			Charles, Seventh Duke of Richmond and Gordon, and owner of the Goodwood Racecourse, dies at the age of 82.	Jan. 18
The Senate bars Illinois Senator-elect Frank L. Smith from taking up his seat by a vote of 61 to 23.... William T. Cosgrave, president of the Executive Council of the Irish Free State, arrives in New York.	U.S. Marines state that they believe General Augusto Sandino survived their bomb attack on the previous day, and news of his death was a ruse to cover his escape.	A tornado strikes Cincinnati, Hamilton and Washington Court House, OH, killing one man and injuring 35 other people....Texas Corporation announces that it will acquire California Petroleum in a $530 million merger....U.S. Treasury Secretary Andrew W. Mellon speaks out critically of the Federal Reserve System.		British publisher John Murray releases another volume of Queen Victoria's letters.	Jan. 19
William T. Cosgrave, president of the Executive Council of the Irish Free State is greeted by large crowds in Chicago, after being welcomed with a 19-Gun salute.	U.S. Marines continue to drive back Nicaraguan rebels claiming that the fighting is a credit to the use of battlefield aircraft. However there is also confirmation that General Augusto Sandino is still alive. Indeed Admiral D. F. Sellers, the Commander of the U.S. Special Service Squadron, USS *Rochester* writes to General Sandino urging him to lay down his arms.	The Soviet Union sells $100,000 worth of bonds to U.S. investors through the Chase Manhattan Bank.	Commander Charles Burney of the (British) Royal Navy announces plans to build airships which could cross the Atlantic....Edward Kay Roberts, British natural history writer, dies, aged 72....Sir Dyce Duckworth, eminent British consulting physician, dies aged 87.	A gift of $500,000 allows work to begin on the building of a large chapel for Washington Cathedral.	Jan. 20

F	G	H	I	J
Includes campaigns, elections, federal-state relations, civil rights and liberties, crime, the judiciary, education, healthcare, poverty, urban affairs, and population.	Includes formation and debate of U.S. foreign and defense policies, veterans affairs, and defense spending. (Relations with specific foreign countries are usually found under the region concerned.)	Includes business, labor, agriculture, taxation, transportation, consumer affairs, monetary and fiscal policy, natural resources, pollution and industrial accidents.	Includes worldwide scientific, medical and technological developments, natural phenomena, U.S. weather and natural disasters.	Includes the arts, religion, scholarship, communications media, sports, entertainment, fashions, fads, and social life.

	World Affairs	Europe	Africa & The Middle East	The Americas	Asia & The Pacific
Jan. 21	Calvin Coolidge opens a 21-nation Sixth Pan-American Conference in Havana, Cuba.	Peteris Jurasevskis becomes Prime Minister of a caretaker government in Latvia after a long political crisis over Soviet spy rings operating in Riga, taking over from Margers Skujenieks. This is the first conservative administration since Latvia became independent in 1918.	A special flight from Bulawayo, Southern Rhodesia, to Salisbury, is undertaken by the Rhodesian Aviation Syndicate, with letters and newspapers delivered by parachute to Gwelo, Que Que, Gatooma, and Hartley.	General George Washington Goethals, builder of the Panama Canal, and the first civil governor of the Panama Canal Zone, dies, aged 70. His funeral takes place at West Point.	
Jan. 22	Evidence emerges that the League of Nations has had a role in the drafting of the proposed antiwar treaty.	Lieutenant-General Wilhelm Groener is appointed to succeed Herr Gessler as the Minister of Defense....The French government protest at more loans being given to the government of the Soviet Union....The Reverend F. R. Lauria of St. Cuthbert's Church, Darwen, Lancashire, England, ias booed by his congregation during his church service which is felt to be too similar to that conducted by the Roman Catholic Church.	The Turkish government starts an investigation into the American School at Broussa after there are rumors that students are being converted to Christianity in the school....Arguments between the Turkish and Greek governments resurface delaying a prisoner swap under the terms of the Treaty of Lausanne....Because of low levels of the River Nile, the Egyptian government releases 400 million cubic meters of water held by the Sennar Dam.		General Chang Fa-kwei, aged 32, leader of what became known as the Iron Army, is ousted from his power base in the Chinese city of Canton....Political parties in Japan publish their political program for the forthcoming general elections.
Jan. 23		The Polish government criticizes the Lithuanian government over what it claims is the latter country's intransigence over possible negotiations on the future status of the city of Vilna....Former British Prime Minister David Lloyd George visits Lisbon, the capital of Portugal.		Chairman Charles Evans Hughes at the Sixth Pan-American Conference in Havana, Cuba, opposes the emergence of a Latin Union, an idea raised by the Mexican government....The delegates to the conference lay wreaths at the tomb of José Marti, the Cuban revolutionary leader who died in 1895.	Japan signs the Russo-Japanese Convention in Moscow. This fisheries agreement with the Soviet Union, which is ratified on May 23, revises the Fisheries Convention of 1907.
Jan. 24		Romanian foreign minister, Nicolae Titulescu, arrives in Rome, Italy, for the start of a week of meetings with Benito Mussolini and Italian government officials.		A British Company Sacambaya Exploration Company, is floated on the London Stock Exchange and outlines its plans to send an expedition to Bolivia to find the treasure worth an estimated $60 million which it claims was left in the country by the Jesuits when they were ejected in the 18th century.	
Jan. 25		A protocol is signed in Belgrade to try to ease relations between Italy and Yugoslavia, stating that a pact of friendship would be signed on July 27, or dispensed with.... Prince Felix Yusopoff, living in Paris, launches a libel case against Alexander Kerensky who was critical of the prince's account of the murder of Gregory Rasputin in 1916. Kerensky's account was published in *Dni*, the Russian paper in Paris.		Getúlio Vargas becomes governor of Rio Grande do Sul Province, Brazil, succeeding Antônio Augusto Borges de Medeiros....Charles Lindbergh flies to Colombia from Colon, Panama.	An unofficial mission from the Nanking government, consisting of C. C. Wu, Sun Fo, Hu Han-min and others leaves for a tour of various countries to prepare the ground for the revision of the "unequal treaties."...The Madras Legislative Council in India carries out its resolution to boycott the Statutory Commission established by the British.
Jan. 26		Nicolae Titulescu issues a press statement saying that there is no contradiction between Romania's support for the Little Entente in the Balkans, and an alliance with Italy.	Charles Lindbergh arrives in the Caribbean port of Cartagena, Colombia, where he is greeted by the city's governor and thousands of people who break through police lines to mob him.	There are major disputes at the Sixth Pan-American Conference held in Havana, Cuba, with Colombia introducing clauses over aviation.... French aviators Captain Dieudonne Costes and navigator Lieutenant-Commander Joseph Le Brix arrive in Guatemala City where they are greeted by a crowd of 3,000.	
Jan. 27	The League of Nations becomes increasingly critical of illegal arms sales as controversy over the Italian arms sent to Hungary attracts more attention.	The Agent General for the Reparations Payment, S. Parker Gilbert, is heckled by a crowd of 10,000 Germans who are critical of his 109,000 mark salary and his employing of 103 staff to run offices to oversee the collection of German monies to pay war reparations from World War I.	Alice Carr, from Georgia, U.S.A, is lost in the Assyrian desert after going there with $10,000 in funds for Assyrian relief. She left Baghdad for Smyrna, via Mosul, but never arrived in Mosul. She is later found wandering in the desert by a British army officer and some Assyrian soldiers—she had been waylaid by desert wolves.	Charles Evans Hughes draws up plans to mollify moves being mooted by Mexico....There are reports of fighting at Mazatlan, Mexico.	The Nanking government issues a proclamation which is interpreted as meaning that they will be taking control of the Maritime Customs from the Peking government. The acting Inspector-General, A.H.F. Edwardes, is invited to visit Nanking to discuss this.

A	B	C	D	E
Includes developments that affect more than one world region, international organizations and important meetings of world leaders.	*Includes all domestic and regional developments in Europe, including the Soviet Union.*	*Includes all domestic and regional developments in Africa and the Middle East.*	*Includes all domestic and regional developments in Latin America, the Caribbean, and Canada.*	*Includes all domestic and regional developments in Asian and Pacific nations (and colonies).*

U.S. Politics & Social Issues	U.S. Foreign Policy & Affairs, Defense	U.S. Economy & Environment	Science, Technology & Nature	Culture, Leisure & Lifestyle	
New York Governor Al Smith, in a speech to the New York State Bar Association, argues in favor of a four year term for governors.	The U.S. government reiterates that its marines are in Nicaragua at the request of the Nicaraguan government and will leave if requested.	In a speech by Saloman de la Sekva, the New York representative of the Nicaraguan Federation of Labour, Nicaragua has more money invested in "Wall Street" than Wall Street has invested in Nicaragua....An extension of time is given to those who failed to claim money owing on Irish bonds.	A dog which was adrift on an ice floe near Detroit for three days is rescued.	Arthur Baecht, a violinist, makes his debut at New York Town Hall with a recital of music by Norwegian composer Edvard Grieg.	Jan. 21
Calvin Coolidge welcomes William T. Cosgrave, president of the Executive Council of the Irish Free State to Washington, DC on a state visit....Presidential hopeful Herbert Hoover declares his opposition to the end of prohibition, and his supporters start planning the campaign for him to gain the Republican nomination....Prosecutors recommend charges are laid against Florence E. S. Knapp, Dean of the College of Home Economics at Syracuse University, and former Secretary of State for the State of New York, for the embezzlement of $118,707 which was illegally spent.	Senator William Borah, Republican Chairman of the Senate Foreign Relations Committee, is critical of the U.S. government plans to massively enlarge its navy.			Evidence in Britain from the Registrar-General responsible for Births, Deaths and Marriages, provides information that some types of cancer are more prevalent among poorer people.	Jan. 22
Senator Thomas Heflin of Alabama continues his anti-Roman Catholic attacks on New York Governor and presidential hopeful Al Smith.	U.S. marine officers in Nicaragua claim that they have crushed the revolt of General Augusto Sandino, seizing the stronghold of the rebel leader at El Chipote; and it is announced that General John A. Lejeune will return to the United States on February 1.			Prince Frederick Hohenzollern, heir to the late Prince William of Sigmaringen, announces that the art collection of Prince William will be sold to American collectors.	Jan. 23
The U.S. Senate continues with their hearings over the Teapot Dome scandal....Some 21 prisoners dig their way out of a prison in Detroit, with 19 of them escaping to Canada.	Calvin Coolidge criticizes the idea of massively enlarging the U.S. Navy claiming that it is leading to increased talk of war, and also nervous Latin American countries are worried about possible increased U.S. intervention.			William Fox buys a controlling interest in 250 theaters in the west of the United States, capable of seating 350,000, and valued at $100 million.	Jan. 24
Florence E. S. Knapp resigns as Dean of the College of Home Economics at Syracuse University, as allegations over corruption scandal mounts.	General John A. Lejeune flies over the U.S. Marines in Nicaragua praising their high morale and once again claiming victory for the U.S. intervention in Nicaragua.	It is also revealed that bankers who rejected stock held by J. Ogden Armour in Universal Oil Products Company, and returned it to his widow, would have been able to sell the stock for $30 million....Gales are experienced in New York, with water driven over the sea wall.		It is announced that the largest taxed estate in New York State is that of Anna M. Harkness, widow of Stephen V. Harkness, one of the original partners of John D. Rockefeller, who left assets worth $107.052,494. Harkness added $8,712,453 to the estate following the death of her husband in 1926, and had given $31 million in gifts over six years.	Jan. 25
As criticism of presidential hopeful Al Smith being a Roman Catholic mounts, it emerges that Herbert Hoover, although a Quaker, was married to his Episcopalian wife in 1899 at Monterey, California, by a Roman Catholic priest, Reverend Raymon Maria Mestries.		The North Atlantic seaboard of the United States is battered by a massive gale.	Plans are unveiled in London, England, to establish a new world record for the flying of seaplanes. The airplane, known as the *Supermarine Napier S-5* monoplane will be similar in design to that which won the Schneider Cup in Venice in 1927.	The Kresge Foundation, established by Sebastian B. Kresge, announces that it will build a massive orphanage at the cost of $725,000.	Jan. 26
William T. Cosgrave, president of the Executive Council of the Irish Free State, in Philadelphia, Pennsylvania, honors the Liberty Bell hailing the city as the birthplace of Liberty.			The first landing by a dirigible, a helium-filled airship, on the landing deck of an aircraft carrier, is made on the *Los Angeles* near Saratoga, off the Atlantic Coast.	J Alfred Spender, former editor of the *Westminster Gazette*, as the senior Walter Hines Page Fellow in Journalism of the English-Speaking Union, continues his attack on the commercial press saying that they are destroying journalism....The Louvre art gallery in Paris announces that it has acquired one of the few pieces of decoration from the Parthenon in Athens, Greece, which was not taken by Lord Elgin to the British Museum to form the Elgin Marbles.	Jan. 27

F	G	H	I	J
Includes campaigns, elections, federal-state relations, civil rights and liberties, crime, the judiciary, education, healthcare, poverty, urban affairs, and population.	Includes formation and debate of U.S. foreign and defense policies, veterans affairs, and defense spending. (Relations with specific foreign countries are usually found under the region concerned.)	Includes business, labor, agriculture, taxation, transportation, consumer affairs, monetary and fiscal policy, natural resources, pollution and industrial accidents.	Includes worldwide scientific, medical and technological developments, natural phenomena, U.S. weather and natural disasters.	Includes the arts, religion, scholarship, communications media, sports, entertainment, fashions, fads, and social life.

	World Affairs	Europe	Africa & The Middle East	The Americas	Asia & The Pacific
Jan. 28		Edvard Bull becomes Minister of Foreign Affairs for Norway, replacing Ivar Lykke; Fredrik Monsen becomes Minister of Defense, replacing Ingolf E. Christensen; Christopher Hornsrud becomes Minister of Finance, replacing Fredrik Ludvig Konow; and Cornelius Holmboe becomes Minister of Justice, replacing Knud Iversen Øyen.		Latin American states at the Sixth Pan-American Conference at Havana, Cuba, rejects the urging of Chairman Charles Evans Hughes, and upholds the right of American nations to have revolutions.	The Chinese New Year begins with the end of the Year of the Rabbit and the start of the Year of the Dragon.
Jan. 29	French writer and journalist Jules Sauerwein writes of his gloom over the failure of world disarmament after World War I.	Rumors spread around the Soviet Union that there was an attempted military revolt in favor of Leon Trotsky after there are reports of Moscow being shelled and General Tuchatschowski, an opponent of Josef Stalin, heading toward zones of fighting near the Baltic States.... Lithuania and Germany sign a treaty providing for arbitration over the future of Klaipeda (Memel).		Charles Lindbergh flies from Bogota, Colombia, over the Andes into Venezuela in an 11-hour flight through wind and fog, for Caracas, the capital of Venezuela....Captain Dieudonne Costes and Lieutenant-Commander Joseph Le Brix arrive to a massive welcome at Mexico City.	
Jan. 30	The League of Nations announces the appointment of a Spanish member to the Preparatory Commission of the Economic Conference signifying that Spain might rejoin the League.	Field Marshal Douglas Haig, commander-in-chief of British Forces on the Western Front in World War I, dies, aged 66....Gustav Stresemann, the former German chancellor, reaffirms in a speech in the Reichstag that the evacuation of the Rhineland would be a local consequence of the Locarno Treaty.		The railway train on which William T. Cosgrave, president of the Executive Council of the Irish Free State, is traveling to Ottawa, Canada, is accidentally derailed 23 miles from the city....Charles Lindbergh is given a hero's reception in Caracas, Venezuela.	
Jan. 31		The Liquidation Commission, which had succeeded the Inter-Allied Commission in Austria is withdrawn....It is revealed that more than 10,000 French citizens had left the Rhineland....The envoys of Poland leave the Soviet Union suddenly after not having resolved problems over trade negotiations.	The governments of Persia and the Soviet Union ratify treaties on neutrality, fisheries and customs agreements of October 1, 1927.		
Feb. 1		Austrian National Socialists protest against a stage performance by African-American singer Josephine Baker....James McNeill becomes Governor-General of the Irish Free State, the last to use that title....The German newspaper *Das Deutsche Tageblatt* leaks French war plans in the event of a Franco-Italian war.	The British Egyptologist Howard Carter reveals that he has found Canopic jars holding the viscera of the Pharaoh Tut-ankh-amen as he comes toward the end of his searches in the tomb of the Egyptian king from the XVIIIth dynasty.	Héctor F. López ends his term as Governor of Guerrero Province, Mexico....Charles Lindbergh attends the races in San Juan, Puerto Rico.	
Feb. 2		French foreign minister, Aristide Briand asks the German government to make some proposals for the settlement of the Rhineland issue.	A locust plague hits Wady Musa, near Petra.	Charles Lindbergh, speaking in San Juan, Puerto Rico, raises the idea of the West Indies being a stepping stone for air travel in the Americas....*The Annals of Niagara*, by William Kirby, a record of Canadian pioneer history and achievement is published in New York by The Macmillan Company.	The Central Executive Committee of the Kuomintang meets in Nanking, excluding the Communist members from the Fourth Plenary Session, which takes place on the following day.
Feb. 3	French foreign minister Aristide Briand states that he envisages the United States joining with Europe in a fiscal scheme to reduce world debt.	The French government starts a crack-down on gigolos preying on vulnerable single women in Paris.... The Greek government of Prime Minister Alexandros Zaimis resigns after a cabinet crisis.	Reports reach London that English explorers Thomas Glover and his wife, who had gone to Central Africa to make films, were both killed in French West Africa.	In fighting at Guadalajara, Mexico, a Roman Catholic priest, Crescencio Esparza, and 45 rebels are killed, following a battle between 600 armed rebels led by Esparza and Luis Guizar Morfin.	The 4th Plenary Session of the Kuomintang Party is held at Nanking with a view to reorganizing the Nationalist administration. It meets for a week and during that time forms a Government Council and a Military Council, both with small standing committees....Sir John Simon and other members of the Indian Statutory Commission arrive in Bombay where all business closed as a protest. Rioting also breaks out in Madras.
Feb. 4		The notorious German multiple murderer and robber, Johannes Heln, is taken prisoner by a lone farmer in Bavaria after terrorizing many people in the district for weeks.	Gbagidi IX Nyumoan, Ruler of Savalu, in Benin, French West Africa, dies, and is succeeded by Gbagidi X Bahinon.		Large protests take place in Madras, India against the Indian Statutory Commission of Sir John Simon, but plans to organize a widespread closing of shops fails as the British send many more soldiers into the city.

A	B	C	D	E
Includes developments that affect more than one world region, international organizations and important meetings of world leaders.	Includes all domestic and regional developments in Europe, including the Soviet Union.	Includes all domestic and regional developments in Africa and the Middle East.	Includes all domestic and regional developments in Latin America, the Caribbean, and Canada.	Includes all domestic and regional developments in Asian and Pacific nations (and colonies).

U.S. Politics & Social Issues	U.S. Foreign Policy & Affairs, Defense	U.S. Economy & Environment	Science, Technology & Nature	Culture, Leisure & Lifestyle	
Supporters of Irish Republican Eamon de Valera argue with William Cosgrave in Chicago.... The admission of guilt by William Edward Hickman of the murder of Marian Parker is declared to be able to be used in evidence in Hickman's trial in Los Angeles despite the defendant's repudiation of the confession.		Storms lash New York City and many places along the North Atlantic seaboard, with the steeple of Queens Church toppling to the ground.	*The Neurotic Personality*, by R. G. Gordon, is published in New York by Harcourt, Brace & Co, describing new diagnoses and treatments for psycho-neuroses.	Artist Hans Stengel commits suicide in Greenwich Village, aged 34.... The heirs of French writer Emile Zola demand that his letters are published including those sent to the De Goncourt Brothers which are believed to be defamatory to some living Frenchmen.	Jan. 28
Supporters of Republican presidential candidate Herbert Hoover claim that they have much support in New York for Hoover's bid for the presidency.			A test radio beacon is used to try to help aviators taking mail from one city to another.	A new shrine to St. John is unveiled at the Cathedral of St. John the Divine in New York.	Jan. 29
Robbers in Chicago steal $40,000 from a bank vault, $40,000 in diamonds from a jewelry shop, and $17,000 in jewelry from two private homes, highlighting the increasing problems over crime in the city.	The U.S. submarine *S-3* is found off the coast of Florida after losing contact with land for two days.... The U.S. Navy draws up plans for dirigibles to carry airplanes.	The U.S. government starts an investigation into the sale of bonds to U.S. investors by the Soviet Union.	Johannes Andreas Grib Fibiger, Danish scientist and recipient of the Nobel Prize in Medicine or Physiology in 1926, dies, aged 60.	The Gobelin tapestries in Berlin put together for the Hohenzollern family, the Prussian royal family and later the German Imperial family, go on show to the public in Berlin after being repaired in Vienna.	Jan. 30
Frank O. Lowden, former governor of Illinois, enters the presidential primary for the Republican Party.		The U.S. Senate passes the Jones bill by 53 to 31 and as a result ends the plans by the U.S. government to sell off its trade fleet.	The Collier Trophy for 1927, awarded by the National Aeronautic Association, is given to Charles L. Lawrance of the Wright Aeronautical Corporation for his work on building airplane engines.	Scotch Tape is first marketed by the 3-M Company....Hugh Jennings, the famous baseball player, dies in Scranton, Pennsylvania....The London *Daily News* absorbs the *Westminster Gazette*.	Jan. 31
W Barton French, aged 35, son of the late Seth Barton French, the New York banker, commits suicide at Santa Fe, New Mexico....Al Smith as governor of New York sends the case of Florence E. S. Knapp, Dean of the College of Home Economics at Syracuse University, to the prosecutors.		The likelihood of a Senate investigation into the recent coal strike increases, as attention focuses on the working conditions of miners in Ohio, West Virginia and Pennsylvania.	Dr. Herbert Evans in the United States discovers Vitamin F.	The South African cricket team wins the fourth test match by four wickets....American buyers purchase two Dürer paintings, one of which is a self-portrait and is reported to have changed hands for 1 million marks.	Feb. 1
Presidential hopeful Al Smith states that he will not interfere in the rights of states to decide to retain Prohibition.	U.S. Marines in Nicaragua give accounts of their capture of El Chipote, the jungle headquarters of General Augusto Sandino, which they captured a week earlier.	New York bank rates are increase to 4 percent, surprising stock brokers and investors at the New York Stock Exchange.		The Architectural League of New York opens its 43rd annual exhibition at the Fine Arts Building, New York City....Elizabeth Corbett's *Walt*, a new biography of poet Walt Whitman, is published in New York by Frederick A. Stokes Company.	Feb. 2
The U.S. Senate orders the arrest of Colonel Robert W. Stewart, Chairman of the Board of Directors of the Standard Oil Company of Indiana, after he refuses, for a second time, to answer questions put by the Senate Committee on Public Lands and Surveys.	At the Sixth Pan-American Conference in Havana, Cuba, the U.S. and Mexican governments clash with the latter arguing that there should be no restrictions placed on governments in the Americas censoring the press.	Major fire at Fall River, Massachusetts, leads to damage amounting to millions of dollars.	Mechanical tests are made on the plane that Antarctic explorer Richard Byrd will be taking with him on his next Polar expedition. These ensure that the plane can cope with low temperatures....The telecommunications company Marconi predicts that radio telephony across the Atlantic will become more common and prices charged will soon fall.		Feb. 3
Calvin Coolidge gives a speech at the dedication of the new National Press Club in Washington, DC.... Coolidge criticizes the trends in American journalism which see the press not declaring any conflicts of interest, or whether they support foreign causes.	Latin American countries at the Sixth Pan-American Conference in Havana, Cuba, are highly critical of the U.S. attitude to its right to intervene in Central America and the Caribbean.	Prominent businessman Edward C. Delafield, President of the Bank of America, after divorcing his wife in Reno, Nevada, in November, marries Clelia C: Benjamin of New York.	Hendrik Antoon Lorentz, Dutch physicist, dies, aged 74.	British bibliophile Edmund Dring, in the *Manchester Guardian* newspaper, raises his theory on the identity of "W H" called the "onlie begetter" in one of British playwright William Shakespeare's sonnets.	Feb. 4

F	G	H	I	J
Includes campaigns, elections, federal-state relations, civil rights and liberties, crime, the judiciary, education, healthcare, poverty, urban affairs, and population.	*Includes formation and debate of U.S. foreign and defense policies, veterans affairs, and defense spending. (Relations with specific foreign countries are usually found under the region concerned.)*	*Includes business, labor, agriculture, taxation, transportation, consumer affairs, monetary and fiscal policy, natural resources, pollution and industrial accidents.*	*Includes worldwide scientific, medical and technological developments, natural phenomena, U.S. weather and natural disasters.*	*Includes the arts, religion, scholarship, communications media, sports, entertainment, fashions, fads, and social life.*

	World Affairs	Europe	Africa & The Middle East	The Americas	Asia & The Pacific
Feb. 5		Newspapers in the Soviet Union publish information on the planned anti-war treaty of U.S. Secretary of State Frank B. Kellogg, although they do not mention any ban on submarines....French authorities plan to allow French Marshals to be buried in the Invalides in Paris.	A full report published in Cairo by British Egyptologist Howard Carter reveals that there are 18 boats in the tomb of the XVIIIth dynasty boy Pharaoh Tut-ankh-amen.	Charles Lindbergh flies over the Columbus Lighthouse at Santo Domingo, Dominican Republic and praises the memorial to the Genoa-born sailor and navigator who landed at Santo Domingo in 1492.	
Feb. 6	The Committee of Jurists of the League of Nations is charged with the duty of preparing for a conference on the Codification of International Law, meets in Geneva until February 15....The Permanent Court of International Justice in the Hague holds its 13th (extraordinary) session.		The German government opposes the move of the seat of the League of Nations from Geneva, Switzerland, to Vienna, Austria.	The Mexican government jails 35 people for attending mass in private houses, contrary to a law on the exercise of religion in the country.... Charles Lindbergh flies from Santo Domingo, Dominican Republic, to Port au Prince, Haiti, flying over the Citadel of La Ferriere of King Henri Christophe, in the north of Haiti.... The Haitian postal authorities issue a postage stamp commemorating the local coffee industry.	Some 50,000 people flee as the Nanking government prepares to attack Peking....Meetings are held in China to establish a Customs Accord for the port of Shanghai.
Feb. 7	The Afghan King Amanullah announces that he will visit Germany to study German industrial development.		King George V, in his official speech following the state opening of the British Parliament, mentions the draft of the new arbitration treaty between Britain and the United States.	Fighting in Nicaragua causes thousands to flee with rebels under General Augusto Sandino managing to capture the hacienda of the President of the House of Deputies.	Leaders of Indian political parties reject the suggestions by Sir John Simon that the Indian Statutory Commission should hold joint sittings with representatives of the Indian legislatures.
Feb. 8		The full details of the U.S.–French arbitration treaty are published.... Cabinet crisis in Germany leads for political instability while leaders in Alsace raise the issue of self-rule.		Charles Lindbergh arrives in Havana, Cuba, where he is greeted by 100,000 Cubans, ending his travels through Central America, Colombia, Venezuela and the Caribbean.... The Mexican government reports that it has defeated the rebels at Guadalajara.	Tukoji Rao Holkar, the former Maharajah of Indore, in India, manages to get support from Hindus in his state to his proposed marriage to Nancy Ann Miller of Seattle, Washington, after Miller reveals that she has converted to Hinduism at Poona.
Feb. 9	Dr. Nicholas Murray Butler, President of Columbia University, and the Carnegie Institute Endowment for International Peace suggests a reduction in naval strength would contribute heavily to world peace.	The Italian government of Benito Mussolini announces that it will reopen the San Remo Casino which will provide a venue in Italy for gamblers who, prior to this, had to either bet illegally or go to Monte Carlo.		As Cuban people flock to see Charles Lindbergh, he works on his plane and turns down invitations to various events to spend some time with the U.S. Ambassador Noble B. Judah.	The Chinese Nationalist government in Nanking reaffirms its anti-Communist stance with the Central Executive Committee of the Kuomintang, the Chinese Nationalist Party, urging for what will become the Northern Expedition, and shows continued support for Chiang Kai-shek.
Feb. 10		The Polish Government signs a Concordat in Rome with the Vatican....William T. Cosgrave, president of the Executive Council of the Irish Free State arrives back in Southampton after his time in North America....The Romanian foreign minister Nicholas Titulescu raises the prospect of his government seeking a loan from Western Europe.	The Egyptian government announces that it will launch a campaign against the locusts on the Sudan-Egyptian frontier in an effort to save much of their corn crop.	A mine explosion and fire in gold mine at Timmins, Ontario, Canada, results in 47 miners being trapped in mine shafts. 11 men die in this accident....At a third ceremony in Havana, Cuba, Charles Lindbergh is cheered by 50,000 people.	
Feb. 11		The Soviet government complains over the payout of $984,000 to Serge Ughet, financial attaché to the Russian Provisional Government of Alexander Kerensky, over munitions destroyed in the explosion at Black Tom, New Jersey in 1916. Ughet had remained in the United States after the second Russian Revolution of 1917 and is declared to be the custodian of all Russian property in the United States.	A tablet dated to 1470 B.C.E. is found on the banks of the Lake of Galilee between the towns of Tiberias and Capernaum. Dating from the period of Tothmes III, it states that the Pharaoh had repelled the Mittani.	Herman Bernard Cornelis Schotborgh is appointed administrator of the Dutch possession of Bonaire, Netherlands Antilles, taking over from William Rufus Plantz who stood down four days earlier.	

A	B	C	D	E
Includes developments that affect more than one world region, international organizations and important meetings of world leaders.	Includes all domestic and regional developments in Europe, including the Soviet Union.	Includes all domestic and regional developments in Africa and the Middle East.	Includes all domestic and regional developments in Latin America, the Caribbean, and Canada.	Includes all domestic and regional developments in Asian and Pacific nations (and colonies).

U.S. Politics & Social Issues	U.S. Foreign Policy & Affairs, Defense	U.S. Economy & Environment	Science, Technology & Nature	Culture, Leisure & Lifestyle	
Construction workers in Kansas City work proclaim that they will work harder to ensure that the city is ready to receive the Republican National Convention in June.	Following earlier criticism by Saloman de la Sekva, the New York representative of the Nicaraguan Federation of Labour, on the lack of U.S. investment in Nicaragua, it is revealed that "Wall Street" has invested $185,000 of the total $12 million invested in the country.	10 men are recovered from an ice floe in Lake Erie, after having been adrift for a day....Servants are involved in picketing Park Avenue Apartments in a strike by members of the Building Service Employees International Union.			Feb. 5
Republicans in the New York state legislature continue to attack the programs of presidential hopeful Al Smith reducing the amount which can be spent on parks.	The U.S. government presses for the Monroe Treaty to be formally recognized.	Federal authorities close three Miami banks following the collapse of the Dade County Security Company.		The woman purporting to be Anastasia, the only surviving daughter of Tsar Nicholas II of Russia, arrives in the United States on the *Berengaria* (Cunard line) to pursue her claims. Known at the time as Anastasia Tchaikovsky, she later becomes dubbed the "Anna Anderson" claimant because of a name she uses to evade some persistent press reporters.	Feb. 6
Suggestions are made in the press that New York Governor and presidential hopeful Al Smith should not attend the Democratic National Convention in Houston, Texas.	The United States signs an arbitration treaty with France.		Australian aviator H.J.L. "Bert" Hinkler leaves Croydon Airport, London in his Avro Avian, for the first solo flight to Australia, arriving in Rome, Italy, where he lands by accident at a military airfield and is immediately arrested....The National Institute of Social Scientists re-elect William C. Redfield as their president.	Choir singer Grace Moore from Jellicoe, Tennessee, is hailed after her opera debut in New York.... The Church of England Houses of Bishops and Clergy in London, approve the revised Church of England prayer book.	Feb. 7
The U.S. Senate passes the Robinson Bill authorizing a medal to commemorate the achievements of Charles Lindbergh.	The British government asks the U.S. Marines to help protect the lives and property of British subjects in Nicaragua.	Francis F. Leman, president of the Staten Island Civic League raises the idea of an airport on Staten Island.	Aviator Bert Hinkler leaves Rome for Malta....The first transatlantic television image is received at Hartsdale, New York....Scottish inventor J. Blaird demonstrates the use of color in television.	The South Africa cricket team wins the final test match by eight wickets....The German press is heavily critical of a British film on the life and execution of British nurse Edith Cavell in 1915 after the Germans had found her guilty of spying in World War I.	Feb. 8
Southern Methodists pass a resolution against New York governor and presidential hopeful Al Smith.... Frank L. Smith, who was denied his seat in the Senate over not declaring donations from a utility company, resigns from his seat and is immediately reappointed by Governor Lea Small of Illinois.... Murderer Edward Hickman is sentenced to death for the murder of Marian Parker, a 12-year-old girl he kidnapped on December 15, 1927.	Nicaraguan rebel leader General Augusto Sandino promises that "blood will flow" if his supporters clash with U.S. Marines as the rebels sweep south toward the location of many U.S. coffee plantations.		Bert Hinkler continues his journey from Malta to the North African Coast, and then to Palestine, and to Basra, arriving there on February 12.	During a showing of the film *The World War* in Berlin, Germany, some viewers hiss when the Kaiser appears on the screen.	Feb. 9
Senator Frank B. Willis of Ohio offers himself for the Republican nomination for the U.S. presidential election, promising to maintain Prohibition.	U.S. Marines claim that they are closing in on Nicaraguan rebel leader General Augusto Sandino.	U.S. Marines using airplanes fail to locate General Augusto Sandino in Nicaragua.	The radio-telephone network connecting Berlin, Germany, to New York and Washington was tested with trans-Atlantic discussions held with telephone services provided by the American Telephone and Telegraph Company.	Harry Relph, the British comedian known as Little Tich, dies, aged 59.	Feb. 10
	Debates continue in Washington, DC, about whether or not the U.S. government should massively increase the size of its navy.	American oil companies which have invested in France raise concerns about the changes of laws there, and also the new higher French tariffs....Calvin Coolidge hosts another breakfast meeting to discuss flood controls in the southern states.	Celebrations are held at Fort Myers, Florida, where inventor Thomas Alva Edison celebrates his 81st birthday....French electrical engineers Georges Claude and Paul Boucherot, at a meeting of the French Engineering Society at the Sorbonne, Paris, raise the idea of using Arctic currents to cool the tropical zone....French aviators Captain Dieudonne Costes and navigator Lieutenant-Commander Joseph Le Brix get a hero's welcome in New York after their recent flight across the Atlantic.	The Olympic Winter Games open at St. Moritz, Switzerland.... The Moscow Opera ask Feodor Chaliapin, the basso of the Metropolitan Opera Company, New York, to return to give more performances in the Soviet Union.... Professor Allan Nevins writes a new biography of 19th-century U.S. explorer and presidential candidate John C. Frémont.	Feb. 11

F	G	H	I	J
Includes campaigns, elections, federal-state relations, civil rights and liberties, crime, the judiciary, education, healthcare, poverty, urban affairs, and population.	*Includes formation and debate of U.S. foreign and defense policies, veterans affairs, and defense spending. (Relations with specific foreign countries are usually found under the region concerned.)*	*Includes business, labor, agriculture, taxation, transportation, consumer affairs, monetary and fiscal policy, natural resources, pollution and industrial accidents.*	*Includes worldwide scientific, medical and technological developments, natural phenomena, U.S. weather and natural disasters.*	*Includes the arts, religion, scholarship, communications media, sports, entertainment, fashions, fads, and social life.*

	World Affairs	Europe	Africa & The Middle East	The Americas	Asia & The Pacific
Feb. 12		A heavy hail-storm in England kills 11 people....13 members of a British exploration party in northern England die in an explosion in a wrecked mine they are exploring....Pope Pius XI celebrates the sixth anniversary of his coronation in the Sistine Chapel in the presence of King Gustavus V of Sweden and his wife Queen Victoria, formerly Princess Victoria of Baden.	Archaeologists searching for remains of the Sumerian city of Ur in Iraq announce that they have found crowns, rings, vases and other treasures. Their expedition is jointly run by the University of Pennsylvania and the British Museum.	Charles Lindbergh leaves Havana to fly back to the United States, landing at St. Louis.	The Chinese Communists start taking power in Canton and parts of southern China with the repudiation of all the pre-1923 debt incurred by the city of Canton, amounting to $42.5 million.
Feb. 13		King George V of Britain names the Prince of Wales as the Master of the Merchant Navy.	The construction of a railway line from mineral-rich Katanga province in the Belgian Congo is completed through Rhodesia to the port of Beira in Portuguese East Africa. It will provide easy access for natural resources from the Belgian Congo to the sea.		Agdanbuugiyn Amar becomes Chairman of the Council of People's Commissars taking over from Balingiyn Tserendorj Beyse.
Feb. 14		Bernhard Adelung becomes State President of Hesse, Germany, replacing Karl Ulrich.			The Nationalist Nanking government draws up plans to send 300,000 troops against the Warlord government based in Peking.
Feb. 15		British politician the Earl of Oxford and Asquith (formerly Herbert H. Asquith), British prime minister from 1908 to 1916, dies at Abingdon, England, aged 75....The first Norwegian Socialist government collapses and Johan Ludwig Mowinckel becomes Prime Minister of Norway, taking over from Christopher Hornsrud.	Shaykh Taj ad-Din al-Hasani becomes acting Head of State of Syria, taking over from Damad-i Shahriyari Ahmad Nami Bay.	Delegates to the Sixth Pan-American Conference in Havana, Cuba, marked the thirtieth anniversary of the sinking of the USS Maine in Havana harbor, the event that started the Spanish-American War of 1898.	The Nanking government promulgates a new trade-mark law requiring that all trademarks registered in Peking have to be re-examined by October 18, 1928.
Feb. 16		British judges signal that they will accept legal separation but Justice Hill states that he prefers divorce.... Delays in the Seville Show in Spain are announced.	A proclamation of the end of the "State of Siege" in Damascus, Syria.	Luis C. Caviglia becomes Chairman of the National Council of Administration in Uruguay, replacing veteran politician José Batlle y Ordóñez....Uruguay and Brazil sign two conventions in Montevideo, Uruguay's capital, regarding the use of funds from the boundary settlement and the establishment of a joint labor institute.	A treaty of friendship is signed between Afghanistan and Latvia. It will be ratified on July 6.
Feb. 17		General Theodorus Pangalos, former dictator of Greece, is brought to Athens, the Greek capital, and put on trial for treason....The German government rents 55 rooms in the Prince Albrecht Palace for the Afghan King to use during his stay in the German capital.	In Transjordan, 120 tribesmen are killed in a raid by rebel Wahhabi supporters of Sheikh Feisalk Ed Dowish.	Socrates Sandino, brother of Nicaraguan rebel leader General Augusto Sandino, makes a speech attacking imperialism at a gathering of the All-America Anti-Imperialism League in New York.	A treaty of friendship signed between Afghanistan and Switzerland, ratified on April 20....The Czechoslovak government refuses to join the embargo on the sale of weapons to China unless it is binding on all states.
Feb. 18		Baron Zubkov and Princess Victoria, sister of the ex-Kaiser of Germany, outline their plans to fly to the United States....Italian leader Benito Mussolini decides to send police to the Mediterranean island of Sardinia to end banditry on the island.		At the Sixth Pan-American Conference in Havana, Chairman Charles Evans Hughes talks down the likelihood of U.S. intervention.	The Indian Assembly at Delhi passes a motion of no confidence in the Indian Statutory Commission.
Feb. 19		The German government announces that it will intervene to stop a strike in the iron and steel industry.... The British government appoints Sir W. G. Tyrrell to become British Ambassador to Paris taking over from Lord Crewe.	French companies outline a plan to build a railway across the Sahara and request a French government grant of 12 million francs to survey the route and draw up a detailed proposal.		Ripudaman Singh ends his reign as the Maharaja of Nabha, India.

A	B	C	D	E
Includes developments that affect more than one world region, international organizations and important meetings of world leaders.	Includes all domestic and regional developments in Europe, including the Soviet Union.	Includes all domestic and regional developments in Africa and the Middle East.	Includes all domestic and regional developments in Latin America, the Caribbean, and Canada.	Includes all domestic and regional developments in Asian and Pacific nations (and colonies).

U.S. Politics & Social Issues	U.S. Foreign Policy & Affairs, Defense	U.S. Economy & Environment	Science, Technology & Nature	Culture, Leisure & Lifestyle	
Herbert Hoover formally announces that he will offer himself as a candidate for the U.S. presidency by permitting his name to be entered for the Republican Party primary in Ohio. He states that he supports the policies of Calvin Coolidge and will be "glad to serve the American people."...The Ku Klux Klan announces that they will establish a National Headquarters near the St. Matthew's Roman Catholic Church in Washington, DC.	U.S. Marines kill five rebel supporters of General Augusto Sandino in Nicaragua.		Lady Heath leaves Cape Town, South Africa, in an Avro Avian III, in an attempt to make the first solo flight by a woman from South Africa to England.	Literary critic and poet Maurice Rostand, son of Edmond Rostand, French playwright, declines to duel with Pierre Weber a young dramatist who challenged him after Rostand criticized Weber's work.... French artist Maurice Vlaminck slashes several paintings he finds in Paris which have his name on them but which he claims were not painted by him.	Feb. 12
U.S. Senator Reed Owen Smoot eulogizes former U.S. President Abraham Lincoln in the Senate.	U.S. Secretary for the Navy Curtis Wilbur continues to argue for plans to massively enlarge the U.S. Navy....The U.S. Naval Reserve announces that it has received 2,500 applications for enrolments.	A fire which followed the derailment of 17 freight cars at Balloch, New Hampshire, results in the death of four people and injuries sustained by many more.			Feb. 13
Senator Charles D. Hilles of the Republican National Convention urges that Calvin Coolidge seek another term as president.	Calvin Coolidge urges Congress to support the enlargement of the navy saying that the U.S. Navy desperately needs more cruisers.	French tariffs on imports are introduced and found to have little effect on U.S.-French trade.	Richard Byrd announces that he will take 100 dogs with him on his trip to the South Pole....Ernesto Schiaparelli, Italian archaeologist and Egyptologist, dies aged 71.	The explorer Frank Mitchell Hedges loses his libel suit brought after the British *Daily Express* newspaper claimed that a recent road hold-up on Hedges was planned to raise his profile, and that his stories of his time in Central America were exaggerated.	Feb. 14
The U.S. Senate votes by 46 to 31 for a power enquiry launched by the Board of Trade.	U.S. Marines start a major operation to try to track down and either capture or kill Nicaraguan rebel leader General Augusto Sandino.	Merger plans between various banks are mooted on Wall Street.... A plane with 19 on board crashes into a bay near Miami, Florida, with all surviving although one is injured by the propeller.	The newly built Short flying boat, known as the *S8 Calcutta*, is flown for the first time by John Lankester Parker, at Rochester, Kent, England.		Feb. 15
Lou Hoover, wife of Herbert Hoover, starts campaigning on behalf of her husband....The house of Judge John Sbarbaro in Chicago is wrecked in a bombing connected with Chicago organized crime networks.	At the Sixth Pan-American Conference in Havana, Cuba, Chairman Charles Evans Hughes pledges the United States to non-aggression in the Americas.		Radiophone contact between Britain and the United States continues with 1500 applauding speakers in London....The McGill Pathological Hospital in Montreal, Quebec, Canada, announces that it has discovered nerves in human cancers.	Prince Paul Dmitri Romanoff Ilyinski is christened in London, England. He is the son of Princess Anna Ilyinski, formerly Audrey Emery, daughter of John Emery, an American citizen.... Eddie Foy, American vaudevillian, dies, aged 71.	Feb. 16
Leading businessman with coal interests, Robert Livingston Ireland, is found murdered in a New York Hotel.	The U.S. postal authorities move to stop parcel post with Cuba as the Cuban government notes that the parcel post convention between the two countries will expire on March 1.	Calvin Coolidge announces that he believes that his tax cuts are in danger of being thwarted by Congress....Stocks fall in price at the New York Stock Exchange....The U.S. liner *Leviathan* runs ashore on the sandbank at the entrance to Southampton Water but is refloated after two hours.	Australian aviator Bert Hinkler leaves Calcutta, India, for Rangoon, Burma, in his bid to be the fist man to fly solo from London to Australia.	Archaeologist Professor Alfredo Trombetti of the University of Bologna announces that he has managed to decipher a Etruscan artifact....French archaeologist M. Pelliot makes a speech at the French Academy of Inscriptions stating that the Chinese used xylographic printing long before Germany.	Feb. 17
Herbert Hoover prepares for the battle for the Republican nomination fighting the Ohio primaries against Frank O. Lowden, former governor of Illinois and James Eli Watson of Indiana, and Charles Curtis.		The Ford Motor Company states that it has reached an output of 800 new cars every day.	Emmanuel de Martonne's *A Shorter Physical Geography* is published in an English-language edition in New York by Alfred A. Knopf.	A Gold Emblem is awarded by the National Education Association at a meeting in Boston to Evangeline Lindbergh, a longtime teacher and mother of the famous aviator....The Oxford University Press announces the publication of the *New English Dictionary*, which they had started in 1887.	Feb. 18
Mayor Walker of Greensboro, MD, promotes New York governor and presidential hopeful Al Smith in his state.			British automobile-racing driver, Malcolm (later Sir Malcolm) Campbell sets a new land speed record reaching 206 miles per hour at Daytona Beach, Florida.	The publication of the 1928 edition of the Club Members of New York, issued annually since 1915, shows that there are now 40,000 club members as against 400 in the 1915 edition.	Feb. 19

F	G	H	I	J
Includes campaigns, elections, federal-state relations, civil rights and liberties, crime, the judiciary, education, healthcare, poverty, urban affairs, and population.	*Includes formation and debate of U.S. foreign and defense policies, veterans affairs, and defense spending. (Relations with specific foreign countries are usually found under the region concerned.)*	*Includes business, labor, agriculture, taxation, transportation, consumer affairs, monetary and fiscal policy, natural resources, pollution and industrial accidents.*	*Includes worldwide scientific, medical and technological developments, natural phenomena, U.S. weather and natural disasters.*	*Includes the arts, religion, scholarship, communications media, sports, entertainment, fashions, fads, and social life.*

	World Affairs	Europe	Africa & The Middle East	The Americas	Asia & The Pacific
Feb. 20	The U.S. envoy Charles Evans Hughes blocks a resolution barring the intervention in the internal affairs of Latin American States. The Sixth Pan-American Conference, being held at Havana, Cuba, ends soon afterwards....The Arbitration and Security Committee of the League of Nations is held in Geneva meeting until March 7, drawing up general and bilateral arbitration and non-aggression treaties.	The British government announces that they favor money to be held collectively to fight war against aggressors....The 21st Earl of Erroll, High Commissioner for the Rhineland, dies, aged 51.	The Kingdom of Transjordan, essentially a buffer state between Palestine and Arabia, is given nominal autonomy by the British government, following the signing of a treaty which takes place in Jerusalem.		Parliamentary elections in Japan—the first held under universal suffrage—leads to a hung parliament with the Seiyukai Party gaining 218 seats, the Minsei Party with 217 seats, and 30 other seats being held by seven other parties and independents....The Nanking government in China announces that the personnel of the Salt Inspectorate would be restored to their positions.
Feb. 21		Air convention between Austria and Czechoslovakia, signed on February 15, 1927, is finally ratified....Benito Mussolini announces the incorporation of the fascist militia into the regular Italian army.		Esteban Baca Calderón becomes interim Governor of Nayarit Province, Mexico, replacing Francisco Ramírez Romano....The Bishop of Tamaulipas, José Armora, was arrested by the Mexican government....Nicaraguan rebels fire on a U.S. Marine scouting plane.	The seaplane carrier HMAS *Albatross* of the Royal Australian Navy is launched....Members of the Diplomatic Corps in Peking decide to urge their governments to ask the Great Powers to prohibit the export of arms and munitions to China in line with the Arms Embargo of 1919. The German minister declares that his government is immediately ready to accede to this demand.
Feb. 22		The King of Afghanistan arrives in Berlin to a warm welcome from the German government.		The liquor trade in the West Indies falls dramatically as the United States introduces new anti-Prohibition measures, confirming the prevailing view that much of the liquor exported to the West Indies is then smuggled into the United States.	
Feb. 23		The Austrian National Assembly debates the issue of the South Tyrol, held by Italy since World War I, but claimed by Austria....The League of Nations orders Hungary to stop the sale of machine guns....Alexander Subkov, the husband of Princess Victoria, the sister of the Ex-Kaiser of Germany, is injured in a brawl in Berlin.		The Cuban postal authorities offer to raise the limit on the value of goods posted between Cuba and the United States, which will benefit the Cuban cigar industry.	Pratap Singh is proclaimed the Maharaja of Nabha, India.
Feb. 24		The Norwegian and Soviet governments sign an industrial property convention....A diplomatic rift between Italy and Austria sees Italian leader Benito Mussolini recalling his envoy from Vienna....French and German delegates to the League of Nations argue over Hungarian weapons sales....The Italian cargo steamer *Alcantara* sinks in dense fog in the English Channel, after colliding with a Russian training vessel.		The State of Vera Cruz in Mexico reveals that it is heavily in debt to the tune of 4.5 million pesos.	Sir Neville Reginald Howse becomes minister of home affairs in Australia, taking over from Charles William Clanan Marr.
Feb. 25		The Soviet union announces that it is giving tools and seed to its grain farmers, as well as extending them credit, to increase the size of the harvest....The Italian leader Benito Mussolini requests direct talks with Austria to end mounting tension.		The Haitian and British governments sign a commercial agreement which comes into force on March 1....Affonso Alves de Camargo becomes governor of Paraná Province, Brazil, succeeding Caetano Munhoz da Rocha.	
Feb. 26	At a meeting of the Workers' International Executive, held at Zurich, Switzerland, among other speeches, Mr. Brockway of the British Independent Labour Party tells how the Soviet Union occupied Georgia.	The Italian government announces that it will oppose a planned Inquiry by the League of Nations into whether Italy and Hungary violated the Treaty of Trianon in sales of machine guns impounded at the start of the year.		U.S. aviators James Doolittle and Ed McMullen fly from Ilo, Peru, to La Paz, the capital of Bolivia, where they are greeted by the U.S. Chargé d'affaires and members of the Bolivian government and the local aviation school, as well as many others.	Negotiations held at the city of Dairen end with an agreement between representatives of the Peking and Nanking governments regarding the future administration of the Chinese postal services, by which the powers of the foreign director-general would be shared by Chinese officials.

A	B	C	D	E
Includes developments that affect more than one world region, international organizations and important meetings of world leaders.	Includes all domestic and regional developments in Europe, including the Soviet Union.	Includes all domestic and regional developments in Africa and the Middle East.	Includes all domestic and regional developments in Latin America, the Caribbean, and Canada.	Includes all domestic and regional developments in Asian and Pacific nations (and colonies).

U.S. Politics & Social Issues	U.S. Foreign Policy & Affairs, Defense	U.S. Economy & Environment	Science, Technology & Nature	Culture, Leisure & Lifestyle	
Missouri Senator James A. Reed starts his campaign for the Democratic Party nomination at a large rally in Dallas, Texas.	The Governor of New York at the suggestion of the Battlefields Advisory Council, authorizes the purchase of the site of the battles of Saratoga in September and October 1777, when the Americans under Horatio Gates and Benedict Arnold defeated the British under General John Burgoyne during the American War of Independence. The site was purchased for $90,000.	Teapot Dome oil scandal case ends with six men being found guilty of contempt of court.		American paleontologists and anthropologists claim that the tooth found in an ancient river bed in Nebraska, and believed to be that of an ancient ape, is actually that of a wild pig.	Feb. 20
Presidential hopeful Herbert Hoover is awarded the Medal of the American Institute of Mining and Metallurgical Engineers, which denies that there was any political motivation in the award....A third judge receives a letter containing the poisonous substance silver nitrate....Harry F. Sinclair and three others are convicted in a jury shadowing case.	The Naval Court of Inquiry into the loss of the U.S. submarine S-4 blames both the Coast Guard destroyer, Paulding, and also on the late Commander Roy K. Jones of the S-4.	Vacuum Oil pay a 100 percent stock dividend and their capital value of their stock increases to $360 million.		Basil M. Hastings, the British dramatist and critic, dies, aged 46.	Feb. 21
Dr. Murray Butler of Colombia University states that he believes that the Democrats could win the November elections....Governor Alvan T. Fuller of Massachusetts states that he believes that it will be a race between Herbert Hoover and Al Smith.			Australian aviator Bert Hinkler lands at Darwin in his Avro Avian after completing his record-breaking 15½ day solo flight from London—the first solo flight from England to Australia....Frank Lockhart is serious injured at Daytona Beach, Florida, when his car skids during his attempt to achieve a new land speed record.	Moves are made to rescind a New York State law which requires that cemeteries are given 24 hours notice of any burials. This rule is seen as discriminating against the burial practices of Orthodox Jews for whom a burial should take place within 24 hours of death.	Feb. 22
Presidential hopeful Herbert Hoover declares himself unequivocally in favor of the continuance of Prohibition which he calls the "great experiment."	The Naval Committee of the House of Representatives decides to authorize the construction of only 15 cruisers and one aircraft carrier, far less than many people thought was adequate to defend the United States if war broke out.		Nervousness of air travel is highlighted when the King of Afghanistan, in Berlin, declines an opportunity to fly while he is visiting the Tempelhof Flying Field.		Feb. 23
Calvin Coolidge gives in to the federal government paying most of the cost of flood controls for the southern states, but Herbert Hoover declares himself undecided on whether he feels that federal authorities should pay for this.	Calvin Coolidge states his dislike of the new Navy Bill which calls for the building of 15 cruisers and one aircraft carrier. Coolidge feels that this will mean that the navy cannot be expanded to suitable levels for the defense of the United States.		Charles Lindbergh announces in Detroit, MI, that he and Major Thomas Lanphier have tested a new type of motor which uses electromagnetism rather than fuel.	The New Gallery of New York exhibits the work of Archibald Motley in its first show to feature an African-American artist....J.D. Rockefeller, Jr., wins the Honor Medal from the New York Chapter of the American Institute of Architects.	Feb. 24
A train near Chicago is held up and two mail pouches containing $133,000 are stolen from it. This consisted of $80,000 sent by the Federal Reserve Bank in Chicago to the First National Bank of Harvey, and $53,000 being sent from the First National Bank of Chicago also to the First National Bank of Harvey.		A fire breaks out in Henry Miller's Theatre in New York, but is quickly extinguished with no injuries.	Bell Laboratories introduce a device which ends the "fluttering" on television images....Charles Jenkins Laboratories in Washington, DC becomes the first holder of a television license from the Federal Radio Commission....U.S. pilot Harry Brooks is lost at sea near Melbourne, Florida.	A three-day sale at the American Art Galleries of Chinese and Korean art objects from the collection of Gisaku Tomitta of Seoul, Korea, and from the Yamanaka collection of Boston netts $59,852 for 661 items....William E. Barton's Abraham Lincoln and Walt Whitman is published by Bobbs-Merrill Company in Indianapolis, Indiana.	Feb. 25
25 people are arrested in Chicago in connection with the massive train heist on the previous day. The Police announce that they have located $17,000 of the money.	The U.S. Navy sends the dirigible Los Angeles to the Panama Canal Zone.		The plane of U.S. aviator Harry Brooks is found near Melbourne, Florida, but the seas were too rough to allow it to be recovered.	Members of the Protestant Episcopal Church in the United States sign a petition to fight Roman Catholic influence which they term Romanism in the Episcopal Church....John Philip Sousa, bandmaster and composer, is awarded a medal by the Society of Arts and Sciences in Boston, Massachusetts.	Feb. 26

F	G	H	I	J
Includes campaigns, elections, federal-state relations, civil rights and liberties, crime, the judiciary, education, healthcare, poverty, urban affairs, and population.	Includes formation and debate of U.S. foreign and defense policies, veterans affairs, and defense spending. (Relations with specific foreign countries are usually found under the region concerned.)	Includes business, labor, agriculture, taxation, transportation, consumer affairs, monetary and fiscal policy, natural resources, pollution and industrial accidents.	Includes worldwide scientific, medical and technological developments, natural phenomena, U.S. weather and natural disasters.	Includes the arts, religion, scholarship, communications media, sports, entertainment, fashions, fads, and social life.

	World Affairs	Europe	Africa & The Middle East	The Americas	Asia & The Pacific
Feb. 27	U.S. Secretary of State Frank B. Kellogg resumes his correspondence with the French foreign minister, Aristide Briand about the proposed anti-war treaty.	Prince Lichnowsky, the German ambassador to Britain at the outbreak of World War I, dies, aged 67.	Italian soldiers manage to defeat Senussi rebels in Cyrenaica in bitter fighting in the Libyan desert. It leads to the Italians controlling two more strategic oases.	Adrien Juvanon becomes Governor of St. Pierre and Miquelon, taking over from the interim Governor Charles Nirpot.	12 senior Korean Communists representing the eight provinces of Japanese-occupied Korea, and the Koreans in Japan and Manchuria, meet on the outskirts of Seoul to form a new Korean Communist Party....To commemorate the ninth anniversary of Afghan independence, the postal authorities in Afghanistan issue a stamp showing the Tughra and the Crest of King Amanullah. A later stamp showing the same design is subsequently printed but not issued because the king was deposed.
Feb. 28	Argentina delegate on the League of Nations' Committee on Arbitration and Security protests against Article 21 of the Covenant of the League arguing that the Monroe Declaration is a unilateral declaration, not a regional understanding.	The British Chancellor of the Exchequer, Winston S. Churchill, announced a balanced budget even though he states that treasury receipts are £120 million less than expected....Captain Ernst Lombos, a Hungarian army officer who was designated by the Hungarian War Office to destroy its illegally held machine guns, is found walking in the streets of Budapest, deemed to be insane, and committed to a mental asylum.	The British government recognizes the Transjordania mandate as independent.	Roman Catholic Bishop Hayes visits San Juan, the capital of Puerto Rico.	
Feb. 29	The League of Nations in Geneva, Switzerland, approves the most recent Note on the anti-war treaty by U.S. Secretary of State Frank B. Kellogg.	German and Austrian governments sign a treaty in Vienna regarding mutual assistance to the unemployed. The treaty comes into force on the following day....Marshal Armando Diaz, the Italian commander who defeated the Austro-Hungarians in 1917, dies in Rome, aged 67....It is announces that the Portuguese general election will take place on March 25.			The Indian Budget is introduced with no changes in taxation to the existing system.
Mar. 1		Herman Adriaan van Karnebeek becomes Governor of Zuid-Holland, Netherlands, his predecessor, Emile Claude Baron Sweerts de Landas Wyborgh, having died on January 3.	The Egyptian government decides to reject a treaty with the British.... The South African government confirms the discovery of a new diamond field near Alexander Bay, at the mouth of the Orange River.	Joseph Oscar Auger becomes Mayor of Quebec, Canada, taking over from Télesphore Simard....The Mexican government announces that they have killed 68 rebels in renewed fighting in the State of Jalisco....French pilot Jean Mermoz takes off from Buenos Aires, Argentina, for Rio de Janeiro, Brazil, for the first part of the new airmail service between South America and France run by Aéropostale, the French company.	The Japanese government appeals to the Soviet Union to prohibit export of arms to China....The Chinese postal authorities issue a series of postage stamps showing Marshal Chang Tso-lin, "the Old Marshal"—these stamps are only available for postage in Chihli and Shantung provinces and inn Manchuria and Sinkiang....Henry L. Stimson arrives in Manila as governor-general of the Philippines.
Mar. 2		Benito Mussolini announces that he totally rejects the idea of democracy and will push through with new constitutional changes.	A large crowd of Europeans in Durban, Natal, South Africa, try to lynch an African who was involved in the desecration of a local cemetery.	The Mexican government announces that they hope to raise their oil production which was curtailed in recent troubles, and this would be able to pay off much of their debt.	The government of India denies that there are any particular constraints on U.S. movie producers distributing their films in India as many U.S. film companies believe that most Indians tend not to watch American movies.
Mar. 3		Benito Mussolini in the Italian Parliament criticizes the Austrian parliamentary debate on February 23, over South Tirol claiming that the issue is "purely cultural and an internal affair of Italy."	A Franco-Spanish agreement is signed in Paris regarding the application of the Tangier Statute of 1923 which increases French powers in the administering of Tangier.		
Mar. 4		The Austrian and German governments react angrily to Benito Mussolini's speech a day earlier....The former Crown Prince of Germany starts selling off many of his assets....British former prime minister Ramsay MacDonald denies that he had any part in the Zinoviev Letter.	Sarwat Pasha of Egypt presents a note explaining the reasons for rejecting the draft Anglo-Egyptian Treaty of Alliance, and resigns from office. The British state their objection to the Public Assemblies Bill before the Egyptian Parliament.... The British send a Gurkha battalion to Kuwait from India to defend the Sheikhdom against attacks by Wahhabi rebels.	Nicaraguan elections resume with the Liberals stating their platform.	A Japanese, a Chinese and a Mongolian, riding horses, reach the Japanese port of Shimonoseki after completing a 3,000 mile horse ride from Manchuli on the Mongolian-Siberian border which they left on January 3.

A	B	C	D	E
Includes developments that affect more than one world region, international organizations and important meetings of world leaders.	Includes all domestic and regional developments in Europe, including the Soviet Union.	Includes all domestic and regional developments in Africa and the Middle East.	Includes all domestic and regional developments in Latin America, the Caribbean, and Canada.	Includes all domestic and regional developments in Asian and Pacific nations (and colonies).

U.S. Politics & Social Issues	U.S. Foreign Policy & Affairs, Defense	U.S. Economy & Environment	Science, Technology & Nature	Culture, Leisure & Lifestyle	
The crime wave in Chicago is officially blamed on the inefficiency of the police in a report made to the National Crime Commission.	Three aviators from the new aircraft carrier *Lexington* were reported as missing near the Virginia-Maryland coast....At the battle of Em Bramadero in Nicaragua, the U.S. Marines succeed in making some advances but are forced to retreat when rebel leader General Augusto Sandino musters a large force to face them.		Bert Hinker flies from Darwin to Bundaberg after his first solo flight from London to Australia.	A memorial to the Spanish painter Francisco Goya is completed at the Monclea Park, Madrid, Spain's capital.	Feb. 27
Republican Assemblymen in New York try once again to sabotage the legislative program of presidential hopeful and New York Governor Al Smith.	The U.S. dirigible *Los Angeles* leaves the Panama Canal Zone to return United States bases in Cuba.			Smokey the Bear is created....The Dolly sisters, one married to the son of a Canadian tobacco magnate, win 30 million francs (about $1.25 million) at the Cannes Casino, the largest loss sustained by the casino since 1920.	Feb. 28
New York delegates to the Democratic National Convention are named.	Five U.S. Marines are killed and eight others were wounded in an ambush by Nicaraguan rebels loyal to General Augusto Sandino....The U.S. government again sends a Note to the French government agreeing with their plan to introduce a treaty to outlaw war.				Feb. 29
A major scandal in Washington, DC erupts with Will H. Hays, Chairman of the Republican National Committee in 1920, Postmaster General in the cabinet of President Warren Harding from 1921 until 1922, and after that President of the Motion Picture Producers and Distributors of America Inc, admits that Harry F. Sinclair gave $260,000 to the Republican Party.	Morgan J. O'Brien, a member of the U.S. delegation to the Sixth Pan-American Conference at Havana, Cuba, raises the idea of a canal across Nicaragua.		Frederick Hochstetter, head of the Hochstetter Research Laboratories of Pittsburgh, Pennsylvania, comes to New York to promote his fuel-less motor.	Denver-born musician Paul Whiteman and his orchestra record *Ol' Man River* for Victor Records....The Transcontinental Footrace begins in Los Angeles with 55 men running from there to New York in 81 days....Andrew Payne of Oklahoma wins the Bunyon Derby.	Mar. 1
Charles Dewey Hilles, the Republican National Committeeman for New York once again raises the suggestion of drafting Calvin Coolidge for the forthcoming U.S. presidential election.	In fighting in Nicaragua it is revealed that in recent battles with rebel supporters of General Augusto Sandino, many of the rebels used guns captured from previous attacks with U.S. Marines, and the five killed two days earlier were all shot with Thompson Automatic guns.	The *Chicago Daily News* announces that it will be building a new 25-storey headquarters at the cost of $8 million.	The U.S. government tells the German government that it might help meet some of the costs of Trans-Atlantic Zeppelin flights planned for later in 1928.	Lewis Melville's biography *William Makepeace Thackeray* is published in New York by Doubleday, Doran & Co.	Mar. 2
Democrat politician Thomas J. Walsh of Montana announces that he will enter the presidential race in Wisconsin and South Dakota.		General Motors, in a show of economic strength, paid $89,175,000 in dividends with one third of the total trading at the New York Stock Exchange being in General Motors' shares.	A new radio tube is used by the General Electric Company in Schenectady, New York, to transmit energy, and in this experiment, fry an egg and bake an apple.	Prince Joachim Albrecht of Prussia, the second cousin of the ex-Kaiser of Germany, cancels his plans to conduct a concert by the New York Symphony Orchestra....The first American edition of Hillaire Belloc's biography *Danton 1729-1794* is published in New York by G. P. Putnam's Sons.	Mar. 3
Calvin Coolidge begins the last year of his term as president....Harvey Parnell becomes Governor of Arkansas, taking over from John E. Martineau.	The U.S. government states is disapproval for the enlarging of the Panama Canal.		A home made aircraft crashed killing five in San Diego after avoiding crashing into another aircraft.	Sadi Kirchen, the lawyer who defended British nurse Edith Cavell who was executed for treason by the Germans in 1915, announces in Brussels that *Dawn*, the new film on her life would be screened in Belgium in a few weeks. It sparked major controversy in Germany after it was first screened in Britain.	Mar. 4

F	G	H	I	J
Includes campaigns, elections, federal-state relations, civil rights and liberties, crime, the judiciary, education, healthcare, poverty, urban affairs, and population.	*Includes formation and debate of U.S. foreign and defense policies, veterans affairs, and defense spending. (Relations with specific foreign countries are usually found under the region concerned.)*	*Includes business, labor, agriculture, taxation, transportation, consumer affairs, monetary and fiscal policy, natural resources, pollution and industrial accidents.*	*Includes worldwide scientific, medical and technological developments, natural phenomena, U.S. weather and natural disasters.*	*Includes the arts, religion, scholarship, communications media, sports, entertainment, fashions, fads, and social life.*

	World Affairs	Europe	Africa & The Middle East	The Americas	Asia & The Pacific
Mar. 5	The 49th Session of the Council of the League of Nations opens; it ends on March 10....The anti-war treaty proposed by U.S. Secretary of State Frank B. Kellogg meets with much support.	The National Socialist German Action Party—the Nazis—win a majority in the Bavarian state elections in Germany....The general elections in Poland result in Marshal Pilsudski gaining the largest block of seats in the Sejm, the Polish parliament....Prince Cyril and Prince Josias, brothers of King Boris of Bulgaria, protest to the League of Nations about the seizure of their assets in Bulgaria....Labour Party resolutions in British parliament for further investigations into the Zinovieff letter are defeated 326 to 132.	The British government gives a large subsidy to King Ibn Saud to protect him against attacks by Wahhabi tribesmen and also to try to get him to put pressure on the Wahhabi tribes not to attack Kuwait or Iraq any more.		Sir Miles Lampson and General Huang Fu start negotiations in Shanghai to settle the Nanking incident of March 1927. 20 days later Lampson leaves for Peking....Lord Sinha, formerly the Right Honorable Sir Satyendra Prassano Sinha, dies, aged 65. He was the first Indian raised to the British peerage.
Mar. 6		Spanish Prime Minster Miguel Primo de Rivera y Orbaneja, marqués de Estella blames the death of Canovas del Castillo for the Spanish-American War of 1898....Scandal erupts in France and Britain after it is revealed that a pearl necklace valued at £50,000 was lost in the post between Paris and London despite being sent in a registered packet.	British colonial soldiers mobilized in Transjordan to protect the border against soldiers loyal to King Ibn Saud....The British also prepare a major fleet of aircraft to go to Arabia.		Korean Communists in Japanese-occupied Korea form a women's group, the *Kun-u-hoe*....Fighting in southern China results in 50,000 refugees fleeing into the port city of Swatow as news is received in Peking that the Chinese Communists killed 3,000 Christian villagers near Swatow.
Mar. 7	French foreign minister, Aristide Briand announces that he favors the Havana Accords for a treaty with the United States.	The Hungarian delegation to the League of Nations rejects the idea of an inquiry into arms sales.... An earthquake rocks southern Italy causing damage in eastern and northern Sicily and also in Calabria, and causing the death of one person....A French court at Douai orders the extradition to England of Lord Terrington.	George Stewart Symes becomes British Resident in Aden, replacing John Henry Keith Stewart....The British warning of a possible "holy war" in the Middle East worries the Egyptian government.	The Nicaraguan Senate passes an amended draft of the electoral law....The Bolivian government takes control of the civilian airline Lloyd Aéreo Boliviano in the "best interests of the defense of the country."	
Mar. 8		Vasil Zakharka becomes Chairman of the Belorussian Rada (in exile), after the death of Pyotr Krecheuski.	The Turkish government announces that they will found a national bank, using jewels which belonged to the House of Ottoman to fund it. These jewels are valued at $50 million.	The League of Nations urges the Brazilian government to reconsider its decision to reign from the League two years previously....Rioting between students and Venezuelan police result in the deaths of six policemen.	
Mar. 9		The League of Nations Council officially invites Spain to reconsider its resignation from the League....The Soviet Union announces a crackdown on dissidents in the country.... British Chancellor of the Exchequer Winston Churchill circulates a memorandum regarding his planned changes to the rates system.	Lady Mary Bailey flies from England to fly to Cape Town, South Africa.	The elections in Nicaragua are criticized in the U.S. Senate.	The inaugural ceremony of the Armidale Teachers' College, New South Wales, Australia, is held. It subsequently becomes the Armidale College of Advanced Education, and then the University of New England....Sir Ludovic Charles Porter KCSI KCIE OBE, prominent Indian Civil Servant, dies, aged 58.
Mar. 10	A Committee of the League of Nations, made up of the Netherlands, Finland and Chile, ask for more time in their investigation into the Szent Gotthard weapons smuggling incident.	Nicholas Titulescu, the Romanian foreign minister, expresses his disquiet at the intrusion of the League of Nations.		A large landslide at the city of Santos, in the state of Sao Paulo in Brazil, results in the death of over 200 people.	
Mar. 11		Massive storms in the British Isles cause traffic chaos, with trains colliding in a blizzard.	British and American archaeologists in Iraq uncover what they believe to be the oldest yet discovered tomb of a king from the Sumerian city of Ur. It had been plundered many centuries ago and the bodies of the guards were found at the doors. However many archaeological finds were made including a large number of gold and stone objects overlooked by the tomb robbers.	A fire in a Mexican mine at Teziutlan, in the State of Puebla, kills nine and traps another 17 miners.	

A	B	C	D	E
Includes developments that affect more than one world region, international organizations and important meetings of world leaders.	*Includes all domestic and regional developments in Europe, including the Soviet Union.*	*Includes all domestic and regional developments in Africa and the Middle East.*	*Includes all domestic and regional developments in Latin America, the Caribbean, and Canada.*	*Includes all domestic and regional developments in Asian and Pacific nations (and colonies).*

U.S. Politics & Social Issues	U.S. Foreign Policy & Affairs, Defense	U.S. Economy & Environment	Science, Technology & Nature	Culture, Leisure & Lifestyle	
Presidential hopeful and New York governor Al Smith tries to push through the halving of direct sales tax in New York State.		There is another large rise at the New York Stock Exchange of the price of General Motors shares, adding $40 million to the total worth of the company.			Mar. 5
The case of corruption against Florence E.S. Knapp, Dean of the College of Home Economics at Syracuse University, is finally dropped after the prosecutor finds no proof of Knapp having committed any crime.	U.S. Secretary of the Navy Curtis Wilbur criticizes the British attitude to U.S. naval policies.	Calvin Coolidge plans for a $225 million tax cut as preparations for the budget are finalized.	U.S. aviator Charles A. Levine manages to fly nonstop from Mitchel Field, NY, in Havana, Cuba, in 14 hours.	The Rockefeller family, through the Laura Spelman Rockefeller Memorial, gives $5 million to the Great Smoky Mountains National Park Fund....Right Honorable Dodgson Hamilton Madden, Irish judge and Shakespearean scholar, dies aged 87.	Mar. 6
The Democrats raise enough money to pay their debts incurred in the 1924 presidential election, and the Democratic National Committee foresees a surplus of $250,000 at the start of the 1928 presidential campaign.	The Senate Foreign Relations Committee votes to continue U.S. military commitments to Nicaragua.				Mar. 7
New York governor and presidential hopeful Al Smith considers naming Ottinger as a prosecutor as he wants to reopen the case surrounding Florence E. S. Knapp, Dean of the College of Home Economics at Syracuse University.	A number of Latin American countries and U.S. groups praise Chairman Charles Evans Hughes for his work at the Sixth Pan-American Conference at Havana, Cuba.			Riots take place in Havana, Cuba, during the Seventh Latin Press Congress.	Mar. 8
A number of Republican candidates try to form an alliance to prevent Herbert Hoover from getting the Republican Party nomination for the presidential elections.	The French government goes to court to try to seize the $5,201,000 in gold held in the United States in the name of Soviet Union.	Leading capitalist Rodman Wanamaker, head of the Wanamaker stores in New York, Philadelphia, London and Paris, dies in the Ventnor district of Atlantic City, New Jersey, aged 65....General Motors stock again rises dramatically at the New York Stock Exchange....The Robert E Lee, a Boston steamer, is wrecked in a storm but all 150 passengers remain on board until rescue vessels arrive.	Lester J. Hendershot of West Elizabeth, Pennsylvania, is given a 2,000-volt electric shock during an experiment to develop his motor which can run without the use of fuel.	Eleanor Roosevelt, wife of Franklin Delano Roosevelt, urges for more women to go into business to change the view held of them in society in the April issue of Red Book Magazine.	Mar. 9
A new scandal erupts over whether Will H. Hays, Chairman of the Republican National Committee in 1920, Postmaster General in the cabinet of President Warren Harding from 1921 until 1922, and after that President of the Motion Picture Producers and Distributors of America Inc, sent Andrew W. Mellon some $50,000 in oil bonds to cover a gift to the Republican Party.		There are major rises in the sales of radio sets throughout the United States leading to rises in Radio Corporation stock at the New York Stock Exchange.	Richard Byrd publishes his plan to map Antarctica as a part of his $500,000 expedition.	An English-language translation of Francis Carco's Perversity, translated by Ford Maddox Ford, is published in Chicago, Illinois, by Pascal Covici....Emmanuel Hertz of New York announces that he has four previously unpublished letters by U.S. President Abraham Lincoln in his collection of Lincolniana, and allows them to be published in the New York Times on March 11.	Mar. 10
Consternation around the United States as newspapers publish details of life on the coalfields of Central Pennsylvania and around Pittsburgh with details of bad housing, school shootings and brutality by the Coal and Iron Police against striking miners.			Scientists in the United States and elsewhere acclaim the planned Antarctic expedition of Richard Byrd.	Bartlett Cormak's melodramatic play on Chicago life, The Racket, is published in New York by Samuel French.	Mar. 11

F	G	H	I	J
Includes campaigns, elections, federal-state relations, civil rights and liberties, crime, the judiciary, education, healthcare, poverty, urban affairs, and population.	Includes formation and debate of U.S. foreign and defense policies, veterans affairs, and defense spending. (Relations with specific foreign countries are usually found under the region concerned.)	Includes business, labor, agriculture, taxation, transportation, consumer affairs, monetary and fiscal policy, natural resources, pollution and industrial accidents.	Includes worldwide scientific, medical and technological developments, natural phenomena, U.S. weather and natural disasters.	Includes the arts, religion, scholarship, communications media, sports, entertainment, fashions, fads, and social life.

	World Affairs	Europe	Africa & The Middle East	The Americas	Asia & The Pacific
Mar. 12		Malta officially becomes a British Dominion with the granting of internal self-rule....The Soviet Union continues its hard-line policy with arrests of more dissidents.		The German airline Luft Hansa considers running flights to Brazil.	The *Daily Mail* in Bombay highlights problems over plans by the former Maharajah of Indore to marry Nancy Ann Miller of Seattle, Washington, after Miller claimed to have converted to Hinduism In a new twist, Shankara Charya Kurtkoti claims that only he has the rights to initiate converts from Bombay to the Himalayas.
Mar. 13		Kurt Gustav Hans Otto Freiherr von Reibnitz is reappointed as Minister of State of Mecklenburg-Strelitz, Germany, taking over from Karl Schwabe.		The Nicaraguan Chamber of Deputies rejects the amended draft of the electoral law passed by the Senate on the previous week.... Eileen Vollick becomes the first Canadian woman licensed to fly as a pilot.	Representatives of the Washington Treaty powers protest to the Peking government that the agreement made at Dairen on February 26, contravenes the conditions agreed at Washington.
Mar. 14	The Conference for the Abolition of Prohibitions and Restrictions on the Exportation of Hides and Bones is held in Geneva sponsored by the League of Nations to help international trade in hides and bones.	Austria and Switzerland ratify their convention of October 24, 1927, against double taxation....The Romanian government intimates that it might follow the lead of the Bank of France and try to get court orders to seize some Soviet assets in the United States and possibly elsewhere.	George Eastman, the camera manufacturer from Rochester, NY, flees from a burning train in Egypt, and is brought to Cairo on a relief train.	Nicaraguan rebel leader General Augusto Sandino, writing to a friend, Froylán Turcios in Tegucigalpa, Honduras, confirms that he has retaken El Chipote.	
Mar. 15		Norway celebrates the centenary of its great playwright Henrik Ibsen with the opening of the Ibsen Exposition held at the University Library, Oslo, and opened by King Haakon....The Italian government of Benito Mussolini modifies the electoral system for the forthcoming Italian general elections.... Alexander Subkov (Zoubkoff), the husband of Princess Victoria of Schaumburg-Lippe, and sister of the former Kaiser Wilhelm II of Germany, is deported from Germany.		The Columbian and Peruvian governments ratify the boundary treaty between the two countries which had been signed on March 24, 1922....The League of Nations asks Costa Rica to consider returning to the League, having left on January 1, 1927, in disagreement over the reference to the Monroe Doctrine in Article 21 of the League's Covenant.	
Mar. 16	The French government announces that they are moving closer to agreement on the anti-war treaty of U.S. Secretary of State Frank B. Kellogg.	The Romanian post office issues a large number of postage stamps of King Michael who had become king in the previous year....British Admiralty announces that a Court of Inquiry has been held at Malta concerning the incident on the *Royal Oak* and as a result of this, Rear-Admiral Collard, Captain Dewar and Commander Daniel were all suspended from duty.	Mustafa an-Nahhas Pasha becomes Prime Minister of Egypt, taking over from Abdel Khalek Sarwat Pasha.	The Mexican and U.S. governments sign in Washington, DC a treaty for the examination of live stock at the Mexican–U.S. frontier....The Nicaraguan Congress adjourns after failing to pass a measure to once again lengthen the life of parliament.	*The Australians at Rabaul*, by S. S. Mackenzie, is published in Sydney, Australia, by Angus & Robertson. It is the tenth volume in the official history of Australia's involvement in World War I, edited by C. E. W. Bean at the Australian War Memorial in Canberra.
Mar. 17		The Bulgarian government announces that they will accept foreign loans on terms prescribed by the League of Nations.		U.S. economist W. W Cumberland of the State Department, assisted by Thomas A. Barrows of New York, ends his three-month survey of Nicaragua concluding that the country's economy is fundamentally sound.	Nancy Miller marries Tukoji Rao Holkar, the former Maharajah of Indore in a massive ceremony at Barwaha, India, involving elephant parades through the city.
Mar. 18		A large Memorial concert is held in Oslo to commemorate the 100th anniversary of the birth of Henrik Ibsen....Grand Duke André of Russia loses his fortune on the gambling tables at the Monte Carlo Casino.			The Nanking government issues two mandates: one orders the arrest of people responsible for the Nanking incident, and announces the execution of some of those involved in it, and the other offering general protection for foreign lives and property.
Mar. 19	The Preparatory Commission for the Disarmament Conference at Geneva discusses the Russian disarmament proposals.	The King and Queen of Afghanistan, during their time in Southampton, visit the British fleet and King Amanullah travels on a British submarine.	Official negotiations begin between the Italian and French governments over the role of the Italians in North Africa, particularly their part in the administration of the International Zone at Tangier, Morocco, and over the juridical status of the Italians in Tunisia.		

A	B	C	D	E
Includes developments that affect more than one world region, international organizations and important meetings of world leaders.	*Includes all domestic and regional developments in Europe, including the Soviet Union.*	*Includes all domestic and regional developments in Africa and the Middle East.*	*Includes all domestic and regional developments in Latin America, the Caribbean, and Canada.*	*Includes all domestic and regional developments in Asian and Pacific nations (and colonies).*

U.S. Politics & Social Issues	U.S. Foreign Policy & Affairs, Defense	U.S. Economy & Environment	Science, Technology & Nature	Culture, Leisure & Lifestyle	
New York Governor and presidential hopeful Al Smith tries to reopen the case concerning Florence E. S. Knapp, Dean of the College of Home Economics at Syracuse University, by ordering a special jury to sift through the evidence.		The St. Francis Dam, north of Los Angeles, California, fails, resulting in the death of between 400 and 450 people in Santa Paula, Ventura County....Radio Corporation shares continue to rise on at the New York Stock Exchange.	Captain G. S. Wright of the Scientific Research Department of the British Admiralty, and survivor of the ill-fated Robert Falcon Scott expedition to the South Pole, offers a word of caution to Richard Byrd.		Mar. 12
Andrew W. Mellon, Secretary of the Treasury, and William M. Butler, Chairman of the Republican National Committee defend their silence over the scandal involving oil shares....The Norris bill for the government operation of the Muscle Shoals is passed by the Senate.		The New York Stock Exchange launches an enquiry into the rapid price rises continuing to be seen by Radio Corporation stock.	British aviator Captain Walter Hinchcliffe and the Hon Elsie Mackay, the daughter of Lord Inchcape, start their flight across the Atlantic heading for Mitchel Field, NY.	Rudolph Friml's musical, The Three Musketeers, premieres in New York City.	Mar. 13
Democrats continue their attacks on Andrew W. Mellon, Secretary of the Treasury, and William M. Butler, Chairman of the Republican National Committee over their involvement in the scandal with not disclosing the donation of oil shares.		Rescue work continues on trying to locate survivors from the collapse of the St. Francis Dam, north of Los Angeles, CA.	The plane with Captain Walter Hinchcliffe and the Elsie Mackay is now long overdue and it is feared that they have crashed at sea.	The U.S. Census Bureau issue a provisional estimate for the U.S. population on July 1, 1928, at 120,013,000.	Mar. 14
Calvin Coolidge rejects the concept of statehood for Puerto Rico and highlights the benefits on the island between 1897 and 1928.			With no news about the plane flown by Captain Walter Hinchcliffe and the Hon Elsie Mackay, it is presumed that they were lost at sea.	In New York, 25,000 people including many of Hungarian descent, turn up to see the unveiling of a statue of Hungarian national hero Lajos Kossuth. At the ceremony Irene Berko was dressed as Hungary, and Margaret Vitarius was dressed as Columbia.	Mar. 15
In the territory of Hawaii, support for both Al Smith and Herbert Hoover is noticeable according to Governor Wallace R. Farrington.	The United States sends 1,000 more marines to Nicaragua, raising the number there to 3,700. According to the U.S. government, this was largely to honor a pledge by Calvin Coolidge to ensure free elections took place in October.	U.S. taxation authorities state that they expect income tax yields to be considerably higher with $38.5 million collected in Lower Manhattan alone.		Josef Bard's novel Shipwreck in Europe, about an American in Vienna, is published in New York by Harper Brothers.	Mar. 16
	The U.S. House of Representatives pass the Navy Bill by 287 to 58.		Debates continue over the theory of evolution against the Biblical teaching of Creation and these are highlighted in a speech by Dr. Robert A. Millikan of the California Institute of Technology at Passadena, CA.	Some 200,000 people attend the St. Patrick's Day Parade in New York City.	Mar. 17
Republicans and Democrats see the Ohio primaries as the crucial test for their candidates for nomination for the presidential elections.	Planes carrying U.S. Marines are hit by ground fire by Nicaraguan rebels loyal to General Augusto Sandino.	The Grace Liner, Santa Teresa, disabled during its voyage from Valparaiso to New York, remains adrift in the high seas....An earthquake shakes the Adirondack region and damages buildings at Saranac Lake, NY.		The Letters of Joseph Conrad 1895–1924, edited by Edward Garnett, are published in Indianapolis, Indiana, by Bobbs-Merrill Company.	Mar. 18
New York governor and presidential hopeful Al Smith asks for the New York State legislature to grant a four-year term to future governors.		After Spanish newspapers declared that U.S. films unsettle the Spanish public, interests connected with the Spanish film industry campaign against the screening of U.S. films in their country.	Sir David Ferrier MD FRS, a British pioneer in the field of neurology, dies, aged 85.	The first performance of Amos & Andy takes place on the radio, on NBC Blue Network, WMAQ Chicago.	Mar. 19

F	G	H	I	J
Includes campaigns, elections, federal-state relations, civil rights and liberties, crime, the judiciary, education, healthcare, poverty, urban affairs, and population.	Includes formation and debate of U.S. foreign and defense policies, veterans affairs, and defense spending. (Relations with specific foreign countries are usually found under the region concerned.)	Includes business, labor, agriculture, taxation, transportation, consumer affairs, monetary and fiscal policy, natural resources, pollution and industrial accidents.	Includes worldwide scientific, medical and technological developments, natural phenomena, U.S. weather and natural disasters.	Includes the arts, religion, scholarship, communications media, sports, entertainment, fashions, fads, and social life.

	World Affairs	Europe	Africa & The Middle East	The Americas	Asia & The Pacific
Mar. 20	The delegation from the Soviet Union criticizes the League of Nations Disarmament Commission, but even though it allies itself with the German and the Turkish delegations, the British, French and Italians vote down the Soviet proposals.	Even though sick, an American woman, Mme Helen Dupuy, continues to run *Le Petit Parisien* newspaper (250,000 copies daily). The newspaper was left to her by husband Paul Dupuy when he died.... Confirmation reaches Vienna that Romanian nationalist students had attacked Jewish synagogues in Grosswardein and other towns in Transylvania in December.		The Canadian Cabinet refuses to reveal whether or not they will grant clemency to convicted murderer Doris Palmer McDonald who, along with her husband George C. McDonald, was found guilty of the murder of a taxi driver Adelard Bouchard.	A Japanese aviation company considers sending one of its aviators on a flight from Hokkaido to Alaska.
Mar. 21		In London, the Prince of Wales somersaults off his horse during a race, landing on his feet uninjured.... Plans are mooted in Belgium to end burials owing to the pressure on land.		President Adolfo Diaz of Nicaragua issues a decree appointing General McCoy as Chairman of the National Board of Elections and conferring on the Board powers to supervise the elections.	The Mau League of Samoa press their case for independence to the League of Nations through British Conservative member of parliament Patrick Bernard Malone.
Mar. 22	The Soviet Union's foreign minister Maksim M. Litvinov attacks his country's critics at the League of Nations Disarmament Commission.... The Conference of Exports for the Coordination of Higher International Studies is held in Berlin, hosted by the League of Nations, to improve the study of international relations. It lasts three days.	Protests by peasants in the Soviet Union over food shortages.... Sahak Mirzoyevich Ter-Gabrielyan becomes Chairman of the Council of People's Commissars, Soviet Union, taking over from Sarkis Saakovich Ambartsumyan.		An earthquake in Mexico City causes extensive damage in the central part of the city, including some structural damage to the U.S. Embassy where the bedroom of U.S. Ambassador Dwight W. Morrow is damaged.	
Mar. 23	The Soviet Union withdraws its plans for universal disarmament and the British Chancellor of the Duchy of Lancaster, Lord Cushendun, announces that negotiations are being undertaken between representatives of various governments to remove difficulties in the way of a Disarmament Convention.	The Spanish government withdraws its resignation letter indicating that it wished to leave the League of Nations, but does not receive a permanent seat on League Council.	J G. McDonald's biography *Rhodes*, about South African pioneer Cecil Rhodes, is published in New York by Robert M. McBride & Co.		
Mar. 24	The International ionary Conference, held at the Mount of Olives, Palestine, opens. It ends on April 8....The Preparatory Commission session of the League of the Nations closes with Lord Cushendun presenting a note from the British government on the issue of naval disarmament.	The Italian leader Benito Mussolini announces that he has completed dictating the first half of his autobiography, which will be ready for sale in the bookshops by the end of the year. An English language edition is being prepared by R. W. Child....Mr. Goldstein, one of the six German engineers taken prisoner by the Soviet Union, returns to Germany but sheds little light on why the engineers had been arrested in the first place.		The Columbian and Nicaraguan governments sign a treaty at Managua, capital of Nicaragua, settling the issue of sovereignty of the Great and Little Corn Islands and the Mosquito Coast. They become parts of Nicaragua, confirming the U.S. lease on Little Corn Island.	
Mar. 25		Pope Pius XI criticizes the French right-wing royalist group Action Française....General elections in Portugal result in interim president, General António Óscar de Fragoso Carmona being elected as president....In a military exercise off Gibraltar, the British Royal Navy states that its new aircraft carrier fared well....The Italian government reveals that 80,000 boys have enrolled in the Fascisti, a pro-Mussolini youth group.	A meeting between different Church groups in Jerusalem makes a plea for Christian unity.		In India there are worries that the Standard Oil battle with Royal Dutch Shell would dramatically affect the price of oil in British India.... The British negotiations with the Chinese Nationalist government in Nanking over attacks on foreigners in their capital, break down without progress to a mediated solution.
Mar. 26		The convention of March 11, 1927, between Austria and Hungary, settling the border delineation is ratified....Pope Pius XI at the Vatican confirms that he has received a petition asking for the canonization of two Englishmen, Cardinal John Fisher and Thomas More who were both executed for treason in 1535, and who had already been beatified.		General Alvaro Obregon in Mexico proposes introducing the Prohibition in that country stating that he feels that alcohol is the enemy of the country.	The National Academy of Art (later renamed the China Academy of Art) is founded at Hankow (Hangzhou), China.

A	B	C	D	E
Includes developments that affect more than one world region, international organizations and important meetings of world leaders.	*Includes all domestic and regional developments in Europe, including the Soviet Union.*	*Includes all domestic and regional developments in Africa and the Middle East.*	*Includes all domestic and regional developments in Latin America, the Caribbean, and Canada.*	*Includes all domestic and regional developments in Asian and Pacific nations (and colonies).*

U.S. Politics & Social Issues	U.S. Foreign Policy & Affairs, Defense	U.S. Economy & Environment	Science, Technology & Nature	Culture, Leisure & Lifestyle	
Richard W. Lawrence, in charge of the New York City campaign for Republican presidential hopeful Herbert Hoover is nominated as president of the National Republican Club.	A message in red crayon written on a piece of cardboard was recovered from the pocket of a sailor on the ill-fated *S-4*, as U.S. naval divers recover the last of the bodies from the submarine which sank on December 17.	Treasury officials note that the total receipts for income tax are already $17 million above those for 1928.	Charles A. Levine, who flew with Clarence D. Chamberlin across the Atlantic is given his own flying license to allow him to fly alone.		Mar. 20
Calvin Coolidge refuses to be drafted for the presidency in Wyoming...."Diamond Joe" Esposito, a Republican ward boss in Chicago is shot and killed while walking home. His two bodyguards with him are both uninjured.... The New York State Senate end Al Smith's plans for introducing a four year term for the governor of New York.	Some 360 marines leave U.S. bases in the Panama Canal Zone to fly go to Corinto, Nicaragua, to boost the U.S. numbers fighting the rebel leader General Augusto Sandino.	In connection with the growing oil scandal, a search of the estate of the late Warren Harding, U.S. president from 1921 until his death in 1923, fails to find any oil stock.	Charles Lindbergh is presented the Medal of Honor by Calvin Coolidge for his first Trans-Atlantic flight in May 1927....Although he had previously refused to get into an air plane in Berlin on February 23, King Amanullah of Afghanistan accepts a British offer to be flown over London, being the first royal person to be flown over the British capital.	The *New York Times* states that 26 European operas are actively recruiting U.S. singers.	Mar. 21
The U.S. Senate sidetracks a move to attack Treasury Secretary Andrew W. Mellon.		A large increase in trading on the New York Stock Exchangesees the prices of stock rise with 3,873,890 shares sold.	*The Economic World* by Thomas Nixon Carver is published in New York by A. W. Shaw Company.	Noel Coward's musical *This Year of Grace* premieres in London.... *Crowell's Dictionary of English Grammar*, by Maurice H. Weneen, is published in New York by Thomas Y. Crowell Company.	Mar. 22
New York governor and presidential hopeful Al Smith manages to get many of his bills though the New York State legislature, which passes those on trivial matters, holding back any of real importance.	U.S. Secretary for the Navy Curtis Wilbur seeks new laws to help the U.S. Navy maintain a stockpile of oil for use in case of emergencies.	John D. Rockefeller urges that there should be a broader basis for the inquiry into the coal industry in evidence he gives at the Senate Interstate Commerce Committee.... On the 11th day on which more than 3 million shares changes hands, prices on the New York Stock Exchange continue to rise.	*Urban Land Economics* by Herbert B. Dorau and Albert G. Hinman is published in New York by The Macmillan Company.	Six selected stories by Algernon Blackwood are published in *The Dance of Death* in New York by The Dial Press.	Mar. 23
A fist fight was narrowly averted in the U.S. Senate when Senator Millard E. Tydings, Democrat, of Maryland, rose from his chair after being called a liar by Senator R. Robinson, Republican, of Indiana, and had to be physically restrained by other senators....George Creel's biography *Sam Houston: Colossus in Buckskin*, is published in New York by Cosmopolitan Book Corporation.		Shares in General Motors rise to $192 which is seen on the New York Stock Exchangeas a vote of confidence in John J. Raskob and what he has managed to achieve for the company.	Charles Lindbergh notes that he is getting tired of being in the limelight but does not intend to retire from his high-profile lifestyle.	Tenney Frank's new biographical and critical study, *Catullus and Horace*, is published in New York by Henry Holt & Co. Alice Glasgow's *The Twisted Tendril*, a biographical novel of John Wilkes Booth, is published in New York by Frederick A. Stokes Company.	Mar. 24
The western part of the Bronx in New York was threatened when a fire broke out in a nearly-completed seven-storey apartment on the hill at Shakespeare Avenue and Jessup Place.	Large celebrations are held in the Nicaraguan capital Managua, and other cities in the country when it is revealed that the U.S. Marines will supervise the forthcoming elections. The move is attacked by the rebel Sandanista movement of General Augusto Sandino, with 2,000 pro-U.S. demonstrators march through Managua waving U.S. flags and relics of aviator Colonel Charles Lindbergh's visit earlier in the year.		Two passengers and a pilot suffer some injuries when their place crash-landed at Pitman, New Jersey....Dr. Hugh J. M. Playfair, British gynecologist and physician, dies, aged 63.		Mar. 25
The homes in Chicago of Judge John A. Swanson and U.S. Senator Charles S. Deneen, who campaigned in favor of Prohibition, are both bombed.		The number of shares exchanging hands at the New York Stock Exchange reaches 4,202,820.		Clarence H. Mackay, chairman of the board of the Philharmonic Society of New York and Harry Harkness Flagler, the president of the Symphony Society of New York, announce that their two societies are merging. Willem Mengelberg will be the conductor and Arturo Toscanini will direct.	Mar. 26

F	G	H	I	J
Includes campaigns, elections, federal-state relations, civil rights and liberties, crime, the judiciary, education, healthcare, poverty, urban affairs, and population.	Includes formation and debate of U.S. foreign and defense policies, veterans affairs, and defense spending. (Relations with specific foreign countries are usually found under the region concerned.)	Includes business, labor, agriculture, taxation, transportation, consumer affairs, monetary and fiscal policy, natural resources, pollution and industrial accidents.	Includes worldwide scientific, medical and technological developments, natural phenomena, U.S. weather and natural disasters.	Includes the arts, religion, scholarship, communications media, sports, entertainment, fashions, fads, and social life.

	World Affairs	Europe	Africa & The Middle East	The Americas	Asia & The Pacific
Mar. 27		Julian Szymanski becomes Marshal of the Polish Senate; and Ignacy Daszynski becomes Marshal of the Sejm (Parliament), taking over from Maciej Rataj.		The United States government accepts the new Mexican oil-land laws, ending a longstanding dispute between the two countries.	In Western Australia, the United Party decides to revert to its former name and becomes the National Party....Georgiy Chicherin of the Soviet Union states that his country would not join the international embargo on selling weapons to China, but it would not export weapons to Chinese factions.
Mar. 28		France reduces the length of military service to one year....Sir Douglas Hogg, later Lord Hailsham, is appointed Lord Chancellor in Britain after the resignation of Viscount Cave. Sir Thomas Inskip is appointed attorney-general and Boyd Merriman is made solicitor-general.		Vital Henrique Batista Soares is appointed Governor of Bahia Province, Brazil, replacing Francisco Marques de Góes Calmon.	Work starts in Tokyo, Japan, to build a mansion for Prince Chichibu to receive him and his fiancée after their marriage.
Mar. 29		George, First Viscount Cave, British Lord High Chancellor dies, and is succeeded as Chancellor by Douglas McGarel Hogg, Baron Hailsham who takes over as the most senior law official in the country.		The Mexican government claims to have killed 106 rebels in two battles in the State of Guanajuato. The major part of the fighting took place near the village of San Francisco Rinson.	
Mar. 30		The Lithuanian and Polish governments hold a conference at Königsberg....The Italian government announces that all non-Fascist youth movements must be dissolved in 30 days....In a test case, Samuel Schwartz from Zehden, Germany, asks the German airline Deutsche Luft Hansa for rent for the airspace above his house, claiming that his property rights include all the ground beneath his property, and also all the space above it.	Nahhas Pasha, the new Egyptian Prime Minister, presents a note declaring that the British note of March 4 constituted a departure from the rules of diplomatic intervention.		The Netherlands government and the British government sign a treaty for frontier delimitation in Borneo....The Nanking government and the U.S. government exchange notes recording the settlement of the Nanking incident....The German Reichstag passes a bill prohibiting the export of arms to China.
Mar. 31	The Conference on Emigration and Immigration, held at Havana, Cuba, opens. It ends on April 16....The 1928 edition of *The Statesmen's Year-Book*, edited by Dr. M. Epstein, is published in London.	The Swedish and Soviet governments exchange an agreement concerning the rights and obligations of the Soviet commercial delegation in Moscow....The Reichstag, the German Parliament, is dissolved ahead of forthcoming general elections.	The Egyptian government publicly states its objection to Britain interfering in its internal affairs.	Benjamín de la Mora becomes interim governor of Aguascalientes Province, Mexico, taking over from Isaac Díaz de León.	The first Australian Grand Prix motor race is held on Phillip Island, Victoria.
Apr. 1	French politician Raymond Poincaré states that he wants an international meeting to discuss plans to settle the massive war debts and reparations.	Marino Rossi and Nelson Burgagni become the Captains-Regent of San Marino....Emil Keller becomes President of the Government Commission of Aargau Canton, Switzerland, for the fourth time, replacing Albert Studler.	An earthquake shakes the Turkish port city of Smyrna leaving at least 60 Turks dead.	Bram Rutgers becomes Governor-General of the Dutch colony of Suriname, replacing Aarnoud Jan Anne Aleid baron van Heemstra....George Ian MacLean is appointed Gold Commissioner of the Yukon Territory, Canada.	Chiang Kai-shek crosses the Blue River beginning the Northern Expedition to defeat the warlords and put the whole of China under the control of the Nationalist Kuomintang government in Nanking.
Apr. 2	Dr. Gustav Stresemann, the German foreign minister, demands that restrictions be placed on arms sales to China as both sides continue to arm themselves ahead of the Northern Expedition reaching Peking....The French foreign minister Aristide Briand starts holding talks with M. Claudel, the French Ambassador to Washington, DC, prior to discussions with U.S. Secretary of State Frank B. Kellogg.	The Romanian government decides to press its claim for Russian gold held in the United States, to prevent it falling into the hands of the Soviet Union.			A rubber factory in Singapore, valued, with stock, at $250,000, is burned down in a fire—it is the third big fire in Singapore since early March.
Apr. 3		A Court martial is held at Gibraltar which finds Commander Daniel of the *Royal Oak* guilty of four charges of "acts subversive to naval discipline" and orders him to be dismissed from his ship and severely reprimanded.	*Social Life in the Cape Colony in the 18th Century*, by Colin Graham Botha, is published in Cape Town by Juta & Co Ltd. It provides a detailed account of life in early South Africa and is received in the Cape Town Press with much acclaim.		An agreement is reached between the Shanghai Municipal Council and the Chinese Ratepayers' Association.

A	B	C	D	E
Includes developments that affect more than one world region, international organizations and important meetings of world leaders.	Includes all domestic and regional developments in Europe, including the Soviet Union.	Includes all domestic and regional developments in Africa and the Middle East.	Includes all domestic and regional developments in Latin America, the Caribbean, and Canada.	Includes all domestic and regional developments in Asian and Pacific nations (and colonies).

U.S. Politics & Social Issues	U.S. Foreign Policy & Affairs, Defense	U.S. Economy & Environment	Science, Technology & Nature	Culture, Leisure & Lifestyle	
Following bomb attacks in Chicago on the previous day, police are sent to guard the homes of all the city's politicians.	Senator Kenneth McKellar of Tennessee urges for the building of a canal through Nicaragua as he claims that the Panama Canal can no longer take the number of ships. He introduces a bill into the Senate for $200 million.	The number of shares exchanging hands at the New York Stock Exchangereaches 4,790,270, with the tickertape lagging by 33 minutes. Shares in General Motors fall by 18 dollars.	Charles Lindbergh manages to avert a near crash of his plane, which contained two New York members of the House of Representatives, during a sightseeing flight over Washington, DC....The first semi-permanent radio telephone link between the United States and the French capital, Paris, is opened.	Dr. A.S.W. Rosenbach, an American investor, pays $15,000 for a collection of books relating to the British writer Daniel Defoe, author of *Robinson Crusoe* when they are sold at Sotheby's in London....Leslie Stuart, British composer of musical comedies and song dies, aged 62.	Mar. 27
The Supreme Court of the United States, by Charles Evans Hughes, a series of lectures at Columbia University under the George Blumenthal Foundation, is published in New York by Columbia University Press.		J L. Rutledge, a pilot with Pacific Air Transport, parachutes from his plane near Orinda, California, after it runs out of fuel. He later retrieves the mail and delivers it to the Orinda Post Office....20 are hurt in a train crash on Long Island....In a fire at Port Washington, Long Island, a dozen speed boats are destroyed as is Harold Vanderbilt's airboat—total losses run to $250,000.		Composer Giuseppe Ferrata dies at the age of 63.	Mar. 28
With rising political tensions in Chicago following bombings, a request is made for 4500 special deputy U.S. marshals to be used to guard the polls at the primary elections there when they are held on April 10.	A study of U.S. policy in Central America, entitled *Machine-Gun Diplomacy*, written by J.A.H. Hopkins and Melinda Alexander is published in New York by Lewis Copeland Company.	The committee investigating the oil scandal searches for more people who might hold oil stock.		*Ashenden*, a book of spy stories by British writer Somerset Maugham, based on his experiences in Russia in World War I, is published in London, and is then published by Doubleday, Doran & Co, in New York on March 30.	Mar. 29
Candidates supporting Senator Charles S. Deneen, a dry reformer in Chicago, are threatened and attacked by supporters of Chicago mobsters. Men close to Al Capone, who is no longer living in Chicago, appear to have been implicated in these and other attacks....Senator Frank B. Willis, a possible Republican candidate for the presidential elections collapses while addressing his supporters at Gray Chapel, Ohio Western University, Delaware, Ohio, and dies soon afterwards.			Italian air force Major, Mario di Bernardi, broke his own world speed record over 300 miles per hour reaching 318.57 miles per hour in a Macchi M-52*bis* being flown near Venice, Italy....Transatlantic aviator George Heldeman and Detroit aircraft manufacturer Eddie Stinson landed their plane at Jacksonville, Florida, after having been in the air for 53½ hours, creating a new world record....Richard Byrd states that he will be using a new camera to map the Antarctic.		Mar. 30
The third count in the Texas Democratic Party Primary gives victory to New York governor and presidential hopeful Al Smith.		Sales of 2,430,900 shares on the New York Stock Exchangeresults in many prices falling and the tickertape lagging by 58½ minutes....After a wounded World War I veteran Jimmie Degan is charged with having a shortage of $7,627 in his accounts, his local township, East Newark, rallies to pay his debts.	*Skyward*, an autobiographical account of the career of Richard Byrd, is published in New York by G. P. Putnam's Sons.	*The Gangs of New York* by Herbert Asbury is published in New York by Alfred A. Knopf.	Mar. 31
Calvin Coolidge orders an inquiry into the leases of the Salt Creek Field to Harry F. Sinclair....Republican opponents of presidential hopeful Herbert Hoover try to form a common front against his bid for the party's nomination.			Lottie Moore Schoemmel, aged 47, of New York swum at Miami for 32 hours, adding one hour to the existing world record.	Eight people die in New York from drinking poisonous liquor....Richard C. Carton, British dramatist, dies, aged 75.	Apr. 1
The campaign team of the late Senator Frank B. Willis decides whether or not to throw in their lot with presidential hopeful Herbert Hoover....New evidence if found for the prosecution of Florence E. S. Knapp, Dean of the College of Home Economics at Syracuse University, and former secretary of state for New York State, after previous attempts to bring her to trial came to nothing.	A Mexican newspaper *Grafico* claims that several Mexicans were killed while attempting to cross the U.S.–Mexican border illegally.		Theodore William Richards, American chemist, and recipient of the Nobel Prize for Chemistry in 1914, dies, aged 60....Karl Hartmann, the oldest taxi driver in Berlin, Germany, starts his planned drive to Paris, the French capital.	George Eastman, the camera manufacturer from Rochester, Pennsylvania, urges for a reform in the Gregorian Calendar.	Apr. 2
A brazen robbery of bank couriers in Riverside, New Jersey, results in five armed robbers stealing $4,000.		Treasury Secretary Andrew W. Mellon advises of a $182 million tax cut in the new budget based on massively increased income tax returns.		The manuscript for Lewis Carroll's *Alice in Wonderland* sells for $75,259 to Dr. A.S.W. Rosenbach, an American book connoisseur who outbids the British Museum which drops out as the price during the auction mounted.	Apr. 3

F	G	H	I	J
Includes campaigns, elections, federal-state relations, civil rights and liberties, crime, the judiciary, education, healthcare, poverty, urban affairs, and population.	Includes formation and debate of U.S. foreign and defense policies, veterans affairs, and defense spending. (Relations with specific foreign countries are usually found under the region concerned.)	Includes business, labor, agriculture, taxation, transportation, consumer affairs, monetary and fiscal policy, natural resources, pollution and industrial accidents.	Includes worldwide scientific, medical and technological developments, natural phenomena, U.S. weather and natural disasters.	Includes the arts, religion, scholarship, communications media, sports, entertainment, fashions, fads, and social life.

	World Affairs	Europe	Africa & The Middle East	The Americas	Asia & The Pacific
Apr. 4		Charles Channel, 52, of Chicago, after a successful night gambling at the Casino in Cannes, France, throws 40,000 francs from his hotel room window creating a riot in the street below as onlookers tried to grab the money....Sir John A. Kempe, private secretary to former British prime minister Benjamin Disraeli, dies, aged 82.	The British authorities in Egypt state that as negotiations for the treaty of alliance had broken down, relations would be returned to the *status quo ante*.		A treaty of friendship signed between Afghanistan and Japan signed in London....The Netherlands government is given, by arbitration, the Palmas Island, near the Philippines after a long running dispute with the United States. It becomes a part of the Netherlands East Indies....The British government announces that it will be lifting the restrictions placed on the export of rubber from Malaya and Ceylon on November 1.
Apr. 5	The ionary Council meeting in Jerusalem unanimously adopts a world statement reaffirming earlier statements by the World Conference on Faith and Order made at Lausanne, France, in 1927.	Count István gróf Bethlen de Bethlen, Prime Minister of Hungary, visits Milan, Italy, for discussions with Benito Mussolini....Another court martial, held in Gibraltar, finds Captain Dewar guilty of "acts subversive to naval discipline" and orders him to be dismissed from his ship and severely reprimanded.	Amir Lashkar Abdollah Khan Tahmaspi, Minister of Public Works in Persia, is killed during a tour of inspection near Khoeamabad.		Manuel Quezon, the President of the Senate in the Philippines, announces that he will attend by the Democratic National Convention at Houston, Texas, and the Republican National Convention at Kansas City, during his forthcoming visit to the United States.
Apr. 6		Another volume in the Economic and Social History of World War I is published for the Carnegie Endowment for International peace. *The Economic Policy of Austria-Hungary during the War*, by Dr. Gustav Gratz and Professor Richard Schuller is published at New Haven, Connecticut, by Yale University Press....Rumors spread that Leon Trotsky is taking up residence in Latvia.	Following archaeological work in Egypt, French savant Dr. J. C. Mardrus predicts that there will be a curse if the sarcophagus of Queen Hotep Heres, the mother of Cheops, is opened as is planned.	Weapons destined for Nicaraguan rebel leader General Augsto C. Sandino are seized in Porto Cortez, Honduras.	
Apr. 7	The ratified revision in the International Sanitary Convention of January 17, 1912, takes place in the United States.	Princess Victoria, the sister of the Ex-Kaiser of Germany, and her husband Prince Subkov, leave Germany for Belgium....Following the point-to-point steeplechase in Oxton, England, the Prince of Wales acted as a medical orderly when he saw a rider competing for the Royal Navy Cup being injured.			The Nationalist government of China recalls Chiang Kai-shek to lead an offensive in northern China to oust Chang Tso-lin from Peking....The six independent members of the Japanese Diet meet to decide to which party they will give their support—the six making up the balance of power in the Diet.
Apr. 8	The Vatican announces that the second volume of the Vulgate, being worked on for the previous 21 years by Cardinal Francis Aidan Gasquet, an 82-year-old Benedictine scholar, is nearly complete, and will be made public at Easter to Roman Catholics around the world.	In a fight at Belfort, France, the French Minister of Public Works, André Tardieu, is punched on the nose by a rival....Italian Air Service, owned by the Cosulich Steamship Line announces that it will be massively increasing the number of its air routes in Europe.	The U.S. banker J. P. Morgan arrives at Stamboul, Turkey, in his yacht, for his tour of the Golden Horn. He spends the evening with his cousin Joseph C. Crew, the U.S. Ambassador to Turkey.		
Apr. 9	The U.S. State Department announces that it will start to approach the British, German, Italian and Japanese government for a treaty to outlaw war.	The Turkish National Assembly, meeting at Angora (modern-day Ankara), refuses to recognize Islam as the official religion of the Turkish Republic. This enshrines the secular nature of the country.		The Brazilian government restates its stance that it will not reconsider its decision to resign from the League of Nations.	
Apr. 10	The International Cold Storage Congress meets under the auspices of the International Institute of Agriculture, based in Rome, Italy. Its meetings continue until April 15.	A large international people smuggling ring is broken at Benevento, Italy, with the head and five of his accomplices arrested while they are stowing away illegal immigrants onto a ship heading for the United States....There are severe floods in Soviet Armenia and other parts of Transcaucasia.	King Fuad of Egypt states that he is considering an official visit to Washington, DC, once he has received a formal invitation.	The U.S. and Columbian governments reach an agreement over the sovereignty of Serrano and Quita Sueno Banks and Roncador Cay, with Columbia taking possession of Roncador Cay....U.S. aviator James H. Doolittle is forced down in a storm while visiting Chile....A revolt in the armed forces in Caracas, Venezuela, is blamed on Communist agitation.	The Japanese government orders the dissolution of Communist organizations in Japan.

A	B	C	D	E
Includes developments that affect more than one world region, international organizations and important meetings of world leaders.	*Includes all domestic and regional developments in Europe, including the Soviet Union.*	*Includes all domestic and regional developments in Africa and the Middle East.*	*Includes all domestic and regional developments in Latin America, the Caribbean, and Canada.*	*Includes all domestic and regional developments in Asian and Pacific nations (and colonies).*

U.S. Politics & Social Issues	U.S. Foreign Policy & Affairs, Defense	U.S. Economy & Environment	Science, Technology & Nature	Culture, Leisure & Lifestyle	
With mounting tensions in Chicago, where Mayor William Hale Thompson was entangled in charges of support for the Ku Klux Klan, and involvement in bomb attacks, the mayor, with his banner "America First" opposes the deployment of 500 special deputies to guard the polls in the forthcoming primary elections.	Handbills are found in Nicaragua advising people to kill all Americans they encounter—including U.S. civilians working in the country, not just U.S. Marines.			Police reveal that the $250,000 pearl necklace which "disappeared" in transit from Cartiers in Paris, France, may have ended up in the United States....Dr. A.S.W. Rosenbach gives the British a two-week option to purchase the *Alice in Wonderland* manuscript from him if they want to prevent it going to the United States.	Apr. 4
The Sinclair trail for conspiracy to defraud the government starts....Florence E. S. Knapp, Dean of the College of Home Economics at Syracuse University is finally indicted six times and stands accused of grand larceny and false audit....Chauncey M. Depew, Senator and orator at the unveiling of the Statue of Liberty in New York Harbor, dies, aged 94.		A massive wave hits the U.S. liner *Leviathan* during a voyage to New York, causing considerable damage to the ship....Floods and tornadoes hit the southwest with seven people killed.		Mercedes Gleitze swims across the Straits of Gibraltar.	Apr. 5
Election agents decide to keep the late Senator Frank B. Willis on the ballot for Ohio in their battle to ensure that Herbert Hoover does not get the Republican nomination for the presidency leading to a debate over whether dead people can remain on the ballot papers.		Massive storms in the south-west of the United States isolate Omaha....Henry Ford, on a visit to Britain, arrives in Southampton, and claimed that bread lines do not exist in the United States where there is work for anybody who actually wants to work.		*Dr Johnson and Company*, a biographical sketch of Dr. Johnson and his literary circle by Robert Lynd, is published in New York by Doubleday, Doran & Co.	Apr. 6
New York governor and presidential hopeful Al Smith defeats E. T. Meredith in the Iowa Caucuses. The bomb attacks in Chicago are used by critics of Mayor William Hale Thompson to show the state of lawlessness in the city.		Grass fires at Deepwater, NJ, threaten the Du Pont Powder Plant.		An old statue of Charles II, missing from the Southwark Town Hall, London, England, since 1825 is found in a heap of rubbish after a search by Rev T. P. Stevens, vicar of St. Matthew's Church, Southwark, and a keen antiquarian.	Apr. 7
New York governor and presidential hopeful Al Smith is cheered in Asheville, North Carolina, after winning a landslide in Iowa....Churches in Illinois urge voters to reject support for Mayor William Hale Thompson.			Richard Byrd names Dr. Francis D. Coman of Johns Hopkins University as the physician on his forthcoming truip to Antarctica.	The first Karastan rug, a machine-made rug which is woven through the back, is produced at Leaksville, NC.	Apr. 8
Grant Reed becomes Mayor of Anchorage, Alaska, taking over from William Clayson....Hawaii endorses Republican presidential hopeful Herbert Hoover....It is revealed that there are 8,000 guards deployed for the Chicago primary due on the following day....It is also claimed that the Ku Klux Klan were involved in many lynchings and attacks on African Americans in Pittsburgh.	The battleships *Arkansas* and *Wyoming*, which, along with a dozen destroyers, had been involved in exercises off the coast of Cuba, return to U.S. waters.			Orders for the demolition of the Women's Chronic Division Building at the Kings County Hospital in New York are given after a report found it to be a major fire-trap....Mae West makes her debut in New York City with her play *Diamond Lil*.	Apr. 9
The so-called "Pineapple Primary" for the Republican Party held in Chicago, Illinois, preceded by assassinations and bombings. It results in the defeat of supporters of Mayor William H. Thompson of Chicago, with Al Smith losing heavily. On the same day an African American attorney opposing Thompson is killed and a supporter of U.S. Senator Charles S. Deneen is shot.		Following a flood of U.S. cars into Czechoslovakia, and a Czechoslovak government ban, the government ease the ban permitting the import of 800 U.S. automobiles annually.	George Chisholm Williams, one of the first X-ray pioneers, dies in London. He had worked with Professor Roentgen who discovered X-Rays, and was presented with the Carnegie Bronze Medal in 1927 for his work.	Death of English novelist Stanley John Weyman, nicknamed the Prince of Romance, aged 72. A barrister, he wrote a large number of best-selling historical romances.	Apr. 10

F	G	H	I	J
Includes campaigns, elections, federal-state relations, civil rights and liberties, crime, the judiciary, education, healthcare, poverty, urban affairs, and population.	Includes formation and debate of U.S. foreign and defense policies, veterans affairs, and defense spending. (Relations with specific foreign countries are usually found under the region concerned.)	Includes business, labor, agriculture, taxation, transportation, consumer affairs, monetary and fiscal policy, natural resources, pollution and industrial accidents.	Includes worldwide scientific, medical and technological developments, natural phenomena, U.S. weather and natural disasters.	Includes the arts, religion, scholarship, communications media, sports, entertainment, fashions, fads, and social life.

	World Affairs	Europe	Africa & The Middle East	The Americas	Asia & The Pacific
Apr. 11		The Italian leader Benito Mussolini states that he will have a permanent government with the Fascist Grand Council controlling it for years to come....Two trains collide outside Paris resulting in 15 people being killed and 32 injured. The engineer who passed the signal is arrested.			The British and Chinese electors in the city of Tientsin reach agreement over the running of the British concession in the city.
Apr. 12		Assassination attempt on King Victor Emmanuel III in Milan, Italy, results in the death of 17 bystanders, with 40 wounded in a bomb explosion in Milan.		The Mixed Boundary Commission is constituted by the U.S. President to establish the provisional boundary between Guatemala and Honduras....The Military Geographical Institute is founded in Ecuador.	Vietnamese Communist activist Ho Chi Minh complains to Jules Humbert-Droz, a Swiss Communist, that the Communist International (Comintern) is neglecting any plans for a revolution in Vietnam.
Apr. 13	U.S. Secretary of State F. B. Kellogg submits his plan for the arbitration of disputes to prevent war to the Locarno Powers (Belgium, France. Germany, Great Britain and Italy).	Italian authorities in Milan arrest scores of people in their efforts to try to find the perpetrators of the previous day's bomb attack.... In Greece, supporters of General Theodorius Pangalos, try to seize power as the general is sent to the Izzeddin Prison on the island of Crete.		Bolivian industrialist and copper baron Simon I. Patino offers to place $100 million at the disposal of the Bolivian government for public works projects in the country.	
Apr. 14		An earthquake in Bulgaria results in the death of 50 people and devastates several towns....A postal sorter at the Paris Post Office is arrested for the theft of the £50,000 necklace being sent to London, and the necklace is recovered.	The Portuguese and Belgian governments conclude an agreement over the point of junction on the River Luao of the railways from the Belgian Congo to Portuguese West Africa (Angola).		The Chinese Nationalist forces finally start moving north.
Apr. 15		General António Óscar de Fragoso Carmona confirmed as President of Portugal, after 17 months as interim President....The Portuguese government and the Vatican sign a protocol regarding Portuguese jurisdiction in the East....Viscount Trematon, heir to the Earl of Athlone and nephew of the Queen of the United Kingdom, dies aged 20.... Benito Mussolini tries to organize an accord with the Vatican....French Communists clash with police in Paris.			The U.S. Fleet in Asia which includes the light cruisers *Richmond*, *Marblehead* and *Cincinnati* arrive in Shanghai, China.
Apr. 16	The British delegation to the Opium Commission of the League of Nations claims that the French have massively increased their imports of opium and the manufacture of morphine in the last few years.	Official statistics in Monaco state that gamblers lost 154 million francs at the Monte Carlo Casino in 1927, which was seven million less than in the previous year....King Boris of Bulgaria visits the area around Cirpan, hit by an earthquake on April 14.			
Apr. 17	The Soviet Union at the Disarmament discussions accuse Britain of encircling them.	Official celebrations took place in Spain to observe the 100th anniversary of the death of painter Francisco Goya....The British government announces the Admiralty decision over the *Royal Oak* with Rear-Admiral Collard being placed on the retired list and Captain Dewar and Commander Daniel having their court martial sentences confirmed....The Polish government sacks their official hangman for drunkenness, incurring large debts and leading a dissolute life. The government also decide to remove the permanent gallows at prisons, with temporary ones to be erected when needed.		There are reported outbreaks of the bubonic plaque in the Atlantic ports of Colombia as these are sealed to prevent the spread of the disease.	German explorer Dr. Emil Trinkler, returning from Chinese Turkestan, announces that he has found a buried city. He brought back many treasures which confirmed the existence of a buried city—Swedish explorer Dr. Sven Hedin is currently in the region in search of just such a city.

A	B	C	D	E
Includes developments that affect more than one world region, international organizations and important meetings of world leaders.	Includes all domestic and regional developments in Europe, including the Soviet Union.	Includes all domestic and regional developments in Africa and the Middle East.	Includes all domestic and regional developments in Latin America, the Caribbean, and Canada.	Includes all domestic and regional developments in Asian and Pacific nations (and colonies).

U.S. Politics & Social Issues	U.S. Foreign Policy & Affairs, Defense	U.S. Economy & Environment	Science, Technology & Nature	Culture, Leisure & Lifestyle	
The U.S. Federal Court bars a court suit to stop the Ku Klux Klan from conducting business in Pennsylvania.	Politicians in Puerto Rico continue to agitate against the decision made by Calvin Coolidge not to give the island statehood.		The overseas telephone service from Paris, France, to the United States, is extended to reach Canada....Irish aviator James Fitzmaurice speaks of his plans for his forthcoming transatlantic flight on a German plane heading for New York.	Following his earlier announcement on February 11, Alfredo Trombetti of the University of Bologna restates that he has managed to decipher the Etruscan script, although his claims were criticized at the time and later found to be false.	Apr. 11
The U.S. Senate again passes the Farm Relief Bill (the McNary-Haugen Bill) by a vote of 53 to 23....Calvin Coolidge continues to try to stop plans to draft him for the forthcoming presidential elections.		Sir Alfred Mond of Imperial Chemical Industries announces that financiers from the United States and the United Kingdom merge to form the Finance Company of Great Britain and America.	The Germans develop a driverless motor-car which is propelled by rockets and is shown to be capable of achieving speeds of 430 miles per hour in tests at Ruesselsheim.	*The Times Literary Supplement* in London, in a review of Somerset Maugham's *Ashenden*, is heavily critical of the way in which the British secret service acted in World War I.	Apr. 12
New York governor and presidential hopeful Al Smith continues his campaigning in the south....Political commentators predict that Republican presidential hopeful Herbert Hoover to win the Indiana Primary, even though scandals there shake the Republican power brokers in the state.			Captain Hermann Köhl, Baron von Hünefeld (Germany) and Commandant James Fitzmaurice (Irish Free State) complete the first East-West Atlantic crossing flying from Ireland to Labrador, Canada, having left on the previous day.		Apr. 13
Florence E. S. Knapp, Dean of the College of Home Economics at Syracuse University, hiding in Middlebury, Vermont, finally accepts the subpoena calling her before the Grand Jury in Albany, New York. She had barricaded herself into a dormitory at the school when she was assailed by a large crowd of onlookers when officials first tried to serve the subpoena on her several days earlier.		A train in Long Island kills three people when it hit their car at a crossing late in the evening, minutes after the watchman who manned the crossing had ended his shift.	French aviators Captain Dieudonné Costes and navigator Lieutenant-Commander Joseph Le Brix land at Le Bourget Airport near Paris, ending their 45,000 km round-the-world flight.		Apr. 14
Senator Thomas Heflin is rebuked in North Carolina for his continual attacks on Democratic Party presidential hopeful Al Smith....Senator Gerald P. Nye of Wisconsin refuses to apologize for his attacks on Al Smith.			Australian explorer and aviator Captain Hubert Wilkins and U.S. pilot Lieutenant Carl Ben Eielson leave Point Barrow, Alaska, in a Lockheed Vega, to make the first flight across the Arctic.	Calvin Coolidge extols the career of the seventh U.S. President Andrew Jackson as he accepts for the Country a statue of him for Washington, DC. Coolidge's long speech involved him classifying Jackson "among the great," highlighting his role as a soldier and explorer before he became president.	Apr. 15
Robbers attack passengers as their train leaves Chicago in yet another incident of lawlessness blamed on Mayor William Thompson.			Commentators continue to applaud the transatlantic flight by aviators Captain Hermann Köhl, Baron von Hünefeld from Germany, and Commandant J. Fitzmaurice of the Irish Free State, as their wives head to the United States to join them.	An exhibition of Old Masters paintings was held at the galleries of M. Knoedler & Co Inc in New York with paintings by Vermeer, Christus, Van Dyck, Rembrandt and Reynolds for sale.	Apr. 16
As the results of the early primaries for the Democratic Party nomination are tallied, it becomes clear that Al Smith is winning....The Republican Club vote to continue their support for Prohibition....Alan Fox from the Hoover State headquarters reveals that presidential hopeful Herbert Hoover had turned down a British title and a seat in the British war cabinet in World War I because he did not want to give up his American citizenship.		As the oil scandal widens, another son-in-law of Albert B. Fall gives evidence of the hiding of large sums of money.		Tests start on the Mona Lisa painting in the Louvre museum in Paris to prove conclusively whether or not it is genuine.	Apr. 17

F	G	H	I	J
Includes campaigns, elections, federal-state relations, civil rights and liberties, crime, the judiciary, education, healthcare, poverty, urban affairs, and population.	*Includes formation and debate of U.S. foreign and defense policies, veterans affairs, and defense spending. (Relations with specific foreign countries are usually found under the region concerned.)*	*Includes business, labor, agriculture, taxation, transportation, consumer affairs, monetary and fiscal policy, natural resources, pollution and industrial accidents.*	*Includes worldwide scientific, medical and technological developments, natural phenomena, U.S. weather and natural disasters.*	*Includes the arts, religion, scholarship, communications media, sports, entertainment, fashions, fads, and social life.*

	World Affairs	Europe	Africa & The Middle East	The Americas	Asia & The Pacific
Apr. 18		José Vicente de Freitas becomes Prime Minister of Portugal.... Another earthquake in Bulgaria causes more damage to the country panicking people in the capital, Sofia, and badly damaging Philippopolis....David, Baron Dalziel of Wooler, pioneer of motor cabs in Britain, dies aged 75.	The United Palestine Appeal raises $1 million in contributions from New York alone....A French company, U.L.F. Company and a British one, J. D. White, get the contract to build the Trans-Persian Railway, subject to the approval of the Majilis, the Persian parliament.	Senor Montes de Oca, the Mexican Minister of Finance, announces that the finances of his country are in a much better state than outside observers believed.	The agreement between the Shanghai Municipal Council and the Chinese Ratepayers' Association is ratified by foreign ratepayers at their annual general meeting, and the resolution also agrees to the admittance of Chinese to public parks in the foreign settlements in China.
Apr. 19		The Austrian and German governments reach an agreement over the assimilation of railway traffic regulations between the two countries. This comes into force on October 1....The French Communist deputy Jacques Doriot, on the run from the police, is arrested late in the evening at Lille.		Fighting takes place at Jalisco, Mexico between government soldiers and rebels.	Japan occupies the Shantung Peninsula in China, and orders an additional 5,000 soldiers to be dispatched to Shantung to secure the railway zone under its control.
Apr. 20	The French government note, embodying the proposals to outlaw war, is issued and there are several differences between this and U.S. proposals.	King Boris of Bulgaria pleads for aid for his impoverished country suffering from several recent earthquakes.		Angle Ortiz Gallarza, the second in command of the rebel band of Maximillano Vigueras, a highway robber in Mexico, is hanged at the roadside after being captured by Mexican authorities.	Three companies of Japanese soldiers leave Tientsin for Tsinanfu, in spite of protests by the Peking government....Purnachandra Bhanj Deo, the Maharajah of Mayurbhanj, India, dies.
Apr. 21	Aristide Briand, French foreign minister, puts forward his draft treaty for outlawing war.	Large celebrations take place in Rome to commemorate the 2,681st anniversary of its foundation....The Albanian postal services inaugurate their airmail service from Vlorë to Brindisi, Italy.		The Peruvian government have their third submarine launched at New London, Connecticut....The New York Times publishes reports on Confederate settlements in Brazil to where former Confederate soldiers, their families and supporters move at the end of the American Civil War.	The Nanking government also protests at the increase in the number of Japanese soldiers in Shantung.... Japanese police in Pyongyang, arrest Korean Communist leader Pak Hyong-byong, along with 50 of his supporters who had recently created a break-away Communist Party.
Apr. 22		An earthquake in Corinth, Greece, results in the destruction of 200,000 buildings, and hundreds of thousands of people are made homeless....The first round of elections in France results in a victory for the National Union of the Left, with 200 deputies being elected....The Soviet Union reaffirms that it will continue to follow the trade policy outlined by Vladimir Lenin.		Mining companies in Canada draw up plans to prospect in remote parts of the country by plane, following the successful flight of Captain Hubert Wilkins and U.S. pilot Lieutenant Carl Ben Eielson.... Naturalists led by Dr. Townsend of the New York Aquarium save 100 big tortoises from The Galapagos Islands, taking them to Balboa, Panama, to take part in a project to try to save the species.	Massive numbers of casualties from the fighting in Shantung, China, overwhelm hospitals in Tsingtao and other cities....Many other Chinese flock to Manchuria....The Prelude to Battle by Manfred Gottfried, a story set in Mongolia, is published in New York by John Day Company.
Apr. 23		Authorities in Corinth, Greece, appeal for aid to help them recover from the devastating earthquake.... Anton Rintelen becomes Premier of Steiermark, Austria, taking over from Hans Paul.			Pratapchandra Bhanj Deo becomes the Maharajah of Mayurbhanj, India.
Apr. 24		Alfred Cerné becomes Mayor of Rouen, France, taking over from Louis Dubreuil....Further earthquake shock waves strike Corinth, Greece....General Pieter Wrangel, one of the White Russian leaders during the Russian Civil War dies, aged 50....British Chancellor of the Exchequer Winston Churchill introduces his budget to the House of Commons in London.			The Australian government sells the Commonwealth Shipping Line to a British group. They also announce that they will raise a film tax.... Chinese Nationalist forces secure Tsinan.
Apr. 25		A giant French motor flying boat, the Richard Penhoet, plunges into the seat at St. Nazaire, killing one of the crew, with three others being injured.	The Maker of Modern Arabia, a biography of King Ibn Saud, written by Ameen Rihani, an American poet of Syrian birth, and who interviewed Ibn Saud, is published in Boston, Massachusetts, by Houghton Mifflin Company.	Sir William H. Clarke is appointed as High Commissioner in Canada.	The first Japanese soldiers dispatched from Japan itself arrive at Tsinanfu on the Shantung peninsula.

A	B	C	D	E
Includes developments that affect more than one world region, international organizations and important meetings of world leaders.	Includes all domestic and regional developments in Europe, including the Soviet Union.	Includes all domestic and regional developments in Africa and the Middle East.	Includes all domestic and regional developments in Latin America, the Caribbean, and Canada.	Includes all domestic and regional developments in Asian and Pacific nations (and colonies).

U.S. Politics & Social Issues	U.S. Foreign Policy & Affairs, Defense	U.S. Economy & Environment	Science, Technology & Nature	Culture, Leisure & Lifestyle	
Al Smith heads for victory in the California Democratic Party Primary.	Some U.S. senators move to prevent any of the $364 million allocated in the Naval Appropriations Bill from being spent in Nicaragua....U.S. Marines in Nicaragua capture a supply base they claim was being used by rebel General Augusto Sandino.		Irish aviator Commander James Fitzmaurice writes of his adventures during the recent transatlantic crossing in *The Times*, in London.	In his will, the late Chauncey M. Depew leaves $1 million to Yale University....Following the gift of $50,000 from S.R. Guggenheim, the Hebrew Union Fund states that it holds $1.5 million for its endowment.	Apr. 18
Some Republicans still feel that drafting Calvin Coolidge for the presidential elections would give their party a better chance of defeating New York governor, Al Smith....Harry F. Sinclair, the man at the center of the oil scandal, on trial at the Supreme Court in the District of Columbia, finally changes his defense.		Winds lash New York and drive waves over the Battery Wall.	Irish aviator James Fitzmaurice claims that with a wireless set on board his plane, he and Hermann Köhl would have reached New York more easily, resulting in many other aviators deciding to put radio sets on their aircraft....British entrepreneur, 1st Baron Eversley, pioneer of the sixpenny telegrams, dies, aged 96.		Apr. 19
Calvin Coolidge comes out angrily against attempts to draft him forbidding the use of his name in another ballot....Judge Franklin W. Taylor from Brooklyn chided jurors in a rebuke over their decision to free a motorist who, through reckless driving, killed Robert Wotherspoon, aged 8.		The U.S. Senate postal cuts save $38,650,000.	German aviators Baron Gunther von Hünefeld and Captain Herman Köhl remain on Greenely Island awaiting repairs after the crash landing of their aircraft.	*The Harvest Wagon* by English painter Thomas Gainsborough, from the collection of Judge Elbert H. Gary, was bought at auction by Sir Joseph Duveen for $360,000, some $90,000 more than was previously paid for a single painting.	Apr. 20
As the primaries continue, it becomes clear that Herbert Hoover will be able to easily win the Republican Party nomination....The Ku Klux Klan considers standing candidates in New Jersey.		The Sinclair trail for conspiracy to defraud the government ends with Harry F. Sinclair being acquitted of the oil lease fraud with the jury retiring for two hours.	Australian explorer and aviator Captain Hubert Wilkins and U.S. pilot Lieutenant Carl Ben Eielson arrive in Spitsbergen, Norway, after making the first flight across the Arctic. U.S. Secretary of State Frank B. Kellogg congratulates the two aviators....The Visagraph is introduced to help blind people read.		Apr. 21
Al Smith attends another rally in North Carolina where 5,000 people cheer him as he meets supporters in Salisbury.			*The Times* in London publishes the official version of the flight of Hubert Wilkins....Day Keech establishes a new land speed record of 207 miles per hour at Daytona Beach, Florida.	It is revealed that private benefactions to 975 institutes of higher education in the United States actually exceed their total income from fees....*Nationalism: A Cause of Anti-Semitism*, by Samuel Blitz, is published in New York by Bloch Publishing Company.	Apr. 22
Al Smith tells reporters that he was really happy with his visit to the South and their support for him.	The Nicaraguan nationalist rebel, General Augusto Sandino, captures American-owned Bonanza and La Luz gold mines, the largest in the country, taking five U.S. civilians as prisoners and destroying much of the mining equipment. The Nicaraguan government announces their total surprise by this action.	U.S. House of Representatives votes down the Flood Bill amendments.		Writer Sinclair Lewis, newly divorced, announces that he will be marrying Dorothy Thompson, the daughter of a Methodist minister in London.	Apr. 23
Republican presidential hopeful Herbert Hoover wins the Ohio primary.	Reports reach the United States that George B. Marshall, thought to have been captured when rebels loyal to General Augusto Sandino took the La Luz mines, was killed during the fighting.	There are reports in the United States that U.S. interests are organizing a oil deal with the Soviet Union....The Flood Control Bill is finally passed by the House of Representatives.	The fathometer, used to measure underwater depths, is patented....Plans begin for a regular flight for airmail deliveries from Spain to New York....The American Geographical Society honors Hubert Wilkins by awarding him the Samuel Finley Breese Morse Gold Medal.	The books from the collection of the late Judge Elbert H. Gary are sold for $18,945, a set of books by Rudyard Kipling selling for $1,000. This brings the total money raised from the sale of his collection to $2,318,708....J.T. Burke, born in Limerick, Ireland, and a veteran of both the Crimean War and then the American Civil War, who was a chief clerk for 51 years in the U.S. Lighthouse Service, dies, aged 92.	Apr. 24
Herbert Hoover continues to draw much support from Republican primaries and establishes an unassailable lead on his opponents.	The U.S. Senate votes, by a majority of three, to reject a proposal to withdraw U.S. Marines from Nicaragua.		Frank Lockhart is killed instantly when his car crashes at Daytona Beach while he is trying to establish a new land speed record....U.S. aviator Flouyd Bennett, dies of pneumonia in Quebec, Canada.	Sir George Rowland Hill, former president and honorary secretary of the Rugby Union, dies, aged 73.	Apr. 25

F	G	H	I	J
Includes campaigns, elections, federal-state relations, civil rights and liberties, crime, the judiciary, education, healthcare, poverty, urban affairs, and population.	Includes formation and debate of U.S. foreign and defense policies, veterans affairs, and defense spending. (Relations with specific foreign countries are usually found under the region concerned.)	Includes business, labor, agriculture, taxation, transportation, consumer affairs, monetary and fiscal policy, natural resources, pollution and industrial accidents.	Includes worldwide scientific, medical and technological developments, natural phenomena, U.S. weather and natural disasters.	Includes the arts, religion, scholarship, communications media, sports, entertainment, fashions, fads, and social life.

	World Affairs	Europe	Africa & The Middle East	The Americas	Asia & The Pacific
Apr. 26	There is a sharp attack in a French newspaper, *Journal des Débats*, on the state of the disarmament talks.	The Spanish and Swedish governments sign a treaty of arbitration, conciliation and judicial settlement....Further earthquake shocks are felt throughout the Balkans.... Margot Asquith, widow of the late Earl of Oxford and Asquith (formerly Herbert H. Asquith), British prime minister from 1908 to 1916, is paid $50,000 for writing a novel, *Octavia*, about a 17-year-old heroine, in a style said to closely resemble Jane Austen.		Mexican Minister of Finance Luis Montes de Oca, in an extensive interview with The *New York Times*, tries to rebuild confidence in the Mexican economy.	
Apr. 27		Bela Kun, the Hungarian Communist leader is arrested by the Vienna police....Oliviera Salazar becomes minister of finance of Portugal and is invested with wide powers, becoming prime minister four years later, and ruler of Portugal until 1968....The French government announce plans to build statues to Sou-Lieutenant Charles Eugene Jules Marie Nungesser, François Coli and Charles Lindbergh to commemorate the first three to fly from France across the Atlantic to North America.	A train is derailed near Worcester, 120 miles from Cape Town, South Africa, with eight people killed and seven injured....*The Marsh Arab: Haji Rikkan*, an account of the life of the Marsh Arabs of Iraq is published in Philadelphia, Pennsylvania, by J. B. Lippincott Company, having been published in London by Chatto and Windus at the end of 1927.		Dr. K. St. Vincent Welch is appointed as the aerial medical officer for the Northern Territory, Australia, with the planned introduction of the Australian Flying Doctor Service.
Apr. 28		The Norwegian government announces that they will have large celebrations to honor Australian aviator Captain Hubert Wilkins and U.S. pilot Lieutenant Carl Ben Eielson when they reach Oslo.			The Peking and Nanking governments both inform the Portuguese government that both of them propose to revise the Sino-Portuguese Treaty of 1888 within the next six months....Relief organizations seek $500,000 to deal with those made homeless and/or destitute in the recent fighting in China.
Apr. 29	The French government welcomes changes made by U.S. Secretary of State Frank B. Kellogg in his proposed anti-war treaty.	Austrian authorities holding Bela Kun, the Hungarian revolutionary, announce that they are examining his papers to find out whether he is planning any plots against the governments of either Austria or Hungary.....The second ballot in the French general elections takes place, with a resounding victory for Raymond Poincaré.	The British in Egypt send an ultimatum demanding that the Egyptian Parliament withdraws the Public Assemblies Bill within 48 hours and allow freedom for public meetings in Egypt.	Archaeologists in Mexico find the mummified bodies of more than 100 men, women and children in a cave near San Juan Nepomuceno, and announce that there is another unexplored cave nearby.	
Apr. 30	British secretary of state for foreign affairs Sir Austen Chamberlain announces that the British government welcomes the U.S. proposals regarding an antiwar treaty; and the German government announce that they would immediately sign the new treaty.	Piotr Pawel Dunin-Borkowski stands down as Governor of Lwowskie, Poland....The German government welcomes U.S. proposals for the conclusion of an international treaty against war.	The British send five warships to Egypt from Malta, and the Egyptian Parliament withdraws the Public Assemblies Bill....Lady Mary Bailey arrives in Cape Town, South Africa, at the end of her flight from England.		In response to the increased number of Japanese soldiers at Tsinanfu, the Northern forces withdraw and cut the railway lines between Tsinanfu and Tsingtao, thereby isolating the 2,500 Japanese soldiers at Tsinanfu.
May 1		Trial in France of Alsatian conspirators who wanted autonomy and campaigned for a separate status for Alsace....The Austrian and Jugoslav governments sign a convention in Belgrade, regarding judicial relations....Paul de Cocatrix becomes President of the Council of State of Valais Canton, Switzerland, replacing Oscar Walpen; and Heinrich Mousson becomes President of the Government of Zurich Canton, Switzerland, replacing Fritz Ottiker.	The Egyptian government replies to the British ultimatum.	General Sir Arthur Currie wins a libel case against a Canadian newspaper which accused him of sacrificing lives at the battle of Mons in 1914 and awards him £100, completely exonerating him.	Chiang Kai-shek's Chinese Nationalist forces enter Tsinanfu.
May 2		Gaston Veil becomes Mayor of Nantes, France, taking over from Paul Bellamy....Lady Maud Hoare, wife of the British Secretary of State for Air, Sir Samuel Hoare, opens the newly revamped Croydon Airport, London, which is claimed to be the first custom-built airport in the world.	The British warn the Egyptians that of the Public Assemblies Bill is revived, the British will intervene in Egypt. However, the British ships which left Malta two days earlier, are directed to take a different course.		The Warlord "government" in Peking sends planes to bomb Shanghai.... Chinese Communist Mao Tse-tung reports to the Kiangsi Provincial Communist Party Committee and to the Central Committee of the Communist Party about developments in China.

A	B	C	D	E
Includes developments that affect more than one world region, international organizations and important meetings of world leaders.	Includes all domestic and regional developments in Europe, including the Soviet Union.	Includes all domestic and regional developments in Africa and the Middle East.	Includes all domestic and regional developments in Latin America, the Caribbean, and Canada.	Includes all domestic and regional developments in Asian and Pacific nations (and colonies).

U.S. Politics & Social Issues	U.S. Foreign Policy & Affairs, Defense	U.S. Economy & Environment	Science, Technology & Nature	Culture, Leisure & Lifestyle	
	U.S. Marines are sent to eastern Nicaragua to prevent the rebel leader General Augusto Sandino from withdrawing to that part of Nicaragua.			Madame Tussaud's waxwork museum opens in London....*Stonewall Jackson: The Good Solder—a Narrative*, by Allen Tate, is published in New York by Minton, Balch & Co.	Apr. 26
The Republican leader Martin Madden dies of a heart attack in Washington, DC, aged 72. He had been a member of the House of Representatives for Illinois for 23 years.		The U.S. Department of Justice sues several film distributors, charging 10 corporations and 32 trade boards with conspiracy to violate the Sherman Anti-Trust Act.	U.S. aviator Floyd Bennett is buried with national honors....Sir William S. Church, eminent British physician, dies aged 90.	Hillaire Belloc's *A History of England* is published in New York by G. P. Putnam's Sons.	Apr. 27
Herbert Hoover enters the Republican primary for West Virginia.	The U.S. Navy, in battle array, heads for Honolulu, Hawaii.	The U.S. government announces that the number of Civil War pensioners now stands at 79,300. It had been 745,822, but deaths—1283 in March 1928 alone—have considerably reduced the numbers.... A snowstorm sweeps over the east and the south of the United States, with three drowned during a gale in New Jersey.		Two dancers in Moscow, Agnessa Koreleva and Natalie Aksenova, both aged 20, after having fallen in love with a scenery painter, leap to their death during a performance. The two were unable to resolve their love affairs. The audience panics at the final curtain call when the two ballerinas, plunged from the uppermost part of the stage.	Apr. 28
The funeral for Congressmen Martin B. Madden is held in Washington, DC.	Nicaraguan rebel leader General Augusto Sandino writes to Henry J. Amphlett, the British administrator of the La Luz mine in Nicaragua, informing him of the destruction of the American-owned mine. Amphlett narrowly escaped the capture of the mine by Sandino on April 23.		The U.S. Congress votes to give the aviators from the *City of Bremen* medals.		Apr. 29
The U.S. Senate vote unanimously to allow full scrutiny of campaign funds....The Californian Primaries are held with victories for both Al Smith for the Democrats and Herbert Hoover for the Republicans.		In the oil bond scandal, Harry F. Sinclair announces that he received $757,000 in profits from the Continental Trading Company.	Aviators Captain Hermann Köhl, Baron von Hünefeld and Commandant James Fitzmaurice receive a massive ticker-tape parade through New York.	Jacques Schnieder, donor of the Schneider Trophy for seaplanes (first awarded in 1911), dies, aged 50.	Apr. 30
Frank White stands down as Treasurer at the Department of Treasury....Walter E. Batterson becomes Mayor of Hartford, Connecticut, taking over from Norman C. Stevens.		Pitcairn Airlines (established on April 19, 1936) begins its first service. With the contract to fly U.S. mail from New York City to Atlanta, Georgia, it has one small-wing single engine aircraft. It later expands and changes its name first to Eastern Air Transport and then to Eastern Air Lines.	British aviator and aircraft designer Lawrence Wackett in a Widgeon II, accompanied by Pilot Officer H. C. Owen and A. C. W. K. Tompkins leaves Richmond, New South Wales, Australia, intending to fly to Singapore.	Sir Ebenezer Howard, prominent British urban planner and pioneer of the garden city, dies, aged 78.	May 1
Police are involved in a raid on an illegal brewery next door to the home of Chief Ed J. Carey in Emeryville, California. They find 5,000 gallons of unbottled beer, and 3,000 bottles of beer. District Attorney Earl Warren files a federal complaint against Carey....The hearings over the Teapot Dome Scandal conclude.		The U.S. Treasury announces that public debt has been cut by a billion dollars a year, with outstanding Liberty Bonds being $9,638,383,450.			May 2

F	G	H	I	J
Includes campaigns, elections, federal-state relations, civil rights and liberties, crime, the judiciary, education, healthcare, poverty, urban affairs, and population.	Includes formation and debate of U.S. foreign and defense policies, veterans affairs, and defense spending. (Relations with specific foreign countries are usually found under the region concerned.)	Includes business, labor, agriculture, taxation, transportation, consumer affairs, monetary and fiscal policy, natural resources, pollution and industrial accidents.	Includes worldwide scientific, medical and technological developments, natural phenomena, U.S. weather and natural disasters.	Includes the arts, religion, scholarship, communications media, sports, entertainment, fashions, fads, and social life.

	World Affairs	Europe	Africa & The Middle East	The Americas	Asia & The Pacific
May 3	The International Commission for the Co-ordination of Agriculture, with its headquarters at the International Institute of Agriculture, in Rome, Italy, meets for the first time.	King and Queen of Afghanistan arrive in Moscow....*The Fascist Dictatorship in Italy*, by Gaetano Salvemini, is published in London by Jonathan Cape.		Medical agreement signed between the Argentine and Danish governments at Buenos Aires about reciprocal medical care....The Canadian Dominion House of Commons is critical of a vote of £30,000 to refurbish the Quebec residence of the governor-general.	Chinese Nationalist and Japanese soldiers clash at Tsinanfu in the Shantung Peninsula, with looting of some houses and businesses of Japanese in the city. During the altercations, Japanese soldiers surround the office of Huang Fu, Minister of Foreign Affairs of the National Government, and raid it.
May 4		An official at the Soviet Legation at Warsaw, Poland, is shot and wounded....The HMS *Bacchus* from the British Royal Navy is damaged during a collision with a Greek steamer in the English Channel.	Banker J. P. Morgan ends his visit to the Near East and returns to the United States.	Nicaraguan rebel leader General Augusto Sandino writes to the Patriotic League of National Defense of Quetzaltenango, Guatemala, asking for help....The 24th anniversary of the opening of the Panama Canal is marked by a ceremony at Balboa, Panama.	Fighting between Chinese Nationalist and Japanese soldiers in Tsinanfu continues with Japanese commander, Fukuta, sending an aide-de-camp to the office of Chiang Kai-shek stating that the Japanese were keen not to extend the fighting.
May 5	The United States signs an arbitration treaty with Germany.	The Soviet Minister in Warsaw presents a note of protest to the Polish government about the official being injured on the previous day.	Gaston Heenen is appointed Governor of Katanga, Belgian Congo, taking over from Léon Guilain Bureau who stepped down on January 21....Alan Cobham and his crew arrive in Devon, England, after completing the Sir Charles Wakefield Africa Survey.		Fighting in Tsinanfu finally comes to an end....Stephen Shepard Allen becomes Governor of Samoa, taking over from Sir George Spafford Richardson....Yashwant Rao becomes the Raja of Sandur, India.
May 6	Alfred Faure-Luce's *Locarno: A Dispassionate View*, translated from French, is published in New York by Alfred A. Knopf. On the same day, *The Mirage of Versailles*, by Herman Stegemann, and translated from German, is also published in New York by Alfred A. Knopf.	Massive demonstration of 200,000 people at Alba Julia, Romania, demanding the overthrow of the Bratianu government, and its replacement with a "responsible" government.			
May 7	The Chinese government ask the League of Nations to help resolve the problems in Tsinan by ordering an inquiry into events there and the cause of the flare-up....The Conference for the Protection of Literary and Artistic Works is held in Rome, Italy, and attended by 53 nations. It ends on June 2 with amendments adopted to the Berne Copyright Convention of 1886.	In Romania, airplane bombers hover over crowds of thousands of peasant protestors with Prince Carol of Romania, on a visit to Britain, is told that his presence in England is not welcome....Georgiy Chicherin presents a note of protest to the Polish Minister in Moscow over the shooting of the Russian official in Warsaw three days earlier....The age for women being allowed to vote in the United Kingdom lowered from 30 to 21.		The Costa Rican and Mexican governments sign an extradition treaty.	Japanese reinforcements reach Tsinanfu from Tsingtao, and with the presence of these, the Japanese military authorities led by General Kurota, Chief of Staff of the Japanese Sixth Division, demand of Chao Shih-hsuan, acting Commissioner for Foreign Affairs in Shantung, the withdrawal of the Nationalists from Tsinanfu and the punishment of officers connected with the looting of Japanese houses and businesses a few days earlier.
May 8		Prince Carol of Romania makes a plea to be able to remain in Britain while Sir William Joynson-Hicks, the British Secretary of State for Home Affairs, outlines, in the House of Commons, the reasons why he must leave the country.	Negotiations begin at Jeddah between Ibn Saud and Sir Gilbert Clayton with a view to settling the outstanding questions regarding Najd, Iraq and Transjordan.	Cleto González Víquez becomes President of Costa Rica, taking over from Ricardo Jiménez Oreamuno.	When the Nationalist soldiers refuse to comply with the Japanese requests, the Japanese attack, leading to the death of up to 1,000 Chinese soldiers and civilians. The Japanese government announces its decision to send a division of between 15,000 and 18,000 men, to Shantung.
May 9		Italy avoids stating whether or not it supports the anti-war treaty proposed by U.S. Secretary of State Frank B. Kellogg....Piotr Pawel Dunin-Borkowski becomes Governor of Poznanskie, Poland, replacing Adolf Rafal Jan hrabia Bninski.	James L. Clark of the Carlisle-Clark expedition of the American Museum of Natural History, leaves New York to begin a long expedition to the Sudan and East Africa.	Charles Evans Hughes, who was the head of the U.S. delegation to the 6th Pan-American Congress in Havana, Cuba, earlier in the year, urged Latin American countries to keep their faith in the Monroe Doctrine.	The Chinese Nationalists evacuate all parts of Tsinanfu except for a small garrison which holds out in the walled city. This leads to the Japanese bombarding the walled city. Warlord Chang Tso-lin then announces that in view of the Japanese aggression at Tsinanfu, he has ordered his men to suspend their fighting with the forces of Yen Hsi-shan and Feng Yu-hsiang....Britain immediately dispatches warships to China.

A	B	C	D	E
Includes developments that affect more than one world region, international organizations and important meetings of world leaders.	Includes all domestic and regional developments in Europe, including the Soviet Union.	Includes all domestic and regional developments in Africa and the Middle East.	Includes all domestic and regional developments in Latin America, the Caribbean, and Canada.	Includes all domestic and regional developments in Asian and Pacific nations (and colonies).

U.S. Politics & Social Issues	U.S. Foreign Policy & Affairs, Defense	U.S. Economy & Environment	Science, Technology & Nature	Culture, Leisure & Lifestyle	
The House of Representatives passes the McNary-Haugen Bill.		The Farm Bill finally passes in the House of Representatives 204–121, but Calvin Coolidge is expected to use his right to veto to prevent it becoming law.			May 3
	Rear Admiral S.S. Robison, who has been commandant of the 13th Naval District and the Bremerton Navy Yard, with headquarters at Seattle, for 13 years, is appointed as Superintendent of the Naval Academy at Annapolis, replacing Rear Admiral Louis M. Nulton.	Calvin Coolidge opposes the revamped Flood Bill and is likely to veto it.	Almon Elias Culberton, a geologist and the pioneer of Russian oil, helping establish the School of Mining, and working on the Grozny Oil Fields, dies, aged 72....The Second Laboratory Conference on the Serology of Syphilis is hosted by the League of Nations in Copenhagen, capital of Denmark.	Comedian Hennie Youngman marries Sadie Cohen after they originally met in a Kresge's 5 and 10 cent store in Brooklyn....Major General William J. Behan, 87, former mayor and postmaster of New Orleans, and the 1905 Commander of the United Confederate Veterans, dies in New Orleans.	May 4
With the Democratic and Republican National Conventions approaching, Al Smith now has 555 delegates—only 178 short of two-thirds for nomination; and Herbert Hoover has 436 delegates—only 109 less than he needs for nomination.		The U.S. government loses $30 million in a tax suit in a stock levy from the Ford Motor Company.	*Meteorology* by David Brunt, is published in New York by Oxford University Press.	Barry E.O. Pain, British novelist and humorist, dies, aged 63.	May 5
Florence E. S. Knapp, Dean of the College of Home Economics at Syracuse University attempts to tell her side of the story about census work and payments to relatives.	The Police Department in New York bans the colors, the armed escort and the band of the 16th Infantry of the United States, together with the color guard of the Veterans of Foreign Wars from a march to the tomb of U.S. President Ulysses S. Grant on the 108th anniversary of the birth of General Grant.		British aviator Lawrence Wackett arrives in Darwin en route to Singapore, but has problems when he takes off from Darwin airport.		May 6
Herbert Hoover sweeps to the lead in voting in the Republican primary in Maryland.	Some 18 men from the War Department dredge *Navesink* are lost in the bay after the dredge crashes into the Lamport & Holt freighter *Swinburne*, in the Narrows off Clifton, Staten Island.	The Flood Control Bill is finally revised to conform to the views of Calvin Coolidge to prevent him exercising his right of veto.		The Pulitzer Prize for fiction for 1928 is awarded to novelist Thornton Wilder for his book *The Bridge of San Luis Rey.* The Pulitzer Prize for cartooning is awarded to Nelson Harding of the Brroklyn Daily Eagle for his cartoon: "May his Shadow Never Grow Less." Pulitzer Prize for Biography is awarded to Charles Edward Russell for his book *The American Orchestra and Theodore Thomas.* Eugene O'Neill wins the Pulitzer Prize for Drama/ Plays (with *Strange Interlude*), and Edwin Arlington Robinson wins the Pulitzer Prize for the Best Verse for his poem *Tristram.*	May 7
The jury hearing the case of Florence E. S. Knapp, Dean of the College of Home Economics at Syracuse University, disagree, with, reportedly six favoring acquittal, and a new trial is ordered....Ralph H. Oyler, chief of the Federal Narcotic Division finds $250,000 worth of cocaine at the Fordham Branch of the Colonial Bank.					May 8
Herbert Hoover receives a setback in his presidential bid in Indiana with Vice-President Charles Dawes expected to pick up a majority of the votes.		John D. Rockefeller, speaking as a shareholder in the Standard Oil Company of Indiana, calls on Colonel Robert W. Stewart to resign as Chairman of its Board of Directors.		A massive orchid show is held in New York with entries from around the world including some from Sir Jeremiah Colman of London and Gurney Wilson, Secretary of the Orchid Committee of the Royal Horticultural Society of England. Of particular note is a rare orchid collection from Central America brought by A. A. Hunter of Balboa.	May 9

F	G	H	I	J
Includes campaigns, elections, federal-state relations, civil rights and liberties, crime, the judiciary, education, healthcare, poverty, urban affairs, and population.	*Includes formation and debate of U.S. foreign and defense policies, veterans affairs, and defense spending. (Relations with specific foreign countries are usually found under the region concerned.)*	*Includes business, labor, agriculture, taxation, transportation, consumer affairs, monetary and fiscal policy, natural resources, pollution and industrial accidents.*	*Includes worldwide scientific, medical and technological developments, natural phenomena, U.S. weather and natural disasters.*	*Includes the arts, religion, scholarship, communications media, sports, entertainment, fashions, fads, and social life.*

	World Affairs	Europe	Africa & The Middle East	The Americas	Asia & The Pacific
May 10		At a grand ceremony in Britain, Westminster Abbey was full for the investiture of the new Knights of Bath....Riots and demonstrations continue in Romania with a fourth foreign correspondent arrested for writing anti-government articles.	Capitulations, by which foreign residents enjoyed extraterritorial protection, are abolished in Persia, along with a new customs tariff. The Persian government also reaches a provisional agreement with Great Britain on commercial relations and the status of British nationals in Persia.		The Nationalists in the walled city of Tsinanfu hold out in spite of a massive Japanese barrage against them.
May 11		The Austrian and Italian governments sign an air navigation convention....Grigory Naumovich Aronshtam becomes 1st Secretary of the Turkmen Communist Party taking over from Halmurad Sakhatmuradov....The British Divisional Court holds that it is illegal to use a hall for the playing of progressive whist or knock-out competitions.	The Persian government reaches a provisional agreement with France over commercial relations with them and the status of their nationals in Persia.		The Japanese army announces that it is finally in control of all of Tsinanfu, including the walled city....The League of Nations Secretariat announces that it has received a telegram from the Nanking government complaining that the territorial integrity and political independence of China as been violated by Japanese aggression.
May 12	A large international exhibition is held at Cologne, Germany, to commemorate the "printed word."	Following a vote in the Italian parliament, Benito Mussolini reduces the Italian electorate from 12 million to 3 million with his new regulations that remove the right for women to vote, and restricts the franchise to males aged 21 or over, and who pay union dues, or taxes, or a payment of 100 lire....German statesman President Paul von Hindenburg asserts that he does not belong to any political party.			
May 13		In France, large celebrations take place to commemorate Joan of Arc, the medieval French heroine who defeated the English but was eventually captured and executed by them....Nikolai Bukharin addresses the Congress of the Communist Youth Organization in Moscow.	The *New York Times* runs a long article extolling the virtues of a trouble-free lifestyle in Palestine.		The Nanking government publishes a telegram addressed to Calvin Coolidge asking the attitude of his government to the incident at Tsinanfu and the role of the Japanese forces there.
May 14	The International Institute of Agriculture meets at Geneva; the meeting ends on May 19.	The Spanish government decides to massive increase the size of their navy....The German foreign minister Dr. Gustav Stresemann falls ill, leading to alarm in Germany....The German railroads decide to end first class travel.	The Persian government promises Germany that it will get "Most Favored Nation Status" over commercial relations with them and the status of their nationals in Persia.		Baron Gowrie, formerly Brigadier-General Hon. Sir Alexander Gore Arkwright Hore-Ruthven becomes governor of South Australia.
May 15	Calvin Coolidge ratifies the arbitration treaty between the United States and Germany....Rumors circulate that U.S. Secretary of State Frank B. Kellogg is to be awarded the Nobel Peace Prize in November.	The condition of Dr. Gustav Stresemann, the German foreign minister, continues to deteriorate with his kidneys ceasing to function well.	The Persian government promises the U.S. government that it will get "Most Favored Nation Status" over commercial relations with them and the status of U.S. nationals in Persia.		The Royal Flying Doctor Service of Australia starts operations from Cloncurry, Queensland, founded by Reverend John Flynn, with the help of the Australian Inland Mission and Qantas. The first flight is made by aviator Arthur Affleck and Sydney surgeon Dr. Vincent Welch....The Japanese War Office instructs the Japanese commander at Tsinanfu regarding terms demanded by the Nanking government.
May 16	The Fifth International Seed Testing Congress opens under the auspices of the International Institute of Agriculture, based in Rome, Italy. Its meetings last until May 19.	Prince Carol of Romania leaves Britain after being told that his presence in the country is not welcome.		Horatio Columbres, a 35-year-old Argentine student and dancing instructor shoots dead Maria Montero, a dancer whom he is in love with, and then commits suicide by shooting himself.	
May 17		With the German general elections approaching, it seems likely that the Nationalists might gain control of the Reichstag.		U.S. Aeronautical Commissioner J. D. Summers heads to Chile to advise the Chilean government on civil aviation issues.	Western powers grow nervous as fighting moves to Tientsin where there are 2,195 Americans and equally large numbers of British and French citizens.

A	B	C	D	E
Includes developments that affect more than one world region, international organizations and important meetings of world leaders.	Includes all domestic and regional developments in Europe, including the Soviet Union.	Includes all domestic and regional developments in Africa and the Middle East.	Includes all domestic and regional developments in Latin America, the Caribbean, and Canada.	Includes all domestic and regional developments in Asian and Pacific nations (and colonies).

U.S. Politics & Social Issues	U.S. Foreign Policy & Affairs, Defense	U.S. Economy & Environment	Science, Technology & Nature	Culture, Leisure & Lifestyle	
Al Smith's election campaign is now stated to have spent $92,090, and is examined by the Senate Special Committee investigating Presidential nomination campaign funds. All the names of Smith's principle donors are published—William F. Kenny heads the list with $10,000 in 1927 and $40,000 in 1928.	*The Bankers in Bolivia*, a study in U.S. foreign investments by Margaret A. Marsh, is published in New York by The Vanguard Press.		Hubert Wilkins and Carl Ben Eielson leave Spitsbergen to head to a round of functions in various European capitals.	The Rockefeller family fight a zoning dispute in New York....Sir Joseph Duveen buys the painting "Madonna and Child" by Raphael Santi, for $750,000 from Lady Desborough.	May 10
It is revealed that $250,000 has been spent by Herbert Hoover....Treasury Secretary Andrew Mellon claims in an interview that Hebert Hoover would be able to defeat Al Smith.	*Our Cuban Colony*, by Leland H. Jenks, a history of U.S. relations with Cuba, is published in New York by The Vanguard Press.		Charles Lindbergh celebrates the anniversary of his flight across the Atlantic quietly.	*The Grub Street Journal* by James T. Hillhouse, a history of the 18th-century periodical, is published in Durham, NC, by Duke University Press.	May 11
Treasury Secretary Andrew Mellon continues his speeches in favor of Herbert Hoover declaring his former cabinet colleague as being "closest to the standard" set for the presidency....It is now revealed that the election fund of Herbert Hoover is $300,000.	*The American Secretaries of State and their Diplomacy*, edited by Samuel Flagg Bemis is published in New York by Alfred A. Knopf, the third book on U.S. foreign policy in three days.			Dr. S.C. Kohs of Brooklyn, in a speech at Cincinatti, OH, makes a speech saying that 250,000 Jews are "lost to the faith."...The British literary scene are trying to raise enough money to ensure that the manuscript of Lewis Carroll's *Alice in Wonderland*, bought by American collector Dr. A.S.W. Rosenbach, does not leave the country.	May 12
	The Chinese government implores Calvin Coolidge and the U.S. government to come to their aid in the fighting with Japan.	Firemen and volunteers battle a forest fire at Worcester, Massachusetts.			May 13
George S. Graham, Chairman of the House Judiciary Committee claimed that overcrowding in federal prisons was bad and conditions were "inhuman."		New York State government in Albany drew a check for $33,723,734 for the appropriation for support of New York common schools—up to that point, the largest bank check ever issued....10 men from a fishing trip drown in the Moosehead Lake, near Greenville, Maine.	A 48-hour airmail service is inaugurated between New York and Madrid, Spain.	Regulations are introduced in New York City to reduce the number of street vendor carts....A Berlin court acquits Frau von Pathelff-Kellman, supporter of the Anastasia claimant.	May 14
Calvin Coolidge signs the Flood Control Bill into law, and the U.S. government announces that work will begin soon....Hoover picks up six more convention seats from Alabama.	The U.S. Ambassador to Japan Charles MacVeagh presents the Japanese government with a lock of hair from Commodore Matthew Galbraith Perry who "opened" Japan in July 1853.		Explorers from the Stoll-McCracken Museum Expedition in Alaska find hummingbirds.	The release of the animated short "Plane Crazy," which features the first appearances of Mickey Mouse and Minnie Mouse....Dr. Lough, the "floating college head" of New York University is ousted and sues for $100,000 in damages.	May 15
Al Smith's supporters, led by William F. Kenny, state their determination to donate more to Smith's presidential bid.		AT&T gives rights worth $155.4 million to stockholders in the mass issuing of new shares.		Major-General Sir Edward Calllwell, British soldier and writer, dies, aged 69....The British critic and poet Sir Edmund W. Gosse dies, aged 78.	May 16
Moves are made to nominate Colonel William J. Donovan of Buffalo, assistant to the Attorney-General John G. Sargent as a possible Republican vice-presidential running mate for Herbert Hoover.	A U.S. marine is killed in Nicaragua, along with five rebels supports of General Augusto Sandino in a shoot-out at Puerto Cabezas....The U.S. Navy is involved in a large military exercise near Oahu, HI.	Complaints are made that golf is being taxed out of existence in the new budget.	Lady Heath arrives at Croydon Airport, London, after completing the first solo woman's flight from Cape Town, South Africa to England.	Four paintings by Rembrandt are sold at auction by Christie's, in London for $755,000....Dr. Chaim Weizmann, President of the World Zionist Organization who was chosen to investigate the Zionist Organisation of America (ZOA) after allegations were made in a newspaper *The New Palestine*, exonerates the ZOA.	May 17

F	G	H	I	J
Includes campaigns, elections, federal-state relations, civil rights and liberties, crime, the judiciary, education, healthcare, poverty, urban affairs, and population.	Includes formation and debate of U.S. foreign and defense policies, veterans affairs, and defense spending. (Relations with specific foreign countries are usually found under the region concerned.)	Includes business, labor, agriculture, taxation, transportation, consumer affairs, monetary and fiscal policy, natural resources, pollution and industrial accidents.	Includes worldwide scientific, medical and technological developments, natural phenomena, U.S. weather and natural disasters.	Includes the arts, religion, scholarship, communications media, sports, entertainment, fashions, fads, and social life.

	World Affairs	Europe	Africa & The Middle East	The Americas	Asia & The Pacific
May 18	William "Bill" Haywood, founder of the International Workers of the World, dies in Moscow.	The Vatican officially denies that King Alfonso of Spain is seeking an annulment of his marriage to Queen Victoria....In electioneering in Germany, Nazis kill one Republican, and Communists kill one of their opponents....In the Soviet Union a trial opens of 52 people charged with prisoners charged with "class crimes." U.S. journalist Walter Duranty covers the case.			The Japanese government hands the Peking and Nanking governments a memorandum on Japanese policies in China and Manchuria, ordering Chang Tso-lin to withdraw his troops to Manchuria of Japan would "close Manchuria to him." The Japanese are worried that Chang might reach an accommodation with Chiang Kai-shek and warn the warlord that if he does not return to Manchuria quickly, he might not be able to control the situation there.
May 19	The British government announces its support for the anti-war proposals of U.S. Secretary of State Frank B. Kellogg.	F. A. Wilson, an English woman, is murdered in the pine forest at Le Touquet, France.		Eduardo Henrique Girão is appointed acting governor of Ceará, Brazil, replacing José Moreira da Rocha.	The Chinese government signs a treaty of friendship and trade with Poland. At the same time Chiang Kai-shek leads his soldiers from the Tientsin-Pukow Railway at Hsuchow to the Peking-Hankow Railway at Chengchow where the soldiers meet with the men of Generals Feng Yu-hsiang and Pai Ch'ung-hsi.
May 20	The British government reply to the U.S. proposals to have an antiwar treaty stating that they support them providing it will not violate the Treaty of Locarno.	The general election in Germany for a new Reichstag leads to a swing to the left, and result in the Nazi Party getting 2.6 percent of the vote, coming in ninth.		General Luis Mena, who had been acting President of Nicaragua in 1910, is assassinated at Pnelova while supporting the election campaign of presidential nominee Maria José Moncada.	The U.S. government hands a note to the Nanking Minister for Foreign Affairs calling for his attention to investigating the murders of American missionaries during the advance of the Nationalists in Shantung.
May 21		In Hamburg, Germany, a cloud of phosgene gas, large enough to be capable of killing all the people in Hamburg, hangs over the city harbor with the League of Nations expected to investigate....In London, England, the Royal Navy chief of staff Admiral Sir Charles Madden circulates his refutation of the claim by Lord Trenchard, the Marshal of the Royal Air Force, that the British should use their air force to attack enemy citizens in time of war.			The Japanese start massing troops at the Manchurian border to control the flight of any soldiers from the warlord army of Chang Tso-lin.... Members of the Chinese community around the world start organizing, with the establishment of The Anti-Japanese Association of Chinese Residents in New York and various other groups.
May 22	At an international chess masters' tournament in Trencianske Teplice, Czechoslovakia, Rudolph Spielmann of Austria wins some of the early rounds after beating Walter of Czechoslovakia.	Investigations in Hamburg, Germany, link the German Army to the large amount of poisonous phosgene gas which appeared over the city's harbor....The Austrian and Polish governments ratify the convention of November 24, 1926, regarding the ending of double death duties for residents of both countries, especially those living in southern Poland which had been a part of the Austro-Hungarian Empire.	Negotiations in Jeddah between Ibn Saud and the British representative, Sir Gilbert Clayton, are suspended over disagreements with the status of Transjordan.	Francisco Lopez Merino, Argentine poet, commits suicide in Buenos Aires, aged 23....Demonstrations take place in Rosario in northern Argentina where 400,000 people are protesting against the government allowing in cheap imports costing many jobs in this important industrial center.	The Japanese government seems to indicate that they would prefer the Nationalist Kuomintang Party ruling Peking than warlord Chang Tso-lin.
May 23	Boris Kortisch from Serbia wins another chess game at the international chess masters' tournament in Trencianske Teplice, Czechoslovakia after defeating Baldur Hoenlinger of Germany.	The Italian North Pole Expedition, in the airship *Italia*, drops the Italian and Milanese flags on the North Pole.		A bomb attack by anti-fascists on the Italian Consulate in Buenos Aires, Argentina, results in the death of 22, with another 41 injured, many being badly mutilated. A six-year-old boy playing with another suitcase outside the consulate averts a second explosion.	The Peking government of Chang Tso-lin seeks a truce as its forces fall back. It promises that its soldiers will protect all foreign citizens in the capital.
May 24	Boris Kostich is declared the winner at the end of the international chess masters' tournament in Trencianske Teplice, Czechoslovakia.	Throughout Italy celebrations take place to commemorate the 13th anniversary of the country entering World War I....A French court convicts four Alsatians who wanted autonomy and campaigned for a separate status for Alsace through the Heimatsbund.		Captain Emilio Carranza, in a replica of the *Spirit of St Louis* of Charles Lindbergh, flies from San Diego, California, to Mexico City in preparation for a flight to Washington, DC.	General Chen Chien, a member of the radical faction of the Chinese Nationalist (Kuomintang) Party is arrested and is then reported to have been executed immediately.

A	B	C	D	E
Includes developments that affect more than one world region, international organizations and important meetings of world leaders.	Includes all domestic and regional developments in Europe, including the Soviet Union.	Includes all domestic and regional developments in Africa and the Middle East.	Includes all domestic and regional developments in Latin America, the Caribbean, and Canada.	Includes all domestic and regional developments in Asian and Pacific nations (and colonies).

U.S. Politics & Social Issues	U.S. Foreign Policy & Affairs, Defense	U.S. Economy & Environment	Science, Technology & Nature	Culture, Leisure & Lifestyle	
	Captain Robert S. Hunter dies of wounds he incurred in his fighting in Nicaragua against the rebels of General Augusto Sandino.	The U.S. Commerce Board allows the Chesapeake & Ohio Railway Company—Marquette merger but states that the Erie Railroad has to be excluded from the deal.	*Christianity in Science* by Frederick D. Leete is published in New York by The Abingdon Press.	The will of Ellsworth M. Statler, the owner of the Stattler Hotels, leaves $15 million to establish a foundation for hotel research.	**May 18**
Calvin Coolidge at a speech at Andover Academy states that spiritual training is important and that U.S. citizens must ensure that they do their duty to their country.... Alabama Senator Thomas Heflin continues with his attacks on Al Smith and William F. Kenny.	In a major study of U.S. diplomacy, Beckles Wilson's *Ambassadors to France 1777–1927* is published in New York by Frederick A. Stokes Company.	There is a big explosion at the Mather Mine in Pennsylvania caused by fire damp. Some 195 of the 273 miners are killed.		The first "frog Jumping" Jubilee is held at Angel's Camp, California, and draws 51 frogs....*The Assassination of Christopher Marlowe* by Samuel A. Tannenbaum, is published in New York by The Tenny Press.	**May 19**
	As fighting in Nicaragua escalates again, rebel leader General Augusto Sandino writes to the U.S. section of the All-America Anti-Imperialist League in New York City thanking them for medical supplies which they sent him.				**May 20**
Allegations that Democratic Party presidential hopeful Alfred E. Smith had established a large "slush fund" in North Carolina to circumvent the regulations on financing campaigns prove unfounded with only $3500 found in the state.... Calvin Coolidge prepares to veto the Farm Bill.		The U.S. Senate passes a Tax Bill with tax cuts of $205,875,000.	The British House of Commons discusses a report that the Imperial Cable and Wireless Conference, meeting in London, will recommend the transfer of post office cables and beam wireless stations within the British Empire to a new company formed from a merger of all empire cable and wireless communications entities.	Clarence Hackney, wins the Professional Golf Association championship in Philadelphia.	**May 21**
Lieutenant-Colonel Theodore Roosevelt criticizes the election bid of Democratic Party hopeful Alfred E. Smith....Huey P. Long becomes Governor of Louisiana, taking over from Oramel H. Simpson....The U.S. House of Representatives overrides two of the eight bills vetoed by Calvin Coolidge....The second trial of Florence E. S. Knapp, former New York Secretary of State, is delayed when she falls ill.		The U.S. Congress passes the Jones-White Act which subsidizes American shipping and mail contracts.		The Stoll McCracken Expedition, on the schooner *Morrissey*, is involved in archaeological work in Alaska, working along the shore of the Bering Sea, where they find ancient burial caves. The Expedition also takes aboard its schooner, Father Demetrie Hotowski, of Beikofski, a famous Alaskan Russian priest and big-game hunter.	**May 22**
Republican donors from New York State and elsewhere raise the amount of money in Herbert Hoover's campaign fund to $310,000....Calvin Coolidge vetoes the Farm Relief Bill calling it a deceptive, price-fixing scheme. The numbers in the Senate who support the bill are clearly not enough to override the presidential veto.				Irish playwright George Bernard Shaw, in a newspaper interview, is critical of the American people, especially in the way that rich Americans are buying much of Europe's heritage, and shipping it back to the United States....The *War Cry*, the newspaper of the Salvation Army announces that General Bramwell Booth, the founder and head of the Salvation Army, has been ordered to take a complete rest and relief from all public engagements.	**May 23**
The U.S. Senate overrides another four vetoes by Calvin Coolidge.		John D. Rockefeller announces that his proposed Mines Act will solve many of the problems facing miners at pits in West Virginia, Ohio, and Pennsylvania.	After their success on the previous day, the Italian North Pole Expedition, in the airship *Italia*, crashes, leading to the stranding the crew of 16 including General Umberto Nobile.		**May 24**

F	G	H	I	J
Includes campaigns, elections, federal-state relations, civil rights and liberties, crime, the judiciary, education, healthcare, poverty, urban affairs, and population.	*Includes formation and debate of U.S. foreign and defense policies, veterans affairs, and defense spending. (Relations with specific foreign countries are usually found under the region concerned.)*	*Includes business, labor, agriculture, taxation, transportation, consumer affairs, monetary and fiscal policy, natural resources, pollution and industrial accidents.*	*Includes worldwide scientific, medical and technological developments, natural phenomena, U.S. weather and natural disasters.*	*Includes the arts, religion, scholarship, communications media, sports, entertainment, fashions, fads, and social life.*

	World Affairs	Europe	Africa & The Middle East	The Americas	Asia & The Pacific
May 25		Moves for the union of the Church of Scotland and the United Free Church increase as the members of the Synod of the Church of Scotland vote unanimously in favor, and a vast majority of the members of the United Free Church do the same.	The Second Afghan-Turkish Treaty was signed raising the level of relations between the two countries.		Jean Marchat becomes French Resident in Wallis and Futuna....The Peking government replies to the Japanese memorandum, rejecting it....A treaty of friendship signed between Afghanistan and Turkey at Angora, Turkey.
May 26	U.S. Secretary of State Frank B. Kellogg invites the governments of the British Dominions (Australia, Canada, New Zealand and South Africa) to become original parties to his treaty to outlaw war.	A pilot and two passengers are killed when a Luft Hansa plane flying from Dortmund to Frankfurt caught fire and crashed near Elberfield. One passenger, Frau Benzkefer from Düsefldorf, survives.			Chinese government representatives in Paris sign a Treaty with representatives of the Greek government.
May 27		The Italian Minister to Belgrade, Yugoslavia, issues the first of four protests about anti-Italian attacks in Croatia and Dalmatia....The annual conference of the British Legion starts at the Yorkshire port Scarborough, and continues until May 29.			Major-General Sir Richard H. Ewart, Indian Army officer, dies, aged 63.
May 28	Dr. Alexander Alekhine, in an interview with The New York Times from Scarborough, England, states that he will defend his world chess championship title which he won at Buenos Aires, Argentina.	Charles E. Montague, the British journalist and novelist, dies, aged 61....Former Chicago resident Eddie Guerin who was imprisoned by the French at Devil's Island is jailed in London as a loiterer.	The Mixed Frontier Commission set up under the Anglo-Iraqi-Turkish Treaty of June 5, 1926, completes its work.		The Japanese government sends an official note on the Tsinanfu incident to the League of Nations denying any responsibility of their soldiers.... Martanda Bhairava Tondaiman, the Raja of Pudukkottai, India, dies.
May 29		The Shahkta trial begins in the Soviet Union with more engineers accused of sabotage.			The Nanking government rejects the Japanese memorandum.
May 30	The 11th Session of the International Labor Conference held at Geneva, Switzerland, opens, under the chairmanship of Carlos Saavedra Lamas from Argentina. It ends on June 16 with a Draft Convention being adopted establishing methods of fixing minimum wages and recommendations regarding the application of the convention.	Further demonstrations take place in Belgrade, Yugoslavia, in protests against the role of Italy and Italian interests in the country. Students burn an picture of Italian leader Benito Mussolini but one of them is later killed by the police....The leading British peer Henry Pelham Pelham-Clinton, Duke of Newcastle, dies, aged 63.	The Italo-Turkish Pact of Neutrality and Conciliation is signed in Rome, being the first political treaty that the Turkish Republic had concluded with a Western Great Power. It has to be renewed after five years.		The Liberal Party defeats the Australian Labor Party in the Tasmanian state elections, signaling an end to the political career of Joseph Lyons who had premier for five years. John Cameron McPhee becomes premier of Tasmania.
May 31		Greek politician Eleutherios Venizelos becomes the premier of Greece again, to head a new Liberal government....Violent scenes in the Jugoslav People's Assembly, the Skupstina, over Italy's role in the country....The new French Chamber of Deputies meets following elections in the previous week.	The new South African flag is hoisted throughout South Africa for the first time. Some riots take place in Cape Town.		The Japanese commander at Tsingtao demands the withdrawal of all Chinese troops to a distance of seven miles from the city by the following day.
Jun. 1			Guido Corni becomes Governor of Italian Somalia, taking over from Cesare Maria de Vecchi, Conte di Val Cismon.		Captain Filchner, a German explorer, returns to Northern India after visiting Tibet where he was surrounded by the entire Tibetan garrison of Lhasa, only managing to escape when the British, to whom he had smuggled out a note, managed to get permission from the Dalai Lama for him to leave.

A	B	C	D	E
Includes developments that affect more than one world region, international organizations and important meetings of world leaders.	Includes all domestic and regional developments in Europe, including the Soviet Union.	Includes all domestic and regional developments in Africa and the Middle East.	Includes all domestic and regional developments in Latin America, the Caribbean, and Canada.	Includes all domestic and regional developments in Asian and Pacific nations (and colonies).

U.S. Politics & Social Issues	U.S. Foreign Policy & Affairs, Defense	U.S. Economy & Environment	Science, Technology & Nature	Culture, Leisure & Lifestyle	
A court battle begins with 900 people demanding two-thirds of the estate left by John Jacob Astor when he died in 1848....The U.S. Senate is involved in a filibuster lasting 20 hours and 40 minutes. The action, to prevent the Muscle Shoals Bill, fails to prevent the bill being passed.	In spite of the persecution of Jews in Romania, the United Romanian Jews of America welcomes the forthcoming U.S. loan to Romania in the hope that it might result in better understanding between the two countries.				May 25
U.S. postal services issue a postage stamp showing George Washington at prayer, commemorating the 150th anniversary of the encampment by Washington at Valley Forge.	The Senate votes 44 to 22 to dismiss the bull to build more warships at the cost of over $100 million.	A U.S. mail pilot is killed in flight from New York to Atlanta. The plane comes down near Richmond, VA.	A British scientific expedition sets out from England to complete research work on the Great Barrier Reef off the north-east coast of Australia.	The Bronx Zoo in New York announces that it has had 2,750,704 visitors in 1927, with 51 human births in the zoo, and 181 deaths....E. J. Odell, the British actor and "Bohemian" dies, aged 93.	May 26
U.S. farmers in the Western corn belt start protesting in Kansas City....The New York Times reports on its front page that in Chicago, "the king of the city's bootleggers and vice lords" has been hired by a number of companies and unions to protect their interests.... Florence E.S. Knapp, former New York Secretary of State, collapses in court under the stress for which she was being treated.		*Administrative Powers Over Sons and Property* by Ernst Freund is published in Chicago, Illinois, by The University of Chicago Press.		The Roland Garros Tennis Court is opened in south-west Paris, France....*John Bunyan: Pilgrim and Dreamer*, by William Henry Harding, is published in New York by Fleming H. Revell.	May 27
A new edition of the correspondence of Peleg Sanford, governor of Rhode Island in the 17th century, is published by the Rhode Island Historical Society, in Providence.	Captain Robert Hunter of the U.S. Marines dies fighting the Nicaraguan rebels loyal to General Augusto Sandino.	The U.S. Senate filibuster of the Boulder Dam Bill goes on all night.	British aviator Lawrence Wackett flies from Darwin to Broome, in Australia.	*The Feathered Serpent* by well-known writer Edgar Wallace, a mystery novel, is published in New York by Doubleday, Doran and Co.	May 28
The U.S. Congress signs the Revenue Act reducing income tax....Calvin Coolidge kills the bill for the government operation of Muscle Shoals by using a pocket veto. Coolidge also vetoes the McNary-Haugen Bill for a second time....The first session of the 70th Congress ends.			Fritz van Opel reaches speeds of up to 200 kilometers per hour in an experimental rocket car.		May 29
A gang of bandits hold up 200 guests at the Indianapolis Speedway, netting between $150,000-$200,000.		Chrysler and Dodge are involved in a $450 million merger.	A rescue mission is dispatched to rescue the Italian North Pole Expedition.	*The Ghetto Messenger* by Abraham Burnstein, a novel illustrating aspects of Jewish life in New York, originally published in The *Jewish Daily News*, is published in New York by Bloch Publishing Company....The novel *Dawn*, written by Captain Reginald Berkeley, about the life of World War I nurse Edith Cavell is published in London by the London Book Co, and in New York by J.H. Sears & Co.	May 30
Calvin Coolidge chooses his cabin in Wisconsin as the Summer White House....H.T. Tate is appointed as Treasurer at the Department of Treasury.			Australian Aviators Charles Kingsford Smith and Charles Ulm, with Americans Harry Lyon and Jim Warner leave Oakland Aerodrome, San Francisco, in a Fokker FV11b-3M "Southern Cross" to make the first flight across the Pacific.	A team of scholars from Harvard University defeat Yale University in the Putnam Prize.	May 31
A bank manager in New York City is robbed of $16,000 on Dyckman Street.		A total of $67,541,834 in New York City taxes are paid in one day.	Charles Kingsford Smith and the other Australian aviators arrive in Honolulu, Hawaii, during their Trans-Pacific flight....The (British) Royal Air Force Far East Flight consisting of four Supermarine Southampton II flying boats arrive in Broome, Australia, completing the first formation flight from England to Australia, via Singapore.		Jun. 1

F	G	H	I	J
Includes campaigns, elections, federal-state relations, civil rights and liberties, crime, the judiciary, education, healthcare, poverty, urban affairs, and population.	Includes formation and debate of U.S. foreign and defense policies, veterans affairs, and defense spending. (Relations with specific foreign countries are usually found under the region concerned.)	Includes business, labor, agriculture, taxation, transportation, consumer affairs, monetary and fiscal policy, natural resources, pollution and industrial accidents.	Includes worldwide scientific, medical and technological developments, natural phenomena, U.S. weather and natural disasters.	Includes the arts, religion, scholarship, communications media, sports, entertainment, fashions, fads, and social life.

	World Affairs	Europe	Africa & The Middle East	The Americas	Asia & The Pacific
Jun. 2	The Australian government states that it will support the proposed antiwar treaty of U.S. Secretary of State Frank B. Kellogg.	Investigations by the League of Nations show that the poisonous phosgene gas which created problems in Hamburg, Germany, was manufactured during World War I, and seems to have been missed by the Inter-Allied Commission for Destroying War Materials.		The governments of Chile and Paraguay in Montevideo, Uruguay, finally ratify the Extradition Treaty signed between the two countries in 1897.	Under pressure from the Japanese, Chang Tso-lin announces his intention of withdrawing to Manchuria and starts evacuating Peking.
Jun. 3			Iraq concludes a provisional commercial agreement with Persia.		The train Peking with warlord Chang Tso-lin on board leaves Peking for Mukden. At Tientsin, two Japanese liaison officers get off the train.
Jun. 4	The 50th Session of the Council of the League of Nations opens in Geneva; it ends on June 9.	In the Soviet Union, Communist Party general-secretary Josef Stalin complains that much of the grain crop is being withheld by peasant farmers, and foreign commentators tend to agree with this.		Juan Rincón Rincón becomes Governor of Tamaulipas, Mexico, replacing Emilio Portes Gil, who later becomes President of Mexico.	The Commonwealth Savings Bank of Australia established as a separate entity....Chang Tso-lin, "The Old Marshal," one of the most powerful warlords in China, and the main military force in the Northern Coalition and the Peking government, is fatally wounded when his train is badly damaged by a bomb placed in it probably by Japanese extremists.
Jun. 5		The Norwegian and U.S. governments signed a Treaty of Friendship, Commerce and Consular Rights at Washington....Italian leader Benito Mussolini, in a speech to the Senate in Rome urges for an alliance between Italy, Greece and Turkey, proclaiming Italy to be a friend of all nations....The Albanian government presents its complaints regarding Albanian properties in Greece to the League of Nations.	The Sultan of Morocco discovers an item of his treasure in the house of his ex-Palace Chamberlain who expresses his amazement at the precious plate being there. He was seeking treatment from a doctor at the time and swore that he had no idea how the gold and silver plate, jewels and pearls ended up in his house, although he did state that a few small items had been given to him as presents by the King's late father.	The governments of the United States and Honduras ratify the extradition treaty signed on February 21, 1927....The U.S. representative on the Mixed Boundary Commission to establish the Guatemala-Honduras border recommends arbitration and suggests that the dispute is submitted to the Central American Tribunal.	Food is brought to the house in Mukden where Chang Tso-lin is said to have been lightly injured. However some historians believe that he died in the car being taken from the railway bombing on June 4, with others believing that he lived on until June 7. Chang Tso-lin's eldest son Chang Hsueh-liang, in Tientsin, is rushed back to Mukden disguised as a woman....Wu Taiqin becomes Military Governor of Heilongjiang, China.
Jun. 6		The German Socialists prepare to form a coalition government as Dr. Gustav Stresemann makes a recovery from his recent hospitalization.		A truce between the Mexican government and the Roman Catholic Church seems likely as both sides indicate that they are prepared to compromise on some of the main areas of difference.	Tensions mount in Peking as locals and foreigners await the arrival of the Chinese Nationalist forces.... Charles Edward Herbert becomes Administrator of Norfolk Island.
Jun. 7		The French politician Raymond Poincaré cautiously predicts that the French Franc will continue to retain its value.	A treaty of friendship signed between Egypt and Afghanistan signed in Cairo, and ratified on December 10.	Pope Pius XII takes up the plan to get the Mexican government and the Roman Catholic Church there to resolve their differences peacefully....José Júlio Cansanção is appointed acting Governor of Alagoas State, Brazil, replacing Pedro da Costa Rêgo.	The Japanese Diet publishes its investigations into the fighting at Tsinanfu stating that 3254 Chinese were killed and 1450 were wounded. They do not list the Japanese casualties (15 dead and 15 wounded) until December....An assassination attempt on Prince Tanaka, the prime minister of Japan, fails when a man tries to stab him when he was en route to Utsunnomiya. The man is arrested.
Jun. 8		Eugen Bolz becomes the State President of Württemberg, Germany, replacing Wilhelm Bazille....The governor of Rome arrives in London to visit the Lord Mayor in the British capital.		The New York police ask the Canadian police to help in their hunt for the missing girl Grace Budd.	The Nationalist forces from Shansi enter Peking ending the Fengtian Warlord Government of Chang Tso-lin. Chiang Kai-shek seeing the end of the Northern Expedition then asks the Nanking government to relieve him of his duties as Commander-in-Chief of the National Revolutionary Army and also as Chairman of the National Military Council.
Jun. 9	U.S. Secretary of State Frank B. Kellogg and French foreign minister Aristide Briand announce that they are near the end of their planned antiwar treaty.	France convenes a National Assembly with a Nationalist majority....*The Hungarian-Romanian Land Dispute* by Francis Deak is published in New York by Columbia University Press.	France convenes a constituent assembly in Syria. The majority of members were Syrian Nationalists and they draft a constitution which does not recognize the French mandate. As a result, the French High Commissioner rejects the draft constitution and prorogues the assembly.		Warlord and Chinese Nationalist troops prepare to confront each other in Tientsin.

A	B	C	D	E
Includes developments that affect more than one world region, international organizations and important meetings of world leaders.	*Includes all domestic and regional developments in Europe, including the Soviet Union.*	*Includes all domestic and regional developments in Africa and the Middle East.*	*Includes all domestic and regional developments in Latin America, the Caribbean, and Canada.*	*Includes all domestic and regional developments in Asian and Pacific nations (and colonies).*

U.S. Politics & Social Issues	U.S. Foreign Policy & Affairs, Defense	U.S. Economy & Environment	Science, Technology & Nature	Culture, Leisure & Lifestyle	
IWith preparations ready for the Republican National Convention in Kansas City, posters showing presidential hopeful Herbert Hoover are put up around the city.				*The Woman Who Rode Away,* a series of short stories by D. H. Lawrence, is published in New York by Alfred A. Knopf.	Jun. 2
Political commentators in the United States compare the forthcoming Republican National Convention in Kansas City to the one in Chicago in 1912 when Theodore Roosevelt led an "insurgency" against William Howard Taft.			German scientists in Berlin announce that they have found a Death Ray which can be used medically to destroy cells.	*The Mind of Leonardo da Vinci* by Edward McCurdy is published in New York by Dodd, Mead & Co.	Jun. 3
Former New York governor William Sulzer denies that he was the source for campaign funds for presidential hopeful Alfred E. Smith....Frank E. Edwards becomes Mayor of Seattle, taking over from Bertha K. Landes.			Five women dying from radium poisoning win a court battle with the United States Radium Corporation at Orange, NJ.	Yale University Divinity School celebrates 106 years since its foundation....Some 4300 degrees are conferred at Columbia University.	Jun. 4
U.S. presidential hopeful Herbert Hoover moves one step closer to the Republican nomination with 22 more delegates.			Australian Polar explorer Hubert Wilkins says that he will not race U.S. explorer Richard Byrd to the South Pole.	Gennaro Papi, the conductor of the Metropolitan Opera Company in New York for 14 years, is detained at Ellis Island on immigration grounds.	Jun. 5
Herbert Hoover manages to pick up another 33 delegates for the Republican National Convention putting him even closer to getting the Republican nomination.		The Boeing Airplane Company announces that it has placed an order for 105 Pratt & Whitney 500-horsepower Hornet engines, and 10 of their 400-horsepower ones....The state of Alabama expedites hurricane relief.	Large numbers of people continue to flock to the *Southern Cross* airplane of Australian aviator Kingsford Smith as it remains on the ground at Suva, Fiji.		Jun. 6
Calvin Coolidge fails to sign the Muscle Shoals Bill into law....The delegation from Tammany Hall, New York, state that they will travel quietly to the Democratic National Convention in Houston, Texas.			In the court battle waged by five women over the doses of radium they received, it is revealed that Dr. S.A. von Soshocky, the inventor of the radium paint used, himself, has been suffering from an overdose of radium.		Jun. 7
As preparations continue for the Republican National Convention at Kansas City, Herbert Hoover has 477½ delegates, as against Frank O. Lowden, former governor of Illinois, who has 230½ with 81 pledged to other candidates, and 300 unpledged or unassigned—these include about 200 who were part of the "Draft Coolidge" attempt.		*Economic Problems,* written by Fred Rogers Fairchild and Ralph Theodore Compton, is published in New York by The Macmillan Company....The New York Telephone Company publicly states that it will bar any phone-tapping uses of its equipment.	Australian Aviators Charles Kingsford Smith, Charles Ulm and two others leave Suva, Fiji, for Brisbane in Australia.	Irish playwright George Bernard Shaw admits during an address to the Conference of the Chief Constables' Association, of the British police force, that he had never managed a single car journey without at least once going over the speed limit.	Jun. 8
Kansas City prepares to receive as many as 50,000 visitors for the Republican National Convention.			Australian Aviators Charles Kingsford Smith, Charles Ulm, Harry Lyon and Jim Warner, arrive in Brisbane, Australia, having completed the first trans-Pacific flight.	*The Complete Sayings of Jesus,* arranged by Arthur Hinds, is published at Williamsburg, MA, by D. H. Pierpont & Co.	Jun. 9

F	G	H	I	J
Includes campaigns, elections, federal-state relations, civil rights and liberties, crime, the judiciary, education, healthcare, poverty, urban affairs, and population.	Includes formation and debate of U.S. foreign and defense policies, veterans affairs, and defense spending. (Relations with specific foreign countries are usually found under the region concerned.)	Includes business, labor, agriculture, taxation, transportation, consumer affairs, monetary and fiscal policy, natural resources, pollution and industrial accidents.	Includes worldwide scientific, medical and technological developments, natural phenomena, U.S. weather and natural disasters.	Includes the arts, religion, scholarship, communications media, sports, entertainment, fashions, fads, and social life.

	World Affairs	Europe	Africa & The Middle East	The Americas	Asia & The Pacific
Jun. 10		The crash of an express train which leaves the rails at Nuremberg results in the death of 22 people with many more being injured....English writer D. H. Lawrence and his wife Frieda leave for a trip to south-eastern France and Switzerland.		The Ministry of Interior in Mexico warns all local municipalities about the need to hold the forthcoming presidential and local elections in a fair manner.	Yen Hsi-shan arrives in Peking, and Chiang Kai-shek announces his resignation from all military offices, as he steps down as commander of the Nationalist Army....There is widespread rejoicing in Sydney Australia, over the flight of aviators Charles Kingsford Smith and Charles Ulm.
Jun. 11		Medical doctors begin a strike in Vienna, Austria....The Reparations Agent, acting on the behalf of the Allied governments, makes the demand for the final settlement of German liabilities and indemnities incurred after World War I....Evidence emerges that the Soviet Union is continuing to give financial support to the Communist Party of Great Britain.		James Horace King ceases to be Minister of Soldiers' Civil Re-establishment and becomes Minister of Pensions and National Health, in the Canadian government.	The Royal Australian Air Force introduces the DH60 Circus Moths to replace the Avro 504Ks as elementary training aircraft. The initial 20 Moths are imported but another 14 are made in Australia....General Sheng Chen, a commander of the Chinese Nationalist Third Group Army leads his men into Peking, while in Tientsin, the city braces itself again for a possible battle between the supporters of various warlords and those of the Nationalist (Kuomintang) Party.
Jun. 12		Former British Prime Minister the Earl of Oxford and Asquith (formerly Herbert Asquith), left $45,480 in his will, with $12,500 left to children of friends.		The Columbian and Mexican governments sign an extradition treaty....Álvaro Correia Paes is appointed Governor of Alagoas State, Brazil, replacing the acting governor, José Júlio Cansanção.	Shansi soldiers supporting the Nanking government enter the city of Tientsin. Allied Kwangsi troops under General Pai Tsing-hsi arrive in Peking from Hankow....The Tokyo War Office finally confirms the death of Chang Tso-lin.
Jun. 13		Wilhelm Marx offers his resignation as German Chancellor but remains until another cabinet is formed....British writer D. H. Lawrence and his wife Frieda arrive at the Hotel des Touristes at Saint-Nizier de Pariset, Savoie, France....Eminent British peer First Marquess of Lincolnshire KG PC GCMG, former cabinet minister and Lord Great Chamberlain, dies, aged 85.	The Egyptian government and the authorities of the Levant States under French Mandate (Syria and Lebanon) conclude a provisional commercial agreement....The Turkish government makes arrangements to pay back the Ottoman Empire's public debt to bondholders.		
Jun. 14	The Italian newspaper *Il Impero* denies rumors that Pope Pius XII is ill.	Emmeline Pankhurst, leader of the campaign for women's suffrage in Britain dies, aged 70....Dr. Gustav Stresemann asks the new German government to retain him as foreign minister in spite of his party not taking part in the new coalition.		Students take over the medical faculty at the University of Rosario, Argentina....Brazil's membership of the League of Nations expires two years after its original announcement.	Mr. C. T. Wang is appointed Minister of Foreign Affairs in the Chinese Nationalist government, replacing general Hwang Fu.
Jun. 15	The Permanent Court of International Justice holds its fourteenth session in The Hague....U.S. Secretary of State Frank B. Kellogg announces that the anti-war treaty may go to world powers for signing next week, as South Africa announces its support.	The Polish Parliament, the Sejm, votes on a new budget. They also send cruisers to Danzig to warn against German interference there.	Murray Bisset becomes Acting Governor of Southern Rhodesia, replacing Sir John Robert Chancellor....Four protocols supplementing a treaty of friendship signed between Persia and Afghanistan at Tehran, the capital of Persia....Representatives of the Turkish and Persian governments also sign a treaty to improve relations in the region.		Joseph Lyons, following his defeat in the election of May 30 resigns from state parliament, and A. G. Ogilvie becomes Labor leader....The Directorate of Posts is moved from Peking to Nanking with the understanding that Nanking will become the new capital of China.
Jun. 16		The Soviet government demands that the Polish government places more restrictions over the admitting of Soviet refugees into Poland....Anti-Italian demonstrations take place at Sebenico and Spalato in Yugoslavia, continuing on to the next day.	Frederick Thomas, the African American citizen who introduced jazz into Turkey dies in a French Hospital in Constantinople.		Takeji Kawamura becomes Governor-General of Japanese-occupied Formosa (Taiwan), replacing Mitsunoshin Ueyama....Chinese Communist Mao Tse-tung writes a report on the current status of the Chinese Communist Red Army.

A — Includes developments that affect more than one world region, international organizations and important meetings of world leaders.

B — Includes all domestic and regional developments in Europe, including the Soviet Union.

C — Includes all domestic and regional developments in Africa and the Middle East.

D — Includes all domestic and regional developments in Latin America, the Caribbean, and Canada.

E — Includes all domestic and regional developments in Asian and Pacific nations (and colonies).

U.S. Politics & Social Issues	U.S. Foreign Policy & Affairs, Defense	U.S. Economy & Environment	Science, Technology & Nature	Culture, Leisure & Lifestyle	
As the Republican National Convention is about to open, several delegates switch from Frank O. Lowden, former governor of Illinois, to Herbert Hoover, but commentators feel that Andrew W. Mellon, Secretary of the Treasury, will be able to clinch the Convention for Hoover or prevent him getting the nomination.			Daniel Murphy, 23, is fatally injured at Mount Pleasant, PA, when he stands too close to a whirling plane propeller just before the plane is about to take off for an aerobatic parachute display.	In baseball, the Reds manage to stop the Giants 3–0....Argentina and Uruguay tie in the Olympic Soccer Final 1–1. Another match is scheduled for June 13.	Jun. 10
Petticoat Lane, Kansas City, is bedecked with flags and banners with the Republican National Convention in the local Convention Hall about to take place. Commentators now expect Herbert Hoover to win 600½ ballots on the first vote, many more than the 545 he needs to win nomination instantly.			At Wasserkuppe Mountain, Germany, the sailplane *Ente*, powered by two Sander rocket motors, becomes the first rocket-powered air plane to fly, covering three-quarters of a mile, piloted by Friedrich Stamer....In a publicity stunt in Britain, Gordon Olley, a pilot with Imperial Airways, flies his A. W. Argosy racing the London and North Eastern Railways' Flying Scotsman train on the 390 mile route from London to Edinburgh. The Argosy has to stop twice en route to refuel, taking 84 minutes, but still beats the train by 15 minutes.		Jun. 11
Presidential hopeful Herbert Hoover is nominated on the first ballot at the Republican National Convention at the Civic Auditorium in Kansas City, MO.			U.S. aviatrix Mabel Boll flies from St. John's, Newfoundland, arriving at Harbor Grace with her pilots Oliver Le Boutillier and Arthur Argles.	An exposition of printmakers is held in Birmingham, Great Britain, to promote the arts. It is sponsored by the League of Nations.	Jun. 12
The battle over farming support delays the Republican National Convention which is all set to choose Herbert Hoover as the Republican Party's presidential candidate with new figures expecting that Hoover will win 659½ votes.			Millions of people around the United States listen to the events at the Republican National Convention by radio, with the National Broadcasting Corporation (NBC) hooking up 69 radio stations.... General Nobile gives an interview about the crash of the Italian airship *Italia* over the North Pole.		Jun. 13
The Republican National Convention, meeting at Kansas City, nominates Herbert Hoover as its presidential candidate after he wins on the first ballot. After months of speculation, and then several anxious weeks of counting the possible votes, Hoover gets 837 votes, as against 74 for Lowden, and 64 to Curtis.	Basil Miles, the U.S. Administrative Commissioner to the International Chamber of Commerce in Paris since 1922, dies, aged 50.		News reaches rescuers that several men lost from the Italian airship *Italia* are still alive.	The British House of Commons rejects, for a second time, the new 1928 Church of England Prayer Book by 266 to 220 votes....Twelve hundred British Congregationalists visiting sites connected with the Pilgrim fathers, arrive in Boston and visit Plymouth Church.	Jun. 14
The Republican Party officially names Herbert Hoover as their presidential candidate for the November 1928 presidential elections after he wins the ballot by 837 votes to 247. He chooses Senator Charles Curtis of Kansas as his vice-presidential candidate.		Floods in Arkansas cause 700 families to flee with nearly half a million acres of along the White River and its tributaries being put under water.	Two ice-breakers are sent to the North Pole to rescue the last survivors of the *Italia*.	Phillips Andover Academy celebrates 150 years since its foundation.	Jun. 15
At a rally of 10,000 members of the Ku Klux Klan and their supporters at Jamesville, near Syracuse, NY, Senator Thomas Heflin announces that he will fight to the end to prevent the United States "becoming the tail to the Roman Catholic kite," attacking Democratic presidential hopeful Alfred E. Smith....Calvin Coolidge spends the day fishing and strolling in the woods.		The Ford Motor Company celebrates its 25th anniversary.	*A History of Medieval Political Theory in the West*, written by S.R.W. Carlyle and A.J. Carlyle, is published in New York by G. P. Putnam's Sons....The ship taking Richard Byrd to the Antarctic stops in Norway.	The new Hotel La Salle at 225 Hyde Street, Sam Francisco, opens. The six-story hotel has 150 guest rooms, each of which has its own bathroom.	Jun. 16

F	G	H	I	J
Includes campaigns, elections, federal-state relations, civil rights and liberties, crime, the judiciary, education, healthcare, poverty, urban affairs, and population.	Includes formation and debate of U.S. foreign and defense policies, veterans affairs, and defense spending. (Relations with specific foreign countries are usually found under the region concerned.)	Includes business, labor, agriculture, taxation, transportation, consumer affairs, monetary and fiscal policy, natural resources, pollution and industrial accidents.	Includes worldwide scientific, medical and technological developments, natural phenomena, U.S. weather and natural disasters.	Includes the arts, religion, scholarship, communications media, sports, entertainment, fashions, fads, and social life.

	World Affairs	Europe	Africa & The Middle East	The Americas	Asia & The Pacific
Jun. 17		The Greek government plans to use the navy against striking workers.		There is widespread damage in Mexico City as the Mexican capital is hit by an earthquake, along with many other parts of the country. However there are few casualties although a child is killed in the capital.	The Nanking government issues a manifesto demanding a revision to the "Unequal Treaties."... Sir Alexander Phillips Muddiman, Governor of the United Provinces, India, dies in office.
Jun. 18		The Italian government gives 5 million lire to the Albanian government for the building of railways in Albania; another 5 million is subsequently handed over. Some of the money is used to bankroll President Ahmed Zog's election campaign for the Constituent Assembly.		The death toll from the earthquake in Mexico rises to three....Antonio Barcelo, president of the Puerto Rican senate was stabbed with a chisel at the close of a demonstration at City Hall, San Juan. His attacker is identified as Justo Matos, 35, a "maniac anarchist."...A ship is blown up at Barranquilla, Colombia, and 51 people from the ship are believed to have been eaten by alligators soon afterwards.	The Chinese Communist Party begins its Sixth Party Congress in Moscow, Russia, under the patronage of Nikolai Bukharin, owing to the congress of the Communist International (Comintern) being held there soon afterwards.
Jun. 19		The Briotish House of Commons elects a new Speaker, after the resignation of Right Honorable John H. Whitley. The new speaker is Edward A. Fitzroy.		The death toll from the earthquake in Mexico is now known to have reached 19.	Korean Communist Yi Song-tae, editor of the *Choson ji Kwang* journal is arrested by police in Japanese-occupied Korea.
Jun. 20	The Little Entente Conference is held at Bucharest, Romania. It ends two days later....Dr. James Scott Brown of the Carnegie Endowment for International Peace, New York, has his speaking engagement at Heidelberg University, Germany, cancelled after Dr. Brown, a specialist in international law, signs a report with 13 other scholars claiming that Germany alone was the cause of World War I.	Punica Rasic, a deputy from Montenegro, shoots and fatally wounds Stefan Radic, the founder of the Croatian Peasant Party, and former minister of education, along with his nephew Paul Radic and Dr. George Basaritchik during a parliamentary session in Belgrade, Yugoslavia's capital, and injures three others....Edward Algernon FitzRoy is appointed Speaker of the House of Commons, in Great Britain, taking over from John Henry Whitley.			T V. Soong, brother-in-law of Chiang Kai-shek and Nationalist Minister of Finance, calls an economic conference at Shanghai, which is attended by officials, bankers and merchants....Chang Hsueh-liang, the eldest son of Chang Tso-lin is proclaimed Governor of Fengtien Province....Wan Fulin becomes Military Governor of Heilongjiang, China, taking over from Wu Taiqin.
Jun. 21	The U.S. government proclaims the International Sanitary Convention of January 17, 1912, which it ratified in April.	The Shakhta Trial of engineers in Moscow continues with evidence put forward that the engineers were responsible for sabotage.	The Egyptian and Palestine authorities conclude a provisional commercial agreement which comes into effect immediately.		Foreign consuls at Mukden are officially notified in the morning that Chang Tso-lin had died, which probably took place on June 7....The Nationalist government declares that the name of the former capital of Peking will be changed to Peiping....The middle part of the British Admiralty Dock for Singapore, being built in Tyne, England, is completed and starts its journey to Singapore.
Jun. 22	A Fourth Session of the Committee of Jurists of the League of Nations is held at Geneva.	Rallies are held by Nationalist Croats to honor the two slain deputies....Rioting in the Greek city of Salonika, results in the death of seven Communists and the injuring of 20 other people.			A Royal Commission reports on its inquiries into corruption in connection with a contract for a plant at Sydney....Thousands of people in Japan hail the future Princess of Japan, Setsu.
Jun. 23	An explanatory note of the proposed Kellogg-Briand Pact is sent to the governments of Britain, Germany, Italy and Japan, as well as the French allies and the governments of Australia, Canada, New Zealand, and South Africa.	The British Post Office reveals that in spite of seals on mail bags being intact, robbers had managed to steal about $500,000 worth of goods from them.		Sir William St. John Carr, pioneer of the South African Rand dies, aged 80.	

A	B	C	D	E
Includes developments that affect more than one world region, international organizations and important meetings of world leaders.	Includes all domestic and regional developments in Europe, including the Soviet Union.	Includes all domestic and regional developments in Africa and the Middle East.	Includes all domestic and regional developments in Latin America, the Caribbean, and Canada.	Includes all domestic and regional developments in Asian and Pacific nations (and colonies).

U.S. Politics & Social Issues	U.S. Foreign Policy & Affairs, Defense	U.S. Economy & Environment	Science, Technology & Nature	Culture, Leisure & Lifestyle	
Democratic Party hopeful Alfred E. Smith's supporters urge Franklin Delano Roosevelt to go for the governorship of New York....Senator Thomas Heflin rallies more members of the Ku Klux Klan, this time at Hurtsville, AL, where he claims that Democratic Party hopeful Alfred E. Smith is "soaking wet," and "unfit to be president."			Aviator Amelia Earhart starts her attempt to become the first woman to successfully fly across the Atlantic Ocean, arriving in Wales, United Kingdom, on June 18.		Jun. 17
Governor Albert C. Ritchie withdraws from the contest for the nomination for the Democratic Party for the presidential election....A dynamite bomb placed by the "Purple Gang" explodes in Detroit, Michigan, injuring 12 people, and badly damaging the county building.	The U.S. government sends a fifth plane to Nicaragua for use by the U.S. Marines fighting rebel forces loyal to General Augusto Sandino.	Herbert N. Straus, President of the Republican Business Men's Committee Inc., and a delegate to the Republican National Convention, urges all businessmen to support Republican presidential candidate Herbert Hoover.	The keel is laid for the biggest ship in the world at Harland & Wolff's shipyards in Belfast, Northern Ireland.		Jun. 18
Supporters of Democratic Party presidential hopeful Reed tries to form a block to prevent rival presidential hopeful Alfred E. Smith from getting the Democratic Party nomination.			In the British southern port of Southampton, aviator Amelia Earhart is given a rapturous welcome....With Norwegian polar explorer Roald Amundsen being overdue on his rescue operation for men from the Italia, some fears are expressed that he might have crashed.	Some 70,000 watch the rowing crew from the University of California beat those from Columbia....The Irish-American novelist Donn Byrne, author of Messer Marco Polo, is killed in a car crash near his Irish residence of Coolmain Castle, Bandon, County Cork, Ireland.	Jun. 19
Although it appears that presidential hopeful Alfred E. Smith will probably not get the Democratic Party nomination on the first ballot, Norman E. Mack, Democratic National Committeeman, predicts that Smith will easily win on the second ballot....At Houston, Texas, Robert Powell, a young African-American who killed Detective A. W. Davis in a shoot-out, is lynched by five men, one in uniform, being hanged from a wooden bridge about six miles from Houston.	The U.S. War Department announces that it is commissioning a detailed study of camouflage for possible use on uniforms and military equipment.		Roald Amundsen, Norwegian adventurer and the first man to reach the South Pole, is believed to have died in a plane crash during a rescue mission for the Italian North Pole Expedition, aged 56.		Jun. 20
James Sweeney, a convicted murderer in New Jersey, who only narrowly escaped being sent to the electric chair, and ended up with a sentence of life imprisonment, is cleared of the murder which was made owing to mistakes by witnesses. However the New Jersey court ruled that he could not be released until September because his application for a pardon from the Court of Pardons, Trenton, New Jersey, was "not properly drawn."		The Norwegian and the French governments send ships to search for Polar explorer Roald Amundsen who has not been heard of for three days after flying to the North Pole to rescue some of the survivors of the ill-fated Italian airship, Italia.	Cunard states that it will introduce a Third Class on its liners going from Britain to India, with a $150 one-way fare.		Jun. 21
There is a massive surge in support for Democratic Party hopeful Alfred E. Smith as preparations begin for the Democratic National Convention in Houston, TX....Moses A. Gunst, millionaire cigar retailer and former San Francisco police commissioners, died in Burlingame, CA, aged 75.		Italian fliers drop supplies to the Italian airmen on the North Pole.	It is reported in the New York Times that three days earlier Mary Pickford had her curls cut off as she wanted to move from her "little girl" roles to adult roles.	In the large lottery in Spain, Zoila M. Valle, a drug clerk at San Pedro Sula, Spanish Honduras, arrives in Spain, en route for Paris, after winning the prize of $125,000.	Jun. 22
Moves to try to stop New York governor and presidential hopeful Alfred E. Smith from winning the Democratic Party nomination collapsed as his rivals were unable to agree on their strategy for the Democratic National Convention at Houston, TX.	The U.S. press receives a latter from the Nicaraguan rebel leader General Augusto Sandino in which he writes an open letter to the U.S. government from El Chipote. Sandino condemns U.S. foreign policy in Central America, urging for the U.S. government to pull out its marines.	Financial commentators urge that the Democrats do not try to change tariffs at the Democratic National Convention at Houston, TX.	The German rocket car being developed in Hanover, Germany, is wrecked in a test after obtaining a speed of 156 miles an hour on rails....John Kirkland Wright's The Geographical Basis of European History is published in New York by Henry Holt & Co.	The Diary of David Garrick, edited by Ryllis Clair Alexander, is published in New York by Oxford University Press. It records his first trip to Paris in 1751 and was transcribed from the original manuscript for this edition.	Jun. 23

F	G	H	I	J
Includes campaigns, elections, federal-state relations, civil rights and liberties, crime, the judiciary, education, healthcare, poverty, urban affairs, and population.	Includes formation and debate of U.S. foreign and defense policies, veterans affairs, and defense spending. (Relations with specific foreign countries are usually found under the region concerned.)	Includes business, labor, agriculture, taxation, transportation, consumer affairs, monetary and fiscal policy, natural resources, pollution and industrial accidents.	Includes worldwide scientific, medical and technological developments, natural phenomena, U.S. weather and natural disasters.	Includes the arts, religion, scholarship, communications media, sports, entertainment, fashions, fads, and social life.

	World Affairs	Europe	Africa & The Middle East	The Americas	Asia & The Pacific
Jun. 24	U.S. government sends draft diplomatic treaty to outlaw war to fourteen other countries, with U.S. Secretary of State Frank B. Kellogg announcing that the signing of the treaty is near.	French government, with the aim of repudiating 80 percent of the national debt, devalues the franc by 500 percent from 19.3 cents to 3.9 cents to the franc, or to 25.5 to the \$1. The move hits people with rented houses hard....The Soviet and Turkish governments exchange the convention of January 8, 1927, regarding the Aras and Arpatchai Rivers.			The Sino-American Treaty is signed restoring Chinese tariff autonomy.... British soldiers arrive at Tongshan to protect the lives and property of British and other foreign employees of the Kailan Mining Administration.
Jun. 25			King Fuad dismisses Mustafa an-Nahhas Pasha as Prime Minister of Egypt and sets about choosing a new prime minister.	The Companie General Aeropostale flies from Montevideo, capital of Uruguay, to France, stopping at Rio de Janeiro and Natal, inaugurating a new airmail service between Uruguay and France.	Eight stowaways found at Colombo on the *Jervis Bay* are convicted and sent to jail.
Jun. 26	The antiwar treaty of U.S. Secretary of State Frank B. Kellogg is submitted to the Japanese government.	Polish prime minister Józef Pilsudski harangued his cabinet, with all his ministers then submitting their resignations.			Chiang Kai-shek leaves Nanking for Peking, and on the way there meets with Li Tsung-jen, Feng Yu-hsiang and Yen Hsi-shan....The Nanking government informed the Peking-based director general and co-director of posts that they must move from Peking to Nanking.
Jun. 27	The Third Session of the Arbitration and Security Committee of the League of Nations meets until July 4 to draw up further model conventions....The World Dairy Congress meets at the Central Hall, Westminster, England, with nearly 2,000 delegates from 45 countries attending. One of the highlights is the detailed description of the Hungarian Dairy Experimental Farm run by Dr. O. Gratz, together with the scheme of registering of dairies and butter-churning facilities in Hungary, a model to be followed by other countries.	Kazimierz Bartel becomes Prime Minister of Poland, taking over from Józef Pilsudski; Kazimierz Bartel stands down as Deputy Prime Minister of Poland, and Stanislaw Car becomes the Polish Minister of Justice, replacing Aleksander Meysztowicz....Captain Alfred Loewenstein, the Belgian millionaire financier dies, aged 59.	Muhammad Pasha Mahmoud Pasha becomes Prime Minister of Egypt, taking over from Mustafa an-Nahhas Pasha.		
Jun. 28		German Socialist leader Hermann Mueller appointed as German chancellor, taking over from Wilhelm Marx. Oskar Hergt steps down as Vice-Chancellor of Germany, with no successor appointed until March 30, 1930....Captain Lemborun of the Danish army is arrested on the Danish-German border as a spy.		The Great Gorge and International Railway in Canada switches to one-man crews for its trolleys in Canada.	As Mexico heads to its presidential elections, General Alvaro Obregon remains the only candidate.
Jun. 29	The League of Nations hosts the Second International Conference for the Abolition of Prohibitions on the Exportation of Hides and Bones, held in Geneva.	Lord Terrington, a member of the British House of Lords, is jailed for taking \$270,000 held by him as a solicitor, and embezzling it.		The Cuban and Mexican governments sign a Radiotelegraphic convention.	Alice Tisdale Hobart's *Within the Walls of Nanking*, about China, is published in New York by The Macmillan Company.
Jun. 30		An accident at a coal mine near Saint Etienne results in the death of 48 miners.	The Belgian Congo issues a large series of postage stamps to commemorate the exploration of the region by Henry Morton Stanley.	Aristeu Borges de Aguiar becomes governor of Espírito Santo Province, Brazil, succeeding Florentino Ávidos.	

A	B	C	D	E
Includes developments that affect more than one world region, international organizations and important meetings of world leaders.	Includes all domestic and regional developments in Europe, including the Soviet Union.	Includes all domestic and regional developments in Africa and the Middle East.	Includes all domestic and regional developments in Latin America, the Caribbean, and Canada.	Includes all domestic and regional developments in Asian and Pacific nations (and colonies).

U.S. Politics & Social Issues	U.S. Foreign Policy & Affairs, Defense	U.S. Economy & Environment	Science, Technology & Nature	Culture, Leisure & Lifestyle	
A large series of thefts take place from mail bags on the Leviathan as it sails between New York and Southampton.	The U.S. State Department allows medals received by U.S. servicemen from 25 countries to be worn by army officers and announces that it will hand out medals it holds to General John Pershing, Commander of the American Expeditionary Force ion World War I, and a number of other generals who served in the war.		The German-designed driverless car propelled by rockets runs for 30 feet and then explodes....A Swedish airplane rescues some of the Italian North Pole Expedition, including General Umberto Nobile.		Jun. 24
Political commentators expect presidential hopeful Alfred E. Smith to win the Democratic Party nomination on the first ballot in the Democratic National Convention at Houston, Texas. It is also announced that Franklin Roosevelt will be Smith's floor chief at Houston.	The Democratic Party refuses to reveal its policy on whether or not the United States should join the League of Nations.	Floods in Arkansas and Tennessee put 600,000 acres under water with troops guarding the levee. Some 4250 families are affected by this disaster.			Jun. 25
It seems increasingly likely that Alfred E. Smith will win the Democratic Party nomination on the first ballot at the Democratic National Convention at Houston, TX.	There is huge consternation in Belgium over King Albert's proposed unveiling of an inscription at the Louvain Library which will be critical of Germany. With Herbert Hoover keen on winning support from the German American community, he is also critical of the inscription.				Jun. 26
New York governor and presidential hopeful Alfred E. Smith is nominated to be the choice of the Democratic Party for the forthcoming presidential elections amid wild cheers on the convention floor at Houston, Texas. Senator Joseph T. Robinson urges tolerance but this leads to fist fights among delegates.		Juan T. Trippe of Pan American Airways takes over all the major Latin American routes establishing the airline as the dominant one in the Caribbean and South America. It has exclusive landing rights in Cuba and runs a regular mail service from Key West to Havana.			Jun. 27
The Democratic National Convention, meeting at Houston, Texas, nominates New York governor, Alfred E. Smith as its presidential candidate, and Senator Joseph T. Robinson of Arkansas as its vice-presidential candidate. Smith gets 849 votes, with the Democrats adopting a policy in favor of continuing with Prohibition.			Aviators Charles B. Collyer and John Henry Mears in the City of New York start their journey to fly around the world in a west-east direction.	Hugh Walpole's biography of Anthony Trollope is published in New York by The Macmillan Company.	Jun. 28
At the Democratic National Convention at Houston, TX, New York Governor Alfred E. Smith becomes the first Roman Catholic nominated by a major party for the U.S. president when his nomination is confirmed....Two African Americans are lynched in Lincoln County issippi after being arrested for assaulting white residents. A mob attacked the prison and seized James and Stanley Bearden. One of the men was tied to the back of a car and taken off to a nearby bridge where he was hanged, and the other was hanged on another bridge.			Sir Arthur E. Shipley's Hunting under the Microscope is published in New York by The Macmillan Company.	A translation of Maurice Bedel's novel, Jerome or the Latitude of Love, which won the Goncourt Prize in France, is published in New York by The Viking Press.	Jun. 29
	The number of people in the Enlisted Reserve Corps is said to be 5,464.	The U.S. Treasury states that the cash balance in the general fund, exclusive of the gold reserve against United States notes and trust funds, held for the redemption of gold and silver certificates, and Treasury notes of 1890, after deducting current liabilities is $265,526,981.	The German government announces that they will try out a Zeppelin in a new trans-Atlantic service.	The Age of Reason by Philip Gibbs, A novel about life in London, is published in New York by Doubleday, Doran & Co.	Jun. 30

F	G	H	I	J
Includes campaigns, elections, federal-state relations, civil rights and liberties, crime, the judiciary, education, healthcare, poverty, urban affairs, and population.	Includes formation and debate of U.S. foreign and defense policies, veterans affairs, and defense spending. (Relations with specific foreign countries are usually found under the region concerned.)	Includes business, labor, agriculture, taxation, transportation, consumer affairs, monetary and fiscal policy, natural resources, pollution and industrial accidents.	Includes worldwide scientific, medical and technological developments, natural phenomena, U.S. weather and natural disasters.	Includes the arts, religion, scholarship, communications media, sports, entertainment, fashions, fads, and social life.

	World Affairs	Europe	Africa & The Middle East	The Americas	Asia & The Pacific
Jul. 1	European jurists claim that they have worked out most of the details of the proposed anti-war treaty of U.S. Secretary of State Frank B. Kellogg.	Gustav Adolf Bay becomes President of the Government of Basel-Land Canton, Switzerland, replacing Albert Grieder....Johann Matthäus Alphons Edwin Rukstuhl becomes Landammänner of Sankt Gallen Canton, Switzerland, replacing Alfred Riegg.		General Alvaro Obregon is elected as president of Mexico, and will take office on December 1....João de Deus Pires Leal becomes governor of Piauí Province, Brazil, succeeding Matias Olímpio de Melo.	The Nanking government denounces the October 26, 1866, treaty between the Chinese Imperial government and the Italian government, and proposes the negotiation of a new "equal" treaty....The Société d'Études et d'Enterprises Aériennes en Indochine et en Extrême Orient (S.E.A.I.E.), an airline for French Indochina, is formed from the Société Indochinoise d'Études d'Aviation Commerciale et Postale, to provide air services in French Indochina.
Jul. 2	The Committee on Arbitration and Security discusses the German government's proposals for security.... The British Commonwealth Labour Conference opens at the House of Commons with delegates from Australia, British Guiana, Canada, Ceylon, India, the Irish Free State, Newfoundland, New Zealand, Palestine, South Africa, Southern Rhodesia, and Trinidad, with J.R. MacDonald as president.			The British cruiser Dauntless runs on a shoal outside Halifax, Nova Scotia, but is refloated with none of the crew being lost.	The sum of $173,000 deposited in the Bank of China in the name of the District Salt Inspectors at Tientsin is transferred to the credit of the Nanking government without the consent of the Tientsin salt inspectors.
Jul. 3	The Soviet Union embarks on a major project to buy wheat from countries around the world.	A school teacher in Rome, Italy, tries to rob a statue of St. Peter in the Vatican of its tiara, robes and ornaments.		A violent storm hits Toronto, Canada, killing three men and injuring four others....The Mexican government announces that its revenues surpassed its expectations, and tries to move toward portraying itself as more financially secure for locals and investors.	Chiang Kai-shek, Li Tsung-jen, Feng Yu-hsiang and Yen Hsi-shan, the four generals who led the Northern Expedition, enter Peking and are cheered by the inhabitants. Later that day Chiang Kai-shek visits the tomb of Chinese nationalist hero Sun Yat-sen in the Western Hills.... Sir David Yule Baronet, the famous Indian merchant dies, aged 69.
Jul. 4		Eleftherios Venizelos becomes Prime Minister of Greece, taking over from Alexandros Zaimis....Hungary and Italy sign a commercial treaty to replace the provisional treaty signed on July 20, 1928....The Vukicevic government in Yugoslavia resigns.			Reso Tours, a combination of the Australian Railways and the Australian Aerial Services Ltd arrange for two aircraft to transport airmail letters to Central Australia.... Chinese Communist Mao Tse-tung writes a report to the Hunan Provincial Committee of the Chinese Communist Party.
Jul. 5		British judge Mr. Justice Rowlatt rules that banks must give information regarding customers to the Income Tax Commissioners.... German aviators Captain Hermann Köhl, Baron von Hünefeld, in Ireland with their co-aviator James Fitzmaurice, announce that they will shorten their visit to Ireland in order to meet the ex-Kaiser Wilhelm II at Doorn.			A major exhibition of masks from the Netherlands East Indies island of Java is exhibited at the American Museum of Natural History in New York. These masks represent the gods of Java and were given by anthropologist G.D. Pratt.
Jul. 6	The International Liberal Conference opens in London.	Franz Slama becomes minister of justice in Austria, taking over from Ignaz Seipel who was in office for only three days.		Storms hit the Chilean coast causing significant damage to property.	A formal service is held at the monastery in the Western Hills near Peking where Sun Yat-sen was buried. Chiang Kai-shek weeps openly in front of the tomb.
Jul. 7		Eleutherios Venizelos forms a new cabinet in Greece....A statue of the World War I French commander, Marshal Ferdinand Foch is unveiled at Cassel....In a power struggle in British politics, some commentators force the return to power of David Lloyd George.	Jongintaba David a Dalindyebo becomes Paramount Chief of the abaThembu tribe, South Africa, taking over from Sampu Jongilizwe a Dalindyebo who died on the previous day.	A Chilean army transport ship, Angomas, founders off the Coast of Chile with 80 passengers and 215 crew members on board, as storms continue to lash the Chilean coast.	The Nanking government denounces the treaty which the Kingdom of Denmark signed with the Imperial Chinese government on July 13, 1863 and states that a new "equal" treaty should be negotiated.....Fan Yaonan is appointed Governor of Xinjiang, China, taking over after the death of the previous governor, Yang Zeingyin.

A	B	C	D	E
Includes developments that affect more than one world region, international organizations and important meetings of world leaders.	*Includes all domestic and regional developments in Europe, including the Soviet Union.*	*Includes all domestic and regional developments in Africa and the Middle East.*	*Includes all domestic and regional developments in Latin America, the Caribbean, and Canada.*	*Includes all domestic and regional developments in Asian and Pacific nations (and colonies).*

U.S. Politics & Social Issues	U.S. Foreign Policy & Affairs, Defense	U.S. Economy & Environment	Science, Technology & Nature	Culture, Leisure & Lifestyle	
Republican Party presidential candidate Herbert Hoover announces that he will make his first major speech on July 16 at Leland Stanford University....Six thousand people cheer Democratic Party candidate Alfred E. Smith as he returned to New York City....Frankie Yale, one-time business partner of Al Capone, is shot dead in Brooklyn on orders of Capone.		A volcanic eruption destroys the town of Legaspi, in the province of Albay in the Philippines, with thousands fleeing their homes. The U.S. administration sends in supplies to help the people with U.S. army aviators dropping urgently needed material from aircraft.		John G. B. Lynch, the British novelist and caricaturist, dies at the age of 44....Avery Hopwood, the American dramatist, dies, aged 46.	Jul. 1
Calvin Coolidge promises that he will do his best to help the presidential campaign of Republican candidate Herbert Hoover....Alfred E. Smith declines an offer to address 25,000 members of the Ku Klux Klan at Queens where Senator Thomas Heflin will be speaking.		The number of loans for stock purchases in the United States declines....Four die in storms in the western states with damage in Minnesota, Wisconsin and the Dakotas put at $1 million.	Physicians around the world pay tribute to the pioneering work of William Harvey who made his discoveries about the circulation of the blood exactly 300 years earlier.	An extra 125 customs guards are deployed in New York to try to enforce Prohibition regulations.	Jul. 2
J M. Phillips, the alleged head of the Queens Sewer Ring, facing charges of corruption, dies at Atlantic City from a kidney disease.		Communists demonstrate against U.S. capitalism at the offices of J. P. Morgan, with 16 arrested by police after a short melee.	A British yacht hears a report that the missing Norwegian Polar explorer Roald Amundsen is alive—the report is found to be false several days later....Following the death of Honorable Elsie Mackay in the Hinchcliffe attempt to fly across the Atlantic, her parents Lord and Lady Inchcape announce that they are giving Britain £500,000 ($2.5 million) in memory of their daughter....Italian aviators Captain Arturo Ferrain and Major Carlo del Prete take off from Montecello Flying Field in Rome, flying to Brazil.	John Ayscough (Monsignor Bickerstaffe-Drew) dies, aged 70.	Jul. 3
Senator Thomas Heflin from Alabama, and Arthur H. Bell, the Grand Dragon of the Ku Klux Klan of New Jersey, speak at Queens, New York....Calvin Coolidge talks of how he manages to hook six trout on his birthday.		The U.S. Treasury offers long-term bonds which have 3 percent interest....Some 23 people are drowned in storms which lash New York.	Italian aviators Captain Arturo Ferrain and Major Carlo del Prete pass the Cape Verde Islands on their way for Brazil.	Jean Lussier becomes the first person to go over the Niagara Falls (at Horseshoe Falls) in a rubber ball. His padded ball, which he had built himself, contains oxygen tanks and weighs 750 pounds....*Bambi: a Life in the Woods*, by Felix Salten, translated from German, with a foreword by British writer John Galsworthy, is published in New York by Simon & Schuster.	Jul. 4
The funeral of slain gangster Frankie Yale is held in New York and attended by 100,000 people, with one of the largest amount of floral tributes known at a gangster funeral, exceeding even that of Dion O'Banion in Chicago in November 1924....The conviction of William Edward Hickman of the murder of Marian Parker is upheld.		The Belgian financier Alfred Lowenstein fell from his private plane, into water in the English Channel in what is believed to have been committing suicide after his stock crashed affecting the European and then the U.S. stock markets.	Italian aviators Arturo Ferrain and Carlo del Prete land their Savoia S64 on a beach near Natal in Brazil after completing their 4466-mile non-stop flight from Rome.	Mummies dating back to the stone age are found on the Aleutian Islands by members of the Stoll McCracken Expedition aboard the schooner Morrissey....*The Complete Works of Percy Bysshe Shelley*, edited by Roger Ingpen and Walter E. Brock is published in New York by Charles Scribner's Sons....Three thousand people hail the opening of the Lewisohn Stadium at with the New York Philharmonic-Symphony Orchestra playing.	Jul. 5
The Republican Party states its support for the continuation of Prohibition.		The world's largest known hailstone falls at Potter, Nebraska.	S. Brodetsky's biography of Sir Isaac Newton, the famous British scientist, is published in Boston by John W. Luce & Co.	The Third Tallinn Philatelic Exhibition is held in the capital of Estonia.... The first all-talking movie film, *The Lights of New York*, has its premier in New York.	Jul. 6
Herbert Hoover continues his presidential election campaign by traveling to Iowa.		U.S. capitalist Henry Ford is honored by the Romanian government which conferred on him the Grand Order of the Crown of Romania in a ceremony held at Detroit, with the citation read by Andrew Popovich, Secretary of the Romanian Legation in Washington, DC.	American aviators John H. Mears and Charles G. Collyer fly into Kazan, Russia, after leaving Moscow.	The first volume of the History of the Byzantine Empire, by A. A. Vasiliev, translated from the Russian, is published in Madison, WI, by the University of Wisconsin....At Haus Doorn, Netherlands, ex-Kaiser Wilhelm II of Germany admits his great love of movies.	Jul. 7

F	G	H	I	J
Includes campaigns, elections, federal-state relations, civil rights and liberties, crime, the judiciary, education, healthcare, poverty, urban affairs, and population.	Includes formation and debate of U.S. foreign and defense policies, veterans affairs, and defense spending. (Relations with specific foreign countries are usually found under the region concerned.)	Includes business, labor, agriculture, taxation, transportation, consumer affairs, monetary and fiscal policy, natural resources, pollution and industrial accidents.	Includes worldwide scientific, medical and technological developments, natural phenomena, U.S. weather and natural disasters.	Includes the arts, religion, scholarship, communications media, sports, entertainment, fashions, fads, and social life.

	World Affairs	Europe	Africa & The Middle East	The Americas	Asia & The Pacific
Jul. 8		An exhibition is held in Turin, Italy, to commemorate the 400th anniversary of the birth of Emmanuel Philibert, Duke of Savoy, and also the 10th anniversary of the Italian victories of 1918. A series of 10 postage stamps is issued by the Italian postal authorities to commemorate the event.		It is revealed that only four people from the Chilean army transport *Angamos* have survived.	The Nanking government issues interim regulations whereby nationals of countries whose "Unequal treaties" had formerly allowed these nationals to have extraterritorial jurisdiction would now be subjected to Chinese laws.
Jul. 9		Wojciech Maria Agenor Goluchowski is appointed as Governor of Lwowskie, Poland; and Henryk Józewski is appointed Governor of Wolynskie, Poland, replacing Wladyslaw Józef Mech.		The Chilean warship *Angomoa* sinks in the Arauco Gulf, with the death of 290.	After two days in office, Fan Yaonan is replaced by Quan Shuren as Governor of Xinjiang, China.
Jul. 10	France gives its qualified support to the anti-war treaty of U.S. Secretary of State Frank B. Kellogg.	Countess Mercedes de Castellanos, the former fiancée of Spanish politician Miguel Primo de Rivera y Orbaneja, marqués de Estella, announces that she will take holy orders and retire to a convent.	A German-American syndicate gets the contract to build railway lines in Persia, worth approximately $65 million.		The Japanese government announced that 7,000 Japanese army reservists in Shantung will start to withdraw in 10 days....The Dutch and U.S. governments conclude an agreement regarding petrol exploration in the Netherlands Indies.
Jul. 11		The French cabinet expresses its approval for the anti-war pact.... The House of Commons in London debates the gift of the Inchcape family following the death of Hon. Elsie Mackay with concern mounting for whether or not the family her co-aviator Captain Walter Hinchcliffe have had provision made for them.... American academic James Brown Scott is assailed in Berlin over his criticism of the German role in starting World War I.			The Chinese Minister in Washington asks the U.S. government to appoint plenipotentiaries for treaty negotiations....The Chinese Communist Party ends its Sixth Party Congress in Moscow, Russia. Among the members elected to the politburo are Zhou Enlai and Xiang Ying.
Jul. 12		The Soviet icebreaker *Krasin* saves the remainder of the Italian North Pole Expedition....German accepts the anti-war pact proposed by U.S. Secretary of State Frank B. Kellogg.		José Moreira da Rocha is appointed acting governor of Ceará, Brazil, replacing the acting governor, Eduardo Henrique Girão.	
Jul. 13		A Macedonian, Momchilo Ivanovicth attempts to assassinate Jirajin Lazitch, the head of the State Department of Police in Yugoslavia.		The U.S. State Department in Washington, DC announces that Chile will resume diplomatic relations with Peru following the intervention of U.S. Secretary of State Frank B. Kellogg....Mexico goes into mourning over the death of aviator Captain Emilio Carranza on the previous day.	The Nanking government announces the termination, as of July 7, of three conventions with the French in 1886, 1887 and 1895 regarding control of trade on the Chinese-Indochinese frontier. The French government replies that the Chinese do not have the right to abrogate the conventions as the two countries were negotiating new conditions.... Sir Austen Chamberlain states in the British House of Commons that the British government regards Manchuria as a part of China.
Jul. 14		In France, Bastille Day is celebrated but in a more somber style than in previous years....Four French mountaineers die in a fall from the Breithorn with their relatives watching....Lithuania announces that it is breaking diplomatic relations with Poland again....George Cretziano, the Romanian minister in Washington, DC, claims that the Romanian government is working to end anti-semitism in the country.		The body of Captain Emilio Carranza is brought to Mexico and lies in state in Mexico City.	The Danish government declares its willingness to renegotiate the treaty of July 13, 1863, but denies the Chinese right of abrogation.

A	B	C	D	E
Includes developments that affect more than one world region, international organizations and important meetings of world leaders.	Includes all domestic and regional developments in Europe, including the Soviet Union.	Includes all domestic and regional developments in Africa and the Middle East.	Includes all domestic and regional developments in Latin America, the Caribbean, and Canada.	Includes all domestic and regional developments in Asian and Pacific nations (and colonies).

U.S. Politics & Social Issues	U.S. Foreign Policy & Affairs, Defense	U.S. Economy & Environment	Science, Technology & Nature	Culture, Leisure & Lifestyle	
Republican Presidential candidate Herbert Hoover returns to Cedar Rapids, Iowa where 75,000 people come to hear him speak....Leading feminist Crystal Eastman dies of nephritis, aged 47, after writing in *The Nation* magazine that no self-respecting feminist would ever accept alimony—she had been married and divorced twice.	The Japanese government announced that Katsuki Debuchi, the vice minister of foreign affairs will be the next Japanese Ambassador to Washington, DC, taking over from Tsuneo Matsudaira whose daughter will be marrying the brother of Emperor Hirohito.	Three people die in sweltering heat in New York City, with millions leaving the city for the beaches.		Longlands wins the Grand National Hurdle, the most famous horse race in Britain....*The Tower*, a collection of poems by W. B. Yeats, is published in New York by The Macmillan Company....John D. Rockefeller buys St. Joseph's Normal School, conducted by the Christian Brothers at Pocantico Hills, NY....A report by the Committee of Fourteen claims a massive increase in vice in New York, citing widespread examples of corruption, drunkenness, and prostitution.	Jul. 8
Democratic presidential candidate Alfred E. Smith meets with farm lobby groups, while Republican candidate Herbert Hoover heads to Illinois.		On another very hot day in New York City, six more people die.		New York Police Commissioner Joseph A. Warren denies that vice in New York is as bad as portrayed in a recent report by the Committee of Fourteen.	Jul. 9
Leaders of the Democrat Party meet in New York to plan for the presidential election in November....In Trenton, New Jersey, the state legislature moves to oust Thomas A. McDonald as Superintendent of the Hudson County Election Bureau.		The Chicago Federal Reserve Bank advances the rediscount rate from 4.5 percent to 5 percent.		Mayor Jimmy Walker of New York is critical of the role taken by Hollywood in the presidential campaign.	Jul. 10
Herbert Hoover announces that he will discuss the important issue of Farm Aid when he gets to Palo Alto....John J. Raskob, a close ally of Democrat presidential candidate Alfred E. Smith is elected as Chairman of the Democratic National Committee.	Major Ross E. Rowell of the U.S. Marines pays tribute to the work of the marines in Nicaragua.	The New York Stock Exchange experiences its greatest fall since 1914, with stock in General Motors losing heavily....American Airways Inc. of New York gets the airmail contract from the U.S. Postal Service for Central America, the southern Caribbean and British Guiana.	Aviators Charles B. Collyer and John Henry Mears in the *City of New York* arrive in Tokyo on their attempt to fly around the world in a West-East direction....A flier over the Arctic reports that he can see the missing three men from the Italian airship *Italia*....Morris M. Titterington, one of the pioneers of the aviation industry is killed in a plane crash near Snyders, Pennsylvania.		Jul. 11
Chairman Hubert Work of the Republican National Committee states in a press conference that most German-Americans will vote for Republican presidential candidate Herbert Hoover.		The Bank Rediscount Rate in New York is raised to 5 percent, matching the rise experienced in Chicago.	Leading Mexican aviator Captain Emilio Carranza is killed when his plane crashes in the New Jersey Pine Barrens while he is returning from a goodwill flight to New York City.	A television show is broadcast in the Bell Telephone Company Laboratories in New York showing tennis players.	Jul. 12
The Democratic Party rejects the ides of having a "Southern base" during the presidential election campaign, leading to criticism in the South that the Democratic Party is becoming too Northern in its focus....German organizations in Wisconsin announce that they will be supporting Alfred E. Smith in the forthcoming presidential elections....Gunmen in Chicago shoot dead a member of the Plumbers' Union who had refused to give in to mob intimidation.			Harvey Baum: a Study of the Agricultural Revolution, by Edward S. Mead and Bernard Ostrolenk, is published in Philadelphia, Pennsylvania, by the University of Pennsylvania Press.	Austin Harrison, the journalist and author, dies, aged 55.	Jul. 13
Herbert Hoover completes his last day of work as Secretary of Commerce having resigned to concentrate on his election campaign, bids farewell to his department, and heads to the West to begin campaigning....In Chicago an accidental discharge of water into a sewer drowns a number of workmen.	To commemorate Bastille Day in the United States, a monument to the French who supported the Americans in the American War of Independence is unveiled at Newport, Rhode Island.		The Russian icebreaker *Maligin* starts searching for lost Norwegian Polar explorer Roald Amundsen.	*George Eliot's Family Life and Letters*, including many letters which had never before been published, by Arthur Paterson, is published in Boston, Massachusetts by Houghton Mifflin Company....Edwin W. Marland, President of Marland Oil Company, and one of the wealthiest men in the South-West of the United States, marries his niece and adopted daughter. They were married at the home of the bride's parents who had earlier expressed surprise when they heard of the impending marriage.	Jul. 14

F
Includes campaigns, elections, federal-state relations, civil rights and liberties, crime, the judiciary, education, healthcare, poverty, urban affairs, and population.

G
Includes formation and debate of U.S. foreign and defense policies, veterans affairs, and defense spending. (Relations with specific foreign countries are usually found under the region concerned.)

H
Includes business, labor, agriculture, taxation, transportation, consumer affairs, monetary and fiscal policy, natural resources, pollution and industrial accidents.

I
Includes worldwide scientific, medical and technological developments, natural phenomena, U.S. weather and natural disasters.

J
Includes the arts, religion, scholarship, communications media, sports, entertainment, fashions, fads, and social life.

	World Affairs	Europe	Africa & The Middle East	The Americas	Asia & The Pacific
Jul. 15		A massive heat wave in Paris, London and Brussels results in a number of deaths with policemen supposed to have been directing traffic sheltering in nearby shade.... Leipzig police in Germany uncover an international passport fraud.		Massive crowds, estimated as high as 50,000 people, in Mexico City greet presidential candidate General Alvaro Obregon following his win in the presidential elections.	
Jul. 16	The British government finally drops its reservations about the anti-war treaty of U.S. Secretary of State Frank B. Kellogg.	A rail crash in Munich kills ten people....Mieczyslaw Seydlitz is appointed acting Governor of Pomorskie, Poland....English holiday makers in France are sent to prison for drunkenness and assault at Boulogne.		General Alvaro Obregon in Mexico City announces that he will not change government policy over the Mexican government's hostility to the power of the Roman Catholic Church....International and local observers in Nicaragua prepare for the forthcoming election.	
Jul. 17	The Sixth Congress of the Third International of the Communist Party is held on Moscow, and continues until September 2. Purged Russian Communist, Leon Trotsky, sends a plea to the congress.	Giovanni Giolitti, five times premier of Italy between 1892 and 1921, dies aged 85....The French authorities in Rouen unveil a statue of Joan of Arc in the city where she was burned to death as a witch by the British in 1431—she was canonized in 1920.		General Alvaro Obregon, president-elect of Mexico, is assassinated during an official luncheon at the La Bombilla restaurant, Mexico City by José de Leon Toral, a Catholic seminary student who opposed the anticlerical policies of Obregon, managing to get into the restaurant disguised as a newspaper artist wanting to sketch Obregon.	
Jul. 18		The Vatican totally condemns the murder of president-elect General Alvaro Obregon in Mexico.		The man who murdered General Alvaro Obregon in Mexico admits that he assassinated the politician for religious motives....The Costa Rican government, in response to a request to rejoin the League of Nations, requests an interpretation of the reference to the Monroe Doctrine in Article 21 of the Covenant of the League.	The Japanese Consul-General at Mukden, Manchuria, advises Chang Hsueh-liang that he should reconsider any agreements between Manchuria and the Nanking government....Sir James Fairfax KBE, leading Australian newspaper proprietor, dies, aged 65.
Jul. 19		The Prince of Wales in Britain inspects the British fishing fleet at Grimsby....Scotland asks for quotas to be introduced to reduce immigration from Ireland.	King Fuad of Egypt issues a royal decree suspending the Egyptian Parliament for three years, and suspending freedom of the press.	The governments of Honduras and the United States ratify the Treaty of Friendship, Commerce and Navigation originally signed on December 7, 1927....The Guatemalan government accepts the idea of arbitrating their border dispute with Honduras.	The government of China annuls all the already-expired "Unequal Treaties" which the Chinese Empire was forced to sign with Western powers during the 19th century.... The Japanese government announces its terms for the settlement of the Tsinanfu incident....The Nationalist government informs the Japanese consul at Nanking that the Sino-Japanese Treaty of July 21, 1896, would be abrogated on the following day.
Jul. 20		In Britain, the conviction of Oscar Slater for the murder of Marion Gilchrist at Glasgow in 1908 is set aside by the Scottish Court of Criminal Appeal and Slater is later offered, and accepts, £6,000 in compensation.		The Mexican government announces that the man who assassinated president-elect General Alvaro Obregon will go on trial in public.	A boat mail train runs off the rails some 30 miles from Madras after the rail lines had been tampered with. Elsewhere in India there is rioting owing to a railway strike over the Indian Statutory Commission.
Jul. 21		Two days of demonstrations in favor of Anschluss with Germany begin in Vienna held at the German singer's festival.		The Mexican Side of the Texas Revolution, by "the chief Mexican participants," is published for the first time in English translation, in Dallas, TX, by P. L. Turner Company.	
Jul. 22		A revolt in Portugal is crushed with seven people being killed, and 30 wounded as artillery shells an army barracks in Lisbon, with three ministers being seized....A memorial to the missing in the Soissons sector during World War I is unveiled in France.			

A	B	C	D	E
Includes developments that affect more than one world region, international organizations and important meetings of world leaders.	Includes all domestic and regional developments in Europe, including the Soviet Union.	Includes all domestic and regional developments in Africa and the Middle East.	Includes all domestic and regional developments in Latin America, the Caribbean, and Canada.	Includes all domestic and regional developments in Asian and Pacific nations (and colonies).

U.S. Politics & Social Issues	U.S. Foreign Policy & Affairs, Defense	U.S. Economy & Environment	Science, Technology & Nature	Culture, Leisure & Lifestyle	
A massive crowd in Chicago turns out to meet Republican presidential candidate Herbert Hoover....Democratic Party presidential candidate Alfred E. Smith suggests that Owen D. Young of the General Electric Corporation should run for New York governor.		Commodore Sir James T. W. Charles, chief of Cunard's company fleet dies, aged 62....The Ford Motor Company is revealed to be negotiating to buy Menlo Park, the scene of many of Thomas A. Edison's early discoveries.		Dr. Darru C. McKown, announcing that automobiles and trains are too slow, too dirty and too noisy, buys himself a small aeroplane to fly to lecture engagements.	Jul. 15
Frank Hague, the Mayor of Jersey City and a Vice-Chairman of the Democratic National Committee comes under attack over a profit of $198,000 made on a Jersey land deal....Republican Presidential candidate Herbert Hoover visits the Republican President Calvin Coolidge.	Jordan D. Hill, 24, a former West Point graduate, announces that he plans to travel by canoe from the Harlem River at Lincoln Avenue in New York, to Colon in Panama.			A playground is opened in New York on 147th Street, between Seventh and Eighth Streets, where African-American children can play....Lottie Venne, the British actress, dies, aged 76.	Jul. 16
Herbert Hoover leaves Calvin Coolidge to continue visiting different parts of the United States in his bid for the presidency.	Calvin Coolidge and other U.S. politicians express their shock at the assassination of incoming Mexican president, General Alvaro Obregon.		Dr. James B. Murphy of New York and Dr. Archibald Leith of London, Britain, announce that they have a new theory into how cancer is caused.		Jul. 17
Democratic Party presidential candidate Alfred E. Smith announces that he will increase his campaigning in New York state....Following a change in the nature of prison parole in New York State, the authorities issue figures showing that 21 percent of those being paroled re-offended in their first year out of prison.	The retiring British Ambassador to Paris, Lord Crewe, makes a speech in favor of the continued U.S.–British bond of friendship.		Katherine Locke of Youngstown, Ohio, returns to the United States from her trip across Saharan Africa to Timbucktu.	A Kelmscott Press edition of Geoffrey Chaucer is sold at Sothebys in London for a record $20,000.	Jul. 18
Democratic Party presidential candidate Al Smith announces that he will merger various government departments if elected in order to reduce expenditure and reduce waste....A prisoner in the Bronx Jail kills a prison guard and then another prisoner before killing himself when he realizes that he will not escape....The Ku Klux Klan announces that it will ban parades until after the presidential elections in November.	The Cuban government sends a marble urn containing material from the Maine memorial in Havana to the U.S. government.		New York beggar Daniel Sugrue, is jailed for begging despite having $20,000 in his bank account.	The American music teacher and pianist Oliver Denton is killed in a fire in Paris, France.	Jul. 19
It is announced that Roy O. West will become the new Secretary of the Department of Interior.		American companies plan airmail routes to China.	Morris R. "Dinger" Daugherty, a legless and one-armed aviator, flies from West Virginia to Long Island, arriving just ahead of a bad storm.		Jul. 20
Plans are introduced to fingerprint all people who violate prohibition laws.		The U.S. government refunds $10.5 million to automobile dealers with the elimination of the 3 percent automotive excise tax.	Aviators Charles B. Collyer and John Henry Mears in the Empress of Russia arrive at Victoria, Vancouver Island, at the end of their flight around the world in a West-East direction....British automobile-racing driver, Malcolm Campbell wins the 200 Mile Race at Brooklands, by 12 minutes and 12 seconds, averaging 78.34 miles per hour.	Ellen Terry, British stage actress, dies in Kent, England, aged 80....The Cornish Miner, a British history work covering Cornish miners from pre-Roman times to the present day, by A. K. Hamilton Jenkin, is published in London by George Allen & Unwin.	Jul. 21
Newspapers suggest that the cost of the U.S. presidential campaign in 1928 may be more than $10 million, with $8 million being spent by the two major parties, and lobby groups for the ending of prohibition, for its continuance, and from farming groups, are expected to add another $2 million to he cost of the election.		A small earthquake rocks St. Louis, MO, and nearby places.	Aviators Charles B. D. Collyer and John Henry Mears in the City of New York end their journey around the world in 23 days and 15 hours, the previous record being 28 days and 14 hours.		Jul. 22

	World Affairs	Europe	Africa & The Middle East	The Americas	Asia & The Pacific
Jul. 23		Portuguese authorities arrest some 240 people after an attempt to overthrow the government fails....The Industrial Transference Board in Britain publishes a report declaring that 200,000 miners might not be able to find any more employment in the coalfields.		Guatemala announces that it will accept arbitration in its border dispute with Honduras.	The Chinese Nationalist Forces take control of the city of Chefoo.
Jul. 24		The French government state their opposition to the concept of Germany merging with Austria.		The Nicaraguan government announces that the rebel leader General Augusto Sandino has fled possibly into Honduras.	The United States sends a note to the Nanking government announcing that it is ready to negotiate a treaty providing for Chinese tariff autonomy, showing its support for the Nanking government....The leaders of the Indian railway strike are arrested by the British.
Jul. 25		The Archbishop of Canterbury reigns with the prospect of the Archbishop of York, the Rt. Rev. Cosmo Lang, taking over....Poland prepares a diplomatic note to lodge against Lithuania over their long-running border dispute.	A new Tangier Agreement proposed by the French and Spanish governments is signed by representatives of the British, French, Italian and Spanish governments, giving the Spanish wider powers....The Transjordania National Pact signed.		The United States signs a revised tariff treaty in Peking and recalls its troops from China....The Portuguese government agrees to the negotiation of the Sino-Portuguese Treaty of 1888 but rejects the Chinese right to abrogate the treaty....The Indian States Committee, meeting in London, hears the case made by the Indian princes for more satisfactory political relationships with the Indian government.
Jul. 26	The Indian Native Princes meeting in London adjourn their talks on future political developments in India.	German fishermen in Hamburg start a strike....The Austrian government announces that it is not going to press ahead with plans to merge with Germany.	Representatives of France, Great Britain and the Hijaz (Arabia) meet at Haifa, Palestine, to discuss the possible rebuilding of the Hijaz Railway wrecked in World War I....Joseph C. Grew, the U.S. ambassador to Turkey jumps into the Bosphorus in an attempt to save an elderly veiled Turkish lady who fell from the ferry on which they were all traveling. He manages to get her back onto the ferry, but she dies soon afterwards.	William Culberton, the former U.S. Minister to Romania, sails for Santiago, Chile where he will become the U.S. Minister to Chile replacing Miles Poindexter who is competing for a U.S. Senate seat for Washington State.	
Jul. 27		A new government formed in Yugoslavia, led by Father Korosec of the Slovene Clerical Party....The British judge Mr. Justice Maugham rules that it is not lawful for Birkenhead Corporation to require any person, as a condition of employment, to be a member of a trade union.		The government of Honduras refuses to submit its border dispute with Guatemala to the Central American Court but suggests arbitration by the U.S. President of the Chief Justice of the U.S. Supreme Court....Some 56 soldiers of General Augusto Sandino surrender in Nicaragua as the government believes that it is finally about to crush the Sandino rebellion.	
Jul. 28		Anton Korosec becomes Prime Minister of Yugoslavia, taking over from Velimir Vukicevic, with non-Croatian politicians hailing the move....Wiktor Lamot becomes Governor of Pomorskie, Poland, replacing Mieczyslaw Seydlitz.	The General Council of the Zionist World Organization, meeting in Berlin, votes to accept the Joint Palestine Survey Commission and start preparing for the establishment of Jewish settlements in Palestine.		
Jul. 29	The French announce their disappointment with some of U.S. Secretary of State Frank B. Kellogg's plans over the treaty to outlaw war as a way of solving international disputes.	Italian Fascist leader Benito Mussolini celebrates his 45th birthday in private with his family at the family farm in Carpena, Italy....The French traffic police in Paris announce that they will ban the use of motor horns by car drivers between 1 and 5 a.m.			The Nanking government sends a telegram to the U.S. government expressing its hope that all outstanding treaty questions could be sorted out as quickly as those over tariffs, a measure that is welcomed by the U.S. government on the following day....The French government announces their support for the new Nationalist government in China.
Jul. 30	The British Secretary of State for Foreign Affairs, Sir Austen Chamberlain, announces his support for U.S. Secretary of State Frank B. Kellogg but also wants an Anglo-French Navy Accord.	A large chemical fire in the Polish city of Lodz results in 50,000 people having to flee their homes in the residential suburbs of Fuks and Hagria.		At the committal hearings of José de Leon Toral in Mexico City for the murder of president-elect General Alvaro Obregon, the assassin claimed that he killed the politician for religious reasons.	

A	B	C	D	E
Includes developments that affect more than one world region, international organizations and important meetings of world leaders.	Includes all domestic and regional developments in Europe, including the Soviet Union.	Includes all domestic and regional developments in Africa and the Middle East.	Includes all domestic and regional developments in Latin America, the Caribbean, and Canada.	Includes all domestic and regional developments in Asian and Pacific nations (and colonies).

U.S. Politics & Social Issues	U.S. Foreign Policy & Affairs, Defense	U.S. Economy & Environment	Science, Technology & Nature	Culture, Leisure & Lifestyle	
Senator George H. Moses of New Hampshire becomes ice-Chairman of the Advisory Committee assisting the Republican presidential candidate Herbert Hoover.	U.S. Secretary for the Navy Curtis Wilbur tells Calvin Coolidge of the great advances in the democratic process made in Nicaragua with U.S. support.		Aviators Charles B. Collyer and John Henry Mears receive a hero's welcome in New York City.		Jul. 23
The sheriff's office in New York seizes $480,000 in jewels from the Wanamakers, with news of a family dispute looming....The State Executive Committee of the Democratic Party in Texas refuses to change its stance banning African Americans from taking part in its primaries preventing J.B. Grigsby from doing so.	The U.S. Navy tests out its latest aircraft carrier the USS *Saratoga*.... The U.S. government recalls 1,350 marines from China as hostilities there die down.		A number of airships fly over the city of Los Angeles.		Jul. 24
Roy O. West of Illinois becomes Secretary of the Department of Interior, replacing Hubert Work.... The U.S. postal service issues an airmail postage stamp showing a beacon on the Rocky Mountains. Although it is the 11th stamp issued for airmail purposes, it is the first that is not allowed to be used for normal mail.		U.S. Secretary of State Frank B. Kellogg announces that he hoped the United States will have good relations with the new Nationalist government in China.	Francis Birtles arrives in Melbourne, Australia, after driving from London, England, to Australia, in a 14 horsepower Bean motor car.	"Big" Bill Tilden confirms that he will be playing in the Davis Cup against French tennis players.	Jul. 25
The suspected swindler, Maria Josephine Leslie, connected with the sale of $238,000 worth of jewelry from the Wanamaker family for $91,000 is apprehended in a private sanitarium in Greenwich, CT.		The Ford Motor Company sends a motor ship *Lake Ormoc* from Detroit to Brazil with the aim of setting up a massive rubber plantation of up to 6 million acres.		Boxer Gene Tunney defeats Tom Henney in match in New York with the referee stopping the contest in the 11th round.	Jul. 26
Republican presidential candidate Herbert Hoover arrives in San Francisco where he is cheered by a large crowd.	The U.S. government starts talks with the new Nationalist government in China over tariff autonomy.	General Motors announces that its sales have increased by 26.4 percent, with a net half-year earnings set at $161,267,974.		British Cricketer Alfred Percy "Tich" Freeman becomes the only bowler to take 200 first-class wickets before the end of July.	Jul. 27
A pamphlet entitled *Can a Catholic be President?*, by Reverend B. L. Conway, is published in New York by The Paulist Press, answering accusations by Charles C. Marshall.	More than 300 American schoolboys, from every state in the Union sail for Denmark, Norway, and Sweden on a goodwill mission.	*The Annual Cyclopedia of Insurance in the United States,* edited by H. R. Hayden, is published in New York by G. Reid Mackay.		The Official Opening Ceremony is held for the 1928 Summer Olympic Games in Amsterdam. On the first day, the track and field events for women start.	Jul. 28
Calvin Coolidge hails the "unity of the nation."...Democratic Party presidential candidate Al Smith unveils his plans to aid state parks.				U.S. athletes win the opening events at the Olympic Games in Amsterdam.	Jul. 29
Some 120 National Guardsmen in New Bedford, Massachusetts, fix bayonets to disperse a crowd of 10,000 people who surrounded the Central Police Headquarters following the arrest of 256 strikers from a textile mill.	The Chinese government hail the diplomatic note received from the U.S. government saying that it will pave the way for better understanding between the two countries.	Plans continue for the Chrysler Corporation to merge with Dodge Brothers Inc.	George Eastman shows the first color motion pictures in the United States.		Jul. 30

F	G	H	I	J
Includes campaigns, elections, federal-state relations, civil rights and liberties, crime, the judiciary, education, healthcare, poverty, urban affairs, and population.	Includes formation and debate of U.S. foreign and defense policies, veterans affairs, and defense spending. (Relations with specific foreign countries are usually found under the region concerned.)	Includes business, labor, agriculture, taxation, transportation, consumer affairs, monetary and fiscal policy, natural resources, pollution and industrial accidents.	Includes worldwide scientific, medical and technological developments, natural phenomena, U.S. weather and natural disasters.	Includes the arts, religion, scholarship, communications media, sports, entertainment, fashions, fads, and social life.

	World Affairs	Europe	Africa & The Middle East	The Americas	Asia & The Pacific
Jul. 31		General Umberto Nobile and the crew from the airship *Italia* return to Rome and are greeted by large crowds....The Peasant Party in Yugoslavia splits causing a political crisis.		At the hearings into the role of José de Leon Toral in Mexico City in the murder of president-elect General Alvaro Obregon, the assassin sits impassively, scorning the large crowd of onlookers as he was committed for trial.	A former official in the Sydney Electricity Department in Australia is sentenced to six months in gaol and fined £500 on a charge placed under the Secret Commissions Act.
Aug. 1		Croatian deputies in the Jugoslav Parliament form their own assembly in Agram....The British and French governments reach an agreement over naval disarmament....The British newspaper the *Daily Mail* turns one of their aircraft, a de Havilland DH61 powered by a Bristol Jupiter engine, into an office....The British government announces that it will be spending $60 million for new bridges in London, with the moving of Charing Cross Railway Station to the south bank of the River Thames, and the retention but enlargement of Waterloo Bridge.	Talks resume in Jeddah between Ibn Saud and Sir Gilbert Clayton over problems the Arabian government has with the establishment of Transjordan. Talks break down a week later.		The National Reconstruction Committee announces that it will convert Nanking into the capital of China....The Central Executive Committee of the Kuomintang is postponed for a week, in the absence of a quorum....The Japanese government issues a statement, dated the previous day, in which they threaten "decisive measures" if Japanese nationals were deprived of any treaty privileges granted in the Sino-Japanese Treaty of July 21, 1896, which was abrogated by the Chinese in the previous month.
Aug. 2		A French express train is derailed at Le Mans station resulting in the death of six people and 16 others being injured....Lord Byng in Britain is appointed the new head of the Metropolitan Police, London at New Scotland Yard.	A 20-year treaty of friendship and arbitration between Abyssinia and Italy signed at Addis Ababa, the capital of Abyssinia. This gives Ethiopia a free zone in the Italian-controlled port of Assab in return for the concession of constructing several roads.		The Bombay Legislature in India passes a motion for the appointment of a committee to cooperate with the Indian Statutory Commission of Sir John Simon.
Aug. 3		The ashes of "Big Bill" Hayward, U.S. Communist and former leader of the Industrial Workers of the World, are interred beside Lenin's Tomb in Red Square, Moscow.		Panama prepares for elections with troops being called out to guard polling stations.	The Right Honorable Syed Ameer Ali, a distinguished Muslim Indian judge, dies, aged 79.
Aug. 4	*Oriental Exclusion,* by R. D. McKenzie, is published in Chicago, Illinois, by the University of Chicago Press. It details the Chinese and Japanese migration to the United States west coast, and the discrimination against many of the Chinese and Japanese there. A similar volume, *Resident Orientals of the American Pacific Coast,* by Eliot Grinnell Mears, is also published in Chicago by the University of Chicago Press.	Pacifists and Communists demonstrate in Berlin under the palace window where Kaiser Wilhelm II proclaimed the start of Germany's involvement in World War I in 1914....Franz Josef Hoop becomes head of government of Liechtenstein, running the principality for the next seventeen years.		Mexican newspapers hail U.S. Ambassador Dwight W. Morrow as a man who has done much to improve relations between the two countries.	The new Chinese nationalist government is formally recognized by the League of Nations.
Aug. 5	International Socialist Congress opens in Brussels, Belgium.	The Tirana *Telegraph* in Albania issues an editorial against the existing republican form of government, and hints its support for the establishment of a monarchy to ensure the country retains its independence....A committee of the Jugoslav Parliament votes to accept a friendship treaty with Italy.... Some 11,000 British war veterans go to Flanders for a service at the Menin Gate attended by Edward, Prince of Wales.		The Mexican government announces that it has a budget surplus of 10 million pesos against a deficit of 25 million in the previous year.... Florencio Harmodio Arosemena is elected President of Panama in elections held with his opponent Boyd being credited with only having received one vote.	
Aug. 6		The Italian government announces that one of their destroyers, the *Giuseppe Missouri,* accidentally collided with their own submarine the *F-14.*	The Soviet and Turkish governments sign four treaties at Angora regarding pasture rights, frontier communications, the settlement of disputes and the inspection of cattle.		

A	B	C	D	E
Includes developments that affect more than one world region, international organizations and important meetings of world leaders.	Includes all domestic and regional developments in Europe, including the Soviet Union.	Includes all domestic and regional developments in Africa and the Middle East.	Includes all domestic and regional developments in Latin America, the Caribbean, and Canada.	Includes all domestic and regional developments in Asian and Pacific nations (and colonies).

U.S. Politics & Social Issues	U.S. Foreign Policy & Affairs, Defense	U.S. Economy & Environment	Science, Technology & Nature	Culture, Leisure & Lifestyle	
Democratic Party presidential candidate Alfred E. Smith urges for a full investigation into the merger of the New York City gas companies.... The *Chicago Tribune* claims that the gun used to kill Frankie Yale on July 1 was traced to Chicago and the linked the shooting to gangster Al Capone....An enquiry reveals that four men trying to collect evidence on a night club breaking prohibition laws spent $60,000 to get evidence, including buying champagne at $42 a bottle.					Jul. 31
Leading Republicans call for a $4 million campaign fund to ensure that they will win the forthcoming presidential elections.	U.S. Ambassador to Mexico, Dwight W. Morrow urges that the U.S. government continues to support the Mexican government.		The British aviator Captain Frank Courtney in his Dornier-Napier flying boat leaves Horta in the Azores for his flight to the Americas.		Aug. 1
William A. Wilson, 47, a former employee of the Farmers' Loan and trust Company shoots himself dead inside the Harvard Club following his wife seeking a divorce, ending their marriage of 19 years.			The British aviator Captain Frank Courtney crashes his Dornier-Napier flying boat, after it catches fire, and is saved by a steamer in the middle of the Atlantic while flying from the Azores for Newfoundland.	Plans are unveiled for a proposed 15-volume *Encyclopedia of Social Science* which will be edited by a staff headed by Dr. Edwin R. A. Seligman, Professor of Political Economy at Columbia University.	Aug. 2
Democratic Party presidential candidate Alfred E. Smith repudiates the Equalization Fee.	The United States buys its own embassy in Paris following the signing of a deed in Paris by Andrew W. Mellon, Secretary of the Treasury.	Plans to hold a 1932 Exposition in New York to commemorate the 200th anniversary of the birth of George Washington are unveiled by Grover Whalen. It is expected to bring much needed trade benefits to New York City in particular and U.S. industry in general.		Ray Barbuti in the 400m race in the Amsterdam Olympics saves the U.S. team from defeat by winning his race in 47.8 seconds.	Aug. 3
Calvin Coolidge issues a warrant for the arrest of Henry M. Blackmer, an oil operator and the missing witness in the Teapot Dome Oil Case....Norman Thomas launches the Socialist Party's campaign for the U.S. presidential elections with himself as the party's presidential hopeful.	An important diplomatic history, *American Policy Toward Russia since 1917*, by Frederick Lewis Schuman, is published in New York by International Publishers.	Nicaraguan rebel leader General Augusto Sandino sends an open letter to "the rulers of Latin America" outlining his cause and detailing his opposition to U.S. foreign policy in Central America.	A search is undertaken in the Atlantic for Polish aviators Ludwik Idzikowski and Kazimierz Kubala.	*The Happy Mountain*, a novel by Maristan Chapman about life in the Tennessee Mountains, is published in New York by The Viking Press.	Aug. 4
Democratic Party opponents of Democratic Party presidential candidate Alfred E. Smith meet in a conference in Birmingham, AL, to discuss their election strategies....The Republican National Committee tries to stop the rumors that are spreading that Republican Party presidential candidate Herbert Hoover is anti-German.			Polish aviators Ludwik Idzikowski and Kazimierz Kubala flying from Paris to New York crash at sea and are rescued by a German ship *Samos*, 60 miles from the Spanish coast.	Sir Alogy wins the Australian Hurdle horse race....El Ouafi, an Algerian, wins the marathon in the Olympic Games.	Aug. 5
Calvin Coolidge sets the U.S. budget at $3.7 billion, which is some $208 million below the safety limit which had previously been set.	The new U.S. budget shows $659 million being spent on the army and navy.		Polish aviators Ludwik Idzikowski and Kazimierz Kubala tell of their rescue at sea in the Atlantic.		Aug. 6

F	G	H	I	J
Includes campaigns, elections, federal-state relations, civil rights and liberties, crime, the judiciary, education, healthcare, poverty, urban affairs, and population.	*Includes formation and debate of U.S. foreign and defense policies, veterans affairs, and defense spending. (Relations with specific foreign countries are usually found under the region concerned.)*	*Includes business, labor, agriculture, taxation, transportation, consumer affairs, monetary and fiscal policy, natural resources, pollution and industrial accidents.*	*Includes worldwide scientific, medical and technological developments, natural phenomena, U.S. weather and natural disasters.*	*Includes the arts, religion, scholarship, communications media, sports, entertainment, fashions, fads, and social life.*

	World Affairs	Europe	Africa & The Middle East	The Americas	Asia & The Pacific
Aug. 7		Some 31 submariners are found to have died during the collision on the previous day between an Italian cruiser and a submarine.... The British prime minister J. Ramsay Macdonald raises the prospect of the British government resuming diplomatic relations with the government of the Soviet Union.			
Aug. 8	The Pan-Pacific Women's Conference opens in Honolulu, Hawaii, with women from 13 states coming. Sending delegations are the United States (mainland), Hawaii, Australia, New Zealand, China, Japan, Canada, The Philippines, Samoa, Tahiti, Fiji, India, and the Netherlands East Indies.	Croat deputies withdraw from the Jugoslav Parliament to establish their own separatist assembly in Zagreb following the death of Stefan Radic, the founder of the Croatian Peasant Party, and former minister of education from injuries sustained on June 20....Edward, Prince of Wales, salutes 13,000 British war veterans and family members outside the Cloth Hall at Ypres after a Service of Remembrance at the Menin Gate.		Honduras refuses to allow international arbitration in its dispute with Guatemala at the Central American Tribunal in spite of special pleading by the U.S. government.	The Fifth Plenary Session of the Central Executive Committee of the Kuomintang, the Chinese Nationalist Party, meets in Nanking for a week of discussions.
Aug. 9	The Australian and New Zealand delegates to the Pan-Pacific Women's Conference in Honolulu, Hawaii, arrive a day late, missing the first plenary meetings.	Italian diver locates 400,000 pounds sterling in diamonds in the Belgian steamship *Elizabethville*, which had been sunk during World War I....The Right Honorable Sir James T. Agg-Gardner, the oldest member of the British House of Commons, dies, aged 81.	A conference is held at Jeddah, Saudi Arabia, to settle the question of the borders of Iraq.	Violent storms lash the coasts of Haiti and Cuba.	The British and Nanking governments reach an agreement, signed at Nanking, over the settling of the Nanking Incident of 1927....Sir Geoffrey Fitzhervey de Montmorency becomes Governor of the Punjab, India, taking over from Sir William Malcolm Hailey who is appointed Governor of the United Provinces.
Aug. 10			Habib Pacha Es-Saad becomes prime minister of Lebanon, taking over from Béchara El-Khoury.		
Aug. 11		A new biography of Dostoyevksy, by J. Meier-Graefe, is published in New York by Harcourt, Brace & Co.			The Japanese Prime Minister Baron Giichi Tanaka abandons his week-end retreat to meet with senior advisers over events in Manchuria.
Aug. 12	The *New York Times* publishes a League of Nations survey showing that $3.5 billion is spent each year on arms, with armies with a total of 5.5 million soldiers being maintained. It shows that sea power has declined but there are still 5,047,300 tons of warships.	Some 70 attacking bomber planes over-fly London to show the increasing power of the Royal Air Force....Leos Janaceck, Czech composer of many operas including *Jenufa* and *Katya Kabanova*, dies aged 75.		Former British prime minister Ramsay MacDonald meets with William Mackenzie King, prime minister of the Dominion of Canada, at Fort William.	The Japanese government offers aid to Chang Hsueh-liang, the "Young Marshal" who took over Manchuria after the assassination of his father by the Japanese. However they state that it is on the condition that he does not form an alliance with Nanking.
Aug. 13		Sir Alexander John Godley becomes Governor of the British colony of Gibraltar, taking over from Sir Charles Carmichael Monro....The Jugoslav parliament votes to accept a friendship treaty with Italy.		Travel writer Richard Halliburton announces that he will swim the Panama Canal, starting from the Atlantic entrance at Cristobal, through to Balboa on the Caribbean, a total distance of 50 miles.	Chang Hsueh-liang, the "Young Marshal," accepts the Japanese "advice" and their promised support and states that he will not support the new Chinese Nationalist government....A glacial dam bursts in the Himalayas causing a massive flood of the Indus Valley in India.
Aug. 14		The British government announced the appointment of a Royal Commission to inquire into police methods....The British bus companies start a sleeper service between London and Liverpool dramatically reducing the number of people making the journey by train.		Honduras finally announces that it will accept international arbitration over its disputed border with Guatemala.	The Fifth Plenary Session of the Central Executive Committee of the Kuomintang, the Chinese Nationalist Party, ends with plans drawn up for the future of China, and the isolating of the rivals of the Nationalists, such as the Communists.

A	B	C	D	E
Includes developments that affect more than one world region, international organizations and important meetings of world leaders.	Includes all domestic and regional developments in Europe, including the Soviet Union.	Includes all domestic and regional developments in Africa and the Middle East.	Includes all domestic and regional developments in Latin America, the Caribbean, and Canada.	Includes all domestic and regional developments in Asian and Pacific nations (and colonies).

U.S. Politics & Social Issues	U.S. Foreign Policy & Affairs, Defense	U.S. Economy & Environment	Science, Technology & Nature	Culture, Leisure & Lifestyle	
The American Federation of Labor's Executive Council announces that they will be non-partisan in the forthcoming U.S. presidential election after supporters of Democratic Party presidential candidate Alfred E. Smith urged for them to declare their support for Smith.		Tropical storms strike the Florida coast causing wide devastation, with high winds sweeping through Palm Beach and leaving two ships sending distress signals.	The Romar, a massive plane and the largest hydro plane in the world, makes its first test flight in Germany for Luft Hansa.	British golfers announce that they are, at last, prepared to accept the new golf ball which had been developed in the United States in 1925.	Aug. 7
Cornelius Callahan, 28, the Assistant Secretary of the Bancitaly Corporation on Wall Street was accused of stealing $467,000 from the bank.		Hurricanes continue to inflict damage on the Florida coastline destroying many fruit trees and disrupting telephone communications.	Australian aviators Charles Kingsford Smith and Harry Ulm, along with H.A. Litchfield and T.H. McWilliams fly from Point Cook, near Melbourne, to Perth, Western Australia, in the "Southern Cross" completing the first nonstop trans-Australian flight.	Antonin Sova, a Czech poet, dies.	Aug. 8
The Board of Directors of General Motors announces that they will not accept the resignation of Pierre S. Du Pont as their Chairman, in spite of his wishes to do so and fight against the continuance of Prohibition.	The United States government draws up plans to reoccupy its consulates in China which it evacuated earlier in 1928 and in late 1927, owing to the troubles after the March 1927 "Nanking Incident."	A new storm lashes the coast of Florida with a hurricane north of Tampa.			Aug. 9
Democratic Party presidential candidate Alfred E. Smith attends the funeral of a close friend George E. Brennan, the Democratic Leader in Illinois....Pierre S. Du Pont announces his backing for Alfred E. Smith in the forthcoming presidential elections.	Nicaraguan rebel leader General Augusto Sandino writes an open letter describing the battle on the Coco River when his men managed to drive back the U.S. Marines.	A train crash on a train traveling between Chicago and New York results in 30 injured, 16 having to be taken to hospital.		The University of California crew wins the rowing championships at the Olympic Games in Amsterdam....C.F. Fox, a prominent golfer and styled the "Grand old lady of golf" dies in Philadelphia.	Aug. 10
Herbert Hoover formally accepts the Republican Party nomination for the November presidential elections, cheered by 60,000 supporters at the football stadium at Stanford University, Palo Alto, California. He highlights the increasing prosperity of the United States, and offers hundreds of millions of dollars in farm aid.	An important military history, The War Department in 1861, by A. Howard Meneely, is published in New York by Columbia University Press.	Four people are found dead in storms which batter the coast of South Carolina.	Australian aviator Charles Kingsford Smith flies the Southern Cross plane from Melbourne to Perth in 23 hours, 24 minutes.	Postal authorities in San Francisco seize and confiscate five copies of D. H. Lawrence's novel, Lady Chatterley's Lover.	Aug. 11
An inquiry is ordered into the Atlanta Federal Prison in Georgia after allegations that rich inmates were being given favorable treatment. The press highlight that probable witnesses might include Dorothy Knapp, Earl Carroll and Warren T. McCray, ex-governor of Indiana.		It was revealed that a forger managed to get seven checks, totaling $104,000, cashed at the Manufacturers Trust Company in the last month....Some 100 people are rescued following gales striking the coast between Long Island and New Jersey.		The Ninth Olympic Games closes in Amsterdam. During the 800 meter races several women collapsed leading to a 32-year ban on women running more than 200 meters in the Olympics. The United States wins the unofficial points championship with 437 points.	Aug. 12
Anti-Prohibition supporters of Republican Party presidential candidate Herbert Hoover state that they recognize that he will not end Prohibition, but that they have reconciled themselves to this....U.S. postal services issue two postage stamps of George Washington both overprinted "Hawaii 1778–1928" to commemorate the 150th anniversary of the discovery of Hawaii by Captain Cook.	U.S. Secretary of State Frank B. Kellogg criticizes the policies of the new Mexican government, especially over their continued holding of land which had been seized during the Mexican Revolution.	Gales continue to lash the coast of Florida, with gales destroying property in Florida and also the Bahamas.		Fernand de la Tombelle, French composer, dies aged 74.	Aug. 13
Pierre S. Du Pont donates $50,000 to the presidential election bid of Alfred E. Smith.		John D. Rockefeller jnr announces that he will establish the Dunbar National Bank of New York, which will open for business on September 17, and will cater to African-Americans.	The body of the missing British explorer John Hornby was found in Hudson Bay with clear evidence that he and two aides had died from starvation.	The Front Page by Ben Hecht and Charles MacArthur premieres in New York City.	Aug. 14

F	G	H	I	J
Includes campaigns, elections, federal-state relations, civil rights and liberties, crime, the judiciary, education, healthcare, poverty, urban affairs, and population.	Includes formation and debate of U.S. foreign and defense policies, veterans affairs, and defense spending. (Relations with specific foreign countries are usually found under the region concerned.)	Includes business, labor, agriculture, taxation, transportation, consumer affairs, monetary and fiscal policy, natural resources, pollution and industrial accidents.	Includes worldwide scientific, medical and technological developments, natural phenomena, U.S. weather and natural disasters.	Includes the arts, religion, scholarship, communications media, sports, entertainment, fashions, fads, and social life.

	World Affairs	Europe	Africa & The Middle East	The Americas	Asia & The Pacific
Aug. 15	Calvin Coolidge, U.S. president, speaking at Wausau, Wisconsin, states that he believes the proposals in the Kellogg-Briand Treaty represent the greatest hope for peace "ever given in the world."		Conference on the Hijaz Railway, taking place at Haifa, Palestine, ends without any agreement on the rebuilding of the railway.	José Patricio Guggiari becomes President of Paraguay, taking over from Eligio Ayala....An expedition in Canada finds the bodies of three British explorers who had been missing since 1926. They are in a lonely cabin in the Hudson Bay region.	The *Hsin Hsu-Tung* ship sinks off Chusan Island, China....Following strikes at cotton mills in Bombay, India, hold a conference which agrees to appoint a board of enquiry to look into wages.
Aug. 16	The United States Arbitration Treaty with Austria is signed. It is ratified by Calvin Coolidge on January 4, 1929.	The Soviet Union introduces compulsory military service....Russian trawlers raise the British submarine *L55* which had been sunk by Russian destroyers in Kaposky Bay.			The Nanking government undertakes not to discriminate against any Japanese in judicial moves.
Aug. 17		Riots in Dalmatia in spite of pleas by Croatian politicians to "give peace to the ashes of Stefan Radic," cause massive instability in parts of Yugoslavia....The French World War I hero Marshal Joseph Jacques Cesaire Joffre announces that he will have his first holiday in 14 years, and visit Canada....German President Paul von Hindenburg goes hunting for chamois in Bavaria, in spite of being aged 80.		Marcos Torres, the rebel "supreme chief" in the State of Colina was killed with his assistant José Managa, when surprised in a private home where they were writing private letters. Their bodies were exhibited in the public square soon afterwards.	The Nanking government and the representatives of the German government sign a treaty at Nanking providing for reciprocity in customs and other issues....Evidence emerges of Communist Mongolian soldiers in Manchuria.
Aug. 18			Charle Bullock's study on the native tribes of Southern Rhodesia, *The Mashona*, is published in Cape Town by Juta & Co Ltd.	The Brazilian and Venezuelan governments sign a frontier treaty at Rio de Janeiro....A storm in Haiti kills 200 people and leaves 10,000 homeless, with torrential rain battering the country destroying many crops.	Chinese forces face Mongolian Communist forces along the Chinese-Manchurian border.
Aug. 19		British Liberal and Labour politician Viscount Haldane, formerly R. B. Haldane, dies, aged 72....The Liberal Party of Premier Eleuthérios Venizelos wins a majority in the Greek parliament in general elections....The Polish government and the Lithuanian government draw closer together on their border disputes.		The Panama Canal sees a decline in traffic in the first half of August.	
Aug. 20		The final results of the Greek elections show that Eleuthérios Venizelos has managed to win 228 of the 250 seats in the Greek Chamber of Deputies, swamping his Royalist opponents....Hugo Stinnes, son of a dead German millionaire, is arrested in Berlin and charged with fraud in connection with war bonds.		General Frank McCoy, Supervisor of the Elections in Nicaragua concludes a 12-day tour of the countryside with an optimistic assessment for Nicaraguan democracy.	In Manchuria, Buriat tribesmen from Mongolia take part in further raids....Sir Herbert James Stanley becomes Governor of Ceylon, taking over from writer and colonial administrator Sir Hugh Charles Clifford.
Aug. 21		The German police in Berlin arrests an international gang of forgers who have been defrauding banks around Europe....Albanian officials confirm that Ahmed Zog will be the King of Albania by the end of the week....Sir Felix Pole, the general manager of the Great Western Railway in Britain, reveals, in an interview in the *Daily Mail*, that the railways in Britain lose $5 million each month.		Simon Fraser Tolmie becomes Premier of British Columbia, Canada, succeeding John Duncan MacLean....More details are revealed in the Brazilian newspapers over the fate of Colonel Fawcett who died in 1925 in the Amazon forests.	
Aug. 22		The Soviet Union barred a visit from a British warship that sought to enter the territorial waters of the Soviet Union to recover bodies from the submarine *L-55*.		The first meeting of the Mixed Claims Commission dealing with disputes between Mexico and Great Britain, held in Mexico City....The people involved in the assassination of Mexican president-elect General Alvaro Obregon are taken to Mexico City Jail.	Pierre Pasquier becomes Governor of French Indo-China, replacing Maurice Antoine François Monguillot.

A	**B**	**C**	**D**	**E**
Includes developments that affect more than one world region, international organizations and important meetings of world leaders.	Includes all domestic and regional developments in Europe, including the Soviet Union.	Includes all domestic and regional developments in Africa and the Middle East.	Includes all domestic and regional developments in Latin America, the Caribbean, and Canada.	Includes all domestic and regional developments in Asian and Pacific nations (and colonies).

U.S. Politics & Social Issues	U.S. Foreign Policy & Affairs, Defense	U.S. Economy & Environment	Science, Technology & Nature	Culture, Leisure & Lifestyle	
Democratic Party presidential candidate Alfred E. Smith attacks the Republican plans to reduce funding for national parks....George K. Morris, the Chairman of the Republican State Committee died from a cerebral hemorrhage, in his suite at the Hotel Drake in New York.		As storms continue to lash the Georgian coast, farmers fear that the lowlands of Georgia might be at risk from floods.		Henry Poole, the British sculptor, dies, aged 55.	Aug. 15
Murderer Carl Panzram is arrested in Washington, DC after killing about 20 people; he is executed on September 5, 1930.	The U.S. Navy selects Oakland municipal airport as the site for a U.S. Naval Reserve aviation base.	The New York City authorities decide to build an elevated highway along the Hudson Shore.	Natural Color Pictures Inc. of Newark, Delaware, state that they have been able to make motion pictures in color, although there are still some problems to be overcome, notably over the color orange.		Aug. 16
Republican Party presidential candidate Herbert Hoover demands more action for the Boulder Dam (which is later renamed the Hoover Dam)....U.S. courts jail British conman Francis Willis Harland who purported to be a British nobleman with the name Viscount Beauclerc Duprez, as he wooed wealthy American ladies.			Roy Chapman Andrews of the Fourth Central Asiatic Expedition to the Gobi Desert reveals that he has located some tools in the Gobi Desert that are probably 150,000 years old. Altogether he found enough to fill 90 packing cases with specimens of human and animal fossils, and stone implements.	Margaret Mead's *Coming of Age in Samoa* is published in New York by William Morrow & Co.	Aug. 17
Senator Charles Curtis makes a long speech accepting the Vice-Presidential nomination of the Republican Party....U.S. Secretary of State Frank B. Kellogg leaves New York after the signing of the Kellogg-Briand Treaty.			German medical researchers led by Professor Esau of Jena, publish their findings that short-wave radio waves might be helpful in treating tuberculosis cases.	The famous British historian and statesman Right Honorable Sir George Otto Trevelyan dies, aged 90.	Aug. 18
Dr. Nicholas Murray Butler, President of Columbia University, rejects the stance of Republican Party presidential candidate Herbert Hoover on Prohibition and the future role of the U.S. Navy....Moves start to get Colonel Herbert H. Lehman of the banking firm of Lehman Brothers, and also Finance Director of the Democratic National Committee to stand for nomination for the governorship of New York.	The U.S. Ambassador to Mexico, Dwight W. Morrow, visits Oaxaca City where he sees a cypress tree which is said to have been more than 3,000 years old when Columbus first arrived in the Americas.			The American Booksellers Association starts a campaign to stimulate the same of more books, and heavily promotes map books and atlases.	Aug. 19
Democratic Party presidential candidate Alfred E. Smith outlines his election plans including visiting many states and making 20 major speeches....Republican Party presidential candidate Herbert Hoover spends his birthday returning to West Branch, IA, where he was born.	Colonel George Harvey, the former U.S. Ambassador to London, dies, aged 64, in Dublin, NH.		The German government announces that it will upgrade its plans to build airships believing that they will become economically viable for paying passengers some time in the future.		Aug. 20
Presidential hopeful Herbert Hoover delivers a major campaign speech at West Branch, Iowa, outlining his program to deal with farm relief and the development of inland water systems....Democratic Party presidential candidate Alfred E. Smith meets Mary Timmer who helped name him, and who he had not seen since he was 13.		William H. Coats, a leading thread maker and the Chairman of J. and P. Coats, died in London, Britain.			Aug. 21
William F. Whiting becomes Secretary of Commerce in the U.S. Government, taking over from Herbert Hoover who stood down on July 14. The appointment surprises many political observers....Democratic Party presidential candidate Alfred E. Smith announces that he will change the Liquor Law with major alterations in the Volstead Act and the 18th Amendment.	Rumors spread in Nicaragua that General Augusto Sandino has formed vigilante groups to upset the forthcoming elections, in the hope that they might be cancelled and disrupt U.S. foreign policy goals for the country.		It is announced that technology in New York is sufficient for all voting in the entire state will be by voting machines....Captain Franz Roner details his rowing across the Atlantic from Lisbon, Portugal, to St. Thomas, in the Virgin Islands, in the Caribbean.		Aug. 22

F	G	H	I	J
Includes campaigns, elections, federal-state relations, civil rights and liberties, crime, the judiciary, education, healthcare, poverty, urban affairs, and population.	Includes formation and debate of U.S. foreign and defense policies, veterans affairs, and defense spending. (Relations with specific foreign countries are usually found under the region concerned.)	Includes business, labor, agriculture, taxation, transportation, consumer affairs, monetary and fiscal policy, natural resources, pollution and industrial accidents.	Includes worldwide scientific, medical and technological developments, natural phenomena, U.S. weather and natural disasters.	Includes the arts, religion, scholarship, communications media, sports, entertainment, fashions, fads, and social life.

	World Affairs	Europe	Africa & The Middle East	The Americas	Asia & The Pacific
Aug. 23	The 25th Conference of the Inter-Parliamentary Union was held at the Reichstag, Berlin, Germany, and was opened by M. Brabec, vice-president of the Czechoslovak Senate, with Professor Schücking from Germany elected as president.	The Jugoslav government moves against Croatian nationalists trying to marginalize them....German foreign minister Gustav Stresemann announces that he will not be attending the next session of the League of Nations in Geneva.		The Panama Canal Company announces that, in its last fiscal year, it made a surplus of $10,881,070, out of revenue of over $18 million.	Some 175 people are arrested in Tokyo, Japan, to face charges of *lese majeste*.
Aug. 24	A conference for the British Empire Parliamentary Union is held in Canada with delegates from Australia, India, the Irish Free State, Newfoundland, South Africa, Southern Rhodesia, New Zealand and the United Kingdom arriving in Montreal, Quebec, Canada, and then touring throughout Canada.	The exiled Soviet Communist politician Leon Trotsky, and former Minister of War, in exile in Central Asia, sends a letter to the Communist International Congress in which he stressed his views on the advocacy of a purely proletarian revolution in China, and that this might, inevitably, alienate the Chinese peasantry in favor of getting support from the urban workers.			Hon Sir William Portus Cullen becomes Lieutenant-Governor of New South Wales, Australia....Japan renews its arbitration treaty of May 5, 1908, with the United States—it has had to be renewed every five years.
Aug. 25		The Albanian Constituent Assembly meets in Tirana, the nation's capital, and starts discussions on whether Albania should become a monarchy.			A sacred white elephant, which had been in London Zoo in 1927, dies in Calcutta, India, and on the same day his mahout Pa Wa goes insane in his flat over the Tapir House in London Zoo, murdering his roommate, another mahout. Pa Wa is arrested soon afterwards.
Aug. 26		World leaders start arriving in Paris for the signing of the Kellogg-Briand Pact.			Relations between the Nationalist Chinese government and the Soviet Union get even worse with the Soviet Union anxious to exert its control over Central Asia....Rear Admiral Alfred Meyer-Waldeck, the commander who defended Tsingtao in 1914 against a combined Japanese-British attack dies, aged 64.
Aug. 27	The Kellogg-Briand Pact is signed at the French Foreign Office in Paris by France, Germany, Great Britain, the Soviet Union, the United States and 10 other countries (later signed by 50 other states), becoming the first treaty to outlaw aggressive wars.	Marie Emile Fayolle, Marshal of France who served in World War I, dies, aged 70.		The Argentine postal authorities issue a series of postage stamps to commemorate the 100th anniversary of peace between the Empire of Brazil and the United Provinces of the Rio de la Plata (Argentina).	Electrification in Sydney, Australia, is extended to cover Homebush....The King of Afghanistan, in an effort to modernize the country, insists that headmen who attend the next triennial parliament must wear frock coats and felt hats rather than flowing robes and turbans.
Aug. 28	The Pan-American Geography and History Institute is founded.	Several women in Paris after preventing, by the police, from presenting a petition to the Peace Pact delegates asking for a Treaty of Equal Rights for women....The Soviet Union refuses to join discussions on the limiting or military supplies.	Plans to expand the Firestone Rubber Plantations in Liberia are denounced as being yet another way of exploiting the people of Liberia.	Outgoing Panamanian President, Rodolfo Chiari, holds a reception at the Presidential Mansion in honor of General Meriwether L. Walker, Governor of the Panama Canal Zone, and Walker.	Delegates to an All-party conference at Lucknow, British India, vote for the introduction of "Dominion Status" for India which will result in self-government. Radical members wanting independence break away....Jacob Johnson, the leader of Australia's seamen's union is jailed on charges of attempting to intimidate seamen to leave a steamship during a strike of cooks.... L.K.S. Mackinnon is re-elected as Chairman of the Victorian Racing Club in Melbourne, Australia.
Aug. 29	The Fourth Conference of European Minorities opens in Geneva, Switzerland, and lasts for three days.		Lucien Eugène Geay becomes acting governor of Benin, French West Africa, replacing Gaston Léon Joseph Fourn.	Club Deportivo Motagua is founded in Honduras.	Australian Iron and Steel Ltd started production at its blast furnace at Port Kembla, New South Wales....A clause in the award given to waterside workers in Australia is amended to remove a preference given to employment by members of the Waterside Workers' Federation after they go on strike.
Aug. 30	The 51st Session of the Council of the League of Nations opens; it ends on September 8. It makes some out of the Monroe Doctrine, although this is challenged by Costa Rica which claims that the Monroe Doctrine is a unilateral statement of U.S. policy not a treaty.	In the morning, the Albanian Constituent Assembly offers Ahmed Zog, leader of the Mati clan and president of Albania, the Crown, and in the evening, Zog comes to the assembly to accept the throne, as King Zog I.		As preparations begin for the November 4 elections in Nicaragua, the authorities decide to ban the sale of alcohol in the period before the voting, and also make it illegal to carry alcohol on one's person during the same period.	Radical members from the All-Party conference at Lucknow, British India, form the Independence of India League, with Jawaharlal Nehru making a request for the end of British rule and independence for India.

A	B	C	D	E
Includes developments that affect more than one world region, international organizations and important meetings of world leaders.	*Includes all domestic and regional developments in Europe, including the Soviet Union.*	*Includes all domestic and regional developments in Africa and the Middle East.*	*Includes all domestic and regional developments in Latin America, the Caribbean, and Canada.*	*Includes all domestic and regional developments in Asian and Pacific nations (and colonies).*

U.S. Politics & Social Issues	U.S. Foreign Policy & Affairs, Defense	U.S. Economy & Environment	Science, Technology & Nature	Culture, Leisure & Lifestyle	
Thousands of messages are received by Democratic Party presidential candidate Alfred E. Smith supporting his speech on the previous day in which he outlined his platform for the forthcoming presidential elections.			Mail from New York starts being regularly delivered to Paris by plane.	Rosa Ponselle, the dramatic soprano of the Metropolitan Opera Company was knocked unconscious by a golf ball at the Lake Placid Golf Course.	Aug. 23
Democratic Party presidential candidate Alfred E. Smith goes to New Jersey where he is cheered by 100,000 supporters.		A subway train in Times Square, New York is derailed resulting in the deaths of 17 passengers and with injuries sustained by many other people.	Commander Richard Byrd sails for the Antarctic in the bark *City of New York* under the command of Captain Frederick C. Melville.... There is massive consternation in Durban, South Africa, after two extremely rare white rhinoceroses are shot dead while wallowing in a river.	Hilda Sharp, aged 18, becomes the second woman to swim the English Channel....The Argentine and American polo teams compete at Talbott Field, Roslyn, in New York State.	Aug. 24
Some 150,000 people chanting "Al" greet Democratic Party presidential candidate Alfred E. Smith as he tours New Jersey....The Republican Party increases its drive for votes in Pennsylvania.	Calvin Coolidge confers with Major-General Charles P. Summerall, Chief of Staff of the Army, at Superior, WI.			*Park Avenue*, a novel about New York society life by Willis Vernon-Cole, is published in New York by the Writers' Guild of America.	Aug. 25
Henry H. Curran, President of the Association Opposed to the Prohibition Amendment offers his support for Democratic Party presidential candidate Alfred E. Smith.		A U.S. Treasury deficit of $94,279,346 is foreseen in the budget for 1929.	Three stowaways are found on the bark *City of New York* on which Commander Richard Byrd is traveling to the Antarctic....Walter W. Ahlschlager, architect for the Chicago Tower skyscraper, planned to be 88 feet taller than the Woolworth Building in New York, unveils his plans.	May Donoghue finds the remains of a snail in her ginger beer drink and begins the *Donoghue v. Stevenson* law suit.	Aug. 26
Democratic Party presidential candidate Alfred E. Smith leaves New Jersey and is advised to go on a nationwide tour....John J. Raskob, Chairman of the Democratic National Committee predicts that Smith will get 309 (of 531) electoral college seats.	Mexican authorities contact the U.S. government for help tracking down six Mexicans believed to have been involved in plots to assassinate president-elect General Alvaro Obregon, and who took part in the bombing of the Mexican Chamber of Deputies and the headquarters of the Obregon election campaign in Mexico City.	Serious floods hit the Rondout Valley on the Hudson River in New York State.			Aug. 27
Walter J. Maddock becomes Governor of North Dakota, taking over from Arthur G. Sorlie.	Members of the U.S. Justice Department failed to apprehend the Mexicans wanted for their involvement in plots to assassinate president-elect General Alvaro Obregon, and two bombings in Mexico City.		Canadian aviators Clennell Haggerston "Punch" Dickins and Lieutenant-Colonel C.D.H. MacAlpine leave Manitoba, Canada, on the first flight across the Barren Lands to survey northern Canada. They flew in a Fokker Super Universal.	The first national Girl Scout camp is held at White Plains, NY.	Aug. 28
Democratic Party presidential candidate Alfred E. Smith announces that he will spend most of his election campaign touring the United States but will not visit the Pacific Coast.... Republican party organizers try to reduce the cost of the campaign to keep it under $3 million.	U.S. Secretary of State Frank B. Kellogg heads to Ireland on the U.S. cruiser *Detroit*.	Poland grants U.S. businessman W. Averell Harriman large mining concessions in Upper Silesia; five mines there being said to have been purchased for $25 million.	Captain Heinen, a Zeppelin expert, takes up U.S. citizenship and continues his work on airships.		Aug. 29
Senator Joseph T. Robinson makes a long speech accepting the Democratic Party's nomination for the election as vice-president during a downpour at Hot Springs, AR.	The Royal Australian Navy's flagship, *Australia*, arrives in Boston on a goodwill visit....U.S. Marines in Nicaragua skirmish with supporters of rebel General Augusto Sandino and two rebels are killed.		American scholar Roy Chapman Andrews of the Fourth Central Asiatic Expedition to the Gobi Desert faces Chinese government seizure of his archaeological and anthropological finds from the Gobi Desert as he tries to get them out of China.		Aug. 30

F	G	H	I	J
Includes campaigns, elections, federal-state relations, civil rights and liberties, crime, the judiciary, education, healthcare, poverty, urban affairs, and population.	*Includes formation and debate of U.S. foreign and defense policies, veterans affairs, and defense spending. (Relations with specific foreign countries are usually found under the region concerned.)*	*Includes business, labor, agriculture, taxation, transportation, consumer affairs, monetary and fiscal policy, natural resources, pollution and industrial accidents.*	*Includes worldwide scientific, medical and technological developments, natural phenomena, U.S. weather and natural disasters.*	*Includes the arts, religion, scholarship, communications media, sports, entertainment, fashions, fads, and social life.*

	World Affairs	Europe	Africa & The Middle East	The Americas	Asia & The Pacific
Aug. 31	The Soviet Union accepts the Kellogg-Briand Pact; and Austria, Brazil, Bulgaria, Cuba, China, Panama, Portugal and Romania sign the treaty, with Luxemburg, the Netherlands, Switzerland and Uruguay announcing their intentions of signing it at some stage in the future.	Germany completes its fourth year of payments under the Dawes Plan, paying £87 million....The Irish government warmly greet U.S. Secretary of State Frank B. Kellogg during his visit to Dublin.	Sebastião José Barbosa becomes acting Governor of the Portuguese Central African islands, São Tomé and Príncipe, taking over from José Duarte Junqueira Rato.	Some Latin American countries at the League of Nations continue their criticism of the Monroe Doctrine.	
Sep. 1	*The Protection of Minorities,* an important work covering the Minorities Treaties under the League of Nations, by L. P. Mair, and with an introduction by Gilbert Murray, is published in London, England, by Christophers.	Coronation in Tirana, Albania, of Zog I, who assumes the title, "King of the Albanians." Italy offers its immediate recognition to the new government....The Ministries of War and Navy in The Netherlands are merged to create a Ministry of Defense with Johan Marie Jacques Hubert Lambooy, previously Minister of War and Minister of the Navy, being appointed to run the new ministry.	The Council of the League of Nations adopts a resolution recognizing that the Treaty by which the British had created Transjordan is in conformity with the principles of the mandate for Palestine....The General Post Office in Addis Ababa is opened at an official ceremony.	Plutarco Calles renounces the office of president for all times, and states that he will not contest future elections.	The Australian state of New South Wales and the Australian Capital Territory both vote in a referendum against the prohibition of liquor....A storm hits the Indian city of Lahore causing much damage and many deaths as houses collapse.
Sep. 2		Maurice Bokanowski, the French Air Minister, falls to his death from a burning plane near Toul, Lorraine, France....British civil aviation celebrates the start of services nine years earlier....The German government is anxious to raise the issue of wartime indemnities with the French.			In referendums held in the Australian Capital Territory and in New South Wales, both areas reject the idea of introducing Prohibition. In the Australian Capital Territory only 193 votes are cast in favor of the proposed new laws.
Sep. 3	The Ninth Assembly of the League of Nations begins with 50 countries being represented....The Belgian government expresses its worry about the new Naval Accord being discussed.	The Trade Union Congress in Britain opens at Swansea with 619 delegates from 160 organizations representing a membership of 3,814,842. It lasts until September 8....Mass demonstrations break out in Tirana, the Albanian capital, and in the port city of Durres (Durazzo) in support of the newly-installed King Zog.	The Prince of Wales, wearing khaki, practices his shooting at Fering-on-Sea prior to leaving for Africa where he intends to hunt big game.	Some 580 Sandanistas who had supported the Nicaraguan rebel General Augusto Sandino, surrender to U.S. Marines....Alberto Díaz de León Bocanegra becomes interim governor of Aguascalientes Province, Mexico, taking over from Benjamín de la Mora.	Chinese Nationalist army commander Chiang Kai-shek issues a press statement rejecting the mounting personal criticism of him and claims that he has "hijacked" the Chinese Revolution....Nationalist Chinese marines under the control of Captain Lin Shu-kuo are involved in an attack on pirates at Hinghwa Bay in Fukien Province.
Sep. 4	During a plenary session of the League of Nations Assembly, there are no speakers, even after President Zahle asks several times whether any of the representatives present wanted to speak....Hinni Forchmammer, President of the National Council of Danish Women is elected as Vice-Chairman of the League of Nations Assembly committee which handles social and humanitarian questions. It is the first time a woman has been elected to such a position in the League.	Greece and Hungary offer their official recognition of the new government in Albania....The enteric fever which has been raging in Greece is reported in Yugoslavia....The British War Office announces that it is stepping up its defenses to deal with possible gas attacks.		Juan Enrique Velasco and two other revolutionaries are killed in a battle with government soldiers near Guayaquil, Ecuador....Jose de Tomasco, a student from the Mariano Moreno National College in Buenos Aires, emerges as the winner of the Argentine oratory competition sponsored by the newspaper *La Nacion* of Buenos Aires. He speaks on "The Reborn and Free Civilization of the Argentine Republic."	Dr. C. T. Wang, the Chinese Nationalist Foreign Minister intimates that there might be a restoration of diplomatic links between China and Japan.
Sep. 5		Germany offers to give concessions to the Allies if they leave the Rhineland.	The Prince of Wales leaves London for his big game shooting holiday in Africa....The Ethiopian postal authorities issue a series of postage stamps of Prince Tafari and Empress Zauditu.	The Bolivian army, to stake their government's claim on the Chaco desert, then held by Paraguay, build Fortin Vanguardia, a military outpost some 15 miles from the Paraguayan Fortin Galpon.	
Sep. 6	The British government admits that there is little chance of getting countries to agree to the Naval Accord.	Russia signs the Kellogg-Briand Pact....Negotiations continue about whether or not the Allied Powers will concede the Rhineland.	The Prince of Wales and the Duke of Gloucester leaves England for West Africa....About 1,000 members of the Italian Fascisti youth organization arrive in Constantinople, Turkey, to seal a friendship pact between the two countries.		British aviators Captain C. D. Barnard and Flying Officer E. H. Alliott arrive at Croydon Airdrome, London, having left India four and a half days earlier—making their flight the fastest from India to England.

A	**B**	**C**	**D**	**E**
Includes developments that affect more than one world region, international organizations and important meetings of world leaders.	*Includes all domestic and regional developments in Europe, including the Soviet Union.*	*Includes all domestic and regional developments in Africa and the Middle East.*	*Includes all domestic and regional developments in Latin America, the Caribbean, and Canada.*	*Includes all domestic and regional developments in Asian and Pacific nations (and colonies).*

U.S. Politics & Social Issues	U.S. Foreign Policy & Affairs, Defense	U.S. Economy & Environment	Science, Technology & Nature	Culture, Leisure & Lifestyle	
Publishing millionaire William Randolph Hearst predicts the defeat of Democratic Party presidential candidate Alfred E. Smith, largely because of his stance on Prohibition.				Bertolt Brecht and Kurt Weill open their *The Threepenny Opera* at the Theater am Schiffbauerdamm in Berlin.....The Walker Cup is retained by the United States 11-1, with the French doubles team losing.	Aug. 31
Al Smith's Tammany Hall, by William H. Allen is published in New York by the Institute for Public Service. It covers many aspects of the recent history of Tammany Hall, coming out just before the presidential election.	The New York Stock Exchange records the sale of 2,119,860 shares, the highest turnover figures for Saturday trading since April 28.		Polar explore Richard Byrd leaves New York for the Antarctic, leading his First Antarctic Expedition.	U.S. boy scouts plant 3,000 Lincoln Highway posts at one mile intervals across the length of the road from Times Square to the Legion of Honor at San Francisco.	Sep. 1
Democratic Party presidential candidate Alfred E. Smith begins his journey crossing the United States by train, taking with him the largest library ever assembled for active use on a train....William L. D'Olier, President of the Sanitation Corporation of New York found shot dead, with police suspecting suicide.		Subway fumes in New York force hundreds to flee the subway, with 111 overcome with partial asphyxiation.	Aviators Parker D. "Shorty" Cramer and R. J. "Bert" ("Fish") Hassell, are rescued in Greenland....German aviators Johann Risticz and Hans Zimmermann, holders of the endurance flight record, leave Germany to make the first nonstop journey flight to China.	Archaeologists in the Orkney Islands, off the north coast of Scotland, led by V. Gordon Childe, Professor of Archaeology at the University of Edinburgh, uncover a new alphabet in carvings at the site of a double burial.	Sep. 2
Mayor Harry A. Mackey gives the police a 24 hour ultimatum to "clean up" Philadelphia....Senator Joseph P. Robinson begins an attack on the "whispering campaign" undertaken by Democrats unhappy at the nomination of Democratic Party presidential candidate Alfred E. Smith.	Congressman Albert Johnson, Chairman of the House Immigration Committee unveils his plans to modify the immigration bills to place more restrictions on Canadians and people from Latin America from working and settling in the United States.		Scottish bacteriologist Alexander Fleming discovers that the mold Penicillin has antibiotic effects, research that led to Australian scientist Howard Florey being able to purify it....German aviation designer Count Zeppelin designs his new zeppelin airship running off ten tons of gasoline rather than the new gas fuel which experts had expected him to use....The dogs being used by Richard Byrd howl dreadfully as they are put on the train at Montreal, Canada.	*The Letters of Robert Burns*, selected with an introduction by R. Brimley Johnson, is published in New York by Dodd, Mead & Co.	Sep. 3
Republican Party presidential candidate Herbert Hoover announces that he will "invade" the southern states on October 17....Florence E. S. Knapp, former New York Secretary of State, is sentenced to 30 days in jail following her conviction on May 26 of grand larceny. She was found guilty of "padding" the payroll when she was organizing the 1925 New York State census.		Bookmakers announce that they have only taken $10,000 worth of bets on the forthcoming presidential elections, most being 2 to 1 bets on the victory of Herbert Hoover. During the Wilson-Hughes presidential election campaign of 1916 some $10 million was placed in bets.... Seven people are killed in a mail plane crash in Pocatello, Idaho.		Fraulein Marie Schumann, daughter of the composer Robert Schumann, dies in Geneva, aged 87.	Sep. 4
Republican Party presidential candidate Herbert Hoover announces that he has received more large contributions for the presidential election, with his total fund standing at $683,418....Florence E. S. Knapp continues her appeal against her prison term for grand larceny.		The Goodyear-Zeppelin Corporation announces that it is going to start designing a new airship.	Contestants in the Wrigley Marathon Swim in Toronto, Canada, complete the competition in an attempt to win the $25,000 prize money. The last of the 199 contestants, Georges Michel, a "corpulent" Paris banker who has previously swum the English Channel, is pulled form the water at the end of the competition.	Sir William Bragg as President of the British Association for the Advancement of Science told a meeting in Glasgow, Scotland, that man has a soul, contradicting a statement by his predecessor.	Sep. 5
After a much-publicized crackdown on crime in Philadelphia, it is revealed that Mr. "Boo Boo" Hoff, allegedly in charge of bootlegging alcohol in the city, has been the main purchaser of machine guns.		Speculation on the stock exchange and an increase in gold exports result in a rise in U.S. interest rates to the highest level since 1924.	Scientist Douglas Johnson, Professor of Physiography at Columbia University, concludes that Manhattan Island may still be sinking into sea, but at such a slow rate that it does not matter. He also suggests that Manhattan Island could become a state on its own.	British writer and thinker H. G. Wells has his most recent work, *The Open Conspiracy*, published in New York by Doubleday Doran, in which he outlines his view of the new Utopia.	Sep. 6

F	G	H	I	J
Includes campaigns, elections, federal-state relations, civil rights and liberties, crime, the judiciary, education, healthcare, poverty, urban affairs, and population.	*Includes formation and debate of U.S. foreign and defense policies, veterans affairs, and defense spending. (Relations with specific foreign countries are usually found under the region concerned.)*	*Includes business, labor, agriculture, taxation, transportation, consumer affairs, monetary and fiscal policy, natural resources, pollution and industrial accidents.*	*Includes worldwide scientific, medical and technological developments, natural phenomena, U.S. weather and natural disasters.*	*Includes the arts, religion, scholarship, communications media, sports, entertainment, fashions, fads, and social life.*

	World Affairs	Europe	Africa & The Middle East	The Americas	Asia & The Pacific
Sep. 7	The French government introduces a resolution to the League of Nations wanting to increase the number of judges on the International Court of Justice.	During a quick visit to Marseilles, the Prince of Wales and the Duke of Gloucester visit the Queen Alexandra Memorial Hospital....A Polish businessman, having left a package of stocks and bonds worth $37,000 in a taxi, rewards the taxi driver who returned to the hotel with the parcels on the following day with a "tip" of $11.50.	Turkey announces that it will sign the Kellogg-Briand Pact.	The government of Costa Rica thanks the League of Nations for its response over the interpretation of the Monroe Doctrine....Dr. Pierre Bougrat, a convicted murdered in France, escapes from Cayenne, French Guiana, a year after being sent there as a convict, after a trial in which he promised he would escape from any prison to which he was sent.	The Mukden government in northern China announces that it will support the Japanese.
Sep. 8	In spite of the United States officially not participating in the League of Nations, U.S. jurist Charles Evans Hughes is elected to become a judge of the World Court.	The French government announces that it will massively expand its defenses under a new plan drawn up by Marshal Philippe Petain....Lithuania and Poland continue their confrontation on the city of Vilna.		It is announced that the first airmail service from the United States to Mexico will start on October 1.	
Sep. 9	The International Aeronautical Exposition and the National Air Races open, and last for eight days, on a former barley field near Los Angeles. Cash prizes offered total $80,000.	A car overturned and crashes into spectators during a motor race in Milan, resulting in the death of 19 people with 36 injured....Commemorations are held in the Soviet Union and elsewhere for the 100th anniversary of the birth of Count Leo Tolstoy, author of War and Peace and Anna Karenina....Police in Paris arrest 800 Communists who are protesting against the Kallogg-Briand Pact....Prince Ludovico Pontenziani resigns from his position as Governor of Rome which he has held since April 1926.		The British Prime Minister Ramsay MacDonald urges for closer cooperation between the British and Canadian governments in a speech made at Ottawa....The Mexican aviator Colonel Roberto Fierro arrives in Balboa, Panama, after having left Costa Rica, in his flight through Central America.	Pai Tsung-hsi, commanding the Kwangsi troops, attacks the remnants of the Chihli and Shantung armies along the Peking-Mukden Railway between Tientsin and the Manchurian border.
Sep. 10	Spain is elected to a non-permanent seat of the Council of the League of Nations, and is declared re-eligible in three years' time; Persia and Venezuela are also elected to the Council....French foreign minister Aristide Briand, in a speech at the Assembly of the League of Nations, says that Germany cannot be described as disarming itself....Charles Evans Hughes from the United States is elected a Judge of the Permanent Court of International Justice.	Koço Kota becomes prime minister of Albania for the first time....Alexandria Tolstoy, the daughter of the famous Russian writer Leo Tolstoy, author of War and Peace, asks the government of the Soviet Union whether she can resign all her educational positions except that of custodian of the Tolstoy Museum at Yasnaya Polyana after Communists start a campaign of vilification against her.	Turkey imports a number of typewriters with the Latin alphabet and they are out to use at Angora with Turkish typists eager to get work at the new foreign embassies there.	The Argentine government of Marcelo T. de Alvear nationalizes oil.	The Australian waterside workers reject an arbitration award and remain on strike.
Sep. 11	At the International Flower Show in Antwerp, Belgium, which also marked the 100th anniversary of the founding of the Antwerp Horticultural Society, the new "Cuba" rose was unveiled for the first time.	A conference is held at Geneva, Switzerland, to discuss the evacuation of the Rhineland.	The South African and Portuguese governments, with many migrant workers in South African mines coming from Portuguese East Africa (Mocambique, now Mozambique), sign a treaty regulating the problems of transport and labor recruitment....The Prince of Wales and the Duke of Gloucester arrive in Alexandria, Egypt.		An investigation by the government of British India into Standard Oil Company reveals that it was not guilty of price-fixing.
Sep. 12	The 52nd Session of the Council of the League of Nations opens; it ends on September 26.	The German government, angry at actions by French foreign minister, Aristide Briand, cancels French concessions in the Rhine....The new Albanian government officially recognized by the United States....The Spanish government arrest 2,000 in an attempt to maintain public order....Police in Beja, Portugal, uncover a bomb factory.		Sir Austen Chamberlain, the British Secretary of State for Foreign Affairs, arrives in Bermuda for a holiday....The Australian ship H.M.A.S. Australia arrives in Jamaica. En route for the Panama Canal.	Months of strikes begin in Australia after waterside workers reject a new award handed down by Justice George Stephenson Beeby of the Commonwealth Arbitration Court....The Nanking government proposes a new treaty with the Norwegian government dealing with customs issues and other matters.
Sep. 13	The Congress for the International Democrats for Peace holds its eighth congress in Bierville and Geneva, Switzerland....Pope Pius XII makes another plea for Christian Unity in an encyclical issued by the Vatican.	The German steel maker Krupp signs a large contract with the Soviet Union for the continuation of the Manich agricultural concession in the Northern Caucasus, the largest agricultural concession in the Soviet Union.		A severe hurricane strikes many of the islands of the West Indies, causing much damage, especially San Juan on the island of Puerto Rico....Sir Austen Chamberlain, the British Secretary of State for Foreign Affairs, on holiday in Bermuda, denies that he is resigning from the British government.	There is renewed fighting in China around the northern Chinese city of Tientsin.

A	B	C	D	E
Includes developments that affect more than one world region, international organizations and important meetings of world leaders.	Includes all domestic and regional developments in Europe, including the Soviet Union.	Includes all domestic and regional developments in Africa and the Middle East.	Includes all domestic and regional developments in Latin America, the Caribbean, and Canada.	Includes all domestic and regional developments in Asian and Pacific nations (and colonies).

U.S. Politics & Social Issues	U.S. Foreign Policy & Affairs, Defense	U.S. Economy & Environment	Science, Technology & Nature	Culture, Leisure & Lifestyle	
Charles C. Beckman, the captain of the police detectives in Philadelphia is arrested in the well-publicized crackdown on crime in the city.... Methodists in Ohio pledge to support Republican Party presidential candidate Herbert Hoover over his stance on Prohibition.		John Coolidge, son of Calvin Coolidge, starts work at New Haven Railroad, wanting no special favors because of his father's position.	A massive gathering of 300 planes is held at Mines Field, CA, for the start of the National Air Exposition which has attracted 200 companies.	Dr. Eugene Stock, the British historian and former Secretary of the Church ionary Society, dies, aged 92....Sir Henry Dickens, son of writer Charles Dickens, speaks out critically on Carl E. Bechogfer Roberts's book, This Side of Idolatory.	Sep. 7
U.S. Secretary of State Frank B. Kellogg states that he is unhappy that Republican Party presidential candidate Herbert Hoover is using the Kellogg-Briand Pact as an election issue....The Democratic National Convention reveals that it has assigned $510,000 to radio advertising.			The German government announces that its Zeppelin will soon be flying to the United States and will carry mail on its journey....A bonfire seen on Edge Island, Norway is found not to be connected with the lost members of the crew of the Italian airship, the Nobile.	n a ceremony at Peterskirk, the Netherlands, a bronze tablet is unveiled to the memory of John Robinson, the pastor at the English Church in Leyden who is regarded as the "Father" of the Pilgrim movement to America—the tablet is paid for by the General Society of Mayflower Descendants.	Sep. 8
Democrat Franklin D. Roosevelt speaks at Bridgeport, Connecticut, in favor of Democratic Party presidential candidate Alfred E. Smith.... Investigators in Philadelphia find that photographs and files of many criminals have vanished from police records.	The October issue of the influential Foreign Affairs journal suggests that the Kellogg-Briand Pact might lull the United States into a false sense of security.			A crowd of 85,265 at the Yankee Stadium watch the American League games in which the Yankees defeat the Athletics....Henri Berraud's My Friend Robespierre, translated from French, is published in New York by Macaulay.	Sep. 9
The Philadelphia police department continues its heavily publicized attack on gangsters and their influence within the department.			Australian aviators Charles Kingsford Smith and Charles Ulm fly the "Southern Cross" plane from Australia to New Zealand, making the first Trans-Tasman flight....U.S. Aviator Earl Rowland finished first in the Air Derby, wining $5,000 as his plane lands at Mines Field, CA.	At a festival dating from the reign of Empress Maria Theresa (reigned from 1740 until 1780), a philosophy student called Dell at a competition in Prague, manages to consume 101 plum dumplings at a single session, beating the next competitor who manages to eat only 88.	Sep. 10
Democratic Party presidential candidate Alfred E. Smith calls for a meeting of New York Democrats to decide on who should stand in the election for the state governor....Murdered Chicago gangster Antonio Lombardo was buried in his home town.			Charles Kingsford Smith and Charles Ulm arrive in New Zealand after their 14 hour flight from Australia.		Sep. 11
Calvin Coolidge returns to Washington, DC....Democratic Party presidential candidate Alfred E. Smith continues to find himself facing a "whispering campaign" against his candidacy and demands that the Democrats behind this support his bid.			The Hollywood Film Studio, Warner Brothers, bus the Stanley Theatres giving them control of 4,000 theatres across the United States and making their company worth about $100 million.	Actress Katherine Hepburn makes her stage debut in The Czarina.	Sep. 12
Republican Party presidential candidate Herbert Hoover announces that in his time in Newark, he will be staying with Thomas Alva Edison.... Colonel Theodore Roosevelt offers to campaign for Herbert Hoover in the western United States.		A hurricane sweeps over several Southern states and the West Indies causing much damage, and resulting in many people killed, with heavy casualties in Puerto Rico where initial reports state the number killed as being as high as 1,000.		Italo Svevo, an Italian writer, dies.	Sep. 13

F	G	H	I	J
Includes campaigns, elections, federal-state relations, civil rights and liberties, crime, the judiciary, education, healthcare, poverty, urban affairs, and population.	Includes formation and debate of U.S. foreign and defense policies, veterans affairs, and defense spending. (Relations with specific foreign countries are usually found under the region concerned.)	Includes business, labor, agriculture, taxation, transportation, consumer affairs, monetary and fiscal policy, natural resources, pollution and industrial accidents.	Includes worldwide scientific, medical and technological developments, natural phenomena, U.S. weather and natural disasters.	Includes the arts, religion, scholarship, communications media, sports, entertainment, fashions, fads, and social life.

	World Affairs	Europe	Africa & The Middle East	The Americas	Asia & The Pacific
Sep. 14	Walter C. Teagle, President of the Standard Oil Company of New Jersey states that he would like an accord with other oil companies.	Laurent Eynac becomes Minister of the newly created Air Ministry in France….On the same day, as many as 400 fighter planes make an aerial display of strength over Paris to show that they can protect the French capital in time of war….The Soviet Union announces that it will extend the number of foreign concessions in the country to encourage more foreign capital….The Jugoslav government arrests 40 anti-Jewish activists in a crackdown on anti-Semitism in the country.			The Chinese Nationalist forces emerge victorious in a battle with the forces of General Chang Tsung-chang, the last of the Northern anti-Nationalist forces south of the Great Wall of China. The Nationalists take about 20,000 prisoners as General Chang's soldiers are routed.
Sep. 15		Italy and France pay $10,625,000 and $20 million respectively to Britain to pay off their war debts.		The hurricane in the Caribbean strikes The Bahamas, leaving 40 dead and also causes more destruction to Puerto Rico. The Red Cross immediately offers $50,000 in aid relief for Puerto Rico.	The Australian Dockers' Federation instructs its men to resume work under the new arbitration award but the men refuse and remain on strike….A typhoon hits the cities of Hankow and Nanking in China, killing more than 50 people.
Sep. 16		Augustinus Bernardus Gijsbertus Maria van Rijckevorsel becomes Governor of Noord-Brabant, Netherlands, his predecessor, Arthur Eduard Joseph van Voorst tot Voorst, having died on July 27….Further meetings are held about the possible German evacuation of the Rhineland, linking it with the payment of more reparations to France.			The remnants of the troops of the Northern Coalition/Peking government, retreats beyond the Lwan River….Mustapha Jaafar becomes the *Menteri Besar* ("Chief Minister") of Johore, Malaya, replacing Abdullah Jaafar….The Indian Assembly refers the Public Safety Bill to a Select Committee for further debate.
Sep. 17		German Communists try to hold up the enlarging of the German navy.		The Canadian and U.S. governments exchange notes regarding the reciprocal exemption from taxation on income from shipping companies…. The U.S. Consul to Colon, Panama, George M. Hanson was found dead in his bedroom above the Consulate, with death believed to be by natural causes.	
Sep. 18		In spite of many disagreements over the title of the Albanian King, Zog I, as "King of the Albanians" inferring rule over the Albanians in Kosovo, the Jugoslav government recognizes the new Albanian government.		In Puerto Rico, there is more storm damage with soldiers patrolling the streets of San Juan and other towns to prevent looting.	The Indian Council of State agrees to elect three members to sit with the Indian Statutory Commission of Sir John Simon….At Dairen in Manchuria, a group of North Chinese warlords enlist some 200,000 men, using 30 million Mexican dollars, to try to maintain their power base.
Sep. 19		Evidence emerges in Germany that it has secretly build 12-motor planes, known as Dornier 10s, and has a 150 foot craft, which has sleeping quarters for 33.		The British Secretary of State for Foreign Affairs, Sir Austen Chamberlain, arrives in Colon, Panama.	
Sep. 20		Law promulgated in Italy legalizing the Fascist Grand Council and making it the organ of government, with its President to be the Prime Minister of Italy….Romania recognizes King Zog I as "King of the Albanians."…With rising unemployment in Britain, the British Prime Minister Stanley Baldwin sends letters to 150,000 employers asking for them to give work to unemployed miners.		Mexican senators indicate that they will support Emilio Portes Gil as their provisional president.	Air Marshal Sir John Salmond of the British Royal Air Force submits his report to the Australian government on the role of the Royal Australian Air Force.

A	B	C	D	E
Includes developments that affect more than one world region, international organizations and important meetings of world leaders.	Includes all domestic and regional developments in Europe, including the Soviet Union.	Includes all domestic and regional developments in Africa and the Middle East.	Includes all domestic and regional developments in Latin America, the Caribbean, and Canada.	Includes all domestic and regional developments in Asian and Pacific nations (and colonies).

U.S. Politics & Social Issues	U.S. Foreign Policy & Affairs, Defense	U.S. Economy & Environment	Science, Technology & Nature	Culture, Leisure & Lifestyle	
Democratic Party presidential candidate Alfred E. Smith prepares for his tour of the western United States.	Calvin Coolidge announces that he will ignore the French-British Naval Accord.	Following the damage in San Juan, Puerto Rico, U.S. President, Calvin Coolidge, sends aid as Red Cross Relief Units try to help those injured in the tornado....A tornado strikes Rockford, Illinois, and killed 50–100 people, with another 150 injured.		Businessman and philanthropist Robert H. Ingersoll leaves between $500,000 and $1 million in his will to establish the Robert and Roberta Ingersoll Foundation to help boys with scholarships to see them through school.	Sep. 14
Advisers of Republican Party presidential candidate Herbert Hoover feel confident that the western United States will give him a victory in the forthcoming presidential elections....Author and educator Dr. Henry Van Dyke declares his support for Democratic Party presidential candidate Alfred E. Smith....In an unexpected move, Dr. John A. Hawkins, former Exalted Cyclops of the Ku Klux Klan in Pennsylvania declares his support for Al Smith.	After criticism of U.S. aid to the Philippines, Senator Manuel Quezon of Manila defends the program of aid introduced by Governor General Henry L. Stimson.	The U.S. government is involved in paying off a large section of the Liberty Loan, debts incurred in World War I.	Scottish bacteriologist Alexander Fleming, makes public his discovery, by accident, that the mold penicillin has antibiotic effects.	British cricketer Alfred Percy "Tich" Freeman sets an all-time record for the number of wickets taken in an English cricket season....*The Daughter of the Hawk*, by British writer C. S. Forester, is published in Indianapolis, IN, by Bobbs-Merrill Company.	Sep. 15
Republican Party presidential candidate Herbert Hoover starts campaigning in the eastern United States....Some 149 prominent authors in the United States declare their support for Democratic Party presidential candidate Alfred E. Smith.		The Okeechobee Hurricane, otherwise known as the Hurricane San Felipe Segundo, kills about 2500 people in Florida.	Am African-American stowaway is found in the ship of Richard Byrd as it heads for the Antarctic.		Sep. 16
Presidential hopeful Herbert Hoover delivers an important campaign speech at Newark, New Jersey, highlighting his program on dealing with unemployment, with 20,000 people joining a parade to the Newark Armory....The Chairman of the Democratic National Convention, John J. Raskob predicts that Democratic Party presidential candidate Alfred E. Smith will get 309 votes in the Electoral College—the winner needing 266....In a brazen robbery in the Bronx, New York, two armed men in uniforms pass themselves off as security guards and collect $18,000.		Calvin Coolidge orders a speeding up of food being sent to Puerto Rico.	The Germans delay a test of their new Zeppelin airship.		Sep. 17
Republican Party presidential candidate Herbert Hoover makes a plea for national unity in Newark, New Jersey; while Democratic Party presidential candidate Alfred E. Smith, in Omaha, Nebraska, condemns the stances taken by Hoover on tariffs.		The storms in Florida are estimated to have killed another 200 to 400 people, with the coast of North Carolina and South Carolina lashed.	Spanish aviator Don Juan de la Cierva flies across the English Channel in his C8L Mark II Autogiro from Croydon Airport, London, to Le Bourget, Paris, being the first cross-Channel flight in a rotary-win aircraft.	The British sportsman, the Earl of Durham, dies, aged 73.	Sep. 18
Democratic Party presidential candidate Alfred E. Smith continues to meet with people in Omaha, Nebraska, attempting to win the support of farmers for the forthcoming presidential elections.	The British and French governments continue to try to get the United States to take part in the Naval Accord.	The estimates for the number killed in Florida rise to 400 with gales lashing the coasts of New Jersey.			Sep. 19
Calvin Coolidge visits Plymouth Notch, Vermont, where his former homestead is located....Democratic Party presidential candidate Alfred E. Smith attacks intolerance and the whispering campaign organized by the Republican National Convention, to the cheers of crowds in Oklahoma City, Oklahoma.		The death toll in Florida mounts to 800 with outbreaks of diseases expected to result in more deaths.	The Okeechobee Hurricane, otherwise known as the Hurricane San Felipe Segundo, dissipates.		Sep. 20

F	G	H	I	J
Includes campaigns, elections, federal-state relations, civil rights and liberties, crime, the judiciary, education, healthcare, poverty, urban affairs, and population.	*Includes formation and debate of U.S. foreign and defense policies, veterans affairs, and defense spending. (Relations with specific foreign countries are usually found under the region concerned.)*	*Includes business, labor, agriculture, taxation, transportation, consumer affairs, monetary and fiscal policy, natural resources, pollution and industrial accidents.*	*Includes worldwide scientific, medical and technological developments, natural phenomena, U.S. weather and natural disasters.*	*Includes the arts, religion, scholarship, communications media, sports, entertainment, fashions, fads, and social life.*

	World Affairs	Europe	Africa & The Middle East	The Americas	Asia & The Pacific
Sep. 21		The German government proposes inviting Owen D. Young to redraft the Dawes Plan regarding Germany's repayment of the reparations imposed after World War I....France recognizes the new Albanian government.			Stanley Melbourne Bruce, the prime minister of Australia, states that the waterside workers' strike is getting worse.
Sep. 22	The German delegation walk out of an arms control meeting held in Geneva, Switzerland.	Adolf Hitler holds a meeting of Nazi Party leaders in Munich in which he urges them to be critical of Gustav Streseman's achievements in foreign policy....Great Britain recognizes the new Albanian government....Italy signs a Friendship Treaty with Greece.		The American Legation in Bogota, Colombia, sends a message asking for clarification of the rights of U.S. oil companies in the country, and receives no reply, with tensions mounting after the Argentine nationalization of foreign oil interests.	The Australian government passes a law to protect free labor on the water front to allow dock companies to employ non-union labor.
Sep. 23	The Congress for the International Democrats for Peace ends its eighth congress in Bierville and Geneva, Switzerland.	A large fire in the Novadades Theater (built in 1860), Madrid, Spain, results in 45 dead (the death toll is later put at 110) and 200 wounded (later raised to 350)....Italian leader Benito Mussolini and Greek Prime Minister Venizelos sign a Italian-Greek Friendship Pact in Rome....The government of the Soviet Union becomes increasingly critical of peasant farmers whom it accuses of holding back vast amounts of grain needed in the towns and cities.	Dr. Welter of the German Archaeological Institute, involved in archaeological excavations at Balata and on Mount Gerizim, the former to the east of the town of Nablus, uncovers evidence of a 3,600 year old city, and also a Christian church dating from 384 c.e., built on the site of a Samaritan church.	In the Caribbean, devastated by the recent storms, there is a large scale outbreak of influenza with 15,000 ill from the disease in Puerto Rico alone....Prince George, the second son of King George V of Britain, travels on a relief ship in the British West Indies....U.S. Ambassador to Mexico Dwight W. Morrow narrowly escapes a bandit attack on a village located on the road between Mexico City and the Morrow country retreat at Cuernavaca.	
Sep. 24		The Nationalists in the German parliament ask for a referendum to end the Weimar Republic....French police arrest Milan Jorich, a one-eyed Serbian burglar for the thefts from the homes of W. K. Vanderbilt and other prominent Americans in the French capital....The Geneva State Council in Switzerland follows the lead taken by the Federal Council in Berne in rejecting the right for women to vote in Swiss elections.	An incident takes place at the Wailing Wall in Jerusalem during the Day of Atonement Ceremonies after police try to remove a partition separating men and women during a prayer service.	Voter registration continues smoothly in the three northern provinces of Nicaragua where the rebel general Augusto Sandino had drawn strong support....General Pedro Savedra, a former lieutenant in the Zapata army in Mexico is shot dead in Cuernavaca while he was visiting the house of the governor Ambrosio Puete.	The Nanking government announces that from this day local Chinese collectorates would pay into specific banks a proportion of receipts amounting to the sum required to service foreign loans secured on the Salt Gabelle....The Indian Assembly, with the casting vote of the president, following a tied vote, defeats a motion to consider a bill providing for the expulsion from India of Communists and "other dangerous agents."
Sep. 25		The Reichsbank in Germany discloses that there has been an attempt to fake large numbers of German bonds to defraud it of millions of marks.		Emilio Portes Gil is elected provisional president of Mexico, to replace Plutarco Calles in November....Student demonstrations take place in Bogota, capital of Colombia, against the United States.	A British Economic ion, sent by the British Government, arrives in Australia to begin its report on the state of the Australian economy....Northern warlords based in the north Chinese city of Mukden in Manchuria, fail in their plans to organize a counter-attack against the Chinese Nationalist forces....Chinese Nationalist Foreign Minister Dr. C. T. Wang announces that he will raise the rank of the legations in Washington, DC, London and Paris, to embassy level.
Sep. 26	Twenty-three members of the League of Nations sign an act embodying the Kellogg-Briand Treaty against war....The Assembly of the League of Nations closes after adopting the League Budget for 1929 amounting to £1,080,000.	The Italian Fascist leader Benito Mussolini warns about the falling birth rate in Italy in an interview in the Fascist magazine *Gerarchia*. He speaks of the eventual domination of the world by Blacks and Asians, and mentions the riots in Harlem, NY, in July 1927 as evidence of this.		The Panamanian government signs commercial treaties with the British and the U.S. governments....William Miller Collier, the retiring U.S. Ambassador to Chile tells a luncheon meeting in London that U.S. foreign investment in Latin America has made it prosperous. He mentions that the Ecuadorian port of Guayaquil was "once the pest hole of the world" but is now a wealthy and entrepreneurial city.	Chinese pirates disguised as passengers seize the steamer *Anking* and kill two English officers.
Sep. 27		The British Conservative Party Conference at Yarmouth hears resolutions to safeguard the iron and steel industries but Stanley Baldwin, the prime minister, announces that he will not introduce tariffs.		William Barlas becomes Magistrate of the British South Atlantic territory of South Georgia and South Sandwich Islands.	

A	B	C	D	E
Includes developments that affect more than one world region, international organizations and important meetings of world leaders.	*Includes all domestic and regional developments in Europe, including the Soviet Union.*	*Includes all domestic and regional developments in Africa and the Middle East.*	*Includes all domestic and regional developments in Latin America, the Caribbean, and Canada.*	*Includes all domestic and regional developments in Asian and Pacific nations (and colonies).*

U.S. Politics & Social Issues	U.S. Foreign Policy & Affairs, Defense	U.S. Economy & Environment	Science, Technology & Nature	Culture, Leisure & Lifestyle	
Calvin Coolidge gave a brief speech at Bennington, VT, where he spoke of his deep affection for his native state....Daniel E. Pomeroy, vice-chairman of the Republican National Convention denies running a whispering campaign against Democratic Party presidential candidate Alfred E. Smith.	U.S. Secretary of State Frank B. Kellogg starts drafting a Naval Accord reply to the British and French governments.			The first issue of the magazine *My Weekly Reader* is launched.	Sep. 21
		Florida expects floods as waters rise in Okeechobee....It is confirmed that 450 people died in Pelican Bay with National Guardsmen finding 200 dead bodies.	*The Conquest of Life*, a popular explanation of the theories of the author, Dr. Serge Voronoff, is published in New York by Brentano's.	*Abraham Lincoln*, a two volume biographical study by Albert J. Beveridge covering the life of the former president until 1858, is published posthumously in Boston, MA, by the Houghton Mifflin Company.	Sep. 22
Casper Holstein, a wealthy Harlem African-American is released after being kidnapped by a White gang who hold him for a reported $50,000 ransom.		Relief workers find another 200 dead in Pelican Bay, Florida, as they worry about the possibility of disease spreading.	Sir Horace Darwin KBE FRS, a famous British scientist and inventor, dies, aged 77.		Sep. 23
Democratic Party presidential candidate Alfred E. Smith criticizes corruption in the Republican Party and speaks of the deafening silence of his Republican adversary Herbert Hoover to these charges....Norman Thomas, the Socialist candidate for the U.S. presidency returns to New York where he is greeted by thousands of Socialists.	The 23rd Annual Convention of the First Catholic Slovak Union of America is held in New York.	The Relief Fund to raise money for Florida reaches $1.5 million.	The German government announces that Zeppelins will tour the United States later in the year with Zeppelin designer Dr. Hugo Eckener refusing to comment on the probable route.		Sep. 24
Democratic Party presidential candidate Alfred E. Smith makes a number of election speeches at Butte, where he is greeted by a crowd of 25,000....As the anti-corruption enquiries at the Philadelphia Police Department continue, 23 police are formally connected by gangsters in a Grand Jury investigation....A Grand Jury is also empanelled to decide on the death of William L. D'Olier, President of the Sanitation Corporation of New York, who was found dead on September 2.	Calvin Coolidge insists on an open discussion on the Anglo-French plans for a reduction in the size of the U.S. naval forces.	The company Motorola is founded as the Galvin Manufacturing Corporation (it changes its name to Motorola in 1947)....The Yellow Cab Company in New York announces that it is considering buying the entire taxi network of Berlin, Germany....Some 45,000 in Florida seek aid from the Red Cross.			Sep. 25
The train taking Democratic Party presidential candidate Alfred E. Smith visits the "Wheat Belt" with Smith in North Dakota.... Newspaper advertisements appear in some New York newspapers urging that a Protestant should be nominated for Governor of New York in the forthcoming elections.		An autumn chill sets a 57 year record for the temperature in New York with the frost likely to damage crops in the northern states.	The Radio Corporation of America requests the right to begin a domestic service in the United States.	The Canadian women's polo team loses the first game of their series against the Westchester County Women's Polo Team.	Sep. 26
Calvin Coolidge states that he will speak out in favor of Republican Party presidential candidate Herbert Hoover....Democratic Party presidential candidate Alfred E. Smith at St. Paul, in front of a crowd of 10,000, attacks Herbert Hoover's record on tariffs.			Sir Henry A. Wickham, a pioneer of the rubber industry, dies, aged 83.	Australian singer Nellie Melba makes her final appearance in opera in Australia with a matinee in Melbourne.	Sep. 27

F	G	H	I	J
Includes campaigns, elections, federal-state relations, civil rights and liberties, crime, the judiciary, education, healthcare, poverty, urban affairs, and population.	*Includes formation and debate of U.S. foreign and defense policies, veterans affairs, and defense spending. (Relations with specific foreign countries are usually found under the region concerned.)*	*Includes business, labor, agriculture, taxation, transportation, consumer affairs, monetary and fiscal policy, natural resources, pollution and industrial accidents.*	*Includes worldwide scientific, medical and technological developments, natural phenomena, U.S. weather and natural disasters.*	*Includes the arts, religion, scholarship, communications media, sports, entertainment, fashions, fads, and social life.*

	World Affairs	Europe	Africa & The Middle East	The Americas	Asia & The Pacific
Sep. 28	The Franco-British accord on naval limitations is rejected by the U.S. government.	The Prussian authorities lift a public speaking ban on German Nazi politician Adolf Hitler.	The Prince of Wales and the Duke of Gloucester arrive at Mombasa in Kenya....*Sons of Africa*, by Georgina A. Gollock, is published in New York by Friendship Press.		U.S. Government announces its recognition of the Nationalist Government in Nanking, China, as the government of the whole of China....Strikers on the dockyards in Melbourne, Australia, bomb the homes of two workers. There are also riots in Adelaide with the enrolling of special constables.
Sep. 29		The French Marshal Joseph Jacques Cesaire Joffre reveals for the first time, in his memoirs, how he went by car to the British commander General French to try to get the British to participate in the First Battle of the Marne in 1914....A British play called *The Eternal Flame*, in which the "Unknown Soldier" rises from his grave in Westminster Abbey and speaks to the audience is heavily criticized in the British media.		The oil fields in Vera Cruz, Mexico, are badly damaged by heavy rains which lead to flooding.	A tin-dredging company for British Malaya is formed by the Anglo-Oriental Corporation of London.
Sep. 30		The French Prime Minister Raymond Poincaré insists that the German government must pay its war reparations.	The Prince of Wales, representing the Navy, wins a golf competition in Mombasa, Kenya.		
Oct. 1		The Soviet Union begins its first five-year plan abandoning its more capitalistic New Economic Policy....Salomon Arvid Achates Lindman becomes Prime Minister of Sweden, taking over from Carl Gustaf Ekman, forming a conservative ministry in Stockholm....Domenico Suzzi Valli and Francesco Pasquali become the Captains-Regent of San Marino.	The Prince of Wales and the Duke of Gloucester arrive in Nairobi, Kenya, where they are greeted by large crowds.	Florencio Harmodio Arosemena becomes President of Panama, following his election on August 5, taking over from Rodolfo Chiari.	The Standing Committee of the Central Executive Committee of the Kuomintang, the Chinese Nationalist Party, adopt a set of six governing principles for inclusion in political education, enshrining the role of the Kuomintang in the administration of the education of the military.
Oct. 2	José Maria Escriva founds the Roman Catholic group *Opus Dei*.	Large avalanche at Mount Arbino near Bellinzona, Switzerland, destroys large tracts of farmland....The Right Reverend Herbert Hansley Henson, Bishop of Durham and leading British cleric, predicts that England might become "Pagan" with the availability of easier divorce procedures and greater access to birth control.	A parade of Jews from the Orthodox Agudah Israel, planned to be held in Jerusalem is banned by the British District Commissioner of Jerusalem following his earlier banning of a Muslim demonstration.		The Nanking official news agency announces that the Nanking government has confirmed the appointment of A.H.F. Edwardes as Officiating Inspector-General of the Maritime Customs and has appointed F. W. Maze as Deputy Inspector-General....A conference of unions is held at Melbourne and advises striking dockyard workers not to take out licenses under the new Australian government scheme.
Oct. 3		The French submarine *Ondine* collides with a Greek steamship off the coast of Spain, resulting in the death of 43 people....Spanish Dictator Miguel Primo de Rivera y Orbaneja, marqués de Estella, announces that there will be a rapid growth in the Spanish economy....Floods devastate parts of Belgium after dikes break in Nieuport and Zeebrugge.	The Prince of Wales and the Duke of Gloucester in Kenya visit the "native camp" where they meet with representatives of all the tribes in British East Africa.	The Minister of Finance in Chile confirms that the American copper mining interests in his country covered by the Chile Exploration Company and the Braden Copper Company will both be subjected to claims for back-tax.	Nationalist government in China introduces a new Chinese Constitution with Chiang Kai-shek becoming president—ratified a week later.
Oct. 4	The *Theses on the Colonial and Semi-colonial Countries* of veteran Finnish Communist Otto Wilhelm Kuusinen, is published in the *Imprecor* newspaper urging the Communist International to become more active in colonial struggles as capitalism there is becoming a "spent force."	A plebiscite held in German against building new battleships fails....German Erich von Ludendorff makes a speech denouncing freemasonry....Tensions rise in Vienna, the capital of Austria, with Socialists taking part in a large demonstration and their enemies organizing a counterdemonstration.			The Organic Law of the National Government of the Republic of China is promulgated at Nanking....John Earl Baker, director of the Red Cross China Famine Relief in 1920-21 highlights the plight of 2.5 million Chinese facing starvation....The Australian prime minister declines to alter his government's policies over the dockyard strike and decides to adopt a "fighting" policy.

A	B	C	D	E
Includes developments that affect more than one world region, international organizations and important meetings of world leaders.	Includes all domestic and regional developments in Europe, including the Soviet Union.	Includes all domestic and regional developments in Africa and the Middle East.	Includes all domestic and regional developments in Latin America, the Caribbean, and Canada.	Includes all domestic and regional developments in Asian and Pacific nations (and colonies).

U.S. Politics & Social Issues	U.S. Foreign Policy & Affairs, Defense	U.S. Economy & Environment	Science, Technology & Nature	Culture, Leisure & Lifestyle	
A gunman in Rahway, New Jersey, snatches $10,000 in a mail raid with an African American porter found tied to a tree and telling of his kidnapping by thugs who abused him before tying him up.	The U.S. government rejects the Anglo-French Naval Accord because it feels it will present an artificial limit on the number of U.S. ships, in spite of a possible change in circumstances.		Richard Byrd spends the weekend with his family before setting out for the Antarctic....Zeppelin engineer Dr. Hugh Eckener states that he is satisfied by new tests on blue gas to be used as fuel on his new Zeppelins.		Sep. 28
The *Washington Post* published a letter by Willie W. Caldwell, a member of the Republican National Committee for Virginia, in which she denounces Democratic Party presidential candidate Alfred E. Smith for his Roman Catholicism. Republican Party presidential candidate Herbert Hoover immediately repudiates the "Anti-Roman" letter.	The U.S. government is told, by the French government, the entire naval agreement between the British and the French in the hope that they might agree to sign the Accord.			The second volume of *The Memoirs of Raymond Poincaré*, translated and adapted by Sir George Arthur, is published in New York by Doubleday, Doran & Co, having originally been published in France in French on December 18, 1927....A U.S. Polo team defeats that of Argentina at Meadow Brook, Long Island.	Sep. 29
Supporters of Republican Party presidential candidate Herbert Hoover claim that he will win the vast majority of the electoral college seats from the southern states....Herbert Hoover's finance committee states that it has sought funds from Americans in Europe.		Five people are killed in a train crash on Long Island.		The Roosevelt Prizes for 1928 are awarded to aviator Colonel Charles Lindbergh, diplomat Charles E. Hughes and Frank M. Chapman, the Curator of Ornithology at the Natural History Museum.	Sep. 30
The Democrats in New York, in a surprise move, draft Franklin Delano Roosevelt to be their candidate in the forthcoming elections for the state governor. The announcement is met with large cheers from Democrats meeting at Rochester.		American Tobacco and U.S. Rubber were removed as components of the Dow Jones Index at the New York Stock Exchangeand are replaced by American Tobacco Class B. and the North American Company....The Newark Municipal Airport in New Jersey is officially opened.			Oct. 1
Democratic Party presidential candidate Alfred E. Smith states his great elation at having Franklin Roosevelt succeed him as Governor of New York.	Coolidge rejects the idea suggested by French Prime Minister Raymond Poincaré that the issue of French debts to the United States should be linked with the unpaid German debts to France.	Clarence W. Barron, the publisher of The *Wall Street Journal*, dies at the Battle Creek Sanatorium, aged 73.			Oct. 2
Calvin Coolidge and Republican Party presidential candidate Herbert Hoover are cheered when they appear together on the campaign trail....New York Gubernatorial candidate Franklin Delano Roosevelt, in an article in the October issue of *Women's City Club Magazine* highlights the importance of the role of women in politics.	The French Prime Minister Raymond Poincaré stated his surprise at the response to his debt ideas and their rejection by Calvin Coolidge.			Argentina defeats the United States at polo, 10–7 in a fast-moving game at Westbury, Long Island.	Oct. 3
Campaign advisers for Republican Party presidential candidate Herbert Hoover announce that $1,074,870 was added to the Hoover election fund in September alone....An investigation in Long Island finds that $900,000 was "creamed off" in bribes in work on four sewer contracts....New York gubernatorial candidate Franklin Delano Roosevelt denies publicly that Smith forced him to stand in the forthcoming elections.			Lady Heath in Britain achieves the altitude record (23,000 feet) in her plane....The Zeppelin Company reveal that the fare in a Zeppelin from Germany to America will cost $12,000, with Dr. Robert Reiner of Weehawken, New Jersey, living at Würzburg, immediately booking a seat.	Mae West is indicted with the rest of the case of *Pleasure Men* for indecency during a show at the Biltmore Theatre, New York.....The managers of the Drury Lane, London, production of *Show Boat* won a court battle with a New York company which claimed that African-American singer Paul Robeson should be performing for them in the United States not in the British capital.	Oct. 4

F	G	H	I	J
Includes campaigns, elections, federal-state relations, civil rights and liberties, crime, the judiciary, education, healthcare, poverty, urban affairs, and population.	*Includes formation and debate of U.S. foreign and defense policies, veterans affairs, and defense spending. (Relations with specific foreign countries are usually found under the region concerned.)*	*Includes business, labor, agriculture, taxation, transportation, consumer affairs, monetary and fiscal policy, natural resources, pollution and industrial accidents.*	*Includes worldwide scientific, medical and technological developments, natural phenomena, U.S. weather and natural disasters.*	*Includes the arts, religion, scholarship, communications media, sports, entertainment, fashions, fads, and social life.*

	World Affairs	Europe	Africa & The Middle East	The Americas	Asia & The Pacific
Oct. 5		The Austrian government draft 12,000 soldiers into the capital of Vienna as the Socialists keep up their protests. Many people flee from factories and hospitals prepare extra beds for people injured in the street fighting....After a leak, an unauthorized summary of the naval compromise between Britain and France is published in a French newspaper.		A British parliamentary commission sails for Buenos Aires to check on the hygiene methods used by Argentine cattle slaughterers sending meat for the British market.	Chinese Communist Mao Tse-tung writes the draft resolution of the Second Congress of the Sian Communist Party Organizations active in the Hunan-Kiangsi border region.
Oct. 6	Canada criticizes the United States and Britain for blocking efforts to bring about arms control.	King Zog I of the Albanians celebrates his 34th birthday, which becomes a national holiday....Yugoslav Communist activist Josip Broz (later Marshal Tito) is sentenced to five years in jail.		The Mexican Roman Catholic church leaders ask the government for new Church laws urging for cooperation between the Church and the state, pointing out the union of the Catholic Church and state in four European countries: Belgium, Italy, Poland, and Spain, and in eight Latin American ones: Argentina, Bolivia, Colombia, Costa Rica, Ecuador, Paraguay, Peru, and Santo Domingo.	Chiang Kai-shek is elected as president of China....Air Vice-Marshal Sir John Salmond recommends a drastic improvement in the equipment being used in the Australian Air Defenses.
Oct. 7		Some 10,000 soldiers guard the Austrian capital with bayonets drawn to keep back Socialist demonstrations and counter-demonstrators....The Royal Flemish Engineers' Organization is established in Belgium....The Pyrenean Principality of Andorra announces that it will modernize itself and establish a casino-based economy similar to that at Monte Carlo in Monaco.	Ras Tafari (Haile Selassie) is crowned King of Abyssinia in a ceremony at Addis Ababa....The Duke of Gloucester leaves Nairobi for a long hunting expedition.		The Chinese government announces the formation of a Central Bank of China and issues a short term loan designed to restore the value of the currency....An explosion on a train from Allahabad to Bombay causes the death of four passengers, with another eight injured.
Oct. 8		King Haakon VII of Norway arrives at Appleton House, Sandringham, visiting the British Royal Family....Right Honorable Charles Andrew, the last Irish Master of the Rolls, dies, aged 73.			
Oct. 9		In the falling of a seven-story building in Prague, the Czech capital, 100 people are believed to have been buried with 13 bodies found and many others unaccounted for....The Greek Prime Minister Eleutherios Venizelos visits Belgrade, the Jugoslav capital.			The Sino–French settlement of the Nanking Incident of March 1927 is agreed by an exchange of notes....Reports reach Shanghai that 200,000 Chinese were killed in the province of Kansu in renewed fighting between warlords and Muslims....On the rest of China, flags are placed in all the major cities in preparation for Chiang Kai-shek to become the president of China.
Oct. 10	The Japanese government announces that they will send 1,000 colonists each year to Brazil.	The Italian Fascist leader Benito Mussolini states, in a press conference, that the Italian press is free....Workers in Prague pull out a body from the wreckage of the building collapse after the man was buried in rubble for 30 hours.		Isidro Ayora, provisional president of Ecuador, becomes interim President, and declared an amnesty for all political exiles....The Chilean government announces the suspension for four months of the Tacna-Arica Boundary Commission. Arica is eventually awarded to Chile, and Tacna to Peru, with Bolivian complaints met with partial control of a railway outlet to the Pacific from La Paz to Arica.	On the anniversary of the 1911 Revolution, a new government of China if formed on the basis of the Organic Law of October 4. Chiang Kai-shek becomes chairman of the National Government of China, with Tan Yankai becoming president of the Executive Yuan.
Oct. 11		Members of the British Liberal Party speak out at its conference in Great Yarmouth about the increased spending on weaponry in spite of treaties and accords to limit these.			Sir John Simon of the Indian Statutory Commission and other members of the commission, arrive in Bombay. The Australian prime minister declares that his government would take action unless the seamen's union ensures the manning of interstate vessels, and the union agrees to stop bans on these vessels.

A	B	C	D	E
Includes developments that affect more than one world region, international organizations and important meetings of world leaders.	Includes all domestic and regional developments in Europe, including the Soviet Union.	Includes all domestic and regional developments in Africa and the Middle East.	Includes all domestic and regional developments in Latin America, the Caribbean, and Canada.	Includes all domestic and regional developments in Asian and Pacific nations (and colonies).

U.S. Politics & Social Issues	U.S. Foreign Policy & Affairs, Defense	U.S. Economy & Environment	Science, Technology & Nature	Culture, Leisure & Lifestyle	
Democratic Party presidential candidate Alfred E. Smith confronts Reverend Manning E. Van Nostrand with spreading rumors of that Smith was intoxicated during a radio broadcast that he had to be held up by two advisers, and counsel for Smith serve an affidavit on the minister....The Democrats reveal that they raised $876,420 in a month.				Lord Allenby, the British general who defeated the Turks in Palestine in World War I, is presented with the Gold Medal of New York City at a ceremony in New York.	Oct. 5
Presidential hopeful Herbert Hoover delivers an important campaign speech at Elizabethton, TN, before 50,000 people, outlining his program in dealing with ways in which the federal government would help the southern states.	U.S. Secretary for the Navy Curtis Wilbur signs a contract with the Goodyear Zeppelin Corporation of Akron, OH, for the manufacture of two giant dirigibles.		Despite the cost of $12,000 per person, some 18 people book flights on the Zeppelin.	The U.S. polo team defeat the Argentine team at Meadow Brook Club, Long Island.	Oct. 6
Republican Party presidential candidate Herbert Hoover returned to Washington, DC, after visiting Tennessee....Democratic Party presidential candidate Alfred E. Smith continues to criticize Hebert Hoover over the Republican's views on tariffs.		Six plane crashes take place throughout the United States, with eight killed and 11 injured.	Two of the Americans who have booked Zeppelin flights for $12,000 each also take out $1 million life insurance policies.	The French Academy of Philately is established.	Oct. 7
The Mayor of New York sends the police department on raids on 20 speakeasies....New York gubernatorial candidate Franklin Delano Roosevelt states that he will oppose any move to revive the New York Dry Laws....Louis Marshall of the American Relief Administration issues a statement that prompt action by Herbert Hoover managed to stop the massacring of Jews in Pinsk, Russia.	The U.S. Supreme Court upholds the rights of Canadians to cross the U.S.-Canadian frontier every day for employment....Harold J. T. Horan of New York, the Paris correspondent of the Universal Service, working for Hearst newspapers, was arrested by the U.S. Secret Service in a crowded street in Paris and accused of leaking information on the Anglo-French Naval Accord.		Aviation authorities reveal that there were 390 plane crashes in the last six months, with 153 killed, and 275 injured.	Thieves break into the house of Count von Hardenberg in Darmstadt, Germany, and are believed to have stolen papers relevant to the claims of the women who said that she was Anastasia, the daughter of Tsar Nicholas II.	Oct. 8
Democratic Party presidential candidate Alfred E. Smith and New York gubernatorial candidate Franklin Delano Roosevelt confer on election strategies as there is a massive rise in people registering to vote for the forthcoming elections....Norman Thomas, the Socialist candidate for the U.S. presidency denies that his standing will help Republican Herbert Hoover by drawing votes away from Smith.				Marcel Pagnol's play *Topaz* is premiered in Paris....Two paintings by Rembrandt van Rijn are brought to New York after having been purchased in London in May 1927 for $500,000. They both came from the collection of the late Sir George Lindsay Holford.	Oct. 9
Democratic Party presidential candidate Alfred E. Smith greets Babe Ruth on his return to New York.		Stock prices soar on the New York Stock Exchange, with $450,000 being paid for a seat on the Stock Exchange.	Dr. Hugo Eckener announces that there will be 60 people on the first Zeppelin flight which will make the journey from Germany to the United States in 50 hours.		Oct. 10
Andrew W. Mellon, Secretary of the Treasury, makes an extended address urging for Americans to elect Republican Party presidential candidate Herbert Hoover to continue the prosperity of the United States....Herbert Hoover spends the day campaigning in Boston.	The U.S. and French governments find some problems in the Kellogg-Briand Pact, with the French still anxious on the Anglo-French Naval Accord to be signed by the United States.		The *Graf Zeppelin* passes Barcelona and then heads over the Atlantic Ocean....The journey is described in detail by people aboard using radio communications....The American Telephone and Telegraph Company announces that telephone service will soon connect New York and Madrid.		Oct. 11

F	G	H	I	J
Includes campaigns, elections, federal-state relations, civil rights and liberties, crime, the judiciary, education, healthcare, poverty, urban affairs, and population.	Includes formation and debate of U.S. foreign and defense policies, veterans affairs, and defense spending. (Relations with specific foreign countries are usually found under the region concerned.)	Includes business, labor, agriculture, taxation, transportation, consumer affairs, monetary and fiscal policy, natural resources, pollution and industrial accidents.	Includes worldwide scientific, medical and technological developments, natural phenomena, U.S. weather and natural disasters.	Includes the arts, religion, scholarship, communications media, sports, entertainment, fashions, fads, and social life.

	World Affairs	Europe	Africa & The Middle East	The Americas	Asia & The Pacific
Oct. 12		The former British Prime Minister, David Lloyd George, denounces the Anglo-French Naval Accord as a "most sinister event."		Hipólito Irigoyen becomes president of Argentina for the second time, replacing Marcelo T. de Alvear.... William Lyon Mackenzie King, the Canadian Prime Minister, on a visit to Britain, presents King George V with a gold medal to celebrate the 60th anniversary of the Canadian Confederation in a ceremony at Buckingham Palace, London.	
Oct. 13		Lord Birkenhead, the Secretary of State for India, resigns from the British cabinet to go into business....The French foreign ministry investigating the leak of the Anglo-French Naval Accord links Harold J. T. Horan of the Hearst newspapers with M. de Noblet, a diplomat attached to the Foreign Office and Roger Deleplanque, a Parisian journalist. Horan is expelled from France....10 people die in three train crashes in England....Dowager Empress Marie of Russia dies, aged 80....New evidence emerges that the Soviet Union is building up her merchant navy.			
Oct. 14		In an announcement by Count Bethlen, the Hunagrian Prime Minister, made at Oedenberg in West Hungary, he states that the Hungarian government has decided to choose its next king by referendum, to fill the throne made vacant by King Karl's abidctaion in 1918....Italian Fascist leader Benito Mussolini announces aid grants to farming families.			The British government agree to hold a meeting of the Princes of India with a view to the establishment of a Federated India, or even a United States of India.
Oct. 15		A massive strike involving 200,000 workers takes place in Lodz, Poland to try to get employers to raise pay rates....Alexandre Mari ends his term as Mayor of Nice, France.	The Prince of Wales arrives in Uganda where he is welcomed by warriors in war canoes....Charles Grey, brother of the British peer Viscount Grey if Falloden, is gored to death by a buffalo while hunting on the shore of Lake Tanganyika, in Kenya.	The Right Reverend Edwin V. Byrne, the Ronan Catholic Bishop of Puerto Rico appeals for more aid for the island which was badly damaged in the recent storms.	The Koninklijke Nederlandschh-Indische Luchtvaart Maatschappij (K.N.I.L.M.), the airline for the Netherlands East Indies, is granted a Dutch Royal Charter to operate air routes in the East Indies....General Erich von Ludendorff demise that he has accepted an offer by General Feng Yu-hsiang to reorganize the Chinese army.
Oct. 16		The Albanian Parliament votes an annual salary for King Zog of 500,000 Gold francs ($96,500), which is more than Calvin Coolidge who is paid $75,000 a year. In addition the Albanian government will pay 100 Gold francs to each Prince in the Royal Family, and also to the mother of the King.		Harry Burgess becomes Governor of the Panama Canal Zone, taking over from Meriwether L. Walker.	The Reverend Dr. Frank C. Laubach from Manila speaking at Bridgeport, Connecticut, condemns racism in the United States.
Oct. 17		Foreign residents in France express worries that under the new proposed taxation law in France they will face double taxation....The first person to be sentenced to death in Italy since the Unification of the Kingdom, Michele della Maggiore, is found guilty of murdering two Fascisti on May 10.	Some 4,000 warriors and tribesmen in Uganda gather to meet the Prince of Wales.	The Argentine training ship Presidente Sarmiento, is anchored in the Hudson River, New York.	Sydney, Australia, and the island of Java in the Netherlands East Indies are connected by a radio link for the first time....The German aviator Baron Ehrenfried Gunther von Huenefeld leaves Shanghai for his flight to Tokyo....Some 70 people drown in a ferry collision off Taku, near Tientsin.
Oct. 18		Discussions in London between S. Gilbert Parker, Agent General for Reparations Payments; Prime Minister Stanley Baldwin; Winston Churchill, the Chancellor of the Exchequer; and representatives of the British Foreign Office and Treasury draw up a new plan for German war reparations.			The Standing Committee of the Kuomintang, the Chinese Nationalist Party, agrees to allow Chang Hsueh-liang, son of Chang Tso-lin to become a member of the State Council....Viscount Peel is appointed as the British Secretary of State for India.

A	B	C	D	E
Includes developments that affect more than one world region, international organizations and important meetings of world leaders.	Includes all domestic and regional developments in Europe, including the Soviet Union.	Includes all domestic and regional developments in Africa and the Middle East.	Includes all domestic and regional developments in Latin America, the Caribbean, and Canada.	Includes all domestic and regional developments in Asian and Pacific nations (and colonies).

U.S. Politics & Social Issues	U.S. Foreign Policy & Affairs, Defense	U.S. Economy & Environment	Science, Technology & Nature	Culture, Leisure & Lifestyle	
Democratic Party presidential candidate Alfred E. Smith, in a speech at Nashville, Tennessee, challenges his opponent Herbert Hoover to clearly state his views on farm aid.	Radio commentator Walter Lippmann states that he prefers Democratic Party presidential candidate Alfred Smith's views on foreign policy to those of Republican rival Herbert Hoover.		The first iron lung respirator is used at the Children's Hospital in Boston, MA.	*Lamentations* by Alter Brody, an anthology of four folk plays about American Jewish life, is published in New York by Coward McCann.	Oct. 12
Democratic Party presidential candidate Alfred E. Smith's promise of a tariff "to protect all classes" is cheered by crowds in Louisville, Kentucky....Joseph Mundo, a Brooklyn bootlegger, is shot dead as gangland violence mounts.		The American Red Cross is praised for its efforts in the relief operation in Florida.	Charles Kingsford Smith and Charles Ulm fly back to Australia from New Zealand, arriving at Richmond, New South Wales....The *Graf Zeppelin* reaches Bermuda, with French newspapers claiming that travel by Zeppelin is unsafe.	Well-known British writer, and author of *Chrome Yellow*, Aldous Huxley has his latest book *Point Counter Point* published by Doubleday, Doran & Co. of New York....R. H. Barrow's book *Slavery in the Roman Empire*, is published in New York by The Dial Press.	Oct. 13
Registration for voting in U.S. presidential elections close, with large numbers of women enrolling, but seven nuns in New York barred from voting....Democratic Party presidential candidate Alfred E. Smith speaks at the log cabin where Abraham Lincoln was built at Louisville, KY....The Republicans spend heavily buying advertising in the southern states.		Bankers gather at Atlantic City, New Jersey for the Annual Convention of the Investment Association.	The *Graf Zeppelin*, is expected at Lakehurst where 65,000 people gather. However it is delayed in winds off Bermuda, and there is a traffic jam eight miles long at Lakehurst as people leave in the evening.		Oct. 14
Presidential hopeful Herbert Hoover delivers an important campaign speech at Boston, Massachusetts, on international trade and tariffs....Democratic Party presidential candidate Alfred E. Smith at St. Louis, MO, speaks to a massive crowd, with some 200,000 people lining the streets.	Calvin Coolidge congratulates Dr. Hugo Eckener and President Paul von Hindenburg over the safe arrival of the *Graf Zeppelin*.		The world's largest airship, the *Graf Zeppelin*, commandeered by Dr. Hugo Eckener, and with 20 passengers on board, arrives in Lakehurst, NJ, after leaving Friedrichshafen, Germany, on October 11—a journey lasting 111.5 hours. One of the passengers, the only woman, was Lady Grace Drummond representing the Hearst newspaper group, and she becomes the second woman to cross the Atlantic Ocean by air, and the first in an airship.		Oct. 15
Democratic Party presidential candidate Alfred E. Smith claims that the view of Calvin Coolidge bringing prosperity to the country is a myth.	The U.S. Army reveals that it has been considering plans for its own airships bigger than the *Graf Zeppelin*.	Walter P. Chrysler, President of the Chrysler Motor Corporation of Detroit plans a 68-story building in New York.	Calvin Coolidge greets Dr. Hugo Eckener in Washington, DC. Many of the 28,124 letters and 37,950 postcards carried by the Zeppelin are delivered in the United States.	The French comedian Maurice Chevalier arrives in New York to make a new movie film.	Oct. 16
Republican campaign officials deny that Republican Party presidential candidate Herbert Hoover ever changed his nationality or renounced his U.S. citizenship....Large crowds in Chicago come out to meet Democratic Party presidential candidate Alfred E. Smith.		Venture capitalists hope that Dr. Hugo Eckener will establish his dream of an Ocean Airship Line.	Some 20,000 people visit Lakehurst to see the *Graf Zeppelin* in the hangar there....Charles Smith of New York, and President of the American Association for the Advancement of Atheism is jailed in Little Rock, Arkansas, for failing to pay a fine incurred for speaking against the proposed anti-Evolution law being put to a referendum in the state.	British painter Sir Frank Bernard Dicksee, president of the Royal Academy, dies, aged 85....It is announced that the library of the music composer Jerome Kern will be auctioned at the Anderson Galleries in New York.	Oct. 17
Democratic Party presidential candidate Alfred E. Smith replies to Secretary of the Treasury Andrew W. Mellon's critique of Smith's statements by Calvin Coolidge over prosperity.			No news is received about the British aviator, Commander H.C. MacDonald, with a vigil by friends and supporters at Croydon Airport, London.		Oct. 18

F	G	H	I	J
Includes campaigns, elections, federal-state relations, civil rights and liberties, crime, the judiciary, education, healthcare, poverty, urban affairs, and population.	*Includes formation and debate of U.S. foreign and defense policies, veterans affairs, and defense spending. (Relations with specific foreign countries are usually found under the region concerned.)*	*Includes business, labor, agriculture, taxation, transportation, consumer affairs, monetary and fiscal policy, natural resources, pollution and industrial accidents.*	*Includes worldwide scientific, medical and technological developments, natural phenomena, U.S. weather and natural disasters.*	*Includes the arts, religion, scholarship, communications media, sports, entertainment, fashions, fads, and social life.*

	World Affairs	Europe	Africa & The Middle East	The Americas	Asia & The Pacific
Oct. 19		British Chancellor of the Exchequer Winston Churchill visits France for an 11-hour meeting in Paris, where he discusses the reparations question with Raymond Poincaré.			The Chinese foreign minister, C.T. Wang and Mr. Yada, the Japanese Consul-General in Shanghai, open conversations for the settlement of the Nanking and Tsinanfu incidents and other outstanding questions.
Oct. 20		Prince and Princess Boris Gargarine of Russia arrive in New York after having left Bulgaria, traveling Third Class in the Cunard ship *Aquitania*....Six Jews are beaten in further anti-Semitic attacks in Budapest, Hungary's capital....A 100-mile gale causes storms in the British Isles.		Mexican President Emilio Portes Gil plans to introduce a radical labor law.	The Chinese Nationalist government confirms that it has approached Henry Ford, and also Owen D. Young, Professor Jeremiah Jenks, Professor E.R.A. Seligman of Columbia University, and R.N. Harper, banker, to serve as economic advisers to them....A Japanese destroyer collides with a torpedo boat off the north coast of Japan.
Oct. 21		Negotiations start on the Anglo-French plan for the repayment by German of its war reparations....French Prime Minister Raymond Poincaré opens a tunnel through the Vosges Mountains.		It is announced that Major Edward A. Burke, the former State Treasurer of Louisana, who died in Tegucigalpa, Honduras on September 25, has left half his property to the Honduran government....Charles Lindbergh speaks of his intention to go to hunt in Mexico.	A small riot took place following allegations of cheating at the examinations for Magistrates for the Chinese Province of Kiangsu, held in Nanking.
Oct. 22	The League of Nations meets in Geneva to discuss ways of removing double taxation and tax evasion.	The French and British governments publish notes on their respective navies....The Czechoslovak government issues a series of postage stamps to commemorate the 10th anniversary of their country's independence....Gales strike the British Isles causing widespread damage.		Plans for an air-rail service from New York to Cuba are unveiled....João Pessoa Cavalcânti de Albuquerque becomes governor of Paraíba Province, Brazil, succeeding João Suassuna.	Andrew Fisher, the prime minister of Australia 1908–09, 1910–13 and 1914–15, dies, aged 66....The National Bureau of Registration in Nanking announces that the time-limit for the re-examination of trade-marks which had been registered in Peking, was being extended until April 18, 1929.
Oct. 23	A meeting of the Red Cross held at The Hague discusses ways of controlling the use of gas in warfare.	The Duke of York in Britain unveils a memorial table to the late World War I commander Douglas Haig at St. Columba's Church, Pont Street, London.		The Argentine and Brazilian governments ratify the frontier convention of December 27, 1927, between the two countries....The Mexican and Panamanian governments sign an extradition treaty.	
Oct. 24		The German government proposes a $1 billion loan in a rescheduling of their war reparations....Alexander Subkov, the husband of Princess Victoria, the sister of the Ex-Kaiser of Germany, arrives in Paris to take part in a circus act....A peasant in the Polish village of Smity, near Kovel, kills six other villagers following a row during a public meeting, before being arrested.	The Supreme Muslim Council of Jerusalem sent a telegram to the British King, George V, hailing him as "a symbol of Christian civilization," and being critical of the Jewish use of the Wailing Wall in Jerusalem.	Politicians in the Mexican parliament criticize the Mexcian Federation of Labor, the Crom.	Rajagopala Tondaiman becomes the Raja of Pudukkottai, India.
Oct. 25		A Simplon express train crashes on the Paris-Bucharest line some 90 miles from Bucharest, resulting in the deaths of 31 people, and leaving 50 injured....S. Parker Gilbert, Agent General for Reparations Payments, reports that there is some agreement over the possible rescheduling of the Geman war reparations to France and Britain....King Michael of Rumania, at the age of seven, reviews his soldiers in Bucharest....British retired Rear Admiral Ernest A. Taylor urges for a larger British Royal Navy.		The Argentine government states its displeasure with Britain over the British government's claims of parts of the South Orkney Islands.	The Chinese Nationalist government announces a lull in negotiations with the Japanese government over outstanding issues between the two countries.

A	B	C	D	E
Includes developments that affect more than one world region, international organizations and important meetings of world leaders.	Includes all domestic and regional developments in Europe, including the Soviet Union.	Includes all domestic and regional developments in Africa and the Middle East.	Includes all domestic and regional developments in Latin America, the Caribbean, and Canada.	Includes all domestic and regional developments in Asian and Pacific nations (and colonies).

U.S. Politics & Social Issues	U.S. Foreign Policy & Affairs, Defense	U.S. Economy & Environment	Science, Technology & Nature	Culture, Leisure & Lifestyle	
Calvin Coolidge speaks at the dedication of the battlefield memorial at Fredericksburg and Spotsylvania County. He tells the crowd about the prosperity of the United States.		The General Electric Company signs a major contract to provide electricity in the Soviet Union.	Mrs. John Quincy Adams, wife of the late Major John Quincy Adams of the Marine Corps, and Gertrude T. Baskin of Montreal, using a car which they could not sell second-hand in the United States, arrived in Paris after having left Turkey for a journey around Europe.	Terrence and Benjamin Waldman, aged four and a half and 14 months respectively, grandsons of Benjamin Guggenheim, and heirs to the family fortune, fell to their deaths from the roof of a three-story building in Madison Avenue in New York.	Oct. 19
Republican Party presidential candidate Herbert Hoover starts campaigning in Washington, DC, with Democratic Party presidential candidate Alfred E. Smith traveling by train through Indiana.	The third and fourth (of four) volumes of *The Intimate Papers of Colonel House*, arranged by Charles Seymour, is published in Boston, MA, by Houghton Mifflin Company. It provides an in depth account of the early days of the U.S. secret service....The British and the French governments say that they will continue with their scheduling plans for German war reparations regardless of the attitude of the U.S. government.		Inventor Thomas Edison is decorated by Calvin Coolidge at West Orange, New Jersey, with the president speaking on the radio and stating that Edison is the embodiment of the finest traditions of American citizenship.	*The Making of Buffalo Bill*, by Richard J. Walsh, is published in Indianapolis, IN, by Bobbs-Merrill.... U.S. postal services issue a postage stamp of George Washington overprinted with "Molly Pitcher" to commemorate the 150th anniversary of the Battle of Monmouth in New Jersey at which Pitcher (Mary Ludwig Hayes) was the heroine.	Oct. 20
Democratic Party presidential candidate Alfred E. Smith returns to New York State greeting crowds in Albany, with Republican Party presidential candidate Herbert Hoover speaking as Madison Square Garden in New York City....New York gubernatorial candidate Franklin Delano Roosevelt expresses his contentment at how well his election campaigning has gone so far.		AT&T is removed from the Dow Jones Index....The postal service investigates reports that 60 or 70 diamonds were found in the remains of a plane which crashed into the woods near Polk, PA.		Marathon runners Joie Ray and El Ouafi meet in the Garden Marathon in Madison Square Garden in New York....Dr. Hugo Eckener and the "Zeppelin Party" move to Chicago, with 150,000 visiting the *Graf Zeppelin* at Lakehurst on October 21, the first Sunday since it arrived.	Oct. 21
Republican presidential candidate Herbert Hoover speaks on "rugged individualism" as his major philosophy in a major policy speech to supporters at Madison Square Garden highlighting the successes of the Calvin Coolidge administration.		The London Stock Exchange sees much activity with last minute selling by speculators.			Oct. 22
Republican Party presidential candidate Herbert Hoover makes a speech in which he calls his opponent Alfred E. Smith "a dangerous man."...Smith hits back at Hoover's claims that he (Smith) will introduce "state socialism."...Charles Evans Hughes makes a strong speech at St. Joseph, Missouri endorsing Herbert Hoover.				French historian and writer François V. Alphonse Aulard dies, aged 80.... George Barr McCutcheon, author of *Graustark*, *Brewster's Millions* and many other novels, dies during a lunch at the Dutch Treat Club, Hotel Martinique in New York.	Oct. 23
Al Smith once again attacks Herbert Hoover's retort that the Democrats will introduce "state socialism," in a speech at Worcester, Massachusetts....Franklin Delano Roosevelt denies that he will introduce "socialism" is he is elected.... The Protestant weekly newspaper *The Christian Herald* burns 100,000 copies of its November 3 issue because of a cartoon on the front cover which is derogatory to Al Smith.	John Sullivan, the President of the New York State Federation of Labor criticized Republican Party presidential candidate Herbert Hoover's record in Asia claiming that he employed, during his business career, coolies in China, serfs in Russia and slaves in Burma, profiteering out of the misery of others....U.S. Secretary of State Frank B. Kellogg states that he is very happy at the progress with the forthcoming elections in Nicaragua.			In a much publicized attempt, A British eccentric scientist Dr. Mansfield Robinson attempts to communicate with the planet Mars but when no response is received, he claims that the Martians did not get his message as it was sent too late at night, and that they might have been asleep....The artist Arthur B. Davies, former president of the American Painters and Sculptors Society, dies, but the news is not made public until December 17.	Oct. 24
Democratic Party presidential candidate Alfred E. Smith returns to New York City where a large crowd greet him, with Republican Party presidential candidate Herbert Hoover refusing to respond to his recent attacks....It is revealed that the Democratic Party Fund now stands at $3,065,038....Customs officials find 1,300 bottles of cognac on the French liner *France*, in New York.	British Field Marshal Viscount Allenby, writing in *The Cavalry Journal* in Washington, DC, urges for the retention of the cavalry.	An American group of investors, led by James A. Talbot of Richfield Oil, acquires control of the U.S. airplane business of Anthony Fokker.... General Motors reports record earnings, with $79,266,639, being the highest quarter earnings ever by any industrial company in peace time.	Professor Charles Nicolle, Director of the Pasteur Institute in Tunis, French North Africa, is awarded the 1928 Nobel Prize for Medicine or Physiology for his research work in connection with the spotted typhus fever which was particularly prevalent in World War I.		Oct. 25

F	G	H	I	J
Includes campaigns, elections, federal-state relations, civil rights and liberties, crime, the judiciary, education, healthcare, poverty, urban affairs, and population.	Includes formation and debate of U.S. foreign and defense policies, veterans affairs, and defense spending. (Relations with specific foreign countries are usually found under the region concerned.)	Includes business, labor, agriculture, taxation, transportation, consumer affairs, monetary and fiscal policy, natural resources, pollution and industrial accidents.	Includes worldwide scientific, medical and technological developments, natural phenomena, U.S. weather and natural disasters.	Includes the arts, religion, scholarship, communications media, sports, entertainment, fashions, fads, and social life.

	World Affairs	Europe	Africa & The Middle East	The Americas	Asia & The Pacific
Oct. 26	King George V sends a message of his good wishes to the 10th anniversary meeting of the League of Nations Union....British writer Rudyard Kipling speaks out in favor of world cruises which he says aid peace efforts....A convention in The Hague, The Netherlands, raises the ides of banning the use of poisonous gas on civilians in war.	British Prime Minister Stanley Baldwin denies that he wants an naval race with the United States.... A railway accident at Recca Station in Rumania results in 31 killed and 50 others injured....The Communist Party of the Soviet Union, in Pravda, states that the Soviet government is displeased by "trade without recognition" and wants diplomatic recognition to be extended by the U.S. government.			Count Uchida returns to Tokyo pleased with his reception in Britain and the United States, and urges the Japanese government to recognize the new Chinese Nationalist Government in Nanking.
Oct. 27		On the eve of the sixth anniversary of his 1922 March on Rome, the Italian Fascist leader Benito Mussolini burns the debt certificates covering $7,364,000 in public debt handed over by patriotic citizens.		A bitter election battle breaks out in Puerto Rico over the next governor.	The government of the Kingdom of Siam and the Kingdom of the Netherlands sign an arbitration and conciliation treaty.
Oct. 28		French police fire on Royalist demonstrators at Pons, near La Rochelle, and one Royalist is killed and another badly wounded during a demonstration against the unveiling of a statue of Emile Combes who was Prime Minister of France when Roman Catholic monasteries and schools were closed down....French Prime Minister Raymond Poincaré states that it will negotiate on war reparations but must get enough to pay its debts and also for war damages.			The Chinese government issues a manifesto detailing a program of internal reform.
Oct. 29		French exporters state that they want a new treaty, preferably a permanent treaty, with the United States to make the export of their goods to America to be easier.	Hon Sir Lewis Lloyd Michell, friend and confidante of Cecil Rhodes, dies, aged 86.	In the first peaceful elections in Honduras for many years, the Liberal Party candidate, Vicente Mejía Colindres, is elected president with 62,319 votes, defeating the National Party's candidate Tiburcio Carias Andino (47,745 votes). Mejía was the first opposition candidate to win the nation's presidency in a free election.	The Melbourne International Exhibition is held in Australia, the postal authorities issuing a stamp showing a Kookaburra.
Oct. 30		Bronislaw Franciszek Nakoniecznikow-Klukowski becomes Governor of Stanislawoskie, Poland, taking over from Aleksander Adam Morawski....The Bulgarian postal authorities issue a series of postage stamps showing a profile view of Tsar Boris III.		Brigadier General McCoy, chief of the election board in Nicaragua, states that he believes that the rebel General Augusto Sandino will have no role to play in the forthcoming Nicaraguan elections.	The members of the Indian Statutory Commission led by Sir John Simon arrive in Lahore where they are met with large hostile crowds which have to be charged by the police on several occasions....The Japan Air Lines is formed from a merger of Tozai Regular Air Transport Society and Kawanishi Japan Air Lines.
Oct. 31		The Polish Parliament, the Sejm, meets to discuss the budget.... France opposes the new German plans to reschedule debt.		The Mexican Treasury has urged for a reduction in government expenditure....The Ecuador postal authorities issue a series of overprinted fiscal stamps for postal use to commemorate the opening of the railway from Quito, Ecuador's capital, to Otavalo in the north of the country.	
Nov. 1		The *Graf Zeppelin* lands in Germany after completing 4,400 miles in 69 hours....William Peel, Viscount Peel is appointed Secretary of State for India in the British government, taking over from Frederick Smith, Earl of Birkenhead, who stood down on October 22.	President Mustafa Kemal Ataturk opens the Turkish Parliament with a speech that is broadcast all over Turkey.	The First Pan Am flight to Costa Rica lands in San José, the Costa Rican capital.	The Bank of China opens, under new management, in Shanghai.

A	B	C	D	E
Includes developments that affect more than one world region, international organizations and important meetings of world leaders.	Includes all domestic and regional developments in Europe, including the Soviet Union.	Includes all domestic and regional developments in Africa and the Middle East.	Includes all domestic and regional developments in Latin America, the Caribbean, and Canada.	Includes all domestic and regional developments in Asian and Pacific nations (and colonies).

U.S. Politics & Social Issues	U.S. Foreign Policy & Affairs, Defense	U.S. Economy & Environment	Science, Technology & Nature	Culture, Leisure & Lifestyle	
The Republican Party Fund stands at $4,141,080....Charles E. Hughes finally defines "state socialism" in a speech in Buffalo, NY....Democratic Party presidential candidate Alfred E. Smith goes to Pennsylvania for campaigning. Smith sends a replacement letter to two New York boys who had sent him a four-leaf clover a month earlier to wish him good luck, but had his reply to them stolen when they took it to school.		The General Electric Company through its British subsidiary the British Thomson-Houston Company, obtains control of the Metropolitan-Vickers Electrical Company.	The Pickwick Stage System files documents to establish their own passenger airline service which will connect San Francisco, San Diego and Chicago using a tri-motored 12-passenger Bach monoplane.		Oct. 26
Democratic Party presidential candidate Alfred E. Smith condemns the comments of Charles Evans Hughes in a speech in Philadelphia, again highlighting the policy of Hoover on tariffs.	The U.S. Navy plan to build large airships at Akron, Ohio, with the construction of two large Zeppelins to start quickly....The French offer a change in the Naval Accord to make it more acceptable to the United States.				Oct. 27
It is revealed that 43 million are qualified to vote, 14 million more than in 1924, largely as a result of far more women registering....Secretary of the Treasury Andrew Mellon urges Republican voters to ensure that Republican Party presidential candidate Herbert Hoover is elected and has a Republican-controlled Senate and House of Representatives....Al Smith moves to Maryland to campaign.	Gangland murdered Vincent McCormick is found to have fled to France and enlisted in the French Foreign Legion.		The *Graf Zeppelin* starts its flight from Lakehurst to Germany with 63 people on board, including three U.S. Navy officers....The California Institite of Technology at Pasadena announces that it will build a 200-inch telescope at Mount Wilson, larger than any other telescope in the world.		Oct. 28
Democratic Party presidential candidate Alfred E. Smith during a speech in Baltimore claims that the Dry League and the Ku Klux Klan are the allies of the Republican Party to a large crowd in Baltimore, Maryland.		The New York Stock Exchange reveals that during October some 91,964,445 shares have traded, with two more days of trading.	Clarence Terhune, a 19-year-old golf caddy, is found to have stowed away on the *Graf Zeppelin*. Authorities at Lakehurst are embarrassed at how he managed to get on board without being noticed.... Professor Hale, the "Grand Old Man of Astronomy" is attributed withy the plans for the massive telescope under construction at Pasadena, California.		Oct. 29
Democratic Party presidential candidate Alfred E. Smith in a speech in Newark, appeals to trade unionists to support him....Republican Party presidential candidate Herbert Hoover speaks in the west on his Farm Aid plans....Protests throughout the United States over people having been removed from the electoral roll with the end of the "protest period," in which they can raise objections to their removal.	Robert Lansing, the former U.S. Secretary of State, and aide to Woodrow Wilson during World War I, dies, aged 64.		The Zeppelin heads across the Atlantic Ocean to Europe, with massive crowds going to Friedrichshafen to welcome the returning airship.		Oct. 30
Democratic Party presidential candidate Alfred E. Smith pledges that he will support organized labor and the trade union movement, replying to attacks by Charles Evans Hughes on the Democrat Party's policies on water power.	Senator William Borah of Idaho predicts that the election of Herbert Hoover will lead to a new and closer understanding between the United States and Latin America.		The Zeppelin which arrived at Lakehurst, New Jersey on October 15, arrived back in Friedrichshafen, Germany, in a journey lasting 71 hours. The French cheer the airship as it flies over the French coast. On its arrival, the teenage stowaway, Clarence Terhune, is invited to meet with Countess von Brandenberg-Zeppelin, daughter of Count Zeppelin, after which the U.S. Consul in Stuttgart, John E. Kehl takes charge of the youth. Some 101,683 pieces of mail were carried by the Zeppelin on its return flight.		Oct. 31
Republican Party presidential candidate Herbert Hoover heads to California to rally Republicans there.	Major-General Mason M. Patrick advocates significant changes in the U.S. air defenses in his book *The United States in the Air*, which is published in New York.	New York authorities plan to rebuild the Queensboro Bridge at a cost of $6 million.		William Leonard Courtney, a distinguished critic and author, dies, aged 78.	Nov. 1

F	G	H	I	J
Includes campaigns, elections, federal-state relations, civil rights and liberties, crime, the judiciary, education, healthcare, poverty, urban affairs, and population.	*Includes formation and debate of U.S. foreign and defense policies, veterans affairs, and defense spending. (Relations with specific foreign countries are usually found under the region concerned.)*	*Includes business, labor, agriculture, taxation, transportation, consumer affairs, monetary and fiscal policy, natural resources, pollution and industrial accidents.*	*Includes worldwide scientific, medical and technological developments, natural phenomena, U.S. weather and natural disasters.*	*Includes the arts, religion, scholarship, communications media, sports, entertainment, fashions, fads, and social life.*

	World Affairs	Europe	Africa & The Middle East	The Americas	Asia & The Pacific
Nov. 2		The British Labor Party makes massive gains in the municipal elections across the country....In London, King George V states that he will make Randall Thomas Davidson, the Archbishop of Canterbury a peer on his retirement....Dean Inge in London urges the removal of the Bishop of London....Berlin historian Arthur Rosenberg blames the defeat of Germany in World War I on General Erich Ludendorff.		The trial of José de Leon Toral for the murder of General Alvaro Obregon, the president elect of Mexico, started in Mexico City with the defendant describing how he was tortured at police headquarters after his arrest.	In escalating tensions in Australia on the Melbourne wharves, Union demonstrators are fired on as they attack volunteer laborers resulting in the death of one waterside worker and the wounding of four others.
Nov. 3		The French prime minister, Raymond Poincaré, is locked in talks over the repayment of World War I loans.... The Spanish government reorganizes its ministries....Some 120 are injured in rioting in Lvov, Poland, with 60 Ukrainains arrested for their involvement in a counter-protest against official celebrations celebrating the 10th anniversary of the town holding out against the Ukranian forces.....The first women's club is founded in Lisbon, Portugal.	In Turkey the country, in line with the laws introduced by Kemal Ataturk, changes from the Arabic to the Roman alphabet....The Palestine-Egypt provisional commercial agreement was promulgated in Jerusalem.	There are celebrations in Balboa and other parts of Panama to celebrate the 25th anniversary of the creation of the Republic of Panama.	Chinese pirates attack a British-owned ship after it left Hankow. They killed one person and looted the cabins of passengers.
Nov. 4		The French Radical Party breaks with the Raymond Poincaré government....Sir William Pulteney unveils a war memorial at La Ferté sous Jouarre to British soldiers who were killed in the first three months of World War I in 1914.... Vintila Bratinu, effective ruler of Romania, steps down as prime minister, which takes effect a week later....King George V entertains the Queen of Spain and her daughters in Britain....All over Italy, Armistice festivals are held to commemorate the defeat of Austria at the battle of Victorio Veneto in 1866.		Presidential elections held in Nicaragua under U.S. supervision result in General José María Moncada Tapia of the Liberal Party being elected by a large majority with U.S. Marines guarding polling stations around the country.	
Nov. 5	In a speech at the International Institute for Educative Cinematography at Frascati, Italy, Italian fascist leader Benito Mussolini claims that the three greatest inventions in the history of the world have been moveable type, photography and the motion picture.	Raymond Poincaré and his cabinet resign owing to the Radical-Socialist Congress instructing their members in the cabinet to withdraw.....In London, King George V opens the British Parliament....Right Honorable Arthur Nicholson, First Baron Carnock, a distinguished British diplomat, dies, aged 79.		The Ministry of Finance in Mexico City proposes a new deal to pay off Mexican debts.	Blanche Tobin, a New Zealand missionary to China, who was kidnapped in Kwangsi province in September, is released unharmed.... Warlord Chang Tsung-chang "disappears" in Dairen, Manchuria.
Nov. 6		Karl Riedel becomes Minister President of Thüringen, Germany, taking over from Richard Leutheusser....Léon Perrier steps down as the French Minister of Colonies....Lava from the Mount Etna volcano on the island of Sicily causing much damage and destroying many houses.	In South Africa, the new cabinet of General J. B. M. Hertzog is sworn in.	It is announced that Canada has achieved a record potato crop.	The Japanese Emperor, Hirohito, and Empress Nagako leave Tokyo for Kyoto, going by train, in a journey that took two days. They spend the first night at Nagoya.
Nov. 7	The Anglo-French Naval Accord is declared to be "dead" in the British House of Lords.	*The Times* in London congratulates Herbert Hoover on his election as president....French Premier Raymond Poincaré is muted in his views over the election victory of Herbert Hoover.		Sir Frederick Gordon Guggisberg becomes Governor of British Guiana, taking over from Sir Cecil Hunter-Rodwell.	Eilhelm Schmidt of Deutsche Luft Hansa presents his plans for the founding of a German-run airline in China to Li Ching Tung of the Chinese Foreign Ministry in Nanking, China.
Nov. 8		It is revealed that large numbers of Sicilian peasants died in the lava flow from Mount Etna.		At the end of his trial in Mexico City, José de Leon Toral is sentenced to death for the assassination of Mexican president-elect General Alvaro Obregon. A nun who helped him is sentenced to 20 years in prison.	Emperor Hirohito and his Empress arrive in Kyoto for the coronation.

A	B	C	D	E
Includes developments that affect more than one world region, international organizations and important meetings of world leaders.	Includes all domestic and regional developments in Europe, including the Soviet Union.	Includes all domestic and regional developments in Africa and the Middle East.	Includes all domestic and regional developments in Latin America, the Caribbean, and Canada.	Includes all domestic and regional developments in Asian and Pacific nations (and colonies).

U.S. Politics & Social Issues	U.S. Foreign Policy & Affairs, Defense	U.S. Economy & Environment	Science, Technology & Nature	Culture, Leisure & Lifestyle	
Calvin Coolidge openly proclaims his support for Republican Party presidential candidate Herbert Hoover whose victory is mentioned as "assured" on the front page of The *New York Times*....Hoover makes a speech at St. Louis.... Democrats in New York cheer Democratic Party presidential candidate Alfred E. Smith.		The Aeronautical Bureau of the Department of Commerce announces that it has issued the 10,000th airplane number.		Conductor L. Stokovski conducts a premiere of Dmitri Shostakovitch's *First Symphony* in Philadelphia.... Reverend Francis J. Finn, a Roman Catholic educator and an author of boys' adventure stories dies in Cincinnati, OH, aged 70.	Nov. 2
Large crowds cheer Republican Party presidential candidate Herbert Hoover as he makes appearances in Kansas and Colorado....Democratic Party presidential candidate Alfred E. Smith greets his supporters at Madison Square Garden in New York.			Albert Einstein in Berlin announces that he is on the "verge of a great discovery" and is critical of press intrusion into his research.	A complete edition of the plays of John Galsworthy is published in New York by Charles Scribner's Sons....Between 3 p.m. and 4 p.m., several hundred women dressed in furs valued collectively at $1 million, strolled down Fifth Avenue.	Nov. 3
Democratic Party presidential candidate Alfred E. Smith makes a final appeal to voters on the radio.... Republican Party presidential candidate Herbert Hoover speaks to cheering supporters in Utah.... Prominent pastor, Reverend Dr. S. Parkes Cadman condemns the criticism on sectarian grounds of Al Smith....Arnold Rothstein, a notorious gambler and gangland figure, in New York, is shot dead in the Park Central Hotel in Manhattan, over a poker game.		Bonfils, the publisher of The *Denver Post* and The *Denver Morning Post* announces that it has bought The *Denver Evening Post* but also sold The *Denver Morning Post* to The *Rocky Mountain News*.	The British aviator D'Arcy Greig manages to reach 319.57 miles per hour in a seaplane....U.S. aviators Captain Charles B. Collyer and Harry Tucker, trying to set a west-east speed record for the United States die when their Lockheed Vega crashes into Canyon Creek....American polar explorer Richard Byrd reaches Wellington, New Zealand, en route for the Antarctic....It is announced that Orville Wright will be the guest of honor at the International Civil Aeronautics Conference in Washington, DC.	The play, *Peter Pan, or the Boy Who Would not Grow Up*, the first appearance of the play in book form, by James Barrie, is published in New York by Charles Scribner's Sons.	Nov. 4
Republican Party presidential candidate Herbert Hoover, in a speech at Palo Alto, California, urges everybody to vote "as a duty to the nation."...Democratic Party presidential candidate Alfred E. Smith urges voters to remember his pledges to farmers over tariffs.			Australian aviators S.J. Moir and H.C. Owen fly from Wyndham, Australia, for London but abandon the flight after crashing near Athens. Captain Frank Hurley is a photographer for the flight, and is later a prominent Australian photographer in World War II.		Nov. 5
U.S. presidential election results in Republican candidate Herbert Hoover easily defeating Democrat candidate Alfred Smith, with 444 electoral college seats as against 87 for Smith. Hoover succeeds in winning Virginia, Texas, Tennessee and Florida, formerly largely Democratic Party territory, and even defeats Smith in New York State.....In New York, Franklin Roosevelt is elected governor by a slim plurality.			The U.S. presidential election results are heard by people around the world as they are broadcast on 100 radio stations....A special radio set is installed in Sing Sing Correctional Facility, Ossining, NY, the prisoners to listen to the results.	Swedes start a tradition of eating Gustavus Adolphus pastries to commemorate the 17th-century ruler who is accredited with creating the modern Sweden....Statesman wins the Melbourne Cup, Australia's most important horse race. It was ridden by J. Munro and trained and owned by W. Kelso.	Nov. 6
The defeated Democrat candidate Alfred E. Smith states that he will not contest the U.S. presidency again....African American Republican candidate Oscar de Priest is elected as a Representative for the First Illinois District.	Lieutenant Colonel Benjamin Mendes of the Columbian Army, arrives in New York en route for Washington, DC, to improve military ties between Colombia and the United States.	Shares on the New York Stock Exchange go up with 4,894,670 shares traded, the second largest turnover in its history.			Nov. 7
New York State Attorney-General Albert Ottinger queries the New York state gubernatorial election results which give the victory to Franklin Roosevelt by 23,616 votes.		Some 5,037,330 shares are traded on the New York Stock Exchange in what becomes known as the "Hoover Market."		*Treasure Girl*, a musical by George and Ira Gershwin premieres in New York City.	Nov. 8

F	G	H	I	J
Includes campaigns, elections, federal-state relations, civil rights and liberties, crime, the judiciary, education, healthcare, poverty, urban affairs, and population.	Includes formation and debate of U.S. foreign and defense policies, veterans affairs, and defense spending. (Relations with specific foreign countries are usually found under the region concerned.)	Includes business, labor, agriculture, taxation, transportation, consumer affairs, monetary and fiscal policy, natural resources, pollution and industrial accidents.	Includes worldwide scientific, medical and technological developments, natural phenomena, U.S. weather and natural disasters.	Includes the arts, religion, scholarship, communications media, sports, entertainment, fashions, fads, and social life.

	World Affairs	Europe	Africa & The Middle East	The Americas	Asia & The Pacific
Nov. 9	The International Education Board donates £700,000 to Cambridge University, Britain, for their university library and the development of research projects.	Iuliu Maniu starts establishing a new Cabinet in Romania, as the Peasants' Party controls the new government....British businessman Alfred C. Thompson, chairman of the Prudential Assurance Company, dies, aged 70....The Soviet Union, in their first comment on the election victory of Herbert Hoover, declares him an "anglophobe."			Ceremonies begin at Kyoto for the coronation of Emperor Hirohito.
Nov. 10		Lava flows in Sicily from Mount Etna engulf the railway line....The Romanian regents dissolve the Romanian parliament paving the way for elections.	A strike surrounding the Mexican newspaper *Exzcelsior* continues in Mexico City.		Hirohito is enthroned as Emperor of Japan in a ceremony in Tokyo, with only the Emperor and the Premier playing an active role in the proceedings....The Chinese government confirms the appointment of F. Hussey Freke as the Associate Chief Inspector of the Salt Gabelle.
Nov. 11		French politician Raymond Poincaré forms a new government excluding the Radical Party....Attacks on Jews take place in Vienna, the capital of the Austrian Republic.	The Prince of Wales attends the Armistice Day ceremony at Nairobi.		The British reopen their Consulate-General in Nanking.
Nov. 12		Iuliu Maniu, the new premier of Romania, is harassed by his political enemies....Father Anton Korosec, Prime Minister of Yugoslavia, gives in to demands of the Croat Peasant Party over autonomy for Croatia....The Polish government holds a special review of its soldiers.			The final rites take place in Kyoto for the coronation of Emperor Hirohito....The Chinese and Norwegian governments agree on a new tariff autonomy treaty.
Nov. 13		The danger of new lava flows from Mount Etna recedes, as Italians turn their attention to Mount Vesuvius near the wrecked Roman city of Pompeii.		The Nicaraguan government announces that José María Moncada Tapia will become president on January 1, with the official proclamation expected on December 15.	
Nov. 14		The British government claims that some people in Germany have hidden weapons from World War I....The Pact of Friendship between Yugoslavia and Italy was ratified in Rome, along with the terms of the Belgrade Convention of August 1924.	Edward, The Prince of Wales, leaves Nairobi, Kenya.		A boycott of Japanese goods starts in Tientsin, China....General elections in New Zealand result in the United (Liberal) Party under Joseph Ward winning 29 seats in the New Zealand Parliament, as against 28 for the Reform Party and 19 for the Labour Party. It takes nearly a month until a coalition government is formed.
Nov. 15		The French Chamber of Deputies passes a vote of confidence in the government by 334 to 129.		The Brazilian and Columbian government sign a frontier treaty at Rio de Janeiro.	
Nov. 16	Former British Prime Minister David Lloyd George talks of the great danger faced by the world if arms limitation does not start in earnest.	The Italian Senate approves the Fascist Labor Charter....Polish police arrest 40 Ukranians in Lvov.		The British Colonial Office waive their rights to Bouvet and Thompson Islands in the south Atlantic.	The Chinese minister of finance issues an official announcement that regulations governing Salt Administration had been revised putting it under the exclusive control of the Ministry of Finance....The Chinese government requests food aid with 12 million people going hungry....A goodwill flight squadron of the British Royal Air Force leaves Manila and arrives in Hong Kong on the following day.

A	B	C	D	E
Includes developments that affect more than one world region, international organizations and important meetings of world leaders.	Includes all domestic and regional developments in Europe, including the Soviet Union.	Includes all domestic and regional developments in Africa and the Middle East.	Includes all domestic and regional developments in Latin America, the Caribbean, and Canada.	Includes all domestic and regional developments in Asian and Pacific nations (and colonies).

U.S. Politics & Social Issues	U.S. Foreign Policy & Affairs, Defense	U.S. Economy & Environment	Science, Technology & Nature	Culture, Leisure & Lifestyle	
U.S. President-elect Herbert Hoover announces that he will embark on a good-will mission to Latin America.	Herbert Hoover announces that before his inauguration he will visit eleven Latin American nations to cement closer relations between his administration and other countries in the Western hemisphere.	Stock on the New York Stock Exchange continues to go up in price with 4,999,140 shares exchanging hands.		Percy P. Gilpin, well-known British racehorse trainer, dies, aged 70.... *The Sword of State: Wellington After Waterloo*, by Susan Buchan, is published in London by Hodder & Stoughton, and in Boston, Massachusetts, by Houghton Mifflin Company....Princess Murat, formerly Helena McDonall Stallo of Cincinnati, Ohio, is granted a divorce from her husband Prince Michael Joachim Murat.	Nov. 9
An enthusiastic crowd in Warm Springs, Georgia, urge Franklin Roosevelt to contest the 1932 U.S. Presidential elections for the Democratic Party....Police raid the strong boxes of the recently murdered gangster Arnold Rothstein and uncover evidence of his involvement in many gangland murders.	The governments of Brazil and Argentina publicly state that they would welcome a visit by U.S. President-elect Herbert Hoover.... The Nicaraguan government also extends an invitation to him to visit Managua.	Some 3,260,090 shares are traded when trading is allowed for only two hours on Saturdays.		The Helsinki Philatelic Exhibition opens in the capital of Finland, and lasts until November 18....George Reid Clifford, a U.S. aviator in World War I, has *My Experiences as an Aviator in the World War* published in Boston, Massachusetts, by Richard G. Badger.	Nov. 10
In his Armistice Day speech, Calvin Coolidge explains that the United States has rejected the Anglo-French naval pact because it meant that the principle of limitations of combatant vessels would effectively be abandoned.	The U.S. Navy take over the last of the 74 F3B-1 fighter bombers which were ordered from the Boeing Airplane Company....Coolidge calls for more cruisers to be built to bolster the U.S. Navy.	Treasury statistics show that 283 Americans had incomes of more than $1 million in 1927, a rise on previous years, although there was a fall in those earning over $5 million.			Nov. 11
Calvin Coolidge unveils a new plan to reschedule war loans from European countries.	U.S. Secretary for the Navy Curtis Wilbur urges for an enlargement of the U.S. Navy.	Some 5,745,000 shares are traded on the New York Stock Exchange, but the value of the stock is below $10 million for the first time in several weeks....The ocean liner *Vestris* sinks off the Virginia Cape with 328 on board, with the loss of 111 lives.	A telephone connection between the United States and Hungary was inaugurated by U.S. Secretary of State Frank B. Kellogg. Mr. A. Silberman of New York was the first person to call Hungary from New York.	Professor Wilhelm von Bode urges the ex-Kaiser of Germany not to sell some of his art collection by public auction, worrying that some of the best pieces may go to the United States.	Nov. 12
Defeated U.S. presidential candidate Alfred E. Smith tries to rally his supporters and start planning for the 1932 election....Clarence Terhune, the first air stowaway, who went from New York to Germany on the Zeppelin, returned to the United States on the French liner *Ile de France*. He said that he planned to spend a few days in New York before returning to his job as a golf caddy.	40 marines leave Panama (having just arrived from Nicaragua) to return to the United States, the first of the marines to return from Nicaragua.		It is announced that the awarding of the Nobel Prize for Physics is to be held over for one year. Professor Heinrich Wieland of Munich, Germany, is awarded the Nobel Prize for Chemistry for 1927, for his investigations into gall acids; and Professor Adolf Windaus of Gottingen, Germany, a member of the Germany Academy of Natural Sciences, is awarded the Nobel Prize for Chemistry for 1928 for his wok on the study of vitamins.	Norwegian writer Sigrid Undset wins the Nobel Prize for Literature for 1928, the third Norwegian to win the award. Her main book, *Kristin Lavransdatter*, was published in 1920, and most of her work deals with Scandinavia during the 13th and 14th centuries. In addition the Swedish Academy announces that Henri Bergson, the French author and philosopher is awarded the Nobel Prize for Literature for 1927, the prize having been held over from the previous year.	Nov. 13
A memorial to John Purroy Mitchel, Mayor of New York, who died during World War I, is unveiled at the corner of Fifth Avenue and Ninetieth Street, New York.		The 205 survivors of the *Vestris* arrive in New York telling of their experiences of the shipwreck. Coverage of this fills most of the first 16 pages of the *New York Times*....The arsenal at the First National Film Studio at Burbank, California, is blown up in an accidental explosion, but 40 actors nearby are all unhurt.			Nov. 14
John MacVicar, the Mayor of Des Moines, dies.	The U.S. government announces a federal enquiry will be held in New York into the loss of *Vestris*.	Press coverage of the sinking of the *Vestris* continues to dominate the newspapers, with more bodies recovered from the wrecks.			Nov. 15
Police searching through the papers of slain gangland identity Arnold Rothstein discover $4 million in loot....J. Novotny, a sporting goods dealer in St. Paul, Minnesota, is named as the man who sold the gun used to kill Rothstein. The man who bought the gun had identified himself as a tourist and hence did not require a permit for the purchase of the firearm.	The Spanish government expresses its fears over Calvin Coolidge's plan to reschedule European war debt.	All records on the New York Stock Exchange are broken with 6,641,250 shares changing hands.	Australian adventurer and aviator Herbert Wilkins flies from Deception Island in the South Shetlands, making the first flight across Antarctica.	*College Life of the Old South*, by E. M. Cosister, is published in New York by The Macmillan Company. It describes the story of the growth of the University of Georgia.	Nov. 16

F	G	H	I	J
Includes campaigns, elections, federal-state relations, civil rights and liberties, crime, the judiciary, education, healthcare, poverty, urban affairs, and population.	*Includes formation and debate of U.S. foreign and defense policies, veterans affairs, and defense spending. (Relations with specific foreign countries are usually found under the region concerned.)*	*Includes business, labor, agriculture, taxation, transportation, consumer affairs, monetary and fiscal policy, natural resources, pollution and industrial accidents.*	*Includes worldwide scientific, medical and technological developments, natural phenomena, U.S. weather and natural disasters.*	*Includes the arts, religion, scholarship, communications media, sports, entertainment, fashions, fads, and social life.*

	World Affairs	Europe	Africa & The Middle East	The Americas	Asia & The Pacific
Nov. 17		The birthday party was held in London, England, for a woman who turned 100, and who was unaware of World War I having been fought.... Storms sweep through Western Europe killing 39 people.	Festivals which have been held in Abyssinia (Ethiopia) to commemorate the coronation of Ras Tafarai as the "King of Kings" begin to subside. Some of these festivals started on October 7.	Sir Richard Squires becomes Prime Minister of Newfoundland and Labrador, Canada, taking over from Frederick C. Alderdice who resigned. He had held the position from August.	Australia holds a general election for the House of Representatives and half of the Senate returning the Bruce-Page government with a reduced majority.
Nov. 18		Iuliu Maniu, the new prime minister of Romania, declares that he wants to model his country on the United States....Viscountess Grey of Fallodon, British poet, essayist and society hostess, dies, aged 57.			Sino-Japanese talks held in Nanking about resolving the Nanking and Tsinanfu incidents break down with the Japanese refusing to withdraw soldiers from Shantung.
Nov. 19		An aide of Leon Trotsky, B. Bajanoff, after escaping to Paris, described the leader of the Soviet Union, Joseph Stalin, as illiterate and ignorant of government and diplomatic procedures, but intent on wanting to rule the world....The Polish government considers taking more loans on advice from Charles S. Dewey, the American financial adviser to the Polish government.		Nicaragua requests a $12 million loan from the United States. It believes that these loans could be used to massively develop some of the infrastructure of the country.	The latest issue of *Time* magazine is published with Emperor Hirohito of Japan on the front cover.
Nov. 20		The French government want experts to serve on a commission about the war debts but have trouble finding any who will serve on the body.... Archaeologists connected with the Louvre Museum in France claim that is it unlikely that the arms of the statue Venus de Milo are in Athens harbor which is being dredged by the Greek authorities.		Pedro Tello Andueza becomes interim governor of Campeche Province, Mexico, taking over from Silvestre Pavón Silva.	
Nov. 21		Dr. Cosmo Gordon Lang, the Archbishop of York, is elected as the Archbishop of Canterbury at a meeting of the Synod of the Church of England in London....In a hold-up of bank messengers in Marseilles, France, gunmen escape with $16,000 shooting dead one of the bank employees and injuring two others.		Captain Jordan, the Bolivian aviator who was listed as missing, is found alive and well in San José in eastern Bolivia.	The government of Edmund Hogan in Victoria, Australia, is defeated over its handling of the waterfront dispute....The British steamers sailing between Shanghai, Hong Kong and Singapore appoint army ratings to serve as permanent anti-piracy guards....Lieutenant-Colonel James Hare, a survivor of the Siege of Delhi at the Indian Mutiny of 1857, dies, aged 92.
Nov. 22		The British ruler, King George V, is confined to bed with a congested lung, and his wife, the Queen, takes over official duties.... A violent shoot-out takes place in a club in Sofia, capital of Bulgaria, between a Macedonian chieftain who threatened civil war and the former Bulgarian Generalissimo Chekoff....The French government finally appoint experts for a panel to look into the war indemnities and war loans....A decision by the Kings Bench of the British High Court found that newspaper football competitions were illegal.		Appeals against the death sentence and the sentence of 20 years imprisonment, respectively, on José de Leon Toral and the nun Madre Concepcion de la Llata are heard in Mexico City following their conviction for their role in the killing of Mexican president-elect General Alvaro Obregon.	Edmund Hogan, Australia, resigns as premier of Victoria, and is replaced by Sir William McPherson of the National Party....The Chinese and Belgian governments sign a provisional treaty in Nanking for tariff autonomy and the conditional abolition of extra territoriality....Shinwari tribes attack Jalalabad in the east of Afghanistan in a protest against the reforms of King Amanullah.
Nov. 23		The Bulgarian government sends soldiers to hunt down Macedonian revolutionaries led by Ivan Michailoff....Franz Josef Schmitt becomes State President of Baden, Germany, taking over from Adam Remmele....A settlement is reached in Germany after the lock-out of the iron and steel workers in the Ruhr valley.	After a sensational trial, Dr. Benjamin Knowles is sentenced to death at Kumasi, Gold Coast (Ghana) for the murder of his wife.		Feng Yu Liang, the Chinese Army Minister, thwarts the German plans to set up a German-run airline in China.

A	B	C	D	E
Includes developments that affect more than one world region, international organizations and important meetings of world leaders.	*Includes all domestic and regional developments in Europe, including the Soviet Union.*	*Includes all domestic and regional developments in Africa and the Middle East.*	*Includes all domestic and regional developments in Latin America, the Caribbean, and Canada.*	*Includes all domestic and regional developments in Asian and Pacific nations (and colonies).*

U.S. Politics & Social Issues	U.S. Foreign Policy & Affairs, Defense	U.S. Economy & Environment	Science, Technology & Nature	Culture, Leisure & Lifestyle	
	The British government assures the U.S. government that there is not an arms race as regards the size of the navies of the respective two countries.	Some 3,105,216 shares traded in two hours on the New York Stock Exchange.		The Boston Garden is officially opened....Notre Dame loses its first football game in nearly 25 years.... *Schubert, The Man*, by Oscar Bie is published in New York by Dodd, Mead & Co, having previously been published in Berlin in 1925.	Nov. 17
New York State Attorney-General Albert Ottinger finally concedes victory to Franklin D. Roosevelt in the New York gubernatorial elections.	U.S. President-elect Herbert Hoover begins his trip to Latin America saying farewell to friends at Palo Alto, CA.	The American Federation of Labor urges for more people to join trade unions.		Mickey Mouse makes an appearance in *Steamboat Willie*, the first sound cartoon, which has its premiere at the Colony Theater in New York City. It was the first successful sound-synchronized animated cartoon.	Nov. 18
The New York Police Commissioner Joseph A. Warren declares that he will find the people who killed gangland figure Arnold Rothstein.	U.S. President-elect Herbert Hoover leaves for a goodwill tour of Latin America, receiving a 21-gun salute on his departure on the battleship *Maryland*.				Nov. 19
	Herbert Hoover heads for Mexico but announces that he will not be visiting Panama.	Some 6,503,230 shares exchange hands on the New York Stock Exchange, smashing previous records.	It is revealed in Copenhagen, Denmark that the Norwegian polar explorer Roald Amundsen was bankrupt at the time of his death and his medals were sold to pay off his debts.	The Spanish government have announced that the exact replica of the *Santa Maria* of Christyopher Columbus, which is being made, will be used as a centerpiece of the Ibero-American Exposition in Seville which is being opened on March 15, 1929.	Nov. 20
Herbert Hoover has stated that he would set up a $3 billion find to aid employment....With 15 suspects arrested in Omaha, NE, some 50,000 people stayed up all night—one in each house—at the suggestion of the local police chief Pazanowski after a machete murder of three people.		Share prices on the New York Stock Exchangefall on another day when 6 million shares exchange hands.	The German authorities in Berlin state that they are undecided whether to have a Zeppelin flight over the Arctic, according to Captain Walter Bruns, the Secretary General of the Aero Arctic Society.	Paul Plouret, the Parisian fashion designer speaking in Ottawa, Ontario, says that the "jupe culotte" or trouser skirt will become the new fashion statement around the world.	Nov. 21
New York governor-elect Franklin D. Roosevelt announces that he would prefer an outdoor investiture ceremony at Albany when he becomes governor of the state on January 1, 1929.		Share prices on the New York Stock Exchange rise and it is revealed that a seat on the Exchange costs $530,000.		*Bolero* by Maurice Ravel has its debut in Paris....George Bernard Shaw, at a meeting of the Fabian Society in London, hurls scorn on many British and world politicians claiming that the future of civilization would see a struggle between technologists.	Nov. 22
New York district attorney Banton announces that he hopes to bring indictments in the case of the death of Arnold Rothstein.		All previous records are smashed at the New York Stock Exchange which records 6,954,020 shares changing hands in one day, with the price of seats on the New York Stock Exchange going up to $550,000, $20,000 more than on the previous day....Thomas F. Ryan, a major financier of Wall Street, who was born to a poor family in Virginia, dies, aged 77.	Nobel laureate Dr. Robert A. Millikan is robbed at Grand Central Terminal losing his briefcase which contained the first chapters of a manuscript that the scientist from the California Institute of Technology was writing. He had just arrived from Schenectady when a thief stole the briefcase while he was sending a telegram....Lieutenant Benjamin Mendez of the Colombian Air Service, trained in the United States, leaves for his first flight back to Colombia.	*Found in Bagdad*, by Charles E. Sheppard, is published in New York by Walter Neale, covering a number of legal and other topics.	Nov. 23

F	G	H	I	J
Includes campaigns, elections, federal-state relations, civil rights and liberties, crime, the judiciary, education, healthcare, poverty, urban affairs, and population.	Includes formation and debate of U.S. foreign and defense policies, veterans affairs, and defense spending. (Relations with specific foreign countries are usually found under the region concerned.)	Includes business, labor, agriculture, taxation, transportation, consumer affairs, monetary and fiscal policy, natural resources, pollution and industrial accidents.	Includes worldwide scientific, medical and technological developments, natural phenomena, U.S. weather and natural disasters.	Includes the arts, religion, scholarship, communications media, sports, entertainment, fashions, fads, and social life.

	World Affairs	Europe	Africa & The Middle East	The Americas	Asia & The Pacific
Nov. 24		The condition of the British King George V improves....Britain and France offer to intervene in Bulgaria to prevent the government from collapsing under threats from Macedonian separatists....A biography of the mother of Tsar Nicholas II of Russia, *The Life and Tragedy of Alexandra Feodorovna*, by Baroness Sophie Buxhoeveden, is published in New York by Longmans, Green & Co.	Sir Cecil Hunter-Rodwell becomes Governor of Southern Rhodesia, taking over from Acting Governor Murray Bisset.	A gale lashes Central America causing damage in Tegucigalpa, the capital of Honduras. There ae also heavy floods in San José, the capital of Costa Rica, and floods in parts of El Salvador.	
Nov. 25		Bohumil Vlasák is appointed Minister of Finance in Czechoslovakia, taking over from Karel Englis.			Chinese Communist Mao Tse-tung writes a long and detailed report on the difficulties faced by the Communists in their dealings with the Chinese Nationalist Kuomintang Party. It remains one of Mao's longest reports from the period before he became Communist Party leader and displays an extensive knowledge of events in China during this period.
Nov. 26	The Economic Statistical Conference, attended by 41 states, is held at Geneva. It ends on December 14 with the signing of a Convention and final Act which streamline the collection and publication of economic statistics.	The health of the British King George V is declared to have improved considerably....The British government announces a rise in the unemployment rates....Admiral Reinhardt Scheer, former German naval commander, dies, aged 65.			Emperor Hirohito in Japan finally finishes all the rites surrounding his accession to the Imperial Theone of Japan.
Nov. 27		Frank H. Butler, founder of the British Royal Aero Club, dies, aged 72.	The Prince of Wales reaches Dar es Salaam, Tanzania ready to hasten back to Britain with the news of his father's illness.	President-elect Herbert Hoover meets with President-elect José María Moncada Tapia in Managua, capital of Nicaragua, and they discuss tactics against the rebels of General Augusto Sandino.	The Chinese and Italian governments sign a treaty in Shanghai on tariff autonomy and the conditional abolition of extra territoriality....Gales lash the Philippines with 200 people killed on the islands of Leyte and Samar.
Nov. 28	With Dr. Gustav Stresemann unwell, and with Sir Austen Chamberlain, the British foreign minister, recovering from illness, the next council meeting of the League of Nations to be held on December 10, is moved from Geneva, Switzerland, to Lugarno, Italy.	The health of the British King George V stabilizes....The French government announces that they will cut their army back to 598,000 by 1930....Kazimierz Moszynski is appointed Governor of Tarnopolskie, replacing Mikolaj Kwasniewski.	The Egyptian and the Persian governments sign a Treaty of Friendship at Tehran.	Ramiro Bojórquez Castillo of the Institutional Revolutionary Party becomes interim governor of Campeche Province, Mexico, taking over from Pedro Tello Andueza.	Sir Austen Chamberlain, the British foreign secretary, explains in the House of Commons that in view of the obligations of the Washington Treaties and the important role of the British and Japanese in China, the British and Japanese governments have agreed informally to maintain contact by means of constant communication and consultation by their ministers in Peking.
Nov. 29		Iuliu Maniu, the new prime minister of Romania, announces that he will be introducing reforms to the courts, the civil service and the army which will be all made independent of executive control. He also plans to revise laws on investment to encourage foreign capital into the country....A storm in Belgium causes $5 million in damage to the Belgian lowlands.	Sir Edward Brandis Denham is appointed governor of Gambia, British West Africa, taking over from Sir John Middleton.	The Mexican government picks soldiers to help with the presidential inauguration on the following day.	Charles Lydiard Aubrey Abbott becomes minister of home affairs in Australia, taking over from Sir Neville Reginald Howse.
Nov. 30		The British government reports that 872 people have been killed in car accidents over the previous nine months.		Emilio Portes Gil of the Institutional Revolutionary Party of Mexico, becomes President, taking over from Plutarco Elías Calles who officially stepped down on the previous day. A crowd of 25,000 witness the inauguration.	
Dec. 1	U.S. Secretary of State Frank B. Kellogg declines to accept British prime minister Stanley Baldwin's answer to the invitation for a conference of Congress members and British members of parliament to discuss Anglo-American naval affairs.	Hugo Celmins becomes Prime Minister of Latvia, presiding over a cabinet made up from members of the Peasants' League, taking over from the caretaker administration of Peteris Jurasevskis....Otto Ender becomes President of the Bundesrat, the Austrian Federal Council, taking over from Richard Steidle....Jean Boissonnas becomes President of the Council of Geneva Canton, Switzerland, replacing Alexandre Moriaud.		A large earthquake hits the Chilean town of Talca, with more than 200 people killed....Adalberto Tejeda Olivares becomes Governor of Veracruz, Mexico, replacing Heriberto Jara Corona....José Eustasio Rivera, Colombian writer, dies, aged 40.	A new Chinese tariff is promulgated, coming into force on February 1. The Japanese instantly reject the tariff with the Japanese Consul-General returning it expressing surprise at the revision of the treaty without the prior consent of the Japanese.

A	B	C	D	E
Includes developments that affect more than one world region, international organizations and important meetings of world leaders.	*Includes all domestic and regional developments in Europe, including the Soviet Union.*	*Includes all domestic and regional developments in Africa and the Middle East.*	*Includes all domestic and regional developments in Latin America, the Caribbean, and Canada.*	*Includes all domestic and regional developments in Asian and Pacific nations (and colonies).*

U.S. Politics & Social Issues	U.S. Foreign Policy & Affairs, Defense	U.S. Economy & Environment	Science, Technology & Nature	Culture, Leisure & Lifestyle	
It is announced that there will be 50 witnesses called in connection with the murder of gangland identity Arnold Rothstein.	Dr. Parker T. Moon, professor of international relations at Columbia University, in a speech to the Foreign Policy Association, claims that the Monroe Doctrine is merely an excuse to justify imperialism and U.S. intervention in Latin America. He states that he does not believe that there is any real threat to the Monroe Doctrine but it is a convenient reason every time a justification for an invasion is needed.	Milton S. Hershey, the chocolate manufacturer, announces that he will be donating $2 million to build a community center in the town of Hershey, near Harrisburg, PA.		The first volume of the *Dictionary of American Biography*, covering Abbe to Barrymore, edited by Allen Johnson, is published in New York by Charles Scribner's Sons, after having been prepared under the auspices of the American Council of Learned Societies.	Nov. 24
	The *Maryland*, taking U.S. President-elect Herbert Hoover, approaches Honduras.		It is announced from San Antonio, TX, that Colonel Charles Lindbergh is safe after his plane was forced down while flying from Tampico, Mexico, to New York.		Nov. 25
New York governor-elect Franklin D. Roosevelt urges more state expenditure on social works programs.	U.S. President-elect Herbert Hoover arrives at Amapala, Honduras, on the first stop of his Latin American goodwill tour.			*Holiday* by Philip Barry has its premiere in New York City.	Nov. 26
	Nicaraguans turn up in large numbers to cheer U.S. President-elect Herbert Hoover who arrives in Corinto, a small port on the Pacific coast of Nicaragua.		Plans are unveiled for a Zeppelin flight over the North pole in 1930 with the Norwegian polar explorer Fridtjof Nansen to head the Aero-Arctic Society project.		Nov. 27
	Massive crowds turn out in Puenta Arenas in Costa Rica to greet the U.S. president-elect Herbert Hoover who then travels by train to San José, the Costa Rican capital where even larger crowds gather to hear him….U.S. Secretary for the Navy Curtis Wilbur denies that the United States is entering into a naval race with Britain and France.		U.S. polar explorer Richard Byrd plans to leave Dunedin, New Zealand for Antarctica.		Nov. 28
Large crowds in Staunton, Virginia, turn up to hear Calvin Coolidge.	U.S. President-elect Herbert Hoover and his party, on the USS *Maryland*, head for Guayaquil, Ecuador….The Argentine government announce plans to start installing hundreds of thousands of electric lights around Buenos Aires for Herbert Hoover's impending visit.		South African diamond millionaire and philanthropist Sir Otto Beit gives $225,000 for radium to be used in the cancer hospitals.	Gabrel Wells, a New York collector, buys a bible and a prayer book which had belonged to the 18th-century British lexicographer Dr. Samuel Johnson.	Nov. 29
	Herbert Hoover watches an initiation ceremony by "Neptune" of crew members on the USS *Maryland* who had not crossed the equator, as the ship heads for Ecuador.	The New York Stock Exchange marks its sixth day with share trading exceeding 6 million.		Arthur W. Gore, British lawn tennis champion, dies, aged 60….Sir John Murray KCVO, head of the important British publishing house, dies, aged 76.	Nov. 30
				Elizabeth and Essex by Lytton Strachey is published in New York by Harcourt Brace & Co. The first edition in an edition limited to 1,000 copies, of which 750 are available in the United States, are distributed by Random House of New York.	Dec. 1

F	G	H	I	J
Includes campaigns, elections, federal-state relations, civil rights and liberties, crime, the judiciary, education, healthcare, poverty, urban affairs, and population.	*Includes formation and debate of U.S. foreign and defense policies, veterans affairs, and defense spending. (Relations with specific foreign countries are usually found under the region concerned.)*	*Includes business, labor, agriculture, taxation, transportation, consumer affairs, monetary and fiscal policy, natural resources, pollution and industrial accidents.*	*Includes worldwide scientific, medical and technological developments, natural phenomena, U.S. weather and natural disasters.*	*Includes the arts, religion, scholarship, communications media, sports, entertainment, fashions, fads, and social life.*

	World Affairs	Europe	Africa & The Middle East	The Americas	Asia & The Pacific
Dec. 2		King Boris of Bulgaria, the lowest paid monarch in the year, gets a 50 percent pay rise, raising his salary to $43,000.	The Prince of Wales leaves Africa on the cruiser *Enterprise*....Dr. Knowles appeals against his conviction for the murder of his wife.	Southern Chile is rocked by a serious earthquake which destroys many towns in the far south of the country.	After a foreigners' club is destroyed in a bomb explosion, police arrest a number of men in possession of bombs in Melbourne, Australia.
Dec. 3		The condition of the British King George V gets worse with crowds beginning to gather outside Buckingham Palace....Heinrich Walther becomes President of the National Council, Switzerland, replacing Rudolf Minger; and Oscar Wettstein becomes President of the Council of States, Switzerland, replacing Émile Savoy.	Sir Alexander Ransford Slater, the Governor of the Gold Coast, granted a reprieve for Dr. Knowles.... The Duke of Gloucester catches the train from Rhodesia to Cape Town from where he will return to Britain by ship.	The death toll of the Chilean earthquake is put at 284, with the injured in Talca alone put at between 300 and 500, with $12 million in damage to property.	
Dec. 4		The British King George V announces names his counselors who will act for him....August Rei, originally the leader of the Socialists, and later the Social Democrats, becomes President of Estonia, taking over from Jaan Tönisson of the Estonian People's Party....The financier Mme Marthe Hanau, is arrested in Paris, France, where she is charged with fraud....A French swindler manages to cheat thousands of investors out of $20 million.		Rescue work in southern Chile, in areas hit by the earthquake, are made worse by heavy rainstorms.... With aviator Alberto Santos-Dumont returning to Rio de Janeiro, Brazil, a large seaplane with six Brazilians on board crashes while flying out to greet him. Santos-Dumont immediately cancels all planned celebrations of homecoming. Altogether, 14 are killed.	The Japanese navy displays its strength and power off the coast of Yokohama with 180 vessels on show for Emperor Hirohito.
Dec. 5	The British Empire Marketing Board donates $50,000 to Cambridge University, Britain, a donation matched by the British government.	Wilhelm Miklas chosen as the second president of the Austrian Republic in succession to Dr. Michael Hainisch. He won the presidency on the third ballot.		A Paraguayan army unit located at Fortin Galpón, near Bahia Negra, under the command of Major Rafael Franco, acting on his own initiative, attacks Fortín Vanguardia garrisoned by Bolivian soldiers. Some Bolivian solders are killed and 21 are taken prisoner. Largely fought over the possible presence of oil in the Chaco desert, this leads to massive fighting in 1932 in what becomes known as the Chaco War.... A massive strike hits Colombia with 12,000 laborers refusing to work	
Dec. 6		Wilhelm Miklas steps down as President of the Nationalrat, the Austrian National Council, to prepare for his appointment as President of the Austrian Republic.... French government ministers cleared of involvement in the $20 million swindle revealed in Paris two days earlier.	Sir John Robert Chancellor becomes High Commissioner for Palestine, taking over from Sir Harry Charles Luke, acting High Commissioner since August....Edward, Prince of Wales reached the Suez Canal returning to Britain to see his father....The Ford Motor Company concludes a deal with the Turkish government about a 25 year concession in Constantinople.		Chinese Communist Mao Tse-tung formulates the resolutions of the Sixth Congress of Communist Party Representatives from the Fourth Red Army....British plans to enlarge the naval base at Singapore are drastically reduced....The Afghan government places a bounty on the head of rebel leader Ameer Amanullah.
Dec. 7	Calvin Coolidge states that he wants to see a strong antiwar pact before he leaves office.		The Prince of Wales on his way back to Britain, takes the train to Cairo. The illness of King George V also results in the Duke of Gloucester leaving Cape Town on the *Balmoral Castle*.	Demonstrations start in Paraguay's capital, Asunción, in support of the events along the Paraguayan-Bolivian border.	Joseph Gordon Coates, the prime minister of New Zealand, resigned after his government loses a vote of no confidence.
Dec. 8	The office of Calvin Coolidge announces that he has received 1,000 messages supporting his strong antiwar pact.	Italian fascist leader Benito Mussolini derides the anti-war pact....Tryggvi Thórhallsson becomes Minister of Finance, Iceland, taking over from Magnús Kristjánsson.	The Prince of Wales re-embarks on the HMS *Enterprise* at Port Said.	The Bolivian army counter-attacks and recaptures Vanguardia but fails to retake Galpón....An air mail route from Chicago to Buenos Aires, Argentina, is announced.	Sir Frederick Sykes becomes Governor of Bombay, India, taking over from the acting governor, Sir Henry Staveley Lawrence.
Dec. 9		British soldier Sir Arthur Paget dies in Cannes, France.	The widow of the former U.S. ambassador to Turkey Oscar S. Strauss announces that she will go on a Museum expedition and safari hunt in Africa in January 1929.	The Colombian army kills 15 in fighting with strikers in Bogota, the capital, and other parts of the country.	Tomasi Kulimoetoke I of Wallis and Futuna, dies.

A	B	C	D	E
Includes developments that affect more than one world region, international organizations and important meetings of world leaders.	Includes all domestic and regional developments in Europe, including the Soviet Union.	Includes all domestic and regional developments in Africa and the Middle East.	Includes all domestic and regional developments in Latin America, the Caribbean, and Canada.	Includes all domestic and regional developments in Asian and Pacific nations (and colonies).

U.S. Politics & Social Issues	U.S. Foreign Policy & Affairs, Defense	U.S. Economy & Environment	Science, Technology & Nature	Culture, Leisure & Lifestyle	
Calvin Coolidge is involved in a hunting competition at Staunton, Virginia,. But does not manage to hit any of the quail.	U.S. President-elect Herbert Hoover arrives at Guayaquil, Ecuador.		Colombian aviator Lieutenant Benjamin Mendez, flying to Colombia, crash lands his plane in the bay near Colon, Panama, and is rescued.	Hallam, the Second Baron Tennyson, biographer of his father, the Poet Laureate, dies, aged 76.	Dec. 2
The second session of the 70th Congress opens.	U.S. President-elect Herbert Hoover heads for Peru on the USS *Maryland*.			A seaplane sinks near Cap Arcona, Rio de Janeiro, Brazil, with Brazilian aviator, Alberto Santos-Dumont being rescued alive.... Archaeologists at Olynthus, Greece, uncover bathtubs and vanity boxes in a city which was sacked in 348 B.C.E.	Dec. 3
Calvin Coolidge makes his last annual message expressing great confidence in the continued prosperity of the United States.	The Naval Committee of the House of Representatives support the proposal for a conference with Calvin Coolidge delivering his farewell message to Congress and urging for the passage of the Fifteen Cruiser Bill.				Dec. 4
The police disperse the Sicilian gangs' meeting in Cleveland, Ohio	Some 100,000 Peruvians cheer "Viva Hoover" in Lima as U.S. President-elect Herbert Hoover visits the capital of Peru.	Calvin Coolidge submits his budget to Congress calling for a total expenditure of £756 million.	Richard Byrd reaches Antarctic waters.	At Brisbane, Australia, England wins the first test match against Australia by 675 runs.	Dec. 5
Charles Evans Hughes, in a speech to the New York branch of the Federal Bar Association urges for fewer jury trials to be held in the United States.		Money funds "at call" reach 12 percent as stock prices fall an average of $6.20 in trading on the New York Stock Exchange in Wall Street.		Treasures owned by Mme Cécile Sorel are auctioned in Paris.	Dec. 6
New York governor-elect Franklin D. Roosevelt announces that he will remove "Smith Republicans" from their offices in New York State.... Narcotics worth $2 million, connected with slain gangland leader Arnold Rothstein are seized from a New York hotel.		At the New York Stock Exchange in Wall Street, 6,185,000 shares are traded with money at call falling to 9 percent.			Dec. 7
	U.S. Marines in Nicaragua try to reach an accommodation with rebel leader General Augusto Sandino with his mother sending her son a letter urging him to give up the rebellion.	There is a massive fall in the share price of Radio Corporation of America which loses 72 cents a share (to $2.96), reducing the total capitalization of the company by $83,188,800		*Mary Shelley*, by Richard Church, a new biography in the "Representative Women Series," is published in New York by Viking Press.	Dec. 8
Rumors spread that U.S. President-elect Herbert Hoover will transfer the enforcement of Prohibition to the Justice Department....Public sentiment urges for an enquiry into the investigation into the shooting of gangland identity Arnold Rothstein.		Five prisoners in Sing Sing Correctional Facility, Ossining, New York, are killed by smoke inhalation with 1,600 moved into a prison yard.	The ship of U.S. polar explorer Richard Byrd heads into ice floes in Antarctic waters.	Yeshiva College at 186th Street and Amsterdam Avenue, New York is opened and dedicated, with 20,000 people attending the ceremony.	Dec. 9

F	**G**	**H**	**I**	**J**
Includes campaigns, elections, federal-state relations, civil rights and liberties, crime, the judiciary, education, healthcare, poverty, urban affairs, and population.	*Includes formation and debate of U.S. foreign and defense policies, veterans affairs, and defense spending. (Relations with specific foreign countries are usually found under the region concerned.)*	*Includes business, labor, agriculture, taxation, transportation, consumer affairs, monetary and fiscal policy, natural resources, pollution and industrial accidents.*	*Includes worldwide scientific, medical and technological developments, natural phenomena, U.S. weather and natural disasters.*	*Includes the arts, religion, scholarship, communications media, sports, entertainment, fashions, fads, and social life.*

	World Affairs	Europe	Africa & The Middle East	The Americas	Asia & The Pacific
Dec. 10	The 53rd Session of the Council of the League of Nations opens; it ends on December 15....The Sixth Pan-American Conference on Conciliation and Arbitration, opens in Washington, DC, with Calvin Coolidge addressing the delegates.	Wilhelm Miklas becomes President of Austria, replacing Michael Hainisch.		Bolivia severs relations with its neighbor Paraguay, and the Sixth Pan-American Conference on Conciliation and Arbitration, at the opening session in Washington, adopts a resolution urging for the peaceful settlement of the border dispute and appoints a committee to consider measures for conciliation which could be adopted.	Sir Joseph Ward becomes Prime Minister of New Zealand, taking over from Joseph Gordon Coates.
Dec. 11		Edward, Prince of Wales, returns to London and meets woth his father whose condition improves slightly.		The League of Nations sends telegrams to the governments of Bolivia and Paraguay urging them to solve their dispute peacefully.... Police in Argentina's capital Buenos Aires manage to foil an assassination attempt on president-elect Herbert Hoover.	Electrification in Sydney, Australia, is extended to cover Hornsby.... Ölziytiyn Badrah, Bat-Ochiryn Eldev-Ochir and Peljidiyn Genden take over the running of Mongolia as joint secretaries of the Central Committee of the Mongolian People's Revolutionary Party.
Dec. 12	The International Civil Aeronautics Conference opens in Washington, DC, and lasts for three days. Calvin Coolidge addresses it on the opening day.	The Peasants' Party wins the Romanian general elections.... Thomas Westropp Bennett becomes Chairman (Cathaoirleach) of the Seanad Éireann, Irish Free State, replacing James Henry Mussen Campbell, Baron Glenavy....M. Klotz, the former French finance minister, resigns from the Senate after being accused of fraud and forgery.		The Bolivian government sends a telegram to the League of Nations placing the responsibility for the fighting of December 6, entirely on Paraguay. The Paraguayan government also sends a telegram denying responsibility.	Aviators Charles Kingsford Smith and Harry Ulm form the Australian National Airways Ltd in Sydney.... The Chinese and the Danish governments sign a treaty in Nanking on tariff autonomy and the conditional abolition of extra territoriality.
Dec. 13		Alfred Gürtler becomes President of the Nationalrat, the Austrian National Council....The foreign ministers of Britain, France and Germany, meeting at Lugano, Italy, agree on the status of the Rhineland.		Rebels in Mexico abduct 22 girls from the town of Jilotepec and carry them back to their base.	Large student riots take place in Nanking against the Japanese. The house of C.T. Wang, the foreign minister, is attacked and badly damaged.
Dec. 14		American-born British parliamentarian Lady Nancy Astor urges the end of arms talks in a speech to the Overseas League luncheon in London.		The Sixth Pan-American Conference on Conciliation and Arbitration offered to mediate in the dispute. In La Paz, the Bolivian government announces that it is calling up its reserves. At the same time Bolivian infantry take the towns of Boqueron and Mariscal Lopez, actions that resulted in the deaths of 15 Paraguayans. The Bolivians then withdraw.	Attack on Kabul, capital of Afghanistan by about 3,000 tribesmen from Kohistan, in continuing protests against the reforms introduced by King Amanullah. They aim to storm the city and kill the king and although they do capture the Koh-i-Lula forts in the northwest of the city, where they seize more weapons, Royalist soldiers hold them back as they approach the Legation quarter, threatening the British Legation.
Dec. 15		The fever of the British King George V moderates....The German foreign minister Dr. Gustav Stresemann Bangs on the table during a meeting of the League of Nations as the Polish foreign minister August Zaleski accused the Germans of infiltrating soldiers into Silesia.		Further fighting between the Bolivians and Paraguayans takes place along the frontier between the two countries with Bolivian airplanes dropping bombs on Bahia Negra, although none of these explode. The League of Nations once again sends messages to both governments reminding them of their mutual obligations under the Covenant of the League to settle their disputes by arbitration.	During the night, staff at the British Legation in Kabul stockpile weapons in the Legation's bathroom and during the day start collecting and packing their possessions for an evacuation.
Dec. 16		The condition of the British King George V improves....Jean Médecin becomes Mayor of Nice, France.		The Paraguayan government announces a general mobilization of its armed forces.	Aeroplanes of the Royal Afghan Air Force, piloted by White Russian émigrés, start bombing rebel bases outside Kabul.

A	B	C	D	E
Includes developments that affect more than one world region, international organizations and important meetings of world leaders.	Includes all domestic and regional developments in Europe, including the Soviet Union.	Includes all domestic and regional developments in Africa and the Middle East.	Includes all domestic and regional developments in Latin America, the Caribbean, and Canada.	Includes all domestic and regional developments in Asian and Pacific nations (and colonies).

U.S. Politics & Social Issues	U.S. Foreign Policy & Affairs, Defense	U.S. Economy & Environment	Science, Technology & Nature	Culture, Leisure & Lifestyle	
	U.S. President-elect Herbert Hoover arrives in Chile and is welcomed in Valparaiso and then in Santiago, the Chilean capital.	The White Star Liner *Celtic* hits a rock near Roche's Point, Queenstown Harbor, Ireland. All the 254 passengers are reported safe—25 of them are survivors of the sinking of the *Vestris*.	Richard Byrd reports that his ship is nearing pack ice.	The design for the monument to the Unknown Soldier planned for Washington, DC is chosen....Charles Rennie Mackintosh, a Scottish architect and a major influence in the Art Nouveau movement in Scotland, dies, aged 60.	Dec. 10
	A plot against the life of U.S. President-elect Herbert Hoover is uncovered in Buenos Aires, Argentina, with plans drawn up by conspirators to blow up his train. Meanwhile Hoover makes a very conciliatory speech in Santiago, Chile, calling the country a friend, not a rival, and urging it to use foreign loans to develop the country.		Richard Byrd "rediscovers" Scott Island.		Dec. 11
U.S. postal services issue two postage stamps showing airplanes for the 25th anniversary of the flight by the Wright brothers on December 17, 1903, and for the International Civil Aeronautics Conference which opens in Washington, DC....Gunmen in New York managed to get $104,500 in a raid on a lightly-armored delivery vehicle taking pay to companies in the city. Seven gang members armed with revolvers and sawn off shotguns managed to make good their escape.	U.S. President-elect Herbert Hoover crosses the Andes into Argentina, arriving at Mendoza from where he will be catching the train to Buenos Aires.		In a demonstration to see how paratroopers could operate, a six-man machine-gun team jumps from a six-plane formation over Brooks Field, TX....Calvin Coolidge extols the pioneers of aviation in a speech at the International Civil Aeronautics Conference.		Dec. 12
	Massive crowds turn out at Buenos Aires to greet U.S. President-elect Herbert Hoover....Calvin Coolidge sends a message to King George V of Britain expressing his satisfaction on the improvement of the king's health.			George Gershwin's musical, *An American in Paris*, holds its premiere at the Carnegie Hall in New York, with the New York Philharmonic Orchestra playing under the direction of Walter Damrosch....The design of the clip-on tie is registered.	Dec. 13
	The U.S. Senate is critical of elements of the Kellogg-Briand Anti-War Treaty.	Radio Corporation of America takes over the Victor Talking Machine Company in a $116 million deal....The bill to build the Boulder Dam (later renamed the Hoover Dam) passes the Senate.	Scientists in Chicago working on poison gas reveal the horrifying consequences of its use in war....Colonial Airways reports that it has carried 1,295 passengers a total of 165,809 flying miles without any casualties and claims this demonstrates the safety of air travel.	The British publishers Jonathan Cape lose their appeal in London against the pulping of *The Well of Loneliness* by Radclyffe Hall. Writer Rudyard Kipling attends the hearing and states he was prepared to give evidence on behalf of the government to urge the book's suppression. The book is said to glorify vice, the author being a lesbian and the main character in the story being Stephen Gordon, a "male lesbian."	Dec. 14
Calvin Coolidge presents the Schiff Flying Trophy to Lieutenant J.E. Dyer of the Navy at a ceremony in the White House.	The Argentine press hail U.S. President-elect Herbert Hoover as a friend of their country.	The aviation companies Pratt and Whitney, and the Chance Vought Corporation merge withy the Boeing Airplane and Transport Corporation of Seattle.	The International Conference of Medicine is held at Cairo, Egypt....The *Daneville Commercial News*, published in Illinois, becomes the first newspaper in the world to be printed on paper made from recycled cornstalks....The Russian Arctic explorer Ktrasinki reports that he found the skeleton of Peter Tessem, a member of the crew of the *Maud* of Roald Amundsen in the 1918–19 expedition to Dixon Island.		Dec. 15
Calvin Coolidge announces that he will take a rest after he retires from the White House and has no immediate plans for his life after being president....New York police reveal that the man they want to question over the shooting of gangland identity Arnold Rothstein has fled to Havana, Cuba.	Large crowds turn out in Montevideo, the capital of Uruguay, to cheer U.S. President-elect Herbert Hoover with guns from the old fort on the crest of Montevideo harbor and the ships in the harbor giving a salute.	Henry Ford makes moves to expand significantly the Ford Motor Company into Britain.	Dr. Charles Mayo moves to Chicago to head a leading cancer research facility in Cook County, IL.		Dec. 16

F	G	H	I	J
Includes campaigns, elections, federal-state relations, civil rights and liberties, crime, the judiciary, education, healthcare, poverty, urban affairs, and population.	Includes formation and debate of U.S. foreign and defense policies, veterans affairs, and defense spending. (Relations with specific foreign countries are usually found under the region concerned.)	Includes business, labor, agriculture, taxation, transportation, consumer affairs, monetary and fiscal policy, natural resources, pollution and industrial accidents.	Includes worldwide scientific, medical and technological developments, natural phenomena, U.S. weather and natural disasters.	Includes the arts, religion, scholarship, communications media, sports, entertainment, fashions, fads, and social life.

	World Affairs	Europe	Africa & The Middle East	The Americas	Asia & The Pacific
Dec. 17	German papers use the impending conflict between Paraguay and Bolivia as a reason to challenge the effectiveness of the League of Nations. The German government also denies sending the Bolivians arms.	After disturbances in Monte Carlo, Monaco, for nearly a week, Prince Louis of Monaco urges the population of the small Western Mediterranean principality to end their differences which might shake the political stability of the country.		As the Chaco dispute escalates, and Paraguayan soldiers are mobilized, the Paraguayan government announces its acceptance of the Sixth Pan-American Conference mediation offer.	With fighting escalating in Afghanistan, King Amanullah and Queen Souriya fled as a section of the army turned against them. Rebels approach the British Legation in Kabul, and the British decide to organize an airlift, the first in history.
Dec. 18		Following the resignation of Luigi Federzoni, the Minister of the Colonies, in a move that surprised many people in Italy, Benito Mussolini increases his power in the cabinet by holding seven portfolios. This makes him Minister of Foreign Affairs, Minister of Internal Affairs, Minister of the Army, Minister of the Navy, Minister of Aeronautics, Minister of Corporations and Minister of the Colonies, giving himself an effective majority in the cabinet of 13.		Bolivia also announces its acceptance of the Sixth Pan-American Conference mediation offer.	
Dec. 19	The League of Nations announces that its Arms Commission will meet between April 8 and April 15, 1929.	Pope Pius XII begins celebrations for the 50th anniversary of his original ordination as a priest.... The Albanian Parliament in Tirana ratifies the Kellogg-Briand Anti-war Treaty.			The Chinese and Dutch governments sign a tariff autonomy treaty, and the Chinese and Portuguese governments sign a tariff and extra-territoriality treaty.... The Chinese government abandons plans to establish a German-run airline in China.... Lieutenant-General Sir Michael Frederic Rimington KCB CVO, dies, aged 70....Rebels in Afghanistan seize forts near Kabul.
Dec. 20		Police in Paris investigating fraud in the French capital arrest a brother of Maxim Litvinoff, the foreign minister of the Soviet Union, and charge him with placing into circulation false Russian promissory notes valued at 24 million francs (about $938,400)....There is a large gas blast in Wrest Central London resulting in 17 people having to go to hospital for treatment.	Lieutenant-Colonel Sir Pieter C. S. Bain, South African publicist, dies, aged 59....Rumors sweep the Turkish city of Constantinople over a possible planned coup d'état with 150 people arrested including a number of senior generals.		The Chinese government agrees on new tariff arrangements with the British and Swedish governments.... The British minister to China, Sir Miles Lampson, formally presents his credentials to Chiang Kai-shek thereby signifying the British government's recognition of the Nanking government.
Dec. 21	Rev Marshall Hartley, former president and secretary of the Wesleyan Conference, dies, aged 82.	A French judge is shot in his rooms in Paris, but survives with his attacker, an Alsatian, surrendering to the police....Marshal Count Luigi Cadorna, Italy's commander-in-chef during World War I, dies, aged 78.... *The Chronicle of the Reign of King Pedro III of Aragon, 1276–1285*, by Bernat Desclot, translated into English for the first time from Catalan by F. L. Critchlow, is published in Princeton, NJ, by Princeton University Press.			Mikaele Tufele becomes ruler of Wallis and Futuna in the Pacific.... British planes fly to Kabul on a reconnaissance mission to plan for the evacuation of Legation personnel and others from the Afghan capital....Authorities in Chungking, China, declare that a state of war exists with warlords attacking.
Dec. 22		Oskari Mantere becomes President of Finland, taking over from Juho Emil Sunila. Significant changes in the cabinet in Finland results in Aimo Kaarlo Cajander replacing Jalo Lahdensuo as Minister of Defense; Hugo Relander replacing Juho Niukkanen as Minister of Finance; Toivo Kivimäki replacing Matti Aura as Minister of the Interior; and Anton Kotonen replacing Torsten Malinen as Minister of Justice.... The German government announces that it has reached an agreement with the Allies over the membership of the Committee of Experts established to deal with the issue of the wartime reparations.			The Australian Capital Territory ends its prohibition of the sale of liquor....The Chinese and French governments sign a treaty in Nanking on tariff autonomy. They also draw up plans for reducing the size of their army with Chiang Kai-shekl calling a military conference for December 26.

A	B	C	D	E
Includes developments that affect more than one world region, international organizations and important meetings of world leaders.	*Includes all domestic and regional developments in Europe, including the Soviet Union.*	*Includes all domestic and regional developments in Africa and the Middle East.*	*Includes all domestic and regional developments in Latin America, the Caribbean, and Canada.*	*Includes all domestic and regional developments in Asian and Pacific nations (and colonies).*

U.S. Politics & Social Issues	U.S. Foreign Policy & Affairs, Defense	U.S. Economy & Environment	Science, Technology & Nature	Culture, Leisure & Lifestyle	
	Under Secretary of State J. Reuben Clark drafts a memorandum in which he declares that the United States will not again claim the right to intervene in the internal affairs of any Latin American country as an international policeman, in effect leading to the repudiation of the Roosevelt Corollary to the Monroe Doctrine.	The Boeing Airplane Company merges with Pratt & Whitney Aircraft and Chance Vought to form the United Aircraft and Transport Corporation.		News is made public that the artist Arthur B. Davies,. Former president of the American Painters and Sculptors Society, died on October 24.	Dec. 17
Packing cases containing cocaine and morphine valued at £800,000 are seized on the docks of New York.	The Senate Foreign Relations Committee vote 14 to two to send the Kellogg Pact to the U.S. Senate.		The ship taking U.S. Polar explorer Richard Byrd is caught in a bad storm in Antarctic waters.		Dec. 18
In a robbery at the Brooklyn home of Frank Bailey, banker and chairman of the Board of the Prudence Bond Company, thieves escaped with jewelry valued at $100,000.	U.S. President-elect Herbert Hoover ends his Latin American goodwill tour by calling at Rio de Janeiro. He also announces that he will no longer be visiting Cuba, eliminating his stop at Havana, which will then bring him back to the United States on about January 7. He said he then plans to spend some time in Utah relaxing before he becomes president.		U.S. aviator Harold Pitcairn flies the first American auto-gyro in Philadelphia, PA.	In Sydney, Australia, England wins the second test match against Australia by eight wickets.	Dec. 19
	U.S. President-elect Herbert Hoover announces that he will make three speeches in Brazil.	The directors of the Waldorf-Astoria Hotel announce that they have sold it to the Bethlehem Engineering Corporation, along with the Astor Court Office Building.	The first international dog-sled mail leaves Minot in Maine, for Montreal in Canada....Richard Byrd hails the flight of Australian Captain Hubert Wilkins who flew over Graham Land.	Gabriel Wells, the New York book dealer, announces that he has purchased the London firm of Henry Sotheran & Co of London.	Dec. 20
New York police commissioner Grover A. Whalen abolishes the homicide squad.	The largest gathering during the Latin American goodwill visit of U.S. President-elect Herbert Hoover takes place in Rio de Janeiro where 200,000 people greet him in the Brazilian capital.	U.S. Congress passes the Boulder Dam Project Bill committing the federal government to this major project to produce hydroelectric power, approving the construction of The Boulder Dam in Colorado—it is later renamed The Hoover Dam.... Three major banks on Wall Street merge making the Manufacturers' Trust Company among the five largest trust companies in New York.	The German government extends its telephone service to Argentina, with every German telephone subscriber being able to call Buenos Aires. However calls cost 180 marks (about $43) for the first three minutes, which is still much cheaper than calls from Berlin to New York which cost 307 marks.		Dec. 21
New York police commissioner Grover A. Whalen speaks pout publicly voicing his criticism of the lack of progress in the investigation into the shooting death of gangland identity Arnold Rothstein.	U.S. President-elect Herbert Hoover tells the Brazilian people of the bond between the United States and Brazil with "peace through affection."			*Married Sweethearts*, a romance set in the Rocky Mountains by Alfred Osmond, is published in Provo, UT, by the author....The New England Society in New York celebrates its 123rd anniversary.	Dec. 22

F

Includes campaigns, elections, federal-state relations, civil rights and liberties, crime, the judiciary, education, healthcare, poverty, urban affairs, and population.

G

Includes formation and debate of U.S. foreign and defense policies, veterans affairs, and defense spending. (Relations with specific foreign countries are usually found under the region concerned.)

H

Includes business, labor, agriculture, taxation, transportation, consumer affairs, monetary and fiscal policy, natural resources, pollution and industrial accidents.

I

Includes worldwide scientific, medical and technological developments, natural phenomena, U.S. weather and natural disasters.

J

Includes the arts, religion, scholarship, communications media, sports, entertainment, fashions, fads, and social life.

	World Affairs	Europe	Africa & The Middle East	The Americas	Asia & The Pacific
Dec. 23		The Soviet and Turkish governments ratify the Railway Convention of July 9, 1922....British authorities announce that King George V is improving in health but remains less inclined to eat. However the new Archbishop of Canterbury Dr. Cosmo Gordon Lang, falls unwell and is treated by the king's doctor.			In response to the increasing lack of safety in Kabul, Afghanistan's capital, an evacuation of foreign women and children starts (finished on December 24) by air plane—using eight RAF Vickers Victoria transport aircraft and a Handley Page Hinaidi—taking the evacuees to Peshawar, in British India.
Dec. 24		German President Paul von Hindenburg announces that he will be celebrating a quiet Christmas.... In Britain, the Royal Family announce that they will be celebrating Christmas as a family.	Christian pilgrims from around the world arrive in Bethlehem, Palestine, to celebrate Christmas Eve at the Church of the Nativity.	A brewery strike in Brazil mars Christmas celebrations in Rio de Janeiro as the heat increases the demand for beer.	Sir Charles Ollivant KCIE, important British civil servant in India, dies, aged 82.
Dec. 25	Calvin Coolidge gives his Christmas address and offers to participate in discussions on World War I debt and reparations in a move which is greeted enthusiastically in Europe.			A Convention demarcating the Brazilian-Bolivian frontier is signed at Rio de Janeiro....The Mexican President Emilio Portes Gil ordered the abolition of summary executions in Mexico.	More refugees flee Kabul as the rebels close in on the Afghan capital.
Dec. 26		The Right Honorable Mark Lockwood, Baron Lambourne, former British member of parliament and horticulturalist, dies, aged 81.			Rebels attacking Kabul, Afghanistan's capital, are driven back by forces loyal to Afghanistan's reformist king, Amanullah.
Dec. 27		The British delegation to the Colonial Commission of the Communist International (Comintern) publishes a dissenting view to the official Comintern *Theses on the Colonial and Semi-Colonial Countries.*			The Chinese and Spanish governments sign a treaty in Nanking on tariff autonomy and the abolition of extra territoriality.
Dec. 28		The Swedish postal authorities draw up plans for a nighttime airmail flight between Sweden and the United States....The Romanian royal family announces that toys given to King Michael of Romania, aged seven, which are not wanted will be given to the poor.		Hugh Havelock McLean is appointed Lieutenant Governor of New Brunswick, Canada, succeeding William Frederic Todd....Lieutenant Benjamin Mendez of the Colombian Air Service, trained in the United States, resumes his flight to Colombia....Maximiliano Vigueras, a captured Mexican bandit who had been a prominent highway robber, is sentenced to death by firing squad.	The Indian National Congress adopts a resolution threatening the establishing of a non cooperation movement if the British government does not accept the draft of a Dominion status constitution by 1929....The Royal army in Afghanistan makes for Kabul to come to the aid of the King.
Dec. 29		In Belgrade the Jugoslav cabinet is locked in crisis talks with newspapers speculating the possible resignation of Anton Korosec.	Sir Charles Metcalfe, Bart., an important Rhodesian railway engineer, dies, aged 75.	The Pan American air company is granted exclusive airmail rights by the Honduran government....The Honduran newspaper *El Democratia* in Tegucigalpa, publishes a long article stating that Nicaraguan rebel leader General Augusto Sandino plans to launch a major offensive soon....The Paraguayan government accepts the conciliation plan in their dispute with Bolivia over the Chaco desert.	Chang Hsueh-liang, son of murdered warlord Chang Tso-lin, announced his support for the Nationalist Government of Chiang Kai-shek by declaring his adoption of the Three Principles of Sun Yat-sen, and also hoisting the Nationalist flag in Manchuria for the first time. As a result Manchuria submits to the authority of Chinese Nationalist government.
Dec. 30		The French ocean liner *Paul Lecat* is seriously damaged by fire while in the dry dock at Marseilles....As the Yugoslav crisis gets worse, the country's prime minister Anton Korosec, is forced to submit his resignation.			The British continue to rescue more people from Afghanistan with the wife of the Italian Minister being among the latest evacuees.
Dec. 31		The chimes of Big Ben are heard for the first time on British radio.... Maksim Litvinov proposes to the Polish government and the Lithuanian government a separate "Kellogg Pact"....Philipp Etter steps down as Landammänner of Zug Canton, Switzerland....Ludwik Darowski ends his term as Governor of Krakow Province, Poland, and is replaced on the following day by Mikolaj Kwasniewski.		A Special Committee of the Sixth Pan-American Conference announces that both the Paraguayan and Bolivian governments have accepted the protocol of conciliation drawn up by the Committee. However it does not stop tensions escalating....Sir Jean Lomer Gouin is appointed Lieutenant Governor of Quebec, Canada, taking over from Narcisse Perodeau....Alejandro R. Vega ends his term as Governor of Sinaloa, Mexico.	Kasagama Kyebambe IV of Tonga, dies....A conference opens in Nanking to discuss the disbandment of the various Chinese armies and their merger into a single national army....Chiang Kai-shek makes a speech ion which he hails the great changes in China during the year, with C.T. Wang, the foreign minister, speaking from Nanking, urging the ending of all extraterritorial rights in China.

A	B	C	D	E
Includes developments that affect more than one world region, international organizations and important meetings of world leaders.	Includes all domestic and regional developments in Europe, including the Soviet Union.	Includes all domestic and regional developments in Africa and the Middle East.	Includes all domestic and regional developments in Latin America, the Caribbean, and Canada.	Includes all domestic and regional developments in Asian and Pacific nations (and colonies).

U.S. Politics & Social Issues	U.S. Foreign Policy & Affairs, Defense	U.S. Economy & Environment	Science, Technology & Nature	Culture, Leisure & Lifestyle	
To try to improve the image of the New York police force, New York police commissioner Grover A. Whalen, sends police in a massive series of raids arresting 100 crime suspects....Outgoing New York Governor Alfred E. Smith assures Governor-elect Franklin D. Roosevelt that there is a surplus of $25 million.	U.S. President-elect Herbert Hoover stes out to return to the United States in the USS *Utah*.	Republicans in New York urge Calvin Coolidge to name New York State Attorney-General Albert Ottinger for the Federal Trade Board.		The National Broadcasting Company sets up a permanent network throughout the mainland United States....Stacy Aumonier, writer of short stories, dies, aged 41.	Dec. 23
Calvin Coolidge lights the Community Christmas Tree in Sherman Square, Washington, DC.				Sir William T.T. Dyer KCMG, CIE, FRS, former director of Kew Botanical Gardens in London, England, dies, aged 85.	Dec. 24
A 26-year-old man in Atlantic City, New Jersey is shot dead with a pistol in a duel fought in the street.... Calvin Coolidge leaves Washington DC, for the southern states.	U.S. President-elect Herbert Hoover crosses the equator on his return voyage to the United States at the end of his goodwill trip around Latin America.		The ship of Richard Byrd enters the Ross Sea....It is announces that the U.S. postal services will begin air mail service to Costa Rica in 1929.		Dec. 25
New York Governor-elect Franklin Delano Roosevelt picks Albert C. Conway of Brooklyn to be the Superintendent of Insurance of New York State.			Richard Byrd and some of his crew land on floating ice to celebrate a belated Christmas on land....The Radio Board in Washington, DC, grants 551 short wave licenses.		Dec. 26
There is a massive crackdown on crime in New York.	Herbert Hoover speaks of wanting the United States to be a strong naval power.	John D. Rockefeller Announces that he has bought $100 million worth of real estate in New York City. Part of it will be used for a new opera.	Some 5,000 scientists from the American Association for the Advancement of Science meet in New York.		Dec. 27
The wife of Calvin Coolidge is involved in a pheasant hunt at Sea Island Beach, GA....Governor-elect Franklin D. Roosevelt announces that Edward J. Flynn is to be named as state secretary, which is seen as a threat to the power of Tammany Hall. Roosevelt also announces that he will not be reappointing Belle Moskowitz (Henry Moskowitz) who had been a longtime adviser to Al Smith.			Byrd continues his expedition to Antarctica....Red Cross advises about possible outbreak of an influenza epidemic....Lucien Howe, a noted ophthalmologist, dies in Belmont, MA, aged 80. He had given $250,000 to endow a laboratory at Harvard.		Dec. 28
U.S. President-elect Herbert Hoover states that he will defer fully to Calvin Coolidge on all matters that come up before the handover of power on March 4, 1929....Calvin Coolidge also agrees to make his New Year's message on the radio.		The U.S. government moves against Sinclair oil interests over the Salt Creek Field in Wyoming which was alleged to have made them a profit of $35 million (20 million barrels of oil).		The United States features *The Jazz Singer* and the *Red Dance*, the first sound films ever shown in Australia, are released in, respectively, the Lyceum Theatre and the Regent Theatre in Sydney.	Dec. 29
Police in New York round up 454 crime suspects in a crack down on illegal alcohol....A dinner is held in Albany to farewell outgoing Governor Al Smith.		The Ford Motor Company announces that it will be hiring 30,000 more workers to allow its factories to run six days a week, raising their output to 6,500 cars a week.	Dr. Eugene Lyman Fisk of the Life Extension Institute claims that science can lengthen the lifespan of humans which is not fixed.		Dec. 30
U.S. President-elect Herbert Hoover continues back to the United States on the USS *Utah*.	The U.S. Marines in Nicaragua hail the campaigns in 1928 as having crushed the revolt of rebel leader General Augusto Sandino, and led to the successful elections in the country. It is also revealed that over the Christmas period marines helped with the mail deliveries, transporting letters to Costa Rica and elsewhere.	The U.S. postal authorities announce that they had a $2 million increase in postal receipts in 1928.		Some 92 couples in New York get married on the last day of the year.	Dec. 31

F	G	H	I	J
Includes campaigns, elections, federal-state relations, civil rights and liberties, crime, the judiciary, education, healthcare, poverty, urban affairs, and population.	Includes formation and debate of U.S. foreign and defense policies, veterans affairs, and defense spending. (Relations with specific foreign countries are usually found under the region concerned.)	Includes business, labor, agriculture, taxation, transportation, consumer affairs, monetary and fiscal policy, natural resources, pollution and industrial accidents.	Includes worldwide scientific, medical and technological developments, natural phenomena, U.S. weather and natural disasters.	Includes the arts, religion, scholarship, communications media, sports, entertainment, fashions, fads, and social life.

1929

Wall Street scene after the October 1929 stock market crash.

	World Affairs	Europe	Africa & The Middle East	The Americas	Asia & The Pacific
Jan.	To settle problems with reparations, the Young Commission is formed. Americans Owen D. Young and J.P. Morgan head the commission.	Armand Colin publishes the first issue of *Annales d'Histoire Economique et Sociale*. Expelled from the Soviet Union, Trotsky moves to Turkey and requests asylum in France and Germany.	The Trans-Sahara Road opens. It ties Algiers and Lake Chad. The ceremonies run through April.... Britain sends the Hylton-Young Commission to examine conditions in Africa. The commissioners recommend tighter relations between British east and central Africa.	The United States and Canada develop a plan to preserve Niagara Falls, which has been crumbling for decades.... The General Act of Inter-American Arbitration requires Pan American Union states to arbitrate disagreements. It models on the Paris Pact of 1928.	
Feb.	An international commission begins working on a revised World Court. The US representative is Elihu Root, who insists that court rulings apply to the United States only with U.S. consent.	Italy and the Vatican sign the Lateran Treaty. Italy recognizes the sovereignty of Vatican City and defines the status of the church in Italy.... Germany accepts Kellogg-Briand, the Pact of Paris.... Signers of the Litvinov Protocol include Poland, Romania, Latvia, Estonia, Turkey, and the Soviet Union. The Protocol is similar to Kellogg-Briand.	France adjourns the Syrian assembly indefinitely. The assembly is too strongly nationalist for France.		American Samoa organizes as U.S. territory. The United States has occupied part of Samoa since the year after dividing the archipelago with Germany in 1899.
Mar.		Greece and Yugoslavia settle their dispute over the Free Zone of Saloniki. They also sign a treaty of friendship.	The change of government in Britain allows resumption of Anglo-Egyptian talks, which continue through April.	Generals Jose Gonzalo Escobar and Jesus Maria Aguirre attempt a coup in Mexico. They fail.	The Chinese boycott works. Japan agrees to withdraw troops from Shantung and pay damages, but not indemnities.
Apr.	The Young Commission submits its reparations recommendations. Germany submits counter-proposals.			The Dominican Republic invites Charles Dawes to examine its finances and suggest reforms.	The first nonstop flight from England to India is a success.
May	Norway annexes the Arctic Ocean's Jay Mayen Island, northeast of Iceland.	British general elections produce a hung parliament with Labour winning 288 seats and Conservatives holding 260. With 59 seats, Liberals control the balance of power.	Britain and Egypt agree on use of the Nile. Sudan will get Blue Nile water, but White Nile water is Egypt's to use.		
Jun.	The Young Plan is submitted with a significant reduction of total German reparations. Diplomats assume this plan will be permanent.	Conservatives concede rather than rely on Liberals in a shaky coalition. Ramsay MacDonald forms a new Labour government.... Macedonians from Yugoslavia begin cross-border raids into Bulgaria. Tensions between the two governments close their border.		Mexico's Cristoro War ends. After Ambassador Morrow brokers a deal between church and state, churches reopen.... Chile and Peru sign an accord ending the Tacna-Arica dispute, which has been ongoing since 1910.	
Jul.	Kellogg-Briand goes into effect. It was signed in August 1928 by most major powers.	Aristide Briand replaces Prime Minister Raymond Poincare, who resigns due to poor health.... France votes to pay war debts to the United States with reparations received from Germany.			
Aug.	Germany accepts the Young Plan and the allies agree to evacuate the Ruhr by 1930. the Young Plan requires Germany to pay at least 660 million marks a year but reduces the total reparations by 1.7 billion from the Dawes Plan.		Palestinians riot in Safed, Gaza, and Hebron. The cause is a simmering dispute with Jews over access to the Wailing Wall. In a week of rioting, Arabs kill 133 Jews and British-led police kill 116 Arabs. Wounded total 339 Jews and 232 Arabs.... Egypt and Britain sign a treaty ending British control but allowing a continuing British presence.	The Chaco War between Bolivia and Paraguay continues after both sides reject an agreement developed by the Pan American Union.	Elected president of the next Congress, Gandhi declines, suggesting Nehru in his stead.
Sep.	Evacuation of the Ruhr begins..... The League agrees to a conference to revise the World Court statute to allow wider membership.	Briand presents a plan for a United States of Europe. The league discusses it but nothing results.... In Finland the steamboat *Kuru* sinks. Lost lives total 136.... Antanas Smetona ousts Augustinas Voldemaras in a Lithuanian coup.... Bulgaria and Yugoslavia resolve their border problems.	Violence breaks out between Arabs and Jews in Palestine. It will continue for several months as Arabs claim Jewish discrimination.	Ramsay MacDonald begins a long visit to the United States and Canada. The trip lasts until November 1.	Nehru is elected president for the Lahore Congress.

A	B	C	D	E
Includes developments that affect more than one world region, international organizations and important meetings of world leaders.	*Includes all domestic and regional developments in Europe, including the Soviet Union.*	*Includes all domestic and regional developments in Africa and the Middle East.*	*Includes all domestic and regional developments in Latin America, the Caribbean, and Canada.*	*Includes all domestic and regional developments in Asian and Pacific nations (and colonies).*

U.S. Politics & Social Issues	U.S. Foreign Policy & Affairs, Defense	U.S. Economy & Environment	Science, Technology & Nature	Culture, Leisure & Lifestyle	
The Seeing Eye begins operations in Nashville, TN. The organization trains dogs to help the blind.	The United States ratifies the Pact of Paris because the agreement is weak. The pact does not limit self defense, violate the Monroe Doctrine, or require the United States to take military action against aggressors.	The U.S. and Canada agree to work together to keep Niagara Falls from deteriorating further.	The *Lexington* and *Saratoga*, modern aircraft carriers, participate in fleet exercises.	Tintin, the cartoon character created by Herge, debuts. Eventually he will appear in 200 million comic books in 60 languages....Elzie Crisler Segar's *Popeye* also debuts....*In Old Arizona* is the first talking feature filmed outdoors.	Jan.
Chicago is site of the St. Valentine's Day Massacre. Seven rivals of Al Capone are gunned down.	The United States authorizes construction of 15 cruisers in the 10,000 ton class. The construction is due to the failure of the 1927 reduction talks.	Astrologer Evangeline Adams predicts that the stock market will rise in coming months. Among her clients are actors and J.P. Morgan.	Congress establishes Grand Teton National Park.	Eugene O'Neill's *Dynamo* premiers....The first Academy Award nominations are announced.... Charles Rigoulet of France becomes the first person to clean and jerk 400 pounds.	Feb.
	In his inaugural, Hoover asks the Senate to accept the World Court under the Root restrictions.	Congress establishes the Court of Customs and Patent Appeals.		A part-talkie version of *Showboat*, based on Ferber's novel rather than the play, debuts in Palm Beach. Reviews are negative and box office receipts poor.	Mar.
	Canada protests the Coast Guard's sinking of *I'm Alone*, a suspected rum runner in the Gulf of Mexico. The two nations agree to arbitrate but friction persists as the United States threatens punitive agricultural tariffs.				Apr.
Atlantic City, NJ, is the site of the purported formation of the National Crime Syndicate. Hosted by New York's Lucky Luciano, the meeting included most U.S. mobsters. Some deny the syndicate ever existed.		Wall Street installs the first automatic electronic stock quote board. The NYSE also adds 6,000 feet of floor space.	The first regularly scheduled television broadcasts occur three times a week.	The American League indicates it will not select a most valuable player any longer.	May
	The U.S. Navy establishes general standards for aircraft ignition, reducing interference with long range radio function.	The new Atlantic City Convention Center hosts its first trade show, electric light industry.	The first public demonstration of a color television by H.E. Ives and colleagues of Bell Laboratories, sends pictures of roses and an American flag from New York to Washington, DC.		Jun.
		Successful airplane hook-ons to a dirigible occur for the first time.	Robert Goddard launches a liquid fuel rocket containing a camera, barometer, and thermometer.	Scotland Yard raids the Mayfair Gallery and seizes a dozen "indecent" nude paintings of D.H. Lawrence.	Jul.
		A brokerage office opens shop aboard trans-Atlantic liners so that passengers can play the stock market during the week at sea.	The BBC makes the first broadcast of James Logie Baird's 30-line color television technology....Germany's *Graf* Zeppelin makes an around-the-world flight.	*Amos 'n Andy* debuts after Gosden and Correll abandon Sam 'n Henry in a salary dispute. *Amos 'n Andy* is the first syndicated program.	Aug.
Alger Hiss begins working as law clerk for Justice Oliver Wendell Holmes.	The United States reverses its policy and joins the World Court.	Values on Wall Street reach record highs. Some issues are triple their 1928 values.	Lt. Gen. James Doolittle makes the first flight totally by radio-controlled instruments.		Sep.

F	G	H	I	J
Includes campaigns, elections, federal-state relations, civil rights and liberties, crime, the judiciary, education, healthcare, poverty, urban affairs, and population.	*Includes formation and debate of U.S. foreign and defense policies, veterans affairs, and defense spending. (Relations with specific foreign countries are usually found under the region concerned.)*	*Includes business, labor, agriculture, taxation, transportation, consumer affairs, monetary and fiscal policy, natural resources, pollution and industrial accidents.*	*Includes worldwide scientific, medical and technological developments, natural phenomena, U.S. weather and natural disasters.*	*Includes the arts, religion, scholarship, communications media, sports, entertainment, fashions, fads, and social life.*

	World Affairs	Europe	Africa & The Middle East	The Americas	Asia & The Pacific
Oct.		Briand's government falls....Britain resumes relations with the Soviet Union...Alexander renames the Kingdom of the Serbs, Croats, and Slovenes to Yugoslavia. His goal is to crate a national identity to replace historical ethnic divisions.	Having gained backing from tribal leaders on both sides of the border, Nadir Khan takes Kabul. He becomes king, and the deposed Habibullah is executed.	Canada begins appointing women to its Senate after the Famous Five, aka the Valiant Five, petition the Privy Council. The council rules that women are persons under the law.	Britain announces that it will begin a series of roundtable discussions with the goal of eventual Indian dominion status.
Nov.	The League begins a conference on the treatment of foreign nationals. The conference continues into December....The Bank of International Settlements begins operations in Switzerland. The BIS is responsible for collecting and distributing reparations.	Allied troops complete troop withdrawals from the Rhineland.	Britain recognizes Nadir Khan.	A 7.2 submarine earthquake off Newfoundland in the Grand Banks breaks 12 transatlantic cables. It triggers a tsunami that kills 28 on the Burin Peninsula coast.	To economize and better reflect its pacifism, Australia ends compulsory military service.
Dec.	The League holds its third conference on easing trade and import restrictions.	Yugoslavia outlaws Slovenian Sokol clubs....Turkey and the Soviet Union sign a neutrality agreement....Germany holds a referendum on the Young Plan. German acceptance of the plan is a blow to nationalists.	France's parliament votes to continue funding troops in Syria, frustrating those who seek an end to French activity in the mandate.	Haiti remains unstable. The United States sends additional troops.	At Lahore's All India Congress, nationalists demand independence....Russia and China sign an agreement that ends their dispute over the Chinese Eastern Railway.

A	B	C	D	E
Includes developments that affect more than one world region, international organizations and important meetings of world leaders.	Includes all domestic and regional developments in Europe, including the Soviet Union.	Includes all domestic and regional developments in Africa and the Middle East.	Includes all domestic and regional developments in Latin America, the Caribbean, and Canada.	Includes all domestic and regional developments in Asian and Pacific nations (and colonies).

U.S. Politics & Social Issues	U.S. Foreign Policy & Affairs, Defense	U.S. Economy & Environment	Science, Technology & Nature	Culture, Leisure & Lifestyle	
The Alien Train starts collecting illegal aliens in Seattle and adds more as it moves east, finally bringing 250 to New York for deportation.	MacDonald meets with Hoover. Afterward, Britain issues a call for a meeting in 1930 of Japan, France, Italy, the United States and Britain to discuss disarmament.	With the opening of a store in Milford, DE, J.C. Penney becomes the first chain with stores in all 48 states....The stock market collapses. On Black Thursday, 13 million shares sell. On Black Tuesday, five days later, a 16-million-share sell off seems to be the bottom of the market.		*Look Homeward, Angel* by Thomas Wolfe is released.	Oct.
The Senate censures Sen. Hiram Bingham for having a lobbyist on his payroll...Albert Fall fails to overturn his conviction in Teapot Dome.	The Ambassador Bridge opens, linking Windsor, Ont., and Detroit, MI. The bridge will come to carry the largest trade volume of any U.S. border crossing.	The stock market reaches bottom. The collapse has erased $30 billion in value.	Vladimir Zworykin of RCA demonstrates cathode ray tube television technology that offers 60 lines....Richard Byrd, Bernt Balchen, A.C. McKinley and Harold June fly over the South Pole. They are the first to do so.	Count Basie records *Blue Devil Blues* as pianist for Walter Page's Blue Devils. The recording for Kansas City's Vocalion Records is the first of Basie's career.	Nov.
Hoover authorizes 19 new veterans hospitals with over 4,000 beds.	The United States joins the World Court after World Court members accept U.S. conditions.	Hoover announces that the worst of the crash is over and that the American people have confidence in the economy.		Among the artists featured at the opening of New York's Museum of Modern Art are Cezanne, Van Gogh, Seurat, and Gauguin....On New Year's Eve, Guy Lombardo plays *Auld Lang Syne*. It is the first time for this perennial. A Lombardo recording continues to be the first song at the Times Square celebration.	Dec.

	World Affairs	Europe	Africa & The Middle East	The Americas	Asia & The Pacific
Jan. 1		King George's health is reported to have slightly improved....German President Von Hindenburg and Chancellor Mueller tell foreign diplomats that Germany should be freed from foreign occupation in the Rhineland provinces.	After three years in power, the Labor Party is defeated in the elections for the Municipal Council of Tel Aviv....Ibn Saud, King of Hedjaz and Nejd, expresses his wish to abdicate, but reconsiders his decision when delegations of prominent chieftains ask him to remain king.	Data on the last months of 1928 show better economic conditions for Puerto Rican workers, thus tempering the destructive effects of the tragic September 1928 storm. ...Waiting for instructions from his government, the Bolivian Envoy refuses to sign the peace protocols with Paraguay devised by the special committee of the Pan-American Conference on Conciliation and Arbitration....General José Maria Moncada is inaugurated president of Nicaragua.	The Philippines announce a delegation to Washington to oppose the Sugar Bill which is deemed as damaging the nation's agriculture....Peace negotiations begin in Afghanistan between King Amanullah and the rebels.
Jan. 2	Radio messages from world leaders wish success to Herbert Hoover in the new year when he will become the new U.S. president.	King Alexander of Yugoslavia accepts the resignation of Prime Minister Koroshetz over the Serbo-Croatian crisis.			Chinese President Chiang Kai-shek announces his drastic plan to cut the army by two-thirds.
Jan. 3		The German Industrial Federation for Foreign Trade demands that Allied governments reconsider their policy on German reparations payments....Romania is allowed to enter Soviet-Polish negotiation for their antiwar pact.			
Jan. 4		Strong blizzards sweeps through France, killing 11 people and disrupting communications.... Slovak leader Tuka is arrested in Czechoslovakia on charges of high treason.		In his last speech before his term expires, Honduran President Paz Barahona thanks the United States for their moral support during the civil war.	
Jan. 5		King Alexander I of Yugoslavia suspends the Constitution and dissolves the Parliament, making its kingdom a dictatorship under the premiership of General Zhivkovich....The persistence of cold weather in France causes more deaths.		Delegates at the Pan American Conference in Washington, DC sign the General Act of Inter-American Arbitration. The act calls for conciliation and arbitration of disputes in the Western Hemisphere.	Chinese President Chiang Kai-shek appeals to the China Famine Relief to raise money to avoid the deaths of thousands Chinese from starvation.
Jan. 6		Grand Duke Nicholas of Russia, a second cousin to the last Czar and possible heir to the throne, dies in his exile at Antibes....Economic data about 1928 show a steady rise in Soviet industrial production while agricultural production makes only slight improvements.	A number of ancient chambers used as tombs for Jewish Kings are discovered during excavations in Jerusalem.		
Jan. 7	The Allied Reparations Commission announces it will appoint an international committee of experts to draw up a final settlement of the reparations problem....The League of Nations continues to select members for its commission on the revision of the statutes of the World Court. A revision of the statutes would encourage the United States to join the court.	Croats welcome King Alexander's decision to suspend the Constitution and express hopes that the King's Cabinet will put an end to the country's racial tensions.		The Calbuco volcano erupts in Chile causing panic and damages in the surrounding region.	The Japanese government expresses fears that American reservations against the antiwar Kellogg Pact may strengthen opposition to the treaty in Japan on patriotic grounds....Afghan rebels shell the capital Kabul in renewed fighting.

A	B	C	D	E
Includes developments that affect more than one world region, international organizations and important meetings of world leaders.	Includes all domestic and regional developments in Europe, including the Soviet Union.	Includes all domestic and regional developments in Africa and the Middle East.	Includes all domestic and regional developments in Latin America, the Caribbean, and Canada.	Includes all domestic and regional developments in Asian and Pacific nations (and colonies).

U.S. Politics & Social Issues	U.S. Foreign Policy & Affairs, Defense	U.S. Economy & Environment	Science, Technology & Nature	Culture, Leisure & Lifestyle	
Franklin Roosevelt is inaugurated governor of New York, promising "a new era of good feeling" in his address....George U. Harvey is inaugurated Borough President of Queens. He is the first Republican in that post since the consolidation of Queens within the greater city....Governor Bilbo of Mississippi says he has neither the time nor the money for lynching enquiries.	S. Parker Gilbert, Agent General for Reparations Payments, denies Germany reductions in war reparations payments, saying that the country's economic conditions allows to meet its obligations.		Henry Fairfield Osborn, the President of the American Association for the Advancement of Science, claims that the discovery of the transparency of space does not modify the concept of God....The American Association of University Professors closes its fiftieth annual meeting announcing it will fight the spread of anti-evolution legislation and other attempts to limit the freedom of teaching in science.	John D. Rockefeller and his family announce a month's holiday in Egypt.	Jan. 1
William Randolph Hearst announces a $25,000 prize for the best plan to repeal the Eighteenth Amendment and suggest a more liberal measure to obtain temperance.	The U.S. Senate agrees to give precedence to the discussion of the Kellogg antiwar pact.	The American stock market starts the New Year making large gains. Professionals expect the year 1929 to be one of memorable record for the market....The Ford Motor Company Plant in Detroit starts to recruit 30,000 more workers to increase its production by 20 percent.	The United States and Canada reach an agreement for a joint preservation of Niagara Falls....A violent storm on the Hondo coast in Japan kills almost 60 people and destroys several hundred houses.	The painter Archibald Motley Jr. and the poet Claude MacKay are among the twelve African-Americans to receive the Harmon Foundation's Awards for outstanding creative work in the arts, education, religion and business done by African Americans.	Jan. 2
William S. Paley becomes CBS president....The Court of Appeals declares speakeasies "public nuisances," thus allowing local authorities to prosecute them on that ground.	Senator Borah, Chairman of the Senate Committee on Foreign Relations, backs the multilateral antiwar treaty, arguing that it does not threaten neither American security nor the Monroe Doctrine....General Italo Balbo, Italian Undersecretary for Aviation, is officially received by New York Mayor Walker. Antifascist demonstrators are dispersed from an impressive display of police forces.	The gross public debt is cut by more than $700 million in a year.		Fox Theaters Corporation announces its plan to build a skyscraper of 52 stories on Broadway which should include offices and a motion picture theater....The U.S. Army plane Question Mark shatters the world's record for sustained flight by refueling....The Laura Spelman Rockefeller Foundation merges into the Rockefeller Foundation, constituting the largest single philanthropic organization.	Jan. 3
	During a four-hour long debate, senators question Borah, Chairman of the Senate Committee on Foreign Relations, on the multilateral antiwar treaty, fearing that it may contradict the Monroe Doctrine and interfere with the American right to protect citizens and properties in foreign countries.	The U.S. Treasury announces it will pay $26 million to the United States Steel Corporation as a settlement for taxes wrongly collected from it in 1917....The merger between Radio Corporation of America and the Victor Talking Machine Company is approved by the directors of the two companies.		Data about 1928 show that the European motion picture bloc, formed to counter Hollywood dominance on European markets, has succeeded to reduce the number of American films in Europe.	Jan. 4
Chicago's business, financial and industrial interests suggest that the city should be headed by James O'Leary, a banker and former President of the U.S. Chamber of Commerce. This is seen as a solution to the political and economic chaos that plague the city.		The Democrats attack Secretary of the Treasury Andrew Mellon for the huge tax refunds given to several corporations and demand a Congressional investigation.	Violent blizzards in the west and southwest regions of the United States cause five deaths.	William Lloyd Evans, professor of Chemistry at Ohio State University wins the Nichols medal for his research on the chemistry of carbohydrates.	Jan. 5
Eight gunmen raid the Fox Folly Theater in New York, holding up 2,500 people.		New York Governor Franklin Roosevelt creates an informal commission to investigate the state's agricultural problems....A survey of the Employment Service predicts a general growth in industry, agriculture and employment for 1929.	A strong gale sweeps over New York City and the nearby areas, delaying liners.	The sports promoter George L. Rickard dies at a hospital in Miami Beach....William Fox announces a plan to build office buildings with incorporated movie houses in all major American cities.	Jan. 6
President-elect Herbert Hoover consults with several Republican politicians for the formation of his future cabinet.	Opposition to the ratification of the Kellogg antiwar treaty in the U.S. Senate diminishes as the debate unfolds.		An intense cold wave affects the East, South and Middle West of the United States, with temperatures below zero in many cities.	The adventure strip of Tarzan appears for the first time....The U.S. Army plane Question Mark ends its record-breaking flight after 150 hours, 40 minutes and 15 seconds.	Jan. 7

F	G	H	I	J
Includes campaigns, elections, federal-state relations, civil rights and liberties, crime, the judiciary, education, healthcare, poverty, urban affairs, and population.	Includes formation and debate of U.S. foreign and defense policies, veterans affairs, and defense spending. (Relations with specific foreign countries are usually found under the region concerned.)	Includes business, labor, agriculture, taxation, transportation, consumer affairs, monetary and fiscal policy, natural resources, pollution and industrial accidents.	Includes worldwide scientific, medical and technological developments, natural phenomena, U.S. weather and natural disasters.	Includes the arts, religion, scholarship, communications media, sports, entertainment, fashions, fads, and social life.

	World Affairs	Europe	Africa & The Middle East	The Americas	Asia & The Pacific
Jan. 8	The Salvation Army opens its first international meeting to decide the Army's leadership and the control of its worldwide properties.	The French Parliament resumes its session in a climate of uncertainty about the future of the government led by Poincaré....The Hungarian and Turkish governments sign a neutrality and arbitration treaty.... The British William Francis Hare, Viscount of Ennismore, renounces his wealth and his title because of his Socialist creed.		Canada rejects most of the measures proposed by the United States for a joint cooperation to halt the smuggling of liquor....Nicaraguan President José Maria Moncada creates a new force, directed by General Feland, to complete the cleaning of the northern part of the country from bandits.	The last American marines stationed at Tientsin, China, for emergency service began preparations to return home.
Jan. 9	General Bramwell Booth, leader of the Salvation Army, tells the Army's international meeting that he has appointed a committee of five people to replace him as General until his health recovers.	Michael MacWhite becomes the new Irish Free State Minister at Washington....The new Yugoslav regime warns country's officials that any attempt to serve any party interest will be prosecuted.			A. H. F. Edwardes resigns as Chief of Customs in China. The Nationalist government appoints F.W. Maze as his successor....Three thousand angry Japanese peasants riot in Gifu, northeast of Kyoto, to protest against the deviation of water supplies from their rice fields.
Jan. 10	The High Council of the Salvation Army asks General Bramwell Booth to resign as world leader.	The European Allied governments name their representatives on the international commission for German war reparations....Yugoslav premier General Zhivkovich says that democracy has only been temporarily suspended, not abolished indefinitely....Tytus Filipowitz is appointed Polish ambassador in Washington.	Joint excavations in Ur by the University of Pennsylvania and the British Museum uncover relics of burial rites of Sumerian kings.		Sino-Japanese negotiations reach a deadlock on the issues of the Japanese occupation of Shantung and of the provisional tariff which the Chinese governments intends to adopt.
Jan. 11		French Prime Minister Poincaré wins the confidence vote by 75 votes, a larger majority than it was expected....All Yugoslav labor unions are ordered to suspend their activities.		Colonel Charles A. Lindbergh becomes technical adviser to the Pan-American Airways and announces the extension of the airmail service as far as the Panama Canal.	Manchurian ruler Yang Yu-ting is arrested and executed by Chinese forces for his opposition to the union with Nanking....King Amanullah of Afghanistan stops his plan of Western reforms and yields to the rebels' requests.
Jan. 12		Gudrun Carlson is appointed American Trade Commisioner at Oslo, Norway....Albert Voegler, Germany's second main delegate for the Reparations Committee, criticizes the report of S. Parker Gilbert, Agent General for Reparations Payments, according to which Germany's economic situation allows the country to meet its reparations payments in full....Turkey's Poet Laureate Abdul Hak Hamid is elected Deputy.		The Chilean government notifies the United States of its intention to adhere to Kellogg's multilateral treaty against war.	Japanese officials fear that Manchurian ruler Yang Yu-ting's execution may precipitate trouble in the region and change the situation for the worse for Japan....Following the mutiny of his army, King Amanullah of Afghanistan surrenders power to a council of 50 high officials.
Jan. 13		General Jacob A. Slaschoff, former leader of the White Army during the Russian civil war, is killed in his Moscow apartment.			T. V. Soong, the Finance Minister of the Chinese Nationalist Government, urges the centralization of financial resource to prevent the bankruptcy and disintegration of the federation.
Jan. 14		Negotiators of the Italian government and the Vatican reach a territorial and financial agreement to settle the dispute between the Pope and the Italian state since the annexation of Rome....King Oscar of Norway announces the wedding of Crown Prince Olaf and Princess Martha of Sweden....Jan Ciechanowski, Polish Minister to the United States, resigns.	In spite of rumors about his resignation, King Ibn Saud of Hedjaz remains in a strong position and threatens the peace of the Middle East region.		King Amanullah of Afghanistan abdicates in favor of his older brother Sirdar Inayatullah....A disastrous earthquake takes place in the Chinese region of Suiyuan, north of Peking.

A	B	C	D	E
Includes developments that affect more than one world region, international organizations and important meetings of world leaders.	Includes all domestic and regional developments in Europe, including the Soviet Union.	Includes all domestic and regional developments in Africa and the Middle East.	Includes all domestic and regional developments in Latin America, the Caribbean, and Canada.	Includes all domestic and regional developments in Asian and Pacific nations (and colonies).

U.S. Politics & Social Issues	U.S. Foreign Policy & Affairs, Defense	U.S. Economy & Environment	Science, Technology & Nature	Culture, Leisure & Lifestyle	
After a political struggle of more than one year, the House of Representatives sustains the right of James M. Beck to a seat as representative of the First District of Pennsylvania....President-Elect H. Hoover continues consultations in Washington for the formation of his future cabinet....Opponents to Oklahoma Governor Henry S. Johnston gain key posts in the state legislature at its first meeting, paving the way for a wide investigation in the state administration.			The Hamburg-American Line plans the building of a liner which will travel at a speed of more than 30 knots.	An rare books and manuscripts auction at Jerome Kern's bookshop in New York marks a new high record for a single session of a book sale....The Carnegie Corporation sets aside funds to continue its scholarships for future fine arts teachers during 1929 and 1930.	Jan. 8
President-elect Hoover consults with President Calvin Coolidge and Secretary of State Kellogg over the selection of his cabinet....The LaFollette wing of the Republican Party loses control of the Wisconsin State Legislature.	The House of Representatives passes an amendment prohibiting the use of wartime Liberty motors in new airplanes for the army.	Henry Ford publishes the book *My Philosophy of Industry* which praises the introduction of machineries in all productive fields and in everyday life....Farmers' organizations urge the increase of tariffs on vegetable oils and fats up to 100 percent.	The Fokker aviation firm plans a nonstop round-the-world flight with refueling in the air....Biologist Albert Fischer claims that cancerous cells are the primary agents of the spread of the disease.	A new record is set at Jerome Kern's book auction: a copy of Henry Fielding's *Tom Jones* is sold for $29,000....Pope Pius appoints the bishops of Rochester and Sacramento dioceses.	Jan. 9
The House of Representatives fails to reach a vote on the Fenn bill which is designed to reapportion its membership.	Senators fail to agree on a time to vote on the Kellogg antiwar treaty.	A delegation of the National Grange urges President-elect Hoover to call for an extra congressional session for a discussion of new farm legislation....John D. Rockefeller begins his fight to remove Colonel Robert Stewart from the chairmanship of the Standard Oil Company of Indiana....William C. Durant announces his retirement from active management of the Durant Motors.			Jan. 10
Prohibition agents seize thousands of gallons of liquer in California.... The House of Representatives passes the Fenn bill for its reapportionment, ending a prolonged political battle....The Senate Appropriations Committee recommends an increase of $25 million for the enforcement of prohibition measures.		An American Army transport plane crashes near Harrisburg killing seven people....The liner President Adams grounds on a reef outside the entrance of the Panama Canal. No one is hurt....Colonel Robert Stewart, chairman of the Standard Oil Company of Indiana, appeals to the employees to re-elect him countering John D. Rockefeller's attempts to oust him.	Albert Einstein states that he has expanded his theory of relativity to unite the laws of field of gravitation and electromagnetism.	Eight hundred copies of Radclyffe Hall's lesbian novel *The Well of Loneliness* are seized by New York police.	Jan. 11
The police use tear gas bombs to end a mutiny in the Philadelphia County Prison at Holmesburg....Efforts to pass a farm relief bill in the remaining weeks of the Congress session fail, so an extra session is now inevitable....Secretary of the Treasury Andrew Mellon says he cannot use the $25 million increase in the funds for the enforcement of prohibition laws passed by the Senate Appropriations Committee....Three men are arrested in Florida in an investigation of alleged threats against President-elect Hoover.		Colonel Robert Stewart, chairman of the Standard Oil Company of Indiana, says he has the full confidence of the employees and the stockholders of the company, in spite of John D. Rockefeller's campaign to oust him....Midwest Senators successfully prevent the survey of the proposed Nicaragua Canal and the enlargement of the Panama Canal. They claim that the inland waterway system should have the priority.	A particularly strong cold wave from the Rocky Mountains hits the middle west regions.		Jan. 12
The legendary frontiersman Wyatt Earp dies in Los Angeles....Prisoners continue to demonstrate in the Philadelphia County Prison at Holmesburg shouting for food.	Senators Moses. Reed and Bingham critical of the multilateral Kellogg's antiwar treaty announce harsh opposition to its ratification.	The Electrical Contractors' Association grants a five-day week and a 10 percent increase to the Electrical Workers Union.		Painter and sculptor Emil Fuchs commits suicide in his New York apartment.	Jan. 13
President-elect Hoover the Speaker of the House of Representatives Longworth discuss the arrangements for an extra session of Congress.	The Senate continues to debate Kellogg's antiwar multilateral pact without reaching an agreement for its ratification.	President Calvin Coolidge issues an executive order declaring Oakland an official port of entry....The United States Supreme Court rules against the Chicago Sanitary District's right to divert 85,000 cubic feet of water per second from Lake Michigan for drainage and navigation.	The north and a large section of the United States suffer from severe cold.	American Broadway impresario Florenz Ziegfeld considers the project to build a London theater for his productions.	Jan. 14

F	G	H	I	J
Includes campaigns, elections, federal-state relations, civil rights and liberties, crime, the judiciary, education, healthcare, poverty, urban affairs, and population.	*Includes formation and debate of U.S. foreign and defense policies, veterans affairs, and defense spending. (Relations with specific foreign countries are usually found under the region concerned.)*	*Includes business, labor, agriculture, taxation, transportation, consumer affairs, monetary and fiscal policy, natural resources, pollution and industrial accidents.*	*Includes worldwide scientific, medical and technological developments, natural phenomena, U.S. weather and natural disasters.*	*Includes the arts, religion, scholarship, communications media, sports, entertainment, fashions, fads, and social life.*

	World Affairs	Europe	Africa & The Middle East	The Americas	Asia & The Pacific
Jan. 15	General Bramwell Booth refuses to retire as the leader of the Salvation Army.	Vladimir Matchek, leader of the Croatian Peasant Party, voices reservations against the new Yugoslavian regime.		Nicaraguan President Moncada states that he will send troops in the northern part of the country to counter the actions of General Augusto Sandino....U.S. Secretary of State Kellogg instructs all consuls in Mexico to impose more strict requirements for the examination of prospective immigrants.	Shinwaris rebels continue to fight in the surroundings of Kabul, refusing to recognize the new Afghan King.
Jan. 16	The Council of the Salvation Army votes General Bramwell Booth unfit to remain leader with a large majority of 55 to eight....The governments of the six countries involved in the war reparations committee (U. K., France, Germany, Belgium, Japan and Italy) approve the American proposal to appoint J. P. Morgan and Owen Young as U.S. representatives on the committee.	In spite of having suspended Constitutional rights, King Alexander of Yugoslavia states that he is working to create a free and democratic country....European nations express their satisfaction for the ratification of the American Senate of Kellogg's antiwar treaty....Polish Foreign Minister August Zaleski expresses distrust of Germany because of its intense propaganda for a revision of the eastern frontiers.		General Feland will direct operations against rebel forces in Northern Nicaragua. His force will be formed by marines, Nicaraguan National Guards and volunteers. The government of Honduras denies that the country is on the brink of a rebellion and confirms that President-elect Colindres will take office on February 1 as planned.	The Minister of War of the Chinese Nationalist government Feng Yu-hsiang suggests that China should have a less aggressive attitude against the Japanese so that a settlement between the two countries can be reached.
Jan. 17		A violent snowstorm affects many European nations reaching as far south as Rome....The Slovak's People Party condemns the arrest of Slovak patriot Bela Tuka.	The British Hilton-Young Commission on Africa recommends a tighter union between the British colonies in East and Central Africa.	A strong earthquake shatters the city of Cumana in Venezuela....Paraguay declares it is ready to accept the Bolivian offer to settle the Chaco dispute in the World Court.	Rebel leader Bacha Sakao overthrows Afghan King Sirdar Inayatullah.
Jan. 18		Soviet dictator Stalin bans his political adversary Trotsky from the Politburo.		In Guatemala, General Ubico revolts against the central governments and captures two towns in the northwest region of the country.	Sirdar Inayatullah, deposed Afghan King, is taken by a British plane and brought to Peshawur, in British India....The Chinese conference on disbandment accepts Premier Chiang Kai-shek's proposal of drastically reducing the Chinese Nationalist Army....China and Japan announce they have reached an agreement in their tariff negotiation.
Jan. 19	The League of Nations considers a revision of the permanent and non-permanent seats in its Council in favor of making all seats elective.	King Alexander of Yugoslavia signs a decree reorganizing the law courts and the judiciary system in view of a tighter union of the country....A Royalist demonstration in Paris quickly becomes a riot.		The last detachment of marines who supervised the November elections in Nicaragua begin their journey back to the United States....Changes in the regulations of the Belem prison in Mexico cause a riot by prisoners....As the revolt grows in Guatemala, martial law is declared throughout the country.	The Western Afghan tribe of the Surianis rebels against the officials in the district and kills all of them except for the governor.
Jan. 20	It is announced that the session of the Experts' Committee on reparations payments will officially discuss only German debts to the Allies. The issue of the Allies' debts to the United States will not be discussed.	M. Matchek, leader of the Croat Peasant Party, criticizes the composition of the new Yugoslav cabinet for the presence of Serbian supremacists.		Government forces successfully regain the towns occupied by rebels in Northern Guatemala....Puerto Rico political leaders will ask the future Hoover administration an elective governor.	
Jan. 21		King Victor Emmanuel of Italy sings two decrees presented by Premier Mussolini for the dissolution of the Chamber of Deputies and the establishment of the Grand Council of Fascism.	Arab raiders kill Rev. Henry A. Bilkerd during an ambush against an American party in Iraq....The Iraqi Government resigns in protest against Great Britain, breaking the negotiations between the two countries for a military agreement.	Guatemala government reports that state forces have regained all the territories previously held by rebels and have thus ended the revolt....Three American marines die in a clash with Nicaraguan rebels.	The Krakatoa volcano in Indonesia shows increased activity with eruptions becoming increasingly violent....Japanese Premier and Foreign Minister Baron Tanaka hopes to maintain friendly relations with the United States and China, in spite of the American exclusion of Japanese immigrants and Chinese interests in Manchuria.

A	B	C	D	E
Includes developments that affect more than one world region, international organizations and important meetings of world leaders.	Includes all domestic and regional developments in Europe, including the Soviet Union.	Includes all domestic and regional developments in Africa and the Middle East.	Includes all domestic and regional developments in Latin America, the Caribbean, and Canada.	Includes all domestic and regional developments in Asian and Pacific nations (and colonies).

U.S. Politics & Social Issues	U.S. Foreign Policy & Affairs, Defense	U.S. Economy & Environment	Science, Technology & Nature	Culture, Leisure & Lifestyle	
Secretary of the Treasury Andrew Mellon says that before the extra $25 million approved by the Senate Appropriations Committee can be spent wisely a survey of needs is necessary.	The U.S. Senate ratifies Kellogg's antiwar Pact, also known as the Pact of Paris....The crew of the U.S.S. *Mallard*, a navy mine sweeper and rescue vessel, is detained on the ship after the cut of the combination hawser and the communication cable securing the submarine to the mother ship.	The fight between John D. Rockefeller, Jr. and Colonel Robert Stewart over the control of the Standard Oil Company of Indiana provokes a dramatic increase in the stock value of the company....The Marble Industry Employers' Association denies the Marble Helpers' Union the five-day week and a $2 rise per day.		The Metropolitan Museum receives a collection of 200 important paintings from the will of Mrs Louisine W. Havemeyer, the widow of Henry O. Havemeyer, president and one of the founders of the American Sugar Refining Company.	Jan. 15
President-elect Hoover announces the appointment of a non-partisan commission to investigate the prohibition enforcement within a short time after he assumes office.... Defeated Democratic presidential candidate Alfred E. Smith broadcasts a radio appeal to raise $1.5 million to cover the party deficit.	Senators begin the discussion of a bill authorizing the construction of 15 new cruisers an airplane carrier.	The Amagansett Flier, a Long Island express train, kills four people at an unguarded crossing....Charles M. Schwab, one of the leading American industrialists, places his stock-holdings in the hands of trustees.	Richard Byrd explores 1,200 miles of unknown Antarctic land during a flight of an hour an twenty minutes.		Jan. 16
W. Griffen Gribbel, the shell-shocked son of a prominent Philadelphia financier, kills a police inspector and seriously wounds his chauffeur....Democratic Party militants express their support of Alfred E. Smith's appeal to pay the party deficit....Democratic Senator Harris attacks Secretary of the Treasury Mellon for his refusal to allocate an extra $25 million to the enforcement of prohibition laws.	During an impressive ceremony at the White House, President Coolidge signs the Kellogg antiwar treaty (Pact of Paris).	John D. Rockefeller, Sr., announces his support to his son's battle to oust Colonel Robert Stewart as the Chairman of the Standard Oil Company of Indiana....Two passenger trains and a freight train crash on the Pennsylvania Railroad causing the death of four trainmen.	British scientist A.S. Eddington offers a new view of the electron as a convenient hypothesis with no real existence.	The first *Popeye* character appears in a cartoon strip....The steamer *Mauretania* breaks its own record for a transatlantic crossing, improving it by 2 hours and 2 minutes.... Chamber Syndacate, the official body of the French film industry, sends a commission to the United States to study the motion picture industry.	Jan. 17
Governor of Oklahoma Henry S. Johnston is impeached by the House of Representatives on charges of corruption....More than 3,000 letters of donations are sent to the headquarters of the Democratic Party in response to the plea of Alfred E. Smith....Representative Box of Texas announces his resignation from Democratic Party whip at the end of the current Congress.	Owen D. Young and J.P. Morgan informally accept their appointment to the international commission on German war reparations.		More than a hundred journalists and publishing houses pressure scientist Albert Elnstein to give more details about his new enlargement of the relativity theory....A tornado in the Midwest regions causes the death of 10 people and injures about 30.		Jan. 18
President-elect Hoover continues to work on his future cabinet.... Leaders of the prohibitionist front challenge Secretary of the Treasury Andrew Mellon's decision not to use the extra $25 million for the enforcement of prohibition set aside by the Senate Appropriations Committee.	Owen D. Young and J.P. Morgan are officially appointed to the international committee on German reparations.	The Undersecretary to the Treasury Ogden Mills defends the Treasury policy on tax refunds....Acadia National Park, ME, is established.	"Eric Robot," a British mechanical man, makes its American debut in New York.		Jan. 19
Republican leaders urge President-elect Hoover to appoint Dwight W. Morrow to the post of Secretary of State in his future cabinet.	The bill authorizing the construction of 15 new cruisers an airplane carrier suffers from filibuster in the Senate.	The Dollar Steamship liner *President Garfield* runs aground on the Bahama reef. All the passengers are put on board of the Muson liner Pan America....Two officers and three crew members of the destroyer Whitney drown after a collision the Canal tug Mariner in Panama canal.		New York Nationals beat the Brooklyn Wanderers, winning the final of the American Soccer League.	Jan. 20
The Senate confirms Roy O. West Secretary of the Interior with a vote of 53 to 27....Secretary of the Treasury Andrew Mellon argues that the extra $25 million for the enforcement of prohibition set aside by the Senate Appropriations Committee would do more harm than good.	Republican Senators agree on a plan to prioritize the cruisers bill against filibustering.	Democrat Senator Bruce sends the Ways and Means Committee and the Finance Committee a proposal for the reform of the Tariff Commission rejecting flexible tariff provisions.			Jan. 21

F	G	H	I	J
Includes campaigns, elections, federal-state relations, civil rights and liberties, crime, the judiciary, education, healthcare, poverty, urban affairs, and population.	*Includes formation and debate of U.S. foreign and defense policies, veterans affairs, and defense spending. (Relations with specific foreign countries are usually found under the region concerned.)*	*Includes business, labor, agriculture, taxation, transportation, consumer affairs, monetary and fiscal policy, natural resources, pollution and industrial accidents.*	*Includes worldwide scientific, medical and technological developments, natural phenomena, U.S. weather and natural disasters.*	*Includes the arts, religion, scholarship, communications media, sports, entertainment, fashions, fads, and social life.*

	World Affairs	Europe	Africa & The Middle East	The Americas	Asia & The Pacific
Jan. 22		Leon Pollier, chairman of the board of directors of the French Sugar Company, is arrested in Paris for fraud against the government....A fire breaks out at the Lenin Institute in Moscow on the fifth anniversary of Lenin's death. It is quickly extinguished so that Lenin's manuscripts are saved....The health of King George improves and the British King is now able to eat solid food....Four hundred houses are destroyed because of a fire in the European sector of Constantinople.	An ancient synagogue is discovered north of Jerusalem.	During the elections for State and local offices, 44 people are killed in the Mexican state of Hidalgo.	Former Afghani King Inayatullah leaves Peshawur, in British India to join his brother in Kandahar and resume fighting for their kingdom....Japanese Premier and Foreign Minister Baron Tanaka opens the session of the Japanese Diet (parliament).
Jan. 23	The Vatican confers the knighthood of Malta to 22 Americans....The Soviet Union and the Imam of Yemen sign a treaty of friendship and commerce.	The Soviet police arrests 150 sympathizers of Leon Trotsky on suspicion of plotting against the official government....The Italian government refuses to renew the Treaty of Friendship with Yugoslavia.	Jews and Muslims disagree in Palestine over mutual claims of ownership of Rachel's tomb, a holy site for both faiths.		2,000 tribesmen welcome the return of deposed King Inayatullah to the Afghan town of Kanhahar.
Jan. 24		French Premier Poincaré rebukes Alsatian deputies for their stance on the region's independence....The Reichstag resumes its session for the examination of the budget....All remaining political parties in Yugoslavia are dissolved. Their archives and funds are confiscated.	The Italian government definitely ends the Senussi rebellion in Libya and unites the provinces of Tripoli and Cyrenaica under a single colonial government.		
Jan. 25		Italian Premier Benito Mussolini officially thanks the American government for the rescue of the crew of the steamship Florida. The Italian Council of Ministers also announces the building of 13 new warships....Germany and Soviet Russia sign a treaty to submit all disputes between them to a joint commission.		Latin American diplomats are concerned over the large Bolivian purchases of weapons in Europe. They fear this may lead to a recrudescence of the conflict with Paraguay.	Three thousand Shantung soldiers at Lungkow mutiny, plunging the city in a state of terror for several hours....Japan and China resume negotiations at Naking to settle the Sino-Japanese crisis due to the Japanese occupation of the Shantung region....Hostility against the new Afghan King Bacha Sakao spreads through the country.
Jan. 26		British Foreign Minister Sir Austen Chamberlain expresses his favorable opinion to naval parity between the United Kingdom. and the United States...Important public works begin in Tirana, Albania, in preparation for the coronation of King Zog set for April....The heaviest snowstorm in 30 years causes damages all over central and eastern Europe.	Raids by Wahabis are reported along the Kuwaiti frontier. These are part of the strategy of Wahabi King Ibn Saud to seek a pretext for war with neighboring countries.		Chinese military chiefs agree to let the central government to control all the finances of the armies of the country.
Jan. 27		The deposed German Kaiser celebrates his seventieth birthday with a grand display of wealth....The Greek Parliament orders an investigation into the crimes of former dictator General Theodore Pangalos and three of his ministers.			Afghan King Bacha Sakao forms a government under the premiership of Kabir ed Din, stepbrother of King Amanullah.
Jan. 28		British Foreign Secretary Sir Austen Chamberlain declares that the British government intends to ratify the Kellogg's antiwar treaty.		The selection for thePan American Commission of Inquiry for the Chaco dispute is completed.	Former Afghan King Amanullah rescinds his act of abdication after appeals from Afghans to resume supreme power in the country....A the Sino-Japanese conference to discuss the withdrawal of Japanese forces from the Shantung region, Japan refuses to commit to a precise date....Philippine political leaders ask the United States to maintain the same tariff or grant independence to their country.

A	B	C	D	E
Includes developments that affect more than one world region, international organizations and important meetings of world leaders.	Includes all domestic and regional developments in Europe, including the Soviet Union.	Includes all domestic and regional developments in Africa and the Middle East.	Includes all domestic and regional developments in Latin America, the Caribbean, and Canada.	Includes all domestic and regional developments in Asian and Pacific nations (and colonies).

U.S. Politics & Social Issues	U.S. Foreign Policy & Affairs, Defense	U.S. Economy & Environment	Science, Technology & Nature	Culture, Leisure & Lifestyle	
President-elect Hoover visits Miami greeted by a large crowd....The radio plea of former presidential candidate Alfred E. Smith brings $100,000 worth of donations to the Democratic Party....The Senate approves the Harris amendment to give an extra $24 million for the enforcement of prohibition to be spent at the President's discretion....The House committee appointed to investigate the country's penal system suggests the building of more federal prisons and criticizes the federal prisons system.	The filibuster against the cruiser bill ends in the Senate....Forty thousand men of the Navy and land forces of the Army begin war games operations in the Panama Canal.	President Coolidge believes he will leave a small surplus to President-elect Hoover, thus covering the entire state deficit....Seventeen people are killed and fourteen injured in a collision between a Lake Shore electric express car and a Greyhound Company bus near Bellevue, Ohio....The American Farm Bureau Federation asks the abrogation of the reciprocal trade agreement between Cuba and the United States and imposition of duties on Cuban sugar.		Columbia University leases its properties between Fifth and Sixth Avenues in New York to John D. Rockefeller, Jr. for the establishment of its monumental center.	Jan. 22
Dwight W. Morrow announces that he will remain Ambassador to Mexico and will not become Secretary of State in the future Hoover administration....The Harris amendment to give an extra $24 million for the enforcement of prohibition goes to the examination of the House of Representatives.	The cruiser bill is given priority over all other bills in the Senate.	The 32 crew members of the sinking Italian freight *Florida* are rescued off Virginia Capes by the U.S. steamship *America*.	The new British Fairey monoplane Question Mark is shown to the public for the first time.		Jan. 23
Republican leaders of the House of Representatives predict that the extra funds for the enforcement of prohibition set aside by the Senate will encounter more opposition in the House.		After a lapse of five years, Bethlehem Steel Corporation resumes payment of dividends to its stockholders....Colonel Robert Stewart issues his first official statement in the battle with John D. Rockefeller Jr for the Standard Oil Company of Indiana saying that he, not Rockefeller, was responsible for the dramatic expansion of the company.	Einstein's new electro-gravitational theory reduces all physics to one law.		Jan. 24
	President Coolidge speaks against including an amendment by Senator Borah to the cruiser bill to introduce an international agreement on maritime law in case of war....Major Lester Gardner, president of the Aeronautical Chamber of Commerce, praises President Coolidge for his policies which have favored the expansion of the aviation sector.	Members of the New York Stock Exchange are asked to create 275 additional seats to enlarge the brokerage personnel....The Stock Exchange soars, with stocks realizing net gains up to 16 points.			Jan. 25
Democratic leaders express their faith to be able to obtain the approval of the House for the extra $24 million for the enforcement of Prohibition.		Gerald P. Nye, chairman of the Public Lands Committee, accuses of corruption in the Senate Colonel Robert Stewart, whose chairmanship of the Standard Oil Company of Indiana was challenged by John D. Rockefeller, Jr....The British steamer Silver Maple launches an SOS off the coast of Boston.	Eight firemen are hurt in a fire which destroys the Central Pier in Atlantic City.	Banker Otto Tremont Bannard leaves $2 million to Yale University....The task of indexing and cataloguing the sixty thousand manuscripts which will be held in the new Vatican Library nears completion. Vatican professionals have been aided by American experts from the Carnegie Endowment for International Peace.	Jan. 26
President Coolidge will veto the extra $24 million for the enforcement of prohibition if the measure is passed by the House of Representatives.	President-elect Hoover wishes the American navy to be second to none. The statement gives hope to the supporters of the cruisers bill which is being examined in the Senate.	General Motors distributes over $13 million in cash and stock to its employees....The Bureau of Agricultural Economics of the Department of Agriculture warns farmers against over production to keep the level of gross income of agriculture stable.	The flood control board announces the preparation of plans worth $30 million for the Mississippi River flood control.	Thousands New Yorkers cheer Captain George Fried and the crew of the *America* for their spectacular rescue of the Italian freighter *Florida*.	Jan. 27
President-elect Hoover resumes his pre-inauguration talks with Republican leaders.	President-elect Hoover denies to have views different from President Coolidge on the cruisers bill.	The banking company Dillon, Reed & Co. purchases 10,000 shares of the Bank of Manhattan, the largest single bank shares transfer in years....President Coolidge reviews the economic successes of his administration in a speech before the 60th meeting of the business organization of the government. He wishes that future administrations continue to maintain constructive economy in all branches of government.		The site offered to the Metropolitan for the new Opera House is priced at $3.6 million. Negotiations on this issue between John D. Rockefeller and the Metropolitan continue.	Jan. 28

F	G	H	I	J
Includes campaigns, elections, federal-state relations, civil rights and liberties, crime, the judiciary, education, healthcare, poverty, urban affairs, and population.	Includes formation and debate of U.S. foreign and defense policies, veterans affairs, and defense spending. (Relations with specific foreign countries are usually found under the region concerned.)	Includes business, labor, agriculture, taxation, transportation, consumer affairs, monetary and fiscal policy, natural resources, pollution and industrial accidents.	Includes worldwide scientific, medical and technological developments, natural phenomena, U.S. weather and natural disasters.	Includes the arts, religion, scholarship, communications media, sports, entertainment, fashions, fads, and social life.

	World Affairs	Europe	Africa & The Middle East	The Americas	Asia & The Pacific
Jan. 29		The Prince of Wales visits the coal fields in Durham and is appalled by the poverty in which miners live.... The United States State Department issues a strong complaint to the French Foreign Office concerning the proposed increase in taxation of American business interests in France.	The trial of former premier Mustafa Nahas Pasha begins in Egypt.... Britain states it has no intention to violate Tanganyika's independence and annex it to Kenya and Uganda in a single colony.	The Labor Department of the Mexican Ministry of Industry and Commerce reveals a deep crisis in Mexican mining centers.	
Jan. 30	A British court overrules the decision of the High Court of the Salvation Army to oust General Bramwell Booth as its leader....Allied nations agree on suggesting to the Experts' committee on reparations that Germany's reparations to the United States should be included in the settlement.	The Soviet government expels Leon Trotsky from the Soviet Union, thus ending his long-term dispute with Stalin following the death of Lenin....Discontent against Premier Voldemaras grows in the Lithuanian Army....The Spanish King Alfonso unexpectedly returns to Madrid to confer with Prime Minister Primo de Rivera regarding the revolt that was suppressed.			British Foreign Secretary Sir Austen Chamberlain says that the British Government has no intention of interfering in the civil war in Afghanistan.
Jan. 31		An attack against the papal nuncio in Spain fails....The Prince of Wales ends his three-day tour of the Northern coal fields. He praises miners for their courage in facing a life of hardship....German political parties enter negotiations for a stronger political coalition to present a united front during the next reparations conference.			The Japanese government declares that the position of his envoy at the Nanking Sino-Japanese conference is one of conciliation and expresses its hopes for a settlement....Afghan King Bacha Sakao concentrates his troops in Kabul. Conflicts break out with forces still loyal to former King Amanullah.
Feb. 1	Pope Pius XI announces he will call the Ecumenical Council of the Catholic Church next year. It will be the first since 1870, the year which marked its adjournment and the Vatican's loss of temporal power with the rise of the Italian state.	British reactions to U.S. Senator Borah's proposal to organize an international conference for the establishment of maritime laws in time of war continue to be negative....Czech Premier Sverhia resigns and Minister of War Udrzal is appointed in his place....French Premier Poincaré ends his three-day Parliamentary speech on the Alsatian situation, but fails to persuade the autonomist deputies.			Former Afghan King Amanullah and the current King Bacha Sakao open negotiations for a peaceful settlement of their disputes.
Feb. 2	The retired Archbishop of Canterbury Lord Davidson urges Salvation Army leader Bramwell Booth to retire from his position....The League of Nations Secretariat places on the agenda for the next council meeting in March the problem of minorities across Europe.	The Norwegian government annexes Peter Island in the South Atlantic Ocean....War hero Colonel T. E. Lawrence of Arabia arrives in London from India....A serious revolt breaks out in Spain in Valencia when the commanding officer refuses to obey orders from the prime minister.			British and American diplomats visit the Chinese Nationalist government in Nanking, renewing hopes in the Chinese that diplomatic relations will be established again.
Feb. 3		Riots against Spanish dictator Primo de Rivera continue in Valencia. Part of the city's garrison attempts to free former premier José Sanchez Guerra....Britain, France, and Germany plan a parley for October to plan a future European economic union....One of the coldest waves in 50 years hits central and eastern Europe.	A University of Pennsylvania archeological expedition in Beisan, Palestine, uncovers an altar used by Mekal worshippers nearly 3,500 years ago.		
Feb. 4		Discontent and disorders spread throughout Spain against the regime of Primo de Rivera....King Alexander of Yugoslavia announces negotiations with Croats to hear their complaints....Forty-four people die across Europe due to the unprecedented cold wave that is affecting the Continent....Famine in Bessarabia causes the death by starvation of thousands.		American marines capture Manuel Maria Jiron, one of generals of the Nicaraguan rebels led by Sandino.	Prince Hediatullah, the eldest son of former Afghan king Amanullah, returns to Afghanistan from Paris and argues that his father has almost regained his kingdom.... Violent riots erupt in Bombay against Pashtuns who are believed to kidnap children and offer them for human sacrifices.

A	B	C	D	E
Includes developments that affect more than one world region, international organizations and important meetings of world leaders.	Includes all domestic and regional developments in Europe, including the Soviet Union.	Includes all domestic and regional developments in Africa and the Middle East.	Includes all domestic and regional developments in Latin America, the Caribbean, and Canada.	Includes all domestic and regional developments in Asian and Pacific nations (and colonies).

U.S. Politics & Social Issues	U.S. Foreign Policy & Affairs, Defense	U.S. Economy & Environment	Science, Technology & Nature	Culture, Leisure & Lifestyle	
Ray Lyman Wilbur, president of Stanford University is first suggested for the position of Secretary of the Interior in the future Hoover Administration....President-elect Hoover and defeated Democratic Presidential candidate Alfred E. Smith meet in Florida. Smith wishes Hoover success with the presidency.	President Coolidge says he does not want to postpone work on all the new cruisers if the bill is approved by Congress.	Pennsylvania Railroad grants wage increases to 36,000 employees.... President Coolidge informs the Senate that diplomatic negotiations will be undertaken with Canada regarding customs preferences on American imports routed through Canadian ports.	Albert Einstein publishes his pamphlet "A New Field Theory" where he fuses gravitation and electrodynamics....The General Electric Company announces the first production of a bolt of artificial lightning of 5,000,000 volts.	The first seeing-eye Dog Guide School in the United States was founded in Morris Township, NJ, by Dorothy Harrison Eustus.	Jan. 29
President-elect Hoover seems to have decided the formation of his cabinet, but this will not be disclosed until March 4th, the day of his inauguration.	Owen D. Young and J. P. Morgan, American members of the committee of experts on German reparations, meet with President Coolidge in view of their participation to the first meeting.	The consumption of cigarettes in the United States exceeds 100 billion for the first time generating a massive increase in the tax collections on their manufacture.		Frank B. Jewett, director of research and development for the American Telephone and Telegraph Company, wins the Edison Medal for his contribution to electrical communication.	Jan. 30
The House of Representatives votes 240 to 141 against the allocation of an extra $24 million for the enforcement of prohibition....The Governor of the Philippines Henry L. Stimson announces he will sail for the United States in time to arrive for Hoover's inauguration. This leads to speculation about his possible role as Secretary of State in the Hoover cabinet.		Supreme Court Justice Aaron J. Levy signs an order restraining the Electrical Contractors' Association and the Electrical Workers' Union from implementing their agreement for the five-day week and a 10 percent wage increase.	The first direct telephonic communication between Paris and Buenos Aires is inaugurated.	A group of American politicians and society leaders put forward the name of Secretary of State Kellogg as a candidate for the 1928 Nobel Prize for Peace.	Jan. 31
Investigations in the administration of suspended Oklahoma Governor Henry S. Johnston unravel favoritism and corruption....The National Woman's Party advocates an amendment to the U.S. Constitution to provide women with equal rights to men.		President Coolidge dedicates the bird sanctuary in Mountain Lake, Florida, to the people of the United States....As the proxy battle between John D. Rockefeller, Jr. and Colonel Robert Stewart goes on, the stock value of the Standard Oil Company of Indiana rises sharply.		Weightlifter Charles Rigoulet of France achieves the first 400 pound "clean and jerk" as he lifts 402-1/2 pounds....Architect Thomas Hastings presents to the public his plan to enlarge the Senate Chamber in the National Capitol at Washington....Columbia Pictures and the Victor Talking Machine Company announce a joint partnership to produce short sound films.	Feb. 1
The Senate refuses to yield to the House request to block the extra $24 million of funds for the enforcement of prohibition....President-elect Hoover resumes conferences with party leaders on his future administration.	Reparations experts Owen D. Young and J.P. Morgan sail for France to take part to the meeting of the international committee for German reparations....President Coolidge is determined to fight the clause in the cruisers bill which forces the construction of the ships within a specific time limit. As a compromise he offers the construction of four ships within the first year.	The Senate Public Lands Committee rejects the report drawn by Senator Walsh harshly condemning the cancellation of Salt Creek oil contract.		Muriel Vanderbilt starts divorce procedures against Frederic Cameron Church Jr. on grounds of nonsupport.	Feb. 2
President-elect Hoover holds conferences with Republican southern leaders to rebuild the party in the region....Henry L. Stimson, Governor General of the Philippines, accepts the position of Secretary of State in the future Hoover cabinet.		The Electrical Workers' Union organizes a strike in New York against the Supreme Court decision to deny the 5-day workweek.		The Federal Council of Churches of Christ in America appeals to American pastors to preach sermons against social drinking the day before Hoover's Inauguration Day.	Feb. 3
	The Senate rejects two proposals to defer the time limit the construction of the ships described in the cruisers bill. The rejection is seen as a defeat of President Coolidge who had strongly argued for a deferral of the construction.	To oppose John D. Rockefeller's move against Colonel Robert W. Stewart in the dispute for the chairmanship of the Indiana Standard Oil Company, the board of directors gives out $310 million in cash and stock dividends....837 separate issues are dealt in the New York Stock Exchange, the largest market in its history.		Colonel Charles Lindbergh flies from Miami to Belize, the first part of his journey inaugurating the new mail line between the United States and Panama.	Feb. 4

F	G	H	I	J
Includes campaigns, elections, federal-state relations, civil rights and liberties, crime, the judiciary, education, healthcare, poverty, urban affairs, and population.	Includes formation and debate of U.S. foreign and defense policies, veterans affairs, and defense spending. (Relations with specific foreign countries are usually found under the region concerned.)	Includes business, labor, agriculture, taxation, transportation, consumer affairs, monetary and fiscal policy, natural resources, pollution and industrial accidents.	Includes worldwide scientific, medical and technological developments, natural phenomena, U.S. weather and natural disasters.	Includes the arts, religion, scholarship, communications media, sports, entertainment, fashions, fads, and social life.

	World Affairs	Europe	Africa & The Middle East	The Americas	Asia & The Pacific
Feb. 5		Irish Republican leader Eamon De Valera is arrested while trying to cross the Ulster border defying his exclusion ban....The German Cabinet denies Russian revolutionary Leon Trotsky a visa to enter Germany....Russian scientist Ivan Pavloff comes into conflict with the Soviet government....The revolt against the Spanish government is defeated without bloodshed.	The French government adjourns indefinitely the Syrian Constituent Assembly due to the prevalence of nationalist factions.		An all-night conference between Chinese and Japanese ministers makes good progress towards a compromise for the Tsinan-fu incident of May 1928. Japanese negotiators express their willingness to withdraw from the Shantung.... Riots between Hindu and Pashtuns in Bombay continue killing 19 and injuring 104.
Feb. 6	Former French President of the Reparations Board Louis Dubois criticizes American policy on the debt agreement....Pope Pius XI informs all nuncios, internuncios and apostolic delegates that full agreement has been reached with the Italian State over the Roman Question.	The German government accepts the terms of the Pact of Paris and renounces war as an instrument of state policy. This acceptance will play an important part in the charges at the Nuremberg Trials....A breakdown in electricity paralyses the traffic and industry in Paris.... Polish Government parties present a proposal for a new Constitution in Parliament....Spanish Queen Mother, Maria Christina, dies.		José de Leon Toral, assassin of Mexican President-elect Alvaro Obregon, is denied a delay in his execution.	Violent Hindus-Pashtuns riots continue in Bombay and armed British patrols are unable to stop them.
Feb. 7	Cardinal Gasparri, Vatican Secretary of State, announces to the assembled diplomatic corps accredited to the Holy See that an agreement with the Italian State has been reached to settle the Roman Question.	Britain announces the construction of two new cruisers....The French Chamber of Deputies denies the Communist Deputy André Marty admittance to his seat....The persistence of cold weather in Central Europe causes the worst grip epidemic in 10 years which leads to the death of hundreds of Czechs.... Yugoslavia removes all restrictions along its Bulgarian borders.			Clashes between Hindus and Pashtuns continue in Bombay, causing hundreds of casualties.
Feb. 8	The League of Nations will examine the Treaty between Italy and the Vatican and try to apply it to its status in Switzerland. The League will ask for extraterritoriality, immunity for its officials, a radio station and an airport.	The solemn funeral of the Spanish Queen Mother takes place in Madrid....Irish Free State leader Eamon De Valera is sentenced to one month in prison....The Labor Party wins a by-election in Britain, electing the ninth woman in Parliament.	Auguste Henri Ponsot, French High Commissioner in Syria, prorogues the Constituent Assembly because of disagreements on the Constitution.	Former Panama Minister Eusebio Morales dies in a car crash.	A peace parade of Pashtuns, Hindus and Muslims in Bombay breaks up into violent riots....Sino-Japanese negotiations reach another impasse on the Shantung question.
Feb. 9	The experts of the international committee on German reparations informally offer the chairmanship to American delegate Owen D. Young.	Delegates from Estonia, Latvia, Poland, Romania and the Soviet Union sign in Moscow the Litvinov Protocol in which the nations renounce war....King George waves to British subjects while on his way to Bognor on the Sussex coast, his health improved....The Spanish dictator Primo de Rivera approves drastic measures to counter opposition to his regime....Severe weather conditions isolate entire cities and villages in Central Europe and the Balkans.	Restoration of the Citadel of David in the Holy City begins in Jerusalem.	José de Leon Toral is executed for the assassination of Mexican President-elect Alvaro Obregon.	The discussion of a non-confidence motion against the Tanaka cabinet is suspended in the Japanese parliament when disorders break out in the Chamber....The Chinese government welcomes a commission of 16 American economic experts who will try to stabilize the currency of the nation and to change from the silver to the gold standard....After a week of clashes between Hindus and Pashtuns, more than 100 people are reported killed and more than 600 injured.
Feb. 10	The League of Nations welcomes the proposal of Senator Capper for an economic boycott of the violators of the Kellogg Treaty.			The train where Mexican President Emilio Portes Gil is traveling is bombed. The President is uninjured....U.S. Marine headquarters in Managua deny that Nicaragua is entirely pacified and that all the Sandino bands have been confined outside the country.	Rioting continues in Bombay between Muslims and Hindus. Sven more people are killed, 75 are wounded and 500 arrested. Hundreds of Hindus flee from the city.
Feb. 11	The international committee on German reparations begins its work in Paris, trying to revise the Dawes Plan to allow the German government to meet its reparation payments requirements. American delegate Owen D. Young will act as chair.	The Italian and Vatican governments sign the Lateran Treaties, ending decades of conflicts between the two states. The Vatican is recognized as an independent state and the Treaties also regulate the activities of the Catholic Church in Italy.		Acting Secretary of the Interior Canales demands that all Catholic priests living in Mexico send their addresses to the government within 15 days.	Governor General Henry L. Stimson pays tribute to the friendly cooperation of Filipino leaders in his farewell address to the Philippine Legislature.

A	B	C	D	E
Includes developments that affect more than one world region, international organizations and important meetings of world leaders.	Includes all domestic and regional developments in Europe, including the Soviet Union.	Includes all domestic and regional developments in Africa and the Middle East.	Includes all domestic and regional developments in Latin America, the Caribbean, and Canada.	Includes all domestic and regional developments in Asian and Pacific nations (and colonies).

U.S. Politics & Social Issues	U.S. Foreign Policy & Affairs, Defense	U.S. Economy & Environment	Science, Technology & Nature	Culture, Leisure & Lifestyle	
The offices of the Italian-American anti-Fascist daily *Il Nuovo Mondo* are raided and its mechanical equipment badly damaged....Maryland House of Delegates rejects the state Prohibition enforcement bill.	The Senate passes the Cruisers Bill which commits the government to build 15 cruisers within three years.	Following the news of a 50 percent stock dividend, the shares of the Indiana Standard Oil Company boom.	Earth tremors shake towns in New Hampshire and Maine, but no damage is reported.	Captain Frank Hawks sets a new record flight spanning the United States in 18 hours and 15 minutes in spite of a harsh storm....J. P. Morgan donates two office buildings worth of $2 million to New York Hospital.	Feb. 5
	The House of Representatives begins the examination of the Cruisers Bill....Major General John Lejeune, commandant of the Marine Corps since 1920, announces his retirement when his term expires.	By a unanimous vote, the Senate blocks the sale of the United States and American Merchant Lines to private interests....The Federal Reserve Board issues a formal statement restraining the use of Federal Reserve Credit Facilities to avoid speculative credit.		Colonel Charles Lindbergh completes his three-day flight from Miami to Panama, delivering for the first time the air-mail to the Canal Zone....Hundreds of visitors attend the opening of the New York Aviation Show at the Grand Central Palace, the first to take place in New York in seven years.	Feb. 6
Gordon Stewart Northcott is convicted for the murder of three youths at his ranch and is sentenced to the death penalty....The deadlock between the Senate and House of Representatives over the extra $24 million for the enforcement of Prohibition.	The House of Representatives passes the Cruisers Bill which goes to President Coolidge for signing.... Major General Wendell C. Neville is appointed to succeed Major General John Lejeune as Commandant of the Marine Corps.	After the Federal Reserve Board warns against the expansion of speculative loans, the stock market declines sharply.	A group of New York bankers reveal plans for the construction of the largest airdrome in the United States at Roosevelt Field.		Feb. 7
Former District Attorney Asa Keyes of Los Angeles is convicted of corruption....President-elect Hoover states that he will not be involved in any local dispute on the enforcement of Prohibition as his program on the issue is of national scope....A supporter of Hoover sends $1,000 to the Democratic Party to help rebuild it as the party of opposition.	President Coolidge remains firm in his conviction that the time constraint in the cruisers bill is wrong.	The selling of shares on the stock market continues....In spite of a reduction in tax rates, income tax returns have grown between 1924 and 1927. This is due to the growth of incomes.	Oklahoma and Texas are swept by a strong blizzard which sends the temperatures near zero.	The United States Lawn Tennis Association reinstates William Tilden six months after suspending him for violation of the player-writer provision. Tilden had written articles on the Wimbledon Tourney.	Feb. 8
President-elect Hoover continues to add people to his cabinet: Walter F. Brown accepts the role of Postmaster General.		Senator Smoot of Utah, chairman of the Senate Finance Committee, states that he is in favor of revising only tariffs linked to farm products.			Feb. 9
	Senator Arthur Capper suggests to complete the Kellogg multilateral antiwar treaty with economic embargoes against those nations which violate its conditions.	In the dispute for the control of the Standard Oil Company of Indiana, John D. Rockefeller charges Colonel Robert W. Stewart of misconduct in connection with the Continental Trading Company transactions.		William R. Moody, the son of famous evangelist Dwight L. Moody, resigns from the chairmanships of the bible schools in Northfield, MA, after 35 years in that position.	Feb. 10
The thirty-first Council of the Union of American Hebrew Congregations opens its session in San Francisco.	Representative Porter proposes restrictive procedures against violators of the Kellogg Treaty....The Senate ratifies the new treaty between the United States and the Chinese Nationalist Government recognizing the Chinese rights to complete control of their customs tariffs.	The stock market recovers almost half the ground lost last week....The Senate adopts the Heflin resolution asking the Federal Reserve Board to check illegitimate speculation on the stock market.	Eight passengers are injured in the collision between their Albany-bound train and a following relief train.	Miss Evelyn Trout sets a new record in both the number of miles and hours flown continuously by a woman....Henry Ford makes a $5 million donation to the Edison Museum.	Feb. 11

F	G	H	I	J
Includes campaigns, elections, federal-state relations, civil rights and liberties, crime, the judiciary, education, healthcare, poverty, urban affairs, and population.	*Includes formation and debate of U.S. foreign and defense policies, veterans affairs, and defense spending. (Relations with specific foreign countries are usually found under the region concerned.)*	*Includes business, labor, agriculture, taxation, transportation, consumer affairs, monetary and fiscal policy, natural resources, pollution and industrial accidents.*	*Includes worldwide scientific, medical and technological developments, natural phenomena, U.S. weather and natural disasters.*	*Includes the arts, religion, scholarship, communications media, sports, entertainment, fashions, fads, and social life.*

	World Affairs	Europe	Africa & The Middle East	The Americas	Asia & The Pacific
Feb. 12	Pope Pius XI receives the applause and cheering of the over 200,000 people crowding St. Peter's Square for his first blessing after the signing of the Lateran treaty....Hjalmar Schacht, first German delegate to the international commission on war reparations, asks for a reduction in the annuity of $600 million that Germany should pay.	The harsh spell of cold weather continues throughout Europe.... British Chancellor of the Exchequer Winston Churchill predicts economic and social breakdown if the Labor Party wins the general election.		Mexican President Portes Gil and his predecessor Plutarco Elias Calles receive threatening letters.	After the violent clashes of the previous weeks, the city of Bombay almost returns to normal. Hindus, however, continue to leave the city.
Feb. 13	Edward J. Higgins succeeds Bramwell Booth as the new General of the Salvation Army.	Soviet exile Leon Trotsky arrives in Constantinople in Turkey with his family under another name....The French government criticizes the resolution of U.S. Representative Porter to introduce harsher penalties for the violators of the Kellogg Treaty....Low temperatures are still recorded in most parts of the European Continent.		Six men try to assassinate Venezuelan President Juan Vincente Gomez, but are killed by the escort.	Forty ruling Indian princes state they oppose independence from Britain.
Feb. 14	Britain announces its intention of holding renewed parley with the United States on navies limitation....The international commission for war reparations suspends its session for a day to give the opportunity to the Allies delegates to study the German proposal for annuity reduction.	Austrian police raid the headquarters of the Social Democratic Party, seizing a large arsenal of weapons and ammunitions....In a by-election, the Labor Party retains its seat in Wansbeck (Newcastle) and greatly increases its majority.		Governor Towner exhorts the legislators of Puerto Rico to limit public expenditure to restore the country's economy.	Rebel forces in Chefoo decide to face the Chinese Nationalist army rather than withdrawing and thus prepare for the battle.
Feb. 15	British Ambassador in Washington, Sir Esme Howard, confirms that Britain will try to call an international conference on the limitation of naval armaments after the general election.	King George continues his recovery....Harsh weather causes coal and food shortages throughout Europe....The French Chamber votes against conceding a general amnesty to political prisoners....The police raid against Socialist headquarters in Vienna is suspected to be a political plot to stop the growing rapprochement between the Christian Socialists and the Social Democrats.	Berlin newspaper Lokal Anzeiger publishes reports of an alleged slave trade still present in British African colonies.	The entire military escort of a train from Yurecuaro to Mexico City is killed when the train is bombed by rebels.	
Feb. 16	British Foreign Office denies the statement made by Sir Esme Howard, Ambassador in Washington, about the British intention to call an international conference on the limitations of naval armaments.	Spanish dictator Primo de Rivera may soon restore constitutional rights and ends his regime....The Soviet regime decides to bring the only foreign-owned factory in the Union to trial for bribery.			Manchurian government leasers fear a rebellion in the Barga district due to taxes and trade restrictions....The Chinese Nationalist government blames the Japanese occupation of Shantung for the Chefoo revolt.
Feb. 17	Vatican officials applaud Italian Prime Minister Benito Mussolini when a movie of the signing of the Italo-Vatican Treaty of Conciliation is shown at a reception. It is the first time an Italian Prime Minister has been applauded in the Vatican.	Members of the House of Commons ask the British government to answer questions about the naval parley prospected by British Ambassador in Washington, Sir Esme Howard....Austrian Social Democrats announce a march in Vienna in protest against the police raid on their headquarters. The march will take place on Sunday at the same time than an already planned Fascist march.		Bolivian forces advance eighty miles into Chaco territory, a move which could revive tensions with Paraguay over the Chaco dispute.	The Chinese Nationalist Government organizes the Mongolian and Tibetan Affairs Committee to bring the two regions under its control.
Feb. 18	The international committee on war reparations begins the discussion of how much annuity Germany may be able to pay.	Exiled Soviet leader Leon Trotsky asks Germany to grant him a visa to enter the country....Austrian Social Democrat and Fascist leaders agree not to arm their followers for their rival demonstrations to take place on Sunday....The Prince of Wales addresses an audience of British manufacturers criticizing them for making products unsuitable overseas....Heavy floods begin in Greece as seven rivers overflowed their banks.	British Foreign Office objects to the proposed trip of the dirigible Graf Zeppelin over Egypt and Palestine for "diplomatic reasons."	Miguel de la Mora, spokesman for Mexican bishops, denies government accusations of Catholic complicity in recent rebel violence, condemning it as a violation of Christian morality....The Tiete River continues rising due to heavy rains and makes thousands of Brazilians homeless....Bolivian Foreign Office denies charges that its troops have advanced into the disputed Chaco territory.	

A	B	C	D	E
Includes developments that affect more than one world region, international organizations and important meetings of world leaders.	*Includes all domestic and regional developments in Europe, including the Soviet Union.*	*Includes all domestic and regional developments in Africa and the Middle East.*	*Includes all domestic and regional developments in Latin America, the Caribbean, and Canada.*	*Includes all domestic and regional developments in Asian and Pacific nations (and colonies).*

U.S. Politics & Social Issues	U.S. Foreign Policy & Affairs, Defense	U.S. Economy & Environment	Science, Technology & Nature	Culture, Leisure & Lifestyle	
Abraham Lincoln's birthday is celebrated throughout the United States with a series of ceremonies and meetings....Representative La Guardia presents a resolution recommending the impeachment of Judge Francis A. Winslow.	President Coolidge is cautious in judging the resolution put forward by Senator Capper calling for economic embargoes against those nations which violate the conditions of the Kellogg Treaty.			Charles Lindbergh announces his engagement to Anne Morrow, the daughter of Dwight Morrow, U.S. Ambassador to Mexico....Actress Lily Langtry, once described as the world's greatest beauty, dies in Monte Carlo at 74.	Feb. 12
Secretary of Agriculture William M. Jardine announces that he will retire from his post and will not seek re-appointment in the Hoover Administration.....President Hoover is officially declared President at a joint session of the House and the Senate to count the electoral vote.	President Coolidge signs the Cruiser Bill authorizing the construction of fifteen 10,000-ton cruisers and one airplane carrier.	John D. Rockefeller considers K. R. Kingsbury, president of the Standard Oil Company of California, for the succession to Colonel Robert W. Stuart as chairman of the Standard Oil Company of Indiana.		Hundreds of telegrams felicitate Miss Anne Morrow for her engagement with Charles Lindbergh.	Feb. 13
The San Valentine's Day Massacre takes place in Chicago in a garage of the Moran gang. The gang is killed by members of Al Capone's rival gang....President Coolidge appoints Irvine L. Lenroot and Finis J. Garrett as judges of the Court of Customs Appeals....Secretary Mellon suggests a compromise between the House and the Senate to appropriate an additional $2,5 million for prohibition enforcement.	President Coolidge puts off funding for the Cruiser Bill.	The directors of the Federal Reserve Bank decide to leave the rediscount rate unchanged after a long and tense debate.	Four gas explosions in underground electric cable conduits damage the downtown shopping district of Boston, injuring 26 people.	Yale University announces the establishment of the Institute of Human Relations which aims to carry out research into human behavior in all its stages.	Feb. 14
President Coolidge orders a study to determine the historical basis for the the national origins quota provision of the immigration law.	Former Secretary of State Elihu Root sails for Europe where he will take part in the works of the League of Nations to revise the statute which created the Permanent Court of International Justice in 1920. Root will seek to create the conditions for the U.S. inclusion in the World Court.	The Federal Advisory Council asks all Federal Reserve banks not to use Federal Reserve credit in stock market speculation. Stock market prices drop shortly after the announcement.		Police arrest the author and twelve actors of the show My Girl Friday performed at the Republic Theater in New York. The police consider the play obscene....Newspaper founder and leading figure of American journalism Melville E. Stone dies in New York at 81 years of age.	Feb. 15
Following the San Valentine's Day Massacre, Chicago police Commissioner William Russell announces war against illegal liquor selling, which, to him, was closely linked to the massacre.	Secretary of state Kellogg gives his approval to the general principle of the Porter resolution empowering the president to place a military embargo on foreign countries engaged in domestic or international conflict.	Stock prices drop steadily, with declines from two to 21 points. The drop is brought about by the threat to refuse extension of credit to speculators.	The Research Department of the New York Skin and Cancer Hospital announces a new treatment against eczema, based on the removal of arsenic from the system.	Screen star Alma Rubens is revealed as a drug addict by a narcotic investigation.	Feb. 16
President Coolidge will retire in his hometown of Northampton, Ma, after stepping down as president.		The Federal Reserve Board makes public a study which discourages the use of federal reserve money for speculative purposes.... Representative Black states his intention of introducing a bill to forbid officials and directors of the Reserve Board and Reserve Banks to buy and sell securities considered speculative.	Airplane passengers watch a movie during their flight for the first time in the history of aviation.	Composer Deems Taylor reveals he has abandoned two years of work on the second American opera commissioned to him by the Metropolitan Opera Company.... John D. Rockefeller purchases the Wakefield estate, where George Washington was born, for the sum of $115,000.	Feb. 17
Two resolutions offered in the House of Representatives ask for a searching investigation of the judicial conduct of Judge Francis A. Winslow....Senators Reed and Borah animate a passionate debate on Prohibition laws.	Secretary of State Kellogg addresses the Foreign Service School of Georgetown University claiming that world public opinion rather than sanctions should be the main reliance of the multilateral treaty against war.	The stock market recovers much of the losses recorded in previous days.		Double Olympic champion and runner Percy Williams is defeated for the first time in his career by Jack Edler at the New York Athletic Club games.	Feb. 18

F	G	H	I	J
Includes campaigns, elections, federal-state relations, civil rights and liberties, crime, the judiciary, education, healthcare, poverty, urban affairs, and population.	Includes formation and debate of U.S. foreign and defense policies, veterans affairs, and defense spending. (Relations with specific foreign countries are usually found under the region concerned.)	Includes business, labor, agriculture, taxation, transportation, consumer affairs, monetary and fiscal policy, natural resources, pollution and industrial accidents.	Includes worldwide scientific, medical and technological developments, natural phenomena, U.S. weather and natural disasters.	Includes the arts, religion, scholarship, communications media, sports, entertainment, fashions, fads, and social life.

	World Affairs	Europe	Africa & The Middle East	The Americas	Asia & The Pacific
Feb. 19		British Prime Minister Baldwin avoids defeat by adjourning the parliamentary session when a group of fellow Conservatives threaten to vote against the proposal of limiting compensation for Irish loyalist to $5 million. They demand that the compensation should be of at least $7 million....King Alfonso of Spain dissolves his artillery corps due to the recurring disaffection among its officers....The judicial reform of the French government passes in the Chamber with a meager majority of only six votes.		The president of the Argentine Agrarian Federation opposes the increase of duties on agricultural tools produced in the United States and exported to Argentina. The Argentinean government is thinking of raising tariffs on those tools should the United States increase tariffs on cattle and agricultural products.	The Chinese Nationalist government bars the American-owned newspaper North China Star from mails. This is seen as a threat to all foreign correspondent who do not write approvingly of the government.
Feb. 20	The international committee of experts on war reparations suggest the establishment of an international clearing house for all reparations debt payments.	Spanish dictator Primo de Rivera announces that the eighteen regiments involved in the recent plot against former Prime Minister Sanchez Guerra have been disbanded by royal decree....The decision to reduce pensions above 12,000 marks creates a political storm in Germany.		The Chilean newspaper Mercurio announces the official settlement of the long-standing Tacna-Arica dispute. The city of Tacna will go to Peru and the city of Arica will go to Chile....Mexican President Portes Gil issues a final warning to the press for its attitude toward his administration.	War Lord Chang Tsung-chang, former Governor of Shantung, rallies former troops to revolt against the Chinese Nationalist government.
Feb. 21	Albert Thomas, director of the International Labor Office, encourages the League of Nations to make its ideals of race equality known in the Far East to stop the appeal of Communism in the region.	The Senate of the Irish Free State ratifies the Kellogg treaty.	South Africans applaud to the Prince of Wales's scolding of British manufacturers for not taking into account South African needs in the planning of their products.	The Chilean Foreign Office denies that a settlement of the Tacna-Arica dispute has been reached as reported in the Chilean newspaper Mercurio....The Mexican Minister of Finance announces that the state has cleared $500,000 of old debts for merchandise supplied to the government.	Chinese Nationalist forces clash with anti-Nationalists fifteen miles west of Chefoo, causing the first battle in the new Shantung uprising.
Feb. 22	The Vatican paper Osservatore Romano attacks the Rotary movement as hostage to the interests of Freemasonry.	The lower house of the Irish Free State ratifies the Kellog treaty....Eastern Europe continues to be affected by bad weather, with cold temperatures and heavy snow.		Two American mining engineers are kidnapped and killed in Mexico.	Loyal Nationalist troops and the forces of Chang Tsung-chang engage in violent battles in the Shantung Peninsula. Nationalist troops, although outnumbered, inflict serious losses to the rebels due to their better organization....The House of Peers passes a resolution rebuking Japanese Premier Tanaka for his handling of the resignation of Rentaro Mizuno, Minister of Education.
Feb. 23	Delegates to the international commission on war reparations consult with their respective governments over German claims not to be able to pay satisfactory annuity.	Austria is threatened by floods due to the rising water of its rivers and lakes....Members of the Conservative Party criticize their own Home Secretary for his statements challenging "the right of every man to do as he likes with his own." According to fellow conservatives, these opinions may cost the party thousands of votes in the coming election.		Mexican government promises to act quickly to capture the killers of the two American mining engineers.	Chinese rebels seize Hunan defeating the forces of the Nationalist government....Filipinos crowd the streets of Manila to salute the departing Governor Henry L. Stimson who will have the post of Secretary of State in Hoover Administration.
Feb. 24	Delegates from Germany want to keep the transfer clause of the original Dawes plan in the new reparation settlement. The clause, which Allies would like to drop, states that marks shall not be transferred abroad for reparation payments if this endangers the international value of German money.	In spite of fears of disorders, the contrasting parades of Social Democrats and Fascists take place peacefully in Vienna....Spanish political leaders against the dictatorship of Primo de Rivera ask audience to King Alfonso....Hundreds of British unemployed march in London converging in Trafalgar Square....French film producers ask the United States for a subsidy to continue to show American film in France.			Chinese Nationalist troops inflict heavy losses to the rebels in Shantung Province.
Feb. 25	The delegates on the international committee on war reparations are optimistic about concluding their work within a month.	Exiled Soviet leader Leon Trotsky publishes the first in a series of articles in the Western press denouncing his own persecution and Stalin's repudiation of Lenin's legacy....Spanish dictator Primo de Rivera removes the governor of Seville without giving reasons for his action.	The South African Parliament rejects the Natives Representation bill, thus leaving unaltered the electoral registers.		15,000 soldiers, led by General Chu Pan-tsao, join the Shantung revolt against Chinese Nationalist troops....Sir Francis Humphrys, British Minister to Afghanistan, is the last Briton to leave Kabul due to the impending invasion of the city by the forces of Amanulah who is seeking to regain his throne.

A	B	C	D	E
Includes developments that affect more than one world region, international organizations and important meetings of world leaders.	Includes all domestic and regional developments in Europe, including the Soviet Union.	Includes all domestic and regional developments in Africa and the Middle East.	Includes all domestic and regional developments in Latin America, the Caribbean, and Canada.	Includes all domestic and regional developments in Asian and Pacific nations (and colonies).

U.S. Politics & Social Issues	U.S. Foreign Policy & Affairs, Defense	U.S. Economy & Environment	Science, Technology & Nature	Culture, Leisure & Lifestyle	
The Senate passes the Jones Bill which makes the maximum penalty for major prohibition violation $10,000 or five years in jail or both....Five convicts escape from Ohio Penitentiary. Two of them are captured the same day....The House adopts a resolution calling for an investigation into the judicial conduct of Francis Winslow.	Secretary of State Kellogg sends an official note to all the governments which have signed the World Court protocol to begin an informal exchange of views about U.S. inclusion in the court.	The Baltimore and Ohio Railroad asks the Interstate Commerce Commission permission to control 10 railroads directly and five others jointly.	A medical diathermy machine is first used in Schenectady, NY....A fire traps 900 passengers in a Hudson tube train, holding them for an hour and a half in smoke-filled cars.	French pilot Dieudonné Costes is forced to interrupt his record flight from France to Indo-China by a faulty feed pipe....Yale University receives a gift of $2 million from the General Education Board of New York City for a new medical and pediatrics laboratory.	Feb. 19
President-elect Hoover confers with President Coolidge on the political situation and makes plans to call a special session of Congress in mid-April.	Fears of filibuster emerge in the Senate against the naval appropriation bill.	A three-day holiday is declared for the stock market....Investigations begin on the Hudson tube fire which caused injuries to more than 200 passengers.	Explorer William Byrd claims a new vast territory of Antarctica for the United States.	Former Broadway actress Mabelle Corey announces her likely marriage to Don Luis de Bourbon, first cousin of the King of Spain.	Feb. 20
With eleven days to go before his inauguration, President-elect Hoover is still unsure on who will fill the post of attorney general in his administration.	Secretary of Commerce Whiting announces that Colonel Lindbergh has been appointed as technical adviser to the aeronautics branch of the Department of Commerce....Filibuster against the naval appropriation bill is defeated in the Senate and discussion begins.	The merger between the National Bank of Commerce and the Guaranty Trust Company creates the largest bank in the United States.		New York Magistrate Hyman Bushel rules Radclyffe Hall's The Well of Loneliness obscene and declares it printed and distributed in violation of the penal law.	Feb. 21
A report presented by Senator Reed recommends that William S. Vare should be denied his seat due to the scandals which characterized the 1926 election.	The Senate approves a provision in the naval appropriation bill to recall all U.S. Marines from Nicaragua....Congress approves a resolution to establish a commission to formulate a new government for American Samoa.				Feb. 22
The House strikes out of the Deficiency Bill the funds asked for the renovation of the Summer White House and for the employment of two aides for President-elect Hoover....Representative Somers files an affidavit charging misconduct against New York Federal Judge Grover M. Moscowitz.	The Senate reverses its decision to cut funds for U.S. Marines in Nicaragua after pressures from President Coolidge and Secretary of State Kellogg.	A report on the railway consolidation bill, prepared by a subcommittee of the Senate Interstate Commerce Committee, is presented to the Senate by Senator Fess. The report recommends consolidation of carriers into a limited number of efficient systems capable of giving the public good service at reasonable rates.		George Haldeman completes the first nonstop flight from Canada to Cuba.	Feb. 23
President-elect Hoover has completed the selection of seven members of his cabinet. He still has to fill the positions of Attorney General and the Secretaries of Agriculture and Labor.	Senator Tydings announces a resolution in the Senate to ask the President to organize a conference of all nations which ratified the Kellogg Treaty renouncing war.			Charles D. Lindbergh flies to Mexico to visit his fiancée, the American Ambassador's daughter....The police block the performance of A. Gavrilov's Ballet Moderne, dispersing a large audience.	Feb. 24
Former world heavy-weight champion Jack Dempsey is shot at in Miami, but is uninjured....Accused Federal Judge Francis A. Winslow appears before the Grand Jury voluntarily....The House refuses again to appropriate an extra $24 million for prohibition enforcement.		The Senate approves the Edge resolution for the construction of an interoceanic canal through Nicaragua. The resolution goes to the House....Stock of the U.S. Steel Corporation soars as the corporation plans a reduction of its debts.	A heavy windstorm sweeps through the village of Duncan, Mississippi, killing at least 15 people and leaving the business section of the city in ruins.		Feb. 25

F	G	H	I	J
Includes campaigns, elections, federal-state relations, civil rights and liberties, crime, the judiciary, education, healthcare, poverty, urban affairs, and population.	Includes formation and debate of U.S. foreign and defense policies, veterans affairs, and defense spending. (Relations with specific foreign countries are usually found under the region concerned.)	Includes business, labor, agriculture, taxation, transportation, consumer affairs, monetary and fiscal policy, natural resources, pollution and industrial accidents.	Includes worldwide scientific, medical and technological developments, natural phenomena, U.S. weather and natural disasters.	Includes the arts, religion, scholarship, communications media, sports, entertainment, fashions, fads, and social life.

	World Affairs	Europe	Africa & The Middle East	The Americas	Asia & The Pacific
Feb. 26	Delegates of the international committee for war reparations still wait for a German proposal concerning the Reich annuity to be paid to the Allies.	In his second article written for the Western press, exiled Communist leader Leon Trotsky denies he had tried to start a civil war in Russia, the charge which caused his expulsion from the country....The impossibility of forming a new coalition government in Germany precipitates the country on the brink of dictatorship....The French Chamber begins discussing the Kellogg Treaty....The government policy of rural socialization in the Soviet Union encounters the opposition of a faction within the Communist Party.			The many revolts against the Chinese Nationalist government give rise to fears about the possibility of Communist uprisings in the country....General Nadir Khan arrives in Afghanistan to work as a mediator between the country's conflicting forces.
Feb. 27	German delegates in the international commission on war reparations split over the figure they should propose for their country to pay as annuity reparation.	The Turkish government signs the Litvinov Protocol, renouncing war as an instrument of state policy....In his third article written for the Western press, Leon Trotsky describes Stalin as a mediocre politician....German chancellor Mueller appeals to all the parties in his former government to form a new coalition....British Conservative leader Baldwin attacks Labor's proposed policy of nationalization before a crowd of 30,000.		Eight prominent Havana professionals are arrested for an alleged plot to kill Cuban President Machado. The assassination would have been followed by a plea for American direct intervention into the country's government....Canadian Premier Taschereau reveals a failed attempt to blow up his office.	Missionaries report the uprisings of 20,000 Muslim fanatics in Kansu, a western province of China.
Feb. 28		Britain and the Soviet Union sign an agreement to settle the two country's long-standing dispute on oil....Sixty people are arrested in Budapest as Communist conspirators....A cold wave in Central Europe causes concerns over coal supplies....In his fourth and last article former Soviet leader Leon Trotsky predicts the demise of the present Soviet government....The Fascist Grand Council publishes the list of 400 names to be submitted to voters for the General Election of March 24....German Chancellor Mueller warns the parties that they refusal to form a coalition endangers German democracy.	The new High Commissioner for Iraq, Sir Gilbert Clayton, hopes to restore order in the country soon and to stop the Wahabi raids.	The eight men arrested in Cuba and charged with conspiracy against President Machado deny that they had planned an assassination plot.	The rebel Governor of Shantung announces the appointment of his government which will be led by Marshal Tuan Chi-jui.
Mar. 1		The French Chamber of Deputies ratifies the Kellogg Treaty with an overwhelming majority....David Llyod George, the leader of the Liberal Party, tells the 500 candidates in the British parliamentary elections that he is certain of their victory....In spite of the political crisis of his coalition, the German Chancellor Mueller does not resign and prepares to present his budget....Soviet leader Stalin explains his decision to exile Leon Trotsky because of his counter-revolutionary views.		Cuban Government leaders announce that a plot against President Machado has been prevented thanks to drastic police action.	The Nationalist Chinese Government officially protests to the Japanese Government for its alleged participation in the disorders in the Shantung province.
Mar. 2	The eleven signatories of the Kellogg Treaty for the Renunciation of War deposit the ratifications of the treaty at the U.S. State Department in an official ceremony.	The Republic of Andorra complains about Spanish interference in its internal affairs in violation of the Republic's traditional liberty....France and Spain begin a serious dispute over the claims of French oil companies whose holdings were confiscated by the Spanish government due to the establishment of a State monopoly on oil....Doctors order a long rest for British King George.			A brigade from Shantung rises in Peking but is quickly suppressed by the Nationalist Army.
Mar. 3		Italian General Umberto Nobile is condemned for the wreck of the dirigible Italia during its Arctict expedition the previous year....Britain announces its intention to add seven new air squadrons.		The Mexican Army revolts in eight Mexican states, seizing Vera Cruz and Nogales. Rebels, led by General Gonzalo Escobar, demand the resignation of President Portes Gil.	

A	B	C	D	E
Includes developments that affect more than one world region, international organizations and important meetings of world leaders.	Includes all domestic and regional developments in Europe, including the Soviet Union.	Includes all domestic and regional developments in Africa and the Middle East.	Includes all domestic and regional developments in Latin America, the Caribbean, and Canada.	Includes all domestic and regional developments in Asian and Pacific nations (and colonies).

U.S. Politics & Social Issues	U.S. Foreign Policy & Affairs, Defense	U.S. Economy & Environment	Science, Technology & Nature	Culture, Leisure & Lifestyle	
President-elect Hoover offers the position of Attorney General to William D. Mitchell, a Democrat....President Coolidge says the end of his presidency lifts a considerable burden from him. He regards his best achievements the three tax-reductions, the settlement of the war debt and the antiwar Kellogg Treaty.		President Coolidge signs a measure establishing Grand Teton National Park in Wyoming....The directors of the United States Steel Corporation approve capital readjustment to eliminate the corporation funded debt....The Ford Motor Company launches an intensive campaign to recapture and expand its former sales in Europe.			Feb. 26
Democrat William D. Mitchell accepts the position of Attorney General in the incoming Hoover Administration....The action of filibuster by Senator Dill keeps the Senate in session for fourteen hours. Dill prevents the appropriation of $150,000 for a survey of a Nicaraguan canal route.			French aviator Joseph Lebrix crashes his plane during an experimental mail plane flight between France and French Indo-China.	Jack Sharkey defeats Young Stribling in a heavyweight match at Flamingo Park, Miami Beach, before a crowd of 35,000 people....Colonel Charles D. Lindbergh and his fiancée Miss Anne Morrow have a serious accident when their plane crashes. However, neither of them is seriously injured.	Feb. 27
President Coolidge appoints John H. Woolsey and Alfred A. Wheat to be judges respectively in the Southern and Eastern District of New York....The House passes the Jones Bill in the same form already passed by the Senate. The bill establishes a $10,000 fine or five years' imprisonment for Prohibition violation....President-elect Hoover completes the selection for his Cabinet. No southern politician is included.		The stock market makes large gains as the approach of Hoover's Inauguration spreads optimism....The stocks of the First National Bank go up $950 in two days.		Representative Fiorello LaGuardia marries former secretary Miss Marie Fisher.	Feb. 28
The House of Representatives and the Senate end their long dispute on how much money should be appropriated to enforce the laws on prohibition. A total of just over $3 million is agreed in addition to the funds already appropriated....President-elect Hoover selects former Missouri Governor Arthur M. Hyde as Secretary of Agriculture in his Cabinet....President Coolidge announces that he will not give a farewell address to the nation.	Future Secretary of State Henry L. Stimson meets Chinese Cabinet Ministers in Nanking.	The belief in an extended "Hoover boom" in securities produces sharp rises on the stock market.		Jimmy McLarnin knocks out Joe Glick at the beginning of the second round before a crowd of 20,000 at Madison Square Garden.	Mar. 1
President Elect Hoover chooses Robert Patterson Lamont as Secretary of Commerce in his Cabinet....President Coolidge signs the Jones Bill, increasing the penalties for violation of Prohibition laws.		The steamer Richard Peck grounds on Conanicut Island in Narragansett Bay.	Bitter cold weather continues to sweep over all of Europe.		Mar. 2
Washington prepares for the inauguration of President Hoover. The inauguration draws thousands of people to the capital.		Haley Fiske, President of Metropolitan Life, the largest financial institution in the world, dies....Fox Theaters Corporation announces that it has acquired control of Loew's Inc. The transaction brings to Fox 450 more motion picture theaters.		Babe Ruth starts training with the Yankees after several weeks in Florida.	Mar. 3

F	G	H	I	J
Includes campaigns, elections, federal-state relations, civil rights and liberties, crime, the judiciary, education, healthcare, poverty, urban affairs, and population.	Includes formation and debate of U.S. foreign and defense policies, veterans affairs, and defense spending. (Relations with specific foreign countries are usually found under the region concerned.)	Includes business, labor, agriculture, taxation, transportation, consumer affairs, monetary and fiscal policy, natural resources, pollution and industrial accidents.	Includes worldwide scientific, medical and technological developments, natural phenomena, U.S. weather and natural disasters.	Includes the arts, religion, scholarship, communications media, sports, entertainment, fashions, fads, and social life.

	World Affairs	Europe	Africa & The Middle East	The Americas	Asia & The Pacific
Mar. 4	The League of Nations Council begins its fifty-fourth session in Geneva....The conference of debt experts for German war reparations agrees on the proposal of its chairman, Owen D. Young, to create a new international body to replace the Reparation Board.	Twenty-eight workers, mostly women, are killed in an explosion in a military arsenal in Sofia, Bulgaria.		The revolt expands in Mexico and rebels gain vital border cities.	Nine villages surrounding the capital of Shantung are destroyed by a brigade of troops of unknown allegiance....Mahatma Gandhi is arrested following his participation to a demonstration supporting the boycott of foreign cloth.
Mar. 5	The League of Nations Council cannot agree on a resolution on the protection of minorities in European nations and thus postpones the discussion of the issue.			The rebels make new important gains in Mexico. U.S. President Hoover decides to support Mexican President Portes Gil against the rebels.	The forces of the Chinese Nationalist government are defeated in clashes with Hankow troops in Hunan.... Mahatma Gandhi is released on bond to appear in answer to charges linked to his participation to the boycott demonstration.
Mar. 6	The international commission of experts on German war reparations cannot agree on the amount the Reich should pay.	The Bulgarian and Turkish governments sign a Treaty of Friendship, settling several disputes between the two countries....More than 100 people are killed by a great landslide in the Valley of St. Vincent in Madeira Islands....Irish Nationalist leader Eamon de Valera is released from jail....Spanish dictator General Primo de Rivera says he will govern the country for two more years, but calls his dictatorship a transitory measure.	The British Cabinet discusses the possible unification of the territories of Kenya, Uganda and Tanganyika under a new British protectorate.	Mexican federal troops recapture important strategic positions, including the city of Monterey.... Nicaragua rebel leader Augustus Sandino flees from the country.	
Mar. 7		French Premier Poincaré defers the discussion of several measures for religious orders thus averting a likely crisis of his government of national union....The Labor and the Conservative Parties challenge the pledge of Liberal Premier Lloyd George to end unemployment with recourse to public works rather than increasing taxation....The Conference of the Communist Party in Moscow plans a more rigid socialization campaign and the tightening of party unity.	Wahabi tribes invade the regions along the Transjordanian and Iraq frontiers.	Federal troops regain positions in the Southeastern and Eastern parts of Mexico, while rebels progress in the North and West. U.S. troops are put on guard as fighting develops along the border and refugees pour into Texas.	
Mar. 8	The international commission of experts on German war reparations recommends the establishment of an international bank to act as payment trustee.	French Premier Poincaré is harshly criticized by the Left minority in Parliament for his support to the passage of measures on behalf of religious orders....The Polish Minister of Finance Gebrjel Czechowicz resigns before the beginning of an investigation into excess expenditures.	Negotiations resume between the Egyptian and the British governments.	Federal and rebel troops continue their fierce battle for the control of Mexico. U.S. President Hoover agrees to sell arms to the Mexican government.	
Mar. 9	The League of Nations Council ends its fifty-fourth session expressing its "ardent desire" to include the United States in the World Court.... The Pope tells Vatican diplomatic corps that the Lateran Treaties with the Italian State have met with international approval.	As Danube floods threaten thousands of Czechs, army soldiers check the river to keep it from inundating villages and towns.... Spanish students strike against the decision of dictator Primo De Rivera to close down the artillery school at Segovia....Soviet officials deny that the rule of Stalin is endangered by the discontent of peasants for his agricultural policies.		Violent clashes between loyal and rebel forces continue in Mexico.... General Manuel Maria Jiron, a leader of the Sandino forces, is executed in Nicaragua.	General Li Tsung-jen, the Hankow government leader, states his support for the Chinese nationalist government and denies his supposed hostility against Premier Chiangkai-Shek.
Mar. 10	The establishment of an international bank for war reparations is opposed by Nationalist and Socialist parties in both France and Germany.	Italian dictator Benito Mussolini celebrates the Lateran Treaties before a crowd of four thousand Fascist chiefs....British authorities consider a bill to make the Prince of Wales Regent to act for his father during his convalescence.		Mexican federal forces recapture Canitas from the rebels.	Nadir Khan, the pretender to the Afghan throne, is arrested in the Khost country. Former King Amanullah begins his march on the capital to defeat Habibullah.

A	B	C	D	E
Includes developments that affect more than one world region, international organizations and important meetings of world leaders.	Includes all domestic and regional developments in Europe, including the Soviet Union.	Includes all domestic and regional developments in Africa and the Middle East.	Includes all domestic and regional developments in Latin America, the Caribbean, and Canada.	Includes all domestic and regional developments in Asian and Pacific nations (and colonies).

U.S. Politics & Social Issues	U.S. Foreign Policy & Affairs, Defense	U.S. Economy & Environment	Science, Technology & Nature	Culture, Leisure & Lifestyle	
Herbert Hoover is inaugurated 31st President of the United States. In his address he stresses his support for Prohibition and for world peace.					Mar. 4
Following the decision of President Hoover not to submit to the Senate the name of Secretary to the Treasury Mellon for confirmation, the Senate adopts a resolution calling for an investigation into the appointment. Several senators question whether Mellon can hold over from the previous administration and if his commercial involvements disqualify him from holding a Cabinet position.	Elihu Root delivers a proposal at the League of Nations Council in Geneva for U.S. admission to the World Court.	The supporters of John D. Rockefeller in the dispute with Robert W. Stuart over the chairmanship of the Standard Oil Company of Indiana state their certainty of victory....Fox Theaters Corporation announces the acquisition of two new chains of theaters, bringing Fox 113 more cinemas.	In a successful test, the submarine salvage tender *Ortolan* provides ventilation to the submarine *S-29*, which is simulating lying disabled on the bottom of the sea.		Mar. 5
President Hoover confers with Attorney General Mitchell on the establishment of a board for a more effective enforcement of Prohibition.		The Ford Motor Company announces that it will offer its shares on European markets soon....After a final check-up of proxies, supporters of John D. Rockefeller are confident to have ousted Colonel Robert W. Stewart from the management of the Standard Oil Company of Indiana.			Mar. 6
President Hoover calls Congress for an extra session beginning on April 15 to discuss measures for agricultural relief and legislation for changes in the tariff....President Hoover resumes the custom begun by President Harding but abandoned by President Coolidge to admit vice-presidents to Cabinet meetings.		Colonel Robert W. Stewart is overwhelmingly defeated by the forces of John D. Rockefeller in the fight over the chairmanship of the Standard Oil Company of Indiana.			Mar. 7
President Hoover states his intention to redistribute and simplify the entire Federal machinery of justice. This will be one of the tasks of the commission for the study of law enforcement that the President intends to appoint....Secretary of Commerce Robert P. Lamont resigns from the Association Against the Prohibition Amendment.	In his inaugural address, President Herbert Hoover urges the U.S. Senate to accept membership in the World Court.		The Master's Voice Gramophone Company acquires all of Guglielmo Marconi's patents and inventions.	Lucius M. Boomer, president of the Waldorf-Astoria Company, announces that work on a new Waldorf-Astoria Hotel will start in the Fall on Park Avenue in New York City.	Mar. 8
President Hoover will not proceed slowly in its appointment of the law enforcement commission to make sure to have an impartial group.	President Hoover appoints David S. Ingalls Assistant Secretary of the navy in Charge of Aviation.	A fire in Staten Island causes damages for over $100,000.	Colonel Charles A. Lindbergh inaugurates regular daily air mail service between Mexico and the United States.	The University of Notre Dame confers the Laetare Medal, the most notable distinction that can be give to a lay Catholic in the United States, to former New York Governor Alfred E. Smith.	Mar. 9
President Hoover's caution in making appointments disappoints office-seekers, particularly those Democrats who bolted their party's presidential ticket to support Hoover.			Colonel Lindbergh finishes his air mail round trip between Brownsville, Texas, and Mexico City, Mexico.		Mar. 10

F	G	H	I	J
Includes campaigns, elections, federal-state relations, civil rights and liberties, crime, the judiciary, education, healthcare, poverty, urban affairs, and population.	Includes formation and debate of U.S. foreign and defense policies, veterans affairs, and defense spending. (Relations with specific foreign countries are usually found under the region concerned.)	Includes business, labor, agriculture, taxation, transportation, consumer affairs, monetary and fiscal policy, natural resources, pollution and industrial accidents.	Includes worldwide scientific, medical and technological developments, natural phenomena, U.S. weather and natural disasters.	Includes the arts, religion, scholarship, communications media, sports, entertainment, fashions, fads, and social life.

	World Affairs	Europe	Africa & The Middle East	The Americas	Asia & The Pacific
Mar. 11	The League of Nations holds its second Conference for the Scientific Study of International Relations.... League of Nations jurists begin to study Elihu Root's proposal for the admission of the United States to the World Court. They accept it as basis for negotiation.	The Balfour Committee on British industry issues its final report after four years' work. It recommends mergers to increase the size of business units and make them more competitive....King Boris of Bulgaria is the first royal person to visit Vienna since Austria has been proclaimed a republic.		Mexican federal forces arrest several rebel leaders and continue their offensive against the rebels.	Chinese authorities strengthen security measures as they fear the outbreak of Communist disorders on the anniversary of Sun Yat-sen's death and the beginning of the third Kuomintang Congress in Nanking.
Mar. 12	Diplomatic talks between France, Britain and the United States advance the possibility of calling a naval limitation conference this year.	The National University of Dublin refuses to give George Bernard Shaw a honorary degree.... According to German sources, the Soviet Commissar for Foreign Affairs George Tchitcherin has been exiled....British Prime Minister Lloyd George presents his Public Works Scheme to solve Britain's unemployment problem....Spanish police opens fire against university students striking against Primo De Rivera's dictatorship.		The massive surrender of rebel soldiers and generals leads Mexican President Portes Gil to declare the revolt virtually broken.	A violent dust storm sweeps over Peking discouraging demonstrations for the anniversary of Sun Yat-sen's death.
Mar. 13		Following his indictment for the failure of his North pole expedition, Italian General Umberto Nobile resigns from air service to clear himself....Switzerland grants Leon Trotsky a temporary visa for medical treatments....The Tory Party welcomes the reported industrial gains as an important weapon against the Labor Party in the coming British general election....More fighting between striking students and police forces erupts in Madrid and Barcelona.		The Mexican government reports defections in rebel ranks throughout the country.	
Mar. 14		Italian dictator Mussolini urges Parliament to ratify the Lateran treatises without delays....Widespread purges within the Communist Party are reported in Russia....French Premier Poincaré obtains two confidence votes from Parliament on the issue restoring financial aid and privileges to religious orders.		Mexican rebels start a counterattack on Naco, while federal troops converge on Torreon....Brazilian and Paraguayan troops clash over the disputed Island of Margarita in the Paraguay River.	Military clashes along the Kiangsi-Hunan border continue in China while Nationalist and Hankow troops make large-scale movements.
Mar. 15	Owen D. Young, the chairman of the international commission on war reparations, states that almost all differences between the members are resolved. The creation of an international bank to act as trustee for German payments is in sight.	The French Chamber of Deputies discusses in a tense session the responsibility of the death of 200 soldiers in the army of the Rhine due to an influenza epidemic the previous month. Poincaré's government obtains another vote of confidence....Leon Trotsky charges the United States with causing international political tensions.		Mexican rebel and federal forces get ready for the battle of Torreon. Loyal troops regain control of Durango City.	The third Kuomintang Congress opens in Peking. Martial law is enforced to prevent disorders.
Mar. 16		The Italian Fascist Party issues a Decalogue for the youth, stating that the Premier Mussolini is always right....Sweden ratifies the Kellogg pact....Russian workers' newspapers attack Trotsky for giving interviews to the capitalist press.		Mexican rebel troops evacuate Torreon as federal troops approach the city.	President Chiang Kai-Shek orders 6,500 troops to leave the Chinese capital for Kiukiang as part of the tensions between the Nationalist government and Hankow forces.
Mar. 17	Pope Pius XI tenders his first diplomatic luncheon to the Vatican Diplomatic Corps.	Queen Marie of Rumania visits her son, former Crown Prince Carol, in Paris. Official sources deny that the visit aims to place the ex-Crown Prince on the throne.	The Cairo Museum displays the first installment of objects brought from Tut-ankh-Amon's tomb in Luxor.	The battle between Mexican rebel ad federal troops breaks out in Torreon. Rebel forces are reported to fight just to cover their retreat.	

A	B	C	D	E
Includes developments that affect more than one world region, international organizations and important meetings of world leaders.	Includes all domestic and regional developments in Europe, including the Soviet Union.	Includes all domestic and regional developments in Africa and the Middle East.	Includes all domestic and regional developments in Latin America, the Caribbean, and Canada.	Includes all domestic and regional developments in Asian and Pacific nations (and colonies).

U.S. Politics & Social Issues	U.S. Foreign Policy & Affairs, Defense	U.S. Economy & Environment	Science, Technology & Nature	Culture, Leisure & Lifestyle	
Prohibitionist leaders seek to have Mrs. Mabel Walker Willebrandt, Assistant Attorney General, in charge of the Hoover Administration's program for law enforcement.	Secretary of State Kellogg announces that the United States will never recognize Mexican rebels as belligerents....Preisdent Hoover announces he will retain Brigadier General Frank T. Hines director of the Veterans Bureau.	The Supreme Court orders the Treasury to pay $45 million to the railroads over the retroactive application of increased rates for post transportation....General Motors buy 76 percent of the total shares of Opel, thus getting a decisive influence on the German automobile market.	Colonel Richard Byrd names part of the Antarctica region that he is exploring after British Captain Robert Falcon Scott.	The English racing driver H. O. D. Segrave establishes a new world's automobile speed record driving at an average of 231 miles an hour at Daytona Beach....New York banker Jules S. Bache, the owner of one of the finest private art collections in the world, acquires Raphael's Portrait of Giuliano de Medici for $600,000.	Mar. 11
The Beth Israel Hospital opens in New York.	President Hoover considers General Charles G. Dawes for a European ambassadorship.	President Hoover announces his intention of banning government oil lands from sale or leasing.	A team of astronomers from the University of Pennsylvania obtains further support to link the phenomenon of Aurora Borealis to spots on the sun.	Philanthropist Asa Griggs Candler, the founder of the Coca-Cola business, dies in Atlanta, GA.	Mar. 12
Several raids are made on Broadway under the new ones law which provides five-year sentences and $10,000 fines for Prohibition violations.	The United States and Cuba begin negotiations for a new reciprocity treaty which could result in a sharp cut in tariff rates.	The Interstate Commerce Commission finds the New York Central, Baltimore & Ohio and New York, Chicago & St. Louis (Nickel Plate) railroads guilty of lessening competition. It orders the railroads to divest themselves of their holdings of 51 percent of the stock of the Wheeling & Lake Erie Railroad whose purchase was made without the Commission's consent.	William Beebe, Ocean explorer, sails for his thirty-second expedition to find any kind of deep sea-life in the Bermudas.	Lee Bible, dirt track racer, dies in a car crash at Daytona Beach while attempting to set a new world's automobile speed record.	Mar. 13
President Hoover issues an Executive Order to give publicity to refunds of income taxes in excess of £20,000.	Former Secretary of State Charles Hughes confers with President Hoover on U.S. admission to the World Court	Secretary Mellon urges investors to buy bonds....The purchase of Opel Works by General Motors and Ford's plans for expansion on the European market create intense rivalry between the two companies.	The town of Elba in Alabama is submerged by a flood caused by the sudden rise of the waters of the Pea River and White Water Creek.	A few days after setting a new world's speed record, British driver H.O.D. Segrave retires from auto racing.	Mar. 14
President Hoover announces his intention not to appear in person in front of Congress for his address on tariff adjustment and farm relief. The custom of appearing in person before Congress was reintroduced by President Wilson and followed by Presidents Harding and Coolidge.... George W. Olvany resigns as leader of Tammany Hall on the ground of ill health....Secretary of Interior Wilbur plans a new government policy towards Indians which will favor their rehabilitation and their assimilation.		Because of the soaring stock market, experts expect gains in tax receipts, leading the Treasury surplus to $50 million....Floods continue to spread over large areas in Alabama, Georgia and Florida. 15,000 people are threatened with death....General Motors offers to buy more Vauxhall shares in its attempt to expand its influence on European markets....As part of his oil conservation policy President Hoover announces the review of 20,000 outstanding oil development permits to determine their legal status.	Professor C. Leonard Woolley claims to have discovered material evidence supporting the biblical accounts of the deluge in Mesopotamia.		Mar. 15
The Department of Justice demands the resignation of John W. Snook, warden of Atlanta penitentiary, over the planting of spies in the prison.		Roy A. Young, Governor of the Federal Reserve Board states he has no intention of advancing rediscount rates.	Heavy floods continue to threaten citizens of Alabama and Florida. About 20,000 people are affected.	Irish immigrants celebrate St. Patrick's Day throughout the United States. A procession of more than 15,000 people takes place in New York.	Mar. 16
James A. Foley refuses to run for the leadership of Tammany Hall.		Federal Reserve Bank reports indicate that the government will obtain a higher revenue from taxes compared to the previous year..... Thirteen people are killed in a plane crash in the Jersey meadows.	Alabama Governor Bibb Graves issues a statement appealing for a minimum relief fund of $250,000 to relieve the suffering of Alabama flood refugees.	Loiuse McPhetridge sets a new women's endurance flight record of 22 hours, 3 minutes and 12 seconds.	Mar. 17

F	G	H	I	J
Includes campaigns, elections, federal-state relations, civil rights and liberties, crime, the judiciary, education, healthcare, poverty, urban affairs, and population.	Includes formation and debate of U.S. foreign and defense policies, veterans affairs, and defense spending. (Relations with specific foreign countries are usually found under the region concerned.)	Includes business, labor, agriculture, taxation, transportation, consumer affairs, monetary and fiscal policy, natural resources, pollution and industrial accidents.	Includes worldwide scientific, medical and technological developments, natural phenomena, U.S. weather and natural disasters.	Includes the arts, religion, scholarship, communications media, sports, entertainment, fashions, fads, and social life.

	World Affairs	Europe	Africa & The Middle East	The Americas	Asia & The Pacific
Mar. 18	The committee of jurists appointed by the League of Nations for the admission of the United States to the World Court accepts Elihu Root's proposal.			Mexican rebels in the north of the country issue a peace plea, but the central government refuses to negotiate with them....Venezuelan President Juan Vincente Gomez denies the insistent reports of disorders and unrest in the country.	Tensions between Hankow and Nanking forces erupt again along the Hunan-Kiangsi border in China.
Mar. 19	The Young commission on war reparations reach an impasse while it tries to determine how much the German annuities should be.	Czech troops rescue 2,000 people from flooded villages....The Louvre opens three new rooms devoted to the 19th-century French School, including the Impressionists.... Thousands of people welcome the arrival to Oslo of Princess Martha of Sweden, the future Crown Princess of Norway.		Rebel forces further retreat as federal troops advance. The Mexican government announces that it plans to ask the extradition as bank robbers of rebel leaders who cross the U.S. border.	Hankow rebels win battles along the Hunan-Kiangsi front and take more than 500 prisoners from the Chinese Nationalist Army.
Mar. 20	The Young Commission on war reparations accepts the three final reports of its subcommittees. The exact figures of how much Germany should pay for reparations, however, are still undecided.	Marshall Ferdinand Foch, the French supreme commander of the Allied armies during the First World War, dies in Paris at 77 years of age.... German spas bar the admission of Leon Trotsky as patient arguing that his presence would drive tourists away....Two thousand families are forced to evacuate their homes on the right bank of the Danube due to heavy floods.	More objects from the Tut-Ankh-Amen's grave are displayed at Cairo Museum.	Rebel forces attack federal troops in Mazatlan on the Mexican west coast. General Aguirre, leader of the rebel forces in Vera Cruz, is arrested.	Police forces launch a surprise offensive against Communist labor leaders in India....General Chiang Kai-shek, president of the Chinese Nationalist government, issues a long manifesto attacking Hankow Generals and threatening a civil war.
Mar. 21	Allied governments fix at $420 million the minimum which Germany should pay as her first annuity payment for war reparations.	Crown Prince Olaf of Norway marries Princess Martha of Sweden....The Liberal Party wins a Cheshire seat in a by-election from the Conservative Party in the United Kingdom		General Aguirre, Mexican rebel leader, is executed. 6,000 federal troops move from Torreon to Mazatlan to counter the attack by rebel columns.	Tensions between the Chinese Nationalist Government and Hankow forces make the prospect of a civil war increasingly likely.... The Viceroy vetoes a debate in the Legislative Assembly o the arrest of thirty-one Communists in India.
Mar. 22	The international commission of experts on war reparations fears U.S. opposition to the Allies' intention of using the Reich's payments for direct remission to the United States to meet the debt payments.	British Foreign Minister Austen Chamberlain objects to the visa fee abolition for American visitors to the U.K....French Premier Poincaré wins the two final votes on the restoration of financial benefits for religious missions....Italian dictator Mussolini issues an "order sheet" to all militants asking them to vote in favor of the plebiscite taking place on Sunday....The Labor Party wins a seat in North Lancashire from the Conservatives in a by-election.	Hafez Bey, Foreign Minister of Egypt, arrives in Berlin to discuss King Fuad's visit planned for the middle of May.	Mexican rebels attack federal forces in the Pacific Coast port of Mazatlan, but are repulsed.	Chinese Nationalist Premier Chiang Kai-shek sends 70,000 troops to the Hankow front in preparation for a military attack.
Mar. 23	Pope Pius is presented with several palms celebrating the newly-reached agreement with the Italian State for the Palm Sunday celebrations....Elihu Root leaves the League of Nations in Geneva for Paris. His proposal has brought the United States nearer to the admission to the World Court.	Italian Fascists celebrate the tenth anniversary of the foundation of Fascism and urge citizens to vote in the election tomorrow. The Fascist Party will be the only party in the polls.		Mexican rebels are repulsed in repeated attacks at Mazatlan where the battle with federal troops continues to rage.	Both houses of the Japanese Parliament pass a new and higher tariff schedule on lumber, which will mainly affect wood from Northwest America....Chinese Nationalist troops clash with Wuhan forces near Kiukiang.
Mar. 24	Elaborate ceremonies mark the beginning of the Holy Week in the Vatican....Owen D. Young, chair of the war reparation committee, announces his intention to conclude a quick agreement between the former allied nations and Germany on the amount the Reich should pay for reparations.	The Fascist Party receives more than 99 percent of the votes in Italian national elections....A huge crowd pays homage to the corpse of Marshal Foch at the Arch of Triumph in Paris....Nine shots are fired during a demonstration in Monte Carlo. Citizens demand more rights from the Prince.	The dirigible *Graf Zeppelin* takes off for its five-day non-stop flight over the Mediterranean and the Holy Land.	Repulsed by Mexican federal defenders at Mazatlan, rebels withdraw after heavy casualties. Federal reinforcements arrive to raise the city's siege.	After 10 months of negotiation, the Chinese Nationalist government and Japan reach a settlement for the Tsianan-fu incident. Japanese troops will withdraw from Chinese territory and a commission will be established to consider compensation of citizens of both countries who suffered during the incident.

A	B	C	D	E
Includes developments that affect more than one world region, international organizations and important meetings of world leaders.	Includes all domestic and regional developments in Europe, including the Soviet Union.	Includes all domestic and regional developments in Africa and the Middle East.	Includes all domestic and regional developments in Latin America, the Caribbean, and Canada.	Includes all domestic and regional developments in Asian and Pacific nations (and colonies).

U.S. Politics & Social Issues	U.S. Foreign Policy & Affairs, Defense	U.S. Economy & Environment	Science, Technology & Nature	Culture, Leisure & Lifestyle	
New York Mayor James Walker summons several district leaders to discuss the future leadership of Tammany Hall. Although the mayor does not have a candidate, he wishes to see a leader elected who would be friendly to his administration.	Eugene P. Carver, commander in chief of the Veterans of Foreign Wars, announces that the bodies of American war dead buried in Russia will be returned to the United States as soon as their graves are located.		The Alabama River causes more severe floods in Western Alabama.	According to a survey of the Continental Insurance Company, diamonds worth $4,000,000,000 are owned in the United States.... Richard F. Hoyt, chairman of the board of directors of the Madison Square Garden Corporation, announces the appointment of William F. Carey as president.	Mar. 18
	Opposition to the admission of the United States to the World Court emerges in the Senate.			Rodman Wanamaker leaves an estate appraised at over $58 million, the largest ever left by a Philadelphian.	Mar. 19
Oklahoma Governor Henry S. Johnston is found guilty by the Senate Court of Impeachment on a charge of general incompetence ad is removed from office....Former President Coolidge visits New York, leaving his home in Northampton, Massachusetts, for the first time since his retirement from the Presidency....President Hoover says he will not draft legislative measures and the send them to Congress urging their passage.	Senator Borah attacks U.S. admission to the World Court. He describes the court as merely a department of the League of Nations and denounces its authority to issue advisory opinions concerning international disputes....The Navy Department approves the building of fifteen 10,000 ton cruisers according to the Congress authorization.	Nineteen people are killed in the crash of two express trains of the Canadian National Railways in Ontario.	Floods wash levees along the Mississippi River north of Quincy, Illinois, forcing dozens of families to evacuate their homes.	Colonel Charles Lindbergh ad his fiancée Miss Morrow announce their wedding in June.	Mar. 20
Four bombs are found at Grand Central Station post-office in a parcel addressed to Chicago. On a closer inspection, however, they turn out to be simply the exhibits of an amateur lecturer on crime....The Caucus summoned to elect the new leader of Tammany Hall fails to agree on a common candidate.... Louisiana House of Representatives censures Governor Huey P. Long on the allegation of offering positions in state departments in exchange for votes.		Twenty-one miners are killed ad 10 more are missing following a explosion in Kilnoch mie near Pittsburgh....John D. Rockefeller buys the entire village of East View in New Jersey paying almost four times its assessed value. The village will be entirely demolished and then used for the new main line of the Putnam division of the New York Central Railroad.		The opera Fra Gherardo with the music and libretto by Ildebrando Pizzetti has it's American premiere at the Metropolitan.	Mar. 21
President Hoover issues a proclamation putting into operation the national origin quotas of the immigration act on July 1. National origins therefore become the basis of the immigration quotas, although Hoover states he is strongly against this criteria....Former President Calvin Coolidge leaves New York and asks journalists to respect his privacy.		President Hoover puts out of commission the yacht Mayflower, saving $300,000 a year to the U.S. treasury....Stock prices drop seven points as fears of drastic action by the Federal Reserve Board to curb speculation lead to strong sales.	Heavy Spring storms sweep southern states, killing six people and leaving heavy property damage.	Baritone Titta Ruffo severs his contract with the Metropolitan Opera Company and announces his intention to devote most of his time to sing in sound movies....The granddaughter of German General Von Kluck makes her Hollywood debut with the Metro-Goldwyn production of 1813, a film about the liberation of German states from Napoleon....Mrs. M.A. Gemmell's Gregalach wins the British Grand National competition.	Mar. 22
In the debate for the election of the new Tammany Hall leader, it becomes clear that former Governor Smith will have a decisive role. Senator Robert F. Wagner appears the most likely candidate although he states he does not want the job.	President Hoover seems reluctant to encourage Congress to revise tariffs upward in such a way that this would disturb the commercial relation between the United States and Europe....The British schooner I'm Alone, an alleged rum runner, is sunk by U.S. Coast Guard craft off the Louisiana coast.	Income taxes in the first twenty-one days of March exceed the total of the whole month of the previous year. The predicted surplus for the fiscal year is $150 million.	Tornadoes and heavy rains cause new floods and more deaths in Tennessee, Mississippi, Alabama, Georgia and Kentucky.	Twelve-year-old violinist Yehudi Menuhin sails for Europe where he will perform in several cities.	Mar. 23
Former President Calvin Coolidge positively assesses his administration saying he has made no feuds and has won many friends....The committee to select the successor to George W. Olvany as leader of Tammany Hall receives the suggestion to elect a triumvirate to lead the organization.				William Fox announces that the Fox Film Corporation will only produce dialogue and musical pictures. The announcement comes after 18 months of preparation and an expenditure of $15 million on new studios, machinery and technical experimentation.	Mar. 24

F	G	H	I	J
Includes campaigns, elections, federal-state relations, civil rights and liberties, crime, the judiciary, education, healthcare, poverty, urban affairs, and population.	Includes formation and debate of U.S. foreign and defense policies, veterans affairs, and defense spending. (Relations with specific foreign countries are usually found under the region concerned.)	Includes business, labor, agriculture, taxation, transportation, consumer affairs, monetary and fiscal policy, natural resources, pollution and industrial accidents.	Includes worldwide scientific, medical and technological developments, natural phenomena, U.S. weather and natural disasters.	Includes the arts, religion, scholarship, communications media, sports, entertainment, fashions, fads, and social life.

	World Affairs	Europe	Africa & The Middle East	The Americas	Asia & The Pacific
Mar. 25	Owen D. Young points out to the members of his international war reparations commission that, having finished all their preliminary work, they should now discuss the exact figures of German reparations.	Spanish dictator Primo de Rivera publishes an unofficial statement indicating that he wishes to retire from active politics soon....Italian diplomacy resumes actions to extend its influence over Balkans nations. Italian Foreign Minister Dino Grandi announces a visit to Budapest in mid-April.		Mexican rebels retreat from Mazatlan ending their attack. Federal troops advance in their operations to recapture the Northern regions of the country.	Chinese Nationalist President Chiang Kai-shek and his staff leave the capital to move to Kiukiang to lead Nationalist forces against the Wuhan army.
Mar. 26	Dr. Schacht, German representative in the Young Committee, informally suggests an annuity of 1,300,000,000 marks for war reparations. Allies find the figure 500 million marks under their demands.	Allied Forces Supreme Commander Marshal Foch is buried in Les Invalides in Paris after a magnificent ceremony....Alanson B Houghton, American Ambassador to England, retires with a farewell dinner in London....The North German Lloyd liner Europa is badly damaged by fire....Soviet authorities issue new labor regulations to tighten discipline on the workplace. Three warnings lead to the worker's dismissal.		Federal troops led by General Calles continue their advance in the Northern part of Mexico forcing rebels to retreat.	Chinese Nationalist troops are defeated by rebel forces in Chefoo. Nationalist President Chiang Kai-shek declares war against Kwangsi rebel forces.
Mar. 27		The governments of Greece and Kingdom of the Serbs-Croats-Slovenes sign a Treaty of Friendship, settling the controversial issues of the Saloniki free zone.		Isidro Ayora is elected President of the Republic of Ecuador by the National Assembly....The federal troops headed by General Calles continue their advance pushing Mexican rebels on the retreat.	Chinese rebels take the city of Chefoo without encountering resistance from the defeated nationalist forces.
Mar. 28	Owen D. Young firmly asks German delegates to make an official offer regarding the Reich's war reparations. Failure to do this will lead to the end of the committee's works.	A Roman galley dating back to the era of Emperor Caligula is recovered from Lake Nemi, Italy....The Soviet newspaper Pravda publishes a report of the disorders caused in the countryside by the central government's decision to extract grains from peasants with harsh measures.	A dozen Israelite houses from between 1100 and 1200 B.C.E. are uncovered just north of Jerusalem by excavations led by Professor William F. Bade of the Pacific School of Religion.	Mexican rebels clash with the advancing troops of General Calles, but retreat after a brief fight.	The Japanese government orders its troops to prepare the withdrawal from the Shantung province due to the effective Chinese boycott of Japanese goods and the settlement of the Tsinan incident....The defeated Nationalist forces at Chefoo reform their ranks in preparation for another attack against the rebels who now occupy the city.
Mar. 29	Tensions within the Soviet Communist Party affect the apparent unity of the Communist International, which splits in various factions.	France and other European nations which produce no oil are worried for the restrictions on the oil production approved by the American Petroleum Institute....Former Crown Prince Carol states he is not going to try to return to Rumania to regain his throne....The French Senate ratifies unanimously the Kellogg treaty to outlaw war. The Chamber had already approved the treaty.		Mexican rebels at Chihuahua put on a staunch resistance against the federal troops led by General Calles. The leader of the rebels, General Escobar, attacks American Ambassador Dwight W. Morrow as a propaganda agent for the Mexican government.	Chinese Nationalist troops defeat Wuhan forces and capture the city of Hupeh.
Mar. 30	The League of Nations makes an official announcement showing optimism for the prospects of world peace.	German President Von Hindenburg gives 445,000 marks (about $100,000) of his fund collected in honor of his birthday to war widows and war maimed.	Pilgrims of every race crowd the city of Jerusalem in preparation for the Easter celebrations.	A violent battle near Chihuahua ends with the retreat of rebel forces. Both the rebels and the Mexican federal forces suffer great losses.	General Chiang Kai-shek, leader of the Chinese nationalist Government, is confident of defeating the Wuhan rebellion within two weeks.
Mar. 31		The citizens of Monte Carlo protest against the Prince and ask that France should proclaim their country a protectorate....American Ambassador to France Myron T. Herrick suddenly dies in Paris.		Rebel forces claim to have defeated a large force of Mexican federals near Escalon and to have taken more than 400 prisoners.	A coup d'état brings Canton under the influence of the Chinese Nationalist government.

A	B	C	D	E
Includes developments that affect more than one world region, international organizations and important meetings of world leaders.	Includes all domestic and regional developments in Europe, including the Soviet Union.	Includes all domestic and regional developments in Africa and the Middle East.	Includes all domestic and regional developments in Latin America, the Caribbean, and Canada.	Includes all domestic and regional developments in Asian and Pacific nations (and colonies).

U.S. Politics & Social Issues	U.S. Foreign Policy & Affairs, Defense	U.S. Economy & Environment	Science, Technology & Nature	Culture, Leisure & Lifestyle	
A committee of lawyers and members of the Louisiana House of Representatives meets to draft impeachment proceedings against Governor Huey P. Long....Jersey City Mayor Frank Hague bars inquiry into his bank funds.	Secretary Mellon justifies the sinking of the British rum-running schooner *I'm Alone* by applying the notion of "continuous pursuit" included in the International Code. British authorities will protest officially.	Due to a dense fog, a Ryan monoplane crashes into a tree on South Mountain, Pennsylvania, killing its pilot and three passengers....The stock market experiences one of its sharpest drops in history as rumors about the tightening of the country's credit leads speculators to sell their holdings.	The Spanish plane *Jesus del Gran Poder* crosses the Atlantic Ocean in a 36-hour flight from Spain to Brazil....Four miners are buried under a snowslide in Gunnison, Colorado.	Representatives of big film studios such as Paramount, Metro-Goldwyn-Mayer and Warner Brothers are reluctant to follow Fox in the exclusive production of sound films. They point out that many theaters are not yet equipped to show sound films and that the foreign market still privileges silent movies.	Mar. 25
Impeachment proceedings are introduced against Governor Huey P. Long in the Louisiana House of Representatives. The impeachment resolution charges Long with inducing a murder plot against Representative J. Y. Sanders....President Hoover urges his Republican Party to reorganize in the South and select respectable leaders.	As the rum-running schooner *I'm Alone* is of Canadian registry, Canada, rather than Britain, will take a more active part in the diplomatic protest against the United States for the sinking of the ship.	The stock market crashes as loan rate mounts, but then recovers in the last hour of trading.			Mar. 26
Jersey City Mayor Frank Hague charges State Counsel to have entered fake evidence of $200,000 graft....Al Capone is charged with contempt of Federal Court for faking illness to avoid appearing before the Federal Grand Jury.		The stockmarket recovers after the sharp crash of the previous day....Directors of the American Petroleum Institute adopt a resolution to limit oil production to the average output of 1928.	League of Nations experts point out the dangers of using x-ray treatments in the cure of cancer.	Golfer Horton Smith wins the North and South open with a score of 287. This is Smith's seventh major conquest of the Winter golf season.	Mar. 27
Michigan legislature repeals by unanimous vote the inclusion of violators of prohibition law in the statute that make life imprisonment mandatory for fourth-time offenders....Congressman M. Alfred Michaelson is indicted on charges of violating the national prohibition act....Because of President Hoover's concerns over effective law enforcement, Attorney General Mitchell launches a vast enquiry into the accomplishments of U.S. attorneys and marshals.	Colonel Henry L. Stimson takes the oath of office as Secretary of State.	Senator Carter Glass, former Secretary of the Treasury and one of the authors of the Federal Reserve act, demands the resignation of Charles Mitchell as a Class A directors of the New York Reserve bank for his aid to stock market borrowers....Radio subsidiary R.C.A. Communications is sold to the International Telephone and Telegraph Corporation.		Pilot Martin Jensen sets a new world's solo duration record landing after more than 35 hours.	Mar. 28
Broker George R. Christian, responsible for the 1924 bankruptcy of Day & Heaton, is arrested by the police in Texas after a five-year hunt....Henry J. Allen, former Governor of Kansas, is chosen as Senator for that State to succeed Vice President Curtis....Federal authorities issue a warrant for the arrest of Representative Alfred Michaelson for breach of prohibition laws. Another representative, William M. Morgan, is accused of having brought liquor into New York upon his arrival on the liner *Cristobal*.	The new Secretary of State Henry Stimson tanks his predecessor Frank Kellogg for his cooperation in the transition from one administration to the other. He also announces that he will continue his predecessor's policies.	Several senators support Senator Glass's call for an investigation in the speculative activities on the stock market....Delegates on the American committee for the British General Electric Company protest against the proposed substitute financial scheme.	Captain Hubert Wilkins plans to launch an exploration of the Antarctic in July.		Mar. 29
Following President Hoover's recommendation, the Interior Department cancels all oil exploration permits obtained for speculation without any intention of operation.		Former Senator Robert L. Owen comes to the defense of Charles E. Mitchell, President of the National City Bank of New York, for offering funds to borrowers after the stock market crash last week....Secretary of the Treasury Mellon states he is in favor of reducing income taxes when public debt and interest charges are cut.	The London to Karachi air service begins transporting both mail and passengers.		Mar. 30
United States Attorney Tuttle begins an investigation to understand whether Republican Representative William M. Morgan has imported or transported liquor in violation of Prohibition laws.	Senator Hiram W. Johnson strongly criticizes Elihu Root's plan to make the United States a member of the World Court.	Charles E. Mitchell, president of the National city Bank, asks for a six percent Federal Reserve rediscount rate, a one percent increase.			Mar. 31

F	G	H	I	J
Includes campaigns, elections, federal-state relations, civil rights and liberties, crime, the judiciary, education, healthcare, poverty, urban affairs, and population.	*Includes formation and debate of U.S. foreign and defense policies, veterans affairs, and defense spending. (Relations with specific foreign countries are usually found under the region concerned.)*	*Includes business, labor, agriculture, taxation, transportation, consumer affairs, monetary and fiscal policy, natural resources, pollution and industrial accidents.*	*Includes worldwide scientific, medical and technological developments, natural phenomena, U.S. weather and natural disasters.*	*Includes the arts, religion, scholarship, communications media, sports, entertainment, fashions, fads, and social life.*

	World Affairs	Europe	Africa & The Middle East	The Americas	Asia & The Pacific
Apr. 1	General Charles Dawes, former vice president, spends time in Puerto Rico, visiting with Governor Horace Towner and inspecting the local troops. Dawes is leading a commission that is en route the Dominican Republic to assist that nation with creating a new, efficient budget.			Mexican Federalists and rebels clash in 18 hour battle at Jimenez, Mexico. Heavy fighting also occurs in La Cruz, along the Pacific Coast and rebel airplanes bomb Naco, Sonora....Brazilian government allocates $750,000 to fight yellow fever epidemic....Two Uruguayan pilots missing on extended flight from Montevideo to New York.	Chinese Nationalist troops kills over 2000 rebels fighting under Marshal change Tsung-Chang at Ninghaichow.
Apr. 2	Thousands of letters of sympathy from all over the world pour into the American Embassy in Paris and the city of Paris proposes to name a street or square in the Bois du Bolougne neighborhood in honor of Ambassador Myron Herrick, who died in office on March 31.	Germans pay first half of the yearly interest of approximately $36 million on World War I war debt for the fifth straight year.	The newly created Transjordanian government opens its first Legislative Assembly....Wahabi raiders kill 400 Howeitat Arabs in Transjordania.	Mexico's rebel army bombs hits Naco, Arizona by mistake, while Federal troops win battle at Jimenez....Former Vice President Charles G. Dawes and other members of commission arrive in the Dominican Republic to help develop a budget and encourage economic stability.	
Apr. 3	U.S. Vice President Charles Curtis protests the ruling by the former Secretary of State that his sister, Dolly Curtis Gann, should be seated after the wives of foreign dignitaries in Washington, DC. This question of etiquette arises because Gann is acting as official hostess for the widowed vice president at formal events.	Monsignor Ignaz Seipel resigns post as Chancellor of Austria due to criticism by others of his dual, and potentially conflicting, roles as government official and priest.	British Air Minister, Sir Samuel Hoare, arrives in Alexandria, Egypt as a passenger on the first England-to-India airmail service. His landing, in an amphibian plane, was the first of many planned passenger flights to use Alexandria as a transfer point from Europe to points in the Middle East and Africa.	Rebels in Chihuahua, Mexico take heavy losses, in part due to 75 lb. bombs provided to Federal Army by United States....Airmail delivery is delayed in the Panama Canal Zone because there is no cooperative agreement between U.S. mail services and Scadta, the new German-Colombian company that is distributing mail between Central and South America.	J. J. Mantell, former vice president of Erie Railroad announces he will become a consulting manager for the Chinese Nationalist railroads. He will survey over 12,000 miles of railway, including the Chinese Eastern Railway in Manchuria, which is jointly run by China and Russia.
Apr. 4		German doctors deny that germ warfare was planned or employed in World War I.		In Mexico, two Federal pilots are killed when their plane is shot down by rebels based at Naco, Sonora.	
Apr. 5	The first meeting of the International Journalist's Federation meets in Prague to discuss issues of professional conduct and protection for journalists working in foreign countries.	A French warship, the *Tourville*, begins its journey from Brest, France to the United States. It is bringing the body of the late Ambassador Myron Herrick for funeral and burial in Ohio.			Chinese Nationalist army regains control of Hankow, signaling collapse of Kwangsi rebellion. In Shantung (Shandong) province, however, warlord Marshal Chang Tsung-Chang captures city of Chefoo (Yuntai).
Apr. 6			The death toll of Bahuti tribesmen from Congo famine reaches thousands as aid supplies from Belgium are hampered by transport and supply problems.	U.S. troops clash with Mexican rebels along border in Arizona, leading to the death of one U.S. soldier. As a result of fighting in the region between rebels and Mexican troops, a bomb is again accidentally dropped on Naco, Arizona.	Members of the Sino-Japanese Commission meet in Shanghai to discuss the withdrawal of Japanese troops from Shantung (Shandong) Province, China.
Apr. 7	The first westward flight of England to India's airmail service begins.	Monaco's Prince Louis agrees to hold elections and return to constitutional regime....Swedish, Norwegian, and Finnish pulp paper industry leaders meet in Stockholm to regulate production rates.	An Egyptian Agricultural Syndicate in Cairo requests that President Herbert Hoover refrain from imposing U.S. tariffs on cotton to protect local industry....Italian troops in Libya kill 160 rebel tribesmen and 15 soldiers in a confrontation.		100 people are injured in Lahore, India during a riot that started during a funeral for Hindu author Mahasha Rajpal. He was murdered by Ilam Din, a Muslim who objected to the author's writings against Islam.

A	B	C	D	E
Includes developments that affect more than one world region, international organizations and important meetings of world leaders.	Includes all domestic and regional developments in Europe, including the Soviet Union.	Includes all domestic and regional developments in Africa and the Middle East.	Includes all domestic and regional developments in Latin America, the Caribbean, and Canada.	Includes all domestic and regional developments in Asian and Pacific nations (and colonies).

U.S. Politics & Social Issues	U.S. Foreign Policy & Affairs, Defense	U.S. Economy & Environment	Science, Technology & Nature	Culture, Leisure & Lifestyle	
Morehouse College, Spelman College, and Atlanta University agree to form an affiliation that will affect approximately 900 students. Morehouse and Spelman will primarily provide undergraduate training, while Atlanta University will serve as a graduate and professional school.		Stocks drop almost five percent, while call loan money rates rise 15 percent....National City Bank and Farmers' Loan and Trust Company agree to $2 billion merger, creating largest U.S. bank in capital funds. Farmer's Loan and Trust will be renamed City Bank Farmers Trust Company and concentrate on trust management, while transferring commercial operations to National City Bank.	Nine people die in the United States as 60 mile-per-hour winds strike 13 midwest and northeast states.		Apr. 1
A Wisconsin referendum to repeal state enforcement of prohibition laws is passed....The Louisiana House of Representatives begins review of 19 charges of impeachment filed against Governor Huey P. Long.	The State Department meets to decide any possible measures to take regarding the bombing of Naco, Arizona by Mexican rebel aircraft. Secretary of State Henry Stimson meets with President Herbert Hoover to confirm that strong retaliatory measures are possible.	Employers of home demolition workers announce they are forming a new union and will no longer deal with the House Wreckers Union, Local 95, which serves the 1,600 workers who are now on strike. The newly proposed union will not be recognized by the American Federation of Labor as the work force already has union representation.	The Mayon volcano in the Albay Province of the Philippines is erupting.		Apr. 2
	Matthew Woll, vice president of the American Federation of Labor, urges the Secretary of State to continue to refuse recognition of the Soviet Union, and states they are not a national government....Secretary of State Henry Stimson is made chairman of the Pan American Union to fill the spot held by the former Secretary Frank Kellogg. In a separate address Stimson warn U.S. residents that those who willingly participate in the Mexican rebellion will have no legal or other support from America.	National Guard troops brought to restore peace among workers striking at Gastonia, North Carolina textile mills. Workers are seeking a 40 hour work week and better wages. Employees at four South Carolina mills also go on strike.	The War Department gives permission to the New York State Department of Public Works to build two new bridges over navigable streams, one over Mott Creek on Long Island and the other across Twelve Mile Creek in Niagara County.		Apr. 3
An underground brewery is found and dismantled by Prohibition agents in Detroit, Michigan.	A U.S. Coast Guard vessel fires at, and narrowly misses, the Juan, a fruit-bearing Norwegian steamship in the Chesapeake Bay. After stopping, the ship was boarded by Guardsmen searching for liquor, although none was found.	The Brooklyn Chamber of Commerce announces that, based on U.S. Department of Commerce figures, the borough of Brooklyn is responsible for two percent of the nation's manufactured goods.	Albert Einstein submits additional work, including further equations, on Unitary Field Theory and Hamilton Principle, to Prussian Academy of Science in Berlin....Former Senator Nathan Straus, Jr. imports French tuberculosis vaccine made of "killed" form of virus for experimental trials.	New Moon, a musical by Sigmund Romberg, opens in London....The first National A.A.U. Greco-Roman Wrestling Championship is held and the heavyweight division is won by J. Manger.	Apr. 4
A report from Treasury Department reveals that 135 citizens and 55 Federal agents have been killed as a result of Federal agent-involved Prohibition enforcement efforts, but this total does not include state or local deaths.	The Secretary of War announces that Jewish soldiers will be granted leaves to celebrate the Passover holiday at home....Lawyers of the State Department are examining British claims of national sovereignty over regions in Antarctica as a result of the creation of Commander Richard Byrd's expedition and research station there.			Mary Pickford's first talking movie, Coquette, opens today in New York....Glenna Collett wins North and South Golf Championship for fifth time....Walter Spence wins the National A.A.U. Swim Championship.	Apr. 5
Members of the Louisiana House of Representatives vote 58 to 40 to impeach Governor Huey P. Long on first of 19 charges. He is charged with attempting to suppress the freedom of the press by threatening a Baton Rouge newspaper publisher.		A book published today notes that state of Louisiana is the leading producer of furs in the country, including those of muskrats and mink.	Two days of tornadoes and storms kill 27 in three upper U.S. Midwest states and Canada....Boeing Air Transport division announces radio communications between pilots and ground-based stations will begin operating along Chicago to Pacific Coast routes.	An hour long program of music and speeches is transmitted 12,000 miles by radio from New York to Commander Richard E. Byrd's Antarctic Expedition in Little America.	Apr. 6
A dynamite bomb addressed to New York Governor Franklin D. Roosevelt is discovered and accidentally discharged at a New York City post office.				New York's Hakoah All-Stars win U.S. Open Cup soccer championship for Eastern Soccer League....Fans rush the field in eighth inning of New York Yankees versus Oklahoma City Indians game to get Babe Ruth's autograph. The game ends in cushion fight among many of the 18,000 fans.	Apr. 7

F	G	H	I	J
Includes campaigns, elections, federal-state relations, civil rights and liberties, crime, the judiciary, education, healthcare, poverty, urban affairs, and population.	Includes formation and debate of U.S. foreign and defense policies, veterans affairs, and defense spending. (Relations with specific foreign countries are usually found under the region concerned.)	Includes business, labor, agriculture, taxation, transportation, consumer affairs, monetary and fiscal policy, natural resources, pollution and industrial accidents.	Includes worldwide scientific, medical and technological developments, natural phenomena, U.S. weather and natural disasters.	Includes the arts, religion, scholarship, communications media, sports, entertainment, fashions, fads, and social life.

	World Affairs	Europe	Africa & The Middle East	The Americas	Asia & The Pacific
Apr. 8	Nicholas Murray Butler, President of the Carnegie Endowment for International Peace, announces that 12 representatives from American newspapers will be sent on a visit to Japan, China, Manchuria and Korea. The purpose of the trip, which begins in May, is to foster international cooperation and contacts.		The Fourth Palestine and Near East Exhibition opens in Tel-Aviv to showcase local and foreign products.	U.S. military planes attempting to bomb suspected rebel camps along the Nicaraguan border mistakenly destroy town of Las Limas, Honduras.	Pro-Communist supporters detonate two small bombs at the Indian Legislative Assembly in Delhi, wounding five people....General Chiang Kai-shek announces that China's boycott of Japan will end.... Philippine workers digging a tunnel for an aqueduct near Manila uncover a 9,000 foot long gold vein worth an estimated $20 million.
Apr. 9	Delegates from 35 nations meet in Geneva as part of a conference to develop methods for prevention of counterfeiting.			Mexican rebels retreating from Juarez, Chihuahua kidnap an El Paso, Texas airplane mechanic. The unit has three remaining aircraft.... Canadian Minister Vincent Massey protests the March 22 sinking of the ship *I'm Alone* by the U.S. Coast Guard in the Gulf of Mexico. The ship's crew is freed from jail due to insufficient evidence they were smuggling alcohol.	
Apr. 10	Members of the diplomatic corps in the United States meet at the British Embassy in Washington, DC and agree to give Dolly Curtis Gann the same rank as her brother, Vice President Charles Curtis for purposes of social engagements.	The International Federation of Spiritualism asks British Parliament to abolish the law making an amendment to the witchcraft law so that those who believe spirits exist and believe they can be communicated with are not subject to legal punishment....Italian Premier Mussolini attempts to create a treaty of friendship with France as a result of encouragement by Britain's Foreign Minister.		The Honduran Government files protests with U.S. and Nicaraguan Legations over bombing and raids along the Honduras–Nicaragua border.	
Apr. 11	Leon Trotsky, the exiled former Soviet military leader, is denied entry into Germany.	Members of the Soviet Union's Central Executive Committee pass a law to prevent churches from performing welfare and charitable activities. The law also restricts attendance at religious services to members of a congregation.	The American Consul General in Cairo, Egypt meets with representatives of Egypt's General Agricultural Syndicate who request that he transmit their concerns about the proposed cotton tariff to the U.S. government.		
Apr. 12	Allied forces from World War I present Germany with a revised $24 billion bill combining war debt and reparations that is to be paid over 58 years.	A British outbreak of smallpox kills five and sickens 30 others. The disease is thought to have been carried by a sailor returning to England from Bombay.			All four crew members of the airplane *Southern Cross* are found alive after days of searching in the Australian bush for the downed plane. The crew, who completed an historic trans-Pacific flight, was attempting to fly from Sydney to London.....The Curtiss-Robertson Airplane Manufacturing Company will send 40 planes and pilots to begin commercial airmail and aviation service in China....Over 1,000 alleged Communists have been executed in Canton, including students from Sun Yat-sen University.
Apr. 13	Hjalmar Schacht, Reichsbank director, states that Germany will not pay the recently proposed amount to the Allies for war debt and reparations and will instead remain under the Dawes war debt repayment plan.	Kasimir Bartel resigns his post as premier of Poland.		Mexican rebels that remain in Sonora offer to surrender to Federal troops.	
Apr. 14		Over 70,000 attend a parade to demonstrate their loyalty to General Primo de Rivera, the dictator of Spain....Casimir Switalski, Poland's former Minister of Education, becomes the new premier and appoints three new cabinet members.	The German Junkers Luftverkehr Company begins air service between Baghdad and Tehran. This route can connect passengers and mail to the India-to-England routes.		The city of Tsing-Tao, China passes from control of the northern faction's Governor Chao Chi to that of the Nanking Nationalist Government.

A	B	C	D	E
Includes developments that affect more than one world region, international organizations and important meetings of world leaders.	*Includes all domestic and regional developments in Europe, including the Soviet Union.*	*Includes all domestic and regional developments in Africa and the Middle East.*	*Includes all domestic and regional developments in Latin America, the Caribbean, and Canada.*	*Includes all domestic and regional developments in Asian and Pacific nations (and colonies).*

U.S. Politics & Social Issues	U.S. Foreign Policy & Affairs, Defense	U.S. Economy & Environment	Science, Technology & Nature	Culture, Leisure & Lifestyle	
The U.S. Coast Guard fires 50 shots at two fishing boats, assumed to be rum-runners, off New York coast. No liquor is found on board.			A newly invented Handley-Page Interceptor slot on airplane wings is demonstrated. It helps to stabilize planes when engines stall in flight.		Apr. 8
Former Vice President Charles G. Dawes accepts the post of Ambassador to Great Britain.	The State Department announces it will be publishing a book that reviews the historical background of the Monroe Doctrine. It was prepared by J. Reuben Clark, the Under Secretary of State, for use by the members of Congress in their deliberation on the Kellogg antiwar treaty last fall.	The U.S. Department of Commerce announces that the United States is now the world leader in aircraft manufacturing.	James Gray explains the process by which food is converted into food and how this activity can be measured.		Apr. 9
On its first voyage as a privately owned vessel, the *Leviathan*, operated by the newly formed United States Lines, Inc. will serve liquor out of its medicinal stores once the ship passes three miles beyond the coastline. Passengers on their way to Cherbourg and Southampton can drink in their cabins or the smoking or dining room. In addition, the ship's crew will purchase liquor in Europe for distribution on the return trip.	The U.S. Shipping Board meets today and agrees on revisions to uniform rates for freight transported between the North Atlantic and Australia and New Zealand.	Former President Calvin Coolidge accepts an unpaid position on the board of directors for New York Life.	Over 50 dead and 200 are injured as tornadoes strike Arkansas.		Apr. 10
Louisiana Governor Huey P. Long is formally impeached on the charge of attempting to bribe legislators.		Sixty-five thousand women sign petitions against an Illinois ruling requiring beauty parlor operators to be licensed as barbers.		A printing press exhibit featuring rare books, prints, and typefaces from Germany begins at the Grolier Club in New York City.	Apr. 11
	The State Department releases a notice that it has not sought to establish an official diplomatic relationship with the Holy See in Vatican City, Italy. This notice was made in response the large numbers of citizens who have urged the Secretary of State, Henry Stimson, to refrain from such an action.		High waters in Great Lakes cause shore damage in Michigan, Wisconsin, Ohio, and Ontario....C. Francis Jenkins releases plans to record television footage from military airplanes to aid in battles.	Sir James Barrie donates all profits from publication and presentations of *Peter Pan* to London's Hospital for Sick Children.	Apr. 12
Democrats and Republicans disagree on the topics to be covered during the special session of Congress called by President Herbert Hoover that will begin on April 15. Republicans believe that only the farm bill and tariff legislation should be considered as those were the originally intended areas of focus.		James Davis, Secretary of Labor, announces that employment figures were increasing in all sectors except the building trades, as loans for new construction are subject to high interest rates.	New England is hit by a blizzard that brings both record snowfall inland and high waves along the coast.		Apr. 13
A U.S. Coast Guard vessel in Florida shoots over 200 machine-gun bullets at a suspected rum-running boat and stray shots hit surrounding houseboats nearly wounding one person.		Members of the U.S. House Committee on Agriculture finalize the draft of the farm bill to present it to the special session of Congress on April 15. The focus of the bill is providing farm relief by establishing a Federal Farm board, encouraging cooperative marketing, and by eliminating the equalization fee.	Commander Richard Byrd declares that the use of airplanes is invaluable to exploration of polar environments such as during his present Antarctic expedition. He notes that flying by relying on instruments occurs about 60 percent of the time when the surface and horizon become indistinguishable.	Charles Frederick William Grover-Williams wins the first Monaco Grand Prix race in a Bugatti 35B.	Apr. 14

F	G	H	I	J
Includes campaigns, elections, federal-state relations, civil rights and liberties, crime, the judiciary, education, healthcare, poverty, urban affairs, and population.	Includes formation and debate of U.S. foreign and defense policies, veterans affairs, and defense spending. (Relations with specific foreign countries are usually found under the region concerned.)	Includes business, labor, agriculture, taxation, transportation, consumer affairs, monetary and fiscal policy, natural resources, pollution and industrial accidents.	Includes worldwide scientific, medical and technological developments, natural phenomena, U.S. weather and natural disasters.	Includes the arts, religion, scholarship, communications media, sports, entertainment, fashions, fads, and social life.

	World Affairs	Europe	Africa & The Middle East	The Americas	Asia & The Pacific
Apr. 15		Britain abolishes the 325 year-old tax on tea....The Yugoslavian dictatorship officially bans the radical Croat newspaper founded by Stefan Raditch and also retires 36 military officers.		Members of Puerto Rico's Legislature vote to give women the right to vote if they can read and write. This right will become effective in the 1932 elections....A Federal gunboat prevents Mexican rebels from reaching and supporting the main rebel group in Sonora.	China retakes control of Tsinan-fu, capital of Shantung (Shandong) province from Japan....U.S. citizens in Kanchow in the Kiangsi Province are advised to leave due to Communist uprisings and siege of the city.
Apr. 16	At the Preparatory Disarmament Commission meeting in Geneva, the Chinese delegate proposes a resolution to end all compulsory military training. Maxim Litvinoff, the Soviet Union delegate, calls for a reduction of troops and stringent limitations on naval ship size.	Health ministers in France decree that all visitors coming from England must show proof they have been immunized for smallpox within the past two months.... Aleister Crowley, an expert on black magic and founder of a religion, is expelled from France....Spanish dictator Primo de Rivera tightens regulation of the press by requiring newspapers to publish certain government sponsored news items.		Airmail is flown from Miami to Peru in a record setting six and a half days. This is the first commercial flight on what is the longest regular air route in the Americas.	In China, Wuhan rebels fight with national Nanking troops along the Yangtze River.
Apr. 17	The German Reich offers to pay $396 million annually for a total of $6.16 billion over 37 years to cover Allied war debts, but not reparations....Leon Trotsky, the exiled former Soviet leader, is banned from entering Norway due to government concerns about ensuring his safety.		Persia ratifies the Kellogg antiwar treaty....A Belgian pilot and all but one of his crew is missing after their plane crashes at Kibanga Bay in the Belgian Congo. The remaining crew member is seriously wounded and doesn't know what happened to his crewmates.	Mail and passenger air service begins between the Panama Canal Zone and Colombia....Two U.S. Marine airplanes bring vaccines to assist with prevention of a smallpox outbreak in Nicaragua.	
Apr. 18	Discussion ends at the Reparations Conference in Paris as the delegates cannot reach a compromise on the amount of the first payment to be made by the Germans to the Allied forces of World War I.	Philip Snowden, a leader in Britain's Labor Party, states that the issue of war reparations will be an important factor in the country's upcoming elections.			Shanghai's city council votes to allow the city to sell its municipally owned electric company to the American and Foreign Power Company, which will allow the city to pay off its debts. The sale is expected to be made for $50 million, making it one of the largest foreign investments in China.
Apr. 19	Lord Revelstoke, chairman of the expert subcommittee considering the German reparations offers at the multi-national conference in Paris dies suddenly. His death allows the committee to deliberate the issue for additional days.	The British General Electric Company, Ltd. gives up a plan to sell stocks exclusively to British citizens. 60 percent of the company's stocks are presently controlled by Americans This plan was led by Sir Hugo Hirst who believes that British companies should be run by British citizens.		General elections are not held in Venezuela as planned because current leader General Juan Vicente Gomez is running unopposed. He had feared a coup attempt and has been strengthening his troops by conscripting over 4,000 men off the street.	
Apr. 20		France opens a conference at the Ministry of Fine Arts to debate whether to tighten restrictions on American movies to a 3:1 quota system. At present there is a 7:1 quota so that for every seven American movies imported by France, the United States must produce, purchase or distribute a French film. This quota is enacted after an initial number of movies have been released each year.	The military forces of Emir Habibullah Kalakani, current leader of Afghanistan, battle with supporters of former King Amanullah Khan at a point about 40 miles south of Kabul. The former king is directing his troops from Kandahar and promises amnesty to those opposed to him if he is returned to power.		The Nationalist Government of China threatens to stifle the foreign press as a result of criticism of governmental policies from U.S. newspapers in northern China. Chinese language papers are already censored.
Apr. 21	Hjalmar Schacht and Albert Voegler, the German delegates to the current World War I war debt and reparations conference repeat that Germany can not pay the newly requested $396 million per year unless the nation's productivity levels increase.			Mexican General Juan Andreu Almazan leads 10,000 Federal troops south toward the Pulpito Pass of the Sierra Madre to attack the rebels in the State of Sonora, their last remaining stronghold. The army is marching carefully as the rebels are believed to have laid mines as they are rumored to possess 300 pounds of nitroglycerine.	

A	B	C	D	E
Includes developments that affect more than one world region, international organizations and important meetings of world leaders.	Includes all domestic and regional developments in Europe, including the Soviet Union.	Includes all domestic and regional developments in Africa and the Middle East.	Includes all domestic and regional developments in Latin America, the Caribbean, and Canada.	Includes all domestic and regional developments in Asian and Pacific nations (and colonies).

U.S. Politics & Social Issues	U.S. Foreign Policy & Affairs, Defense	U.S. Economy & Environment	Science, Technology & Nature	Culture, Leisure & Lifestyle	
Members of Congress begin a special session at the request of President Herbert Hoover to discuss tariffs and farm aid. Many of the initial bills call for an end to Prohibition, while others seek to modify the Volstead Act to apply to all American ships in response to the *Leviathan's* liquor sales.	Secretary of State Henry Stimson meets with a delegation from the Philippines who ask for continued support for their country as he did when serving as Governor General of the island nation. He reiterated his opinion that there should be no tariffs imposed on Philippine sugar.	The U.S. National Guard is sent to quiet strikers at textile mills in Gastonia, NC where workers are attempting to unionize. A new strike begins at a textile plant in Elizabethton, TN.	Cambridge Scientist A. S. Eddington announces in a radio lecture that space is not empty but that the universe is comprised of an interstellar cloud.	An Architectural and Allied Arts Exposition opens at Grand Central Palace in New York, drawing over 10,000 visitors daily to see works of contemporary artists.	Apr. 15
			The American Engineering Council announces a plan to install uniform traffic signals throughout the country.	Ohio's Cleveland Indians become the first major league baseball team to wear numbers on the back of their jerseys as part of the league's new uniform regulations....Paul Robeson sings a collection of African-American spirituals to a full theater in Vienna, Austria.	Apr. 16
Wisconsin State Assemblymen votes to repeal the state's Prohibition act.	Secretary of State Henry Stimson appears before the Republican members of the House Ways and Means Committee to protest any changes to the free trade agreement with the Philippines. He notes he is acting in the capacity as the former governor, and not as a member of the current administration as he speaks against imposition of tariffs on sugar imports.	Textile workers at the Pineville Mill in Charlotte, NC, vote to end their strike without having achieved unionization.		N. Y. Yankee player, George Herman "Babe" Ruth is married to Claire Hodgeson, a former member of the Ziegfeld Follies at a 6:30 a.m. ceremony....Raoul Monty, a Frenchman, crosses the English Channel on a hydro-cycle in a new record time of five hours, 57 seconds.	Apr. 17
A jury convicts New York publisher D. S. Friede, for selling a copy of Theodore Dreiser's story *An American Tragedy* to a vice squad officer in violation of Boston's obscene book law....President Herbert Hoover nominates 11 new Federal Circuit judges, including eight who had been nominated by former President Calvin Coolidge but had failed to win Senate confirmation.		A large group of masked men destroy the Gastonia, NC, headquarters of the National Textile Workers Union, which is affiliated with the Communist Party in America.		Charles A. Llindbergh's birthplace in Detroit, MI is bought by the Swedish Engineering Society of Detroit to preserve it as a memorial and use as the group's headquarters.	Apr. 18
U.S. Customs Agents prevent rumrunners from stealing champagne and cognac from the *Ile de France*. The would-be thieves gained access to the ship by sliding down ropes from the roof of the dock to the ship deck, but manage to escape authorities by means of a small boat intended to remove the liquor from the ship.	Four naval pilots are killed when two Vought Corsair planes collide in mid-air over Coronado, CA, as they were returning to base from gunnery practice.		Ludwik Silberstein presents a revised estimate of the radius of the universe as 3.25 x 1,019 miles.	Lou Hoover gives a radio address, achieving a new milestone for First Ladies....Canadian Johnny Miles wins the Boston Marathon with a new record of two hours, 33 minutes, and 8.8 seconds.	Apr. 19
Missouri men kidnap an African-American man who had been in jail on charges of robbery and assaulting women. The man was severely beaten and then returned to the jail.		In order to promote greater use of water transit, particularly as run by the government owned Inland Waterways Corporation, the U.S. Interstate Commerce Commission rules that a new set of combined barge-to-rail routes must be developed. The rates for these combined transport modes are to be cheaper than the rail-to-rail rates presently in use.	Bologne, Italy experiences the seventh earthquake in six days, which damages property. Many citizens are sleeping outside their homes in fear of collapsing buildings....F.S. Hammett announces a new avenue for cancer research that focuses on a chemical, issulfhydryl, that controls the growth of malignant tumors by cell division.	French pilot Maryse Bastie sets a French women's endurance record with a flight of 10 hours, 30 minutes.	Apr. 20
President Herbert Hoover denounces the feasibility and utility of the export debentures plan submitted in Congress' farm relief bill. He states that it will not help farmers, but will instead provide money to the exporters, over-stimulate crop production and reduce the national treasury for no foreseeable long-term gains.		National Guard troops withdraw from the Loray Mill region in North Carolina.	Three days of tornado strikes in Arkansas and Mississippi leave 22 dead....A Mississippi River levee near Canton, MO, breaks....Flooding occurs in New York and northern Pennsylvania.		Apr. 21

F	G	H	I	J
Includes campaigns, elections, federal-state relations, civil rights and liberties, crime, the judiciary, education, healthcare, poverty, urban affairs, and population.	Includes formation and debate of U.S. foreign and defense policies, veterans affairs, and defense spending. (Relations with specific foreign countries are usually found under the region concerned.)	Includes business, labor, agriculture, taxation, transportation, consumer affairs, monetary and fiscal policy, natural resources, pollution and industrial accidents.	Includes worldwide scientific, medical and technological developments, natural phenomena, U.S. weather and natural disasters.	Includes the arts, religion, scholarship, communications media, sports, entertainment, fashions, fads, and social life.

	World Affairs	Europe	Africa & The Middle East	The Americas	Asia & The Pacific
Apr. 22	British diplomats are happy to hear U.S. Ambassador Hugh Gibson's speech at the Preparatory Disarmament Commission meeting in Geneva as he reveals a new plan for achieving naval disarmament between Great Britain and the United States.	France ratifies the Kellogg-Briand pact to renounce all war.		All rebels in Coahuila, Mexico surrender, giving the Federal army control of the state....Juan Bautista Perez is nominated as provisional president of Venezuela until a new general election can be held in two weeks.	The Emir of Afghanistan, Habibullah Kalakani, denounces former King Amanullah Khan as an unbeliever whose attempts to modernize the nation by building co-educational schools and removing veil requirements for women were heretical. Amanullah responded by calling the Emir menial, as he had previously been the king's water boy.
Apr. 23		Great Britain's three political parties all agree that U.S. Ambassador Hugh Gibson's plans for naval disarmament reductions are worth considering.		Charles Dawes and the rest of his commission leave the Dominican Republic after presenting President Vasquez a 200 page plan to reduce the nation's debt by reorganizing government finances and installing a new budget....Mexican rebels kill or capture 700 Federal troops in Sonora, claiming victory in that state.	115 of 209 people on board the *Toyo Kuni Maru* die after it sinks within minutes of hitting rocks off Hokkaido, Japan.
Apr. 24	Spain halts the importation of all fruits and plants from the United States, Canada, Japan and New Zealand to prevent the spread of agriculture-born disease. In addition, U.S. and other cotton supplies are prohibited to stop the spread of the boll weevil and boll worm.	Yugoslavia ratifies the Kellogg antiwar treaty....36 students are stabbed during a battle between Christians and Jews at Lemberg, Austria....Critics of Spain's leadership speak out on the decreasing value of the peseta, due to excessive internal debt and high levels of current spending.		Six new pyramids are discovered at San Juan Teotihuacan, Mexico.	
Apr. 25		A plan was released today at the All-Russian Communist Conference in Moscow setting forth an ambitious five year goals for industrialization of the Soviet Union. Highlights of the plan include a new automobile factory manufacturing, extensive train lines, and improved electrical capabilities.		A Mexican Federal Army airplane accidentally bombs the American Consulate at Ciudad Obregon, but no injuries are reported.	
Apr. 26	The first nonstop flight from England to India is completed. Members of Britain's Royal Air Force fly over 4,100 miles before landing at Karachi, setting a British record for a nonstop flight. As a result of bad weather, the trip ends 1,170 miles short of their target city of Bangalore, which would have also set a long distance flight record.	The first part of an antireligion law goes into effect in the Soviet Union today. It prohibits religions from collecting money for, and performance of, any charitable works. No books or educational activities of a nonreligious nature are allowed in churches.		Mexico's Federal troops re-occupy the town of Navojoa, Sonora. General J. G. Escobar, head of the rebellion, resigns his post and attempts to reach America for asylum....Government representatives from Peru and Chile meet to make finalize agreements regarding their longstanding, 51-year border dispute. It is expected that Province of Tacna will soon belong to Peru, while Arica will be given to Chile.	A case of meningitis occurs on a liner from the Philippines, forcing a quarantine of the passengers upon arrival in Honolulu, HI.
Apr. 27	Members of the Preparatory Disarmament Commission meeting in Geneva agree to not limit a country's right to maintain trained military reserve units. This decision was supported by those countries that have a mandatory draft while others felt it weakened the goal of disarmament.	Britain's smallpox outbreak spreads to Paris....In Cologne, Germany, Georg Zapf announces the invention of a new telephone cable that is strong enough for undersea use to connect the telephone systems between continents.	The Zionist Congress agrees on a constitution for Palestine that will guide the future actions of an extended Jewish agency to control the state. The agency is expected to be comprised of Zionist and non-Zionist supporters.	Mexican rebels groups are dividing and dispersing throughout the southern part of Sonora state.	Marshal Feng Yu-hsiang's resignation from the post of Minister of War for China's Nanking Nationalist Government is accepted by President Chiang Kai-shek.
Apr. 28	Leaders of Belgium and France unveil a monument in Flanders to the 21,000 British and 18,000 French soldiers who were killed in the first gas attack by the Germans in World War I.		The Booker T. Washington Institute opens in Kakata, Liberia as the nation's first vocational institution. It is founded by U.S. missionary and philanthropic groups and will provide courses in agriculture, auto mechanics, carpentry, and masonry.	Venezuelan revolutionary troops, under command of Genera Arevalo Cedeno, take control of the town of Orza.	

A	B	C	D	E
Includes developments that affect more than one world region, international organizations and important meetings of world leaders.	Includes all domestic and regional developments in Europe, including the Soviet Union.	Includes all domestic and regional developments in Africa and the Middle East.	Includes all domestic and regional developments in Latin America, the Caribbean, and Canada.	Includes all domestic and regional developments in Asian and Pacific nations (and colonies).

U.S. Politics & Social Issues	U.S. Foreign Policy & Affairs, Defense	U.S. Economy & Environment	Science, Technology & Nature	Culture, Leisure & Lifestyle	
In a speech to members of the Associated Press at New York, President Herbert Hoover identifies crime and law enforcement as the biggest issues facing the country. He denies that the liquor prohibition is mainly responsible for crime and instead blames an attitude of lawlessness on the part of criminals and the lax or poor enforcement and actions by police and lawyers.		President Herbert Hoover sets aside over 4,000 acres of natural stone arches and other unusual features in Utah's canyon lands to the National Park Service for protection and recreation.	Residents of Bologne, Italy and the surrounding region are distressed by the 22nd earthquake in a 10-day period.	Communist leader Erich Mühsam's play, *Sacco and Vanzetti*, about the famous U.S. trials and execution of the two men opens today in Berlin. It is intended as a statement against capital punishment.	Apr. 22
The National League of Women Voters adopts a resolution that women should be able to choose or retain their nationality independently of their husbands. They will submit the resolution to for international discussion at the Hague in 1930....John F. Curry is elected the new leader of Tammany Hall, which will mean much support for New York City Mayor James Walker.			Members of the National Academy of Sciences present the Agassiz Medal for Oceanography to J. Stanley Gardner of Cambridge University for noteworthy zoological research and the James Craig Watson Medal to William de Sitter of the University of Leiden for contributions in astronomy.	The American Academy of Arts and Letters awards gold medals for literature to Edith Wharton, for excellence in stage diction to Julia Marlowe, and a new award for excellence in radio diction to Milton J. Cross.	Apr. 23
The annual convention of the American Newspapers Publishers' Association begins today with a protest from members against the Minnesota statue that permits judges to suppress or cease newspaper operations at their own discretion.	President Herbert Hoover is identified as the inventor of the algebraic method for objectively measuring naval assets that is currently being presented by Ambassador Hugh Gibson to the Preparatory Disarmament Commission in Geneva.		A tornado in eastern Texas kills 7.	*Madame X*, starring Ruth Chatterton and produced by Lionel Barrymore, opens in New York....American pilot Elinor Smith, age 17, sets a U.S. women's endurance record with a flight of 26 hours, 21 minutes, and 32 seconds.	Apr. 24
The United States and Canada will submit the case of the Coast Guard's March 22 sinking of the *I'm Alone* to an international arbiter under the Ship Liquor Treaty of 1924. The United States maintains that it fired at the ship after a legal pursuit, while Canada claims that the treaty did not provide for the extension of U.S. territory into international waters.... The U.S. House of Representatives passes the farm relief bill without the debenture plan.		Aviation heads from the War, Naval, and Commerce Departments meet and agree that a new southern airmail route would be beneficial for fast transcontinental troop transport in event of a war. They support a proposal from the Southern Airway Association to create a new route serving cities between Washington, DC, and Los Angeles.	Tornadoes in Georgia and South Carolina kill 52 people and cause much property damage.		Apr. 25
	Meningitis is found among soldiers aboard a U.S. Army transport ship bringing troops to assist with the elimination of Nicaragua's rebellion. The entire ship of soldiers is quarantined as they pass through the Panama Canal.		Italians test a method for the undersea evacuation of submarine crews by use of metal tubes that attach to torpedo tubes. Each crewmember dons diving gear, crawls through the pressurized tube, and then shoots up to the surface.		Apr. 26
The Louisiana House of Representatives formally serves Governor Huey P. Long with impeachment charges on five of the original 19 counts. He is accused of using government funds for personal entertainment, attempting to bribe legislators, attempting to suppress freedom of the press, misuse of state funds and general incompetence. His response on receiving notice of the charges was to laugh and immediately begin preparing for an expected May trial.	Charles F. Adams, Secretary of the Navy, reports that about one-third of all fatalities among Naval and Marine Corps airplanes are caused by tail spins. He notes that the death rates have recently been reduced relative to the increasing hours of flight time by new innovations including the use wing slots, parachutes, rescue boats, and more efficient flight inspections.	A Senate Judiciary Committee meets to determine whether Secretary of the Treasury Andrew Mellon should be disqualified from office since he holds stock in large corporations that may pose a conflict of interest with his post....Representatives from beach cities and state government meet for the first time in New Jersey to plan for beach pollution cleanup and to figure out how to prevent New York garbage boats from dumping waste along the shore.		British golfers win the Ryder Cup.	Apr. 27
Raymond F. C. Kieb, New York State's Commissioner of Corrections, announces that Auburn Prison is installing a cafeteria style system to feed inmates in a more timely and cost effective manner. Other state prisons including Attica and Sing Sing will soon adopt the system.		Senator Burton K. Wheeler of Montana calls for a Congressional investigation into working conditions at textile mills in North and South Carolina in response to recent strikes.	The crest of the Mississippi River floodwaters reach St. Louis, MO, at a level only one foot below the great 1927 flood stage. Thousands of acres of farmland have been inundated, particularly near the Mississippi and Missouri River confluence.	Thirty people die in one day in car crashes across the United States.... Two new luxury ocean liners are being built for the Canadian Pacific Railway company. They are expected to be in the 40–70,000 ton range and cut the time needed to cross the Atlantic Ocean to five days.	Apr. 28

F	G	H	I	J
Includes campaigns, elections, federal-state relations, civil rights and liberties, crime, the judiciary, education, healthcare, poverty, urban affairs, and population.	*Includes formation and debate of U.S. foreign and defense policies, veterans affairs, and defense spending. (Relations with specific foreign countries are usually found under the region concerned.)*	*Includes business, labor, agriculture, taxation, transportation, consumer affairs, monetary and fiscal policy, natural resources, pollution and industrial accidents.*	*Includes worldwide scientific, medical and technological developments, natural phenomena, U.S. weather and natural disasters.*	*Includes the arts, religion, scholarship, communications media, sports, entertainment, fashions, fads, and social life.*

	World Affairs	Europe	Africa & The Middle East	The Americas	Asia & The Pacific
Apr. 29	Egypt deports two men who worked for a Russian cotton agency due to suspicions that they were illegally spreading Communist propaganda in the country.			Puerto Rico's Governer Horace M. Towner signs a bill abolishing the death penalty as it was not found effective in deterring murders.	
Apr. 30	French government officials send a message through the Paris press to warn German leaders that there is no future reparations conference planned and so they would do well to accept either the new war debt and reparations proposal or agree to continue under the original Dawes Commission agreement.	Edward Windsor, Prince of Wales, and British Premier Stanley Baldwin lay the cornerstone of the $1 million Eastman Dental Clinic that will serve the poor in London when it is completed. The country's leaders thank benefactor George Eastman of Rochester, NY, and citizens of the United States for their generosity.	The Nathan and Lina Straus Health Centre opens in Jerusalem, Palestine and will be run by the Hadassah medical organization. Former Senator Straus' goals for the center are to reduce infant mortality rates and to improve preventative medicine.	All Mexican rebels remaining in Nogales, Sonora offer to surrender and the Federal Army regains control of the region.	Writers for the Japanese press state that the current limitations on battle cruiser size under the 1922 Washington Treaty that limits the capital ship tonnage ratio of 5-5-3 is too small to insure the nation's security. These complaints are brought up by the press and not government officials because Japanese delegates are attending the Preparatory Disarmament Commission meeting in Geneva, where naval reductions are being considered.
May 1	The U.S. State Department announces that the Arms Embargo Treaty of 1919 is voluntarily ended. The agreement was made between America, Great Britain, France, Japan, and other nations in order to prevent the sales of weapons to China during its destabilizing civil war.	Thousands of people in many European cities march in May Day parades to celebrate the International Labor Day. More than 20 die in clashes between police and pro-Communist supporters in Germany, Austria, and Lithuania and over 3,400 demonstrators are arrested in Paris....A jury finds over 150 people guilty of suspected Mafia activity after a 9-month trial in Sicily, Italy.		Over 30,000 pro-union supporters march in an International Labor Day parade and several hundred demonstrators protest America's foreign policies at the U.S. Consulate in Mexico City, Mexico....Over 1,500 rebels surrender to Federal troops at Agua Prieta, Mexico.	China's President Chiang Kai-shek calls a special meeting of the State Council in Nanking to discuss whether to begin war preparations against Marshal Feng Yu-hsiang in the Shantung (Shandong) Province.
May 2	Members of the Preparatory Disarmament Commission meeting in Geneva, Switzerland disagree on how to limit army material stocks of rifles, tanks, and other equipment.	The work of the late French architect Albert Eiffel is honored with a monument established at the foot of the tower he designed in France.	Tel Aviv, Palestine, founded as the first Hebrew city, celebrates its 20th anniversary....A general assembly of judges votes to allow all cases against non-Turkish foreigners in Egypt to be heard by an international mixed court instead of through the local court system.	Archbishop Leopold y Ruiz, chairman of the Catholic Bishops in Mexico, requests that the government of Mexico change the laws restricting the practice of Catholicism that led to the last two years of rebellion.	China sends a request to the United States requesting to end the law of extraterritoriality, which allows U.S. citizens in China the right to avoid prosecution under Chinese jurisdictional sovereignty.
May 3	Prince Henry, Duke of Gloucester, while visiting in Tokyo, makes Japanese Emperor Hirohito a Knight of the Order of the Garter, England's highest honor. In return, the Emperor makes the Prince a member of Japan's Grand Order of the Chrysanthemum.			The son of the former governor of Sonora State attempts to assassinate Plutarco Elias Calles, Mexico's Commander in Chief and former President at a reception....General J. Gonzalo Escobar, leader of the Mexican rebels, flees to El Paso, Texas....Venezuela's Congress unanimously re-elects General Juan Vicente Gomez to continue to serve as president until 1936.	At least six are killed and 60 injured during fights between Hindus and Muslims in Bombay, India.
May 4	A Spaniard, a Mexican, and two Texans are arrested with $750,000 in money allegedly stolen from the Mexican government and banks are arrested in New York City. They are charged with attempting to help the Spanish citizen escape the country by ship with the money.	Austria's new Chancellor, Ernst Streeruwitz, and Cabinet members from the Christian Socialist party assume office.		General Juan Vicente Gomez declines the presidency of Venezuela, a post to which he was unanimously reelected on May 3.	
May 5		Germany disbands the Red Front Army as a result of the four day long May Day riots between the police and the pro-Communist supporters in Berlin.		Brazilian President Washington Luis announces in a speech to Congress that the nation has achieved a budget surplus of approximately $23.6 million, although bankers in London concurrently note they are loaning the Brazilian government 5 million pounds sterling to help stabilize the local currency.	Emir Habibullah Kalakani, current leader of Afghanistan, defeats the troops of former King Amanullah Khan near Mukkar and captures military supplies.

A	B	C	D	E
Includes developments that affect more than one world region, international organizations and important meetings of world leaders.	Includes all domestic and regional developments in Europe, including the Soviet Union.	Includes all domestic and regional developments in Africa and the Middle East.	Includes all domestic and regional developments in Latin America, the Caribbean, and Canada.	Includes all domestic and regional developments in Asian and Pacific nations (and colonies).

U.S. Politics & Social Issues	U.S. Foreign Policy & Affairs, Defense	U.S. Economy & Environment	Science, Technology & Nature	Culture, Leisure & Lifestyle	
Two thousand teachers from the United States and Canada attend the 36th annual convention of the International Kindergarten Union in Rochester, NY....Former President Calvin Coolidge finishes writing the fifth and final installment of his autobiography, which is being published by Cosmopolitan Magazine.	J.C. Penney, store founder, sends a radiogram to President Herbert Hoover asking for the United States to send aid to China for famine relief.	The Interisland Airways Company has been organized in Hawaii to provide passenger service between Honolulu, Molokai, Maui, Hawaii, and Kauai, using amphibian aircraft.		The White House announces it is having new technology installed so that the president, his family, and guests can hear talking motion pictures.	Apr. 29
A joint panel from the New York County Medical Society and the Diphtheria Prevention Commission announce a plan to put 30 temporary stations in city parks this summer to administer diphtheria vaccines to children.		U.S. Steel Corporation sets a peace time production record for April and the first quarter profits exceeded $60 million.	An increase in lighting led to the beginning of nighttime flights between the west and east coast, which will reduce arrival times for airmail. The Transcontinental Air Service will leave New Jersey at 9:35 p.m. and arrive in San Francisco 31 hours later. Additional flights will be made to Los Angeles.	*Paris Bound*, a new play by American Philip Barry, opens at the Lyric Theater in London. The playwright was formerly an attaché for the American Embassy in England....E. Gerard Issinger commutes to work in New York City by flying his Travelair plane from his suburban Philadelphia home three times each week.	Apr. 30
William A. DeGroot, U.S. Attorney for the Eastern Division of New York, is ordered to quit his post by President Herbert Hoover for failure to aggressively prosecute prohibition cases....In New York City, over 27,000 Socialist and labor supporters gather at Madison Square Garden and 5,000 pro-Communists parade through the city.		August Heckscher makes a gift of $4 million to support public playgrounds, child care centers, and dental clinic in New York boroughs.	At least 10 people die and dozens are injured in tornadoes and thunderstorms in Arkansas and Georgia.	The Waldorf-Astoria Hotel in New York City closes after 36 years in order to make room for the building of the Empire State Building. A new hotel is planned at a location 15 blocks north....Sir John Sandeman Allen, a member of Britain's House of Commons complains that British children should not watch American talking movies in order to preserve their own national identity and accents.	May 1
		President Herbert Hoover encourages Eastern railroads to accept a lower rate on the freight rate for exported wheat in order to reduce some of the nation's wheat stockpiles....Fox Film Company's president, William Fox, announces that U.S. investments in the movie industry exceed $1.75 billion annually, with over $750 million coming from ticket sales.	Tornadoes and storms extending from the U.S. southeast to Pennsylvania injure hundreds and kill 38, including 11 children attending school in Rye Cove, VA....The Spanish Royal Mail liner *Cristobal Colon*, carrying 1,000 passengers, hits the American Levant Line's *River Orontes* freighter in a fog near New York City's harbor. None are injured as the liner tears a hole in the freighter and pushes it into shallow waters where it sinks.	Charles Scribner's Sons of New York publishes the second volume of the *Dictionary of American Biography*. It includes histories of 670 famous or noteworthy citizens ranging from Billy the Kid to Alexander Graham Bell.	May 2
State and Federal courts indict 96 people in one day including 15 accused of corruption and 81 accused of Prohibition violations.		The Secretary of the Department of the Interior allows oil and gas prospecting to begin on lands where reliable geological surveys have been conducted.	Pilot Parker Cramer completes a record flight from Nome, Alaska to New York City in 48 hours, 28 minutes. He believes that this will eventually prove to be the safest route to Asia....The village of Kidderville, NH, is destroyed when the Balsams Dam on the Mohawk River collapses due to heavy rainfall and high floodwaters....Over 2,000 are killed by earthquakes in Northwest Persia.	Over $600,000 is brought in during an auction at Christie's in London of paintings by masters such as Anthony Van Dyck, Rembrandt, Goya, and Titian.	May 3
Through a voting process, members of the Senate Judiciary Committee refuse to find Andrew Mellon ineligible to be Secretary of the Treasury as a result of his ownership of corporate stocks. The Senate will now consider the matter.		Executives for the Building Trades Employers' Association and Building Trades Council announce that over 150,000 New York City building trade workers will receive a 10 percent pay raise and be granted a five-day work week to be effective by September.		A suspected gang of international thieves steal a package containing $125,000 in diamonds by substituting pebbles for the gems while they were in the mail between Portuguese East Africa and Antwerp, Belgium.	May 4
		Over 800 militia, police, and National Guard members are assembled to protect the Elizabethton, TN, rayon plants, which plan to resume business on the next day.	The first Canadian telephone conversation between a moving passenger train, the Canadian National flier, and the rail company's station in Toronto, which then broadcast the voices over the railroad's radio station.	An exhibit of artwork created by Japanese school children is exhibited at the American Museum of Natural History in honor of the Japanese Children's Day festival.	May 5

F	G	H	I	J
Includes campaigns, elections, federal-state relations, civil rights and liberties, crime, the judiciary, education, healthcare, poverty, urban affairs, and population.	*Includes formation and debate of U.S. foreign and defense policies, veterans affairs, and defense spending. (Relations with specific foreign countries are usually found under the region concerned.)*	*Includes business, labor, agriculture, taxation, transportation, consumer affairs, monetary and fiscal policy, natural resources, pollution and industrial accidents.*	*Includes worldwide scientific, medical and technological developments, natural phenomena, U.S. weather and natural disasters.*	*Includes the arts, religion, scholarship, communications media, sports, entertainment, fashions, fads, and social life.*

	World Affairs	Europe	Africa & The Middle East	The Americas	Asia & The Pacific
May 6	Delegates to the Preparatory Disarmament Commission meeting in Geneva begin a recess in order to review proposals for naval arms reductions....André Lafond, editor of the French Journal de Rouen, wins the $500 Ralph B. Strassburger prize given to an author whose writings make a significant contribution to French-American relations.	An unknown assassin escapes after fatally shooting one person and wounding two others in a failed attempt to kill Augustin Waldemaras, the premier of Lithuania.			
May 7	Sir Eric Drummond, Permanent Secretary of the League of Nations, releases the agenda for the September meeting which notes that members will discuss the protocol for American adherence to World Court decisions, the results of the Preparatory Disarmament Commission, and a draft treaty for financial assistance during wartime.		Government representatives from Great Britain and Egypt sign the Nile Waters Agreement, which gives Egypt access to 48 billion cubic meters of annual flow from the Nile River and the entire flow during the dry season from January 15 to July 15, while 4 billion cubic meters annually are reserved for the Sudan.	Mexican President Portes Gil offers to parley with Archbishop Leopold y Ruiz, chairman of the Catholic Bishops, and other church representatives to settle the three year old disputes that arose when the government passed laws that were seen as anti-Catholic and which led, in part, to the recent rebellion.	Leroy Webber, U.S. Consul at Chefoo (Yuntai), China, is traveling to the Yellow River delta region to negotiate for the release of Marie Monsen, a Norwegian missionary who was kidnapped by the pirates who attacked the steamship Peking in April....China's National Government announces that decapitation will no longer be used as a method for executions.
May 8	Gianni Albertini heads an Italian rescue party that begins travel to the Arctic Ocean to search for the missing crew of the Italia, a dirigible that crashed on the ice pack. They will also search for Captain Roald Amundsen who led a rescue expedition for the missing Italia crew by air and is now missing.	Members of the Norwegian Parliament vote to annex Jan Mayen Island, which is used primarily as a base for Arctic Ocean whale hunters....Over 200,000 people watch a parade of religious and civil dignitaries and participate in the 500th anniversary of the victory led by St. Joan of Arc in Orelans, France.		For the first time 39 women including a nun, are sent along with 34 men to serve prison time at the Tres Marias Islands penal colony off Mexico's Pacific Coast....A Hudson Bay Railway Company trains with 14 patients suffering from typhoid is stuck for a second time due to a blizzard in Manitoba, Canada.	
May 9	Heads of all three leading political parties in Britain express their dissatisfaction with the current proposal by American Owen Young for World War I war debt settlements now being discussion n Paris. Under the Young plan, Britain would only receive enough money to pay her debts to America, with no reparations for the rest of the nation's losses and expenditures.	The Dowager Queen Marie and the boy King Michael and citizens of Romania celebrate the tenth anniversary of the reunification of the nation by honoring the 500,000 Rumanian soldiers who died in World War I.			Kwangsi rebels are gaining control of Canton, China where the local Kwangtung defenders, though loyal to the Nanking Nationalist Government, are not strong enough to prevent the takeover. A British gunboat has been ordered to the region to evacuate American women and children from the region.
May 10	Greece agrees to pay the United States $15 million to settle World War I war debts and will repay over 20 years an additional $12 million that has been loaned by the United States to the Refuge Settlement Commission that provides assistance to Greek war refugees.	In a move that disturbs the nation's pro-Socialist leaders, the Austrian government overrules a ban by Vienna's Mayor Karl Seitz and will instead allow members of the Nationalist, paramilitary group Heimwehr to march in an upcoming parade.		The United States relaxes its arms embargoes imposed on Honduras and Nicaragua to permit shipments of barbed wires, machetes, chemicals, and pharmaceutical products. Items used for military purposes such as ammunition, aircraft, and weapons are still restricted.	American Consul Leroy Webber helps broker the surrender of the city of Fushanhsien, China, which was held by rebel leader Marshal Chang Tsung-Chang, to the Nanking Nationalist Government. Elsewhere in China, however, the rebel Kwangsi troops are closing in on the city of Canton (Guangzhou), which is only lightly defended by Nationalist forces.
May 11	The League of Nations Economic Consultative Committee's annual report states that both North and South America lead the world in the volume and value of world trade in 1929. It also expresses concerns about impacts from the United States' recent tariff and farm bills on world trade.	Italy's Premier Benito Mussolini presents the 1928 Kellogg peace pact to the nation's Parliament for discussion and ratification.	Persian authorities note that pro-Communist supporters are increasing their activity in Abadan.		The Indian Government announces that, to improve their working conditions, a gradual reduction of the 32,000 women working in underground mines must begin on July 1st with a total elimination expected to occur by July 1, 1939....Abdur Rahmin, leading troops belonging to Emir Habibullah Kalakani, current leader of Afghanistan, capture the important trade and agricultural town of Herat in western Afghanistan
May 12	The Yugoslav government complains that the current proposal made by Owen Young at the World War I war debt parley in Paris is not acceptable as it would lower the amount of reparations to be paid to their nation by Germany.	Swiss citizens vote against a law that would have given local cities and towns the right to control or prohibit liquor sales in their districts.		Over 8,000 people join Mexico's President Portes Gil at Mexico City's Colonia Train Station to welcome back Secretary of War and Commander-in-chief Plutarco Elias Calles who has spent three months directing Federal troops in fighting against rebels on several fronts across the country.	The city of Canton (Guangzhou), China agrees to pay $285,000 per month to rebel Kwangsi troops to prevent them from attacking and looting the city. In addition, the city agrees to let the rebels continue their opium trade along the West River.

A	B	C	D	E
Includes developments that affect more than one world region, international organizations and important meetings of world leaders.	Includes all domestic and regional developments in Europe, including the Soviet Union.	Includes all domestic and regional developments in Africa and the Middle East.	Includes all domestic and regional developments in Latin America, the Caribbean, and Canada.	Includes all domestic and regional developments in Asian and Pacific nations (and colonies).

U.S. Politics & Social Issues	U.S. Foreign Policy & Affairs, Defense	U.S. Economy & Environment	Science, Technology & Nature	Culture, Leisure & Lifestyle	
President Herbert Hoover appoints Charles Evans Hughes, Jr., son of the former Secretary of State, to be the Solicitor General of the United States....Harry F. Sinclair, former oil magnate, is sentenced to 90 days in jail on contempt of court charges arising during his testimony on the Teapot Dome oil leasing scandal in front of a Senate committee in 1924.		C. M. Keys is named chairman of the board of the newly formed Curtiss Airports Corporation, a division of the Curtiss-Keys Group, which plans to build and operate airports in 15 cities across the country.	Naval Lieutenant Thomas Settle sets new long distance and endurance records for his 900-mile, 42-hour hot air balloon flight from Pittsburgh, PA, to Prince Edward Island, Canada during the National Aeronautic Association's national elimination balloon race.	For the first time, John Phillip Sousa leads his 52-piece band playing many of the famous marches he composed in a live performance broadcast over the radio....The Prix of Rome award in painting is given to John M. Sitton of Greenville, SC, and in sculpture to Sidney B. Waugh of Amherst, MA.	May 6
Three henchmen of gangster Al Capone are killed in Indiana in retaliation by opposing mob forces.	U.S. troops guarding the Mexican border during the recent Mexican rebellion are ordered to return to their home duty stations.		C. Leonard Wooley, archeologist, describes how a ziggurat found at the ancient city of Ur indicates that Sumerians in the 4th century B.C.E. understood architectural elements such as the arch, apse, column, and dome.		May 7
34 Democratic and 13 Republican Senators vote to return the debenture export plan back to the farm relief bill in defiance of the wishes of President Herbert Hoover.			Naval Lieutenant Apollo Soucek flies a Wright Apache airplane to a record setting altitude of 39,140 feet where the temperatures were 76 degrees below zero Fahrenheit.	William F. Bade, professor at Berkeley's Pacific School of Religion, finds remains of an Early Bronze age settlement dating from before 3000 B.C.E. at Tel Nasbeh, Palestine.	May 8
Members of both the Puerto Rican legislature and a local farmers' association complain to President Herbert Hoover that Governor Horace Towner is failing to act on important bills due to his travels to Washington, DC.	Major Walter Prosser, head of the U.S. Army's Pictorial Service, announces that talking movies will soon be used to train troops.	The U.S. Department of Agriculture estimates that 595 million bushels of winter wheat will be ready for sale on July 1, an amount that is 16 million bushels more than the previous year. This large wheat crop is problematic as the government is trying to get rid of the current wheat surplus by encouraging railroads to reduce freight rates on wheat exports.	Five groups of scientists gather at the U.S. Naval Observatory in Iloilo, Philippines, to study the total solar eclipse and to confirm Albert Einstein's theory that rays of light from stars will be bent by gravitational attraction as they pass the sun.	After 19 years of planning, the Spanish-American Exposition opens today in Seville, Spain featuring pavilions showcasing cultural exhibits from countries in the Americas and Europe....A 600 member chorus sings Camille Saint-Saëns' opera *Samson and Delilah* on the opening night of the three-day Westchester County, NY, music festival.	May 9
	The U.S. Army prepares for several days of simulated aerial war games and bombing runs by flying 21 planes from their base in California to a staging area in Ohio.	Farm groups complain to members of the U.S. Senate and House that the current tariff bill does not have high enough import duties imposed on certain products such as oils, fats, fruits, starches, and cotton from other countries, particularly the Philippines, and so the bill does not adequately assist American farmers.	U.S. President Herbert Hoover recognizes and rewards the work of three men in the development of a "lung" type underwater breathing device that enables crews of sunken submarines to escape. For this work, Lieutenant Charles B. Momsen and Chief Gunner Clarence L. Tibbals receive Distinguished Service Medals and civilian engineer Frank H. Hobson is awarded an extra year of pay by the Navy.	U.S. golfer, Walter Hagen, wins the British Open Championship in Muirfield, Scotland. His winning score of 292 makes it the second consecutive year and fourth time in his career that he places first in this event...Jockey Louis Schaefer, riding Dr. Freeland, wins the Preakness Stakes at Pimlico race track in Baltimore, MD.	May 10
A conflict between T. T,. Shields, the conservative head of the Board of Trustees, and Des Moines University president, Harry Wayman, leads to the firing of all faculty members and rioting by the students that destroys some of the building on this Fundamentalist Baptist campus in Iowa.		Members of the Committee on Recent Economic Changes, chaired by President Herbert Hoover, release a report stating that the present demand for stock market loans will unfavorably impact the stability of the New York financial market.	The Liggett Candy Store in New York City showcases a new money-changing machine that can tell the difference between good quarters and slugs or unacceptable coins. Camco, a so-called robot, was created by the Consolidated Automatic Merchandising Corporation to produce five nickels in exchange for a quarter and it will speak to customers if it detects a bad quarter.	The seventh annual exhibition of the American Institute of Graphic Arts opens at the Grolier Club in New York, featuring the 50 best designed books of the last year.	May 11
The Association Against the Prohibition Amendment states that prohibition laws cost Americans $936 million in 1928 due to the loss of Federal and local revenue and the costs of Federal enforcement.			H.H. Sheldon, professor at New York University, announces in a report for the Smoke Nuisance Committee that analysis of the air above New York City is polluted with dust, dirt, poisonous gases such as carbon monoxide and sulfuric acid, and bacteria, against which he believes most city dwellers develop immunity.	Pulitzer Prizes for the best American writing in 1928-29 are awarded to Julia Peterkin for the novel *Scarlet Sister Mary*, to Burton J. Hendrick for the biography *The Training of an American*, to Fred Albert Shannon for *The Organization and Administration of the Union Army 1861-1865*, and to Stephen Vincent Benet for the narrative poem *John Brown's Body*.	May 12

F	G	H	I	J
Includes campaigns, elections, federal-state relations, civil rights and liberties, crime, the judiciary, education, healthcare, poverty, urban affairs, and population.	*Includes formation and debate of U.S. foreign and defense policies, veterans affairs, and defense spending. (Relations with specific foreign countries are usually found under the region concerned.)*	*Includes business, labor, agriculture, taxation, transportation, consumer affairs, monetary and fiscal policy, natural resources, pollution and industrial accidents.*	*Includes worldwide scientific, medical and technological developments, natural phenomena, U.S. weather and natural disasters.*	*Includes the arts, religion, scholarship, communications media, sports, entertainment, fashions, fads, and social life.*

	World Affairs	Europe	Africa & The Middle East	The Americas	Asia & The Pacific
May 13	Belgian and German experts explain to the League of Nations Economic Committee that overproduction of sugar beets and sugar cane is responsible for the world's current beet sugar crisis....American Charles Evans Hughes, former U.S. Secretary of State, becomes the newest judge as the Permanent Court of International Justice opens its 16th session at the Hague.	Leaders of the Tory, Liberal, and Socialist political parties in Great Britain forbid all candidates running for Parliament from talking about prohibition questions during the pre-election period.		Canada's Sir Henry Drayton rules that sailors on the Great Lakes cannot consider their ships to be homes so that they do not come in conflict with the liquor control acts, which might lead to confiscation of the ships when in U.S. ports.	
May 14	President Herbert Hoover disapproves of the plan to make the U.S. Federal Reserve Bank System responsible for handling the transactions associated with World War I war debt reparations as will be instituted through an International Bank of Settlements.	The 50th anniversary of the liberation of Bulgaria from Turkish rule is celebrated by thousands gathered in the city of Sofia.	Approximately $32 million is earmarked by Egypt's government for irrigation and other public works, which will help increase production of cotton and other important crops.		
May 15	In an effort to reduce the beet sugar crisis, the League of Nations announces that countries with high production rates will reduce their exports of the product until the industry stabilizes.			Air mail service begins between the United States and Nicaragua via Pan-American Airways.	In India, striking workers break into four cotton mills and refuse to leave while police clash with strikers near other mills.
May 16		The Greek Senate, consisting of 120 members, meets in Athens for the first time since 1862....British film censors warn film makers to avoid objectionable language and scenes including those that show mockery of religious figures, degradation of Far East citizens, and intoxication of girls and women....Over 30,000 attend the opening of the Polish National Exhibition at Posen.		The last major rebel leader in Sonora State, Mexico, Genera Ruben Yucupicio, surrenders to Federal forces.	Nearly 200,000 are involved in a battle for the city of Canton, China, which is being defended by the local Kwantung forces against the attacking Kwangsi Army....In Japan, Tokyo police forces blame pro-Communist supporters for instigating student riots at Imperial and Waseda Universities, a charge the students deny and instead blame police interference at a meeting.
May 17		An editorial in the current issue of Economic Life magazine accuses the Soviet Union of mismanagement and poor distribution plans for allowing as much as 25 percent of the fresh meat, egg, and dairy supply to rot before reaching urban markets, a situation at odds with the praises awarded during the last month to the Socialist system by the All Russian Soviet Congress.		President Herbert Hoover announces that the 46 year long border dispute between Chile and Peru is settled with the province of Tacna going to Peru and Arica province will belong to Chile.	In Canton (Guangzhou), China, the local Kwangtung forces are repelling the attacking Kwangsi forces away from the city and have recaptured the town of Weichow.
May 18	The League of Nations Refugee Advisory Committee agrees to extend the position of High Commissariat for another 10 years in order to assist the remaining 1million refugees from World War I, particularly former Russian and Armenian residents who can only obtain passports and other documentation through the League.			Mexico's National Railways estimate that $30 million is needed to recoup revenue losses and to rebuild bridges and rail tracks destroyed during the recent rebellion.	China's President Chiang Kai-Shek sends a message to Marshal Feng Yu-hsiang asking for a truce between the two and offering safe passage for Feng to Nanking to discuss his current military campaign against the Nationalist forces.
May 19	U.S. President Herbert Hoover agrees to the proposed changes made by Owen Young to the World War I debt reparations bill as being negotiated in Paris which would extend the years Germany would have to make payments to the Allied forces.	An Italian shipyard outbids American, British, and French companies and is awarded a contract to build two torpedo destroyers, two submarines, and two submarine chasers for the Turkish government.		U.S. Ambassador to Mexico Dwight Morrow is negotiating with the Mexican government to determine whether to allow California and Texas to deport 20,000 people believed to have crossed into the United States in violation of immigration rules.	The U.S.S. Guam arrives at Wuchow (Wuzhou), China to evacuate Americans from the city, which the Canton Government plans to attack to rid the area of Kwangsi rebels.

A	B	C	D	E
Includes developments that affect more than one world region, international organizations and important meetings of world leaders.	Includes all domestic and regional developments in Europe, including the Soviet Union.	Includes all domestic and regional developments in Africa and the Middle East.	Includes all domestic and regional developments in Latin America, the Caribbean, and Canada.	Includes all domestic and regional developments in Asian and Pacific nations (and colonies).

U.S. Politics & Social Issues	U.S. Foreign Policy & Affairs, Defense	U.S. Economy & Environment	Science, Technology & Nature	Culture, Leisure & Lifestyle	
	Charles Edward Weir, an African-American, passes the mental examinations required for entrance into the Naval Academy. He was one of three men nominated for admission to the academy by the only African-American currently serving in Congress, Illinois Representative Oscar De Priest.	The May 4th agreement for a five-day work week and 10 percent pay raise made by the Building Trades Employers Association and the Building Trades Council is rescinded. Additionally, the employers are planning a lockout that will force over 75,000 mechanics from their jobs as a result of a dispute between the two organizations over sympathetic strikes supporting the Electrical Workers Union, Local 3.	A Chinese and a Danish pilot make the first long distance plane trip between England and China by traveling in three segments over a two month period....U.S. President Herbert Hoover has temporarily set aside 144,000 acres in southern Nevada along the Moapa and Virgin River valleys that contain ancient Pueblo and Paiute archeological sites.	New York's Metropolitan Museum of Art exhibits the newly acquired marble altar frontal relief, *Descent from the Cross*, sculpted by the French Renaissance artist Jean Goujon....Egypt's Edmond Soussa wins the International Amateur 18.1 Balkline Billiards Tournament for the third year in a row.	May 13
The trial of Louisiana Governor Huey P. Long on impeachment charges begins today at the Louisiana State Senate where lawyers for the governor claim the procedure to violate the state's constitution.		U.S. Senators vote 54 to 33 in favor of the farm relief bill that includes the export debenture plan and pass it on for consideration by the House of Representatives.....New York's Supreme Court files a restraining order preventing the Building Trades Employers Association from forcing a lockout of over 75,000 mechanics which would have affected $100 million in current construction projects.	A committee on navigation recommends that the International Convention for the Safety of Life at Sea now meeting in London continue to monitor iceberg activity in the North Atlantic and to adopt regulations requiring certain ships to provide regular weather reports and to create a code of lighted signals on ships to prevent collisions.		May 14
Wisconsin State Senators pass a bill that would rescind the prohibition enforcement laws as approved by an April referendum from the state's citizens and deliver the bill to Governor Walter J. Kohler.	Ground troops and 200 planes are participating in the U.S. Army's aerial combat war games practice over Ohio.		Leaking steam causes an explosion in a basement storage room containing x-ray and photographic film at the Cleveland Clinic Hospital and releases several deadly poisonous gases. 125 patients, nurses, and doctors die and over 100 are injured from the gases, smoke, and fire.		May 15
Governor Huey P. Long is freed from all impeachment charges as his trial is adjourned today when 15 Louisiana State Senators vow to acquit him because they believe the trial is illegal under the state's constitution....Chicago mob boss Al Capone is arrested in Philadelphia on charges of carrying a concealed weapon and immediately begins serving a one year prison sentence.		The Equitable Trust Company and Seaboard National Bank merge to form the fifth largest bank in the United States with assets of over $859 million....General Motors Corporation buys 40 percent of the stock of Fokker Aircraft Corporation, giving it a controlling interest of the world's leading airplane manufacturer.	The *Graf Zeppelin* dirigible makes an emergency landing in France after two crank shafts break 750 miles into its second journey from Berlin to the United States....Members of Commander Richard Byrd's Antarctic Expedition realize that the aurora phenomenon affects wireless radio reception and transmission.	The first Academy Awards given by the Academy for Motion Picture Arts and Sciences are given during a banquet at the Hollywood Roosevelt Hotel to movies made in 1927 and 1928. Awards are given to *Wings* for best picture, Emil Jannings for best actor, and Janet Gaynor for best actress.	May 16
	Dwight F. Davis, former Secretary of War, has accepted the post of U.S. Governor General of the Philippines.	Through a test vote, members of the House of Representatives rebuke the Senate for including the export debenture plan in the farm relief bill because all legislation involving revenues are required by the U.S. Constitution to be initiated in the House.	Days of rain cause River Drave and River Kolubra to flood, inundating much of Serbia and interrupting railroad service to Belgrade.	Joyce Wethered of England wins the women's British Open Golf Championship played at St. Andrews, Scotland.	May 17
		The Montclair (NJ) Building Trades Council announces that bricklayers and carpenters will be given pay raises and a five-day work week, which is hoped to relieve unemployment....The U.S. Department of Agriculture releases figures showing farm laborers earn a salary nearly equivalent to that of factory workers if the value of food and shelter provided at most farms is included as income. A large geographical difference of $50 is found in the farm hand incomes between the southeast and western states.	German Pilot E. Starke sets a new flight record by flying an Heinkel Seaplane at 173.284 miles per hour.	Members of the American Library Association meeting in Washington, DC award President Herbert Hoover with a lifetime membership to the organization in recognition of his collection containing two million manuscripts, papers, and records pertaining to World War I....Clyde Van Dusen, ridden by jockey Linus McAtee, wins the 55th Kentucky Derby held at Louisville, KY in 2 minutes, 10.8 seconds.	May 18
		$3,500 is sent for relief to the families of textile strikers in Elizabethton, TN and Greenville, SC, by the Emergency Committee for Strikers' Relief, which is jointly supported by the League for Industrial Democracy and the American Federation of Labor.	Jean Du Rand makes a parachute jump from 18,700 feet above Minnesota, setting a new world record for women in this category.	King Alfonso opens the International Exposition held at Barcelona, Spain....Two people are killed and 62 injured when fans stampede the bleacher exits at Yankee Stadium to avoid a rain shower during a Yankee–Red Sox game.	May 19

F	G	H	I	J
Includes campaigns, elections, federal-state relations, civil rights and liberties, crime, the judiciary, education, healthcare, poverty, urban affairs, and population.	Includes formation and debate of U.S. foreign and defense policies, veterans affairs, and defense spending. (Relations with specific foreign countries are usually found under the region concerned.)	Includes business, labor, agriculture, taxation, transportation, consumer affairs, monetary and fiscal policy, natural resources, pollution and industrial accidents.	Includes worldwide scientific, medical and technological developments, natural phenomena, U.S. weather and natural disasters.	Includes the arts, religion, scholarship, communications media, sports, entertainment, fashions, fads, and social life.

	World Affairs	Europe	Africa & The Middle East	The Americas	Asia & The Pacific
May 20	The first meeting of the International Academy for the History of Science begins in Paris, France. Attendees discuss methods for supporting international cooperation in research and teaching in this field.	Svetozar Pribicevic, leader of Yugoslavia's Independent Democratic Party is arrested in Belgrade as an enemy of the dictatorship of King Alexander Karadordevic....Two Irish Nationalist Party members are elected to Great Britain's House of Commons for the first time since 1922.		Canada's House of Commons approves a treaty for the preservation and conservation of Niagara Falls and River....Cuba's new President Gerardo Machado y Morales is inaugurated in Havana.	Partly as a result of the effective Chinese boycott against its goods, Japan completes the evacuation of all military troops from China's Shantung (Shandong) Province.
May 21	Belgium and Sweden are the first two nations to agree to the League of Nations peace treaty, which requires that, beginning in 90 days, all signatory nations will go through the League for arbitration of new international disputes between countries.	The governments of Czechoslovakia, Yugoslavia, and Rumania renewed treaties that bind the three nations into the Little Entente and add to their agreement an arbitration pact.		Honduran Minister Plenipotentiary to the United States states that conditions of peace are now established and he welcomes American businesses to invest in his country.	Over 200,000 Nationalist troops are mobilized to prevent Marshal Feng Yu-hsiang's rebel soldiers from crossing the borders of the Honan Province where they are currently assembled.
May 22	The Bolivian government agrees to buy 15 million boxes of matches from the Soviet Union, making this the first agreement between a Soviet commercial enterprise and a South American nation.	Turkey expels Samuel Halevi for publicly protesting the nation's treatment of Jews.			The Japanese government is seeking a date to formally install Kenkichi Yoshizawa as Foreign Office Minister to Nanking, China to continue the reestablishment of trade and treaties between the nations.
May 23	A committee of three national representatives to the League of Nations from Great Britain, Spain, and Japan refuse to agree to a German plan that would have made the League responsible for oversight of the treatment of 40 million people who are considered minorities within their countries. Instead the League will only act if a member of the League Council identifies a violation of a treaty on minorities that is currently in effect.	The Soviet Union's State Political Department executes three men, who formerly held high rank in the nation, for obstructing railway and gold and platinum mining operations. These activities were seen as counter-revolutionary attempts at restoring capitalism by the present Communist leader....Vladko Macek, leader of the Croat Peasant Party, is released after several hours of police interrogation in Zagreb, Yugoslavia for suspected activities with the banned Peasant International Party.		Panamanian officials state they will not ratify the 1926 mutual aid treaty with the United States because it contains a clause that transfers a section of land presently in the city of Colon to Canal Zone jurisdiction.	
May 24		For the third week in a row, a bridge in Croatia is dynamited as a protest by the Croats against the policies of Yugoslavian dictator King Alexander Karadordevic.	Persian troops are gathering in the city of Tehran and the Shiraz region to prevent raids and rebel actions from members of the Kash Gai tribe.		Amanullah Khan, the deposed king of Afghanistan, announces he will cease efforts to return to power, but instead is seeking asylum in Europe.
May 25	Members of the French Cabinet discuss whether to ratify the Mellon-Berenger plan for repayment of $4 billion in war debt to the United States, although final agreement will have to wait until the German war debt and reparations conference ends.	Berlin police order the pro-Communist newspaper, *Rote Fahne*, banned for four weeks after it publishes articles that blame police for mishandling of the May Day parades that ended in riots and multiple deaths.			At a conference in Simla, India a leading publicist, Chin Tamani calls for Indians to demand self-rule throughout the country's states and provinces.
May 26		Candidates for the Liberal Party win the majority of seats in Belgium's elections for positions in the Chamber of Deputies and the Senate, including the first female Deputy. Voting in this election was compulsory for the nation's 2.5 million men and only those widows who have not yet remarried, because women do not have the right to vote.		The U.S. district director for immigration in New York prohibits all non-native born Canadian citizens from commuting into the United States to work, a rule that affects naturalized Canadian citizens, British subjects, and others.	The body of revolutionary Chinese leader Sun Yat-sen is carried on a cortège through of Peking on the way to the railway station where it be transported to Nanking for entombment in a $3 million mausoleum.
May 27	The U.S. State Department declines, despite a repeated invitation, to send a representative to the annual conference given by the League of Nations' International Labor Office, which will discuss issues of forced and white collar labor.	Italy's King Victor Emmanuel III signs the Lateran Treaties, establishing the Vatican as a sovereign nation.			

A	B	C	D	E
Includes developments that affect more than one world region, international organizations and important meetings of world leaders.	Includes all domestic and regional developments in Europe, including the Soviet Union.	Includes all domestic and regional developments in Africa and the Middle East.	Includes all domestic and regional developments in Latin America, the Caribbean, and Canada.	Includes all domestic and regional developments in Asian and Pacific nations (and colonies).

U.S. Politics & Social Issues	U.S. Foreign Policy & Affairs, Defense	U.S. Economy & Environment	Science, Technology & Nature	Culture, Leisure & Lifestyle	
President Herbert Hoover appoints 10 male lawyers and one female college president to serve on the newly created National Law Enforcement Commission, which will examine the current status and failings of judicial process and law enforcement.			The naval rescue ship U.S.S *Mallard* and submarines *S-12* and *S-20* participate in a simulated rescue of a sunken submarine, the *S-11*, which was located through the use of a new acoustic device called an SC tube. The ships also tested systems for providing food and then raising a sunken submarine.		May 20
U.S. Senators argue whether newspapers have the right to publish how individual congressmen vote in confirmation hearings on presidential appointees, which some feel violates the normally secret nature of the sessions.	Planes in the U.S. Army's Air Corps drop flares representing bombs on Fort Jay in New York City as part of a war games simulation testing the ability to make non-stop, refueled flights from a base in Ohio.	The Advisory Council to the Federal Reserve Board recommends that Federal Reserve Banks be allowed to raise the rediscount rate on loans to six percent to bring them close to commercial loan rates.	Flooding along the Mississippi River and tributaries has inundated thousands of acres in Missouri and threatens to collapse levees in Kentucky, Tennessee, and Missouri.		May 21
All newspapers are barred from the Senate floor after the United Press Association is excluded and one of its reporters subpoenaed by the Senate Rules Committee for revealing the voter identities of the confirmation hearing of Senator Lenroot to a federal judgeship.			Flooding along the Tigris and Euphrates Rivers covers thousands of acres in Mesopotamia and the Basra to Baghdad rail line is washed out in two places....The Curtiss Flying Service, Inc. begins 60 minutes flights between New York City and Atlantic City, NJ aboard a Sikorsky amphibian plane.	Missourian Horton Smith wins the French Open Golf Championship in St. Cloud, France with a new record of 273 strokes on 72 holes.	May 22
Colonel Theodore Roosevelt accepts the position of Governor of Puerto Rico, which was recently offered by President Herbert Hoover.			Columbia University announces that a collaborative group of geographers, geologists and engineers determined that the east coast of the United States was not sinking at rates of one to two feet per year as had been hypothesized by geologists, but instead there were local variations in mean sea level along the shore.		May 23
	The Navy Department assigns five former mine sweepers to ports scattered across the globe to act as rescue vessels, particularly for submarine disasters.		Construction crews break ground on New York City's first elevated highway, which will extend 14–18 feet above the ground for a length of 4.1 miles across the west side.	RCA Photophone, Inc. demonstrates the first three-dimensional movie using a Spoor-Berggren duplex lens camera.	May 24
House of Representative members walk out of a joint committee meeting with Senators and refuse to sign the farm relief bill containing the export debenture plan. To induce the Senators to accept the bill without the debenture plan, the House offers them a three month recess and a promise to discuss the tariff bill in the fall.			Over 60 people are killed as more than 1,000 homes are destroyed by an earthquake centered near the city of Sivas in central Turkey....The first direct delivery of air mail from Peru to the United States on Pan-American-Grace Airways, Inc. arrives in 6.5 days, which is eight days shorter than travel by ship.	The first installment of Ernest Hemingway's *A Farewell to Arms* is published in the newly released June issue of *Scribner's Magazine*.	May 25
			A new air endurance record is set by the crew of the *Fort Worth* who complete a nonstop 172.5 hour flight at Forth Worth, Texas....French pilots set a new speed record by traveling an average of 112 miles per hour during a 3,125 mile flight.		May 26
The U.S. Supreme Court votes 6-3 to refuse naturalization to a Hungarian pacifist, Rosika Schwimmer, who sought U.S. citizenship but refused to agree to fight for the nation. In a separate vote, the court upholds the use of the pocket veto by the president to prevent legislation from being enacted when Congress adjourns before the usual 10-day bill signing limit expires.		Trading on the New York Stock Exchange drops prices to very low levels on news that the Federal Reserve Banks may raise the rediscount loan rate and in reaction to a projected loss of $70 million on wheat at the Chicago Stock Market.	Members of the life saving appliances committee at the International Convention for the Safety of Life at Sea meeting in London recommend that all ships carry lifeboats sufficient to evacuate all persons from the ship and that they be easily accessible in an emergency.	Colonel Charles Lindbergh, famous aviator, marries Anne Spencer Morrow, daughter of Dwight Morrow, the U.S. Ambassador to Mexico, at her family home in New Jersey.	May 27

F	G	H	I	J
Includes campaigns, elections, federal-state relations, civil rights and liberties, crime, the judiciary, education, healthcare, poverty, urban affairs, and population.	Includes formation and debate of U.S. foreign and defense policies, veterans affairs, and defense spending. (Relations with specific foreign countries are usually found under the region concerned.)	Includes business, labor, agriculture, taxation, transportation, consumer affairs, monetary and fiscal policy, natural resources, pollution and industrial accidents.	Includes worldwide scientific, medical and technological developments, natural phenomena, U.S. weather and natural disasters.	Includes the arts, religion, scholarship, communications media, sports, entertainment, fashions, fads, and social life.

	World Affairs	Europe	Africa & The Middle East	The Americas	Asia & The Pacific
May 28		Statements by Premier Eleutherios Venizelos that Greece needs to build sufficient naval power in order to compete with the developing naval capabilities of Turkey is seen as a serious blow to diplomatic efforts to create a three-way alliance between Italy, Greece, and Turkey.	Representatives from the U.S., Great Britain, and Iraq complete a final draft of a treaty between the three nations that recognizes the sovereignty of Iraq.		Nadir Khan, nephew of deposed King Amanullah Khan, declares himself the new Emir of Afghanistan with the intent of taking over rule from the current Emir, Habibullah Kalakani.
May 29	Germany agrees to pay $27 billion in war debt and reparations over the next 59 years to the Allied nations of World War I in a plan that will supersede the present Dawes debt plan....The Soviet Union denies charges by China's Nationalist Government that it is financially and militarily supporting Marshal Feng Yu-hsiang who is leading the Kwangsi revolt in China.			The New York, Rio, and Buenos Aires Lines, Inc. and Pan-American Airways plan new air routes from New York to Buenos Aires that will have stops in Brazil.	Marshal Feng Yu-hsiang declares war on Chinese President Chiang Kai-shek and the Nanking Nationalist government.
May 30	Representatives from 14 nations attend the annual conference given by the League of Nations' International Labor Office.	Great Britain's Labor Party wins a large number of seats in the national elections, achieving a plurality, and Ramsay MacDonald is voted the new prime minister.			A bomb is exploded in Kabul, Afghanistan in an attempt to assassinate Emir, Habibullah Kalakani. The leader is not injured, but Syed Hussein, the Minister of War is killed.
May 31	Italy announces that a battle near Tripoli between Italian troops and a rebel tribe has resulted in 454 deaths.	Members of the Italian government react unfavorably to the election gains made by Great Britain's Labor Party, which will alter future foreign policy decisions.		Federal troops, with the assistance of aircraft, take control of rebel strongholds in Jalisco State, Mexico.	
Jun. 1	Germany agrees to pay an unconditional annual annuity in the amount of $158.4 as part of the war debt payments to the World War I Allied nations.	Pro-Nationalist students at Vienna University in Austria verbally and physically attack a group of Jewish students on campus.	Iraq's Baghdad Museum is forming a committee to determine how best to sell cultural antiquities from its collection to European and American buyers in order to preserve their historical value.		The body of revolutionary leader and educator Sun Yat-sen, who died in 1925, is entombed in a $3 million memorial on Purple Mountain near Nanking, China.
Jun. 2		Turkey's National Assembly approves a bill that will raise tariffs on almost all goods, including used clothing, by 25 percent in order to promote Turkish industry....Members of Austria's Heimwehr, the Nationalist militia, disrupt a Socialist children's parade, which results in a brawl between the two political groups, injuring many people on both sides....Arrests of leaders such as Svetozar Pribitchevitch and suspicious military shootings of Croats are leading to increasing tensions between Croats and Serbs in Croatia.		Police in Rio de Janeiro, Brazil arrest two men accused of spreading rumors that two local banks were nearly bankrupt, which caused panic among depositors, and they noted the unfounded bank closing reports have become a common problem.	
Jun. 3		Members of the Greek Senate and Chamber re-elect Admiral Paul Kondouriotis to be president of Greece.		Chilean and Peruvian dignitaries meet in Lima, Peru to ceremoniously sign the Tacna-Arica Treaty, which had been ratified on May 17. Under the agreement, Chile keeps the province of Arica while granting Peru $6 million, the Tacna region, a harbor in the Bay of Arica, and access to the rail station....The American Association of Railroad Superintendents opens its 36th annual convention in Mexico City, Mexico.	

A	B	C	D	E
Includes developments that affect more than one world region, international organizations and important meetings of world leaders.	Includes all domestic and regional developments in Europe, including the Soviet Union.	Includes all domestic and regional developments in Africa and the Middle East.	Includes all domestic and regional developments in Latin America, the Caribbean, and Canada.	Includes all domestic and regional developments in Asian and Pacific nations (and colonies).

U.S. Politics & Social Issues	U.S. Foreign Policy & Affairs, Defense	U.S. Economy & Environment	Science, Technology & Nature	Culture, Leisure & Lifestyle	
		The U.S. House of Representatives passes the far-reaching Hawley tariff bill and send it to the Senate for consideration....The Ford Company asks the League of Nations' International Labor Office to provide wage scales for countries in Europe so employees at factories planned in various cities will earn approximately an equivalent wage.	Marvel Crosson sets a new altitude record for women by flying to 24,000 feet.	*On With The Show*, the first all color, full-length talking motion picture debuts in New York.	May 28
Wisconsin's Governor Walter Kohler signs a bill that repeals the state's prohibition enforcement law; although he warns the federal prohibition laws are still in effect.	The U.S. Coast Guard plans to use seaplanes along coastal areas to assist with airplane rescue operations at sea.		Robert Fahy sets a new record for solo endurance flights with a time of 36 hours, 56 minutes, and 36 seconds.	Arturo Toscanini, conductor with Milan's La Scala Opera Company retires from a 40-year-long career in opera to focus on concerts.	May 29
			An earthquake near the town of Villatuel, Argentina kills 20 and destroys much of the town with surrounding provinces also suffering property damage and casualties.	The Indianapolis 500 race is won by Ray Keech, with an average speed of 97.585 mph in his car, Simplex Special.	May 30
President Herbert Hoover disapproves of any plan that would give the Senate a long recess without discussion of the Hawley tariff bill, which he would like to see signed into law by September.		Soviet officials sign an agreement with Henry Ford who will help build an automobile factory at Nizhni Novgorod, Russia. In addition, the Soviets will purchase $30 million worth of Ford automobiles over a four year period.	Researchers from the Carnegie Institute's Genetics Department discuss how humans can altar species characteristics through controlled environmental and breeding experiments on corn, fleas, doves, mice, fish, and weeds.	Erich Maria Remarque's novel about World War I, *All Quiet on the Western Front*, is released in the United States. Little, Brown and Co., the publisher, changed several words and deleted two scenes to remove content it deemed vulgar or objectionable to Americans....The Society of American Magicians holds their annual conference, privately at a New York City hotel, to share knowledge about performing tricks.	May 31
Democratic members of the House of Representative vow to fight the reapportionment bill recently passed by the Senate because it would give illegal immigrants representation in Congress.	President Hoover meets with Adams, Secretary of the Navy to discuss plans for naval reductions.		The New York City's Health Department's plans to drain swamp and riverside areas for mosquito extermination exceed $100,000 in projects for the upcoming summer.		Jun. 1
New York City's Department of Hospitals announces new policies to prevent hospital and morgue employees from notifying particular undertakers of a death so that they could retrieve the body and arrange funeral services without consent or notification of the next of kin.			Delegates from 18 nations sign the new ship safety code created at London's International Conference on the Safety of Life at Sea that includes rules requiring all ships over 1,600 tons to carry radios, nations must collaborate on sharing of weather information, and ship stability must be assessed before use....Passengers and crew aboard the Anchor ocean liner *Cameronia* spot icebergs much further south in the North Atlantic than is normal for the season."...Policemen in Detroit, MI, have significantly improved arrest records and response time to crimes by using newly invented radio-dispatch units in their patrol cars.	American Helen Wills wins the singles event of the French Tennis Championship at Paris for the second year in a row.	Jun. 2
A New York city toxicologist announces that a man has died of poisoning from drinking alcohol that had been denatured with aldehol by the government to render it unfit for consumption.		Over $300 million is made at the Chicago Stock Market on wheat and grains upon hearing that Congress planned to add $100 million for wheat aid to the farm relief bill under discussion.		*Honky Tonk*, starring Sophie Tucker in her first movie role, opens at the Warner Brothers Theater in New York....Nineteen year-old actor Douglas Fairbanks, Jr., marries actress Joan Crawford In New York.	Jun. 3

F	G	H	I	J
Includes campaigns, elections, federal-state relations, civil rights and liberties, crime, the judiciary, education, healthcare, poverty, urban affairs, and population.	Includes formation and debate of U.S. foreign and defense policies, veterans affairs, and defense spending. (Relations with specific foreign countries are usually found under the region concerned.)	Includes business, labor, agriculture, taxation, transportation, consumer affairs, monetary and fiscal policy, natural resources, pollution and industrial accidents.	Includes worldwide scientific, medical and technological developments, natural phenomena, U.S. weather and natural disasters.	Includes the arts, religion, scholarship, communications media, sports, entertainment, fashions, fads, and social life.

	World Affairs	Europe	Africa & The Middle East	The Americas	Asia & The Pacific
Jun. 4	All sides approve the World War I war debt and reparations bill, known as the Young Plan, after Belgium agrees to negotiate directly with Germany to settle a question about the redemption of German marks used during the war.	Great Britain's Prime Minister Stanley Baldwin gives his resignation to King George, ending the Conservative Party's five-year control of the nation's government.		The Canadian Parliament postpones signing a sockeye salmon treaty with the United States because not all members of the Marine and Fisheries Committee agrees that the treaty's provisions will help preserve the salmon industry.	Chinese authorities arrest N.K. Kuznetzoff, the Soviet consul General at Mukden and two other officials on suspicion they were carrying papers confirming a conspiracy between the Soviet Union and the Chinese rebel leader Marshal Feng Yu-hsiang.
Jun. 5	The U.S. State Department rejects the latest French Film Board offer of a 4:1 film quota, under which plan the United States would have to produce, buy, or distribute one French film for every four U.S. movies that France imports.	Ramsay MacDonald begins a new term as Prime Minister of Great Britain....Paris postal carriers end their 24 hour strike, in which they demonstrated their disapproval of a government tax. The strike also successfully demonstrated that police officers who had been pressed into duty to deliver the mail were not as efficient as the carriers.		In response to recent student protests at the National University, Mexico's Chamber of Deputies vote to allow President Emilio Portes Gil to declare the school autonomous from government interference.	The U.S. State Department requests permission from China for Roy Chapman Andrews, of the American Museum of Natural History, to bring prehistoric Gobi Desert fossils to the United States for study.
Jun. 6	300 delegates from North America, Europe, and the Middle East meeting in Hamburg, Germany at the first international conference of Jewish women establish a world federation to be headquartered in New York. The group seeks to establish equality for women in Jewish communities, the abolition of university quotas on Jewish students, and meetings with rabbis to change Jewish divorce practices.	King Zog of Albania agrees to dedicate the new American diplomatic building in Tirana and attend the inaugural dance, his first, to celebrate with the American delegate Charles C. Hart.		After over 25 year of control, the Liberal Party loses the majority of seats in Saskatchewan's provincial elections in Canada....Mexico's Federal troops engaged in an eight hour battle with religious rebels in the Los Altos region of Jalisco.	China's leader's decree that all fossil hunting expeditions and other archeological excavations will be regulated by the Nationalist Government in Nanking according to plans being developed by the country's Ministries of Education, Foreign Affairs, and the Interior.
Jun. 7	Experts meeting at the Paris talks on World War I war debts sign the 50 page Young Plan report and begin to arrange the Bank of International Settlements as a non-political entity. Germany agrees to pay a total of approximately $8.9 billion, which is less than the original Dawes plan figure.	Italian Premier Benito Mussolini and Pope Pius XI ratify the Lateran Treaty, making the Pope a leader of the sovereign nation of Vatican City and ending the 59 year separation of the Catholic Church and the Italian State....Ramsay MacDonald, the new Prime Minister of Great Britain, names his Cabinet appointments, which include Minister of Labor Margaret Bondfield, who is the first female Cabinet member.	Sugar producers in the African Gold Coast announce smaller than expected production, causing concern that warehouse stocks may not be able to cover international contracts.		Japanese Naval officers hope for an increase in naval ships beyond that limited by the Washington 5-5-3 ratio that limits Japan's naval strength to 60 percent of that of the United States and Great Britain, while citizens instead plead for an arms reduction among the three naval superpowers.
Jun. 8	Analysis of the Young Plan indicates that 65 percent of the German payments to Allied nations will be transferred to the United States from other nations to pay off war debts, while the remaining 35 percent will be used to repair war damages, primarily n France.	Italy sends a squadron of 36 hydroplanes to deliver a message of friendship and peace to Bulgaria, which is seen by surrounding countries as inciting the nation to reclaim Macedonia.	Eighteen Merrille tribesmen are killed in a clash with British soldiers from the King's African Rifles near the Sudanese border in British East Africa.		Bandits kidnap five British missionaries and one child in southeastern Honan, China, according to the China Inland Mission.
Jun. 9	Lichtenstein's Prince Ferdinand Androeas and Hungary's Count de Almasy are reported missing in Sudan after attempting to drive from Wadi-Halfa to Cairo along the Nile.	Over 500,000 watch a parade in Vienna, Austria that celebrates the nation's commercial and industrial activities....Police in the Soviet Union arrest 200 businessmen and city officials on corruption charges relating to a fish pricing scam in Astrakhan that netted $7.5 million.		An armed band of hundreds of insurgents briefly kidnap the governor of the Dutch West Indies at Willemsted, Curacao, during a raid on the town's garrison to steal ammunition and armaments to support rebellious activities in Venezuela.	
Jun. 10	The 55th League Council session of the League of Nations opens today in Madrid, Spain.	Great Britain's Prime Minister Ramsay MacDonald shows a talking motion picture to introduce the members of his Cabinet. This is the first time such technology is used in this way in politics.	Legislation is pending in Africa's Gold Coast that would allow cocoa farmers to form cooperatives to grow and distribute better cocoa, a crop for which they currently produce half of the global supply.	A Dutch Naval destroyer is sent to the Dutch West Indies to maintain stability in the region after Venezuelan rebels raided the island of Curacao.	

A	**B**	**C**	**D**	**E**
Includes developments that affect more than one world region, international organizations and important meetings of world leaders.	Includes all domestic and regional developments in Europe, including the Soviet Union.	Includes all domestic and regional developments in Africa and the Middle East.	Includes all domestic and regional developments in Latin America, the Caribbean, and Canada.	Includes all domestic and regional developments in Asian and Pacific nations (and colonies).

U.S. Politics & Social Issues	U.S. Foreign Policy & Affairs, Defense	U.S. Economy & Environment	Science, Technology & Nature	Culture, Leisure & Lifestyle	
U.S. Senators engage in heated debate on the high value of broker's loans made through the stock market and a call for investigation into the actions of the Federal Reserve Board that has led to recent huge losses on the Chicago and New York Stock Exchanges.	Dwight F. Davis takes the oath of office to become the new Governor General of the Philippines.	The Actor's Equity Association declares that talking motion picture actors must now be covered by an Equity contract, as with worker's unions, that limits the workweek to 48 hours and requires payment for rehearsals and overtime.	Naval Lieutenant Apollo Soucek sets a new altitude record for seaplanes by flying to a height of 38,560 feet.		Jun. 4
A U.S. Senator introduces a bill for consideration that would require newspapers to disclose ownership information after Congress learns that the International Paper and Power Company sought to purchase dozens of papers.		The House and Senate conference committee agree to remove the export debenture plan from the farm relief bill, which is in accordance with the wishes of President Herbert Hoover.	The Carnegie Institute announces that two of its scientists, Bailey Willis and N.L. Bowen, are traveling around the globe in order to investigate causes of seismic activity....Earthquakes occur in Bulgaria and Argentina.	The horse Trigo wins the English Derby at Epson Downs, an event in which thousands of people participated via a multi-national sweepstakes.	Jun. 5
Representatives from the House pass the Census Reapportionment Bill that was already approved by the Senate, although they remove amendments that had taken away rights of representation from illegal immigrants and disenfranchised southern African Americans.		Workers from Chicago's Building Construction Employers' Association end their 4.5 day strike today after winning a raise from $12 to $13 per hour that is effective until June 1, 1930.		An American colt, Reigh Count, wins the Coronation Cup Stakes race at Epsom Downs, England.	Jun. 6
U.S. Representative Homer Hoch submits a resolution that would amend the Constitution so that only U.S. citizens, as counted by the decennial Census, are accounted for during Congressional apportionment procedures, instead of the current accounting that includes all persons.		The Farm Relief Bill is passed by the U.S. House of Representatives.... Five people, including four policemen, are shot in a confrontation between police and striking textile workers from the Loray Mill at Gastonia, NC.	Charles Darwin's home, Down House located near Orpington, Kent, in England, has been restored and is opened as a public museum.		Jun. 7
Over 25,000 people and an elephant gather to celebrate the 75th anniversary of the founding of the Republican Party at Ripon, WI.			A new ocean trench, 28,380 feet deep, is discovered in the Pacific Ocean between Japan and Guam by the Carnegie, a magnetic survey ship operated by the Carnegie Institute. It is named the J. A. Fleming Deep....The first radio beacon in the eastern U.S. is established at Mitchel Field, NY to guide Army airplanes at night or in foggy conditions.	The Atlantic prize for best biography, offered by the editors of Atlantic Monthly, Atlantic Monthly Press and Little, Brown & Co., is awarded to Harriet Connor Brown for the book Grandmother Brown's Hundred Years, 1827–1927.	Jun. 8
Two striking textile workers charged in the shooting death of the Gastonia, NC Chief of Police escape being lynched by an angry mob through the actions of police officers who transfer the workers to a jail at an undisclosed location.		The Assistant Secretary of Commerce announces that Congress's passage of the Census Reapportionment Bill specifies the 1930 population census will begin on November 1 while an extensive secondary census of domestic trade will begin next January.		American teams win first place in both the five-man and two-man team events at the International Bowling Tournament at Stockholm, Sweden.	Jun. 9
President Herbert Hoover, holding a trowel used by George Washington to inaugurate the Capitol building, lays the cornerstone of the new Department of Commerce building in Washington, DC. In an accompanying speech, the president applauds the economic successes of the country since the time of Washington.	12,000 troops in the U.S. Army's Hawaii Department begin two weeks of war games designed to simulate an attack by foreign ships on the defenses of Oahu.	Representatives from the nation's oil companies and government officials from oil-producing states meet at an oil conservation conference in Colorado Springs, CO to discuss eliminating wasteful economic and processing practices in the $11 billion industry.	Two people are killed and property is damaged when two tornadoes strike rural areas in Minnesota and Wisconsin.	New Yorker Mike Shirghio wins the singles event at the International Bowling Tournament at Stockholm, Sweden....A French archeological expedition announces the discovery of the fortress and palace of Assyrian King Tiglath-Pileser III dating to 780 B.C.E. near Arslan Tash, Mesopotamia (Syria).	Jun. 10

F	G	H	I	J
Includes campaigns, elections, federal-state relations, civil rights and liberties, crime, the judiciary, education, healthcare, poverty, urban affairs, and population.	Includes formation and debate of U.S. foreign and defense policies, veterans affairs, and defense spending. (Relations with specific foreign countries are usually found under the region concerned.)	Includes business, labor, agriculture, taxation, transportation, consumer affairs, monetary and fiscal policy, natural resources, pollution and industrial accidents.	Includes worldwide scientific, medical and technological developments, natural phenomena, U.S. weather and natural disasters.	Includes the arts, religion, scholarship, communications media, sports, entertainment, fashions, fads, and social life.

	World Affairs	Europe	Africa & The Middle East	The Americas	Asia & The Pacific
Jun. 11	C.T. Wang, China's Foreign Minister, claims that no members of the Nanking Nationalist government ordered raids on the Soviet Consulate offices at Harbin, Manchuria or the arrest of Soviet diplomats. Instead, in an apology to the Soviet Union, Wang blames local officials for misunderstanding orders from the Nationalist leaders to arrest Communists.	The Rumanian government and Krueger & Company, a Swedish engineering firm, sign a $12 million contract to build a 52 mile long canal connecting Bucharest to the Danube River and to construct a power station near the city.		Venezuelan insurgents attack the town of Coro, Venezuela, but flee after several hours of fighting with federal troops.	
Jun. 12		French politician Joseph Caillaux encourages members of the French Parliament to quickly ratify the Mellon-Bérenger and Churchill-Caillaux World War I war debt accords so that the nation can avoid have to pay the United States $400 million in August.		Mexico's President Emilio Portes Gil meets with two Catholic bishops to settle a three-year-old conflict that resulted from anti-Catholic regulations made by the previous president's administration.	
Jun. 13	Members of the League of Nations' Council, meeting in Madrid, Spain, agree to adopt resolutions to assist ethnic or racial minorities, including the granting of greater representation on the League's Minority Committee and responding to claims of mistreatment by member nations.		8,000 troops of the French Foreign Legion are ordered to rescue the French military outpost of Ait Yakoub, Morocco, which is under attack from 3,000 Moorish tribesmen. 81 people have died in fighting that has included ground combat and aerial bombing runs by the French....After months of fighting, rebel chiefs surrender to Italian troops at Barka in Cyrenaica, Italian North Africa.		
Jun. 14	Germany's Foreign Minister Gustav Streseman brings a petition to the League of Nations Minority Committee to have the League settle a dispute on the status of two men, whose nationality became questionable after World War I as Germany believes they are minority citizens of Poland while the Polish government asserts they are German and therefore their property may be confiscated.		The Nationalist Party wins the majority of votes in South Africa's elections and General James B.M. Hertzog is reelected as premier.	The Nicaraguan government grants permission for the United States to send a battalion of Army Engineers to survey a potential route for an inter-oceanic canal through Nicaragua, which is a right given to America by the Bryan-Chamorro treaty of 1914.	
Jun. 15	The International Alliance of Women for Suffrage and Equal Citizenship celebrates its 25th anniversary at a conference in Berlin. Delegates from 48 nations urge that all countries should grant women and men equal work, voting, and parental rights and opportunities....The Soviet Union is deploying troops along its borders with Manchuria and Mongolia in response to accusations by China that it supports the Chinese rebel leader Marshal Feng Yu-hsiang.	Germany's Minister of Defense, Wilhelm Groener, complains to the Reichstag that under disarmament treaties signed after World War I, the nation is outnumbered by the larger number and better equipped troops in surrounding countries and is unable to defend itself properly....The Soviet Union mandates that factories will operate 360 days each year, with shut-downs only allowed on five Bolshevist holidays, although workers will retain a 5.5-day work week.			
Jun. 16		Bramwell Booth, son of the founder of the Salvation Army and its second General, dies near London.			
Jun. 17	The Permanent Court of International Justice opens its 17th session at the Hague.	Seven people die when a British Imperial Airways passenger plane crashes into the English Channel.			Japan's Premier, Baron Giichi Tanaka promises to support naval arms reductions to promote international peace and reduce national taxes.

A	B	C	D	E
Includes developments that affect more than one world region, international organizations and important meetings of world leaders.	*Includes all domestic and regional developments in Europe, including the Soviet Union.*	*Includes all domestic and regional developments in Africa and the Middle East.*	*Includes all domestic and regional developments in Latin America, the Caribbean, and Canada.*	*Includes all domestic and regional developments in Asian and Pacific nations (and colonies).*

U.S. Politics & Social Issues	U.S. Foreign Policy & Affairs, Defense	U.S. Economy & Environment	Science, Technology & Nature	Culture, Leisure & Lifestyle	
Ten New England residents plead guilty to operating an alcohol still in which they were distilling a chemical insecticide used on trees as the source of alcohol.		The Standard Oil Company of Indiana and 51 associated oil companies are found guilty in United States District Court of violating the Sherman anti-trust law by refusing to share a patented process for extracting gasoline from crude oil, a corporate practice that inhibited competition and inflated gasoline prices.		England's National Gallery pays $1.06 million to acquire two paintings, the *Vendramin Family* by Titian and the *Wilton Diptych*.	Jun. 11
Four men abduct W. B. Kinne, Idaho's Lieutenant Governor, from his vehicle and then assault two men who attempt to rescue him, and eventually leave all three men tied to a tree.		Officials at J.P. Morgan and Company assist with negotiations to merge at least six large public utilities located in New York State, creating a new company worth at least $500 million.	A Newark Air Service plane uses a hook system designed by inventor Lytle S. Adams of Seattle to retrieve an airmail bag of airmail platform positioned above the deck of the liner *Leviathan*. This pickup occurred when the ship was at sea and it is expected that this new technology will shorten down the time for mail arriving from Europe by two days.		Jun. 12
Representative John C. Schafer calls for a Congressional investigation into Prohibition enforcement policies after recent shooting deaths of unarmed civilians by federal officers.		Persia's Minister to the United States complains to the State Department that the increased rates proposed in the Hawley tariff bill on hand-made woven rugs and carpets imported from Persia will be harmful to trade policies with the United States. This message and similar complaints from six other nations are forwarded to the Senate Finance Committee to consider as the members deliberate the bill.	George E. Vincent, president of the Rockefeller Foundation, releases a report describing efforts made by the organization to combat yellow fever, hook-worm, and malaria throughout the world....H.C. Rentschler, director of research at the Westinghouse Lamp Company, demonstrates for the first time a new invention to measure the intensity of ultra violet rays, which is expected to help treat diseases such as rickets.	Florenz Ziegfeld, famous for creating musical comedies, signs a deal with Samuel Goldwyn to produce musical movies.	Jun. 13
		President Herbert Hoover estimates that the government will end the fiscal year on June 30 with a $110 million surplus instead of the expected $17 million deficit due to increases in income tax payments and customs duties.	Universal Aviation Corporation begins the first transcontinental combined air and rail service, cutting down travel between coasts to 2.5 days....A three-person crew from France and one American stowaway fly 3,128 miles non-stop across the Atlantic Ocean from Maine to Spain, stopping short of their goal of France when they run out of fuel.	Playwright George Bernard Shaw's newest production, *The Apple Cart*, which heavily satirizes European political intrigues, opens in Warsaw, Poland with President Ignacy Moscicki in attendance.	Jun. 14
Doctors from many nations meet at the International Hospital Congress in Atlantic City, NJ, where speakers call for more clinics to serve psychiatric patients as well as for smaller general hospitals to provide more individualized care.	Secretary of War James Good warns Tennessee's Governor Henry Horton that National Guard troops may not use Federal equipment or uniforms while serving in their regular jobs as Tennessee State Police, as happened when police were called to protect a textile mill from striking workers at Elizabethton, TN.	President Herbert Hoover signs the farm relief bill, known as the Agricultural Marketing Act, which creates the Federal Farm Board. He asks for $150 million of the $500 million fund created by the bill to be made immediately to help farmers, especially to stabilize the price of wheat....The fire and police departments of Hackettstown, NJ, stop a riot between striking hosiery mill workers staging an automobile parade and strike-breakers.	Southern China, including Hong Kong, is suffering from a severe drought.	The World Congress of Librarians opens in Rome, Italy with a speech by Premier Benito Mussolini. Attendees will visit libraries, view exhibits of rare books, and some will meet with Pope Pius XI, who has worked extensively in libraries.	Jun. 15
J.G. Hardgrove, a Milwaukee attorney, determines that the Eighteenth Amendment prohibits U.S. companies from manufacturing and distributing liquor, but that States are not regulated and two Wisconsin congressmen draft legislation to permit the state to make and sell liquor to its citizens.			Detroit, MI, policemen are testing portable radios for dispatching officers that only weigh four pounds.	Hebrew University at Mt. Scopus, Palestine, opens the new Wolfsohn Library with a collection of 200,000 books.	Jun. 16
Assistant Secretary to the Treasury, Seymour Lowman, announces he plans to prohibit all Federal Customs agents patrolling the Canadian border from using so-called riot guns, or sawed-off shotguns, to stop suspects. The rule is a result of a series of shootings related to Prohibition enforcement.		The New York State Banker's Association begins its annual meeting at Toronto, Canada, where the main subject is the actions of the Federal Reserve Board to control stock market speculation....The directors of Chase and National Park Banks announce they will merge, creating a pool of $340 million in capital.	The northern part of New Zealand's South Island is shook by a one minute long earthquake that kills nine people and destroys much property....Japan's Komagatake volcano erupts in Hokkaido, spewing ash and lava that sets the nearby forest on fire and destroys villages.	Francis Boucher's painting *The Birth and Triumph of Venus*, newly acquired along with 65 other early prints by the Metropolitan Museum of Art in New York, goes on display.	Jun. 17

F	G	H	I	J
Includes campaigns, elections, federal-state relations, civil rights and liberties, crime, the judiciary, education, healthcare, poverty, urban affairs, and population.	Includes formation and debate of U.S. foreign and defense policies, veterans affairs, and defense spending. (Relations with specific foreign countries are usually found under the region concerned.)	Includes business, labor, agriculture, taxation, transportation, consumer affairs, monetary and fiscal policy, natural resources, pollution and industrial accidents.	Includes worldwide scientific, medical and technological developments, natural phenomena, U.S. weather and natural disasters.	Includes the arts, religion, scholarship, communications media, sports, entertainment, fashions, fads, and social life.

	World Affairs	Europe	Africa & The Middle East	The Americas	Asia & The Pacific
Jun. 18	America's new ambassador to Great Britain, Charles Dawes, gives a speech in Scotland to British and foreign diplomats calling for all countries to agree to the Kellogg antiwar treaty to promote world peace.	Polish Socialists demonstrate in Warsaw against the rise of Fascism and totalitarian regimes....France's Foreign Minister Aristide Briand complains to the League of Nations that Austria is secretly stockpiling ammunitions from World War I and is maintaining armed forces, a charge that is believed aimed at the Heimwehr, the nation's Fascist militia.		Mexico's President Emilio Portes Gil and two Catholic bishops resolve differences between the government and church by agreeing to a new interpretation of the anti-Catholic laws passed in 1926 and send the settlement to Pope Pius XI for approval.	American engineer Ernest P. Goodrich and architect Henry Murphy complete the initial planning phase for the rebuilding of Nanking into a modern capital for China. The plans call for construction of new roads, buildings, and a train station. Sun Fo, China's Minister of Railways, also announces plans for the completion of the Canton to Peking and the Lunghai rail lines.
Jun. 19	Members of the U.S. Congress approve a request to defer, for nine months, a $400 million payment that is owed by France for war surplus supplies.	Hungary's Lower House ratifies the Kellogg antiwar treaty....Italy's Ministry of the Interior rules that the nation's two official anthems, the *Royal March* and the Fascist hymn *Giovenezza*, may only be played in public on specific holidays.		Eleven Cubans, including a police informant, are missing after an alleged attempt to illegally transport them and a quantity of liquor to the United States. Only the captain and bloodstains remain onboard the *Del Rio* after the trip from Havana to Florida.	Troops of Emir Habibullah Kalakani, current leader of the rebellion, gain control of the town of Jadjalak and recapture Nagar....China announces that the agreement with Curtiss' Aviation Exploration Company to build a national airline will proceed as planned but the airways will now be regulated under the Ministry of Communications, instead of Railroads.
Jun. 20	Japan's acting Consul General presents a bronze miniature model of the newly rebuilt library at Tokyo Imperial University to John D. Rockefeller, Jr., who provided 4 million yen to restore the building after it was destroyed by 1923 earthquake and fire in 1923.		An Italian expedition led by Lidio Cipriani finds a rare rock painting in the region of Marandellas, Rhodesia (Zimbabwe) that depicts an image of a Bushman fighting Bantu tribesman superimposed over a drawing of a person in native Arab dress.	Brazil's Federal Minister of Railways grants permission to the Ford Industrial Company to build a radio station at Boa Vista in Para State.	
Jun. 21	The International Alliance of Women for Suffrage and Equal Citizenship end its conference in Berlin by resolving to fight against the use of poison gas during war time and to promote activities to bring about world peace.	Britain's Foreign Minister Arthur Henderson is given the nation's authority to prepare to re-establish diplomatic relations and to work out a trade agreement with the Soviet Union....Six hundred Bulgarians are arrested by Yugoslavian police in connection with plots to bomb the railroad near Vranja.		The Mexican Government and the Roman Catholic Church agree on new interpretations of church-related legislation to ease the tensions that resulted in three years of rebellion known as the Cristero war. A key part of the agreement is the right for bishops to maintain control over registration of priests.	China's President Chiang Kai-shek and leader of the rebellion, Marshal Feng Yu-hsiang, are negotiating a truce by means of telegrams.
Jun. 22	Prime Minister Ramsay MacDonald notes that Great Britain will accept the optional clause of statutes of the World Court, which states that the Court can hear all cases brought against the nation. This statement will be officially presented at the League of Nations Assembly in September, when Britain will join the 44 nations that have already adopted the optional clause.	A group of French war veterans, the National Confederation of Former Combatants announce they will march in protest of the government's ratification of the war debt accords, which they find insulting to their service for the country....Albania grants a monopoly on all oil sales to the Italian company Agip for a price of $300,000.		Officials at Costa Rica's Department of Vital Statistics announce that trafficking of narcotics such as opium and cocaine is increasing. They warn the Public Health Department that drug treatment programs are becoming necessary.	Chinese police raid a gambling resort in Shanghai and arrest 170 Chinese and 50 foreign nationals.
Jun. 23	German officials hope that the Allied war debt and reparations agreements and disarmament discussions indicate the troops of British and French soldiers will soon evacuate the Rhineland region they have occupied since the end of World War I.	The shooting of four Bulgarians by Yugoslavian border guards leads to requests by the Bulgarian government for inquiries by the League of Nations into border aggressions.		At a speech given to the National Women's Party in Washington, DC, Maximo Soto-Hall, editor of the Argentinean journal *La Prensa*, urges U.S. women to help fellow women in Central and South America to achieve constitutional and legal rights.	
Jun. 24	British Ambassador to Belgium, Hugh S. Gibson, and American Ambassador to Great Britain, General Charles Dawes, meet in London to discuss naval arms reductions.	Two boys and one girl commit suicide in Tagil, Soviet Union after the local newspaper accused them and their families of becoming too bourgeois to belong to the Communist Youth organization, which results in criticism of the paper's extreme position.		In response to the new agreement made between the Catholic Church and Mexico's government, religious rebels have ceased fighting in the Mexican states of Jalisco, Michoacan, and parts of Guanajuato.	

A	B	C	D	E
Includes developments that affect more than one world region, international organizations and important meetings of world leaders.	Includes all domestic and regional developments in Europe, including the Soviet Union.	Includes all domestic and regional developments in Africa and the Middle East.	Includes all domestic and regional developments in Latin America, the Caribbean, and Canada.	Includes all domestic and regional developments in Asian and Pacific nations (and colonies).

U.S. Politics & Social Issues	U.S. Foreign Policy & Affairs, Defense	U.S. Economy & Environment	Science, Technology & Nature	Culture, Leisure & Lifestyle	
U.S. Commissioner Walker rules that Prohibition enforcement agents cannot search a person without having a warrant allowing such a search....Federal agents indict 140 people accused of running a national operation to distribute fake liquor bottles and wood shavings for flavoring, and selling counterfeit internal revenue tax stamps....District Court Judge James Lenihan reminds residents of the Canal Zone at Panama that liquor possession is illegal after finding many workers violate the law.		In order to slow down the high rates of speculation in the stock market, two Senator prose an amendment to the tariff bill under consideration that would tax stock transfers if the purchase and sale transactions occur within a 60-day period.	Rising floodwaters on the Buller River threaten to sweep away the town of Murchison, New Zealand, which has already been devastated by the previous day's earthquake....New York City's Board of Alderman enact a rule that bans all nitro-cellulose x-ray film to prevent an accident similar to that of the Cleveland Clinic where over 100 people died in May from poisonous gas fumes when a film storage room caught fire.		Jun. 18
Members of the Senate spend their last day in session before a two month recess discussing whether Prohibition enforcement should be administered under the Internal Revenue Service or the Judicial, Treasury, or Labor Departments, and how to slow the rate of Prohibition-related killings by federal agents.	The U.S. State Department announces new national quotas for admission of immigrants to the country that will become effective on July 1. Decreasing amounts are given for Germany, Ireland, Sweden, and Norway, while a larger number of immigrants will be allowed to come from Great Britain.		Pilots at Mitchel Field, NY, begin testing airplanes submitted to the Daniel Guggenheim Fund's $150,000 contest to determine which has the best improvements in aerodynamic safety with the least impact on efficiency....Pilots unsuccessfully attempt cloud seeding over Hong Kong by dropping a chemical called deolin on clouds over the drought-stricken region.	All copies of the June issue of *Scribner's Magazine* are barred from newsstands in Boston, MA, because it contains the first installment of Ernest Hemingway's *A Farewell to Arms*, which the city's police chief has determined to be antiwar propaganda and salacious....The William Randolph Hearst and Metro-Goldwyn-Mayer motion picture companies form a merger.	Jun. 19
A U.S. Senate subcommittee meets to arrange to make the proposed tariff bill, now in discussion by the Senate Finance Committee, more favorable for farmers as they believe it currently gives unfair financial preferences to industries.	Assistant Secretary of War, F. Trubee Davis, signs $5 million in contracts for 162 new planes for the Army Air Corps....Secretary of State Henry Stimson begins an investigation into a shooting of a Federal customs patrol boat by a rum-runner vessel on the Detroit River.	Officials at J.P. Morgan & Company announce a plan for a $430 million merger of food products corporations including: Fleischmann Company, Royal Baking Powder Company, W.W. Gillette Company, Ltd., and Chase & Sanborn.	The American Brazilian Association honors Dr. Carols Chagas for his work identifying Chagas disease and for modernizing the public health and nursing systems in Brazil.		Jun. 20
	Chicago's Superior Court Judge Joseph Sabath re-examines the status of the state's first two couples granted probationary, trial divorces and grants one couple a final divorce while the other couple chooses to remarry.		Milton Humason and Francis Pease of Mount Wilson Observatory present evidence to the American Association for the Advancement of Science that three new stars are located approximately 50 million light years from Earth and two of them are moving at over 4,000 miles per second.	Yale University's freshmen, junior, and varsity crew teams beat Harvard University's teams in front of a crowd of 75,000....Attendees at the annual convention for Educational Film Exchanges discuss how to promote and sell talking motion pictures to non-English speaking countries.	Jun. 21
The National League of Women Voters releases statistics indicating that the number of women holding political office, from local to national posts, has risen each year since women were granted voting rights in 1920.	At Camp Dix, NJ, both reserve and regular officers are monitoring the daily progress of the war games simulation taking place throughout the mid-Atlantic region to train ground and aerial combat forces.	The War Department grants permission to fill a portion of Lake Ponchartrain at New Orleans to build a new air terminal for land and sea plane arrivals.	The Parsippany, NJ, workshop where Thomas Alva Edison invented the electric light bulb is presented to Henry Ford, who intends to move it to the Edison Institute in Dearborn, MI....Approximately 250,000 cubic yards of material fall into the Panama Canal during a landslide at the Gaillard Cut, although dredging operations permit ship transport to continue.		Jun. 22
The National Association for the Advancement of Colored People requests that President Herbert Hoover's Law Enforcement Commission seek to establish stricter laws and better enforcement against lynching, mob violence, segregation, and peonage.		President Herbert Hoover begins reviewing possible candidates for the position of Chief of the Army Corps of Engineers to oversee the construction of the Mississippi River flood control projects that were initiated after the devastating Mississippi Valley Floods of 1927.	Spanish pilot Ramon Franco and three crewmen attempting to fly around the world are reported missing during the journey between Portugal and the Azores.		Jun. 23
Jersey City (NJ) Mayor Frank Hague is arrested on contempt of court charges for the New Jersey State Legislature related to an investigation into $400,000 that he allegedly spent while in office.		U.S. wool producers present arguments to the Senate Finance Committee that the tariff on imported wool should be higher than it is currently stated on the tariff bill as approved by the House of Representatives in order to protect domestic suppliers.	Seven members of a research party led by Captain Harold White for the Chicago's Field Museum of Natural History arrive in Nairobi, Kenya Colony, British East Africa, after passing through Abyssinia collecting information on weather, giraffes, locusts, and cultural practices.	Columbia University's eight-man crew team wins the Poughkeepsie Regatta varsity race with a crowd of 125,000 watching....U.S. Secretary of War James Good and Secretary of the Navy Charles Adams agree to enter into talks to restore the annual Army-Navy Football game that has not been played recently because the Naval Academy restricts its players to three years, while the Army's West Point campus refused to do the same.	Jun. 24

F	G	H	I	J
Includes campaigns, elections, federal-state relations, civil rights and liberties, crime, the judiciary, education, healthcare, poverty, urban affairs, and population.	Includes formation and debate of U.S. foreign and defense policies, veterans affairs, and defense spending. (Relations with specific foreign countries are usually found under the region concerned.)	Includes business, labor, agriculture, taxation, transportation, consumer affairs, monetary and fiscal policy, natural resources, pollution and industrial accidents.	Includes worldwide scientific, medical and technological developments, natural phenomena, U.S. weather and natural disasters.	Includes the arts, religion, scholarship, communications media, sports, entertainment, fashions, fads, and social life.

	World Affairs	Europe	Africa & The Middle East	The Americas	Asia & The Pacific
Jun. 25		Senator Cesare Maria de Vecchi visits with Pope Pius XI during the first official visit from an Italian ambassador to the newly established state of Vatican City.	A Persian emissary announces he has brokered a settlement between Persia (Iran) and the Hedjaz peoples (Hejaz, Saudi Arabia), as represented by King Ibn Saud....The Egyptian government refuses to sell its cotton stock as promised, which causes prices to drop and the market to become more unstable.	A Mexican aviator drops a bomb on a suspected rebel group, but instead accidentally kills 15 Federal soldiers and wounds another 16 in the State of Jalisco.	
Jun. 26	Diplomats from Japan, France, Italy, Great Britain, and the United States meet in London to discuss plans for a formal naval arms reduction conference. In the planning process, they are discussing whether naval experts will meet to agree on a strength assessment method before civilian negotiators take over and also which type of vessels will be considered.	The Soviet Union, with the help of the Red Cross, has agreed to repatriate 900 people of Swedish birth who are now living near Odessa to Sweden's Scania region.		Mexico's government hands control over 11 Catholic churches, including the national shrine of Guadalupe, back to priests designated and properly registered by bishops.	China's President Chiang Kai-shek announces that rebel leader, Marshal Feng Yu-hsiang, will resign from his post and leave the country. The President appoints his Minister of the Interior, General Yen Hsi-shan, to take control over the Northwest Provinces in Feng's place....Japan's Privy Council approves the Kellogg antiwar treaty and submits it to the Emperor for ratification.
Jun. 27	Emperor Hirohito ratifies the Kellogg antiwar treaty, making Japan the 15th nation to sign the pact, which will now become effective in one month.	Austria's newspaper *Arbeiter Zeitung* reports that as early as recently as 1927, the Austrian government had plans to use the Heimwehr, the Fascist militia, to aid Italy in its fight against Yugoslavia over Tirana. The presence of militia groups in Austria causes concern for European diplomats seeking peace.		Mexico's Catholic community celebrates its first mass in three years after the Church leaders and the nation's President eliminate anti-Catholic interpretations of legislation passed in 1926.	China's recent rebel leader, Marshal Feng Yu-hsiang is named to a newly created position of Special Investigative Commissioner of Foreign Economic Affairs for the Nanking Nationalist government, which title he can assume one he turns over control of his troops and lands to General Yen Hsi-shan.
Jun. 28	At the London disarmament talks the United States requests that Great Britain dismantle its West Indian Naval Base as a gesture of good faith to promote peace with America....Germany's Reichstag approves a new rule requiring that domestic supplies comprise 40 percent of all wheat ground in the nation's mills, a move that will significantly impact trade with the United States, a major wheat exporter to Germany.			Canada's Minister of Trade and Commerce, James Malcolm, promises retaliatory action if the upcoming U.S. tariff bill significantly penalizes Canadian exports with the United States.	Japan's Nippon Yusen Kaisha steamship line notes it is planning two more ships to be built to the same specifications as the 584 foot long *Asama Maru*, which is expected to begin service between China and the United States starting in October.
Jun. 29		Members of Bulgaria's Parliament fight against a bill that would give amnesty to government officials in charge of the nation's pre-World War I regime and allow them to return to the country if they are serving exile or internment sentences of less than 12 years.		Nicaraguan rebel leader Augusto César Sandino is granted asylum in Merida, Mexico, but he gives a speech from the city of Vera Cruz in which he blames U.S military interference for political problems in Honduras, Salvador, and Guatemala.	China's Minister of Finance, T.V. Soong, denies rumors that the nation will seek loans from foreign countries to establish financial stability and instead insists that a planned Ventral Bank of China will soon be operational.
Jun. 30	Delegates from 46 nations meet in Geneva to revise the 1906 agreement on treatment of prisoners of war and address whether captured ambulance drivers should be considered prisoners or civilian medical personnel.	Franciscan monks restoring the Rock of Cashel at Tipperary, Ireland celebrate mass in the cathedral for the first time in 300 years.		Cuba begins to send would-be immigrants, primarily from eastern Europe, to detention camps outside Havana for failing to have proper authorization to live in the country.	
Jul. 1	A Sino-British naval agreement is signed at Nanking. Britain will help China to develop its navy and train its cadets.	King George returns to Buckingham Palace after seven months of severe illness. Thousands people welcome him home....British Premier MacDonald plans to create 20 more Labor peers to strengthen the government's position in the House of Lords....Charles Prestwich Scott resigns as the editor of the Manchester Guardian, Britain's leading liberal newspaper, after holding the position for 57 years.			Japanese Prime Minister Tanaka tenders the resignation of his Cabinet to Emperor Hirohito.

A	B	C	D	E
Includes developments that affect more than one world region, international organizations and important meetings of world leaders.	Includes all domestic and regional developments in Europe, including the Soviet Union.	Includes all domestic and regional developments in Africa and the Middle East.	Includes all domestic and regional developments in Latin America, the Caribbean, and Canada.	Includes all domestic and regional developments in Asian and Pacific nations (and colonies).

U.S. Politics & Social Issues	U.S. Foreign Policy & Affairs, Defense	U.S. Economy & Environment	Science, Technology & Nature	Culture, Leisure & Lifestyle	
Harry P. Fletcher, U.S. Ambassador to Italy, resigns his post to be effective in October.	A newly designed Army observation plane, to be built by the Fokker Aircraft Corporation in West Virginia, will look essentially like flying wings....Immigration and border patrol officials announce the arrest of Detroit, MI resident Russell Scott, who is accused of helping to smuggle almost 1,000 illegal immigrants into the United States in a two-year period.	President Herbert Hoover signs the Colorado River compact that has now been ratified by six of the seven states, which makes the Boulder Dam agreement effective, which outlays $165 million to create the dam on the Colorado River near Las Vegas, NV.	Reporters flying in a plane over New Jersey states speak by radio telephone with colleagues at their offices in London, during the first trans-Atlantic airplane-to-ground telephone conversation.	Princeton University's golf team beats Yale in play-offs to win the intercollegiate title for the third year in a row.	Jun. 25
		William N. Jardine, former Secretary of Agriculture, testifies to the Senate Finance Committee that the proposed sugar tariff of $3 per 100 pounds for most countries, would help protect sugar beet farmers in the United States.		The U.S. Ambassador to Great Britain, Charles Dawes, refuses to wear the traditional silk knee breeches to the royal court at Buckingham Palace in England, defying a tradition held by recent diplomats to the country and instead wore evening clothes.	Jun. 26
U.S. Senator Arthur R. Gould, Jr., of Maine admits to making wine from grape juice and elderberry plants and that his disapproves of Prohibition even though Maine has outlawed alcohol in some form for 75 years.		President Herbert Hoover asks Alexander Legge, president of International Harvester Company to give up his business activities and serve on the newly created Farm Board.	A color television is demonstrated for the first time at Bell Laboratories in New York City. Images of the American flag, a watermelon, and geraniums are among the first images shown on the postage stamp sized screen....Captain Frank Hawks sets a new cross-country record by flying nonstop from New York City to Los Angeles in 19 hours, 10 minutes, and 28 seconds.	German boxer Max Scmeling defeats Basque heavyweight Paulino Uzcudun in a 15-round benefit fight at Yankee Stadium that raised $180,000 for the Milk Fund.	Jun. 27
Hubert Work, chairman of the Republican National Convention, denies he allowed the use of his name to be published in a fund-raising letter distributed by the *National Republic* magazine to generate money for an education program to defeat Communism and radical activities in America.		All 18,000 building trade employees in Pittsburgh, PA, are granted a five day work week and the City Wage Board of Cincinnati considers granting the same benefit to its building tradesmen.	Major flooding in the Kauktam and Arakan regions of India destroys entire villages, leaving over 10,000 people homeless....U.S. Secretary of the Navy Charles Adams releases a report from Commander Richard Byrd detailing mountain ranges and other geographical features newly discovered in Antarctica.		Jun. 28
Assistant Attorney General Mabel Walker Willebrandt, known for aggressive prosecution of Prohibition laws, resigns from her post amid speculation she was asked to leave by the White House.		R.H. Macy & Company announces it has bought the Newark firm of L. Bamberger & Company, making it the largest department store in the United States with total sales of $125 million per year....One hundred and fifty businessmen sail from New York to Amsterdam to attend the International Chamber of Commerce's fifth annual congress.	Spanish pilot Ramon Franco and three crewmen are rescued by the British Navy after surviving for seven days floating in their seaplane after it crash-landed in the Atlantic Ocean 100 miles from the Azores.	Minor C. Keith, founder of the United Fruit Company, wills his extensive collection of Aztec gold jewelry and figures to the American Museum of Natural History.	Jun. 29
Philadelphia police raid the home of Chinese immigrants and confiscate $10,000 worth of opium.	Kenneth McKellar, a U.S. Senator examining the role of Republican patronage, declares that, in order to improve efficiency and enforcement, all Federal functions pertaining to customs, judicial actions, Prohibition, and immigration along the Mexico–U.S. border should be under control of one person who reports to the president.		The German Institute for Physics awards the Max Planck Medal to Albert Einstein for contributions to the field.	Bobby Jones wins the U.S. Open Golf Championship with 141 strokes at the Winged Foot Club in Mamaroneck, NY.	Jun. 30
The U.S. Immigration law of 1924 goes into effect.	Secretary of State Stimson suggests that any naval armament limitation arrangement between the United States and Great Britain should maintain the parity in naval strength between the two governments.	As call money on the Stock Exchange rises to 15 percent, several stock prices fall provoking considerable losses....Republican leaders in the Senate reassure President Hoover that the heavy duties of the Tariff Bill approved by the House will be drastically reduced.		American cartoonist Elzie Segar creates the character Popeye.... Aviator Wilmer Stultz dies when his plane clashes on the outskirts of Mineola.	Jul. 1

F	G	H	I	J
Includes campaigns, elections, federal-state relations, civil rights and liberties, crime, the judiciary, education, healthcare, poverty, urban affairs, and population.	Includes formation and debate of U.S. foreign and defense policies, veterans affairs, and defense spending. (Relations with specific foreign countries are usually found under the region concerned.)	Includes business, labor, agriculture, taxation, transportation, consumer affairs, monetary and fiscal policy, natural resources, pollution and industrial accidents.	Includes worldwide scientific, medical and technological developments, natural phenomena, U.S. weather and natural disasters.	Includes the arts, religion, scholarship, communications media, sports, entertainment, fashions, fads, and social life.

	World Affairs	Europe	Africa & The Middle East	The Americas	Asia & The Pacific
Jul. 2		The new British Parliament opens its session with the reading of the King's Speech....Vasil Radoslavoff, Bulgarian Prime Minister during the First World War, hopes to be able to re-enter his country soon as the National Parliament has approved an amnesty.	From his exile in Egypt, former King Amanullah of Afghanistan states that he hopes to return to his native country as a simple farmer within a year.	The Peruvian Congress ratifies the Tacna–Arica settlement with Chile which settles 45 years of controversy....Bolivia and Paraguay accept the arbitration of a neutral committee for their dispute in the Chaco region.	Yuko Hamaguchi is appointed Japanese prime minister after Baron Tanaka's resignation.
Jul. 3		British Premier MacDonald is criticized within his own party by the extreme Left which does not consider his government radical enough.		The leader of the religious rebels, Aristeo Pedroza, is killed with 23 other people at Guadalajara.	A volcanic outburst takes place on Ambrym Island in the New Herbrides archipelago.
Jul. 4	Pope Pius plans his first exit from the Vatican for July 25th.	A group of leading American Communists is detained in Moscow due to orders from the Communist International....British Premier MacDonald confirms that he aims for naval parity with U.S. to be maintained....The Cabinet of Portuguese Premier Vincente de Freitas submits its resignation to President Carmona.			
Jul. 5		Sir Austen Chamberlain, former British Foreign Secretary, demands that the Labor government resume diplomatic relations with the Soviet Union only after precise guarantees against Third International Propaganda....The new Spanish Constitution is presented to the Parliament. It makes suffrage universal and keeps Catholicism as state religion....A violent storm breaks out in central Europe causing the death of 38 people.	King Fuad of Egypt is received by the League of Nations Secretariat without the formalities expected for a monarch's visit.	At the convention of the Anti-Reelectionist Party, delegates vote a resolution to organize the national exploitation of oil and electrical reserves, preventing them to fall into the hands of foreign engineers.	
Jul. 6		In spite of the approval of the majority of the Deputies, French Premier Poincaré refuses to have the ratification of the French debt settlements....Portuguese President Carmona requests General Ivens Ferraz to form a new government.	Sir John Chancellor, High Commissioner for Palestine, states that the increasing tourist traffic in the Holy Land is helping Palestine to meet its unfavorable trade balance.	Tolls collected at the Panama Canal for the current fiscal year are the highest on record....A survey of Mexico's economic and financial situation reveals that the country has made considerable progresses toward stability.	Heavy rains in the central and lower Yangtse Valley end months of drought in China. Yet, the failure of crops continue to provoke serious food shortages.
Jul. 7		A Thanksgiving service takes place in Westminster Abbey for the recovery of King George V.		A huge demonstration is held in Santiago, Chile, in support of the Tacna–Arica settlement with Peru.	Colonel Dwight Filley Davis is inaugurated ninth American Governor General of the Philippine Islands in Manila.
Jul. 8	The fifth biennial congress of the International Chamber of Commerce opens in Amsterdam, Holland. Delegates are angry at the American upward revision of duties.	Industrial leaders of the Rhineland region attack the Young Plan for war reparations. They consider the plan to be completely beyond the economic and financial capacity of Germany....Diplomatic relations between Italy and the Holy See are fully established with the visit of the first Papal Nuncio, Borgongini Duca, to King Victor Emmanuel at the Quirinal Palace....A plot to overthrow the government of Premier Julius Maniu is discovered in Bulgaria.	South Africa plans the development of a diplomatic service. A Minister Plenipotentiary is sent to London and similar appointments are to be made to the United States, France, Germany, and Holland.		The Chinese Nationalist Government continues its campaign to suppress the publication of American newspapers and the sending of unfavorable reports. Chinese Foreign Minister C. T. Wang demands the deportation of *New York Times* correspondent Hallett Abend.
Jul. 9	Thirty-Eight nations, including Britain, France, Belgium, Italy, and all Latin American countries protest against the high rates in the new U.S. Tariff Bill.	The House of Commons rejects the Tory's attack against the decision of the new Labor government to abolish safeguarding duties....British submarine *H-47* sinks in the Irish Sea after a collision with a companion submarine, the *L-12*.		Mexican rebels fail to seize the village of Pihuamo in the State of Michoacan. Four insurgents are captured and executed....Mexican President Portes Gill calls for a special session of congress to debate the special labor code.	The new Japanese government states in its program that it will favor arms reduction.

A	B	C	D	E
Includes developments that affect more than one world region, international organizations and important meetings of world leaders.	*Includes all domestic and regional developments in Europe, including the Soviet Union.*	*Includes all domestic and regional developments in Africa and the Middle East.*	*Includes all domestic and regional developments in Latin America, the Caribbean, and Canada.*	*Includes all domestic and regional developments in Asian and Pacific nations (and colonies).*

U.S. Politics & Social Issues	U.S. Foreign Policy & Affairs, Defense	U.S. Economy & Environment	Science, Technology & Nature	Culture, Leisure & Lifestyle	
President Hoover intends to organize a national conference on the health of children at the White House for the following year.		Leading industrialist Alexander Legge accepts the presidency of the Farm Board offered by President Hoover....In spite of the 15 percent call money, stocks make one of the largest advance of the year.		The phone number of the White House changes for the first time since 1900.	Jul. 2
Special Extradition Commissioner Francis A. O' Neill dismisses the Mexican government's application for the extradition of Salvador Ateca, a rebel agent, on charges of theft and embezzlement.		Chairman Smoot expresses doubts as to whether the Senate Finance Committee will be able to complete examining the Hawley-Smoot bill before the Senate returns to work in August....As call money drops to six percent, the prices of shares soar.	Dunlop Latex Development Laboratories create foam rubber.... A fire breaks out in Mill Valley, CA, destroying 100 homes.	The Hungarian government informs American film companies that they should either subsidize the developing motion picture industry of Hungary or stop operating in that country.	Jul. 3
New York Governor Franklin Delano Roosevelt denounces the ever-growing aggregations of capital and the partnership of government and business. Roosevelt is acclaimed by Democratic militants as the next president....President Hoover intends to reorganize and coordinate executive bureaus to improve efficiency in government.		American stocks reach record levels in London....The examination of the Tariff Bill in the Senate Finance Committee proceeds slowly because of the wide discontent caused throughout the country by the heavy duties imposed.			Jul. 4
Four Prohibitionist raiders are charged with murder in Oklahoma City for the killing of a farmer and his brother-in-law....One man dies and hundreds are injured when the Public Service Company of New Orleans tries to resume street car service and break off the strike.	The U.S. government announces that it will not interfere with the alleged detainment of several American Communist leader in Moscow unless it receives a direct appeal from them. Soviet authorities deny that none of the leaders is being detained.	President Hoover calls the six member of the Farm Board that he has already appointed for a first meeting on July 15th.		Cleveland Pilots Byron K. Newcomb and Roy L. Mitchell establish a new world record for a refueling duration flight....London detectives raid the Warren Galleries in London and seize the works of writer D.H. Lawrence on exhibition....U.S. champion Helen Wills wins Wimbledon for the third successive time.	Jul. 5
The Democratic National Committee attacks President Hoover as an autocrat....The chairman of the Republican National Committee, Hubert Work, argues that the party should firmly support President Hoover's stance in favor of Prohibition.		Henry Ford declares he is in favor of a big power trust, a nation-wide monopoly that will make electricity as "common as air."			Jul. 6
		The Democratic minority plans strong opposition to the Tariff Bill approved by the House when it comes to the Senate....The State of New York maintains the first place in income and miscellaneous taxes collected in the fiscal year 1929.	Two French amateur climbers freeze to death while attempting to reach the summit of Mont Blanc.	John D. Rockefeller celebrates his 90th birthday.	Jul. 7
President Hoover confers with New York Republican Party leaders and expresses his hopes that the party will be able to win the next gubernatorial election.		President Hoover selects William F Schilling as a member of the new Farm Board to represent the dairy cooperative interests.	A sharp earthquake causes $100,000 property damage in the Los Angeles area of East Whitmiles.		Jul. 8
Republican Senator Borah says he is against the flexible provisions of the new Tariff bill as they give the President too wide an authority to raise and lower tariff rates.			The Dornier Company exhibits its newest airplane at its Swiss plant. The plane impresses visitors for its overwhelming size.	American banks begin to distribute new size currency....President Hoover says he is indifferent to sound films and prefers newsreels and detective films.	Jul. 9

F	G	H	I	J
Includes campaigns, elections, federal-state relations, civil rights and liberties, crime, the judiciary, education, healthcare, poverty, urban affairs, and population.	Includes formation and debate of U.S. foreign and defense policies, veterans affairs, and defense spending. (Relations with specific foreign countries are usually found under the region concerned.)	Includes business, labor, agriculture, taxation, transportation, consumer affairs, monetary and fiscal policy, natural resources, pollution and industrial accidents.	Includes worldwide scientific, medical and technological developments, natural phenomena, U.S. weather and natural disasters.	Includes the arts, religion, scholarship, communications media, sports, entertainment, fashions, fads, and social life.

	World Affairs	Europe	Africa & The Middle East	The Americas	Asia & The Pacific
Jul. 10		Premier Poincaré is defeated when the Foreign Affairs Commission of the French Parliament votes in favor of ratifying the debt accord with the United States and Great Britain with reservation that France should never pay more in debt settlement than the amount it receives from Germany. Premier Poincaré was in favor of unqualified acceptance and if the Parliament maintains the reservation he announces that he will resign.		Former Mexican Foreign Minister Candido Aguilar makes an appeal for international peace and for the cessation of further bloodshed in the country. He maintains that more than one million Mexicans have died since the 1910 revolution against the dictatorship of Porfirio Diaz.	Ying Kao, Chinese Vice Consul at San Francisco, is suspended from his role as his wife is implicated in a case of opium smuggling.
Jul. 11	The delegates at the fifth congress of the International Chamber of Commerce admit China to full membership. This is an important step in the development of closer financial and economic relations between China and the rest of the world.	French President Doumergue considers signing the debt agreement with Great Britain and the United States before Parliament approves it. In this way the agreement would be ratified without attaching any conditions….Home Secretary J.C. Clynes announces that Soviet exile Leon Trotsky will not be admitted to Britain.	A confederation of tribes rebels against the government of King Ibn Saud in Arabia. Violent battles between the tribesmen and the King's troops break out.		Chinese officials dismiss the Russian general manager of the Chinese Eastern Railway together will all Russian heads of departments. Owned by the Russians, the Railway operates in Manchuria.
Jul. 12	Circles of the League of Nations discuss the possibility of creating a custom union throughout Europe.	Italy awards gold medals to the American fliers who have made the transatlantic journey on the Pathfinder….The Tories back Labor proposal to spend about $5 million a year to aid the development of colonies.		Canadian Minister to Washington Vincent Massey protest to the U.S. State Department against the planned tariffs for shingles, lumber and feeder cattle.	Soviet troops advance to the border between Eastern Siberia and Manchuria after Chinese officials have replaced Russian managers of the Chinese Eastern Railway with their own officials.
Jul. 13		The doctors of the British court decide to operate King George to clear the abscess in his right chest….Belgium and Germany reach an agreement for the reimbursement of Belgium for German marks left in the country in exchange for Belgian francs confiscated during the First World War.	Almost 400 die in Persia due to heavy floods at Tabriz, near Teheran.	The Communist Party and the Anarchist Labor Federation work together to organize a general strike in Argentina in sympathy with the striking Rosario port workers….The Mexican Presidential campaign starts without causing any trouble.	The Soviet Union sends an ultimatum to China over the Chinese Eastern Railway dispute. If the Chinese do not accept to negotiate, Russia threatens to use "other means" to solve the situation.
Jul. 14	The French and British governments cannot agree on where to hold the international conference on War Reparations.	Demonstrations in the Soviet Union demand drastic action against the Chinese seizure of the Chinese Eastern Railway….Germany, Italy, Poland, Czechoslovakia, Yugoslavia, Rumania, Greece, Belgium and Austria express their approval of French Foreign Minister Aristide Briand's proposal for an economic United States of Europe.		The Argentine truck drivers' union votes a twenty-four-hour strike in solidarity with the port workers at Rosario.	Japanese Minister to China Kenkichi Yoshizawa praises the Chinese government in the Shantung Province from where Japanese forces withdrew the previous month.
Jul. 15		King George is successfully operated on his chest….More popular demonstrations are held in Moscow against the seizure of the Chinese Eastern Railway by Chinese officials….The British government works to resume diplomatic relations with the Soviets. Russia is asked to give guarantees against Third International propaganda in Britain.			At a hearing of the senate Finance Committee, Manuel Roxas, Speaker of the Philippines House of Representatives, demands that Congress fix a definite date for granting independence to the Philippines. He also opposes higher duties on Philippines products…. Chinese authorities ignores the ultimatum issued by the Soviets over the Chinese Eastern Railway dispute.
Jul. 16		French Premier Poincaré scores an important victory when the Chamber of Deputies rejects a motion to adjourn the ratification of the war reparations plan with a large majority. Those in favor of including reservations in the plan withdraw their motions, another success for the prime minister.		The Chilean transport *Abtao* sinks off the coast near Topocalma due to a violent storm. 48 people are missing, only two are found alive.	The Chinese Nationalist Government at Nanking replies to the Russian ultimatum over the Chinese Eastern Railway by asking the release of all Chinese prisoners in Russia and that the Soviet government protects Chinese citizens in Russia from aggression. Both Russian and Manchurian troops mobilize in the region.

A	B	C	D	E
Includes developments that affect more than one world region, international organizations and important meetings of world leaders.	Includes all domestic and regional developments in Europe, including the Soviet Union.	Includes all domestic and regional developments in Africa and the Middle East.	Includes all domestic and regional developments in Latin America, the Caribbean, and Canada.	Includes all domestic and regional developments in Asian and Pacific nations (and colonies).

U.S. Politics & Social Issues	U.S. Foreign Policy & Affairs, Defense	U.S. Economy & Environment	Science, Technology & Nature	Culture, Leisure & Lifestyle	
		The chairman of the Senate Finance Committee Smoot dismisses the international protests against the new tariff bill as "complaints of interested parties."	The transatlantic plane Pathfinder lands in Rome completing its adventurous voyage from the United States.		Jul. 10
The Bishop of Washington announces the building of a new cathedral which will cost $3 million....Psychiatrist and health experts at the convention of the American Medical Association in Portland recommend a thorough mental hygiene program for the nation.	American Ambassador in London Dawes meets British Premier MacDonald to resume talks on armaments reduction.	President Hoover confers with Republican Senate leaders on the Tariff Bill.		Edith Quier wins the golf Griswold Trophy in Eastern Point, Connecticut, thus preventing Dorothy Campbell Hurd to win it for the third successive time.	Jul. 11
Philip and Hudson Clarke, New York bankers, are arrested for the failure of their bank.		President Hoover appoints the eighth member of the Farm Board, Charles S. Wilson, and confers with the Board's chairman, Alexander Legge....The Governor of Minnesota Theodore Christianson warns Hoover that the new Tariff Bill may alienate farmers from the Republican Party....The Stock Exchange makes its widest advance since early spring.	Tests are made aboard the ship Berengaria to telephone from the ship to the shore.	Loren Mendell and Roland Reinhart set a new record in endurance flight, remaining in the air for 246 hours.	Jul. 12
Republican Speaker of the New York Assembly, Joseph A. McGinnes assures Governor Roosevelt that the Legislature would support his plans for the developments of new hospitals.	President Hoover and Secretary of the Navy Adams promote Smedley D. Butler, a veteran of fifteen campaigns and the youngest officer of the Marine Corps, to the rank of Major General.	The American Federation of Labor launches a nationwide campaign to establish the right of labor unions to carry out legitimate union activities in the south without having to fear retaliation.		Film star Adolphe Menjou signs a contract with the American Sound Recording Company for a new series of feature films in which he will star.	Jul. 13
A citizens' committee of 682 political and business personalities is formed to ask New York Mayor James J. Walker to run again for mayor at the next election....The Board of Temperance, Prohibition and Public Morals of the Methodist Episcopal Church denies having taken part in political campaigns as charged by Massachusetts Representative Tinkham.		The United Textile Workers of America launches a plan to organize 100 of the biggest textile mills in the South....Press clippings indicate a strong opposition in Western States to the higher tariffs passed by the House of Representatives.		French transatlantic flier Captain Dieudonné Coste is forced to interrupt his flight to New York as he has encountered a steady west wind which has caused him to use more fuel than expected....On his transatlantic flight to New York the Polish plane Marshal Pilsudski crashes in the Azores.	Jul. 14
The American Civil Liberties Union and the International Labor Defence make public their plans for defending the fifteen leaders of the Gastonia textile strike who will go on trial for the murder of O. F. Aderholt, Chief of Police of Gastonia.	President Hoovder reviews in Baltimore the Veterans of the Rainbow Division who fought in the Champagne trenches.	The Farm Board, established to help the agricultural sector, holds its first meeting....Rail stocks make impressive gains on the market. All other stock prices suffer from the 12 percent rate for call money.	The new Dornier airplane has its first trial flight over Lake Constance.	Famous playwright and poet Hugo Von Hofmannsthal dies....John Van Ryn, Wilmer Allison, William Tilden and Francis T. Hunter are selected as the U.S. Davis Cup team, which will face Germany.	Jul. 15
George W. Wickersham, chairman of the National Commission on Law Observance and Enforcement, a commission for the study of crime and law enforcement, asks the Conference of Governors in session at Groton that federal and state governments should cooperate for the enforcement of Prohibition laws.	American ambassador to Britain Dawes makes a plea for friendship between Britain and the United States at the meeting of the Travel Association of Great Britain and Ireland.	Alexander Legge, president of the Farm Board, announces that the first policy the new board will implement will be the establishment of cooperatives to bring producer and consumer into a more direct contact.		Colonel Charles Lindbergh reacts angrily when he discovers that a sound-camera man has recorded a private conversation using a concealed microphone.	Jul. 16

F	G	H	I	J
Includes campaigns, elections, federal-state relations, civil rights and liberties, crime, the judiciary, education, healthcare, poverty, urban affairs, and population.	Includes formation and debate of U.S. foreign and defense policies, veterans affairs, and defense spending. (Relations with specific foreign countries are usually found under the region concerned.)	Includes business, labor, agriculture, taxation, transportation, consumer affairs, monetary and fiscal policy, natural resources, pollution and industrial accidents.	Includes worldwide scientific, medical and technological developments, natural phenomena, U.S. weather and natural disasters.	Includes the arts, religion, scholarship, communications media, sports, entertainment, fashions, fads, and social life.

	World Affairs	Europe	Africa & The Middle East	The Americas	Asia & The Pacific
Jul. 17		The Liberal Party supports the plan of the Labor government to spend $5 million a year for the development of British colonies.Anton Pavelich, leader of the Croatian Federalist Party, and Gustav Perec are sentenced to death in Belgrade by a special tribunal for the protection of the state.	The British Labor government denies he is planning to place the control of the Suez Canal under the League of Nations.		The Soviet Union breaks diplomatic relations with China over the Chinese Eastern Railway controversy. Chinese and Russian troops clash along the Manchurian border.
Jul. 18	The League of Nations considers whether to intervene officially in the dispute between the Soviet Union and China over the Chinese Eastern Railway. None of its members however takes the step of calling the dispute officially to the attention of the Secretariat.	An unemployed blacksmith's assistant called Anton Leitner is arrested when he levels a loaded pistol at a policeman in Ballhausplatz, Vienna, as the Austrian Chancellor is leaving the square to attend Parliament. This incident gives rise to speculation about a plot to kill the Chancellor.			Russia and China mass troops along the Siberian-Manchurian border. Civilians flee from the danger zone fearing imminent war. Japanese officials offer themselves as mediators.
Jul. 19	Britain agrees with France that the international Conference on War Reparations should take place on neutral ground and suggests Holland.	Egyptian Prince Ibrahim is saved with 33 guests when his yacht sinks off the coast of Norway, near Trondhjem....Soviet Commissar of Railroads Jan Rudzutak confirms Russia's adherence to the Kellogg Pact. He also stresses that, unless attacked, Russia will not invade China.		The strikes of port workers in the Argentine town of Rosario continues. Unions renew talks of a national general strike in support of the Rosario workers.	Soviet and Chinese troops continue to mobilize and to clash along the Siberian-Manchurian border. The Chinese government still offer no reply to Russia's severance of diplomatic relations.
Jul. 20		The French Chamber of Deputies ratifies the war debt agreement with Britain and the United States without reservations. This is a clear victor for the French Premier Poincaré.		Six American border patrolmen are ambushed by a large force of Mexican rum-runners on the Rio Grande....The Argentine Federal Government sends more soldiers to reinforce the troops already mobilized in Rosario to control the strikers.	The Soviet and Chinese governments strongly emphasize their allegiance to the antiwar Kellogg Pact. Yet, in spite of this, minor clashes between troops continue along the Manchurian border.
Jul. 21		German Chancellor Hermann Mueller is operated on for an ulcerated gall bladder. His conditions are critical....Although France has ratified the war debts agreement with the United States and Great Britain without reservations, many politicians and journalists think that war debt payments owed to the United States should be covered by German reparations payments to France.			Military maneuvers continue along the Manchurian border. The Chinese government says it will have to protect itself from Russian propaganda and military attacks.
Jul. 22		Earthquakes and floods strike the region of Northern Anatolia, causing the death of 1,000 persons. Ten thousand are homeless....Central European countries are gripped by an anomalous heat wave.	Uganda Sanitary Inspector Kendall is attacked by members of the Amalekites religious sect who object to inoculation against disease.		Chinese and Russian officials reply to the appeal of U.S. Secretary of State Stimson, assuring that they will not breach the Kellogg multilateral antiwar treaty. Soviet troops patrolling the Amur River seize the Chinese river steamer Ilan.
Jul. 23		The Finance and Foreign Affairs Commissions of the French Senate ratify the debt settlements with the United States and Great Britain.... Iceland is struck by a violent earthquake.		Chilean Parliament ratifies the Kellogg Antiwar Pact.	

A	B	C	D	E
Includes developments that affect more than one world region, international organizations and important meetings of world leaders.	Includes all domestic and regional developments in Europe, including the Soviet Union.	Includes all domestic and regional developments in Africa and the Middle East.	Includes all domestic and regional developments in Latin America, the Caribbean, and Canada.	Includes all domestic and regional developments in Asian and Pacific nations (and colonies).

U.S. Politics & Social Issues	U.S. Foreign Policy & Affairs, Defense	U.S. Economy & Environment	Science, Technology & Nature	Culture, Leisure & Lifestyle	
The appeal of George W. Wickersham, chairman of the National Commission on Law Observance and Enforcement, for cooperation between state and federal governments for the enforcement of Prohibition laws stirs a sharp conflicts between Wet and Dry executives in the Governors' assembly in session at Groton.		Fourteen Florida banks close down in a single day. The invasion of the Mediterranean fruit fly has made it impossible for many citrus growers to meet their obligations with banks.		Babe Ruth collapses during the Yanks–Detroit match due to a painful knee injury.	Jul. 17
New York Mayor James J. Walker announces that he will run again for mayor at the next election....The Governors' Conference shelves the proposal of George W. Wickersham, chairman of a commission for the study of crime and law enforcement, for cooperation between state and federal governments for the enforcement of Prohibition laws. The conference adopts a compromise expressing its support for President Hoover's policy.	American foreign officials declare they were surprised by Russian ultimatum against China and by the Russia's severance of diplomatic relations with China.	The shares of the First National Bank of New York soar more than $500 per share.	A train derails off a bridge in Colorado on the Chicago, Rock Island & Pacific Railroad causing the deaths of at least nine passengers. The bridge had been weakened by heavy floods.	Tommy Loughran retains his title of light-heavyweight champion against James J. Braddock in a 15-round match at the Yankee Stadium.	Jul. 18
Dry leaders in congress look with suspicion at the letter sent by George W. Wickersham, chairman of the National Commission on Law Observance and Enforcement, to the Governors' Conference on the enforcement of Prohibition. According to dry leaders, the letter reveals Wickersham's intentions to modify Prohibition laws.	Secretary of State Stimson reminds both China and Russia that, as signatories of the Kellogg Pact, they are bound to resolve their dispute over the Chinese Eastern Railway by other means than war....President Hoover raises the embargo against the shipment of arms to Mexico.			The American Davis Cup Team beats the German team in the two opening single in Berlin.	Jul. 19
Actors Equity Association files a test case in superior court to rule if members of the organization may close movie contracts without the approval of the association.... Loan clerk Lawrence Sorenson is arrested for the theft of $173,000 in negotiable securities from the Equitable Trust Company....New York Republican leaders consider Supreme Court Justice Harry E. Lewis as a candidate for mayor.		Opposition mounts to the introduction of a sliding scale of duties on sugar into the new tariff bill.	The first mountain-climbing locomotive, "Old Peppersass," derails and blows up during a ceremony for its presentation to the state of New Hampshire. Many state governors are present at the ceremony and their lives are put at risk, but none are injured.	President Hoover states that the label of "Hoover's Apricots" on apricots sold in New York City is illegal, as the president is not the sole owner of the ranch where they are grown.	Jul. 20
Fiorello LaGuardia confirms that he will run as a candidate in the primary election for the New York Mayor regardless of the results of the Republican convention....The Department of Commerce announces that birth rate decreased while death rate increased during 1928.				The U.S. Davis Cup team beats Germany 5–0 in Berlin.	Jul. 21
1,300 prisoners riot at Clinton Prison at Dannemora, New York, in an unsuccessful effort to escape. Three are killed and twenty hurt.	The New York Stock Exchange suffers a sharp decline.	The Senate Finance Committee begins examination of the new Tariff Bill approved by the House and whose higher tariffs have caused wide discontent throughout the nation and the world.	The showing of the first American talking films in Berlin is put off due to the legal battle between the Western Electric Company and the German Klangfilm Company regarding infringement on patent rights.	The merchant ship Bremen arrives at the Ambrose Channel Lightship from Cherbourg breaking all records for a transatlantic crossing by a merchant ship....The U.S. Davis Cup Committee announces that Francis T. Hunter will be replaced by George M. Lott in the American Davis Cup team that will play against France.	Jul. 22
A conservative group of teachers at Princeton Theological Seminary announces their intention to open a new seminary in contrast to the liberal climate of the institution....Supreme Court Justice Harry E. Lewis does not accept the offer of New York Republican leaders to run as a candidate for mayor.	Secretary of State Stimson is satisfied by the Russian and Chinese replies to his plea not to breach the antiwar Kellogg treaty....President Hoover declares he is in favor of limiting military expenditure.	The Standard Oil Company intends to take over the Pan-American Petroleum and Transport Company....Republican Senator Borah states that the proposed flexible provisions of the tariff bill are unconstitutional.		Jonce I. McGurk announces that he has bought for an American client Houdon's marble bust of George Washington....The autograph and typewritten manuscript of George Bernard Shaw's "You Never Can Tell" is auctioned at Sotheby's for $6,000....American playwright Eugene O'Neill marries actress Carlotta Monterey in Paris.	Jul. 23

F	G	H	I	J
Includes campaigns, elections, federal-state relations, civil rights and liberties, crime, the judiciary, education, healthcare, poverty, urban affairs, and population.	Includes formation and debate of U.S. foreign and defense policies, veterans affairs, and defense spending. (Relations with specific foreign countries are usually found under the region concerned.)	Includes business, labor, agriculture, taxation, transportation, consumer affairs, monetary and fiscal policy, natural resources, pollution and industrial accidents.	Includes worldwide scientific, medical and technological developments, natural phenomena, U.S. weather and natural disasters.	Includes the arts, religion, scholarship, communications media, sports, entertainment, fashions, fads, and social life.

	World Affairs	Europe	Africa & The Middle East	The Americas	Asia & The Pacific
Jul. 24	The Kellogg Pact outlawing offensive war is promulgated in Washington almost a year from its signing in Paris in August 1928. Representatives of 43 nations attend the ceremony....Britain suggests that the international conference on the Young Plan should take place at the Hague.	British Prime Minister Ramsay MacDonald announces in the House of Commons that Britain will suspend the expansion of its military fleet....The French Senate begins discussing the war debt settlements with the United States and Great Britain.	Baron Lloyd of Dolobran is dismissed from his post as British High Commissioner for Egypt. This is the first political crisis between the Labor government and officials appointed by the previous conservative government.		Russia and China begin diplomatic talks over the Chinese Eastern Railway dispute.
Jul. 25	British and American oil leaders meet in London to discuss an American proposal to increase the price of gasoline....The French government approves the British proposal that Holland should be the nation chosen for the international conference on war debt reparations.	The French government praises the British and American decisions to stop the enlargement of their naval fleets....President Hoover's move to stop the enlargement of U.S. fleet greatly helps British Premier MacDonald to silence criticism that he is conceding too much to the United States in talks to organize an international naval parley.	Professor Smeath Thomas of Cape Town University discloses the discovery of a 10,000 square-mile field of sodium nitrate in South Africa.		Chinese officials face a conundrum in the Chinese Eastern Railway dispute. If the Chinese government agrees to negotiate on Russian terms, it may lose domestic prestige. If it does not, it will have to face war against a much better equipped army.
Jul. 26	Two thousand teachers from 50 countries gather in Geneva for the Congress of the World Federation of Education Associations.	French Premier Raymond Poincaré offers his resignation to the President of the Republic due to health problems. His Cabinet, however, asks him to stay....Thirteen people are killed when an explosion occurs on board the British cruiser Devonshire.		Most of the buildings in the Ecuadorian town of Moyurgo are destroyed a violent earthquake which causes the death of sixty people....Foreign business leaders warns Mexican President Portes Gil that if his new labor code passes, it will make conditions for large investments in Mexico unstable....Argentine police arrest more than 100 strikers in the town of Rosario.	After the seizure of the Chinese Eastern Railway, China reassures foreign nations with interests in the country that these will be respected.
Jul. 27	A new code on prisoners of war and a convention on the treatment of sick and wounded in time of war is approved in Geneva....The Sixteenth Biennial Zionist Congress gathers in Zurich to discuss the final ratification of the pact with non-Zionist forces for the creation of a joint Jewish Agency for Palestine.	The Council of Monaco adopts a resolution asking Prince Louis to take into account the complaints on his policies or face a referendum for the creation of a republic allied to France....French Premier Poincaré confirms his resignation. President Doumergue asks Aristide Briand to form a new cabinet.		Provisional Mexican President Portes Gil says he is confident that the next presidential election will take place without disorders.	China announces that diplomatic negotiations with Russia for the seizure of the Chinese Eastern Railway will be held in Berlin.
Jul. 28	Chaim Weizmann, president of the World Zionist Organization, urges the formation of a Jewish Agency for Palestine consisting of Zionist and non-Zionist.	The French Premier Briand tries to form a new cabinet with the support of the Radical groups that had left the previous Poincaré's government.		The text of a complementary protocol to the general Tacna–Arica agreement between Chile and Peru is made public. It states that no part of the territory covered by the treaty can be ceded to a third power and that no international railway line can be constructed on the land.	
Jul. 29		The strike of 500,000 Lancashire cotton mill workers begins against the owners' proposal to cut weekly salaries by 12.5 percent....French Radicals refuse to enter Briand's cabinet. The Prime Minister retains most of the ministers of the Poincaré government. He keeps for himself the role of Foreign Minister....Professor Voitetch Tuka is tried for high treason by Czech authorities.			
Jul. 30	The Labor and Socialist International in Zurich adopts a resolution asking for an embargo of arms against China and Russia if the two countries come to war.	Yugoslavia officially refuses to ratify the Pirot conventions for the settlement of the border dispute with Bulgaria.			

A	B	C	D	E
Includes developments that affect more than one world region, international organizations and important meetings of world leaders.	Includes all domestic and regional developments in Europe, including the Soviet Union.	Includes all domestic and regional developments in Africa and the Middle East.	Includes all domestic and regional developments in Latin America, the Caribbean, and Canada.	Includes all domestic and regional developments in Asian and Pacific nations (and colonies).

U.S. Politics & Social Issues	U.S. Foreign Policy & Affairs, Defense	U.S. Economy & Environment	Science, Technology & Nature	Culture, Leisure & Lifestyle	
	President Hoover stops the building of three cruisers planned in the American naval program.	Three banks belonging to the Hobart Trust Company, whose president is former U.S. Senator Edward L. Edwards are closed down by the State Department of Banking and Insurance because their continued operation was considered unsafe.			Jul. 24
The Connecticut Supreme Court of Errors outlaws more than 1,500 legislative acts over the last 10 years because Governors failed to sign them within the constitutional period of three days from final adjournment of the Assembly....Eight motorists die in the Californian desert.	President Hoover selects Senator Walter E. Edge as Ambassador to France to replace the late Myron T. Herrick....Colonel Paul V. McNutt, national commander of the American Legion, protests the against President Hoover's decision to suspend the construction of fighting cruisers.	The Hobart Trust Company goes into receivership, an action which blocks the plan to free the deposits of the bank and its branches through their sale to a group of citizens who had guaranteed full payments to creditors.	A report issued by the Commerce Department shows that more than 6,000 planes will be licensed in the United States during 1929.	The speedboat Bogie breaks the 59-year-old record of Robert E. Lee for the New Orleans-St. Louis run.	Jul. 25
North Carolina Governor O. Max Gardner sends his confidential adviser Judge Nat Townsend to confer with the prosecution in the trials of the fifteen Gastonia textile strike leaders accused of murdering Police Chief O. F. Aderholt.	President Hoover responds to criticism against his decision to stop the construction of cruisers arguing that his move aims to build a climate of cooperation with Great Britain in view of a future naval parley.	The Farm Board created by President Hoover suggests creating a grain-marketing corporation to stabilize grain market and develop the agricultural sector....Harry W. Weinberger, the founder of the Hobart Trust Company, threatens to file a $5 million damage suit against New Jersey governor and officials for the closing down of his company.	Lufthansa takes possession of three huge airplanes constructed at the Rohrbach works in Berlin to start regular transatlantic freight and mail route from Germany to Brazil.	Twelve leading producing companies of sound pictures lower their rental prices for independent exhibitors....The French Davis Cup tennis team wins the first two matches against the United States.	Jul. 26
Connecticut Governor J. H. Trumbull calls a special session of the State's General Assembly on August 6th to re-enact the bills declared void by the Connecticut Supreme Court of Errors....New York Governor Franklin Delano Roosevelt requests Attorney General Hamilton Ward to state definitely if the Niagara-Hudson power merger violates any statute. The Attorney General had previously submitted a noncommittal report on the merger.	Secretary of State Stimson supports President Hoover's decision to stop building fighting cruisers, arguing that it is not an unpatriotic decision.	Farmer and cooperative groups representing 650,000 grain growers unanimously select a committee of sixteen to organize a grain marketing corporation as suggested by the Farm Board....Budget experts begin to draft the government's $4 million budget for the 1931 fiscal year.		Playwright Eugene O'Neill files answer to the $1 million plagiarism suit brought against him by Georges Lewys. According to Lewys, O'Neill's "Strange Interlude" largely borrows from her novel "The Temple of Pallas Athene." O'Neill denies having ever heard of the novel before the suit.	Jul. 27
The federal government plans the construction of a town along the Colorado River for the families of workers of the Boulder Dam. The houses will be leased only to those who commit not to breach Prohibition Laws....A riot breaks out at Auburn Prison and four prisoner manage to escape.	President Hoover is confident that diplomatic talks between the United States and Britain will result in the organization of a naval parley in London before the 1931 conference already scheduled under the Washington treaty of 1921.	The flood of the Missouri River threatens the town of Corning.... After the announcement of a plan to reorganize Samuel Insull's Middle West Utilities Company, the stocks of the company make sensational gains.		France retains the Davis Cup, defeating the United States three to two.	Jul. 28
President Hoover addresses the planning committee for the Child Welfare Conference declaring that the issues of child education and welfare reach "to the root of democracy itself."...Governor Roosevelt orders a sweeping investigation to determine the responsibilities for the Dannemora and the Auburn riots....Sixteen strikers ask that the Gastonia trial should take place in another county.	American and British diplomats continue talks for the organization of a naval parley.	The American Institute of Cooperatives convenes in Baton rouge to form a national farmers' cooperative organization, the National Chamber of Agricultural Cooperatives, with a membership of more than two million farmers.	New York is struck by an intense heat-wave which cause three deaths.	Charles A. Lindbergh discovers a lost Mayan city while flying over the Yucatan jungle.	Jul. 29
New York Republicans insist that Supreme Court Justice Lewis should be the candidate for Mayor....New York Governor Franklin Roosevelt argues that prisons are antiquated and should be modernized as "a simple act of humanity"....Judge M. V. Barnhill moves the trial of the 16 Gastonia strikers to Charlotte.	President Hoover states that his decision to stop the construction of more cruisers seeks to establish naval parity with Britain by agreement rather than by competitive building.	United States Steel Corporation announces that its net earnings have reached the highest peak in time of peace....Attorney General Hamilton ward replies to Governor Franklin Roosevelt saying that the power merger in the formation of the Niagara Hudson Company did not breach any antimonopoly statutes.		The St. Louis Robin, piloted by Dale Jackson and Forest O' Brine, sets a new world's record for endurance flight. The plane lands after 420 hours, 21 minutes and 30 seconds in the air, exceeding the previous record by 173 hours 37 minutes and 58 seconds....The Yankee continue their winning streak beating the Chicago White Sox. It is their sixth consecutive victory.	Jul. 30

F	G	H	I	J
Includes campaigns, elections, federal-state relations, civil rights and liberties, crime, the judiciary, education, healthcare, poverty, urban affairs, and population.	Includes formation and debate of U.S. foreign and defense policies, veterans affairs, and defense spending. (Relations with specific foreign countries are usually found under the region concerned.)	Includes business, labor, agriculture, taxation, transportation, consumer affairs, monetary and fiscal policy, natural resources, pollution and industrial accidents.	Includes worldwide scientific, medical and technological developments, natural phenomena, U.S. weather and natural disasters.	Includes the arts, religion, scholarship, communications media, sports, entertainment, fashions, fads, and social life.

	World Affairs	Europe	Africa & The Middle East	The Americas	Asia & The Pacific
Jul. 31	British and American diplomats agree that at the planned naval conference the limitation of battleships will constitute a crucial topic.	The court set up by the British Board of Trade to investigate the loss of the steamship Vestris the previous November found three man guilty of wrongful acts. They are thus held responsible for the deaths of 112 people....French Premier Briand obtains the vote of confidence by the Chamber of Deputies.	Jews protest against the permission given to Muslims to build a mosque near the Wailing Wall in Jerusalem.		The Soviet government call all the Siberian reserves of the age of 27 or under back into service as tension between China and Russia along the Manchurian border increases.
Aug. 1	The Congress of the World Federation of Education Associations in Geneva adopts a resolution declaring the equality of all children in schools irrespective of race, religious faith, or social position.	Negotiations to restore diplomatic relations between Britain and the Soviet Union end in failure....Communist demonstrations throughout Europe against war on the fifteenth anniversary of the beginning of the First World War fail to attract demonstrators....The Italian Cabinet announces it is ready to accept the Young Plan on war debts if all other nations do so.			Dr. C.C. Wu, Minister Plenipotentiary of the Nanking Government at Washington, denies that China has seized the Chinese Eastern Railway or that it has contravened to Russia's rights in the region.
Aug. 2	The Prince of Wales reviews 50,000 boy scouts from 71 countries in Birkenhead, England.	Italian dictator Benito Mussolini bans Ernesto Belloni, former mayor of Milan, from political and public activity as serious discrepancies are reported in a $30 million loan to the city of Milan from the American Dillon-Read Company.			The Soviet Union and China halt negotiations over the Chinese Eastern Railway as Soviets set firm conditions for a settlement.
Aug. 3	The governments of Hejaz and Nejd and Turkey sign a Treaty of Friendship.		British Foreign Minister Henderson and the Egyptian Premier, Mahmoud Pasha, agree on the terms for a new Anglo-Egyptian treaty. British troops will be concentrated along the Suez Canal....British King George continues his recovery.	Mexico demands that the waters of the Colorado River should be distributed equally between Mexico and the United States after the construction of the Boulder Dam.	Talks between the Soviet Union and China continue at Manchuli over the dispute of the Chinese Eastern Railway. Russians denounce the meager pay and the continuous harassment by the Chinese police and military.
Aug. 4		The Communist organ Pravda issues an appeal to the proletarians in all countries for a world revolution....Austrian police raid the palaces of Prince Von Starhemberg, the leader of the Heimwehr (Fascist) Party. They find weapons and ammunition....60,000 SA and SS storm troopers marched in Munich.			The Chinese Nanking government takes official action against the newspapers The Peking Leader and Le Journal de Peking. A censor is installed in the Leader offices, while Le Journal is confiscated and its circulation is prohibited.
Aug. 5	The delegates to the War Reparations conference at the Hague cannot agree on which nation should chair the meeting.	Playwright George Bernard Shaw criticizes the British Labor government....The Lancashire cotton strike, which affects 500,000 mill workers, continues as workers refuse to negotiate a 12 percent wage reduction.		Communists clash with governmental forces in Colombia, casing 10 deaths....Augusto B. Leguia is re-elected President of Peru for another five-year term.	The Tass News Agency denies that negotiations are progressing between the Soviet Union and China on the dispute of the Chinese Eastern Railway.
Aug. 6	The conference on War Reparations begins at the Hague. English Chancellor of the Exchequer Philip Snowden criticizes the Young Plan on War Reparations, claiming that Britain gets an unfair treatment.	Prince Von Starhemberg, the leader of the Austrian Heimwehr (Fascist) Party, announces he won't allow the confiscation of his properties where the police found weapons and ammunitions....The British ruler King George walks into the gardens of Buckingham Palace. It is the first time he has gone out since his operation in July....Sixteen miners are killed and 200 are injured by Rumanian police at the Lupeni mines in Transylvania.	The British and the Egyptian governments reach an official settlement after years of negotiations. Britain agrees to end its occupation of Egypt and to station its troops along the Suez Canal.	The Mexican Chamber of Duputies approve the Senate's decision that Parliament can make changes to the Constitution to approve Federal labor legislation.	The Chinese Legation in Washigton publishes a memorandum with details of alleged Bolshevik activities in Manchuria that prompted the Chinese to oust Soviet officials from the Chinese Eastern Railway.... Mongolian tribes rebel against the Chinese Nationalist government.
Aug. 7	French Prime Minister Briand argues that the Young Plan for War Reparations should be approved as it is, without any changes.	Three well-known Italian anti-fascists, Francesco Nitti, Carlo Rosselli and Emilio Lussu, escape from the penal isle of Lipari to Paris....Dutch Premier van Beerenbrouck, leader of the Catholic Party, forms a new government.	Sir Percy Loraine is appointed new British High Commissioner at Cairo, Egypt.		In an editorial in the army newspaper The Red Star, the Soviet Union expresses its condemnation of the Chinese seizure of the Chinese Eastern Railway....The Commonwealth Loan Council decides drastic reductions in public works throughout Australia.

A	B	C	D	E
Includes developments that affect more than one world region, international organizations and important meetings of world leaders.	Includes all domestic and regional developments in Europe, including the Soviet Union.	Includes all domestic and regional developments in Africa and the Middle East.	Includes all domestic and regional developments in Latin America, the Caribbean, and Canada.	Includes all domestic and regional developments in Asian and Pacific nations (and colonies).

U.S. Politics & Social Issues	U.S. Foreign Policy & Affairs, Defense	U.S. Economy & Environment	Science, Technology & Nature	Culture, Leisure & Lifestyle	
		The Senate Finance Committee increases the duties approved by the House on milk, cream, poultry, but it refuses to increase those on butter and eggs.		The 49 candidates selected as possible candidates for the Edison scholarship are welcomed by Edison himself, Lindbergh and Ford at West Orange, NJ, for the decisive test.	Jul. 31
Thirty-seven hundred convicts riot in the Federal Penitentiary in Leavenworth, Kansas....New York Republicans name Fiorello LaGuardia as their candidate for mayor.	U.S. Senator Borah appeals to Britain for a reduction of its cruisers.	A violent hailstorm causes damages for more than $1 million in Hartford, Connecticut.	Forty-nine students take part to the selection to win the scholarship offered by inventor Thomas Edision.	Playwright George Bernard Shaw refuses to contribute to the fund to restore St. Mary's Church in Youghal, Ireland.	Aug. 1
	Senator Smoot, chairman of the Finance Committee, announces his plan for a sliding scale of sugar duties.	Dutch oil company Shell plans a massive expansion in the metropolitan district of New York at the expense of the American Standard Oil Company....High-priced shares in the stock market make further gains.	Wilber B. Huston from Seattle is the winner of the first Edison scholarship.	Sammy Mandell defends his title of world's lightweight champion against Tony Canzoneri in Chicago.	Aug. 2
President Hoover refuses to grant clemency to James Horace Alderman who has been sentenced to the electric chair for killing two Florida Coast Guardsmen.	Democratic Senator Claude Swanson attacks President Hoover's decision to suspend work on three 10,000-ton cruisers.	The Federal farm Board urges wheat growers against flooding the market and causing wide fluctuations in prices.			Aug. 3
Bishop James Cannon of the Methodist Episcopal Church denies that he has lent money to the church to advance his political career.			German airship *Graf Zeppelin* lands in New York ending its journey of 5,000 miles across the Atlantic. It betters its previous voyage by 16 hours and seven minutes.		Aug. 4
Republican Party leaders fix the date of September 9 to elect the new chairman of the party's National Committee. They are confident that Claudius H. Huston will be elected.	American veterans pay tribute to the courage of German soldiers in the First World War by laying their wreath in Berlin.	The sharp increase in the price of wheat causes an unprecedented accumulation of bushels....The stocks of the Insull Company drop dramatically on the Chicago stock market....John J. Raskob, former financial administrator of General Motors, makes large investments in the aviation industry.	German airship *Graf Zeppelin* is refueled and prepared for its round-the-world trip.	Carl Laemmle, president of the Universal Pictures Corporation, announces the filming of Erich Maria Remarque's *All Quiet on The Western Front*.	Aug. 5
President Hoover proposes a $5 million program to enlarge four existing prisons and the building of a new penal institution. This measures will help to relieve the overcrowded condition of federal prisons....John Garland Pollard is nominated by Virginia Democrats for Governor in the November election.		Republican Senators in the Finance Committee agree on cutting the duty on passenger carts imported to the United States from 25 to 10 percent.			Aug. 6
George W. Wickersham, the chair of the Hoover Law Enforcement Investigation Commission, is also appointed the chair of the subcommittee on Prohibition.	Congressmen plan to save the cruiser Olympia as a memorial in Washington. The cruiser was used to bring to the Unites States the body of the Unknown Soldier to be buried at Arlington National Cemetery on Armistice Day in 1921.	President Hoover announces the donation to his summer camp in the Blue Ridge Mountains to the Shenandoah National Park.	German airship *Graf Zeppelin* leaves from Lakehurst, New Jersey, for its round-the-world trip, the longest passenger voyage ever attempted by a dirigible.	A record crowd of 46,000 people watch the double header between New York Yankees and the Philadelphia Athletics.	Aug. 7

F	G	H	I	J
Includes campaigns, elections, federal-state relations, civil rights and liberties, crime, the judiciary, education, healthcare, poverty, urban affairs, and population.	*Includes formation and debate of U.S. foreign and defense policies, veterans affairs, and defense spending. (Relations with specific foreign countries are usually found under the region concerned.)*	*Includes business, labor, agriculture, taxation, transportation, consumer affairs, monetary and fiscal policy, natural resources, pollution and industrial accidents.*	*Includes worldwide scientific, medical and technological developments, natural phenomena, U.S. weather and natural disasters.*	*Includes the arts, religion, scholarship, communications media, sports, entertainment, fashions, fads, and social life.*

	World Affairs	Europe	Africa & The Middle East	The Americas	Asia & The Pacific
Aug. 8	Britain threatens to leave the War Reparations Conference if its changes to the Young Plan are overlooked.	New marriage rules enter in force in Italy as result of Lateran Treaties.... Officials of the Ministry of Labor step in as mediators in the negotiations in the Lancashire cotton strike in England.	Arabs conduct a large scale attack against Jews in Palestine....Persian authorities announce that the revolt in the southern region of the country has been suppressed.		Negotiations between the Soviet Union and China over the Chinese Eastern Railway break down. Soviet troops begin military maneuvers.
Aug. 9	The Conference on War Reparations is suspended at the Hague after Britain threatens to leave if its demands for a greater share in German reparations are not met.	The Parliament in Monte Carlo warns Prince Louis that a republic will be declared if he does not allow the referendum over the matter to take place....The Austrian Fascist Party, Heimwehr, holds its first demonstration in Vienna, but only 6,000 people attend.		Pasqual Ortiz Rubio, candidate of the Revolutionary Party for Mexican President, orders the division of his ranch in the State of Michoacan among the peasants in the area.	Strict censorship over the American newspaper The Leader is lifted as it is sold to Chinese interests.
Aug. 10	The French delegation to the Hague Conference on War Reparations demands to meet British premier MacDonald to avoid the collapse of the conference	Ford's European headquarters announce they will raise the wages of their employees....British premier MacDonald meets the leaders of the workers involved in the Lancashire cotton strike.	The Liberian government allows an international commission to investigate over the allegations on the widespread conditions of slavery in the country.	Gonzales Arnao, Spanish Envoy in Mexico City, is arrested during a raid for smuggled wine but is immediately released....Peruvian president Leguia cancels the Lee concession which allowed Americans to use over 12 million acres of land in the basins of the Huallaga and Maranon Rivers.... Industrial companies fear that the new labor laws under consideration in the Mexican Parliament may cause losses in their profits.	
Aug. 11	British Premier MacDonald supports his Chancellor of the Exchequer's demands for a larger share of war reparations to Britain at the Hague conference....The sixteenth Zionist Biennial Congress in Zurich, Switzerland, elects Chaim Weizmann as president.	Germany celebrates the tenth anniversary of the proclamation of the Weimar Republic.	The Iraqi and Persian governments sign a Treaty of Friendship. Persians officially recognize the Iraqi government.	Fourteen Mexican States approve a proposal to alter the national Constitution to permit the enforcement by the Federal Congress of a national labor law.	
Aug. 12	British and French experts at the Hague conference on war reparations hold a series of meetings to reach a compromise which would give Britain a larger share of war reparations without radically altering the Young Plan....The World Advertising Congress is inaugurated in Berlin, aiming at the promotion of amity and peace through advertising.	Violent incidents take place in the morning in the Parisian subway between Communists and workers building a new subway line. Police and troops of the Republican Guard patrol the subway system for the rest of the day....Fascist and Socialist militants clash along the western railway through the Vienna Forest....Sante Pollastri, Italy's most notorious bandit of the 1920s, is extradited to Italy from France.		Rebels in Venezuela attempt to capture the city of Cumana. They are completely defeated although they manage to kill General Emilio Fernandez, President of the State of Sucre.	The Soviet Union threatens the invasion of Harbin, Manchuria, if the dispute over the Eastern Chinese Railway is not settled quickly.
Aug. 13	British Chancellor of the Exchequer Snowden drops his threat to leave the Hague conference on war reparations.	The Italian Fascist government orders the arrest of two relatives of Carlo Rosselli, a notorious anti-Fascist who has successfully escaped from the penal island of Lipari (Sicily) taking refuge in Paris....French Premier Briand states that French troops may withdraw from the Rhineland region by Christmas....The General Labor Union Congress of Spain proclaims its opposition to the dictatorship of General Primo de Rivera and its support of the Republican cause.		Venezuelan rebels plan a new attack on Maturin, the capital of the Mongas province....The Chilean government announces its willingness to negotiate a ship liquor treaty with the United States to improve the country's wine trade....Nicaraguan President Moncada criticizes the press for inciting rebellion against his government.	The Soviet Union amasses his army along the border with Manchuria, preparing a possible invasion....The Batanes Islands, the northernmost group in the Philippine Archipelago, suffer from famine due to crop failure and typhoons.
Aug. 14	Sir Cecil Hurst and Henri Fromageot receive the greatest number of nominations to fill the vacancies on the Permanent Court of International Justice (World Court) bench....The Italian, French, Japanese and Belgian delegations to the Hague Conference on War Reparations hold long meetings to consider the British demands for a larger share in German reparations.	The Bank of England makes an arrangement with the Federal Reserve Bank of New York allowing for the establishment of a $250 million credit within a few hours' notice....Many French newspapers express concerns over governmental plans to evacuate the Rhineland region.		Venezuelan revolutionaries led by General Regulo Olivares cross the Colombian border and invade the Tachira province with 1,700 men.	Eight men are killed in the crash of a Japanese military plane at Takikawa airfield near Tokyo....Chinese Foreign Office officials hold a meeting with President Chiang Kai-Shek to discuss the Russian conditions for a settlement of the Chinese Eastern Railway dispute.

A	B	C	D	E
Includes developments that affect more than one world region, international organizations and important meetings of world leaders.	Includes all domestic and regional developments in Europe, including the Soviet Union.	Includes all domestic and regional developments in Africa and the Middle East.	Includes all domestic and regional developments in Latin America, the Caribbean, and Canada.	Includes all domestic and regional developments in Asian and Pacific nations (and colonies).

U.S. Politics & Social Issues	U.S. Foreign Policy & Affairs, Defense	U.S. Economy & Environment	Science, Technology & Nature	Culture, Leisure & Lifestyle	
Al Capone is moved to the Eastern State Penitentiary from the Holmesburg County Prison after threats from fellow convicts.... Independent candidate John F. Hylan withdraws from the mayoral race in New York.		Directors of the New York Federal Reserve Bank raise the rediscount rate by one percent bringing it to six percent as brokers' loans reach a new high record for the fourth consecutive week....The Federal Farm Board makes a loan of $300,000 to Florida Citrus Growers' Association to fight the Mediterranean fly.			Aug. 8
J. R. Clarke and other directors of the bankrupt firm Clarke Brothers are sentenced to prison just six weeks after the $5 million failure which affected more than 2,000 depositors.	U.S. officials express great concern about Britain's ultimatum at the Hague Conference on War Reparations.	The decision to increase the rediscount rate causes the most severe slump in the stock market since 1911.			Aug. 9
The home of Mr. and Mrs. Hutchinson at Beverly Farms, Massachusetts, is broken into and jewelry worth $250,000 is stolen....Senator Burton Wheeler denounces the poor conditions of Native Americans and argues for their improvement from the federal government.		The stock market regains half of the losses suffered the previous week....Senator Smoot accepts the advice of the Republican members of the Senate Finance Committee and drops his program for a sliding scale of sugar tariffs.		President Hoover celebrates his 55th birthday at his summer camp in Virginia. Many important guests, including aviator Charles Lindbergh, attend.	Aug. 10
The Association Against the Prohibition Amendment summarizes the results of a survey showing the increase of alcoholism and of arrests for drunkenness in spite of prohibition....William Green, President of the American Federation of Labor, declares that membership in the Federation has increased during the previous year.		The United Growers of America is created to effect greater unity between cooperatives and growers' organizations dealing in fruit and vegetables.	A violent electrical storm strikes the New Jersey coast, causing one death and serious damages.	Babe Ruth hits his 500th major league home run against the Cleveland Indians....Brooklyn bullfighter Sidney Franklin is seriously wounded by a bull in Lisbon.	Aug. 11
Republican members of the Senate Finance Committee reach a tentative agreement to lay tariffs upon hides, leather, and shoes.		The record amount of wheat accumulated during the year causes a sharp drop in prices.	Earth tremors greatly varying in intensity are felt over five Eastern states. They are particularly intense in some localities of New York and Pennsylvania.		Aug. 12
A crowd of sympathizers with the striking street-car employees attack the Mayor and members of the City Council of New Orleans, forcing their way into the City Hall. Policemen open fire against the crowd injuring four....William M. Bennett, a supporter of Prohibition, announces his intention to seek the Republican nomination for New York Mayor to oppose LaGuardia...."Wee Willie" Doody, considered Chicago's most dangerous criminal, is captured after a six months' search.				RKO Productions ratifies a new franchise for the sale of sound pictures to independent theaters. Under the new franchise, independent owners must accept all the RKO output, up to fifty-two pictures a year....America's Cup defender, *Resolute*, captures the Vanderbilt Cup.	Aug. 13
Former Ohio Professor James Snook is found guilty of first-degree murder for the killing of Theora K. Hix, a second-year student at the university.	President Hoover discusses the problems of naval armament with members of his cabinet. Hoover's intention is to organize an international naval parley in London before the end of the year to reduce the number of cruisers.		A new bridge worth $5 million spanning the Delaware River between Palmyra, NJ, and the Tacony district of Philadelphia is opened by New Jersey and Pennsylvania officials.		Aug. 14

F	G	H	I	J
Includes campaigns, elections, federal-state relations, civil rights and liberties, crime, the judiciary, education, healthcare, poverty, urban affairs, and population.	*Includes formation and debate of U.S. foreign and defense policies, veterans affairs, and defense spending. (Relations with specific foreign countries are usually found under the region concerned.)*	*Includes business, labor, agriculture, taxation, transportation, consumer affairs, monetary and fiscal policy, natural resources, pollution and industrial accidents.*	*Includes worldwide scientific, medical and technological developments, natural phenomena, U.S. weather and natural disasters.*	*Includes the arts, religion, scholarship, communications media, sports, entertainment, fashions, fads, and social life.*

	World Affairs	Europe	Africa & The Middle East	The Americas	Asia & The Pacific
Aug. 15	The representative of former German Kaiser is forbidden to attend the Hague Conference on War Reparations....The French delegation to the Hague Conference announces that French, Italian, Japanese, and Belgian representatives remain firm in their rejection of British demands for a larger share in German reparations.	After an eighteen-day strike, the Lancashire cotton mills reopen. The mills resume activity at the old rates of pay....The Free Church of Scotland rebukes the Duke and the Duchess of York as well as the British Premier MacDonald for breaking the Sabbath....The French government agrees to the return to France of American treasury agents. This settles a long-standing dispute between the French and the American governments over the application of the American valuation system to French exports.		Colombian Communist militants attack ranches in the Department of Santander and demand a fairer division of land.	Soviet forces take for villages in Manchuria. China sends troops to patrol the borders....The province of Bombay, India, is struck with a severe cholera epidemic which causes the death of more than 1,000 people.
Aug. 16	British Chancellor of the Exchequer Snowden rejects the new offer from the representatives of Japan, France, Belgium and Italy at the War Reparations Conference at the Hague.	Premier MacDonald plans a subsidy to the Lancashire cotton industry for its recovery after the long strike of the previous weeks. He also calls for more cooperation between workers and employers in British industries.	The British paper *Daily Sketch* announces that the Duke of York will be appointed Governor General of South Africa when the present Governor, Lord Athlone, completes his term.	The Inter-American Commission on conciliation between Bolivia and Paraguay over the boundary dispute in the Chaco region considers drawing a line of demarcation from Port Leda on the Paraguay River to El Hito on the Pilcomayo River. The Commission is confident that the proposal could settle the dispute.	Chinese Foreign Minister C. T. Wang notify the signatories of the Kellogg antiwar pact that Russia has invaded Chinese territory in Manchuria and has thus breached the pact.
Aug. 17		Sixteen Polish miners die in a disaster in the Hildebrand colliery near Kattowitz.		Venezuelan rebels claim to have seized the port and the city of Cumana. The government sends troops to recapture the city.....The General Confederation of Mexican Workers warns President Portes Gil that if he goes on with his project for the federalization of labor laws there will be a general strike.	China considers a world-wide appeal for help to repel the Russian invasion of Manchuria or to bring the Soviet Union to arbitrate.
Aug. 18		A tugboat sinks a Spanish steamer in the North Sea causing the deaths of sixteen Spanish sailors....In the Austrian region of Styria, one man is killed and sixty-two are injured in a battle following the breaking up of a Socialist meeting by Austrian Fascist militants.			As clashes between Soviet and Chinese forces continue along the Manchurian border, the Chinese government prepares to send up to 100,000 soldiers in the area.
Aug. 19		The British government announces its decision to withdraw its 6,000 troops from the German Rhineland region in September. This causes further tensions between London and Paris. The French intend to start withdrawal only after the Young Plan for War Reparations is approved....Austrian Socialist Party calls its members to get ready for the defense of their ideals and their party.		The American Popular Revolutionary Alliance asks for the internationalization of the Panama Canal.	Marshal Chang Hsueh-liang, war lord and governor of Manchuria, appeals to the Chinese government in Nanking to send more troops to Manchuria. This is interpreted as evidence that a Soviet invasion is feared.
Aug. 20	German Foreign Minister Stresemann demands that the Conference on War Reparations approves the Young Plan immediately....British Premier MacDonald and American Ambassador in Britain Dawes reveal their plans for an international naval conference.	German officials express their disappointment because French Premier Briand has not given a precise date for German evacuation of Rhineland yet....A military treaty uniting Czechoslovakia, Rumania and Yugoslavia is revealed by a Czech newspaper.	The violent clashes between Arabs and Jews in Jerusalem cause the first dead.	Venezuelan rebels defeat an attempt by federal troops to recapture the city of Cumana....The Argentinean government fears that the general strike called by Communists may cause widespread upheaval.	Concerned over the clashes between Soviets and Chinese in Manchuria, Japan begins to move its troops northward on the South Manchuria Railway and through Korea to the Manchurian border.
Aug. 21	France and Germany join forces in their accusation to Britain of delaying the approval of the Young Plan at the Hague War Reparations Conference.	Belgian troops prepare for the evacuation of the Rhineland region.	The funeral of the first Jewish victim in the riots in Jerusalem stirs strong reactions against the British administration. Demonstrators clash with the police.		The Chinese government states that the occupation of Manchuria is only a first step in the Soviet plan to start a world-wide revolution. Russians are ready to advance into Chinese territory and occupy the city of Harbin.

A	B	C	D	E
Includes developments that affect more than one world region, international organizations and important meetings of world leaders.	Includes all domestic and regional developments in Europe, including the Soviet Union.	Includes all domestic and regional developments in Africa and the Middle East.	Includes all domestic and regional developments in Latin America, the Caribbean, and Canada.	Includes all domestic and regional developments in Asian and Pacific nations (and colonies).

U.S. Politics & Social Issues	U.S. Foreign Policy & Affairs, Defense	U.S. Economy & Environment	Science, Technology & Nature	Culture, Leisure & Lifestyle	
		The Day-Fan Electric Company of Dayton, radio manufacturers, announces its merger with the General Motors Corporation.	American explorer Herbert Spencer Dickey returns from his expedition along the Orinoco River without having discovered any new tribes.		**Aug. 15**
William Bennett announces that he will seek nomination as the Republican candidate for New York Mayor against Fiorello LaGuardia on a Prohibition platform. He aims to "close the speakeasies."	Two dozen vessels and boats are added to the Coast Guard force on the Great Lakes to fight rum-runners along the Canadian frontier.	Faced with strong protests from consumers, the Republican members of the Senate Finance Committee lower the duty on imported sugar.	Scientists at the Bureau of Standards announce the development of a self-extinguishing cigarette.	Aviator Charles A Lindbergh proves himself as daring with cars as he has proved to be with planes: he drives an automobile around a concrete track at Utica reaching a speed of 112 miles per hour.	**Aug. 16**
William Bennett, dry Republican candidate in New York mayoralty race, denounces that the 30,000 speakeasies in New York could all be closed down if authorities really wanted to....Oil magnate Harry F. Sinclair, convicted for contempt, asks for a commutation of sentence on the ground of ill health.		Postal savings business in July shows a great increase as compared with June. This is due to the recent bank failures in Florida and New Jersey. Because of this, the postal savings system is called "a refuge for the timid"....Although the Senate has lowered the tariff on sugar initially voted by the House, the increases are still opposed by a large coalition of interests even within the Republican Party.		President Hoover attends a fair grounds ceremony in Virginia and greets the crowd of 5,000 people with a speech on his passion: fishing.	**Aug. 17**
The Actors' Equity Association calls off its 10 weeks' strike to have all casts selected among members of the association. Equity's President Frank Gillmore blames actress Ethel Barrymore, who expressed her opposition to the proposal, for the failure of the strike....Wealthy Queens builder Richard P. Weber is robbed of $35,000 in jewelry.		Democrats strongly attack the Republican proposal for the revision of tariff rates. They claim that the Republicans' manipulation of the sugar schedule will cause an increase in the burden of living to American families....The heavy increase in personal income taxes produces a sharp rise in federal funds.	A ten-car electric train of the Long Island Railroad crashes into a twelve-ton concrete bumber at the long Beach terminal as brakes fail to check the train speed. 16 people are injured.	The first cross-country women's air derby begins....German yachtsmen win the Hoover Cup in Marblehead, MA.	**Aug. 18**
Two companies of National Guardsmen are sent to Marion, North Carolina, at the Clinchfield Mill where 600 striking workers are preventing non-striking employees to start the mill machinery.	Senator Walter E. Edge is appointed as the next American ambassador to France.	After two months' work the Republican members of the Senate Committee on Finance hand to the committee's Democrats and to the press their revision of the tariff schedules passed in May by the House of Representatives....The United Cigar Store Company is sold for $100 million to the Gold Dust Corporation.		The comedy program *Amos 'n' Andy*, starring Freeman Gosden and Charles Correll, makes its network radio debut on NBC....Aviator Charles Lindbergh teaches his bride how to pilot a plane....Serge Daghileff, famous Russian opera and ballet producer, is found dead in his room at the Hotel Lido-Bains in Venice.	**Aug. 19**
Dr. James Snook is sentenced to death in the electric chair for the murder of Theora Hix. The judge overrules a motion for a new trial.		Senator Smoot, the chairman of the Finance Committee, states that, although the tariffs made public by republican members of the committee were lower than those passed by Representatives, they were still considerably higher than the present law.		Miss Marvel Crosson, a competitor at the woman's national air derby in Phoenix, dies after her parachute fails to open.	**Aug. 20**
Automobile manufacturer Henry Ford praises Prohibition and says he would stop manufacturing cars if it should be repealed.		Three Americans scale Mount Alexander in the Canadian Rockies for the first time.	German dirigible *Graf Zeppelin* is damaged while leaving Tokyo hangar in its round the world trip.	Dwight W. Morrow, American ambassador to Mexico, returns to the United States for the first time since the wedding of his daughter to Charles Lindbergh.	**Aug. 21**

F	G	H	I	J
Includes campaigns, elections, federal-state relations, civil rights and liberties, crime, the judiciary, education, healthcare, poverty, urban affairs, and population.	*Includes formation and debate of U.S. foreign and defense policies, veterans affairs, and defense spending. (Relations with specific foreign countries are usually found under the region concerned.)*	*Includes business, labor, agriculture, taxation, transportation, consumer affairs, monetary and fiscal policy, natural resources, pollution and industrial accidents.*	*Includes worldwide scientific, medical and technological developments, natural phenomena, U.S. weather and natural disasters.*	*Includes the arts, religion, scholarship, communications media, sports, entertainment, fashions, fads, and social life.*

	World Affairs	Europe	Africa & The Middle East	The Americas	Asia & The Pacific
Aug. 22	Worried by the negative effects that the failure of the Hague Conference on War Reparations may have, the French, Italian, Belgian, and Japanese delegations make one more effort to meet the British demands for a larger share of reparations.	Paul Marion, former head of the Communist propaganda bureau in France, resigns from the Communist Party after a visit to the Soviet Union....The Board of Arbitration of the Lancashire Mills votes for a pay reduction for workers....The Austrian government forbids parallel meetings of Fascists and Socialists to prevent further clashes.		The Chilean Cabinet presents its resignation to the president.	The Soviet Union and China continue to amass troops along the Manchurian border. War seems inevitable....Because of a break in the dike on the Yellow River, in West Shantung, crops are destroyed and the suffering of the population increases.
Aug. 23	British Chancellor of the Exchequer Snowden rejects the new offer made by the Allies Powers at the Hague Conference....The Inter-parliamentary Union of Legislators opens its sessions in Geneva to consider the Kellogg peace pact and optional clause for compulsory jurisdiction of the World Court.	A violent storm strikes the Yugoslav town of Skoplje killing 50 people and destroying 50 houses.	More riots break out in Hebron and Gaza in Palestine between Jews and Arabs. Nine Jews and three Arabs are killed and 11 people are injured.	With the exception of street-car crews, workers in the Argentine town of Rosario end their fifteen-month strike....Bolivia requests the aid of the League of Nations to re-organize its health service....Venezuelan rebel forces advance towards the country's capital, Caracas.	Communist troops are instructed to kill all White Guards still present in the Manchurian region.
Aug. 24	American pacifist and social worker Jane Addams opens the sixth international congress of the Women's League for Peace and Freedom in Prague.	The British monarch King George is cheered by thousands of people while he goes to his Sandringham Summer house. He appears to have fully recovered from his illness....Heimwehr leaders say they will fight to compel fundamental changes in Austria's constitution.	Violent clashes between Jews and Arabs break out in Jerusalem. 47 people are killed. Martial Law is proclaimed in Jerusalem and a state of emergency is declared throughout Palestine. British troops are sent from Egypt to put down the riots.	A new Cabinet is formed in Chile....British Ambassador to Mexico Esmond Ovey resigns to take up the post of ambassador to Brazil.	The Soviet Union threatens to declare war against China and invade the Manchurian region if China does not accept its requests.
Aug. 25	The British cabinet holds a meeting at the Hague during the international conference on War Reparations to support the demands of its Chancellor of the Exchequer. The other four powers at the Conference (Italy, France, Japan, and Belgium) offer Snowden a compromise meeting 60 percent of his requests.	The Paris–Warsaw train derails at Bruir in Germany. Eight passengers die in the wreck....The estimated budget for the fiscal year 1929–30 in the Soviet Union shows a steady economic growth....Several political demonstrations by the opposing Socialist and Fascist parties take place in Austria without incidents.	Twelve Americans are killed in Hebron during riots between Arabs and Jews. Arab attacks against government offices and Jews are also reported in Jaffa and Tel Aviv.	Chilean newspapers express their approval for the selections made in the country's new cabinet.	The continuous state of tension between Russia and China along the Manchurian border damages Chinese trade....The newspaper Shanghai Mainichi is closed down by Japanese censorship after reporting the deportation from Shanghai to Japan of a notorious Japanese Communist.
Aug. 26	British Chancellor of the Exchequer Snowden rejects the offer of the other four creditor powers at the Hague Conference on War Reparations. The offer met 60 percent of the British demands....The League of Nations committee for the drafting of a convention on the manufacture of weapons, ammunition and other war materials opens its session in Geneva.	Johann Schober, Police President of Vienna and Former Chancellor of the Republic, issues a statement denying that a Fascist putsch is likely.	More Arab attacks are reported in Palestine. Arab forces clash with British troops landing from warships at Jaffa and try to oppose the advance of marines to Jerusalem. The number of dead and injured mounts hourly.	Honduras notifies the Secretariat of the League of Nations that it will start to re-attend its sessions. The country had not attended since 1923....Provisional Mexican President Portes Gil says the country is united and denies talks of new unrest and riots.	Chinese Foreign Ministers denies that Chinese troops have crossed Siberian borders and raided villages as Soviet authorities maintain.
Aug. 27	Britain and the other four creditor nations at the Hague Conference on War Reparations reach an agreement which grants British Chancellor of the exchequer Snowden 80 percent of his requests. Britain gets an increase of more than $9 million in its share of German reparations. German Foreign Minister Stresemann demands that Allied troops should evacuate the Rhineland region within three months from the approval of the Young plan.	Due to the breakout of Arab violence against Jews in Palestine, Zionists in London present formal demands to the British government asking for compensation, freedom of Jews to carry arms, punishment of guilty Arabs and an official statement of British policy in the region....Violent floods cause severe damages in southern Serbian towns and villages.	Widespread disorders continue to occur in Palestine between Arabs and Jews. British troops fight against Arabs in Haifa. More deaths are reported within both the Jewish and Muslim communities.	Joseph E. Barlow, an American citizen who sued the Cuban government for $9 million for seizure of property, is arrested in Havana and held in jail without bail.	Chinese government circles are confident that Russia is slowly becoming more willing to negotiate for a pacific settlement of the Eastern Chinese Railway.
Aug. 28	The German delegation refuses to agree to the implementation of the Young Plan on War Reparations without receiving precise assurances about a speedy evacuation of the Rhineland region.	Italian Aviator Colonel Francisco de Pinedo resigns from his post as Chief of the General Staff for Aviation....Bulgarian Premier Liaptcheff is fired at by mistake by a peasant....Croatian leader Anton Trumbitch flees from Croatia into Austria in protest against the treatment of Croats under the Yugoslav dictatorship.	Disorders continue in Palestine. Muslims attacks government offices in Tulkare and Nablus. The revolt now targets the British administration. Business in Jerusalem stops completely. Uprisings also break out in Syria.	Joseph E. Barlow, an American citizen arrested in Cuba after suing the government for $9 million for seizure of property, is released on bail.	Unofficial Chinese–Russian negotiators in Berlin recommend M. Zharkoff, former head of the Kazan railway, as general manager of the Chinese Eastern Railway.

A	B	C	D	E
Includes developments that affect more than one world region, international organizations and important meetings of world leaders.	*Includes all domestic and regional developments in Europe, including the Soviet Union.*	*Includes all domestic and regional developments in Africa and the Middle East.*	*Includes all domestic and regional developments in Latin America, the Caribbean, and Canada.*	*Includes all domestic and regional developments in Asian and Pacific nations (and colonies).*

U.S. Politics & Social Issues	U.S. Foreign Policy & Affairs, Defense	U.S. Economy & Environment	Science, Technology & Nature	Culture, Leisure & Lifestyle	
Wisconsin legislature defeats a bill allowing counties to enact Prohibition laws of their own....On the second anniversary of Sacco and Vanzetti execution a crowd of 3,500 workers gathers in Union Square demonstrating on behalf of the striking Gastonia workers.	President Hoover will confer in person with British Premier Ramsay MacDonald in October to organize an international naval parley before the end of the year....Bulgaria is the eleventh member of the League of Nations to register a treaty of arbitration and conciliation with the United States.	Republican Senator Borah urges the repeal of the tariff bill and announces he will work with Democrats to that effect. According to Borah, the bill breaches the pledges of the Republican Party to farmers.		Bert Lown files suit in the Supreme Court against orchestra leader and vaudeville performer Rudy Vallée. Lown claims that Vallée has refused to carry out an agreement to share profits as agreed.	Aug. 22
	American Ambassador in Britain Dawes states that the problem of naval reduction must be solved in a way understandable to the average man, otherwise parliaments may not ratify it.	Contrary to the negative expectations, the stock market rises. Wall Street expected a decline in the market because of the expansion of brokers' loans.		John Coolidge, the son of former U.S. President Calvin Coolidge, announces his marriage to Florence Trumbull, daughter of Connecticut governor for the month of September....American Olympic champion Martha Norelius wins the ten-mile Wrigley marathon in Toronto, Canada.	Aug. 23
Georgia State Prison Commission recommends to Governor L.G. Hardman to deny clemency to Robert E. Burns, former Chicago publisher.		Due to the sharp decrease in the price of wheat, farmers demand loans to the Federal Farm Board to be able to hold their stores until prices start to rise again.... Merchant groups protest against the norm included in the new tariff bill which raises to $200 in the value of personal property that can be brought into the United States from other countries....Henry Ford purchases the Vaucluse gold mines in Orange County, Virginia.		Helen Wills wins the American Women's national tennis title for the sixth time by defeating Phoebe Watson.	Aug. 24
New York Governor Franklin Delano Roosevelt announces his intention to run again for governor in 1930. He says he is confident he will be renominated.		President Hoover puts pressure on Republican leaders to enact tariff legislation before the regular session of Congress in December.		At the national swimming championship in San Francisco, Walter Spence wins the 440-yard senior men's breast-stroke event. John Galitzen won the championship in platform diving. Clarence Crabbe retains its title in the 880-yard freestyle event.	Aug. 25
A crowd of 15,000 Jews marches in New York and protests in front of the British Consulate for the failure of British authorities to protect Jews in the riots that are breaking out throughout Palestine....A Greek immigrant tries to kill the Greek Minister to the United States in Washington, but is disarmed and arrested.	The U.S. Department of State asks the British Foreign Office to ensure the safety of American citizens in Palestine.	President Hoover demands a drastic change in land policy. He suggests restricting the activities of the Federal Reclamation Service and to have the individual states take over irrigation and water rights.	An oil-electric locomotive is tested on a run of 334 miles from Montreal to Toronto.	The first U.S. roller coaster is built....Louise McPhetride Thaden wins first prize in the heavier-plane division of the first women's air derby, while Phoebe Fairgrave Omlie comes first in the lighter-plane category.	Aug. 26
Jersey City Mayor Frank Hague is freed from arrest by Chancellor Fallon and the Court of Errors and Appeals....President Hoover and Secretary of State Stimson receive a delegation of Zionist leaders who express deep concern for the violence against Jews in Palestine.	President Hoover confers with Secretary of State Stimson and Secretary of the Navy Adams on the progresses made in British-American talks for the organization of an international naval parley for the reduction of fighting fleets.	President Hoover explains that his proposal to turn over to the states 200,000 acres of public land is designed as a measure of conservation that would eventually yield a considerable revenue for the states.	Three people are killed in the crash of the second plane which reaches the Boston airport at the end of the first part of the Philadelphia-Cleveland air derby.	Colonel Charles A. Lindbergh joins the performers of the First Naval Squadron in Cleveland, Ohio, and leads them in spectacular maneuvers which thrill the crowd of 30,000 people attending the event.	Aug. 27
Three jurors are selected for the jury of the trial against the Gastonia strikers tried for the murder of O. F. Aderholt, Chief of Police of Gastonia.	The British Foreign Office reassures American Ambassador Dawes that every effort is being made to protect American citizens in Palestine and to restore law and order in the region.	New York Governor Franklin Delano Roosevelt states that cities should cooperate with farms to solve agricultural marketing problems.			Aug. 28

F	G	H	I	J
Includes campaigns, elections, federal-state relations, civil rights and liberties, crime, the judiciary, education, healthcare, poverty, urban affairs, and population.	Includes formation and debate of U.S. foreign and defense policies, veterans affairs, and defense spending. (Relations with specific foreign countries are usually found under the region concerned.)	Includes business, labor, agriculture, taxation, transportation, consumer affairs, monetary and fiscal policy, natural resources, pollution and industrial accidents.	Includes worldwide scientific, medical and technological developments, natural phenomena, U.S. weather and natural disasters.	Includes the arts, religion, scholarship, communications media, sports, entertainment, fashions, fads, and social life.

	World Affairs	Europe	Africa & The Middle East	The Americas	Asia & The Pacific
Aug. 29	The German delegation accepts the conditions offered by the five creditor nations at the Hague international Conference on War Reparations. June 30, 1930 is set as a date for the final evacuation of Allied Troops from the Rhineland region....The League of Nations hosts the Third International Conference for the Abolition of Prohibitions in the Exportation of Hides and Bones....The League of Nations committee responsible for drafting a convention on the control of the manufacture of arms ends without an agreement.	Spanish dictator Primo De Rivera postpones the new session of the Parliament.	British troops seize a Transjordanian Arab leader just outside Jerusalem who was believed to have planned an attack on the city.		Three hundred people die in India in the Dera district of the Indus valley due to heavy floods....The Japanese Navy Department plans a large expansion of its fighting fleet involving the expenditure of $188 million over six to eight years.
Aug. 30	The League of Nations Council proposes to place the question of American membership into the World Court under the formula suggested by American diplomat Elihu Root at the conference of court members beginning on September 4.	British Prime Minister MacDonald announces he will begin his official American visit on October 4th and will stay for three days....French Premier Briand faces strong opposition in his country for his concession to Britain at the Hague Conference on War Reparations....The Spanish government gives up its plan to create a state monopoly on cars.	Arabs attack the city of Safed, killing twenty-two Jews and burning down the whole town. British troops continue to raid Arab villages and make many arrests throughout Palestine. Muslims also riot in Damascus and Beirut.		Fearing an imminent invasion by the better equipped Russian Red Army, the Chinese government agrees to negotiate the far eastern crisis on Russian terms.
Aug. 31	The British and American governments regard the Kellogg pact banning wars as the spirit that should underlie the naval armament treaty that the two countries are trying to bring about.	The German film production company UFA begins producing talkies both in German and English.	Muslim tribesmen invade Palestine from Syria. More fighting breaks out in Haifa.	The Pan American Conference negotiates an Arbitration Convention between the Bolivian and Paraguayan governments to settle the dispute in the Chaco region. Both governments reject the settlement.	Five youths are executed by a fire squad in Shanghai when they are caught distributing Communist propaganda. Authorities try and execute them in less than two hours as an example to other youths coming to the city for the International Youth Movement Day.
Sep. 1		British Chancellor of the Exchequer Snowden receives an enthusiastic welcome in London due to his success at the Hague War Reparations Conference....The French Cabinet praises Prime Minister Aristide Briand for his work at the Hague War Reparations Conference.	The British High Commissioner in Palestine condemns the violence against Jews by Muslims and issues a proclamation promising severe punishment. More attacks take place.	Provisional Mexican President Emilio Portes Gil opens the thirty-third Congress promising free elections and stating that he will not try to retain power at all costs.	A plot to assassinate President Chiang Kai-Shek planned by his own bodyguards is discovered.
Sep. 2	The League of Nations assembly convenes in Geneva, with 53 nations being represented. Gustavo Guerrero, former Foreign Minister of Salvador, is elected president.	British Premier MacDonald states that the aim of the Anglo-American diplomatic talks is the reduction of all armaments....Former Austrian Chancellor Seipel praises the Fascist Heimwehr as a movement for change....A treaty of friendship between France and Poland is ratified in Warsaw.	Riots between Muslims and Jews continue in Palestine. British troops surprise and capture 1,000 tribesmen preparing an attack on Hibbin between Tiberias and Nazareth.	The government of Paraguay accepts the first two of three proposals for the settlement of the Chaco dispute made by the Pan-American Union commission.	Chinese Foreign Minister C. T. Wang states that China will not accept to replace the chairman of the board of directors of the Chinese Eastern Railway as asked by Russia to settle the dispute.
Sep. 3	British Premier MacDonald addresses the League of Nations saying that the Anglo-American agreement on naval armaments limitation is near. He urges a revision of the League covenant and says that Britain will accept the optional clause for compulsory jurisdiction of the World Court.	The political bureau of the Communist Party announces the dismissal of the six main editors of the party newspaper, *L'Humanité*....Ante Korosetz, the only Slovenian member of the Yugoslav Cabinet, resigns.	The statement of the British High Commissioner entirely blaming Muslims for the violent disorders in Palestine stirs angry reactions from Arab leaders. The clashes continue.		The negotiations in Berlin between Russia and China for the Chinese Eastern Railway dispute reaches a deadlock. Chinese authorities do not agree to have a Russian chairman of the company.
Sep. 4	The Conference of World Court members unanimously accept the formula devised by Elihu Root for American admission to the Hague tribunal.	The German dirigible *Graf Zeppelin* returns to Germany from its record-breaking transatlantic flight to an enthusiastic reception....France criticizes the speech of British Premier MacDonald to the League of Nations for its exclusive focus on an Anglo-American agreement which should then be imposed to other nations.	An anonymous proclamation found in Jerusalem calls Arabs to an holy war against Jews.	Bolivia, Peru and Honduras rejoin the League of Nations Assembly.	

A	B	C	D	E
Includes developments that affect more than one world region, international organizations and important meetings of world leaders.	*Includes all domestic and regional developments in Europe, including the Soviet Union.*	*Includes all domestic and regional developments in Africa and the Middle East.*	*Includes all domestic and regional developments in Latin America, the Caribbean, and Canada.*	*Includes all domestic and regional developments in Asian and Pacific nations (and colonies).*

U.S. Politics & Social Issues	U.S. Foreign Policy & Affairs, Defense	U.S. Economy & Environment	Science, Technology & Nature	Culture, Leisure & Lifestyle	
Three more jurors are added to the jury for the trial the Gastonia strikers tried for the murder of O. F. Aderholt, Chief of Police of Gastonia.			The *Graf Zeppelin* returns to Lakehurst, New Jersey, after 21 days four hours, a new world record.		**Aug. 29**
The Veterans of Foreign Wars of the United States demands a national referendum for the repeal or the retention of Prohibition.		Postmaster General Brown considers increasing the first class mail rate.	At least 70 people die when the steamship *San Juan* collides with the Standard Oil tanker *S.C.T. Dodd* and sinks 18 miles off the coast of San Francisco.	Sir George Hubert Wilkins, Australian explorer who completed the round-the-world voyage with the dirigible *Graf Zeppelin*, marries actress Suzanna Bennett in Cleveland, Ohio....Transatlantic pilot Clarence D. Chamberlin wins the 10-lap, 50-mile competition for civilians at the national air races in Cleveland.	**Aug. 30**
Tennessee Governor Henry H. Horton appoints newspaper publisher Colonel Luke Lea senator for the state. Lea replaces the late Lawrence D. Tyson.		A torrent of water sweeps away the Colorado College settlement when the dam at Colorado Springs breaks.		Aviator Thomas D. Reid establishes a new world record in solo flying as he flies for thirty-nine hours. However, two hours later, he crashes in a tree and dies near Cleveland.	**Aug. 31**
	Senator Wagner, member of the Foreign Relations Committee, condemns the murders of Jews in the Wailing Wall area of Jerusalem as premeditated.	Nicholas Butler, president of Columbia University and of the Carnegie Endowment for International Peace, attacks the Tariff Bill as a threat to world peace.	Maddux Air begins the first direct aerial passenger service from San Francisco to New York.	Lieutenant James H. Doolittle, army air racing star, has to use a parachute for the first time in his long career and lands unhurt about five miles from Cleveland Municipal Airport.	**Sep. 1**
		Senate Finance Committee Chairman Smoot defends the changes made by his commission to the Tariff Bill....The New York, Rio and Buenos Aires Line closes a contract to carry 70 percent of all the mail from South American countries to the United States.	The Bull Line steamer *Dorothy* sinks in the Chesapeake Bay after a collision with the American steamship *Eurana*.		**Sep. 2**
A second panel of 300 is examined without completing the selection of the jury at the Gastonia trial of 16 strikers accused of murdering Chief of Police O. F. Aderholt....The administrative committee of the Zionist Organization of America thanks President Hoover for his statement on Palestine situation....Senator Borah announces his intention to run again for the Senate when his term expires. His campaign will be based on increased farm rates and reduced rates on the industrial schedules of the Tariff Bill.	George T. Summerlin is appointed Minister to Venezuela.	Progressive Republicans led by Senator Borah meet to discuss how to oppose the Tariff Bill.	U.S. western states face serious fires due to drought and high temperatures.	Circus owner John T. Ringling refuses to renew his annual Spring lease for the Garden.	**Sep. 3**
New York Governor Roosevelt announces a parley with crime experts and penologists on the conditions of prisons.	President Hoover confers at the White House with the Secretaries of state and of the Navy to discuss the progress in the Anglo-American informal talks on naval reduction.	To oppose the new Tariff Bill, Democrats and Progressive Republican Senators announce their intention of disclosing the business secrets of corporations seeking increased tariff protection....The Dow Jones industrial average marks the peak of the bull market of the 1920s.	The United States are struck by a heat wave which causes extremely high temperature throughout the nation....The City of San Francisco, a transcontinental air transport passenger plane, is struck by lightning and crashes, killing eight people.	King of golf Bobby Jones is defeated by 20-year-old Omaha golfer Johnny Goodman in the opening round of the golf championship in Del Monte, California.	**Sep. 4**

F	G	H	I	J
Includes campaigns, elections, federal-state relations, civil rights and liberties, crime, the judiciary, education, healthcare, poverty, urban affairs, and population.	*Includes formation and debate of U.S. foreign and defense policies, veterans affairs, and defense spending. (Relations with specific foreign countries are usually found under the region concerned.)*	*Includes business, labor, agriculture, taxation, transportation, consumer affairs, monetary and fiscal policy, natural resources, pollution and industrial accidents.*	*Includes worldwide scientific, medical and technological developments, natural phenomena, U.S. weather and natural disasters.*	*Includes the arts, religion, scholarship, communications media, sports, entertainment, fashions, fads, and social life.*

	World Affairs	Europe	Africa & The Middle East	The Americas	Asia & The Pacific
Sep. 5	French Premier Briand addresses the League of Nations assembly stating that France will accept the optional clause for compulsory jurisdiction of the World Court. Briand also proposes a European Federal Union to facilitate economic and political policies. This proposal is discussed in depth but little action is taken to implement it.	The British proposal for naval reduction fails to eliminate the disparity in cruisers between the British and the American fleets.	British troops cease raids against Muslim towns in Palestine. The situation remains tense. Jews accuse the government of inefficiency in handling the riots.		
Sep. 6	France, Italy, Belgium, Denmark and Chile join the British proposal to change the League of Nations covenant....British Foreign Minister Arthur Henderson reassures the League of Nations that disorders in Palestine are under control.	The reactionary German Officers' League criticizes the intention of the Nobel Prize committee to award the literature prize to Erich Maria Remarque for "All Quiet on the Western Front."...Princess Charlotte of Monaco tries to mediate to reach a settlement between her father and the citizens of Monaco who demands the republic to be established.	Seventeen Nationalist Party candidates and fifteen South African Party candidates are elected in the Senate elections.	Paraguay accepts resuming diplomatic relations with Bolivia but voices reservations in accepting the arbitration of the Chaco dispute.	
Sep. 7		One hundred and thirty people, most of them school children, drown in Lake Nasijarvi, near Tammerfors, Finland....Italian Premier Mussolini changes several important officers in the Italian navy....World-famous conductor Arturo Toscanini resigns as the artistic director of the prestigious Italian theater La Scala.	An Imperial Airways air mail liner en route from London to India crashes in flames while landing in Persia.	Argentina protests against the U.S. intention to increase the tariff on flaxseed.	
Sep. 8			Tension mounts again in Jerusalem due to the stabbing of a Jewish youth while he is going to the Wailing Wall.	Mexico's Budget Commission presents the budget for the 1930 fiscal year. A surplus of $3 million is forecast with cuts in most departments except for the funds for the education and roads....Both Bolivia and Paraguay are eager to resume diplomatic relations but they make reservations about accepting arbitration for the Chaco dispute. Neither Bolivia nor Paraguay will accept a tribunal of arbitration formed by their Latin American neighbors.	Russian infantry raids and bombs towns in Manchuria....The number of deaths in the Philippines due to a strong typhoon mount daily.
Sep. 9	German Foreign Minister Gustav Stresemann addresses the League of Nations assembly, stating that Germany will be eager to cooperate with its former enemies. Italian Senator Scialoja accepts the optional clause for compulsory jurisdiction of the World Court.	French Premier Briand gives a luncheon for the 27 heads of the European delegations to the League of Nations. He says that the event represents the establishment of the cornerstone for a European federation.	Clashes continue in Palestine between Jews and Arabs.	Theodore Roosevelt, Jr. is appointed Governor of Puerto Rico.	Simultaneous attacks by Russians are reported against Manchurian towns. Chinese brings in reinforcements....Manuel Quezon, President of the Philippine Senate, announces he will soon retire from public life....Herbert Marler, the first Canadian Minister to Japan, arrives in Tokyo.
Sep. 10	The congress of Agudath Israel, the world organization of orthodox Jews, opens in Vienna.	Britain asks the Soviet Union to fix a date for a diplomatic parley where the two countries could discuss the resumption of diplomatic relations.		A period of prolonged drought causes damages to Argentine crops.	Russian planes bombs Manchurian towns and villages spreading terror....The attempt by the Australian government to abolish federal compulsory arbitration fails.
Sep. 11		Twenty German Fascists allegedly involved in terrorist attacks are arrested in Berlin.			Soviet troops make significant advances along the Manchurian border. Chinese officials concede defeat and set up a new defense line.

A	B	C	D	E
Includes developments that affect more than one world region, international organizations and important meetings of world leaders.	Includes all domestic and regional developments in Europe, including the Soviet Union.	Includes all domestic and regional developments in Africa and the Middle East.	Includes all domestic and regional developments in Latin America, the Caribbean, and Canada.	Includes all domestic and regional developments in Asian and Pacific nations (and colonies).

U.S. Politics & Social Issues	U.S. Foreign Policy & Affairs, Defense	U.S. Economy & Environment	Science, Technology & Nature	Culture, Leisure & Lifestyle	
President Hoover ends his summer vacation and goes back to Washington to speed the approval of the Tariff Bill.....Four witness for the State testify at the Gastonia strike trial. They assert that Chief of Police Aderholt was shot in the back and received 41 wounds.	Secretary of State Stimson accepts the Root formula for U.S. admission to the World Court.	After 19 days of progress, the Stock Market experiences a sharp decline. Experts begin to predict a big slump....The Department of Agriculture issues a formal warning to wheat growers that their contemplated acreage of winter wheat would result in the marketing of the crop on an export basis.		At the golf championship in Del Monte, California, champion Jess W. Sweetser is eliminated by H Chandler Egan, a veteran golfer who won the championship in 1904 and 1905....John D. Rockefeller announces the establishment of a permanent museum of modern art in New York to complement the Metropolitan.	Sep. 5
	President Hoover asks shipbuilding companies to deny the charge that they financed propaganda against naval reduction.	The stock market recovers the heavy losses experienced the previous day.	Wyoming and Nebraska are hit by violent snowstorms.	Oscar F. Willing and Harrison R. Johnston reach the golf final in Del Monte, California. Neither of them had reached the final before.	Sep. 6
The American Communist Party faces serious challenges from its militants on its pro-Arab stand in the Palestine crisis....In the trial against 16 Gastonia strikers, the State puts on four more witness with the aim of strengthening the contention that Chief of Police O. F. Aderholt was murdered by unprovoked strike guards.	Led by Borah, Senators plan an inquiry in the alleged propaganda against naval reduction orchestrated by shipbuilding companies. Washington prepares a counter-proposal for naval reduction to the one sent by the British.	The Department of Commerce reports that car exports for July 1929 show a sharp increase compared with July 1928.	Torrential rains cause floods and serious property damage in New Orleans.	Harrison R. Johnston wins the National Amateur Golf Title in Del Monte, California....British officer and flier Henry R.D. Waghorn wins the Schneider trophy in Calshot, England, and establishes a new world speed record.	Sep. 7
Professor John Dewey of Columbia University announces he will be the chairman of the League for Independent Political Action which aims to establish a new political party in addition to the Republican and Democratic Parties....The Citizens' Union, a group which has repeatedly criticizes the policies of Tammany Hall, state that they will not support Fiorello LaGuardia in his run for New York mayor.		Twelve farm groups ask that the tariffs on agricultural products should be higher than those in the Tariff Bill.		Ethel McGary retains her A.A.U. senior long-distance title, successfully defending it at the Biltmore Shores Yacht Club in Great South Bay, Massapequa.	Sep. 8
President Hoover nominates several district judges....When papers announce that the 16 Gastonia strikers may be acquitted, an anti-Communist mob raids the offices of the National Textile Workers' Union in Charlotte and kidnaps three unionists....Patrolman Walter Lowe kills an African-American student, Ralph Baker, after they argue over a seat in an elevated train.	The U.S. Navy denies having taken an active part in promoting propaganda against naval reductions.	The Senate starts the debate on the Tariff Bill. Senate Finance Committee chairman Smoot accuses the Democratic-Progressive Republican coalition to try filibustering on the bill.		Circus owner John Ringling purchases five more competing circuses of the American Circus Corporation.	Sep. 9
Five members of the National Law Enforcement Commission appointed by President Hoover gathers data in New York on the failure to enforce Prohibition....The three kidnapped members of the National Textile Workers' Union return home. One of them is badly bruised from lashes inflicted by captors.	President Hoover declares he is determined to bring to light the forces behind the propaganda against naval reductions.	The Senate adopts the Simmons resolution authorizing the revealing of corporation income tax facts for tariff-making purposes.		Squadron Leader Augustus H. Orlebar smashes all world speed records flying at 355 miles per hour at Calshot, England.	Sep. 10
Former Police Commissioner Richard E. Enright announces his intention to run for New York Mayor for the newly organized Square Deal Movement....The vote for the expulsion of Senator Vare is deferred until the December session.	The Senate orders immediate inquiry in the allegations that the Navy and shipbuilding companies have made active propaganda against naval reductions....President Hoover confers with the Secretaries of State and of Navy to reply to Britain's latest offer on naval reductions.			Charles A. Lindbergh sets a new speed record flying from St. Louis to New York.	Sep. 11

F	G	H	I	J
Includes campaigns, elections, federal-state relations, civil rights and liberties, crime, the judiciary, education, healthcare, poverty, urban affairs, and population.	*Includes formation and debate of U.S. foreign and defense policies, veterans affairs, and defense spending. (Relations with specific foreign countries are usually found under the region concerned.)*	*Includes business, labor, agriculture, taxation, transportation, consumer affairs, monetary and fiscal policy, natural resources, pollution and industrial accidents.*	*Includes worldwide scientific, medical and technological developments, natural phenomena, U.S. weather and natural disasters.*	*Includes the arts, religion, scholarship, communications media, sports, entertainment, fashions, fads, and social life.*

	World Affairs	Europe	Africa & The Middle East	The Americas	Asia & The Pacific
Sep. 12	Jackson E. Reynolds, president of the First National Bank of New York, and Melvin A. Taylor, president of the First National Bank of Chicago, are selected as the two Americans to sit on the subcommittee to devise the statutes of the Bank of International Settlements.	Italian dictator Benito Mussolini reorganizes his Cabinet, appointing nine new ministers....British Premier MacDonald announces that he will sail for the United States on September 28th. The announcement is interpreted as evidence that a naval limitation agreement between Britain and the United States is in sight....Princess Charlotte's mediation averts the crisis between the Royal Family and the citizens of Monaco.	Police raid the offices of Jerusalem's Hebrew daily Doar Hayom, owned by an American citizen. The daily had published a poem inciting to violence.	A state of siege is declared in Paraguay following a campaign against the government by opposition newspapers....President Chacon suspends some constitutional guarantees in Guatemala.	Fighting between Chinese and Russians resumes at Pogranichnaya and Manchuli along the Manchurian border.
Sep. 13	The European countries represented in the League of Nations work to draw a pact of economic solidarity between them for the free circulation of capital, raw materials, commodities and people. The pact would be open to non-European countries on the basis of reciprocity.	Monaco Prince Louis accepts the requests of his citizens thanks to the intervention of his adopted daughter Charlotte.	In spite of negative predictions, the Muslim Sabbath passes quietly in Jerusalem.	The state of siege declared in Paraguay is aimed against Communist agitators and will make it easier to deport them.	The Nanking government refuses to appoint a new Chinese Eastern Railway manager as asked by Russia to settle the dispute which is causing heavy fighting in Manchuria.
Sep. 14	The League assembly takes the final step for American admission to the World Court by unanimously accepting the Root protocol....The Irish Free State accepts the optional clause for compulsory jurisdiction of the World Court.	British troops begin the evacuation of the Rhineland region....The Polish parties represented in the Lower House refuse to meet the government and attend the budget conference. They urge the President to call a parliamentary session immediately....Spain and France sign a treaty for the development of waterpower in Andorra. The project is the first step to turn the small Pyrenees republic into a modern state.	Twenty-four Arabs are arrested for stealing from the Hulda Jewish labor settlement.		Former Afghan King Amanullah and his Queen Souriya convert to Catholicism....The Chinese refusal to appoint a new general manager for the Chinese Eastern Railway angers Russians who threatens new attacks in Manchuria.
Sep. 15		Italy celebrates the twenty-fifth birthday of Prince Humbert of Piedmont, heir to the Italian throne....Britain begins to withdraw from active service several cruisers in preparation for a treaty agreement with the United States for naval disarmament....Italian dictator Benito Mussolini moves his offices in Venezia Palace.	After three weeks the curfew in Jerusalem is shortened.	Mexico holds imposing celebrations for the 119th anniversary of its independence.	A crowd of 150,000 people watch the arrival of the corpse of Jatindranath Das in Calcutta. Das died in prison after a 61-day hunger strike against the British domination.
Sep. 16	Britain asks the Preparation Committee for the international naval parley to reconsider the exclusion of trained reserves and war supplies from the discussion.	France denies that its troops will replace the British ones in the Rhineland region.		Bolivia and Paraguay resume diplomatic relations but the Chaco territorial dispute keeps the situation between the two countries tense.	
Sep. 17	Japanese Minister to the Navy Kyo Takarabe demands that Britain and the United States reduce the high standards they set for naval parity.	Labor peer Lord Arnold will accompany British Premier MacDonald during its American visit....Austrian Fascist leaders state that their movement, the Heimwehr, will never compromise with the Socialist Party, thus renewing threats of a civil war.	Forty-five Jews arrested in Haifa are charged with premeditated or attempted murder with no bail in connection with the recent clashes with Arabs.	Nicaraguan President Moncada expresses his thanks to the United States for helping to keep his country free.	The Chinese government bans three Japanese newspapers to use the mails....Russia rejects the Chinese offer to appoint a Russian assistant to the general manager of the Chinese Eastern Railway to settle the dispute between the two countries.
Sep. 18		British Premier MacDonald sees the King to discuss his future visit to the United States....France regards with suspicion the Anglo-American agreement on naval reductions fearing a plot against France....The Fascist Party, Heimwehr, demands the resignation of the Austrian government and its replacement with one which includes Fascist leaders.	Arab groups opposed to the Palestinian Grand Mufti, Hadj Amin-el-Hussein, blame him for the recent violent clashes between Arabs and Jews in the region.	The presidential candidate of the Anti-Re-electionist Party, José Vasconcelos, is shot at while campaigning, but is uninjured....Bolivia and Paraguay reply to the American governments which have proposed arbitration for the Chaco dispute.	

A	B	C	D	E
Includes developments that affect more than one world region, international organizations and important meetings of world leaders.	*Includes all domestic and regional developments in Europe, including the Soviet Union.*	*Includes all domestic and regional developments in Africa and the Middle East.*	*Includes all domestic and regional developments in Latin America, the Caribbean, and Canada.*	*Includes all domestic and regional developments in Asian and Pacific nations (and colonies).*

U.S. Politics & Social Issues	U.S. Foreign Policy & Affairs, Defense	U.S. Economy & Environment	Science, Technology & Nature	Culture, Leisure & Lifestyle	
Fourteen men are arrested in Charlotte in connection with anti-Communist violence....The New Orleans streetcar strike enters its tenth week.	The Department of Commerce shows that German borrowings in the United States have largely contributed to the funds used by Germany to pay its war reparations under the Versailles Treaty.	Democratic Senator Simmons charges that the Tariff Bill constitutes a virtual embargo against foreign products.		For the first time since 1924, four American tennis player reach the semi-finals in the men's national championship at the West Side Tennis Club in Forest Hills, NY	Sep. 12
Eight strike leaders are arrested in Gastonia and charged with conspiracy to revolt against the government of North Carolina....The interdepartmental committee named by the President to study the ocean mail situation, recommends that the Postmaster General rejects all pending bids for ocean mail contracts until Congress amends the Merchant Marine Act of 1928.	U.S. government reaches a formal agreement with Britain to call a formal disarmament conference for December. In addition to the United States and Britain, Italy, France, and Japan are invited to take part.	The Niagara Hudson Power Corporation, owned by J.P. Morgan and associates, purchases the Frontier Corporation. Through this purchase the Morgan conglomerate gets control of nearly every important waterpower site in new York State....Democrats and Progressive Republicans strongly attack the tariff Bill in the Senate debate.	The world's largest land plane, built by Anthony H.G. Fokker to carry thirty passengers and a crew of four, takes air for the first time.	William Tilden and Francis T. Hunter wins the semi-finals in the men's national championship at the West Side Tennis Club in Forest Hills.	Sep. 13
Attorney General Mitchell rejects the petition for pardon filed by oil magnate Harry F. Sinclair and his aid Harry Mason Day....Textile worker Ella May Wiggins is shot in Gastonia by anti-Communist demonstrators on her way to a rally of the National Textile Workers' Union.		Democratic Senator Walsh attacks as "ominous" the acquisition of more power resources in New York State by the Morgan interests....Jouett Shouse, chairman of the executive committee of the Democratic National Committee, attacks the Tariff Bill as an unnecessary "monstrosity."		William T. Tilden defeats Francis Hunter in five sets in the final of the men's national championship at the West Side Tennis Club in Forest Hills. He wins his seventh United States championship....Philadelphia Athletics win the American League pennant for the seventh time in their history and the first in 15 years.	Sep. 14
Seven men are charged with the murder of textile worker Ella May Wiggins in Gastonia....New York Board of Transportation announces plans to build more subway lines.	The United States offers the service of Maj. Gen. Frank McCoy for a further study of the Bolivian-Paraguayan territorial dispute in Chaco.	Three Republican senators from the Northern Pacific coast threaten to vote against the Tariff Bill unless it includes a duty on shingles and lumber....Governor Roosevelt states he is firmly against the private development of the St. Lawrence River hydroelectric power by the Morgan interests. He contends that the State must be the agency to use those water-power sites.			Sep. 15
	President Hoover selects Harry F. Guggenheim as the new American ambassador to Cuba.	Senator Borah criticizes the Tariff Bill as unfair to agriculture and as a violation of Hoover's pledges during his Presidential campaign.			Sep. 16
Representative Fiorello LaGuardia wins the New York primary election for the Mayoralty nomination. He has a lead of more than 38,000 votes over former State Senator William M. Bennett.... African Americans erect a shaft in Wonderland Park, Baltimore, with photographs of President Hoover and Representative Oscar de Priest to celebrate the progress of the race.		New York Transit Commission dismisses the Interborough Rapid Transit Company's application for a 10-cent fare on its elevated lines....The Niagara Hudson Power Corporation expresses its willingness to cooperate with the State or other public authorities in the development of water power on the St. Lawrence.		German writers Thomas Mann is rumored to be the favorite for the Literature Nobel Prize.	Sep. 17
The Square Deal Party nominates Richard E. Enright, former Police Commissioner, as candidate for New York Mayor....Anti-Communist violence continues in Gastonia.	In a radio address to the nation, President Hoover discusses the negotiations for naval reductions undertaken by the United States and Britain. The negotiations will preserve national defenses and, at the same time, "relive the world from the hate and fear which flow from the rivalry in building warships."	Republicans call a general caucus of Senators to determine the party's strategy in the future consideration of the Tariff Bill....American Telephone and Telegraph shares soar 14 points above the previous day's closing price.		Charles Lindbergh starts a 10,000 mile flight to the West Indies and to Central and South America.... Chicago Cubs are the new champions of the National League and will meet the Athletics in the next world's series in October.	Sep. 18

F	G	H	I	J
Includes campaigns, elections, federal-state relations, civil rights and liberties, crime, the judiciary, education, healthcare, poverty, urban affairs, and population.	Includes formation and debate of U.S. foreign and defense policies, veterans affairs, and defense spending. (Relations with specific foreign countries are usually found under the region concerned.)	Includes business, labor, agriculture, taxation, transportation, consumer affairs, monetary and fiscal policy, natural resources, pollution and industrial accidents.	Includes worldwide scientific, medical and technological developments, natural phenomena, U.S. weather and natural disasters.	Includes the arts, religion, scholarship, communications media, sports, entertainment, fashions, fads, and social life.

	World Affairs	Europe	Africa & The Middle East	The Americas	Asia & The Pacific
Sep. 19	France, Italy and Japan state they are against discussing again the topic of land force reduction, as proposed by Britain.	Britain recommends the admission of Iraq into the League of Nations and announces it will give up its mandate for Iraq....Vienna is completely deserted as rumors of a Fascist putsch spread throughout the city.	Palestine courts begin trying Arabs for the recent attacks against Jews.	Latin-American countries represented at the League of Nations decide to act in a spirit of continental collaboration when dealing with questions of common interest.	
Sep. 20		Clarence C. Hatry is arrested in Britain following the complete collapse of his companies on the London Stock Exchange....The Austrian government announces it will introduce a bill proposing fundamental constitutional changes. This is interpreted as a concession to Fascist leaders.		The Nicaraguan government appoints Tomas Soley Guell as its representative to the commission which will meet in Washington to discuss the country's financial situation....Mexico is hit by violent storms both on the Pacific and Gulf coasts....The governments of Bolivia and Paraguay face strong domestic opposition for their decision to resume diplomatic relations.	The Japanese Cabinet sends general instructions to its ambassadors in London and Washington on how to behave in the preliminary negotiations for the planned five-power parley on naval reduction.
Sep. 21		After the long dispute with the American film industry, French theater owners start to show American sound pictures which become the newest craze in Paris.		American businessmen in Cuba defend President Machado against charges of a reign of terror....Three men are killed and three are seriously wounded in a riot in Mexico City between supporters of rival candidates for the November presidential election.	Fighting between China and the Soviet Union resumes along the Manchurian border....Chinese Nationalist President Chiang Kai-shek gives formal orders to General Liu Shih to attack the reactionary forces of General Chang Fa-kwei.
Sep. 22		Communist and Nazi factions clash in Berlin during demonstrations against war reparations treaties....The Turkish region of Eastern Anatolia is hit by a violent earthquake.	Jews abandon rituals for the dead in the recent disorders in Palestine not to arouse Muslim fanatics. This is viewed as evidence that the situation remains tense.		Fighting continues along the Manchurian border between Chinese and Russian troops. Russians repulse Chinese attacks....The second election campaign in a year starts in Australia. The main topic of the election is the government's decision to abolish the Federal Arbitration Court and turn arbitration jurisdiction over to the States. The Labor Party opposes this solution and demands Commonwealth jurisdiction.
Sep. 23	A resolution for a close cooperation between the League of Nations and the proposed International Bank for Settlements is withdrawn.	Czech President Masaryk authorizes Premier Udrzal to dissolve Parliament and hold a general election in October if his coalition of five parties cannot reach an agreement.	The Palestine government aims to have quick trials of those involved in the recent riots and encourages refugees from Arab villages to return to their homes.		Nationalist troops advance in the Yangtsze Valley against the forces of General Chang Fa-kwei which are forced to move southward.
Sep. 24		Forty-five people die in the derailment of a trans-Siberian mail train....The French government is against drastically reducing the country's navy as it fears this will weaken its international position....The French Cinema Control Commission unanimously ratifies the Franco-American motion picture agreement....Britain and Russia resume talks for re-establishing diplomatic relations.		One hundred and thirty people are killed and several hundred are wounded in Vera Cruz in riots connected with the municipal elections.	General Ho Ying-ching, one of the most powerful supporters of Chiang Kai-shek's Nationalist government, resigns all his official positions linking him with the government. This is an important defection for the Nationalist government which is also defeated by General Chang Fa-kwei rebel forces.
Sep. 25	The tenth assembly of the League of Nations ends. Its President Gustavo Guerrero of Salvador stresses that the work of the League is the fight against the "most cruel of man's enemies," war" and argues that the League budget is insignificant when compared to the expenditure for battleships.	The Soviet government introduces the non-stop four-day working week....The Austrian government led by Streeruwitz resigns and former Chancellor and Police President of Vienna, Johann Schober, is asked to form a new ministry.	Ibn Saud, ruler of Nejd and the Hedjaz, sends a punitive expedition against 60 rebel tribesmen who are all killed.	Mexican Minister of Industry, Commerce and Labor Ramon P. de Negri argues that the State should take over industries closed down for lack of profit.	Nationalist troops defeat the rebels of General Chang Fa-kwei....The Russian government sends a firm warning to China that the Red Army will act decisively against any further raid on the Russian population along the Manchurian border.

A	B	C	D	E
Includes developments that affect more than one world region, international organizations and important meetings of world leaders.	Includes all domestic and regional developments in Europe, including the Soviet Union.	Includes all domestic and regional developments in Africa and the Middle East.	Includes all domestic and regional developments in Latin America, the Caribbean, and Canada.	Includes all domestic and regional developments in Asian and Pacific nations (and colonies).

U.S. Politics & Social Issues	U.S. Foreign Policy & Affairs, Defense	U.S. Economy & Environment	Science, Technology & Nature	Culture, Leisure & Lifestyle	
Kentucky Governor Flem D. Sampson is indicted of unlawfully and knowingly receiving a gift from a textbook publishing company while he was a member of the State Textbook Commission.	The Senate asks for a commission of investigation on the political and economic conditions in Cuba as President Machado is accused of spreading terror.	The National City Bank announces a merger with the Corn exchange Bank Trust Company which will make it the largest bank in the world.		Representatives of the French and American film industries sign an agreement ending a two-year dispute.	Sep. 19
In a letter read before the International Convention of the Woman's Christian Temperance Union, President Hoover places upon the individual citizen responsibility the successful enforcement of Prohibition law....New York Mayor Walker poses in front of cameras at Fox Studios, using "talkies" technology for his political campaign....18 people die and 47 are seriously injured when a fire breaks out in the Study Club, one of Detroit's leading cabarets and night clubs.....Fiorello LaGuardia accepts nomination as the Republican candidate for New York Mayor. He pledges to reorganize city government to eliminate useless jobs and to solve the rapid transit problem.	In the Senate inquiry on the alleged propaganda against navel disarmament, Clinton Bardo, president of the New York Shipbuilding Company, denies that his company worked for the failure of the naval disarmament conference at Geneva in 1927.	Secretary of State Stimson informs Italy, France and Japan on the progresses for the organization of the international naval reduction parley.	Severe earthquakes occur around the base of the Hualalai volcano on the island of Hawaii. Inhabitants of the island fear a sudden eruption.		Sep. 20
Republican Senator Howell declares that Washington id the city where Prohibition enforcement could be the most efficient as city officials are appointed by the president.... Fifteen people are injured at the car races at the close of the annual Mineola Fair.	At the Senate hearings on the alleged propaganda against naval reductions, Charles Schwab, chairman of the Bethlehem Steel Company, states he supports the idea of a smaller U.S. Navy.			Charles Lindbergh continues his 10,000-mile flight and reaches Puerto Rico.	Sep. 21
Replying to Senator Howell, President Hoover promises to make Washington a model city for Prohibition enforcement....Oil magnate Harry F. Sinclair says he is not discouraged by the rejection of his petition for clemency by the president.	Senator Borah, chairman of the Senate Foreign Relations Committee and sponsor of the enquiry into the alleged propaganda against naval disarmament, announces a second resolution for the investigation of lobbying activities in Congress in connection with the Jones-White Merchant Marine Act.	Fourteen Republican senator representing farm interests ask higher farm rates and reduced industrial duties and threaten to vote against the Tariff Bill if their requests are not taken into account.		Charles Lindbergh reaches Trinidad, where he is welcomed by a huge crowd.	Sep. 22
Senator Shortridge, chairman of the Senate committee investigating propaganda against naval reduction, declares he is in favor of a separate investigation on all lobbying activities in Washington.			Fifty-eight earthquake shocks are felt near the extinct volcano of Hualalai on the Hawaii island. Residents evacuate the area fearing an eruption.	Major John Coolidge, son of former U.S. President Calvin Coolidge, marries Florence Trumbull, daughter of Connecticut Governor John Trumbull in Plainville, Connecticut....Charles Lindbergh arrives in Dutch Guiana, ending his 10,000-mile flight.	Sep. 23
Gutzon Borglum, former sculptor for the Stone Mountain Confederate memorial, is indicted for malicious mischief and larceny for the destruction of his models for the monument in 1925....Senator Brookhart supports Senator Howell's allegations on illegal drinking in Washington when he declares to have attended a function for newly elected and old Senators where liquor was served.		After a promising beginning, the stock market takes a sharp downturn and many issues close with severe losses....Treasury experts begin to work on a tax-reduction program to submit to Congress when it convenes again in December....President Hoover breaks his silence on the Tariff Bill, stating he is in favor of retaining the authority given to the President of increasing or decreasing a tariff rate up to 50 percent.	U.S. Army pilot Lieutenant James H. Doolittle guides a Consolidated NY2 Biplane over Mitchell Field in New York in the first all-instrument flight....Earthquakes in Hawaii spread throughout the island and increasingly grow in intensity.		Sep. 24
Thousand policemen are sent into Chicago's South Side district to prevent rioting after an African American religious leader and a detective are killed.		Democrats and Progressive Republicans accuse Bingham to have hired an industrial lobbyist to draft the Tariff Bill....As the Stock Market experiences a drastic decline, bankers issue unlimited buying orders for pivotal issues, thus sending stocks upward.	British Commander Sir Charles Burney makes known his plans to build a large airship to carry 400 passengers....Southeastern Florida residents take precautions against the possible arrival of a hurricane.	Mrs. Herbert Hoover officially opens a loan exhibition of antique furniture, paintings and art objects held in New York for the benefit of the National Council of Girl Scouts.... The baseball league games are suspended for the death of Miller J. Huggins, manager of the New York Yankees for 12 seasons.	Sep. 25

F	G	H	I	J
Includes campaigns, elections, federal-state relations, civil rights and liberties, crime, the judiciary, education, healthcare, poverty, urban affairs, and population.	Includes formation and debate of U.S. foreign and defense policies, veterans affairs, and defense spending. (Relations with specific foreign countries are usually found under the region concerned.)	Includes business, labor, agriculture, taxation, transportation, consumer affairs, monetary and fiscal policy, natural resources, pollution and industrial accidents.	Includes worldwide scientific, medical and technological developments, natural phenomena, U.S. weather and natural disasters.	Includes the arts, religion, scholarship, communications media, sports, entertainment, fashions, fads, and social life.

	World Affairs	Europe	Africa & The Middle East	The Americas	Asia & The Pacific
Sep. 26	The World Zionist Organization splints into two factions over the recent riots in Palestine. A more radical group, led by Vladimir Jabotinsky, establishes a different organization attacking the moderate policy of Chaim Weizmann.	The Bulgarian and the Serb-Croat-Slovene governments sign an agreement to establish improved border safety and prevent border raids by Macedonian revolutionaries....The Bank of England raises its discount rate from 5.5 percent to 6.5 percent....The French government increases its naval budget for 1930. More than half of its total will be allocated for new constructions....Contrary to all predictions, the new Austrian Cabinets does not include leaders of the Fascist movement, Heimwehr.			Former Minister of Japanese Railways Heikichi Ogawa is indicted and imprisoned for bribery....Several members of the Central Executive Committee of the Kuomintang sign a manifesto demanding the dismissal of Chiang Kai-shek as party leader.
Sep. 27		The Spanish government fines a Barcelona Business House for refusing to enter into commerce with the Italian Chamber of Commerce because of the Italian political regime....The British and the Russian governments reach an agreement to resume diplomatic relations.... Former head of Mussolini's Press Bureau, Cesare Rossi, is condemned to thirty years imprisonment for anti-Fascist propaganda.		More American interests praise the Cuban government of President Machado....The Paraguayan government faces strong opposition for what it is generally considered a defeat before the Chaco Conciliation Committee at Washington.	The Japanese Cabinet accepts the invitation to take part to the 5-power naval parley....The American Red Cross decides against entering upon famine relief in China.
Sep. 28	Fifty nations sign the protocol for American entry into the World Court. Only three more signatories are necessary for final acceptance of the United States into the court.	British Prime Minister MacDonald begins his visit to the United States....Sir William Waterlow is appointed Lord Mayor of London....Austrian police breaks up a Communist meeting in Vienna and confiscates their newspaper.... France announces it will award former U.S. Secretary of State Frank Kellogg the Grand Cross of the Legion of Honor for his achievements for world peace.			The Chinese Nationalist government states that the troops of General Chang Fa-kwei have faced a disastrous defeat at the hands of government troops.
Sep. 29		After 37 days of continuous drought, rain falls over wide areas in Southern and Western England....British political circles hopes that Premier MacDonald and President Hoover will discuss the issue of the freedom of the seas when they meet in Washington....28,000 members of the Austrian Fascist movement, Heimwehr, parades through Vienna, but no clashes with leftists occur.		The Argentine Senate rejects a bill already approved by the lower House to nationalize petroleum lands.	Former Japanese Premier Baron Giichi Tanaka dies of a heart attack. This leaves the Seiyukai Party without leaders as vice president Ogawa is imprisoned on a charge of corruption....Japanese Empress Nagako gives birth to a third daughter. The Royal Household is disappointed as it had wished the birth of a Crown Prince.
Sep. 30		London's police force celebrates its 100th anniversary....The twenty-ninth conference of the British Labor Party begins in Brighton.			
Oct. 1		Russia and Britain complete the first draft terms for reestablishing diplomatic relations. Propaganda is prohibited....Prince Louis of Monaco averts a revolution by agreeing to citizen representation on the privy council and administrative and financial reforms. He also agrees to let Monaco residents work in the casinos.	Tensions seem to be easing as Palestine's Arab executive calls off a scheduled general strike. However, rumors persist of gun smuggling after recent Arab-Jewish riots....Rhodesia and South Africa announce that their trade union will dissolve on December 31.	The League agrees to help Bolivia improve its sanitation system to control malaria and typhus. The Rockefeller Foundation last year rejected Bolivia's request.	
Oct. 2	The 1928 Brussels Agreement on code words in cable and telegrams goes into effect upon ratification by 31 nations.	After 20 years of negotiation, Scotland's two Presbyterian churches end the separation that began in 1843. A small segment of the Free Church membership, the Wee Frees, rejects unification.	Unpopular with King Fuad and the nationalists, Mahmoud Pasha resigns as Egypt's premier. The dictator's resignation paves the way for renewed parliamentary government under the Wafd Party.	Colombia challenges Honduras' 1928 claim to the Roncador and Quitasuena Keys. Colombia asserts that its century old claim of sovereignty over the islands has never before been challenged by Honduras....The United States and four other nations offer to mediate the Chaco dispute. Bolivia and Paraguay both claim the region.	Russian Communists renew ground and air attacks in Manchuria. Japan is the beneficiary of the Russo-Chinese dispute over the Chinese Eastern Railway, which shuts down traffic to Vladivostok.

A	B	C	D	E
Includes developments that affect more than one world region, international organizations and important meetings of world leaders.	Includes all domestic and regional developments in Europe, including the Soviet Union.	Includes all domestic and regional developments in Africa and the Middle East.	Includes all domestic and regional developments in Latin America, the Caribbean, and Canada.	Includes all domestic and regional developments in Asian and Pacific nations (and colonies).

U.S. Politics & Social Issues	U.S. Foreign Policy & Affairs, Defense	U.S. Economy & Environment	Science, Technology & Nature	Culture, Leisure & Lifestyle	
28,000 low-paid New York City workers win an average increase from $100 to $240 a month....For the first time in the history of the House of Representatives, a woman, Edith Nourse Rogers, presides a session.	Drew Pearson, an American newspaper correspondent, testifies before the Senate Naval Affairs Committee that members of staff of naval experts attached to the American delegation helped to bring about the failure of the Three-Power Disarmament Conference at Geneva in 1927.	Senator Borah challenges President Hoover to give his opinion on the rates on industrial products contained in the Tariff Bill.	The hurricane threatening the east coast of Florida swings toward Cuba.	U.S. Secretary of State Stimson invites only men at the dinner in honor of British Premier MacDonald. This represents a marked departure from tradition.	Sep. 26
The National Safety Congress reveals that an average of 91 persons a day were killed in the United States during the previous August, the highest average in the nation's history....President Hoover sends to the Senate the nomination of George A parks for a second term as governor of Alaska.	The Senate Naval Affairs Committee will call to testify members of staff of naval experts attached to the American delegation to evaluate their alleged role in bringing about the failure of the Three-Power Disarmament Conference at Geneva in 1927.	Senator Simmons introduces an amendment to the Tariff Bill to repeal the flexible clause, thus stripping the President of all powers to fix tariff rates. The Tariff Commission would also become a mere fact-finding body to assist Congress.	Nassau, Bahaman capital, is struck by a hurricane which then threatens Miami.	The football season of 1929 opens and most of the larger universities and colleges bring out their new teams.	Sep. 27
Several members of counsel for the State are against asking the death penalty for the 16 Gastonia strikers on trial for the murder of Chief of Police O. F. Aderholt. They would prefer a second degree murder charge.	President Hoover consults Senators Hale and Swanson on the international naval parley and the formation of the American delegation.	President Hoover is confident that the Farm Board that he has appointed will be confirmed by the Senate.	The tropical hurricane which struck Nassau in the Bahamas moves across the southern extremity of Florida....East Georgia towns are hit by heavy floods....More earthquakes take place in the Hawaii and cause damages in the city of Hilo.	General Director Giulio Gatti-Casazza announces that the 1929–30 season of the Metropolitan Opera will open on October 28th.	Sep. 28
North Carolina Governor O. Max Gardner argues in favor of higher wages and shorter hours for textile workers. He also pleads for a closer cooperation between capital, labor, and the state.		The eight Democratic members of the Senate Finance Committee issue a joint statement attacking the flexible provision in the Tariff Bill as striking at the roots of constitutional government.	The hurricanes which brought gales the Southeastern part of Florida moves northward threatening the mouth of the Mississippi River.	The "Thirty-two Club" emerges as the new leading club in Washington. Its membership includes Senators, cabinet members, and former government officials.	Sep. 29
Republican candidate for New York Mayor Fiorello La Guardia charges that Tammany Hall is guilty of "tax racketeering" on a huge scale. According to LaGuardia, improper tax reductions amounting to more than $75 million have been given to Tammany's friends.	William B. Shearer is examined by the Senate Naval Affairs subcommittee concerning his activities on behalf of three American shipbuilding companies during the Geneva disarmament conference of 1927.	Senators predict a slim margin for the vote on the flexible provisions of the Tariff Bill which enable the president to increase or decrease tariffs.	Car manufacturer Fritz von Opel makes the first manned rocket plane flight....The hurricane sweeping northwest from the Gulf of Mexico reaches Pensacola.	Several Ambassadors and diplomats at Washington appoint a single responsible member of staff for liquor after the charges of Senator Howell on the breaches of Prohibition in the capital.	Sep. 30
The Episcopal House of Bishops opens its annual meeting. Attendees, including missionaries from throughout the world, expect to deal with Jim Crow, brought to the fore by a Brooklyn minister's refusal to accept black congregants.		A report that September business failures are fewer indicates that insolvency is light for the year....Cuba Cane Sugar goes into receivership. The $110 million firm was unable to pay a $25 million obligation in July. Low sugar prices are its downfall....Candy makers announce a $3 million, three-year ad campaign.	The C.A. Coffin Association awards Samuel Insull's Chicago, South Shore, and South Bend as a leading electric railway. Before Insull rebuilt it the road was a "pile of junk."		Oct. 1
A textile strike to protest union busting in Marion, NC, turns violent. Three are dead, reportedly shot in the back.	Secretary Stimson announces that Costa Rica has become the 53rd nation to sign the pact against war. Of the 64 nations asked to sign, only two remain uncommitted—Argentina and Brazil....The Senate votes to remove Hoover's power to adjust tariff rates.	Ford denies rumors that it will shut down to change models. The company says sales are satisfactory and it has no plans to introduce new models.	Britain unveils the R-101 dirigible. Capable of 80 mph, the luxury liner has every amenity, including a dance floor and a smoking room.....After a Florida hurricane, gales batter the east coast from the Carolinas to New England, causing floods and grounding vessels. Three die.	Albert A. Capone claims he killed gambler Arnie Rothstein. Capone also claims to be the brother of "Scarface" Al Capone, currently serving time in a Pennsylvania prison. Police plan a sanity hearing.	Oct. 2

F	G	H	I	J
Includes campaigns, elections, federal-state relations, civil rights and liberties, crime, the judiciary, education, healthcare, poverty, urban affairs, and population.	*Includes formation and debate of U.S. foreign and defense policies, veterans affairs, and defense spending. (Relations with specific foreign countries are usually found under the region concerned.)*	*Includes business, labor, agriculture, taxation, transportation, consumer affairs, monetary and fiscal policy, natural resources, pollution and industrial accidents.*	*Includes worldwide scientific, medical and technological developments, natural phenomena, U.S. weather and natural disasters.*	*Includes the arts, religion, scholarship, communications media, sports, entertainment, fashions, fads, and social life.*

	World Affairs	Europe	Africa & The Middle East	The Americas	Asia & The Pacific
Oct. 3	At the Hague, Radio Conference delegates define radio standard wave lengths and set recommended guidelines for licensing amateurs. The wave classes are long, medium, border, short, and ultra short.	The Kingdom of Serbs, Croats, and Slovenes becomes Yugoslavia. To promote unity, the 33 historical provinces are restructured into nine banats named for rivers....Hindenberg takes over the German government to forestall a crisis after the sudden death of Foreign Minister Stresemann....The Italianization of the formerly Austrian Southern Tyrol is complete. For seven years, Tyrolese have been eradicating German influences.	Wafdists back Adly Pasha, who indicates that the nationalists will have a strong voice in his government. Adly calls for calm....Sir Francis Humphreys, who evacuated Europeans during the Afghan civil war, becomes commissioner for Iraq. Plans are for him to oversee the three-year transition from mandate status.	Mexico donates seized rebel estates to the national university. The properties, worth millions, were taken after the March rising.	
Oct. 4		Albania breaks relations with Turkey over a slight to Albania's King Zog. Turkey recalled its ambassador on Zog's accession....Britain raises the school leaving age from 14 to 15, effective January 1.		Bolivia's vice president is under detention. Former president Montes found sanctuary in Chile....Chile denies that it has come to agreement with Japan over nitrate fields. Negotiations over copper earlier failed because Americans dominate Chile's copper production....Nicaragua deports eight for plotting against the government.	
Oct. 5		Britain identifies the 17 ships it will scrap if the five-power agreement passes. Six are inactive and will be replaced if the pact fails....The secretary of the Slovakian People's Party receives 15 years at hard labor giving Czech information to Hungary, which wants the territory back. Czechs, who have just nominated the secretary for parliament, are shocked at the severity of the sentence.	Despite an increase in British troops and police, sniping continues in the six-week-old Arab-Jewish confrontation in Palestine. The police commissioner threatens a renewed curfew while both Arabs and Jews complain about the British government.		
Oct. 6		Twenty-two European nations report balanced budgets. Four are still in deficit, but only Russia is seriously so, $279 million in the red.		Now that the Paraguayan war scare is ended (and perceived by many as a hoax), President Siles' dictatorship is under pressure from those wanting elections and the return of former president Saavedra, exiled by Siles....Uruguay offers to host Chaco talks.	
Oct. 7	Britain issues formal invitations to the five-power naval parley. France indicates it will attend and Japan and Italy are expected to accept shortly.	Yesterday's takeover of Boden Anstalt by Austrian Kredit Anstalt is more than a simple business transaction. A consortium including English, Belgian, and American bankers and Austria's government are prepared to lose tens of millions because loss of the bank could topple the Austrian economy.	Egypt estimates a cotton crop of 7.8 million kantars, up from 6.9 million kantars last year. A kantar is approximately 99 pounds.		An anti-Nanking mutiny at Ichang causes Americans to seek protection on the Yangtze riverbank. A Chinese gunboat quells the rising.
Oct. 8		Marshal Pilsudski cuts short his trip to Italy and returns to fight an imminent no-confidence vote. The right-wing Nationalists have just won municipal and Sejm elections, and the Socialist youth are preparing demonstrations against the government.		Canada and the United States wheat production strains storage as world demand is weak. The crop exceeds 200 million bushels, 56.8 million over the previous record. Exports are down 3.6 million bushels.	On the death of Baron Tanaka, the Japanese opposition Seiyukai Party leaders select 74-year-old Ki Inukai as party leader. The goal is to forestall intraparty competition by younger leaders and preserve a united front for the anticipated collapse of the ruling party next session.
Oct. 9	The Institute of International Law opens its 36th annual meeting at Briarcliff Lodge with Elihu Root presiding.	With the filing of the Franco-Swedish agreement, pacifist Sweden has 21 non-aggression pacts on file with the League of Nations....Prussia's minister orders the disbanding of the Steel Helmets in the Ruhr and Westphalia. The organization is too militaristic.		Lindbergh continues filling in the map with additional Mayan cities. His aerial survey finds four more in a previously unknown area of the Yucatan.	Afghan officials say they planned to remove Shujah Ed-Dowleh, but the civil war intervened. He transferred government funds to his personal account and embassy furnishings are gone. The rebel Habibulah flees Afghanistan. His rule seems at an end with the taking of Kabul by Nadir, representative Amanullah's regime, which England does not recognize.

A	B	C	D	E
Includes developments that affect more than one world region, international organizations and important meetings of world leaders.	Includes all domestic and regional developments in Europe, including the Soviet Union.	Includes all domestic and regional developments in Africa and the Middle East.	Includes all domestic and regional developments in Latin America, the Caribbean, and Canada.	Includes all domestic and regional developments in Asian and Pacific nations (and colonies).

U.S. Politics & Social Issues	U.S. Foreign Policy & Affairs, Defense	U.S. Economy & Environment	Science, Technology & Nature	Culture, Leisure & Lifestyle	
The Marion, NC, sheriff and fourteen others are in jail on murder charges. The governor opens an investigation into allegations of unprovoked shooting.		The stock market has its worst day of the year, with billions lost. Bank, industrial, and insurance stocks lead a sharp decline in the unlisted market. Other issues are sluggish, but chain stores hold firm.	A Metropolitan Life statistician says that the maximum life span is set at 80. He notes that centenarians are rare, with many claims questionable due to the lack of records....France asks Russia for aid in finding the lost flyers, Dieudonne Coste and Maurice Bellonte, who disappeared over Siberia in an attempt to set a distance record. Russia notifies all Siberian stations of a reward for finding them.		Oct. 3
The East Chicago, IL, mayor leads the list of 299 men and women indicted for violating liquor, white slave, auto theft, and narcotic laws. Gary and East Chicago are home to 213 of the 299....After the hostages escape, a Colorado prison riot ends. Twelve prisoners are dead, including the ringleader, a suicide.	British Prime Minister Ramsey MacDonald arrives in Washington, DC to meet with President Hoover.	F.A. Seiberling of Seiberling Rubber reports that European meetings of the Rubber Growers Association last week produced a plan to stabilize rubber prices at a level that promotes production. Rubber producers want to end price fluctuations from 12 cents to $1.20 a pound in a given year.....Stocks drop again on a 5.6 million share day with a lagging ticker.	Coste and Bellonte arrive safely in Manchuria. Their 5,000-mile flight is a record.	A Philadelphia municipal judge cites lack of jurisdiction as he denies Scarface Al Capone's request for parole. Capone and his bodyguard, slippery Frankie Rio, are in prison for carrying guns....Scalpers set the price for World Series tickets at $100 for a pair. They offer to buy tickets for $50. Face value is $33.	Oct. 4
		The markets rally on heavy weekend trading of 2.4 million shares. The NYSE is up 30 points and curb shares rise....Reynolds raises cigarette prices to $6.40 a thousand, ending the cigarette war. The other three major makers follow suit and cigarette prices climb to 15 cents a pack.		The first-ever game between Mexican and American college football teams pits Louisiana College against the University of Mexico. The U.S. team wins 59–0 before 12,000 spectators in Mexico City.	Oct. 5
	After talks with MacDonald, Hoover announces that the naval discussions will convene January 23.	New York produce truck drivers strike, leaving $5 million in perishable food in the system. Pickets and police ring markets and terminals as producers inform the public that prices will rise and government works a plan to feed the people.		Harvard's Institute of Comparative Law, the first of its kind in the United States, provides students a chance to compare U.S. and other legal systems. Johns Hopkins' year-old law institute gets a $450,000 anonymous donation.	Oct. 6
Lawrence Fisher, president of Cadillac Motor Company, protests the Coast Guard's firing on his speedboat on Lake Michigan. The Coast Guard counters that the boat failed to heed an order to stop....Catholic Msgr. John Belford supports Episcopalian William Blackshear in segregating black churchgoers. He notes that a few blacks are okay but in large numbers they get loud and pushy.	The Army Corps of Engineers organizes into geographical districts. Hoover anticipates that projects for the next four years — flood control and river and harbor upgrades — will be more demanding than the building of the Panama Canal.	After four years an advisory commission on prison goods reports to the Commerce Department. Options include barring prison goods from market or identifying them by tags. Prison-made goods cost half the normal price.	Byrd's party is preparing for the weather to break so it can begin trekking across Antarctica....Lindbergh completes the second leg of his aerial survey of Chichen Itza in the Yucatan.	The secretaries of the army and navy are unable to arrange a post-season army-navy game. The navy wants parity....A 100-city radio network is ready to carry the opening game of the Cubs–Athletics series tomorrow.	Oct. 7
The 185,000-member trainmen's union leans toward joining the AFL by year's end. The AFL's William Green is hopeful that all the railway brotherhoods, with 400,000 members, will join and improve labor unity....The New York truck strike ends, and food moves within 20 minutes of the settlement. Losses exceed $1 million.		Chrysler signs to produce two-cycle, nine-cylinder, 1,500-rpm Super Diesel engines for planes, buses, and cars. New Jersey is preparing to test a diesel bus....The U.S. cotton forecast is 14.9 million bales. Forecasts for Texas and the Carolinas are down, but Alabama, Mississippi, and Georgia's projections are up.	Abbe Breuil contends that humankind originated in the Sahara Desert and moved from there nearly simultaneously to South Africa and Europe. His argument rests in part on cave paintings and a prehistoric mine he explores in the Orange Free State and Basutoland.	The first game of the World Series goes to the Athletics 3–1 over the Cubs. Attendance is 51,000.	Oct. 8
William Green of the AFL tells a receptive Canadian audience that American labor supports a ban on immigration.	Hoover and MacDonald jointly announce that war between their nations is unthinkable. They will put the Kellogg pact into effect....The Senate votes 45–36 against Philippine independence....The bodies of 86 members of the Polar Bear Division reach Leningrad. The division fought at Archangel and Murmansk during and after the World War.	After a week of weak demand, call money drops suddenly from six percent to five percent. This is the lowest rate since August 1927....A curb seat sells for $250,000, down $4,000 from the record.		The Athletics crush the Cubs in Chicago, 9–3. Philadelphia scalpers now offer to buy tickets at $130 and sell for $150. Demand is down in Chicago.	Oct. 9

F
Includes campaigns, elections, federal-state relations, civil rights and liberties, crime, the judiciary, education, healthcare, poverty, urban affairs, and population.

G
Includes formation and debate of U.S. foreign and defense policies, veterans affairs, and defense spending. (Relations with specific foreign countries are usually found under the region concerned.)

H
Includes business, labor, agriculture, taxation, transportation, consumer affairs, monetary and fiscal policy, natural resources, pollution and industrial accidents.

I
Includes worldwide scientific, medical and technological developments, natural phenomena, U.S. weather and natural disasters.

J
Includes the arts, religion, scholarship, communications media, sports, entertainment, fashions, fads, and social life.

	World Affairs	Europe	Africa & The Middle East	The Americas	Asia & The Pacific
Oct. 10	Details of the workings of the new world bank are progressing, although the United States is hesitant.			France commits $2 million for a West Indies airline....MacDonald leaves the United States for Canada. He indicates that he intends to disarm Halifax and perhaps the West Indies.	
Oct. 11	In preparation for the 5-power naval talks, Japan indicates it wants to retain submarines. This supports the Italian position. France is suspicious of an Anglo-American entente.... The Institute of International Law declares for universal rights of life, liberty, and property.	After visiting Sing Sing and other American prisons, Denmark's Minister of Justice Zahle prepares a revision to the criminal code of 1666. Aside from abolishing capital punishment (not practiced since 1892), the code decriminalizes infidelity and blasphemy, sets a one-year sentence for animal cruelty, and implements American-style youth prisons.	Prime Minister MacDonald tells American Jews that he intends to carry out the mandate for a Jewish homeland in Palestine. He also supports Jewish immigration—within the capacity of Palestine to absorb the immigrants.		Nadir Khan enters Kabul and asks all tribes to cease fighting. He will not be king. Western governments anticipate a quick return by King Amanullah, currently in Rome.
Oct. 12		Russia struggles to get 80 percent of the grain harvest in by the end of the month. Peasants are balking at government prices well below what the market brings.	The Italian Savoia Society of Philadelphia gives Mussolini $300,000 for construction of a retirement village for Italian-Americans in Tripoli. The village will include a 100-bed home under Libyan governance....South African scientists discover a Neanderthal type skull near Cape Town. They take this as further evidence for the theory that South Africa is the cradle of civilization.	The Tecototlan mayoral election turns deadly as dissidents fire into crowds waiting to vote. They kill eight and wound 138. In other electoral news, National Revolutionary Party candidate Ortiz Rubio says he will continue the current administration's redistribution of land to peasants but will reimburse landowners.	The Chinese war turns against Chiang's Nationalists as Feng, formerly in his pay, joins with Yen. The united Northern forces imperil Chiang.
Oct. 13		A soviet official publishes the contract with Ford Motor Company for construction of an automobile plant in Russia. The soviets have earlier used American tractor and steel companies to expedite major industrial projects....Police charge a crowd of 10,000 unemployed Hungarians demanding work.	At 3.6 million pounds, Transvaal gold production is down slightly for September but sure to set a record for yearly output. Estimated 1929 production is above 1928's 44 million pounds.		Labor takes a preliminary 12-seat parliamentary majority in Australia. The party leads for 43 of 75 seats.... Northerners accuse Chiang of corruption and dictatorship. Chiang acknowledges there is peril from 400,000 troops marching toward Hankow. Chinese bankers elect not to lend the nationalists sorely needed funds.
Oct. 14	The International Law Institute sends a recommendation for an appeals court superior to the Hague to committee for further study.				The anti-nationalist rising spreads. Mukden negotiates a separate peace with Russia over the railway as Chiang's advisors suggest that he shorten his lines, abandon some cities, and prepare for a long battle.
Oct. 15	Cotton prices continue to drop in the U.S. Egyptian and British prices are also declining. U.S. cotton touches 18.15 cents a pound, down 1–4 cents for the day; Egyptian sells for 29.5 cents, down 5 cents from last September....France, Italy, Japan, and Britain formally accept invitations to the naval conference. All five nations are on record as planning to attend.		With Nadir in Kabul and proclaimed Emir, Hababullah refuses to capitulate. He takes Amanullah's brother hostage and demands a ransom.	New York and London bankers refuse to offer Brazil a $9 million loan to help the country through the coffee glut. Warehouses already hold 32 million unsold sacks, and more lands continue to come into production.	Yen captures Feng. Chang remains aloof. Chiang seems to be in a squeeze between north and south. The Chinese civil war continues.
Oct. 16	The International Law Institute announces plans to establish a body to recodify the world's laws.	Germans begin voting in a referendum on repudiation of war guilt and impeachment of ministers supporting Young Plan reparations. Hindenberg opposes, but the referendum is expected to gain the four million votes it needs. Then the Reichstag must act.	Arabs strike in Palestine, closing shops and taking a holiday or visiting mosques. Abraham Goldberg of the World Zionist Organization denies that Jews are leaving Palestine after recent violent disturbances.		

A	B	C	D	E
Includes developments that affect more than one world region, international organizations and important meetings of world leaders.	Includes all domestic and regional developments in Europe, including the Soviet Union.	Includes all domestic and regional developments in Africa and the Middle East.	Includes all domestic and regional developments in Latin America, the Caribbean, and Canada.	Includes all domestic and regional developments in Asian and Pacific nations (and colonies).

U.S. Politics & Social Issues	U.S. Foreign Policy & Affairs, Defense	U.S. Economy & Environment	Science, Technology & Nature	Culture, Leisure & Lifestyle	
The new Protestant Episcopal prayer book eliminates the word "obey" from the wedding ceremony. The book is the work of 15 years.			Geologists agree that the reason the Sour Lake oilfield is sinking is removal of the oil beneath the surface. To date, 50 acres have sunk and are now submerged.		Oct. 10
The AFL votes to unionize the South. Illinois United Mine Worker officials bar entry to UMW officers sent to replace them. John L. Lewis and Illinois district leaders have a longstanding feud....Two recently fired Angelus Temple employees accuse Aimee Semple McPherson of misappropriating funds.	Hoover receives a Polish delegation on the 150th anniversary of Pulaski's death.	Atlantic and Pacific stores raise cigarette prices to two packs for a quarter. Up from 23 cents for two, this price still undercuts Kroger, United Cigar, and other sellers who ask a straight 15 cents a pack.		The Cubs take game three, reviving Chicago betting interest. The Athletics are still favored to take the series....In Philadelphia, Leopold Stokowski conducts Serge Prokofieff's Second Symphony. Some leave during the second movement; others hiss the work.	Oct. 11
				The Athletics tie or set 10 records, including the record for most runs in an inning. They take their third game and lead the series 3–1.... Collapsible umbrellas that fit into handbags are the fashion rage of the season.	Oct. 12
Twenty-five Klansmen attend church in Brooklyn to keep out an expected 100 blacks. Minister Blackshear reaffirms his Jim Crow stance....The new district attorney of Stinnett, TX, prepares to try nine murder cases. All occur in Borger, a three-year-old oil town, now under martial law because of 22 murders in three years and county control by a government crime ring.		On his 25th anniversary in motion pictures, William Fox announces a 25-year, $9 million commitment to bring movies to schools, churches, and hospitals. He also announces the opening of a newsreel-only theater and plans for 16mm home movies. Fox provides Movietone News.		The Hoovers stroll the streets of Washington, DC's business section. Few Washingtonians recognize their president. Escorting them is a single secret service agent instead of the customary four.	Oct. 13
	Senator Smoot blames Sen. Borah for delaying the tariff bill. Borah counters that the tariff is contrary to what Hoover wants it to accomplish. Sen. Brookhart has 100 amendments. The House votes to suspend all work until the Senate acts on the tariff.	General Motors Radio Corporation is a partnership of GM, RCA, Westinghouse, and General Electric. The $2 billion company will sell and distribute radio products, including the new automobile radios to appear in Cadillac and LaSalle and, eventually, all GM cars.	Lieutenant Harry Sutton wins the 1928 Mackay Trophy for most meritorious accomplishment in flight. Sutton tests spinning characteristics of new army aircraft. Another pilot died doing the same tests.	Hoover watches as Connie Mack becomes the first manager to win 4 series titles. Philadelphia scores three in the 9th and beats the Cubs 3–2. The Athletics take the series, 4–1. Betting on the series is the lightest to date....Ginger, Rin Tin Tin's stunt double, dies. Ginger's screen name is Lightning.	Oct. 14
Ex-senator George W. Pepper tells the advertising industry convention that billboard owners must heed public preference in placing billboards and may face federal regulation otherwise. Agriculture Secretary Hyde lauds advertising as promoting business.		Independent manufacturers ask the attorney general to intervene against General Motors Radio Corporation. They claim the venture violates anti-trust laws....Leonard Ayres of Cleveland Trust says the market is a creeping bear, with a select few stocks rising enough to conceal the overall decline during the year. Yale's Irving Fisher says stock prices are at permanent high.	Dr. B.B. Crohn says smoking is more serious to health than drinking. It causes ulcers, hyperacidity, and excitability.	Madison Square Garden authorities announce plans to build a 50,000-seat arena next to Penn Station and over the railroad tracks. The $2 million facility will host boxing, hockey, and bicycling.	Oct. 15
In a massive raid, 130 federal prohibition agents attack 35 separate locations along a 200-mile stretch of the east coast. They capture 32, including the ringleader, after breaking the gang's wireless code and infiltrating.	The September foreign trade surplus is down $13 million from the previous year. Gold imports are $18.9 million, and metal imports to date are the highest for any year since 1924.	Chrysler reports third quarter earnings of $6.6 million, down $3 million from a year earlier. The 9-month profit of $24.7 million is up $3 million from 1928. Chrysler pays a dividend of $1.49 versus last year's $2.29....Kraft-Phenix Cheese buys 10 companies.	At Little America, Admiral Byrd bids farewell to a veteran team headed by dogsled 200 miles deeper into Antarctica. The team will establish new bases.		Oct. 16

F	G	H	I	J
Includes campaigns, elections, federal-state relations, civil rights and liberties, crime, the judiciary, education, healthcare, poverty, urban affairs, and population.	*Includes formation and debate of U.S. foreign and defense policies, veterans affairs, and defense spending. (Relations with specific foreign countries are usually found under the region concerned.)*	*Includes business, labor, agriculture, taxation, transportation, consumer affairs, monetary and fiscal policy, natural resources, pollution and industrial accidents.*	*Includes worldwide scientific, medical and technological developments, natural phenomena, U.S. weather and natural disasters.*	*Includes the arts, religion, scholarship, communications media, sports, entertainment, fashions, fads, and social life.*

	World Affairs	Europe	Africa & The Middle East	The Americas	Asia & The Pacific
Oct. 17	Ramsey MacDonald cites Canada's ties to the United States and the peaceful border. He invites the Canadians to sit in at the naval talks....At Baden, World Bank organizers agree that central banks have veto power over its actions. The United States is satisfied because the Federal Reserve can control the banks without participating in its operations.	Italy and Turkey file a 1928 treaty with the League. Officials find its absolute neutrality provision in conflict with League requirements that all nations must join against an aggressor state.	Sheiks Talab Makara, on trial, denies that he instigated the August 24 Hebron massacre.	Haiti sinks a condemned lighthouse tender. Her navy now consists of 10 motorboats to patrol a 1,000-mile coastline.	Soviet forces enter Manchuria then withdraw. This foray is a further distraction for the Nanking government, already squeezed by multiple rebellious forces.
Oct. 18		Yugoslavians protest the execution of Croatian student Gortan by Italy. Italians protest Yugoslavia. Yugoslavia closes all newspapers protesting the execution.	After several months of quiet, an attack by Moorish tribesmen in the South Atlas Mountains kills 50 French and indigenous troops. A French relief column chases the Moors into the mountains.		
Oct. 19		At Constantinople, Greek Orthodox metropolitans elect a new patriarch. Photius II replaces Basil III, who died in September. By custom, the province of Stamboul serves as the Holy Synod and chooses patriarchs....From exile Trotsky denies recanting. He says the opposition in Moscow is strong.			
Oct. 20	British and European funds are withdrawing from the United States. Now that interest rates have dropped, home markets are more attractive.	Berlin police block planned demonstrations in support of the anti-Young Plan plebiscite. There are no riots....Russia's grain harvest is slowed by a major shortage of tarpaulins and mismanagement of the railroads....Russia declares Tajikistan a Soviet Republic. The million Tajiks are autonomous for the first time in centuries.	Arab raiders at Kfar Veladin, Palestine, fire on a Jewish orphanage. There are no casualties.... Amanullah's brothers are found dead after Hababullah flees Kabul.	The Cuban government arrests four workers for the El Sol newspaper. This is part of a wider crackdown on distributors of "seditious" literature from outside the country. The "plotters" deny they are doing anything illegal.	After widespread protests, Japan cancels plans to reduce salaries of officials making more than $600. The proposed saving of $4 million, supported by rural members, is not worth the loss of the judiciary, many of whom join a generally urban protest.
Oct. 21				Floods on the Uruguay River isolate the Argentine town of Concordia. Three thousand are stranded and the railroad is submerged.	
Oct. 22		Briand loses a chamber vote of confidence. He and his cabinet resign.	White settlers in Kenya express concern about growing discontent among young Masai and Lumba men, who are stealing or burning each other's property. Africans on reservations are unhappy with increased white settlement.	Candidates begin filing for Mexico's presidential campaign. Favored is the government party's Ortiz Rubio. Long shots include Jose Vasconcelos and the Communist General Pedro Triana....After U.S. pacification, Nicaragua records the highest trade in its history. Foreign trade in 1928 is $25 million.	In Peking rickshaw men riot, destroy tram equipment, and injure tram workers. Troops dispel the rioters under martial law. Tram and rickshaw workers have been hostile for some time.
Oct. 23	Canada reports that wheat is piling up. Wheat from Argentina and Australia is cheaper.	French politicians express second thoughts at the ouster of Briand. There is no party with a majority and no clear favorite to succeed him....Early German returns show the anti-Young plebiscite failing. Hindenberg gets credit for the defeat.	The civil war is over and Nadir Khan is the British-recognized ruler of Afghanistan after "Water Boy of the North" Bacha Sakao surrenders. Bacha Sako has been Afghan king for 10 months.	President Ibanez of Chile escapes an assassination attempt. The would-be killer's gun jams three times....Mexico's interior department rules that women have no right to vote.	
Oct. 24	Conferees at Baden Baden deadlock on the powers of the world bank. Tension and distrust rise in the absence of Briand.	At Brussels, Humbert, the Italian crown prince, avoids assassination, then lays a wreath on the tomb of the unknown soldier. The would-be assassin is an anti-Fascist Socialist.	A closed-door British commission investigates the Palestinian riots. A two-member court sentences two Arabs to death, twelve to life in prison, and three to lesser penalties.		Both sides claim victories in heavy fighting as the Chinese civil war continues....Australia's new Labour Prime Minister, James Scullin, introduces himself in a talkie. He explains that immigration restrictions are for the purpose of reducing unemployment.

A	B	C	D	E
Includes developments that affect more than one world region, international organizations and important meetings of world leaders.	Includes all domestic and regional developments in Europe, including the Soviet Union.	Includes all domestic and regional developments in Africa and the Middle East.	Includes all domestic and regional developments in Latin America, the Caribbean, and Canada.	Includes all domestic and regional developments in Asian and Pacific nations (and colonies).

U.S. Politics & Social Issues	U.S. Foreign Policy & Affairs, Defense	U.S. Economy & Environment	Science, Technology & Nature	Culture, Leisure & Lifestyle	
		GM reports September sales are the lowest since February. Cotton drops to 17 cents.		Navy agrees to meet with Army in Washington, DC, to find a compromise that will allow renewal of the Army–Navy game next year. The two schools have differing eligibility rules.	Oct. 17
		Cotton drops to a low for the year before rallying slightly....Hoover appoints a commission to study conditions in the West's public lands. Water is first priority, but other issues include reclamation, overgrazing, and oil and coal conservation.		Critics find *The Radio Girl* a weak vehicle for the talents of Molly Picon....Navy indicates that twice this year it offered to play Army with no restrictions on eligibility.	Oct. 18
Chicago loads two railroad cars with aliens, including Giuseppi "The Spy" Genna. The cars will join the train from Seattle, which has already collected aliens from Kansas City and St. Louis and will bring about 250 aliens to New York for deportation.		The *New York Times* reports that money is plentiful and interest rates low. Easy money for the rest of the year should boost bonds and investments and allow exports of gold....In heavy trading the stock market drops, with leaders taking hits of 5–20 points.	Dr. W.W. Herrick reports that pipe smokers are more susceptible than cigar or cigarette smokers to angina pectoris, a heart disease. Other causes are overeating, obesity, stress, and lack of exercise.	Greta Garbo begins work on her first talking film. The title is *Anna Christie*.	Oct. 19
The Moderation League sends Hoover data showing that deaths from alcoholism rise in dry states. Only Maine shows a decline....The October 16th rum raid nets only six cases. Three special agents were seen at the ringleader's mansion before the raids.		Atlanta and Lowry merges with Fourth National to create the South's largest bank. Resources top $150 million.	New Jersey's highway commission votes $19 million to finish the state superhighway. By linking Camden with the Holland Tunnel, the new road will provide a 100-mile, town-avoiding superhighway from Philadelphia to New York.	A woman swims six miles with her feet tied and her hands cuffed.	Oct. 20
After a three-week trial, a Gastonia, NC, jury deliberates less than an hour and finds seven unionists guilty of killing the city police chief and others in a June labor fight. The defense claims prosecution prejudice in raising the defendants' atheism and communism but praises Judge Barnhill's impartiality.		The farm board offers $100 million in loans to cotton cooperatives to stabilize prices through "orderly marketing." The board promises a comparable to wheat growers later....Yale's Irving Fisher says stock prices are low, even in a high market, and will catch up with values later....New York, Boston, and other cities see heavy trading and sharp drops.	A 12-engine Dornier airplane stays aloft for an hour with 169 passengers. This is a record for the most passengers in any type of aircraft.		Oct. 21
A woman who confesses to killing gambler Arnold Rothstein goes to Bellevue for psychiatric observation.		General Motors combines with Germany's Dornier and Fokker (owned 40 percent by GM) to build flying boats. Dornier is builder of the 169-passenger 12-engine machine.		When an otherwise apathetic Carnegie Hall audience hisses a work by Schoenberg, conductor Stokowski asks the concertgoers to be more open minded. Schoenberg's work is cacophonous.	Oct. 22
		The stock market loses $4 billion. In the final hour, 2.6 million shares change hands, but no brokerage fails. The curb and wheat futures markets also take hard hits.	A Japanese biologist says he can make an infant any color and otherwise alter an individual's racial characteristics. For 15 years he has been researching glandular secretions.	A Carnegie Fund report reveals widespread use of slush funds, improper recruiting, and other abuses in college athletics. Of 130 schools reviewed, only 28 are clean. One is seven athletes gets illegal aid.	Oct. 23
The American Bar Association calls for a standard state criminal code. The ABA wants a more scientific approach, including the use of psychiatric testing, in criminal cases....Universalists resolve that doctors should be free to provide birth control. They say birth control will aid world peace and child welfare and reduce crime.		Wall Street continues in turmoil as 50,000 clerks work through the night to catch up with orders. Crowds gather outside as 1,000 brokers crowd the floor and thousands of accounts are wiped out. Leading bankers call it a technical adjustment. Cotton hits its low point for the year. Wheat struggles too.	Dr. William Beebe ends an exploration of the ocean off Bermuda By diving as deeply as possible and using nets to reach a mile below, he has captured 100,000 specimens from the two-mile-deep ocean.	Two explosions at Consolidated Films in Hollywood kill one and injure six. Fire destroys $2 million worth of film masters—including silents by Douglas Fairbanks, Mary Pickford, Norma Talmadge, and Bebe Daniels. Valuable works—including Douglas Fairbanks talkies—are saved.	Oct. 24

F	G	H	I	J
Includes campaigns, elections, federal-state relations, civil rights and liberties, crime, the judiciary, education, healthcare, poverty, urban affairs, and population.	*Includes formation and debate of U.S. foreign and defense policies, veterans affairs, and defense spending. (Relations with specific foreign countries are usually found under the region concerned.)*	*Includes business, labor, agriculture, taxation, transportation, consumer affairs, monetary and fiscal policy, natural resources, pollution and industrial accidents.*	*Includes worldwide scientific, medical and technological developments, natural phenomena, U.S. weather and natural disasters.*	*Includes the arts, religion, scholarship, communications media, sports, entertainment, fashions, fads, and social life.*

	World Affairs	Europe	Africa & The Middle East	The Americas	Asia & The Pacific
Oct. 25	The League agrees to discussions on a tariff truce.	German reaction to the Wall Street crash is that it will encourage capital to return to Europe. Weak stocks will boost bonds and ease German borrowing. England also sees a return of capital after two years of Wall Street speculation....Daladier attempts to form a cabinet but Briand declines any role. The deadline is tomorrow at 3 p.m.		For the first time an injunction stops Mexico from expelling unwanted foreigners and challenges the constitutional provision for such deportations. Usually sheriffs move so quickly that deportees are out of Mexico before they can challenge their expulsion.	Chiang raises a war chest, orders American planes, prepares for Communist border attacks, and says he is ready to negotiate a settlement.
Oct. 26		Britain expels a Yugoslavian spy who stole the Italian code from the Berlin Italian embassy. Italy banishes to a deserted island the diplomat who succumbed to her blandishments.			
Oct. 27	A Russian ship leaves Vladivostok with the remains of 86 American war dead. The United States declines a Russian offer of military honors.	Daladier forms a new cabinet with Briand as foreign minister. Both Socialists and Conservatives are nonsupportive and expect the cabinet to fall quickly....Russia executes 26 more kulaks for hampering Socialism.	Eight hundred Arabs from Transjordan, Palestine, Egypt, Syria, and Iraq announce that there cannot be peace as long as the Balfour Declaration remains in force. An Arab boycott of Jewish businesses in Palestine remains in effect.	Argentina's grain crop is devastated by drought and unseasonable frosts. Two major producing provinces report crop estimates of 35 percent of last year's.	
Oct. 28		The withdrawal of European capital due to the tumbling U.S. stock market reaches an estimated $100 million....French Socialists delay committing to joining the Daladier government as centrists split over the issue of supporting Socialists. Czech Socialists lead in parliamentary elections over Catholic and Communist parties.			The Kyoto Conference on Pacific relations opens with greetings from Hoover. Old grudges surface: China complains of Japanese interference with the war under Tanaka and Japan complains about U.S. 1924 immigration restrictions....Foochow is in rebellion with two other cities due to follow.
Oct. 29	Stocks slide in Paris, London, Berlin, and Toronto. The market break produces record worldwide phone, cable, and radio traffic.	King Zog jails deputies who present him grievances, and Albania closes two critical newspapers.....Daladier fails to form a cabinet.		Brazil's consul general says that the economy is strong and Brazil needs no loan. Speculation about the economy had lowered coffee prices.	
Oct. 30	The Baden Baden committee establishes statutes and the charter for the world bank. A subcommittee is set to draft reparations rules. All that remains is finding a home for the organization.	Clementel is next to attempt forming a French government. The conservatives like him, and he has commitments from Briand, Loucheur, Cheron, and possibly Tardieu to join his government....The German plebiscite opposing the Young Plan fails when only 1.8 million vote for it. Passage requires 4 million.	Liberia gives wide latitude to a commission investigating slavery. Members are from the United States, the League, and Liberia. Liberia wants to clear allegations arising from investigations of concessionaires, including Firestone Rubber. It also wants examination of charges it provides forced labor to Fernando Po. The investigation is to last 4 months.	Coffee prices drop to their lowest since 1923. Brazil declines to call a moratorium or issue more currency to ease the crisis....Ontario votes for conservatives who promise to continue upholding liquor controls. Incumbent conservatives gain win 90 of the 112 seats, gaining at liberal expense.	Chiang denounces the reds and takes charge of his forces at Hanchow in anticipation of a major offensive. The United States sends six destroyers to China from the Philippines.
Oct. 31	The Bank of England lowers its bank rate to six percent to stem the flow of money from the United States in the aftermath of the crash. The bank sees less pressure on English gold to move to the United States.	After a seven-month break, the Polish Sejm is to reconvene to deal with the budget. Marshal Daszansky cancels the session after 80 armed men enter the chamber, claiming to be there to protect Marshal Pilsukski....Clementel fails to form a government. Tardieu is next to attempt it. Paul Boncour is next if Tardieu fails.	The Arab counsel before the hearing into the riots blames Jews. The Jewish counsel blames the Grand Mufti for spreading falsehoods and provoking unrest for political advantage. Earlier, the head of police had indicated that Arab police were unreliable....King Fuad restores the Egyptian parliament and constitution. Effective date is January 1931.	Workers walk out at the Mexico City Ford plant, asking union recognition and collective bargaining. This is Ford's first-ever strike.... Nova Scotia votes 35 to one to end prohibition and approve government sales.	Australia cancels compulsory military training, instituted in 1911. The government begins examining overall military reform for improved efficiency.
Nov. 1		Poland and Germany cancel war claims totaling $289 million. The way is clear for trade between the two.	Palestine Potash, Ltd, headed by an American and a Briton, forms with $2 million capital. It is ready to begin extracting salts from the Dead Sea, one of the world's richest sources of mineral salts.	Prime Minister Mackenzie-King tells western Canadians to wait and see what the U.S. tariff looks like. Since tariff debates began in the spring, Canadians have agitated for keeping parliament in session so it can retaliate immediately if the United States passes a tariff adverse to Canada....Mexico orders the states to return to Roman Catholics church property confiscated by schismatics in the summer. Schismatics can retain what they held before the disputes. The Mexican state owns all church property.	Hirohito becomes the first Japanese emperor to attend a baseball game. He is among 40,000 spectators as Keio University beats Waseda University.

A	B	C	D	E
Includes developments that affect more than one world region, international organizations and important meetings of world leaders.	Includes all domestic and regional developments in Europe, including the Soviet Union.	Includes all domestic and regional developments in Africa and the Middle East.	Includes all domestic and regional developments in Latin America, the Caribbean, and Canada.	Includes all domestic and regional developments in Asian and Pacific nations (and colonies).

U.S. Politics & Social Issues	U.S. Foreign Policy & Affairs, Defense	U.S. Economy & Environment	Science, Technology & Nature	Culture, Leisure & Lifestyle	
A jury finds Harding's interior secretary Albert Fall guilty of accepting a bribe but not guilty of conspiracy in the oil lease scandals. Fall becomes the first cabinet member convicted of a felony.		G.E., Westinghouse, and RCA-Victor begin a joint radio venture.	A flotilla reaches Cairo, IL, for the christening of the final dam in the Ohio River's new navigation system. Over two decades the federal government spends $118 million on 50 dams to make the river navigable year-round from Pittsburgh to the Mississippi.		Oct. 25
Ex-Florida governor Catta denies that he was involved in a counterfeiting ring but admits he did intervene with current governor Carlton for people the ringleader wanted in government.					Oct. 26
					Oct. 27
	Secretary of State Stimson lifts the U.S. ban on Hungary's Count Karolyis, imposed by Hughes in 1925 after Italy expelled the count. Both Kellogg and Hughes objected to Karolyis playing politics in the United States....Various senators call on Hoover to take a position on the tariff to break the congressional logjam.	An unexpected sell off rocks the market, with over nine million shares traded, including three million in the last hour. The ticker is 167 minutes behind. The curb market falls sharply, as do markets in Chicago, Philadelphia, Boston, Baltimore, and Cleveland. Nationwide losses top $14 billion.	At the Navy Day show in Washington, DC, 12 navy flyers parachute in 10 seconds, setting a new record for parachute jumps from a single plane.		Oct. 28
	Army tests of semi-automatic rifles have winnowed a field of nine to two, American-made Garand and Pedersen .276 caliber weapons.	After a closing rally, brokers say values are sound and the market has bottomed. They disagree on whether the upturn will be slow or sharp.			Oct. 29
	The Budget Bureau cuts the Army and Navy aviation budgets by $4.5 apiece. Airmail also takes a $3 million cut.	Stocks turn upward on a 10 million share day, regaining nearly half of their two-day losses. The exchange declares a two-day holiday to catch up on the paperwork and ease the strain on workers.	Following the American lead, Britain withdraws governmental sponsorship of Schneider Cup participants. The government says the race has gotten out of hand, with this year's British participation costing $5 million, and it has drifted from its original purpose of advancing speed plane technology....Scott's second expedition to the Antarctic interior returns after penetrating 100 miles. Snowmobiles prove satisfactory for transportation.	The Scientific Book Club begins. Geology professor Kirtley Mather of Harvard will chair a committee of distinguished scientists who select books with the aim of reducing the prevalence of pseudo-scientific works.	Oct. 30
Hoover asks a speedy submission of a tariff bill. The Senate acknowledges that the opposition coalition of western populists can block it indefinitely.		The Federal Reserve cuts the prime rate to five percent from six percent to reduce the chance of speculators returning to the United States after the Bank of England lowers its rate....Brokers' loans are down $1 billion, wiping out a 10-month gain. The $5.5 billion total is $1.2 billion below the October 2 record. Sales of shares in October top 141 million.	Mme. Curie tells a cancer society dinner in her honor that radium is extremely dangerous. Only experts should handle it....Martinique's Mount Pelee erupts for the sixth time in 2 weeks. Eight thousand are refugees from the villages at the foot of the mountain.	Yale football records its third consecutive year with $1 million in revenue. After expenses, the department clears $1,424.	Oct. 31
Albert Fall's attempt to overturn his bribery conviction fails. His sentence is a year in jail and a $100,000 fine.	Hoover appoints a commission of Scandinavian-American men to attend next summer's 100th anniversary of Iceland's parliament, the Althing. Sen. Norbeck of South Dakota will present a statue of Leif Erikson.	Ford reduces prices $15–$200 per vehicle. The action surprises dealers and sparks rumors that a new model is imminent....Air service between New York and Buenos Aires begins. The eight-passenger amphibian will take 11 days one way....The Foshay utility holding companies fail. Properties worth $20 million are in receivership. Foshay has subsidiaries in 30 states and Latin America. This is the largest failure ever in the northwest.	A Guggenheim Fund study reveals that the cure for air sickness is adequate cabin ventilation. Air sickness is a problem for only about five percent of flyers.	A Columbia University marketing expert says women will keep short skirts for another five years.	Nov. 1

F	G	H	I	J
Includes campaigns, elections, federal-state relations, civil rights and liberties, crime, the judiciary, education, healthcare, poverty, urban affairs, and population.	Includes formation and debate of U.S. foreign and defense policies, veterans affairs, and defense spending. (Relations with specific foreign countries are usually found under the region concerned.)	Includes business, labor, agriculture, taxation, transportation, consumer affairs, monetary and fiscal policy, natural resources, pollution and industrial accidents.	Includes worldwide scientific, medical and technological developments, natural phenomena, U.S. weather and natural disasters.	Includes the arts, religion, scholarship, communications media, sports, entertainment, fashions, fads, and social life.

	World Affairs	Europe	Africa & The Middle East	The Americas	Asia & The Pacific
Nov. 2		Austrian troops surround a factory where Socialists refuse to work with Fascists. They prevent *heimwehr* forces from interfering. The country is in a Socialist–Fascist struggle....English divorces totaled 4,018 in 1928, up 838 over 1927 due to easier divorce laws. Women seek divorce more often than men do, and women marry as young as 15. Another record is expected for 1929....Tardieu forms a center-right cabinet.	A new road from Behere has imperiled the Cedars of Lebanon. Locals cut off branches to sell to tourists and the forest is becoming a dumping ground.	Russian-immigrant Doukhobors in British Columbia, solid workers but anti-tax pacifists and communal, are on a hunger strike. Last September they protested in the nude against government enforcement of unpalatable laws....Latin American diplomats express disappointment at the failure of Nicaragua's Cordero Reyes to interest other central American countries in joint diplomatic representation. That would have been the first step toward a union of Central America.	The Chinese Red Cross reports that the 10,000 men of General Wang Tai, a bandit controlling 300 square miles of Eastern Honan, have killed 20,000. His men have destroyed 1,600 villages and hold 10,000 for ransom.
Nov. 3		Italy discontinues the draft of American citizens visiting the mother country—in time of peace, at least. Americans can safely visit for three months to a year.	After pressure from cotton interests, the Egyptian government announces that it will buy cotton futures to keep prices from falling.	Argentine farmers flock en masse to Buenos Aires after heavy crop losses of up to 80 percent. The want new loans, extensions, and debt forgiveness....Eruption of Santa Maria sends sand and lava down the Guatemalan mountain. Injuries and deaths are numerous as the flow threatens Quetzaltenanga.	The Chinese rebels score a major victory against Chiang at Hankow. Ten thousand nationalist soldiers desert at Laohokow and begin looting. Refugees crowd Tengchow.
Nov. 4	A League commission rules that Hamburg must lease Elbe River land to Czechoslovakia. The land will give Czechoslovakia an outlet to the sea after waiting 10 years.	The French vacate Coblenz. Before leaving the French general pays homage to fallen Germans at the Coblenz cemetery, where the French troops serve as Rhineland Commission guard of honor.... Russian grain production is at 75 percent of the goal. Russia announces that non-cooperative peasants will suffer jail as well as confiscation of their lands.	A Jerusalem weekly labor newspaper is suspended for publishing a government blacklist of Arabs and Communists. The paper reopens under a new name as a daily.	Eight Arctic flyers, missing for two months, report in from Cambridge Bay in northern Canada. After running short of fuel they landed and received aid from Eskimos....At Kiel 5300 Russians heading for Canada say that the soviets took all their money and food. Another 1500 families are awaiting transport in Leningrad. Canada will pay immigrants' travel.	Japan stands firm for a cruiser quota at 70 percent. Officials indicate they don't understand American concern when there is no chance of a Pacific offensive....At the Kyoto Pacific conference, Japan is defensive about its involvement in Manchuria.
Nov. 5	Forty nations convene at Paris for a conference on aliens' rights. Of interest to Americans abroad are double taxation, landlord-leaseholder relations, the status of branch businesses, and the like. The ultimate goal is free circulation of people, property, and capital.	England's House of Commons beats back a Tory censure resolution. With Labour and Liberals collaborating, it also votes to reestablish diplomatic relations with Russia. Labour members leave the House of Lords over Indian policy.		The Santa Maria volcano's lava flow is six feet high. Lava and gas kill hundreds of Guatemalan villagers. Ash destroys crops.	The rebels take two more of Chiang's cities as desertions and mutinies continue among the nationalist troops.
Nov. 6	The U.S. delegate explains that the Constitution bars the United States from signing the proposed alien rights treaty because it pertains to states' rights. And some states bar sales of land to aliens. China and Egypt do not like the agreement because it gives aliens greater rights than their citizens have.	The 86 members of "Detroit's Own," killed during the war in Siberia, reach Havre, where the French provide a military salute and honors. Their journey home for burial will resume on November 15.		Six thousand Russian Germans are at Kiel and in Russia waiting for Canada to say whether it will receive them. Canadian Mennonites are negotiating with the government.	Tokyo police finish a two-week sweep during which they arrest 825 Communists and seize 6,000 books. Other arrestees are 52 geishas and 20 schoolgirls.
Nov. 7		Tardieu outlines his foreign policy—caution on the Rhine and firmness on holding the empire. Domestically, he promises more public works and lower taxes....In Vienna, the heimwehr drives Jews and Socialists from the university. The deans close the school....in the Rhineland, Maginot says French troops have not vacated but have merely shifted positions.... Spain's Primo de Rivera forms fascisti to counter the army.			Chiang halts the offensive in Honan, saying he will starve out the rebels. He appoints Yen to the nationalist army although Feng continues to charge that Yen sympathizes with the rebels.
Nov. 8	Eight Latin American states caucus at Paris to set a united front on the alien treaty. Delegates agree to a draft authorizing freedom of commerce to aliens....Switzerland is to be the home of the world bank. Delegates prefer Zurich, but no Swiss city is set. Only Belgium objects—and quits the meeting after Brussels loses.	English emigration is down because of the generous dole and the lack of passage money. Emigration to Canada was up in 1928 but that to Australia and New Zealand was down, and Conservatives want government aid to get the 1.23 million unemployed off the dole and out of the country.	With the lifting of the curfew at Jerusalem, all Palestinians are free to move at night. The commission of inquiry is touring Palestinian cities and getting Arab denunciations of Balfour at each stop....Iraqi statehood will not come sooner than 1932. Although Britain wants to end the mandate, there is opposition from the mandate commission, Italy, and Germany.	The Guatemalan volcano has ceased spilling lava. The final death count is between 300 and 700.... Mexican flying ace, Col. Pablo Sidar, returns to a hero's welcome from a 9,000-mile goodwill tour of Latin America. Greeting him are 30,000 fans and the largest flying formation in Mexican history.	

A	B	C	D	E
Includes developments that affect more than one world region, international organizations and important meetings of world leaders.	Includes all domestic and regional developments in Europe, including the Soviet Union.	Includes all domestic and regional developments in Africa and the Middle East.	Includes all domestic and regional developments in Latin America, the Caribbean, and Canada.	Includes all domestic and regional developments in Asian and Pacific nations (and colonies).

U.S. Politics & Social Issues	U.S. Foreign Policy & Affairs, Defense	U.S. Economy & Environment	Science, Technology & Nature	Culture, Leisure & Lifestyle	
			The U.S. assistant trade commissioner to Berlin reports that Germany has found a superior alternative to powder rocket fuel. The carbon-oxygen combination gives four times the power for just a third more cost than equivalent gasoline. Flights now last 40 minutes rather than 40 seconds.		Nov. 2
The Protestant Episcopal Church of the Intercession of Trinity Parish, New York, installs a columbarium in the church crypt. This is the first church in the United States to provide a resting place for the cremated....A rally at Madison Square Garden draws 10,000 supporters of the Communist ticket in municipal elections.		With 254,000 tons of new work, the United States is number two in ships under construction. Work for Matson, Dollar, Porto Rico, and Export lines provides 8,000 new jobs.	A German doctor successfully inserts a catheter through a vein into his heart. He plans direct injection for treatment of heart disease.	Short skirts boost the hosiery market by $43 million a year reports the University of Pennsylvania's Wharton School of Finance and Commerce. The number of hosiery mills rose from 92 in 1919 to 235 in 1928.	Nov. 3
By 54-22 the Senate votes to censure Senator Hiram Bingham for putting a lobbyist on his Senate payroll. This is the third censure in Senate history....Senators Reed and Smoot work with Republican insurgents and Democrats to limit debate on tariff legislation. Their goal is to speed passage.	Hoover congratulates President Florencio Arosomena on Panamanian independence day.	Stocks sag during a shortened session of only three hours. Sales top 6.2 million shares, twice the desired 3-million-share volume. Shortened sessions will continue.	From his base, Byrd sends a second team deep into Antarctica. This three-month trek of 400 miles is to search for fossils in the mountains.	Twelve-year-old Yehudi Menuhin debuts at London's Queen's Hall. The violin prodigy gets an enthusiastic reception.	Nov. 4
Black candidates allege that 50 voting machines are out of order and that unnecessary checking of voter identification denies black voters the franchise. Delays force them to leave for work without voting. Blacks also acknowledge better than expected white support.	The United States and Canada sign an accord that allows each nation's airplanes free passage across the border. Licenses are interchangeable, but those wishing to take photos must have permission....Hoover receives the new minister from South Africa. Only Australia and New Zealand of the Dominion nations lack Washington representation.			Baritone Paul Robeson enjoys a warm reception during his first performance at Carnegie Hall since returning from performing abroad.	Nov. 5
Hoover apologizes to Senator Johnson of California for overlooking him at a dinner for all Senate leaders. The omission had fueled rumors of renewal of the old rift between the two Californians.		The Associated Grocery Manufacturers of America vote to establish cooperative terminals in major cities to eliminate middlemen. One speaker sees the demise of the butcher, fruit seller, and the like at the hands of markets selling chilled meats, frozen milk, vegetables, and fruits....Stocks continue to fall on volume of 5.9 million shares.	Tests of the Sperry stabilizer show the benefits of gyroscopes in keeping a plane's flight level....J.B. Taylor demonstrates the photoelectric cell. He transmits music on a beam of light.		Nov. 6
The New Jersey supreme court rules that "mutton head" is a harmless epithet. Calling even a public official that is not disorderly conduct.	At Goodyear's Akron plant, Admiral William Moffett drives the golden rivet, beginning construction of the world's biggest dirigible. The ship will be 785-feet-long and hold 6.5 million cubic feet of gas. Moffett continued to advocate lighter than air ships after the Saratoga disaster.	Stocks are up on volume of 7.1 million shares.	Byrd's snowmobile fails 80 miles out as the rear end gives way. It will be a fuel depot, and Byrd's teams will rely on dogs.	The Museum of Modern Art opens first to invited guests. The public gets in free tomorrow. On exhibit until December 7 are works by Seurat, Van Gogh, Cezanne, and Gauguin.	Nov. 7
Hoover's budget is $3.8 billion, a cut of $111 million. It provides no increased farm aid but includes flood control and full funding for the air corps....The government is selling new stamps at Washington, DC. A better technique for applying the adhesive makes them stick tighter.		J.A. Goldsmith warns silk manufacturers to beware of rayon. Production of the synthetic totals 137 million pounds, up 300 percent since 1923. Silk people need to be more careful about standards.	An RCA spokesperson quashes the idea of home movie recording. He says cheap recording technology is just a rumor.	Leopold Stokowski asks a Philadelphia audience to stop their "strange beating of hands." The audience applauds his request.	Nov. 8

F	G	H	I	J
Includes campaigns, elections, federal-state relations, civil rights and liberties, crime, the judiciary, education, healthcare, poverty, urban affairs, and population.	Includes formation and debate of U.S. foreign and defense policies, veterans affairs, and defense spending. (Relations with specific foreign countries are usually found under the region concerned.)	Includes business, labor, agriculture, taxation, transportation, consumer affairs, monetary and fiscal policy, natural resources, pollution and industrial accidents.	Includes worldwide scientific, medical and technological developments, natural phenomena, U.S. weather and natural disasters.	Includes the arts, religion, scholarship, communications media, sports, entertainment, fashions, fads, and social life.

	World Affairs	Europe	Africa & The Middle East	The Americas	Asia & The Pacific
Nov. 9	Basle will be the home of the world bank. It has good rail access and assured neutrality....Conferees weaken double taxation language in the draft alien rights document. Experts expect the document to change little.	German liberals tell Tardieu that he misreads the requirement to evacuate the Rhine by zones. The powers, including France, agreed to a withdrawal schedule in August.... Ireland's Dail adds $55,000 funding for Galway College. It won't ban English yet, but it does encourage use of Gaelic.	Former prime minister Smuts tells an oxford audience that England should press settlement of her colonies. Africans benefit from a white presence, there is plenty of land for all, and there is no injustice in it.	Of the 134,000 permits to brew beer at home, 110,000 are from rural Ontario. The government says it has no jurisdiction over the U.S. mail-order sellers of home brewing kits. Home brew is exempt from the 42-cent-a-gallon provincial tax.	The League mandate group is studying sharply dropping population in the Caroline, Marianna, and Marshall Islands under Japanese mandate. Infant mortality is unusually high.
Nov. 10	The League sends a draft tariff agreement to members and non-members. It also sends invitations to a parley on the tariff.	Ismet Pasha receives a vote of confidence. Rumors that the Turkish government is about to fall prove false....Switzerland announces plans to spend $5 million on 105 planes to modernize its air force.		Vasconcelistas and backers of Ortiz Rubio face off in Mexico city. They burn campaign offices and fire 500 shots. Three die and 12 suffer wounds....Costa Rica suffers from banana blight and the new tax law....Fiesta celebrations get out of hand in Quito. A rocket sets the university afire.	Sir Douglas Mawson notifies the Australian government that his vessel has reached Possession Island in Antarctica. This is the spot where a British captain claimed Antarctica for Queen Victoria in 1841.
Nov. 11	Around the world, nations observe Armistice Day. Speeches, parades, ceremonies, and moments of silence are typical remembrances. Hoover proposes free passage for food ships in wartime and backs the World Court.			Brazil's government denies newspaper reports that troop movements are in preparation for the upcoming elections. Transfers are routine and there has been no strengthening of garrisons in opposition strongholds....Mexico says troops will guard its voting sites on election day.	Tungning, Manchuria, is almost in a state of siege by soviet forces, which also are massing at the border. Britain says that China and Russia have to work it out; Britain will not get involved. Britain also returns the Chinkiang concession to China after holding it since 1868.
Nov. 12	Europeans find Hoover's proposed exemption of food ships unacceptable. It violates League advocacy of economic blockade and by aiding outlaws might promote war. League officials see Hoover's backing of the court as a sign that the United States might join in world affairs.	After a court martial fails to convict former conservative president Jose Sanchez Guerra of rebellion, the case moves to the Supreme Army and Navy Council. Premier de Rivera wants Guerra punished.			Shensi Province's Governor Yen calls for an armistice. Chiang declares it a victory but Shanghai bankers think Chiang is losing. Four nationalist leaders are assassinated.
Nov. 13			In anticipation of a Zulu attack, natal shifts troops to protect Durban. Natives have rioted, are boycotting beer halls and eating houses, and refuse to pay poll taxes, levied on blacks only. The Durban government blames native and Russian Communists.	Panama ends the quarantine instituted due to a smallpox epidemic.	Chiang abandons the Honan front and withdraws to Nanking. Rebels are within seven miles of a strategic railway....The British settle Chinkiang claims.
Nov. 14	Hoover drops his proposal for safe passage of food ships in wartime.	Greece announces the establishment of an air service. Venizelos will command it....The Bank of France denies that it is hoarding gold. Recent gold purchases have been due to changes in the dollar and pound. The bank has bought nothing because it has $1.6 billion in gold, sufficient to back 50 percent of French paper.	Palestinian Arabs attack a British post and wound one soldier. Arabs also attack a Jewish official and a suburb of Jerusalem....Four hundred Durban police use tear gas to take 600 black poll tax violators into custody. Violators must either pay or spend a month in jail. Thousands from outlying areas pay the taxes, and single-day collections exceed the previous two months.		Senate President Manuel Quezon and House Speaker Manuel Roxas warn Filipinos not to expect anything from the Independence Mission to Washington, DC next month. Filipino, European, and American businessmen oppose independence without preparation.
Nov. 15	British press reaction to the Hoover food ship idea is favorable. Newspapers call for officials to try new ideas. Officialdom reacted negatively because the idea seemed unworkable....Tardieu and Briand say they will not negotiate on cruisers or submarines. They are unwilling to accede to Anglo-American wishes.	Britain rejects a German plan for immediate return of property seized during the war. Snowden says the matter of war claims has previously been decided by the Hague. Germany must accept the terms or Britain will resume taking reparations out of German property it holds.	Britain recognizes Nadir Khan as king of Afghanistan. To promote friendship with the soviets, Nadir Khan appoints his brother as envoy there.		

A	B	C	D	E
Includes developments that affect more than one world region, international organizations and important meetings of world leaders.	Includes all domestic and regional developments in Europe, including the Soviet Union.	Includes all domestic and regional developments in Africa and the Middle East.	Includes all domestic and regional developments in Latin America, the Caribbean, and Canada.	Includes all domestic and regional developments in Asian and Pacific nations (and colonies).

U.S. Politics & Social Issues	U.S. Foreign Policy & Affairs, Defense	U.S. Economy & Environment	Science, Technology & Nature	Culture, Leisure & Lifestyle	
New Orleans is tired of dynamited cars. Increased robberies and shootings are due to out-of-state gangsters flocking in to the city, and its police dislike their new chief, seen as a political appointee pushing wrong-headed reforms….A Missouri commission says the state needs to issue bonds and raise taxes for a decade. Its rural schools need $75 million in improvements.		Radio sales for 1929 are estimated to top $1 billion, with 4 million sets sold.	The Rockefeller Foundation reports it spent $21.7 million on public health in 1928. Focus was on veruga peruana, hookworm, and respiratory diseases. The foundation has spent $144 million to date.	Paris fashion decrees the muff is back. Especially popular for muffs is raccoon fur. Missouri fur trappers are pleased. Some firms gross $30,000 to $40,000 a year from raccoon pelts.	Nov. 9
New York merchants ask the outlawing of pushcarts. The places they congregate are generally dirty and disorderly, say the merchants.	Honduras accepts Secretary Stimson's offer. It agrees to send a delegate to Washington, DC, so the United States can mediate its border dispute with Guatemala.	The stock-tracking "Fisher Average" is 25 percent below the first week of September.		The Catholic Actors Guild votes to oppose Sunday evening performances. Its officers so notify Actors' Equity.	Nov. 10
	Minister John Van A. MacMurray notifies Nanking that the United States is willing to negotiate extraterritoriality. The United States has significant concerns, though, about the safety of its citizens over the past few months.	Stocks break again, with 1.76 million shares sold the final hour. The total for the rest of the day is 1.6 million. Philadelphia suspends trading. Chicago is closed for the holiday.	The United States and Canada open the Ambassador Bridge over the Detroit River. The structure is the world's largest suspension bridge. American and Canadian crowds meet at the middle.		Nov. 11
Letters reveal that a lobbyist for the Southern Tariff Association proposed that Republicans run Northern blacks as Democrats to make the South Republican. The lobbyist denies all knowledge of the letters. Senator Caraway demands another lobbyist identify "backward states" he wants excluded from tariff debates.	Guatemala joins Honduras in accepting the United States offer to arbitrate the border dispute in the banana region.	Post office officials ask $1.5 million to provide airmail service down the east coast to Latin America. The target is seven-day service to Rio. Current east coast service extends only to Paramaribo, Dutch Guinea. Rio receives mail through a route from Chile….Stocks set new lows, wheat and corn drop, and Liverpool says the bottom has arrived.	Nobel Prizes for science go to Britain's Prof. Owen Richardson and France's Duc du Broglie in Physics. Arthur Harden of Britain and Hans von Euler of Switzerland win in chemistry.	Alekhine bests Bogulkubov and retains his chess championship. Alekhine promises to take on Nimzowitch or Capablanca, from whom he took the title in 1927….Germany's Thomas Mann receives the Nobel Prize for literature.	Nov. 12
Detroit immigration officials break up an immigrant smuggling ring. Canadians hide undocumented Europeans on ferries and wait until the ferries dock for the night on the U.S. side. The ring has smuggled 50 in three months….Boston breaks up an interstate white slave ring. Indictments are handed down for six men and six women.	The United States sells 25 vessels to the Soviet Union for $1.155 million. The ships, in dry dock for seven years, are the basis for a Russian merchant marine.	The exchange opens an inquiry into short selling as the exchange hits a new low despite an offer by Rockefeller to buy a million shares of Standard Oil at 50. Cincinnati hits a record low although the exchange is buying.			Nov. 13
Senator Caraway says lobbyists are the third house of congress. They serve only themselves, prey on the public, and promote disregard for the law.	The Senate defeats a motion to adjourn and continues working on tariff legislation. "Young Republicans" ignore the leadership's desire to quit.	Congressional leaders agree to pass a personal and business income tax cut of one percent in December and pass on the surpluses immediately instead of waiting for 1930 tax cuts. Giving business and consumers more money will avoid a depression….General Motors says it will pay an extra 30 cent a share dividend.		The American Council of Learned Societies publishes Volume 3 of *Dictionary of American Biography*. Volume 1 appeared in 1928. Cost of producing the 16-million-word, 20-volume, project is $50,000.	Nov. 14
At Platte City, MO, the winning husker husks 25.27 bushels, half a bushel more than the second place finisher.	In an all-night session, the Young Republicans push 44 amendments to the tariff bill. No roll call vote slows the proceeding.	The New York federal reserve cuts its rediscount rate to 4.5 percent….A cross-country air-rail ticket on Transcontinental Air Transport drops from $338.10 to $267.43. The price includes meals except dinner and breakfast on the Pennsylvania Railroad….Hoover asks national leaders to find ways to improve business.	Experiments at a Western Electric Plant indicate that fear of the boss can impair a worker's efficiency. The test involves eliminating the old-style scolding boss.		Nov. 15

F	G	H	I	J
Includes campaigns, elections, federal-state relations, civil rights and liberties, crime, the judiciary, education, healthcare, poverty, urban affairs, and population.	Includes formation and debate of U.S. foreign and defense policies, veterans affairs, and defense spending. (Relations with specific foreign countries are usually found under the region concerned.)	Includes business, labor, agriculture, taxation, transportation, consumer affairs, monetary and fiscal policy, natural resources, pollution and industrial accidents.	Includes worldwide scientific, medical and technological developments, natural phenomena, U.S. weather and natural disasters.	Includes the arts, religion, scholarship, communications media, sports, entertainment, fashions, fads, and social life.

	World Affairs	Europe	Africa & The Middle East	The Americas	Asia & The Pacific
Nov. 16		Czechoslovakia bans Erich Marie Remarque's *All Quiet on the Western Front* from military libraries....Austrian Chancellor Schober says the heimwehr threat is under control. There will be no revolution....German students prepare to protest if they lose their right to duel. Already upperclassmen cannot force freshmen to drain a beer in a draught.			
Nov. 17	Germany, with $1.87 billion in exports during the first half of the year, passes England as the world's number two exporter. Britain has moved from first to third in 15 years. The United States became number one in 1914. Both Britain and Germany export significantly less than they did before the war.	Communists cut into Socialist strength in Berlin elections. They benefit from complicity by several social democrats in a recent scandal. In other cities, Socialists fare well while nationalists lose ground to Adolf Hitler's Fascists, competing in local elections for the first time.	Egypt announces a reduction of 50 percent in port duties for passenger steamers. The goal is to increase tourism, and the major beneficiaries are American cruise lines.	Ortiz Rubio wins the Mexican presidency. Violence kills 19. Vasconcelists claim fraud and intimidation, while the administration cites a quiet election.	Tokyo gets a $48.9 million credit from U.S. and British banks. This allows the end of the gold embargo in January.
Nov. 18		Bulgarians in Sofia halt work and demonstrate for 2 hours in front of the French and British legations. They are protesting reparations....France launches *Surcouf*, the world's largest submarine at 328 feet. The craft can fire 14 torpedoes simultaneously and carry a small plane.	Students hiss the president of Hebrew College in Jerusalem when he calls for forbearance. They applaud a speaker who rejects kindness toward Arabs.	United Fruit Company contracts with Ecuadorans to grow bananas. This decreases Ecuadoran dependency on cacao, which is slumping. United Fruit is backing off investments in Costa Rica and Colombia.	
Nov. 19		The government closes the Barcelona and Madrid exchanges early. Stocks are slumping.	A Metropolitan Museum of Art team unearths the tomb of Queen Meryet Amun of Egypt. The tomb, dating to between 1480 and 1440 B.C.E., was robbed around 1049 B.C.E....Nazi Bey Suadi forms a new Iraqi cabinet. Sir Abdul Musin committed suicide last week after being charged with treason for working with the British.		In Manchuria, Soviets take Manchuli and Dalainor in heavy fighting that includes the use of aircraft and artillery against the railway. Reportedly, 2,000 Chinese die.
Nov. 20	Fifty nations agreed to accept a modified World Court. Belgium is the first to sign the protocol. The protocol on admission of the United States to the court has no signatures. They wait for the United States to sign.	Shoreditch asks government aid for a birth control clinic. The English borough says birth control is a class privilege, and poor women should have it too.		Prospectors in Ecuador find an idol and many skeletons. They think they are close to finding the $15 million in gold and jewels the Incas paid Pizarro to ransom Atahaulpa.	Chang, the Manchurian warlord, says the soviets have violated a peace agreement. Thus, the Chinese are unprepared. Fierce fighting continues.
Nov. 21		Germany and France begin negotiations on the status of the coal-rich Saar. Germany is inclined to guarantee French interests in return for a speedy return of the region....Russia claims a group tied to Petlura and Russian emigres is plotting overthrow of the Ukrainian government.	The Jewish press scores Dr. Magnes of Hebrew University for seeking an end to the effort to make Palestine a Jewish state. The Jewish Legion says his work with Arabs and anti-Zionists and his idea for making Palestine a peaceful center for all religions is treason.		
Nov. 22	The draft protocol on the treatment of foreigners grants aliens the right to serve as attorneys for other aliens but not to represent them in court. Latin America objects to reciprocal treatment of businesses because there is no Latin American interest in the United States comparable to American interests in Latin America.	Briand spells out to deputies that French troops will not leave the Saar until Germany signs the Young Plan....Austrian Socialists reveal that the heimwehr has plans to take over Innsbruck. The plan includes use of trench mortars, machine guns, and poison gas.....Russia decrees that failure to return from abroad when ordered is punishable by death....Spain's Supreme War Tribunal orders Sanchez Guerra freed.		Discovery of chromite near Lake Nipigon, Canada, is a boost to U.S. steel production. An alloy used in making stainless steel, chromite mostly comes from Rhodesia.	Chiang quits the front, promises reforms, and asks a $4 million loan. His troops retreat to safeguard Canton.

A	B	C	D	E
Includes developments that affect more than one world region, international organizations and important meetings of world leaders.	*Includes all domestic and regional developments in Europe, including the Soviet Union.*	*Includes all domestic and regional developments in Africa and the Middle East.*	*Includes all domestic and regional developments in Latin America, the Caribbean, and Canada.*	*Includes all domestic and regional developments in Asian and Pacific nations (and colonies).*

U.S. Politics & Social Issues	U.S. Foreign Policy & Affairs, Defense	U.S. Economy & Environment	Science, Technology & Nature	Culture, Leisure & Lifestyle	
Hoover gives the go-ahead to Secretary Wilbur to organize a committee for a war on illiteracy. The problem became apparent during the wartime draft....Pilgrims, including the Boston mayor and archbishop, flock by the tens of thousands to Malden, MA, cemetery. They claim miracle cures at the grave of Father Patrick Power, dead almost 60 years.	The chief of the Army Chemical Service reports that tests with artillery firing tear gas shells have gone satisfactorily. Also, field laboratories will accompany armies to test enemy gases. In field tests, tanks are able to keep up with the infantry.			Professor Snedden says there should be three types of college: one for pre-professionals, one for the socializers, and one for the serious student. The current arrangement frustrates the serious student.	Nov. 16
Two rabbis, a Unitarian, and Harry Emerson Fosdick attack the new cult of humanism as unnecessary and inadequate. First Humanist Society of New York founder Charles Francis Potter issued a list of 22 religious leaders committed to destroying his secular religion.	The annual air corps survey reveals a severe shortage of hangars and insufficient reserve training. Only 600 of 4000 reservists are qualified for their missions.	A credit survey reveals that large stores take back 2.5 percent of what they sell. Also, half of grocery purchases are on charge accounts.	The S.P.C.A. calls for an end to muzzling, required by law as a measure against rabies. The society says muzzling is unfair to animals as well as ineffective against rabies. Leash laws are preferable.	Finnish–American Athletic Club's William Carlson wins the national seven-mile walking championship in 55 minutes, 27.5 seconds. He won the Met walk last week. The U.S. seven-Mile dates to 1879....In a chess exhibition, Alexhine plays 26 simultaneous games and wins all. Bogoljubow loses four, ties two, and wins 20.	Nov. 17
	Secretary Stimson encourages the Pan American Conference on Customs Procedures and Port Facilities to standardize and simplify. He says a customs union is a first step toward solidarity in the Pan American Union.	The stock market is quiet in slow trading. Only 2.7 million shares change hands.	An earthquake rocks the East Coast from New York to Nova Scotia. A thirteen-foot tide washes over Boston's waterfront, and winds reach 78 mph at block island. The quake breaks 10 of the 21 undersea cables to Europe. The tidal wave kills 26 in Newfoundland.	The Amateur Athletic Union votes to use starting blocks, but not until the International Amateur Athletic Federation agrees. President Avery Brundage decries commercialism in sport. Actors Equity votes to reject the managers' plan for Sunday performances.	Nov. 18
After a record Socialist vote in the recent New York mayoral election, Norman Thomas says he will surrender the label "Socialist" if that brings in labor and farmers. He doubts they are ready to join a national "New Party."	Gen. Fuqua says the infantry suffers poor morale due to low pay. Housing is also inadequate, and slow promotions hamper reserve officer career progression.	Senate Democrats say they have 48 votes to adjourn without finishing the tariff. They say the "Young Guard" have lost....Stocks rise on volume of 2.7 million. The curb exchange is up sharply.	The National Academy of Sciences hears a report of the creation of a new plant through use of radium. It also hears a report about tracking the retreat of a glacier through examination of mud. Other reports deal with enzymes and living culture vaccination.		Nov. 19
The leadership bests the "New Guard." The senate votes 49-33 to adjourn and reconvene in December....Harry Sinclair leaves prison after completing a 6-month contempt sentence.			Paul Bartsch's wife, Signe, sues the biologist for divorce. She contends that he treats her as a specimen. She also says he keeps animals in the house and drives away young female associates by talking biology to them.	Show of Shows debuts. The talkie has a cast of 77 contemporary stars such as Barrymore and old-timers including Ben Turpin.	Nov. 20
The Cayuga Indians ask New York for permission to return from Canada. The tribe, currently 1,500 members-strong, has been in Canada since 1795. Governor F.D. Roosevelt promises to see what he can do....A judge in Marion, NC, rules that rebellion is an inappropriate charge in a labor dispute. The neighboring county, citing the AFL's Southern unionization plan, charges union leaders with rebellion in the violent August textile strike.		Business leaders meet with Hoover at the White House. Ford springs a surprise, announcing wage increases. His statement upstages Hoover's, which announces the creation of a business council and says business agrees not to cut wages and labor not to request increases.	Byrd announces the discovery of a new Antarctic mountain range with peaks of 10–15,000 feet. The range stretches 150 miles.	Florenz Ziegfield signs Fred and Adele Astaire to star in Tom, Dick, and Harry. Book is by Noel Coward with music by Vincent Youmans.	Nov. 21
New York's attorney general rejects the Cayuga petition for a reservation in new York. He says they gave up their land in 1797 and got paid for it.	Stimson says he would like to bring the 1,200 troops home from Nicaragua. He cites pressure from the Nicaraguan government, both conservatives and liberals, to have the Marines stay.	Ford announces it will shut down all its factories for a "readjustment." The shutdown is not seasonal.	Amelia Earhart sets a woman's speed mark on a Los Angeles course. Reaching 197 mph, she averages 184.17 mph.		Nov. 22

F	G	H	I	J
Includes campaigns, elections, federal-state relations, civil rights and liberties, crime, the judiciary, education, healthcare, poverty, urban affairs, and population.	Includes formation and debate of U.S. foreign and defense policies, veterans affairs, and defense spending. (Relations with specific foreign countries are usually found under the region concerned.)	Includes business, labor, agriculture, taxation, transportation, consumer affairs, monetary and fiscal policy, natural resources, pollution and industrial accidents.	Includes worldwide scientific, medical and technological developments, natural phenomena, U.S. weather and natural disasters.	Includes the arts, religion, scholarship, communications media, sports, entertainment, fashions, fads, and social life.

	World Affairs	Europe	Africa & The Middle East	The Americas	Asia & The Pacific
Nov. 23		Belgian merchants blame the worst slump in the diamond market since 1914 on women's fantasies about driving American cars. Speculation on the stock market is another cause....Clemenceau dies after 88 hours in a coma.	Ibn Saud, king of the Hedjaz and Nejd, has crushed the bandits in his kingdom and stabilized the border with Iraq. The hope is that Britain will demolish the line of forts between the two countries. The forts annoy the Saudis.		Australia raises tariffs on leather, auto bodies, gasoline, and cigars.
Nov. 24				A filaria epidemic in mostly-black St. Kitts in the British West Indies is complicated by elephantiasis. Within the past few months, 40 of 375 victims have died.	Faced with the Soviet menace, the warring Chinese factions stop fighting and establish a united front. The Russians are west of Manchuria's Khingan Range and threatening Harbin.
Nov. 25		The final vote on the for a German plebiscite on the Young Plan and war guilt is 4,135,300. After initial expectations of failure, the measure passes by 8,000 votes.		A Guatemalan historian, Maximo Soto-Hall, says "America" derives from Nicaragua's Amerrique Peak and the city of Americopan, not Amerigo Vespucci. His source is 16th-century historian Julius Marcau.	Chiang claims victories in Honan and Hupeh, with 40,000 men lost to the enemy. He turns toward Canton. Refugees pour into Harbin.
Nov. 26			Locusts from the Atlas Mountains plague Morocco. The French Foreign legion is using cavalry and aircraft to fight the locusts, and both Christians and Muslims are praying for a wind shift to take them elsewhere.	Ecuador's economy measures include cutting the army budget by a million sucres ($200,000) and closing legations and embassies to avoid paying salaries. Only Peru and the United States will retain paid diplomats....Mexico projects a 1930 budget surplus after cutting the military $6.5 million. The $57,000 will go to education.	Japanese reports say that Feng's retreat is due to a $5 million bribe from Chiang. Yen also may have taken a bribe. Fighting ceased suddenly after the rebels visited Chiang.
Nov. 27		Belgian Socialists refuse to work with any party until after elections. This prevents the Catholics from forming a coalition and leaves Belgium without a government.... Norwegian police investigate a polyandrous cult. The Dissenters share everything communally and do not believe in explaining themselves to authorities.	King Nadir announces Afghanistan will have prohibition and Islamic law. He also promises to restore infrastructure and the military and to continue Amanullah's foreign policy.	The Dominican Republic announces plans to create a Great Columbus Library. The library's goal is to have complete historical data on all nations of the western hemisphere. Site is undetermined.	Russia says that Manchuria has agreed to revert to the status quo on the railroad issue. Fighting stops and rumors spread that Soviet troops have withdrawn.
Nov. 28		Germany prepares wartime camps for prisoners of war and Polish refugees to receive 4,000 Russian peasants. The German commissioner will evaluate the peasants for potential colonization in Germany or the Americas....The reichsrat passes a bill strengthening protections against acts endangering the government and authorizing the return of the Kaiser. It goes next to the Reichstag.			The viceroy's secretary says only state governors can address state matters. Thus, interest groups with state issues will not attend the conference on the status of India.
Nov. 29	The League conference on facilitating delivery of newspapers proposes that all European states open their borders so airplanes can drop bundles of papers. Current international law prohibits dropping bundles. Hachette is experimenting with three planes in France.	New foreign minister Julius Curtius the vote for a plebiscite a nationalist ploy to sow confusion and that it is incompatible with German interests, and that it usurps Reichstag prerogative. The Reichstag is expected to defeat the plebiscite demand.		Canadian industrial and commercial activity, measured by employment, sets a new record. Strongest sectors are logging, construction, telephone and telegraph. Coal output for October is down from October 1928.	
Nov. 30		France and Belgium withdraw their troops from zone 2 of the Rhineland. The German republic's flag waves as Germans celebrate and at least a few Belgians express doubts.			The Nanking finance minister abolishes "tax farming." The practice promotes corruption and squeezing of the people. It conflicts with the efficiency and integrity the party seeks.

A	B	C	D	E
Includes developments that affect more than one world region, international organizations and important meetings of world leaders.	*Includes all domestic and regional developments in Europe, including the Soviet Union.*	*Includes all domestic and regional developments in Africa and the Middle East.*	*Includes all domestic and regional developments in Latin America, the Caribbean, and Canada.*	*Includes all domestic and regional developments in Asian and Pacific nations (and colonies).*

U.S. Politics & Social Issues	U.S. Foreign Policy & Affairs, Defense	U.S. Economy & Environment	Science, Technology & Nature	Culture, Leisure & Lifestyle	
Kentucky prepares to make whisky for the first time in a decade as the state licenses three distilleries to replenish its supply of medicinal whisky. Prescription whisky costs $6 a pint. Pre-Prohibition whisky cost $4.50 a quart.			Dr. Vladimir Zworykin of Westinghouse laboratories touts his new cathode ray tube, which unites picture and sound. By eliminating neon tubes and whirling disks, it brings "radio vision" nearer to home use.	Negligees are fashionable in chiffon and marquisette. Pastels are most popular, but strong colors appeal too. Fur and lace top off the seductive nightwear.	Nov. 23
	The Surgeon General reports that the army alcoholism rate is the lowest since 1921 but the death rate is up. Air fatalities and respiratory disease are also up.	State governors commit to spend millions on roads and other construction. Governor Roosevelt promises President Hoover that New York will build prisons and hospitals to the limit of its income.	A Jockey Club examination of 1034 races shows that there is no advantage to the pole position. Horses win equally from inside and outside positions.	Beatrice Lillie entertains at the Palace. The veteran comedienne is noted for distinctive arch mannerisms that set apart her act's nonsense songs and skits.	Nov. 24
The shrine at Malden cemetery closes pending an investigation ordered by the cardinal. Seeking a last chance cure, 150,000 flock to the priest's grave.	The Army's annual report shows actual strength of 137,000. Desertions are down for the second year. The report attributes the decline to the implementation of IQ testing two years ago and improved quality of recruits as a result.	In preparation for a scheduled strike in January, the 45,000-member International Ladies Garment Workers union begins organizing 4,000 black seamstresses, who earn less than 40 percent of union wage. The ILGWU will use black organizers working from a Harlem office.	The Department of Commerce reports the United States has 9,319 registered airplanes and 8,907 pilots. Students number 27,997 and mechanics 7,705. Of the registered planes, 6,215 are licensed, while the other are identified but not licensed.		Nov. 25
		The Southern Pacific, Great Northern, and Northern Pacific announce plans to spend $100 million in 1930. New orders include cars, rails as the railroads prepare to extend a line or lay a second set of rails.	The U.S. Department of Agriculture reports that doctors are having success in treating aplastic anemia with embryonic calves liver. The first tests of the liver treatment were in March 1929.	The Theater Guild Studio announces plans to present three experimental plays. The first is the Soviet play Red Dust....Wellesley women opt for long skirts. Radcliffe and Smith wear long skirts in the evening but retain short skirts for daytime wear.	Nov. 26
	The Army aviation chief says the air service is short of training planes. He wants more equipment. Promotions are slow too....The labor department is considering taxing aliens $18 per border crossing. The levy would affect the 6700 Canadians who work in Detroit. And the department wants to discourage Detroit's 250,000 aliens from moving to Canada and commuting. Similar problems are prevalent at Buffalo, El Paso, and other border towns.	Oklahoma takes over 12 banks that collapse due to a liquidity problem brought on by 1920s deflation. State bank officials are quick to explain that the failures have nothing to do with the recent stock market collapse.	Electrical engineer Dr. E.E.Free says the all-electric house of 1950 will be windowless and sound-proof with individual climate controls for each room. It will be affordable for moderate income families and healthier than current houses.	Fox and Warner Bros. are sued for anti-trust violations. The two studios combined control 65 percent of movie production.	Nov. 27
			Byrd heads out to fly over the South Pole. His principal worry is whether his heavily laden plane can climb over the 14,000 foot peaks.	Ernie Nevers sets a professional mark by scoring 40 points in a football game. The Cardinals beat the Bears 40–6 to win the Chicago city championship.	Nov. 28
	New York pays respects to 75 returned soldiers, buried in Siberia for 11 years, as they transit to final rest in Michigan. Commissioners reveal the hard work they did in overcoming native resistance....In London, ambassadors Dawes of the United States and Matsudaira of Japan begin talks on naval reduction preparatory to the full naval discussions.		On an 18-hour flight with Bernt Balchen at the controls, Byrd crosses the South Pole through Glacier Pass at 11,500 feet. The British set aside the land dispute to celebrate with the Americans.	Al Jolson announces he will give up legitimate theater. He will devote his attention to the movies and concerts.	Nov. 29
The Harlem Tenant Association forms. The group is devoted to improving run down neighborhoods and reducing the incidence of tuberculosis, several times higher than it should be.	The army simplifies maneuvers. Previous complex war games have intruded on civilians.	A national survey completed last week points to a good Christmas for radio sales and a banner 1930. The stock market is not a factor now that the radio has moved from luxury to necessity.	A group of 300 dinosaur footprints near Flagstaff, AZ, is believed to be the largest ever found. The area also includes good samples of cliff dwellings.		Nov. 30

F
Includes campaigns, elections, federal-state relations, civil rights and liberties, crime, the judiciary, education, healthcare, poverty, urban affairs, and population.

G
Includes formation and debate of U.S. foreign and defense policies, veterans affairs, and defense spending. (Relations with specific foreign countries are usually found under the region concerned.)

H
Includes business, labor, agriculture, taxation, transportation, consumer affairs, monetary and fiscal policy, natural resources, pollution and industrial accidents.

I
Includes worldwide scientific, medical and technological developments, natural phenomena, U.S. weather and natural disasters.

J
Includes the arts, religion, scholarship, communications media, sports, entertainment, fashions, fads, and social life.

	World Affairs	Europe	Africa & The Middle East	The Americas	Asia & The Pacific
Dec. 1		A week's worth of dropping values on the Paris bourse despite government and bank intervention brings comparisons to the Wall Street crash. At worst, the boom is over. Gold continues to flow from the United States to Paris because interest rates are better and because French firms have to meet year-end obligations. Italy and England are feeling economic pressures.			
Dec. 2	France presents U.S. and French notes to Russia requesting peace in Manchuria. The act is a first test of the Kellogg-Briand peace pact.	Yugoslavia arrests employees of the railroad ministry for passing Yugoslavia's mobilization plans to Italy. The workers are mostly Russian immigrants in low-level jobs....The Labour government tells the Commons that it plans to socialize transportation. This is the government's first proposal for public ownership of a resource....Rome police recover St. Peter's jewels, including the ring of the fisherman. The jewels were taken in 1925.	Egypt estimates its cotton crop at 355,660 metric tons. Last year's crop was 352,600 metric tons, and the 5-year average is 319,100 tons. A metric ton is 2,204 pounds.		
Dec. 3	The American charge in Geneva meets with League officials concerning the United States joining the world court. Expectations are for a quick senate ratification of the court treaty.	Former Belgian premier Jaspar tells the king he is ready to form a cabinet. The previous cabinet resigned over the question of what language to use at the University of Ghent. The new government will face the same economic and cultural problems that toppled the old one.	The Grand Mufti of Jerusalem, at hearings into the August riots, contends that Britain promised Arab independence before the war and again for service during the war. He also says Arabs own the Wailing Wall. Arabs shoot the sixth Jewish doctor since the riots.	An American-owned 143-mile gas pipeline opens between Zapata County, TX, and Matamoras, Mexico. Capacity is 21 million cubic feet a day....Vasconcelos crosses into Mexico from Arizona and claims he was cheated in the presidential election.	Fighting resumes as the rebels march on Canton. Nationalist troops mutiny at Pukow, refusing orders to march....Manchuria and Russia sign the protocol ending the dispute over the railway. Status reverts to that of 1924 after China yields on the issue of Chinese managers and Russia promises to appoint Chinese to other positions.
Dec. 4		The House of Lords votes 43 to 21 to reject the government's move to resume diplomatic relations with Russia. The Lords reject arguments that there will be protection against spying and that recognition will improve trade.		Uruguay, which has been mediating the Chaco dispute, announces that Bolivia and Paraguay are ready to renew diplomatic relations. They will exchange ministers when they exchange Forts Vanguardia and Bouqueron.	After looting Pukow, Chinese mutineers hijack trains and move north. Their number is estimated at 15,000....Reports of an agreement in Manchurua prove premature. In Mukden, Chang rejects the terms offered by Moscow to settle the railway dispute.
Dec. 5	The League agrees to change the date of its opening session to accommodate the five-power naval discussions. Most members agree, but many regret the precedent of accommodating to one nation's demands.	The Czechs agree to a new cabinet under Udrzal. Socialists will have a third of the portfolios....Hjalmar Schacht of the Reichsbank says that Germany cannot meet demands on top of Young Plan reparations. Citing overlapping Dawes and Young assessments, he lists additional demands from England, Poland, Belgium, and elsewhere.		The U.S. Marine commander declares martial law in Haiti. Customs workers are on strike, and the colonel anticipates disturbances by labor and students. Unrest has bothered Haiti for several weeks.	
Dec. 6	The Woman's Party convention opens. The party will take its demands for equal women's rights to Hoover and the Hague....The international labor office opens meetings to discuss protections for white-collar workers and find a definition of "trade secret." It will also deal with protection of musicians from talking pictures and radio.		In Jerusalem the government tells newspapers not to print anything that might inflame Arabs or Jews. If necessary, the government will impose censorship.	Mexican railway workers go on strike. Mexican troops are sent to preserve order and prevent the use of strikebreakers.....In San Antonio, Vasconcelos says he won 95 percent of the vote. He says his revolt is funded and he will not ask any American for money.	Australian coal miners reject a proposed agreement. The stage is set for a strike....The presence of Soviet troops makes Manchurian Mongols feel safe. They declare independence.
Dec. 7			Ibn Saud protests that the Kuweiti sheik is supplying and providing sanctuary to rebels under Feisal al Dawash. Saud wants the British to intervene in their Kuwaiti protectorate.	The NAACP says that Haitians are oppressed and freedom of press is a joke. The economy is a shambles, the constitution was enacted through fraud, and the president was elected illegally in 1922 and remains in office only due to the United States.	Shanghai, Nanking, Canton, and Hankow are under martial law and Chiang is isolated as the mutinous force swells to 50,000. Chiang must divert 70,000 questionably loyal nationalist troops to face the rebels.

A	B	C	D	E
Includes developments that affect more than one world region, international organizations and important meetings of world leaders.	Includes all domestic and regional developments in Europe, including the Soviet Union.	Includes all domestic and regional developments in Africa and the Middle East.	Includes all domestic and regional developments in Latin America, the Caribbean, and Canada.	Includes all domestic and regional developments in Asian and Pacific nations (and colonies).

U.S. Politics & Social Issues	U.S. Foreign Policy & Affairs, Defense	U.S. Economy & Environment	Science, Technology & Nature	Culture, Leisure & Lifestyle	
Rev. Harry E. Fosdick says Christianity has become too complex. People have to get back to a personal relation with Jesus. Rev. J. Fulton Sheen says the trend toward pre-Christian belief in human self-sufficiency is creating intellectual dwarfs.		Secretary Hyde approves use of $73 million of 1931 funds for 1930 road construction. This provides a total of $101 million for the states and Hawaii. States must provide matching funds.	Drought in the Pacific northwest is causing power shortages. Seattle and Tacoma officials ask the state to appoint an administrator to oversee rationing.	Now playing at the Palace are Fred Waring and his Pennsylvanians, Bert Wheeler, Lulu McConnell, and Buck and Bubbles....Twelve thousand fans turn out for the start of a six-day bicycle race.	Dec. 1
Congress returns. The first priority is passing the tax cut. Hawley asks that the cut be $160 million....The Department of Justice reports 21,000 dry law violators served an average 147-day jail or prison term in fiscal year 1929. The department prosecuted 57,000 cases. A significant backlog persists.	Secretary of State Stimson denies that he is negotiating with Dr. Wu. He does acknowledge that they have had informal talks over extra-territoriality.	The post office reports a deficit of $85 million, up from $32 million in 1928. Postmaster General Brown blames $32 million of the deficit on franking privileges and air and ocean mail subsidies....The Loughead brothers incorporate a new aircraft company in California. Inventors of a hydraulic brake, they sold their other company, Lockheed Aircraft, to Detroit Aircraft, earlier in the year....Julius Rosenwald says Sears Roebuck has opened negotiations for J.C. Penney.	Storms dump four inches of snow on New York City and pound a ship to pieces. Great Lakes shipping shuts down.	Kid Chocolate, the Cuban featherweight phenomenon, signs for two Madison Square Garden bouts in 1930. Opponents remain to be determined....An indoor polo league forms in New York City.	Dec. 2
A petition to put repeal of prohibition on the Massachusetts ballot garners 32,000 signatures. If the legislature fails to act, the issue will be on the November 1930 ballot....Assistant district attorney Lehman closes without action an inquiry into the Utopia Benevolent Association. The association proposes to help elderly and orphaned blacks by establishing resorts in upstate New York.		Ford raises its minimum wage to $7 a day. Both Canadian and U.S. workers get the increase....The head of J.C. Penney denies merger rumors. He says he has no interest in merging with any mail order house....Sam Insull continues expanding his utility empire. He buys a majority stake in Texas-Pecos Power.	A French scientist says iodine-fed oysters are cleaner and safer....One hundred Columbia students sign up for a test of the psychological effects of coffee. The 36 selected receive $1 an hour for drinking coffee.		Dec. 3
The president of the American Patriotic Societies says 41 percent of annual immigration is from the western hemisphere. F.H. Kennicutt asks a ceiling of 5,000 for Mexican immigration rather than the current 51,000.	Foreign Secretary Litvinof implies that Stimson interfered in the Manchurian negotiations between Mukden and Moscow and delayed the resolution of the dispute. Stimson replies that the United States had no ulterior motive but was simply using Kellogg principles to bring peace. And the United States has a right to work toward peace.	Ford begins recalling all laid off workers. The company expects to achieve record output in the near future....Citing a huge anticipated surplus, Hoover asks a $3.8 billion budget for 1931, down from $4 billion this year. He warns that excessive spending will threaten tax cuts.	Highlighting the 25th Automobile Salon are "chameleon" cars that change color in different light. The custom-built European and American cars change from blue to black, tan to yellow, and grey to blue and can change shades within a color.	George Jessel contracts to appear as Joseph in the Biblical production "P.S.—He Got the Job." He is abandoning films for the legitimate theater.	Dec. 4
A new cigarette price war causes United Cigar Stores to add four more brands to the 12-cent-a-pack category.		The American Petroleum Institute asks controls on gasoline. It says that output is approaching the point of being economically unviable.		F.R. Rogers of the New York state health department calls for an end to scholastic sports championships, a rein on coaches' powers, and a reduction on the amount of money spent on sports. He says excessive emphasis on sports causes strain and is bad for athletes' health.	Dec. 5
After 2½ years, the Senate rules that Vare cannot take his seat. Sen. Nye says no person involved in the 1926 campaign will be allowed to fill the seat....Secretary Wilbur appoints Dean James Bond of Kentucky Normal and Industrial Institute to a commission to examine the condition of black secondary education.	The U.S. warning to China and Russia to avoid war has six new supporters. Twenty nations now support a peaceful resolution.	Secretary Hyde reports that farm income at $12.5 billion is the highest since 1925. Farm values are up $400 million. Dr. Ralph E. Diffendorfer of Methodist foreign missions sees the U.S. farmer moving toward peasant status.		Goucher College, a women's school in Maryland, permits students to smoke....Baseball's minor leagues agree not to sign athletes still in school. Owners express interest in having a team in Havana and decry the practice of owning multiple franchises, i.e. the farm system.	Dec. 6
The president of the Independent Retail Tobacconists' Association asks his 360 active and 2,000 inactive members to hold prices at 15 cents a pack. He also asks Federal Trade Commission aid to keep the large companies from driving small stores out of business by selling at a loss.			Gale winds of 108 mph strand ships off Britain, sinking one with a loss of 21 lives. An Italian ship carrying $70 million of art to London is missing but later turns up safe.	The Big Ten denies the University of Iowa's second plea for reinstatement after the conference bans the school for subsidies to athletes. The Big Six announces an investigation of rumors of subsidies at member schools.	Dec. 7

F	G	H	I	J
Includes campaigns, elections, federal-state relations, civil rights and liberties, crime, the judiciary, education, healthcare, poverty, urban affairs, and population.	*Includes formation and debate of U.S. foreign and defense policies, veterans affairs, and defense spending. (Relations with specific foreign countries are usually found under the region concerned.)*	*Includes business, labor, agriculture, taxation, transportation, consumer affairs, monetary and fiscal policy, natural resources, pollution and industrial accidents.*	*Includes worldwide scientific, medical and technological developments, natural phenomena, U.S. weather and natural disasters.*	*Includes the arts, religion, scholarship, communications media, sports, entertainment, fashions, fads, and social life.*

	World Affairs	Europe	Africa & The Middle East	The Americas	Asia & The Pacific
Dec. 8		Greece announces it will build two cities to house immigrants from Russia....Spain ends censorship of the foreign press after six years. After a prisoner amnesty and a new foreign loan, the De Rivera government feels stronger and more secure.		Haiti is quiet as authorities hold strike leaders and a U.S. warship arrives. Protests continue against the president as officials deny press censorship. The Society of United American Countries scores the killing of Haitians and backs Hoover's call for an inquiry.	
Dec. 9	The German publication *Die Bank* publishes an editorial claiming that the Wall Street stock market crash was an inevitability that should have occurred much sooner, and was delayed only through the actions of idealistic banking firms.	Russia grants Gillette a concession to build a razor factory. W. Averell Harriman had abandoned a manganese concession in 1928. Russia usually prefers technical assistance and routinely violates concession terms.			
Dec. 10	European opinion is favorable to the Root protocol committing the United States to the world court. The Senate has not yet agreed, and the United States is not signing the provision making observance of court rulings mandatory.	Eamon de Valera, in the United States to seek funds for a new newspaper, says he expects an Irish republic in the future. He also says his party will eventually take power through elections....The Upper Thames breaks its banks and runs three miles wide. Floods threaten London as Oxford gets food by boat.	The curator of the Greco-Roman museum at Alexandria says that Egypt should unearth the tomb of Alexander, not Howard Carter. Egyptian Prince Omar Tousoun recently said that Arabic records locate the tomb under the mosque of Nebl Daniel, the tomb of the prophet Daniel.	Ontario premier Ferguson asks producers of newsprint and publishers to meet and work out a compromise. He says the price increase is not anti-American; the province's three major mills are American owned. Quebec premier Teschereau says the price is fair. The U.S. justice department will not get involved unless someone proves price fixing....With the Haitian crisis cooling, Hoover orders the aircraft tender *Wright* to divert to Guantanamo.	Drought and sandstorms force the abandonment of cattle ranches in Central Australia. Cattle drives that evacuate animals to the Adelaide market require airdrops of hay for the animals. Birds wait at the drop sites for the next herd of cattle.... The battle for Chiang's capital is on. Rebels begin attacks 40 miles away.
Dec. 11		Belgium is still working on the language issue. The current compromise proposal makes Flemish the official language of the University of Ghent.	The British House of Lords votes 43–13 to condemn the labor government's proposal to withdraw troops into the desert and allow Egyptian control of Cairo and Alexandria. Lord Lloyd, recently resigned high commissioner to Egypt, says the move will risk the Suez Canal and communication with India and allow Communist influence in Egypt, as in Palestine and China.	Wireless service between the United States and Peru begins.	Chiang kai-Shek holds off the rebels at Canton. At Shanghai, foreign nationals flee disturbances....Nadir Khan sends forces to Koidaman in northwest Afghanistan to quell a rising. Thirty-eight rebels have already been executed in Kabul.
Dec. 12		British troops leave the Rhineland.... Copenhagen University awards a doctorate in astronomy for the first time in 34 years.		Dutch West Indians are persecuting Venezuelan refugees. Allegedly, the West Indian junta sends Venezuelans unsympathetic to the government back to Venezuela, whose government they have fled....As priests officiate after being barred by the government for three years, the Shrine of Guadalupe attracts 200,000 pilgrims. Many of the devout make the four-mile trip on their hands and knees.	Chiang kai-Shek's forces win at Canton, Honan, and Anhwei. The Reds control Kiangsi.
Dec. 13	Nineteen of the 26 nations working to reduce tariff barriers sign a treaty that establishes freer but not free trade effective January 1. The agreement is for six months because most nations say they will drop out July 1 if Poland and Czechoslovakia do not join. The United States is signatory.		The French government votes funds for the army in Syria, defeating those who want an end to the mandate in Syria. Sixte Quentin says the mandate is too costly. War minister Maginot counters that the mandate is a commitment France must keep as a matter of national honor.		The House of Representatives applauds when commissioner Camilo Osias enters debate on agricultural funding to plead for Philippine independence. Representatives Leonidas Dyer, Joseph Edwards, and Charles Hooper say the Philippines are ready for self-rule....Chiang kai-Shek's forces win on all fronts.
Dec. 14		In preparation for legislation restricting types of work foreigners can perform, Turkey's parliament issues a list. Foreigners cannot be chemists, bootblacks, veterinarians, customs inspectors, pharmacists, guides, watchmen, and more. It supplements a 1914 law that barred foreign doctors, lawyers, chauffeurs, waiters, and street merchants.	The Arab boycott of Jewish merchants spreads from Palestine to Syria. Jewish merchants are entering bankruptcy, and Armenian merchants are buying Jewish stores.	Motilone Indians in western Venezuela attack, rob, and fade into the jungle. American oil crews cannot catch them because they are more adept at operating in the jungle and protected by the Venezuelan government. The oil companies bring in bloodhounds and wolfhounds to pursue the Motilones.	

A	B	C	D	E
Includes developments that affect more than one world region, international organizations and important meetings of world leaders.	Includes all domestic and regional developments in Europe, including the Soviet Union.	Includes all domestic and regional developments in Africa and the Middle East.	Includes all domestic and regional developments in Latin America, the Caribbean, and Canada.	Includes all domestic and regional developments in Asian and Pacific nations (and colonies).

U.S. Politics & Social Issues	U.S. Foreign Policy & Affairs, Defense	U.S. Economy & Environment	Science, Technology & Nature	Culture, Leisure & Lifestyle	
The American Bible Society presents Hoover with a bible in commemoration of its 120th anniversary. The ABS handed out a million Bibles in 71 languages in New York City alone in 1928.	Raymond Leslie Buell's study for the Foreign Policy Association finds less democracy in Haiti than in Puerto Rico. The association backs Hoover's request for a commission to find a new U.S. policy to prepare Haiti for 1936 independence....The National Patriotic League says Stimson's use of Kellogg is a mistake. The Soviets will take advantage of it to convince the Russian people the United States is a threat.	American publishers hold an emergency meeting after learning that paper will rise $5 a ton. The additional cost will total $20 million a year.	With a phone call to the ship *Leviathan*, ship-to-shore service begins. The *Leviathan* is 200 miles out to sea.	Columbia's freshmen are the smartest in 10 years. The upper quartile scores 91.5 on the Thorndike test. Average since 1922 is 89.6 on a 120-point scale. Columbia's Dean Willet Eccles says the average for all college freshmen is 85 and high school seniors average 72.	Dec. 8
		The national Chamber of Commerce broadcasts a comprehensive business survey to 900,000 businesses. The report, input to the national business advisory board, finds overproduction only in automobiles and radio.		French critics say foreign films are a menace to French language and culture. U.S. films are the greatest threat of all.	Dec. 9
Congressman Frederick Zihlman (R-MD) and Warren Harding's Controller of the Currency Daniel Crissinger are among the officials of the F.H.Smith brokerage firm indicted for mail fraud. Zihlman, protesting innocence, says he will not invoke Congressional immunity....A National Miners' Union strike in Illinois' Taylorville coalfields brings out 3,000 miners. To keep the strike from spreading, elsewhere in Illinois troops guard Peabody mines, and law enforcement arrests union officials. The NMU is a newly formed radical rival of the UMWA.	The navy board votes to recommend that Congress spend $5 million to create a dirigible base on a 1,700-acre tract at Sunnyvale near San Francisco. The minority prefers 2032-acre Camp Kearney, near San Diego.			The U.S. State Department tells Americans not to believe promises that they are heirs to the Blake and Drake fortunes. The fortunes are myths spread by hustlers, to whom several hundred Americans each year pay large sums for "legal fees."	Dec. 10
Pennsylvania Governor Fisher appoints Grundy, a high-tariff lobbyist, to the seat denied to Vare. Grundy and Vare, along with Pinchot, are expected to compete in the 1930 primary....In western Kentucky, 15,000 miners vote for UMWA representation. Illinois UMWA miners prepare to cross the picket lines of the rival union's strikers.	The United States is reluctant to grant a license to nationalist China to buy arms and ammunition. The United States worries that a nationalist victory will end extraterritoriality....Admiral Hughes, Chief of Naval Operations, says the navy needs small arms and a radio-controlled target ship. The lack hampers training of gunners and landing parties.	Reports to the radio board reveal that 168 radio stations made a profit for the year while 149 took losses. Stations vary in wattage from 100 to 50,000. Operating costs range from under $10,000 to almost $500,000, but smallest wattage does not necessarily mean smallest cost.			Dec. 11
The navy agrees to let the city of Tacoma, WA, use the carrier *Lexington* as a supplemental power source for 30 days. Drought in Washington has produced critical shortages of electricity.	Poland welcomes the new U.S. ambassador. In return it will raise the status of its representative to Washington.	After U.S.-based International Paper Company indicates that it will not be raising its paper prices, Canadian firms abandon their plans for a $5-a-ton increase. The U.S. publishing industry is victorious.	Millions of Americans tune in as Marconi sits before a London microphone and tells how he made the first transatlantic signal. NBC carries the 28th anniversary event on its 59-station network....University of Chicago bacteriologist Isadore Falk, after studying 3,400 possibilities, identifies the flu bug as pleomorphic streptococcus. He has no vaccine, but 14 of his assistants came down with the bug.	The University of Iowa names 14 players in five sports as partakers of the unauthorized fund. Amounts taken by the now ineligible players range from $15 to $80.	Dec. 12
New York promises 100 inspectors to clean up health violations in Harlem starting 16 December, less than a week after the Harlem Renters' Association reports violations in 75 percent of the 1500 tenements it has inspected. Harlem has 175,000 people in 5,000 houses.			The 1929 Chandler Medal goes to Irving Langmuir, president of the American Chemical Society and head of the General Electric research laboratory. Langmuir's work is in the behavior of the electron.	Edwin Rudolph sets world records at the World Pocket Billiards Championship in Detroit. He has an unfinished string of 111 and wins a 4-inning match, 125 to minus 2.	Dec. 13
Princeton seminary faculty issue a statement that they teach the Bible's divinity and the miracle birth of Jesus and will require new faculty to sing a statement agreeing to that teaching. They are responding to rumors and false statements that they are moving away from historical conservative Presbyterian principles.	Navy Secretary Adams wants Marine Maj. Gen. Smedley Butler to explain his December 5 speech. Reportedly, Butler said the United States declared opposition candidates outlaws in order to guarantee victory to its chosen candidate in Nicaragua.		A Stuttgart, Germany, ice rink debuts "Opal ice." Made of water with chemicals added, the artificial ice is reusable, durable, and simple to produce. It costs $6 a square meter, less than 10 percent the cost of ammonia-based ice used in rinks such as Madison Square Garden.		Dec. 14

F	G	H	I	J
Includes campaigns, elections, federal-state relations, civil rights and liberties, crime, the judiciary, education, healthcare, poverty, urban affairs, and population.	*Includes formation and debate of U.S. foreign and defense policies, veterans affairs, and defense spending. (Relations with specific foreign countries are usually found under the region concerned.)*	*Includes business, labor, agriculture, taxation, transportation, consumer affairs, monetary and fiscal policy, natural resources, pollution and industrial accidents.*	*Includes worldwide scientific, medical and technological developments, natural phenomena, U.S. weather and natural disasters.*	*Includes the arts, religion, scholarship, communications media, sports, entertainment, fashions, fads, and social life.*

	World Affairs	Europe	Africa & The Middle East	The Americas	Asia & The Pacific
Dec. 15		Gold continues to flow into France, which gains another $32 million in November. The year's total is $370 million.		Argentina's *La Prensa* says that the problems in Haiti have come about during the U.S. Marine presence. The paper is in the middle of a campaign to get the United States out of Haiti. Haitians request that the Marines remain at least through the April elections. They distrust President Borno.	The largest Christian celebration in Asia ends as 40,000 Filipinos close the National Eucharistic Congress. The meeting calls for religious education in the schools. The men's conference votes to ask independence, but the priests' conference takes no stand on the issue.
Dec. 16		London newspapers and the boxing commissioner call for cancellation of the Primo Carnera – Franz Diener fight. Carnera is 6'10" and 283 pounds, and some fear he will kill an opponent. He does—in 1933. He wins this fight in six rounds.			
Dec. 17				Argentina closes the gold exchange office because the exchange rate of the peso is fluctuating and Argentina is losing gold. Most South American currencies and bonds are weak.	
Dec. 18		Russia and Turkey sign a two-year pact of friendship. Russia compares it to the prewar Entente Cordiale between France and England.	The Arab boycott of Jewish merchants continues, but Arab sheiks want to resume agricultural production. Sheiks promise to protect those who return from the cities to farms and villages. Palestine issues a blasphemy law prescribing a year in jail for anyone speaking offensive words about another religion.		Cuneiform writings discovered at Alishar in Asia Minor, previously thought to be Hittite, date to 1,000 years earlier. They are Assyrian, possibly from the time of Hammurabi, and they extend the borders of the known Assyrian realm.
Dec. 19		Labor barely wins a preliminary vote on the coal industry reform bill. Few liberals back labor and many Tories boycott. The fragility of the labor government is apparent, should liberals and Tories unite against it.	In Nigeria, native unrest prevents the landing of the mail boat at Calabar. At Opobo troops prevent women from looting the factories and trading station. When pressed against the walls by the crowd of women, troops open fire and kill 20.		
Dec. 20		The Prince of Wales receives ambassador Grigorie Sokolnikov. Britain and the Soviet Union resume diplomatic relations, broken in 1927.... Yugoslavian authorities arrest 2,000 Croatian members of the Raditch Group.	British troops in Egypt capture Chief Lafofa, whose recalcitrant attitude earlier brings about a punitive expedition by Sudanese forces. The dissidents wound a British officer and kill a trooper.	The Chaco negotiations stall as Paraguay backs out of the fort exchange, refusing to rebuild a fort for Bolivia. Rumor is that Paraguay is building new forts.	The Russian army reopens the Chinese Eastern Railway from Hailar to Manchuli. Trains from Hailar to Moscow now run daily.
Dec. 21				A Brazilian judges order enforcement of the nation's child labor laws. They reject requests for child labor in munitions plants and exemptions from limits on daily hours.	The Blue Ribbon Decoration of the Emperor of Japan goes to Princeton's A.G. Fletcher. The award recognizes his 20 years working at the Taiku, Korea, leper hospital, funded primarily by Princetonians.
Dec. 22		Yugoslavia arrests 11 Croatian leaders of the Students and Farmers Party for bombing a Zagreb hotel and cathedral. Croatians also attack a train....A Nationalist-led referendum on rejection of the Young Plan falls well short of the 21 million votes needed. Barely six million Germans turn out.	The Wafd (Nationalist) Party wins 155 of 235 seats in Egyptian parliamentary elections. With a strong majority, Wafd's Nahas Pasha can form a government.		An attempt to assassinate Indian viceroy, Lord Irwin, by throwing a bomb through a train window fails. Indians are on the eve of the Indian National Conference meeting in Lahore, and Sikh-Hindu tensions are high.

A	B	C	D	E
Includes developments that affect more than one world region, international organizations and important meetings of world leaders.	Includes all domestic and regional developments in Europe, including the Soviet Union.	Includes all domestic and regional developments in Africa and the Middle East.	Includes all domestic and regional developments in Latin America, the Caribbean, and Canada.	Includes all domestic and regional developments in Asian and Pacific nations (and colonies).

U.S. Politics & Social Issues	U.S. Foreign Policy & Affairs, Defense	U.S. Economy & Environment	Science, Technology & Nature	Culture, Leisure & Lifestyle	
Connecticut announces plans to test 25–30 mph speed limits at Stratford to establish the safest for a heavily traveled city highway. The state denies it is setting a speed trap for New Yorkers....New York begins purging its list of corporations. It has 90,000 that are five years delinquent in paying fees. The state estimates that 95 percent are defunct.		The National Bureau of Economic Research reports that national income is $89 billion for 1928. The increase between 1920 and 1929 is $23.5 billion, and income is triple that of 1909. The United States experienced recessions in 1914 and 1921.	Dr. Davidson Black of Canada, discoverer of the 10 skeletons and an intact skull near Peking, says Peking Man may be as important a find as Java Man and Piltdown Man. He estimates the skull to be a million years old and says the grouping of the 10 shows communal life similar to that of modern man. Others say the age is closer to 200,000–250,000 years.	Musical comedy star Bert Lahr signs to appear in George White's *Flying High*, opening in Boston. Debuting on Broadway in 1927, Lahr appeared in *Hold Everything*, a major hit of 1928–29. *Flying High* became Lahr's first feature film in 1931....The Green Bay Packers' 12–0–1 record is the best in the eight-year history of pro football.	Dec. 15
	The Senate votes 53–21 to ratify the French debt agreement. France promises to repay $4 billion over 62 years.	Christmas spending for luxuries is matching 1928. Fewer shoppers are buying $100,000 jewelry, $1,000 radios, $25,000 furs, and other ultra-luxury items though....U.S. Steel buys Atlas Portland Cement. It becomes the largest cement maker with a 36.5 million barrel annual output.		The National Hockey League prohibits players from crossing the opposing blue line ahead of the puck. The game becomes less wide open offensively.	Dec. 16
A coal mine blast at McAlester, OK, kills 59 men. Rescue crews save three and retrieve 23 bodies, leaving 36 in the gas-filled shaft 3500 feet below. Thirty-four of the dead are Mexican and 15 are African American.	A Texas sheriff attempts to arrest former president Calles for an old Texas murder. Mexico cites diplomatic immunity and closes the Nuevo Laredo customs house, stopping a $3.5 million a year exchange, greater than Vera Cruz's $2.5 million. Gov. Moody asks Stimson to intervene. Mexico denies retaliation.	Republic Steel is the product of a four-company merger in the Midwest that creates the third-largest U.S. steel company, valued at $350 million. Number one is U.S. Steel, with Bethlehem number two.	A Royal Air Force plane takes off for Capetown. The goal is a 55-hour flight that will set a new record. The men carry arms for the event they are forced down....Dr. Ales Hrdlicka of the Smithsonian says the Peking bones may not be very old. The missing skulls hint of more modern headhunters.	George M. Cohan signs to write, produce, and direct for United Artists starting in April. His first star will be Al Jolson.	Dec. 17
Canon Chase of the Federal Motion Picture Council of America demands a Congressional investigation of the movie industry. He says the Hays organization provides a screen behind which improper movies proliferate—and movies cause crime. If Congress fails to investigate, federal oversight is necessary, says Chase.	The House approves asking Hoover to appoint a commission to investigate Haiti.		Wreckage of the RAF plane is found in Tunisia. Tribesmen report, and French officials confirm, that the two flyers are dead. Presumably they hit the mountains.		Dec. 18
Hoover names Columbia economics professor Wesley Mitchell to head the commission to study "Changes in National Life." With Rockefeller Foundation money, the commission will collect health and other data on Americans.....A spokesman for hays says chase is a leader without an army. He has appeared before Congress already, and when he called a rally only 18 people came.	Gov. Moody again asks state department intervention. Surely Washington cannot allow an affront from a "friendly" country. Stimson hints that maybe the problem is Moody's to fix.	Stock exchange bonuses for 1,800 employees average 10 percent. Banks and brokerages announce Christmas presents.		Ralph Greenleaf wins the world pocket billiards championship 125-69 over Edwin Rudolph. The final takes 18 innings. Winner's prize totals about $8,000.	Dec. 19
To decrease overproduction, the United Textile Workers of America asks a universal 48-hour workweek for all textile workers. Some locations already have 48- or 44-hour weeks. The rival National Textile Workers Union strikes at Mystic, CT.		Chrysler announces that prices will rise $20 to $100 on January 1. The increases are to preserve the quality of the product.	A cold wave from the midwest reaches New York and lifts the heavy fog that has paralyzed transportation for a week. Ships sail and airmail flies. Trains from the west are late because of midwestern snowdrifts.	Chorus girl Agnes O'Laughlin sues orchestra leader Rudy Vallee for breach of promise for reneging on his marriage proposal. She asks $200,000. He says they are just friends....Katherine Fogarty drops her $500,000 breach of promise suit against Gene Tunney. The ex-heavyweight champion counter sues.	Dec. 20
Athens, GA, imposes a $25 fine for hitchhiking. Male University of Georgia students have bypassed the trolley in favor of a free lift to class, and their example has influenced children to try the risky practice.		W.T. Grant's director of research reports on the company's test stores. The 260-store chain uses five stores to test layouts, merchandise selection and arrangement, and other elements to make the most efficient store for a given size.	Dr. Lawrence Gould of the Byrd expedition reports that Roald Amundsen's Carmen Land, claimed by Norway, does not exist. Amundsen was in Marie Byrd Land, claimed by the United States.		Dec. 21
The 4-year-old Fascisti League of North America shuts down. Count Ignazio Thaon de Revel says that the 12,000-member organization has achieved its goals of publicizing fascism and Mussolini's Italy and fighting communism. The count denies the league is violent and an agent of Italy.	London's *Sunday Chronicle* reports that the United States is holding 500 Englishmen in violation of Jay's Treaty of 1794, which guarantees free passage across the border. It alleges the United States regards border crossers as violators of immigration law and treats them as common criminals.			A St. Louis promoter says the National Hockey League has agreed to expand to his city in 1930. The new franchise will cost $50,000.	Dec. 22

F	G	H	I	J
Includes campaigns, elections, federal-state relations, civil rights and liberties, crime, the judiciary, education, healthcare, poverty, urban affairs, and population.	*Includes formation and debate of U.S. foreign and defense policies, veterans affairs, and defense spending. (Relations with specific foreign countries are usually found under the region concerned.)*	*Includes business, labor, agriculture, taxation, transportation, consumer affairs, monetary and fiscal policy, natural resources, pollution and industrial accidents.*	*Includes worldwide scientific, medical and technological developments, natural phenomena, U.S. weather and natural disasters.*	*Includes the arts, religion, scholarship, communications media, sports, entertainment, fashions, fads, and social life.*

	World Affairs	Europe	Africa & The Middle East	The Americas	Asia & The Pacific
Dec. 23		Berliners buy 620,000 Christmas geese worth $2 million in 48 hours. Berlin bans frozen Russian geese because open-air freezing is regarded as unsanitary.	The final tally shows that the Wafd and associated independents hold all but seven seats. Wafd has 206 and independents 19 seats.		
Dec. 24	Unable to come up with a formula to combine disarmament with outlawing war, conferees drop the idea of using Kellogg as a basis for negotiations. Hoover and MacDonald remain confident of a successful outcome.	Russians ignore Christmas. Earlier in the year many soviets abandoned weekends in favor of the "unbroken working week," which becomes mandatory next year." Besides, orthodox Christmas is a week off.	Bethlehem's 1,500 pilgrims include 300 Canadians and Americans. The numbers are down considerably from prior years.	Argentina struggles. A poor wheat crop raises prices for other grains and limits exports. London bankers offer a $5 million loan to stabilize the peso. An assassin fails to kill President Irigoyen.	
Dec. 25	A shortwave Christmas celebration includes U.S., British, Dutch, and German programs in five languages.		France reports that births in Equatorial Africa exceed deaths—finally. France quadrupled the medical budget and doubled the medical staff that tested 2.4 million and treated almost 100,000 Africans for sleeping sickness in four years.	San Blas Indians threaten to burn a refueling station because they are tired of airplanes flying over their jungle home. They have already chased off employees at Puerto Escoses, Panama....Brazil announces it will borrow $60 million to save the coffee industry.	
Dec. 26	Chanukah begins. Jews begin the Eight-day feast of lights.			Cuba announces that its first labor conference will take place in mid January. U.S. unionists will observe.	The Indian National Congress opens by adopting Gandhi's call for a boycott and civil disobedience because the conference on India's status is unacceptable. Crowds throng in Lahore, and the police arrest eight.
Dec. 27		The Tardieu government withstands attacks from rightist nationalists to win an overwhelming 342–17 vote of confidence. The left parties abstain because they support Briand, Locarno, and naval talks.			The Nanking government issues its final decision to eliminate extraterritoriality. The United States says it violates treaties.
Dec. 28	The United States will not participate in next year's negotiations of German reparations to international community. Pending Senate approval, he U.S. and Germany arrange for Germany to pay Young Plan reparations directly to the United States rather than having the money go through the international commission.	Belgians attribute the deaths of carrier pigeons to the eating of plants unnaturally stimulated by artificial fertilizer. They also argue that these foods are unsafe for humans.		A gold rush begins in Ontario after a woman finds two gold nuggets worth $10 each in the craw of her Christmas turkey. Neighbors begin digging up gravel beds in the area.	
Dec. 29		Poland forms a new government. The Greek government is close to collapse as two members resign and cite growing anarchy. Rumor in Bucharest is that Nicholas' mother, Marie, will become regent.		Ecuador's efforts to shrink its budget run into obstacles as the president's opponents of block war department reductions. There will be less money for public works, sanitation, and education.	Nine to twelve thousand Sikhs march for land and entry into Gandhi's Nationalist Party. Lahore already has 50,000 delegates.
Dec. 30		France's total increase in gold reserves for the year is $370 million....Germany reports two million unemployed, an increase of 900,000 in a year.			India inaugurates airmail as the first leased Jupiter leaves New Delhi. Mail is light as service begins to Jodhpur, Hyderabad, and Karachi, with links to London....Indian liberals reject independence in favor of home rule within the empire.
Dec. 31	Spain requests a seat at the naval talks. She wants to participate in the talks on the Mediterranean. Authorities arrest three Italians with explosives intended for naval talks delegates.	Today is the last day that Bosnians can enter polygamous marriages. The ban will grandfather current polygamists. The practice has waned with economic decline and practitioners are mostly well-to-do Muslims and an occasional Christian who converts to take a second wife.		Ulen and Company signs a contract to build a $2 million dam as part of a major irrigation effort in Chile. The company has built two other dams and is building a tunnel through the Andes in Chile and a road in Colombia.	

A	B	C	D	E
Includes developments that affect more than one world region, international organizations and important meetings of world leaders.	Includes all domestic and regional developments in Europe, including the Soviet Union.	Includes all domestic and regional developments in Africa and the Middle East.	Includes all domestic and regional developments in Latin America, the Caribbean, and Canada.	Includes all domestic and regional developments in Asian and Pacific nations (and colonies).

U.S. Politics & Social Issues	U.S. Foreign Policy & Affairs, Defense	U.S. Economy & Environment	Science, Technology & Nature	Culture, Leisure & Lifestyle	
Hoover signs a bill authorizing 19 new veterans' hospitals with 4491 additional beds. Cost is just under $20 million. Hoover also asks a study of the centralization of veterans' hospitals under a single agency.	The Labor Department official in charge of immigration says illegal entry is a crime. The Britons who fill U.S. jails deserve to be there.				Dec. 23
Union plasterers become the first AFL brotherhood to recommend a six-hour day. Forty percent of New York's 10,000 plasterers are unemployed. Employers cite delays and higher costs in rejecting it. Non-AFL-affiliated railroad brotherhoods broached a six-hour day in March.				A fire in Hoover's White House office causes $50,000 to $60,000 in damage. Cause is an electrical short....Hoover lights the national Christmas tree....The NAACP protests the U.S. Lawn Tennis Association rejection of applications from two African-American players to compete in junior championships. The USLTA denies it discriminates in requiring players to be members of clubs belonging to the USLTA.	Dec. 24
Dr. Shirley Wynne asks the Federal Radio Commission to bar the airwaves to quack doctors. She notes that the FRC gives access to health-menacing ads and claims that newspapers decline to publish.	For one day the border between Nogales, AZ, and Nogales, Mexico, is two blocks north. The INS moves its border station to allow the Nogales Christmas celebration for poor children to include those on both sides of the border.		The Curtiss Tanager plane wins a $10,000 Guggenheim prize and becomes eligible for the $100,000 grand prize by becoming the first to meet the 18-point criteria for the "Safe Plane" competition. The contest, begun two years ago with 100 entrants, will end around the first of the year.		Dec. 25
The Society of Penal Institutions reports that Mississippi's prisons are profitable but plagued by politics. They also, like Louisiana's, rely too much on the lash. Oklahoma's are overcrowded. Texas prisons need a complete overhaul.	Hoover visits Ortiz-Rubio at the Mexican embassy. By not requiring the Mexican president to visit him, he breaks a precedent dating to George Washington.			A national fraternity official says college drinking is declining. It is more common in the west and south than in the east....A Kentuckian with 13 bullets in his body survives in the snow long enough to name those who lynched him. The six, relatives of the man he murdered, surrender peacefully.	Dec. 26
New York City okays "flivver" taxicabs to help ease its congestion problem. Already in use in Philadelphia, the smaller cars are less comfortable but cheaper to operate.			Reconstruction of the French cable is almost complete. It was broken with others during the recent earthquake.		Dec. 27
Alabama's Grand Dragon says the Klan is not involved in politics. Yesterday the Birmingham News published a Klan letter decrying the state Democratic Party's decision to bar as candidates anyone who bolted the party in 1928.	Lieutenant Jimmy Doolittle arrives in New York, halfway through a round-trip flight from Albuquerque, NM. Doolittle is on a Guggenheim grant to test instrument flying through fog.		University of Chicago anthropologist Fay Cooper-Cole tells the American Association for the Advancement of Science there is no such thing as racial purity or superiority. What populizers refer to as race is actually language or nationality. At least half of Scandinavians are not "Nordic," and Nordic superiority is a myth.	Frances Alda, prima donna, gives her farewell performance, Puccini's Manon Lescaut, at New York's Metropolitan Opera. Alda debuted at the Met in 1908.	Dec. 28
Chicago police raid the "Bugs" Moran offices and prevent an extortion try. They arrest members of three Chicago gangs—Aiello, Capone, and Moran—for racketeering and mail fraud.	Hoover says goodbye to Ortiz-Rubio as the Mexican president-elect heads for Canada.				Dec. 29
The first estimate of the upcoming census is that the U.S. population has grown 17 million in the decade. Projection is that the new total is 122 million.....The annual NAACP survey of lynching reports the 1929 total as 12, up from 11 in 1928. Four are white. One is female. All occur in the south.		New York's Standard Oil sues Standard Oil of Rhode Island to bar the company from using Standard, Standard Oil, or Standard Oil Company. The dummy Rhode Island corporation is the work of Harry Starr and Aaron Shapiro, who have incorporated Standard Oil of several other states.		Linguist Sir William Craigie says that most Americans know 60,000 words. Unfortunately, most don't know how to use most of them. Shakespeare knew 15,000 but knew how to use all of them.	Dec. 30
		The Union Tobacco Company ends its cigarette and cigar business and becomes a stock holding company. The American Tobacco Company will reclaim the brands it has leased to Union for three years—including Herbert Tareyton, Three Castles, Melachrino, and Capstan cigarettes and various smoking tobaccos.		Sergei Rachmaninoff returns to the United States. Also due shortly are Mischa Elman and Sergei Prokofieff. Thirteen-year-old Yehudi Menuhin returns from a European tour. He will play Carnegie Hall again in January before returning to Europe in April.	Dec. 31

F	G	H	I	J
Includes campaigns, elections, federal-state relations, civil rights and liberties, crime, the judiciary, education, healthcare, poverty, urban affairs, and population.	*Includes formation and debate of U.S. foreign and defense policies, veterans affairs, and defense spending. (Relations with specific foreign countries are usually found under the region concerned.)*	*Includes business, labor, agriculture, taxation, transportation, consumer affairs, monetary and fiscal policy, natural resources, pollution and industrial accidents.*	*Includes worldwide scientific, medical and technological developments, natural phenomena, U.S. weather and natural disasters.*	*Includes the arts, religion, scholarship, communications media, sports, entertainment, fashions, fads, and social life.*

INDEX

The index refers to all daily entries, which are keyed to page numbers and column headings.

К